MTV

Best of Mexico

1st Edition

by Sara Lieber, Liza Monroy, Ann Summa, Jeff Spurrier, and Rachel Tavel

Wiley Publishing, Inc.

Sara Lieber

Sara Lieber's (Cancún and Yucatán chapters) passion for travel writing was first sparked during a solo trip aboard an airplane as a 6-year-old. Since then she has traversed the U.S. twice by car and once on foot, always making sure to leave plenty of time to enjoy the hidden spots along the way. A Pittsburgher by blood and a Californian at heart, Sara recently relocated from the Bay Area to the Big Apple in pursuit of new horizons and has since found an endless supply of sites to explore within the five boroughs. In 2002, she walked 2,186 miles from Georgia to Maine as a thru-hiker on the Appalachian Trail during a semester off from Pomona College, where she received her B.A. in English and Creative Writing. In her spare time she likes to weld steel, cast bronze, and just generally make things out of metal. She currently works as an editorial assistant at Oxford University Press in New York City.

Liza Monroy

Liza Monroy (Mexico City chapter) is a 27-year-old writer and freelance journalist. Her articles and essays have appeared in the *New York Times*, the *New York Times Magazine*, the *Los Angeles Times, Newsweek, Jane*, the *Village Voice, Time Out New York*, and the travel writing anthologies *Mexico, A Love Story* and *Greece, A Love Story*. The daughter of a U.S. diplomat, she has lived, worked, and studied in Mexico, Italy, Holland, and the Czech Republic. Liza's first novel, *Mexican High*, will be published in 2008. She is a graduate of Emerson College, where she double-majored in film and creative writing. Currently, Liza resides in New York City, where she teaches writing at Mediabistro and is working on a memoir. Her website is www.lizamonroy.com.

Ann Summa

Ann Summa (San Miguel de Allende, Costa Chica, and Oaxaca chapters) has worked as a photo-journalist for national publications from *People* magazine to the *Los Angeles Times*. A book of her punk rock work is slated to be published by Greybull Press. Based in L.A., she travels frequently to her home in San Miguel Allende, and rides a bike 600 miles every year for AidsLifeCycle (www.aidslifecyle.org) to raise money in memory of her friend Lance Loud.

Jeff Spurrier

Jeff Spurrier (Best Of, Basics, North Baja, Los Cabos & Southern Baja, Mazatlán, Puerto Vallarta, and Appendices chapters) has traveled extensively in Mexico for *Outside* magazine, the *Los Angeles Times, Details,* and other publications. His *Irreverent Guide to Los Angeles* is currently in its fourth edition. When not in Los Angeles he can be found either biking in the desert near his home in San Miguel de Allende or camping on his plot of jungle land in Nayarit.

Rachel Tavel

Rachel Tavel (Acapulco and Ixtapa & Zihuatanejo chapters) is a native New Yorker with an unrelenting itch to travel. In 2005 she graduated from Bowdoin College with a major in Spanish and a minor in archaeology, but much of her college career was spent on the water as a rower for Bowdoin crew. After graduating, Rachel worked at American Express Publishing, writing and drooling over the photos in *Food & Wine* and *Travel + Leisure* magazines. She is most inspired by people-watching in foreign countries and her favorite indulgence is fabulous food. Rachel has visited more countries than states and has spent extended time studying in Spain, exploring Argentina (her mother's homeland), and volunteering with children in Costa Rica. In the future, Rachel plans to combine her adoration for food and travel with her love for writing and hopes to someday write a column called "Travels with Tavel."

Published by:
Wiley Publishing, Inc.
111 River St.
Hoboken, NJ 07030-5774

ISBN: 978-0-7645-8775-7

Editors: Stephen Bassman and Jennifer Reilly

Production Editor: M. Faunette Johnston

Cartographer: Liz Puhl

Cover & Interior Design: Eric Frommelt

Production by Wiley Indianapolis Composition Services

For information on our other products and services or to obtain technical support, please contact our Customer Care Department within the U.S. at 800/762-2974, outside the U.S. at 317/572-3993 or fax 317/572-4002.

Wiley also publishes its books in a variety of electronic formats. Some content that appears in print may not be available in electronic formats.

Manufactured in the United States of America

5 4 3 2 1

Table of Contents

List of Maps

Acknowledgments

Sara Lieber would like to thank: Her editors Jennifer Reilly and Stephen Bassman, as well as Naomi Black, Anita Carrillo from AeroMexico, her parents for their unwavering support of her increasingly elaborate journeys outside of ordinary terrain, her sister Molly for holding down the fort in NYC so that she had something to come back to when the trip was over, and her "flan-addict" sister Anne—the coolest, most beautiful travel companion in the world.

Liza Monroy would like to thank: Consul General Peggy Gennatiempo for her skills at maneuvering through potholes; Alex; Grandma; Lydia Gregory; the fantastic Rafael Micha for all his expertise on what's hip, new, and creative in Mexico; Diane Hauke; the Citizen Services section at the U.S. Embassy in Mexico City; the inspirational, inimitable Susan Shapiro; Jennifer Lyons; the poetry of Nick Flynn (which reads especially well in Plaza Garibaldi); and all the wonderful editors I've been fortunate to work with both on this book—Jennifer Reilly and Stephen Bassman—and throughout my writing career. **Jeff Spurrier** and **Ann Summa** would like to thank Cilla Zweig for helping with research. **Rachel Tavel** would like to thank: My friends and family for supporting and encouraging me throughout my adventures; Christian Berger Trauwitz and Alejandro Villarejo Hernandez for their hospitality in Taxco; Naomi Black for opening the door; and Lola the Laptop for keeping me company in Mexico. Finally, the **editors** would like to thank David Baird, Emily Hughey Quinn, Shane Christensen, Jennifer Polland, and Alexia Travaglini, and of course Faunette Johnston and Liz Puhl, for all their invaluable help. Also, thanks to all the stringers for their help with the Basics chapter.

An Invitation to the Reader

In researching this book, we discovered many wonderful places—hotels, restaurants, shops, and more. We're sure you'll find others. Please tell us about them, so we can share the information with your fellow travelers in upcoming editions. If you were disappointed with a recommendation, we'd love to know that, too. Please write to:

MTV Best of Mexico, 1st Edition
Wiley Publishing, Inc.
111 River St.
Hoboken, NJ 07030-5774

An Additional Note

A Note on Prices

The MTV Guides provide exact prices in each destination's local currency. The rates of this exchange as this book went to press are listed in the table below. Exchange rates are constantly in flux; for up-to-the-minute information, consult a currency-conversion website such as www.oanda.com/convert/classic.

Peso $	US $	UK £	Canadian $	Australian $	New Zealand $
1 peso ($1)	US$11	£0.05	C$.10	A$.11	NZ$.13

Star Ratings, Icons & Abbreviations

Every hotel, restaurant, and attraction listed in this guide has been ranked for quality, value, service, amenities, and special features using a star-rating system. Hotels and restaurants are rated on a scale of zero (recommended) to three stars (exceptional). Attractions, shopping, and nightlife are rated according to the following scale: zero stars (recommended), one star (highly recommended), two stars (very highly recommended), and three stars (must-see). In addition to the star-rating system, we also use three feature icons that point you to great deals, in-the-know advice, and unique experiences. Throughout the book, look for:

The most-happening restaurants, hotels, and things to do—don't leave town without checking these places out

When cash flow is at a trickle, head for these spots: no-cost museums, free concerts, bars with complimentary food, and more

Savvy advice and practical recommendations for students who are studying abroad

The following abbreviations are used for credit cards:

AE	American Express	DISC	Discover	V	Visa
DC	Diners Club	MC	MasterCard		

The Best of Mexico

I love Mexico. I am totally besotted, head-over-heels, foolishly in love with the entire country. Because of this, I'm quick to recognize that this is not a country that can be easily categorized—the land is too big and beautiful and the culture is simply too superlative. For some, a best could be a night spent in a graveyard in Mexico City on the Day of the Dead, drinking hot chocolate and quietly talking to families cleaning graves; for others it's the crispy crunch of a ceviche tostada from a street stand in Ensenada, or grabbing a rail before vanishing into the curl at the Mexican pipeline, or dropping down a tricky single track in the shadow of a pyramid in the Yucatán, or the first touch of a masseuse's hands on shoulders burning from a week of kayaking in the Sea of Cortez, or crawling home at dawn after an all-night dancing session almost anywhere in the country.

Mexico can be all things to all people if you open yourself to it. It excels at many things, and delights all five senses—it's very much a sensualist's delight, warm, tropical, and spicy when you want it, or soothing when you don't. While its beach resorts are what seduce initially, you should head inland, even just a few miles, to get a full sense of *Mi tierra,* which means so much more than the simplistic English translation "my earth." *Mi tierra* encompasses everything from a landscape defined by the sun and storm, to childhood memories, to the prick and smell of nopales. It means love, refuge, honor, and home. And it symbolizes the very essence, if you will, of the country itself.

Calling Mexico *mi tierra* is no hyperbole. This land has a soul and a depth that demands a relationship from those who walk, work, or play upon it. As a tourist, you'll get but a hint of its richness. You can surf its waves, rescue its turtles, fly through its trees, or cycle up its dirt roads into the Sierra Madre, and at the end of it say you've tasted some of the flavor of Mexico. But you'll want to come back again and again to get a true feeling for *mi tierra,* and to be able to call it that yourself.

While I encourage you to seek out your own favorite things in Mexico, what follows is an abbreviated list of this amazing country's best activities, places, tastes, and moments to get you started.

Best Only-in-Mexico Experiences

- All the world may be a stage, but some parts have richer backdrops than others. Mexico's **town plazas** are the perfect settings for watching everyday life unfold. Alive with people, these open spaces are no modern product of urban planners, but are rooted in the traditional Mexican view of society. Several plazas are standouts.

  One look tells you how important **Oaxaca**'s *zócalo* (see chapter 14) is to the local citizenry; the plaza is remarkably beautiful, grand, and intimate all at once. **Mexico City**'s Alameda (see chapter 3) has a dark, dramatic history—heretics were burned at the stake here during the colonial period—but today it's a people's park where lovers sit, cotton-candy vendors spin their treats, and the sound of organ grinders drifts over the changing crowd.

  San Miguel de Allende's Jardín (see chapter 4) is the focal point for meeting, sitting, painting, and sketching. During festivals, it fills with dancers, parades, and elaborate fireworks. And El Centro in **Mérida** (see chapter 6) on a Sunday simply can't be beat.
- Mexicans have such a passion for **fireworks** and such a cavalier attitude toward them that it's a good thing most buildings here are stone and cement, or the whole country would have burned down long ago. Practically every festival includes a display. The most lavish are the large constructions known as *castillos,* and the wildest are the *toros* that men carry over their shoulders while running through the streets, causing festival-goers to dive for cover. Some of the best displays go off in **San Miguel de Allende** (see chapter 4).
- Wherever there's a seafront road, you'll find a **malecón** bordering it. This is generally a wide sidewalk for strolling, complete with vendors selling things like pinwheels and cotton candy. In some places, it has supplanted the plaza as a centerpiece of town life. The best examples are in **Puerto Vallarta** (see chapter 9), **Mazatlán** (see chapter 10), and **La Paz** (see chapter 8).
- Nothing reveals the soul of a people like music, and Mexico boasts many kinds in many different settings. You can find brassy, belt-it-out **mariachi music** in the famous **Plaza de Garibaldi** in Mexico City (see chapter 3). For something far punkier, you can pay a visit to **MultiKulti** in Tijuana (p. 328). This collective operates out of a burnt-out movie theater off Revolución, in a roofless amphitheater that books punk bands as well as DJs and speakers like Chiapas rebel Subcommandante Marcos.

Best Beach Vacations

- **Puerto Vallarta** is the only place in Mexico where authentic colonial ambience truly mixes with resort amenities. The spectacularly wide Banderas Bay here offers 42km (26 miles) of beaches. Some, like Playa Los Muertos—the popular public beach in town—abound with palapa restaurants, beach volleyball, and parasailing. See chapter 9.
- The best overall beach value in Mexico, **Puerto Escondido,** is principally known for its world-class surfing beach, Playa Zicatela. The surrounding beaches all have their own appeal; colorful fishing pangas dot the central town beach, parked under the shade of palms leaning so far over they almost touch the ground. Puerto Escondido offers unique accommodations at excellent prices, with exceptional budget dining and nightlife. See chapter 13.
- The side-by-side resorts **Ixtapa/Zihuatanejo** offer beach-goers the best of both worlds: Serene simplicity and resort comforts. For those in search of a back-to-basics beach, the best and most beautiful is Playa La Ropa, close to Zihuatanejo. The wide beach at Playa Las Gatas, with its restaurants and snorkeling sites, is also a great place to play. The luxury hotels in Ixtapa, on the next bay over from Zihuatanejo, front Playa Palmar, a fine, wide swath of beach. See chapter 12.
- Despite extensive damage from October 2005's Hurricane Wilma, **Cancún**'s legendary beaches are back to their own splendid selves, thanks in large part to a US$19-million, government-sponsored beach renewal program. In terms of sheer beauty, Cancún and the coastline of the Yucatán state of Quintana Roo have always boasted Mexico's best beaches. The powdery, white-sand beaches boast water the color of a Technicolor dream; it's so clear you can see through to the coral reefs below. Cancún also offers the widest assortment of luxury beachfront hotels, and more restaurants, nightlife, and activities than any other resort destination in the country. See chapter 5.
- Fronting some of the best beaches on Mexico's Caribbean coast, **Tulum**'s small palapa hotels offer guests a little slice of paradise far from crowds and megaresorts. The bustling town lies inland; at the coast, things are quiet and will remain so because all these hotels are small and must generate their own electricity. If you can pull yourself away from the beach, nearby are ruins to explore and a vast nature preserve. See chapter 6.
- There's only one main beach at **Isla Mujeres**—Playa Norte—but it's superb. From this island, you can dive El Garrafón reef, snorkel offshore, and take a boat excursion to the Isla Contoy national wildlife reserve, which features great birding and a fabulous, uninhabited beach. See "Isla Mujeres" in chapter 6.
- **Playa del Carmen** is Mexico's hip beach destination with a dash of third-world chic. Above all, it's easy and low key. You walk to the beach, you walk back to the hotel, you walk to one of the many good restaurants. Next day, you repeat. The beaches are white sand; the water is clear blue and perfect for swimming. If you feel the urge to be active, not far away are ancient Maya ruins, Cozumel, and the megaresort of Cancún, offering all the variety that you might want in a beach vacation. See chapter 6.
- The state capital **La Paz** borders a lovely beach, dotted with colorful playgrounds and lively open-air restaurants.

Take a cue from the local residents, though, and pass on swimming here in favor of the exquisite beaches just minutes from downtown. La Paz's beaches and the islets just offshore have transformed this tranquil town into a center for diving, sea kayaking, and other adventure pursuits. See chapter 8.

- Dramatic rock formations and crashing waves mix with wide stretches of soft sand and a rolling break at **Los Cabos.** Though some beaches here are more appropriate for contemplation than for swimming, that doesn't have to be a bad thing. Start at Playa Palmilla by San José del Cabo, and work your way down the Corridor to the famed Playa Amor in Cabo San Lucas. See chapter 8.

Best Hostels

- While Mexico doesn't have the quantity of backpacker hostels that Europe does, there are still outposts of civilized group communalism happening in places, like the **Oasis** (p. 450) in Puerto Vallarta where $130 will get you a safe cozy bunk, or the **Paulina Youth Hostel** (p. 625) in a modernized colonial-era building, newly remodeled and upgraded, in the heart of Oaxaca city.
- In Puerto Escondido, check out the **Hotel Mayflower** (p. 600). Like the best hostels anywhere, you probably won't get any sleep and the accommodations are less than, ahem, resortlike, but the ambience is totally casual, and it's affordable if not dirt cheap. Most important, it's popular with travelers from all over the world who come to share travel tips, stories, and food.

Best Hotels That Don't Feel Like Hotels

Mexico is filled to the brim with wonderful small hotels. Some are B&Bs with just a half dozen rooms, while others are slightly larger and boast world-class restaurants and spas. In both cases, the experience of staying at a small hotel is the polar opposite of staying at one of the country's massive resorts. The boutique hotels sometimes cost a little more but are well worth it; they bring home the essence of the place where you're staying, melding both historical ambience with creature comforts.

- **Casa Natalia** (p. 371), in Baja's San José, is a perfect example, since it manages to be both high-end and minimalist, and soothing and seductive.
- Over in La Paz, **Angel Azul** (p. 421), is inexpensive and down-home friendly, but with great amenities, as are **Casa Bentley** (p. 435), in Todos Santos; **La Casona** (p. 96), in Mexico City; **Casa Catrina** (p. 628), in Oaxaca; the **Melville** (p. 496) and **Casa de las Leyendas** (p. 495) in Mazatlán; and **Posada Corazon** (p. 162) and **Villa Scorpio** (p. 161), in San Miguel de Allende. There are more, of course. Delve into the "Sleeping" sections of each chapter for info.

Best Resorts

- One of the dangers of visiting the Pacific Coast in late summer is the chance that your trip will involve a hurricane. If you're lucky, you'll be trapped at **Majahuitas** (p. 454), an impossibly perfect all-inclusive miniresort snuggled into a tiny protected cove on the cusp of Puerto Vallarta's Cabo Corrientes. It's

Best Caffeinated Concoctions

Chocolate and coffee are Mexican specialties, the former native and the latter imported. Oaxaca is the center for all things chocolate in Mexico, from the casual evening hot cocoa drink, unique for its cinnamon overtones at places like **La Soledad** (p. 634) to seven kinds of mole served at restaurants all over the city.

When it comes to coffee, it seems the entire country is searching for the best buzz. Mazatlán, Puerto Vallarta, and Oaxaca are hot spots for local organic growers and roasters and have excellent small coffee bars, although you won't find super cheap cups, since much of the country's coffee is still grown for export.

totally off the grid, every grid—electrical, mental, and cosmological. This rustic yet high-end spot is so remote, the only mechanical sound you'll hear is the occasional put-put of a water taxi passing off shore. That's a very good thing.

- In Cancún, **El Rey del Caribe** (p. 192) is another grid-free possibility, a hacienda-style hotel in the jungle, smothered in orchids, with a vegetarian-friendly menu, solar-powered electricity, and a full-service spa. It perfectly straddles the line between old and new Mexico. You want tai chi classes with your cable channels? *No problemo.*
- **La Casa Que Canta** (p. 564) is one of the *world's* best resorts, in my opinion. On the bay of Zihuatanejo, nestled amid banana trees and palms framing the sea, it's a romantic never-never land, complete with infinity pools and blue-flash sunsets.
- **One&Only Palmilla** (p. 385) is currently the most popular Mexican resort with the Hollywood crowd; the completely renovated Palmilla has regained its spot as the most deluxe hotel in this seaside playground known for sumptuous accommodations and great golf. The exceptional spa, fitness center, and yoga garden, as well as a restaurant under the direction of renowned chef Charlie Trotter, are added bonuses.

Best Eating

Don't worry. Eating from street stands is an essential part of visiting Mexico and it's safe if you take precautions (see "Health & Safety," in "Basics")—plus you'll never find a cheaper, better sidewalk meal this side of Bangkok.

- Ensenada's **Mariscos La Guerrerense** (p. 346) makes ceviche like nowhere else—13 types from shrimp to octopus, clam, and sea urchin, all on small crunchy tortillas and served with a whole zoo of startling homemade sauces. They keep the fish on ice and have been on the same street corner for nearly 50 years, for a good reason.
- **Hangman's** in San José del Cabo (p. 373) is an example of what happens when a street stand grows up and puts on a tarp roof. Off the beaten path yet populated with locals and visiting surfers in the know, it feels more like a circus setting than a place to eat. Amazing turkey tacos, charro beans, and flor de calabaza sauces are all on the menu. It doesn't get more real or savory than this.
- In the Yucatán on Isla Mujeres, the **Playa Lancheros Restaurant** (p. 226) is the sort of place where everyone digs in with their fingers, plucking apart spiced fish prepared in the Tikin Xic

style (like whole red snappers rubbed with bitter orange and chiles and baked in wood-fired ovens).

- In Oaxaca, everyone stops by **Tlayudas del Libres** (p. 636) after a night of drinking for amazing *tlayudas*, huge handmade tortillas crisped on live coals, plastered with black beans (seasoned with avocado leaf) and salsa, and topped with *tasajo* (half-dried salted beef).
- **El Tacón de Marlín,** next to the airport in Puerto Vallarta (p. 457), has amazing smoked marlin, stuffed into a grilled burrito with sweet-sour mayo dressing and a side of jicama. After tasting one, you might want to book another flight just to know you'll be coming back for more soon.

Best Reasons to Stay Up 'til Dawn

- Mexico has countless amazing bars and clubs, but let's start with Mexico City's **Pervert Lounge** (p. 109). Doesn't the name just say it all? Here you can dance to electronica, acid-jazz, and trip-hop until dawn with models and geeks, students, and bohos. It's a tiny place, totally decked out in Barbie dolls, trash containers, stuffed animals, and assorted pack rat craziness.
- In Cancún, the party scene has been taken to a whole new level at places like **Coco Bongo** (p. 201). Foam, lasers, neon confetti, and trapeze artists are all mixed up with a deafening soundtrack and thousands of sweating strangers pressed up against you.
- Acapulco's **Palladium** (p. 531) is another madhouse that's open way-late—this one comes with a dress-to-impress look and view of the bay that is the perfect backdrop to grooving and grinding.
- Mazatlán is where **Señor Frog's** (p. 502) insanity began: Super-tall drinks, conga lines, table dancing, thong contests, they've got it all. There are Señor Frog's all over Mexico these days, and they differ in quality—this is the country's best.
- In Cabo San Lucas, **Squid Roe** (p. 403) or the **Giggling Marlin** (p. 403) are the places to stop by for a fast tray of vodka-Jello before you get hung by your ankles in the harness for some gravity-defying tequila shots. (It's the marlin's revenge, get it?) Both are definitely places to party 'til you, well . . . you know.

Best Sightseeing

- The **Museo Nacional de Antropologia** in Mexico City (p. 117) is like the Louvre—except the art and culture here are way older. This is where you should come if you really want to touch the soul of Mexico. Its staggering 53,000-plus item collection shouldn't be missed.
- For what many consider the best art library in Mexico, head to the **Instituto de Artes Graficas de Oaxaca** (p. 644). This world-class collection of artist (and Oaxaca native) Francisco Toledo has more than 30,000 volumes on art, movies, and architecture, which Toledo has essentially donated to local citizens to use.
- Prefer to sightsee outdoors? Then check out the cliff-divers of Acapulco's **La Quebrada** cliff in Old Town (p. 538). Every night on the half-hour, starting at 7:30, the divers step onto the small platform over the sea, torches in hand, and

leap into the darkness. This is an iconic tourist stop, so retro yet still so real (because if they time it wrong and miss the swell, then, ouch).

- The **Museo Dolores Olmedo Patino** (p. 121) was Patino's home but is now a rambling display case for a huge collection of Diego Rivera and Frida Kahlo art; the **Frida Kahlo Museum** in Kahlo's original home, as well as the **Leon Trotsky Museo,** in the house where he was assassinated, also showcase the museum-in-a-house style of museum that's so popular in Mexico. All of these *museos* are in Mexico City; see chapter 3.
- At the other end of the country, just a few miles from San Diego, the **Centro Cultural Tijuana** (p. 332) is the kind of place one should expect from a unique border city like Tijuana—a rich and well used performance space and museum. It helps that the building itself is brilliant, a fat Death Star–like structure (boasting an OMNIMAX theater) where everyone from ballet divas to border outsider artists makes appearances.
- Acapulco's **La Casa de las Máscaras,** the House of Masks (p. 537), gives a whole new depth to the masks that lucha libre wrestlers wear. Here you'll see more than 1,000 samples of the still vibrant mask-making tradition in Mexico on display. You don't have to limit your masked endeavors to this museum, though. From Mexico City's **Arena Mexico** to **carnaval** in Mazatlán, masks pop up all over the place. To fully understand the Mexican psyche, why not try one on yourself? Masks are on sale at almost all markets throughout the country.

Best Archaeological Sites

- **Teotihuacán** is so close to Mexico City, yet centuries away. You can feel the majesty of the past in a stroll down the pyramid-lined Avenue of the Dead, from the Pyramid of the Sun to the Pyramid of the Moon. Imagine what a fabulous place this must have been when the walls were stuccoed and painted brilliant colors. See chapter 3.
- A grand ceremonial city built on a mountaintop overlooking the valley of Oaxaca, **Monte Albán** offers the visitor panoramic vistas; a fascinating view of a society in transition, reflected in the contrasting methods of pyramid construction; and intriguing details in ornamentation. See chapter 14.
- No matter how many times you see **Uxmal,** the splendor of its stone carvings is awe-inspiring. A stone rattlesnake undulates across the facade of the Nunnery complex, and 103 masks of the rain god Chaac project out from the Governor's Palace. See chapter 6.

Best Way to Secure Good Karma

Between June and November, sea turtles return to the beaches of their birth to lay their eggs in nests on the sand. With poaching and natural predators threatening these species, communities along Mexico's Pacific coast have established protected nesting areas. Many are open for public viewing and participation in the egg collection and baby-turtle release processes. Turtles are found along the Yucatán coast, in Baja Sur, in Puerto Vallarta, and along the Costa Chica up to Oaxaca.

- Stand beside the giant serpent head at the foot of El Castillo pyramid at **Chichén Itzá** and you can't help but marvel at the architects and astronomers who positioned the building so precisely that shadow and sunlight form a serpent's body slithering from the peak to the earth at each equinox (Mar 21 and Sept 21). See chapter 6.

Best Overall Playing Outside

- Want to get your game on? **Valle de Bravo,** a couple of hours west of Mexico City (p. 139), is the best place in the country for **mountain biking, hang gliding, rock climbing** that almost equals Everest, **sailing,** and **horseback riding.** All that, and you'll also get Aztec sweat lodges in fab modern architecture après-play.
- If that doesn't get your heart pumping, try the ultimate free fall, **sky diving** into a picture-postcard-worthy landscape over **Cabo San Lucas** (p. 410).
- If being jet-propelled over the ocean by the wind is your thing, **Los Barriles** (p. 430) in southern Baja has become a mecca for **windsurfing** in recent years.
- From Cabo San Lucas to La Paz, and continuing north, the Sea of Cortez is a sea **kayaker**'s dream. It has dozens of tiny coves and impressive inlets to pull into and explore, under the watchful gaze of sea lions and dolphins. Professional outfitters provide gear, guides, and instruction for novices. See chapter 8.
- The coral reefs off the island of **Cozumel,** Mexico's premier **diving** destination, are among the top five dive spots in the world. See chapter 6.
- The Yucatán's coastal reef is part of the second-largest reef system in the world and affords excellent diving. Especially beautiful is the **Chinchorro Reef,** 32km (20 miles) offshore from Majahual or Xcalak. You can also dive in the clear, cool water of the many caverns and ***cenotes*** (sinkholes, or natural wells) that dot the interior. See chapter 6. Other excellent dive sites are in and around **Puerto Vallarta** and off **Los Cabos.** See chapters 9 and 8.

Best Biking

- Not all the joys of Mexico are on the sands. Some are out in the mud on a mountain, weaving between the cornfields, sliding sideways on tricky singletrack, and climbing into the Sierras. **San Miguel de Allende** (p. 177), has more than 1,280km (800 miles) of tracks that crisscross the high plateau.
- Over in Baja, the contrast between resort and reality get put into stark display on a 2-hour climb out of **Los Cabos** (p. 407), that finishes with a screaming downhill run back to town. You'll ride with Club Cactus, a loose assortment of shredders and shlubs, locals and tourists. Nobody gets left behind, since it's all in good fun.
- Like a little brew with your biking? The annual **Rosarito fun ride** (p. 314) attracts thousands of cyclists of every shape and size to ride the free highway (closed to cars for this event) along the mountains bordering the sea with the final goal—plenty of cerveza—being a definite motivating factor.

Best Surfing

- There's a good reason why the first tourists who explored Mexico's beaches were mainly surfers from California. The waves all along the Pacific Coast, from Puerto Escondido in the south to Ensenada in Baja Norte, are beyond outstanding. There are bone-crushers and gentle newbie-friendly sandy bottom breaks, pocket rocket shore breaks, and long board point breaks. They are as diverse as you might expect from a 1,600km (thousand-mile) open ocean coastline. Better yet, the water is mostly bathtub warm, the crowds are small, and the locals are generally welcoming since, unlike in California, there are still plenty of waves for everyone here. The best view for watching the pros do what you can only dream of has to be Puerto Escondido's **Zicatela Beach,** aka the "Mexican pipeline" (p. 612).
- In Cabo, **Old Man's, Zippers,** and **La Roca** (p. 379) are less intimidating. Across the Sea of Cortez in Nayarit and Sinaloa, there are literally scores of breaks, running for hundreds of miles, starting north of Mazatlán (p. 509) and continuing south to Sayulita and Punta de Mita.

Best Shopping

- Whatever you're looking for, you'll undoubtedly find it at **Mexico City's La Lagunilla** (p. 127), or Thieves Market. It's one of the biggest flea markets in the world and has been going for decades. You'll find everything from antiques, coins, clothes, toys, farm equipment, serapes, branding irons, retablas, stuffed animals, photos, to rugs here—it goes on and on. Just watch out for pickpockets: It's called Thieves Market for a reason.
- **Oaxaca's "Los Baules" de Juana Cata** (p. 648) is an amazing little store with the absolute best textile art you'll find anywhere, including high-end private collections. The pieces—felt hats, shawls, pants, and so on—are unique, expensive, and live up to the standards of the most artistic state of Mexico. You can truly wear a piece of history if you buy something from here.
- The **valley of Oaxaca** produces the best weavings and naturally dyed textiles in Mexico; it's also famous for its pottery (especially the black pottery), and colorful, imaginative woodcarvings. See chapter 14.
- Latin American art is surging in popularity and recognition, and **Mexico City's galleries** feature artwork by some of Mexico's best masters and emerging stars, with **Oaxaca, Puerto Vallarta,** and **San Miguel de Allende galleries** also offering excellent selections. See chapters 3, 4, 9, and 14.
- One of the last indigenous cultures to remain faithful to their customs, language, and traditions, the Huichol Indians come down from the Sierra Madre to sell their unusual art to **Puerto Vallarta** boutiques. Inspired by visions received during spiritual ceremonies, the Huichol create their art with colorful yarn or beads pressed into wax. See "Shopping" in chapter 9.

The Basics: Planning Your Trip to Mexico

By now, you've started daydreaming about all the beautiful things you'll see, all the amazing food you'll eat, all the booze you'll consume, and all the romantic things that will happen to you during your trip to Mexico. Guess what? In all likelihood, all of the above will come true without your planning a damn thing. After all, Mexico might be foreign to you, but as a tourist, you're not foreign to Mexico. We want you to be wild and carefree in your approach to travel in Mexico, but to a point. There are plenty of things you should think about and be aware of—from the logistical to the cultural—before you board that plane or bus. We'll start with some overall planning suggestions, and take it down to the nitty-gritty. Read on, and you'll minimize those "I can't believe I didn't think of that" moments that can stress you out and throw a wrench into your otherwise *buen viaje*.

The Regions in Brief

There are more than 9,660km (6,000 miles) of coastline in Mexico (Estados Unidos Mexicanos). From the U.S. frontier to the borders with Guatemala and Belize, the Mexican beach experience varies enormously, moving from arid desert to dense tropical jungle, from the chilly deep blue of north Baja to the bathtub-warm turquoise waters of Tulum. Ensenada, Los Cabos, La Paz, Mazatlán, Puerto Vallarta, Ixtapa/Zihuatenjo, Acapulco, Puerto Escondido, Huatulco, Cozumel, and Cancún: It's impossible to sum up briefly the differences in climate, topography, and culture you will encounter at all these popular destinations. Mexico is huge—it's the 14th largest country in the world, in fact. And if you limit your travels to the coastal resorts, you'll only get a very partial picture of this historically complicated and culturally rich country. The country's beaches are the eye candy, certainly, but they are best appreciated with an understanding of the civilizations that were here thousands of years before that high-rise Marriott or all-night disco moved in.

Cancún & the Yucatán Peninsula

No doubt about it—**Cancún** is a modern mega resort; it's the most popular destination in the country because of its high-quality accommodations and ability to put foreign travelers at ease. The party land that is Cancún is offset by the stunning natural beauty of the entire **Yucatán peninsula,** though—home to several barrier reefs extending all the way down the "Riviera Maya" to Belize. The peninsula borders the dull aquamarine Gulf of Mexico on the west and north, and the clear blue Caribbean on the east. It covers almost 217,560 sq. km (84,000 sq. miles) with nearly 1,600km (1,000 miles) of shoreline.

Yes, you can have a rowdy spring break in one of the all-inclusive hotels in Cancún if that's what you want, but if you love snorkeling, diving, and Maya ruins, the Yucatán peninsula is still the place to be. Your options are wide open: Soak in history at the ruins of **Tulum, Coba, Chichén Itzá,** and **Uxmal;** dive at **Cozumel;** snorkel in **Isla Mujeres;** visit the gorgeous colonial city of **Mérida;** or just hang out in pretty **Playa del Carmen.**

The Mainland

If you want to truly begin to understand Mexico, leave the beaches for a while and spend some time inland. The mainland's colonial cities, like **Puebla, San Miguel de Allende,** and **Taxco** are great places to encounter the country's post-Columbian-era history. These colonial cities are aesthetically and spiritually dense, intellectually rewarding, and consistently welcoming.

In many ways **Mexico City** is probably the most important and oddly futuristic city in North America. It's confusing, disturbing, chaotic, maddening, seductive, and endlessly surprising—a blend of *Gangs of New York* mixed with *Blade Runner.* **Oaxaca,** on the other hand, is a window into the pure Indian soul of pre-Columbian Mexico—not its past but its still-vibrant present.

Baja

Baja is the world's fourth longest peninsula, a narrow finger of land that split off from the mainland of Mexico back when mammoths roamed the globe. Locals commonly define Baja as an island and in some ways it is—remote from the mainland of Mexico and united only in the last 35 years by the completion of the Transpeninsular Highway (Rte. 1). It is where some of Mexico's most stunning geography is on display, such as the Sea of Cortez, with one of the world's best marine ecosystems. It's also home to the world's busiest border crossing at **Tijuana,** the northernmost city in North Baja, as well as the less sleazy but no less Americanized **Ensenada** and **Rosarito Beach.** In contrast, South Baja truly excels as a vacation haven, offering golf, fishing, diving, and whale-watching in beautiful settings at posh resorts, from **San José del Cabo** and **Cabo San Lucas,** towns with some of the most expensive real estate in the country, to the peaceful town of **La Paz,** to the increasingly hip yet still hippie-friendly **Todos Santos.**

Puerto Vallarta & the Central Pacific Coast

Director John Huston brought **Puerto Vallarta,** or PV, to the world's attention in his *Night of the Iguana* film in the '60s, but remarkably, almost half a century later, the city is still ready for its close-up. PV is that rare resort town that is massively popular with both foreigners and Mexicans

Mexico

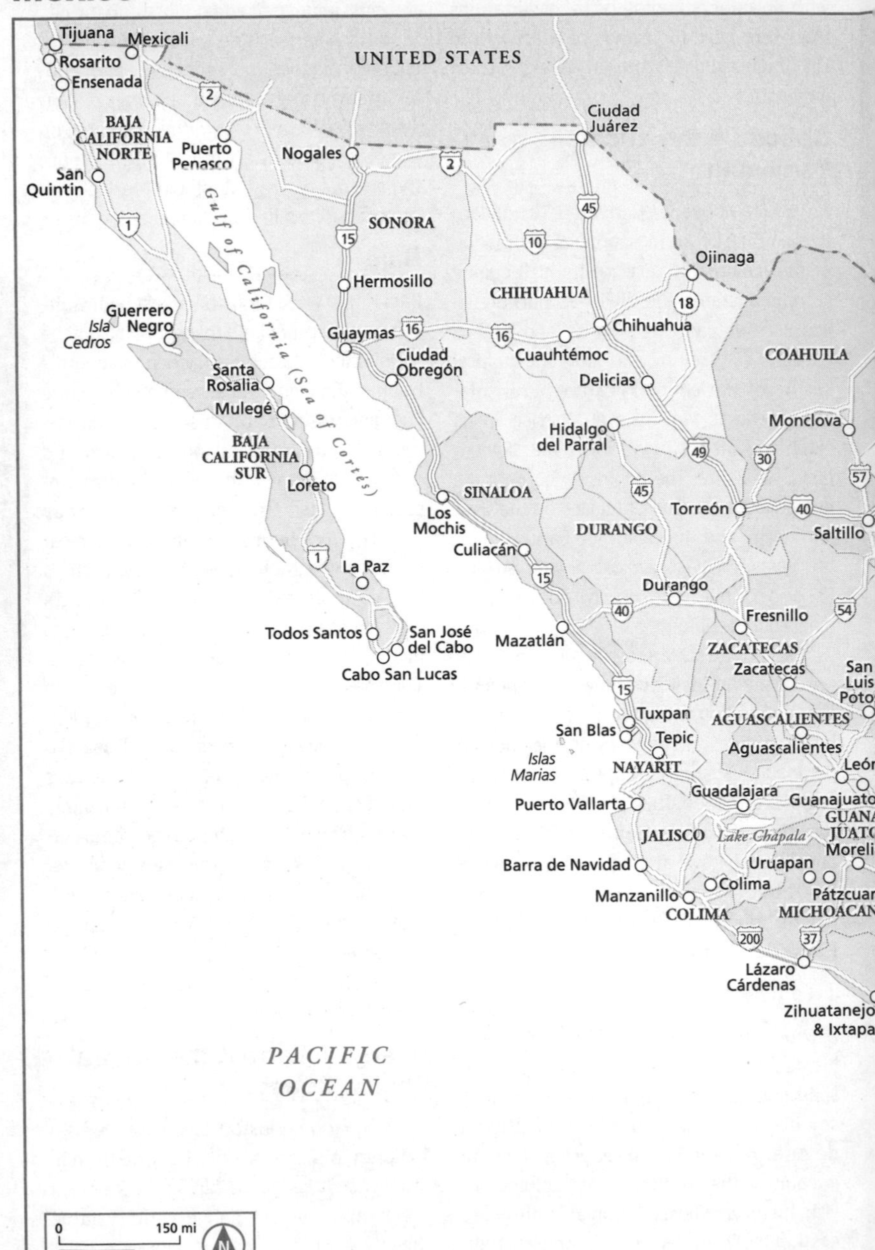

UNITED STATES
Tijuana
Mexicali
Rosarito
Ensenada
BAJA CALIFORNIA NORTE
Puerto Penasco
Nogales
Ciudad Juárez
San Quintin
Gulf of California (Sea of Cortés)
SONORA
Hermosillo
CHIHUAHUA
Ojinaga
Chihuahua
Guerrero Negro
Isla Cedros
Guaymas
Ciudad Obregón
Cuauhtémoc
COAHUILA
Santa Rosalia
Mulegé
Delicias
Hidalgo del Parral
Monclova
BAJA CALIFORNIA SUR
Loreto
SINALOA
Los Mochis
Torreón
Saltillo
DURANGO
Culiacán
La Paz
Durango
Fresnillo
Todos Santos
San José del Cabo
Cabo San Lucas
Mazatlán
ZACATECAS
Zacatecas
San Luis Potos
Tuxpan
San Blas
Tepic
AGUASCALIENTES
Aguascalientes
Islas Marias
NAYARIT
Leór
Puerto Vallarta
Guadalajara
Guanajuato
GUANA JUATC
JALISCO
Lake Chapala
Moreli
Barra de Navidad
Uruapan
Colima
Pátzcuar
Manzanillo
COLIMA
MICHOACAN
Lázaro Cárdenas
Zihuatanejo & Ixtapa
PACIFIC OCEAN
0
150 mi
0
150 km
N

UNITED STATES
Gulf of Mexico
Piedras Negras
Nuevo Laredo
85 D
Monterrey
Matamoros
180
NUEVO LEÓN
85
TAMAULIPAS
Ciudad Victoria
Ciudad Mante
Tampico
SAN LUIS POTOSÍ
San Miguel de Allende
QUERÉTARO
Tuxpan
Poza Rica
HIDALGO
Papantla
Querétaro
Pachuca
180
Mexico City
Xalapa
TLAXCALA
Toluca
Tlaxcala
Veracruz
Cuernavaca
Puebla
MORELOS
PUEBLA
Orizaba
Tehuacán
Taxco
95
GUERRERO
190 D
175
Acapulco
200
Oaxaca
OAXACA
Puerto Escondido
Puerto Ángel
Huatulco
Salina Cruz
Gulf of Tehuantepec
Bay of Campeche
Catemaco
VERACRUZ
Coatzacoalcos
TABASCO
Villahermosa
186
Palenque
Tuxtla Gutiérrez
San Cristóbal de las Casas
CHIAPAS
Comitan
200
Tapachula
GUATEMALA
BELIZE
HONDURAS
EL SALVADOR
Caribbean Sea
Río Lagartos
Isla Mujeres
Progreso
Valladolid
Cancún
Celestún
Mérida
180 D
Cozumel
YUCATÁN
Playa del Carmen
180
Campeche
Punta Allen
QUINTANA ROO
CAMPECHE
Bacalar
Majahual Peninsula
261
186
Chetumal
Escárcega
186

(it's the second-most-visited resort town after Cancún), developed yet environmentally pristine, and a hot spot of fine food and modern art that still manages to exude a completely believable Mexican vibe. For most visitors, Puerto Vallarta is the easiest of the country's beach towns to slip into. The cobblestone streets, red-tiled roofs, endless pastel hues of bougainvillea, and best of all, the expanse of the sweeping Banderas Bay make PV a place with something for everyone: the eco-traveler, the gourmand, the all-night party-hard spring-breaker, the creative wannabe, the veteran old-Mexico hand, the single, the gay, and the tech-nerd. The local culture is mature and approachable, the food truly world-class, and the pace wonderfully casual. Plus it's shrouded by the Sierras and the jungle is never very far away.

A city with a population of nearly 500,000, **Mazatlán** boasts 27km (17 miles) of sandy beaches and a geographically diverse environment. Back in the 1960s, it was *the* spring break hot spot, but it slipped beneath the tourist radar until recently. Still, as a working city, Mazatlán is not dependent on tourism as much as its fishing and its port—the largest on the West Coast after Long Beach—and that makes it a great resort value. Although some developments are edging Mazatlán into the golf-playing, manicured resort that typifies most of Mexico today, it is going there grudgingly—most of Mazatlán remains refreshingly simple.

Acapulco & the Southern Pacific Coast

The mother of all Mexican beach towns is **Acapulco,** some 1,600km (1,000 miles) south of Puerto Vallarta. At one time, it was *the* place for Mexico City elites and Hollywood jet-setters but it quickly became a victim of its own popularity. It just grew too fast, and without proper infrastructure to take care of all the tourism, it got dirty, dangerous, and downright skanky. Today it's undergoing a renaissance of sorts, as a result of slowly cleaning up its act.

Situated on a horseshoe bay, with year-round temperate temperatures, cool kitschy mid-century architecture, ocean-side restaurants, surfer bars on the beach, and kick-ass nightlife, Acapulco still has a certain appeal. Even with all the high rises and hillside development, the mountains this city is built upon remain covered in trees. Fishermen in pangas share the beaches with tourists, families, jet skis, banana boats, parasailers, and giant cruise ships that lumber into the bay, complete cities in themselves. And Acapulco is still a gay-friendly mecca (second only to Puerto Vallarta)—sophisticated in a sense without being snobby.

Just about midway between Puerto Vallarta and Acapulco, in the middle of the Mexican Riviera, are the twin towns of **Ixtapa** and **Zihuatanejo.** While they are always linked like twins in tourist brochures, the two could not be more different. They're only 6km (3¾ miles) away from each other but light-years apart in sensibility. Ixtapa is the high-end all-inclusive resort, while Zihuatanejo is its funky and laid-back opposite. Ixtapa will take care of your every creature comfort; Zihuatanejo requires a bit more work, but the pay-off is deeper.

Ixtapa owes its birth to FONATUR, the government organization responsible for Cancún. It's situated on a 3km-wide (2-mile) beach and boasts a golf course, a marina, and all the manufactured ambience you might want. Just down the road, "Zihuat" has the Old Mexico thing down pat. It's a former fishing village that benefits from the proximity of its high-toned neighbor. Once hippie-friendly, back in the day, let's face it, it's starting to lose its edge. That said, Zihuatanejo is still fairly authentic, and stays true to its fishing village roots (it's just that now the fishermen are mainly gringos).

Costa Chica (Far Southern Pacific Coast)

The surfing town of **Puerto Escondido** is only 2 hours south of Acapulco but it seems a lot farther away because it's so difficult to get there. As a result, it's managed to retain the charm of a typical small, if somewhat scruffy, Mexican beach town. Add to this the international surfing community and their entourage, great and reasonable expat restaurants, and beachside hotels, and you've got a town that's worth the trek.

Two hours south of Puerto Escondido you'll find the Mexican government's latest attempt at a tourist resort development: **Huatulco.** The end result is a place without much of a town center, but the nine bays that make up this resort are still stunningly beautiful; and budget accommodations as well as bigger hotels that offer good packages are both on hand. It's a very good option if you want to soak in nature during the day, then retreat to well-appointed comfort at night.

There are tons of road trip opportunities along this coastline. North of town are unique ecosystems with pristine beaches; inland are coffee plantations, waterfalls, and hiking paths in the rugged Oaxacan mountains; and down the coast are the villages surrounding Puerto Angel and the nude beach of Zipolite. There's an abundance of volunteer opportunities to be had in the area, too.

Visitor Information

See "Nuts & Bolts" later in this chapter for a list of embassies and consulates in Mexico.

The **Mexico Hot Line** (☎ **800/446-3942**) is an excellent source for general information; you can request brochures on the country and get answers to most common questions from the exceptionally well-trained, knowledgeable staff.

More information (15,000 pages' worth) about Mexico is available on the official site of Mexico's Tourism Promotion Board, **www.visitmexico.com**. The **U.S. State Department** (☎ **202/501-4444;** fax 202/647-1488; www.travel.state.gov) offers **Travel Warnings** and a **Consular Information Sheet** on Mexico with safety, medical, driving, and general travel information gleaned from reports by its offices in Mexico.

The **Mexican Government Tourist Board** has offices in major North American cities, in addition to the main office in Mexico City (☎ **55/5278-4200**). In the **United States,** the offices are: Chicago (☎ **312/228-0517,** ext. 14), Houston (☎ **713/772-2581,** ext. 105, or 713/772-3819), Los Angeles (☎ **310/282-9112**), and New York (☎ **212/308-2110**).

The **Mexican Embassy** in the United States is at 1911 Pennsylvania Ave. NW, Washington, DC 20005 (☎ **202/728-1750** or -1600).

In Canada the embassies are at: 2055 Rue Peel, Suite 1000, Montreal, QUE, H3A 1V4 (☎ **514/288-2502**); Commerce Court West, 199 Bay St., Suite 4440, Toronto, ON, M5L 1E9 (☎ **416/925-0704**); 710 West Hastings St., Suite 1177, Vancouver, BC, V6E 2K3 (☎ **604/684-1859**); 1500-45 O'Connor St., Ottawa, ON, K1P 1A4 (☎ **613/233-8988;** fax 613/235-9123).

The embassy in **Australia** is at 14 Perth Ave., Yarralumla, Canberra, ACT 2600 (☎ **02/6273-3963**), and 135 New South Head Rd., Edgecliff, Sydney, NSW 2027 (☎ **02/9326-1292**). The embassy in the

U.S. Embassy Registra

MTV U Art & Cooking Classes

If you feel like exploring your inner Frida or Diego while in Mexico, get in tou with **Mexican Art Tours,** 1233 E. Baker Dr., Tempe, AZ 85282 (☎ **888/783-1331** or 480/730-1764; fax 480/730-1496; www.mexicanarttours.com). Led Jean Grimm, a specialist in the arts and cultures of Mexico, these unique to focusing on the authentic arts and cultures of Mexico are accompanied by compelling speakers who are themselves respected scholars and artists. Itineraries include visits to Oaxaca, Chiapas, Guadalajara and Puerto Vallarta, Mexico City, and other locales. Special tours include a Day of the Dead tour, and one on the art of Mexican masks.

If you'd prefer to eat your way through your trip, then try **Culinary Adventures,** 6023 Reid Dr. NW, Gig Harbor, WA 98335 (☎ **253/851-7676;** fax 253/851-9532; www.marilyntausend.com) instead. It specializes in a short but select list of cooking tours in Mexico. They feature well-known cooks and travel to regions known for excellent cuisine. The owner, Marilyn Tausend, is the co-author of *Mexico the Beautiful Cookbook* and *Cocinas de la Familia (Family Kitchens).* In Tlaxcala, **Mexican Home Cooking School** (Apdo. 64, Tlaxcala; ☎ **246/468-0978;** www.mexicanhomecooking.com) is run by Estela Silva, who works off Puebla-inspired recipes learned via her grandmother, Dona Eulogia Silva Castillo. Expect an emphasis on mole. Finally, in the Yucatán, there's another reason to stay in Mérida: the **Los Dos Cooking School** (Calle 68, no. 517; ☎ **999/928-1116;** www.los-dos.com), which is world famous as the first cooking school dedicated solely to Yucatecan cuisine.

San Miguel de Allende and Oaxaca are particularly good spots to base yourself in for cooking sessions; see those chapters for info on particular classes.

THE BASICS

U.K. is at 41 Trinity Square, Wakefield House, London EC3JN 4DJ (☎ **020/748809392**). The embassy in **Ireland** is at 43 Ailesbury Rd, Ballsbridge, Dublin 4 (☎ **01/260-0699**). The embassy in **New Zealand** is at 111-115 Customhouse Quay, 8th Floor Wellington (☎ **04/472-5555**).

Getting In & Out

See "Nuts & Bolts" at the end of this chapter for info on how to obtain passports and visas.

Passports

As of 2007, the U.S. requires that all citizens traveling by air to and from Mexico have a valid passport. The same rules will soon apply to travel to Mexico via land or sea—possibly as early as January 2008. Before that law goes into effect, you can simply bring a birth certificate and driver's license if traveling via car or cruise ship (though having a passport certainly doesn't hurt). At press-time, the U.S. government was also considering allowing visitors traveling to Mexico via land or sea to use a PASS card, a less expensive alternative to a passport. Check http://travel.state.gov for updates.

The U.S. State Department also advises American citizens to register with a U.S. embassy or consulate once you arrive in Mexico. Or you can pre-register online at https://travelregistration.state.gov. You'll d to have your itinerary, passport number, and the name, address, and phone number of an emergency contact. Once you get to your destination, you can again go online to register or go in person to the nearest embassy or consulate. In accordance with the Privacy Act, information on your welfare or whereabouts may not be released to inquirers without your expressed written authorization. If you do lose your passport, recording this information makes it a lot easier to get a new one quickly. Another reason to register is so that you can be contacted in case of an emergency such as a hurricane.

Tourist Cards & Visas

You don't need a tourist card if you're staying within the border zone (20–30km/12–19 miles of the frontier, depending on the location) and remaining in Mexico for less than 72 hours. If you're staying longer or going deeper into the country, you'll need to get an FM-T **tourist card,** available from Mexican consulates and handed out automatically if you're arriving by air. Tourist cards are generally good for 90 days, single entry only. Just take care *not* to lose the tourist card. While it is almost pro forma to get one, not having one to turn in at the time of your departure can be a real headache.

If you want to stay longer on a tourist **visa**—up to 180 days, and enter multiple times—you'll need to present proof of "sufficient funds," or US$50 a day in a bank account covering the length of stay. If you have a tourist card that lasts for less than 180 days, you can renew it at an immigration office (Instituto Nacional de Migración) as long as you have a passport that's valid for a minimum of 6 months. Tourist visas and cards are available only to people entering Mexico on holiday, for reasons of health, or to engage in "scientific, artistic, or sporting activities which are neither remunerative nor lucrative."

Typically, students need not apply for anything other than a tourist card unless staying for longer than 6 months, in which case a **student visa** may be required. A student visa is good for 1 year. Generally it will take a few days—depending on nationality—to issue a visa.

What Can I Bring?

When you enter Mexico, Customs officials will likely be tolerant as long as you have no illegal drugs or firearms. You're allowed to bring in two cartons of cigarettes or 50 cigars, plus 1kg (2¹/₄ lb.) of smoking tobacco, two 1-liter bottles of wine or hard liquor, and 12 rolls of film. A laptop computer, camera equipment, and sports equipment that could feasibly be used during your stay are also allowed. The underlying guideline is: Don't bring anything that looks as if it's meant to be resold in Mexico. You can see a list of the most common items not allowed for entry into Mexico at http://matamoros.usconsulate.gov/matamoros-esp.

You are supposed to enter the "Merchandise to Declare" lane at the Customs checkpoint even if items are duty-free (by your estimation). This is more a factor when driving into Mexico, since failure to declare personal effects means your vehicle can be seized along with your "smuggled" goods.

Mexican Customs officials are strict regarding the importation of used clothing, textiles, or other used goods intended for donation, even if they're going to charitable organizations. You'll need to hire a Customs broker to shepherd the goods through. Check with the Aduanas (Customs) website, in Spanish only, at www.aduanas.sat.gob.mx/webadunet/body.htm.

According to the State Department, "possession of any amount of prescription

What to Pack for a 2-Week Stay at the Beach

"Backpacker" is a figurative term. You can be a young, carefree, budget-oriented traveler even if you carry a rolling suitcase. In most cases, a rolling bag is just as convenient to carry around as a backpack, and it can be easier to keep organized. However, when it comes to climbing stairs and covering longer distances on foot, the classic backpack can't be beat.

To maximize the space in any bag, the key words are **rolling** and **compartmentalizing.** Rolling your clothes will keep you more space-efficient and you'll fit more. As for compartmentalizing, you want to be able to access those things that you need most, more readily, and others not so much. Put toiletries and the like near the top or in their compartment. Keep film, camera, and so on in a separate compartment that is easily accessible, and make sure you have a separate compartment for dirty clothes. Another thing to keep in mind is that **you don't have to look like a schlep to be a backpacker!** Nice(r) clothes don't necessarily take up more room, so pack some wrinkle-free clothes that'll make you look presentable when you hit the town. Lastly, we all know that shoes can take up the most room in our bags. Keep this in mind when you're contemplating wearing your Uggs in Mexico.

When choosing a backpack, note that there are straps on the outside for larger items such as shoes, sweatshirts, coats, and blankets. Use those and keep the inside of your bag free for anything fragile that you might need to protect. And remember: Since you may want to bring a few things home, it doesn't hurt to leave a few compartments empty or pack an extra, empty bag for the goodies. And if you arrive in Mexico and realize you forgot to pack socks, never fear: There are plenty of places to shop here!

Here's a sample packing list to get you started:

- Clothes, but not too many. 2 to 3 shorts, 1 sarong, 1 to 2 bathing suits, 5 T-shirts or tops, 1 to 2 long-sleeved cotton shirt/blouse for dress or sun protection, 1 cotton skirt or dress for gals (or an extra pair of pants for

medicine brought from the United States, including medications to treat HIV and psychotropic drugs such as Valium, can result in arrest if Mexican authorities suspect abuse or if the quantity of the prescription medicine exceeds the amount required for several days use." They further warn against buying your prescription drugs in Mexico.

What Can I Take Home?

Returning **U.S. citizens** who have been away for at least 48 hours are allowed to bring back, once every 30 days, US$800 worth of merchandise duty-free. You'll pay a flat rate of duty on the next US$1,000 worth of purchases. Any dollar amount beyond that is subject to duties at whatever rates apply. On mailed gifts, the duty-free limit is US$200. Be sure to keep your receipts or purchases accessible to expedite the declaration process. ***Note:*** If you owe duty, you are required to pay on your arrival in the United States—either by cash, personal check, government or traveler's check, or money order (and, in some locations, a Visa or MasterCard).

To avoid paying duty on foreign-made personal items you owned before your trip, bring along a bill of sale, insurance policy, jeweler's appraisal, or receipts of purchase.

guys), 1 pair of jeans, 1 pair of lightweight long pants, 1 light sweater or windbreaker (depending on season), and 1 dressy top and pant set for a club/restaurant should do you fine.

- Comfortable shoes, but again don't go crazy. All you really need is 1 pair of flip-flops, 1 pair of dressier sandals, and 1 pair of tennis shoes (bike shoes if you plan to ride).
- Underwear and non skimpy sleepwear (like sweats, for hostels).
- Snorkeling gear if you intend to do a lot of it, because rental gear may not fit.
- Sunglasses and wide-brim hat or baseball cap.
- Small flashlight.
- Basic medicine kit (p. 40).
- Trail mix (expensive in Mexico), ground coffee (if you're particular), and tea (even if you're not particular—it is hard to find decent tea in Mexico).
- Camera and memory card—film and batteries can be purchased in Mexico if needed, but it's best to bring those, too.
- I-Pod charger and other electronic chargers, plus currency converters, if needed (Mexico uses the same currency as the U.S.).
- Extra bag to bring stuff home in.
- ATM and/or credit cards, and some cash to keep you going upon arrival.
- Passport. See "Before You Leave: The Checklist" later in this chapter for tips on what other IDs and paperwork to bring.

And what to leave behind:
Anything you would hate to lose, including valuable or expensive-looking jewelry, irreplaceable family objects, unnecessary credit cards, and unnecessary IDs, like Social Security cards, regularly carried in your wallet.

Or you can register items that can be readily identified by a permanently affixed serial number or marking—think laptop computers, cameras, and CD players—with Customs before you leave. Take the items to the nearest Customs office or register them with Customs at the airport from which you're departing. You'll receive, at no cost, a Certificate of Registration, which allows duty-free entry for the life of the item.

U.S. CITIZENS

For more specifics on what you can bring back and the corresponding fees, download the invaluable free pamphlet *Know Before You Go* online at **www.cbp.gov**. (Click on "Travel," and then click on "Know Before You Go! Online Brochure".) Or contact the **U.S. Customs & Border Protection (CBP)**, 1300 Pennsylvania Ave. NW, Washington, DC 20229 (☎ **877/287-8667**), and request the pamphlet.

CANADIAN CITIZENS

For a clear summary of Canadian rules, write for the booklet *I Declare*, issued by the **Canada Border Services Agency** (☎ **800/461-9999** in Canada, or 204/983-3500; **www.cbsa-asfc.gc.ca**).

THE BASICS

U.K. CITIZENS

For information, contact **HM Customs & Excise** at ☎ **0845/010-9000** (from outside the U.K., 020/8929-0152), or consult their website at **www.hmce.gov.uk**.

AUSTRALIAN CITIZENS

A helpful brochure available from Australian consulates or Customs offices is *Know Before You Go*. For more information, call the **Australian Customs Service** at ☎ **1300/363-263**, or log on to **www.customs.gov.au**.

NEW ZEALAND CITIZENS

Most questions are answered in a free pamphlet available at New Zealand consulates and Customs offices: *New Zealand Customs Guide for Travellers, Notice no. 4*. For more information, contact **New Zealand Customs,** The Customhouse, 17–21 Whitmore St., Box 2218, Wellington (☎ **04/473-6099** or 0800/428-786; **www.customs.govt.nz**).

When to Go

How Much Time Do I Need In Mexico?

Airfares to Mexico are generally cheap and its hotels offer great bargains year-round. So the question you should ask yourself isn't how long you should spend here but how long do you have? If you're too stressed to go away longer than a long weekend, you can easily take a 3-day jaunt to Tijuana or Cancún. If you have more time to spend, you can just as easily use up a couple of weeks roaming the Pacific coast, looking for secret spots. Mexico has a way of silencing any inner ticking clocks and it's flexible enough so that you can stretch out your trip. On your first day here, you may remember obligations back home, the second day less so, and by the third day you probably won't remember them at all.

Seasons

Traditionally, late fall through early spring are the high seasons in Mexico, with tourist levels peaking around Thanksgiving, Christmas, New Year's, and Easter. January through March see the heaviest influx of folks from Canada and the northeastern U.S.

The slowest periods in Mexico are late summer and early fall (excluding the days before and after Mexican Independence Day on Sept 15). During this low-season period, you can expect hotel costs to drop 20% to 50%. Since July and August are the traditional vacation periods for Americans, Europeans, and Mexicans, you won't find as many deals at the beach resorts then as you'll encounter in September. In Mexico City and San Miguel and other interior cities, there is less of a difference between high- and low-season prices. Prices are almost always high and then higher around peak holidays.

Mexico has two main climate seasons: **rainy** (around May to mid-Oct) and **dry** (mid-Oct to Apr). The rainy season can be of little consequence to the dry, northern regions of the country. Southern regions typically receive tropical showers, which begin around 4 or 5pm and last a few hours. Though these rains can come on suddenly and be quite strong, they usually end just as quickly. **Hurricane season** particularly affects the Yucatán peninsula and the southern Pacific coast, especially June through October. **Norte season** runs from late November to mid-January, when the jet stream dips far south and creates northerly winds and showers in many resort areas. These showers usually only last for a couple of days.

Elevation is another important factor to keep in mind. High elevation cities such as Mexico City can be surprisingly cold; temps can drop close to freezing at night in winter even in San Miguel de Allende, which is at a lower elevation.

THE CASE FOR NOT GOING IN SUMMER

Mid-summer to early fall is hurricane season (see above). Regular storms also regularly knock out basic transportation links like highways and ferry service during this period. In addition, May to August in northern states like Baja and along the southern U.S. border can be incredibly hot. Along the coasts, July to September are not only the hottest months, they're also the most humid. In Puerto Vallarta, for instance, the temperature ranges from the low 60s (mid-teens Celsius) to the mid-90s (mid-30s Celsius), but the humidity is almost always brutal. Finally, because less tourists visit during late summer, restaurants and clubs all along the Pacific, from Cabo to Puerto Escondido, either close up for the months of August or September or use this time to renovate and upgrade.

THE CASE FOR GOING IN SUMMER

In our opinion, mid to late fall or spring are the perfect times to visit Mexico, no matter where you're headed. On the other hand, outdoor options abound in the summer. From May to August, surfers flock to Mazatlán and Puerto Escondido for the south swell, divers head to La Paz for the hammerheads, and mountain bikers go to Valle de Bravo and San Miguel for the hard-packed trails. Summer is also the best time to bargain for everything from hotel rooms to car rentals to massages, especially along the coasts. Just keep in mind that May to mid-June is the end of dry season all along the west coast and inland, so during those months, everyone is waiting for rain. When the rains begin in late June, everyone's mood improves. Now wouldn't you prefer to be around for that?

THE BASICS

Mexico's Average Daily Temperature & Average Rainfall

		Jan	Apr	July	Oct
Acapulco	Temp. (°F)	72/88	73/90	77/90	75/90
	Temp. (°C)	22/31	22/32	25/32	24/32
	Rainfall	6mm	1mm	256mm	159mm

		Jan	Apr	July	Oct
Cancún	Temp. (°F)	67/83	73/89	75/90	74/87
	Temp. (°C)	19/28	23/32	24/32	23/31
	Rainfall	8mm	41mm	109mm	218mm

		Jan	Apr	July	Oct
Mexico City	Temp. (°F)	43/66	52/77	54/73	50/70
	Temp. (°C)	6/19	11/25	12/23	10/21
	Rainfall	13mm	20mm	170mm	51mm

Fiestas Mexicana

Before traveling, it's wise to take into account Mexico's numerous fiesta days. If you want to escape the mob, don't go; if you love culture and tradition, they are an experience not to be missed.

In January, there's **Three Kings** (Jan 6). February has **Constitucion Day** (Feb 5), **Flag Day** (Feb 24), and **Carnaval** (late Feb or early Mar). March/April has **Semana Santa,** Easter Week, probably the most important holiday period in the year, culminating with

Día de Los Muertos

While many people think Día de Los Muertos, or the Day of the Dead, is on October 31, it's actually celebrated on November 2. Most people also celebrate November 1 as a Day of the Dead. November 1 is reserved in homage to those who have died over the years, while November 2 is reserved for those who have died in the preceding year. The history of the celebration is based in the cosmology of the Mesoamerican civilizations in which the dead were thought to still be around the living. According to this philosophy, death is a part of life and rather than hide from it or fear it, Mexicans celebrate it as a cosmic joke. November 2 is a major national holiday, marked by candy skulls, special "Dead Bread," skeletons, and visits to graveyards. People build special altars in their homes for the dead, scatter paths of marigold petals leading up to the front door to lead the dead home, and spend the night drinking and eating in graveyards. The altars contain the dead person's favorite food, which the spirits are thought to enjoy.

parades and processions throughout the country.

In late April or early May, Mexico City usually hosts the **Vive Latino** concert festival—a fine excuse for dancing, drinking, and diving into some of Latin America's best music. The festival, which features everything from indie rock to punk acts, usually lasts for 1 or 2 days, depending on the number of live acts lined up each year. Check out www.vivelatino.com.mx for info.

May has **Labor Day** (May 1) when all the unions make their annual demands, **Cinco de Mayo** (May 5), which celebrates the defeat of the invading French at the battle of Puebla, **Mother's Day** (May 10) when the women who really run the country are celebrated, and **St. Isidore's Day** (May 15) for the blessing of the animals. May/June sees **Corpus Christi** (on the first Thurs after Trinity Sun) which celebrates the presence of Christ in the Eucharist, celebrated mainly in Veracruz.

At press time, there was no official website up and no firm date for **Tijuana's Gay Pride parade,** but check out **www.gaymexico.net/tijuana.html** for the latest news and info. The parade usually takes place on either the first or second Saturday in June. In past years, crowds have lined Avenida Revolución and cheered on the couple of hundred marchers. The annual gay pride parade in **Mexico City,** also normally held in June, is a much bigger affair, and runs along Paseo de la Reforma to the *zócalo* main square.

In September comes **Independence Day** (Sept 15), which is the traditional start of the fall-winter fiesta season, celebrated via parades, fireworks, and the shouting of *"El Grito"* by the President (and local mayors).

October brings the **Festival Internacional Cervantino,** a major art/cultural festival that is based in Guanajuato but spills over into San Miguel de Allende. Late October and early November (Oct 31–Nov 2) brings **Día de los Muertos;** see the box above for info. December kicks off with the **Virgin's birthday** (Dec 12), celebrated throughout Mexico, such as at the Basilica in Mexico City. It's followed by the **Pomades** (Dec 16–24), which re-create the journey of Mary and Joseph in search of a birthing room for Jesus—it's marked by nighttime parades, piñatas, and hot chocolate. And then there's **Christmas Eve** (Noche Buena) and **Christmas Day,** a time for masses, dinner at home, family fights, and opening presents—just like in the States.

[illegible]ndividual chapters in this book fo[illegible]letails about local festivals, or for info on national festivals celebrated in a special way in that area.

M[illegible]y, Money, Money, Money (Money!)

Th[illegible]cy in Mexico is the peso. The u[illegible]urrency sign $ is used to indicate pesos in Mexico, and so is used in this book. If the cost mentioned is in U.S. dollars, the symbol used is US$. Paper currency comes in denominations of 50, 100, 200, and 500 pesos. Coins come in denominations of 1, 2, 5, 10, and 20 pesos, and 20 and 50 centavos (100 centavos = 1 peso).

The current exchange rate for the U.S. dollar, and the one used in this book, is around $11 pesos; at that rate, an item that costs $11 pesos would be equivalent to US$1. Rates fluctuate, though, so make sure to check the exchange rates at **www.oanda.com/convert/classic** to see how your money will hold up during your stay in Mexico.

There is a value-added tax of 15% (Impuesto de Valor Agregado, or IVA) on almost everything in Mexico, including restaurant meals, bus tickets, and souvenirs. This charge decreases in the port cities of Cancún, Cozumel, and Los Cabos, where the IVA is 10%. In addition, there is an added 2% hotel bed tax added on top of the 10% to 15% IVA. The prices you see online and in advertisements for hotels and restaurants usually do *not* include the IVA. Plan accordingly.

ATMs & Banks

All large airports in Mexico have currency-exchange counters ***(casas de cambio).*** Though they don't give out the best rate, hitting one of these up upon arrival is better than changing money at home before your trip—do that, and you'll get the absolutely worst rate.

Banks offer better rates and are usually open weekdays from 9am until 5pm, and until 2pm or so on Saturday. In larger resorts and cities, you can usually exchange dollars anytime during business hours. Typically banks charge up to 1.5% of the transaction value when you withdraw cash but in addition some banks also apply a "foreign exchange charge" that can be up to 2.75% of the transaction value.

There are **ATMs** throughout Mexico. Be sure to check what the fee is for using the system, though, because they are sometimes exorbitant. The **Cirrus** (☎ **800/424-7787;** www.mastercard.com) and **PLUS** (☎ **800/843-7587;** www.visa.com) networks are worldwide; check the back of your bank card to see what network you're on, and don't forget to check your balance before you leave. If you're really anal, you can call or check online for ATM locations at your destination.

While ATMs are ubiquitous throughout Mexico, that doesn't mean they're totally risk free. There have been instances of ATM robberies, particularly in Mexico City, but less often at the beach resorts. Some guidebooks advise only using machines that are inside buildings, during the day,

Change Is Good

Getting change can sometimes be a problem if you have large bills, so do try to collect small bills. It's never a bad idea to walk out of the airport with some local currency in your pocket. You'll definitely want enough small pesos for taxi drivers who may not have change; it's also a good idea to carry small U.S. bills for emergencies and tips.

THE BASICS

but that's not really a practical approach. Just be sensible and take note of your surroundings, particularly if it's late and you're alone.

Credit Cards

Credit cards are another safe way to carry money. They provide a convenient record of all your expenses, and they generally offer relatively good exchange rates. You can also withdraw cash advances from your credit cards at banks or ATMs, provided you know your PIN. If you don't know yours, call the number on the back of your credit card and ask the bank to send it to you. It usually takes 5 to 7 business days, though some banks will provide the number over the phone if you tell them your mother's maiden name or the last four digits of your Social. It's also not a bad idea to call your credit card company to let them know of your upcoming trip—that way, you won't run the risk of having your card frozen for unusual activities.

MasterCard, Visa, and American Express cards are commonly accepted in Mexico,

Money Matters

Six Little Ways to Save Some Pesos

1. ***Habla español:*** Don't know what that means? Learn. The easiest way to lose money in Mexico is to not be able to haggle your way to a better price. If you don't speak Spanish, bring a friend who does. You'll be surprised how much you can save.
2. **Ask before entering:** Taxis are relatively cheap in Mexico, but so are the taxi drivers. Meaning, they will know that you are a tourist who doesn't know the set rates and will probably ask you for more than you really should pay. Ask someone at the front desk of your hostel or hotel how much a cab *should* cost to your destination before hailing one. Then ask the cab driver when you get in and make sure the two prices match up. Whenever possible, take the bus or walk.
3. **Fill 'er up!:** You're going to be drinking a lot of bottled water during your trip. Small convenience stores sell large bottles of water for almost the same price as the small bottles. Stock up on some big ones so then you can just keep refilling your small bottle. Not only will you save money, you'll also be doing the environment some good.
4. **Visit museums on Sundays or other free days:** Many of Mexico's museums, like the Museo Nacional de Antropologia in Mexico City, are free on Sundays, so plan your time accordingly. Granted, museums here don't cost *that* much to begin with, but neither does beer. You do the math.
5. **Strategize your meals:** Eat a large breakfast—it's the cheapest meal you can buy here—and then look for a late lunch at a *comida corrida* place to tide you over for most of the day. For dinner, you can simply have antojitos or snacks, and what you save can be contributed towards drinks.
6. **Work it if you're a woman:** Many bars and clubs in Mexico host ladies' nights, where you can drink for free or pay much less than usual. Shop around before deciding where to imbibe.

Rachel Tavel

What Things Cost in Mexico

As you'll see in this handy box, you can fill your stomach in Mexico for very little money with tacos, and you can get drunk cheaply with cerveza. *(*Note that prices can increase at fancy establishments, though.)*

Cappuccino + pastry	22 pesos
Bus/metro ticket	50 pesos
Small bottle of water	11 pesos
Can of soda	11 pesos
Fish or meat taco (takeout)	22 pesos
Mole dish*	44–88 pesos
Hot chocolate	11–33 pesos
Corona	11–33 pesos
Tequila shot	22–33 pesos
Postcard + int'l postage	11 pesos

and as in the U.S., most storefronts will post the logos of the cards they accept in the windows. Do note, however, that small businesses in Mexico (even in big cities) far prefer cash payment and will often lie about their credit card machine being out of order if they sense that you have enough cash to cover the purchase. Stand your ground, and you'll be amazed how quickly these credit card machines can spontaneously fix themselves! Deep down, shopkeepers know that the rest of the world's money is card-based, and they'd rather not lose the sale altogether.

Some places do add on a surcharge if you use a credit card—anywhere from 5% to 10%. Also keep in mind that many banks now assess a 1% to 3% "transaction fee" on all charges you incur abroad (whether you're using the local currency or U.S. dollars). But credit cards still may be the smart way to go when you factor in things like exorbitant ATM fees and the higher exchange rates and service fees you'll pay with traveler's checks.

Traveler's Checks

While your parents and the State Department will insist you take Traveler's Checks, know that trying to cash them will be a headache. Banks will take them, of course, but it will be a lengthy process and really, the rate won't be so great. Once upon a time they were essential, but that's not the case anymore. The only reason to take traveler's checks with you is if you don't have an ATM card, since personal U.S. checks are rarely accepted by Mexican hotels or banks.

You can buy traveler's checks at your bank before you leave or by calling **American Express** (☎ **800/807-6233** or 800/221-7282 for card holders); **Visa** (☎ **800/732-1322;** or AAA members can obtain Visa checks for a US$9.95 fee [for checks up to US$1,500] at most AAA offices or by calling ☎ 866/339-3378); and **MasterCard** (☎ **800/223-9920**).

Definitely keep a record of the serial numbers for your traveler's checks separate from your checks—you need to have those numbers to get your money back if you lose the checks.

Getting There

By Plane

Most major flights from North America to Mexico will take from 3 to 6 hours depending on how far south you're going (and how far north you're coming from). It's not advisable to arrive late at night if you have to travel by bus or car upon arrival since Mexican roads at night are extremely dangerous; try to book your flight to arrive accordingly.

Airfare to Mexico is most expensive at Christmas and Easter, and hotel rooms are also difficult to reserve at that time of year, so book in advance for the best rates. See "When to Go" earlier in this chapter for more advice on when to travel.

The main airlines operating direct or nonstop flights from the United States to Mexico include **Aero California** (☎ 800/237-6225; www.aerocalifornia.com), **AeroMexico** (☎ 800/237-6639; www.aeromexico.com), **Air France** (☎ 800/237-2747; www.airfrance.com), **Alaska Airlines** (☎ 800/252-7522; www.alaskaair.com), **America West** (☎ 800/327-7810; www.americawest.com), **Ameri-can Airlines** (☎ 800/223-5436; www.aa.com), **Continental** (☎ 800/537-9222; www.continental.com), **Delta Airlines** (☎ 800/221-1212; www.delta.com) **Frontier Airlines** (☎ 800/432-1359; www.frontierairlines.com), **Mexicana** (☎ 800/531-7921; www.mexicana.com), **Northwest/KLM** (☎ 800/225-2525; www.nwa.com), **Taca** (☎ 800/400-8222; www.taca.com), **United** (☎ 800/538-2929; www.united.com), and **US Air-ways** (☎ 800/428-4322; www.usairways.com). **Southwest Airlines** (☎ 800/435-9792; www.iflyswa.com) serves the U.S. border. The main departure points in North America for international airlines are Atlanta, Chicago, Dallas/Fort Worth, Denver, Houston, Las Vegas, Los Angeles, Miami, New York, Orlando, Philadelphia, Phoenix, Raleigh/Durham, San Antonio, San Francisco, Seattle, Toronto, and Washington, D.C. See individual [illegible]s for airlines that service your desti[illegible].

A great perk of flying **AeroM**[illegible]s opposed to domestic U.S. airlines is [illegible]plimentary drink cart, which offe[illegible]ited free beverages of everythi[illegible] Coca-Cola to the finest hard-to-find brands of scotch and tequila. Also, AeroMexico employs five-star chefs to create their free meals, including special vegetarian, kosher, and low-carb meals. (**Mexicana** does this as well, but AeroMexico does it better.)

Mexico charges an airport tax on all departures, which may or may not be included in the price of your ticket. Be prepared to pay a US$24 tax on international flights. Taxes on each domestic departure within Mexico are around US$17, unless you're on a connecting flight and have already paid at the start of the flight. Mexico also charges an US$18 "tourism tax," and if your ticket price does not include it, be sure to have enough money to pay it at the airport upon departure.

It doesn't hurt to reconfirm your flight even though Mexican airlines say it's not necessary.

BOOKING YOUR FLIGHT ONLINE

You can often find the best rates for tickets online with websites like **Travelocity** (www.travelocity.com, or www.travelocity.co.uk); **Expedia** (www.expedia.com, www.expedia.co.uk, or www.expedia.ca); and **Orbitz** (www.orbitz.com). A great site, **Kayak** (www.kayak.com) uses a sophisticated search engine that compares the lowest fares from many online sites including the three above.

Many airlines now offer online-only fares that even their phone agents know nothing about. For more on websites of airlines that fly to and from your destination, go to the "Getting There & Getting Around" section in individual chapters.

Last-minute deals can also be found via weekly e-mail services provided directly by the airlines. Most of these are announced on Tuesday or Wednesday and must be purchased online; many such as United are valid for travel that weekend. Sign up for weekly e-mail alerts at airline websites or check mega-sites that compile comprehensive lists of last-minute specials, such as Smarter Travel **(www.smartertravel.com).** For last-minute trips, **www.site59.com** and **http://us.lastminute.com** offer air-and-hotel package deals for much less than the major-label sites (however, it may not be that big of a bargain if based on double occupancy). If you do book a package, be sure the operator has a consumer-protection program; if they go out of business you will be out of luck.

Some More Sites to Surf for Bargains

- www.cheapflights.com
- www.hotwire.com
- www.opodo.co.uk
- www.priceline.com
- www.sidestep.com

OTHER CASH-SAVING TRAVEL IDEAS

- Check the travel section of local alternative newspapers for promotional specials or fare wars. You'll rarely see fare wars at peak travel times, but if you can travel in the off-peak months, you may get lucky. There are many agencies, for example, in Los Angeles that cater to immigrant communities that offer cheap charter fares to Mexico. ***Beware:*** Bucket shop tickets are usually nonrefundable or rigged with stiff cancellation penalties, often as high as 50% to 75% of the ticket price, and some put you on charter airlines, which may leave at inconvenient times and experience delays.
- Several reliable consolidators are worldwide and available online. **STA Travel** (☎ **800/781-4040;** www.statravel.com) is the world's top consolidator for students, but their fares are competitive for travelers of all ages. **ELTExpress** (☎ **800/TRAV-800;** www.flights.com) has excellent fares worldwide. They also have "local" websites in 12 countries. **FlyCheap** (☎ **800/FLY-CHEAP;** www.1800flycheap.com), owned by package-holiday megalith MyTravel, has especially good fares to sunny destinations. **Air Tickets Direct** (☎ **800/778-3447;** www.airticketsdirect.com) is based in Montreal and leverages the currently weak Canadian dollar for low fares; they also book trips to places that U.S. travel agents won't touch, such as Cuba.
- Most major airlines offer air/land packages to Mexico, including **American Airlines Vacations** (☎ **800/321-2121;** www.aavacations.com), **Delta Vacations** (☎ **800/221-6666;** www.deltavacations.com), **Continental Airlines Vacations** (☎ **800/301-3800;** www.covacations.com), and **United Vacations** (☎ **888/854-3899;** www.unitedvacations.com). Travel packages are also listed in the travel section of your Sunday newspaper or in national travel magazines such as *Arthur Frommer's Budget Travel Magazine.*

By Car

Driving is not the cheapest way to get to Mexico, but it is the best way to see the country. Even so, you may think twice about taking your own car south of the border once you've pondered the bureaucracy involved. If you decide to drive from the States and into mainland Mexico you must have a **Temporary Importation of Vehicle permit** (see "Car Permits," below), which you can get at the border or in advance of your trip. An easier option is to

THE BASICS

How to Stay Comfortable up in the Air

- With a little advance planning you can have a more comfortable flight, whether you're taking a fairly short flight from America or a longer one fr the U.K. or Australia. A great site to start your research at is **www.seatg com**. For international airlines, the research firm Skytrax has posted a lis average seat pitches at **www.airlinequality.com**.
- Emergency exit seats and bulkhead seats have the most legroom. Emergency exit seats are usually left unassigned until the day of a flight (to ensure that someone able-bodied fills the seats); it's worth getting to the ticket counter early to try to get one. Bulkhead seating (the row facing the wall at the front of the cabin) also has more legroom, but keep in mind that there are no seats under which you can put your carry on bags, and baby bassinets are often put here, so you may end up sitting next to a crying baby.
- Try for an aisle seat in a center section toward the back of coach to score two seats for yourself in a three-seat row. If you're traveling with a companion, book an aisle and a window seat. Middle seats are usually booked last, so it's possible you'll get three seats to yourselves.
- Ask about entertainment options. Many airlines offer seatback video systems where you get to choose your movies or play video games—but only on some of their planes. (Boeing 777s are your best bet.)
- Avoid the last row of any section or the row in front of an emergency exit, as these seats are the least likely to recline. Avoid seats near highly trafficked toilet areas. And avoid seats in the very back of many jets—these can be narrower than those in the rest of coach. You also may want to reserve a window seat so that you can rest your head and avoid being bumped in the aisle.
- Get up, walk around, and stretch every 60 to 90 minutes to keep your circulation going.
- Avoid alcohol and drink plenty of water before, during, and after your flight to keep hydrated and fight the lack of humidity in airplane cabins.

rent a car once you arrive and tour around a specific region.

See "Getting Around," later in this chapter, for specific tips on driving in Mexico. In addition, check with the U.S. State Department (see "Visitor Information," earlier in this chapter) for warnings about dangerous driving areas.

CAR PERMITS

If you're planning on driving to Mexico, you have to get a temporary import permit or risk having your car confiscated by Mexican Customs officials. To acquire a permit, you have to bring **a passport, valid international credit card (for bond purposes), the title for the car, a current car registration certificate, a current driver's license, a temporary importation application,** and pay a **processing fee** to either a Banjercito branch located at a Mexican Customs office at the port of entry, or to one of the Mexican consulates located in Austin, Chicago, Dallas, Houston, Los Angeles, Sacramento, San Bernardino, or San Francisco. Mexican law also requires the posting of a bond at a Banjercito (Mexican Army Bank) office to guarantee the departure of the car from Mexico within the time period determined at the time of the application. You can do this by using a credit card (American Express, Visa, or MasterCard). With a credit card, you are required to pay only a US$23 car-importation fee. The credit card must be in the same name as the car registration. If you do not have a major credit card (American Express, MasterCard, or Visa), you must post a bond or make a deposit equal to the value of the vehicle.

Important reminder: Someone else may drive, but the person (or relative of the person) whose name appears on the car-importation permit must *always* be in the car.

For more information, check out the Embassy of Mexico website at http://portal.sre.gob.mx/usa or call the **Embassy of Mexico** at ☎ **202/736-1000.** For up-to-the-minute information, another great source is the Customs office in Nuevo Laredo, or *Módulo de Importación Temporal de Automóviles, Aduana Nuevo Laredo* (☎ **867/712-2071**).

RETURNING TO THE UNITED STATES WITH YOUR CAR

You *must* return the car documents you obtained when you entered Mexico when you cross back with your car, or at some point within 180 days. (You can cross as many times as you wish within the 180 days.) If the documents aren't returned, heavy fines are imposed (US$250 for each 15 days late), your car may be impounded and confiscated, or you may be jailed if you return to Mexico. You can only return the car documents to a Banjercito official on duty at the Mexican aduana building *before* you cross back into the United States. Some border cities have Banjercito officials on duty 24 hours a day, but others do not; some do not have Sunday hours.

By Ship

Numerous cruise lines serve Mexico. Some (including whale-watching trips) cruise from California to the Baja Peninsula and ports of call on the Pacific coast, or from Houston or Miami to the Caribbean (which often includes stops in Cancún, Playa del Carmen, and Cozumel). Several cruise-tour specialists offer substantial discounts on unsold cabins if you're willing to take off at the last minute. One such company is **The Cruise Line,** 150 NW 168 St., North Miami Beach, FL 33169 (☎ **800/777-0707** or 305/521-2200).

By Bus

Taking a bus from the States to Mexico is certainly cheap, but it's an arduous process—you'll have to first wait some time at the border before crossing and then transfer buses once in Mexico. **Greyhound-Trailways** (or its affiliates; www.greyhound.com; ☎ **800/231-2222**) offers service from around the United States to the Mexican border, where passengers disembark, cross the border, and buy a ticket for travel farther into Mexico.

By Train

There really isn't a national rail service in Mexico, though trains do service the Cooper Canyon and Jalisco regions. In 2006, the government announced plans to build railways connecting Mexico City to its outskirts, but that's a ways off from completion.

As with bus service, we recommend you pay for the highest class of travel available. Primera Especial class is recommended for day trips and the top-of-the-line Pullman compartments for overnight travel. Pullman service offers sleeping compartments suitable for one *(camarin)* or two *(alcoba)*. Each converts to a comfortable sitting room during the day.

For more info on taking trains in Mexico, visit www.mexlist.com/railways.htm.

House Swapping

House swapping is becoming a more popular and viable means of travel; you stay in their place, they stay in yours, and you both get an authentic and personal view of the area, the opposite of the escapist retreat that many hotels offer. Try **HomeLink International** (www.homelink.org), the largest and oldest home-swapping organization, founded in 1952, with over 11,000 listings worldwide (US$75 for a yearly membership). **HomeExchange.org** (US$50 for 6,000 listings) and **InterVac.com** (US$69 for over 10,000 listings) are also reliable. Our favorite organization is **Couchsurfing.com**, though, because they don't charge membership fees. As long as you're willing to share your home space with fellow travelers, you can use the site to get free lodging while in Mexico—there's a long list of possibilities listed all over the country, and members skew younger and hipper than the other sites.

Staying There

Accommodations in Mexico include everything from a handful of hostels to low-end cabañas or palapas without any amenities to speak of, to standard hotel rooms, to condos that may rent by the week or month. Basically, you have many options, so read on below to help sort through them all.

Note: Air-conditioning isn't included in most hostels, cabañas, or palapas in Mexico and it's not necessarily a given in many midscale hotels. In general, this is a not a problem, though. Cooler nights and a well-placed ceiling fan are often more than enough to keep things chill, unless if we mention otherwise in reviews.

Camping

If you're really looking to save on accommodations, camping is definitely an option in some towns, especially along the northern Pacific Coast, around Mazatlán, and in Baja. It'll cost about US$3 to US$20 to pitch a tent fitting two, or US$10 to US$20 for two people with a car. Really the difference is less than US$10 a day to camp versus stay in a palapa or cabaña (read on for info) if you look around, though. Also keep in mind that not all beaches are *safe* for camping even if you can stay there. Try to check with the local tourist office or police before pitching a tent anywhere. It's also worthwhile getting a copy of *The People's Guide to RV Camping in Mexico* by Carl Franz if you'd like more info on campsites than what's mentioned in the chapters throughout this book.

Hostels

With prices starting at US$10 a night, dorm beds in hostel-style accommodations offer the cheapest option for staying in Mexico, if you rule out camping. Hostel booking policies vary dramatically. Some allow reservations and allow you to pay by credit card; others don't accept reservations and you have to pay cash. The best way to find out is to call the hostel first from home a few days before you're thinking of staying there (most don't book far in advance). If you're a member of **Hostelling International** (www.hihostels.com) you can often book days or even weeks in advance, though many private hostels won't let you do so. Once there, you'll notice that hostels vary in what services they offer. Lockouts, when the whole place is closed during the day, used to be the norm. That's not the case now, but you should always ask. Many hostels also have laundry facilities (but not detergent), lockers (but not locks), kitchens (but no food), beds (but no bedding)—you get the picture. Ask, ask, and ask again. It's best not to be surprised.

For additional info about Mexican hostels, get in touch with **Hostelling Mexico, A.C.,** Guatemala 4, Colonia Centro, Mexico D.F. (☎ **555/518-1726;** www.hostellingmexico.com), or the **Associacion Mexicana de Albergues Juveniles, A.C.** (www.hostels.com/en/mx.htm), which are organizations affiliated with Hostelling International.

Cabañas & Palapas

Palapas are open sided, thatched roof buildings that dot many of the country's beaches. For only about US$2 to US$10, you can usually rent a hammock and stay in one—or bring your own hammock and pay less. Beachside palapas are great budget options because they allow the breeze to flow through and they feel exotic and romantic (as long as the bugs stay away). Cabañas are slightly fancier options—they're essentially hut dwellings with beds and cost about US$10 to US$35 a night. Some include amenities like fans and fridges.

Posadas

Bed-and-breakfasts, or *posadas,* are pretty common in Mexico these days. Rooms vary from US$75 for singles and US$100 for doubles, but like bed-and-breakfasts in other parts of the world, whatever price you pay includes breakfast. In addition to the highlights we've listed here, check out www.inncrawler.com for links to info on posadas in Mexico.

Hotels

Mexican hotels start at the lowest common denominator (a Motel 6 or one-star hotel) and work up from there (a five-diamond resort). The hotel rating system in Mexico is based on a "Stars and Diamonds" system and hotels can qualify to be rated from one to five stars or diamonds. Some perfectly fine hotels aren't certified; at the same time, some rated hotels are, well, less than star or diamond worthy. The guidelines relate to service, facilities, and hygiene more than to prices.

Five-diamond hotels meet the highest requirements: The beds are cushy and the room well kept, the bathrooms work and are clean, amenities like a hair dryer are on hand, all facilities are renovated regularly, and your rental car won't get broken into. Five-star hotels are essentially the same but without the bragging rights; the level of service is not that much different and while the elevators may not be quite as fast or clean, really, who cares? Four-star hotels are less expensive and more basic, but they are still super clean and safe. You'll probably be able to brush your teeth out of the tap (See p. 37 for tips on drinking water here, though) and there will be plenty of hot water. Three-, two-, and one-star hotels are a case of you get what you pay for. Bathrooms are kept relatively clean and linens are washed daily, and you can expect a minimum standard of service. Two- and one-star hotels generally provide bottled water rather than purified water.

The nonprofit organization Calidad Mexicana Certificada, A.C., known as **Calmecac** (www.calmecac.com.mx), is responsible for hotel ratings. For additional details about the rating system, visit Calmecac's website.

Picking the Beach Resort That's Right for You

Each of Mexico's beach resorts has its own distinct character, so following is a *very* brief rundown to get you started on choosing the right one for you. Check out

Rooms to Die (Splurge?) For

Why bother staying in a cookie cutter impersonal chain ho[...] a completely personalized experience where the hotelier g[...] The boutique hotel experience in Mexico is the only way t[...] get the most bang for your buck. Located in unique or idy[...] **Boutique Hotels** (www.mexicoboutiquehotels.com) speci[...] ties that are always different, and always worth the money. Most of the members of this group have fewer than 50 rooms, and the accommodations can consist of anything from entire villas to *casitas* (apartments or homes), bungalows, or a combination. Mexico is not as cheap as it once was, but if you're ready to splurge even a little—the difference in price is truly minimal—these are the places to do it. All are highly recommended.

the individual chapters throughout this book for more specific information.

If you're looking for an easy introduction to Mexico's beaches while enjoying world-class shopping and amazing nightlife in a pampered environment, **Cancún** is your beach. If underwater diving is your most important criteria for choosing a beach instead of nightlife, then **Cozumel** is a good option—it's considered by many to be one of the world's top diving spots. Nearby **Isla de Mujeres** is a viable alternative if you like snorkeling.

If you love getting away from it all, a town like **Playa del Carmen** along the Riviera Maya is the natural choice—Playa attracts outdoorsy types looking for a combination of simplicity and variety (it's close to Maya ruins and colonial cities).

If you're an avid golfer, head to **Puerto Vallarta**—though it has first-class golf resorts, it also has an ideal mix of great restaurants and bars and outdoor options from mountain biking to surfing; it's really a great choice for anyone.

Nearby **Mazatlán** is another good outdoorsy option—it probably best represents the golden beaches, fresh seafood, and inexpensive accommodations that typified spring-breakers' opinions of Mexico in the first place.

If you can't decide between a modern beach resort and a typical Mexican seaside village, then consider **Ixtapa** and **Zihuatanejo.** Ixtapa is a model of modern infrastructure and services while Zihuatanejo is the quintessential Mexican village—since they're within less than 7km (4⅓ miles) of each other, you can probably stay at both.

Acapulco is a good choice if you want to dine at midnight, dance till dawn, and sleep all day on the sun-soaked beach—it's known for its sultry beaches for tanning during the day and its glitzy discos for partying at night.

The resort found farthest south along Mexico's Pacific coastline, **Huatulco** is the perfect place for those travelers who want to enjoy pristine beaches and jungle landscapes but would rather view them from a luxury-hotel balcony. Located just north along the Pacific coastline from Huatulco, **Puerto Escondido** is known for its great surf, breathtaking beaches, friendly locals, and inexpensive prices. It's definitely the place for surfers, but, since it's not a planned development, it's also great for those looking for a funky, relaxed attitude.

In terms of everything from taxis to dining out, Los Cabos is much more expensive than other Mexican beach resorts—that's

To All-Inclusive or Not?

Staying at an all-inclusive resort definitely has its perks: You'll be right on the beach; you can eat and drink unlimited amounts at a pre-paid price; and you won't have to worry about money during a week of sweet excess. On the other hand, an all-inclusive makes it easy never to leave the hotel grounds and explore all that the town has to offer. (Why would you when everything outside costs money and everything in the hotel is free?) Before you choose which way to go, it is important to decide what kind of vacation you have in mind. If you just want to go from hotel to beach and back again without a worry in the world, an all-inclusive may be what you need. If you'd like to soak in some authentic culture, though, an inclusive won't be for you.

because everything needs to be trucked down the peninsula. That said, the quaint town of **San José del Cabo,** the high-energy tourist enclave of **Cabo San Lucas,** and the 29km (18-mile) stretch of highway connecting the two, **The Corridor,** has great sport-fishing, golfing, and beaches and incredibly hip nightlife. It's also one of the most Americanized parts of Mexico—it can sometimes feel like an extension of Southern California. Does that sound like a good thing to you? If so, then Northern Baja's **Ensenada** and **Rosarito Beach** might be up your alley—though close enough to the border to be pretty Americanized, they're friendly beach towns; Rosarito has great surfing, and Ensenada is known for its fishing.

Booking Your Hotel Online

Shopping online for hotels is generally done by either booking through the hotel's own website or through an independent booking agency (or a fare-service agency like Priceline; see below). There are many Internet hotel agencies competing for your business, which is great if you have the patience and time to shop and compare the online sites for good deals. Remember that hotels at the top of a site's listing may be there just because they paid money to get the placement. Many of these places are generic American-style places; stay in one of them, and you may as well stay in Florida. Or just stay home. Of the major three sites, **Expedia** (www.expedia.com) offers a long list of special deals and "virtual tours" or photos of available rooms so you can see what you're paying for. **Travelocity** (www.travelocity.com) posts unvarnished customer reviews and ranks its properties according to the AAA rating system. **Trip Advisor** (www.tripadvisor.com) is another excellent source of unbiased user reviews of hotels. While even the finest hotels can inspire a misleadingly poor review from picky or crabby travelers, the body of user opinions, when taken as a whole, is usually a reliable indicator.

Other reliable online booking agencies include **Hotels.com** and **Quikbook.com.** An excellent free program, **TravelAxe** (www.travelaxe.net), can help you search multiple hotel sites at once, even ones you may never have heard of—and conveniently lists the total price of the room, including the taxes and service charges. Another booking site, **Travelweb** (www.travelweb.com), is partly owned by the hotels it represents (including the Hilton, Hyatt, and Starwood chains) and is plugged directly into the hotels' reservations systems—unlike independent online agencies, which have to fax or e-mail reservation requests to the hotel. If that e-mail or fax gets lost, though, you may arrive at your hotel only to be told that they have no reservation. To be fair, many of the major sites are improving in service and ease of use, and Expedia will soon be able to plug directly into the reservations systems of many hotel chains. Get a confirmation number and bring along a printout of any online booking transaction just in case.

Saving Pesos on Accommodations Before You Go

The rack rate is the maximum legal rate that a hotel can charge for a room. Almost no one pays this price, however, except during peak season or on holidays. To get a better deal:

- **Book early.** If you make a habit of showing up at hotels without a reservation, you may get stuck paying more than what you like. Since the best-value accommodations in good locations tend to be fairly well known, try to book early. We've listed the best budget hotel and hostel options in this book, but many of them are small, with fewer than 20 rooms. If you wait too long to call or e-mail for a reservation, rooms (and others in the same price range) could be gone, and all that's left might cost 50% to 100% more.
- **Book online.** Some of the hote listed in this book offer Internet discounts, so check their websit the best rates and special seaso offers. Conversely, other hotels rooms to Priceline, Hotwire, or E at rates lower than the ones you through the hotels themselves. Shop around. And if you have special requests—a quiet room, a room with a view—call the hotel directly and tell them after you've booked online.
- **Location, location, location.** You'll usually save some money if you're willing to settle for a bed away from the charming heart of town, or a few blocks from the beach. Always keep in mind that the cheapest room may be the one *without* a view. See "Getting the Best Room" later in this section for tips on getting a quality vs. cheap room.
- **Travel midweek or off season.** Resort hotels are most crowded, and therefore most expensive, on weekends, so better discounts can be had for midweek stays. In contrast, business hotels in downtown locations are busiest during the week, so you can often expect discounts over the weekend. Almost all Mexican hotels have

Rent Your Own *Casita*

If you're staying in town 3 nights or more, consider booking a house or apartment. You can find many great, reasonably priced places online that may include mountain bikes or kayaks or snorkel equipment. Renting a home is especially a good option if you're going with friends, and a great way to save money on food since most places have kitchens. It may not be the best way to meet other people, but you can stay in a prime location for a fraction of what a hotel room would cost and spend your extra cash at clubs meeting locals. And just think of how much fun you can have shopping at the local market, and cooking some of your own meals.

One good option for renting is Vacation Rentals by Owner (**VRBO;** www.vrbo.com). They have over 33,000 homes and condominiums for rent worldwide, including a large selection in Mexico.

high-season and low-season prices, and booking the day after "high season" ends can result in discounts.

Saving Pesos When You're There

- Hotels can charge astronomical rates for in-room calls; get a Ladatel card instead and make calls from public phones on the streets. Find out how much your cell will cost as well before you start running up charges that will definitely ruin your trip. See p. 47 for phone tips.
- Most hotels that have Internet access (in-room broadband or Wi-Fi, or a public terminal in a common area), won't charge you for it; but it doesn't hurt to check. If there's a charge when you log on, you'll get a page telling you that you need to pay a certain fee per hour or per day.
- Hitting up the minibar is a no-no, unless you stock it yourself. Those little bottles of whiskey and beers will cost you a fortune, so buy your own snacks and drinks on the sly and store them in the minibar.
- Always ask about local taxes and service charges, which can increase the cost of a room by 15% or more. Smaller, family-run hotels include the tax (IVA) in the room charge, while larger, more expensive hotels often tack the IVA charge on top of the already exorbitant room rate, so check it out before you check in.
- If you get a surprise charge that wasn't mentioned at check in or prominently posted in the room, or a "resort fee" for amenities you didn't use, you can often make a case for getting it removed. Tell them you're going to complain to the local tourism board and they may change their mind.

Getting the Best Room

Usually rooms in the back of the hotel or on a corner are quieter; corner ones can also have more light and be larger. That is unless you're staying on a busy street and want to stay up all night observing the scene. When you make your reservation, find out if the hotel is renovating; if it is, get a room away from the construction. Also consider asking about nonsmoking rooms, rooms with views, and rooms that face an interior garden or pool. And if you really hate your room, don't be shy—ask nicely to see another one. Most places really don't care about switching your spot.

When making your reservation, you may want to ask basic questions like if you'll need to share a room or bathroom (in hostels); if there's a safe or place to keep valuables; if there's air-conditioning or fans/ mosquito nets; if breakfast is included; if there's a fridge you can use; if there's a shuttle from the airport and, and if not, how to get from there to the hotel. You may also want to ask what the check-in/check-out time is and if they have Internet access—either a public terminal in the lobby or Wi-Fi throughout the property.

Health & Safety

Staying Healthy

Although there are no required vaccinations when entering Mexico, it is important that you are up to date with all immunizations as defined by the Advisory Committee on Immunization Practice (ACIP). Major vaccinations include Tetanus, Hepatitis B, MMR, and chickenpox if necessary. It is also always a good idea to see your doctor 4 to 6 weeks prior to your departure for a regular check-up and to make sure you

Before You Leave: The Checklist

Here are a few things you might want to do before you walk out th ensure that you have the most efficient and drama-free trip to Me love the idea of packing a bag and heading to paradise, but it nev take a moment to check into details.

- Don't forget your passport as well as your tickets and your confirmation number, and the credit card you purchased your tickets with if you have e-tickets. It's also a good idea to bring along copies of your airline tickets and passport—just don't pack them with the originals.
- Leave copies of your itinerary and your passport with a friend or relative in the U.S. And it can't hurt to bring the name of someone at home to contact in case you have a serious illness or an accident.
- Remember to bring your student ID card, ISIC card, or any other ID cards that could entitle you to discounts, and make copies of them (again, keep them separate from the originals).
- Make a point of finding out where the U.S. Embassy or consulate is located in the cities you're visiting. Luckily for you, we've listed all the embassies in the cities we covered in this book; if you're going anywhere else, look up the address online (http://mexico.usembassy.gov). The U.S. Embassy site is also worth a visit to find out about travel warnings.
- You really don't need to book museums, theater tickets, or special events in advance in Mexico, but for special cases, we've listed the website info throughout this book. If you want to go deep-sea fishing or take another outdoor adventure, though, you should definitely try to book that in advance. See "Adventure Tours & Resources" below for some options.
- How's the weather? Look it up (www.weather.com) and pack accordingly. See the "What to Pack for a 2-Week Stay at the Beach" box earlier for more tips on packing.
- Check the current exchange rate at www.oanda.com/convert/classic.
- Check your daily ATM withdrawal limit (it's usually 3,000 pesos at Mexican banks). Write down your credit card PINs, in case of emergency.
- It's a good idea to notify your bank/credit card companies that you will be traveling in Mexico to avoid automatic account freezes for suspicious activity.
- If you purchased traveler's checks, remember to write down the check numbers someplace separate from the checks.
- Think about how you're going to keep your money. Do you have a money belt or a safe, accessible place to store it? Take small locks for your suitcase or knapsack so you can lock valuables inside if there isn't a safe in your room.
- Bring any emergency drug prescriptions (although you can pretty much get prescription drugs in Mexico over the counter) and extra glasses and/or contact lenses and a small bottle of lens fluid, which can be hard to find.
- If using a mobile phone from the U.S., call your provider to find out the rates and how to unlock it so that you can use it with local SIM cards, available at TelMex outlets (see p. 46 under "Phone Home").

have enough prescription medications to last your entire stay.

For more information, contact the **International Association for Medical Assistance to Travelers** (IAMAT; ☎ **716/754-4883** or, 416/652-0137 in Canada; www.iamat.org) for tips on travel and health concerns in the countries you're visiting, and for lists of local, English-speaking doctors. The United States **Centers for Disease Control and Prevention** (☎ **800/311-3435;** www.cdc.gov/travel) provides up-to-date information on health hazards by region or country and offers tips on food safety. The website **www.tripprep.com**, sponsored by a consortium of travel medicine practitioners, may also offer helpful advice on traveling abroad. You can find listings of reliable clinics overseas at the **International Society of Travel Medicine** (www.istm.org).

If you suffer from a chronic illness, consult your doctor before your departure. For conditions like epilepsy, diabetes, or heart problems, wear a **MedicAlert identification tag** (☎ **888/633-4298;** www.medicalert.org), which will alert doctors to your condition and give them access to your records through MedicAlert's 24-hour hotline.

For the latest information about travel advisories and conditions, check with the Consular Affairs home page, http://travel.state.gov. You can also call from abroad to the **Overseas Citizens Services** call center at ☎ **202/501-4444.**

For info on pharmacies in Mexico, see "Nuts & Bolts," p. 71.

DIRTY WATER

Well, where should we begin? If you have never been to Mexico before, you should expect to be a little, well, looser than usual. Because of the new bacteria that will be going into your system, you can expect to have a little bit of an upset stomach now and again. This is *not* Montezuma's Revenge. This is normal. Food poisoning (often called Montezuma's Revenge or *turista*) is marked by severe projectile vomiting and uncontrollable diarrhea. You'll know the difference. The more frequently you go to Mexico, the less often minor stomach upsets will occur. And the longer you stay in Mexico the more likely you'll get sick upon returning. It's a no-win situation.

But how can you try to prevent getting sick? The U.S. Public Health Service recommends the following measures for preventing travelers' diarrhea: **Drink only purified water** (boiled water, canned or bottled beverages, beer, or wine). **Choose food carefully.** In general, avoid salads (except in first-class restaurants), uncooked vegetables, undercooked protein, and unpasteurized milk or milk products, including cheese. Choose food that is freshly cooked and still hot. In addition, something as simple as **clean hands** can go a long way toward preventing turista.

Basically, you can lessen your chances of getting ill by paying attention to what (and who) you put in your mouth. Don't feel shy about asking if the ice cubes in your drink are from purified water. Dry off the tops of cans before you open them. Avoid brushing your teeth with tap water. Don't kiss the street dogs.

As for fruit and veggies, the general rule of thumb is that if you can't peel it, then purify it. You can buy "gotas" at most markets, which are iodine drops that you add to water, to use for soaking the fruit. Take special care to separate leaves of lettuce; berries also need extra purification since they retain so much water from the ground.

If you're spending more than 6 months in Mexico and are traveling outside major resort areas, it's a good idea to go to a local

Beach Health & Safety

Ever had "surfer's flu"? During rainy season, the polluted rivers feeding into the bays near beach towns or cities can give you a nasty viral infection. It's best not to go into the water after a heavy rain if the water is stirred up or muddy.

Although most of Mexico's beaches don't have lifeguards, some like Zicatela Beach and La Punta in Puerto Escondido and the city beaches in Mazatlán have added stands. Many of the lifeguards are volunteers so, although they take CPR courses every 6 months from the local Red Cross, they're simply not professionals. Watch for those red warning flags on the beach, folks, and don't take a chance. At experienced surfing spots, don't venture into the water at the main break without a board even if it looks shallow, because the undertow can often reportedly suck you under and not let you up for a kilometer. And don't drink or smoke anything that makes you think you really can swim out there. Mother Nature always wins.

If you do get caught in a rip, don't fight it. Float on your back and stay calm; as the current pulls you forward, paddle with it. As it pulls you back, just let it go. Eventually you will work your way out at an angle as it curves out to sea. Try to continue swimming parallel to the beach. Never attempt to swim directly out of a strong current as you will just exhaust yourself. Recently in Puerto Escondido, a man was pulled out to sea and could not be found; he appeared 24 hours later since the current carried him back to Puerto.

Finally, when picking a beach keep in mind the following color coding for the tide levels:

White = Perfect conditions (with the exceptions of some towns, like Mazatlán)
Green = Safe waters
Yellow = Use caution (experienced surfers only)
Red or Black = Don't even think about it

Ann Summa

clinic and get checked for amoebas, which can attack your system without any visible symptoms for months or even years.

If you *do* get a nervous belly, be sure to keep hydrated; drink lots of water and Gatorade or Pediolyte, an electrolyte replacement fluid that you can find in most pharmacies. A doctor may prescribe Lomatil or Imodium but we recommend taking these only in case of emergency. You can probably control sickness simply by taking Pepto-Bismol and eating plain white rice with salt (and black sesame if you can find it). Ride it out for a few days and you'll probably be fine.

BUGS, BITES & OTHER WILDLIFE CONCERNS

Scorpion and snakes, oh my. Lots of wild critters are crawling around Mexico, so take a small flashlight and wear good shoes when going to the bathroom outdoors at night. Shake out your pillows and check your bed and clothes before jumping into them, too.

You probably won't ever see an *alacrán* (scorpion) during your visit, but wear long pants and protective shoes when you're out hiking just in case. If one still stings you, go immediately to a doctor. In Mexico you can buy scorpion toxin antidote at any drugstore. It is an injection and it costs around US$25. Buying some in advance is a good idea if you plan to camp in a remote area where medical assistance can be several hours away.

While hiking, also wear long pants and good shoes in order to avoid bites by potentially lethal snakes like the blue coral. If you're unlucky enough to get bitten by one of those, you can get antivenom and a syringe at most pharmacies. We recommend that you get to a doctor as quickly as possible, though.

Malaria & Dengue Fever

You're in the lush tropics and jungle here, so mosquitoes (and every other kind of bug) come with the territory. What's that buzzing sound, you ask? Maybe malaria, maybe dengue fever, maybe just a bite that will fester and turn into a nasty ulcer that goes down to the bone. Mosquitoes are part of the environment and they do carry diseases, possibly malaria in the backwoods parts of Campeche, Chiapas, Guerrero, Michoacán, Nayarit, Oaxaca, Quintana Roo, Jalisco, Sinaloa, Sonora, Durango, Chihuahua, and Tabasco. But generally you don't need to worry about malaria in resort areas along the Pacific and Gulf coasts.

One natural way to avoid bites is to take complex B12 with B6 at 200mg for a week; then you can cut back. Also, stay someplace clean, and check that bottles and cans aren't left out by your sleeping area—they collect rainwater and breed mosquitoes. And always use a topical mosquito repellent containing DEET such as Bayer Autan. If you can stand the smell, you can also try mosquito coils, which burn like incense and contain chemicals that repel mosquitoes. You can pick up mosquito coils just about everywhere here; they're sold in stores under the name Raid-O-Litos.

Other ways to avoid being bitten include wearing long-sleeved shirts and pants, especially during twilight (the peak feeding time). At night, sleep under a mosquito net or with a fan directly on you. Mosquito bed nets *(mosquiteros)* are available in Mexican markets and stores, and tucking one under your mattress will provide protection against scorpions and spiders as well.

Some doctors recommend taking the anti-malarial drug chloroquine before your trip, but this seems like overkill to us. If you're only headed to resorts and major cities, you'll be safe if you simply take all the precautions mentioned earlier.

If you get bitten and simply want to ease itching, try an "itch-stick" or sting gel; calendula is a great natural remedy for itching. Other natural remedies include applying lime juice (some swear by this!) or citronella oil which should be re-applied every 30 minutes (bring with you or buy in a large Mexican city).

HIV/AIDS

Although locals may deny it, AIDS is still a problem in Mexico. Though it's much more prevalent in small villages due to many factors, including lack of education and lack of money for protection, AIDS is also prevalent in beach cities. And although prostitution is somewhat regulated (sex workers have semi-required check-ups in Oaxaca city, for example) that doesn't mean sex is safe here. It's warm, you aren't wearing a lot of clothes, you're drinking too much, and inhibitions are down, but don't be stupid! Use protection. Remember that condoms that are not latex are less effective against disease transmission and pregnancy and should be avoided.

As with any destination, you should always avoid shared needles for tattoos, piercings, or injections of any kind. Always make sure that you watch the establishment open a fresh needle—again, it's not worth the risk.

AIR QUALITY/ALTITUDE SICKNESS

If you're having trouble breathing, you're either at a high altitude or in Mexico City, where the air quality is funky on a *good* day. It's typically full of ozone, hydrocarbons, industrial pollutants, and a daily dose of 600 tons of fecal dust thanks to the fact that as many as 3 million of the city's inhabitants have no sewage system. Fifty years ago the air here was among the world's cleanest, with an average visibility of about 11km (7 miles). Now visibility is less than 1.6km (1 mile), if that. Ozone levels are twice as high here as the maximum allowed limit for 1 hour a year.

Not much can be done about the poor air in Mexico City, but you can take steps to help **elevation sickness,** which results from the relative lack of oxygen and the decrease in barometric pressure that characterizes high elevations (more than 1,500m/5,000 ft.). Symptoms include shortness of breath, fatigue, headache, insomnia, and even nausea. Mexico City is at 2,100m (6,888 ft.) above sea level, as are a number of other central and southern cities. At high elevations, it takes about 10 days to acquire the extra red blood corpuscles you need to adjust to the scarcity of oxygen. To help your body acclimate, drink plenty of fluids, avoid alcoholic beverages, and don't overexert yourself during the first few days. If you have heart or lung problems, talk to your doctor before going above 2,400m (7,872 ft.).

SHOULD YOU GET SICK . . .

Just about every major beach resort area will have adequate medical care. There have been complaints that health care facilities in beach resorts have overcharged or provided unnecessary care but this is the exception, more than the rule. In addition, any foreign consulate can provide a list of area doctors who speak English. Many hospitals also have walk-in clinics for emergency cases that are not life-threatening; you may not get immediate attention, but you won't pay the high price of an emergency room visit. We list hospitals and emergency numbers under "Nuts & Bolts," in most chapters.

If you're injured in an accident and need immediate medical attention, call the **Mexican Red Cross** at ☎ **55/5395-1111,** 55/5557-5758, 55/5557-5759, or 55/5557-5760. While the service is free, the Red Cross does request that patients give a donation. The Red Cross ambulance will deliver the patient to the nearest Red Cross hospital, which provides basic care.

In extreme medical emergencies, a service from the United States will fly people to American hospitals. **Global Lifeline** (☎ **888/554-9729,** or 01-800/305-9400 in Mexico; www.globallifeflight.com) is a 24-hour air ambulance.

Basic Medicine Kit

- Bug spray that contains DEET or natural bug repellent
- Prescription medicines (and copies of the prescriptions)
- Contact lens solutions
- Toothbrush and dental floss
- Pepto-Bismol and other toiletries
- Sunblock and lip balm

COVERING HEALTH CARE COSTS

It's always good to make sure that you have a U.S. (or other home country) health insurance policy and that you have checked with them to see how they may or may not cover medical attention in Mexico. Most health plans (including Medicare and Medicaid) do not provide coverage, and the ones that do often require you to pay for services upfront and reimburse you only after you

Diving Tips: So That's Why They Call It the Bends

Ever wonder why they call recompression sickness the bends? Contrary to popular opinion, it doesn't make you double over in pain. When your body is placed under a lot of pressure, the gasses in it condense, and if you go deep enough, these eventually become liquids. If you surface too quickly without doing the standard safety stops on the way up (or if you're dehydrated or hung over) the nitrogen that has become liquid doesn't have enough time to dissipate, and so it forms bubbles in your joints as you surface—the same way bubbles rise to the top of a Coke bottle when you open it. The nitrogen bubbles cause joint pain in victims of recompression sickness, which makes them unable to stretch bent joints straight without excruciating pain. Divers who have the bends tend to keep all of their joints awkwardly bent, hence the name. The reason recompression sickness or "the bends" is so dangerous is because if one of those nitrogen bubbles enters your brain or heart it could cause a stroke or heart attack and become life-threatening. So even if you are experiencing mild joint pain after a dive, take it seriously and make a trip to the nearest hyperbaric chamber.

Sara Lieber

return home. As a safety net, you may want to buy travel medical insurance, particularly if you're traveling to a remote or high-risk area where emergency evacuation is a possible scenario. If you require additional medical insurance, try **MEDEX Assistance** (☎ **410/453-6300;** www.medexassist.com) or **Travel Assistance International** (☎ **800/821-2828;** www.travelassistance.com; for general information on services, call the company's Worldwide Assistance Services, Inc., at ☎ **800/777-8710**).

Staying Safe

CRIME

You will probably feel physically safer in most Mexican cities and villages than in any comparable place at home. The crime rate is, on the whole, much lower in Mexico than in most parts of the United States, and the nature of crimes in general is less violent. Random, violent, or serial crime is fairly unheard of in Mexico. However, crime in Mexico has received attention in the North American press over the past several years. Many feel this unfairly exaggerates the real dangers, but it should be noted that crime rates, including taxi robberies, kidnappings, and highway carjackings, have risen in recent years. Check the U.S. State Department advisory (http://travel.state.gov) before you travel to read up on any notable "hot spots."

In case of emergency, call ☎ **555/250-0123,** the 24-hour hotline of the **Mexican Ministry of Tourism.** They also have a national toll free number (☎ **800/903-9200**). Or you can call the Mexican "911": In Mexico City, dial ☎ **060;** in the rest of Mexico, dial ☎ **066.**

Cabo, Mazatlán, and Puerto Vallarta all have their own tourist police whose only job is to keep the tourists coming. So many people depend upon the tourist dollar that muggings, robberies, rapes, and murders are rare. Even though **Tijuana** had 400 murders in 2006 and **Acapulco** suffered from a spate of killings in 2006, both are considered safe for tourists. (In fact, both destinations have made extra efforts to reinforce security in 2007.)

That doesn't mean you can wander around drunk on a deserted beach at night. Use your common sense. You can generally trust people whom you approach for help or directions—but be wary of anyone who approaches you offering the same. The more insistent the person is, the more cautious you should be. Travelers should also exercise caution in traveling Mexico's highways, avoiding travel at night, and using toll *(cuota)* roads rather than the less secure "free" *(libre)* roads whenever possible. There *have* been robberies on buses, particularly second- and third-class buses that don't use the *cuota* (toll) roads. One route that the U.S. Embassy warns about is the bus from Acapulco to Ixtapa or Huatulco. It is also advised that you should not hike alone in backcountry areas, nor walk alone on lightly frequented beaches, ruins, or trails.

The most severe crime problems have been concentrated in **Mexico City,** where taxi robberies from non-licensed cabbies and pick pockets (especially on the Metro), and purse snatchers are fairly common. Though there's been a wave of "express" kidnappings here that involve snatching somebody just long enough to empty out an ATM account, those are generally targeted at the very wealthy. You can avoid being a victim by staying in safe areas, not wearing flashy jewelry, and not always trusting a man in uniform. If you suspect that the "policeman" who's shaking you down is not a real cop, ask for identification. Insist on going to the station. Finally, although you will pay more for an airport taxi from Mexico City's Benito Juarez International Airport, it's a good idea at the start of your trip when you're disoriented and tired. Definitely avoid the use of the **green Volkswagen taxis,** many of which have been involved in "pirate" robberies, muggings, and kidnappings.

CONSUMER CRIME

American citizens should exercise caution when considering time-share investments and be aware of aggressive tactics used by some time-share sales representatives. Buyers should be fully informed and take sufficient time to consider their decisions before signing time-share contracts, ideally after consulting an independent attorney. Mexican law allows time-share purchasers 5 days to cancel the contract for unconditional and full reimbursement. U.S. citizens should never sign a contract that includes clauses penalizing the buyer who cancels within 5 days.

A formal complaint against any merchant should be filed with **PROFECO,** Mexico's federal consumer protection agency. PROFECO has the power to mediate disputes, investigate consumer complaints, order hearings, levy fines and sanctions for not appearing at hearings, and do price-check inspections of merchants. All complaints by Americans are handled by PROFECO's English-speaking office in Mexico City at ☎ **55/5211-1723.**

For info on how to spin the time-share experience in your favor, see the "Sharing My Time with Only You" box, p. 404).

Bribes & Scams

As is the case around the world, there are the occasional bribes and scams in Mexico, targeted at people believed to be naive—such as the telltale tourist. For years Mexico was known as a place where bribes, called *mordidas* (bites), were expected; however, the country is rapidly changing. Frequently, offering a bribe today, especially to a police officer, is considered an insult, and it can land you in deeper trouble.

If you believe a **bribe** is being requested, here are a few tips on dealing with the situation. Even if you speak Spanish, don't utter a word of it to Mexican officials. That way you'll appear innocent, all the while understanding every word.

When you are crossing the border, should the person who inspects your car ask for a tip, you can ignore this request—but understand that the official may suddenly decide that a complete search of your belongings is in order. If faced with a situation where you feel you're being asked for a *propina* (literally, "tip"; colloquially, "bribe"), how much should you offer? Usually US$3 to US$5 or the equivalent in pesos will do the trick. Many tourists have the impression that everything works better in Mexico if you "tip"; however, in reality, this only perpetuates the mordida attitude. If you are pleased with a service, feel free to tip, but you shouldn't tip simply to attempt to get away with something illegal or inappropriate, whether it is crossing the border without having your car inspected or not getting a ticket that's deserved.

Whatever you do, **avoid impoliteness;** under no circumstances should you insult a Latin American official. Extreme politeness, even in the face of adversity, rules in Mexico. In Mexico, gringos have a reputation for being loud and demanding. By adopting the local custom of excessive courtesy, you'll have greater success in negotiations of any kind. Stand your ground, but do it politely.

As you travel in Mexico, you may encounter several types of **scams,** which are typical throughout the world. One involves some kind of a **distraction** or feigned commotion. While your attention is diverted, a pickpocket makes a grab for your wallet. In another common scam, an **unaccompanied child** pretends to be lost and frightened and takes your hand for safety. Meanwhile the child or an accomplice plunders your pockets. A third involves **confusing currency.** A shoeshine boy, street musician, guide, or other individual might offer you a service for a price that seems reasonable—in pesos. When it comes time to pay, he or she tells you the price is in dollars, not pesos. Be very clear on the price and currency when services are involved.

Breaking the Law

Remember. You are in Mexico, and if you commit a crime, you are subject to full prosecution under the Mexican judicial system. This is a system based on Roman and Napoleonic law which means 1) You are guilty until proven innocent and 2) There is no trial by jury or writ of habeas corpus. Sentencing may take 10 months and you are not allowed bail until after that (as long as you get fewer than 5 years). And if you do get into trouble, you'll have plenty of company. More Americans are arrested in Mexico—more than 1,000 a year—than in any other country worldwide. They also hold the most incarcerated Americans—more than 800 at any given time. If you are busted, you have the right to talk to an American consul (if you request it), but they can't do much other than notify your chagrined relatives and make sure you are treated "fairly." In addition, your request may take months to actually go through.

So, let's say you are headed for prison. Well, good luck with that. You'll be paying thousands for your own food, medical care, and of course, protection from the other inmates. And according to the U.S. Embassy, Mexican police regularly obtain information through torture even though the law prohibits it: Since the beginning of 2002, 18 American citizens have died in Mexican prisons, including four apparent homicides.

The three laws you might casually break are the laws against public drunkenness (which is often forgiven), drinking alcohol in public (illegal in some places), and urinating in public which is not only illegal, but often prosecuted and very offensive to locals. Just hold it, please.

A word about **illegal drugs.** Possession of and trafficking in illegal drugs is a federal offense. For trafficking there is no bail. Possession can mean a 25-year sentence in

We Visit the U.S. Embassy to Find Out How You Can Avoid Ending Up There

The Citizen Services section of the U.S. Embassy is an interesting place. My mother used to work there and always came home with a story, usually about schizophrenics who ran away and out of medicine or a drug-addicted heiress demanding a plane ticket home. I went back to the old office to find out how Americans traveling in Mexico can avoid ever needing to go there. Here are some helpful tips from a current officer to keep in mind if by unfortunate chance you *do* end up with a stolen passport or missing credit card:

- In cities like Mexico City, take taxis from *sitios* (authorized stands) only. Tourists taking green-and-white cabs have been robbed and even kidnapped for a couple of days to avoid maximum-withdrawal bank rules.
- Keep your stuff closed and firmly in your arms in crowded areas like the subway, and consider a money belt. Place valuables in your hotel safe if possible.
- Groping can be an issue for women in the Metro, especially during rush hours. At certain stops, there are designated standing areas and Metro cars for women and children—look out for these.
- Always carry your passport, but leave copies in your hotel safe or locker. When you have to carry all your documents on your person, you may wish to put them in various places rather than all in one wallet or pouch.
- Put your name, address, and telephone numbers inside and outside of each piece of luggage. Use covered luggage tags to avoid casual observation of your identity or nationality. If possible, lock your luggage.
- If you are robbed or assaulted, file a police report immediately. Citizen Services can't follow up for you if a police report hasn't been filed.
- Don't do drugs. Drug penalties are very harsh—you could stay in jail for up to 25 years. See "Breaking the Law" above for more info.
- If you're stopped by police, get a name and badge number in order to avoid being a victim of police corruption or even police impostors.
- The Mexican Constitution prohibits political activities by foreigners, so avoid demonstrations and protests.
- Travel in pairs or groups whenever possible. And leave flashy jewelry or anything else that'll make you look too obviously wealthy at home.

Liza Monroy

a Mexican prison. Even a small amount can mean a 10-month sentence—served mainly while waiting to go to trial. If dope is found in your car, you lose it. Possession of controlled substances, such as those like Valium that require a prescription, is a gray area. Depending on the quantity of drugs you have, you may be charged with trafficking. If you buy antibiotics over the counter (which you can do in Mexico) and still have some left, U.S. Customs probably won't hassle you.

U.S. Customs officials are also on the lookout for diet drugs that are sold in Mexico but illegal in the U.S. Possession could land you in a U.S. jail.

Military and law enforcement checkpoints aimed at detecting narcotics, alien smuggling, and firearms traffic are located at various places throughout Mexico. Areas known to possess these checkpoints include the Yucatán peninsula, Chiapas, Oaxaca, and Guerrero. Many checkpoints will have a red flag marker and are operated by uniformed officials; however, others will not be marked and are manned by police/military officers not in uniform. These checkpoints have "spiked devices" that are sometimes used to deflate tires of vehicles attempting to evade these checkpoints.

Getting Wired

With Your Own Computer

Our advice is that you unplug and just immerse yourself in local culture while in Mexico, but if you really must check your MySpace page regularly, you'll find lots of Wi-Fi spots where you can log on without charge. The only catch is that, when wireless signals are located in a cafe, it's common courtesy to buy a coffee in exchange for the service.

We've listed Wi-Fi spots in the destination chapters throughout this book, but you also might want to visit the website **wifi411.com**, which has a remarkably comprehensive list of all the wireless Internet networks throughout the world (including Mexico). Select your desired city, and then select "All Networks" and "All Locations," and you'll get dozens of results.

Before hauling along your laptop, though, it's a good idea to make sure that at least some of the places you'll be staying offer Wi-Fi coverage on the property. Or if you have a wireless card, just open your laptop and see what happens. With so many unprotected wireless networks in such proximity, you'll often be able to get online automatically. We've been in many a non-wired hotel where we've managed to poach off a neighboring network (from the apartment across the street or law offices next door) that wasn't password-protected.

That said, hotels that offer Wi-Fi often have some convoluted password-protected network that may be down half the time. As a result, hotels that offer the somewhat more old-fashioned broadband/Ethernet cable connection can be more reliable. Fortunately, most business-class hotels in Mexico offer dial-up access for laptop modems. In addition, major Internet Service Providers (ISPs) have **local access numbers** around the world, allowing you to go online by placing a local call. The **iPass** network also has dial-up numbers around the world. You'll have to sign up with an iPass provider, who will then tell you how to set up your computer for your destination(s). For a list of iPass providers, go to www.ipass.com and click on "Individuals Buy Now."

You've Got Mail

If you don't already have one, you may want to open a free, Web-based e-mail account with Yahoo or GMail, which you can access from any computer in the world with an Internet connection. If you already have an AOL account, you can log onto www.aol.com and check your AOL mail from there; if you have an Earthlink account you can log onto www.webmail.earthlink.net to access your account.

Note that Mexican keyboards usually don't have a functioning @ symbol; ask which keys you will need to hold down to get that symbol (such as alt + 64 in Baja).

THE BASICS

Wherever you visit, bring a connection kit of the right power and phone adapters, a spare phone cord, and a spare Ethernet network cable—or find out whether your hotel supplies them to guests.

Without Your Own Computer

Chances are your backpack is stuffed enough without having to squeeze in your laptop (and worry about its theft). If you decide not to bring your computer along, don't fret. Almost all hostels and some budget hotels also have at least one Internet terminal set up for guests' use. Some places offer this service for free; others charge anywhere from US$5 to US$15 per hour.

If your hotel does not have a public computer, you'll find many Internet cafes even in small towns across Mexico. Many boast great views of the ocean, so you can sit and watch burros roam by while chatting with your friends back home.

For each destination in this book, we've listed the addresses of some of the country's best Internet cafes. You can also try www.cybercaptive.com and www.cybercafe.com for more suggestions.

Phone Home

Yes, you can totally get through your trip without having a cellphone, but let's face it—it's incredibly handy to have at least one between you and your traveling companions for when you need to make hotel reservations, coordinate travel plans with other people, and, of course, for when you meet someone cute at an *antro* (club) and need to exchange numbers.

Mexico, like most of the world, is on **GSM** (Global System for Mobiles), a big, seamless network that makes for easy cross-border cellphone use throughout Europe and dozens of other countries worldwide. In the U.S., T-Mobile, AT&T Wireless, and Cingular use this quasi-universal system; in Canada, Microcell and some Rogers customers are GSM, and all Europeans and most Australians use GSM. If your cellphone is on a GSM system, and you have a world-capable multiband phone such as many Sony Ericsson, Motorola, or Samsung models, you might be able to make and receive calls in Mexico. The frequency in the country is different, however, so call your wireless operator and ask if "international roaming" can be activated on your account. Unfortunately, per-minute charges can be high—as much as US$1 to US$1.50. When you speak to your service provider, make sure you check to see if there is a per-month charge for international calling capability. T-Mobile, for example, doesn't charge you a per-month fee; Cingular does. If your provider does charge you for this service, remember to call and cancel it when you return from your trip.

If you'll be traveling for awhile, find out how to unlock your phone so that, upon arrival, you can buy a SIM card with a local provider. With this new card, you'll get a new, local number—and much lower calling rates.

If you don't have a GSM phone, you can always **rent a mobile phone** for your trip. There are dozens of cellphone rental outfits on the Web—including www.planetfone.com, www.worldcell.com, www.cellhire.com, www.cellularabroad.com, and www.rentcell.com—which are all pretty competitive with each other. You'll fill out an online form (or call their toll-free customer service line) and provide your credit card number, and they'll ship you a box that contains your rental cellphone, extra battery, charger, and dorky cases, to the address of your choice. When you've returned from your trip, you just put everything back in the same packaging and ship it back to them in the pre-addressed and pre-paid FedEx or UPS package. The

Telephone Tips: From Your Cellphone or a Pay Phone

Mexico's telephone system is slowly but surely catching up with modern times. All telephone numbers have 10 digits. Every city and town that has telephone access has a two-digit (Mexico City, Monterrey, and Guadalajara) or three-digit (everywhere else) area code. In Mexico City, Monterrey, and Guadalajara, local numbers have eight digits; elsewhere, local numbers have seven digits. To place a local call, you do not need to dial the area code. Many fax numbers are also regular telephone numbers; ask whoever answers for the fax tone *("me da tono de fax, por favor").*

Many cellphone numbers in Mexico have a 044 prefix. This prefix is only to be used when calling the number locally. When calling from a long-distance location, the 044 is omitted. To call a local cellphone, dial 044 + the seven-digit number; to call a long distance cellphone dial 01 + area code + seven digits. To dial it from the U.S., dial 011-52, plus the three-digit area code and the seven-digit number.

The **country code** for Mexico is **52.** (Individual city and town area codes are listed in destination chapters throughout this book.)

To call Mexico: If you're calling Mexico from the United States:

1. Dial the international access code: 011.
2. Dial the country code: 52.
3. Dial the two- or three-digit area code, then the eight- or seven-digit number. For example, if you wanted to call the U.S. consulate in Acapulco, the whole number would be 011-52-744-469-0556. If you wanted to dial the U.S. Embassy in Mexico City, the whole number would be 011-52-55-5209-9100.

To make international calls: To make international calls from Mexico, first dial 00, then the country code (U.S. or Canada 1, U.K. 44, Ireland 353, Australia 61, New Zealand 64). Next, dial the area code and number. For example, to call the British Embassy in Washington, you would dial 00-1-202-588-7800.

For directory assistance: Dial ☎ **040** if you're looking for a number inside Mexico. ***Note:*** Listings usually appear under the owner's name, not the name of the business, and your chances of finding an English-speaking operator are slim to none.

For operator assistance: If you need operator assistance in making a call, dial ☎ **090** to make an international call, and ☎ **020** to call a number in Mexico.

Toll-free numbers: Numbers beginning with 800 within Mexico are toll-free, but calling a U.S. toll-free number from Mexico costs the same as an overseas call. To call an 800 number in the U.S., dial 001-880 and the last seven digits of the toll-free number. To call an 888 number in the U.S., dial 001-881 and the last seven digits of the toll-free number. For a number with an 887 prefix, dial 882; for 866, dial 883.

whole process couldn't be easier—just remember to do it at least a week in advance of your trip. Phone rental isn't cheap, however. You'll usually pay around US$50 per week, plus airtime fees of anywhere from 15¢ to a dollar a minute. (Most have free incoming calls, however.) The bottom line: Shop around for the best deal.

If you don't plan on taking a mobile phone with you or renting one while abroad, you can still make phone calls from public telephones. Just beware phones advertising cheap calls to the States or Europe; they may incur huge tariffs on your credit card or your home phone or to whomever you're calling. Your best bet is to use a Ladatel card which costs about US$5 per minute and is pre-paid, so you won't get any nasty surprises when you get home. They're sold at most pharmacies throughout the country.

Finally, if you have Internet access, you might consider checking out Voice Over Internet Protocol (or VoIP) services like **Skype** (www.skype.com) or **Vonage** (www.vonage.com), which let you make free international calls if you use their services via your laptop or in a cybercafe. The people you're calling must also use the service for it to work; check the sites for details.

Getting Around

By Bus

BETWEEN CITIES

The days of sweating in long distance buses, packed not only with people but also pigs and chickens, is nearly a thing of the past in Mexico. **Primera Plus** (first class) buses are now used by several major carriers and make leaving the driving to others a pleasure of sorts. These buses have 30 or so seats that recline almost to sleeping positions, have air-conditioning, lights that actually work, TV monitors playing videos, and black-out curtains. Some bus tickets even include free lunch (a sandwich and Coke), and all are equipped with fairly clean bathrooms so you don't have to hold it for hours after eating.

Unfortunately, although these new bus lines are still fairly economical, some of the runs may cost as much as flying on one of the country's budget airlines (read on for info on that). But if the country's budget airlines don't have good deals to where you want to go, taking a first-class bus is still a *lot* cheaper than renting a car and paying for gas and insurance.

Second-class buses are especially cheap, but you'll have to be prepared for them to stop for practically anyone waving them down in the road—and to get crowded, quickly. The seats will not be as clean or comfortable as first-class buses; and there will seldom be a bathroom on board (there will be pit stops however; public restrooms often charge US$3 or so for "toilet paper"). You'll need to bring your own food, and just forget about videos and curtains. Many of these buses also travel along winding roads that, in addition to taking a lot longer, are bumpy enough to be nausea-inducing.

You can reserve tickets in advance for both first- and second-class buses and even pick your seat online without having to go to individual bus stations. **Autotransportes del Oriente** (Ado; ☎ **800/950-0287;** www.adogl.com.mx/en) services Mexico City, Oaxaca state, and Yucatán, among other regions. **Grupo Estrella Blanca** (☎ **800/507-5500;** www.estrellablanca.com.mx), which includes carriers **Elite** (☎ **669/981-3811**), **Transportes del Norte** (☎ **669/981-2335**), and **Transportes del Pacifico** (☎ **669/982-0577**), services Mexico City, the Pacific Coast, the northeast, and the northwest. **Estrella de Oro** (☎ **525/549-8520;** www.autobus.com.mx) services the Pacific Coast and Mexico City. **Omnibus de Mexico** (☎ **01/800-011-6336;** www.odm.com.mx) services various parts of Mexico, as does **ETN** (☎ **01-800/800-0386;** www.etn.com.mx). **Autotransportes Baja California** or **ABC**

(☎ **664/621-2424;** www.abc.com.mx) services Baja California. Other bus companies are listed in individual "Getting There & Getting Around" sections throughout this book. To see a round-up of all carriers, check out www.differentworld.com/mexico/common/pages/bus_info.htm.

Note that a good rule of thumb for any bus travel within Mexico is to add at least 1½ hours to the expected time of arrival. Many buses leave at least a half-hour after the predicted time (which is great if you're someone who is always running into the station at the last minute, but not so great if you're an early bird). Never cut close an important arrival based on a predicted bus arrival time, as they can even arrive up to 3 hours later than predicted.

IN THE CITIES

Mexico's local buses are funky, noisy, and smoky but they sure are plentiful and cheap. Bus stops are often marked by blue signs with the image of a bus on them. You can also get a bus to stop by simply holding your hand up and waving. You pay the driver or his assistant if there is one when you board; have your change ready since they don't accept large bills. The rate for short rides in most places is $4 to $5.

Though city buses have regular stops, most stop in between these official stops, depending on the needs of the passengers. If you need to get off, you can yell *"bajan!"* (getting off) or push the *"timbre"* (bell) button if there is a working one. Or go up front and let the driver know your corner is approaching.

By Budget Airline

Several relatively new regional carriers, such as AeroMexico's **Aerolitoral** (☎ **800/800-2376;** www.aerolitoral.com); **Aero Mar** (☎ **555/133-1111;** www.aeromar.com.mx); **Avolar** (☎ **800/328-6527** in U.S.; www.avolar.com.mx); Mexicana's **Click Mexicana** (☎ **800/11-CLICK;** www.clickmx.com); **Interjet** (☎ **551/102-5555;** www.interjet.com.mx); Ryanair-affiliated **Viva Aerobús** (www.vivaaerobus.com); and **Volaris** (☎ **551/102-8000;** www.volaris.com.mx) offer budget flights from Mexico's east and west coast cities and to places in between. These are a good bet if you're traveling long distances and don't want to waste valuable beach time in a bus or car. Note that prices are often quoted in pesos on the websites.

If you're traveling a short distance, you might also consider taking an **"air taxi,"** or a small plane that fits about 10 to 15 passengers. Oaxaca is one destination that offers air taxi service to towns a couple of hours away; for example, **Aero Tucan** (Alcalá 201-204; ☎ **951/501-0530** or 951/501-0532 in Oaxaca; ☎ **958/587-2427** in Huatulco; or ☎ **954/582-3461** at the airport in Puerto Escondido; www.aero-tucan.com) flies from Oaxaca to nearby Huatulco and Puerto Escondido. Air taxi service is also common in Baja and along the Pacific Coast down to Manzanillo. **Aero Calafia** (☎ **624/143-4302;** www.aerocalafia.com) is the most reliable of the operators in that region.

Be sure to pack light (often 20 lb. max), or you'll get charged an extra fee for overweight baggage on air taxis. (It doesn't hurt to look into the carry-on restrictions for standard budget airlines, too.) Also check out the "Getting There & Getting Around" sections throughout this book for more information on airlines servicing your destination.

By Car

Driving in Mexico will either give you a great sense of freedom or a nervous breakdown. Although it can be really fun, the predominance of amphetamine-fueled truck and bus drivers with death wishes combined with mountainous narrow roads without shoulders can also make it a trying experience.

If you decide to drive, keep in mind that Mexico charges some of the highest tolls in the world for its network of new toll roads; as a result, they are rarely used. Generally speaking, though, using toll roads cuts travel time. Older toll-free roads are generally in good condition, but travel times tend to be longer.

For information concerning Mexican driver's permits, vehicle inspection, road tax, mandatory insurance, and so on, contact the **Mexican Secretariat of Tourism (SECTUR)** at ☎ **1-800-44-MEXICO,** or visit its website at http://mexicotravel.com. Consult with the Mexican Embassy or the nearest Mexican consulate in the United States for additional, detailed information prior to entering Mexico. For travel in the Baja California peninsula, travelers can also consult www.traveltobaja.net.

It is illegal to drive without a seat belt or use a cellphone while driving in Mexico.

DRIVING TIPS

The best advice we can give you for driving in Mexico is to drive defensively and drive during the day. About 80% of accidents in Mexico occur at night because some drivers still drive without their lights on—sometimes because they think they're "saving" the battery, sometimes because they say they can see better. The absence of shoulders on many of the smaller roads makes matters worse—you can come up over a rise at 100kmph (62 mph) and smack right into someone who is broken down in the middle of the road with no lights on.

Slower traffic always **stays to the right** in Mexico. Left lanes are reserved for passing. You will see many other drivers passing over solid yellow lines, at the tops of hills, on mountainous roads with blind curves. Maybe they have a death wish or really excellent brakes, or a huge insurance policy. Who knows? There are almost no major highways with decent shoulders (or guard rails) on them in Mexico, and there's a reason why there are all those pretty crosses on the road. Stay to the right, use your turn indicators, and be patient.

Also watch the other cars for **turn signals.** If an approaching car flashes its lights at you, this means there is danger ahead of you. Slow down. If you come to a narrow bridge, the first car to flash its lights gets to go first. A left turn signal (especially from a truck you can't see around) means "Clear up ahead, safe to pass." Usually when someone is turning left, they will actually pull off to the right then cross over to their turnoff when the road is clear; this is a good rule to follow. If you try turning left using your signal, the person behind you could interpret it as "safe to pass" and, then, blammo. A right turn indicator means "not safe to pass"; or that the driver is turning right. We like to extend our arms out the windows in addition to the turn indicator just to be clear.

Signage especially on the highways can be poor or nonexistent; turn-offs can either not be marked or suddenly appear four lanes over to the right. There are many access roads paralleling the main highways going through cities which can give you an opportunity to turn around. There are also left hand exits which may not be marked as so; if you are in the fast lane and it suddenly splits off, *usually* it's best to get over. Again, try to figure out where you're going before you head off; no matter what, you will probably get lost driving through bigger cities, so give yourself extra time.

A person standing by the side of the road making a downward patting motion at you means "slow down NOW." Three stones set in the road across the lane means be prepared to stop at once. If you do have to slow quickly, put on your flashers at once. Warn the people behind you. You should *not* expect that buses, cabs, or other drivers will stop at stop signs, stoplights, or any other indicated signage, though.

In Mexico a car **turning** at a four-way stop has the right of way; although most believe the stop sign to be "just a suggestion." Use caution entering a *glorietta* (round-about) used in many intersections especially in larger cities. But do remember that "he who hesitates is lost" and just go for it; circle the island with the frantic flow and merge over at your turn. Again remember that public transportation vehicles, specifically taxis and city buses, often do not comply with traffic regulations, including observing speed limits and stopping at red lights.

While speed limits are much lower here generally than you'll find back home, they are not enforced as a rule. There are few patrol cars or radar traps. Really the most effective speed control device is the low-tech speed bump, ***topes,*** usually indicated by signage just before you see them. The sign shows two round mountain tops, and a stretched-out M. Whenever you are approaching a village of any size, know that you should be watching for topes and slow down.

Driving through ***vados*** (arroyos, or dips in the road) can be very dangerous. You will not be able to see a car passing into your lane hidden by the arroyo and it could be full of water if it's been raining. Treat arroyos as blind curves. They are indicated by a yellow triangular sign of a rectangle with two wavy horizontal lines running through it. While you're driving in the rain, you should slow down and go *slowly* through any standing water.

SAFETY

Banditos, who may use stones, tree trunks, or other cars to block the roads in order to hijack cars (and buses), do pop up sometimes along smaller back roads. Most incidents occur at night so try to avoid driving then, especially along back roads. It's also dangerous to drive from 1pm on Saturday until late Sunday night because of the amount of drunk drivers on the road. That warning goes double for Semana Santa and the week between Christmas and New Year's.

Be prepared to encounter **military and police checkpoints** on any major highway. These checkpoints are looking for drugs and guns and you may be asked to pull your car over to an inspection pit. Always be polite, take off your sunglasses, and have your rental agreement ready. Usually you'll just be waved on through.

GAS

There's one government-owned brand of gas and one gasoline station name throughout the country—**Pemex** (Petroleras Mexicanas). There are two types of gas in Mexico: *magna,* 87-octane unleaded gas, and *premio,* 93 octane. In Mexico, fuel and oil are sold by the liter, which is slightly more than a quart (1 gallon equals about 3.8 liters). Many franchise Pemex stations have bathroom facilities and convenience stores—a great improvement over the old ones.

When filling up at the gas station ("lleno, por favor") always make sure the meter is set to zero before the nozzle is put in; if necessary get out to watch. There are some who will fill you up on top of what the last guy paid. And be sure to give the attendant a small tip ($2–$10); they will usually clean your windshield and check oil, water, and tire pressure if you ask (or as part of the service).

RENTING A CAR IN MEXICO

You'll need a major credit card, and obviously, a driver's license, to rent a car in Mexico. You'll get the best price if you reserve a car at least a week in advance before your trip. U.S. car-rental firms include **Advantage** (☎ **800/777-5500** in the U.S. and Canada; www.arac.com), **Avis** (☎ **800/331-1212** in the U.S., 800/879-2847 in Canada; www.avis.com), **Budget** (☎ **800/527-0700** in the U.S. and Canada; www.budget.com), **Hertz** (☎ **800/654-3131** in the U.S. and Canada; www.hertz.com), **National** (☎ **800/227-7368** in the U.S. and Canada; www.nationalcar.com), and **Thrifty** (☎ **800/847-4389** in the U.S. and Canada; www.thrifty.com), which often offers discounts for rentals in Mexico. For European travelers, **Kemwel Holiday Auto** (☎ **800/678-0678;** www.kemwel.com) and **Auto Europe** (☎ **800/223-5555;** www.autoeurope.com) can arrange Mexican rentals, sometimes through other agencies. These and some local firms have offices in Mexico City and most other large Mexican cities. You'll find rental desks at airports, all major hotels, and many travel agencies.

Car-rental costs are high in Mexico because cars are more expensive. The basic cost of the 1-day rental of a Volkswagen Beetle at press-time, with unlimited mileage (but before 15% tax and US$15 daily insurance), was US$48 in Cancún, US$52 in Mexico City, US$44 in Puerto Vallarta, US$48 in Oaxaca, and US$38 in Mérida. Renting by the week gives you a lower daily rate. (Just be sure to bring a printout of your reservation—showing the rates you were promised along with your reservation number.)

In order to keep the costs down, just be sure to carefully check out *any* damage or blemishes to the car once you get it. You'll be asked to sign a paper showing prior damage. If the car comes back in a different condition, you will be expected to pay an absurd repair cost. If you do get a small scratch from say, a palm frond, stop by a body shop or car wash and have them rub it out with a paste. Actually, it's not a bad idea to get the car completely cleaned before return, especially if you have been doing a lot of off-road driving.

Insurance

You may be asked to agree to third party insurance, running as high as US$15 a day when you pick up your car. It will do you no good to argue that your credit card (such as American Express Platinum) or your hometown car insurance company (such as AAA) has insurance protection coverage for travel. In places like Puerto Vallarta, you'll be required to have proof from the credit card company and even then you will probably be told it doesn't work in Mexico. Call your credit card company before you leave and find out what they cover and what they don't.

The standard insurance included with many car rental contracts in Mexico provides only nominal liability coverage, often as little as the equivalent of US$200. Because Mexican law permits the jailing of drivers after an accident until they have met their obligations to third parties and to the rental company, renters should read their contracts carefully and purchase additional liability and comprehensive insurance if necessary.

ACCIDENTS

When possible, many Mexicans drive away from minor accidents, or try to make an immediate settlement, to avoid involving the police. Foreigners who don't speak fluent Spanish are at a distinct disadvantage when trying to explain their version of the event. Three steps may help the foreigner who doesn't wish to do as the Mexicans do: If you were in your own car, notify your Mexican insurance company, whose job it is to intervene on your behalf. If you were in a rental car, notify the rental company immediately and ask how to contact the nearest adjuster. (You *did* buy insurance with the rental, right?) Finally, if all else fails, ask to contact the nearest Green Angel, who may be able to explain to officials that you are covered by insurance. **Green Angels,** or *Angeles Verdes,* patrol the highways and offer assistance to stranded motorists. They drive green trucks and the drivers are often bilingual mechanics. You can reach them anywhere in Mexico at ☎ **01-55/5250-8221** daily 8am to 8pm, Mexico City time. Before you call for assistance, take care to note where you are (on which road and how far you are from the last big town). They do not charge for their labor, only for gas, parts, and oil. You will be expected to pay in cash. You can also try **Infotur** at ☎ **01-55/5250-8221** for assistance; they're open daily 24 hours a day and usually have English operators.

By Taxi

For anyone who is uncomfortable driving in Mexico, taking taxis is a convenient, comfortable alternative. Taxis also usually cost much less than the price of a rental car for a day, and they're faster than any bus. Fares for short trips within towns are generally preset by zone, and are quite reasonable compared with U.S. rates. (Los Cabos is one exception.) For longer trips or excursions to nearby cities, taxis can generally be hired for around US$10 to US$15 per hour, or for a negotiated daily rate.

You Talking to Me?

Tips on Talking to Your Taxi Driver

Taxi drivers are some of the highest paid free agents in Mexico, due to a hearty supply of tourists and pricey, unregulated fares. Many of them speak English and are happy to offer advice on beaches and drink specials. However, avoid their restaurant tips, as many of the worst chain restaurants pay taxi drivers to refer them. For tips on where to dine, you'd be better off speaking with the receptionist at your hotel, or a local you meet on the street who doesn't have any hidden financial motives.

If you think your taxi driver is dropping you off at the wrong restaurant, simply speak up. It also doesn't hurt to bring a map in the car with you to point out exactly where you want to go.

Sara Lieber

One bonus of taking taxis is that you have a Spanish-speaking person with you in case you run into trouble; many drivers also speak some English.

Taxis are the preferred way for getting around most resort towns, where you can either have your hotel call for one or simply

Colectivos, Aurigas & Pulmonias

Your options for getting around Mexico aren't just limited to standard planes, cars, boats, and buses. In most towns, you'll have the chance to ride around in *colectivos* (shared vans, with cheaper fares than taxis) and *aurigas* (same concept as colectivos, but you'll ride in a pickup truck). And in places like Isla Mujeres and Mazatlán, you can tool around in *pulmonias* (golf carts). Finally, all along the coasts of Mexico, private boats, called *lanchas* or *pangas,* are available for hire as water taxis. See the individual "Getting Around" sections throughout this book for more info on all the funky transportation options in the country.

Jennifer Reilly

hail one on the street by the town's ferry or bus stations. In cities like Mexico City, however, only take taxis from *sitios* (authorized stands). The unauthorized green-and-white cabs there are unsafe; some tourists have been kidnapped after taking one.

By Boat

A number of ferries connect Baja with the Mexican mainland, and there are lots of ferries running off the Yucatán peninsula. Specific info is provided in destination chapters, but you can also visit www.goyoura.com for info.

Tips for Student Travelers

If you want to break out your student ID card for discounts, head to Europe, not Mexico. Here, higher education is not a given; consequently student discounts, cheap tickets, or any kind of support from the state or private institutions is rare.

That said, deals aimed at student travelers can still be had here. A number of cheap backpacking tours are offered, including one through **Bamba Experience** (☎ **555/584-4401;** www.backpackingmexico.com)—their tours are a wonderful, safe, and economical way to experience the hippie/Maya trail.

Hostels are still rare in many cities with the exception of Oaxaca and Mexico City, but they are starting to pop up in more cities like Puerto Escondido, La Paz, and San

MTV U Spanish Classes

In addition to being a great place to study art and cooking (see the "Art & Cooking Classes," box on p. 16), Mexico is of course an excellent spot to learn Spanish. **San Miguel de Allende** (p. 152) is famous for its Spanish schools, though you can take other classes there as well and get U.S. university credit. For a more formal course, **Taxco** has the Centro de Enseñanza Para Extranjeros (CEPE) which is the oldest language school for foreigners in Latin America and offers more traditional courses like history that are tailored to those whose first language isn't Spanish. For more information, contact CEPE at ☎ **762/622-0124** or 762/662-3410, or go to www.cepetaxco.unam.mx (Centro de Enseñanza Para Extranjeros, Ex Hacienda el Chorrillo, Av. Universidad 3002).

Oaxaca (p. 618) has about six language schools, including the well-reputed Instituto Cultural Oaxaca A.C. program. For total immersion, you may want to pick a town with few foreigners so you won't get tempted to be lazy. Why not take a class at the beach like **Puerto Escondido** (p. 596) or **Mazatlán** (p. 489) where you can also learn to surf or volunteer locally? For the largest choice in schools, consider **Cuernavaca,** 50 miles outside Mexico City. For a quarter-century, this town has been a language school mecca for foreigners from all over the world.

Another good way to learn Spanish is by doing a semester abroad here; many university-level programs in Mexico are taught in Spanish. If you'd like more info on academic programs in the country, check out **www.studyabroad.com** and the **Council on International Educational Exchange** (7 Custom House St., Third Floor, Portland, ME 04101; ☎ **207/553-7600;** www.ciee.org/study).

Miguel de Allende. The **Mexican Youth Hostel Network,** or Red Mexicana de Albergues Juveniles (www.hostellingmexico.com), offers a list of hostels that meet international standards in Mexico City, Oaxaca, and surrounding areas. The **Mexican Youth Hostel Association (Asociación Mexicana de Albergues Juveniles;** www.hostels.com), offers a list of hostels in Mexico City, Zacatecas, Guanajuato, Puerto Escondido, Uxmal, Palenque, Tulum, Cancún, and Playa del Carmen.

Cheap alternative accommodations like palapas and cabañas, as well as package deals on resorts, are so common here that you probably won't miss the abundance of hostels, though. See p. 30 under "Staying There" for details.

Just in case you stumble upon that rare institution that accepts one, you might as well get an **International Student Identity Card (ISIC),** and try for discounts at some hostels and museum entrance fees. It also provides you with basic health and life insurance and a 24-hour help line. The card is available from **STA Travel** (☎ **800/781-4040** in North America; www.sta.com or www.statravel.com; or www.statravel.co.uk in the U.K.), the biggest student travel agency in the world. If you're no longer a student but are still under 26, you can get an **International Youth Travel Card (IYTC)** from the same people, which entitles you to some discounts (but not on museum admissions). **Travel CUTS** (☎ **800/667-2887** or 416/614-2887; www.travelcuts.com) offers similar services for both Canadians and U.S. residents.

Tips for Travelers with Disabilities

Although we hope that having a disability won't stop you from traveling here, Mexico is sadly lacking in facilities. The few escalators in the country are often out of order; many stairs don't have handrails; nor are restrooms made for travelers with disabilities. If one is actually large enough to accommodate a wheelchair, it may be difficult to access. Plus, you'll have to contend with cobblestone streets and huge curbs without ramps in the colonial cities, and with uneven sidewalks with gaping holes in wealthier resorts like Cabo San Lucas. Finally, although Mexican airports are upgrading their services, you may still have to board by either descending stairs to a bus that takes you to the plane (which you board by climbing stairs), or by walking across the tarmac to your plane and ascending the stairs. Deplaning presents the same problem in reverse.

All of the above things can make Mexico seem like one giant obstacle course to travelers in wheelchairs or on crutches. Help is around if you look, though. Airports have well-hidden elevators or escalators, and airlines can arrange wheelchair assistance to the baggage area. There are porters outside of baggage claim at airports and bus stations who can help you get a taxi, and will wait while you change money. Many deluxe hotels now have rooms with bathrooms for people with disabilities; we have noted hotels that are wheelchair friendly in the individual listings.

If all this seems daunting, remember that people here are friendly and generally eager to help the disabled. Recently due to the efforts of a local disabled citizen, Puerto Vallarta renovated the majority of its downtown sidewalks and plazas with ramps that accommodate wheelchairs (as well as baby strollers).

Happily there are many travel agencies that offer customized tours and itineraries for travelers with disabilities. Among them are **Flying Wheels Travel** (☎ **507/451-5005;** www.flyingwheelstravel.com); **Access-Able Travel Source** (☎ **303/232-2979;** www.access-able.com); and **Accessible Journeys** (☎ **800/846-4537** or 610/521-0339; www.disabilitytravel.com). **Avis Rent a Car** has an "Avis Access" program that offers such services as a dedicated 24-hour toll-free number (☎ **888/879-4273**) for customers with special travel needs; special car features such as swivel seats, spinner knobs, and hand controls; and accessible bus service.

Organizations that offer assistance to disabled travelers include **MossRehab** (www.mossresourcenet.org); the **American Foundation for the Blind (AFB;** ☎ **800/232-5463;** www.afb.org); and **SATH** (Society for Accessible Travel & Hospitality; ☎ **212/447-7284;** www.sath.org). **AirAmbulanceCard.com** is now partnered with SATH and allows you to pre-select top-notch hospitals in case of an emergency.

The community website **iCan** (www.icanonline.net/channels/travel) has destination guides and several regular columns on accessible travel. Also check out the quarterly magazine ***Emerging Horizons*** (www.emerginghorizons.com), and ***Open World*** magazine, published by SATH.

Tips for Gay & Lesbian Travelers

Mexico is a conservative country, with deeply rooted Catholic religious traditions. Pro-gay celebrities like talk show hosts Christina (sort of like Mexico's Oprah), have helped open things up a bit; but especially outside of the major cities or resort areas, homophobia is not uncommon. Public displays of same-sex affection are rare and still considered shocking for men. Although women in Mexico frequently walk hand in hand, and men greet each other with *abrazos,* or bear hugs, full-on kissing and such could offend locals. However, gay and lesbian travelers should not experience any harassment, assuming they give the appropriate regard to local culture and customs.

Acapulco used to be the most gay-friendly resort in Mexico but these days, Puerto Vallarta is the most welcoming and accepting destination in the country. It boasts many gay hotel rooms and nightclubs and is frequently cited as the number one gay beach destination in Latin America.

As Mexico's largest city, Mexico City has a gay scene that's almost as huge as Puerto Vallarta's. Cancún and Ensenada are starting to become more gay friendly, as is San Miguel Allende, where internationally famous artists (who happen to be gay) are building up the scene slowly. Tijuana used to have a notorious reputation for frowning upon gay nightlife, but gay activists have made progress in recent years, by establishing AIDS clinics and launching an annual gay pride parade.

We've listed a number of gay nightlife and sightseeing options wherever possible throughout this book; however, some towns simply don't have much of a gay nightlife scene, or any at all. Perhaps that will change now that some places in Mexico, such as Mexico City, started recognizing same-sex unions in early 2007. For info on the current gay nightlife scene throughout the country, check out www.gaymexico.com.mx.

Many agencies offer tours and travel itineraries to Mexico specifically for gay

Traveling Sola, Amiga?

As a woman traveling alone in Mexico, you will meet unique challenges but it's well worth it. Traveling alone forces you out of your own little world and enables you to make friends with people from all walks of life. And I actually feel safer in most cities in Mexico than I do in some American cities—that's because the majority of people you'll encounter in Mexico will be sweeter and more helpful to tourists. Take some common sense safety precautions and I promise you that you'll have the time of your life. Following are a few tips to keep in mind to help that happen:

- Pretend to be married. I know this may seem retro, but so is machismo. Mexico is still basically a conservative Catholic country and saying that you're hitched can make your life much easier. Just be prepared for taxi drivers to quiz you about how many children you have. The punch line is: "Well I could give you so many children" wink, wink. Pretend like you don't understand, lie, or don't answer. If you tell them you're a lesbian they'll become even more interested.
- Ditch miniskirts, itsy-bitsy bikinis, and short shorts. Bring a sarong or something to cover up; don't go off the beach in just your swimsuit. I switched my minidress in Mexico for a robe which covered me head to foot and was able to have much more meaningful experiences with men and women who were no longer distracted by my unintentional rudeness in choice of clothing. And remember, not only can you not run very fast in stilettos, streets in Mexico can be real ankle twisters. Leave the heels at home.
- Figure out where you're going before you leave your hotel, but don't be shy about asking for directions—just approach other women or families.
- If you feel like someone's following you, duck into a store or doorway; don't be afraid to ask for help (just think twice before asking the police). Use some caution at ATMs—they're best used in daylight. And avoid walking around alone at night, especially when drunk.
- Try to travel light. This will let you move more quickly; and you won't have to set your luggage down, leaving it unattended. Don't carry your passport and other valuables but leave them locked in the hotel. Don't wear a fanny pack or it'll mark you as a tourist; instead, distribute what you have in secure pockets on your person. And don't pull out a huge wad of bills to pay for something.
- Check your hotel room to be sure the doors and windows lock; or if they have a night watchman *(velador)* on duty (even the most humble places usually do). Don't walk on unlit streets or on the beach alone at night; spend a couple of bucks and take a taxi to your door.
- Check out the award-winning website **Journey-woman** (www.journeywoman.com), a "real-life" women's travel information network where you can sign up for a free e-mail newsletter and get advice on everything from etiquette to safety.
- Finally, walk tall and proud like you know what the hell you're doing! Exude confidence, not fear, and you won't attract those preying on the weak. 'Cause you aren't weak: You've got the guts to travel alone, after all.

Ann Summa

and lesbian travelers. Among them are **Above and Beyond Tours** (☎ **800/397-2681;** www.abovebeyondtours.com); **Now, Voyager** (☎ **800/255-6951;** www.now voyager.com); and **Olivia Cruises & Resorts** (☎ **800/631-6277;** www.olivia.com). **Pato Enterprises** (www.gaymexico.net) was one of the first gay travel consultants online and has many economical hotel rooms and information about where to travel in Mexico.

Gay.com Travel (☎ **800/929-2268** or 415/644-8044; www.gay.com/travel or www.outandabout.com) provides regularly updated information about gay-owned, gay-oriented, and gay-friendly lodging, dining, sightseeing, nightlife, and shopping establishments in Mexico.

In Puerto Vallarta, Susan Weisman's travel service **Bayside Properties** (☎ **322/223-4424;** www.baysidepuerto-vallarta.com) rents gay-friendly condos, villas, and hotels for individuals and large groups. Her services are customized to individual needs, and she can offer airport pickups and in-villa cooks.

The International Gay and Lesbian Travel Association (IGLTA; ☎ **800/448-8550** or 954/776-2626; www.iglta.org) is the trade association for the gay and lesbian travel industry, and offers an online directory of gay- and lesbian-friendly travel businesses; go to their website and click on "Members." **The Gay and Lesbian Times** (www.gaylesbiantimes.com) is another excellent site with travel articles and information.

Tips for Eco-Tourists

Eco-Tourism Sites

The **International Ecotourism Society** (TIES) defines eco-tourism as "responsible travel to natural areas that conserves the environment and improves the well-being of local people." Although "eco" has become somewhat of a buzzword in Mexico and seems to be attached to every kind of tourist outfit, including things that definitely are *not* ecological, we have to applaud and encourage the many new organizations trying to make Mexico more eco-friendly.

Here are a few sites to check out for info on eco issues in Mexico:

- **www.ecotourism.org**: The International Ecotourism Society website lists helpful eco-friendly travel tips, statistics, and touring companies and associations.
- **www.worldwildlife.org**: A good site to find volunteer opportunities if you're interested in the environment, with info on overfishing and bottom trawling the Gulf of California, and tips on protecting dolphins, migrating monarchs, and turtles, as well as wilderness habitats.
- **www.planeta.com**: This "global journal of practical eco-tourism" is fun to read and informative—perhaps that's why it's Carl Franz's favorite website (he's the author of the *People's Guide to Mexico*). The site also has forums and news about Oaxaca.
- **www.amtave.org**: The Association Mexicana de Turismo de Aventura y Ecoturismo (AMTAVE) is a national organization that monitors the country's professional eco-tourism and adventure outfitters. It also promotes the involvement of local communities in eco activities.
- **www.emeraldplanet.com**: This travel agency based in Latin America uses tourism to help generate revenue in

protected areas; visit the site for info on eco-trips to Mexico.

- **www.ecotravel.com**: Part online magazine and part eco-directory, you can search for touring companies in several categories (water-based, land-based, spiritually oriented, and so on) on this site.
- **www.nrdc.org**: Has a wealth of information about endangered places in their BioGems section, and is working actively in Mexico to protect the gray whale and vaquita dolphin; link to www.savebiogems.org for more info.

In addition to the websites listed above, check out **Conservation International** (www.conservation.org) which, with *National Geographic Traveler,* annually presents **World Legacy Awards** (www.wlaward.org) to those travel tour operators, businesses, organizations, and places that have made a significant contribution to sustainable tourism. We've also indicated resorts that are self-sustaining in the individual chapters throughout this book. For tips on conserving fuel and energy during your stay in Mexico, see Appendix C, p. 699.

Swimming with Dolphins

Although the sport is highly advertised in many resort cities, the ethics of swimming with dolphins are being questioned by organizations such as Greenpeace and the Humane Society. Often, dolphins are penned up in overcrowded conditions that aren't exactly healthy or enchanting for *them;* and reportedly many of the organizations don't adhere to international regulations for the treatment of animals. For more information see the **Whale and Dolphin Conservation Society** (www.wdcs.org) and **Tread Lightly** (www.treadlightly.org); and consider tours which take you out to sea to experience the animals in their natural state (see Puerto Escondido in "Playing Outside," p. 645).

Swimming & Diving with Sharks

You'll have a number of opportunities to dive or snorkel with nurse sharks in Mexico. These look exactly like "regular" sharks to the untrained eye. However, because of the way that their jaw is built, they cannot bite you unless you intentionally provoke them. In order not to disturb the natural environment where you're diving or snorkeling, of course, you'll not only want to avoid provoking them—you'll also want to steer clear from the nurse sharks as much as possible.

Around destinations like Ensenada, you'll also have a chance to cage dive with regular sharks. This sport entails being submerged underwater in an impenetrable cage that lets you get up close and personal with great whites and, if done sensitively, in small groups, it doesn't harm the animals in any way. Many operators entice sharks over to the cage by offering them food they shouldn't be eating, though—not exactly the best way to just let creatures be in their natural environment. Make sure the operator you choose to go out with is a reputable one, and visit www.responsibletravel.com for more info.

Bullfighting

Just so you have no misconceptions about going to a bullfight here, know in advance: The bull will be tortured and killed, there will be lots of blood, and the animal will be dragged unceremoniously out of the ring by a team of horses. (If it's any consolation, he is then taken to a butcher.) That said, going to a fight is a quick way to understand Mexico's Spanish colonial past, and to see machismo on full display. Bullfights are held in towns as different as Tijuana and Puerto Vallarta, and they offer a colorful spectacle like no other: a brass

Volunteer Opportunities

We've listed volunteer options throughout this book, but for general info on and listings for volunteer opportunities in Mexico, visit the websites **www.volunteer abroad.org** or **www.idealist.org**. Also see "Getting In & Out" on p. 16 for info on obtaining a student visa.

As Mexico works to develop its eco-tourism potential, more and more volunteer opportunities are opening up. In addition to chocking out the sites listed under the "Eco-Tourism" section above, here are some general tour organizations to keep in mind: **One World Workforce** (P.O. Box 3188, La Mesa, CA 91944; ☎ **800/451-9564**) arranges 1-week "hands-on conservation" trips that offer working volunteers a chance to help with sea turtle conservation at Bahía de Los Angeles, in Baja (spring, summer, and fall), and along the Majahuas beach 100km (62 miles) south of Puerto Vallarta (summer and fall). **Earthwatch** (3 Clocktower Pl., Suite 100, Box 75, Maynard, MA 01754; ☎ **800/776-0188;** www.earthwatch.org) sets up 1- to 3-week volunteer sessions throughout the country that promote ecological conservation. The **Centro Ecologico Akumal** (CEA; Apartado Postal 2, Akumal, Quintana Roo 77760; ☎ **984/875-9095;** www.ceakumal.org) recruits volunteers for turtle and reef monitoring, along with other eco-research projects throughout Mexico.

The Archaelogical Institute of America (656 Beacon St., Fourth Floor, Boston, MA 02214; ☎ **617/353-9361;** www.archaeological.org) offers info on how to volunteer for field digs throughout the country.

ESPWA (Hope; P.O. Box 2071, Rouseau, Commonwealth of Domnicia; ☎ **767/449-0322;** www.espwa.org) provides volunteer opportunities ranging from archaeological, to public health, to environmental causes.

band playing, the costumed matador's macho stare, men shaking their heads at less-than-perfect swipes of the cape, and overly made-up, bloodthirsty women chanting *"ole,"* waving their white hankies, throwing roses, jackets, and hats at the matador's feet. There is also the extremely miniscule chance that, if the bull puts up a good enough fight or sticks his horn through the matador's leg, he will be spared for breeding purposes. It does happen, if only rarely.

To read more about the implications of attending a bullfight, visit www.peta.org.

Climbing Ruins

We've included a number of Maya archaeological sites throughout this book, but, at a number of them (like Chichén Itzá), you'll discover that the pyramids are roped off so that tourists can't climb them. Keep in mind that this has been done in the name of sustainable development; many of these sites have been so trammeled upon over the years that they're nearly falling apart. That shouldn't discourage you from climbing ruins like the ones at Uxmal—just be respectful of their long history while you are.

Adventure Tours & Resources

Mexico is huge and its geography diverse, with more than 7.2 million hectares (18 million acres) of national parks, preserves, and biospheres reserves. Since there are far fewer outdoor rules and regulations (that are followed, anyway) than you might be accustomed to back home, you can definitely have a *wild* wilderness experience here. That doesn't mean you should do anything too stupid, though; there aren't any helicopters that can airlift you out if you get stuck on a cliff or get your arm stuck between boulders somewhere.

But my, what options there are. You can mountain bike from village to village through the Oaxacan Sierras or on the high plateaus surrounding San Miguel de Allende. Or hang glide and parasail in Valle de Bravo near Mexico City. Kayak for days in Baja's Sea of Cortez (also called the Gulf of California), and also hike from the desert to alpine meadows in this region.

Seven mountain ranges can be scaled in Baja alone. The Copper Canyon, a section of the Sierra Madre of northwestern Mexico, is five times bigger than the Grand Canyon and is home to some amazing hiking and horseback riding. Surfing is awesome all along the Pacific Coast. Snorkeling and diving in the Caribbean off the Yucatán (or in its underground rivers via cenotes) is some of the best in the world.

With all these possibilities on hand, the point is that you shouldn't just hole up in your resort. Get out there and do *something.* Following are some operators that can help you do just that.

Diving 101

A word of warning: Do not go on a dive with any tour company that mixes drinking and diving on the same vessel. Diving is inherently dangerous and a five-star PADI outfit (or PADI resort) will have a one dive instructor to four divers ratio, and they won't approve of drinking and diving. Also, you will likely be approached by vendors in the street who will offer a bargain dive package, but if it sounds too good to be true, it probably is. Most likely, you'll be signing up for a 3-hour timeshare lecture.

PARKS Most national parks and nature reserves are understaffed or unstaffed. Reliable Mexican companies (such as AMTAVE members; see below) and many U.S.-based companies offer adventure trips.

OUTDOORS ORGANIZATIONS & TOUR OPERATORS **AMTAVE** (Asociación Mexicana de Turismo de Aventura y Ecoturismo, A.C.) is an active association of ecotour and adventure tour operators. It publishes an annual catalog of participating firms and their offerings, all of which must meet certain criteria for security, quality, and training of the guides, as well as for sustainability of natural and cultural environments. For more information, contact AMTAVE (☎ **800/654-4452** or 55/5688-3883; www.amtave.org).

The **Archaeological Conservancy,** 5301 Central Ave. NE, Suite 402, Albuquerque, NM 87108 (☎ **505/266-1540;** www.americanarchaeology.com), presents one trip per year led by an expert, usually an archaeologist. The trips change from year to year and space is limited; make reservations early.

Baja Expeditions, 2625 Garnet Ave., San Diego, CA 92109 (☎ **800/843-6967** or 858/581-3311; fax 858/581-6542; www.bajaex.com), offers natural-history cruises, whale-watching, sea kayaking, camping, scuba diving, and resort and day trips out of Loreto or La Paz, Baja California, and San Diego, California. Small groups and special itineraries are Baja Expeditions' specialty.

Expediciones México Verde (☎ **279/832-3730;** www.mexicoverde.com.mx), under the leadership of Agustín Arroyo, offers a tour covering the original route of Cortez—though unlike Cortez and his henchmen, you're not on horseback or on foot. Highlights include the ruins of Zempoala; the cities of Veracruz (where you learn the local dance borrowed from Cuba, *danzón*), Xalapa and its excellent Museo de Antropología, Puebla, Tlaxcala, and Mexico City; river rafting (if you desire); plus cultural experiences in food, history, and literature. Trips can be customized.

Mexico Travel Link Ltd., 300-3665 Kingsway, Vancouver, BC V5R 5W2 Canada (☎ **604/454-9044;** fax 604/454-9088; www.mexicotravel.net), offers cultural, sports, and adventure tours to Mexico City and surrounding areas, Baja, Veracruz, the Copper Canyon, the Maya Route, and other destinations.

Mountain Travel Sobek, 6420 Fairmount Ave., El Cerrito, CA 94530 (☎ **888/687-6235** or 510/594-6000; www.mtsobek.com), takes groups kayaking in the Sea of Cortez, whale-watching in Baja, and river rafting, hiking, and camping in Veracruz. Sobek is one of the world's leading ecotour outfitters.

Natural Habitat Adventures, 2945 Center Green Court, Suite H, Boulder, CO 80301 (☎ **800/543-8917** or 303/449-3711; www.nathab.com), offers naturalist-led natural history and adventure travel. Expeditions focus on monarch butterfly watching in Michoacán and gray whale–watching in Baja.

Naturequest, 30872 S. Coast Hwy., Suite PMB, Laguna Beach, CA 92651 (☎ **800/369-3033** or 949/499-9561; www.naturequesttours.com), specializes in the natural history, culture, and wildlife of the Copper Canyon and the remote lagoons and waterways off Baja California. A 10-day hiking trip ventures into rugged areas of the canyon; a less strenuous trip goes to Creel and Batopilas, in the same area. Baja trips get close to nature, with special permits for venturing by two-person kayak into sanctuaries for whales and birds.

Oaxaca Reservations/Zapotec Tours, 4955 N. Claremont Ave., Suite B, Chicago, IL 60625 (☎ **800/446-2922** outside Illinois, or 773/506-2444; fax 773/506-2445; www.oaxacainfo.com), offers a variety of tours to Oaxaca City and the Oaxaca coast (including Puerto Escondido and Huatulco). Its specialty trips include Day of the Dead in Oaxaca and the Food of the Gods Tour of Oaxaca. The coastal trips emphasize nature, while the Oaxaca City tours focus on the immediate area, with visits to weavers, potters, markets, and archaeological sites. This is also the U.S. contact for several hotels in Oaxaca City that offer a 10% discount for reserving online.

Tour Baja, P.O. Box 827, Calistoga, CA 94515 (☎ **800/398-6200** or 707/942-4550; fax 707/942-8017; www.tourbaja.com), offers sea-kayaking tours in the Loreto area. Owner Trudi Angell has guided these trips for more than 20 years. She and her guides offer firsthand knowledge of the area. Kayaking, mountain biking, and pack trips as well as sailing charters combine these elements with outdoor adventures.

Sea Kayak Adventures, 1036 Pine Ave., Coeur d'Alene, ID 83814 (☎ **800/616-1943** or 208/765-3116; fax 208/765-5254; www.seakayakadventures.com), features kayak trips in both the Sea of Cortez and Magdalena Bay, with a focus on whale-watching. This company has the exclusive permit to paddle Magdalena Bay's remote northern waters, and they guarantee gray whale sightings. Trips combine paddling of 4 to 5 hours per day, with hiking across dunes and beaches, while nights are spent camping.

Sea Trek Sea Kayaking Center, P.O. Box 561, Woodacre, CA 94973 (☎ **415/488-1000;** fax 415/332-8790; www.seatrekkayak.com). Alternating sea-kayaking trips between Alaska and Baja for 20 years has given Sea Trek an intimate knowledge of the peninsula's coastline. Eight-day trips depart from and return to Loreto, and a

Teaching English

If you're looking to work while in Mexico, why not teach English? The pay is decent and you'll probably pick up some Spanish during the lessons. Some training is necessary for placement, though: Most schools require you to have a Teaching English as a Foreign Language (TEFL) certificate. **Dave's ESL Café** (www.eslcafe.com) is a good place to hunt for advice on the subject, as well as to get info on how to obtain a work visa. You should also check out the **Office of Overseas Schools** (U.S. Department of State, Room H328, SA-1, Washington D.C., 20522; ☎ **202/261-8200;** www.state.gov/m/a/os), which has a thorough list of agencies that can place you in Mexican schools.

12-day expedition travels from Loreto to La Paz. An optional day excursion to Bahía Magdalena for gray whale–watching is available. Full boat support is provided, and no previous paddling experience is necessary.

Trek America, P.O. Box 189, Rockaway, NJ 07866 (☎ **800/221-0596** or 973/983-1144; fax 973/983-8551; www.trekamerica.com), organizes lengthy, active trips that combine trekking, hiking, van transportation, and camping in the Yucatán, Chiapas, Oaxaca, the Copper Canyon, and Mexico's Pacific Coast, and a trip that covers Mexico City, Teotihuacán, Taxco, Guadalajara, Puerto Vallarta, and Acapulco.

Tips on Shopping

Although haggling has long been accepted and even expected in Mexican shops and markets, the practice is beginning to change. You would never haggle in an expensive shop in Mexico City that has prices clearly marked, but if someone approaches you on the beach with jewelry it's all but expected. At such spots, you can try to bargain someone down (if they engage you, that is) to about a third less than the asking price; if the original price is way more than you can afford, don't even start bargaining.

When you're buying food in markets, or when the asking price seems really reasonable, don't bargain. Most sellers in the market will charge you the same as they are charging locals; if you notice someone next to you getting a cheaper price, you can always ask for it. Just don't be a *codo* (cheapskate)—remember the sellers are trying to make a living.

What to Buy

You're going to come across a lot of amazing, cheap *artesanías* (handicrafts) during your visit, so plan on doing at least a little shopping. In addition to browsing the markets, we recommend stopping by at least one store affiliated with Fonda Nacional para el Fomento de las Artes **(FONART)**, a government organization that helps village craftspeople and operates stores throughout Mexico. Look for listings for their shops throughout this book.

It's worth noting that San Miguel is especially well known for its crafts, Mexico City for its galleries, Oaxaca for its textiles, and Puerto Vallarta for its Huichol (indigenous Indian) art, so you'll want to target those things in those destinations. See the individual chapters for more specifics.

Some other must buys include the following:

- ***Guayaberas:*** Traditional men's shirts from the Yucatán, which are smart and comfy for the tropics.
- **Hammocks:** You might want to invest in one of these if you're crashing on the beach a lot. Mérida has great ones.
- ***Huipils:*** Looser versions of guayaberas for women; they can be quite elaborately woven and embroidered.
- **Leather goods:** *Huaraches* (sandals) are the one must-buy leather product, but you'll find lots of cheap but nice leather bags and belts for sale, too.
- ***Milagros:*** Little silver or alpaca charms usually sold outside of churches.
- **Pottery:** Pottery from the states of Oaxaca, Puebla, and Michoucan is of the best quality.
- ***Retablos:*** Small paintings on tin or other material done in homage to saints or holy objects.
- ***Rebozos:*** Long shawls for either the shoulders or for carrying objects.

Sweat It in Style

Don't fret if you're not up for adventure activities in Mexico. In addition to its tons of relaxing beaches, the country has loads of spas to help you truly unwind. (Check out the individual chapters throughout this book for specific options.) Our favorite spa experience in the country is the *temazcal,* which has been around for centuries, but is recently coming into its own in up- and down-scale spas and resorts, including the **Jardín Botanico** (www.laneta.apc.org/charco/project.htm) in San Miguel Allende, the **Casa Catrina** (www.casacatrina.com.mx) in downtown Oaxaca, the **Espacio Meditativo Temazcalli** (☎ **954/582-1023;** www.temazcalli.com) in Puerto Escondido, **Rodavento** (www.hotelsboutique.com/rodavento) in Valle de Bravo, **Xquenda** (☎ **958/583-4448;** www.huatulcospa.com) in Huatulco, and **Casa Sagrada** (www.casasagrada.com) in Teotitlan near Oaxaca.

A pre-Hispanic traditional bath of therapeutic cleansing which purifies the body and the soul, temazcals were once constructed of mud plastered over bent sticks but now are more commonly made of brick. Specifically, volcanic rock is heated until red-hot and is placed in the center of an igloo-type construction, which represents the womb, or Mother Earth. (In theory, the dark, hot, and humid interior of the temazcal holds us and protects us just like our mother did.) If you get a more traditional bath, a conch shell may be sounded to signal the beginning of the bath. Then hot stones are brought in and the door is closed, sealing off the light and sealing in the heat. Herbs are thrown on the stones to create a curative vapor, and water is poured on them to make a steam bath. During your session, your body temperature may reach as high as 104°F (40°C). Once you enter you really aren't supposed to leave, but if it gets too hot your "guide" will usually crack the door.

The rest of the temazcal experience depends on where you have your treatment. At Casa Catrina, you'll sit on benches inside the saunalike temazcal and rub honey all over your body, then beat yourself with fresh herbs, and cool off with herbed and eucalyptus-scented water poured from gourds. But the treatment at Casa Sagrada is less spalike and more spiritual; its 6-hour traditional healing art session includes a class in pre-Hispanic energy practices.

- ***Serapes:*** Traditionally used for warmth in the mountains, these hand-loomed blankets have a slit in the middle for your head; sew up the middle and they become beautiful little rugs or wall-hangings. Also look out for other woolen goods.

Shopping Tips

It may be difficult to find any specialized art products in beach towns, so it's best to bring your own supplies. Ditto for things like photography supplies; color negative film is in plentiful supply but chrome is more difficult to find. Just forget about larger format film or supplies for developing film and printing. You'll also pay a premium for higher tech items like memory cards or flash cards, or most electronics.

Keep in mind these few gestures while shopping: Wagging your finger back and forth like a primary school teacher means "No thank you." Use this gesture for kids selling Chiclets, time-share salesmen, taxi drivers, beach jewelry salesmen—anyone trying to sell you something when you're just trying to relax. Holding your hand flat and wagging left and right in succession, means *"mas o menos,"* or more or less. A finger put on the elbow means "cheap," or *"codo."*

You can tell whether something is really amber or not by its clarity; if it is completely clear, it is probably poured resin. Real amber is mottled with dark spots and comes in many different colors, shapes, and sizes.

Pure 100% silver is too soft to make jewelry with, so jewelry makers mix it with other metals to make it pliable—look for the percentage of pure silver used that's listed on any silver objects.

Never buy gold in the street. Most vendors will tell you that what you're considering buying is from Chiapas if it's stamped with a "C," but in reality, it's probably from China. If it's too good to be true, that means it probably is and that it'll turn your skin green. You can always scratch the piece with a coin to see if it's got copper inside (although you may be forced to buy it then).

You don't need to shell out for Sammy Hagar's tequila; you can always find it cheaper in supermarkets than at his bar Cabo Wabo (p. 403). And it's best to buy perfume in duty free shops where there's a larger selection and you won't pay duty.

Recommended Books, Movies & Music

Before you head off to Mexico, you might want to treat yourself to some Mexican culture to whet your appetite. Following is a list of quality books, movies, and music that should help set your mood to the tune of Mexico.

Books

HISTORY & CULTURE *The Life and Times of Mexico* by Earl Shorris offers a decidedly in-depth analysis of Mexican history. It's really the only text you'll ever need if you're seeking to learn the history of the country, from the rituals of Aztecs to the 70-year-rule of the PRI.

2012: The Return of Quetzalcoatl by Daniel Pinchbeck is a nonfiction narrative that will appeal to fans of *The Celestine Prophecy.* While it doesn't all take place in Mexico, the book's foundations lie in the Aztec belief in five circles of life—in which the world is created and destroyed five times by the gods. Pinchbeck also delves into other Mesoamerican beliefs and ideologies. Quetzalcoatl, the god who gives this book its title, is said to have been born in Tepoztlan (p. 134), so this is a good backpack stuffer for while you're there.

If you want to learn about Mexican *corridas,* or ballads, check out *True Stories from Another Mexico* by *Los Angeles Times* award-winning journalist Sam Quiones. The chapter on Chalino is enlightening, and the Mazatlán drag queen chapter is a must-read before traveling to that city.

Mexico, One Plate at a Time, by celebrity chef and Mexico aficionado Rick Bayless, offers a fun analysis of Mexican food. Bayless has written some great regular cookbooks as well.

Exuberantly designed and photographed, *Paso del Nortec: This is Tijuana* contains essays about Tijuana and growing up on the border from Nortec collective members. In addition to its amazing photos and graphics, cultural music analyses and music glossaries help make the tome a standout.

Like Water for Chocolate by Laura Esquivel is a classic tale of Mexican cooking and family obligations. See the movie, too.

Guillermo Arriaga, the screenwriter for *Amores Perros,* is a brilliant writer of *literatura,* too. If you can read Spanish, pick up these books on your trip: *Retorno 201* was the name of the street Arriaga grew up on, and the book is filled with his impressions of Mexico City back then; *El Bufalo de la Noche* is a novel about a young man reeling from his best friend's suicide. Both books are due to be published in the U.S. by Atria, so keep an eye out for the English versions soon.

Stones for Ibarra, by Harriet Doer, has provided fantasy-fodder for generations of gringas looking to expatriate to Mexico. By tracing the story of one woman's search for herself in Mexico after the death of her husband, it delivers a romanticized tale of cultural immersion.

For contemporary culture, start with Octavio Paz's classic, *The Labyrinth of Solitude,* which still generates controversy among Mexicans.

Our Word Is Our Weapon is a collection of writings by Subcomandante Marcos, leader of the Zapatista movement. For more on politics, *Basta! Land and the Zapatista Rebellion* by George Collier, et al, is also recommended.

Some of our other historic and cultural favorite reads include anything written by Carlos Fuentes, Mexico's leading leftie intellectual; *Hasta No Verte* by Elena Poniatowska; and anything by Luis Alberto Urrea, who is the master of heart-wrenching works about third-world realities.

TRAVEL *Incidents of Travel in the Yucatán, Vol. I and II* by John L. Stephens are travel classics as well as fascinating archaeology reads. The two volumes describe Stephens's discoveries in the Yucatán in the mid–19th century. Stephens found and described 44 Maya sites, and his account of these remains the most authoritative in existence.

Mexico, A Love Story is an essay collection by women who have deep ties to the country (including a piece by the writer of the Mexico City chapter). The stories, which cover the emotional spectrum from fun to serious, perfectly illuminate the spell Mexico casts over travelers and locals alike.

We're a bit biased, of course, but our very own Liza Monroy's first novel, *Mexican High,* will be published in the summer of 2008 by Spiegel & Grau, an imprint of Random House. The fast-paced novel tells the story of a girl who spends a year at an exclusive prep school in Mexico City, giving us a look into the lives of its wealthy teenagers.

A must-read for first-time visitors, *The People's Guide to Mexico* by Carl Franz and Lorena Havens is a quintessentially hippie guidebook. Even though it refuses to reveal any place names (to keep unspoiled places that way), it still provides expert cultural and practical advice about visiting Mexico.

The Baja Adventure Book by Walt Peterson is an oversized yet thorough manual detailing Baja's campsites, along with info on where to launch boats and kayaks, off-roading, hiking, climbing, sailing, wind surfing, surfing, bike riding, diving—basically, you'll get info on just about everything active travelers could want. There are decent maps, too. It's an essential resource if you're driving the peninsula.

NATURE *A Naturalist's Mexico,* by Roland H. Wauer, is a fabulous guide to birding. *Peterson Field Guides: Mexican Birds,* by Roger Tory Peterson and Edward L. Chalif, is another excellent guide to the sport. *A Hiker's Guide to Mexico's Natural History,* by Jim Conrad, covers flora and fauna and tells how to find the easy-to-reach as well as out-of-the-way spots he describes.

Movies

CLASSICS For some takes on old school Mexico, check out Elia Kazan's 1952 classic, *Viva Zapata!,* which was written by John Steinbeck and stars Marlon Brando as the early-20th-century Mexican revolutionary Emiliano Zapata. Or rent the HBO flick *And Starring Pancho Villa as Himself* with Antonio Banderas, which is a true story about how revolutionaries allowed a Hollywood film company to tape Pancho Villa in actual battle. Then there's the deservedly famous Orson Welles flick *Touch of Evil* about drugs and corruption in Tijuana (even though it preposterously stars Charlton Heston as a Mexican).

Luis Buñuel's stylish 1950 film *Los Olvidados* chronicles a group of young hoodlums living in the slums of Mexico City. It was filmed partially in the Plaza de La Romita, a charming, somewhat hidden section of Colonia Roma.

Directed brilliantly by John Huston, the Academy Award–winning classic *Night of the Iguana* is a must watch if you're visiting Puerto Vallarta or Acapulco. Starring the luscious Ava Gardner as a down-on-her-luck hotel owner in the '50s, the film fired fantasies for many a gringa pursuing the good life, beach boys and all, south of the border. The filming required a whole village (Mismaloya, p. 467) to be built to accommodate sets and crew. If you can find a copy of the making of the film, watch that, too. It presents a slice of PV history before it became the sprawling resort it is now.

CONTEMPORARY FILMS Anyone planning a trip to Mexico should watch the brilliant *Y Tu Mama También* directed by Alfonso Cuaron. It chronicles a pair of teenage boys who end up on an impromptu road trip to a fictional destination with a sexy older woman they randomly met at a wedding. Much of the film deals with the country's poverty, immigration, and social class issues. And the sites explored on film can be visited in real life. Explore the Costa Chica and you'll find that hidden virgin beaches, a la the mythical "La Boca del Cielo," do exist down unexpected dirt roads.

Frida, starring and produced by Salma Hayek, is a wonderful Frida Kahlo biopic. Watch it and you'll learn everything you need to know about the famous artist, her world-shattering accident, and her relationships with men like Diego Rivera and Leon Trotsky. The exquisite cinematography also perfectly captures Mexico's inherent spirit of magic realism.

In *Amores Perros,* the director of *21 Grams* and *Babel* (Alejandro Gonzalez Inarritu) presents three connected stories about different ways of life in Mexico City that become intertwined at the site of a car accident. Taken together, the stories offer a great glimpse into contemporary Mexican society. Inarritu's Academy Award–nominated *Babel* is another tour de force; its Mexican border scene is realistic, exhilarating, and frightening all at once.

Director Robert Rodriguez's breakout (and arguably his best) film, *El Mariachi,* is set in a small central Mexican town. Made on a shoestring budget, this somewhat cheesy action flick is at least highly entertaining. His *Once Upon a Time in Mexico* isn't as great but it's fun to see scenes of San Miguel Allende, where it was filmed. Ditto the Brad Pitt and Julia Roberts vehicle, *The Mexican.*

Man on Fire stars Denzel Washington alongside Dakota Fanning, as a bodyguard in Mexico City and the little girl he is hired to protect, respectively. There are some great scenes shot around the city, even though the plot is pretty depressing.

Sexo, Pudor y Lagrimas by director Antonio Serrano offers a gritty, unflinching look at the battle of the sexes in Mexico City in the '90s. It was the second film to emerge from the new era of Mexican cinema, after *Like Water for Chocolate.*

Tijuana Makes Me Happy, directed by Dylan Verrechia with music by Pepe Mogt from Nortec Collective, shows a thankfully bright and realistic picture of Tijuana. The film's goal is "to break down the preconceived notion of Tijuana as a city of sin by showing the humanity of its people: their struggle, the strength of character, and the love of life that flourishes within." Something must be working—the film has won Latin film awards and was screened in 2007 at the Slamdance festival.

If you want more info on what's happening now in border towns, rent *Traffic,* starring Academy Award–winner Benicio del Toro. It includes some powerful scenes focusing on the drug war at the Tijuana border. Or get a hold of the 2002 documentary *Tijuana Remix,* which celebrates the city's culturally unique and idiosyncratic qualities. You can also get a great "tourist guide" online via a short film called *Tijuana es Addiccion* made by local Jacinto Astiazaran (www.turnhere.com/city/tijuana/all/films/252.aspx).

Finally, we can't overlook the fact that a number of Mexican films were nominated for Academy Awards in 2007, including Inarritu's *Babel;* Guillermo del Toro's *Pan's Labyrinth,* a beguiling fantasy set in Franco-era Spain; and Cuaron's *Children of Men,* an apocalyptic tale set in London and starring Clive Owen. You'll want to keep an eye on all three of these directors. Let's hope they do more movies about their native country soon.

Music

Yes, you can rock out to plain old rock in Mexico. But why limit yourself, when you can take in sounds as varied as troba (acoustic folk), reggaeton (rap 'n' reggae), cumbia (4/4 beat popular dance music), norteño (a type of ranchera, or country 'n' western music, featuring lots of accordions and banjos), nortec (a techno spin on norteño music), or corridos (sentimental ballads, heavy on guitar-strumming)? And we haven't even mentioned better-known types of music, like salsa, merengue, rumba, and mariachi.

All of the following music recommendations should help you create an appropriately varied Mexican playlist for your iPod, though not all of the *musicos* (musicians) are actually from Mexico—some are just huge artists here.

At press time, **MySpace Mexico** was in its beta stage, but by the time you read this, it'll be up and running. That means you can use it to listen to music by the artists listed below—and to hear tunes by cutting edge indie bands like Mexico City's **Los Dynamite** (the most popular of a

THE BASICS

Mariachi Bands

So you always thought mariachi music was really cheesy and embarrassing especially when it's blasting while you're trying to eat dinner in a Mexican restaurant, right? Well get over yourself. Mariachi music is the essence of Mexico, so you'll be missing out if you tune it out. Originating in the State of Jalisco during the 19th century, mariachi music was introduced by the Spanish to play in church. But the *criollos* (Mexican-born Spaniards) had different ideas. First hired to sing at haciendas after the revolution, mariachis got their start roaming the countryside and singing *corridos* (topical songs about politics, gossip, good and bad deeds). As the country changed, so did the songs, which began to incorporate waltzes, polkas, and new instruments like trumpets. Today the genre also uses harps, guitars, and violins to play what are essentially pop songs addressing universal themes of love lost, love bought through prostitution, drunkenness, death, joy, and despair.

Still strolling gardens and squares as they have been for the last 2 centuries, mariachis can be found throughout Mexico, but one of the best spots to hear them do their thing is the Plaza Garibaldi (p. 119) in Mexico City. And if for some reason you haven't heard of mariachis before, you can't miss them—they look a little like Mexican cowboys dressed up for a special occasion, with tight studded trousers and elaborate cropped jackets. If you want to impress your girlfriend or boyfriend, try to grab one for a serenade. Here's a list of the most popular mariachi songs to request:

Amor Eterno

Cielito Lindo

El Becerro

Hermoso Carino

Jarabe Tapatio

Mexico Lindo & Querido

Mujeres Divinas

Te Voy a Olvidar

Volver, Volver

recent spate of Mexican bands whose songs are mostly in English).

The Tijuana Sessions by the Tijuana and San Diego–based Nortec collective of musicians, DJs, artists, graphic artists, and filmmakers, is *the* soundtrack to modern Tijuana. A mix of electronica, and snare drum and bass, layered over norteño beats, the music alternates between jittery and dreamy. It's a sophisticated blend of traditional, pop, and techno music with some truly unique elements thrown in.

Kinky is the self-titled album by the Monterrey, California, band Kinky—it's an earful of norteño music, but given a unique, Americanized twist.

"Me gusta la playa, me gustas tu . . . Me gusta la mar, me gustas tu . . . Me gusta la vecina, me gustas tu." So goes the refrain for **Manu Chao**'s internationally popular ditty "Me Gustas Tu" on his *Proxima Estacion, Esperanza* album. The song is not only danceable, it's a brilliant way to learn some Spanish.

The French-Latin signer Manu Chao used to be in the band Mano Negra before he launched his successful solo career. A French band with a Spanish name, **Mano Negra** became really big in Mexico in the late '80s and early '90s. With a talent like Manu Chao at the helm, it's no wonder. Any of their albums are worth a listen.

The soulful Julieta Venegas has garnered comparisons to musicians like Bjork and Fiona Apple because of her creative, fresh songs and sexy-quirky personal style. She's composed for films and sings everything from punk-influenced pop to soulful ballads. She grew up between Tijuana and California but calls Mexico City home today. Her latest album is *Limón y Sal.*

If you like The Pixies, you'll probably be into **Café Tacuba**'s music. They've been together since 1989 and took their name from the old (1920s) Centro Historico cafe of the same name. Pixies comparisons aside, their music is hard to classify—they're influenced by their country's indigenous music as much as folk, punk, bolero, and hip-hop. They're on the soundtrack of both *Amores Perros* and *Y Tu Mama Tambien,* and of their five albums, we most recommend *Re* (1994).

If you like rural northern border music at all, you're gonna love **Los Tigres del Norte.** The Tigers catchy melodies backed by hopped up accordion and bass guitars make for ideal road trip music.

Flaco Jimenez is a Grammy Award–winning artist whose Tex-Mex style of norteño music may be more palatable to "Western" ears than Los Tigres. Often a guest artist on Los Lobos' LPs, his beautiful voice and fabulous accordion playing just make us happy.

Spawned out of the Los Angeles punk music scene, **Los Lobos** may be Angelenos but they have deep roots in Mexico. Their spin-off group **Los Super 7,** whose albums include guest artists' interpretations of traditional Mexican ballads, is a must for any road trip. Their beautiful *La Pistola y el Corazon* will surely get you in the mood to travel south.

For some poppy music, try any of **Selena Quintanilla Perez**'s albums. Though this Mexican-American singer was murdered at the age of 23, her brand of *Tejano* music, or pop music originating from northern Mexico and southern Texas, is still immensely popular.

Recommended Websites

Here's a list of sites you might want to bookmark as you plan your trip to Mexico, and to call up as you sit at an Internet point in Mexico City or Puerto Vallarta.

- **www.foreignword.com**: Translations from English to Spanish.
- **www.mexperience.com**: A 5-year old website that specializes in travel, real estate, and general lifestyle issues. In 2005, this won a Silver Lens Award from President Vicente Fox.
- **www.mexconnect.com**: This highly recommended site has lots of specialized columns and some of the best forums on the country you'll find anywhere.
- **www.ourmexico.com**: Includes forums and features and "the most comprehensive directory of Mexico travel sites on the Internet." Or so they say; it does provide a very thorough and useful list of links on Mexico.
- **www.mexonline.com**: The oldest of the Mexico websites, Mexonline was started in 1993 back in the Internet's Stone Age. Yet it remains trustworthy, reliable, and totally up-to-date, with links to maps, city guides, and real estate info.

Nuts & Bolts

Addresses In many small towns, shops and businesses don't have street numbers (throughout this book, s/n indicates *"sin numero,"* or "without number"). Cross streets are indicated wherever possible in those cases. If a cross street isn't provided, you just have to ask someone for directions when you get to the neighborhood. For instance, if an address is listed as "Playa Zipolite, s/n," that means you have to look for it on Playa Zipolite.

ATM Networks See "Money, Money, Money, Money (Money!)," p. 23.

Business Hours In general, businesses in larger cities are open between 9am and 7pm; in smaller towns many close between 2 and 4pm. Most close on Sunday. In resort areas it is common to find stores open at least in the mornings on Sunday, and for shops to stay open late, often until 8 or even 10pm. Bank hours are Monday through Friday from 9 or 9:30am to anywhere between 3 and 7pm. Increasingly, banks open on Saturday for at least a half-day. Most bars and clubs get kicking around 10pm and stay open until 2 or 3am.

Cameras & Film Film costs about the same as in the United States. Tourists wishing to use a video or still camera at any archaeological site in Mexico or at many museums operated by the Instituto de Antropología e Historia (INAH) must pay US$4 per camera at each site visited. Also, use of a tripod at any archaeological site requires a permit from INAH. It's courteous to ask permission before photographing anyone. It is never considered polite to take photos inside a church in Mexico.

Climate See "When to Go," earlier in this chapter.

Doctors & Dentists Every embassy and consulate can recommend local doctors and dentists with good training and modern equipment; some of the doctors and dentists speak English. See the list of embassies and consulates under "Embassies & Consulates," below. Hotels with a large foreign clientele can often recommend English-speaking doctors.

Drugs Places to buy drugs are called *tiendas.* Busts happen periodically and you don't want to be around a tienda when one does (that's why all the happening dealers now use cellphones and make deliveries). See "Health & Safety" earlier in this chapter for info on drug penalties.

Drugstores *Farmacias* (pharmacies) will sell you just about anything, with or without a prescription. Most pharmacies are open Monday through Saturday from 8am to 8pm. The major resort areas generally have one or two 24-hour pharmacies. Pharmacies take turns staying open during off hours; if you are in a smaller town and need to buy medicine during off hours, ask for a *farmacia de turno.*

Electricity The electrical system in Mexico is 110 volts AC (60 cycles), as in the United States and Canada. In reality, however, it may cycle more slowly and overheat your appliances. To compensate, select a medium or low speed on hair dryers. Many older hotels still have electrical outlets for flat two-prong plugs; you'll need an adapter for any plug with an enlarged end on one prong or with three prongs. Many better hotels have three-hole outlets (*trifásicos* in Spanish). Those that don't may have loan adapters, but to be sure, it's always better to carry your own.

Embassies & Consulates Info on the three **U.S. embassies** below can be found at http://mexico.usembassy.gov:

Mexico City: Mexico American Embassy, Paseo de la Reforma 305, Colonia Cuauhtemoc, Mexico 06500; D.F.; ☎ **555/080-2000** or 5511-9980.

Mérida: American Consulate, Paseo Montejo 453, Yucatán; ☎ **999/925-5011.**

Tijuana: American Consulate General, Tapachula 96, Baja California; ☎ **664/622-7400.**

U.S. Consular Agents have been designated to assist U.S. citizens in serious emergencies. Each consular agent listed below is supervised by one of the above-listed offices and may be contacted through it or by calling the consular agent's direct number.

Acapulco: Hotel Continental Emporio Costera Miguel Aleman 121—Local 14; ☎ **744/484-0300** or 744/469-0556.

Cabo San Lucas: Bulevar Marina Local C-4, Plaza Nautica, Col. Centro; ☎ **624/143-3566.**

Cancún: Plaza Caracol Two, Second Level, No. 320-323, Bulevar Kukulcan, Km 8.5, Zona Hotelera; ☎ **998/883-0272.**

Cozumel: Plaza Villa Mar en El Centro, Plaza Principal (Parque Juárez between Melgar and Calle 5), second floor, Locales #8 and 9; ☎ **987/872-4574.**

Ixtapa/Zihuatanejo: Hotel Fontan, Bulevar Ixtapa; ☎ **755/553-2100.**

Mazatlán: Hotel Playa Mazatlán, Playa Gaviotas #202, Zona Dorada; ☎ **669/916-5889.**

Oaxaca: Macedonio Alcala No. 407, Interior 20; ☎ **951/514-3054** or 951/516-2853.

Puerto Vallarta: Zaragoza #160, Col. Centro, Edificio Vallarta Plaza, Piso 2 Int. 18; ☎ **322/222-0069.**

San Miguel de Allende: Dr. Hernandez Macias #72; ☎ **415/152-2357** or 415/152-0068.

The Embassy of **Australia** in Mexico City is at Rubén Darío 55, Col. Polanco (☎ **555/1101-2200**). It's open Monday through Friday from 9am to 1pm.

The Embassy of **Canada** in Mexico City is at Schiller 529, Col. Polanco (☎ **555/724-7900**); it's open Monday through Friday from 9am to 1pm. At other times, the name of a duty officer is posted on the door. Visit www.dfait-maeci.gc.ca for addresses of consular agencies in Mexico. There are Canadian consulates in Acapulco (☎ **744/484-1305**); Cancún (☎ **998/883-3360**); Monterrey (☎ **818/344-2753**); Oaxaca (☎ **951/513-3777**); Puerto Vallarta (☎ **322/293-0098**); San José del Cabo (☎ **624/142-4333**); and Tijuana (☎ **664/684-0461**).

The Embassy of **New Zealand** in Mexico City is at Jaime Balmes 8, fourth floor, Col. Los Morales, Polanco (☎ **55/5283-9460;** kiwimexico@compuserve.com.mx). It's open Monday through Friday from 8am to 3pm.

The Embassy of the **United Kingdom** in Mexico City is at Río Lerma 71, Col. Cuauhtémoc (☎ **55/5242-8500;** www.embajadabritanica.com.mx). It's open Monday through Friday from 8:30am to 3:30pm.

The Embassy of **Ireland** in Mexico City is at Bulevar Cerrada, Avila Camacho 76, third floor, Col. Lomas de Chapultepec (☎ **55/5520-5803**). It's open Monday through Friday from 9am to 5pm.

The **South African** Embassy in Mexico City is at Andrés Bello 10, ninth floor, Col. Polanco (☎ **55/5282-9260**). It's open Monday through Friday from 8am to 3:30pm.

Emergencies In case of emergency, dial ☎ **065** from any phone within Mexico. The 24-hour **Tourist Help Line** in Mexico City is ☎ **01-800/987-8224** or 55/5089-7500, or you can now simply dial ☎ **078.** The operators don't always speak English, but they are always willing to help. The tourist legal assistance office (Procuraduría del Turista) in Mexico City (☎ **55/5625-8153** or -8154) always has an English speaker available. Though the phones are frequently busy, they operate 24 hours.

Holidays See "When to Go," p. 20.

Language Spanish is the official language in Mexico. English is spoken and understood to some degree in most tourist areas. Mexicans are very accommodating with foreigners who try to speak Spanish, even in broken sentences.

Liquor Laws The legal drinking age in Mexico is 18; however, asking for ID or denying purchase is extremely rare. Grocery stores sell everything from beer and wine to national and imported liquors. You can buy liquor 24 hours a day, but during major elections, dry laws often are enacted for as much as 72 hours in advance of the election—and they apply to tourists as well as local residents. Mexico does not have laws that apply to transporting liquor in cars, but authorities are beginning to target drunk drivers more aggressively. It's a good idea to drive defensively.

It is not legal to drink in the street; however, many tourists do so. If you are getting drunk, you shouldn't drink in the street, because you are more likely to get stopped by the police.

Lost & Found If your wallet is stolen, the police probably won't be able to recover it. Be sure to notify all of your credit card companies right away, and file a report at the nearest police precinct. Your credit card company or insurer may require a police report number or record of the loss. Most credit card companies have an emergency toll-free number to call if your card is lost or stolen; these numbers are not toll-free within Mexico (see the "Telephone Tips" box, earlier, for instructions on calling U.S. toll-free numbers). The company may be able to wire you a cash advance off your credit card immediately, and, in many places, can deliver an emergency credit card in a day or two. **Visa**'s U.S. emergency number is ☎ **800/847-2911** or 410/581-9994. American Express cardholders and traveler's check holders should call ☎ **800/221-7282.** MasterCard holders should call ☎ **800/307-7309** or 636/722-7111. For other credit cards, call the toll-free number directory at ☎ **800/555-1212.**

THE BASICS

Identity theft or fraud are potential complications of losing your wallet, especially if you've lost your driver's license along with your cash and credit cards. Notify the major credit-reporting bureaus immediately; placing a fraud alert on your records may protect you against liability for criminal activity. The three major U.S. credit-reporting agencies are **Equifax** (☎ **800/766-0008;** www.equifax.com), **Experian** (☎ **888/397-3742;** www.experian.com), and **TransUnion** (☎ **800/680-7289;** www.transunion.com). Finally, if you've lost all forms of photo ID, call your airline and explain the situation; they might allow you to board the plane if you have a copy of your passport or birth certificate and a copy of the police report you've filed.

Mail Postage for a postcard or letter is 8 pesos; it may arrive anywhere from 1 to 6 weeks later. A registered letter costs US$1.90. Sending a package can be quite expensive—the Mexican postal service charges US$8 per kilo (2¼ lb.)—and unreliable; it takes 2 to 6 weeks, if it arrives at all. (The mail system here is that bad.) The recommended way to send a package or important mail is through FedEx, DHL, UPS, or another reputable international mail service.

Newspapers & Magazines There currently is no national English-language newspaper. Newspaper kiosks in larger cities carry a selection of English-language magazines.

Passports & Visas For residents of the **United States:** Whether you're applying in person or by mail, you can download passport and visa applications from the U.S. State Department website at http://travel.state.gov. To find your regional passport office, either check the U.S. State Department website or call the **National Passport Information Center** toll-free number (☎ **877/487-2778**) for automated information.

For residents of **Canada:** Applications are available at travel agencies throughout Canada or from the central **Passport Office,** Department of Foreign Affairs and International Trade, Ottawa, ON K1A 0G3 (☎ **800/567-6868;** www.ppt.gc.ca).

For residents of the **United Kingdom:** To pick up an application for a standard 10-year passport (5-year passport for children under 16), visit your nearest passport office, major post office, or travel agency. You can also contact the **United Kingdom Passport Service** at ☎ **0870/521-0410,** or search its website at www.ukpa.gov.uk.

For residents of **Ireland:** You can apply for a 10-year passport at the **Passport Office,** Setanta Centre, Molesworth Street, Dublin 2 (☎ **01/671-1633;** www.irlgov.ie/iveagh). Those under age 18 and over 65 must apply for a US$12 3-year passport. You can also apply at 1A South Mall, Cork (☎ **021/272-525**), or at most main post offices.

For residents of **Australia:** You can pick up an application from your local post office or any branch of Passports Australia, but you must schedule an interview at the passport office to present your application materials. Call the **Australian Passport Information Service** at ☎ **131-232,** or visit the government website at www.passports.gov.au.

For residents of **New Zealand:** You can pick up a passport application at any New Zealand Passports Office or download it from their website. Contact the **Passports Office** at ☎ **0800/225-050** in New Zealand or 04/474-8100, or log on to www.passports.govt.nz.

Police In Mexico City, police are to be suspected as frequently as they are to be trusted; however, you'll find many who are quite honest and helpful. In the rest of the country, especially in the tourist areas, most are very protective of international visitors. Several cities, including Puerto Vallarta, Mazatlán, Cancún, and Acapulco, have a special corps of English-speaking Tourist Police to assist with directions, guidance, and more. For police emergency numbers, turn to "Nuts & Bolts" in the chapters that follow.

Safety See "Health & Safety," earlier in this chapter.

Smoking Smoking is permitted and generally accepted in most public places, including restaurants, bars, and hotel lobbies. Nonsmoking areas and hotel rooms for nonsmokers are becoming more common in higher-end establishments, but they tend to be the exception rather than the rule.

Taxes The 15% IVA (value-added) tax applies on goods and services in most of Mexico, and it's supposed to be included in the posted price. This tax is 10% in Cancún, Cozumel, and Los Cabos. There is a 5% tax on food and drinks consumed in restaurants that sell alcoholic beverages with an alcohol content of more than 10%; this tax applies whether you drink alcohol or not. Tequila is subject to a 25% tax. Mexico imposes an exit tax of around US$24 on every foreigner leaving the country by plane.

Telephone Tips See the "Telephone Tips" box earlier in this chapter.

Time Zone Central Time prevails throughout most of Mexico. The states of Sonora, Sinaloa, and parts of Nayarit are on Mountain Time. The state of Baja California Norte is on Pacific Time, but Baja California Sur is on Mountain Time. All of Mexico observes **daylight saving time.**

Tipping Always tip the gas station attendant who pumps your gas $2 to $10; tip the kid who bags your groceries in a supermarket $2 to $5 as well. Tip porters US$1 per bag, depending on how heavy they are. Tip taxi drivers only if they give good service—the standard is 10% to 15%. Tip restaurant waiters 15%. And always leave a tip in your hotel room for the maid, from $5 to $10 each night depending on the hotel.

Toilets Public toilets are not common in Mexico, but an increasing number are available, especially at fast-food restaurants and Pemex gas stations. These facilities and restaurant and club restrooms commonly have attendants, who expect a small tip (about $5).

Useful Phone Numbers **Tourist Help Line,** available 24 hours (☎ 01-800/987-8224 toll-free inside Mexico; or dial 078). **Mexico Hot Line** (☎ 800/446-3942). **U.S. Dept. of State Travel Advisory,** staffed 24 hours (☎ 202/647-5225). **U.S. Passport Agency** (☎ 877/487-2777). **U.S. Centers for Disease Control and Prevention International Traveler's Hot Line** (☎ 877/394-8747).

Mexico City

B*ienvenidos a la capital.* Ever since I first set foot in Mexico City over 10 years ago, I've been fascinated by *la gran ciudad* (the big city) and return every chance I get. But a lot has changed in the Mexican capital since my first visit—and the time has never been better to visit.

Mexico City is Mexico's Federal District (*Distrito Federal*, or DF) and the Western Hemisphere's oldest urban center; what began in the early 1300s as a community on the shores of Lake Texcoco has morphed into an international megalopolis of 22 million. You already know it as an archaeologist's delight and the numero uno place to score some damn good tacos. But these days, Mexico City is also home to the oldest and largest university in the Americas, a burgeoning fine art and gallery scene, and some of the tastiest nouveau cuisine around. *Chilangos,* as DF-ers call themselves (though they don't always welcome the label from out-of-towners), have always known how to *disfrutar la vida* (read: have a blast), and nightlife aficionados will find the all-hours party scene among the world's best. With new highways elevated above the Periferico, a booming real-estate market, and the arrival of hip boutique hotels that are both affordable and classy, the city hosts international jet-setters and backpackers alike. They arrive in droves to shop its flea markets and chic boutiques, drink in classic cantinas and upscale dance clubs, ride with the working class on the Metro, and emerge to see *fresas* (preppies) cruising their Ferraris down Avenida Presidente Masaryk in ultra-posh Polanco.

Some things haven't changed in the Distrito Federal, or "el DF" (day-effeh), as the city is typically called by its residents, though. At 2,220m (7,400 ft) the city maintains the highest elevation of any major city in North America. Unless you're a sherpa from the Himalayas, don't be surprised if you lose your appetite and feel a little short of breath within your first 24 hours of arrival—give yourself a chance to acclimate while experiencing the mellow side of the city. Like Washington, D.C., Mexico City also remains a federal district, which means it's not part of any state—this gives it a decidedly freewheeling vibe. (During political protests, the overall atmosphere is way more inclined toward street fair than riot gear.)

Whatever you decide to do while in Mexico City, you'll discover that life—like the food—is just spicier here. *Que disfrutes!* (Enjoy!)

Best of Mexico City

- **Best New Hotel in a Happenin' Hood:** You can stroll the sweet chocolate lab, Conde, at **CondesaDF** through nearby Parque Mexico, watch an indie film series, and blast the in-room iPod through the flatscreen wall-mounted TV. Then head up to the roof deck for a quick hot tub dip before reclining on an adjacent lounge-bed while the waiter serves you signature sushi and fresh, unique cocktails. With all its options, CondesaDF is the ultimate place to stay in the city. See p. 94.
- **Best Historic Hotel in a Happenin' Hood: La Casona** is so homey you might never want to leave. With an elegant facade, stained-glass windows, the best breakfast menu in town, and a flair-filled *epoca porfiriana* style, this cozy boutique makes you feel more at home than when you're at *su casa*. It has 29 rooms but feels like a luxe bed-and-breakfast. An added bonus is that the hip Colonia Roma is at your doorstep, and it's within walking distance of neighboring Condesa. See p. 96.
- **Best Artsy Nouveau Cuisine:** At **Aguila y Sol,** renowned chef Martha Ortiz Chapa brings her signature style to traditional Mexican dishes like chiles en nogada and creative desserts with imaginative back stories. She's been a guest chef at hip Hangar 7 in Austria, coauthored a cookbook with Laura Esquivel, is a fascinating conversationalist, and a great source of information about Mexico, its history, people, and cuisine. See p. 102.
- **Best Late-Night Taqueria:** Arguing with a Chilango about where to find the best tacos al pastor is kind of like getting into it with a Roman over the greatest trattoria for fettuccini, or asking a Londoner which pub serves the top fish and chips. It's all good. But these days the PYTs of Mexico City flock to trendy **El Califa** in Condesa after a late night on the town for some DGTs (that's damn good tacos) before hitting the sack (or more *antros,* or dance clubs). Order the tacos al pastor with extra piña and a side of *cebollitas* (small grilled onions in *salsa magi,* which is kind of a Mexican version of soy sauce, also used on pizzas). See p. 99.
- **Best Frida and Diego Fix:** You're going to Xochimilco for a canal ride Venice couldn't hold a candle to (p. 105), so don't pass up seeing the fantastic collection of F&D's patron and close friend Dolores Olmedo at the **Museo Dolores Olmedo Patiño** on the way. See p. 121
- **Best All-Night-Long Dance Club:** Don't let the name **Pervert Lounge**

fool you. It's a hip haven not for perverts but for electronica lovers or anyone looking to have an all-out, all-night, booty-shakin' blast, Mexican jet set and alt-crowd style. See p. 109.

- **Best Bar: El Hijo del Cuervo** is a veritable Coyoacán institution. This "Son of the Crow" has been here forever and shows no sign of slowing down. Great music is the staple, whether it's live Mexican rock or '80s tune-ology blasting through the PA. This is the sort of place where tequila is consumed by the bucket, not the bottle. See p. 106.
- **Best Cultural Center:** Renovated in 1993, **Centro de Cultura Casa Lamm** is a private cultural institute housed in a restored mansion that dates from 1911. As such, it's a unique Belle Epoque survivor in the Roma district where most of its *compadres* have since met the wrecking ball. It hosts fabulous contemporary art exhibits and gives you a great idea of how the other half lived back in *el día* when Roma was, like, totally *fresa*. See p. 116.
- **Best Sorta-Overwhelming Yet Must-See Museum:** With over 53,000 pieces in its collection, the **Museo Nacional de Antropologia** is so big you could spend days exploring it. But don't 'cause then you'd have to go straight back to the airport and miss everything else. Think of what the Louvre is to Paris; that's the equivalent of the Antropologia to Mexico City. See p. 117.
- **Best Weekend Adventure:** Adventure travel company Rio y Montana has created a paradise for adventure lovers in the hills of Valle de Bravo, a lake town and popular weekend getaway (think Hamptons, only without the ocean, colonial-style). If you're into hiking, mountain biking, flying, zip-lining, off-roading, rock climbing, or steaming out your demons in a temazcal (see box, p. 64), the **Rodavento** lodge is a must. See p. 143.
- **Best Weekend Markets:** In **Coyoacán,** you'll spot boys with dreadlocks and girls with tattoos. Plus handcarved wooden pipes, tie-dyed everything, tarot readings, and Aztec dancers with bells on their feet. In short, this plaza rocks, and its weekend market (check it out on Sat) is a neo-hippie, goth, bohemian, rocker, character, burnout, and, yes, tourist haven. The artisans make most of the goods they sell, and you can find funky crystal, amber, and silver jewelry, Bob Marley flags, hand-knit ponchos, and typical Mexican crafts at great prices. Just be sure to bargain your heart out for anything without a price tag. See p. 126.
- **Best Mystical Haven:** Wake up, step outside, and see the clouds lightly draping the Tepozteco, the fantastically hikeable hill crowned with the archaeological site, Tepozteco. With a view to die for of the town and rocky surrounds, **Posada del Tepozteco** in Tepoztlán is absolutely *the* place to come for a drink or romantic meal on the easiest of weekend getaways, even if you're not staying as a guest. See p. 135.

MEXICO CITY

Getting There & Getting Around

Getting into Town

BY PLANE

Tons of major international airlines fly to Mexico City. **AeroMexico** (☎ **800/021-4000;** aeromexico.com), one of Mexico's two main carriers, has good food and service on its fleet of Boeings. **Mexicana** (☎ **800/502-2000;** www.mexicana.com), **American** (☎ **800/433-7300;** www.aa.com), and **Continental** (☎ **800/900-5000;**

www.continental.com) also offer daily flights to Mexico's capital.

Several relatively new regional carriers, such as Mexicana's **Click Mexicana** (☎ **800/11-CLICK;** www.clickmx.com); **Aero Mar** (☎ **555/133-1111;** www.aeromar.com.mx); and AeroMexico's **Aerolitoral** (☎ **800/800-2376;** www.aerolitoral.com) offer budget flights to and from Mexico City. See "Basics" p. 26 for more info.

Note: On your flight into Benito Juárez International Airport, save time at immigration by making sure the forms given to you on the plane are filled out—front *and* back—because cranky officials have been known to send less-thorough travelers to the back of the line.

In the domestic terminal between Gates B and C, a mural by Juan O'Gorman chronicles the history of flight, in case you're feeling ambitious about getting into Mexico City's art scene. Once through immigration, grab your bag and head toward the exit. But wait—you're not home-free yet. At the sliding glass doors, there's a button to press. If you get green (more often than not), then you're good to go. If it pops up red, you're the lucky winner of a random bag search.

To the left of the sliding doors are a bunch of legit money-changing places and ATMs; it's better to cash out now than wait until you get into town. A multi-million-dollar airport expansion project is underway, and flatscreen TVs throughout the terminals explain the upgrades. (The information may not be up-to-date but the TVs sure are pretty.) For **general airport info,** dial ☎ **55/5571-3600** or visit the clearly marked information booth in the international arrivals terminal.

Ignore the guys who approach you within the terminal asking you to take their taxis. Outside the terminals on your left is an authorized **taxi booth** (www.taxisdelaeropuerto.com.mx), which offers the best way to reach your destination, especially if it's late and you've had a long day of traveling. Fares are set by *zona* (zone); to give an idea, at press-time a taxi to the Roma neighborhood was $152. Don't run across the street to the unauthorized cabs to save a few bucks. Mexico affords many places to scrimp and save along the way, and this isn't one of them.

No city buses serve the airport. The nearest **Metro** stop (6am–midnight) is the Terminal Aerea station on the yellow #5 line, located up the sidewalk from the domestic terminal. It's about a 45-minute ride to the Centro. Change to the #1 line at Pantitlan to go downtown. It's a pain in the ass, but if you're saving your pesos for *micheladas* (spiced beer with lime), that's the deal. It's the cheapest subway ride ever, too, at $3.90 per ticket. (Once inside, you can transfer as much as you like.)

BY CAR

Here are the chief thoroughfares for getting out of the city: Insurgentes Sur becomes Highway 95 to Taxco and Cuernavaca. Insurgentes Norte leads to Teotihuacán and Pachuca. Highway 57, the Periférico (loop around the city), is also known as Bulevar Manuel Avila Camacho, to denote street addresses; it goes north and leads out of the city to Tula and Querétaro. Constituyentes leads west out of the city past Chapultepec Park and connects with Highway 15 to Toluca, Morelia, and Pátzcuaro. (Reforma also connects with Hwy. 15.) Zaragoza leads east to Highway 150 to Puebla and Veracruz.

See "By Car" under "Getting Around" for more tips on driving in Mexico City.

BY BUS

It's probably easiest and just as cheap for you to get around Mexico by budget airline (see "By Plane" earlier for info) as by bus. Still, the bus systems here are efficient, cheap, and well-maintained (though the cheapest buses can mean a bumpy and hot ride). Major Mexican bus lines are **ADO** (☎ **01-800/800-0364;** www.adogl.com.mx), with service from southeastern Mexico; **Estrella Roja** (☎ **01-800/712-2284;** www.estrellaroja.com.mx), featuring service from Puebla (see "Road Trips," p. 130); **Omnibus de Mexico** (☎ **01-800/011-6336;** www.odm.com.mx), which arrives from everywhere, including the U.S.; **ETN** (☎ **01-800/800-0386;** www.etn.com.mx), also omnipresent in Mexico; and **UNO** (☎ **01-800/702-8000;** www.uno.com.mx), providing service to el DF from 20-plus destinations in southeastern Mexico and the Gulf region.

See "By Bus" under "Getting Around" for more info on taking buses in Mexico City.

Getting Around

Despite its massive size, Mexico City is fairly easy to navigate. There are Metro stations in all the major neighborhoods (often more than one, as in Centro Historico). **Taxis** are plentiful, though be sure to take one from a *sitio*—official taxi stand—rather than hailing one of the mini-Volkswagens on the street, as drivers have been known to rob tourists since the devaluation of the peso in the 1990s. Sad but true.

A fun way to see the city by bus is via **Turibus** 'cause you can sit on the upper deck and hear cool tunes while you're taken directly to places you want to visit anyway. For more information, see "Sightseeing," p. 112.

At presstime, the Mexican government had announced multi-billion-dollar plans to create a rail system for Mexico City and its outskirts, but it's still a long way from completion.

BY COLECTIVO

Green-and-white microbuses, known as ***colectivos,*** follow routes along main avenues like Insurgentes or Universidad, and often have stations outside the Metro, like at the Coyoacán stop, to transport you to the Coyoacán Plaza. Stops are not official, but by request, so don't be shy about flagging them down. Larger buses cost $4 (no fare cards or tickets—you just pay onboard) and have official stops, and a light-rail system runs on Insurgentes (two lanes of traffic were removed to install it).

BY SUBWAY

I ♥ the Mexico City subway. With Mexico City's thick traffic, it's really just easier to hop on the Metro rather than mess with the bus. Trains, which come, like, every 5 seconds, are quick and reliable, safe, clean, pleasant, and easy; and stations even have art exhibits—serious ones, like architectural artifacts and installations by contemporary sculptors. In fact, subway-riding is *the* best way to see art without ever setting foot in a museum or gallery. It's a ridiculously low $2 to ride, and tickets are sold at taquilla booths located in every station. The directions of trains are marked by their last stop, so check the boards by track entrances to make sure you're heading in the right direction. Example: You're at Auditorio and want to get to Tacubaya. Your train is the one to Barranca del Muerto, end of the line to the south, not Rosario, last stop to the north. Pretty *facil, no?*

Transferring between lines inside a station is free. Transfer points are marked by overlapping colors on the subway map, and the word *correspondencia* tells you what lines you can transfer to (i.e., correspondencia Tasqueña, correspondencia Pantitlan). Hours of operation are 6am to midnight, and 6am to 1am on Saturday nights. Of course, anytime you use public transportation, don't go waving wads of dough in the air. Keep bags and cameras close to your chest, and cards, passports, and cash well-buried in a waist-front flat money belt. Odds are you won't be mugged if you're just going about your business in broad daylight, but it's just good common sense against pickpocketing.

BY CAR

If you are an especially skilled driver, it's a good idea to consider renting a car to get around points outside of town. All the major companies have offices at Benito Juárez airport. **Advantage Rent-a-Car** (☎ **800/777-5500;** www.arac.com) is a particularly friendly and no-hassle company that offers cars to those who are 23 or over. See the box on p. 83 for more info.

That said, brace yourself for some defensive driving. It's actually not *that* crazy—just a little less controlled of an environment than in, say, the States. The drivers aren't as aggressive as they are in, say, Rome, Dublin, or Boston. Instead of road-rage, the issue here is simple inattention, like changing lanes without signaling or driving slowly and not letting you pass. Just keep an eye out at all times, plan your route, and negotiate traffic safely. Avoid rush hour from 8am to 10am in the morning and Friday afternoons, when traffic seriously sucks.

Lots of restaurants, hotels, and even Starbucks and divey taco joints offer **valet parking** to safely stow your steel chariot. Parking is an industry here that employs millions of men, women, and even children who help you *estacionar* (park) and watch your car while you go do your thang-about-town.

Another option is to hire a car and driver. This is less expensive than the same service would run you in the States, but still not for the budget traveler. So if that's you, skip ahead to the next section. Otherwise, here are some suggestions:

My main man **Jesus** (☎ **044/55-1792-1586**) speaks English and is associated with the **Habita** hotel (p. 98), where you can find his red Volkswagen if he's not out with clients. He charges by the hour ($200), or you can negotiate for a day-rate to save a few bucks. A trip to the pyramids of Teotihuacán runs approximately $2,600 for the full day, including tolls. Tipping is appropriate if you feel you've received excellent service; the amount's at your discretion.

Limorent (☎ **55/5277-2304**) also provides a car and driver for approximately $2,900 for the day. Also check with **Transportacion Turistica y Ejecutiva Chapultepec** (☎ **55/5516-0850;** www.mexicolimorent.com.mx) to compare rates.

BY BUS

Mexico City has a bus terminal for each of the four points of the compass: north, east, south, and west. You can't necessarily tell which terminal serves which area of the country by looking at a map, however.

Some buses leave directly from the **Mexico City airport.** Departures are from a booth located outside **Sala D (Gate D),** and buses also park there. Tickets to Cuernavaca and Puebla each run about $120, with departures every 45 minutes. Other destinations include Querétaro, Pátzcuaro, and Toluca.

If you're in doubt about which station serves your destination, ask any taxi driver—they know the stations and the routes they serve. All stations have restaurants, money-exchange booths or banks, post offices, luggage storage, and long-distance telephone booths where you can also send a fax.

Taxis from bus stations: Each station has a taxi system based on fixed-price tickets to various zones within the city, operated from a booth or kiosk in or near the entry foyer of the terminal. Locate your destination on a zone map or tell the seller where you want to go, and buy a boleto.

Terminal Central de Autobuses del Norte Called "Terminal Norte," "Central Norte" (☎ **55/5133-2444** or 5587-1552), Avenida de los Cien (100) Metros, is Mexico's largest bus station. It handles most buses coming from the U.S.-Mexico border. It also handles service to and from the Pacific Coast as far south as Puerto Vallarta and Manzanillo; the Gulf Coast as far south as Tampico and Veracruz; and such cities as Guadalajara, San Luis Potosí, Durango, Zacatecas, Morelia, and Colima. You can also get to the pyramids of San Juan Teotihuacán and Tula from here. By calling the above number, you can purchase tickets over the phone, charging them to a credit card. The operators can also provide exact information about prices and schedules, but few speak English.

To get downtown from the Terminal Norte, you have a choice: The **Metro** has a station (Terminal de Autobuses del Norte, or TAN) right here, so it's easy to hop a train and connect to all points. Walk to the center of the terminal, go out the front door and down the steps, and go to the Metro station. This is Línea 5. Follow the signs that say DIRECCION PANTITLAN. For downtown, you can change trains at La Raza or Consulado (see the Mexico City Metro map on the inside back cover). Be aware that if you change at La Raza, you'll have to walk for 10 to 15 minutes and will encounter stairs. The walk is through a marble-lined underground corridor, but it's a long way with heavy luggage. If you have heavy luggage, you most likely won't be allowed into the Metro in the first place.

Another way to get downtown is by **trolley-bus.** The stop is on Avenida de los Cien Metros, in front of the terminal. The trolley-bus runs down Avenida Lázaro Cárdenas, the "Eje Central" (Central Artery). Or try the Central Camionera Del Norte–Villa Olimpica buses, which go down Avenida Insurgentes, past the university. Just like the Metro, the trolley will not let you board if you are carrying anything larger than a small carry-on suitcase. Backpacks seem to be an exception, but not large ones with frames.

Terminal de Autobuses de Pasajeros de Oriente (☎ **55/5762-5210,** 5133-2424, 5542-7156, or 5542-2009) This terminal is known as **TAPO.** Buses going east (Puebla, Amecameca, the Yucatán Peninsula, Veracruz, Xalapa, San Cristóbal de las Casas, and others) and Oaxaca buses, which pass through Puebla, arrive and depart from here.

To get to TAPO, take a Hipodromo–Pantitlán bus east along Alvarado, Hidalgo, or Donceles; if you take the Metro, go to the San Lázaro station on the eastern portion of Line 1 (DIRECCION PANTITLAN).

Terminal Central de Autobuses del Sur (☎ **55/5689-9745**) Mexico City's southern bus terminal is at Av. Taxqueña 1320, right next to the Taxqueña Metro stop, the last stop on Line 2. The Central del Sur handles buses to and from Cuernavaca, Taxco, Acapulco, Zihuatanejo, and intermediate points. The easiest way to get to or from the Central del Sur is on the Metro. To get downtown from the Taxqueña Metro station, look for signs that say DIRECCION CUATRO CAMINOS. Or take a trolley-bus on Avenida Lázaro Cárdenas.

Terminal Poniente de Autobuses (☎ **55/5271-0038**) The western bus terminal is conveniently located right next to the Observatorio Metro station, at Sur 122 and Tacubaya.

This is the smallest terminal; it mainly serves the route between Mexico City and Toluca. It also handles buses to and from Ixtapan de la Sal, Valle de Bravo, Morelia, Uruapan, Querétaro, Colima, Ixtapa-Zihuatanejo, Acapulco, and Guadalajara. In general, if the Terminal Norte also serves your destination, you'd be better

Con Cuidado! Mexico City Driving Tactics

The Land of Lost Highways

One of the most fun—and oftentimes easiest—ways to sightsee outside of Mexico City is to drive. For renting your *lancha* (slang for car), I recommend **Advantage** (☎ **800/777-5500;** www.arac.com, or book through third-party sites like Expedia or your travel agency). Rates fluctuate constantly depending on demand, but they always try to be among the most competitive on the market. Their service is a little more fun than your average rental car company—cool young locals meet your flight at the gate, bring you to your car, answer your questions, and point you toward good times. Ask for a Nissan Sentra, which is so fuel-efficient that I drove mine well over 966km (600 miles) on three tanks. If you rent your car online, make absolutely sure that you bring a printout of the reservation that includes your rate. And let the company know if you need to cancel a booking.

There are massive road-renovation and construction projects underway all around Mexico City and the surrounding areas. Some of the newer roads are traffic-free, direct, and navigable. If you run into a dead-end where there should be a highway, or mud where there should be concrete, the best thing to do is take it in stride. Remember the saying *son cosas de la vida* (that's life), grab your *Guia Roji,* the ultimate road guide to Mexico, and use your best Spanish to ask a local for directions. Mexicans are incredibly friendly if you make even a small effort to speak the language. And always ask a second opinion after getting directions. For serious matters, like robbery or accidents, the **Federal Highway Police** can be reached at ☎ **55/5677-2227.**

off going there. It has more buses and better bus lines.

ON FOOT

As with New York or London, each of Mexico City's neighborhoods is relatively walkable in itself. Just keep your map handy as the city isn't arranged in a grid or according to any logical system. The most pedestrian-friendly areas are the Centro Historico, Coyoacán Plaza, Condesa and Roma, and around Masaryk in Polanco on through to the Chapultepec Park. But unless you want to cover only a very small area, you'll need to rely on cars, cabs, and the Metro to shuttle between different parts of the city.

Basics

Orientation

PRIMARY NEIGHBORHOODS

This place is mega-huge, so it's mandatory to know exactly where you're going and the route you'll take to get there before setting out. Each of the colonias has its own distinctive look, personality, and history. Some, like the Centro Historico and Coyoacán, invite walking; others are good for bike riding (Condesa); while many, like Lomas de Chapultepec, are best navigated by car—or sometimes *trajinera,* a traditional Aztec boat (Xochimilco). You're likely to spend most of your time in just a few neighborhoods, but others offer the off-the-beaten-path traveler a look into daily life outside the more touristed areas of Mexico City. Here is a rundown of the colonias.

CENTRO HISTORICO The Mexico City mother lode, Centro Historico is where most travelers will want to spend a significant chunk of their time. If you only have time for one place in Mexico City, make it the **zócalo,** the third-largest square in the world (after Tiannamen Square in China and Moscow's Red Square). This remarkable wide open space is marked by a ginormous Mexican flag, the **Catedral Metropolitana,** and **Templo Mayor,** which is the most significant archaeological site in the city. Also check the **ex Colegio de San Idelfonso** with its **Museum of Medicine, Palacio Bellas Artes,** and **Palacio Postal.** Hotels like the Best Western and Gran Hotel de Mexico offer rooftop bar/restaurants to scope an awesome view, and the most concentrated tourism destinations are located in this neighborhood. The Centro Historico is, after all, the spot on which Mexico City was founded, the legendary Tenochtitlan. In 1987, this capital of the Aztec empire was recognized by UNESCO as an artistic and cultural monument.

LA CONDESA & COLONIA ROMA These are greener, *glorieta-* (traffic circle–) ridden versions of SoHo and the Lower East Side, respectively. Young, hip, and happening, Condesa and Roma are home to chic and bohemian nightspots, trendy eateries, indie-designer shopping, and a burgeoning gallery scene. Roma is slightly rougher around the edges than Condesa, but with several new nightspots and raved-about restaurants like **Contramar** (p. 103) and **Lamm** (p. 116), the scene is catching up to Condesa's fast. Condesa, which got its name from Hipodromo de la Condesa de Miravalle, the grounds of an old hacienda on which it was built, is where Art Deco architecture reached its peak in Latin America in the first half of the 20th century. Today it's not only one of the most en-vogue neighborhoods in town, but also home to grand parks, like the **Parque Mexico,** and tree-lined avenues. Roma gets its name not from the Italian city, but because it used to be Potreros de Romita a little over a hundred years ago, before it was renamed. The streets around **Plaza Madrid** and **Plaza Rio de Janeiro** are dotted with bohemian cafes, upscale restaurants, and cultural sights like **Casa del Poeta.**

NORTHERN NEIGHBORHOODS

POLANCO Let's put it this way: Even the Starbucks in this neighborhood (Av. Masaryk and Calle Spencer) has valet parking. Polanco is the Beverly Hills of Mexico City, and Masaryk is its Rodeo Drive (or Fifth Ave.). Located north of **Chapultepec Park,** it's one of the poshest colonias in the city, home to the most sophisticated hotels, fabulous restaurants, and designer stores like Prada and Louis Vuitton. You'll also find galleries, notably the **Sala de Arte Publico Siqueiros** (p. 119), a space dedicated to the famous muralist David Alfaro Siqueiros, as well as tons of nightlife—the jet set gather at **Skyybar** and **Habita** hotel's swanky rooftop lounge (p. 98). The hood is popular with Lebanese, Jewish, and Spanish residents who abandoned living in the city center for the tranquillity of residential life in Polanco. Right in front of Chapultepec Park, the avenue named Ruben Dario is one of the most exclusive addresses in the entire city. Apartments in *los pasteles* (the cakes), the two giant pink towers that define this skyline, reportedly start at $22 million.

ZONA ROSA Touristy but lovely, the "Pink Zone" is a walking neighborhood where you'll find rows of **bars, restaurants,** and **shops.** Its markets, Internet cafes, and cheap all-you-can-eat buffets are a great bet for the budget traveler.

Mexico City & Environs

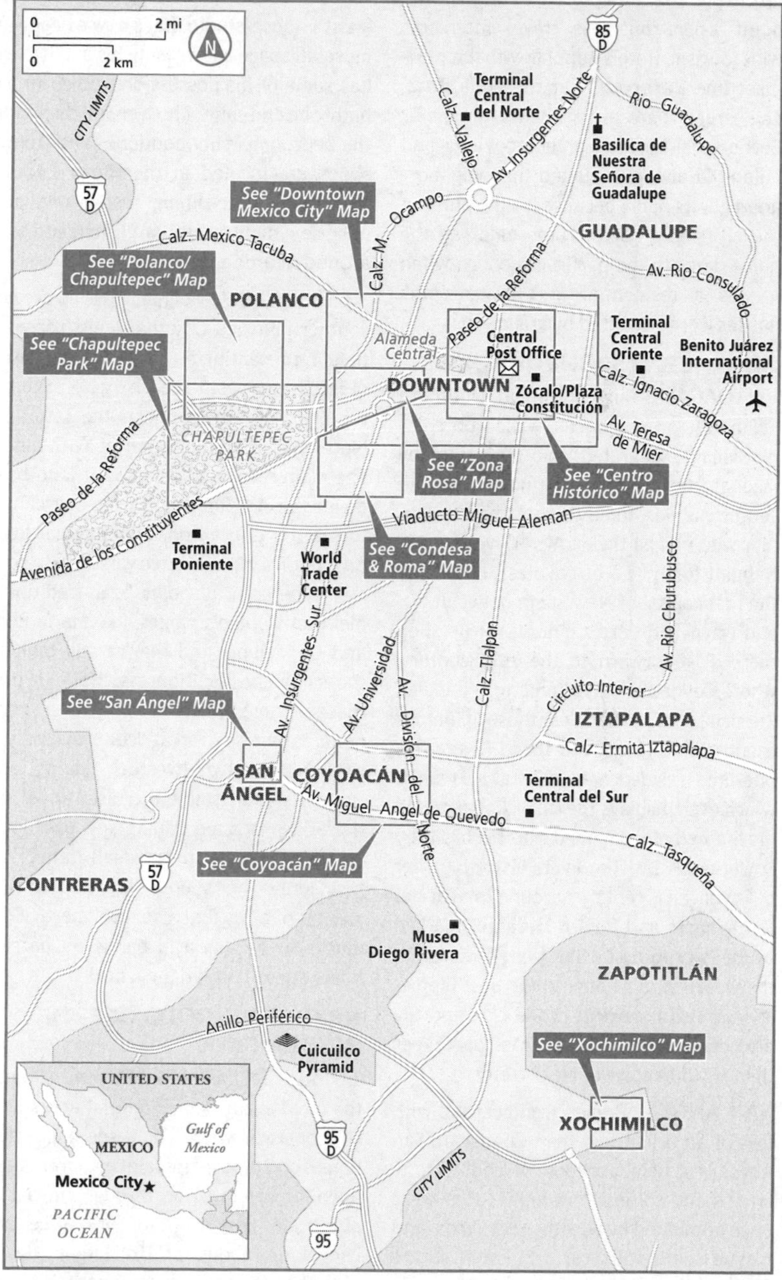

Between the Centro Historico and Bosque de Chapultepec (Chapultepec Park), it's the point where business travel intersects with tourism. Hotels popular with the 9-to-5 set line **Reforma** near the Zona Rosa. The streets here are named after major European cities, like Hamburgo, Viena, and Milan. I'd always assumed this neighborhood got its name because it's the pulse of the city's **gay scene,** but some say the name dates to the porfiriana epoch when it was a residential area whose pink houses were inhabited by aristocrats.

SOUTHERN NEIGHBORHOODS

COYOACÁN This bohemian southern neighborhood was once a walled-off colonial village, separated from the Centro by lakes and fields. At the beginning of the 16th century, it was home to an Aztec community who named their town "Coyohuacan," Nahuatl for "place of coyotes." It became the first capital of New Spain between 1521 and 1523 when Cortez himself set up shop there. Fast forward to the 20th century, where Coyoacán plays home to the exiled Russian Leon Trotsky. Near those of famous friends Frida Kahlo and Diego Rivera, his one-time residence is now a museum—which even displays the ice pick that ended his life by being jammed into his brain by Soviet assassins. The lively historic center of Coyoacán is centered around **Jardín del Centenario** and **Jardín Hidalgo,** marked by the **Parroquia de San Juan Batista.** On the weekend, it's home to the best hippie-style **artisan market** in the city, and the area draws more creative, free-spirit types than any other part of Mexico City.

SAN ANGEL Pricier, trendier, and with less of an urban feel than Coyoacán, San Angel is a neighborhood of cobblestone streets and colonial-era homes that were once populated by wealthy Spaniards (and maybe some still are). It's home to the famous **Bazar Sabado,** an *artesanías* (traditional crafts) market. Here you'll find the **Casa Estudio Diego Rivera,** the artist's house/studio that's now a beautiful museum space showcasing his art. It even has some of his possessions, down to his bathrobe and cane, which are on display in the bedroom. Many boutiques and trendy shops are located in the **Plaza Loreto** area, while fine-dining restaurants and upscale nightspots are concentrated around **Avenida de la Paz.**

XOCHIMILCO Xochimilco is an area of southern Mexico City that feels frozen in time, representing an earlier, simpler way of life. It's easiest to reach by taxi, though the light rail also connects the Tasqueña Metro station to the center of Xochimilco. The main reason travelers visit is to boat down the neighborhood's famous canals to see the ***chinampas*** (floating gardens) on a ***trajinera,*** the Aztec version of a gondola. The colorful boats bear traditional Mexican women's names, like María Rosa and Guadalupe, and they're still built to the same specifications as those in pre-Hispanic times. Many of Xochimilco's residents subscribe to an agricultural lifestyle, raising their own livestock, plants, and fruits. As your trajinera cruises down the UNESCO-protected canals and past local homes, you'll see these small farms, and hear only the sounds of the 150-plus species of birds that also dwell here (if the music of the mariachi bands on passing boats doesn't drown them out).

NEIGHBORHOODS OFF THE BEATEN PATH

LOMAS DE CHAPULTEPEC One of the most exclusive residential areas in el DF, Lomas is where you'll see impressive homes and dine in upscale restaurants and open-air cafes. Drive through on a lazy afternoon and drop in for coffee and chocolate fondue at **Un Lugar de la Mancha** (p. 102), a neighborhood spot that's been popular with local residents for decades. The young jet-setters of the nabe do sushi for lunch on weekdays around 3pm at **Tai Itto** (Everest 630, intersection of Monte Athos and Monte Everest; ☎ **55/5202-1386**). Yoga studios, salons, gourmet grocers, and all the fixin's of finer urban living coexist with the greenness and tranquillity of a suburb. It's so green here that even the streets are named after mountains.

TECAMACHALCO I just love saying the name of this neighborhood. Tecamachalco is farther out and I've never seen it written up in a tourist publication before. It has no tourist attractions whatsoever, which means you'll experience a totally authentic, largely Jewish (locals might refer to the colonia as Tecamachalski), and mostly upper-middle-class Mexican neighborhood. Hit up the lively Anderson Group's (Señor Frog's, Carlos 'n Charlie's) **Tecamacharlies** (Fuente de Trevi 4; ☎ **55/5293-0121**) for dinner and do **Deya Vu** (Av. de Las Fuentes 184; ☎ **55/5294-8292;** opens 11pm), a club with a laid-back vibe and cool DJs ($50 cover). You'll be the only *Norteamericanos* to have discovered it.

BOSQUES DE LAS LOMAS Most tourists never make it out this far—but local youngsters in search of style go to **Interlomas,** a futuristic-looking mall with trendy and classic shops, and, of course, a multiplex. It draws a younger crowd to its cantinas, food court, and arcade. In recent years it's been usurped in popularity by Centro Comercial Santa Fe.

SANTE FE The Toluca highway passes through the Santa Fe district, home to a mega-mall (www.centrosantafe.com.mx) and a major development boom. Newer than Interlomas, the **Centro Comercial Santa Fe** is home to a movie theater (in Mexico City, films from the U.S. are typically subtitled), shops like Zara and Palacio de Hierro, and even a small golf range. Santa Fe is a good stop on your way out of town if you're heading up the Toluca highway.

NEIGHBORHOODS TO AVOID

Mexico City is, in general, no more dangerous than any other large metropolis where you need to exercise precaution and keep a low profile. However, if you like your money, credit cards, hubcaps, and/or general safety, stay away from these rough hoods. **Cuchilla del Tesoro, Lomas de Becerra, Tepito, Colonia Doctores, Colonia Buenos Aires,** and **Ciudad Nezahualcóyotl.** They are all relatively out-of-the-way locales that you would never need to pass through anyhow.

Tourist Info & Offices

In a city this size, dropping in to the **tourism information booths** at major sightseeing destinations will score you maps, tips, brochures, and warm welcomes. Five central locations are:

Aeropuerto: In the arrivals area of Mexico City's international airport. ☎ **55/5786-9002.** Daily 7am–9pm.

Antropologia: Reforma at Gandhi, right in front of the Anthropology Museum in Bosque de Chapultepec. ☎ **55/5286-3850.** Daily 9am–6pm.

Bellas Artes: Avenida Juárez at Angela Peralta, between Bellas Artes and Alameda Central. ☎ **55/5286-3850.** Daily 9am–6pm.

Templo Mayor: Adjacent to Catedral Metropolitana in the Centro. ☎ **55/5512-8977.** Daily 9am–6pm.

Coyoacán: Jardín Hidalgo, which is the plaza just beyond Jardín del Centenario. Daily 9am–6pm; no phone.

In the southern district of **Xochimilco,** the tourist office (☎ **55/5576-0818;** www.xochimilco.df.gob.mx.) is at Pino 36, Barrio San Juan, Centro Historico de Xochimilco.

Recommended Websites

- **www.mexicocity.gob.mx**: Mexico City's official tourism office offers good, solid info, links, and statistics.
- **www.imagenesaereasdemexico.com**: Taken by a helicopter pilot, these aerial shots of Mexico City are some of the coolest photographs of the city ever. And the pic of Interlomas details why it's a mall like no other.
- **www.mexpat.com**: This site is geared toward young foreigners living in Mexico, especially el DF. Check out their forum and chat with other Mexpats about where to go, what to do, and what's hot now.
- **www.craigslist.org**: A newly added Mexico City section features the usual CL fare: bulletin boards for lodging, housing, stuff for sale, dating, meeting up, and more.
- **www.df.gob.mx**: Mexico City's official website offers news and information in Spanish.
- **www.mexicocity.com.mx**: Get more information and statistics about the capital, along with practical info about museums, performing arts, attractions, weather, and more.
- **www.allaboutmexicocity.com**: This fairly comprehensive list of the city's nightlife spots also has museum descriptions, travel advice, and a FAQ section, plus printable maps.

Mexico City Nuts & Bolts

Banks **Banamex** (☎ **800/226-2639** from the U.S. and Canada) is a prevalent chain here, and the typical fee for withdrawal is around $7 to $8. Withdraw a large chunk at once to avoid paying multiple fees, but stash what you're not going to use in your hotel safe.

Embassies/Consulates If your passport, ID, or wallet gets stolen, your embassy's Citizen Services department can help—as long as you file a report with local authorities first (see "Emergencies," below). The **U.S. Embassy** (Paseo de la Reforma 305, Colonia Cuauhtémoc; ☎ **55/5080-2000**) has an officer on duty at all times (main hours 8:30am–6pm). For the **British Embassy** (Río Lerma 71, Cuauhtémoc), dial ☎ **55/5242-8500. Australian Embassy** (Ruben Dario 55, Polanco), dial ☎ **55/1101-2200. New Zealanders** can reach their embassy (Embajada de Nueva Zelandia Jaime Balmes 8, Level 4; Colonia Los Morales, Polanco) at ☎ **52/5283-9460.**

Emergencies Dial ☎ **060** for the **police, ambulance, or fire department.** You can reach the **Rescue and Medical Emergencies Squad** at ☎ **52/5722-8805. ABC Hospital** (also American Hospital, or Hospital Ingles as it's known locally) has emergency lines you can call (☎ **55/5230-8161,** 8162, 8163, or 8164), and the main switchboard is at ☎ **55/5230-8000.**

Internet/Wireless Hot Spots Finding an access point is *so* not an issue here, and they're super-cheap to boot. I like the **Café Internet Java Chat** in the Zona Rosa (Calle Genova 44, near Hamburgo; ☎ **55/5525-6853**), where it's $10 for 20 minutes, $15 for 30 minutes, and $0.50 per additional minute. It's open daily 9:00am to 11:30pm (10:00am–11:30pm on weekends) and has about 10 computers. In Coyoacán, a sweet e-spot is **Intergraff Ciber Café** (Cuautemoc 184-A; daily till 10pm), with Frida Kahlo's portrait and other Mexican folk art on the walls. Rates are $5 for 20 minutes, $8 for 30 minutes, or $15 for an hour (student discount: $6 for 30 min., or $12 per hr.).

Internet inalambrico (wireless) is increasingly popular in Mexico City cafes, and **El Ocho** cafe/restaurant in Condesa (p. 100) is a good Wi-Fi hot spot. ***Note:*** A new wireless security-camera initiative by the city's mayor also means free Wi-Fi city-wide by 2008—a handy byproduct of increased cyber–police presence.

Laundromats Most neighborhoods have more than one *lavanderia,* where you just drop off your laundry and pick it up later in the day. If you'd rather do your own, well, you're SOL because even the divey lavanderias do your wash for you, and for darned cheap. They typically charge by the kilo. In the Centro, **Lavanderia Automatica Esmafga** (Mesones 42; ☎ **55/5709-0278**) is open from 10am to 6pm, Monday through Saturday. Most hotels and hostels offer laundry service for guests as well (though unlike lavanderias they usually charge per item).

Pharmacies Pharmacies are marked by green crosses and are ubiquitous around the city. Sanborn's department stores also have pharmacies. Convenience stores like **OXXO, 7-11,** and **Matador** are seemingly omnipresent, and also sell beverages, beer, junk food, condoms, and film.

Post Offices Mexico City's post offices are open from 9am to 5pm on weekdays, and 9am till 1pm on Saturdays. In the **Zona Rosa,** the PO is at Londres 208, on the corner of Varsovia and Londres. In the **Centro Historico,** don't mistake the Palacio Postal for a place to send your postcard—it's strictly museum-only. Head instead toward **MexPost** (Netzahualcoyotl 109; ☎ **55/5709-9606**). In **Condesa** (Aguascalientes 161) and **Roma** (Alvaro Obregon 31) you can send Auntie Rosemary that shot-glass set, too.

Restrooms Where to do your 1s and 2s is an aspect of visiting Mexico City that's improved dramatically in recent years. These days, major tourism destinations have clean public restrooms clearly marked "WC" and attendants who ensure you have toilet paper and soap. The typical bathroom visit averages only $2 to $4, and the measly sum is well worth it.

Safety Over a year ago, former New York City Mayor Rudolph Giuliani's security consulting firm was hired to bring crime rates down—and preliminary results seem encouraging. Mexico City is safer than you'd think as long as you use precaution and keep your wits about you. This is *not* the place to traipse through the streets loud and drunk late at night—that's like wearing a sign on your forehead that says "rob me now, *por favor.*" For more info on **tourist safety** call ☎ **55/5250-0123** or 01-800/5903-9200.

Telephone Tips Newsstands, grocery stores, and authorized vendors sell **Ladatel phone cards,** which you'll need for the majority of pay phones. They come in various amounts starting from $350. A few coin-operated pay phones still exist, and you may happen upon one. Internet cafes usually offer long-distance calling services too. As a testament to the city's hugeness, telephone numbers in Mexico City have eight digits rather than the usual seven.

The local area code is 55. To call a cellphone, you need to dial 04455, then the eight-digit number.

Sleeping

Mexico City has fewer safe and cheap hostels than your average European capital, though, with the rise of chic young boutique hotels, the options for budget travelers are greater than ever. The Centro Historico offers some dirt-cheap hostel options, and most of the city's inexpensive hotels are found here as well. Since you're dealing in pesos, even luxe accommodations can come at budget-friendly prices. A hotel like CondesaDF, which has a rooftop bar with a hot tub, iPods that play through flatscreen televisions in every room, a killer ambience, and even hosts an independent film series, has a $1,450 per night weekend rate. Not too shabby, huh?

While many museums and important sites are located in and around the Centro Historico, my preference is to stay in a more laid-back, nicer part of town, and then journey downtown for sightseeing during the day. La Condesa and Colonia Roma, the cool kids of Mexico City's neighborhoods, are good bets for both moderately priced hotels and the most worthwhile splurges in la Capital. Polanco is home to some of the big guns, like Camino Real, JW Marriott, and the W, all within walking distance of Chapultepec Park. The charming Cenote Azul is right by the UNAM (Universidad Autonoma de Mexico), and the closest hostel to Coyoacán, San Angel, and the canals and floating gardens of Xochimilco.

Hostels

→ **El Cenote Azul** CIUDAD UNIVERSITARIA Hostels and hotels aren't common around Coyoacán and San Angel due to zoning restrictions, so El Cenote Azul is as close as you'll get. A 2-minute walk from UNAM's campus, this 12-room family-run hostel is a great choice if your primary interests lie in the southern part of the city. Frida Kahlo's Casa Azul, the Museo Casa Estudio Diego Rivera, and Leon Trotsky's house are nearby, as are the nightlife and dining scenes of Coyoacán and San Angel. It's closer to the canals of Xochimilco, too. The hostel is cute and charming with exposed brick that adds a homey touch to the colonial house. Light-filled rooms feature Talavera-tiled floors. Guests can use the full kitchen at their leisure on weekends (for breakfast and dinner only during the week). The proprietors are friendly and helpful to boot—their goal in opening the hostel was to encourage travelers to discover Mexico City. *Alfonso Pruneda 24, at Lázaro Cárdenas. ☎ 55/5554-8730. www.elcenoteazul.com. $100 per person in shared room. MC, V. Amenities: Restaurant; kitchen; TV room. In room: Sheets, towels. Metro: Copilco.*

→ **Hostal Moneda** CENTRO HISTORICO If you're hostelling in Mexico City, this is the primo place to do it. With inexpensive rooms (from $120 per person per night, including breakfast and dinner buffets), in-room lockers, a free downtown walking tour, a free tour of the Anthropology museum, 24-hour Internet, and a round-the-clock, English-speaking front desk, you couldn't ask for more from a hostel. The terrace has a bar with views of the zócalo, and hammocks sweeten the deal. *Calle Moneda 8, Col. Centro. ☎ 55/5522-5803 or 800/221-7265. www.hostalmoneda.com.mx. $320 single, $140 single bed in a 4-person dorm, $130 single bed in a 6-person dorm, $120 single bed in a 10-person dorm. Breakfast and dinner buffet included. MC, V. Amenities: Complimentary airport pickup, concierge, elevator, Internet access, laundry service, rooftop bar with hammocks, safe, 24-hr. front desk. In room: Lockers, sheets, towels. Metro: Zócalo.*

Centro Historico

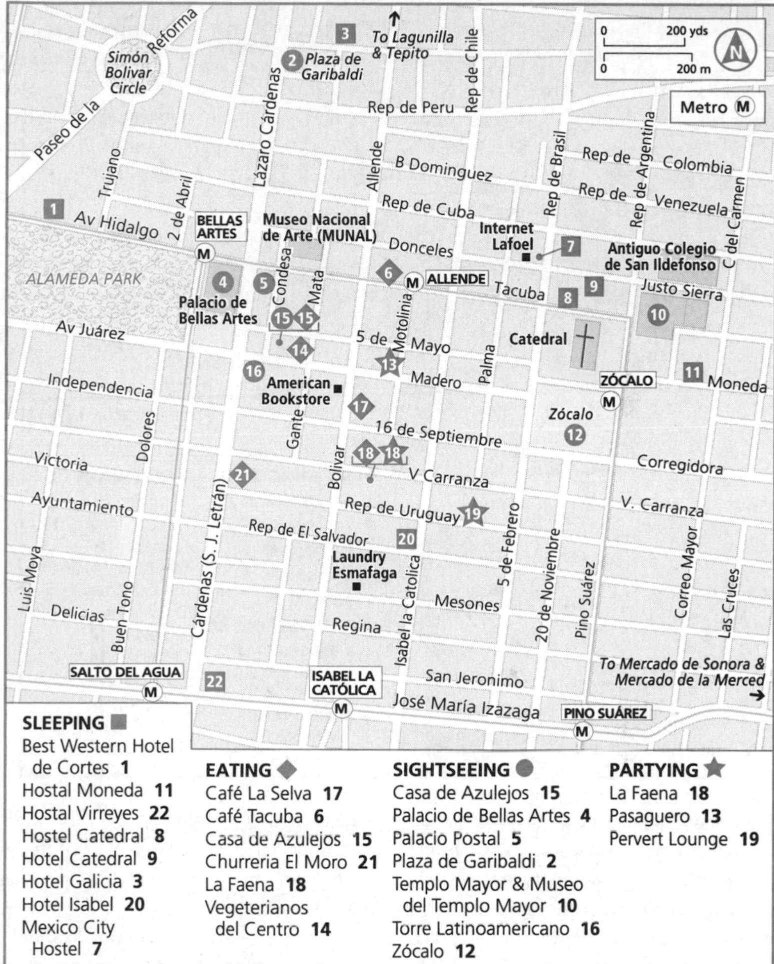

→ **Hostal Virreyes** CENTRO HISTORICO Shared and private rooms are clean, comfortable, and even stylish in this long-popular downtown hostel that's been in business since 1947. This affiliate of the Mexican Association of Youth Hostels is a funky and happening spot cherished by travelers for its marble stairway with blue Talavera tiles, neoclassical architecture, and active nightlife. Mauro Gutierrez, who has been working here for more than 30 years, recalls that, in the hotel's heyday, it was a posh spot for visiting celebrities. It maintains an antique feel with a 1949 Stromberg wall clock and a mural portraying different social classes during the colonial era. Bonus: It has a cinema series showcasing offbeat and cult films. *Av. Izazaga 8, at Lázaro Cárdenas. ☎ 55/2141-8087. www.hostalvirreyes.com.mx. $250 private single or double, $111 single bed in a 4–6 person dorm, or $108 with Hostelling Internacional Cardo or*

Condesa & Roma

Internacional Student ID. Continental breakfast included. MC, V. Amenities: Restaurant/bar, gym, Internet access, laundry service, lockers, money exchange, 24-hr. front desk. In room: TV, sheets, towels. Metro: Salto del Agaua.

➔ **Mexico City Hostel** CENTRO HISTORICO Located in a beautifully renovated colonial house, this hotel's artistic flair makes up for its name's lack of originality, which doesn't seem to do any harm—the hostel draws backpackers from every corner of the world: Norway, England, France, Japan, the U.S. Just a block away from the zócalo and its Metro station, the convenient location is but one of the perks of this budget-traveler's haven. With colorful murals on the walls and impeccably clean rooms centered around an open-air courtyard, it's like staying in an old house. Three private rooms are available in addition to bunk-bed dorms that sleep six to ten, with shared bathrooms. A tasty daily breakfast is included, and tours to places of interest, like the pyramids of Teotihuacán, can be arranged. *Republica de Brasil 8, at Donceles. ☎ 55/5512-3666. www.mexicocityhostel.com. $280 private single or double, $130 single bed in a 6–10 person dorm. Ask about special $90 rate. Breakfast included. No credit cards. Amenities: Kitchen use, laundry service, safe. In room: Sheets, towels. Metro: Zócalo.*

Polanco/Chapultepec

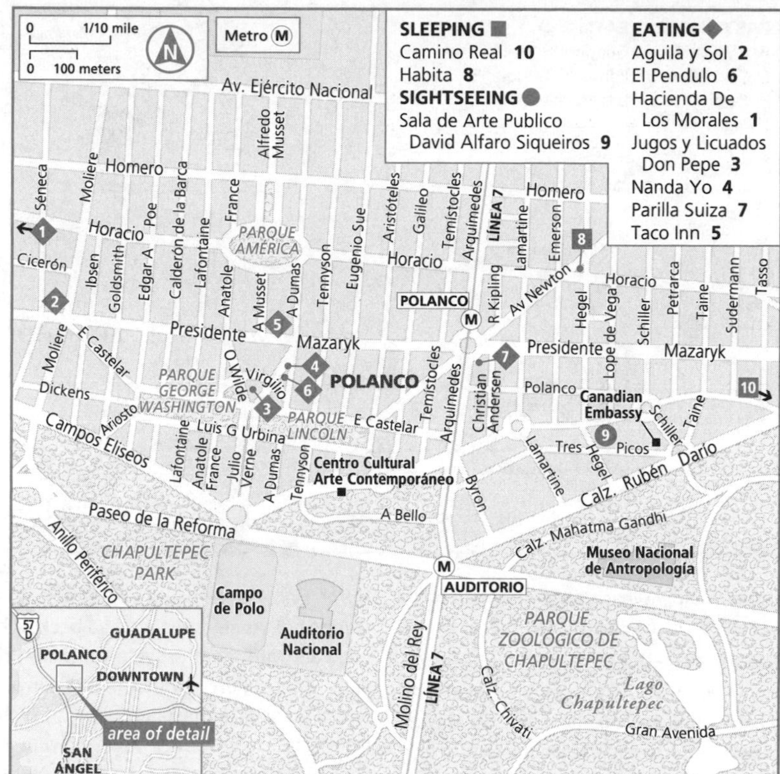

Cheap

→ **Hotel Catedral** CENTRO Owned by the same group as the Mexico City Hostel, the modern, 116-room Hotel Catedral is a simple, clean step up in amenities (and price, too). A travel agency and good restaurant, El Retiro, occupy the ground floor. Unlike at other hotels in Mexico City, local calls are free from your room. The staff is happy to recommend things to see and do in the area. The rooms are standard, relaxing, and functional, some with bathrooms that have Jacuzzi tubs. *Donceles 95.* ☎ *55-5518-5232 or 800-701-8340. www.hotelcatedral.com. $450 single, $520 double. AE, MC, V. Amenities: Restaurant/bar, Internet access, laundry/dry-cleaning service, room service. In room: A/C, TV, phone, safe. Metro: Zócalo.*

→ **Hotel de Cortes** CENTRO For a no-frills, no-fuss place to stay, this small hotel run by Best Western is a good bet. It's located right on Alameda Park—certain rooms overlook it, and they're soundproofed so you can have your view and sleep in, too. Construction of the colonial building, which is a national monument, was completed in 1780. Each of the 19 rooms—small, comfortable, and simple yet inviting—and 10 suites open out onto a courtyard. *Av. Hidalgo 85.* ☎ *55-5518-2181. www.hoteldecortes.com.mx. $750 double. AE, MC, V. Amenities: Restaurant, bar, business*

Zona Rosa

center, laundry service, room service. In room: TV, bottled water, hair dryer. Metro: Bellas Artes.

→**Hotel Galicia** CENTRO If you're in the mood for an authentic neighborhood with plentiful *pulquerias* and taco shops, staying here is a way to experience the grittier side of Mexico City without being in a truly dangerous neighborhood—Garibaldi is significantly safer these days. Hotel Galicia is a pristinely clean, comfortable hotel with all your basic amenities and a retro look that speaks to the 1960s—the decade when it was built. After late nights of Mariachi-listening and Michelada-drinking in the bars that dot the plaza, you'll easily stumble right upstairs. It's within walking distance of Centro Historico as well. *Honduras 11, at Plaza Garibaldi. ☎ 55-5529-7791. www.hgalicia.com. $380–$420 double. MC, V. Amenities: Restaurant/bar, Internet, travel agency. In room: A/C, TV, phone. Metro: Garibaldi.*

→**Hotel Isabel** CENTRO Though it makes an appearance on the U.S. Embassy's list of suggested budget hotels, Hotel Isabel also has a reputation as a favorite of young travelers and backpackers who want an affordable yet more private atmosphere, without forsaking a hostel's social atmosphere. The 75 high-ceilinged rooms either have private or shared bathrooms, and basic amenities like phones and TV—just don't expect anything fancy. Ask the English-speaking staff for one of the rooms around the upper patio, which have natural light coming through a skylight. On the fourth floor, rooms open around a terrace. Both options are more cheerful than the dark inner rooms. *Isabel la Catolica 63. ☎ 55-5518-1213. $150–$250 double. No credit cards. Amenities: Bar/restaurant. In room: TV, phone. Metro: Isabel la Catolica.*

Doable

MTV Best → **CondesaDF** ★★★ CONDESA In a word? Impressive. It's young, it's hip, and it's the most happening hotel in Mexico City today. CondesaDF is not so much a hotel as an experience; the thought

Coyoacán

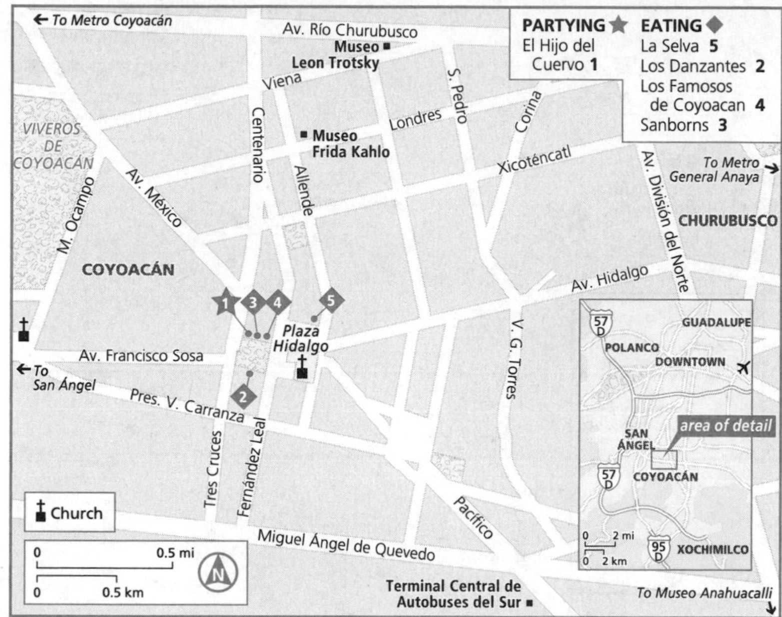

and care that went into every detail is evident from the moment you pass through the doors. The award-winning chic-n-cozy boutique hotel in an Art Deco mansion is the design love child of Paris-based interior designer India Mahdavi, architect Javier Sanchez, restaurateur Jonathan Morr of Bond Street in New York, Ich&Kar graphic designers, and local artist Betsabee Romero. Each of the 40 rooms features a blend of hi-tech and classic design; there's a comfy bed, but also an iPod hooked into a flatscreen TV, which broadcasts a video-art installation. Just a few of the many perks of the hip, unpretentious space include a nightclub downstairs, a film series curated by the organizers of the Festival Internacional de Cine Contemporaneo (International Festival of Contemporary Cinema), and a *hammam* (hot tub) on the roof to soothe even the worst case of jet lag. Missing a furry friend back home? Take the resident chocolate Lab, Conde, for a walk or jog to Parque España or Parque Mexico. Plus, four bikes can be used by guests at no cost, a great way to see one of the city's trendiest neighborhoods. *Av. Veracruz 102, at Parque España. ☎ 55/5241-2600. www.condesadf.com. From $1,400 single/double, $3,000–$3,950 suite. Ask about special weekend rates. AE, MC, V. Amenities: Restaurant/bar, access to local health club, hot tub, roof deck, room service, spa. In room: A/C, TV/DVD, iPod with music selection, hair dryer, minibar, safe, Xbox 360 (on request). Metro: Sevilla.*

→ **Gran Hotel de Mexico** CENTRO The badass downtown building housing the Gran Hotel de Mexico was the first in Mexico City built in Art Deco style. Originally a department store, the hotel boasts a stained-glass ceiling, cool 19th-century cast-iron elevators, a rooftop bar,

San Angel

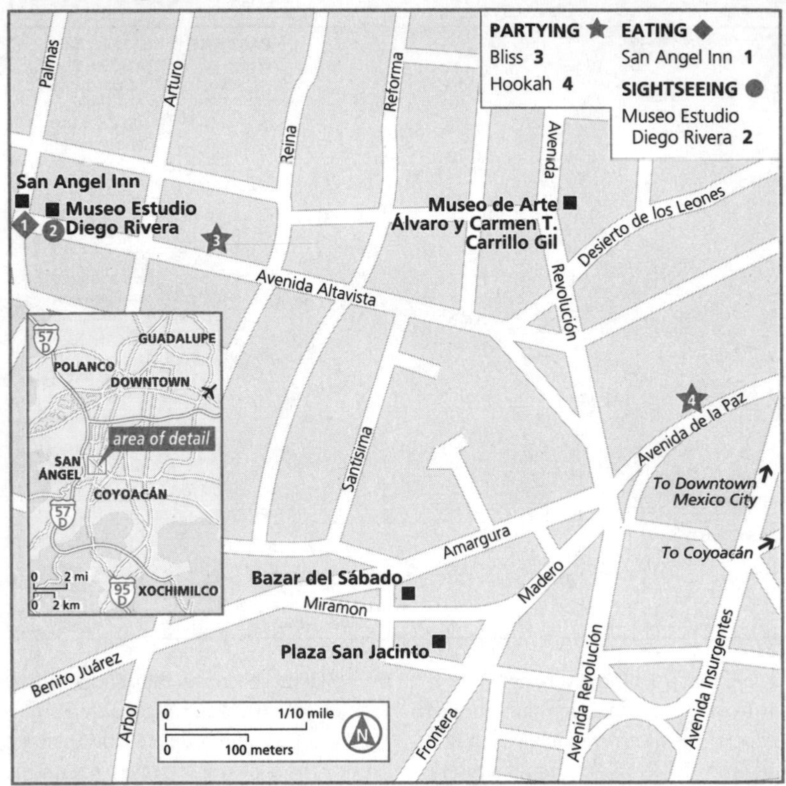

a restaurant with a zócalo view, and rooms that reflect the hotel's style with canopy beds and old-fashioned furniture. Mixing up period pieces with hi-tech—flatscreen televisions, wireless Internet, and a tricked-out gym—brings modern convenience to an old-school experience. If you're not staying here, it's worth dropping in to the majestic lobby to check out the Tiffany ceiling; then head up to the bar for a margarita above the Centro Historico. *16 de Septiembre 82. ☎ 55/1083-7700. www.granhotelciudaddemexico.com.mx. $1,600–$3,500 singles/doubles. AE, MC, V. Amenities: Bar/restaurant, business center, gym, room service. In room: A/C, TV, hair dryer, minibar, safe. Metro: Sevilla.*

MTV Best → **La Casona** ★★★ ROMA A cozy, inviting, and well-designed boutique housed in an old mansion, La Casona has a great breakfast menu, with lots of choices, from American-style bacon and eggs to Mexican specialties. Each of its 29 rooms is a refuge from the bustle outside, a quiet place to retreat after a busy day of sightseeing or long night on the town. The manor's design plays off *epoca porfiriana,* a classic, elegant style that people who feel alienated by the ultra-modern decor of many trendy hotels will appreciate—it's more Parisian charm than South Beach sleek. Ask for room 19 and open the curtains behind the television; a stained-glass

Xochimilco

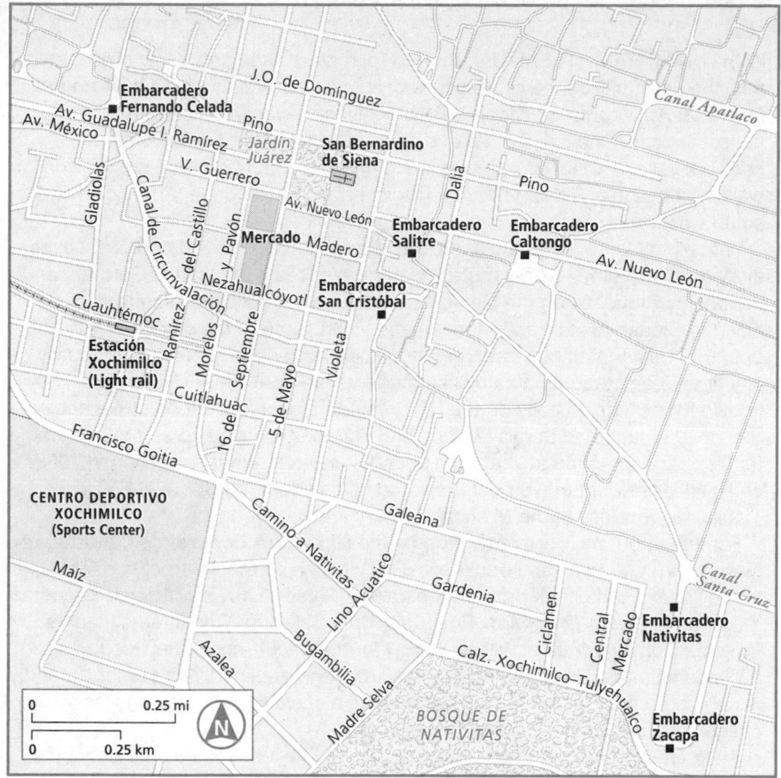

window from across the hall perfectly fits the view from the window frame. The Roma location means you can walk to some of the best restaurants in the city today, like Contramar, and also go on foot to the anthropological museum, Chapultepec Park, and even Zona Rosa and Condesa. On the upper floor, the gym is on the small side, but the rooftop patio is a relaxing place to kick back and watch the city go by. *Durango 200, at Cozumel. ☎ 55/5286-3001. www.hotellacasona.com.mx. $1,400–$2,500 singles/doubles. AE, MC, V. Amenities: Restaurant, business center, gym, room service. In room: A/C, TV, hair dryer, safe, snacks and water. Metro: Chapultepec.*

Splurge

→ **Camino Real** POLANCO The behemoth of DF hotels with 714 rooms and nine restaurant/bars spread over 3.4 hectares (8½ acres), the Ricardo Legorreta–designed Camino Real is worth checking out (or into) for its architecture alone. It has sloped walls with the look of a pre-Hispanic temple, and colors you can't miss even when driving by at night in the rain. A hot spot when it debuted in the late '60s, this hotel was lauded by the Fine Arts Institute of Mexico—maybe because it's home to over 400 works of art by heavyweights like Rufino Tamayo. The bright yellow-and-pink building is directly across

MTV U The University Scene

With UNAM, ITAM, ITESM, Universidad Iberoamericana and a few others in the mix, the university scene in Mexico City is quite vibrant. But the **Universidad Nacional Autonoma de Mexico (UNAM)** is the big man on campus. The largest in Latin America, it even has it's own "city"—Ciudad Universitaria, known locally as CU. The campus is 7.3 million sq. m (79 million sq. ft.), so walking the whole of it is nearly impossible. Bike trails connect the north and south sides.

With all the famous murals and buildings around the UNAM campus—especially the three-dimensional mural covering the library by Juan O'Gorman, and the one by Siqueiros on the Rectoria administrative building—you'll always have an excuse to start up a conversation with some of the students who are bound to be hanging out, studying, gossiping, and playing soccer at virtually any time of day. About half a million students are enrolled at UNAM, which is known for being politically on the left. In 1999, students went on strike because of a government plan to raise tuition and ended up closing down the university for 9 months. Extreme as that may sound, it pales to what happened in 1968, when leftist student movements resulted in a student massacre in Plaza Tlatelolco, courtesy of the Mexican military and secret police.

For info about the university, stop by the **Direccion General de Orientacion** (www.unam.edu.mx; 9am–5pm Mon–Fri), which is to the south of the field next to the library. And check out the free gallery, **Museo Universitario de Ciencias Y Artes CU** (10am–7pm Mon–Fri, 10am–6pm Sat–Sun). The streets leading from the Copilco Metro stop are named for the departments they lead to—Filosofia y Letras, Derecho (Law), Medicina—and are lined with student-friendly super-cheap food, holes-in-the-wall to grab a *chela* (beer), and vendors selling everything from soccer T-shirts to textbooks.

An interesting factoid about university life in Mexico: You have to declare a major before you enter, and if you change your mind you go back to square one, starting over from the first year in your new major. Intense, huh?

from Chapultepec Park, which means easy access to its museums, lakes, and jogging paths. The trendy nightlife scene attracts more locals than tourists: Blue Lounge in the lobby and the open-air Moon Bar, with beds to relax on. Rooms are large with balconies and marble bathrooms. Ask for one overlooking the outdoor pool and garden. If the price prevents you from even staying here, try La Huerta for brunch—a delicious Mexican buffet. (And it wasn't us who told you to sneak out back for a dip in the pool afterward.) The Spanish resto, La Cava, is a good choice for dinner. Over 600 bottles of wine line the walls. *Mariano Escobedo 700.* ☎ *55/5263-8888. www.caminoreal.com. $1,900–$3,000 double. AE, MC, V. Amenities: 6 restaurants, 2 bars, business center, gym, Internet cafe, laundry and dry-cleaning service, spa. In room: A/C, TV, hair dryer, minibar, phone, pool, safe, Wi–Fi ($150 surcharge also includes free parking, daily newspaper, free local calls, and late check out). Metro: Polanco.*

➔ **Habita** POLANCO Habita was the debut of the New-York-City-slash-South-Beach-style boutique hotel in Mexico City; and since its opening in 2000, it has drawn the business and pleasure jet set. Once a '50s apartment building, it has since been wrapped in blue Plexiglas, which made TEN Arquitectos, its designers, in-demand global superstars in their field. The vibe is somewhat reminiscent of The Standard in L.A.—classy, yet young and hip. Sleek, chic, and overtly minimalistic, this is where socialite types sleep, eat, drink, and swim—one of the few rooftop pools in the city is here, though it's more for lounging in to cool off and scope the scene than for actual swimming. Comfortable rooms feature king-size beds and marble-floored bathrooms. Rooms facing Masaryk can get a bit loud, so light sleepers might forfeit the nice balcony for an interior room. The city's PYTs gather at the hotel's AREA bar and AURA restaurant, both of which draw a trendy crowd, especially on weekends. An extra $90 gets you a DVD from the selection in the lobby—don't forget to grab a shot of tequila from the common bottle by the coffee table in the seating area. Ask about special weekend rates or discounts to avoid the steep full price; either way, it's a worthy splurge. *Masaryk 201. ☎ 55/5282-3100. www.hotelhabita.com. $1,950 single, $2,650 double, $3,150 suite. AE, MC, V. Amenities: Bar, restaurant, business center, gym, laundry and dry-cleaning service, pool and solarium, room service, spa. In room: A/C, TV/DVD, hair dryer, minibar, phone, safe, Wi-Fi. Metro: Polanco.*

Eating

From tacos al pastor to the nouveau Mexican revolution sparked by talents like Martha Ortiz Chapa of top-notch Aguila y Sol, conveyor-belt sushi at Nanda Yo, and the hotel Camino Real's outpost of NYC/Las Vegas's Le Cirque, la Capital is an international culinary destination that stands up there with the rest of 'em (New York, Paris, Rome, L.A.). I eat my way through Mexico City every time, searching for the perfect taco, *sincronizada* (ham and cheese quesadilla), or my personal favorite, chicken torta. On the street, I'll still eat the reliably tasty *elote* (corn on a stick) or mango with chile from a vending cart any day—as long as the joint looks clean. See the box on p. 678 of Appendix B for info on some other common Mexican food you'll find in Mexico City.

Breakfast portions here tend to be either small (think pastries and coffee on the run), or large (think a big plate of chilaquiles and huevos rancheros). Eating times tend to be later, with lunchtime as the main meal when you eat *platos fuertes* (main dishes) and drink a cerveza. Lunch heats up around 2pm or later, while dinner is leisurely enjoyed around 9 to 11pm.

Cheap

→ **Cheong Ki Wa** ASIAN In Zona Rosa you'll find this Chinese, Japanese, and Korean buffet, served in a modern open-kitchen atmosphere with a pleasantly gurgling fountain. Sushi, teriyaki, shrimp, and various crunchy fried things are served every day. You can blow all the money you saved at the **Via Spiga** shoe store next door. *Amberes 41, Zona Rosa. ☎ 55/5511-6198. Buffet $75. No credit cards. Daily 11am–3pm. Metro: Insurgentes.*

MTV Best → **El Califa** ★ MEXICAN This is the spot in La Condesa where club kids and night owls gather for scrumptious tacos al pastor, *bistek* (steak), quesadillas, nopales with cheese, *café de olla* (cinnamon coffee), and a full roster of Mexican beers. It's open late, so you can stop in for a snack on your way from one Condesa hot spot to the next. Simple and straightforward with an orange-and-blue color scheme, plastic chairs, and outdoor sidewalk seating, it's the crowd that will keep you coming back. Valet parking is available. The small street is a little hard to find—but the food is so worth it. *Calle Altata 33, at Alfonso Reyes, La Condessa.* ☎ *55/5271-7666. Tacos $9–$52. AE, MC, V. Sun–Thurs 1pm–5am; Fri–Sat 1pm–6am. Metro: Sevilla*

→ **El Ocho Café** INTERNATIONAL Free wireless Internet, a bookshelf with magazines and reading material, menus shaped like frying pans, and a bright, modern, cheerful decor make El Ocho stand out of the Condesa cafe pack. The well-thought-out menu is chock-full of choices like panini, a veggie sandwich, milkshakes, croissants, coffees, breakfasts (huevos El Ocho comes with turkey bacon, refried beans, salsa, and manchego cheese), and even a hookah. There are games like Sudoku at every table and gelato for dessert. It caters to a Norteamericano palate and is just the kind of place that makes you want to settle in and stay awhile. *Ozuluama 14, at Amsterdam, La Condesa.* ☎ *55/5211-9015. Main courses $56–$130. AE, MC, V. Daily 8am–10pm. Metro: Sevilla*

MEXICO CITY

→ **Los Murales** MEXICAN The Zona Rosa is great for a deal, and you can't go wrong with this cheap vegetarian buffet in a pretty room with Mexican murals decorating the walls. The selection changes daily but always includes whole-grain breads, tostadas, soup, pastas, salads, and desserts, along with green tea to refresh weary travelers. A fantabulous bargain. *Liverpool 152, Centro.* ☎ *55/5726-9911. Buffet $85. No credit cards. Daily 9am–4pm. Metro: Insurgentes.*

→ **Parilla Suiza** MEXICAN Fancy-pants types craving cheap eats hit up the all-you-can-eat at Parilla Suiza. This place has been here forever and is counted on by neighborhood locals and young people on dates for tasty inexpensive Mexican food and good times. There's definitely nothing much going on with decor or anything else, but put back a few *chelas* (beers) and chow down on as many tacos as you can take for a solid out-and-about meal. The nopales are recommended, as is the green-and-red chorizo for those with more adventurous tastes. *Masaryk 249, at the corner of Arquimides, Polanco.* ☎ *55/5280-2371. Tacos $20–$75. AE, MC, V. Mon–Fri noon–6pm. Metro: Polanco.*

→ **Taco Inn** MEXICAN A great place to drop in for a quick lunch or snack while exploring the upscale main drag of Presidente Masaryk in all its glitterati glory. The first Taco Inn was created in 1970 on a corner at the Colonia Guadalupe Inn, hence the name. It was a tiny 17-sq.-m (183-sq.-ft.) space intended to "revolutionize the taco industry" through cleanliness, quality service, and mouthwatering tacos—seems they've met their goal. A torta de pastor is a good way to enjoy the signature taco, and even vegetarians can enjoy delicious options like nopalitos, or the less-traditional cactus with tomato, onion, spices, and tortillas. The Inn Vegetariano is another exotic option with sweet and sour sauce, pineapple, onion, cheese, and tortillas. Most dishes are priced below $50. An ice bucket stocked with beers will run you another $50. (Ten pesos a beer . . . please can I go back now?) Note that this stretch of Masaryk is an extremely popular afternoon dining spot for young Mexican yuppies. On the same block, you'll find the likes of Garabatos, a cafe/pastry shop frequented by ladies who lunch, and the laid-back Japanese joint, Mr. Sushi. *Masaryk 360, between Musset and Dumas, Polanco.* ☎ *55/5281-2945. Tacos $18–$29. No credit cards. Daily noon–11pm. Metro: Polanco.*

→ **Vegetarianos del Centro** VEGETARIAN This may be the perfect spot to lunch on your first day in town, as you'll likely be in El Centro anyway and want to avoid a case of *turista,* aka Montezuma's revenge. Chow down on a veggie burger and fries—though the dish is slightly modified from the usual version you'd find in the States, with darker bread, simpler ingredients, and smaller fries, the overall quality of the food is great. You'll find all your healthy staples like cleansing (or stomach-soothing) juices and a variety of salads. The multi-grain bread and horchata water (made from rice milk and cinnamon) that comes with your meal will also help settle your stomach for the taco binges that are sure to come. *Filomeno Mata 13, Centro. ☎ 55/5510-0113. Main courses $40–$70. No credit cards. Daily 10am–8pm. Metro: Zócalo*

Doable

→ **Aura** INTERNATIONAL/FUSION The see-and-be-seen-scene at Aura is as worthwhile checking out as the Asian and Mexican menu. Dinner here is the ideal way to see one of Polanco's most happening spots—it's located in Polanco's Habita hotel—without shelling out the dough to stay the night. Aura has something for everyone, from Italian dishes with Mexican touches, like penne with chipotle and goat cheese or mushroom and asparagus risotto, to sushi—the duck roll is decadent—and favorites like quesadillas and the ubiquitous hotel staple, the club sandwich. Just dress for it, as the other patrons are sure to have donned their Prada. *Presidente Masaryk 201, Polanco. ☎ 55/5282-3100. Main courses $45–$120. AE, MC, V. Daily 7am–11pm. Metro: Polanco.*

→ **Casa Azulejos** MEXICAN A Centro Historico sightseeing destination in itself, Casa Azulejos (literally "house of tiles") is an excellent example of Baroque architecture and was converted into the first Sanborn's, a very popular everything-under-one-roof type of store. There's a pharmacy, souvenirs, toys, cosmetics, electronics, a decadent chocolate shop, and of course, the restaurant, with a grand dining room covered in murals and offering typical Mexican fare. Located in the interior patio of what was once a house named the Blue Palace, eating here is still a royal experience thanks to the waitstaff in traditional dress and pre-Hispanic ambience. The tiles that make the house famous are rumored to have been made in China, but more likely were imported from Puebla, where they would have been made in a factory built by Dominican friars in 1653. The friars would surely have enjoyed the hearty Mexican breakfasts like chilaquiles and molletes. For lunch or dinner, tamales with red or green sauce are an excellent choice, as are the *tacos conchita pibil* (barbecued pork with red onion, beans, and cheese). Not in the mood for Mexican? The favorite standby here is a classic burger with fries or the ubiquitous club sandwich. *Calle Madero 4, at Callejón de la Condesa, Centro. ☎ 55/5512-9820. www.Sanborn's.com.mx/Sanborn's/azulejos.asp. Appetizers $35–$150, main courses $85–$200. AE, MC, V. Daily 7am–1am. Metro: Bellas Artes.*

→ **Fonda El Refugio** MEXICAN Fonda's is such a Mexico City classic that eating here is practically a requirement. Octavio Paz ate here, along with the many Mexican painters, artists, and cartoonists whose work lines the walls of the upstairs rooms. The place screams history, from the old-time black-and-white photographs to the 1968 *New York Times* review (calling Fonda El Refugio "the handsomest Mexican restaurant in the world") that is still printed in the menus. From refreshing aguas like *limonada* (lemonade), *horchata* (rice milk and cinnamon), and *chia* (lemonade steeped with chia seeds to aid digestion) to typical platos fuertes like *filete de pescado a la Veracruzana* (red snapper in yellow pepper sauce with tomato, onion, and capers), the food has remained consistently exquisite throughout all these years. *Liverpool 166, between Florencia and Londres, Zona Rosa. ☎ 55/5207-2732. www.fondaelrefugio.com.mx. Appetizers $30–$115, main courses $105–$155. AE, MC, V. Daily 1–11pm. Metro: Insurgentes.*

➔**Hunan** CHINESE The contemporary paintings and sculptures lining the walls and abundance of plants make for an exotic interior in what's considered by many to be the finest Chinese restaurant in Mexico City. Crispy Hunan shrimp with rice and duck that's cut from the bone tableside are house specialties. Other classic favorites include chicken with asparagus and dishes with exotic sauces like the fermented soybean and chile de arbol. Service is fast and efficient, but arrive early as the restaurant is prone to be packed with the well-heeled Lomas de Chapultepec crowd, especially on Saturday nights. *Paseo de la Reforma 2210, Lomas de Chapultepec. ☎ 55/5596-5011. www.hunan.com.mx. Appetizers $45–$150, main courses $160–$200. AE, MC, V. Mon–Thurs 1:30–11pm; Fri–Sat 1:30pm–midnight; Sun 1:30pm–6pm. Metro: Auditorio.*

➔**Nanda Yo** JAPANESE A super-cool Polanco joint that's the newest and best branch in the funky four-restaurant Kaiten Sushi concept chain, Nanda Yo's design references the traditional Japanese style intended to bring good fortune. You can't miss the entrance: giant photo portraits of ladies in kimonos mark the sleek, modern exterior. Paper mobiles strung with notes and letters of luck dangle above the conveyor belt that circulates various types of sushi that you just grab as you desire. A full a la carte menu is also served, and a lounge upstairs is open nightly for drinks. For an interesting fusion choice, try the rib-eye tacos, or for a roll, do the Pucca, with crab, salmon, spinach, avocado, onion, and chile. The name translates to "What's up?" in Japanese. And what's up is that this place rocks. *Alejandro Dumas 105, just off Presidente Masaryk, Polanco. ☎ 55/5281-8970. www.kaitensushis.com. Sushi $15–$55. AE, MC, V. Mon–Wed 1:30–11:30pm; Thurs–Sat 1:30pm–2am; Sun 1:30–8pm. Metro: Polanco.*

➔**Un Lugar de la Mancha** INTERNATIONAL This popular brunch spot in Lomas de Chapultepec is filled with Don Quixote statues and memorabilia. Lugar has a book and music shop downstairs and is popular with neighborhood youth. It gets packed with brunching families on the weekends. In 11000—the 90210 of Mexico City—it draws a stylish crowd for coffee and tea to its outdoor patio throughout the day. International cuisine takes center stage with specialties like pancakes, salads, and brunch dishes like *Don Belianis de Grecia* (eggs baked in the oven with goat cheese). *Prado Norte 205, just east of Reforma, Lomas de Chapultepec. ☎ 55/5202-8048. Appetizers $40–$125, main courses $90–$150. AE, MC, V. Mon–Fri 8am–10pm; Sat–Sun 9am–10pm. Metro: Auditorio.*

Splurge

MTV Best ➔**Aguila y Sol** ★★★ MEXICAN International celebrity chef Martha Ortiz Chapa's lovely restaurant is built around attention to detail, be it the service, the elegantly crafted dishes, the artistic themes around which the menus are framed, or the artful touches on every plate. It is dressy, high-end, and draws a stylish crowd, yet it is not obscenely pricey. It's consistently rated one of the top restaurants in the city by local publications like *Chilango* magazine, which called it "the temple of high Mexican cuisine," and *Donde Ir* (Mexico City's version of *Time Out*), which ranked it as #1 on a recent list of the Top 10 restaurants in town.

Aguila y Sol has received international attention as well, leading Martha to guest-chef at places like hip Hangar 7 in Salzburg, Austria, design a first-class menu for Lufthansa airlines, and win the Five Diamond Award for her restaurant. The decor here is muted—fancy but comfortable. Ambience is chic but not snobby. Martha creates new specials constantly, drawing inspiration from traditional Mexico and combining it with her signature artistic flair. At press-time, the theme was "Xochimilco chic," which included a dessert of pistachio ice cream floating in its own tiny trajinera on a canal of blue crushed ice. Another series involves an imaginary character named "María," a traditional Mexican woman whose daily activities inspire the dishes. A rich cheesecake dessert was named "María goes to the flower market," and came adorned as a lady carrying home bougainvilleas. Sugar-rimmed tamarindo margaritas are garnished with, appropriately, margarita flowers, and are ultra-tasty.

Don't pass up the ceviche appetizer, which comes with two sauces: a tangy *zapote negro,* which is a fruit, and a tomato-based *sangrita roja* vinaigrette. Martha's next project is to design a "Casa Azul" menu, using Frida Kahlo colors and themes. Passionate about her culture, Martha will tell you that every dish has a history, as do the crafts for sale in the gallery downstairs. *Masaryk 460, Polanco. ☎ 55/5281-8354. Main courses $150–$250. AE, MC, V. Daily 1–11pm. Metro: Polanco*

➔ **Contramar** SEAFOOD Contramar does power lunch right—during any lunch at this spot in Colonia Roma, you're bound to see local trendsetters, movers, shakers, and maybe even Gael Garcia Bernal. It's been one of the trendiest restaurants in Mexico City since it opened over a year ago in one of the hippest colonias of the moment. Not a day goes by that it isn't packed full (so reserve in advance), nor a dish that isn't delightful. The young owner, Gaby Camara, walks around to visit tables, making sure patrons are happy. The shrimp cocktail or tuna tostadas with leeks go great with a Corona or tequila to start; then you can concentrate on one of the daily specials. Keep your eyes peeled for Mexican celebrities or just enjoy the restaurant's underwater color scheme and minimalist fish-bone art. *Durango 200, Roma. ☎ 55/5514-9217. Main courses $130–$300. AE, MC, V. Daily noon–7pm. Metro: Sevilla.*

➔ **Hacienda De Los Morales** MEXICAN This 16th-century hacienda has been here since it was a country residence and el DF wasn't even a gleam in Mama Mexico's eye. My waiter tells me that when the first land-grants were given by the king of Spain, the estate was given to Don Hernan Cortez, chief of New Spain. With food as rich as its history, Hacienda Los Morales is the perfect place for *pollo en mole poblano* followed by a stroll across its lush, leafy grounds. Think of it as a Mexican history lesson with margaritas, which should definitely be sampled here, as they are 100% fresh—no scary fluorescent colors in these babies. Between that and the flavorful dishes, it's no wonder they've won about a gajillion awards. *Vazquez de Mella 525, Polanco. ☎ 55/5096-3054. www.haciendadelosmorales.com. Appetizers $105–$244, main courses $95–$387. AE, MC, V. Daily 1pm–1am. Metro: Polanco.*

➔ **San Angel Inn** MEXICAN The hacienda that was built in 1692 is now known as the most classic restaurant in the region. San Angel Inn is the South's version of Hacienda De Los Morales—upscale, very traditionally Mexican, fancy, and expensive. To start, taste the huitalcoche crepes or the *sopa Azteca*; for main dishes, the most popular is the beef filet marinated in adobo salsa, served with a chile relleno and guacamole. Also recommended is the chicken breast stuffed with cheese and either mango, raspberry, or mandarin sauce—it varies according to what's in season. If you're into wine, talk to the knowledgeable sommelier, who can recommend a perfect pairing. *Diego Rivera 50, at Altavista, San Angel.* ☎ *55/5619-2222. Appetizers $90–$250, main courses $170–$320. AE, MC, V. Mon–Sat 1pm–1am; Sun 1–10pm. Metro: Barranca del Muerto.*

Cafes & Snacks

Other than Starbucks and bookstore/music chains, cafes here tend to be cash-only, and with good reason: They're quite cheap. These grab-n-go places are great for a snack or caffeination refuelation. (With the exception of the *churrerias*, which don't usually do coffee—just hot chocolate. Hey, it's tradition.)

→**Cafebreria El Péndulo** COFFEE SHOP A bookstore/music shop and cafe (hence the Cafe/Librería fusion in the name), El Péndulo is a place to wile the afternoon away, or, if you speak Spanish, join in on one of the public discussions in their series. Other outposts are in Zona Rosa and Condesa. *Alejandro Dumas 81, Polanco.* ☎ *55/5280-4111. www.pendulo.com. Entrees $100–$200. AE, MC, V. Daily 10am–6pm. Metro: Polanco.*

MEXICO CITY

→**Café La Selva** COFFEE SHOP La Selva is a chain cafe with several locations around Mexico City, but the one in the Centro is special because of its setting in an old-fashioned colonial house from the 19th century. The ceiling is about 27m (90 ft.) high and the iced cappuccinos provide a tasty caffeine buzz to get you through your intense sightseeing agenda. The Coyoacán branch is a good choice, too, set back off the Jardín Hidalgo. Try the La Selva—a tasty drink with coffee liqueur. *Bolivar 31, Centro Historico.* ☎ *55/5521-4111. Nothing over $100. No credit cards. Daily 10am–6pm. Metro: Zócalo.*

→**Café Tacuba** COFFEE SHOP Inside this 17th-century colonial house, you can get a traditional Mexican meal as well as coffee and snacks. Popular with locals and travelers alike for live music, it's the spot where the band Café Tacuba (see "Recommended Books, Movies & Music," p. 65) got its moniker. *Tacuba 28, Centro.* ☎ *55/5521-2048. Entrees $40–$150. No credit cards. Daily 8am–11pm. Metro: Zócalo.*

→**Churreria El Moro** COFFEE SHOP This famous old 24-hour churro spot has a beautiful interior and the perfect crispy-fried sugary dough. Dip them in the ultra-rich hot chocolate—heavenly. *Eje Central 42, between Uruguay and Carranza, Centro Historico.* ☎ *55/5512-0896. Nothing over $30. No credit cards. Daily 24 hr. Metro: Zócalo.*

→**Churreria La Parroquia** COFFEE SHOP This cute, historic churros spot is the perfect place for a break while touring Coyoacán, or grab your churro ($2.50) to go from the outside window. Try them filled with *cajeta* (caramel) for more caloric bliss. *Jardín del Centenario s/n, Coyoacán. No phone. Nothing over $60. No credit cards. Daily 10am–11pm. Metro: Coyoacán.*

→**Jugos y Licuados Don Lupe** COFFEE SHOP With different blends of smoothies and fresh juices meant to relieve various conditions from poor digestion to weight loss, Don Lupe's got a cure for what ails ya. Or at least a fresh-fruit breakfast and perfectly blended drink. Service is carry-out only, so you'll have to walk 'n' sip. *Virgilio 9, Loc. 3, corner of Oscar Wilde, Polanco.* ☎ *55/9112-9173. Nothing over $100. No credit cards. Metro: Polanco.*

→**Snob Café** COFFEE SHOP You can't *not* go to the Snob Café: It wins the Funniest Restaurant Name of All Time award. And it

Canal of Love

On Friday and Saturday nights, you can experience MTV Best *lunadas* or moonlight rides ★★★ on candle-lit *trajineras* (colorful gondola-like boats) through the canals of Xochimilco. You'll glide down the watery passageways by candlelight, while listening to mariachis, sipping Coronas, and nibbling *antojitos*. For a romantic date or a party you can't go wrong. If you reserve in advance and ask, the artisans can create your name out of woven-together flowers for the boat. (They usually have women's names like María or Guadalupe.) The trip lasts as long as you want, and yes, there are pitstops along the way.

A designated nature preserve, the canals have been in existence since the days when Aztecs cruised down them in the very same type of boat that visitors ride today. There are several *embarcaderos* (docks where you can board), but the biggest and best is Embarcadero Nativitas, which has a crafts market and family-owned casual and inexpensive restaurants/food stands that serve amazing hangover food: pambazos, quesadillas, and huaraches. I dig the ones with *nopales* (cactus) or the *pambazos* with chicken from Antojitos Paola.

At the entrance to the trajineras, ask for the *servicio de trajineras El Chango* (Mercado de Curiosidades Nativitas-Xochimilco; ☎ 55/5675-5335; $160 per hr; Metro: Line 2 to Tasqueña, light rail to Embarcadero). Some of the "gondoliers" are jewelers who've studied at the nearby Xochipilli school for artisans so you might score a deal on something silver. Mariachis on passing boats will play for about $70 a song. Grab an elote and a michelada, or a candy apple, from vendors' boats, and settle in for the ride. If you have to pee, your guide will likely pull over at the home of a friendly local who's agreed to lend out their bathroom—just one example of how much tourism fuels Xochimilco's economy. (It's second only to agriculture.)

definitely doesn't live up to its name. You can chill over some coffee and dessert at one of the outdoor tables, nicely situated away from the street. The service is relaxed and friendly and a full menu is served as well. As for the name, chalk it up to "lost in translation." *Pasaje Polanco, at Masaryk 360, Polanco.* ☎ *55/5281-0816. Nothing over $150. AE, MC, V. Daily 8am–10pm. Metro: Polanco.*

➜ **Starbucks** COFFEE SHOP Yeah, it's arrived, so you don't have to miss your nonfat caramel no-whip cream-swirled green tea Frappuccino while you're in Mexico. Go, globalization. PS: They've got better sandwiches and cleaner bathrooms than the ones in Manhattan. *Pasaje Polanco and every-freakin'-where. Nothing over $80.*

Partying

Mexico City is nothing if not a party town. Many large clubs charge a cover at the door—the one beneficial side effect of machismo is that the fee is often waived for the ladies—and have an open bar all night long. More traditional cantinas can have a dive-bar ambience and a crowd of old men, while sleek, upscale lounges and laid-back New York City–style bars draw the young scenesters.

Whether dancing up a storm or kicking back with a tequila Cosmo, Chilangos love to party until well after sunup, celebrating the freedom of Mexico's nightlife and bringing the *reventon* (aka fiesta). Nightclubs tend to open around 10pm, but don't really get going until midnight.

Big spenders should consider reserving a table at clubs; you'll get bottle service and avoid the by-the-drink masses who surround the bar. Some common cocktails in Mexico City are the Splash, great if you like amaretto (amaretto and orange juice hit with some grenadine and a cherry), Cuba Libre (known to us gringos as rum-and-coke), and innovative beer mixtures like the Bull (beer, vodka, and *naranjada,* aka orange soda) or michelada (spiced, with lime). If you order a *michelada preparada* (sometimes also called *Cubana,* or prepared), it comes mixed with Worcestershire sauce, Tabasco, and other funky condiments.

To find out what's on tap when you're in town, pick up the excellent mags *Donde Ir* and *Chilango,* which have the latest and greatest news on all things nightlife. You'll spot copies at Sanborn's or any newsstand.

Bars

→ **Bar Milan** JUAREZ Just south of the Zona Rosa in quiet Colonia Juárez, Bar Milan is another longtime favorite staple on Mexico City's bar circuit. Popular among locals for after-work drinks, this bar has the quirky policy that you can't pay in pesos, dollars, pounds, or Yen. Instead, you trade your pesos in at the door for Milagro Money, the bar's own Monopoly-esque paper cash. The vibe is fun and relaxed, with a prevailing funky decor. And while it's not a gay bar, per se, it is definitely gay-friendly, with a mixed crowd bonding over martinis. *Milan 18, General Prim and Locema.* ☎ *55/5592-0338. Metro: Insurgentes.*

→ **Caballo Negro (The Black Horse)** CONDESA A true-to-roots classic British pub in Mexico City. The first and only real-deal bar of its type, it hits all the marks, with darts, bands, and a roomful of expats. One of the pioneers in the recent wave of Euro-style bars and lounges that have opened in the city, they serve green beer on St. Patrick's day and receive fresh Guinness every day. Music is mostly international hits, and a DJ comes in for late night sets. *Mexicali 85, at Tamaulipas.* ☎ *55/5211-8740. www.caballonegro.com. Metro: Juanacatlan.*

→ **El Barsin** CONDESA The name literally translates to "the bar without." Without alcohol, that is. Yup, that's right, it's Mexico City's first cantina sans intoxicants. If you're straight-edge or underage, you can enjoy the traditional cantina atmosphere in a 19th-century casona while sipping unique "mocktail" beverages prepared with extracts of *melaza de caña* (cane juice) or *malta* (malt), with flavors resembling rum and whisky, but without the buzz; I recommend the *Marcianito limon,* non-alcoholic whiskey with mint, lime, and soda ($35). The rooms are homages to Mexican culture, like the Sala Monos, which has a gallery of *historietas,* little stories, like *Chanoc y Los Supermachos,* or the *Salon de Oro,* a tribute to the personalities that formed part of the Mexican cinema's golden age. The snack menu is extensive. *General Francisco Murguia 108.* ☎ *55/5516-1323.*

MTV Best → **El Hijo del Cuervo** ★★★ COYOACÁN A great place to people-watch and soak up the energy of the vibrant Coyoacán plaza, this has been my favorite bar in Mexico City for a long time. Order a tequila and *sangrita* (spicy tomato juice) and sit in the front window, outdoors, or hole up in the dark back room, where live bands sometimes perform on weekends. *Jardín Centenario 17.* ☎ *55/5658-5196. Cover up to $70. Metro: Coyoacán.*

→ **El Under** ROMA Authentic and unpretentious, this cafe/bar was built as a showcase for alternative artistic expression. In the afternoons it offers lunch service with meals made from organic ingredients, cappuccinos, mochas, and herbal teas. (The only alcoholic beverage served is beer.) Come nighttime, goth music, art exhibits, and themed parties are de rigueur. Thursdays bring the experimental film series, and the music is industrial, monster surf, death rock, and punk. Goths, punks, and those with multiple piercings, blue hair, or whatever non-mainstream "thing" will feel very much at home here. *Monterrey 80, at Insurgentes. ☎ 55/5511-5475. www.theunder.org. Metro: Sevilla.*

➔ **La Faena** CENTRO HISTORICO A semi-run-down virtual museum of what once must have been an upscale cantina, this historical dive stands out—besides its special events nights and occasional hipster parties—for the bullfighting memorabilia that is shown off by adorned mannequins in glass cases lining the walls. A painting of a torero startin' somethin' with an unsuspecting bull is the *signatura* painting, and the DJ booth, when there is one, sets up in front of it. For quirky, dilapidated charm, you can't beat La Faena's plastic chairs and non-functional chandeliers. *Venustiano Carranza 49. ☎ 55/5510-2907. Metro: Zócalo.*

➔ **La Jugada** FLORIDA On Insurgentes Sur, patrons at La Jugada have more than 100 ways to be a player. Of dominoes, backgammon, and rummy, that is . . . So hold up, Romeo—this fun bar is the turf of the table-game aficionado. The crowd is laid-back and looking for good times—and better chess opponents. The music is a variety of pop hits in English and Spanish with oldies tossed into the mix here and there. A snack menu offers mostly junk food named after games (papas Boliche, salchichas Histeria, and so on). Best on Thursdays and Fridays. *Insurgentes Sur 1862. ☎ 55/5663-1261. Metro: Insurgentes.*

➔ **Pata Negra** CONDESA A trendy tapas bar, Pata Negra is abuzz with Condesa hipsters and an influx of foreigners, even on rainy Monday nights. Its lively music and tasty small plates are just the right ingredients for a solid, fun night out. Sidle up to the dark-wood paneled bar and order up a sangria; you never know who you might meet at this happenin' hot spot. *Tamaulipas 30, at Juan Escutia. ☎ 55/5211-5563. Metro: Juanacatlan.*

Lounges

➔ **Bengala** ROMA The creative martinis are one main draw of this sophisticated, artsy, and very trendy lounge. Try the Marea Roja (mandarin vodka, Brazilian fruit liqueur, cassis, grape juice, and lemon juice) or the Modjo, which is the house specialty (lime juice, mescal, anis, and pepino). The short menu consists of Asian small plates like steamed dumplings, beef won tons, and shrimp brochettes. Tuesday is jazz night, Wednesday rock or pop, Thursday funk and soul, and Friday different decades. But Saturday may be the best night to come, especially if you're scene-seeking. The music that night will appeal to electronica fans; it's down tempo, house, and chill out. *Sonora 34. ☎ 55/5553-9219. Metro: Sevilla.*

➔ **Cinnabar** CONDESA This trendy-but-totally-unsnobby, chic, and comfortable bar/lounge is perfect for a late-night Thai or Vietnamese treat with your perfectly mixed drink. Specialty cocktails are a highlight here—the list features over 20 choices. I loved the Graffiti—raspberry puree, lime soda, and vodka—but I've got a sweet tooth for girly drinks. The Vanilla Julep—Absolut Vanilla, mint, lemon, a touch of sugar, and soda—is a general crowd-pleaser. For nibbles, the Shia appetizer is the love child of sushi and a bagel, with a crispy sesame crust, smoked salmon, cream cheese, red peppers, and ginger. If you're in the mood for something more filling, try the Pato Cinna, duck rolls with hoisin sauce. The lounge is dimly lit in red, with hardwood floors and dark wood furniture. Settle into one of the couches, or pick a table toward the center for prime people-watching. A Buddha Bar–esque soundtrack tops off the sleek Asian-fusion vibe. *Nuevo Leon 67. ☎ 55/5286-8456. Metro: Juanacatlan.*

➜ **Hookah** SAN ANGEL This Middle Eastern–themed venue in the South is located in a shopping mall. But inside, the spacious setting of Hookah is decorated exotically with tapestries and Swarovski curtains, and there's a posh VIP room you can try to talk your way into. The resident DJ spins electronica nightly. The specialty cocktail, the Hookah, is an interesting blend of Red Bull and light beer but I like the Yemanya, with Malibu rum and Red Bull. The kitchen does Middle Eastern–Mexican fusion. Go on Thursday night, when live belly dancers perform. *Av. La Paz 40, Plaza Gerard. ☎ 55/5616-2914. Metro: Barranca del Muerto.*

➜ **Only You** CONDESA The menu at CondesaDF's rooftop bar encourages you to "meet the sushi" from the adjacent restaurant, and what a fatefully delicious meeting it is. A coconut shrimp roll arrives with a side of tangy coconut sauce on one side and a savory vinegar reduction on the other that mingles to create the perfect sweet-and-sour crunch. Unique cocktails like the Wokka Saki Bellini (a mix of vodka, peach liqueur, and champagne) are worth savoring. A mix of arty local Condesa connoisseurs and hotel guests lounge on beds or share sushi and conversation at the comfy banquette tables. The altitude here means the nights cool down quickly, but the friendly staff and heat lamps make sure you don't. Oh, and they give you a super-cozy Mexican blanket too. *Av. Veracruz 102. ☎ 55/5241-2600. www.condesadf.com. Metro: Juanacatlan.*

Clubs

➜ **Bliss Club** SAN ANGEL This hip-hop and reggaeton club is popular with university students and young locals. Sophisticated, minimalist design adorns the comfortable beige-and-red rooms, and the extensive cocktail menu offers plentiful options that are mixed by hot bartenders. The specialty drink is the Martini Bliss: vodka, Red Bull, blue Curacao, and lemon soda. *Altavista 131. ☎ 55/5550-5529. Cover $100. Metro: Barranca del Muerto.*

➜ **Bulldog Café** SAN JUAN MIXCOAC A longtime favorite among the nightclubs in town, Bulldog typically features late-night rock bands and DJs playing rock-'n'-roll classics. There are two main areas, one upstairs and one downstairs, for drinking, dancing, hanging out, and listening to the (very loud) music. The too-cool-for-school crowd has their own roped-off VIP lounge, and the chill-out room with benches and a hot dog stand means you don't have to leave should the 3am munchies strike. ***Note***: There's no Metro stop in sight, so you'll want to take a taxi to and fro here. *Jardín Centenario 17, corner of Revolución. ☎ 55/5611-8818. Cover varies.*

➜ **The Dance Club @ CondesaDF** CONDESA It's not surprising that happening CondesaDF has its own nightclub, too. After enjoying sushi or drinks on the rooftop, drop down to this somewhat cavernous subterranean space to party up with one of the rotating international DJs; it's a perfect romantic-liaison spot. Call in advance: There's bound to be some kind of film screening after-party or a top DJ taking to the turntables. *Av. Veracruz 102, at Parque España. ☎ 55/5241-2600. www.condesadf.com. No cover. Metro: Sevilla.*

MEXICO CITY

→ **Dos97** CONDESA A dance club for electronica and glam rock lovers, Dos97's DJs spin mostly house, trance, goth, and darkwave music. A large, pared-down space with red vinyl banquettes, candles, muted blue lighting, and an alternative and punk rock crowd, it's a great spot for getting down or just chilling out. *Ámsterdam 297, Celaya and Sonora. No phone. Cover $50–$70. Metro: Sevilla.*

→ **Pasaguero** CENTRO Nightlife downtown is going through a revival thanks to spaces like this one, which mixes up cultural activities with full-on partying. Art openings, themed nights, and fashion launches might be among the flavas on any given night at this more-than-a-club, so call ahead to find out what's on. *Motolinia 33. ☎ 55/5512-6624. Cover varies. Metro: Zócalo.*

Best → **Pervert Lounge** ★★★ CENTRO If you only go out dancing once in Mexico City, let this be the place. With neon-colored Barbies hanging out on lamps lining the walls, Korova Milk Bar–esque furnishings, trippy electronica, and a hilarious name, it's no wonder this lounge has been around since the '90s and shows no sign of slowing down. The crowd is young and funky, and the scene always hip, although definitely not in a snobby-doorman, pricey-cover sort of way. *Uruguay 70, 5 de Febrero and Isabel la Catolica. ☎ 55/5518-0976. Cover varies. Metro: Zócalo.*

→ **Rincón Cubano** ROMA Just a block away from the better-known Mama Rumba, this is a newer, more interesting, Cuban dance club. With live salsa and rumba, lots of good dancers to either join or watch, and what may be the best mojito in Mexico City, it's a prime nightspot for people in their 20s to 40s. The decor and ambience are traditional Cuban. *Insurgentes Sur 300. ☎ 55/5264-0549. Cover $50 on Fri and Sat. Metro: Insurgentes.*

→ **Rioma** CONDESA Your token obnoxious-bouncer, long-line, get-turned-away-for-wearing-the-wrong-shoes nightclub. If you're hot to trot and work your way into this hot spot, you'll find lounge music, techno, and chill-out electronica. The crowd is of course made up of beautiful people, dressed to the nines. It used to be owned by Cantinflas, who was like a Mexican Dane Cook (except older). *Insurgentes Sur 377, Michoacan. ☎ 55/5584-0631. Cover $100. Metro: Sevilla.*

→ **Roots** LOMAS DE SOTELO This nightclub has a large, lit-up facade and two plasma televisions broadcasting the scene inside the gigantic antro. The vibe is casual and relaxed, with three different concepts under one roof: a lounge that serves Mediterranean cuisine; Club Roots, with a stage for live music; and two dance floors, where you can groove with one of the first female DJs in Mexico, Xochitl Lujan, who spins popular hits and kicked-back electronica. The other room is devoted to tunes from the '70s. Come early, around 10pm, because the line gets long fast. With no Metro stop nearby, grab a taxi instead. *Rodolfo Gaona 3. ☎ 55/5580-6106. Cover $250 for men, free for women; varies for concerts or special events.*

Gay Nightlife

Though Mexico has traditionally been a conservative, Catholic country, in fall of 2006, Mexico City's politicians voted to recognize civil unions between gay partners, in a monumental step for gay rights. With the law being officially passed in late winter 2007, gay marriage—and acceptance—is at an all-time high in the city.

For general information on Mexico City's gay scene, most of which centers around the Zona Rosa, be sure to grab a copy of ***SerGay,*** Mexico City's most popular gay magazine, or visit them at www.sergay.com.mx to find LGBT bars, restaurants, and attractions.

→**El Celo 2000** ZONA ROSA This spot, frequented by a 20-something crowd, is one of the most established and popular gay bars in Mexico City. *Londres 104, Zona Rosa. No phone. Metro: Sevilla or Insurgentes.*

→**El Taller** ZONA ROSA El Taller is one of the grittier choices as far as gay bars go, with darkened rooms and lots of cruising. It caters to a varied crowd, ranging from their 20s to 40s, who come to listen to house and trance music. *Florencia 37-A, Zona Rosa. No phone. Metro: Insurgentes.*

→**Living** CUAUHTEMOC Picture Limelight in its heyday—*Chilango* style. A slick, fun, multi-roomed dance club in a huge old church with international DJs near Zona Rosa, Living is Mexico City's premier spot for gay nightlife. You can't miss it; just look for the rainbow flag in front. The Pop Room has an '80s vibe and features, well, pop music, the Main Room is all techno, all the time, while the green Lounge Room is where you can sit and have a conversation with that new cutie you just met on the dance floor. Snack Bar El Gallo is the place to replenish all the calories you burnt off while getting your groove on, and the very pink-and-red private room is a sleek VIP lounge. So many options for living it up, all under one roof. *Paseo de la Reforma 483, at Elba.* ☎ *55/5826-0671. Cover $50. Metro: Insurgentes.*

Performing Arts

Most plays in the city are conducted in Spanish, but there are plenty of performing arts options for non-Spanish-speakers as well. Ballet Folklorico, which features spectacular folk-dancing, is perhaps the most famous performance space in Mexico, and the most popular among travelers. Auditorio Nacional hosts big concerts and international artists.

Spanish speakers seeking theater will be well-served by the weekly listings magazine *Tiempo Libre,* available at newsstands and shops like Sanborn's, or online at www.tiempolibre.com.mx. Conaculta (National Council For Culture and the Arts) also backs theater, so give clicks to their online listing at www.conaculta.gob.mx.

Theaters

→**Auditorio Nacional** CHAPULTEPEC This fantastic, huge auditorium on Reforma near Chapultepec Park has seen shows by everyone from Michael Jackson, U2, and the Pet Shop Boys to operas like *Aida* and performers such as the Three Tenors. Hard Rock Cafe is just up the street for more musical ambience (or a burger) after the show. Check schedules and see who's coming to town at www.auditorio.com.mx. *Reforma 50.* ☎ *55/5280-9250. Admission varies by performance. Metro: Auditorio.*

→**Palacio de Bellas Artes** CENTRO HISTORICO With its Art Nouveau facade, columns, cupolas, statues, and interior murals by David Alfaro Sequeiros, Rufino Tamayo, José Clemente Orozco, and Diego Rivera, you should check out Palacio de Bellas Artes for its own sake. But double up on culture and come see the **Ballet Folklorico de Mexico,** a spectacular display of traditional dance that is enjoyed by locals just as much as tourists. Their website, www.balletamalia.com, has more information and showtimes. *Av. Juárez s/n, Eje Central.* ☎ *55/5512-1410. Admission varies by performance. Metro: Bellas Artes.*

The Gallery Scene

Mexico City's **Condesa** and **Roma** are experiencing a renaissance of their own in the form of a gallery scene that is starting to rival that of Chelsea in New York. The prime spaces all feature jaw-droppingly good contemporary Mexican and international artists. The galleries are perfect for touring on foot, while popping in and out of the pretty parks and chic cafes along the way. To make it walkable, these suggestions pertain to Roma and Condesa only, but be sure to look into a trip to the Colecion Jumex and some galz that are worth seeing in that area, too. Added bonus: galleries are free.

Put these spots on the afternoon's agenda (because there's something so *je ne sais quoi* about gallery-hopping in the pm hours):

- **Casa Lamm** (Centro de Cultura). The mother lode of the new-wave Chilango art scene, in Roma. For the full review, see p. 116.
- **OMR ROMA.** A beautiful light-filled space in a typical early-20th-century Roma house, OMR has two floors dedicated to solo and group exhibitions. The gallery represents a respected selection of new and emerging artists on the scene. A recent exhibit featured Yishai Jusidman's paintings of letters from epistolary manuals of the 17th, 18th, and 19th centuries. Torolab's 2006 installation show featured a fascinatingly creepy treelike structure made out of security cameras—very Big Brother. *Plaza Rio de Janeiro 54, Roma. ☎ 55/5511-1179. www.galeriaomr.com. Mon–Fri 10am–3pm; Sat 10am–2pm.*
- **Galería Nina Menocal.** With a sunny open courtyard and huge exhibition space, this gorgeous gallery is one of the best in show. Among the contemporary Mexican artists are the painter Gustavo Acosta, photographer Martin Soto, and multimedia artist Miguel Ventura. Acosta's enormous canvases showcase scenes from Mexico City, including one stunning painting of the zócalo. Whatever's on, it's bound to be thought-provoking. *Zacatecas 93, Condesa. ☎ 55/5564-7209. www.ninamenocal.com. Call for hr. and prices.*
- **Garash Galería.** They were in between exhibits when I visited, but this emerging contemporary gallery represents cutting-edge young artists, so it's guaranteed to be cool. Just check the website to see what's on before you head over. *Alvaro Obregon 49, Condesa. ☎ 55/5207-9858. www.garashgaleria.com. Mon–Fri 10am–2pm and 3–6pm.*
- **Galería Florencia Riestra.** This small gallery has only a couple of rooms, but merits a quick visit. Expect to see modern art, such as the colorful abstract work of Tatiana Montoya, along with some interesting sculpture. There's a branch in San Miguel de Allende, too. *Colima 166, Roma. ☎ 55/5514-2537. www.galeriaflorenciariestra.com.mx. Call for hr. and prices.*
- **Casa Barragan.** Okay, so it's not technically a gallery, but, the architecture on display is so beautiful, it might as well be. This house was designed and once lived in by Luis Barragan, the Pritzker Prize–winning architect. Today, it's a UNESCO World Heritage site. *General Francisco Ramirez 14, Condesa. ☎ 55/5515-4908. www.casaluisbarragan.org. Call for prices and hr.*

Sightseeing

Given Mexico City's enormity, it won't come as a big shock that there is an overwhelming amount of time-worthy sights, from recently uncovered Aztec ruins in the Centro Historico to the massive Anthropology Museum to a booming gallery scene.

The **Turibus** (see below), a London-style double-decker that makes various stops at places of interest around the city, is a great way to get oriented and see el DF's major monuments and museums. But several of the important museums—**Anthropology, Museo Rufino Tamayo, National History Museum**—are concentrated in the *primera seccion* (first section) of **Chapultepec Park.** You can walk from one to the next till you drop.

Same goes for the sights in and around the Centro Historico. In the south, Frida and Diego fans will appreciate the artists' homes—Frida Kahlo's **Casa Azul, Diego** Rivera's studio house, **Diego Rivera Anahuacalli,** which houses his influential pre-Hispanic art collection, buddy **Leon Trotsky's house,** and, toward Xochimilco, the greatest one of all: **Museo Dolores Olmedo Patiño,** Diego's friend and patron Dolores Olmedo's hacienda, which has been converted into an art museum with some of Mexico's most important works, like Frida's *Self Portrait with Small Monkey.*

Most importantly, when it comes to sightseeing in la Capital, pick your battles.

Free & Easy

Most museums in the city are either free or deeply discounted for students (and teachers, too) with valid ID. But there are tons of other free ways to enjoy Mexico's capital, including taking a free tour with the historical center (p. 115). Here are some more FREE ideas:

- **Subway Art.** The government has a fantastic program to showcase art inside the Metro. From Aztec artifacts to modern light-installations, you can cruise the underground and admire as much as you would in a museum.
- **Chapultepec Park.** If you have a student or teacher ID, you can get into the museums in the vicinity for free. And if not, this is a great place to walk around and take it all in.
- **Museo Dolores Olmedo Patiño.** The Kahlo-Rivera friend and patron's house opens its doors to all every Tuesday.
- **The gallery tour.** Galleries are free. Of course you can't succumb to the urge to snatch up that $45,000 painting . . . it's NOT free. See box, "The Gallery Scene," p. 111.
- **Coyoacán Plaza.** You could spend hours on end here and never get bored with the sights. There are that many people-watching and sightseeing options on offer—tons of bohemian types come here, especially on weekends, just to hang.
- **Zócalo.** The center of Mexico City is free, and there are plenty of sights in the area that can be visited at no cost, like the Palacio Postal and the interior of Palacio Bellas Artes.
- **Alameda Park.** A charming place to wile away an afternoon. Architecture fans will appreciate this area, just west of the zócalo.

The Story of El Grito

On September 16, Mexican Independence Day, crowds gather in the zócalo to watch the president deliver el Grito from the balcony of Palacio Nacional. It's a yearly ritual—except in 2006, when then-prez Vicente Fox went to Hidalgo to avoid the masses of Obrador loyalists. El Grito is Padre Hidalgo's famous rallying cry that launched the quest for Mexico's independence from Spain in 1810. It was originally phrased "Long live Virgen Guadalupe and death to Spaniards!" It has since been rephrased to the more palatable *"Viva Mexico! Vivan los héroes de la patria! Viva la Republica!"* My favorite place to be for Independence Day is the Coyoacán Plaza, because the zócalo's a mess. Coyoacán is crowded as well, but the atmosphere's more fun. Go early to snag a table by the window at El Hijo del Cuervo (p. 106), enjoy some red, white, and green sopes, and avoid the masses.

Unless you live here for awhile, there's no way to see everything the DF has to offer. Note that for students and teachers with ID, most museums are free or discounted.

Festivals/Events

If you're lucky enough to visit during a holiday period, you'll catch a glimpse of the way Mexicans like to party. Fourth of July can't hold a firecracker to the passion with which Independence Day is celebrated in Mexico City. Day of the Dead is another biggie, with its sugar skulls and flower-petal mosaics of the Virgen Guadalupe on grave sites. Here are some of the *dias festivos* you won't want to miss:

Día de la Independencia: This independence national holiday is marked by **El Grito,** when Hidalgo gave the "shout" of independence (see box, "The Story of El Grito," above). Coyoacán, the zócalo, and Plaza Garibaldi are the best spots to see it go down. Downer: The sale of alcohol is prohibited that day. You can consume it, though, and many people drink beer in the streets. September 16.

Cinco de Mayo: You may know this holiday as a night of margaritas and fajitas at the best Mexican resto in your hometown, but here the party lasts for 5 days. May 1 is Mexican Labor Day, and in Mexico any holiday is inevitably accompanied by a *puente* (bridge)—i.e. an excuse to take off a little more school or work. The best place to experience El Cinco is in its birthplace of **Puebla** (p. 144). May 5.

Día de Los Muertos: This is the Day of the Dead, when Mexicans gather to remember their loved ones who have passed. Colorful festivals take place and you can pick up some of the traditional sugar skulls all around town. November 1 and 2.

Semana Santa: "Holy week," as it translates, is huge in Mexico. Two weeks before Easter is the **Xochimilco Festival,** honoring the goddess of flowers, Xochipilli, and Maculxochitl, the goddess of dance. Each year a beauty pageant is held to choose the "most beautiful flower of Xochimilco," a young woman who rides down the canals in lieu of a float/parade type situation. April 1–8.

Spring equinox: On the first day of spring, tons of people drive out to the pyramids of Teotihuacán dressed in white. They climb the pyramid of the sun not only to welcome spring, but to absorb the energy the pyramids are believed to transmit on this magical day. (And the white threads help absorb

Downtown Mexico City

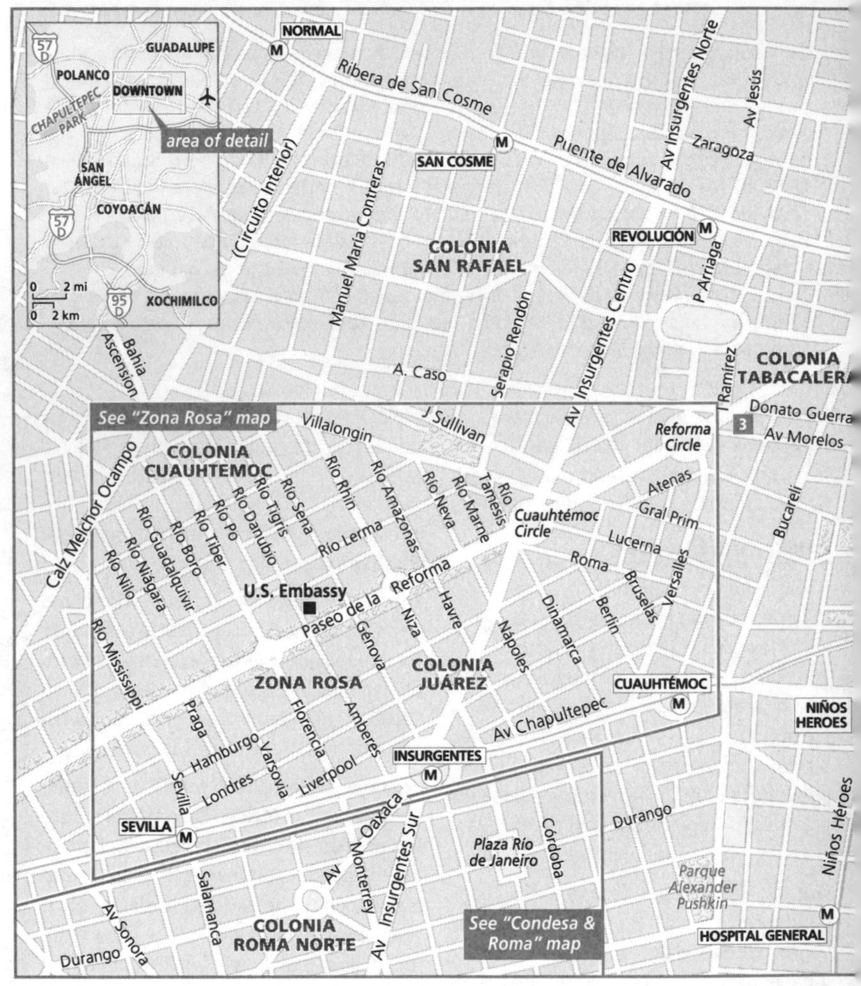

this.) It might sound a little hippie-dippy to some, but the spectacle of thousands of white-clad people scaling a pyramid is a sight to behold no matter what you think of the ritual. End of March.

Tours

The double-decker bus **Turibus** may be the pinnacle of touristy, but when you're sitting on the upper deck, breezing past the Angel de la Independencia and digging some cool tunes, who cares? In the end it's a convenient and fun way to get around to many of the places on your agenda: like the Museum of Modern Art, Condesa, La Feria/Papalote Museo del Niño (the amusement park and children's museum), Masaryk in Polanco, and the zócalo. You can get on and off, spending time at any of the attractions on the bus's hit list. A bus

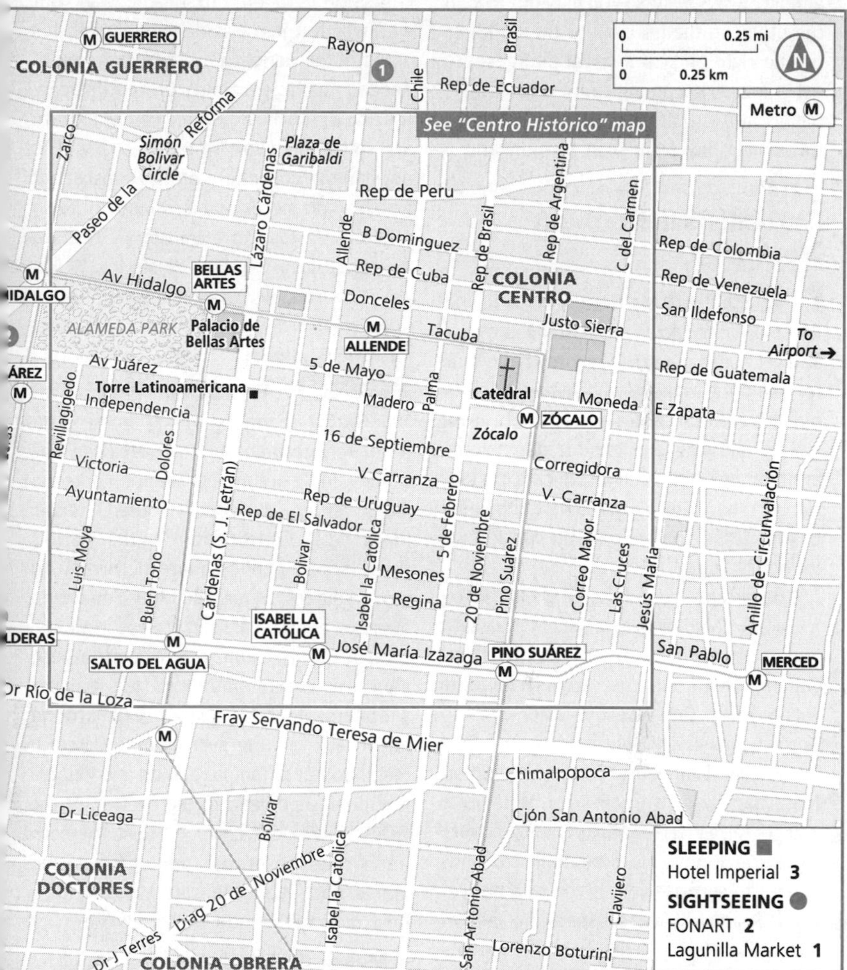

comes by each stop every 30 to 45 minutes and you just show your ticket to get back on. The price for a day tour is $100. Call ☎ **55/5563-6693** for info or visit www.turibus.com.mx.

Free guided tours are also sponsored by the **Mexico City Historical Center** (☎ **55/5345-8000,** ext. 1499), in the 18th-century home of Don Manuel de Heras y Soto, at Donceles and República de Chile. Groups meet each Sunday at 10:45am at a central gathering place for that day's tour, which varies from week to week. These tours might explore a historic downtown street, cafes and theaters, cemeteries, or the colonial churches of Xochimilco. Most tours, which last about 2 hours, are in Spanish; as many as 300 people may be divided among 10 guides. Visitors can ask a day in advance for a guide who speaks their language. The center's phone is almost always busy, so you may opt to visit the office, in the far back of the building, on the right and up a spiral staircase, to get a list of upcoming tours and gathering locations. Office hours are Monday through Friday from 9am to 3pm and 6 to 9pm.

Attractions in Northern Mexico City

MTV Best → **Casa Lamm** ★★★ ROMA When in Roma, do as those in the know do and visit Casa Lamm. If you only have time for one thing in the newly chic-again colonia, this cultural center is it, with a bi-level gallery showing one exhibit downstairs, another upstairs, a modern cafe/restaurant and bar, plus a bookstore (with some English titles, too) where you can lounge for hours.

One recent groundbreaking exhibit by awesome collaborative artists Marisa Lara and Arturo Guerrero, titled Nos-Otros (Us-Others), featured the artists donning Sacha Baron Cohen–esque alter-egos to portray imaginary self-important artists from around the world in a mock-exhibit featuring their own paintings. Whenever you go, the galleries at Casa Lamm are sure to have an innovative, potentially hilarious exhibit to surprise you. If you're a native-level Spanish speaker spending a few months in Mexico City, it's worth looking into their well-respected classes to unleash your creative side. The school here offers certificate programs in writing, literature, art, and other subjects. *Alvaro Obregon 99, Orizaba. ☎ 55/5208-0171. www.casalamm.com.mx. Admission free–$100 for students. Daily 11am–6pm. Metro: Insurgentes.*

FREE → **Coleccion Jumex** SANTA MARIA TULPETIAC Founded in 2001 by Eugenio Lopez-Alonso, the heir to Grupo Jumex, a company best known outside of Mexico for fruit juices, this private art collection is a bit out of the way, but well worth it if you can swing a visit. It's actually the perfect pit-stop when you're headed to the pyramids of Teotihuacán. It's one of the most hoppin' contemporary art spaces in Latin America today. The permanent collection alone consists of nearly 1,500 pieces and is valued at US$80 million. *Antigua Carretera Mexico-Pachuca Km 19.5, Ecatepec, Estado de Mexico. ☎ 55/5775-8188. www.lacoleccionjumex.org. Mon–Fri 10am–5:30pm by appointment only. Free. Metro: Indios Verdes.*

MTV Best → **El Zócalo** ★★ CENTRO HISTORICO Founded in 1325 as the capital of Tenochtitlan, the huge Mexican flag in the middle of this vast square marks the city's center. The zócalo (official name: Plaza de la Constitución) is the world's third largest public square according to most sources, after the Red Square in Moscow and Tiananmen Square in China, though some claim it's second-largest. Measurement competitions aside, it makes a statement about space. Walk around and check out the surrounding Catedral Metropolitana, Templo Mayor, and Palacio Nacional, then head to the rooftop of the Gran Hotel de Mexico or Best Western (more touristy) for the stunning views (and margaritas). Aztec dancers typically perform daily in the square. *Metro: Zócalo.*

→ **Museo de Arte Moderno** CHAPULTEPEC Easily confused with the Tamayo since it's a museo in the same area that also showcases contemporary art, the Arte Moderno is actually a very distinct space. The Museo de Arte Moderno's permanent collection contains Frida Kahlo's *Las Dos Fridas,* one of her most telling self-portraits. You'll also see work by her then-husband Diego Rivera and other significant Mexican and international artists like Leonora Carrington and José Clemente

Orozco. The photography and sculpture collections are impressive as well. *Paseo de la Reforma, Seccion 1. ☎ 55/5553-6233. www.conaculta.gob.mx/mam/mam.html. Admission $15; free for students and teachers with ID. Tues–Sun 10am–5:30pm. Metro: Chapultepec.*

→ **Museo del Caracol** CHAPULTEPEC Right next to the History Museum is the Museo del Caracol (Museum of the Snail), so named because of its spiral structure. Figures and scenes in glass cases illustrate important battles, events, and people, like the Cinco de Mayo combat, the French invasion, and Benito Juárez, respectively. Geared toward school kids, it's a great place to get a quick survey of Mexican history. You should speak at least a little Spanish to go, though, as the explanations of exhibits are all *en Español.* Or ask if an English-speaking staff member is on duty to give you a quick tour with explanations in English. *Chapultepec Park 1a Seccion. ☎ 55/5061-9241. Admission $30; students and teachers with ID free. Tues–Sun 9am–4:15pm. Metro: Constituyentes.*

→ **Museo del Papalote** CHAPULTEPEC This children's museum (which translates to Museum of the Kite) is, well, a Grateful Dead fan's paradise. There's all kinds of fun stuff to do, and it's adjacent to **La Feria,** an amusement park with a rickety-looking old roller coaster. Have fun, kids! *Av. Constituyentes 268. ☎ 55/5237-1781. www.papalote.org.mx. Admission $5 adults, $4 children; IMAX show $6 adults, $5 children. Mon–Fri 9am–1pm and 2–6pm; Sat–Sun 10am–2pm and 3–7pm; Thurs 7–11pm. Metro: Constituyentes.*

→ **Museo del Templo Mayor** CENTRO HISTORICO Once a shrine in Tenochtitlan, the Templo Mayor used to be a complex of almost a hundred buildings flanked by two pyramids. It was unearthed in 1978 by repairmen from the phone company and was, in turn, excavated by archaeologists. Since the anthropology museum was fresh out of room to accommodate new finds, some smarty made an executive decision to build a new museum at the excavation site. Architect Pedro Ramirez Vasquez, of Museo de Antropologia fame, designed this place as well. Here, rather than enclosing the 3,000-plus artifacts behind glass, they're displayed on stands, allowing visitors to see them up close and from every angle. The 1,700-sq.-m (18,300-sq.-ft.) exhibition space occupies four floors around a central courtyard.

As this was famously a sacrificial spot, be sure to check out the skulls of those ancient victims. The centerpiece is an 8-ton disc depicting the moon goddess Coyolxhauhqui. According to myth, she was decapitated by her brother. Nice guy. *Seminario 8, at Republica Guatemala. ☎ 55/5542-4784. Call a month ahead to schedule an English-language tour. Admission $38; students and teachers with ID free. Tues–Sun 9am–5pm. Metro: Zócalo.*

MTV Best → **Museo Nacional de Antropologia** ★★★ CHAPULTEPEC What started in 1910 as the National Museum of Archaeology, History, and Ethnography is now one of the most important anthropology museums in the world—even its home on Reforma, designed by Pedro Ramirez Vasquez, is considered one of the most significant buildings in contemporary Mexican architecture. The Antropología is of mammoth, Louvre-like proportions, but a visit to its famed pre-Hispanic collections is worth clearing the better part of a day for. Even 3 hours will give you a great survey of indigenous cultures in Mexico. From pottery to skeletons to a showcase on a soccer-like sport where the losers were beheaded, the exhibits chronicle the history of the people who have inhabited Mexico: the Aztecs, Maya, and the peoples of the Gulf Coast, Oaxaca, Toltecs, and Teotihuacán.

You can't miss the entrance, marked by a statue of Aztec rain god Tlaloc, which was brought over from a hillside near Texacoco, east of the city. *Paseo de la Reforma at Calzada Ghandi. ☎ 55/5286-5195. www. mna.inah.gob.mx/musei/mna/musei/muna/mna_ing/main.html. Admission $45 9am–5pm, $150 5–7pm; free every Sun for the general public and daily 9am–5pm for students and teachers with ID. Tues–Sun 9am–7pm. Metro: Auditorio or Chapultepec.*

→ **Museo Tamayo Arte Contemporaneo** CHAPULTEPEC Muralist Rufino Tamayo was also an art collector. Originally from Oaxaca, he had a goal of bringing international contemporary art to Mexico. The result is this museum in Chapultepec Park, near the bottom of the hill leading up to the castle. Tamayo and his wife, Olga, brought together work representative of late-20th-century art for the museum's permanent collection, including heavyweights like Picasso, Rothko, Miro, Noguchi, and Latin superstars like Joaquin Torres-Garcia and Fernando Botero. It's an impressive review of the last 50 years in art in a building created to be on display itself. Jazz nights and other events and performances are often featured; check the website for details. There's a gift shop and a funky cafe, too. *Chapultepec Park 1a Seccion, at Ghandi. ☎ 55/5286-6529. www. museotamayo.org. Admission $10. Tues–Sun 10am–6pm. Metro: Chapultepec.*

MEXICO CITY

→ **National History Museum** CHAPULTEPEC The grand MTV Best **Chapultepec Castle** ★★★ built by Emperor Maximilian of Habsburg sits atop a large cliff and reflects all of the pomp and circumstance one would expect from a monarch who, prior to his Mexico gig, spent his days kicking back in a castle overlooking the Gulf of Trieste in Italy, then termed the Austrian Riviera. Walk over to the edge of the cliff for a relatively unobstructed view down Reforma Avenue, built to resemble the Champs-Élysées in Paris. Word is that Emperor Maximilian's jealous wife Carlotta had him build the avenue that way so that she could keep tabs on him—he apparently couldn't keep it in his pants.

The castle is the site of many important events throughout Mexican history, like the final battle of La Intervención Norteamericana (the Mexican American War) in 1847, when one of the Niños Héroes (see box, p. 120) wrapped himself in a Mexican flag and jumped off the cliff rather than surrender to the U.S. army. Porfirio Díaz lived here for over 30 years, and at the end of his dictatorship, presidents of Mexico moved in. It was Lázaro Cárdenas who, in 1939, decided the Chapultepec Castle should be given to Mexico as a museum, and presidents would live at Los Pinos, a mansion in the district, where they have resided ever since.

The museum is divided into two major sections, the Colegio Militar and el Alacazar. The first houses objects and artwork that reflect period living in Mexico City, as well as murals by José Clemente Orozco and David Alfaro Siqueiros. The second features furnishings, jewelry, paintings, and other works from the era when Emperor Maximilian and Carlotta lived in the castle. Check out the Battle of Chapultepec room, with portraits of the Niños Héroes. Weird rule: You're not allowed to take notes inside the museum. The guard wouldn't explain why, so I can only assume this is to encourage you to buy the books for sale in the gift shop. *Castilla de Chapultepec, 1a Seccion. ☎ 55/5516-2848. Admission $38; free for students and teachers with ID. Tues–Sun 9am–4pm. Metro: Constituyentes.*

FREE → **Palacio Postal** CENTRO HISTORICO Most post offices don't make it onto sightseeing lists but the Palacio Postal merits a visit for its splendid Gothic/Arabesque architecture with baroque, neoclassical, and Art Deco touches, designed by Italian architect Adamo Boari in 1908. (He also designed Balacio de Bellas Artes, right across the street.) Filled with antique postal memorabilia, the exhibition rooms chronicle interesting random factoids; for instance, the Servicio Postal Mexicano (SEPOMEX) moves some 760 million pieces of mail each year—who knew? And after a visit here, you too will be able to answer the question "How did the postal stamp get its start?" The most breathtaking part of the museum is the stamp-mosaic *La Tarasca,* an Aztec pyramid scene featuring the deity Quetzalcoatl made out of 48,234 postal stamps used between 1890 and 1934. The year 2007 marks the Palacio's 100th anniversary. *Eje Central at Tacaba.* ☎ *55/5510-2999. Free admission. Mon–Fri 8am–9pm; Sat 8am–6pm. Metro: Bellas Artes.*

→ **Plaza Garibaldi** CENTRO It's worth dropping by Plaza Garibaldi either on a walk from the Lagunilla market to the zócalo, or late at night after the bars close—in a group, mind you; once plagued by petty criminals and drug addicts, the plaza has been cleaned up and has more of a police presence, but it's still a place to use caution. The statues lining the plaza pay tribute to famous mariachis of time past, like Tomás Mendez Sosa from Zacatecas (1926–1995) who wrote the traditional song "Cucurrucucu Paloma," and María de Lourdes, who lent her soaring voice to the mariachi songs.

The bars and restaurants in this area are overpriced tourist traps, so if you want to check them out, it's best to go with a local friend who can assure you won't be overcharged. The large Rincon del Mariachi on the far side of the plaza is a tri-level restaurant and bar with no cover charge. Try some *pulque*—an ancient Aztec smoothie-type beverage with a kick. It's made from *maguey,* a honey-tasting syrup extracted from the center of a cactus . The Pulqueria de Hermosa Hortencia (pulque $6–$26) is filled with old pictures of the plaza and the characters that populated it. The sign outside reads simply "Pulqueria." *Metro: Garibaldi.*

→ **Sala de Arte Publico Siqueiros** POLANCO A tiny gallery tucked away on a quiet side street in Polanco, Siqueiros is a very cool place to see said artist's murals, and it often hosts special exhibits, too. Siqueiros himself was an activist who mentored Jackson Pollock, teaching him the "accidental painting" technique. He loved murals and printmaking since they made his work available to a wider audience and freed it from what he deemed to be entrapment by elitist institutions. Siqueiros was awarded a Lenin Peace Prize in 1966. *Tres Picos 29.* ☎ *55/5203-5888. www.siqueiros.inba.gob.mx. Admission $10. Tues–Sun 10am–6pm. Metro: Polanco or Auditorio.*

MTV Best → **Torre Latinoamericana** ★★★ CENTRO HISTORICO This 44-story tower, built from 1949 to 1956, offers hands-down one of the best views of the city, starting from the glassed-in (and sort of greenhouse-hot) 42nd floor, to the outdoor deck on the 44th floor. The museum on floor 38 has some stunning photographs of the torre after the big quake of 1986. It was one of the only structures left standing among the rubble because the tower was one of the first things designed to withstand a severe earthquake. *Eje Central Lázaro Cárdenas 2 at Calle Madero.* ☎ *55/5518-7423. www.torrelatino.com. Admission $50. Daily 9am–10pm. Metro: Bellas Artes.*

Culture 101: Los Niños Héroes

The large, white, five-columned monument at the entrance to Chapultepec Park by the castle is in remembrance of Mexico's Niños Héroes, five young military cadets who sacrificed their lives defending the Chapultepec Castle. The story is one of the most famous in the country's history. It is said the young fighters' commander ordered the soldiers to surrender, but they resisted the U.S. forces until they were killed by their hand—except for one niño, who wrapped himself in a Mexican flag and leapt over the edge. And so they were known forever as "the boy heroes." Each column in the monument represents one of the young men. Día de Los Niños Héroes de Chapultepec (Day of the Boy Heroes of Chapultepec) is commemorated every year on September 13, the anniversary of the battle.

Attractions in Southern Mexico City

→ **Casa Azul** COYOACÁN Frida Kahlo's house, where she was born in 1907, is by far one of the most popular sights in the south. The Blue House—they should have called it the Blindingly Blue House—has works from Frida's own private collection on display as well as Paul Klee and José María Velasco pieces, Mexican folk art, and pre-Hispanic artifacts. The most fascinating part of the museum is the glimpse into Frida's personal life: her bed, dresses, a wheelchair, what's left of her body cast. Frida was injured in a bus accident when she was a teenager and much of her work reflects the themes of pain and immobility that she felt throughout the rest of her life. The air is so thick with history you can almost feel the ghosts in this house. *Londres 247. ☎ 55/5554-5999. Admission $30. Tues–Sun 10am–6pm. Metro: Coyoacán.*

→ **Museo Diego Rivera Anahuacalli** SAN PABLO TEPETALPA Not to be confused with the Museo Estudio Diego Rivera, the Anahuacalli was designed by Rivera (with help from his pal Juan O'Gorman) to resemble a pre-Hispanic temple and houses his sprawling personal collection of 60,000 pieces from that period. The name *Anahuacalli,* "house of Anahuac" in the Nahuatl language, was appointed by Rivera himself. This stunning, unique building was made in 1942 of volcanic rock with alabaster windows from Puebla. Stone mosaics on the ceilings portray giant skulls (the death god), snakes (Quetzalcoatl), wind gods, and the ongoing cycle of life after death. Diego's work space on the top floor, left pretty much as it was, exhibits sketches for murals he was working on at the time of his death from stomach cancer in 1959—apparently Diego found inspiration for these murals in his vast collection of Aztec ceramics. From the roof, there's a spectacular view of the 40-hectare (99-acre) ecological park below. Its location is a little off-the-beaten path, giving a very hidden-treasure feeling to the whole experience, but you'll be glad you made the effort. Visits are by guided tour only, and leave every half-hour; they can be conducted in English on request. *Calle de Museo 150. ☎ 55/5617-3797. Admission $35. Tues–Sun 1–6pm. Metro: Taxqueña; then tren ligero (light train) to Xotepingo; go west on Xotepingo (Museo) 3 short blocks; cross División del Norte and go another 6 blocks.*.

MEXICO CITY

Best → **Museo Dolores Olmedo Patiño** ★★★ XOCHIMILCO Dolores Olmedo was a patron and friend of Diego and Frida's and dedicated her house, Hacienda La Noria, as a stunning museum brimming with the works of art she amassed over her lifetime. Through the wooden gates is a verdant garden filled with peacocks, swans, and ducks. Olmedo's plaque bears a message for visitors: "Following my mother's example, Professor María Patiño Suarez Vda. De Olmedo, who always told me to 'share all you have with your *compadres,*' I leave this house, with all my collections, the product of all my life's work, for the enjoyment of the Mexican people." You, too. The exhibition spaces are cavernous rooms that used to make up the living area of the house. The bedroom is left somewhat intact with a bed, family photos, and furniture to show how the family lived. Diego Rivera's portrait of Olmedo, accompanied by a photograph of him creating it, is pretty amazing. All the exhibits—from Kahlo to cubism, murals and portraits to Angelina Beloff's illustrations—reflect a deep-seated love of two fabulous things: art and Mexico. One stand-out room holds Diego Rivera's series of 25 Acapulco sunsets, which serve to remind us that life is made up of a collection of moments. *Av. Mexico 5843 La Noria, Xochimilco. ☎ 55/5555-1016. www.museodoloresolmedo.org. Admission $35; students and teachers with ID $20; free on Tues. Tues–Sun 10am–6pm. Metro: Line 2 to Tasqueña, transfer to light rail to La Noria station.*

→ **Museo Estudio Diego Rivera** SAN ANGEL Frida and Diego lived in these Siamese-twin houses, designed by Juan O'Gorman in a clean, functional style that was groundbreaking in the early 1930s. The small house has everything from Diego's giant papier-mâché people sculptures to his bathrobe and slippers. Frida worked here, too, but the exhibits are exclusively Rivera's. A visit to this museum, which takes only about a half-hour to explore, tops off a half-day in San Angel nicely; mix it up with lunch at San Angel Inn (p. 103), within walking distance, or Bazar Sabado (10am–7pm Sat only), if it's a Saturday afternoon (and you don't mind a crowd of older ladies). *Calle Diego Rivera s/n, corner Av. Altavista. ☎ 55/5550-1518. Admission $10; free for students and teachers with ID. Tues–Sun 10am–6pm. By taxi, go up to Insurgentes Sur to Altavista and make a left.*

What Lies Beneath: Why the Zócalo Is Sinking

The Catedral Metropolitana and many other buildings around the Centro Historico are slowly sinking because the area was originally marshland—a city built on water. You can tell by looking up at rooftops—which are at a slant, like a scene from a cubist painting. Walking into a church recently used as the *Harto-espacio* experimental art space (adjacent to the Templo Mayor museum), I felt a gravitational pull toward one side of the room, practically dragging me along. It's surreal, but that's what happens when you fill in a lake to build a city. Not the smartest engineering move, Aztec dudes. In the '90s, a project got underway to save the cathedral from sinking into oblivion. The engineers couldn't stop it from happening—but they implemented a system to make sure it sinks uniformly. It's kind of deep (and very Mexican) when you think about it . . . accepting the inevitable in life.

Twelve Hours in Mexico City

This will be a full day, so get a good night's sleep!

9am: Dash over to Chapultepec Park and visit the National History Museum. Admire the view over Chapultepec from the museum. (Skip the Anthropology Museum even though you'll be tempted, because it takes at least 4 hours and you'd probably rather see more of the city with your limited time.)

10:30am: Descend to the Metro or grab a taxi to the zócalo, where you can visit Catedral Metropolitana, Templo Mayor, and the Torre Latinoamericana.

1pm: Cab it to Roma (or take the Metro to Sevilla), and check out Casa Lamm. Enjoy the Lamm restaurant or walk to a seafood lunch at hot spot du jour Contramar.

3:30pm: Skip Casa Azul and do Museo Dolores Olmedo, which is cooler *and* less touristy. You'll be near Xochimilco, so get thee to the canals for a 1-hour trajinera ride. Wrap things up with a stroll in Plaza Coyoacán.

7:30pm: Dinner at Aguila y Sol. Order up a tamarindo margarita and call it a night!

Playing Outside

The best place for outdoor activities in Mexico City is indoors. Especially during the winter months, when pollution levels are extra-high, you might not enjoy spending so much time outside in the city. Seriously. Flags are even raised in schoolyards to warn about pollution levels—if there's a red flag up, gym classes are held inside.

In other words, don't come here for the great outdoors. Mexico has many amazing beaches, pristine lakes, rugged volcanoes, and Utopian vistas for the outdoor freak—just not in *la ciudad*. It's the cultural capital, so while you'll naturally spend most of your time in urban oases like museums, plazas, bars, and restaurants, everyone needs a breath of fresh air sometimes—even if it's not so fresh.

Chapultepec Park (see below) is the veritable exception to the better-off-indoors rule, since the greenery keeps the air cleaner. There are also some great options for hiking, picnicking, and hanging out among trees very close to the city—you can even go boating at **Xochimilco** (p. 86). But if you're really feeling the call of the wild, you should hop in your car and floor it to greener (and cleaner) pastures. Many of the playing outside options that follow are actually some distance from the city.

Hiking

If you leave the city via the Toluca highway and drive north for about 45 minutes, you'll come to forested areas full of trails perfect for a day spent trekking about. However, don't go alone—it's not dangerous per se, but, as with most things in Mexico, it's always better/safer to do things in groups or pairs.

La Marquesa is a national park up the Toluca highway, with plentiful hiking trails. You can also go ATV-ing or horseback riding here. Its highlight, though, is **El Ajusco**—a 3,930m (12,890-ft.) peak that you can see from the Insurgentes Metro stop on less-smoggy days. It's approximately a 2-hour hike to the top. You can get to the park via Camino Al Ajusco, which dead-ends at the park, or grab a bus at Estadio Azteca's tren ligero (see p. 83 for more bus info).

Chapultepec Park

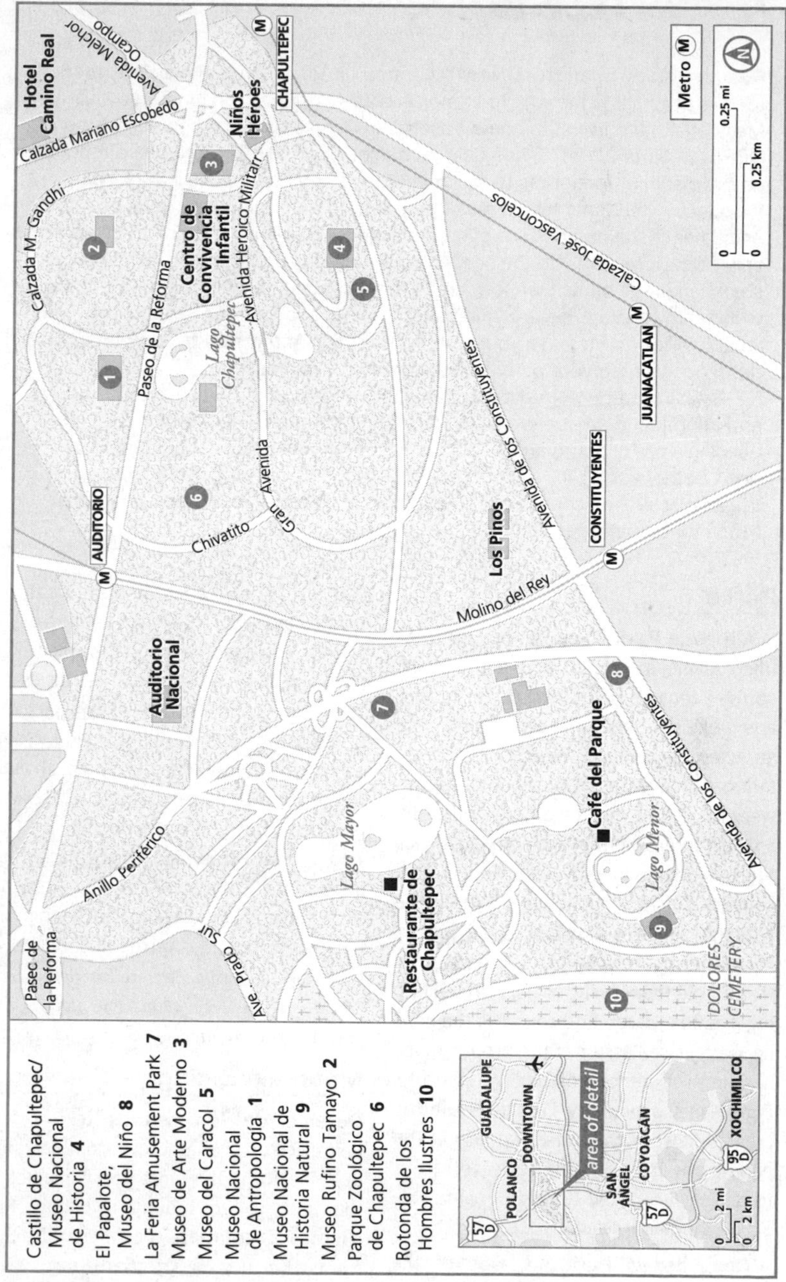

MTV U **Se Habla Español**

Ready to study Spanish? **UNAM's Centro de Enseñanza Para Estranjeros** (CEPE) program is the way to immerse yourself in Spanish language and Mexican culture from the home base of the largest university in Latin America. CEPE (☎ **55/5622-2470**) has been in business since 1921 and has a reputation as *the* place for foreigners to study language and humanities in Mexico. Prospective students take a placement test to determine their level before enrollment—the courses are offered in Spring, Summer, and Fall trimesters and vary from "Intensive," to the hard-core-sounding "Super-Intensive." You can study language on its own, or combine it with the Mexican culture program, which throws in art, history, and literature. The school houses you either with local families (to increase your Spanish-learning immersion by tenfold) or in a dorm (to increase your party immersion by the same).

CEPE is right on UNAM's campus, just a few blocks away from the library and information center. While you're visiting campus, check out the CEPE building's pretty courtyard, and stop by the office to introduce yourself. But don't bother asking for a brochure—they don't have any printed material, and the admissions officer will direct you to their website, www.cepe.unam.mx. Props for saving trees . . .

Parks

→ **Alameda Park** Today the lovely tree-filled Alameda Park attracts pedestrians, cotton-candy vendors, strollers, lovers, and organ grinders. Long ago, the site was an Aztec marketplace. When the conquistadors took over in the mid-1500s, heretics were burned at the stake here under the Spanish Inquisition. In 1592, the governor of New Spain, Viceroy Luis de Velasco, converted it to a public park. Within the park, known as La Alameda, is the **Juárez Monument,** sometimes called the **Hemiciclo** (hemicycle, or half-circle), facing Avenida Juárez. Enthroned as the hero he was, Juárez assumes his proper place here in the pantheon of Mexican patriots. European (particularly French) sculptors created most of the other statuary in the park in the late 19th and early 20th centuries. *Av. Juárez and Lázaro Cárdenas. Free admission. Metro: Bellas Artes.*

→ **Chapultepec Park** ★★ One of the biggest city parks in the world, 220-hectare (543-acre) Chapultepec Park is more than a playground; it's virtually the centerpiece of the city. Besides accommodating picnickers on worn-away grass under centuries-old trees, it has canoes on the lake; jogging and bridle paths; vendors selling balloons, souvenirs, and food; a miniature train; an auditorium; and **Los Pinos,** home of Mexico's president. The park is also home to the **City Zoo** and **La Feria** amusement park. Most important for tourists, it contains a number of interesting museums, including the Museo Nacional de Antropología. *Between Paseo de la Reforma, Circuito Interior, and Av. Constituyentes. Free admission. Daily 5am–5pm. Metro: Chapultepec.*

Mountain Biking

Deserto de los Leones (exit off of Periferico or take a pesero from Barranca del Muerto) is the most popular place in the area to go mountain biking. **San Nicolas Totolapan** (Carretera Picacho-Ajusco Km 11.5; ☎ **55/5630-8935;** www.parquesannicolas.com.mx; admission $20) has trails leading up to Montaña Nrzehuiloya. Unlike Deserto de los Leones, you can rent bikes here.

For biking equipment, head to **Vertimania** (Patriotismo 899; ☎ **55/5615-5230;** www.vertimania.com.mx), a mountain-gear store that has a decent assortment of bikes and accessories (like helmets and clothing) for different budgets. You can also get rock climbing gear and advice here. **Deportes Marti** (Venustiano Carranza 19; ☎ **55/5221-1636;** www.marti.com.mx) is a big and popular chain sporting-goods store that stocks plenty of bike equipment.

Rock Climbing

Escaladromo Carlos Crasolio (18 Tecnicos Mexicanos, Col. Santa María Ticoman; ☎ **55/5752-7574**) is an indoor rock-climbing club, so you don't even have to leave the city. The walls are 12m (40 ft.) high and they have straight verticals as well as inclined practice walls for those of us (ahem) who are less versed climbers. The cave is pretty rad, too.

Outside the city, try **Parque y Corredor Turistico Los Dinamos** (Col. Magdalena Atlitic), a wooded area in the southwest, with volcanic rock formations reaching as high as 30m (100 ft.).

Two hours northeast of Mexico City is the **Parque Nacional El Chico** which is known as one of the best rock climbing areas around. So is **Jilotepec** to the northwest, one of the only places nearby to go **camping.**

Sporting Events

BULLFIGHTING

Overall, bullfighting attendance in Mexico has been on the decline, for reasons that might have something to do with watching an innocent animal get provoked to anger and subsequently stabbed to death. Nonetheless, **Plaza de Toros** (Augusto Rodin 241, Ciudad de Los Deportes; ☎ **55/5611-4413**) remains the largest bullfighting ring in the world. The season to check it out, if you're so inclined, is November through March, before the daily rains begin in late spring. Tickets are $20 to $250. Call ahead for information and schedules.

LUCHA LIBRE

The best place to see traditional Mexican wrestling (watch Jack Black's *Nacho Libre* to get an idea about the sport) is at the **Arena Mexico** (189 Calle Dr. Lavista; ☎ **55/5588-0385**), aka La Catedral de Lucha Libre. It's the most popular wrestling stadium in Mexico and where all the stars come to perform—uh, I mean, wrestle. It's also in Colonia Doctores, one of the neighborhoods we warned you about, so be absolutely sure not to bring any valuables. There's more history, info, and pictures at www.cmll.com. For info on **gay Lucha Libre,** check out www.triplea.com.mx. Tickets run from $100.

Shopping

What's the best thing about shopping in Mexico City? That's easy—the exchange rate. You can find excellent bargains on everything from clothes to traditional crafts. (***Note:*** This does not apply to the designer stores in Polanco, unfortunately. Prada is Prada.) The stereotypical outdoor flea market has made room for a new wave of young independent designers who run boutiques and quirky, interesting shops in Condesa and Roma. Get off designer row on Polanco's **Presidente Masaryk** and slip into the outdoor-mall-style oasis of **Pasaje Polanco** (Masaryk 360), which has a more relaxed atmosphere and less-pricey shopping. An array of shops there specialize

Plaza Shopping: Clothes, Ice Cream & Non-Cheesy Gifts

The area around the city's two plazas, **Jardín Hidalgo** and **Jardín del Centenario,** is the most fun place to be in Mexico City on a Saturday afternoon. If you take the metro to the Coyoacán stop, you're a nice 15-minute stroll from the main plazas. Just out of the Metro station is a mall, **Centro Comercial Coyoacán,** which has a Starbucks, shops like Zara and Berksha (similar to Express), and Pull & Bear, a funky H&M-type clothing store for both women and men.

Back outside, on your stroll along **Avenida Mexico** to the plaza, you'll pass a **Mr. Sushi** chain restaurant (good sushi and inexpensive), several little local cafes, and **Dao** (Av. Mexico 59 at Londres; ☎ **55/5554-5406**) an upscale, trendy new Asian fusion restaurant. It can get pretty crowded in the bustling **artisan markets** around Jardín del Centenario, and more crafts and food in Jardín Hidalgo, but it's forgivable because the place is just so damn cool. This market is the best for picking up non-cheesy gifts for your friends. The vendors are mostly hippie artisans who make their own wares—from amber jewelry to tapestries, hand-carved pipes to onyx figurines. Street vendors sell goodies from cotton candy to elotes, or grab some from **Loncheria María Elena,** right next to the **Sanborn's** (with a solid selection of English magazines) in Jardín del Centenario.

The best place for lunch on the plaza is **Los Danzantes,** notable for its three big colorful masks atop a white awning. Grab a table in the outdoor section, closed off from the rest of the plaza by a wall of cacti. The ice cream places 'round here are known for being especially good, particularly **Sineria Helados, Los Famosos de Coyoacán.** Coffee to go and croissant sandwiches can be had at **La Esquina del Viejo Barrio** right next to the ice-cream shop. For a secret rendezvous, slink down the passageway to the right of **Parroquia de San Juan Batista** (built in 1589) and order a cappuccino La Selva at **La Selva Café:** Their specialty drink of espresso and coffee liqueur can be prepared hot or frozen. For a light bite, get the jicama plate, a healthy share-able snack for two, with jicama, pineapple, and chile. After sunset, there are two major options: **El Hijo del Cuervo** (p. 106) or for a more old-school atmosphere, **Cantina La Guadalupana** on the far side of Jardín Hidalgo. Take the Metro to Coyoacán.

in clothing, like **La Esquina Azul** (see below), which carries trendy street-wear by independent designers, **Crochet,** for knit aficionados, and, for fans of occult merchandise, **Chelterra.** You'll also find a large indoor marketplace selling upscale artesanías, and, yes, a Starbucks.

Arts & Markets

→ **Bazar del Sabado** SAN ANGEL An art market held only on Saturdays, Bazar del Sabado is located in a colonial building right off the main square of San Angel. It's pricey; but if you're looking for the best quality in Mexico, this is where you get what you pay for. *Plaza de San Jacinto. Metro: Barranca del Muerto.*

→ **Chic by Accident** CONDESA Not that you're planning to buy a restored antique couch to lug around Mexico with you, but design fans will enjoy this showroom of restored 20th-century pieces by French-Mexican antiquarian Emmanuel Picault, who designs as well, adding his signature twist to modern Mexican aesthetics. The prices are, as one would expect, astronomical, but those of us who didn't just win the lottery or hit the jackpot in Vegas can enjoy it as a little gallery exhibiting beautifully restored, fun, and eclectic antiques. Check out the lamps, which are especially cool. *Colima 180. ☎ 55/5514-5723. Metro: Sevilla.*

MTV Best → **Coyoacán Plaza** ★★★ See the "Plaza Shopping: Clothes, Ice Cream & Non-Cheesy Gifts" box in this section, for details on this hippie artists' community that is a shopper's heaven. It's great for those who like a little alternative in their retail diet. *Corner of Av. Universidad and Av. Rio Churubusco. Metro: Coyoacán.*

→ **El Chopo** Another Saturday-only market, but you won't find pretty crafts and Talavera pottery at this one. El Chopo is where punks and rockers hang out, in a warehouse district a couple blocks from the Buenavista Metro stop, near the intersection of Eje 1 Norte with Calle Aldama. The market specializes in Mexican punk and hard-core music, mostly bootleg CDs and tapes. You'll also find concert T-shirts, punk jewelry, and even stands that will dye your hair so you'll really blend in with the surroundings. *Eje 1 Norte, Calle Aldama. Sat only. Metro: Buenavista.*

→ **FONART** CENTRO Think of it as a gallery representing the top artisans of Mexico. Run by the National Council for Culture and the Arts, this store offers higher-priced—and certainly high-quality—arts and crafts from around the country. Their mission is to maintain traditional crafts and advance the artists' communities, and from the looks of this place, they're clearly doing a good job of it. *Av. Juárez 89. ☎ 55/5521-0171. Metro: Zócalo.*

→ **La Ciudadela** ★★ CENTRO Right near the lovely Alameda park (4 blocks south, to be precise) is the Ciudadela artisans market, one of Mexico City's top places for crafts from all over the country. A more structured environment than Lagunilla, this "artisanal center" is enclosed in a designated building and well maintained. I mean, what other market has its own website and valet parking? Ceramics, silver jewelry, onyx, candles, bags, toys, masks, figurines . . . it's like we died and went to souvenir heaven. *Calle Balderas at Plaza de la Ciudadela. ☎ 55/5510-1828. www.laciudadela.com.mx. Metro: Balderas.*

→ **La Lagunilla** ★★★ CENTRO Best on Sunday mornings, Lagunilla is chock-full of all flea-markety things imaginable, from trendy hoodie sweatshirts (I picked up one with silver skull decals), and punk-inspired clothing to antique record players, TVs, and radios. The prices are low and can be made even lower by bargaining. Beware of bootleg music, though—you never know if a CD is going to work or not and it's better not to waste your money. (I learned the hard way with a Manu Chao live CD. And, yes, I got what I deserved for supporting piracy.) But anyway, the market's awesome. See if you can find Manuel Bauman, who sets up his booth toward the north side away from the fray. He sells his own mixed-media paintings and artwork featuring *luchadores* (the wrestlers) alongside the *Virgen Guadalupe*, to bless them all the way to victory in the ring. Beware that Lagunilla is a great place to put that money belt to use—it's also known as "Thieves' Market," and for good reason. *La Lagunilla, Eje Norte at Brasil. Metro: Lagunilla.*

→ **Mercado Sonora** CENTRO This is a weird place to visit because it's essentially a witchcraft market. You can buy bizarre powders and potions, lucky charms, and lotions. You'll also see plants and animals and rare exotic birds for sale, but the trade of these often-endangered species is illegal, which is why the market is sometimes raided by police. *Fray Servando Teresa de Mier 419. www.mercadosonora.galeon.com. Metro: Merced.*

Books

Non-Spanish speakers in need of reading material will appreciate **Librería Gandhi** (Av. Juárez 4; ☎ **55/5510-4231**) and **American Bookstore** (Bolivar 23; ☎ **55/5512-0306;** www.americanbookstore.com.mx), two downtown shops with wide selections of books in English. Take the Metro to Zócalo. ***Note:*** When you buy imported publications in Mexico, they're typically twice the price of what you would pay at home.

→ **El Péndulo** POLANCO This cafe/bookstore has a nice selection of titles, for Spanish readers only. You'll see other branches of this small chain throughout el DF. *Alejandro Dumas 81.* ☎ *55/5280-4111. Metro: Polanco.*

→ **Librería Pegazo @ Casa Lamm** ROMA This cultural center has the best bookstore in the city for ambience. Lounge for hours in the sitting area with art books, or pick up a novel to practice your Spanish. Some English selections are also available. *Alvaro Obregon 99, Orizaba.* ☎ *55/5208-0171. Metro: Sevilla.*

Boutiques

WOMEN

→ **Colectivo 7** CONDESA Colectivo 7, a super-cute shop run by a group of indie designers, is the chicest boutique for downtown-girl style in Mexico City today. The clothes and accessories are unusual and stylish, and the colectivo sometimes has great sales. A group of seven young designers (hence the name) started the store to showcase their wares, and one of them will often be manning the cash register. From Sophie Massun's retro '50s-style polka-dot dresses, to cute bikinis and drop earrings, the fashion collective doesn't disappoint. *Amsterdam 92, between Laredo and Parras.* ☎ *55/5553-1793. Metro: Juanacatlan.*

→ **La Esquina Azul** POLANCO In Pasaje Polanco, the outdoor mall on Masaryk, you can browse this tiny, hip women's clothing shop filled with pieces from the unique to the trendy. You'll also find cute accessories, handbags, and lingerie. The name translates to "The Blue Corner," but your wardrobe will be anything but after picking up an item or two here. *Pasaje Polanco Local 36B, Masaryk 360.* ☎ *55/5282-0937. Metro: Polanco.*

→ **Local** CONDESA This smaller boutique is sorta like Colectivo 7's little sister, with beautiful pieces by independent designers for every budget. Local sells everything from jewelry to swimsuits to fancy yoga mat bags. When I visited, I spotted a white cotton dress with the now-trendy black skull pattern that was textured to make it look like it was made out of feathers. Look for stuff by Cata Mont, Carla Fernandez, Malena De La Riva, Claudia Suinaga, and Ximena Fernandez. *Amsterdam 248.* ☎ *55/5564-9148. Metro: Juanacatlan.*

MEN & WOMEN

→ **Kulte** CONDESA As the name implies, this is a cult favorite for edgy brands like NaCo, True Religion, and Burn N Violet. They have a sizable collection of funky T-shirts and customized kicks like Vans, with camo and silver-skull patterns as well as the more traditional checkered design. Cute Paul Frank glasses, unique bags and jackets, and the NaCo T-shirts depicting Mexican inside jokes are too cool. If you're into skateboarding style, you'll gain Kulte status after picking up some fresh looks here. *Atlixco 118.* ☎ *55/5211-7389. Metro: Juanacatlan.*

→ **Soho** POLANCO The store for trendy club-gear for both sexes, each branch in this chain of boutiques looks like it got lost on the way to New York City. You can buy the latest styles inspired by the runway, plus shoes, belts, bags, and other youthful accessories that are ideal for looking the part on a night out on the town in Mexico City. In other words, if you need clothes for your new job in corporate litigation, give this one a pass. *Presidente Masaryk 191. ☎ 55/5281-1707. Metro: Polanco.*

Miscellaneous

→ **Crochet** POLANCO Knitters will love this cute store, which has imported and domestic yarns, coffee and tea, and a table so you can bring your needles and put in some sewing-circle time with friendly locals. In the same shopping plaza, you'll find **Chelterra,** a 15-year-old occult store with tarot cards, incense, candles, and books, charts, and calendars about reiki, chakras, and other alternative-spirituality topics; there's also **Artesanías** (www.lasartesanias.com.mx), a large indoor crafts market. *Masaryk 360. ☎ 55/5280-5385. Metro: Polanco.*

→ **5LEMENTO** CONDESA At this way cool, or, to use the language of the era, "far out" retro and retro-inspired shop, you'll find everything from bikes to vintage martini shakers. For $22,500 you can get yourself a bubble-swing chair to bolt to your ceiling. More realistically, there's a fantastic selection of amusing items like a checkers game with shot glasses, push-down ashtrays in the shape of lipstick, mini-egg frying pans, funky fondue sets, and awesome retro-home items like rugs and a pink-feather rotary phone (for a far-fetched $950). Sidecar- and Manhattan-mixing aficionados will fall for the barware selection and lamps shaped like cocktails. This is a freakin' awesome store even for just browsing. It might be difficult not to leave with something, even if it's not a fuzzy phone. *71 Cuernavaca, at Fernando Montes de Oca. No phone. Metro: Juanacatlan.*

→ **Sanborn's** COYOACÁN It just wouldn't be Sanborn's if they didn't have a little bit of everything. The omnipresent variety store carries an ample selection of everything from some books, magazines, and newspapers in English to a variety of music. You can also find gifts, toys, and a variety of artesanías. *Parque Centenario 5. ☎ 55/5659-8958. Metro: Coyoacán.*

→ **Yug** ROMA This New Age-y hippie store has a foods section vegans will flip for: soy pastor and soy barbacoa! Now even veggies with the strictest regimen can get a taste of traditional Mexican flavors, without the traditional Mexican meat. Dedicated to the promotion of well-being, the store carries a wide selection of spiritual, theological, and self-help literature (in Spanish only . . . another excuse to learn?), New Age music, tarot cards, scented cantles, crystal pendants, and other giftable goodies. *Puebla 326-6. ☎ 55/5553-3872. Metro: Sevilla.*

Music

→ **El Péndulo** POLANCO The cozy bi-level bookstore/record shop and cafe has a decent selection of CDs, especially jazz and Mexican rock. All you old-schoolers can grab your Discman and head to the cafe to chill with your new Café Tacuba disc. *Alejandro Dumas 81. ☎ 55/5280-4111. Metro: Polanco.*

→ **Mixup** ZONA ROSA This outpost of Mexico's own music chain carries every imaginable type of music, from traditional ranchera and mariachis to *gran exitos* (greatest hits) from the top of the pop/rock and alternative music charts. Many hip young Mexicans are into different types of electronica, so if you're a club kid or danceaholic check out the impressive selection of electronic music. *Genova 66. www.mixup.com.mx. Metro: Insurgentes.*

Road Trips: Four Faves near Mexico City

Now that you've experienced the capital, it's time to hit the road. After mastering Mexico City, these side trips will be a breeze. **Teotihuacán** is a must on any traveler's Mexico City agenda, as it's only 45 minutes away and was the Aztec's version of Manhattan. If you only have time for one more, it's a toss up between **Valle de Bravo** and **Tepoztlán,** depending whether you prefer adventure sporting or a bohemian vibe, respectively.

The easiest way to travel to and around the areas in this section is to rent a car and arm yourself with a Guia Roji map. Otherwise, taking the **ADO** (☎ **55/5133-2424** or 01-800/702-8000; www.adogl.com.mx) bus is the next-best option. This company has first-class buses that go to destinations all around Mexico. Depending on where you're headed, you depart from one of four major bus stations in the city: Central del Sur (Metro: Tasquena) or Central del Atapo (Metro: Constitucion 1917) for southern destinations; Central del Norte (Metro: Politecnico) or Central de Observatorio (Metro: Observatorio) for northern.

MTV Best Teotihuacán ★★★

This groovy day trip from Mexico City is easily accessible at just an hour northeast, and scaling the pyramids is always a fun challenge. If you didn't get to the hiking or rock climbing destinations near Mexico City, all the climbing, walking, and sightseeing here is like doing several birds with one stone. Actually, many stones—the **Pyramid of the Sun** alone is five stepped platforms measuring 225m (738 ft.) across each side and 70m (230 ft.) in height. This is the most visited archaeological site in Mexico, and also one of the most researched and excavated.

Experts don't know exactly who built this city, but it's clear they were a huge, influential, and militaristic society. More than 1,200 skeletons have been uncovered among the ruins, and they were most likely the sacrificed (gulp). Around A.D. 750, Teotihuacán was abandoned and set on fire, perhaps the result of a war between Teotihuacán and a nearby city. The Aztecs arrived in A.D. 1200 and set up shop, naming it Teotihuacán—"the place where gods are born." Today, Teotihuacán is a UNESCO World Heritage Site and on the list of the World Monuments Fund's 100 most endangered monuments because of its lack of a conservation plan. So tread lightly . . .

GETTING THERE & GETTING AROUND

BY CAR Drive up Insurgentes Norte to Indios Verdes to the northeast of Mexico City. Get on the Carretera Mexico-Pachuca (the way to la Coleccion Jumex, p. 116, too). Go straight to Pachuca, and after 50 or so kilometers (31 miles) you'll exit to the archaeological zone before hitting a toll booth. Do take the toll road—*cuota*—rather than the free—*libre*—unless you like being stuck in traffic and potholes. There are two toll booths on the way, at $37 each.

BY BUS Take the Metro to Central del Norte bus station (Metro: Politecnico), and board one of the Autobuses Sahagun (at the far northwest end), which leave every 30 minutes from 5am to 6pm. Make sure the bus is bound for Los Piramides and not the city of San Jaun Teotihuacán. The last bus back to Mexico City leaves the entrance of the pyramids at 6pm.

SLEEPING

To be quite honest with you, Teotihuacán is not much of an overnight destination, especially if you are already based in Mexico City. The city is so close that spending the night out here seems a little *loco*

Teotihuacán

because there is absolutely *nada* going on besides the archaeological site. If you're trekking through on your way someplace else, or just too pooped after a day of pyramid-scaling, there are a couple of places to crash, one with an outdoor pool to ease the soreness out of those leg muscles.

→ **Posada Sol y Luna** This charming, 8-year-old family-run hotel has 16 colonial-style rooms and more amenities than you might expect from a place its size. There's a (very small) indoor pool and a stationary bike in case you didn't get enough of a workout on the pyramids. There are crafts by local artisans for sale in the lobby, which has a charming boutique-hotel atmosphere. *Av. Dr. Jimenez Cantu 13. Col. Purificacion. ☎ 594/956-2368. $300 double. MC, V. Amenities: Pool; room service; safe. In room: TV, phone.*

→ **Quinto Sol** This is a clean, comfy, modern beacon of Teotihuacán chic. The 34 rooms have Talavera pottery, TVs, music and, if you spring for one of the four suites, a Jacuzzi. There's an impressive breakfast buffet spread, too. The restaurant has cool art on the colorful walls—an homage to archaeological items of Teotihuacán—plus a full bar, and is as close to the pyramids as you can get without paying the entrance fee. ***Note:*** If it's not high season, try to bargain for your room rate. *Av. Hidalgo 26,*

Barrio Purificacion. ☎ *594/956-1881. www.hotelquintosol.com.mx. $625 single, $761 double, $850–$940 suite. AE, MC, V. Amenities: Restaurant/bar; sun deck; swimming pool with palapa bar; Wi-Fi. In room: TV, phone.*

EATING

→ **Pirámide Charlie's** MEXICAN Calling it "the food that made the Aztecs great" may be a stretch—but points for being cute. This restaurant, unmissable as you head to the pyramids' entrance, used to be one of the bazillion in the Grupo Andersons (Carlos 'n Charlie's, Señor Frog's, and so on) empire; but it's since become independent, despite keeping its name. The menu is a lot like their other menus—mostly Mexican specialties, and food for gringo stomachs too. (Even famous gringo stomachs—U2 ate here once when they visited the pyramids while on a world tour.) Their guacamole is excellent, and I love the *queso fundido* (cheese fondue) ($55) and nopales salad ($48). For entrees, the "drunk fish" in a white wine sauce is tasty ($130) and comes with mashed potatoes and veggies. For more epic appetites, the *puntas de filete* (steak tips) come in a hearty red sauce. *Periferico de las Priamides, between entrances 1 & 2.* ☎ *594/956-0472. Main courses $80–$190. AE, MC, V. Daily 10am–6pm.*

MEXICO CITY

SIGHTSEEING

Exploring the Teotihuacán Archaeological Site

ORIENTATION The ruins of Teotihuacán (☎ **59/4956-0276** or 59/4956-0052) are open daily from 8am to 5pm. Admission is $45. Using a video camera costs $30.

A small trolley-train that takes visitors from the entry booths to various stops within the site, including the Teotihuacán museum and cultural center, runs only on weekends and costs $6 per person.

Keep in mind that you're likely to be doing a great deal of walking, and perhaps some climbing, at an altitude of more than 2,120m (7,000 ft.). Take it slow, bring sunblock and drinking water, and during the summer be prepared for almost daily afternoon showers.

A good place to start is at the **Museo Teotihuacán** ★. This excellent state-of-the-art museum holds interactive exhibits and, in one part, a glass floor on which visitors walk above mock-ups of the pyramids. On display are findings of recent digs, including several tombs, with skeletons wearing necklaces of human and simulated jawbones, and newly discovered sculptures.

THE LAYOUT The grand buildings of Teotihuacán were laid out in accordance with celestial movements. The front wall of the **Pyramid of the Sun** is exactly perpendicular to the point on the horizon where the sun sets at the equinoxes (twice annually). The rest of the ceremonial buildings were laid out at right angles to the Pyramid of the Sun.

The main thoroughfare, which archaeologists call the **Calzada de los Muertos (Avenue of the Dead),** runs roughly north to south. The **Pyramid of the Moon** is at the northern end, and the **Ciudadela (Citadel)** is on the southern part. The great street was several kilometers long in its prime, but only a kilometer or two has been uncovered and restored.

LA CIUDADELA The Spaniards named the Ciudadela. This immense sunken square was not a fortress at all, although the impressive walls make it look like one. It was the grand setting for the Feathered Serpent Pyramid and the Temple of Quetzalcoatl. Scholars aren't certain that the Teotihuacán culture embraced the

Quetzalcoatl deity so well known in the Toltec, Aztec, and Maya cultures. The feathered serpent is featured in the Ciudadela, but whether it was worshipped as Quetzalcoatl or a similar god isn't known. Proceed down the steps into the massive court and head for the ruined temple in the middle.

The Temple of Quetzalcoatl was covered over by an even larger structure, a pyramid. As you walk toward the center of the Ciudadela's court, you'll approach the Feathered Serpent Pyramid. To the right, you'll see the reconstructed temple close behind the pyramid, with a narrow passage between the two structures.

Early temples in Mexico and Central America were often covered by later ones. The Pyramid of the Sun may have been built up in this way. Archaeologists have tunneled deep inside the Feathered Serpent Pyramid and found several ceremonially buried human remains, interred with precise detail and position, but as yet no royal personages. Drawings of how the building once looked show that every level was covered with faces of a feathered serpent. At the Temple of Quetzalcoatl, you'll notice at once the fine, large carved serpents' heads jutting out from collars of feathers carved in the stone walls; these weigh 4 tons. Other feathered serpents are carved in relief low on the walls.

AVENUE OF THE DEAD The Avenue of the Dead got its strange and forbidding name from the Aztec, who mistook the little temples that line both sides of the avenue for tombs of kings or priests.

As you stroll north along the Avenue of the Dead toward the Pyramid of the Moon, look on the right for a bit of wall sheltered by a modern corrugated roof. Beneath the shelter, the wall still bears a painting of a jaguar. From this fragment, you might be able to reconstruct the breathtaking spectacle that must have been visible when all the paintings along the avenue were intact.

PYRAMID OF THE SUN The Pyramid of the Sun, on the east side of the Avenue of the Dead, is the third-largest pyramid in the world. The first and second are the Great Pyramid of Cholula, near Puebla, and the Pyramid of Cheops on the outskirts of Cairo, Egypt. Teotihuacán's Pyramid of the Sun is 220m (722 ft.) per side at its base—almost as large as Cheops. But at 65m (213 ft.) high, the Sun pyramid is only about half as high as its Egyptian rival. No matter—it's still the biggest restored pyramid in the Western Hemisphere, and an awesome sight. Although the Pyramid of the Sun was not built as a great king's tomb, it is built on top of a series of sacred caves, which aren't open to the public.

The first structure of the pyramid was probably built a century before Christ, and the temple that used to crown the pyramid was completed about 400 years later (A.D. 300). By the time the pyramid was discovered and restoration was begun (early in the 20th c.), the temple had disappeared, and the pyramid was just a mass of rubble covered with bushes and trees.

It's a worthwhile 248-step climb to the top. The view is extraordinary and the sensation exhilarating.

PYRAMID OF THE MOON The Pyramid of the Moon faces a plaza at the northern end of the avenue. The plaza is surrounded by little temples and by the Palace of Quetzalpapalotl or Quetzal-Mariposa (Quetzal-Butterfly) on the left (west) side. You have about the same range of view from the top of the Pyramid of the Moon as you do from its larger neighbor, because the moon pyramid is built on higher ground. The perspective straight down the Avenue of the Dead is magnificent.

PALACE OF QUETZALPAPALOTL The Palace of Quetzalpapalotl lay in ruins until the 1960s, when restoration work began. Today, it reverberates with its former glory, as figures of Quetzal-Mariposa (a mythical, exotic bird-butterfly) appear painted on walls or carved in the pillars of the inner court.

SHOPPING

The shopping in Teotihuacán is best for touristy knickknacks. On the walkway into the site, stands offer everything from dresses to wooden children's games. Once inside, vendors hawk their wares, including jewelry, onyx figurines, and "archaeological" trinkets, to the point of harassment. Unless you're buying, the best way to discourage them from following you is with a polite but firm "no gracias." You should bargain here, as you'll definitely find overpriced merchandise.

Tepoztlán

Tepoztlán, or *Tepoz,* as it's called by those in the know, is both a spiritual mecca and weekender's playground in the state of Morelos. Tepoz is the Sedona, Arizona, of Mexico, offering Reiki massages, vegetarian restaurants, tarot readings, spiritual encounters—all with the backdrop of the Tepozteco, a rocky peak that holds the archaeological site of the same name. At 81km (50 miles), it's the second-closest of the side trips to Mexico City (after Teotihuacán); and if you're only doing one quick weekend or overnight away, it may very well be your best bet. The town's compact size means you can pack a lot of activities into a day. Tepoztlán gets it right for mixing local flavor, culture, tradition, and rituals with great restaurants, pampering, and outdoor options.

Start with a morning hike up the Tepozteco and then have an early lunch at a city-class seafood or Hindu-style vegetarian restaurant. Follow this up with a stroll through the bustling marketplace and end the day with a bargain massage or tarot reading. Or, if you have the energy, head out again for an Uruguayan meat dish before mingling with locals over salsa music at Café Latino. Or you could simply sit and contemplate the surroundings, margarita in hand, at the patio bar at Posada Tepozteco, the town's classiest hotel, built in a colonial house. Whatever your pace, this town of expat hippies and long-standing traditions has a lot to offer. So read on . . .

GETTING THERE & GETTING AROUND

BY CAR The fastest way to drive from Mexico City is on the Cuernavaca cuota road, which costs $60. Turn off before the Cuernavaca exit on the toll road heading west to Tepoz ($19). Traffic is horrible going on Fridays and returning on Sundays, so travel on alternative days if you can.

There is a *carretera libre* (free road) from Cuernavaca to Tepoztlán, too. It's less direct, but takes you through farmland and typical little villages.

BY BUS There's a bus every 40 minutes from the Tasqueña terminal in Mexico City (Metro: Tasqueña), 8am to 7pm ($50). The bus company is **Autobuses Pullman de Morelos** (☎ **55/5549-3505**).

BASICS

There is no tourist office in Tepoztlán, but everything of interest is within walking distance. The friendly locals are more than happy to point you in the right direction or give out some tips on what to see and do. Try the Buenos Tiempos cafe (p. 136) as a tourist-office substitute.

SLEEPING

The booming tourism industry in Tepoztlán means demand for lodging is high. Though prices are kinda high overall, there's still plenty of doable options.

→ **Hospedaje Mahe** One of the least expensive places you'll find, Hospedaje Mahe still has all the amenities you'd want in a hotel, albeit simpler. Really close to the center of town on a nice, quiet block, *dueña* (owner) Rosa María Monroy Lopez takes well deserved pride in her hotel, even having a neighborhood artist paint the walls in classically Mexican colors, with different details in each room. Each room has a private bath. Prices are even lower during the week, and at press-time the hotel was in process of upgrading its gym. There's a sizable pool, a garden, and a nice view of Tepozteco and the surrounding hilly area. *Paraiso 12.* ☎ *739/395-3292. $300–$500 double. No credit cards. Amenities: Garden; pool; gym. In room: A/C or fan, TV.*

→ **Posada Bugambilias** This is an interesting guesthouse because it offers a bunch of holistic treatments like a temazcal (p. 64) with a shaman, "energy balancing" reiki, shiatsu massage, tai chi, and other New Age-y stuff. There's plenty of outdoor space and greenery, and a newly constructed terrace with a viewing platform and sitting area where you can take in the sight of the majestic Tepozteco. The rooms are sparse but clean. Ask for either the room with a king-size bed, which is a newer room, or the room with the tree in it. *P. Rodriguez 22.* ☎ *739/395-0450. $650–$800 double. No credit cards. Amenities: Massage services; roof deck. In room: Hair dryer, phone, safe.*

MTV Best → **Posada del Tepozteco** ★★★ This is by far the best hotel in Tepoztlán. Posada del Tepozteco has pretty much no competition and is seriously worth the splurge. The grounds are gorgeously landscaped, with plants, pathways, and greenery everywhere. The building used to be a house (the bar was its living room) and the current management remodeled it in 1993. Rooms are stylish, simple, and in tune with the surroundings—in fact, the whole place has a harmonious vibe going on. Many rooms have stunning views of Tepozteco. The staff is bilingual, and the owner, Alejandro, studied architecture and did some of the designing himself. He's very knowledgeable about the town and a great source of information about local customs, festivals, and eccentricities (fireworks and church bells at the crack of dawn, anyone?).

Within a couple years, the hotel will be completely green, using only solar heat and power. The restaurant, Sibarita, is one of the best (and most $$$) in the area. You may see a few bridesmaids during your stay—Posada del Tepozteco is a favorite for marriages and honeymoons. *Paraiso 3.* ☎ *739/395-0010. www.posadadeltepozteco.com. $1,000–$2,500 double, $3,600 suite. Breakfast included. MC, V. Amenities: Restaurant/bar; pool; spa treatments (offsite); temazcal. In room: TV, coffee, hair dryer, phone, safe.*

→ **Posada Nican Mo Calli** Larger than your typical posada, Nincan Mo Calli is a medium-size hotel that has a bright, cheery lobby with a colorful mural of the town, heated outdoor pool and hot tub, and spacious rooms, many with balconies. Open since 2001, it's a relaxing spot with a big garden in back. The manager, Ricardo, is very welcoming. At press-time, he was in the process of building a breakfast room. *Netzahualcoyotl 4-A.* ☎ *739/395-3152. nincanmocalli@hotmail.com. $850 double. No credit cards. Amenities: Pool. In room: TV.*

EATING

The one thing Tepoztlán has that other small towns don't is a fantastic selection of international cuisine. This is one place you won't find yourself tossing back tacos from street carts. It's important to note, however, that many of the restaurants in the weekend-getaway town are open only later in the week, and some only on weekends; always call ahead to check if you can.

➔ **Buenos Tiempos** CAFÉ A European-style cafe that offers brownies, frozen cappuccinos, and other delectable treats, Buenos Tiempos is a favorite among expats and foreign travelers. Having coffee here, you're bound to meet those people who came to Tepoztlán on vacation and never left. *Av. Revolución 10. No phone. Coffee $50. No credit cards. Daily 10am–7pm.*

➔ **Candombe de los Feos** ★★★ URUGUAYAN Owned by a friendly Uruguayan who used to be a social worker for street kids in Tepito, this restaurant is a must. Everything about the altruist's venture into his country's cuisine is a success. From a large outdoor pool you're welcome to enjoy, to an impressive list of Uruguayan wines and delicious meats and breakfasts, it's a special place you'll be glad you visited. *Av. Tepozteco 24. ☎ 739/395-1291. Main courses $60–$200. MC, V. Fri–Sat 9am–10pm; Sun 9am–8pm.*

➔ **El Ciruelo** MEXICAN "It's where all the *fresas* (preppies) go on the weekend," one local tells me. El Ciruelo is described in many guides as "the best" restaurant in Tepoztlán, but don't believe the hype. It's nice, pretty fancy, and yes, the food is good. But I'd take Muelle 32 or Candombe de los Feos over this place any day, for three reasons: more interesting, more fun, cooler atmosphere. This is more like the place your rich uncle takes you when he's in town. They were also opening a boutique hotel at press-time, which was not ready to be reviewed. *Zaragoza 17. ☎ 739/395-1203. Main courses $98–$190. AE, MC, V. Mon–Thurs 1–7pm; Fri–Sat 1–11pm.*

➔ **La Antigua Casa Huehuecalli** TRADITIONAL This restaurant with a sizable outdoor patio has a section on its menu called "Cocina de la Abuela"—aka Grandma's Kitchen—and it's the stuff to order. From enchiladas de mole to a delicious *pozole* (a thick soup with corn and other ingredients) and chiles rellenos, you can sample Mexican home-cooking to your heart's delight. But what makes the place special is the attached spa, with a full menu of inexpensive services. *Cima 1. ☎ No phone. Main courses $38–$110. No credit cards. Daily 9am–9pm.*

➔ **La Sibarita** INTERNATIONAL/MEXICAN The restaurant in Posada del Tepozteco is one of only two restaurants in town to have been awarded the "distinctivo H" award by the tourism bureau, which means it's certified as having accomplished the highest standard for cleanliness and all the vegetables have been treated with a disinfectant. It doesn't *sound* very appetizing but what it means is no stomach bugs for you. The beautiful scenery and good food are a great combination. Come for a meal on the patio and sip a margarita as the sun sets behind the hills. *Paraiso 2.*

MEXICO CITY

Dias Festivos

September 7—when there's a huge festival for the god of Tepozteco—is a special day in Tepoztlán. The pyramid is lit up at night and revelers climb up with torches (although flashlights are more common now), starting at 7pm. The next day, there's a theater performance at the church, Capilla de Nuestra Señora de la Asunción, in the main plaza. In weeks prior to the festival, a special mosaic is made by several artisans just in front of the church. If you're here in early September, it's a marvel to watch the giant mosaic come together. A new one is made each year—out of beans and nuts, no less—and the result is breathtaking.

Tepoztlán

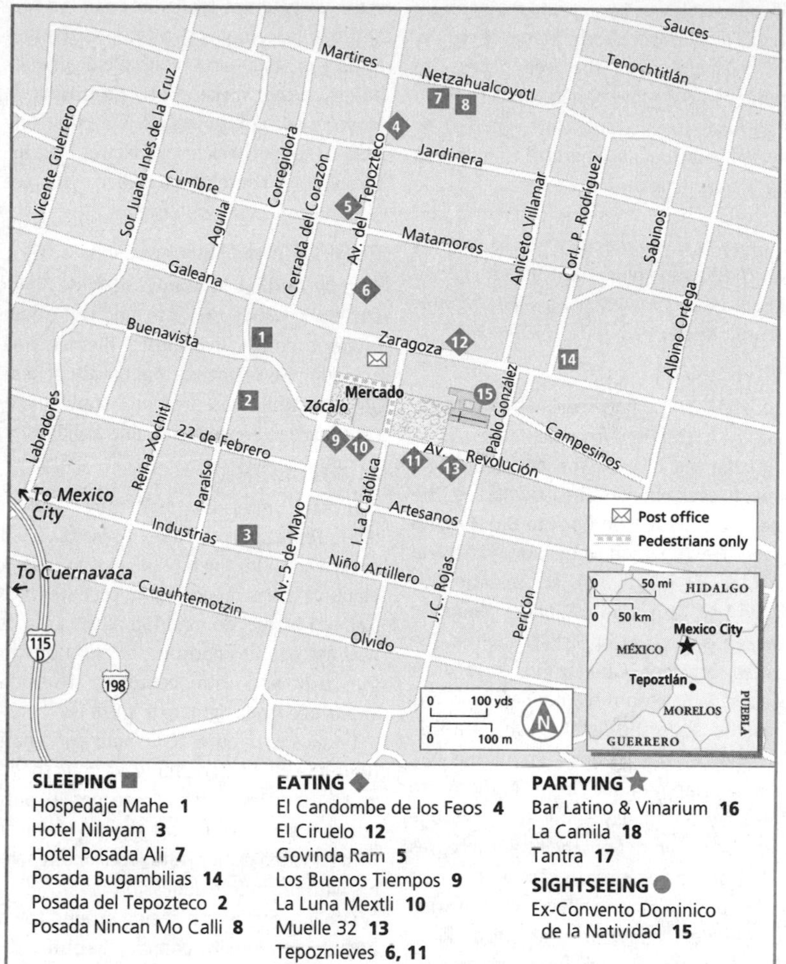

☎ *739/395-0010. www.posadadeltepozteco.com. Main courses $80–$180. AE, MC, V. Mon–Fri 8am–9pm; Sat–Sun 8am–10pm.*

➔**Muelle 32** ★★★ SEAFOOD Another top-notch restaurant in town, especially if you're a seafood fan—you won't want to miss the creative fish dishes. Try the filet "Hindu," which comes in a mango-curry sauce with a side salad of greens, almonds, and shredded coconut in a tangy vinaigrette. For something ultra-decadent, the filet topped with cream cheese, smoked salmon, and caviar ($140) is fantastic. Grab a beer in the bar area with its cool rock floor and seafaring decor, and chat with the owner Gustavo about the menu, which he and his wife designed together. *Revolución 32.* ☎ *739/395-3471. Main courses $60–$160. AE, MC, V. Daily noon–8pm.*

➔ **Tepoznieves** ★★★ DESSERT With close to 100 flavors, you could really fill up on this unique spot's sorbet-type ice cream, not to mention all the free tastes the counter workers love to hand out. From the traditional (coffee, chocolate, vanilla) to the brilliant (tequila, amaretto, mimosa) to the bizarre (carrot, lettuce, avocado), the ice creams here never fail to surprise and delight you. If you like spicy, get the *chamoy con chile* (a salty plum-like fruit with added chile). *Revolución 18. ☎ 721/395-3813. Nothing over $60. No credit cards. Daily 10am–8pm.*

PARTYING

Tepoztlán isn't a huge party town. Maybe people are too tired from the main attraction, the big hike to the archaeological zone, to seek out nightlife adventures. The energetic, though, do flock to **Bar Latino** (5 de Mayo 14, between Zaragoza and Revolución; no phone), an eclectic live music bar with a Son Cubano group on weekends and DJs on Friday nights. The owner, Melchor Campuzano, says tons of Norteamericanos come here, adding that the staff speaks "English, Spanish, Portuguese, and French . . . all the bad words." Happy hour from Monday to Thursday is "all day"—buy two, get one free. From 4pm to 6pm the ratio increases to buy one get one free. Bottoms up.

If you are a more mellow sort, the wine bar, hidden away on the third floor, **Vinarium** (5 de Mayo 14, between Zaragoza and Revolución; ☎ **739/395-1010**), has a terrace with a lovely view of Tepozteco, so you can sip your chardonnay or pinot noir (or champagne for a more romantic eve) and take in the surroundings. They offer wine classes for beginners and connoisseurs alike, and have live music (albeit more relaxed than at Bar Latino) on Saturday nights.

Tantra (Tepozteco 24; ☎ **739/395-7100;** www.tantra-tepoztlan.com) is a cafe and bar that stays open late—sometimes until 3 or 4am—and hosts Mexican rock bands on the weekends. **La Camila** (5 de Mayo 3; ☎ **739/395-7142**) is a cute, tiny blue-lit bar set back from the street in a little shopping center. It's a chilled-out place for a relaxed drink with friends.

PERFORMING ARTS

Stop by **Auditorio Ilhuicalli** (5 de Mayo s/n; ☎ **739/395-0673**) to find out about folkloric dance, live music, theater, and any other performance that may be scheduled for while you are here. Shows typically happen on weekends and holidays.

SIGHTSEEING

You can't miss the star attraction in town, Tepozteco pyramid—it's visible from everywhere in town. The pyramid is a Tlahuica construction that predates the Náhuatl (Aztec) domination of the area. It was the site of important celebrations in the 12th and 13th centuries. Avenida Tepozteco leads right up to the base.

It takes 30 minutes to an hour and a half to do the climb, depending on your speed and fitness level. It's $30 to get in plus another $30 if you want the privilege of using a video camera. Students and teachers with ID get free admission.

Other sights worth seeing around town include the main church, **Capilla de Nuestra Señora de la Asunción** (no phone; free admission; daily 7am–1pm, 5pm–9pm), on the plaza. It was built in the 16th century and features unusual frescoes (look for them over by the altar); and the Dominican monastery **Ex-Convento de la Natividad** (no phone; free admission; Tues–Sun 10am–5pm), a small five-room museum with artifacts and history from the region.

SHOPPING

There's not too much shopping to be done here, but you'll find some items of interest in the crafts market in the main square. The **Pro Arte** (Tepozteco 9; no phone) store is also good for souvenirs: jewelry, pipes, bags, clothing, musical instruments, artwork, mugs, hacky sacks, wallets, frames, maracas, games and puzzles, and other eclectic stuff. Since Tepoz is such a spiritual mecca, there are tons of shops with tarot cards, essential oils, incense, and the like. An interesting one is **Nestinar** (Av. Tepozteco 19; ☎ **739/395-2379**), which specializes in flower essences, to the point of offering "floral therapy" courses and consultations. They have a beautiful selection of tarot decks, I Ching cards, and crystals. **Jacare** (Isabel la Catolica 1; ☎ **739/395-2311**) is a nicer gift shop, with handmade amber jewelry, blown-glass pipes, homemade paper journals, crystals, and a mess of incense.

If you want to buy leather jackets, bags, and accessories, **De Piel Carlos Rueda** (Revolución 9; ☎ **739/395-7398**) has good deals, and all the huarache sandals your feet could desire are at **Huaracheria Yuriyamiris** (Av. Zaragoza 1B; no phone). For Tepoztlán's version of Condomania, head to **El Condon Vagabundo** (Isabel la Catolica 15; no phone), a safe-sex shop with a sense of humor.

Valle de Bravo

Just 147km (91 miles) from of Mexico City (a 3-hr. drive), Valle de Bravo is an excellent choice for a road trip. This beautiful, white-washed lake town (the lake is man-made) is a huge favorite for Mexico City weekenders, especially the elite, who maintain vacation homes here. The nicest are around La Peña, also a primo rock-climbing and hiking spot.

The adventure-travel-lover's paradise is also world-famous for hang gliding and para-gliding. Two major schools here will get you certified and have you making the big leap in no time. Boaters can sail on the lake, or take a tour in a shared boat.

GETTING THERE & GETTING AROUND

BY CAR Take the 134 highway. You'll pass by Nevado de Toluca, a 4,691m (15,386-ft.) inactive volcano where you can grab a break from driving and take a hike.

BY BUS The **Zinacantepec** company (☎ **726/262-0213**) runs buses between Terminal Observatorio in Mexico City and Valle, every hour between 6am and 6pm. Fares are $65 for buses stopping in Toluca, $90 direct.

Look into the Future

Right on the southwest corner of the main plaza stands **Casa Arco Iris** (Av. 5 de Mayo; no phone), a center for holistic therapies of sorts. If you are into hot stone massage, reiki, energy balancing, reflexology, the I Ching, tarot, or any of that esoteric sort of stuff, this is the best place in town for it. The proprietor, Xose Aguirre, has a sort of mystical air about him, maybe because he's a tarot reader and practices indigenous herbal remedies, or it could just be what happens when you live in Tepoztlán for a long time. My tarot reading turned out to be scarily accurate, so I say you trust the guy. You can also pick up essential oils and stomach-calming teas (istafiate is the one that's supposed to get rid of Montezuma's revenge), or get a quickie 15-minute massage for a mere $50 to relieve muscles sore from hiking.

BY FOOT Once you're there, the town of Valle is very walkable. If you get tired, there are plenty of taxis you can just hop in.

BASICS

In a picturesque open-air booth adjacent to the lake, the **tourist office** (no phone) in front of the Embarcadero has brochures on all kinds of things to do in Valle. They can set you up with recommendations from restaurants to sailing.

SLEEPING

→ **El Santuario** This place is more like a retreat for maximum relaxation, an exclusive getaway destination in itself, than a hotel for someone who wants to do a lot of sightseeing. Politicians and Mexican celebrities come here to escape the fray. Each luxurious room has its own minipool, and there's an infinity pool overlooking the lake. The view of La Peña and the town across the water is incredible. The spa offers every treatment under the sun, and the restaurant has a romantic ambience. Come here to totally relax and lounge around in a Feng Shui environment. Get spa treatments, swim, sleep, and chill. If you are looking to be active, its distance from the town and the temptation to linger on the property will challenge your ambitions. Bathrooms feature double showerheads, so grab a partner and do-si-do. *Carretera a Colorines Km 4.5. ☎ 726/262-9100. www.elsantuario.com. $1,500–$2,000 double. AE, MC, V. Amenities: Bar/restaurant; gym; pool; spa; tennis courts. In room: TV, hair dryer, phone.*

→ **Flymexico Club de Vuelo** This little casa de huespedes is right on the lake, with grassy grounds and the bar/cafe **Boga Boga** just paces away. The guest house is small and often completely full (hang gliding and para-gliding instructors have first dibs), but check into it because if there's a room, you gotta grab it. It's cheap and really nice, and if you're planning on doing any gliding, you couldn't ask for a better location. Surrounded by fun young people, fruity cocktails, breakfast, plus leisure and adventure activities, it's just a 10-minute walk (uphill) to the town center. The owners operate the splurge-worthy Meson del Viento, and similar charming touches have been given to this small guesthouse. *111 Cinco de Mayo. ☎ 800-861-7198 or 512/467-2529 from the U.S.; 726-262-0579 from Mexico. E-mail flymexico@prodigy.net.mx for availability and rates.*

→ **Meson del Viento** This special hotel is the nicest place to stay right in town. Each of the cozy, mostly white rooms is named after a different wind: Xaloc, Brisa, Alvis. With wood finished with Talqueado—a varnish typical of this area—and white-washed walls, they have a welcoming, natural, and light feel to them. There's a beautiful outdoor garden with a heated swimming pool. The restaurant's menu features unique traditional dishes, like *Trucha al Eneldo* (trout with a sauce from a local plant). If you're staying here, Omar Torres, the young, 20-something manager, is friendly, helpful, and fun to hang out with, too—have him bring you down to the lakeside lounge at Flymexico's Club de Vuelo. *5 de Mayo 111. ☎ 726/262-0048. www.mesondelviento.com. $1,300–$1,500 double. AC, MC, V. Amenities: Restaurant; bar; Internet access; laundry service; pool; room service. In room: TV, hair dryer, minibar, phone.*

MTV Best → **Rodavento** ★★★ This adventure lodge by Rio y Montaña is so freakin' cool we had to give it its own box (p. 143). The activities they offer are all the things Valle is famous for: ATV-ing, mountain biking, para-gliding, and so on. And the hotel's not so bad either. *Carretera Valle de Bravo Km 3.5. ☎ 726/251-4185. www.rioymontana.com. $1,290–$2,340 double, $2,700–$6,600 for all-inclusive 3-day package. AE, MC, V. Amenities: Restaurant, bar, bike rental, kids club, lake kayaking, rappelling, spa.*

MEXICO CITY

Valle de Bravo

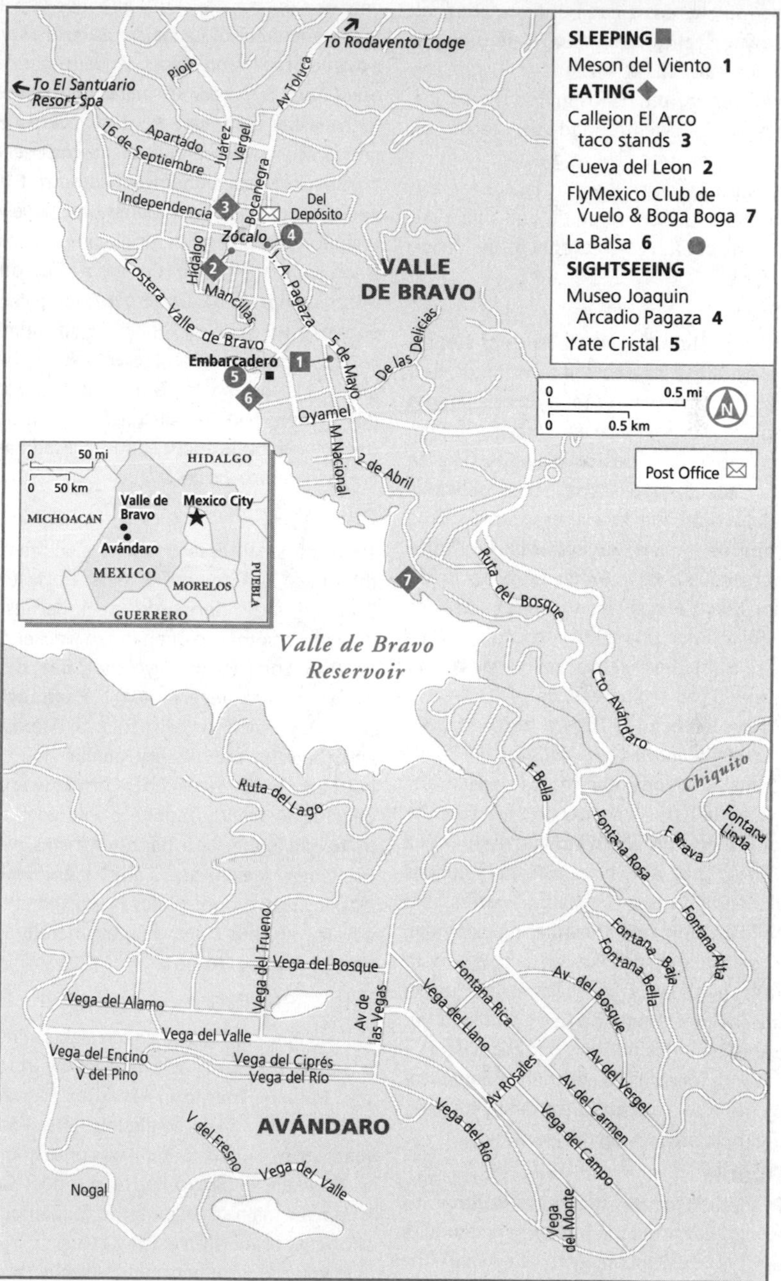

EATING

The food here is great, but there aren't as many eclectic, funky, and international choices as in Tepoztlán (p. 135). The favorites are the restos in Rodavento and Meson del Viento, and the tacos on Callejon el Arco. There are two floating restaurants down by the lake near the boat-tour departure point, and those are touristy but fun—a great spot to sit outside at dusk.

Cheap

Go to **Callejon el Arco** (entrees $10; no credit cards) for a row of taco stands with made-to-order street food. It's cheap and really good. For some awesome ice cream, **Café y Gelato de los Angeles** (Pagaza 322; ☎ **726/262-1403**) has delicious gelatos and Italian espresso drinks. **Los Churros y Las Alcachofas de Valle** (Vergel 104C; ☎ **726/262-1477;** no credit cards; daily 1–6pm) is another spot ideal for a cheap lunch, or a churro y chocolate. They have a salad-bar-esque spread where you can help yourself to seconds.

Los Helechos (Pagaza 200; ☎ **726/262-2835;** entrees $100; MC, V; daily 8am–10pm) is a good choice for vegetarians since you'll find what may very well be the only veggie burger in Valle and other veg dishes. They also have eclectic yummies like elote crepes, a variety of pastas, and pollo en mole rojo, the other type of mole, a red sauce. Artichokes are a specialty in Valle, by the way, so, veggie lovers, be on the lookout. **Boga Boga** (5 de Mayo 311; 11am–8pm), Flymexico's bar and cafe, is a fab spot for a snack, cocktail, or light meal by the lake. You can watch the flyers making their landings on the grassy area.

Doable

In addition to the restaurant at **Rodavento** (p. 140), check out the two barge restaurants on the lake (Embarcadero Municipal), the famous **Pericos** (☎ **726/262-0558;** entrees $85–$125; MC, V; Thurs–Tues 8am–10pm) and colorful **La Balsa** (☎ **726/262-2553;** entrees $100–$200; V; daily 9am–9pm). They're incredibly similar, right down to the dishes they serve. Both have outdoor patios where you can watch the mist settling over the surrounding hills toward the end of the day. They are touristy, but have a unique environment, especially if romance is on your menu. **La Cueva del Leon** (Plaza Independencia 2; ☎ **726/262-4062;** entrees $110–$220; MC, V; daily 8am–11pm) is a colorful restaurant overlooking the plaza; this "lion's den" is a prime spot for doing some people-watching. The *trucha* (trout), salmon fettuccine, and quesadillas are tasty, as are the cocktails.

PARTYING

There's a small assortment of clubs here that Mexico City weekenders flock to. Don't try to go during the week because they don't bother to open til the weekend. **La Pila Seca** (5 de Mayo 100), **Bar des Artistes** (Bocanegra 103), **Pachanga** (Bocanegra at 16 de Septiembre), **Alexia,** and **Camelia** are all very similar—full of hot Mexico City weekenders drinking and dancing to trendy tunes. La Pila Seca is more of a lounge as is Bar des Artistes, but Pachanga, Alexia, and Camelia are your classic antros. Door policy is relaxed, and covers vary but clubs charge generally in the range of $50 to $100.

SIGHTSEEING

Valle is more for sporting than sightseeing, but there's a gallery worth dropping in to: the **Museo Joaquin Arcadio Pagaza** (Pagaza 201; free admission; Tues–Sat 10am–6pm, Sun 11am–7pm) was once home to the Valle de Bravo native and poet for whom the main street is named. Exhibitions showcase primarily Mexican artists.

If you are here between December and February, it's prime season for watching

Rodaventure ★★★

Adventure and eco-travel group Rio y Montaña—the only one of its kind in Mexico—is extremely popular among Mexicans. Their lodge, Best **Rodavento** (Carretera Valle de Bravo Los Saucos Km 3.5; ☎ **726-251-4185;** www.rioymontana.com), in weekender's playground Valle de Bravo provides luxury-level accommodations in settings that harmonize with the natural surroundings. Just a 5-minute drive from the center of town (the hotel can also arrange to pick up guests from the Mexico City airport), Rodavento has the ambience of a boutique hotel but caters to adventure-travel aficionados. Each of the 14 lofted suites with fireplace is a private cabin (sleeps four) built to blend with the landscape. Some of your options for a day's activities are mountain biking, ATV-ing through the local countryside with a guide, speeding down a zip-line, kayaking in Valle's lake, para-gliding, hiking, or taking an outdoor yoga class.

Courses are offered in rock-climbing and para-gliding, and Valle is a major destination for both. Larger groups can take part in a temazcal (see the box on p. 64) in the evening. Each of the rooms in the full-service spa mirrors the cabins: private and built to fit in with the natural surroundings. By night, guests can sip chile-salt rimmed tamarindo martinis (one of about 10 specialty cocktails—they also have a damn good cosmo) by the open stone fireplace in the bar. Then amble over to the dining area for dishes like salmon in sweet 'n' sour apricot and tequila sauce while admiring the view of the small lake and the sound of the pines whispering in the wind.

Founded and owned by architect Waldemar Franco Sol, who designed the lodge himself, and Alfonso de la Parra Cubells, a longtime white-water rafting and mountain-climbing guide, Rodavento and Rio y Montana's other locations are truly a labor of love, as well as devotion to the outdoor-adventure lifestyle and Mexico's ecology. Check out their magazine, *Inhala.* Rodavento is but one of their four properties; others are located in the Veracruz jungle and the ecological reserve of Montes Azules in the Lacandona jungle. A new one—El Jabali—recently opened in the Sierra Gorda area, along a path Franciscan monks once beat through the desert.

the **monarch butterflies** on their migration path from Canada to Michoacan. Go to www.monarchwatch.org to find out about the best places to see the butterflies.

SHOPPING

Pagaza Street is lined with shops selling arts, crafts, clothing, and knickknacks. For professional artisan crafts, head to the **Mercado de Artesanías** by the plaza for a decent selection. The **Arawi** bookstore (Coliseo 101; ☎ **726/262-2557**) has magazines and newspapers in English. Searching for street-wear, cropped jackets, cargo pants? **Gapos' Boutique** (Pagaza 305; no phone) carries inexpensive clothes in trendy styles for both sexes.

PLAYING OUTSIDE

There are so many adventurous activities to keep a traveler occupied in this area. So stop reading and go hang gliding, already.

Flymexico (☎ **726/262-0579;** www.flymexico.com) and **Alas del Hombre** (☎ **726/262-6382;** www.alas.com.mx) both offer certification, have trained professionals who are expert flyers, and have been in business for 15 and 30 years, respectively. You can go **hang gliding or para-gliding,** either in tandem with an instructor, or alone following a rigorous training program.

There are plentiful trails through the pine forests and hills in every direction around Lake Avandaro for hiking and mountain biking. You can rent bikes at **Pablo's Bikes** (Pagaza 103; ☎ **726/262-3730;** $40 per hr., $200 per day). From there, ask about **La Peña,** a spot to the northern end of town where you can hike to a rocky peak with a 360-degree view. **La Torre** (a peak where hang gliders take off) and **Velo de Novia** (a waterfall) are prime mountain-biking destinations—the trails to these two places bring you along winding paths through the woods. For **guided mountain biking trips** organized by Rodavento, contact mtb@rioymontana.com.

Down Calle Ameyal at the lakefront, you can rent sailboats, arrange for water-skiing, or take a boat tour for around $250 to $500 per hour. **Yate Fiesta Valle** (☎ **726/262-0558**) offers hour-long tours on weekends and a night tour on Saturday night, leaving the dock at 9pm for drinking and dancing on the boat. The **Yate Cristal** (☎ **726/262-2553**) is another tour boat at the Embarcadero, offering similar tours.

Puebla

If you're looking to come to Mexico to spend some time studying Spanish, Puebla, the country's fourth-largest city, is an excellent place to do it. More compact, centralized, and walkable than Mexico City, Puebla is a haven of culture, *musica en vivo* (live music), art, architecture, and nightlife. One hundred twenty kilometers (75 miles) from Mexico City, Puebla was declared a UNESCO World Heritage Site in 1987.

GETTING THERE & GETTING AROUND

BY CAR Toll road Mexico 150D runs from Mexico City to Veracruz. It's a 90-minute drive to Puebla.

BY BUS Buses from Mexico City to Puebla leave from Terminal Sur, with service by **Cristobal Colon** (☎ **55/5544-9008;** $130 round-trip; buses from 6am–6pm). Once in Puebla, you'll mostly want to walk the Centro, but for busing it the **Turibus** (☎ **55/226-7289;** www.turibus.com.mx; $70; 9am–9pm) is the best option for seeing sights outside the area around the main square.

BY FOOT The center of Puebla is easy to navigate on foot. It was built by Spaniards around a pre-existing indigenous city as a rest stop between Veracruz and Mexico City, so its construction had a master plan. Much like Manhattan, it's set up like a grid. The streets are numbered and labeled *poniente* (east) or *oriente* (west). The one thing to remember when it comes to getting around is the even-numbered *avenidas* (avenues), which run east and west, are north of the zócalo, while the even-numbered avenidas are south of the zócalo. The *calles* (streets) run north and south. The odd numbers are to the east of the zócalo, the even numbers to the west.

BASICS

Decorated with Tavalera tiles and pottery, the **tourist office** (☎ **222/246-2044;** www.puebla.gob.mx) is located on Av. 5 Oriente 3. Hours are 9:30am to 8:30pm Monday to Saturday, and Sunday 9am to 2pm.

SLEEPING

Puebla has accommodations for every budget, from fancy casonas like Mesones Sacristia, new hipster hangout La Purificadora (from the Grupo Habita, the folks behind CondesaDF), classic-meets-ultra-modern and uber-pricey Casona de la China Poblana, and, totally opposite of all the colonial stuff, the modern NH Puebla with its rooftop pool and bar. If you're hostelling it, you'll find some great international-backpacker havens. All the places to crash are centrally located on the grid.

Hostel

➔ **Hostel Internacional Puebla** This Hostelling International–branded hostel is more similar to a European hostel than quaint Hostal Santa María. Simple, clean facilities in a neo-colonial style house help create a friendly, pleasant atmosphere, and breakfast is included in the rate. Dorm and private rooms are available. *Calle 2 601, between 6 Norte and Boulevard 5 de Mayo. ☎ No phone. hostelinternacionalpuebla@hotmail.com. $110 per person. No credit cards. Amenities: Restaurant; common rooms; Internet access; kitchen; lockers; vending machines. In room: Sheets, towels.*

➔ **Hostel Polanco** The Hostel Polanco was under renovations at press-time, but promises to come back bigger and better in '08. There's an awesome rustic-cowboy style bar in the lobby, with wooden floors and cow skulls and couches and tables for socializing with other hostellers. Two beers tally to only $25, so the price is right, too. If you stay here, bring your own towel as the hostel does not provide them (unusual for Mexico). Spacious shared rooms sleep a maximum of four, and private rooms have queen-size beds. All rooms have private bathrooms. *4 Oriente 403. ☎ 222/232-9560. $110 per person in shared room, $250 for private double room. No credit cards. Amenities: Restaurant/bar; Internet access; laundry room; roof deck; tours; travel agency; TV. In room: Lockers, no towels.*

Cheap

➔ **Hotel Colonial Puebla** One block from the zócalo, the Hotel Colonial de Puebla is housed in a building constructed by Jesuits and used as a monastery until the end of the 18th century; it became a hotel in the mid-1800s. It's now cataloged as a historic monument. The hotel still has an old-school vibe, reflected in the traditional furnishings. The rooms are bright and airy, too. Its restaurant is in an enclosed courtyard with a glass ceiling. *Calle 4 Sur 105. ☎ 222/246-4612. www.colonial.com.mx. $660 double. MC, V. Amenities: Restaurant/bar; room service. In room: TV, phone, safe.*

➔ **Hotel Imperial** An excellent choice for going it on the cheap, and a major step up from a hostel, Hotel Imperial has some cool and quirky details, like an indoor minigolf course. (Yeah, crazy.) There's a free Mexican snack served at 8:30pm, room service, and a breakfast buffet that's included in the rate. *4 Oriente 212. ☎ 222/246-3825. travelbymexico.com/pueb/imperial. $360 double. MC, V. Amenities: Restaurant; game rooms; gym; minigolf; pool. In room: TV, phone, safe.*

Doable

➔ **El Sueño Hotel & Spa** A chic casona that successfully blends the colonial with the modern, this is one of the coolest places to stay in the Centro Historico. The rooms are sparse but warm, with many original details preserved. The restaurant draws a scene on weekends. If you squint, it looks a little bit like a trendy New York City spot. *9 Oriente 12. ☎ 222/232-6489. $120 double. AE, MC, V. Amenities: Bar/restaurant; room service; safe. In room: TV, hair dryer, phone, snacks.*

Splurge

If you don't stay at one of these two sister hotels, do sign up for their excellent cooking class (see "Kitchen Skillz," p. 148): The **Meson Sacristia de las Capuchinas** (9 Oriente 16, Callejon de los Sapos; ☎ **222/232-8088**) is a very quiet small hotel with a private restaurant for guests only. **Meson Sacristia de la Compañia** (6 Sur 304; ☎ **222/232-4513**), on the other hand, is in a louder, more colorful part of town. The building reflects this with its bright colors and lively restaurant.

→ **Camino Real** Puebla's branch of the popular hotel group is markedly different than the usual link on a national chain. This former elitist convent (only wealthy women of pure Spanish ascendance were accepted) was transformed into its current incarnation in 1996. Its rooms are decorated with frescoes, furniture, and art from Mexico's Viceroyal period—the 17th to 19th centuries. With two restaurants, courtyards, and a bar, its colonial meets chic. *Calle 7 Poniente 105.* ☎ *222/229-0909. www.caminoreal.com/puebla. $2,433 double. AE, MC, V. Amenities: 2 restaurants; bar; business center; spa. In room: A/C, TV, minibar.*

→ **Casona de la China Poblana** The super-expensive and luxe Casona is one of the newest, fanciest, and priciest boutique hotels in Puebla. Set, unsurprisingly, in an old casona, what is surprising about China Poblana are the rooms: Sleek, modern, and thoughtfully designed, they're the best of two very different worlds. No guests under 14 are allowed, and it's a very quiet retreat from the world. *Calle 4 Norte at Palafox.* ☎ *222/242-5621. www.casonadelachinapoblana.|com. $2,600–$3,400 double. AE, MC, V. Amenities: Restaurant/bar; laundry service; room service; Wi-Fi. In room: A/C, flatscreen TV, hair dryer, phone.*

EATING

With traditional specialty dishes from the area like chiles en nogada and *pollo con mole poblana,* eating in Puebla is always an experience. Your concept of "Mexican food" might completely change while sampling the local cuisine.

Cheap

→ **Hackl** INTERNATIONAL This restaurant follows the Italian "Slow Food" movement of preparing and eating food the old fashioned way—slowly, that is. But if you're a modernista in a rush, they've got bagels, cheese plates, and other quick bites. Options for vegetarians are extensive, and the prix-fixe dinner menu, while pricier ($425–$560) is a huge meal. *7 Oriente 403, at Plazuela de los Sapos.* ☎ *222/403-6309. www.hackl.com.mx. Entrees $120–$250. No credit cards. Daily 8am–9pm.*

Doable

→ **Hotel Royalty** INTERNATIONAL The outdoor section of the restaurant at Hotel Royalty, which opens out onto the zócalo, is a major destination for people-watching, listening to music, relaxing with a cocktail, and watching the city go by. The food won't amaze your palate—rather, it's the environment that's the real draw. They also have an extensive drinks list, good cappuccinos, and worldly desserts like apple strudel. *Portal Hidalgo 8.* ☎ *222/242-4740. www.hotelr.com. Main courses $65–$110. No credit cards. Daily 7:30am–midnight.*

→ **Meson Sacristia de la Compañia** MEXICAN I recommend their *consome para un enfermo* (soup for a sick person) as a starter—with chicken, garbanzo beans, rice, and secret flavorings, it will cure whatever ails you. (I swear I was coming down with something before I had my first bite—and poof! Walked out feeling

Puebla

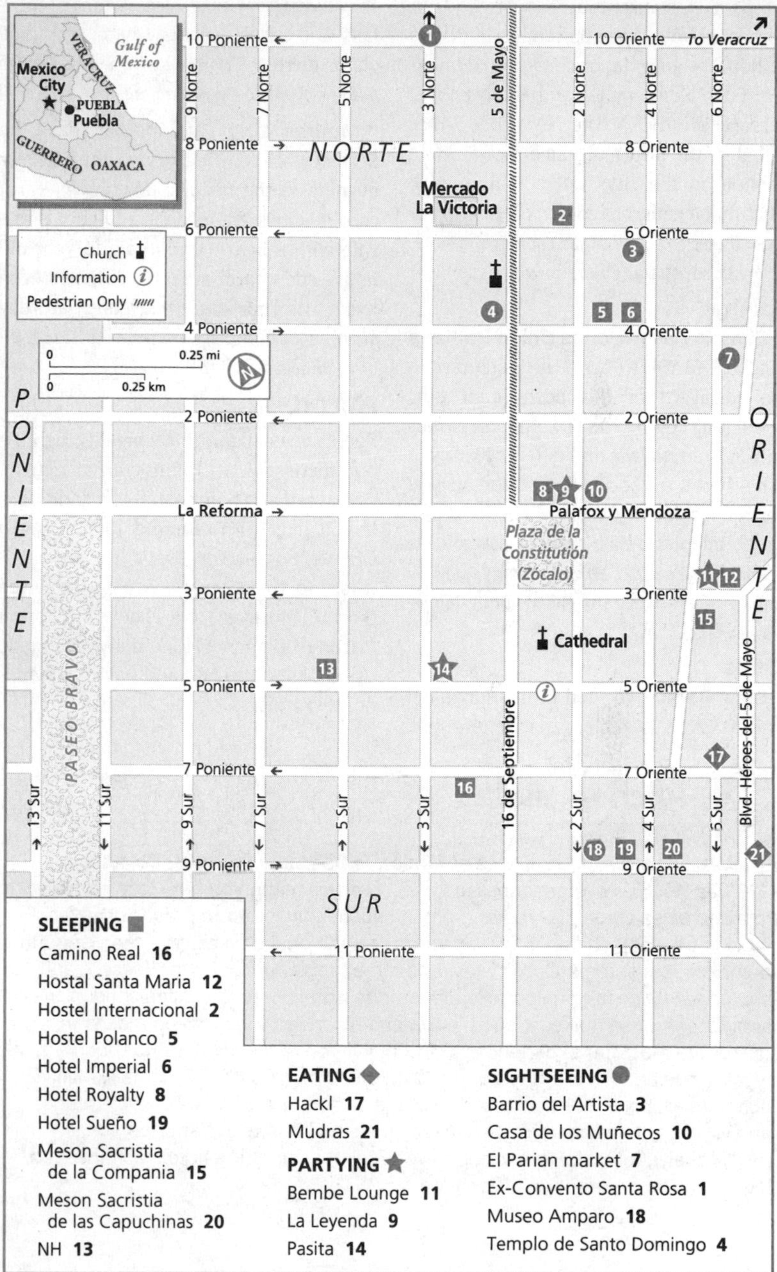

Gulf of Mexico
Mexico City
VERACRUZ
PUEBLA
Puebla
GUERRERO
OAXACA
Church
Information
Pedestrian Only
0 0.25 mi
0 0.25 km
10 Poniente
8 Poniente
6 Poniente
4 Poniente
2 Poniente
La Reforma
3 Poniente
5 Poniente
7 Poniente
9 Poniente
11 Poniente
10 Oriente
8 Oriente
6 Oriente
4 Oriente
2 Oriente
3 Oriente
5 Oriente
7 Oriente
9 Oriente
11 Oriente
To Veracruz
9 Norte
7 Norte
5 Norte
3 Norte
5 de Mayo
2 Norte
4 Norte
6 Norte
13 Sur
11 Sur
9 Sur
7 Sur
5 Sur
3 Sur
16 de Septiembre
2 Sur
4 Sur
6 Sur
Blvd. Héroes del 5 de Mayo
PASEO BRAVO
NORTE
SUR
PONIENTE
ORIENTE
Mercado La Victoria
Palafox y Mendoza
Plaza de la Constitución (Zócalo)
Cathedral
SLEEPING
Camino Real 16
Hostal Santa Maria 12
Hostel Internacional 2
Hostel Polanco 5
Hotel Imperial 6
Hotel Royalty 8
Hotel Sueño 19
Meson Sacristia de la Compania 15
Meson Sacristia de las Capuchinas 20
NH 13
EATING
Hackl 17
Mudras 21
PARTYING
Bembe Lounge 11
La Leyenda 9
Pasita 14
SIGHTSEEING
Barrio del Artista 3
Casa de los Muñecos 10
El Parian market 7
Ex-Convento Santa Rosa 1
Museo Amparo 18
Templo de Santo Domingo 4

okay . . .) But more to the point, this beautiful patio restaurant at the bright, fun Compañia hotel has gourmet-style dishes without the gourmet price tag you'd imagine. Enchiladas, mole, and their typical desserts are delish. The *New York Times* called it "the best multidimensional mole poblano in the city." I'm not quite sure what that means, but good mole, it is. *6 Sur 304. ☎ 222/232-4513. Main courses $75–$110. No credit cards. Daily 7am–10:30pm.*

Splurge

➜ **Ekos @ Casona de la China Poblana** UPSCALE TRADITIONAL The restaurant in the courtyard of this posh hotel puts fine-dining twists on traditional dishes like *chile en nogada* and different kinds of fish. There's a good wine list for all you oenophiles. For all you players in the house, it's an impress-a-date type of place. *Calle 4 Norte at Palafox. ☎ 222/242-5621. Main courses $150–$250. AE, MC V. Daily 8am–closing.*

Cafes

➜ **Café Rentoy** Located in the Barrio del Artista district, this cafe is an excellent spot, especially for jazz brunches on Sundays. They have free wireless access, tons of cocktails, and coffees, snacks, salads, and some platos fuertes. *8 Norte 602. ☎ 222/246-4459. Nothing over $40. Daily 8am–2am.*

➜ **Mudras** A hip cafe and bar that's the perfect place to wile away an afternoon or evening in the historic downtown. Tarot card readings, art for sale, a full bar, and a cafe with a light menu in a 400-year-old house add charm and style. There's even live music Thursday, Friday, and Saturday starting at 8pm. *9 Oriente 1. ☎ 222/298-0035. Snacks $20–$40. Hours vary.*

PARTYING

Puebla doesn't quite have big-city nightlife but there's plenty of nocturnal activity going on if you're in search of a good time. If you like salsa, **Bembe** lounge (Av. 3 Oriente 605 at Los Sapos; no phone) is where to shake your booty. **La Leyenda** (Portal Morelos 106, above Vittorio's Pizzeria; no phone; MC, V; daily 4pm–4am) overlooks the zócalo and has rock bands on weekends.

MTV U Kitchen Skillz

Chef Alonso Hernandez Juárez at **Mesones Sacristia** (☎ **800/712-4028** or 222/232-4513; www.mesones-sacristia.com) will teach you how to make salsa roja and salsa verde (the red and green sauces you'll see on practically every table in Mexico); chalupas; *pipian verde,* a traditional dish with chicken or pork, pumpkin seeds, tomatillos, chiles, and more; *arroz con leche* for dessert; and *agua de jamaica* (a nonalcoholic drink made from jamaica, aka hibiscus, flowers). Chef Alonso makes it seem easy, and his friendly instruction makes this one of the most fun experiences in Puebla. If you're staying for more than a week, you can take a 6-day course ($16,350, including lots of extras like all accommodations, transportation from the airport, museum access, massages, and more). Otherwise, try a 1- or 3-day course ($709–$1,962 per person, respectively), for which you don't have to be staying at the hotel. Visit the website or call them for more information.

Heaven (Av. 5 Sur 105; ☎ **222/309-1919**; nothing over $60), the rooftop lounge at the NH hotel, is a good place to meet friends for a drink to start the evening off. **La Pasita** (Calle 3 Sur 504; no phone) is awesome. They make all their own liquor and have quirky art, cartoons, and random stuff on the walls. There's a noose hanging from the wood ceiling that the bartender says is "for customers who don't pay." So don't forget to pay for your *rompope* (eggnoglike beverage) or *pasita* (flavored liqueur).

If you walk along **Callejon Los Sapos** in the evening, pretty much every establishment lining the street is a bar, many with live music. If really loud is your thing, this is your spot.

The town's upscale clubs and bars are away from the main downtown area, on Juárez between Calles 23 and 29 Sur. **Habit** (no phone), and **Rumba** (no phone) are trendy (dress up). Take the Turibus, because it's a hike to get to this main road from the Centro Historico.

SIGHTSEEING

The historic center of Puebla is where most sightseeing takes place. It's famous, it's fabulous, and it's chock-full of churches, cathedrals, museums, arts, and one very old library.

➔ **Casa de los Muñecos** A local curiosity, the facade of this "Dolls' House" has paneled-tile representations of the local politicians who would not let the owner at the time, Agustin de Ovando y Villavicenico, add a floor to his house, because it would be taller than city hall. These alfresco depictions of them are his revenge. *Calle 2 Norte and Calle 2 Oriente. No phone. Hours vary.*

FREE ➔ **Catedral de la Immaculada Concepción** This large, majestic cathedral in the zócalo is considered to be one of the most beautiful in Mexico, which is saying a lot. Its construction was undertaken in 1575 and finished in 1664 and combines medieval, Renaissance, and baroque architectural styles. There are daily tours at 11am and most of the guides speak English—donations are accepted. *Calle 3 Poniente at 16 de Septiembre. ☎ 222/232-3803. Free admission. Daily 7:30am–2pm and 4pm–8pm.*

➔ **Ex Convento de Santa Rosa** Santa Rosa's kitchen at this former convent is said to be where mole was invented. The convent was founded in 1698 and is now a museum for typical crafts. The Talavera-tiled kitchen has earthenware utensils and cauldrons, poised to conjure images of the Dominican nun Asunción stirring up the first ever mole poblano here. *Calle 3 Norte 1204. ☎ 222/246-2471. Admission $15. Tues–Sun 10am–4:30pm.*

➔ **Ex Seminario Y Biblioteca Palafoxiana** Founded by Bishop Juan de Palafox y Mendoza in 1646, this library that was the first public library in the Americas is now recommended for inclusion in the Memory of the World Register by UNESCO. It houses books like the *Nuremberg Chronicles*, edited in Puebla in 1493. *Calle 5 Oriente 7. ☎ 222/246-3186. www.bpm.gob.mx. Admission $15; $10 students with ID; Tues free. Tues–Fri 10am–5pm; Sat–Sun 10am–4pm.*

➔ **Museo Amparo** ★★ This is the must-visit museum in the city, like Puebla's version of the Museo Nacional de Antropologia—though much, much smaller. It's modernized with recordings that explain the exhibits in different languages, and headsets can be rented for $20. The well-laid-out exhibition rooms showcase a very impressive collection of pre-Hispanic and colonial art, as well as modern art by contemporary Mexican painters and sculptors. Furnishings and artifacts from colonial times demonstrate what it was like to live in 17th-century Puebla. *2 Sur 708.* ☎ *222/229-3850. Admission $35; $25 students and teachers with ID. Wed–Mon 10am–6pm; closed Tues.*

FREE → **Santo Domingo (Capilla del Rosario)** Puebs is all about churches. Seriously, you could spend all day chapel-hopping. Out of all of them, if you're going to see just one, this is the most amazing, so much so that it is called "the eighth wonder" by locals. Enter the Templo de Santo Domingo, walk toward the altar, and to your left is the Capilla del Rosario (Rosary Chapel) in all its baroque glory. The walls are covered in ornate carvings and gold-leaf detail. *Calle 4 Poniente at 5 de Mayo. Free admission.* ☎ *222/232-2715. Daily 7:30am–2pm and 4–11pm.*

→ **Zona Civica del Cinco de Mayo** It's easiest to get to these forts, Loreto and Guadalupe, via the Turibus or a taxi. They're in the designated historical zone of the Cinco de Mayo battle. The Loreto Fort was built in 1821 and was the center of the battle. General Ignacio Zaragoza led 2,000 Mexicans to defend the fort against an attack by 6,000 French troops. Needless to say, they didn't win, but later won back their land. Loreto has the War Museum inside, and the Guadalupe has artillery from the era on display. If you get to visit during the Cinco de Mayo holiday, a major parade and festival kicks off here. *Located on Calzada de los Fuertes.* ☎ *222/229-9800. Admission $25. Tues–Sun 10am–4:30pm.*

SHOPPING

If you want to buy Talavera pottery, you've come to the right place. **Talavera Armando's** (6 Norte 402; ☎ **222/242-3455**) is an excellent workshop. Armando's has factory tours and Talavera pottery of all price levels. Check out the stands and shops along **El Parian,** which was a clothing warehouse in the 18th century. You'll find Talavera, traditional sweets, hammocks, shot glasses, ponchos, souvenirs, tiled mirrors, and a range of other Mexican crafts. **Uriarte** (4 Poniente 911; ☎ **222/232-1598**) is one of the most famous Talavera shops in Puebla, open since 1872.

Definitely head to the artists market and cafes in **Barrio de los Artistas,** a neighborhood that was the brainchild of a group of art students who wanted to turn the area, once called Parian de los Tornos, into a center for the arts. If you've had it with souvenirs and just want to smoke a

Talavera: Puebla's Trademark Pottery

There are many rumors about how Talavera pottery became synonymous with Puebla, but there are actually documents supporting that there were craftsmen from the town of Talavera de la Reina living in Puebla in the 16th century. They were making ceramics and tiles for the many monasteries and churches being built at the time. Tile- and pottery-making were so serious that there were ordinances about the quality of the ceramics and their aesthetic appearance. Some of the rules? Blue was only to be used on the finest-quality ceramic, "master" potters had to sign their products in order to avoid counterfeiting, and regular potters would have to pass an exam before being considered a master.

Cuban, **Entre Muros** (6 Sur 306; ☎ **222/ 232-6043**) is a furniture store that has a humidor room full of an international selection of cigars. For hip vintage and contemporary fashion for men and women, go to **Bulbo** (16 Septiembre s/n, between Calle 7 and 9).

The food market **Mercado de Comida TIpica El Alto** has its own stop on the Turibus tour (p. 114), and that's the easiest way to get to spend some time in this traditional marketplace. Well that and munching on some delicious grub.

In a colonial shopping area, the diagonal street known as **Callejon de los Sapos** runs between Calle 4 Sur at 7 Oriente and Calle 3 Oriente. Street vendors come here to sell their wares, many of which are interesting antiques and cool flea market–type finds. And when you tire of all the shopping, you can hit up one of the bars that line either side of the street.

San Miguel de Allende

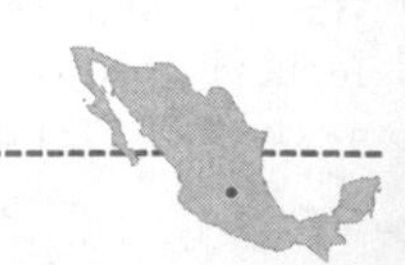

From Inquisitor playground to revolutionary landmark to hippie hangout to its current incarnation as a high-end resort/artist colony, San Miguel has been many things, to many people. For some, this small colonial city is famous for being a fiesta town—it's *the* place where young middle-class Mexicans come to party in the streets, under the glow of all-night fireworks, while their parents enjoy a gourmet meal in the shadow of La Parroquia's spires. For others, it's famous for its somber Semana Santa procession in which the entire town dresses up—the women in black mourning threads, the men in Roman-soldier drag—to follow a glass-covered coffin bearing a life-size statue of Jesus on an hours-long slow-mo parade around town. And for a good number of tourists, the town will always be known as the place where Neal Cassady, the inspiration for Jack Kerouac's beatnik classic *On The Road,* met his end; he died in this colonial mining town in 1968, apparently, a victim of downing one too many tequilas.

Since the late 1970s, San Miguel has been a landmark on the Hippie Trail that winds down through Mexico on the way to Guatemala and points farther south and, to this day, a certain live-fast, die-young ethos lives on in town. Despite its long history of supporting revolutionary pursuits (the fight for Spanish independence began in nearby Dolores), though, San Miguel has always had a puritanical edge. During the Spanish Inquisition, the town served as a colonial judicial center and, in more recent years, the police have deported quite a few longhaired potheads back across the border. This combination of the hippie and the straight-laced is typical of

San Miguel, a decidedly schizoid town. Yes, it can be formal and incredibly religious, but it also loves to party and occasionally embarrass itself. And yes, it's small in scope, but its narrow cobblestone streets offer such a variety of restaurants, shops, and galleries—the art scene here is definitely hopping—that you'll never get bored.

Best of San Miguel de Allende

- **Best Cheap Inn:** Not only will she cook a huge breakfast and comida for you (vegetarian or vegan, even) but Maricela at **Maricela's Home B&B** will happily correct your Spanish too. The rooms are tiny and the design somewhat lacking, but it's a great value in a central location. See p. 160.
- **Best Luxury Inn on a Budget: Casita Quetzal** is a charming off-shoot of the larger, high end Casa Quetzal. You get an equally central location, great design, and the same management and luxury touches (like great bedding) at a fraction of the price. See p. 160.
- **Best Backwoods Lodge in the Middle of Town:** Think *North by Northwest* meets *The Mexican* at the B&B **Posada Corazon.** Built within the Canal family's centuries-old gardens, the breakfast here is superb (and open to the public) with eggs from their hens, wrapped in the hoja santo leaf from their garden, and fruit from their orchards. See p. 162.
- **Best Breakfast:** *Huevos albanil* (eggs poached in red or green sauce) are hard to beat at the **Café de La Parroquia.** They're especially good with *nopales* (steamed cactus) and salsa roja. They also cook up a mean dinner in their front room, **La Brassiere,** which is hosted by the owner's daughter and has wonderful, reasonable fixed price dishes. See p. 163.
- **Best Splurge Restaurant:** Chef Andrea has finally reached his peak after many years in different San Miguel locations with **Ristorante da Andrea (La Landeta),** his gourmet Italian restaurant. In a beautiful setting in an old hacienda on the outskirts of town, it makes for a romantic night out. See p. 166.
- **Best Spot to Linger over Coffee:** It's hard to beat sitting in a courtyard surrounded by giant bamboo, looking up at the bell tower of Las Monjas next door, with an espresso and little lemon cookies at the **Las Musas** cafe at the **Bellas Artes.** See p. 166.
- **Best Excuse for a Drink: The Pamplonada,** or running of the bulls, was imported from Spain and recently attracted crowds of over 50,000 who drank, slept, screwed, and urinated in the streets—oh yeah, and chased full grown bulls around. It's one helluva party. See p. 173.

Getting There & Getting Around

Getting into Town

BY AIR Although there is a small private airport in town, the closest commercial airports are either the Lic Benito Juárez **International Airport in Mexico City** (code MEX; Av. Capitan Carlos Leon s/n, Col. Penon de los Banos, Delegacion Venusiano Carranza; **☎552/482-2400)** which is 3½ hours away, with direct bus service to nearby Querétaro, (45 min. by taxi); or the **León-Guanajuato Airport** (code BJX; 1½ hours by shuttle or taxi).

There is a new airport in Querétaro, but it is so far east that it is only 5 minutes less than going to Leon, and it has far fewer international flights. Taxis to San Miguel from Leon cost about $1,090 (buy your ticket inside at the kiosk) or reserve a shuttle online for $240 through either **Viajes Vertiz** (www.viajesvertiz.com), **Transportadora Turistica Imperial** (see below), or **Viajes San Miguel** (www.viajessanmiguel.com; beware they may be late).

BY CAR From Mexico City, the shortest route is via the Querétaro bypass. Take Highway 57, a four-lane freeway, north toward Querétaro. Past the Tequisquiapan turnoff, exit right at the sign marked "a San Miguel." This toll road bypasses Querétaro and crosses Highway 57 again north of town, where it narrows to two lanes and becomes Highway 111. San Miguel is another 30km (19 miles). As elsewhere in Mexico, driving at night is not advised.

From Guanajuato, the quick route is to go south from the city a short distance on Highway 110, then east on a secondary, paved road passing near the village of Joconoxtle. The turnoff is clearly marked but comes up suddenly, so keep an eye out for it. There will be another left turn into town where this road dead-ends. This road is not safe at night due to unfenced livestock who like to sleep on it.

BY BUS From **Mexico City airport: AeroPlus** buses (☎**555/786-9357**; www.primeraplus.com.mx/iata) leave directly from the airport for Querétaro about every 45 minutes from outside Gate E2 and cost $220. Grab a porter and, for a small tip, he'll take all your stuff over there; or at the E-2 area take the ramp or elevator up one floor and walk down a concourse that crosses over to the passenger pick-up area. Ticketing booths are at the end of the concourse. After buying your ticket, take the elevator to the ground floor. If you have time, grab a hot grilled chicken sandwich from the great torta place on the crossover bridge (near the ticket counter)—otherwise, you're stuck with the Primera Plus cold ham and cheese sandwich that comes with your ticket.

From Mexico City's "Terminal Norte": First-class buses **Primera Plus** (www.primeraplus.com.mx/iata) and **ETN** (www.etn.com.mx) take 3½ to 4 hours. ETN has four buses a day and slightly better service (for slightly more money, at $260); they do stop briefly in Querétaro. Primera Plus has two buses per day ($220). Both have wide reclining seats and video (take your iPod or earplugs in case you hate the movie). **Flecha Amarilla** (www.flecha-amarilla.com) has second-class service with buses leaving every 40 minutes. Another option is to take a bus to Querétaro and change to a second-class bus (or taxi) to San Miguel. Be careful here; the latest scam involves a "porter" grabbing your bag and taking off with it. Check for correct change when you buy your ticket at the kiosk.

From Querétaro: Local buses run to San Miguel every 20 minutes. If you arrive in Querétaro by first-class bus you'll be in Terminal A; walk across the station to Terminal B.

From Guanajuato: ETN has two nonstop super-deluxe buses per day. Primera Plus/Servicios Coordinados has four nonstop buses per day. Second-class buses run every 30 minutes.

To/from Nuevo Laredo: Autobuses Americanos (☎ **415/152-2237**) has a first-class bus leaving at 6:30pm, arriving in San Miguel de Allende between 8 and 9am the next day. The return bus leaves San Miguel at 5:30pm and arrives in Nuevo Laredo around 7am.

The **bus station** in San Miguel is 2km (1¼ miles) west of town on the extension of Calle Canal. Taxis to town are $30 and meet the buses. **Transportadora**

Gringos (or *Gabachos*) in San Miguel

Newcomers complain that San Miguel is too gringo-ized, but only 8% of the 135,000 residents here are foreigners (mostly European, though the Texas twang is really encroaching). However, the concentration of expats (called *gabachos* by locals) can seem quite heavy during high season, especially in the historical center, where native families have been pretty much priced out of their homes by those wielding the almighty dollar (or euro). Don't be too judgmental of those flaunting their cleavage, midriffs, or butts in this still-conservative town; many of them are Chilangos on vacation. And keep in mind that San Miguel is not only a place where locals and foreigners mingle; it is also a place where young and old co-mingle in the majority of public places—restaurants, clubs, shows, openings, and fiestas.

Turistica Imperial (Plaza Principal 18, Interior 7 off the Jardín; ☎ **415/154-5408;** www.transtur-imperial.com) sells bus tickets in advance and provides shuttle service to the airports. You can also take their tourist trolley around town (if you're not too embarrassed). Runs 10am–2pm and 4–8pm.

Getting Around

BY BUS You can take a bus up to Gigante or to the Ancha San Antonio or other areas around town for $4. Most of them start at the plaza in front of the covered market. Bus stops are marked with a blue bus icon sign near street corners; look at the top of the bus to see its destination. Buses to outlying villages (Atotonilco for example) leave from here; there is also a taxi stand.

BY FOOT San Miguel is a walking city; it is almost ridiculous to rent a car, as parking in town is so difficult and everything is within walking distance. However, because of the cobbled streets, high curbs, steep streets, and high altitude, walking can be tough until you adjust to it. Wear walking shoes and forget about stiletto heels unless you're a native (they somehow can maneuver the streets without killing themselves).

BY TAXI Taxis cost $20 to $25 within the gloriettas that mark the edges of the center, or $30 to $40 outside of them. Plan on an extra $10 from the bus station or at night; don't let them overcharge you. A taxi will take you to Atotonilco or the hot springs for $150 to $180, and arrange a pickup time as well. Try **Radio Taxi** (☎ **415/152-4501**); **Sitio Allende** (☎ **415/152-0192**); or **Sitio Central de Autobuses** (☎ **415/152-2635**).

Basics

Orientation

With the historical monument the **Parroquia Church** on one side and the **Presidencia** offices on the other, life in San Miguel swirls around El Jardín, the town square. Pretty much the point of reference for the historical center, it is bounded by Correo, San Francisco, Hidalgo, and Reloj (also spelled Relox). Streets may change names when crossing the axis of the Jardín. Extensions of some streets also change names as they lead out of town (San Francisco becomes "Salida a Queretaro," Canal becomes "Calzada de la

Estacion," Zacateros becomes "Ancha de San Antonio" and then the Salida Celaya). Don't worry, it's a small town; you'll catch on.

Up the hill toward Querétaro is the older neighborhood of **Atascadero.** Adjoining it above the arroyo is the newer wealthier **Los Balcones** with its stunning views of town and the valley beyond. The Centro is surrounded by colonias including **Colonia San Antonio** off the Ancha de San Antonio (beyond the Instituto); opposite is the somewhat suburban newer **Colonia Guardiana. Colonia Independencia** on Westside hills is "up and coming," as is **Colonia Julia** which adjoins it. Many of these colonias are populated by generations of San Miguelenses priced out of their family homes in the Centro.

Tourist Info & Offices

The state tourist information office **(Oficina Consejo Turistico)** is located at Plaza Principal 8, on the opposite side of Jardín from the Parroquia (☎ **415/152-0900** or 152-6500; www.turismosanmiguel.com.mx). Office hours are Monday through Friday 10am to 5pm, and Saturday and Sunday 10am to 1pm. Free monthly tourists publications include ***Inside (Dentro de) San Miguel*** (www.inside-Dentro.com), published quarterly. The English-language newspaper ***Atencion*** also has a wealth of information about local services and events; buy it at the Biblioteca Publica or around town for $8.

Recommended Websites

- **www.internetsanmiguel.com**: This comprehensive site has local homes for rent and other lodging, art schools and classes, Spanish classes and schools, real estate services, a business directory, restaurants, tourist guide, shopping, health and spa services/retreats, and community information.
- **www.portalsanmiguel.com**: This site has a wealth of practical information (how to bring your car in, Visa requirements, medical information), as well as tourist info (hotels, restaurants, things to do) and classes/lifestyle info. They also keep an updated calendar of events, so check here for concert and play info.

San Miguel de Allende Nuts & Bolts

American Express The local office is at **Viajes Vertiz,** Hidalgo 1–A (☎ **415/152-1856;** www.viajesvertiz.com), and offers full travel agency guidance in addition to AMEX services. They offer a $240 shuttle service to the Leon airport and can make bus reservations, air packages, and wedding arrangements for a fee.

Banks & ATMs Several ATMs are located around the Jardín as well as up Calle San Francisco in front of banks there. There's an ATM on the corner of San Francisco and Cuna de Allende (in front of Banamex) as well as at Gigante, the Pemex station on the Salida Querétaro. Beware of "false front" ATM machines; it's wise to keep receipts and check your account regularly.

Dentists Dr. Laura Elias is a bi-lingual dental surgeon, at San Jorge 12, Colonia San Antonio (☎ **415/152-4330** or 415/152-4262; lauraelu@prodigy.net.mx). Her office is open Monday to Friday 9am to 2pm and 4pm to 8pm.

Embassies The **U.S. Consular Agency** is inside the plaza at Hernandez Macias 72 (☎ **415/152-2357** or 044/415-113 9574 for emergency; coromar@unisono.net.mx).

Monday to Friday 9am to 1pm. Also try emergency Consular Agent Philip Maher (☎ **415/152-0068**), and the **Canada National Embassy** in Mexico City, on Schiller 529 (☎ **800/706-2900** for emergencies).

Emergencies American physician **Dr. James Vlasak** can make urgent home or hotel visits (☎ **044/415-101-0163**). If you have more faith in **homeopathy,** try **Dr. Antonio Garcia Gonzalez** (☎ **415/151-0334,** cell). To reach the **Red Cross**, call ☎ **415/152-4121** or 152-4225; for the **Hospital de la Fe**, call ☎ **415/152-2545;** for the **Fire Department**, call ☎ **415/152-2888** or 415/152-3238; and for the **Police,** call ☎ **415/152-0022**.

Internet/Wireless Hot Spots There are Internet cafes all over San Miguel as well as **Wi-Fi** hot spots in many hotels and restaurants (such as the **Posada Corazon,** p. 162). **Unisono** (Hernandez Macias 12, above the Buena Vida) is the oldest Internet provider in San Miguel, and new owner Dave Richards is offering a super high-speed and secure Internet for $10 per hour. Their Wi-Fi extends to the whole plaza downstairs, including the consulate. They also provide short term high-speed Internet rental if you are staying at an apartment or home where you can hook-up.

Laundry **El Chorro** (20 de Enero 110, Col. San Antonio; ☎ **415/154-4951**) is a bit out of the center but the lower prices and quick service reflect that. They charge a mere $10 per kilo and they can return laundry the same day. There are many other laundries throughout the Centro including **Lava Magico** (Pila Seca 15; ☎ **415/152-0899**), which charges $46 for a "full load;" and **La Pila** (Jesus 25; no phone).

Libraries Founded in 1953 and purporting to be the largest bilingual, publicly accessible, privately funded library in Latin America, the **Biblioteca Publica** (Insurgentes 25; ☎ **415/152-0293**) serves more than 700 people a day from the Mexican and foreign communities.

Pharmacies **Farmacias Guadalupe** (Ancha de San Antonio 13; www.farmacias guadalajara.com), is open 24 hours. **Chelos** (Canal 26; ☎ **415/152-1198**), just down from the Jardín, is an expat favorite for everything from Retin-A to Vitamin B shots, to over-the-counter Valium. It's open daily 10am to midnight. Also see "Shopping" on p. 178 for info on places to buy alternative medicine.

Post Offices The post office is located at Correo 16 (☎ **415/152-0089**). There are also two excellent mail services in town: **La Conexion** (Aldama 3 or Av. Independencia 74; ☎ **415/152-1599**), and **Border Crossings** (Mesones 57; ☎ **415/152-2497;** www.bordercrossingsma.com), that provide shipping services, free e-mail, and free (Vonage) telephone service to the U.S. (for members). Both have addresses in Texas where you can have stuff shipped and then it is brought to town on "runs" to the border. You can also use the "karma mail" system where people carry mail north and mail it for you on an honor (or karma) system.

Safety This is a small town, so it's relatively safe especially when compared to sister cities in the U.S. In 2006, however, there was a serial rapist of older women out there (eventually caught after several town meetings). Keep your doors/windows/balconies locked at night. Carry a flashlight at night as some neighborhoods aren't well lit. Be especially careful when out alone during fiestas such as **La Pamplonada** (running of the bulls) that feature heavy drinking. Christmas and Semana Santa are fairly safe times of the year.

Sleeping

The real estate boom in San Miguel is reflected in the price of its lodgings. There are many hotels in the "splurge" range, while cheaper options are sorely lacking. One alternative is to rent a private house or apartment online (**www.internetsanmiguel.com**). You'll also save money on food this way, since most come with kitchens. Because of San Miguel's increased popularity, you may need to book several months in advance.

The prime neighborhood to stay in is the Centro, or the area around the historical center downtown. The Spanish colonial architecture has been kept beautiful in this historical hood: There are no U.S. chain stores; indeed stores aren't even allowed to have English names. There are a couple of budget options here but generally, the further out you go, the cheaper the expenditures such as food and laundry. The center extends west uphill for about a mile into a mostly residential section (Balcones and Atascadera) and then again toward the east downhill; the residential areas tend to have more shops, Internet cafes, schools, and so on (though not as good of a view).

If you're staying in town 3 nights or more, consider booking a house or apartment. You'll find many homes and apartments for reasonable prices online (like the author's at www.jeffspurrier.com/chepito.htm), and many include mountain bikes, kayaks, or snorkel equipment for your use. This is a cheap option if you're traveling with friends—you'll spend a fraction of what a hotel room would cost, and you'll also save on eating out (most places have kitchens).

Hostels

→ **Hostal Alcatraz** ★ CENTRO The best thing about this dormitory-style hostel is its great location, right across the street from one of the best coffee houses in town, Café Etc. (p. 166) and right around the corner from the Biblioteca (p. 157). The dormitories are clean if simple—one side of the space has bunks for four to five women; ditto the other side for men. A good mix of European visitors as well as North Americans stays here; guests often congregate around the central patio with a kitchen. *Reloj 54, Centro.* ☎ *415/152-8543. www.geocities.com/alcatrazhostel. $100 per person shared room. No credit cards. Amenities: Cheap international telephone access; fans; Internet access; kitchen; lockers; sheets; no towels; cable TV (in common room); purified water.*

→ **Iron House Hostal** COLONIA GUADALUPE This place is pretty funky and slightly out of the center of town. Yet the laid-back owner Ricardo makes up for it—he's always ready to show you around town, whether that means taking you to the hot springs or out to salsa. The dormitory-style rooms are small, with two bunks in two rooms, one bunk in another that also has a desk, and a more private rooftop room (the only with a private bath) for a slightly higher price. There's a large but bare front patio and some tables on the roof but not much of a view. *H. Colegio Militar 17D, Colonia Guadalupe.* ☎ *415/154-6108. www.geocities.com/hostelsma. $100 per person in dorms, $250 in private room. No*

San Miguel de Allende Sleeping & Eating

SLEEPING ■
- Casa de Sierra Nevada **17**
- Casita Quetzal **16**
- Dona Urraca **4**
- Hostal Alcatraz **7**
- Iron Horse Hostel **2**
- Mansion Virreyes **10**
- Maricela's Home B&B **25**
- Posada Corazon **23**
- Posada Las Monjas **11**
- Villa Scorpio B&B **12**

EATING ◆
- La Brasserie **22**
- El Burrito Bistro **15**
- Café, Etc. **6**
- Café de la Parroquia **22**
- La Capilla **19**
- Casa Sierra Nevada (Centro) **17**
- Cha Cha Cha **30**
- Dila **28**
- Fellini Gourmet **1**
- Hecho en Mexico **27**
- La Landeta **24**
- Maple **29**
- Media Naranja **3**
- Las Musas **9**
- Ole Ole **5**
- Posada Corazon **23**
- La Posadita **20**
- Rincon de Don Tomas **13**
- San Agustin Chocolates y Churros **14**
- Santa Clara **26**
- TEN TEN Pie **21**
- La Ventana **18**

credit cards. Amenities: Computer to share; shared hair dryer; kitchen; lockers; sheets and pillows; cable TV to share; hot water; purified drinking water; shared bathrooms (in some); Wi-Fi. Mexito-Seguro bus line (get off at the corner of Hidalgo and Calzada de la Luz).

Cheap

Best → **Maricela's Home B&B** ★★ CENTRO You'll feel right at home at Maricela's. A stay at her refurbished Mexican home includes a hearty homemade breakfast and a *comida corrida*. The rooms are tiny but each has a TV with cable, Wi-Fi, and a private bath with a shower. Maricela also cooks vegetarian and vegan meals if you ask, and loves to help you learn Spanish by gently correcting you. You can call home for free using her Vonage hookup in the downstairs living room; there is also a dining room and a rooftop terrace, complete with Astroturf, with a great view uphill of the Parroquia (p. 175). *Jesus 41B, Centro. ☎ 415/152-6631 or in the U.S. 409/209-0030. macahe2000@yahoo.com. $450 single, $650 double. Includes full breakfast and lunch. No credit cards. Amenities: Breakfast room; rooftop terrace; sitting room. In room: Cable TV, ceiling fans, heater, Wi-Fi.*

→ **Posada Las Monjas** CENTRO This former convent, next door to the **Templo de la Concepción** (p. 176) or "Las Monjas" from which it gets its name, is now an art student hang-out. It still retains some of the former building's charm, especially the older rooms at the top of the hotel, which evoke a nun's cell in their minimalism—as in flagstone floors, a single hard bed, and a cross on the wall. Additions made in the '90s are unfortunately motel-ish, but there are still glorious views to be had from the outside terraces. *Canal 37, under the Quebrada bridge. ☎ 415/152-0171. Fax 415/152-6227. $420 singles, $420–$600 double/triple. MC, V. Amenities: Restaurant; bar; laundry service; solarium.*

Doable

Best → **Casita Quetzal** ★★ CENTRO This sister hotel to the much more expensive **Casa Quetzal** (Hospicio #34, Zona Centro; ☎ 415/152-0501) gets you the same location (just around the corner), the same management, and just as much charm at a fraction of the price. Built and designed by artist Cynthia Price, the hotel boasts only three colorful rooms that each express her funky chic aesthetic. Since it's designed for "creative types on a budget," the comfortable hotel has cool amenities like a small sun deck and upstairs terrace, Wi-Fi, high quality bedding and linens, and a large continental breakfast. *Recreo #21b, Centro. ☎ 415/152-3998. Fax 415/152-7162. www.casitaquetzal.com. $800–$1,000 per room. MC, V. Amenities: Breakfast room; cable TV. In room: TV, Wi-Fi (signal clearest on terrace).*

→ **Dona Urraca** CENTRO This new hotel designed by a group of Querétaro architects features lots of glass, simple stone fountains, contemporary furniture, and art. There's a "bio-spa" attached with a lap pool, and spa packages available, with parking behind the hotel. Its colonial exterior makes a nice contrast to the modern interior, but it lacks a patio or outdoor area. *Hidalgo 69, Centro. ☎ 415/154-9770 www.donaurraca.com.mx. $900–$2,000 single to suite. AE, MC, V. Amenities: Restaurant; Wi-Fi. In room: Plasma TV w/Sony House Theater, coffeemaker, fridge, hair dryer, microwave, robes.*

→ **Mansion Virreyes** CENTRO As one of the older hotels in San Miguel, this very centrally located hotel's rooms are clean but have seen better days. All open onto a central patio, which also serves as a restaurant—note that it gets a bit noisy except in the rooftop suite (more money, since it has a kitchen, living room, fireplace, and king-size bed). All guests can

MTV U Going to School in San Miguel

Probably more than any other town in Mexico, San Miguel is known for its Spanish-language and art schools. These schools cater to English speakers and often provide a list of apartments for long-term stays. Rates for language classes are usually hourly and get lower the more hours you take.

Instituto Allende (Calle Ancha de San Antonio 20, 37700 San Miguel de Allende, Gto.; ☎ **415/152-0190;** fax 415/152-4538; www.instituto-allende.edu.mx), put San Miguel on the map in the 1930s. Its founders were Enrique Fernández Martínez, the former governor of the state of Guanajuato, and Stirling Dickinson, an American. Today, it thrives in the 18th-century home of the former counts of Canal, a beautiful place with elegant patios and gardens, art exhibits, and murals. You can wander past classrooms where weavers, sculptors, painters, ceramists, photographers, and students are at work. Much of the craftwork that San Miguel is known for sprang from this institute. The language office maintains a list of local families who rent rooms for stays of a month or more. The institute offers an MFA degree, and the school's credits are transferable to at least 300 colleges and universities in the United States and Canada; noncredit students are also welcome.

Academia Hispano Americana (Mesones 4 (Apdo. Postal 150), 37700 San Miguel de Allende, Gto.; ☎ **415/152-0349;** fax 415/152-2333; www.ahaspeakspanish.com), has a reputation for being a comparatively tougher language school with an emphasis on grammar as well as conversation. Classes are limited to 12 people. The work is intensive, and the school is particularly interested in students who plan to use Spanish in their careers or who feel the need to communicate and understand the other Americas. The school has a continuous program of study of 12 4-week sessions for 35 hours a week. Private lessons are available. It's a member of the International Association of Language Centers.

LanguagePoint (20 de Enero Sur 42, 37750 San Miguel de Allende, Gto.; ☎ **415/152-4115;** www.languagepoint.org), offers instruction and immersion at basic, intermediate, and advanced levels. There are only three students per instructor, and emphasis at the basic level is on gaining a working knowledge of everyday Spanish as a basis for developing language skills.

Also check for classes via **Bellas Artes,** listed under "Performing Arts," below.

The **Centro Bilingue de San Miguel** (Correo 46; ☎ **415/152-5400,** www.geocities.com/centrobilingue) is geared toward the casual student looking to improve or develop Spanish for business, school, or conversation. In trying to integrate cultural experience with learning Spanish, they will take you on field trips in or around San Miguel. They offer private tutoring, in addition to classes for $1000 per week. They can also arrange housing in a hotel or apartment, or a home stay with a Mexican family.

use the roof terrace—it's a great place to watch parades. *Canal 19, a block south of the Jardín. ☎ 415/152-3355 or 152-0851. mansionvirreyes@prodigy.net.mx. $750 single, $950 double, $1,200 suite. Includes tax and full breakfast (in their restaurant). AE, DISC, MC, V. Amenities: Bar; restaurant; telephone; travel info desk; TV. In room: TV.*

→**Villa Scorpio al Puente B&B** ★★ CENTRO This beautiful colonial house is furnished with antiques and has a well-appointed library and study, with spacious rooms on several floors, including one with direct access to the rooftop terrace. An honor system bar, Jacuzzi, and massage room are also on the rooftop (masseuses will come to the hotel), with full breakfast (included) served in a patio dining area on the first floor. *Quebrada 93, at Canal. ☎ 415/152-7575. www.villascorpio.com. $1,250 double; $1,350 for the "sky room" (recommended). Personal check for deposit, no credit cards. Amenities: Jacuzzi; laundry facilities; library; sala. In room: Fireplace, full private bathroom, purified water, Wi-Fi.*

Splurge

→ **Casa de Sierra Nevada** ★★★ JARDIN Known for its attractive (if somewhat heavy) Spanish colonial and Mexican design and its excellent service, the Sierra Nevada perfectly meshes cosmopolitan luxury with a mix of Mexican style. This boutique hotel has 33 rooms, spread throughout its main building and within the five separate colonial mansions of the complex. The main building rooms are a real treat to stay in, with beautiful preserved architectural details, lots of tile and flagstone rock, and hand-painted frescoes. If you rent an entire mansion, you can get several bedrooms on different levels, a living room, dining room, and kitchen looking out at the beautiful street; or rooftop/terrace views of town. Basically, you'll have your own home where you're waited on hand and foot.

Located within a 2-block neighborhood just up from the Jardín, the hotel boasts a pool enclosed within a walled garden and a spa. Room service is available from their restaurant **El Centro** (p. 165). *Hospicio 35, between Diez de Sollano and Recreo. ☎ 415/152-7040 or 800/701-1561 in the U.S. and Canada. Fax 415/154-9703. www.casadesierranevada.com. Second location Santa Elena 2, at top end of the Parque Juárez. ☎ 415/152-7040. $2,880 single, $4,465 suite. Packages available. AE, MC, V. Amenities: 2 restaurants; 2 bars; concierge; dry cleaning; laundry service; in-room massage; large outdoor heated pool; room service until 11pm; spa; tour and activities desk. In room: TV, fridge, hair dryer, minibar, safe.*

MTV Best → **Posada Corazon** ★★★ CENTRO This elegantly rustic '70s lodge-style boutique B&B was created by Cesar and Rosio Canal Arias on the upper part of their family's extensive gardens. One of the rooms of the hotel (called *Carpintero*) has its own swimming pool; others open to the garden or interior area, where breakfast is served. All are stylishly and beautifully decorated with minimalist Mexican crafts mixed with contemporary furniture and design. The extensive use of heavy wood (mesquite) and small mosaic tiles in the open-air bathrooms lends the place a definite lodge-in-the-woods vibe. The breakfast (p. 164) is simple but as gourmet as anything this town has to offer. The library of former resident Tony de Gerez was saved and brought here for guests to enjoy; there are also terraces where you can have breakfast or hook-up to Wi-Fi. *Aldama 9, Centro. ☎ 415/152-0182 or 152-2165, 315/828-6273 in the U.S. www.posadacorazon.com.mx. $1,000–$1,500 single, $1,200–$1,700 double. Breakfast included. Special deals and packages available. MC, V. Amenities: Garden; library; meeting rooms. In room: Fans, hair dryer, Wi-Fi. Pool for room "Carpintero."*

Eating

Although San Miguel is full of restaurants, locals love to complain that there are no good places to eat. It's true that restaurants seem to change hands frequently, but many of those listed here have been around for generations and are consistently good.

There are also lots of good cheap options. I love the *rajas* in front of the Instituto at night, as well as the excellent *huraches* at the Tuesday market. The full-fledged expensive "gourmet" restaurants in the center of town tend to be hit or miss when it comes to the quality of the food, but the beautiful surroundings and attentive service can make for a pretty swell dining experience.

One seasonal specialty to try is *chiles en nogada*—these green pork-stuffed chiles smothered with red pomegranate/white almond sauce are somewhat omnipresent during Independence Day festivals. Otherwise, break out your steak knives—this area of the country is known for its beef. Since there are also many Italian expats in town, you can get great pastas in many restaurants. And though great seafood is harder to come by here than in, say Cancún, because San Miguel is inland, quite a few restaurants cook up a mean fish dish.

Cheap

In addition to the following restaurants, try **El Tomate** (Mesones 62; ☎ **415/151-6057;** all items under $100; no credit cards; Mon–Sat 9am–9pm), which has veggie options like salads and fresh-squeezed juices. For *pozole*, your best bet in town is **La Posadita** (Cuna de Allende 13; ☎ **415/154-7588;** entrees $60–$100; no credit cards; Tues–Sun 8am–10pm), where you can sit on their rooftop terrace and enjoy the view while scarfing down a bowl of delicious but cheap pozole. Finally, it's worth stopping by **La Media Naranja,** (Hidalgo 83; ☎ **044/415-105-0920;** no credit cards; Mon–Sat 9am–6pm), a cool place that offers a great $40 full breakfast including juice and coffee, along with fresh vegetarian fare and online services.

MTV Best → **Café de la Parroquia** ★★★ MEXICAN Few places cook my favorite breakfast, *huevos albanil* (eggs poached in a spicy red or green sauce) better than La Parroquia. Ask for yours with nopales and salsa roja, and with a side of black beans and handmade tortillas. Other great Oaxacan egg dishes, as well as typical Mexican fare like tacos, round out the menu. Since this restaurant sits inside the courtyard of Tecolote bookstore—the best bookstore within hundreds of miles—it gets crowded with locals. It's a scene outside, yes, but that doesn't mean you can't grab a scene inside and tuck into your excellent eggs in comfort. *Jesus 11. ☎ 415/152-3161. Main courses $40–$120. No credit cards. Tues–Sat 8am–4pm; Sun 8am–2pm.*

→ **Cha Cha Cha** MEXICAN Mario and his American wife (graphic artist and event organizer Cece) run this casual home-style Mexican cooking restaurant on the cheap—beers are only $12. It's a bit out of the way if you're staying more in town (it's close to the Instituto in the Colonia San Antiono), but it's worth the trip for a cheap and filling lunch with a young and hip crowd. *Calle 28 de Abril Norte 37 at Rosales, Col. San Antonio. ☎ 415/152-6586. Main courses $10–$100. No credit cards. Tues–Sun 1–7pm. Closed Mon.*

→ **El Burrito Bistro** CALIFORNIA-MEXICAN Hankering for a burrito California style? You'll get fresh ingredients, grilled meat instead of stewed, whole wheat tortillas, and healthy salads and wraps in this colorful joint owned by a San Francisco native. This is a hangout for students from the Academia Language School. *Correo 45, at Chiquitos. ☎ 415/154-8956. Nothing over $80. No credit cards. Mon–Sat noon–9pm. Closed Sun.*

→ **La Brasserie** ★★★ FRENCH-MEXICAN This fabulous bistro takes over the front space of Café de la Parroquia (see above) at night, when it offers high quality and reasonable dinners such as tilapia in a wine butter sauce wrapped in paper, fresh pancetta, and homemade chocolate flan—all served with fresh vegetables, black beans, and rice. The crowd is all ages and types, and you can eat either in the morning patio or their interior room. The a la carte Mexican dishes are average, but why bother with that when a drink, coffee, and dessert are included in the $100 prix-fixe dinner? *Jesus 11, front rooms. ☎ 415/152-3161. Main courses $80–$120. No credit cards. Tues–Sat 5–10pm.*

➜ **Ole Ole** MEXICAN This ex-bullfighter's home-style fajitas are reliably good, as are the brochettes of marinated beef or chicken with bell peppers served over rice. It used to be such a great deal but then like everywhere the prices keep going on up. Large portions, and the delicious fajitas delivered sizzling to your table, still make it a good value. *Loreto 66. ☎ 415/152-0896. Main courses $80–$120. No credit cards. Daily 1pm–9pm.*

MTV Best ➜ **Posada Corazon** ★★★ MEXICAN BREAKFAST This boutique B&B, designed by Cesar and Rosio Canal Arias and situated on the upper part of their family's extensive gardens, serves a wonderful gourmet breakfast that's open to the public. All the organic food on offer is exquisite, from the eggs wrapped in *hoja santo* to the Michoucan-style fresh baked cookies (flavored with oranges from their orchard and using eggs from their hennery). Even the Oaxacan coffee, which includes decaf, a rarity in Mexico, is organic. Bring your laptop and hook-up with their Wi-Fi in front of the sunken living room fire. Or grab a seat in the "lodge" area, designed in a 1970s style using natural indigenous materials such as the pink cantera stone that the Parroquia was built with. It houses the unique library of former San Miguel resident Tony de Gerez, so you'll have plenty of good reading on hand. *Aldama 9, Centro. ☎ 415/152-0182 or 152-2165. www.posadacorazon.com.mx. Breakfast only $60–$100. MC, V. Daily 8am–noon.*

➜ **Rincon de Don Tomas** ★★ MEXICAN Though her restaurant is named in honor of her father, Alicia Reglado uses her mother's recipes to whip up the delicious homemade dishes on offer at this comfy restaurant. Since it's at the west corner of the Jardín, it's a fantastic location for people-watching. Order some of the seasonal specialties, like *chiles en nogada* (beef-stuffed green chiles, covered with a white ground nut sauce and topped with red pomegranate seeds) and *flor de calabasa* soup and get ready to take in the scene. *Portal Guadalupe 2, at San Francisco. ☎ 415/152-3780. Main courses $60–$150. AE, DISC, MC, V. Mon–Sat 8:30am–10pm; Sun 8:30am–9pm.*

➜ **Ten Ten Pie** MEXICAN This longtime local hangout specializes in "a little something to keep you on your feet," which translates to delicious meaty tacos *al pastor* as well as a variety of vegetarian (such as mushroom) options wrapped in soft corn tortillas. The tacos are delicious if somewhat small, and at $12 each they can get expensive. It's probably worth the extra price not to worry about getting sick from a street stand, though. *Cuna de Allende 21, at Cuadrante. ☎ 415/152-7189. Main courses $12–$50. No credit cards. Daily 9am–midnight.*

Doable

MTV Best ➜ **Dila** ★★★ SRI LANKAN Chef Dilshan Madawala's Sri Lankan chicken curry, featured in *Bon Appétit*, is pretty amazing, as is the fish soup, Sri Lanka mixed noodles, biryani, and lamb garam masala curry. Dilshan met his wife Teresa in Switzerland studying Hotel Management and luckily (for you) followed her home to Mexico where they started up a restaurant first in Dolores Hidalgo. He uses European techniques combined with his knowledge of his native cuisine to create a pretty ass-kicking curry. There's equally kicking live music on the weekends—and it's a Wi-Fi hot spot. *31 Ancha de San Antonio. ☎ 415/152-4050. Nothing over $150. Tues–Sat noon–midnight.*

➔ **Fellini Gourmet** ★★ ITALIAN Everything here, from the organic vegetables to the Italian cheese and sausage to the olive oil to the wine, is made with ingredients from the owner and chef Etore's ranch. That results in some amazingly delicious classic Italian ravioli, pasta, pizza, and antipasto. They also have a deli case where you can buy any of the above. The best part is that this restaurant is situated in the circus tent outside of the Aurora arts complex, where special events such as live Brazilian or Cuban bands and the yearly circus "Cirkonvencilon" (see "Performing Arts") are held. Plus, they contribute to the community by sponsoring circus classes for low income children. *La Carpa Circus Tent, Calz. de la Aurora s/n, in front of the Fabrica de la Aurora, Col. La Aurora. ☎ 415/152-4713. rpop@prodigy.net.mx Nothing over $70 (except a $120 bottle of wine.) No credit cards. Daily 1–8pm.*

➔ **Hecho en Mexico** AMERICAN This is one of the most popular restaurants in town, with reliably good seafood and chicken dishes, excellent fresh beet and jicama salad, and monster brownies with ice cream to cure the munchies. The outdoor patio setting that's next to Instituto Allende has the makings for just a bit too much Gringolandia, though. *Ancha de San Antonio 8. ☎ 415/154-6383. enemer100@hotmail.com. Main dishes $60–$120. MC, V. Daily 9am–11pm.*

Splurge

➔ **El Centro at Casa Sierra Nevada** INTERNATIONAL It used to be the best in town, but after losing a succession of excellent chefs and then being purchased by the Orient Express, the food just isn't that great for the price. Yet the El Centro is still a great excuse for getting all dressed up to impress someone for dinner. (Men are required to wear jackets, which they will supply if needed.) Try the salad greens with grilled shrimp or goat cheese, any of the beef, or the fresh salmon baked in an olive crust. Light up the night and really impress your date with tequila crepes flambé. The outside area is much more pleasant than the main dining room, which tends to be a bit formal and stuffy, if elegant. The bar fronting the street is particularly a great place to meet for a drink, filled with happening, if upwardly mobile, young things (as well as rich old folks). *Hospicio 44. ☎ 415/152-7040. Second location "Restaurante en el Parque," Santa Elena 2. www.casadesierranevada.com. Main courses $180–$300. AE, MC, V. Daily 8am–11pm.*

➔ **La Capilla** INTERNATIONAL Adjacent to the Parroquia on Cuna de Allende, this restaurant is like a Mexican take on a '70s steakhouse. Expect everything to be rich, heavy, creamy, buttery, and fatty; there's nothing nouvelle about this place. The thing to get here is beef or pork. The setting is absolutely gorgeous, if somewhat dark, with a burnt chapel ceiling. Downstairs may look dead but that's because everyone is upstairs dining away. This place is a favorite for wedding and birthday parties; men usually wear nice jackets (ties not required), women dresses and shawls. The food isn't completely worth the splurge—you can find equally tasty food at half the price at any number of places around town. Still, the setting is what you're paying for—this is a trippy place to see and be seen. Plan on spending at least US$150 for two, or more if you order from the wine list. *Cuna de Allende 10. ☎ 415/152-0698. www.la-capilla.com. Entrees $30–$285. Wed–Sun 8:30am–noon & 1pm–11pm.*

MTV Best → **Ristorante da Andrea (La Landeta)** ★★★ ITALIAN After many years in different San Miguel locations, Chef Andrea has finally reached his peak on the outskirts of town with this gourmet Italian restaurant in an ex-hacienda. Come for the fresh homemade pasta, such as the ravioli stuffed with huitlacoche when in season, and be sure to try delicious fresh organic salads. This splurge is a special night out, so dress up a bit (there's no formal dress code but no one wears shorts or T-shirts). This is an amazing location, with stone walls and a hacienda feel throughout. You could easily drop $2,180 for a meal you won't forget. Call ahead for reservations. *On the road to Los Rodriguez, off the Salida Queretaro.* ☎ *415/120-3481. Pasta dishes $240–310. No credit cards. Thurs–Sun 1pm–11pm.*

Cafes & Desserts

In addition to the following options, hit up **Santa Clara** *(Ancha de San Antonio 3; no phone; no credit cards; daily 10am–9pm)* for the best ice cream in town. Theirs is really rich and creamy, if expensive at $38 for one scoop. Also stop by **La Ventana** ★ *(Sollano 11;* ☎ **415/154-8701;** *cheap; no credit cards; daily 8am–9pm)* which sells 100% organic beans from Chiapas via a window on Sollano—it's San Miguel's version of a drive- (or walk-) through.

MTV Best → **Café Etc.** ★★ Oaxacan native Juan Ortiz presides over the coffee bar, outdoor tables, and Internet stations at Café Etc—home to arguably the best coffee in San Miguel—with aplomb. Around the corner from the Biblioteca and across the street from the Alcatraz Hostel, the place is homey and funky, with walls covered with political posters, local art, and many homages to Juan. With magazines and newspapers on hand to browse, as well as various teas and coffee roasted locally to suit the taste buds of tourists—what's not to like? There's also a very decent breakfast ($65) with Juan's special basil/tomato omelet, the mid-day *comida corrida*, and desserts like Key lime pie. Juan, who hosts a philosophy group on Tuesdays from 10:30am to 12:30pm, firmly believes that "the magic of San Miguel is that people are friendly and want to talk." Perhaps that's why he lets patrons linger with their cup of coffee, chatting away, for hours. *Relox 37, at Insurgentes.* ☎ *415/154-8636. café_etc@hotmail.com. Nothing over $70. No credit cards. Mon–Sat 8:30am–9pm; Sun noon–6pm.*

MTV Best → **Las Musas** ★★ This cafe in the courtyard of the Bellas Artes (p. 161) doesn't have the best coffee in town, but the setting is perfect for lingering. Order a cup, and take your time to enjoy the fantastic architecture, especially the magnificent dome of the Iglesia de la Concepción which was designed by the same unschooled architect who designed the Parroquia. They also serve pasta, salads, sandwiches, and desserts. *Hernández Macías 75, between Canal and Insurgentes.* ☎ *415/152-0289. All items under $70. No credit cards. Mon–Fri 10am–5:30pm; Sat 10am–2pm.*

→ **Maple** ★★★ Maple makes the best croissants, pastries, bread, and cookies at the most reasonable prices in town—I'm a fan of the giant fantastic apple-filled turnovers. They can sell out so get there early. All food is made according to recipes the bakers developed over the years. It's pretty much take out only, but you can eat in the garden at the Instituto down the street or take your sugary concoctions to any of the coffee places nearby. *Salida Celaya 51A. No phone. Nothing over $30 (except pies $100). No credit cards. Mon–Fri 10am–10:30pm.*

→ **San Agustin Chocolates y Churros** ★ I guarantee that Mexican soap star Margarita Gralia ("Amor en Custoria") and her husband Ariel will get you all hopped up on sugar and caffeine at their place, featuring decadent deep-fried dough rolled in sugar (the churros) and hot chocolate from all over the country—big bubbling vats of it. The cafe is housed in a colonial building in the historical center, and you'll dine (there are full meals, in addition to the sweets) under framed shots of Margarita hanging from the pink frescoed-walls. *San Francisco 21, Centro. ☎ 415/ 152-9102. Churros under $20; meals $30–$120. MC, V. Mon–Thurs 8am–11pm; Fri–Sat 9am–midnight; Sun 9am–11pm.*

Partying

San Miguel excels at happy hours, from rooftop imbibing at the Xipal Bar—where you can say penance while getting drunk—to sipping martinis at Tapas y Tinas. But there's also good live music to be had, and there are a slew of cantinas. I'll never forget seeing a guy stumble out of a cantina at 10am and heave all over the street; if you want to witness this yourself, there's La Cucaracha, a traditional cantina on Zacateros, or el Gato Negro at Mesones 12A. See the Appendix A, p. 681 for more info on cantinas.

Bars and clubs come and go with rapidity here so check first before going—though if one has closed another one has probably sprung up in its place.

Bars & Cantinas

→ **Berlin** Down the street from Mama Mia's, Euro-trash and movie stars on location frequent this German expat's very hip bar and restaurant. This is a great place to celebrate holidays like New Year's Eve, with fixed-price dinners that include drinks. A long black bar takes up most of the front room, with a view of the street; there are also tables in a back room decorated in a contemporary European style. *Umaron 19. ☎ 415/154-9437.*

→ **Le Petit Bar at El Market Bistro** Search for Johnny Depp or other visiting movie stars in one of the two dark rooms of this bar attached to the restaurant El Market Bistro. Reopened in 2006 after a brief hiatus, it promises to be a cultural hub once again and a hangout for a happening international crowd. *Hernández Macías 95. ☎ 415/152-3229. No cover.*

→ **Xipal Bar and Restaurant** This "colonial jewel" built in 1729 (and the former home of Diego Rivera's daughter, Guadalupe Rivera Marin), is now a beautiful if pricey hotel, with a pleasant bar worth a happy hour trip (two beers or margaritas for the price of one). On an upstairs outdoor terrace adjoining the back wall of

Gay Nightlife in San Miguel

With its deep roots in the Catholic Church—reinforced by a certain cowboy machismo—San Miguel was not considered a gay-friendly town until the 1990s, when there was actually a lesbian club here (for about an hour). There are no longer any real gay bars here, though **Mama Mia's** (p. 168), **The Chocolate Lounge** (Mesones 99; no phone), the Irish pub **Limerick** (Umaran 2; **☎ 415/ 154-8642**), and **The Foreplay Lounge** (Hidalgo 79; no phone), are all considered "gay-friendly." There are also periodic gay-centric events happening at **La Carpa** (p. 170) and **Casa de la Cultura** (p. 170), and more and more gay artists and writers are moving here—an encouraging sign.

Airhead

Really got a *cruda* (hangover)? Maybe what you need is a shot of oxygen! In the thin altitude here you could be getting headaches from lack of air, too, honest. **Bambu Oxygen Bar** (Ancha de San Antonio 15, inside Posada la Aldea; ☎ **044/ 415-103-3690;** $50 for 20 min., packages available; Tues–Sun 9am–9pm) provides the solution—air. This bar offers a comfy room to chill out in and breathe in fresh oxygen or "air flavors" including almond (reduces hunger), lemongrass (relieves tension), rosewood (alleviates depression), or juniper (cleans your aura).

the Parroquia, you can get plastered and indulge your Catholic guilt at the same time. Don't stay too late or you may be treated to the church's ear-splitting bell ringing at God knows what hour. *Cuna de Allende 12, upstairs at the Casa Rosada Hotel. ☎ 415/152-0382. Restaurant open 7am–3pm, bar until 11pm.*

Clubs & Supper Clubs

Supper Clubs like Tio Lucas usually have a house band; you buy your dinner (or sit at the bar) and enjoy a ringside seat by the stage with full views of the musicians. Clubs like the Ring are more "traditional" discos—you don't really go there to eat.

→ **La Cava de la Princesa** Set on the bottom floor of a colonial building, this small club space is decorated colorfully with flamingo paraphernalia. This place has been in town for years, with live music from Thursday through Saturday. The sets are usually folk-oriented, with an emphasis on *troba* (acoustic) tunes. The cheesy *espectaculos de imitadores* (Mexican pop star impersonators) night is a hoot. *Recreo 3. ☎ 415/152-1403. Cover $30–$80.*

→ **Mama Mia's** This raucous nightlife institution seems to have endured forever—it certainly has great music if a more hit or miss bar menu and crowd. (It became super touristy a few years ago, but is trying to get back to its roots.) There are four bars on the premises including the weekend-only rooftop bar La Terraza; the Patio Bar downstairs adjoining the restaurant; Leonardo's video sports bar; and Mama's Bar downstairs with live rock (Fri), salsa (Thurs, packed), as well as funk, Latina jazz, and Peruvian folk music/acoustic at the restaurant. Check out Roberto and Trish's free salsa lessons on Tuesday and Wednesday. *Umaron 8. ☎ 415/152-2063 or 415/152-3679. www.mamamia.com.mx. No cover.*

→ **Mechicanos** *The* place to dance salsa in town, Mechicanos gets full of young Mexican kids on the weekends when the DJ spins banda, salsa, rock, and Latin music. The bright red light decor is reminiscent of a bordello but more like Disneyland than something naughty; think Johnny Rockets (burgers, ribs, etc.) meets Gypsy Rose Lee. It's a fun experience in spite of the "tasteful" porn on the walls. *Canal 16. ☎ 415/152-0216. No cover.*

→ **The Ring** Because it boasts a large and airy space, some think this is the best place in town to dance (at least on Tues salsa nights) but others complain that the place is pretty soulless. You be the judge—just note that a shooting happened here in the '90s when the place was inarguably hot. *Hidalgo 25. ☎ 415/152-6789. Cover $80.*

→ **Tio Lucas** This venerable jazz club has been in business for at least 15 years with Robert (Bobby Kap) Kaplan laying down funky jazz licks on Tuesday, Friday, and Saturday. On weekend afternoons, you can

San Miguel de Allende Partying & Sightseeing

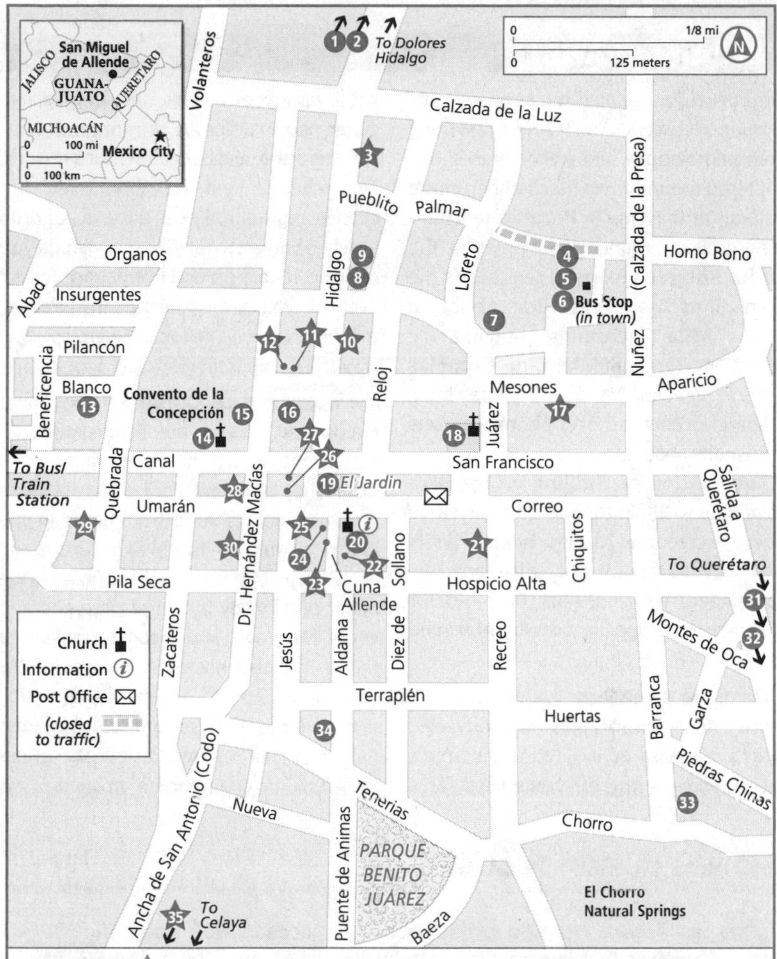

PARTYING ★
Bambu Oxygen Bar **35**
Berlin **28**
Cava de la Princesa **21**
Chocolate Lounge **11**
Foreplay Lounge **3**
La Fragua **23**
Gato Negro **17**
Limerick **26**
Mama Mia **25**
Mechicanos **27**
Petite Bar at Market Bistro **30**
The Ring **10**
Tapas y Tinas **29**
Tio Lucas **12**
Xipal Bar **22**

SIGHTSEEING ●
Bellas Artes **15**
Biblioteca Publica **8**
Casa de la Cultura **33**
La Carpa **2**
Cine Gemelas **31**
Fabrica de la Aurora **1**
Instituto Allende **34**
El Jardin **19**
Jardin Botanico (Charco de Ingenio) **32**
Meditation Center **13**
Mercado de Artesania **4**
Museo Casa de Allende **24**
Oratorio San Felipe **7**
La Parroquia **20**
Plaza Civica **6**
Teatro Angela Peralta **16**
Teatro Santa Ana **9**
Templo de Concepción **14**
Templo de Nuestra Señora de la Salud **5**
Templo de San Francisco **18**
Villa Jacaranda **34**

check out the cool troba of Anita with her accordion. A somewhat older crowd comes here to eat "the best steak in town," while admiring Cece and Polly Stark's colorful extravagant decorative touch. *Mesones 103. ☎ 415/152-4996. No cover.*

Performing Arts

San Miguel has a small but growing performing arts scene. You'll find everything from photography and writer workshops scattered around town, to chamber music festivals at the **Angela Peralta,** to drumming groups or lunar ceremonies at the **Jardín Botanico** (p. 177). Then there's the town's film scene; Spanish flicks are shown at the **Villa Jacaranda** (Aldama 73; **☎ 415/152-1015**), and the **Cine Gemelas** ("Twin Theaters" at the Gigante Mall, Salida Querétaro s/n; no phone)—tickets are usually about $50.

The Biblioteca Publica (p. 157) is a great spot to hit up for info on alternative cinema screenings around town. This is also home to the town's English language newspaper, *Atencion*—your best bet for information on specific goings on around town.

→ **Casa de la Cultura** ★★ Housed in a space that incorporates a converted church, the Casa de la Cultura has an art gallery and a string of rooms used for a wide variety of classes, including piano, guitar, paper cutting art, drawing and painting, literature, and ballet folklorico lessons. The schedule and classes offered can change; register online in advance, or drop by when you get to town to see what they're offering. It's a great and lively space to visit even if you aren't taking any classes, though. *Bajada del Chorro 4. ☎ 415/154-5670. www.iba-etc.org/claboston/index.htm.*

MTV Best → **La Carpa** ★★ This large circus tent houses the Fellini Gourmet restaurant (p. 165) most days, but just as often they also have cool cultural events and "happenings" here. I wandered in one night to find a full-blown Cirque du Soleil–type trapeze thing happening in the midst of a rowdy bunch of partygoers of every race, age, and income bracket. La Carpa has also hosted a Festival of "La Diversidad Sexual," or sexual diversity, along with drag shows and pride parades. Call or e-mail for info on events; prices vary. *Calz. de la Aurora s/n, in front of the*

Movies in San Miguel

In the past decade, San Miguel has become a mecca for Hollywood filmmakers, so much so that there are plans to build a movie studio here. ***The Mexican*** (2001), with Brad Pitt and Julia Roberts, was filmed in San Miguel and the nearby Real de Qatorce. ***And Starring Pancho Villa as Himself*** (2003)**,** the story of Mexican revolutionary Pancho Villa (played by Antonio Banderas), was filmed here and introduced Banderas and wife Melanie Griffith to San Miguel—now they have a home in the area. ***Once Upon a Time in Mexico*** (2003), starring Johnny Depp, Banderas, and Salma Hayek, made residents giddy and crazy at the same time. Whole streets were shut down during filming and residents were not allowed to step outside their homes for entire afternoons; extras were paid a mere $100 to populate the seats in the bullfighting ring for hours. On the other hand, most locals loved that there were movie stars in town. Too bad the movie was so awful.

Fabrica de la Aurora, Col. La Aurora. ☎ *415/ 154-9705 or 152-3620. lacarpa.sm@gmail.com*

➔ **Teatro Angela Peralta** ★★★ The first performance (in 1873) in this beautiful, neoclassical theater was by the most famous Mexican opera singer at that time, Angela Peralta, "the Mexican Nightingale." Today, the theater is still a wonderful place to see theater and dance, or listen to classical or modern music performed by international artists. The Bellas Artes "Festival de Musica de Camara," held annually, features string quartets like the Grammy-winning Turtle Island String Quartet, as well as more traditional international quartets and violinists. The annual Cervantes music festival is also worth checking out for its roster of international performances; call or check *Atencion* for info on what's going on during your visit. *Mesones 63, at Hernandez Macias.* ☎ *415/ 152-2200. Tickets $20–$600.*

Sightseeing

It's difficult to get bored in San Miguel. Though small in size, the town boasts enough sights to warrant taking a walking tour. One to try is the **House and Garden Tour,** sponsored by the Biblioteca Publica. The tour opens the doors of some of the city's most interesting colonial and contemporary houses. Tours leave Sunday at 11:30am from the library at Insurgentes 25 (☎ **415/152-0293**) and last about 2 hours. A $150 donation goes to support various library projects.

The **Centro de Crecimiento,** Zamora Ríos 6, a donation-supported school for children with disabilities, conducts Saturday tours (10am–3pm) to interesting places in the countryside around San Miguel. Donations are $150 per person; tickets are available at Casa Maxwell, a store at Canal 14.

A couple of the most enjoyable walks in town are to the lookout point **El Mirador,** especially at sunset, which colors the whole town and the lake beyond, and to **Parque Juárez,** the town's large and shady park.

Festivals & Events

San Miguel is probably the biggest festival town in Mexico. On any given day, you may be awakened by one of the many saint's day celebrations at 3am at the little chapel right behind your hotel. In addition, Independence Day is celebrated passionately here, as this is where El Grito (p. 113) happened. Celebrations here are also literally explosive. *Castillos* (castles), which are brought out for any and all parties, are fragile looking, elaborate constructions of fireworks, which take the rocket makers months to construct. Watching one of these go off is like witnessing pyrotechnic dominoes—each layer ignites the one above it. It's supremely dangerous, but definitely cool.

In addition to checking out the monthly festival info outlined below, you can find more info on the town's festivals on the websites **www.internetsanmiguel.com** and **www.portalsanmiguel.com**.

January

Tres Reyes Magos or "Three Kings' Day": Kids get "Christmas" presents today (*not* on Dec 25) to commemorate the Three Wise Men. See p. 21. January 6.

St. Anthony's Day: Also called "blessing of the animals," this day is celebrated all over Mexico and is best observed at outlying villages (like Cruz del Palmar, off the road to Guanajuato). January 17.

Natalicio del General Ignacio Allende y Unzaga: Military and civic parades are held to commemorate the birthday of Insurgent hero General Ignacio Allende. January 21.

Departure of Pilgrims for San Juan de los Lagos: Thousands make the 5-day walk to pay tribute to the Virgen de San Juan de Los Lagos, in the state of Jalisco.

Semana Santa (Holy Week)

Semana Santa, or Holy Week, is San Miguel's most significant community event, and you'll probably wind up joining the festivities (or at least watching them), no matter what your religious beliefs are. It typically begins two Sundays before Easter with a display of **El Señor de la Columna,** an incredibly bloody rendition of Jesus). The life-size statue was carved and painted in 1823 for the **Atotonilco Church,** Salida Dolores Km 12, and makes its trip to the San Juan Church in San Miguel two weeks before Easter. Five days later, on **Friday of the Sorrows,** there are special masses at the Oratorio and San Francisco churches, and local families open up their houses to show off their Easter altars.

On **Palm Sunday** there's another public procession starting in the Parque Juárez that leads to the Parroquia, punctuated by strolling bands, more **home altars** (especially along Sollano and at Atotonilco), fireworks, and singing. On Wednesday there's yet another procession, from the Oratorio to the Church of San Rafael. Then on **Holy Thursday,** the Last Supper is celebrated and the truly faithful do their best to visit at least seven churches.

The Mother of All Processions takes place on **Good Friday**—the one day a year when the church bells of San Miguel fall silent—and the entire town shuts down, lining the streets to watch three processions, from San Juan, the Parroquia, and the Oratorio. The women dress in black, representing the "widows of Christ." The men dress either in black mourning suits, acting as pall bearers (of the El Señor de la Columna, once again), or as Roman soldiers. The procession winds around town at a snail's pace, stopping every block or so for a prayer.

On the **night before Easter**, the church bells are again in full force, pealing in the day with an ecstatic abandon. Fireworks erupt from all over town and everyone spills out into the streets to do what San Miguelenses do best—party. Finally, on **Easter Sunday**, masses aren't very crowded, as many locals stay home to nurse hangovers. By evening, everyone returns to the Jardín to watch the last (and biggest) fireworks display of the week send off the festivities with a bang.

You can go, too, to raise money for CASA (p. 180). Log onto www.internetsanmiguel.com/insiders-guide/insiders-guide-jd03.html for info. January 24.

February

Candelaria Day: A religious holiday which gets translated in San Miguel as a fantastic week-long plant fair in Benito Juárez Park. Look for Indian dancers strutting their stuff in front of the Parroquia from dawn until dusk. Log onto www.sanmiguelguide.com/candelaria.htm. February 2.

March

El Señor de la Conquista: Dancers in indigenous costume perform all day in front of the Parroquia to honor the statue of Christ housed there. Log onto www.portalsanmiguel.com/things-to-do/festivals.html. March 5.

Día de Benito Juárez: National holiday to celebrate the birthday of hero and ex-president Benito Juárez. March 21.

April

Día del Niño, or "Kids Day": A very sweet holiday in San Miguel when you'll see young girls dressed as princesses, tulips, buttercups, whatever. April 30.

May

Feast of Santa Cruz: Day of masons and builders. If you're building a home here, this is the day to honor your workers with a big pile of *carnitas* and *mucho cerveza.* Party down. May 3.

Cinco de Mayo: See p. 22. May 5.

June

San Antonio de Padua: This festival actually celebrates spring, but in San Miguel it is one of the year's most fun and creative excuses for a party called **Día de los Locos.** It's marked with a parade of "locos," people from various neighborhoods, businesses, and families who literally go crazy by dressing as political characters, fluffy toys, birds, or simply cross-dressing. The locos then throw candy at regularly dressed folks to get them to join in dancing wildly through the streets. June 19.

August

The Festival de Música de Cámara. This wonderful classical music festival brings international musicians to San Miguel for 2 weeks of concerts and workshops. Classes are taught by visiting quartets, which have included the St. Petersburg String Quartet, the Ying Quartet, and the José White String Quartet, as well as individual musicians including Elinor Freer, Sadao Harada, Joji Hattori, and Jasminka Stancul. Many concerts are in the Angela Peralta Theater (p. 171); there are also free concerts daily in the Jardín, the Public Library, or the Auditorium of Bellas Artes. Admission is $250 to $350 depending on the venue. Early August.

September

September is pretty much a month of festivals. The party starts slowly on September 13 with the **Commemoration of the Death of the Child Heroes,** the excitement escalates to **El Grito** on September 15 (literally "the shout," commemorating Father Hidalgo's famous speech calling people to fight for Independence). On El Grito night, crowds gather in the Jardín to set off giant *castillos.* You can even get up on the stage and dance with half the town. Next up is **Independence Day** on the 16th, when the Jardín is full of parading military bands, officials making speeches, and kids eating ice cream. The following weekend the MTV Best **Pamplonada** (the running of the bulls) descends. Mature bulls are let loose in the streets, lined with drunken crowds who wait for hours to "fight" the bulls—someone gets gored (or shot) every year. It's pretty much an excuse to get drunk for 2 days straight; the town is so overrun with tourists (acting badly) from all over Mexico that most residents just lock themselves inside their homes and watch from their roofs.

Things finally calm down the last weekend of the month, when the **Sanmiguelada,** or **Día de San Miguel Archangel** is held. This is pretty much a quiet family- and town-based affair, except for the fireworks (big, loud ones, of course) set off at 4am for an hour to reenact the battle of Lucifer and St. Michael. The festival also features a spectacular procession of dance groups from all over Mexico wearing traditional costumes and carrying 15m-high (49-ft.) floral arrangements.

October

Feast of San Miguel Arcángel: Stroll by the Instituto Allende to see people getting ready with their fabulous costumes before parading up to the Jardín. The weeklong **Octava,** a series of processions that takes the statue of Saint Michael from the Parroquia to visit other local churches, also starts today. First Sunday of October.

Also during October you must find time to cruise over to the capitol city Guanajuato for the 2-week-long, famous **Cervantino Festival** (www.festival

Free & Easy

San Miguel boasts tons of free things to do and see—you'll just have to time things right. The **Museo Allende** (p. 175) is free on Sundays and, if nothing else, is worth visiting to see the inside of the beautiful baroque building. The **Instituto Allende** (Archa de San Antonio 22, Zona Centro; ☎ **415/152-0190;** www.instituto-allende.edu.mx/) and **Bellas Artes** (p. 161) are free to the public on certain days and are lovely places for strolling, in addition to checking out art. The galleries at **La Fabrica de la Aurora** (p. 175) are a bit formal, but they're still good, free places to view art and try out design workshops. Finally, free art openings are posted on bulletin boards at the entrance to the town's schools and in the *Atencion.* Or you can log onto www.portalsanmiguel to see what artists are showing in town; even if the art's not great, the wine should be free.

Of course, you don't have to pay to go out and watch (or participate in) any of the town's amazing festivals (see "Festivals & Events" earlier) and sites like La Parroquia are always free during open hours.

cervantino.gob.mx/Ficesmas). This festival features music varying from mariachi to opera, theater productions, dancing, and a cinema series. You can buy tickets via Ticketmaster for some shows; check out www.festivalcervantino.gob.mx.

November

All Saints Day and **Día de los Muertos**: San Miguel may not celebrate this day of the dead as fantastically as other cities in Mexico (see "Basics," p. 22), but there's still plenty to offer: You can check out the local cemetery on the Salida a Celaya to see decorations, go by the market to get a candy skull or two, and take a stroll to see various homes and businesses which have their altars on display (like the Museo Allende). November 1 and 2.

Día de la Revolución: On this national holiday, all of Mexico commemorates the Mexican Revolution. November 20.

International Jazz Festival: This annual jazz festival brings in musicians from around the world to the Bellas Artes Theater (and other spots around town) for a weeklong party in homage to jazz. November 25–27.

December

Día de Nuestra Señora de Guadalupe: This religious day is probably most feverishly celebrated in Mexico City, but celebrations do take place at San Miguel's various churches. You may be invited into someone's home to drink atole while they recite an endless Mass. December 12.

Las Posadas: These Christmas celebrations take place on each of the nine nights preceding Christmas, when the Holy Family's search for an inn is reenacted with candlelit processions through the streets. See the *Atencion* for a schedule and location, as the church participants leave from changes nightly. December 16–24.

Navidad (Christmas): During Christmas season, many homes in town display altars or extensively decorated private chapels. You also may come across small fiestas held in nearby ranchos, such as the one at La Banda on Christmas Day. December 25.

Galleries

There are galleries all over town, many in the complex **Pila Seca Tres** (Pila Seca 3;

☎ **415/154-6825;** open Mon–Fri 10am–2pm and 4–6pm; Sat 10am–2pm). It houses several artists such as **Mary Jane Miller** (www.sanmiguelicons.com), who fashions icons using repose technique; **Marjorie Heady** (☎ **415/154-5203**) who creates contemporary sculpture; and **Victor Heady** (☎ **415/152-2141**), a painter.

There are also several galleries around the corner on Jesus, like the **Caracol Collection** (Cuadrante 30 corner of Jesus; ☎ **415/152-1617**); the **Galería de Arte Fotografico** (Reloj 46; ☎ **415/152-2483**); and the **Galería Arte Contemporaneo San Miguel** (Plaza Principal 14; ☎ **415/152-0454;** ssgalsanmig@hotmail.com).

You may have just come from Mexico City, but if you want to go back and buy art there, consider taking a tour with **Anita Middleton**, who does fine art tours there. She not only reps contemporary Mexican artists but also will take you to artists' studios and contemporary art museums to help you find that perfect piece to take home. Call ☎ **415/152-5509** or visit www.anitamiddleton.com for info.

Built in a former 1902 fabric factory, the design center **Fabrica de la Aurora** (Salida a Dolores s/n; no phone; www.fabricalaaurora.com; most shops Mon–Fri 10am–6pm; some on weekends) on the edge of town now houses 13 working artists as well as galleries, fashion ateliers such as Christopher Fallon, furniture and interior designer D'Wayne Youts (two of the founders), and many more shops. The **Cantador Antiguedades** and **La Buhardilla,** both filled with high-quality Mexican antique furniture, paintings, and folk art, are worth the trip alone. Though essentially an art mall, the space feels sophisticated, if a bit pretentious and expensive. There's a real factory full of seamstresses for a jolt of reality, and the large circus tent at the entrance hosts the restaurant Fellini (p. 165). There's a map at the entrance, but the spaces don't have numbers.

Major Attractions

The **Plaza Civica** in front of the Templo de Nuestra (see below), built in 1555, was once the center of the town, not the Jardín. Today, in addition to most of the sites described below, the plaza boasts a daily covered market (behind the church) where you can get fresh and cheap fruit, vegetables, flowers, and dry goods, as well as the **Mercado de Artesanías** (see "Shopping," p. 178).

MTV Best FREE ➔ **La Parroquia** ★★★ Built in the late 17th century as San Miguel's original parish church, the Parroquia became an amazing neo-Gothic fantasy when Zeferino Gutierrez, a master stone mason, was commissioned in 1880 to create a new facade. The current pink swirling incarnation looks like an ice cream cone on acid. On weekends, the cross on top is lit with high wattage light bulbs for an added surreal touch. The inside is not nearly as fun as the outside; still there are things to see, like the crypt beneath the altar. You get to it through a door on the right side but will have to seek out the caretaker to unlock the door. *Plaza Principal on Correo. No phone. Free admission. Daily 8am–2pm and 5–9pm.*

➔ **Museo Casa de Allende** This 18th-century two-story baroque building was the birthplace of Ignacio Allende, and is a perfect example of homes built by colonial nobility. Inside are exhibits intended to explain the roles the area played in the context of national development as well as the history of the region from pre-historic times to recent history. The result is somewhat of a hodgepodge of pre-Columbian art, archaeology, and the area's history centering on Allende's role in the fight for Independence. Though most are

How to Cook Like a San Miguelense

If you want to sharpen your culinary skills in this food-loving town, you have several options for courses, everything from one-shot classes to weeklong extravagant tours.

Victoria Popovsky (☎ **415/152-5912;** flavorsofthesun@yahoo.com) is a veteran of Food TV and was featured on "The Castaways of San Miguel." She demystifies Mexican cooking in her classes "Chiles for Gringos" (which includes a trip to the market), and various Mexican regional classes that incorporate Mexican culinary history, ethno-botany, and food anthropology. Modern classes cook dishes such as goat-cheese-stuffed chicken with roasted chile and almond sauce, and her recipes are clear and easy enough to re-create on your return home. One-shot classes are offered weekly and start at $709 per person (never more than 10 students at a time) during high season.

Kris Rudolph (☎ **415/152-5807;** www.mexicocooks.com) of the **Buen Café** (Jesus 23; ☎ **415/152-5807**) teaches traditional Mexican food courses (one class for $491–$709) and includes appetizers, margaritas, dinner with dessert, and a recipe packet. Classes are held Thursdays from 4 to 7pm. Her **Culinary Adventures of Mexico** also offers one-week intensive culinary tours ($19,075 or $23,980 for singles), in which you stay in a colonial home in San Miguel and participate in hands-on cooking classes, then visit Guanajuato, Dolores Hidalgo, and Pozos.

Chef, caterer, and longtime resident **Patsy Dubois,** Carretera Dolores, on the road to Dolores (☎ **415/185-2151** or 044/415-153-5303 cell; www.patsydubois.com) uses vegetables from her garden and greenhouse and teaches the basics about Mexican food. A 4-hour introductory class is $545, and you get to snack the whole time and perhaps partake in a margarita or two. She can also organize 3-day classes for groups of four to six.

somewhat staid exhibits, it's worth going inside just to see the architectural details of the building. *Cuna de Allende 1, at the Plaza Principal.* ☎ *415/152-2499. Admission $30, free on Sun. Tues–Sun 9am–5pm.*

➜ **Templo de la Concepción** Originally constructed between 1755 and 1842 as part of a complex which housed a convent for the sisters of the Immaculate Conception, this church still puts up nuns—you may catch a glimpse of them around holidays. Since the church adjoins the Bellas Artes (see Las Musas, p. 166), I recommend grabbing a seat in their courtyard to soak in the view of the church's beautiful dome, by Zeferino Gutierrez (the stone mason who created the Parroquia's facade). *Canal at Hidalgo.*

➜ **Templo de San Francisco** This church boasts an amazing Churrigueresque facade with a sharply contrasting neoclassical tower, which was added later by architect Francisco Eduardo Tresguerras. *At San Francisco and Juarez.*

Playing Outside

If you're sick of eating, shopping, and history, you can easily get your heart pumping via one of the many outdoor options in and around town. Following are the best adventure activities.

Ballooning

For a bird's-eye view of San Miguel, Jay Kimball's hot air ballooning tours are really fantastic. They take off daily at sunrise and soar quietly over the Parroquia and rooftops of San Miguel, and on up the Santo Domingo arroyo and finally out to a field where you'll be picked up for the drive back to town. Call ☎ **415/152-6735** (or 310/734-4109 in the U.S.). Cost is $1,908 per person for a 1-hour ride.

Biking

With hundreds of kilometers of single- and double-track in the surrounding countryside, San Miguel is a mountain biking mecca. The best way to explore the area if you don't have your own bike is with Beto Martinez or one of his guides from **Bici Burro,** Hospicio 1 (☎ **415/152-1526;** www.bici-burro.com). A native San Miguelense, the amiable and funny Beto knows every single track out there as well as the history of the nearby small towns and hidden archaeological and religious ruins. His tires are "slimed" to combat the cactus and mesquite thorns, and he is an experienced and well-equipped biker as well as a guide. Six-hour tours include transport, bikes, gloves, and helmets. Some include a soak in the area hot springs afterwards, or an optional lunch. Tours range from $600 to $850.

Brought your own bike and got it tangled in a cactus? You can get it repaired at **Mountain Bike Reparacion de Bicicletas** by Valentin Rodriguez, Av. Independencia 13a, Colonia Independencia (no phone).

Horseback Riding

Coyote Canyon Tours (☎ **415/154-4193;** www.coyotecanyonadventures.com) specializes in horseback riding tours by real wranglers who know the area and are willing to take you hiking, mountain biking, and rock climbing if you show an interest in the outback. **Sol y Luna Tours** (☎ **415/154-5551;** www.solylunatours.com) also has horseback riding and hiking trips to nearby towns.

For some serious horseback riding, try the **3 Senores** (☎ **044/415-101-4976;** www.3senores.com), just over the train tracks from the old train station. As the first stable in San Miguel, the horses here are healthy and well trained. They can take you on 2- to 3-hour trips in the country to

Jardín Botanico

One of the most popular hiking/biking spots in San Miguel is the beautiful **El Charco del Ingenio,** known locally as the **Jardín Botanico.** Open daily from sunrise to sunset, this 88-hectare (220-acre) park surrounds *la presa* (a man-made lake) and offers miles of groomed trails. The area was rescued by the ecological group Cante when the area was slated for condominium development a few years ago; with species of every cacti in Mexico, plus flocks of white egrets, herons, ducks, and other migrating birds, it is one of those places that just makes you happy to be alive—and forever grateful to eco organizations. El Charco is located on a plateau at the top of town above Balcones. Walk to the end of the Cuesta de San José, or take a taxi up and walk back (alternatively it's a couple of kilometers down a dirt road off the Salida Querétaro behind Gigante). Call ☎ **415/154-4715** or 154-8838, or log onto www.laneta.apc.org/charco (check for special guided walks, moon viewings, and monthly temazcal ceremonies). The cost is $30 per day or $500 for a yearly membership.

San Miguel Viejo or other towns depending on your skill level. They also offer classes, boarding, camping tours, and film production services. The cost of an average horseback riding session is $600 per person, including soft drinks/water.

Mind & Body

The **Meditation Center of San Miguel,** Callejon Blanco 4 at Quebrada (☎ **415/152–2659**), is Buddhist-oriented, but all are welcome. Sitting (8am and 8:50am) and walking (8:40am) meditations are held Monday through Friday in this space centered on Zen, Tibetan, and Vipassana traditions. Sunday morning service is conducted by a local branch of the **Self Realization Fellowship** (www.homepage.mac.com/yoganorman/yoga/srfdevotees.html) at 8:30am. Watch for spiritually oriented videos on Thursdays. Guest rooms are available for up to 2 weeks for those trying to go deeper into meditation.

For yoga, try a session with **Norman Popovsky** (☎ **415/152-1852;** www.yoganorman.com), who has studied and taught yoga for more than 35 years. The form of hatha yoga that Norman teaches focuses on meditation and self-improvement. He also offers classes on stress management, yoga therapy, and successful living at $100 per class; most are held from 10am to 11:15am Monday through Friday at the Meditation Center.

Life Path, Recreo 80 (☎ **415/154-8465;** www.lifepathretreats.com), offers retreats that range from 1-day escapes to ongoing open classes on Enneagram, dream interpretation, journal writing, massage therapy, and body-work or acupuncture. Another good (and cheap) alternative medicine option, offering services in acupuncture and hot stone massage as well as a health diagnosis by a licensed naturopath, is **Shanti Revotski and her partner Miguel** (☎ **415/152-5909**).

Swimming

For swimming in town, **Club Deportivo Santo Domingo,** Santo Domingo 46 (spinningsma@hotmail.com), has a beautiful, heated, and partially covered lap pool for $50 per day (cheaper by the week/month) as well as a fully equipped gym with aerobic classes. It's open Monday through Friday 7am to 3pm and 4pm to 8:30pm.

You can't leave San Miguel without visiting the nearby hot springs, about 8 to 10km (5–6 miles) outside San Miguel. **La Gruta** (Carretera a Dolores Km 10; on the left side just after the turn-off to Atotonilco), has a funky underground hot mineral water grotto and used to be my favorite in the area. It's getting crowded and a bit overdeveloped, though. It's still a cool only-in-Mexico experience, though, and cheap, at only $80. If you want to swim laps in a long, warm mineral water pool and then soak in a hot(ter) tub, try **La Taboada** (Carretera a Dolores Hidalgo Km 8; ☎ **415/152-9250**), for $50. There's also a big area for picnicking or rowdy Sunday afternoon volleyball games with the locals.

Shopping

San Miguel de Allende is a shopaholic's dream. There are a great variety of stores here including international fine art spots; shops that specialize in the local regional crafts of tinsmith, ironwork, and glass blowing; and little stationery stores with hand-cut paper decorations as well as quirky '50s posters.

Art & Crafts

Even though San Miguel is very much an art colony, there is also somewhat uneven fine art to be found in the galleries all over town; see "Galleries," above for the best.

La Calaca ★★★, Mesones 93, at Hidalgo (☎ **415/152-3954**), has the town's best (and most expensive) collection of folk art. Owner Evita Avery, who has worked as a museum consultant, is a folk art specialist who travels all over Mexico and Guatemala buying traditional, antique, and contemporary folk art. Her shop is filled with textiles, ceremonial folk art, costumes, Linares family papier-mâché, silver leaf–lacquered gourds, and traditional-style silver jewelry.

Zocolo ★★, Hernandez Macias 110 (☎ **415/152-0663;** www.zocalotx.com), has another wonderful collection of folk art, with a great variety of work from Oaxaca, Puebla, Michoucan, Jalisco, Guerro, and the state of Mexico. This reasonable to expensive store is chock full of great stuff, including great green pineapple ceramics from Michoucan, anima-style home altars, and other (more expensive) museum-quality pieces from master craftsmen. The owners, Rick and Debra Hall, are interested in ritual folk art that can be practical as well as decorative.

Akitsch ★★, Cuna de Allende 12, on the second floor of the Casa Rosada Hotel (☎ **415/152-8123**), is chock full of kitsch goodies as its name implies. You'll find all things Mexican wrestler-related, belt buckle crosses, Guadalupe holy water bottles, hot pink velvet mariachi hats, virgin/sacred heart jewelry galore, and puny tees from Naco.

Fai (Save Children Mexico), Hidalgo 13, Centro (☎ **415/152-3686;** www. savethe childrenmexico.org), has hand-made aprons, rugs, wool shawls, woven and embroidered pillows, mesquite flower honey, and traditional medicine from Guanajuato women's co-ops who receive 50% of each sale.

Other local art services include fine framing at **La Fortuna,** Pila Seca 3 (☎ **415/152-7782**). This is the only place in town that specializes in conservation and preservation of fine art, photographs, and textiles. Framer Karen Clements and her husband Richard use 100% acid-free materials and can get or make any kind of frame you desire.

Bookstores

English and Spanish books can be found at the **El Colibri,** Sollano 30 (☎ **415/152-0751**), which has been in town for years, and has artists' materials and magazines as well as bestsellers, paperbacks, and art and language books.

A better variety can be found at **El Tecolote** ★, Jesus 11, at **La Parroquia Café** (☎ **415/152-7395;** tecolotebooks@yahoo.com). Owner Mary has a great range of art and home design books as well as books on Mexican art and history, Spanish language books, and a discounted used section (mostly novels) in back. **Casa de Papel,** Mesones 57 (☎ **415/154-5187**), has road maps, CDs, photo albums, scrapbooks, cards, and journals.

Home Decor

Because of the huge influx of American expats seeking giant homes in town, the home decorating shops here have grown in proportion. At **Insh'ala,** Aldama 30 (☎ **415/152-8335**), owner Carol Romano has a wonderful collection of art and design items from Morocco and other Arabic-influenced countries, including fine tribal rugs, ceramics, furniture, and sculpture. **Icapalli,** Correo 43 (☎ **415/152-1236;** icpalli@cybermatsa.com.mx), can order you tile from Dolores Hidalgo (the wonderful Angelica Baca has been known to bring back matching tiles to save you the trip), as well as fabrics.

Volunteer Ops

You have several options for volunteering in San Miguel. One of the most worthwhile grass-roots organizations benefiting women and children is **CASA,** (Santa Julia 15, Colonia Santa Julia; ☎ **415/152-0129** or 310/593-4358 in U.S.; www.sanmiguelwalk.com). They run a variety of programs and sponsor **The San Miguel Walk,** a yearly fundraiser held in conjunction with a 5-day pilgrimage to view the Virgin at San Juan de Los Lagos. During this life-changing experience, you'll walk every day with thousands of other Mexican religious pilgrims and disseminate information to combat violence against women.

Numerous groups allow you to work with needy children. You can help out at the local orphanage at **Casa Hogar Santa Julia** (☎ **415/152-3426;** faydugas@aol.com); at the boys' orphanage of **Santuario Hogar Guadalupano** (☎ **415/152-5082**); at the Mexican **Head Start** Program, **Centro Infantil San Pablo** (☎ **415/152-0387;** www.Centroinfantil.org.mx); at **Patronato Pro Ninos,** San Francisco 1, second floor (☎ **415/152-7290;** ppn@unisono.net.mx), which provides medical assistance and free dental care to children in and around San Miguel; or at **Centro de Crecimiento,** Zamora Rios 6 (☎ **415/152-0318;** www.cdecsma.org), a rehab center for disabled children in San Miguel and nearby rural areas. You can also help feed kids at **Feed the Hungry** (☎ **415/152-2402;** www.feedthehungrysma.org).

The **Amigos de Animales** (www.amigosdeanimalessma.org) is dedicated to helping abused animals. Amigos has spayed and neutered over 4,500 animals in the last 3 years, and has developed outreach programs to the poorer communities outside of San Miguel.

The Audubon Society in San Miguel (☎**044/415-103-3791;** www.audubonmex.org), the only Audubon organization in all of Mexico, works actively on water and other ecological issues. There are also plenty of volunteer opportunities at the Jardín Botanico (see p. 177).

Jewelry & Clothes

There are many little shops all over town with embroidered blouses; **El Nuevo Mundo,** San Francisco 17 (☎ **415/152-6180**), has a good if expensive selection and full-tiered cotton skirts from India, but it's rough going if you're looking for something a bit more fashionable or tailored. Although a bit pricey, **Diva,** Hernandez Macias 72 (☎ **415/152-4980;** www.theateroflife.com), has tooled leather purses, hats, and belts; shawls; linen clothing; and jewelry. Go upstairs in the same building to find the **Diva outlet** with last season's offerings (they don't change much), at up to 75% off.

If you like flea markets, go bargain for silver, ceramic, and leather goods at the 3-block long **Mercado de Artesanías** (open daily 9am–8pm) behind the Plaza Civica's **Ignacio Ramirez Market.**

Need a bag to carry all your loot around in? Then stop by **De Todo un Poco** (Mesones 56; no phone), which carries a huge variety of *bolsas* (plastic mesh or hand-woven bags) and other funky/chic plastic ware for $50 to $100.

Pharmacies

San Miguel is a mecca of alternative medicine and treatments. **Farmacia**

Homeopática, Mesones 67 (☎ **415/152-0230**), offers a full supply of homeopathic medicine and also the services of Dr. Antonio Garcia Gonzalez, who offers consultations for $250. The various remedies, at $30 to $100, are at about a tenth of U.S. prices. You can also receive a consultation via e-mail at lucano68@hotmail.com.

Alternatively—as it were—try Alison at **La Victoriana,** Hernandez Macias 72, next to Buena Vida (☎ **415/152-6903;** www.lavictoriana.com), for consultations as well as remedies. The store specializes in natural cosmetics and hair treatments, but also sells and hand-made lace lingerie and children's clothes.

Cancún

Cancún, which means "golden snake" in the Mayan language, is downright reptilian in its design: Its narrow strip of land, most of which is devoted to the Hotel Zone, snakes around the calm turquoise waters of the Caribbean on one side and a crocodile-infested lagoon on the other. This landscape lends a definite indulgent vibe to the coastal city: since visitors are virtually stranded between two powerful bodies of water, there's nowhere to go but to all the luxurious hotels, fantastic restaurants, and pristine beaches. In this sun-drenched city, anything is possible, every amenity you could desire is available, and nothing is too outrageous to try at least once.

If cities were celebrities, Cancún would be the eternal It Girl, always golden, always hot, always in the spotlight wearing the most outrageous outfit on the red carpet. The *Village Voice* recently compared Coco Bongo, Cancún's most regaled nightclub, to a rocking combination of Studio 54 and the best live shows in Vegas, and that's an apt comparison. Where else but Cancún can you find both mediocre joints where you can drink for free (if you're female), and clubs with astronomical covers that you don't mind paying? (And I say that as someone who *never* pays a cover.) Once you are livin' the fantasy, you won't regret that your wallet is 400 pesos lighter, only that you hadn't saved up a little more cash to do it all again tomorrow night.

Any given night in a Cancún club might involve trapeze artists in neon outfits re-enacting the fights of famous comic book heroes, above scantily clad dancing women, while at least one guy in a gorilla suit whacks patrons with a giant balloon to get them to join the conga line. All of this plays out against a never-ending soundtrack of both new and old Top 40 jams. Once your thirst has been properly quenched by your servers (servers in Cancún are *always* at the ready with their tequila shot holsters), all this sensory overload will be just what the doctor ordered. Just don't party so hard that you over-sleep the beach. "Unreal" is the word most commonly uttered by foreigners first confronted with the intense transparent turquoise water here—it makes the Gulf of Mexico look like a cast-off jar of brackish pickle brine.

If Cancun's mix of raging parties for the nighttime and beautiful beaches for the daytime seems fabricated to fulfill the vacation fantasies of tourists, that's because it was. In 1967, the state-sponsored Mexican National Tourist Association systematically chose this area as the best spot for international tourism; the MNTA cited the area's clear waters, soft sands, low frequency of hurricanes, and a location close enough to the U.S. to allow for short, cheap flights south of the border. The idea was that a big spender could be in New York City for lunch, and Cancún by dinner. So, if you are an offbeat backpacker, looking for a city with great hostels, museums, and loads of local flavor, you should probably head somewhere like Mérida, the longtime capital city of the Yucatán. But if you want to have fun in the sun during the day and party like a rock star at night, you won't be disappointed by Cancún's exquisite excess.

Best of Cancún

- **Best Hotel for Avoiding Gringos:** Entering **Hotel Xbalamque** is like descending into a Maya temple then discovering modern luxuries within its historic walls. Tropical birds in hand-woven wicker cages the size of closets line the lobby, and candelabras balance atop mountains of wax drips amid shelves of books in the revolutionary cafe named after Adelita, the wife of Pancho Villa. From warm golden lighting in the rooms to the hot salsa club next door, this truly authentic hotel in the heart of El Centro is a destination for travelers searching for the Mexican heart of Cancún. Exotic and lavishly decorated, Hotel Xbalamque is a refreshing antidote to all of the white-washed American super resorts. See p. 193.
- **Best Ecohotel:** From composting to solar power to vegetarian specialties, **El Rey del Caribe Hotel** has all its earth friendly bases covered, and it doesn't skimp on the little indulgences like air-conditioning that you'd seek out in a less caring resort. Lush jungle vegetation (including over 20 species of rare orchids) surrounds the buildings, borders the pool, and overflows from the inner courtyard. Opportunities for mind-opening learning experiences abound, with workshops available in yoga, tai chi, tarot card reading, and other new age faves. See p. 192.
- **Best Yucatecan Cuisine: Labna** is hands down the best Yucatecan restaurant in Cancún. The menu boasts perfect *panuchos,* mind-altering chile rellenos, fantastic flan, and delicious table salsas, including roasted pumpkin seed pate and olive jalapeño tapenade. Even if the food wasn't that good (and cheap), this high-ceilinged eatery would be worth a visit just to take in the eclectic lighting, which includes lanterns made of giant snail shells, stained glass snakes, and real bird's nests. See p. 197.
- **Best Place to Party Like It's the End of the World:** When the apocalypse nears, run, don't walk, to **Coco Bongo.**

Back to back performances by expert aerialists, dead-on celebrity impersonators, and hot dancers, all take place overhead in front of giant high resolution movie screens while below the wildest crowd in Cancún dances like it's 1999 on the multileveled floor. There is no *official* dance floor, though, so all of the bumping and grinding to the throbbing pop hits takes place on top of tables, chairs, and of course, the giant elevated bar in the center of the room. Cover includes unlimited drinks, so the crowd gets more outrageous as the night wears on. The sensory overload is so intense that when the trigger-happy bartenders squirt you with frozen CO_2 fire extinguishers and booze, you'll be genuinely grateful for the cool down. See p. 201.

Getting There & Getting Around

Getting into Town

BY PLANE It keeps getting easier and easier to fly nonstop to Cancún on many domestic airlines. To compare rates go to any of the competitive travel websites (see "Basics," p. 26) where you can also purchase your tickets directly online. Flights fly into **Aeropuerto International de Cancún** (☎ **998/886-0028**), located south of Cancún on Highway 307, about 24km (15 miles) from the beginning of the Zona Hotelera and 40km (25 miles) from El Centro or downtown.

AeroMexico (☎ **800/237-6639** in the U.S. or 800/021-4000 in Mexico; www.aeromexico.com) offers direct service from Atlanta, Houston, Miami, and New York, as well as connecting service via Mexico City from Dallas, Los Angeles, and San Diego. **Mexicana** (☎ **800/531-7921** in the U.S. or 800/502-2000 or 998/881-9090 in Mexico; www.mexicana.com.mx) flies direct from Chicago, Denver, Los Angeles, Oakland, San Antonio, San Francisco, and San Jose via Mexico City, with nonstop service from Miami and New York.

Regional budget carrier **Click Mexicana** (☎ **800/11-CLICK;** www.clickmx.com), flies from Cozumel, Havana, Mexico City, Mérida, Chetumal, and other cities within Mexico. Other budget carriers that fly to Cancún include **Viva AeroBus** (www.vivaerobus.com) and **AeroMar** (www.aeromar.com).

If you need to confirm departure times for flights into the U.S., here are Cancún-based contact numbers for the major domestic international carriers: **American** (☎ **998/883-4461;** www.aa.com), **Continental** (☎ **998/886-0006;** www.continental.com), and **Northwest** (☎ **998/886-0044** or 998/886-0046; www.nwa.com).

BY BUS Considering the steep cost of renting a car by day (see below), a first-class bus can be an easier and relatively cheap option. **ADO's** (☎ **998/884-4352**) first-class buses are air-conditioned, play movies in both English and Spanish (usually one of each on long trips) with reclining chairs. The **ADO Bus Station** is in El Centro (Downtown Cancún) on the corner of avenidas Ixmal and Tulum (☎ **998/884-1378,** or 800/702-8000 from the U.S.).

Buses run to Cancún from just about every destination in Mexico, from urban and resort centers such as Mérida and Playa del Carmen, to within walking distance of the ruins of Chichén Itzá and Tulum. One ticket for a 4-hour bus ride (with two movies) to or from Mérida is $200, with most rates for closer locations between $40 and $100.

BY TAXI OR SHUTTLE VAN It's not necessary to take a taxi back to your hotel from the airport, as there are reliable **van services** by the airport exits. These vans are much more reasonably priced, with helpful drivers who usually speak English. You may have to make stops at other hotels before you get to yours (so you're looking at an hour ride on the shuttle versus a half-hour taxi ride).

Green Line Shuttle conveniently has a booth right outside the only international exit from the airport, so you have to pass them to leave the airport; you might as well buy a ticket for $90 (fee for all hotel drop-offs) and be on your way. For the return trip back to the airport you will have to take a taxi or a bus, as there are no shuttles from the hotels.

If you opt for a **taxi** to or from the airport, it will set you back $200. Do not pay more than this and negotiate this price upfront. Drivers often take advantage of clueless tourists by charging them up to $300 to $400.

BY CAR To get to the coast by land, the fastest and most well-paved route from most major Mexican cities to Cancún is Highway 180, which you follow east all the way to Cancún. The distance from Mérida is approximately 81km (50 miles), and takes about 4 hours in fair weather. Highway 180 is a two-lane road that splits into 180D, an express toll road between Izamal and Nuevo Xcan. Once you reach Nuevo Xcan, you are about halfway to Cancún. If you're coming from the south, take Highway 307N, which is well-marked with signs to Cancún.

If you're planning on renting a car, it's wise to shop rates for the rental and book before you depart for your trip; you may be able to get a special deal if you're renting for more than 3 days. If you wait until you arrive at the airport, the lowest daily cost for any rental car hovers around $500. All the major rental car companies are at the airport; their representatives speak English.

Reliable rental car companies include **Avis** (☎ **800/527-0700** in the U.S., or 998/886-0221; fax 998/886-0021 in Mexico; www.avis.com); **Budget** (☎ **800/527-0700** in the U.S., or 998/886-0417; fax 998/884-4812 in Mexico; www.budget.com); **Dollar** (☎ **800/800-4000** in the U.S. or 998/884-1326 in Mexico; www.dollar.com); **Hertz** (☎ **800/654-3131** in the U.S. and Canada, or 998/884-1326 in Mexico; www.hertz.com); and **National** (☎ **800/328-4567** in the U.S. or 998/886-0655; www.nationalcar.com).

To drive to your hotel from the airport: Follow signs to Bulevar Kulkulcan, and take that for about 11km (7 miles) to the Zona Hotelera (Hotel Zone), where the majority of luxury hotels are located. You'll see hotels and attractions on both sides of the road. If you are headed to El Centro, home of more affordable hotels, follow Kulkulcan for another 16km (10 miles), all the way through the Zona Hotelera and beyond. This will lead you to Avenida Tulum, the main road in El Centro.

Getting Around

If you haven't rented a car, your two main options for navigating Cancún are taxis and the buses. **Taxis** are easy to come by, but expensive, and they are notorious for charging green tourists extra for their naiveté. A good rule of thumb is to always state the destination and ask the price before you get in. Generally, cab rides within the Zona Hotelera are $50; cabs from the Zona Hotelera to El Centro or vice versa are $100; and cab rides within El Centro are under $20. Do not be afraid to turn down an expensive rate; another cab will whiz by before you know it.

The **buses** in Cancún run frequently and stop at almost all of the hotels in the Zona Hotelera, main intersections in El Centro, and many beach destinations. A ride on the bus only costs $6. Buses will usually

Yachts & You: An Affordable Combo

Nothing makes you feel like a million bucks more than speeding through the surf on a yacht with a beer in your hand, the sun on your skin, and the wind in your hair. Every type of pleasure boat cruise imaginable leaves from Cancún's ports during the day and returns at night, from high speed yachts to smaller catamarans, and a luxurious day trip will only cost you a cool $40. Depending on what your pleasure is, be it snorkeling, shopping on a nearby island, lunch on an isolated beach, or just hours and hours onboard, you'll get it here. Over 50 boats leave Cancún's ports every day, and all you have to do is show up at any of the more frequented beaches or the Embarcadero to get a spot on one. Isla Mujeres is a popular daytime destination (but if you have the time, I recommend a separate trip here for 1 or 2 weeknights in order to absorb its full island appeal).

stop to pick you up wherever you're waiting on the main road in the Zona Hotelera, even if it's not a bus stop, which is handy. The two bus companies that run throughout the Zona Hotelera (and to the edge of El Centro) are the **Hoteles R1** busses ($65) and the **Bus 1** ($111, with air-conditioning).

I don't recommend renting a **moped** or a motorcycle in Cancún unless you are an experienced rider. The traffic is so dangerous that most renters will not sell you insurance. Rentals are available at various shops between Km 3 and 5 on Bulevar Kukulcan for $100 per hour or $500 per day. Many of the moped shops also rent **bikes** and **rollerblades** for $70 per hour or $160 per day.

Basics

Orientation: A Tale of Two Cities (& One Lagoon)

Cancún is not really one city, but two—the older **El Centro,** or downtown Cancún, and the newer strip of the **Zona Hotelera** (Hotel Zone, developed in the 1970s and 1980s). The Hotel Zone is a city in itself, with a style and culture all its own, and all of the happening night clubs, luxury hotels, beaches, and shopping malls are in this area. On the other hand, the restaurants in the Hotel Zone are generally much more expensive and inferior to the restaurants in El Centro. In El Centro you will find cheaper hotels, quality Mexican and Yucatecan restaurants where locals eat, and a lively atmosphere in La Plaza, especially on Sunday night (p. 204). It is easy to stay near your hotel, but far wiser to avoid this trap and absorb the best of what both worlds have to offer.

Geographically speaking, the Zona Hotelera is a thin 7-shaped strip of land which stretches east from El Centro, then south 20km (12 miles) toward the Cancún airport. Bulevar Kulkulcan is the main four-lane road stretching through the Zona Hotelera, and addresses are marked in kilometers (such as "Bulevar Kulkucan Km 9.5"). On both sides on the strip, between the lagoon and the ocean, you'll find swarms of shops, clubs, malls, and mega-hotels.

The **"lagoon side"** of Cancún refers to the area along the western side of Cancún's main strip, so it faces the **Laguna Nichupté,** while the Hotel Zone properties are on the eastern side facing the Caribbean Sea—a big difference if you want to stay *on* the beach. Here you'll find little collections of waterside apartments and condos. If you don't mind a short bus or boat ride to the beach (the lagoon has crocodiles, so it is a strictly look-don't-touch body of water), you can save some serious cash by staying in one of these cute condos. Boating is a favorite pastime of lagoon-siders; many of the hotels are also boat clubs where you can rent a boat to take out for the day if you are a resort guest.

Otherwise, there isn't much of what you'd call a "scene" on the lagoon side; that's why it's cheaper. The only restaurants are the modest ones within the hotels, and activities consist of resort or boat-club-affiliated activities as well. It's a quiet, family-friendly kind of place.

Tourist Info & Offices

The representatives at the **Cancún Visitors and Convention Bureau,** Bulevar Kulkulcan Km 9, Zona Hotelera (☎ **998/884-6531;** www.cancun.info), are informed and accessible. The website is also useful and easy to use. For tour companies, try the following:

→ **Mayaland Tours** In addition to the usual group tours, this unique tour company offers "self-guided tours" where they provide you with a car, an itinerary, a map, and an emergency helpline. The jungle tour—where you take a two-person speedboat through the mangrove channels of the Nichupte Lagoon then cross over to the ocean for a guided snorkel through the coral reefs at Punta Nizuc—is the most popular. *$550. AE, MC, V. Av. Robalo 30, Sm 3. ☎ 998/987-2450. www.mayaland.com/tours.htm.*

→ **Intermar Caribe** Specializes in ocean-centric tours to eco-parks and other popular destinations for snorkeling and other outdoor activities. They also offer one of the lowest rates for a round-trip day trip to Chichén Itzá. The rate to Chichén Itzá including admission to the park, transport, and buffet lunch with entertainment is $65. ***Note:*** Intermar has desks at many of the larger hotels in the Zona Hotelera such as the Marriott, so rates may differ depending on where you are staying. *Av. Tulum 225 at Calle Jabali, Sm 20. ☎ 998/881-0000.*

→ **Olympus Tours** Offers tours to all major sites including ruins, eco-parks, and other attractions. *Starting at $200. Av. Yaxchilan, Lote 13, Sm 17, Mza 2. ☎ 998/881-9030.*

Recommended Websites

- **www.mexicoweb.com/chats/Cancun**: A place to talk to real people with tried-and-true advice from their experiences in Cancún.
- **www.cancun.info**: An official but frank site hosted by the Cancún Convention and Visitors Bureau, with one of the best hotel guides available and detailed information on major attractions and seasonal events.
- **www.go2cancun.com**: Despite the fact that the services and companies recommended on this site have to pay to be included, it is a comprehensive list of many of the most popular destinations, rentals, and hotels in town.
- **www.cancun.com**: Another list of only paying advertisers, but still a good source of information on highlights to explore in Cancún.

Cancún Nuts & Bolts

Banks/ATMs In El Centro, most of the banks are on Avenida Tulum and have ATMs that are open all night. In the Zona Hotelera, the major malls Plaza Caracol and La Isla both have ATMs, as do some of the smaller shopping centers.

Embassies & Consulates The **U.S. Consular Agent,** in Plaza Caracol 2, Bulevar Kukulcan Km 8.5, on the third floor (☎ **998/883-0272**), is open from 9am to 1pm on weekdays. Because it is basically a kiosk at the mall and not a full consulate, they'll send you to the embassy office in Mérida if you have a major problem. Log onto www.yucatantoday.com/culture/eng-consulates.htm for Mérida consulate information.

Emergencies The Mexican equivalent of 9-1-1 is ☎ **060.** The **Red Cross** or Cruz Roja (☎ **065** or **998/884-1616;** www.cruzroja.cancun.com.mx) is open 24 hours next to the Telmex building on Avenida Yaxchilan No. 2, Sm 21, between avenidas Xcaret and Labna. The small emergency hospital **Total Assist** (☎ **998/884-1058** or 998/884-1092; www.totalassist.com) has English-speaking doctors and nurses, is open 24 hours, and accepts payment with all major credit cards.

Internet/Wireless Hot Spots There are Internet kiosks all through El Centro, and **C@conet,** in Kulkulkan plaza, is one of the cheaper providers in the Zona Hotelera. Even most modest resorts in El Centro and the Zona Hotelera have free wireless and a complimentary computer in the lobby with free Internet as well, so make sure that you check before you spend an afternoon in one of these cramped kiosks.

Pharmacies There are pharmacies all over El Centro and the Zona Hotelera, so if you're looking for a particular medication you may want to shop around for the best price before stocking your stash. **Farmacia Roxanna** (☎ **998/885-0860** or 998/885-1351) has a wide selection and will deliver your drugs directly to any hotel in the Zona Hotelera from one of their two locations, Flamigo Plaza and Kulkulcan Plaza.

Post Office The central **Cancún Post Office** (☎ **998/884-1418**) is on the corner of avenidas Xel Ha and Sunyaxchen and is open Monday through Friday from 9am to 4pm.

Safety Despite the many warnings you may hear, Cancún has a relatively low crime rate. On the other hand, if you leave something valuable unattended there is a high chance it won't be there when you return. Mexicans possess a healthy distrust of authority figures, so even if an honest person finds your backpack, they will not turn it into the police. Keep an eye on your stuff and always keep copies of your driver's license and passport in your hotel room when you go out. As in any large city, the best safety is always in numbers—one more reason to stay out with your friends a bit longer.

Telephone Tips The area code in Cancún is **998.**

Sleeping

When choosing where to tuck in at night in Cancún, here are a few tips to keep in mind. If you want to be by the beach, it's worth it to pay extra to be in the Zona Hotelera. If you don't mind taking a bus to the ocean, you'll save a lot of benjamins bedding down in El Centro, and are guaranteed to chow down on spicier, more flavorful food for less *dinero.* If you're looking for a condo or apartment with a kitchen and a low-key vibe, the lagoon side may be just your place. If you do decide to book at one of the mega-resorts in the Zona Hotelera, make sure to inquire about special deals for first time guests, students, and large groups.

El Centro

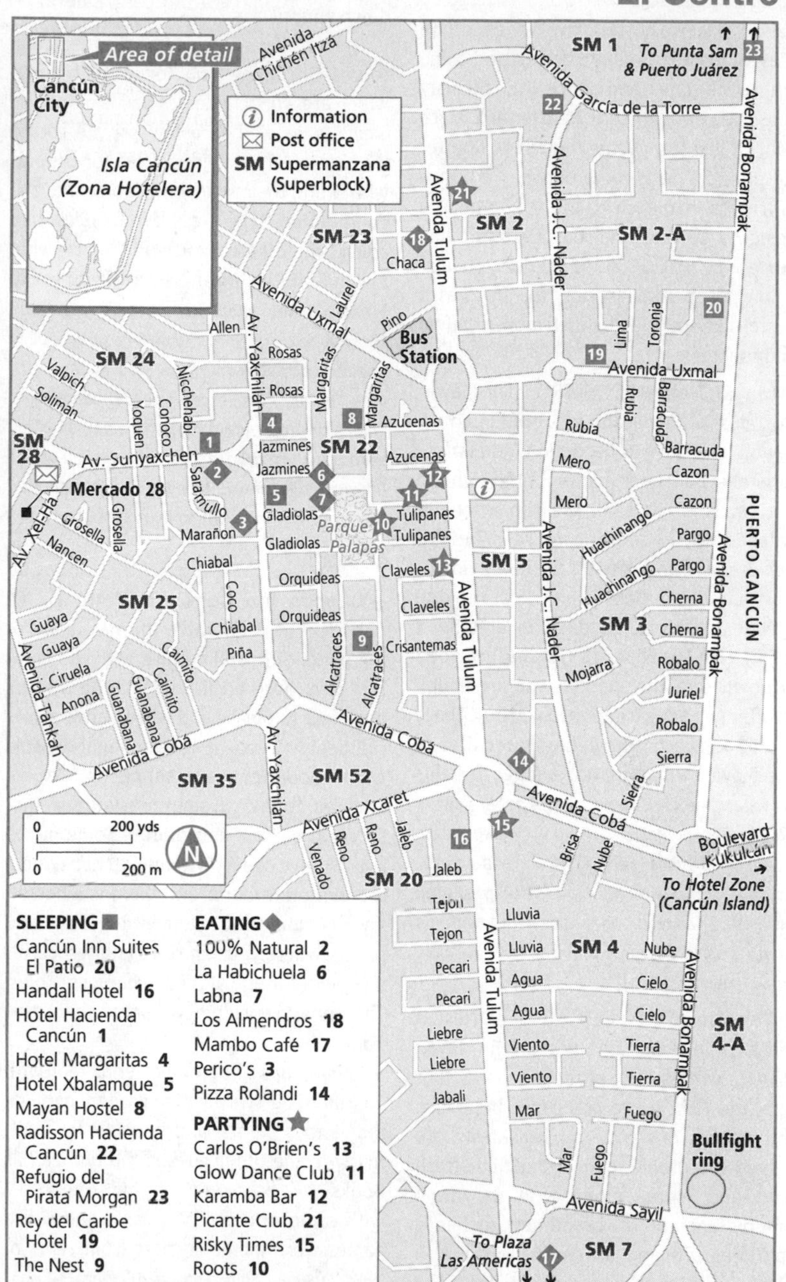
Area of detail
Cancún City
Isla Cancún (Zona Hotelera)
Information
Post office
SM Supermanzana (Superblock)
0 200 yds
0 200 m
N
SLEEPING
Cancún Inn Suites El Patio 20
Handall Hotel 16
Hotel Hacienda Cancún 1
Hotel Margaritas 4
Hotel Xbalamque 5
Mayan Hostel 8
Radisson Hacienda Cancún 22
Refugio del Pirata Morgan 23
Rey del Caribe Hotel 19
The Nest 9
EATING
100% Natural 2
La Habichuela 6
Labna 7
Los Almendros 18
Mambo Café 17
Perico's 3
Pizza Rolandi 14
PARTYING
Carlos O'Brien's 13
Glow Dance Club 11
Karamba Bar 12
Picante Club 21
Risky Times 15
Roots 10
To Punta Sam & Puerto Juárez
To Hotel Zone (Cancún Island)
To Plaza Las Americas
Bus Station
Mercado 28
Parque Palapas
Bullfight ring
PUERTO CANCÚN
SM 1
SM 2
SM 2-A
SM 3
SM 4
SM 4-A
SM 5
SM 7
SM 20
SM 22
SM 23
SM 24
SM 25
SM 28
SM 35
SM 52
Avenida Chichén Itzá
Avenida García de la Torre
Avenida Tulum
Avenida J.C. Nader
Avenida Bonampak
Avenida Uxmal
Av. Yaxchilán
Av. Sunyaxchen
Av. Xel-Ha
Avenida Tankah
Avenida Cobá
Avenida Xcaret
Boulevard Kukulcán
Avenida Sayil

Hostels

Cancún has two hostels, **The Nest** and **The Mayan Hostel.** Both are decent and come with thick gates and souped-up security (this is downtown Cancún after all). Since Cancún is a resort city, though, it's better to split up a hotel room between a bunch of friends than each go in for a bunk at a hostel. I recommend the **Cancún Inn Suites El Patio** (listed under "Cheap," below) over both hostels; the Inn has a hostel-like scene with much more comfort and space.

→ **Mayan Hostel** EL CENTRO The Mayan Hostel is located in the heart of El Centro, so you'll be close to the action (and unfortunately you'll hear it at night through the thin walls). That said, the rooms at the palapa-roofed Mayan Hostel seem kind of out-of-place and grungy for fancy downtown Cancún (unless you can get the one private palapa, a good value at $180 a night). Like The Nest, it's tiny and crowded but owned by nice people who are happy to offer you advice and help you out. There is only one bathroom in the shared area of the Mayan, which is not enough for this traveler. *Margaritas No. 17 Sm. 22, El Centro. ☎ 998/892-0103. Fax 998/892-0103. $90–$180 beds or private rooms. No credit cards. Amenities: Internet; kitchen; laundry; shared bathroom; sheets; telephone (in common area); towels; TV (in common room). In room: Fans; lockers.*

→ **The Nest** ★ EL CENTRO The Nest is much cleaner and sunnier than the Mayan Hostel, with a few attractive perks: For one, the Nest has a great free breakfast; the Mayan doesn't. The breakfasts are served in a dining room and include fresh fruit and coffee along with the usual bready fare, and the brand new kitchen is sparkling with appliances. The Nest is also just a few minutes walk from the main bus station, which is a relief when you have just arrived in town and can't wait to lay down your pack.

The Nest has some air-conditioned bunk rooms (including one for women only) which are worth the extra pesos in the hot weather, as well as a few private rooms that are small but a good value for couples who want their own bathroom and air-conditioning. The Nest even offers free cold purified water (you won't realize what a wonderful luxury this is until you get to Mexico). *Calle Alcatraces 49, Sm 22, M. 11. ☎ 998/884-8967. Fax 998/883-9689. www.hostalalcatraces.com. $110–$180 beds or private rooms. No credit cards. Amenities: Complimentary breakfast; Internet; kitchen; laundry; shared bathroom; sheets; telephone (in common area); towels; TV (in common room). In room: A/C (in some rooms), locker.*

Cheap

→ **Cancún Inn Suites El Patio** ★★ EL CENTRO This adorable inn has many of the perks of hostel culture with the comfort of a more civilized B&B. The owners are eager to please and will arrange a special deal with you if you pay by the week. Accommodations are simple but clean, and you'll find a small restaurant that serves breakfast and dinner. Some of the rooms have their own minikitchens, most are air-conditioned, and there is a hostel-style communal kitchen with a fridge and pantry where you can store your groceries if you opt for one of the kitchenless rooms. The only downside here is that there's no pool or bar.

El Patio has a homey, hacienda feel, with an inner courtyard with a garden, hanging indigenous plants, and benches for chilling with the other guests; the lounge has books for borrowing, a big screen TV with cable, and decks of cards and board games worn at the corners from years of happy use. *Av. Bonampak 51, at Cereza. ☎ 998/884-3500. Fax 998/884-3540. $400–$600 double. Breakfast included. AE, MC, V. Amenities:*

Hotel Zone

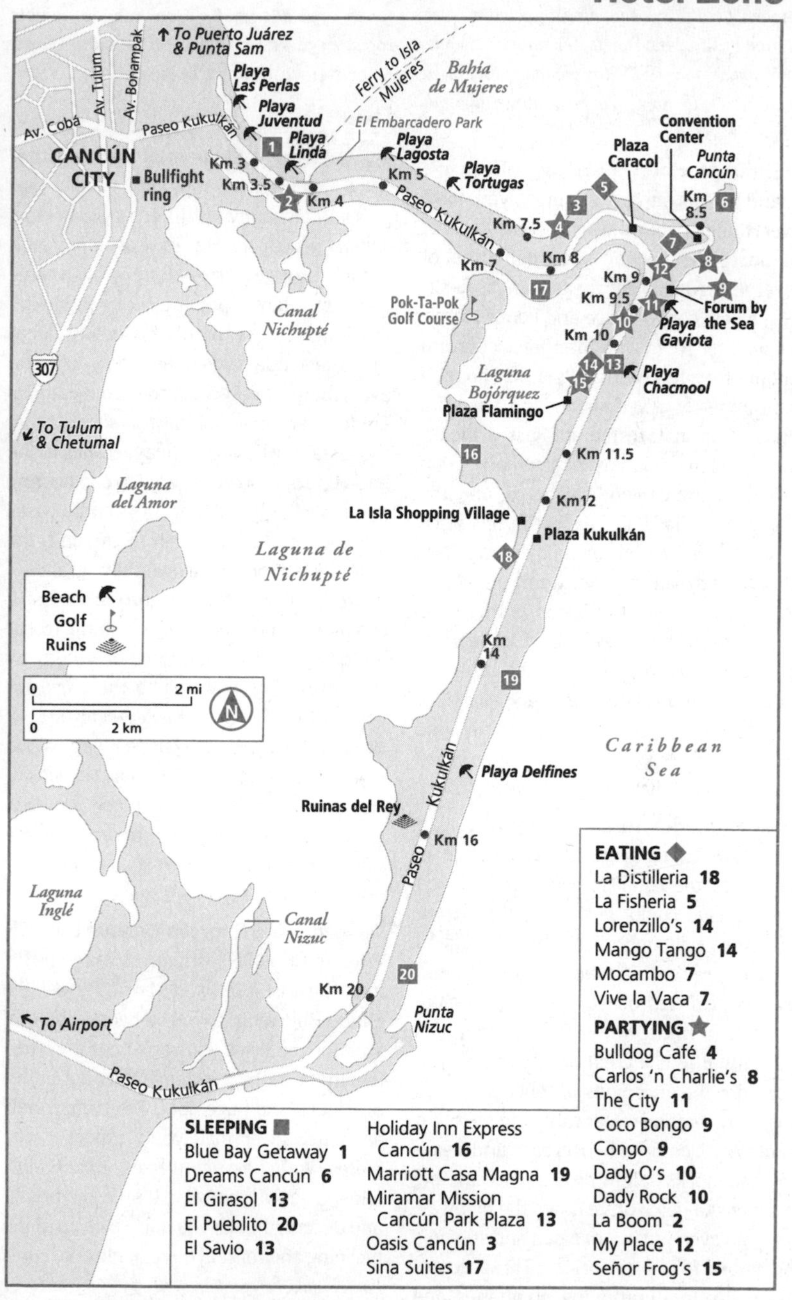

To Puerto Juárez & Punta Sam
Av. Tulum
Av. Bonampak
Av. Cobá
Paseo Kukulkán
CANCÚN CITY
Bullfight ring
Playa Las Perlas
Playa Juventud
Playa Linda
Km 3
Km 3.5
Km 4
Ferry to Isla Mujeres
Bahía de Mujeres
El Embarcadero Park
Playa Lagosta
Km 5
Playa Tortugas
Km 7.5
Km 7
Km 8
Plaza Caracol
Convention Center
Punta Cancún
Km 8.5
Km 9
Km 9.5
Km 10
Forum by the Sea
Playa Gaviota
Playa Chacmool
Canal Nichupté
Pok-Ta-Pok Golf Course
Laguna Bojórquez
Plaza Flamingo
307
To Tulum & Chetumal
Laguna del Amor
Km 11.5
Km12
La Isla Shopping Village
Plaza Kukulkán
Laguna de Nichupté
Beach
Golf
Ruins
0
2 mi
0
2 km
N
Km 14
Caribbean Sea
Playa Delfines
Ruinas del Rey
Km 16
Laguna Inglé
Canal Nizuc
Km 20
Punta Nizuc
To Airport
EATING
La Distilleria 18
La Fisheria 5
Lorenzillo's 14
Mango Tango 14
Mocambo 7
Vive la Vaca 7
PARTYING
Bulldog Café 4
Carlos 'n Charlie's 8
The City 11
Coco Bongo 9
Congo 9
Dady O's 10
Dady Rock 10
La Boom 2
My Place 12
Señor Frog's 15
SLEEPING
Blue Bay Getaway 1
Dreams Cancún 6
El Girasol 13
El Pueblito 20
El Savio 13
Holiday Inn Express Cancún 16
Marriott Casa Magna 19
Miramar Mission Cancún Park Plaza 13
Oasis Cancún 3
Sina Suites 17

Restaurant; fax; Internet in main office; kitchen; laundry machines; private and shared bathrooms; sheets; telephone (in common area); towels; TV (in common room). In room: A/C (in some rooms), minifridge (in some rooms).

→ **Hand All Hotel** EL CENTRO The name "Hand All" is meant to imply you have everything at your fingertips, and you sort of do (depending on your definition of "everything"). You get cheap laundry facilities, a deli, convenience and liquor stores, a computer room with Internet access and phones for a few pesos ($2 per half-hour), a bank and ATM next door, and the delightful Punta Gourmet restaurant just 2 blocks away. But the pool is very small and in an urban-feeling cement courtyard, and the rooms are what you'd expect in this price range: thin sheets, cheap pillows, noisy air-conditioning, and slow-draining plumbing. If you are coming to Cancún primarily to party (as opposed to swim, surf, or be pampered) this is your cheap and centrally located headquarters. *Mza 1. ☎ 998/884-1412. $300–$600 double. MC, V. Amenities: Fax; Internet; laundry and laundry service; liquor store; deli-convenience store. In room: A/C.*

→ **Refugio del Pirata Morgan** ★ ISLA BLANCA Though not officially within El Centro or the Zona Hotelera, this relaxed cabaña club could be your secret retreat from the bright lights of the big city—if you have or are renting a car. Located about a 25-minute drive north of the action (on the main highway towards Punta Sam), this peaceful B&B is a great bargain when you consider the enormous untouched beach, the tasty seafood restaurant, and the quiet rooms with colorful bedspreads and swaying hammocks—all in proximity to the big party just a quick drive down the highway. You can even opt out of a bed and stay in a hammock for hostel prices. Three downsides: No air-conditioning, no phones, and no TVs. *Carretera Punta Sam, Isla Blanca, Km 9. ☎ 998/860-3386. $400 cabaña double room, $50 hammock. No credit cards. Amenities: Restaurant. In room: Fan.*

Doable

MTV Best → **El Rey del Caribe Hotel** ★★★ EL CENTRO Hip, high-minded hippies will be happy at this ecological resort which makes living in harmony with nature a top priority—along with spoiling its guests. Rare blooming exotic plants fill the inner courtyard of this lushly decorated hacienda-style hotel, and you'll find everything from tarot card readings to Tai Chi to alternative health workshops. From the restaurant's veggie-heavy dishes to the back-up solar power energy to composting and recycling, all the earth-friendly bases are covered here, though in the end, the hotel feels more luxurious than "granola." However, if you are not into progressive ecological pursuits (or if you want to eat hot dogs and fries for lunch every day by the pool), this may not be the place for you. *Av. Uxmal at the corner of Nadar, Sm 2-A. ☎ 998/884-2028. Fax 988/884-9857. www.reycaribe.com. $400–$630 double. MC, V. Amenities: 2 restaurants with bar; pool with snack bar and bar; fax; Internet; laundry service; spa; travel desk; Wi-Fi. In room: A/C or fan, TV w/cable, fridge, telephone.*

→ **Holiday Inn Express Cancún** LAGOON What this Holiday Inn Express has going for it and against it is that it's basically just like all the Holiday Inns you've been to before. Still, for the price you can't beat the wireless in the lobby, complimentary hot buffet breakfast, and huge pool. The large rooms are much nicer than you'd expect in the States, with new mattresses, soft sheets, and powerful showers. It's clean, bright, and decent, though you may wake up in the morning and forget you're in Mexico. *Paseo Pok-Ta-Pok #21 and 22. ☎ 998/883-2200 or*

888/HOLIDAY from the U.S. Fax 998/883-2532. $800–$1,000 double. AE, MC, V. Amenities: Restaurant/bar; complimentary breakfast buffet; large pool with snack bar and bar; elevator; Internet available on computer in lobby; laundry service; Wi-Fi in lobby. In rooms: A/C, TV w/cable, fridge, minibar, Wi-Fi Internet.

→ **Hotel Margaritas** ★★ EL CENTRO It's no secret that this little hotel owned by Radisson resorts is one of the best values in Cancún, so make reservations over a month in advance for one of their offbeat, arty bedrooms. Of the many boutique hotels in El Centro, Margaritas follows the Radisson creed of cleanliness and amenities without losing its authentically Mexican spirit. All rooms have quality mattresses with festive bedspreads, brightly tiled floors, and bathrooms with funky interior touches that are saturated with bright blues and reds. *Av. Yachilan 41, Sm 22, Centro. ☎ 998/884-9333 or 800/537-8483 from the U.S. www.interclubresorts.com. $750–$950 double. AE, MC, V. Amenities: 2 restaurants with bars; pool with swim-up bar and snack bar; elevator; fax; Internet; laundry service; travel agent; Wi-Fi. In room: A/C, TV w/cable, fridge, telephone.*

MTV Best → **Hotel Xbalamque** ★★★ EL CENTRO If you're looking to avoid gringos and discover secret treasures, look no further than this richly decorated, Maya-inspired hotel. Everything about Hotel Xbalamque is pure Yucatán, from the wicker cages filled with colorful birds (who are remarkably quiet) in the lobby, to the library cafe with dripping wax candelabras. You will find guests drinking cocktails from the poolside bar and lounging in the cove under the waterfall at the pool in the inner courtyard.

Murals of Maya temples adorn the hallways, and the late-night bar and diner is named after La Adelita, the famous revolutionary wife of Pancho Villa (see "La Adelita: A Woman, Her Guns & Her Coffee," p. 196). In addition to the luxurious sleeping accommodations—with their warm amber lighting and soft linens—the spa attracts international visitors because of its impressive list of Maya treatments. *Av. Yaxchilan No. 31, Sm 22, Mza. 18. ☎ 998/884-9690 or 998/887-3055. www.xbalamque.com. $700–$1,000 double. AE, MC, V. Amenities: 2 restaurants with bars; swim-up bar; salsa bar and club; fax; health club and spa; Internet; laundry service; office suite; travel desk; Wi-Fi. In room: A/C, TV w/cable, telephone.*

→ **Oasis Cancún** ★ HOTEL ZONE As its name implies, the Oasis Cancún is small but refreshing, with plenty of water. The hotel sits on top of a prime swimming beach, yet you don't have to deal with the crowds and whirring jet skis that plague the beaches of larger resorts. Many of the air-conditioned rooms have minikitchens that, like the included buffet breakfast, can be an easy way to save *dinero* on small eats. Located less than a mile from most of the hottest clubs on Bulevar Kulkulcan, Oasis gives you a straight walk home from all the action, which is a true rarity in the Zona Hotelera. *Bulevar Kulkulcan Km 8.5 ☎ 998/883-0800 or 800/221-2222 from the U.S. Fax 998/883-0800. $1,350–$1,450 double. AE, MC, V. Amenities: 3 restaurants; 2 bars; pool with bar; fax; Internet; laundry service; travel desk; Wi-Fi. In room: A/C, TV w/cable, fridge, telephone.*

→ **Radisson Hacienda Cancún** ★★★ EL CENTRO This hotel has the best of both worlds: the affordability and proximity to real Mexican culture of the hotels in El Centro, combined with the services and cleanliness available at the more Americanized hotels in the Hotel Zone. Unlike the majority of other hotels in El Centro, the pool is shimmering, large, and contains a generous sunning area and swim-up bar, yet the restaurant has affordably priced Mexican and European food that is of the quality I would expect in El Centro. Despite being a Radisson, the interior is decorated in authentic hacienda style, with bright yellow walls, grass green furniture, and suns painted on the walls. *Av. Nader 1, Sm 2, Centro. ☎ 998/877-4455 or 800/333-3333 from the U.S. www.radisson.com. $800–$1,250 double. AE, MC, V. Ask about special all-inclusive rates. Amenities: Restaurant; bar; gym with classes; Internet; office suite; large pool; spa; travel agent; Wi-Fi. In room: A/C, TV w/cable, fridge.*

➔ **Sina Suites** ★ LAGOON This is one of the nicer sets of condos on the lagoon side, with stand-out lush gardens and professional staff. Rooms are clean and furnished with flowered bedspreads. Each apartment comes with a full kitchen, air-conditioning, a large bathroom, and cable. There is a wide, clean pool with a snack bar and restaurant beside it. La Isla, a small dining-room-like restaurant, has yellow tablecloths and a rib-sticking, simple menu. Take a 5-minute walk to a shopping center with groceries, laundry, Internet, and a drug store. *Quetzal No. 33, Club de Golf, Zona Hotelera. ☎ 998/883-1017 or 800/712-6704 from the U.S. www.cancunsinasuites.com.mx. $400–$500 double, $1,200–$1,400 master suite. MC, V. Amenities: Restaurant; poolside bar; boat rental; fax; Internet. In room: A/C, TV w/cable, fridge, full kitchen or kitchenette.*

Beachside Vacation Apartments: Two Options

Just west of the main part of Bulevar Kulkulcan, where all the action is, you'll find three narrow white towers that look like they could almost be part of the same resort. Two of these hotels—**El Salvia Condos,** Bulevar Kulkulcan Km 9, Zona Hotelera (☎ **651/481-8744** or 888/841-4184; fax 651/481-1407); and **Condominio Girasol Cancún,** Bulevar Kulkulcan Km 9, Zona Hotelera (☎ **998/883-5045**)—have beach access with double rooms starting at $1,000, making them a favorite with savvy Mexican travelers. All three skyscrapers are officially condos, meaning that people actually own these rooms, furnish them, and rent them out. For most of the rooms that I saw this was a plus as opposed to a minus; owners go above and beyond hoteliers when it comes to decorating their rooms. It also means you might find a room with a DVD player or other nonstandard hotel item, if you're willing to pay a bit extra.

Girasol stands out from the pack a bit because of its pool (right on the beach), its cute adjacent restaurant, and its proximity to restaurants on Bulevar Kulkulcan. El Salvio has the nicest interior rooms, a tour office in front, and the grandest lobby. But both offer clean rooms with ocean views, homey decorations, small marble bathrooms, and a prime location on the beach right next to Coco Bongo and the rest of the party strip. Because these are vacation apartments, there are a wide variety of sizes and styles available, so if you are coming with a large group you can get larger rooms or a full kitchen with a microwave. El Savio has a dream penthouse that comfortably fits eight people and has its own Jacuzzi—for $2,950 a night, which comes out to about $368 (US$34) per person per night for you and your buddies to live like celebrities in Cancún. They also have a penthouse for 12 people and many smaller group rates as well. Book groups at both hotels in advance and note most deals require 5-night minimum stays, though they're eager for business and often willing to negotiate.

SPLURGE

➔**Blue Bay Getaway** ★ HOTEL ZONE This adults-only all-inclusive is a festive place to get treated right. You'll find acres of tropical gardens, a gorgeous swimming beach with calm water, and comfy, country-style rooms with crafty Mexican interiors. I could do without the lackluster nightly "entertainment" which is cheesy at worst and average at best. Despite all the warnings you may hear about the clothing optional beaches, I did not see a single fully nekkid person on the property. *Bulevar Kulkulcan Km 3.5. ☎ 998/848-7900 or 800/211-1000 in the U.S. $1,600–$2,800 double. AE, MC, V. Amenities: 4 restaurants; 4 bars; fax; Internet; 3 swimming pools; spa; watersports; Wi-Fi. In room: A/C, TV w/cable, fridge, telephone.*

➔**Dreams Cancún** ★★ HOTEL ZONE Though most all-inclusive hotels have their ups and downs, the Dreams Cancún is a far superior breed of all-inclusive. This was one of the first hotels built in the Zona Hotelera, and no one spends this kind of money when building hotels these days. This spanning monument to excess sits regally at the tip of Punta Cancún, within walking distance of many clubs and shops, and with views of both the lagoon and the ocean. In terms of creating the mood this place is unstoppable, the classic architecture is stunning, the grounds are gorgeous, and there is a gazebo that extends over the water (weddings are sometimes held here). This also makes the perfect spot for a solo yoga session at sunrise. Inside the rooms, sheets and comforters are so soft you may have to remind yourself not to spend your whole trip in bed. There are no pesky all-inclusive bracelets to wear, and employees are always trying to outdo each other to impress you.

Of course you pay for all of this when you get the bill, but it is truly relaxing to not think about money during your stay, and little pampering touches (a drink offered to you when you arrive, for one) can make you feel like you've finally found paradise. The 24-hour free room service, the all-inclusive minibar stocked with Corona, an arctic air-conditioner, and the free video library also help. With three included restaurants (Oceana for seafood, Himitsu for sushi, and World Café for a buffet), a Seaside Grill snack bar, a salsa club, and more than a few hoppin' bars, you may find it hard to leave this massive fort of indulgences, which is perhaps the only downside of staying in an all-inclusive that has so successfully mastered the art of pampering. ***Note:*** A fourth restaurant, the upscale Paloma Bonita, is not included but worth the splurge if you can afford it. *Bulevar Kulkulkan, Punta Cancún, Aposado Postal 14. ☎ 866/237-3267. Fax 998/848-7000. www.dreams.com. $1,950–$2,750 double. AE, MC, V. Amenities: 5 restaurants; 3 bars; 1 club; 2 pools with swim-up bar; fax; Internet; spa; watersports; Wi-Fi. In room: Digital A/C, TV w/cable, fridge with complimentary minibar.*

➔**El Pueblito** HOTEL ZONE Very popular with families, this resort always has buffets of food waiting to feed hungry children, plus a miniature golf course and a riverlike pool with waterfalls and a huge slide. If you don't mind being surrounded by youngins' (especially at the pool, which is packed during the day with those pesky foam noodles and games of Marco Polo), this is a top-notch all-inclusive with spacious rooms with marble floors and large, luxurious bathrooms. Another plus: El Pueblito is composed of a series of small buildings instead of one gigantic one, which is a nice change from the usual landscape of the Zona Hotelera. Although, combined with the cheering kids in the pool and the buffet meals, the squat buildings arranged in a semi-circle by the water can start to feel a bit too much like summer camp. *Bulevar Kulkulcan Km 17.5. ☎ 998/885-0422. www.elpueblitohotels.com. $2350–$3000 double. AE, MC, V. Amenities: 3 restaurants; 2 bars; snack bar; fax; Internet; 8 tennis courts; Wi-Fi. In room: A/C, TV w/cable, fridge, minibar, telephone.*

→ **Marriott Casa Magna** HOTEL ZONE This hotel resembles many other Marriotts in that it is huge and overbearing; you're staying here because of the location, the frequent traveler points, or occasional bargains that can actually make this the cheapest of the mega resorts. Motorboats dock in the water-filled lobby and will tow you to one of the resort's five restaurants through man-made canals that traverse the compoundlike mega resort. Typical of many Marriots, the lobby is enormous, the restaurants are overpriced, and the rooms are noticeably bare for the hefty full price. Construction is currently in progress on the JW Marriot Cancún, which is being added to the Casa Magna, so make sure to check that the construction is not on the side near your room. *Bulevar Kulkulcan Km 14.5. ☎ 998/881-2000 or 800/228-9290 from*

La Adelita: A Woman, Her Guns & Her Coffee

As you travel around the Yucatán, you'll notice many edgier bars and coffee shops named **La Adelita,** or simply Adelita. This is not a chain but a common tribute to a Mexican revolutionary, **Adela,** the fiery mistress of Pancho Villa, who joined the Mexican revolution and became a symbol of female *Soldaderas*—much in the way Rosie the Riveter is a symbol of WWII in the States. If you keep an eye out for her you'll notice the huge image of La Adelita, plastered over doorways and painted on murals. She holds a sharp hook in one hand and a saw in the other, and peers out at you on eternal lookout for any colonial enemy. Many times she'll even be wearing strings of bullets across her chest and a gun hanging down toward the ruffles of her peasant skirts. Though Pancho Villa was an infamous polygamist (historians count his official wives as numbering over 24), La Adelita is the most beloved of them all for her fearless fight for Mexico (though she was actually his mistress and they probably were never officially married). Here are the lyrics to the most popular folk song that soldiers sang during the revolution, in Spanish and English:

Si Adelita se fuera con otro
La seguiria por tierra y por mar.
Si por mar en un buque de Guerra
Si por tierra en un tren military.
Adelita, por Dios te lo ruego,
calma el fuego de esta mi passion,
porque tea mo ye te quiero rendido
y por ti sufre mi fiel corazon.

If Adelita should go with another
I would follow her over land and sea.
If by sea in a battleship
If by land on a military train.
Adelita, for God's sake I beg you,
calm the fire of my passion,
because I love you and I cannot resist it
and my faithful heart suffers for you.

the U.S. Fax 998/881-2085. www.marriott.com. $1,500–$2,500 double. Ask about packages. AE, MC, V. Amenities: 5 restaurants; 3 bars; snack bar and swim-up bar; fax; Internet; Jacuzzi; 3 pools; spa; Wi-Fi. In room: A/C, TV w/cable, fridge, minibar, telephone.

→ **Miramar Mission Cancún Park Plaza** ★★★ HOTEL ZONE For a typical Cancún vacation of sunbathing by the pool, wading in the surf, and dancing all night, no resort covers all of your bases in one place as well as the Miramar Mission Cancún Park Plaza. It features by far the best pool in Cancún, a double-Olympic-size marvel that stretches through the interior of the hotel all the way to the soft, sandy beach so that you can get your swim on even during the peak of hurricane season. On sunnier days, laying out on the floating, anchored lounge chairs will make you wonder why no one else thought of such an ingenious way to maximize your poolside solar exposure without overheating.

Decor is gently romantic and chic—with lots of soft off-white fabric draped against darkly stained wood furniture—which is probably why it attracts more young couples and less loud families. Other reasons for the late-20s crowd include the biggest Jacuzzi in Cancún (though it can get crowded at prime hours), and a hot club called Batacha where you can party till 4am without having to worry about navigating your way home in the morning. *Bulevar Kulkulcan Km 9.5. ☎ 998/883-1136 or 800/221-2222 from the U.S. www.hotelmission.com. $1,600–$2,000 double. AE, MC, V. Amenities: 3 restaurants; 2 bars; rooftop snack bar; nightclub; fax; Internet; Jacuzzi; indoor/outdoor swimming pool; spa; Wi-Fi. In room: A/C, TV w/cable, fridge, minibar, telephone.*

Eating

Whether in the posh, pretty dining rooms of the Zona Hotelera, the greasy, hissing stalls in La Plaza, or the dimly lit, spicy corners of El Centro, Cancún offers a large variety of dining options, including Mexican, seafood, Italian, and more experiences. In El Centro you will find fresh Mexican and Yucatecan cuisine—some of the most interesting and fiery I've tried in Mexico—at bargain prices (dishes are mostly under $150); the Zona Hotelera is ideal for Caribbean lobster, ceviche, and shrimp Caesar salads (dishes are $120–$350); and the Plaza is your destination to try any- and everything fried, dipped, and served on a stick for a few pesos ($5–$50). Your best bet is to be culinarily adventurous; the burritos, fajitas, and tacos here seem altered to please American palettes, more so than perhaps anywhere else in Mexico.

Do not leave without trying a flaming dessert or entree, as chefs of every stripe take pride in their ability to char their specialties right in front of your eyes.

Cheap

MTV Best → **Labna** ★★★ YUCATECAN Directly next door to La Habituela, the best restaurant in Cancún is hidden inconspicuously behind an almost invisible wall of frosted glass. Once you find the entrance you'll discover a jungle-like environment of tall plants, wall sconces made from giant snail shells, hanging lanterns made of dried vines, and glowing stained glass cobras that snake down the walls between the tables.

Labna had the best free table salsas of any restaurant I visited in Mexico, which is a serious distinction, considering the pride that Mexican chefs take in their table sauces. At Labna, the standard free fare includes a pâté of roasted sunflower seeds and local fresh herbs (I requested three refills of this), an olive and jalapeño tapanade (two refills of this), as well as perfect versions of guacamole, chunky tomato salsa, and red onion and habanero hot sauce. *Panuchos,* tortillas fried with beans on top, then smothered with chicken, cheese, avocado, and tomato, were a satisfying start. Any of the poultry in sauces made from ground squash seeds are slickly delicious, especially the *pollo en pepian.* And, if you like chile rellenos, you should not pass up the ones at Labna, which are a superior species all together. My dining companion for the evening, a self-described "flan-atic," proclaimed the flan the best she'd ever tasted. *Margaritas 29, hidden next door to La Habituela, El Centro. ☎ 998/892-3056. Entrees $70–$140. AE, DISC, MC, V. Daily noon–10pm.*

➔ **Los Almendros** ★★ YUCATECAN For pure, traditional Yucatecan food, this is your one-stop shop. An appetizer called *combinado Yucatecan* (Yucatecan combination) is an excellent introduction to the regional cuisine, as it features generous portions of *poc-chuc* (a special type of pork cutlet), *pavo en eschabeche* (turkey slow cooked in a stew), *cochinita pibil* (pork pieces barbecued with regional spices), and *pollo asado* (spicy roasted chicken), all local favorites that you should sample before you leave the Yucatán. For a main course, the *pavo en relleno negro* (turkey in black pepper sauce) was served in a sauce that was as black, thick, and shiny as wet tar, yet surprisingly smoky and delicious. Los Almendros is an intense experience, not for the weak of palate or stomach. This is strong, spicy stuff. The beverages include Jamaica juice, which is made from fresh flowers. *Av. Tulum Lote, 66 Ticul, El Centro. No phone. Entrees $60–$100. AE, MC, V. Mon–Sat noon–9pm; Sun noon–6pm.*

➔ **100% Natural** VEGETARIAN/MEXICAN This vegetarian heaven is a popular chain but never feels like one once you're sitting on the wooden swings inside, sipping on smoothies and chomping on exotic salads and bottomless baskets of whole-grain bread. If your friends are into fish or fowl, 100% Natural's got lots of Mexican classics with vegetables or free-range versions of your flying and swimming friends. Try the *nopal planchado,* grilled cactus and Mexican cheese with basil dressing and pita bread, or the cristalina soup, a warm combination of wild mushrooms, spinach, and onions with rice noodles, to start. Follow up with a pitcher of cucumber, lemon, and hibiscus agua fresca and some *enchiladas poblanas,* stuffed with poblano pepper, corn, onions, and creamy cheese, then smothered in a green sauce. For dessert, the ginger hot tea and carrot spice cake will make you feel all warm and fuzzy inside before you even start on the tequila for the evening. ***Note:*** As we go to print, they're opening a second location on the main road in the Zona Hotelera, across from Lorenzillos. *Plaza Commercial Suite Terramar, beside plaza Caracol, Local 40-41, El Centro. ☎ 998/883-3636. www.100natural.com.mx. Entrees $20–$120. AE, MC, V. Daily 7am–9pm.*

➔ **Rolandi's Pizzeria** ITALIAN Much more than a cheap pizza place, this 20-year-old institution has a full bar, stained glass windows, and the swanky feel of a fine Italian diner. A popular favorite for years, the thick Sicilian menu includes over 20 different pizzas, and an equally long list of Italian pastas, calzones, and big salads. At the main El Centro location, after 10pm the outdoor garden becomes a lively nightspot, with hanging white lanterns to set the mood. The Pizza Rolandi at Plaza Caracol is more of a lunch spot. *Av. Coba at Av. Tulum, El Centro. ☎ 998/884-4047. www.rolandi.com. Pizzas $60–$150. AE, MC, V. Mon–Sat noon–2am; Sun noon–midnight.*

Doable

→ La Distilleria ★★★ MEXICAN Tequila lovers of the world unite and worship at the altars of your gods. More a museum and temple to everyone's favorite Mexican libation (made from the thick leaves of the agave plant), this place also serves over 150 varieties of tequila, including many rare brands. It's possible to opt out of the short tour of the museum when you arrive, but it only takes a few minutes and provides worthy fodder for dinner conversation while getting saucy during "tequila tastings." (You can order a sampler for the table and taste test 5 or 20 different tequilas as if they were fine wines.) Food choices happen to be adventurous and fresh. *Bulevar Kulkulkan Km 12.65, across from Plaza Kukulkan, Hotel Zone. ☎ 998/885-1086 or 999/885-1087. Entrees $70–$250. Tequilas $40–$5,000. AE, MC, V. Daily noon–11pm.*

→ La Fisheria SEAFOOD There's nothing wrong with developing a healthy ceviche habit while you are in Mexico. This intoxicating concoction made of fresh raw seafood and fish diced-up and soaked in lime juice, cilantro, and salsa is everywhere, and unfortunately difficult to get back home. Just as shopping fatigue sets in at the maze that is Plaza Caracol, La Fisheria appears like a mirage, beckoning with its promise of delicious ceviche, cold beer, and slushy cocktails. You'll leave feeling refreshed, a bit tipsy, and amazed that such a quality seafood restaurant was hiding out in a mall. *In the Plaza Caracol Mall, Bulevar Kulkulkan Km 8.5, 2nd floor, Hotel Zone. ☎ 998/883-1395. Ceviche $70. AE, MC, V. Daily 11am–11pm.*

→ Mocambo ★ SEAFOOD A seafood joint from the owners of La Parilla (a tacky place that taxi drivers are paid to recommend), this restaurant is the better of the two. Set under a giant palapa right on the beach of Playa Caracol, this is a centrally located place to grab an affordable seafood dinner. To begin, the ceviches and shrimp *aguachile* (a Mexican version of shrimp cocktail where the shrimp is served in a cold tomato sauce) were both fresh, and of sharable size. Grilled lobster with black spaghetti (died with squid ink) was a dark, tasty treat. They also prepare lobster just about any way you can imagine, and it's the only restaurant in the Hotel Zone that prices it at under $200. *Past Plaza Caracol on Playa Caracol, overlooking the water, Hotel Zone. ☎ 998/884-5398. Snacks and appetizers $2–$10, entrees $80–$400 (for 3 or more people). MC, V. Daily noon–10pm.*

→ Perico's ★ TRADITIONAL MEXICAN Though the decor is hokey, and the entertainment can be boisterous and imposing, the food is authentic. (I don't want to have a sombrero put on my head and a full mariachi band hanging around my table while I'm trying to eat, but my neighbors at the next table seemed to be really getting off on it.) If you've been craving a dense burrito, some spicy steak fajitas, or even a steaming hot bowl of tortilla soup with just the right amount of shredded chicken and cheese, look no further. Every item on the menu is a certifiable Mexican classic served up with plenty of tortillas, re-fried beans, rice, guacamole, and salsa. *Av. Yaxichilan, El Centro. ☎ 998/883-1395. Entrees $70–$190. AE, MC, V. Daily noon–10pm.*

→ Vive la Vaca ARGENTINE Right smack in the center of the strip between Plaza Caracol and Punta Cancún, this Argentinean eatery has a breezy atmosphere and diverse dining selection that make it an easy stop after shopping or beach-going. You can order anything from grilled Argentine beef to penne with salmon and vodka sauce. *On the island in the middle of Bulevar Kukulcan 8.5, to the right of the Plaza Caracol parking lot, Hotel*

Zone. No phone. Entrees $80–$180. MC, V. Mon–Sat 11am–10pm; Sun noon–8pm.

Splurge

→ **La Habituela** ★★ MEXICAN/SEAFOOD As one of the oldest and most beloved restaurants in El Centro, this local landmark manages to feel swanky and laid-back at the same time. Named after a humble bean, the enchanting courtyard in the back is where residents of Cancún celebrate special occasions such as birthdays and anniversaries. The only restaurant in its price range that is packed with locals and not American tourists, this is not the place to go for a budget entree. Appetizers are practically entree-size, though, and much more interesting. Beginning with the fried whole soft-shell crabs, served with tortillas, guacamole, and a red onion and habenero salsa for $100, many of the other specialty seafood appetizers are equally tempting and substitutable as entrees. If you've got a sweet tooth, for $10 you get four full-size crepes sautéed in a sauce of melted chocolate and fine spirits, then stuffed with the hot, sweet filling of your choice. *Av. Margaritas 25, El Centro. ☎ 998/884-3158. habituela@infosel.net.mx. Entrees $120–$300. MC, V. Mon–Sat noon–10pm; Sun noon–9pm.*

→ **Lorenzillos** ★★ SEAFOOD After you enter past the giant sculpture of a lobster, this outdoor eatery becomes a romantic spot to bring your date for first-class appetizers, cocktails, and dessert while you watch the sun set over the lagoon. One of the oldest restaurants in Cancún, Lorenzillos is a series of hand-built, open-air gazebos that extend out on docks so you can eat amidst the waves. Stained glass, mosaic fountains, and a curvy, multi-hued wooden floor combine to make you feel like you're dining inside a kaleidoscope or a lighthouse. For starters, you can't go wrong with the blue corn fish chowder and shrimp Caesar salad. To sweeten your sunset, the Maya brownie sundae known as *Isla de Sacrificios* (Island of Sacrifices) is cinnamony, and, indeed, worth sacrificing your diet for. *Bulevar Kulkulkan Km 10.5, Hotel Zone. ☎ 998/883-1254. www.lorenzillos.com. Entrees $80–$280. AE, MC, V. Daily 11am–10pm.*

→ **Mango Tango** ★★ INTERNATIONAL If you're looking for gumbo, this joint's got the spicy stew with thick chunks of lobster thrown in. Mango Tango seems to have decided to embrace the two elements of its name full force, the first being to incorporate the fruit of the mango tree into as many dishes as possible, and the second to create a restaurant with live musical performances that actually make people get up and dance—two very worthy causes indeed. *Bulevar Kulkulkan Km 10.5, Hotel Zone. ☎ 998/883-1254. Entrees $120–$250. AE, MC, V. Daily 2pm–2am.*

Partying

Cancún is the unofficial Party Capital of the Western World, so be prepared for the outrageous antics and Vegas-caliber live performances that go on in the Golden City's hottest night spots—though the magnitude of the party scene won't fully hit you until you get past the velvet rope and into one of the high caliber clubs in Cancún, and suddenly realize you've arrived at the biggest party of your life. The best part is that the city never sleeps; if you're up for it you can dance from morning to night, nap, take a dip in a Jacuzzi, and grab a gourmet snack in between without ever having to leave the club.

Clubs

→ **The City** ★★★ HOTEL ZONE Built with the idea that bigger is better, The City has the capacity for 5,000 revelers inside and 15,000 more on its adjoining daylight beach club. Their motto is, "Day or Night, We Never Sleep," and they hold true to their promise for all you 24-hour party people. This massive clubber's club was built in 2004 with all the newest sound and light gadgets, so it's well-equipped to keep you raving all night and well into the next day. Inside there are five levels of debauchery to revel in, including the luxe third floor VIP martini lounge and the mobile stage where 50 Cent and DJ Sasha have performed live.

The inside area boasts nine bars, and outside there's a wave pool for surfing and boogie boarding, a skyscraping waterslide, and a beachside snack bar. If you want to revive between dance breaks, the second floor lounge has comfy couches, tasty desserts, and salty snacks. Special effects include bubbles, CO2, balloon machines, and giant floating snakes. (Yes, giant floating snakes.) *Bulevar Kulkulcan km 9.5. ☎ 998/848-8380. Cover $200, $400 with open bar. Some nights ladies drink free.*

MTV Best → **Coco Bongo** ★★★ HOTEL ZONE Tell any local in Cancún that you're going clubbing and they will say, "Oh, you're going to Coco Bongo," because as far as those in the know are concerned, there is no other club in Cancún. Coco Bongo is like the best of Cirque du Soleil, burlesque, Disneyworld, and MTV all rolled up into one wild night with plenty of cold smoke, crazy lasers, neon confetti, and alcohol thrown in to keep the party bumping. It doesn't matter how old you are; if you're into cult classic movies, pop star impersonators, comic books, music, spectacular special effects, or just video screen close-ups of hot girls, you are guaranteed to have the time of your life.

The show is so fast-paced and mesmerizing that you don't have time to get bored between aerial reenactments of the scene in *Beetlejuice* where Wynona Ryder levitates singing "Shake Señora"; the flawless Beyoncé impersonator; and the Joker and Batman duking it out high over your heads. Even skeptical indie types will be impressed at the quality of the pop shows and the postmodern antics that go on in front of the original movie footage on the mega high-resolution screens.

Not to mention, this is the hottest crowd in all of Cancún. Coco Bongo regularly packs in over 3,000 bodies, all dancing their *culos* off until 5am. (Watch out ladies, that guy with the camera seems to have an obsession with getting exposed thongs up on the big screen.) Seriously though, no matter who you are or what your thing is, there is nothing like this place on the entire earth. Even the bartenders seem to be having the time of their lives. Bring your ID; this club is over 18. *Bulevar Kulkulcan Km 9.5 No. 30, Plaza Forum by the Sea, Segundo Piso. ☎ 998/883-5061. www.cocobongo.com.mx. Cover $400 (including open bar; you can pay $100 more to skip the long line).*

MTV Best → **Congo** ★ HOTEL ZONE The best place to get free drinks (if you're female). You can always count on a few free cocktails to start the night off right if you're a pretty girl at Congo, which is right in the heart of the party strip and provides a great early perch for people-watching before the sun sets. Once it gets dark however, this place becomes a bad dream come to life, complete with pawing men and hired dancers in neon orange hot pants blowing whistles in your ear and trying to get you to join the conga line. That is the club's one trick pony—getting everybody up out of their seats to join the conga line. If this sounds lame to you, you're right—it is, and it gets old incredibly quickly. This does not mean that I didn't return early in the evenings to receive my complimentary cocktails and slurp them down before sunset. *Bulevar Kulkulcan km 9.5. No phone. No cover.*

→ **Dady 'O** ★★★ HOTEL ZONE A frat boy's dream come true, this world-class club holds rocking theme parties every night of the week that don't end until the last scantily clad person stops dancing (usually around 5am, but they never kick anyone out). Theme nights include: a hip-hop party, an oldies karaoke sing-along night, an "old school" rap party, plus theme parties for just about every decade. Dady 'O is particularly renowned for their amateur bikini competitions and sexy beach parties. Expect hot fire performances, fierce samba drumming, daring aerial stunts, jazz saxophone played over house beats, and crazy 3D lasers and holographic special effects. Companies that have held parties here include Playboy and Maxim, to give you an idea of the crowd. *Bulevar Kulkulcan km 9.5. ☎ 998/883-1626. Cover $400 (including open bar).*

→ **Dady Rock Bar and Grill** HOTEL ZONE This is a chill place for an off night after a few too many benders. A side project of the people who brought you Dady 'O, Dady Rock has food, live music, and a more low-key atmosphere, although you still won't find a sober person in the place. More like a bar with a little bit of dancing than a club, it opens at 6pm, serves dinner, and features live DJs and hot local acts later in the evening. *Bulevar Kulkulcan km 9.5. ☎ 998/883-1881. No cover.*

→ **La Boom** HOTEL ZONE Does paying steep covers make you sick? This two-story dance club spins house beats and shoots lasers without the trumped-up charges. Most nights females get in free, and guys pay $150 for an open bar. Though it's off the main drag, you'll make up the taxi fare in an hour of pounding powerful drinks and grinding to even more hard-hitting beats. *Bulevar Kulkulcan km 3.5. ☎ 998/883-1152. Cover $150 guys; females free.*

Live Music

→ **Bulldog Café** ★★ HOTEL ZONE This amazing space has hosted first-class acts such as Guns N' Roses, Shakira, AC/DC, Mana, Naughty by Nature, and Radiohead. Check the schedule for live shows when you're in town. Even on a night of recorded hits, you can still have some "Only in Cancún" type fun frolicking in the VIP hot tub favored by the famous rock stars who have played shows here. The DJs spin the largest selection of music at any club, straying from the Top 40 but keeping the tempo hot enough with underground hip-hop and reggeaton for nonstop dancing. This is by far the best place on the Bulevar Kulkulcan to party like a rock star, and you can even buy drinks by the bottle. Cristal anyone? *Bulevar Kulkulcan km 7.5. ☎ 998/848-9800. Cover $120, $250 for open bar.*

Bars

→ **Carlos 'n Charlie's, Carlos O'Brien's & Señor Frog's** HOTEL ZONE/EL CENTRO If what you're looking for in Cancún are mountains of loaded nachos and toilet-bowl-size margaritas, look no further than Señor Frog's, Carlos 'n Charlie's, and Carlos O'Brien's—all are from the same owners, and each brings you the same whacked-out atmosphere of Jell-O shots, frat boys, and waitresses with tequila shot holsters. These places consistently attract a full house of English speakers under 25, and you won't have to wait in long lines or worry about anyone around you taking themselves too seriously on the sawdust-covered dance floor. Yet you won't find any locals here. ***Tip:*** If you eat some of the monster-size munchies at Carlos 'n Charlies, you can avoid paying cover.

Carlos 'n Charlies: Bulevar Kulkulcan Km 8.5, Hotel Zone. ☎ 998/883-4486. $50, or no cover with food purchase. Carlos O'Brien's: Tulum 29, El Centro. ☎ 998-884-1659. No cover. Señor Frog's: Bulevar Kulkulcan Km 9.5, Hotel Zone. ☎ 998/883-1092. No cover.

➔ **Mambo Café** EL CENTRO There is a Mambo Café in every Mexican city with a dance scene worth its salt, and Cancún is no exception. Take a break from the more American offerings of the Zona Hotelera for one night of live salsa music and venture into this local favorite in El Centro. The best place to pick up new steps by a long shot. The dancers here aren't kidding around, and the music is hot enough to keep them seriously stepping all night long. *Av. Tulum at Plaza las Americas, 2nd floor, Sm 4. ☎ 998/887-7894.*

➔ **My Place Bar and Restaurant** ★★★ HOTEL ZONE If you thought that there was no such thing as a rockin' "Mom 'n Pop" bar, My Place has arrived right smack in the heart of the party strip to prove you wrong. Its owners are a couple from the States who loved the scene in Cancún so much that they quit their jobs, headed south of the border, and started working at hotels for room and board. Everybody in Cancún liked them so much, that they soon had their own club with a posse of waiters and staff who seem more like their family than their employees.

You won't encounter smoke machines, lasers, or half-naked girls here. You will stumble on the biggest selection of beer and quality liquor on the island (at low prices), a huge stage and bar, a long list of quality karaoke songs, and a lot of laughter. Unlike most bars in Cancún, the food is great, making this a fun spot to pre-party with dinner and beer. Pork tenderloin served with mango salsa went well with some fine bourbon, and the half-pound mushroom cheeseburger was great with beer. "The big one" is a special that you can apply to anything from shots to loaded nachos; you get about four times the size of the regular one for only twice the price.

There's also a taco truck outside and a collection of beer bottles that happy patrons bring from their hometowns. (Good luck stashing a bottle from your local microbrewery on the plane these days.) *Plaza El Zocalo, Kukulcan Bulevar Km 9. ☎ 998/883-1300. Entrees $70–$200.*

➔ **Roots** EL CENTRO This swanky spot spins Latin fusion, jazz, and underground hip-hop, with live artists making guest appearances on the weekend. Get your R&B or flamenco on in this high-class bar. *Av. Tulipanes, across the street from Parque de las Palapas, Sm 22. ☎ 998/884-2437.*

Gay Bars & Clubs

Cancún does not have the flourishing gay scene of Acalpulco or even Puerto Vallarta, but the general "anything goes" atmosphere of the city has paved the way for a handful of hot and welcoming clubs with awesome drink specials, even better drag shows, the best techno on the strip, and overflowing energy and enthusiasm. ***Note:*** Because of obvious economic disparities between the U.S. and Mexico, if that guy hitting on you at the club looks impossibly ripped and adorable, there is a good chance he will expect you to pay for his attentions. An easy way to avoid this type of awkward situation is to do the opposite of current U.S. military policy; just ask and tell, and party on.

➔ **Glow Dance Club** EL CENTRO DJs at this dance extravaganza play upbeat house, techno, and disco music with happy hard-core beats to keep you dancing nonstop until 5am. More of a rave than anything else, this place attracts the city's youngest crowd, so check that cutie's age on his ID before you make a brunch date. Glow is an offshoot of the ever popular

Karamba bar and disco, but the Karamba crew has made an investment in this place—you'll find a bar stacked with specialty liquors and elaborate costumes and make-up. Glow feels a bit like Karamba's hipper, sleeker little brother, and you might say the same about the crowd. *Tulipanes 33, Sm 22.* ☎ *998/827-0724.*

→ **Karamba Bar & Disco** ★★ EL CENTRO Karamba has a constantly changing weekly schedule so you never attend the same party twice: Friday night is for go-go boys, Saturday and Sunday belong to strippers, Wednesday and Thursday are for celebrity impersonators, and Monday and Tuesday are usually reserved for lip-synching. This place is known for its performers and usually packs in more locals and partiers than any other gay club, with its star-quality acts and elaborate costumes. Their website offers useful recommendations for gay tourists, including the best beaches and a

Hanging Out at the Parque Las Palapas

The most enjoyable way to mix, meet locals, and find live entertainment in any Mexican city is to head to the central plaza downtown on any night of the week, though Friday and Saturday nights and Sunday during the day are traditionally the most festive—and this rule holds in Cancún as well. The plaza here is **Parque Las Palapas,** located at the intersection of avenidas Tulipanes and Alcatreces in El Centro, and includes an outdoor amphitheater, outdoor food courts, and a park full of vendors.

I strolled into the plaza on a sleepy Tuesday and got to cheer on a professional minor league basketball game. Here, fan dedication and player egos top any major league game in the States, and the plaza provides you with front row seats to these hot, sweaty, intense sports events—a refreshing glimpse of great athletes in peak form, untainted by pursuit of big money. Pay attention to the nicknames on the backs of the players' jerseys, a Mexican tradition; big star athletes usually get dealt the most diminutive names, such as "Little Sausage," "Sweet Cream," and "Muddy Pants."

Weeknights are also prime time to see the acts that didn't make the cut for the coveted weekend line-up; the effect is like a live gong show, with memorable acts that are so bad they're gut-bustingly good. I saw an amateur clown who kept dropping his props and losing his nose, a magician who pulled an angry snapping turtle out of his hat instead of a rabbit, and two teenage girls practically screaming duets of old Céline Dion hits. With colorful lights, upbeat music, and swarms of families milling about, the plaza has a way of feeling like our version of a carnival or amusement park every night.

Sunday night, usually a sleeper night on the party strip, is by far the wildest night in the Parque Las Palapas. Here you'll see all the hottest local live music and dance acts. Cancún's Playa also has a huge outdoor amphitheater which usually fills to the brim with locals munching on the cheap churros, elote, and tacos, so it's a great cheap dinner sampling. (You'll never see so many different fried treats in one place, guaranteed.)

If you saw the movie *Nacho Libre,* you'll recognize the extremely popular and tasty corn on the cob, rolled in lime juice, sour cream, and chili powder on sale here. Want to avoid getting cream and chili all over your face while eating it? Ask for your elote corn in a cup, as smart locals do.

cafe owned by a local gay couple. *Tulum No. 11 at Calle Azucenas. No phone. www.karambabar.com/karamba/en/tips.htm. No cover.*

➔ **Picante Club** ★★★ EL CENTRO Open for 15 years, this is the most established gay bar in Cancún, and Mother Picante who runs the place knows how to translate those years of experience into a real old-school cabaret style show, including drag queens, dance numbers, strippers, singers, and professional lip-synchers who will keep you dancing all night long. She's been doing this a long time, but you can tell she still has a blast emceeing the raucous musical performances, and her enthusiasm is infectious. As are the nightly drink specials, which include free tequila shots on Thursday nights, and two for one beers every day except Saturday. It's open from 9pm until 5am. *Plaza Gallerias Av. Tulum 20, Sm 5. No phone. www.picantebar.com. No cover.*

➔ **Risky Times** EL CENTRO This smaller club is really known for its afterparty, which starts at 3am and usually stars bartenders and performers from the big ticket clubs, who are off duty and ready to relax for real. The name says a lot about the club. It's not hard-core in a creepy way, more in the way that people are serious about hooking up, and they will be doing it on the dance floor, and in more private places throughout the club as well. *Av. Tulum at Av. Coba, Sm 4. ☎ 998/827-0724. No cover.*

Heading to the Beach

The most popular public beaches in Cancún include: Playa Tortugas, Playa Langosta, Playa Linda, Playa Las Perlas, Playa Delphinas, and Playa Caracol. Each has its own personality. **Playa Tortugas** is the #1 party beach, with a Fat Tuesdays bar right on the beach where you can guzzle over 20 colors and flavors of daiquiris from .9m-long (3-ft.) plastic cups. You'll also find every variety of hair braider, souvenir stand, and sports equipment booth. This beach gets packed but you can easily lose the crowds by taking a short walk to some nearby beachside cliffs with shallow caves; this is where locals set up lounge chairs and make makeshift cabañas out of the natural rock overhangs to escape the sun.

Playa Langosta, Playa Linda, and **Playa las Perlas** are all far less crowded than Tortugas, and are better for watersports because you don't have to spend all your time avoiding other people on jet skis. Playa las Perlas is the locals' favorite for escaping the party scene and just chilling in the sun and sand.

Surfers and gay tourists both prefer **Playa Delphinas,** because the rougher (but not too rough) waves deter families and other conservative types who might crash their party.

Playa Caracol is conveniently located right on the tip of Punta Cancún by the party strip, so if you are dining at one of the many restaurants along the water you will see both tourists and locals swimming in the water right next to the shops and clubs. Don't follow their example; Playa Caracol has a dangerous rip tide and has the most drownings of any beach in Cancún.

The greatest thing about beaches in Cancún is that each and every one of them is considered public property, and many of the beaches in front of the bigger resorts in the Zona Hotelera also have the same set-up, with better equipment and less people, so you won't have to worry so much about where you maneuver your canoe.

Equipment rental companies on the beaches in front of the fancy resorts are privately owned, so you don't have to be a

Get On the (Drunk) Bus

The **Party Hopper Tour** is a 7-hour bus trip that goes from club to club, saves you open bar and cover charges, and significantly increases your chances of drunkenly making out in the back of a bus. The tour meets every night at Congo (on Bulevar Kulkulan km 9.5, across from Coco Bongo) at 8pm, then proceeds to Dady Rock at 9:15, Dady 'O at 10:45, and ends up at Coco Bongo from midnight to 3:30am (an escalating party experience, with best for last). The price of this tour changes slightly with the season, but usually stays around US$50. Party Hopper tips—as listed on the fliers that litter the entire city of Cancún—include:

- Write your hotel name on your underwear . . . so you can get home later.
- If the person next to you takes out a plastic bag . . . run!
- Do not take the bus for a joy ride. That is our job.
- Do not give the bus driver anything. He has his own stash.

The **VIP Party Tour** operates under a similar philosophy, except the first stop is the VIP zone at Nectar, then Carlos 'n Charlie's, Dady 'O, and The City (until 3am) for around $600 per person (see the "Partying" section for club reviews). The ticket includes cover charges and open bar fees, plus entrance into the VIP lounge at Dady 'O. This tour meets at the mezzanine of Dady 'O at 8pm. This company doesn't have a website or contact information, but watch for the ubiquitous fliers on the streets.

guest at the hotel to rent one of the premium sailboats on its beachfront. Surprisingly, equipment rentals are often cheaper on beaches in front of posh resorts than on crowded public beaches, because there is less demand for the equipment. My favorite hotel beach to crash is **El Presidente Cancún** (generally considered the most beautiful beach in the Zona Hotelera; Bulevar Kulkulcan km 7.5). You can start walking up the beach from one of the more crowded spots until you find something that suits your fancy, be it watersports galore or simple peace and quiet.

Sightseeing

Cancún may be one of the worst places in Mexico for true sightseeing; the most memorable "sight" in Cancún may be the mesmerizingly clear turquoise waters and baby-powder-fine white sand. Still, you'll find a few worthy options to check out while you give your sun-scorched skin a break from UV rays. Here are a few of the stimulating things you can do in Cancún with your clothes on.

➔ **El Embarcadero (The Marina)** Want a bird's-eye view of paradise? Try a dizzying new outlook on your vacation from the top of **La Torre Cancún,** the spinning observation deck over the Embarcadero amusement park. Then stay and spend the afternoon browsing the city-block-size **Museo de Arte Popular Mexicano** that fills the second floor of the Embarcadero complex. The impressive collection of Mexican folk art such as masks, musical instruments, and *cartoneria* (the art of Mexican papier-mâché) features many of the most beloved Mexican artists and is

Get Your Fest On

Mexico-Caribbean Food Festival: During the first 2 weeks of November, this delicious display of regional cuisine can keep your belly and wallet more pleasantly filled than any other time of the year. Head to the Main Plaza at Parque Palapas in El Centro for tasty treats that include spicy fried oysters, *menudo* (a special beef stew that is slow cooked and served over yellow rice), green chile casserole, and every type of fried finger food from flautas to corn fritters. Most dishes are $10 to $50, closer to $100 for the Camarones Diablo (spicy shrimp sautéed in tomato sauce) or the lobster ceviche.

sure to give you a colorful fresh perspective on the culture and history of Cancún. While at the Embarcadero, you can also buy tickets for any of the eco–theme parks, as well as many boat related activities, from chartering a yacht for the day to joining a guided snorkeling tour. *Bulevar Kulkulcan Km 4. ☎ 998/849-4848. Admission $100. Daily 11am–11pm.*

→ **Museo Arqueológico de Cancún** This small museum is worth its weight in gold (probably literally). Located at the entrance of the Cancún Convention Center, it displays Maya artifacts (such as jade jewelry used in body modification), intricate stone sculptures, gold vessels, and dyed cloth—all of which add new depth to some of Mexico's hollow stone ruins by giving you a peek at the bizarre riches that were found buried inside. *Bulevar Kukulkan. ☎ 998/883-0305. Admission $30. Tues–Fri 9am–8pm; Sat–Sun 10am–7pm.*

→ **Ruinas del Rey (A Maya Ruin)** You must not leave Mexico without seeing one of the major ruins like Chichén Itzá or Uxmal, so don't think because you visited this one that you're getting out of a long bus ride or a day coated in bug spray in the jungle (it'll be worth it). However, if you want a taste of what awaits you before you shell out for the main course, these little ruins in the middle of a golf course should whet your palate for the real thing. If you're a golfer, you can bring your clubs and make a day of it; the ruin is right smack in the middle of the Hilton Hotel's golf course (which has a $160 fee and a separate entrance). *Bulevar Kukulcan Km 17. ☎ 998/883-0305. Admission $45; free on Sun. Daily 8am–5pm.*

Playing Outside

Cancún has many well-equipped professionals with lots of water toys on hand to help you have the time of your life in this gorgeous natural beach environment. Following are some of the best options for playing outside (though just plunking down on a private spot on a beach seems to be good enough for some).

ATVs & Horses: Rough Riding Through the Jungle

Rancho Loma Bonita's (☎ **998/887-5465** or 998/887-5423) offers both horseback riding and ATVs, and the two haven't collided yet despite the popularity of the place. For $720, you get 2 hours to buzz through the jungle on a fine animal or a ridiculous motorized vehicle. Once you reach the beach, you get two more hours of chilling out and swimming, plus a picnic lunch and soda (included). Insurance and a guide also come with the package. **Cancún Mermaid** (☎ **998/886-4177** or 998/843-6517; www.cancunmermaid.com) also offers ATV tours through the rainforest, where you can see more species of wildlife and lush vegetation in an hour than you will in a whole year of city living (though no horses) for $490; you get a 2-hour guided tour, and no food, but they do pick you up at your hotel.

Bullfighting

Bullfights in Cancún aren't cheap, but they are quite a sight if you've never seen a stubborn, 2-ton animal with a small brain duke it out with a wiry, flamboyantly dressed man to a soundtrack of flamenco music, all in front of hundreds of screaming fans. Vegans and PETA card-carrying members will hate this display of animal-cruelty-for-sport's-sake, but adventure-seekers may find that these bullfights—which are bloody, terrifying, and drawn out—carry the same sort of sordid appeal as a car that has burst into flames on the freeway. Your mind knows it's terrible; you can't look away.

Each fight night has dancing followed by four bulls (and the four cowboys who try to tame them). Fights take place at **Plaza del Toros,** Av. Bonampak and Calle Sayil (☎ **998/884-8372;** bull@prodigy.net.mx), Wednesday nights at 3:30pm, and admission is $500. Check with the receptionist at your hotel for tickets, or buy them across the street at Los Almendros (p. 198), where you can also get a spicy meal before the match.

Scuba Diving

If you're a certified diver, you probably have an idea of the magnificent sights that await you in **The Great Mesoamerican Reef,** at Punta Nizuc. This largest reef in the Western Hemisphere (and one of the largest in the world) includes sunken ships that add spice to the already hearty slew of tropical fish, sea turtles, sea horses, octopuses, nurse sharks, and other treasures that lie a little deeper below sea level.

If you have done your homework and logged some advanced diving courses, opportunities for cave and cenote diving abound in the area as well. **El Garrafon Natural Park** (p. 230) and **The Cave of the Sleeping Sharks** (p. 231) are just two of many exciting options within day-trip distance.

Aquaworld (Bulevar Kulkulcan Km 15.2; ☎ **998/848-8300**) is the biggest dive shop in the area, and it sends out boats to the most locations. Whether you are a certified pro or a nervous novice, Aquaworld has English-speaking instructors who will plan a dive to suit your needs; cave dive, explore underwater ruins, or simply learn to buddy breathe correctly for the first time. Dives come with gear, a one-time dive is $700, 4-day certification is $3,000, and there are a lot of interesting combinations of options in between. It's open 24 hours, in case you've always wanted to dive at night. A slightly smaller but no less reputable outfit, **Scuba Cancún,** Bulevar Kukulcan Km 5 (☎ **998/849-7508;** www.scubacancun.com.mx) also does boat trips, resort, and full certification programs. For both companies, remember that if you do the 4-day certification, you won't be able to drink more than a couple of beers at night. A morning hangover is a minor inconvenience on land, but if you take it 12m (40 ft.) underwater it becomes a serious threat to your safety.

Snorkeling

The water in Cancún really has to be seen to be believed. It is at once blue, clear, calm, and warm so you can't stay out of it for long. And snorkeling is one of the best ways to enjoy the waves and see all of the dazzling reefs and tropical wildlife on offer. Even if you stay at your hotel, you will be amazed at the stunning array of fish you'll encounter a few feet from the shore.

If you decide to take a guided tour farther out, my favorite operator is **Cancún Mermaid** (☎ **998/843-6517;** www.cancunmermaid.com). The guides there are super friendly and know where to find all the best sea sightings. A boat trip to the **Great Mesoamerican Reef** (see "Scuba Diving," earlier) costs $500 per person including equipment, lunch, beer, soda, 2 hours on the reef, and round-trip transport to and from your hotel.

Other spectacular spots for snorkeling include nearby **Isla Contoy** and **El Garrofon Natural Park** (p. 230). Most hotels have a travel desk right in the lobby where you can arrange trips or point you toward one of the many agencies in town. Tours usually go for $440 to $650, depending on how long you hang out on the boat and how fancy a lunch you want. ***Tip:*** Many hotels in Cancún have snorkeling equipment that they will lend to you for free or for a small fee, so you can save on renting from an operator.

Swimming with Dolphins

It's easy to snicker at the inescapable ads and promos you'll see for **Dolphin Discovery** (☎ **998/849-4757;** www.dolphindiscovery.com), but deep down you know you want to swim with, pet, and possibly hug a dolphin. Before your swim (in a fenced-in section of the ocean), you get a lecture of neat facts about dolphins; did you know dolphins have more recreational sex than any other mammals (no wonder they're always smiling), that their brains are four times the size of humans', and that many "reputable" scientists believe that we evolved from these sleek, smart creatures? Sessions start at 10:30am, noon, 2pm, and 3:30pm, and range from $870 to $1,530.

Parque Nizuc, Bulevar Kukulkan Km 25 (☎ **998/881-3030**), offers much of the same, although the dolphin swim takes place in an elaborate aquarium instead of the ocean. They also have a water park with some rockin' waterslides included in the price of the swim.

The downside of your little petting session with Flipper? Dolphins living in captivity, even in dolphinariums with the best credentials, get sick easily, and have shorter life spans. Visit the **Whale and Dolphin Conservation Society** (www.wdcs.org) and **Tread Lightly** (www.treadlightly.org) for more information.

Shopping

As one of the major resort destinations in the world, Cancún certainly has first-class shopping—unfortunately much of it is at first-class prices. If you thought that you were coming to Mexico to get killer bargains and steals on luxury goods, think again. Cancún is like the Palm Springs of Mexico, and though there are many designer outlets with exclusive labels, there are no sales.

A general rule for arts and crafts: Buy them elsewhere in Mexico. Cancún is the priciest place to buy Mexican crafts, partly because they are imported from other towns, and partly because the vendors here know what they can get for them. If your time in Mexico is limited to Cancún only (nothing wrong with that), check out the Parque Palapas or Central Plaza of El Centro (see "Hanging Out at the Parque Las

Palapas," p. 204) on a weekend, particularly Sunday, when many artists and vendors hawk their wares. In the Zona Hotelera, you can find similar goods (for slightly higher prices) at Coral Negro.

→ **Coral Negro** ★ This is the best place in the Zona Hotelera to get handmade souvenirs. There is also a Mexican Flea Market (look for the giant painted sign) right next-door. A cheaper, wider variety of crafts and handmade gifts can be found in the main plaza of El Centro on weekend nights, or on Avenida Tulum during the day. *Bulevar Kulkulcan Km 9.5.* ☎ *998/885-2200. www.kukulcanplaza.com.*

→ **Forum by the Sea** This mall is mostly made up of clubs and restaurants, including Rainforest and Hard Rock Cafe. It also has **Tommy Hilfiger, Harley Davidson, Swatch, Levis** (which is much posher and higher priced than in the States), and more **Diesel.** There is an outdoor huge food court with cheaper lunch fare than pretty much anywhere else in the Zona Hotelera. *Bulevar Kulkulcan Km 9.* ☎ *998/883-4425.*

→ **Kulkulcan Plaza** This is my least favorite of the malls, I was overwhelmed by the hundreds of stores filled with absolutely nothing I wanted to buy. That said, you'll find a full movie theater, plenty of restaurants, and a few good crafts stores featuring handmade clothes, shoes, and jewelry. This is more a place to watch movies and eat than anything else. *Bulevar Kulkulcan Km 9.5.* ☎ *998/885-2200. www.kukulcanplaza.com.*

→ **La Isla Shopping Center** This premium mall has all the hottest name brands including **Lacoste, Diesel, Guess, Nine West, DKNY,** as well as some posh lingerie and bikini shops you won't find in the U.S. (If you do yoga, there is a whole **Brasil Sur** store here, which is the coveted favorite brand of most yoga instructors, and very hard to find in the U.S.) You may be surprised to find that familiar favorites like Diesel and Guess have a whole different style down here, one that is more colorful, revealing, and tropical. You won't find bargains, but you will find the newest looks south of the border in revealing cuts and fabrics that never make it up to the States. Guess especially is a lot gutsier and less of what you would expect in an American mall. For guys with posh tastes, La Isla's got upscale brand stores **Lazaro Montero, Paul and Shark,** and even a **Tycoon Store.**

Ladies, if you're looking for lip gloss and lotions to replace all those tubes of "gels" that those bullies at airport security robbed you of, this mall has the best make-up and designer toiletry outlets, and most of them have duty-free price tags. Queen of them all is **Ultrafemme** which has brands like Clinique and Estée Lauder in pretty pastel shades to compliment your new tan. If you have the kind of skin that turns pink instead of brown under the Cancún sun, the selection of fancy self-tanners is a world above what you can find in the States.

The center also has an aquarium, a full movie theater, and a few bars and clubs, though I don't recommend them except for an afternoon cocktail.

Eat lunch at **La Casa de Las Margaritas,** which has great salads including warm wild mushroom with Mexican cheese, and other new twists on classic Mexican dishes. *Bulevar Kulkulkan Km 12.5.* ☎ *998/883-1038. www.laislacancun.com.mx.*

→ **Mayafair Plaza** This place is old school. The main attraction is **Sanborn's,** which is a huge department store sort of like Macy's, except with a much better selection of Mexican pastries and other tasty local foods (check out the crazy wedding cakes!), and the biggest array of English books in Cancún. This is also a great place to pick up CDs of those Latin artists you've just discovered in the clubs. There's also some quality leather stores with those cute handcrafted satchels with the long straps. *Bulevar Kulkulcan Km 10.* ☎ *998/883-2801.*

➔ **Plaza Caracol** ★★ At first you may be disappointed to find that this whale of a shopping center is mostly filled with hundreds of jewelry, swimsuit, and cheesy souvenir shops, but if you adjust your attitude, you're guaranteed to leave with a one-of-a-kind piece of jewelry (you have hundreds to chose from) that you couldn't find on the street or in the States. Every kind of body adornment you can imagine—from handcrafted silver, to rare coral and seashell pieces, to that special belly-button ring you've been looking for your whole life—lies within this huge mall o' jewelry.

If you don't wear jewelry there is one store, **ENVY,** on the bottom floor that carries top fashion houses like Gucci, BCBG, Dolce & Gabana, Chloe, and a slew more for you to drool over, at prices slightly less than what you'd expect (though still steep). It's an enjoyable place to get ideas for knockoffs to actually buy, and if you get really lucky they may be having a blowout sale. There are a few quality lunch places with smashing margaritas if you need a break from the glare of all those glittery earrings and necklaces. You'll find **Ultrafemme** here as well. *Bulevar Kulkulcan Km 10.5.* ☎ *998/883-2945.*

Road Trips: The Yucatán & Tres Rios

Cancún offers lots of accessible road trip options,.which are each great ways to supplement your club-heavy vacation with some authentic Mexican culture.

If you are going to be jetting around Mexico and will be closer to the pyramids of **Chichén Itzá** (p. 301), there is no need to try to make it in a day trip from Cancún (2.5 hr. by car and 3 by tour bus). However, if you are only staying in Cancún, you must visit this breathtaking pyramid. Luckily there are many tour companies based in Cancún who take care of all of the annoying details for you so you can be back on the party strip in time for dinner. **ADO buses** (p. 184) go between Cancún and Chichén Itzá every 2 hours during the day, and cost about $140 round-trip for a first-class bus; a second-class bus is significantly less, but it will take you all day to get there.

For an outdoor adventure, try the eco–theme park of **Xcaret,** often called a "Maya Disneyland" (p. 266), about an hour south of Cancún.

Just 10 minutes from the **Tulum ruins** (p. 268) you'll find the amazing ecological park of **Xel Ha** (p. 268). It's about an hour and a half from Cancún along Carretera Chetumal-Cancún Km 240 (with large signs once you start to get close).

Farther south of Tulum, you'll find the greatest protected collection of flora and fauna in Mexico at **Sian Ka'an** (p. 275), which is 500,000 hectares (1.3 million acres) in size and over 97km (60 miles) long.

Tres Rios

A do-it-yourselfer's alternative to the country's more manicured theme parks, **Tres Rios,** Carretera Cancún, Playa del Carmen Km 40 (☎ **998/887-8077**), about 25 minutes from Cancún, has a wealth of hiking and biking trails through the jungle for more rugged outdoor enthusiasts. This is my favorite of all the eco-parks because of its hands-off approach to letting you enjoy the gorgeous 60 hectares (150 acres) of nature within its boundaries. Tres Rios is so big and full of wildlife and opportunities to explore that you may feel the need to come back for a second or third day to get in all of the kayaking, canoeing, and snorkeling that the three rivers encourage, after you've had your fill of the practically untouched hiking and biking trails through the jungle.

Included in the $220 admission ticket is bike rental, guided canoe trips (or just the canoe if you prefer), kayaks, snorkeling gear, and (for a break between paddling and peddling) a hammock or beach chair. Diving, horseback riding, and private kayaking tours are available for extra fees, but you may want to take a day exploring the jungle on your own, and save the premium activities for a less enticing spot. Many travel agencies push half-day kayaking packages for around $50 that include pick-up and drop-off at your hotel plus lunch and booze, but don't cut your time in half here. Either drive yourself or arrange for a tour company or shuttle service that leaves you there for a full day (9am–5pm). Ask your hotel front desk about tour companies that can arrange a trip here.

The Yucatán Peninsula

Yucatán means "place of richness" in the Aztec language, and the Yucatán peninsula, which is made up of three different states on Mexico's eastern peninsula, is every bit as stuffed with attractions as its name promises. The Maya dominated this region from around A.D. 100 to A.D. 1300, and evidence of their great intellectual and architectural achievements dot the landscape—from the ruins of Chichén Itzá, Tulum, Cobá, and Uxmal to urban museums jam-packed with ancient treasures in towns such as Cozumel. These days, the people of the Yucatán also make the continued influence of the Maya known through their art: From vibrant revolutionary murals on the sides of haciendas in Playa del Carmen to performance artists hustling in Mérida's main square, the peninsula offers countless authentic cultural experiences.

Then there are the peninsula's amazing outdoor opportunities, like the first-rate diving off the island of Cozumel and the snorkeling around the region's other island, Isla Mujeres. The adventure action isn't limited to the islands, though; the region's lush ecosystem makes for a wealth of mind-blowing outdoor options like zip line canopy tours and *cenote* (wellspring) diving. Finally, the nightlife in this area may not be quite as wild as Cancún's (that town is technically part of the peninsula, but it's covered in chapter 5). But groove to a live bolero band in Mérida or work some voodoo in an actual voodoo lounge in Playa del Carmen, and you can't help but realize how rich this region is, in every respect.

Best of the Yucatán

- **Best Ride:** There is only one road that stretches along the coast of the 13km-long (8-mile) Isla Mujeres and this idyllic stretch of asphalt is a place you'll want to return to again and again during your stay on Isla. The empty stretches of open road bordering the water are the perfect place to **rent a moped** without having to worry about the psycho traffic of most other Mexican resort towns. Pristine beaches and cheap seafood shacks dot the scenic loop and make for fun stops along the way. See p. 221.
- **Best Beachfront Hostel:** Playa Norte is the most beautiful beach on Isla Mujeres, and **Pocna Hostel** is right next to its tranquil waves. For under $100 a night, you can relax in a hammock in one of the many private outdoor alcoves, dance to live music barefoot in the bar with $10 pints, and join the most affordable snorkeling and dive expeditions on Isla. And with a restaurant serving up fresh eats for under $20 and a laid-back international party scene, you may want to rest your pack here permanently. See p. 223.
- **Best Tropical Hideaway with a Yoga Vibe:** The paths between the bungalows at **Hotel Na Balam** in Isla Mujeres are paved with the spirals of pink conch shells, free yoga classes are offered every morning in a two-story palapa overlooking the ocean, and despite the resort's success, you'll always feel like you are alone on a deserted island (in the best kind of way). Though it's just a stone's throw away from the pristine Playa Norte beach and a 5-minute walk from town, Na Balam is the definition a peaceful retreat. See p. 224.
- **Best Place to Eat Fish with Your Hands:** At **Playa Lancheros** in Isla Mujeres, the only thing you'll see more often than families ripping apart whole fish with their fingers are children playing happily in the water bordering this beachside seafood-shack. Home of the famous fish Tikin Xic, the pros at Restaurant Lancheros have been baking whole red snappers rubbed with bitter orange and chiles in their massive wood-fired oven for over 50 years. Tikin Xic turns the flesh of the snapper bright red, but the fish is so flavorful, you'll take pride in being caught red handed. See p. 226.
- **Best Home Away from Home:** The friendly folks who run Cozumel's **Condumel Beach Apartments** go out of their way to make sure that you have a stress-free vacation. All of the little details, from the fridge stocked with essentials like beer, sodas, milk, eggs, and (of course) salsa and tequila, to the lending library and the book of coupons for local restaurants left by your bed, help you relax and enjoy snorkeling or swimming in the transparent waters that surround the spacious apartments. See p. 239.
- **Best Place to Eat Authentic Mexican Food: El Moro** is on the other side of Cozumel, far away from the strip of restaurants and shops that border the port and cater to cruise ships. Even if you don't eat from its sublime menu, it's worth a trip here just to experience a decidedly hidden, and authentic, part of the island. See p. 242.
- **Best Hipster Hotel:** Every detail in the rebellious **Hotel Basico** in Playa del Carmen is industrially inclined and undeniably chic, including its young, chiseled guests. Winner of a number of recent prizes for innovative design, Basico is unlike any hotel you've ever

stayed in before. In-room details include a massive bathtub in the center of the room, a complimentary Polaroid camera chained to the king-size bed, and totally exposed pipes. Outdoor perks include free salsa classes in the hopping rooftop bar, with two whirlpools that are filled with hotties at all hours. See p. 257.

- **Best Cheap Hotel for Living It Up:** All the laid-back elements of Playa del Carmen's popular **Siesta Fiesta Hotel** resort and bar combine to make you feel like you're at one giant house party. From the free live music every night, to the mattresses on the floor of the tree-housey rooms, to the low budget, fun crowd the place attracts, to the heavenly piña coladas, you're bound to have a good time during your stay here. See p. 255.
- **Best Place to Get Your Daily Dose of Fruits and Vegetables:** Though old-school Mexican food has many merits, big salads are not one of them. **100% Natural,** a nouveau vegetarian eatery with an outpost in Playa del Carmen, offers new takes on your old favorites like enchiladas and ceviche, while incorporating organic ingredients such as wild mushrooms and whole grains into the mix. Their smoothies and soups are also packed with flavorful, healthy ingredients. See p. 259
- **Best Bar for Drinking in Bed:** At the impossibly hip hotel **Hotel Deseo** in Playa del Carmen you can mingle over mojitos while sharing soft beds with gauzy canopies. Both day and night, this elevated spot overlooking 5th Avenue is the best place to find Playa del Carmen's finest hanging out. See p. 258.
- **Best Voodoo Lounge:** Haven't heard of Santeria, or Latin American voodoo? Luckily, you can get your voodoo on at the decadent nightclub **La Santanera** in the heart of Playa del Carmen. There you can learn spells in the bathroom, dance in front of a giant illuminated crystal ball, and drink potent alcoholic elixirs under spirals of sequined skulls the size of cars. See p. 262.
- **Best Art Museum with Beds:** If you live and breathe art, now you can sleep and eat it too. Both locations of **Hotel Trinidad** in Mérida are recognized by art organizations in Mexico as official art museums. In addition to the installations and paintings that cover every inch of shared space, both unusual sleeping establishments boast rates that fit every budget from backpacker to billionaire. Though it boasts quarters with low ceilings and shared bathrooms to luxury suites that have been featured in design magazines, the most creative thing about Hotel Trinidad is the diversity of the guests it attracts. See p. 288.
- **Best Bed-and-Breakfast:** Staying at **Casa Mexilio** in Mérida is like staying in the home of an old friend. An old friend who happens to be in possession of a lushly restored hacienda with gorgeous Maya artifacts and private suites decorated to mirror the personalities of famous Mexican luminaries, and an old friend who cooks up one very good breakfast. See p. 287.
- **Best Place to Admire Frida Kahlo:** Gabriela Praget, the owner and chef of Mérida's **La Casa de Frida Restaurant and Art Gallery** has created a delightful shrine to the life and work of everyone's favorite Mexican art maven. Unusual prints, photos, and facts about the artist make up the cheerful decor, but the delicately prepared dishes, which feature hard-to-find regional specialties like the Chile en Nogada, are the true works of art. See p. 290.
- **Best High-Tech Cafe:** At Mérida's **El Hoyo Café Restaurant** you may enjoy

The Yucatán Peninsula

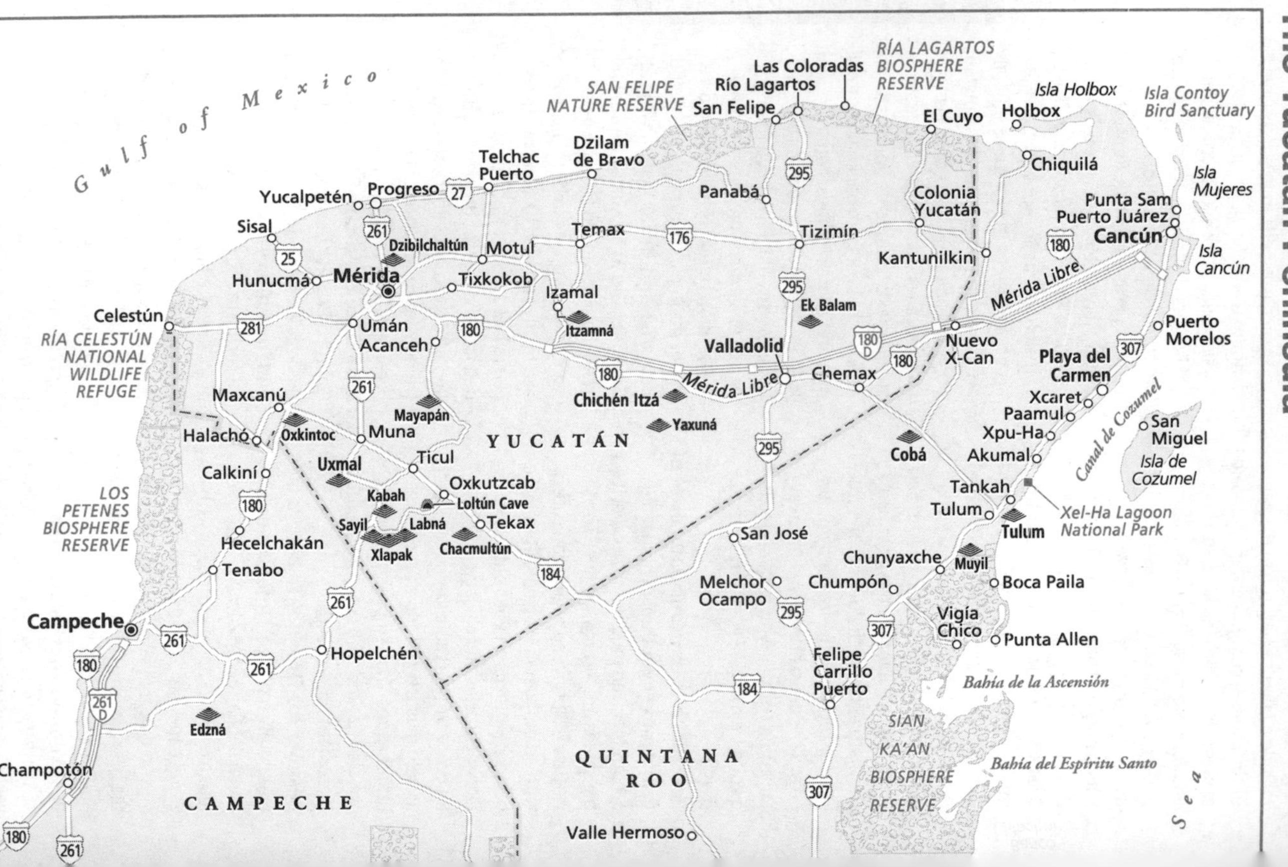

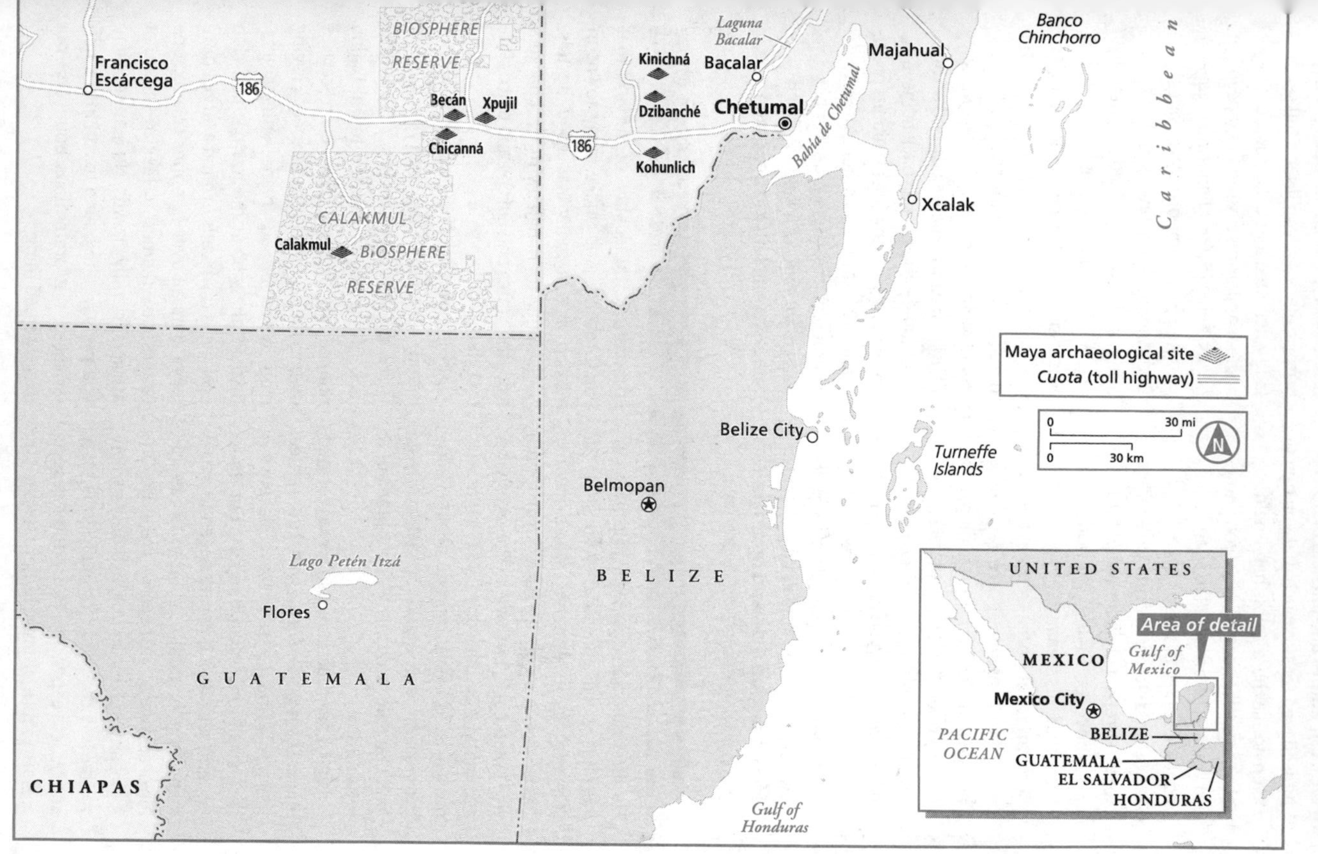
Caribbean
Banco Chinchorro
Maya archaeological site
Cuota (toll highway)
0
30 mi
0
30 km
N
UNITED STATES
Area of detail
Gulf of Mexico
MEXICO
Mexico City
PACIFIC OCEAN
BELIZE
GUATEMALA
EL SALVADOR
HONDURAS
Majahual
Xcalak
Turneffe Islands
Bahía de Chetumal
Laguna Bacalar
Bacalar
Chetumal
Belize City
Gulf of Honduras
Kinichná
Dzibanché
Kohunlich
Belmopan
B E L I Z E
186
Xpujil
Becán
Chicanná
BIOSPHERE RESERVE
CALAKMUL BIOSPHERE RESERVE
Calakmul
Lago Petén Itzá
Flores
G U A T E M A L A
186
Francisco Escárcega
CHIAPAS

the fresh waffles and pitchers of flower-infused iced teas so much that you don't even notice the wireless hand-held phone or Wi-Fi access. Now you know—so you can be prepared to spend a few hours here. See p. 292.

- **Best Popsicles:** In Mérida, an average weather report includes temperatures well above 100°F (38°C). No wonder then, that this steamy city possesses the best variety of frozen treats in the entire Western hemisphere. From milky mango licuados to chocolate dipped ice cream cones, **Janitzio** is the place to fulfill your cold, creamy dreams at prices that allow you to sample more than a few frozen delights. See p. 292.
- **Best Place to Compare Piercings and Tattoos:** Visiting Mérida's magnificent **Museo Regional de Antropología** is much more exciting than the average tattoo parlor. Within the walls of this historic mansion, you'll see a full set of jade-encrusted teeth, diagrams of ancient apparatuses used to shape infant heads, and earrings of enormous gages sculpted from semi-precious stones. Body modification junkies and anthropologically inclined art enthusiasts will be equally impressed. See p. 298.
- **Best Souvenir Store:** Forget all those jewelry stands and street-side embroidered dresses. The pint-size skull-headed miniatures at Mérida's quirky **Miniaturas** will please any and all of your family and friends back home. By irreverently poking fun at famous politicians, rock stars, and other cultural characters, these goods deliver big laughs without taking up too much space in your suitcase. See p. 300.

Isla Mujeres

The first question any local who lives on Isla Mujeres will ask you when you meet is, *"Cuando vas a regresar?"* which means, "When are you coming back?" Not *if* you will come back, but *when.* The overlying assumption is that once you have witnessed Isla Mujeres' serene beauty, laid-back charm, and quirky attractions, you won't be able to depart without plans of a return trip.

Isla's charm actually isn't exaggerated much: The island is such a gem, I guarantee that you'll find it hard to leave. Because it is so small (only 13km/8 miles from tip to tip) and secluded, it has managed to avoid many of the pitfalls of more accessible Mexican towns. The beaches are as beautiful as any in Cancún or Playa del Carmen, yet far less crowded. The seafood is tasty and far less expensive. Many of the resorts are also more affordable here, especially considering the quality of service that you'll receive. And unlike many towns in Mexico, Isla actually has good hostels, good spots to mingle with backpackers from the States and Europe and places farther flung.

Most important of all, a genuinely chill island vibe permeates everything here. There are very few cars on Isla, and this lack of traffic contributes to the calm, relaxed atmosphere. That calm carries over to the nightlife—don't expect a raging club scene or big name entertainers. Instead, the vibe at the few bar and club options in town calls to mind a large house party. Bars all over Isla offer two-for-one caipirinhas—the best in Mexico—and that attracts friendly crowds. No matter where you party, you're bound to run into familiar faces, not pretentious bouncers—not exactly a bad thing.

Isla Mujeres

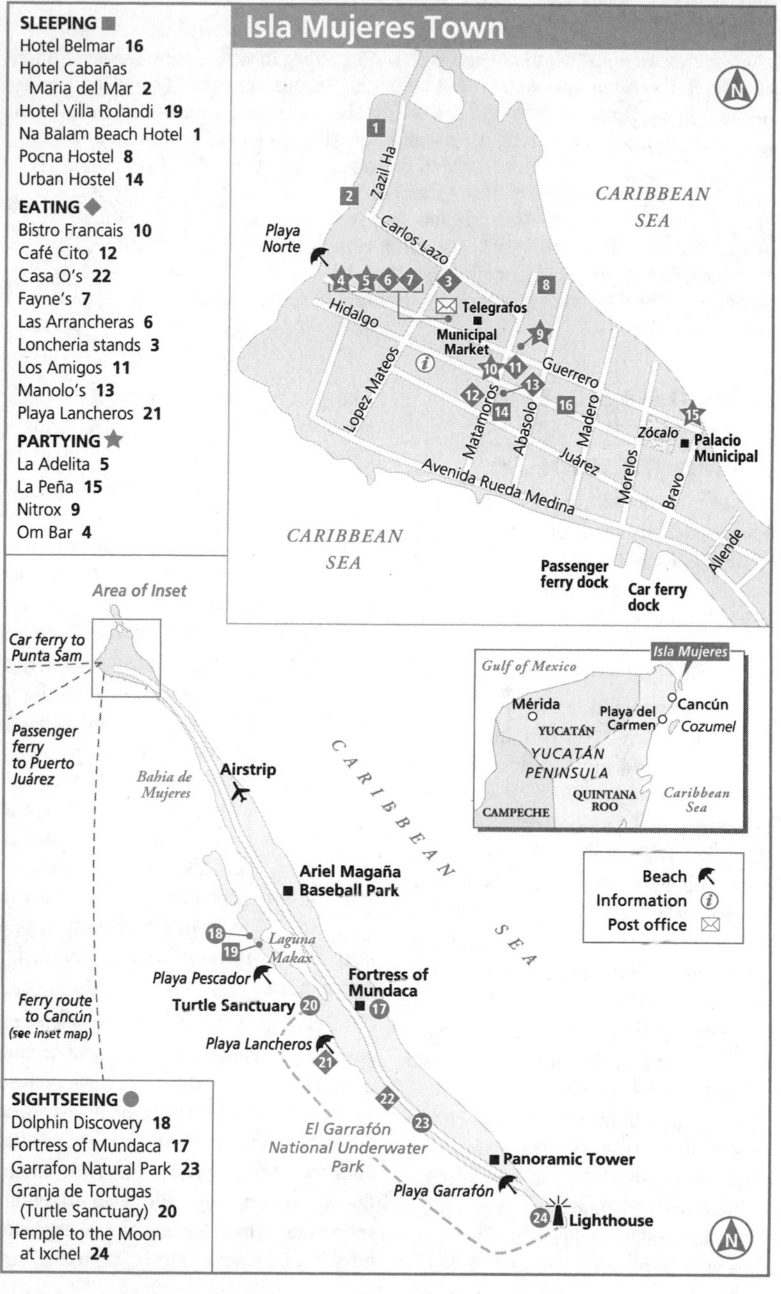

How Isla Mujeres Got Its Name

Isla Mujeres means "Island of Women," but contrary to what many would like to believe, it was *not* once ruled by hot lesbians. Spanish explorer Francisco Hernandez de Cordova renamed the island such after he arrived from Cuba in 1517—his horny sailors made an unexpected stop on Isla after they spotted the temple's alluring sculptures of topless goddesses while at sea. The voluptuous statues were of the goddess of the moon Ixtel, and her cosmic daughter and daughters-in-law Ixchelbeliax, Ixhunie, and Ixhunieta. Sadly, most of these statues were poached by explorers, and what was left of them was destroyed by Hurricane Gilbert in 1988. Locals claim that though her body was stolen, the serene spirit of Ixtel still influences the tranquil tides that seem to supernaturally bless the island.

Getting There & Getting Around

GETTING INTO TOWN

BY BOAT Ferries for Isla Mujeres leave from the dock at Playa Tortugas (☎ **998/877-0618**) just north of Cancún; the trip takes 45 minutes and ferries run about every half-hour. A ticket runs $70 one-way and $140 round-trip.

There are also ferries to Isla Mujeres from the **Playa Linda,** known as the Embarcadero pier in Cancún, but they're less frequent and more expensive than those from Puerto Juárez.

A **water taxi** (☎ **998/886-4270** or -4847; asterix@cablered.net.mx) to Isla Mujeres operates from **Playa Caracol,** between the Fiesta Americana Coral Beach Hotel and the Xcaret terminal on the island, with prices about the same as those from Playa Linda; round-trip fares are $150. Scheduled departures are at 9am, 11am, and 1pm, with returns from Isla Mujeres at noon and 5pm.

Taxis are available at the dock once you arrive in Isla to take you to your final destination. Rates generally run $25 to $45 for anywhere on the island. Moped and bicycle rentals are also readily available as you depart your ferry.

Keep in mind that the time of the latest ferry departure changes often. As a rule, it is good to plan to leave for the Isla on the 3pm ferry at the latest, as the other ones don't always run. Better still, ask the concierge of your hotel to confirm what the schedule is on the morning of your departure to Isla Mujeres.

Also be wary of pirate "guides" who tell you either that the ferry is canceled or that it's several hours until the next ferry. They'll offer the services of a private *lancha* (small boat) for about $400—and it's nothing but a scam. Small boats are available and, on a co-op basis, charge $150 to $250 one-way, based on the number of passengers. They take about 50 minutes and are not recommended on days with rough seas. Check with the clearly visible ticket office—the only accurate source for information.

BY PLANE You can fly into Cancún on any major domestic or Mexican airline (p. 184 in Cancún). Once you have arrived at Cancún Airport International, it is about a half-hour cab or shuttle van ride to the dock for a ferry. If you are arriving late in the afternoon, you will need to either spend the night in Cancún or hire a private boat from the dock to ferry you to the Isla.

See "By Boat" earlier for info on taking ferries or private boats to the island.

BY CAR I strongly recommend against driving a car to Isla Mujeres, since tooling around on a moped or in a golf cart is part of the fun of visiting here. In fact, if you drive a car, you'll detract from the distinct charm of a place where most of the traffic consists of mopeders and bikers.

If you insist on bringing your car, there is a port at **Punta Sam** (no phone) past Puerto Juárez, where you'll find a car ferry that runs five or six times throughout the day between 8am and 8pm; it takes 40 minutes and prices vary. Cars should arrive an hour before the ferry departure to register for a place in line and pay the posted fee, which varies depending on the weight and type of vehicle. The sole gas pump in Isla is at the intersection of Avenida Rueda Medina and Calle Abasolo, just northwest of the ferry docks.

GETTING AROUND

ON FOOT Get ready to walk. Downtown is so small that you can make it from one end to the other in less then half an hour on foot. The entire downtown is designed with pedestrians in mind, and most of the traffic on the main streets is foot traffic. If that doesn't convince you to break out your sneaks, know that if you stay at any of the resorts on Playa Norte (the best beach on the island) you will be less than a 10-minute walk from the town center.

MTV Best **BY MOPED** ★★ Unlike most Mexican cities, Isla Mujeres is the perfect place to rent a moped. Unlike in Cancún or Cozumel, where motorcycle riding is equivalent to a game of Russian roulette due to traffic, Isla Mujeres is the perfect place for motorcycle virgins. The virtually carless, flat, and newly paved roads that border the untouched beaches along the north side of the island all add up to dream conditions for any first-time rider. (Full disclosure: I was once one myself, and couldn't believe how much fun I had whizzing along on the back of a moped here.)

While you won't need a moped to get to town and back, they are great for day trips to the attractions along the coasts of the island. There is really only one main road that circles the island, with dead end turnoffs to beaches and local attractions, so it is virtually impossible to get lost.

Don't rent from a company that doesn't offer insurance and a helmet. I prefer **Ciro's** (Av. Guerrero No. 11 on the corner of Av. Matamoros; ☎ **998/877-0568**), which has the newest models of mopeds. Most moped rentals are about $350 per day or $100 per hour.

BY GOLF CART If you're traveling in a group of three or more and feel more secure in a vehicle with four wheels on the road as opposed to two, golf carts are a safe and sunny way to explore all the Isla has to offer. Plus, you don't have to get dressed to drive—bathing suits seem to be the clothing of choice for golf carters. And keep an eye out for locals riding around in souped-up customized carts. Some have bling that would make Snoop Dogg envious.

For golf cart rentals (like mopeds), there is no reason to rent from someone who doesn't include insurance. I like **El Sol Golf Cart Rental** (☎ **998/877-0791** or 998/877-0068) on Av. Fransico I. Madero 5, because they will deliver to your doorstep, but there are a variety of reputable rental companies on the island. A good price for golf carts is $150 per hour or $450 per day.

BY TAXI The majority of the cars on the island are taxis, which will take you to almost anywhere on the island for $25 to $45. Taxi fares are posted by the street where the taxis park, so be sure to check the rate before agreeing to a ride.

BY BIKE Just 13km (8 miles) from tip to tip and with flat terrain, Isla is a biker's dream. Average bike rentals are about $30 per hour or $70 per day. Many hotels rent bikes, or can point you in the right direction of a good bike shop. Two good ones to try are: **Rentadora María José Bikes** (Av. Madero; no phone) and **Moto Rent Kan-Kin Bikes** (Av. Absalo; no phone).

Isla Mujeres Basics

Isla Mujeres is about 8km (5 miles) long and 4km (2½ miles) wide, with the town at the northern tip. "Downtown" is a compact 4 blocks by 6 blocks, so it's very easy to get around. The **ferry docks** are at the center of town, within walking distance of most hotels, restaurants, and shops. The street running along the waterfront is **Avenida Rueda Medina,** commonly called the **malecón (boardwalk).** The **Mercado Municipal (town market)** is by the post office on **Calle Guerrero,** an inland street at the north edge of town, which, like most streets in the town, is unmarked.

TOURIST INFO & OFFICES

The tourist office (☎ **998/877-0767**) on Av. Rueda Medina 130, is on your left as you reach the end of the pier. It's open Monday through Friday from 9am to 4pm, closed on Saturdays and Sundays. Their publication, *Islander,* is very useful, and one of my favorite local tour guides. It's available at many of the island's hotels.

RECOMMENDED WEBSITES:

- **www.isla-mujeres.net**: The Tourism Board of Isla Mujeres puts out some of the most comprehensive information on the island, from its hotels to local legends to overlooked attractions.
- **www.isladiveguide.com**: This site is the authority on all things scuba on Isla Mujeres, from little known sites to the best instructors.

Isla Mujeres Nuts & Bolts

Banks A number of banks are within a few blocks of the ferry docks, such as **Bital** on Avenida Rueda Median across from Zona Hotelera. Most are open Monday to Friday from 8:30am to 5pm and Saturday from 9am to 2pm.

Emergencies In case your golf cart unexpectedly flips, the **Hospital de la Armada** (☎ **998/877-0001**) on Avenida Rueda Medina at Calle Ojon P. Blanco accepts patients on an emergency-only basis. If you have a more minor health issue, they will send you over to the **Centro de Salud** (☎ **998/877-0117**) on Avenida Guerrero, 1 block before the malecón.

Internet/Wireless Hot Spots Internet access is less prominent in Isla's hotel lobbies than elsewhere in Mexico, since life traditionally moves at a slower pace here. Luckily, **Cyber Isla Mujeres** (Av. Francisco y Madero 17, between calles Juárez and Hidalgo; ☎ **998/877-0272**) offers Internet access from 8am to 10pm, Monday through Saturday. The bottomless cups of free coffee they serve offer a great "perk" while you work.

Pharmacies **Isla Mujeres Farmacia** (☎ **998/877-0178**) has the best selection of prescription and over-the-counter medicines. It's on Calle Benito Juárez, between Morelos and Bravo, across from Rachet & Rome jewelry store.

Post Office The *correo* is at Calle Guerrero 12 (☎ **998/877-0085**), at the corner of López Mateos, near the market. It's open Monday through Friday from 9am to 4pm.

Telephone Tips The area code on Isla Mujeres is **998. DigaMe** (☎ **608/467-4202;** info@digame.com) on Avenida Guerrero between calles Absolo and Matamoros has cellphones for rent with short-term long distance phone plans. If you're just looking to make a few quick calls, there are pay phones that accept change in downtown Isla, and phone cards are dispersed at shops downtown.

Sleeping

Isla Mujeres excels at little resorts, which are vastly cozier than the mega hotels on the mainland, but don't skimp on treats like spas and fresh beachside restaurants. If you had your sights set on Cancún but were shocked by the town's prices, the deals on this sunny, small strip will come as a relief. Because of the great value of most of the island's accommodations, you're also likely to bump into a lot of students and other younger travelers from all over the world. While planning where to stay, keep in mind that it might cost you extra to travel here versus Cancún, though.

HOSTELS

MTV Best → **Pocna Hostel** ★★ Quite possibly the most happening hostel in Mexico, Pocna Hostel is right on a stretch of beautiful beachfront and just steps from the center of town. It also caters to all budgets, boasting an area for camping on the beach as well as swanky air-conditioned private rooms.

Guests party in the beach bar at night and lounge in the hammocks that hang between palm trees during the day. In the large inner courtyard you can sink your toes into the sandy floor while dancing to live music and sampling dollar pints on tap. The fun loving, international crowd that the hostel attracts keeps it packed, so make sure to reserve online well in advance. There's no free continental breakfast, but the kitchen does offer up a variety of hot options all day long for about $20. The staff arranges weekly parties, movie screenings, and theme nights with games. They are also helpful when it comes to arranging diving and outdoor expeditions. *Av. Matamoros 15.* ☎ *998/877-0059 or 998/877-0059. www.pocna.com. $90 joint room, $200 private room. No credit cards. Amenities: Restaurant; bar; Internet; kitchen; laundry; shared bathrooms; sheets; telephone (in common area); towels; TV (common room). In room: A/C (in some rooms), fans, lockers.*

→ **Urban Hostel** In the likely event that Poc Na is full, this intensely painted hostel is your second best bet. Urban Hostel's location right on the main street alongside the bars and restaurants, makes it more of a party scene than a sleeper's dream. Both times I visited, contented groups of hostelers were hanging in the lounge, jamming on their guitars, and eating together on the dining deck amid a lingering cloud of earthy-smelling smoke. There's a hoppin' bar downstairs, and a juice bar next door which provides free coffee and purified water at all hours. The hostel allows guests to work the front desk and do dishes in exchange for a bed, a great arrangement if you're low on funds but less helpful if you're hoping for a wise hostess to give you local tips or help arrange day trips. *Av. Matamoros 9.* ☎ *998/877-1573. $70 bunks, $200 private double. No credit cards. Amenities: Continental breakfast; Internet; kitchen; laundry; shared bathrooms; sheets;*

telephone (in common area); towels; TV (common room). In room: Fans, lockers.

CHEAP

→**Hotel Belmar** The Hotel Belmar is in the center of downtown, directly above one of the town's most popular restaurants, Pizza Rolandi. If you're hoping for an escape from the hustle and bustle of island life, this isn't the place to be—although the scene usually quiets down around 1am. Rooms are clean and simple and come with TVs that carry American stations—a rarity on the island. Ultimately, I recommend either saving money and crashing in a hostel, or paying a little extra to be by the beach if you want a true taste of island paradise. *Av. Hidalgo 110, between Madero and Absolo. ☎ 998/877-0430. www.rolandi.com. High season $560–$900 double; low season $280–$800 double. AE, MC, V. Amenities: Restaurant; bar; laundry service; room service. In room: A/C, TV, fan.*

DOABLE

→**Hotel Cabañas María del Mar** ★ A good choice for simple beach accommodations, the Cabañas María del Mar is on the popular Playa Norte. The older two-story section behind the reception area and beyond the garden offers nicely outfitted rooms facing the beach. All have two single or double beds, refrigerators, and oceanview balconies strung with hammocks. Eleven single-story cabañas closer to the reception area are decorated in a rustic Mexican style. The third section, **El Castillo,** is across the street, by Buho's restaurant. It contains all "deluxe" rooms, but some are larger than others; the five rooms on the ground floor have large patios. Upstairs rooms have small balconies. All have ocean views, and a predominately white decor. There's a small pool in the garden. *Av. Arq. Carlos Lazo 1, on Playa Norte, ½ block from the Hotel Na Balam, 77400 Isla Mujeres, Q. Roo. ☎ 800/223-5695 in the U.S., or 998/877-0179. High season $1,100–$1,210 double; low season $660–$990 double. MC, V. Amenities: Boat for rent; bus for tours; golf cart and moto rentals; outdoor pool. In room: Fridge (in cabañas).*

SPLURGE

→**Hotel Villa Rolandi** ★★ The pet project of the successful owners of the ever-popular Rolandi Pizza chain, Hotel Rolandi is the definition of a splurge. This five-star boutique hotel sends a yacht to pick you up in Cancún and to take you back after the dream of staying here has ended. Each room has its own private hot tub on the balcony, and a gorgeous two-person stained glass shower with 10 jets. The red-brick vaulted ceilings are a marvel in modern construction, and the faux black and white snakeskin headboard somehow gets away with being edgy instead of tacky because of the simple elegance of the rest of the ivory and leather decor. The hotel's mammoth infinity pool is situated right next to a secluded stretch of beach. Both the bar and Italian restaurant in the hotel are first-rate, but pricey enough to encourage you to venture outside the villa. *Fracc. Laguna Mar SM. 7 Mz. 75 Lotes 15 y 16 Carretera Sac-Bajo. ☎ 998/877-0700 or 998/877-0500. www.villarolandi.com. $2,000–$2,900 double. AE, MC, V. Amenities: Restaurant and bar; gym; Internet in office suite; large pool; spa; Wi-Fi in lobby. In room: A/C, TV w/cable, fridge, minibar, private hot tub on balcony, shower with multiple jets.*

MTV Best → **Na Balam Beach Hotel** ★★★ A serene resort with a rustic island vibe, Na Balam works both as a romantic getaway for couples and as a haven for large groups. This popular, two-story hotel near the end of Playa Norte has comfortable rooms on a quiet, ideally located portion of the best beach in town. The large rooms are in three sections; some face the beach, and others are across the street in a garden setting with a swimming pool (open all night). The standard doubles are large enough to fit four of your closest friends. The natural exteriors, in combination with the surrounding lush foliage, swaying hammocks strewn about, and ubiquitous seashell decor, succeed in creating a truly relaxing vibe. If you're into yoga, you won't find a more revitalizing place to practice it than in the elevated palapa. Complimentary yoga classes are offered to guests there every weekday morning at 9am. *Calle Zazil Ha no. 118, Playa Norte. ☎ 998/877-0446 or 998/877-0058. www.nabalam.com. Low season $1,500 double; Dec–Apr $2,420 double. AE, MC, V. Amenities: Restaurant and bar; Internet in lounge; pool; spa; yoga classes. In room: A/C.*

Eating

The roads along the side of town closest to Playa Norte and by the Las Palmas Hotel, at Guerrero 20, are lined with **loncherías,** or breakfast and lunch stands. These stands boast the cheapest eats you'll find on the island—including everything from tacos to barbecued chicken to big breakfasts. Loncherías are probably the best place to try *huevos motulenos,* a local specialty of two sunny side up eggs on top of two fried minitortillas, with a layer of beans in between and covered with shredded Mexican cheese, fresh peas, and cubes of hot ham. Typically, you can get a huge platter of food and a soda for about $30.

At the **Municipal Market,** next to the telegraph office and post office on Avenida Guerrero, obliging, hardworking women operate several little food stands. Some of the island's best full-fledged restaurants—seafood is always a good bet here—are congregated around Hidalgo between Morelos and Abasolo.

CHEAP

➔ **Café Cito** CAFE If you're hankering for a lazy, lingering breakfast, plunk down at one of this cafe's outdoor tables for a spell. In addition to a long list of sweet and savory crepes, you can order Mexican eggs, Cuban sandwiches, and fluffy Belgium waffles topped with fruit. The cappuccinos are divine and, at $15 each, you can afford to get your buzz on. *On the corner of Av. Matamoros and Av. Juárez. No phone. Breakfast $30–$50, lunch $30–$60. No credit cards. Daily 9am–2pm.*

➔ **Fayne's** MEXICAN Infamous for their mango margaritas and other sublime alcoholic slushes, this funky bar and grill also boasts an eclectic menu of Mexican favorites done right, with plenty of fresh fish and ample vegetarian fare thrown into the mix. The walls are painted in wild colors, the bar features a gigantic aquarium, and the local art adorning the interior is done up in bright tints, all of which work together to give the restaurant a festive yet offbeat feel that suits the Isla just fine. *Av. Hildalgo No. 12A, between Av. Matamoros and Guerrero. No phone. Main courses $50–$120. No credit cards. Mon–Sat noon–11pm; Sun noon–9pm.*

➔ **Las Arrancheras** MEXICAN After a few too many margaritas, the cheesy, meaty snacks at Las Arrancheras are just the cure to coat your rumbling stomach. It's open late, so you can smell the smoky barbecue goodness when you're stumbling out of a bar a block away. It specializes in super nachos, quesadillas, and melted cheese bowls filled with spices or chunks of chicken and beef—but no matter what you order, you're guaranteed to sample the best greasy eats in town. Don't expect much ambience, though—the tiny inner area is usually so filled with smoke that you'll probably want to grab one of the few tables scattered out in front. *Av. Hidalgo Norte No. 7, across the street from La Adelita. No phone. Appetizers $20–$50, main courses $30–$70. No credit cards. Daily 2pm–2am.*

→ **Los Amigos** ★ PIZZA This local favorite is an ideal spot for grabbing a slice between bars. Though they offer a variety of vegetarian and Italian dishes, the real reason to stop by is the thin-crust pizza, and there is no better way to enjoy it than by sitting at one of the outdoor tables with a cold beer and listening to the live music from the bar next door. It's open with a full menu for breakfast and lunch; the late night menu features pizza and fries—but the crowd that packs in here around 10pm ain't complaining. *Av. Hidalgo, between Av. Matamoros and Absalo. No phone. Pizzas $20 (per slice) to $100 for a large pie. No credit cards. Mon–Sat noon–2am; Sun noon–9pm.*

MTV Best → **Playa Lancheros** ★★★ SEAFOOD Any worldly traveler knows that to get the best and cheapest seafood, you need to go straight to the source. If you want the local specialty fish Tikin Xic, then, come to this beachside restaurant at Playa Lancheros—the exotic red snapper literally swims the waters here. It's marinated in a bitter orange and chile sauce, then wrapped in a banana leaf and cooked in a massive wood-fired oven the size of a house. The end result is amazing, but the ceviche here is just as good. You can dine at white plastic tables lining the sand along the water under a large thatched palapa, or closer to the shore where there's a dance floor with more tables under a large palapa. But this is more of a serious eating place than a dancing spot—the place gets packed with families who come to stuff themselves and then work off their meal by plunging into the nearby water. *At Playa Lancheros Beach, where Av. Ruida Medina forks into Sac Bajo and Carretera Garragon. No phone. Main courses $30–$90. No credit cards. Mon–Sat noon–10pm; Sun noon–7pm.*

DOABLE

→ **Manolo's** ★★ SEAFOOD The front of this family-owned restaurant boasts a vibrant mural depicting parrots, toucans, and lush vegetation. Walk through its open archways and you'll enter an equally lush-looking palm tree filled inner courtyard, and an interior with postcards from happy customers dangling from its cheerful pink walls. The customers have reason to be happy: Seafood dishes here are exceptional for the price. For starters, the hot seafood soup is just spicy enough, and both the white asparagus and heart of palm salads are fresh and tasty. For main dishes, the fish cooked in coconut curry and the grilled lobster served with garlic drawn butter are both huge portions—but so tasty that they are easy to finish off. All main courses are served with warm, freshly baked bread. *Av. Matamoros #29, Col. Centro. No phone. Main courses $50–$150. No credit cards. Daily 1–9pm.*

SPLURGE

→ **Bistro Francais** SEAFOOD If what you're looking for is good lobster or shrimp and lots of it, this place is for you. The preparation doesn't get more complicated than some added garlic butter, but what they do they do well. Each night, they also have a hand-written list of specials that come with a free beer. I had the special, which was a combo of a lobster tail and nine jumbo shrimp for $170. All beers after the first freebie are a dollar, so drink up. *Av. Hidalgo, between Av. Lopez and Av. Matamoros. No phone. Main courses $130–$190. No credit cards. Mon–Sat 1pm–midnight; Sun 1–8pm.*

→ **Casa O's** ★★ SEAFOOD Hidden from view on a rocky drop-off to the sea, this intimate local favorite is an idyllic venue for special occasions, from catching a romantic sunset to simply sharing a bottle of wine. Though it's casually situated under an open palapa, this place feels quite fancy mainly due to the presentation of the dishes and the gracious attitudes of the waiters. (The restaurant is actually named after the incredibly polite waiters, whose names all end with the letter "O.") Pescado O's, the special snapper served with sautéed shiitake mushrooms and garlic in a brown butter sauce, is so sweet and tender that it practically dissolved once it hit my tongue. The dessert list is equally sweet, including meringue cups filled with white chocolate mousse and drizzled in hot caramel sauce. *Carretera Garafon at the turn-off to María Rankin Beach. Pass the signs for María Rankin and you will begin down a windy stone footpath which will lead you to Casa O's. ☎ 998/888-0170. www.casaos.com. Appetizers $50–$100, main courses $90–$200, desserts $30–$60. MC, V. Daily 1–10pm.*

Partying

It's worth repeating that the party scene on the Isla is significantly smaller than in Cancún. If you want big-time clubs, you'll need to head to the mainland. Otherwise, why not enjoy the relaxed vibe, along with the novelty of bumping into your new friends night after night? Most bars and clubs here are clustered around the north end of Hidalgo.

MTV Best → **La Adelita** ★★★ Named for the mistress of revolutionary Pancho Villa, this low-key bar has barrel wicker chairs with soft cushions, awesome two-for-one caipirinhas, mojitos, margaritas, and just about anything else you'd like to order, including an impressive list of fine tequila and cigars. The waiters at this local hangout seem to love working here, and will offer you a cigarette and a light if you seem so inclined, or a free shot of fine tequila with your cocktail. A huge outdoor seating area attracts a jet-setting crowd of international, young travelers every night, and is the best place on the island to strike up a casual conversation with new friends. From blocks away, you can hear the cover band that plays here almost every night; they are pretty good at switching up the song list so you can come back all week and not get bored. Local groupies show up to sing along to all of their hits. *Av. Hildalgo Norte 12A. No phone.*

→ **La Peña** ★★★ The interior of this bar is so ornate and unusual that even if you can't stay awake until 1am when the party usually gets started, you should stop by for a cocktail earlier in the evening to check out the amazing decor. Every piece of furniture is made from the sculpted and shaped roots of local trees, and for all their twistiness, the wooden thrones and lounges are remarkably comfortable. At least, that's what I thought when I plopped down in one after spending the night dancing in the sand to the best house and jungle music on the island. *Calle Nicholas Bravo, Zona Maritima. ☎ 998/845-7384.*

→ **Nitrox** Specializing in fast-paced electronica, this neon-lit club keeps the tempo up until 3am. Though it normally blasts techno and house favorites, on Wednesday nights, the club switches to salsa music. *Lote 19, Mza. 15 Calle Matamoros. ☎ 998/820-4876.*

→ **Om Bar** If you like your organic green tea spiked with something a little stronger, stop by this Zen-inspired bar for sulfate-free wines, free-trade loose tea by the pot, and a list of invigorating cocktails that incorporate fresh indigenous herbs into the mix. A progressive menu of snacks like vegetarian spring rolls, samosas, and steamed shrimp dumplings goes well with the light beverages. What really rocks are the personal taps on each table, where you can top yourself off as much as you please. The only down side is that the bar's sporadically closed during prime drinking times. *Calle Matamoros between Lotes 15 and 19. ☎ 998/820-4876.*

Heading to the Beach

Playa Norte (sometimes called Playa los Cocos), which extends around the northern tip of the island, is the most popular beach on Isla, but unlike in Cancún, this popularity doesn't translate into large crowds. Expect transparent turquoise water, soft sand, and plenty of beds and hammocks available for rent, cheaply. Since many of the restaurants here offer some of the best seafood and piña coladas on the island, this is the best beach for hanging out and relaxing. Equipment is available for watersports if you're feeling more active.

The second most popular beach on the island is **Playa Lancheros,** on the western end, but this is more a destination for the tasty seafood (p. 226) than the water itself, which is brackish and full of seaweed. The beaches that border **El Garrafon Natural Park** on the southern end of the island are better for scuba and other watersports than for swimming, because the water can get choppy.

Playa Tiburon is the most developed beach on the island, with a big restaurant, souvenir stands, calm water, and a tank where you can swim with (harmless) nurse sharks. (See "Playing Outside," on p. 230, for info.) Since Tiburon is the most developed beach on the island, it's a better place for getting henna tattoos, T-shirts, and hair braids than for relaxing in the surf.

The beaches on the east shore of the island are not safe for swimming despite their serene appearance. Because of bad riptides, many drownings have occurred on the secluded beaches on this side of the island. **Playa Media Luna** (Half Moon Beach), is one such eastern beach that, while gorgeous, is not recommended for swimming.

Sightseeing

FESTIVALS/EVENTS

The Bajada de la Virgin: This event brings out thousands of Virgin Mary believers beginning on November 30 with the Procession of the Virgin and culminating on December 8 with a fiesta that celebrates Mary's life. Locals and visitors hit the streets to feast and enjoy live music and dance. Late November through early December.

Cruz de la Bahia (Cross of the Bay) Festival: On August 17, Isla Mujeres erupts with festivities celebrating the town's founding on this date in 1854. See p. 231 for info on the actual Cross of the Bay. August 17.

MAJOR ATTRACTIONS

→ **Fortress of Mundaca** ★ A visit to this monument to love's labors lost makes for a fun moped or bike trip along the coast. The ruins themselves are quaint compared to Mexico's many Maya temples, but it's cool to see the inscriptions that El Pirata Mundaca carved to the object of his obsession living on in 200-year-old stone. As is common in Mexico, the folks in charge of this historical site have installed a makeshift zoo featuring local wildlife to try to keep your attention once you've perused the old stones. Fortunately, the zoo is one of the best in the country—I spent an hour walking around the historical site, but twice that much time checking out the wild boars, crocodiles, and other examples of local wildlife. *East of Av. Ruida Medina. Follow the main road Southeast from town till you reach the curve at Laguna Makax, then turn left onto the unpaved road to the ruin. No phone. Admission $30. Daily 10am–6pm.*

→ **Granja de Tortugas (Turtle Sanctuary)** If you've only seen small house pets and illustrated pictures of turtles, you'll be dazzled by the array of shell patterns and

The Legend of El Pirata Mundaca

According to folklore, famous 19th-century pirate El Pirata Mundaca chose Isla Mujeres as his place to retire with all of his ill-earned wealth, partly because of its natural beauty, but mostly because it was isolated enough to serve as a safe-haven from his enemies. Upon settling on the island, middle-aged Mundaca fell in love with a local 18-year-old known as La Triguena, or "The Brunette," who, as legend has it, was the most beautiful girl on the island. Despite her persistent lack of interest, El Mundaca was convinced that his massive fortune would win her over, and set to build the most magnificent hacienda ever seen on the island, filled with gardens of exotic plants and stone gates carved with dedications to her unearthly beauty. But money, in this case, couldn't buy love. No one ever lived in the opulent houses; La Triguena married a local boy before construction was completed. Each child she bore with her chosen husband slowly drove Mundaca mad until his death.

Isla Mujeres locals rejoice in the moral of this story—that a beautiful girl chose a simple local boy over a wealthy, morally corrupt old man. (Though he enjoyed a reputation as a pirate, Mundaca's real fortune was made from the human cargoes he brought from Africa to Cuba in the slave trade, many of whom died toiling in the Yucatán's sugar fields in the 1800s.) Today, you can visit the hacienda ruins, where Mundaca's inscriptions to the peasant girl are still legible on the entryways.

colors of the many sea turtles that this farm nurtures. The staff is made up of marine biologists and preservationists whose lives are dedicated to protecting these vulnerable animals from natural predators as well as poachers who illegally kill them to sell their beautiful shells. The scientists at the sanctuary hatch the turtles and keep them in captivity until they are between 5 to 10 years old, when they have grown large enough to increase their chances of survival in the wild.

Before 2005's Hurricane Wilma, the turtles here were kept in cordoned off areas of the ocean, but during the storm the barriers and docks were destroyed. The biologists rescued the turtles during the storm and have kept them in pools ever since. Construction and fundraising are still underway to replace the larger, more natural habitats, so your visit here might help make that happen sooner.

Once you're done with the turtles, venture inside to see the aquarium with rare specimens such as an albino turtle, electric eels, and translucent seahorses. *Follow Av. Ruida Medina south of town. Take the right turn about 30m/100 ft. after the Hacienda Mundaca. There should be a small sign with a picture of a turtle to mark the entrance. ☎ 998/877-0595. Admission $30. Daily 9am–5pm.*

➔ **Temple to the Moon at Ixchel** When compared to the country's more impressive ancient sites, such as Chichén Itzá, this Maya ruin is a letdown—it feels more like an unkempt stone storage shed than a working tourist attraction. It's worth a visit anyway, if only because the site is set on rolling cliffs that overlook the ocean. It's an ideal lunch stop, whether you splurge and go to the fairly expensive restaurant and bar or pack a picnic and sit in the grassy sand.

Perhaps because the government realizes these ruins aren't quite fascinating, an outdoor sculpture park has been added along the winding path to the ruins. This park features an array of sculptures that look impressive jutting out of the tall grass that dots the surrounding cliffs. If you're into sculpture, the admission fee is worth it for the outdoor art museum alone. If you're not, you will probably feel ripped off when you get to the humble ruin. *Carretera El Garrafon, about 4km/2½ miles southeast of Playa Lancheros. ☎ 998/884-9420 in Cancún, 998/877-1100 in the park. Admission $50 to walk to the ruin, entrance to the grounds is free. Daily 9am–7pm.*

Playing Outside

DOLPHIN DISCOVERY ★

The inescapable ads and promos that you'll see in town for Dolphin Discovery (**☎ 998/849-4757;** www.dolphindiscovery.com) are easy to make fun of. But if you're one of those people who has been in love with dolphins your whole life, this may be your only chance to get this close. You'll swim with them in an enclosure at Treasure Island, on the side of Isla Mujeres that faces Cancún, accompanied by some very friendly professionals. They'll tell you lots of neat facts about dolphins during the pre-swim lecture (example: they have recreational sex more than any other mammals—no wonder they're always smiling) and that their brains are four times bigger than ours. The site offers many different packages, but generally the cost is $1,290 per person; call to make a reservation far in advance. Before visiting, you might also want to check out "Basics," p. 59, to read up on the complicated ethics behind swimming with dolphins.

GARRAFON NATURAL PARK ★★

The eco-park Garrafon is run by the same people who manage Xcaret (p. 266), so you can expect a similar environment full of amenities, unusual outdoor activities, and plenty of eating and drinking options. Snorkeling is the big draw here—folks come from Cancún and other mainland cities to view the exotic variety of fish and wildlife that live around the famous Garrafon reef. But if snorkeling isn't your thing, you'll have other ways to view fish in their natural surroundings. Scuba divers of all levels will be happy here; certified, English-speaking PADI instructors are available to lead guided dives on the reef, and a full roster of certification courses are offered, from resort style samples to Open Water, Advanced, and Rescue PADI certification.

Wanna-be astronauts will love the snuba setup, where you can walk on the ocean floor wearing a space-age style helmet attached to a long air tube. I loved paddling in a transparent canoe, which let me take in all the pretty activity going on below me without getting too wet. If you don't like to get wet at all, you can take an underwater submarine called Sea Trek that will bring you down below the waves for a better look.

Dry activities include hammocks and decks for lounging and sunbathing. You can also take in the amazing view of the surroundings via a zip line canopy tour ★★ or from a 50m (164-ft.) Panoramic Tower.

Changing rooms, a pool, a souvenir shop, and snack bars are all on-site, and the activities I've mentioned can be arranged at the park's main tour desk once you arrive. Prices vary, but expect to pay about $150 to $440, depending on how adventurous you're feeling.

El Garrafon Natural Park is on the southern tip of the island on Carretera El Garrafon, about 4km (2½ miles) southeast of Playa Lancheros. Call **☎ 998/884-9420** in Cancún, **☎ 998/877-1100** in the park, for info. Entrance to the park is $290 and it's open daily 9am to 5pm.

ISLA CONTOY

Isla Contoy is a tiny (6km/3¾ mile long) island about 45 minutes from Isla Mujeres that has been turned into a national wildlife preserve and bird sanctuary. It's well worth a trip to snorkel along the empty beaches and observe more than 70 species of tropical birds including flamingos, brown boobies, egrets, and many other rare breeds on their own turf. During the summer months you can sometimes see giant sea turtles making their slow climb up the shore to lay eggs in the sand.

Most trips to the island are taken by small boat with an experienced captain, who will usually fish for your lunch on the way over to the island and then cook the fish over a campfire on Contoy. All the boatmen on the island have unionized, so the price for a day trip is $400 no matter whom you ask. Most dive shops also send boats to the outskirts of the island. A small government museum and restrooms are on the island.

I recommend going out with **Captain Tony Garcia** (Calle Matamoros 7A; ☎ **998/877-0226**), who leads boat tours for $400 per person; the price includes snorkeling and fishing.

PLAYA TIBURON

Tiburon means shark in Spanish, and Tiburon Beach is best known for its tanks of nurse sharks; you can swim in the tanks (safely!) and have your picture taken for $20. The setup is much less formal than the experience you'll have at Dolphin Discovery (p. 230), so there's no specific address or phone number to mention. Before you jump in, though, you might also want to read "Basics," p. 59, for info on the ethics of swimming with these animals.

MORE SNORKELING & DIVING DESTINATIONS

Cave of the Sleeping Sharks: One day in the 1960s, a lobster fisherman was skin diving (without scuba gear) and looking for lobster when he found "a cave of sharks that did not attack." The cave later became the most popular diving destination on the island, due to the many sharks that were sleeping with eyes open under only about 20m (65 ft.) of water. The fisherman, Carlos Garcia Castilla, still fishes for lobster on Isla Mujeres, but unfortunately in the years that have gone by since his discovery, so many divers have descended into the cave that the sharks have found a quieter, more distant spot to take their siestas. Though chances are good that you *won't* see sharks, the caves are wide enough for beginners (with an experienced guide, of course) and worth the trip for the dive alone.

If you want to slightly increase your chances of seeing sharks, you might want to also visit **La Punta,** although the sleeping sharks in this cave are also scarce in this day and age.

Cruz de Bahia (Cross of the Bay): Near the colorful Manchones Reef (see below),

Dive Shops

Isla Mujeres' calm waters and ample reefs are a diver's dream. Many PADI-certified dive shops operate on the small island. Two shops I found to be very professional and friendly include **Coral Scuba Center** (☎ **998/887-0061** or 998/877-0763), on the corner of Matamoros 13A and Rueda Medina, and the **Bahia Dive Shop** (no phone), on Rueda Medina #166, right near the main ferry dock. All shops on the island offer essentially the same rates; one-tank dives cost $550 and two-tank dives cost $700.

Both of these shops offer trips to the diving sites mentioned in this section.

the 1-ton Cruz de Bahia, a bronze cross, is anchored to the ocean floor and rises to a height of 12m (40 ft.). Until quite recently, Isla Mujeres was primarily an island of fishermen, and the cross was placed in 1994 as an underwater marker in homage to all the locals who lost their lives at sea. In the cross's center, where the body of Christ is normally mounted, there is instead a human-size hole, which fish swim through. The best way to approach the site is by diving, but if you're not a diver, you can take one of the many boat tours that visit the site.

Area Reefs: The calm waters surrounding Isla are rich with colorful and undisturbed reefs. Some of the best for diving include: **Tabos** reef, along the eastern coast; the **Manchones** reef, half a mile from the southeastern tip of the island, which is known for shallow water that's perfect for new divers; and **Banderas** reef, between Cancún and Isla, which boasts deeper water and is better for experienced divers because of its sharp current. There is also a small **wreck** 14km (9 miles) off shore of the island that most dive tours visit.

Shopping

Shopping is a casual activity here, with only a few shops of any note. Shop owners will bombard you, especially on Avenida Hidalgo, selling Saltillo rugs, onyx, silver, Guatemalan clothing, blown glassware, masks, folk art, beach paraphernalia, and T-shirts in abundance. Prices are lower than in Cancún or Cozumel, but with such overeager sellers, bargaining is necessary.

The one treasure you're likely to take back is a piece of fine jewelry—Isla is known for its excellent duty-free prices on gemstones and hand-crafted work made to order. Diamonds, emeralds, sapphires, and rubies can be purchased as loose stones and then mounted while you're off exploring. The superbly crafted gold, silver, and gems are available at competitive prices in the workshops near the central plaza. The stones are also available in the rough. **Rachat & Rome** (☎ **998/877-0331**) at the corner of calles Morelos and Juárez, is the grandest store, with a broad selection of jewelry at competitive prices. It's open daily from 9:30am to 5pm and accepts all major credit cards.

The **Casa de Cultura** community center offers a wealth of classes in Mexican paper sculpture, folkloric dance, and other arts. But my favorite thing about it is the Book Exchange, where you can bring in your beach reads and exchange them for new stories to fuel your lazy sunbathing during the remainder of your trip. It's open 9am till 9pm Monday to Friday and is at Casa de la Cultura, Av. Guerrero. Call ☎ **998/887-0639** for info.

Cozumel

Plan on Cozumel living exactly up to your expectations. If you are a diver, as most people who visit Cozumel are, and you've heard that it is one of the top diving destinations in the world (second only to the Great Barrier Reef) you won't be disappointed by the incredible array of reefs easily within reach. During my dives in Cozumel, I saw a turtle, two sharks, an octopus, and many otherworldly flora and fauna. Plus, the water in Cozumel is so warm that you don't need to wear a wet suit, which can feel incredibly liberating if you're an experienced diver who is used to wearing one.

Yet if you are a skeptic, and you've heard of the swarms of cruise-shipper day-trippers who disembark from giant white vessels to ravage the island of its resources and pillage its deserved profits, you will

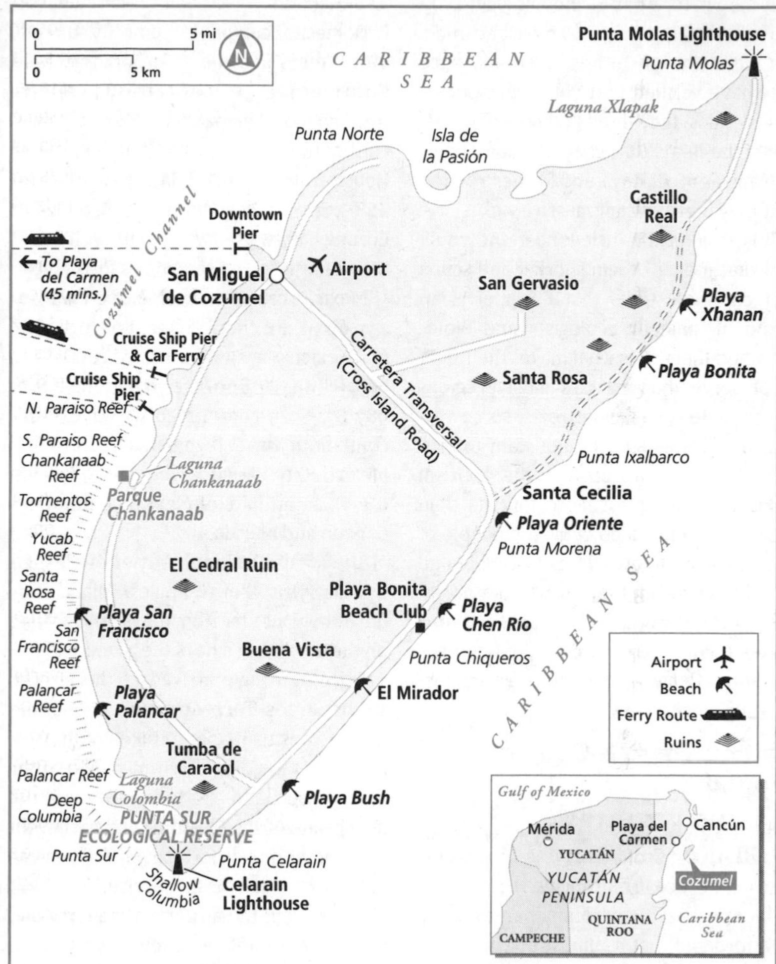

also see your worst suspicions realized. In many ways Cozumel is picture perfect: a small island with a wealth of outdoor delights, a hoppin' town with more top quality shops and restaurants per square mile of walking strip than New York City, and a Caribbean island with a wealth of art and local culture. However, like many other destinations that seem too good to be true, Cozumel has been exploited for its charms. Amid its many cozy bars and restaurants lurks a darker side, made up of overpriced and watered-down bars and dining establishments populated by tourists fresh off the boat and still drunk from last night's open bar.

If you've been on a cruise and enjoyed it, props to you and I hope you don't take too much offense at my jabs at your boat cruising companions. Stay for a while on

Cozumel (*please* don't cheat yourself and only stop in for a day of shopping) and you too will develop an anti-cruiser attitude. Get close enough to any local, and once they have verified that you're not one of the enemies, they'll tell you how they feel about the boats that come in—sometimes as many as 15 per day—and the destruction that they leave in their massive wakes.

Talk to a local a little longer and you'll find that most of them snorkel and scuba in their spare time, that Cozumel is an island of amateur ecologists and biologists, and that this is what makes their fight to preserve their island's most precious resource, its spectacular reefs, so powerful. The Cozumelenos do not want to protect the reefs to protect the tourism industry—they've got more tourists than they know what to do with. The people of Cozumel want to protect their wildlife and its habitat because they love it. They are an entire island of nature lovers, and this makes them a fierce and fascinating people, and Cozumel an equally fierce and fascinating place.

Getting There & Getting Around

GETTING INTO TOWN

BY PLANE Cozumel is one of the best spots in Mexico for all-inclusive hotel and airfare package deals. Many packages are so affordable that it almost doesn't make sense to purchase your ticket and hotel separately, unless you are a diver and have arranged a scuba package with one of the dive hotels in town. For websites catering specifically to all-inclusive packages in Cozumel, see p. 240. Some companies, such as **Funjet** (www.funjet.com), also offer international charter flights, and you may want to look into these, especially if you will be traveling with a large group. During high season there are a lot more flights directly into Cozumel, whereas during low season you may have to stop in Cancún for a connection.

Domestic companies that fly directly into the Cozumel Airport include: **Continental** (☎ **800/231-0856** in the U.S., or 987/872-0487 in Mexico; www.continental.com) with flights from Houston and Newark; **USAirways** (☎ **800/428-4322** in the U.S. or 987/872-2824 in Cozumel; www.usairways.com), with flights from Charlotte and sometimes Pittsburgh.

Mexican carriers **AeroMexico** (☎ **800/237-6639** in the U.S. or 800/021-4000 in Mexico; www.aeromexico.com), and **Mexicana** (☎ **800/531-7931** in the U.S. or 987/872-2945 from Mexico; www.mexicana.com) both have flights that connect in Mexico City. **Aerocaribe** (☎ **987/872-0877**), an affiliate of Mexicana, flies from Cancún and Mérida.

The small **Cozumel Airport** (tel] **987/872-0485**) is 2km (1¼ miles) inland from downtown, not far from the main ferry pier on the northwest side of the island.

Once you have arrived at the airport, **Transportes Terrestres** (no phone) has luxury vans available to take you to your hotel for $40 going downtown, $80 to the north beach, and $80 to $120 to the south beach side of the island. There are booths lined up at the airport exit where you can purchase tickets for the service.

A cab from the airport to the ferry pier or the center of downtown is $50. One operator to call is ☎ **987/872-0041.**

See "By Car" under "Getting Around" for info on renting a car from the airport.

BY BOAT **Ultramar** (☎ **987/869-2775**) and **Barcos Mexico** (☎ **987/872-1508** or 987/872-1588) both have passenger ferries that leave Playa de Carmen for Cozumel every hour on the hour between 5am and midnight. If you are counting on taking a certain ferry, make sure to buy your ticket at least a half-hour in advance. Tickets on

San Miguel de Cozumel

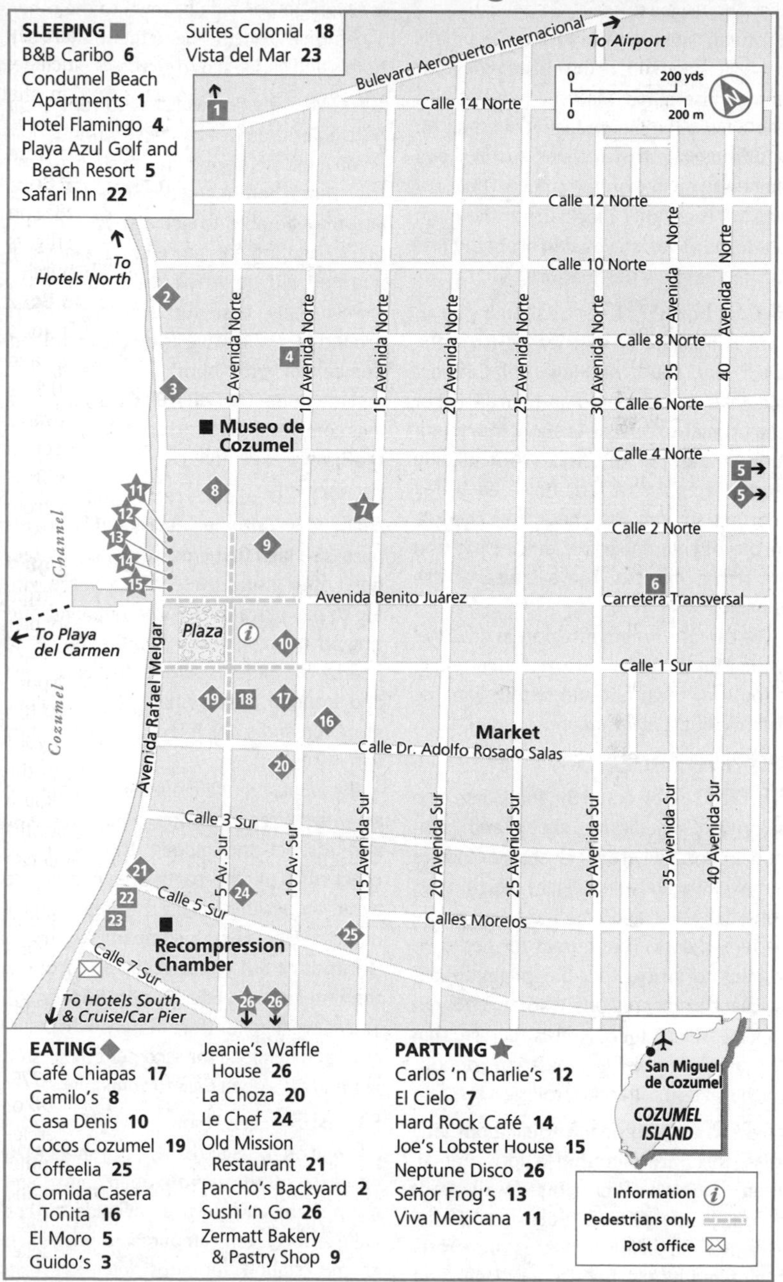

both ferries cost $100, and the boat ride takes about 45 minutes.

You can't miss **Muelle Fiscal,** Cozumel's pier, as it is marked by the clusters of giant white cruise ships that surround it—it's visible from the main plaza. Cabs line up outside during arrival times to take you wherever you like on the island. The ferry terminal is only 1½ blocks from the main square, however, so you can probably just walk to your final destination.

BY CAR FERRY If you're bringing a car, there is a car ferry that leaves from the Calica pier, south of Playa del Carmen; trips take 45 minutes to an hour. A ticket for a normal-size sedan is $800. **Maritima Chancanaab** (☎ **987/872-1706**) usually departs from Calica four times each day from 7am to 9pm. But check the schedule the day of your departure, since early and late ferries may not run because of low demand.

The car ferry comes into port in Cozumel at the **Muelle International** pier, which is south of town but still within walking distance of the main square.

GETTING AROUND

ON FOOT For better or for worse, the majority of restaurants, shops, and night spots in Cozumel are all clustered close to the Avenida Rafael Melgar, which runs along the water and past the ports where the ferries dock. That's great for pedestrians, but not so great for the inhabitants of the island's other regions, who can't benefit from the island's tourist infrastructure. That said, all of Cozumel is pedestrian-friendly, which makes this a good strolling town.

BY TAXI If you need to reach outlying areas, taxis are plentiful—a long line of green and white chariots await your patronage the moment you step off the ferry pier, for instance. Prices are pretty much fixed by the Taxi Drivers Union, so don't try to haggle. Taxi fares average as follows: from the ferry terminal into town is $20; from one side of town to the other, $50; from the north side to the south beach hotels and clubs, $50 to $150.

BY CAR It's not worth it to rent a car here unless you just can't live without one. If you must, it's a good idea to shop around for a rental before you depart home, since you may be able to get a special deal if you're renting for more than 3 days. If you wait till you arrive at the airport, the lowest daily cost for any car hovers around $545, the same as on the mainland. Companies with booths at the airport include **Avis** (☎ **987/872-0099;** www.avis.com) and **Executive** (☎ **987/872-1308;** www.executive-car.com).

BY MOPED I don't recommend renting a moped on Cozumel; the rate of accidents here is so high that most rental companies don't offer insurance (even if you are willing to pay extra for it). I recommend putting off the moped rental until you get to nearby Isla Mujeres, where the lack of cars and tranquil island vibe make it a much more fun and a much less life-threatening activity (p. 221).

If you *must* rent a moped in Cozumel, do so with extreme caution, wear a helmet, and inspect the moped thoroughly to check that all the parts are in order to avoid an accident caused by mechanical defects. One rental company to try is **Rentadora Sol y Mar** (Calle 2, in front of the Hotel Posada Ede; ☎ **987/869-0545**). They have mopeds (fortunately with insurance and helmets) for $250 per day or $100 per hour. It's open 9am to 7pm daily.

BY BUS Even though no buses are allowed on the island, there is a small **ADO** office (☎ **987/872-1706;** open daily 8am–9:30pm) in downtown at Avenida 20 and Calle 2 Norte. You can purchase bus tickets at this station for trips later on your Mexican itinerary, so you can avoid standing in the sort of long lines you'll encounter at the country's other stations.

Cozumel Basics

ORIENTATION

Cozumel is 45km (28 miles) long and 18km (11 miles) wide, and lies 19km (12 miles) from the mainland. Most of the terrain is flat and clothed in a low tropical forest. The only town on the island is San Miguel, which, despite the growth of the last 20 years, still can't be called anything more than a small town.

CITY LAYOUT San Miguel's main waterfront street is **Avenida Rafael Melgar.** Running parallel to Rafael Melgar are other avenidas numbered in multiples of five—5, 10, 15. **Avenida Juárez** runs perpendicular to these, heading inland from the ferry dock. Avenida Juárez divides the town into northern and southern halves. The calles (streets) that parallel Juárez to the north have even numbers. The ones to the south have odd numbers, with the exception of Calle Rosado Salas, which runs between calles 1 and 3.

ISLAND LAYOUT One road runs along the western coast of the island, which faces the Yucatán mainland. It has different names. North of town it's **Santa Pilar** or **San Juan;** in the city it is **Avenida Rafael Melgar;** south of town it's **Costera Sur.** Hotels stretch along this road north and south of town. The road runs to the southern tip of the island (Punta Sur), passing **Chankanaab National Park. Avenida Juárez** (and its extension, the **Carretera Transversal**) runs east from the town across the island. It passes the airport and the turnoff to the ruins of San Gervasio before reaching the undeveloped ocean side of the island. It then turns south and follows the coast to the southern tip of the island, where it meets the Costera Sur.

TOURIST INFO & OFFICES

The **Municipal Tourism Office (☎ 987/869-0212)** is in the Plaza de Sol building in the center of the main plaza, on the second floor. It's open Monday through Friday from 9am to 4pm. There is also a booth run by the same people on the ferry pier; it's open Monday through Friday from 8:30am to 4:30pm.

RECOMMENDED WEBSITES

- **www.cozumel.net**: One of the best websites for tourist info that I've come across, period. It boasts everything you need to know about Cozumel, from ferry schedules, to recommended dive sites and shops, to rental and hotel listings.
- **www.islacozumel.com.mx**: This site has great info on package deals, all-inclusive resorts, and the longest list of hotels online. (It's run by the local hotel association.)
- **www.go2cozumel.com**: If you're looking for ideas on how to organize your vacation time, this travel planning site has great suggestions on the best local attractions and services.
- **www.travelnotes.cc**: An excellent resource for divers and other outdoor adventurers, this site contains over 1,000 pages of photos and info on outdoor activities in Cozumel.

THE YUCATÁN PENINSULA

Cozumel Nuts & Bolts

Banks **HSBC (☎ 987/872-0182)** is at the far end of the main plaza and has a 24-hour ATM. It's open Monday to Saturday from 8am to 7pm. **Banorte (☎ 987/872-0718)** is on Av. 5 Norte, between Calle 2 and Juárez. It's open Monday to Saturday from 10am to 2pm.

Emergencies The **U.S. Consulate** (☎ **987/872-4574**, or for emergencies 987/872-0624; usca@cozumel.net) is on the second level of the Plaza Villa Mar shopping center, in the central Plaza. It's open Monday to Friday from noon to 2pm. For hyperbaric chamber and medical centers, see p. 248. For general emergencies, dial ☎ **066. Red Cross** (☎ **987/872-1058**) is on Av. Sur 20, at Calle Salas and is open daily 7am to 11pm.

Internet/Wireless Hot Spots **Modutel Comunicaciones** (☎ **987/8690-3029**) on Avenida 10 between Calle 2 and Juárez, charges $10 an hour for Internet access. In addition, they have phones and fax machines. It's open Monday to Friday 9am to 11pm, Saturday and Sunday 9am to 10pm.

Telephone Tips The local area code is **630.**

Sleeping

If you want to stay right on the beach, it makes sense to book your trip through one of the many all-inclusives in Cozumel; most of them have packages that include meals and airfare. The hotels in downtown San Miguel generally have more personality than the all-inclusives on the beach, though, plus they are situated right in the center of a town made for foot traffic. Because most of the nighttime party action in Cozumel is in San Miguel, most savvy travelers stay at one of the lower priced hotels there at night and journey over to party at the beach clubs during the day.

Punta Morena and Punta Chiqueros both have isolated, tranquil campgrounds that are never full. In addition to tent sites, Punta Morena has cute cabañas with double beds and private bathrooms for $200.

CHEAP

➜ **B&B Caribo** The owner of this cute, cozy B&B is an excellent host, although sometimes her warm welcome makes this place feel too much like home to be a vacation destination. (You definitely can't rock out at night here.) You can get a great deal, though, especially if you want to rent an apartment for a few weeks or even a month. Everything is also sparkling clean, from the moderately sized rooms (some come with kitchens) to the communal dining room, where you can get amazing free breakfasts. *Av. Juárez 799.* ☎ *987/872-3195. www.visit-caribo.com. $400–$500 double. Breakfast included. No credit cards. Amenities: Breakfast room; massage available; yoga classes. In room: A/C, kitchens (in some suites).*

➜ **Hotel Flamingo** ★★ Right in the heart of downtown, Hotel Flamingo attracts an international and mostly young crowd with its simple, clean rooms, and Aqua, its happening lobby restaurant and bar. It's simply the swankiest place in town in this price range—added perks include Wi-Fi throughout the lobby, a funky blue mosaic decor, good air-conditioning in the rooms, and a swinging scene right in your lobby that usually doesn't get loud enough to reach your room. On the roof, there is a nice deck for sunning with a prime view of the ocean. *Calle 6 Norte 81.* ☎ *529/872-1264. www.hotelflamingo.com. $500–$600 double. MC, V. Amenities: Restaurant and bar; Wi-Fi. In room: A/C, fridge.*

➜ **Safari Inn** The Safari Inn is a small, friendly hotel conveniently placed above the **Aqua Safari** (p. 249), the best dive shop in Cozumel. The 12 rooms here are simple, clean, and comfortable; in keeping with the underwater theme, each has a different plaster relief of an undersea creature on the wall above the main bed. What stands out about this hotel is that some of the rooms have as many as five beds, which are arranged in surprisingly creative ways—they're great for sleeping large groups of friends. It's worth noting that the maids here are very into making complex origami animals out of the fresh towels they leave on your bed. They took serious pride in showing me the folded terry-cloth elephants, hearts, octopuses, and fish. I think it says something good about a place if the maids are having that much fun. *Av. Rafael Melgar at Calle 5. ☎ 987/872-0101. www.aquasafari.com. $400 double, $450 triple, $500 quad. Ask about special dive packages. AE, MC, V. Amenities: Full-service dive shop with dock downstairs; Internet in office; laundry service; free snorkel equipment. In room: A/C.*

→ **Suites Colonial** This simple downtown guesthouse could be a money saving place to crash if you're traveling in a group of three or four. Regular "double rooms" have a double bed plus an extra twin, while the suites have two double beds and a sitting/dining room. The trapped-in-the-'70s decor leaves a lot to be desired; despite appearing clean, rooms smell slightly of all the cigarettes that have been smoked in the rooms in the decades since. A free continental breakfast includes stale pastries and bad coffee. But who says you have to eat here just cause it's free? *Av. 5 Sur 9, Aposado 286. ☎ 987/872-9080. www.suitescolonial.com. $500–$680 double, $600–$800 suite. AE, MC, V. Amenities: Cafe; bar; car rental; laundry service; tour info. In room: A/C, TV.*

DOABLE

MTV Best → **Condumel Beach Apartments** ★★★ Condumel is a magical place. If you are looking for a peaceful, ocean-side resort where you can escape from it all and keep to a budget, you won't find a better deal. When I first encountered the isolated beach hotel—reminiscent of an ancient Maya castle, complete with a stone wall that drops off into 4m (13 ft.) of crystal-clear ocean, I felt transported back in time to a simpler and more serene place. The friendly owner and manager go out of their way to ensure you have a pleasant stay by stocking the kitchens in the large apartments with basics like beer, sodas, milk, eggs, and salsa, and there is a grill right on the beach for guests' use.

Bill Horn, who lives in one of the apartments here and owns the place, also runs the recommended **Aqua Safari** (p. 249), so this is also a great hotel for divers. If you are a serious swimmer or snorkeler, you'll also find that the beach here is a welcome change from the typical wading beaches in Cancún and Playa del Carmen. *Condumel Condo Beach Apartments, Box 142, Cozumel, Quintana Roo, Mexico 7760. ☎ 987/872-0892. www. condumel.com. $1,300–$1,600 condo for 4 people. Ask about special weekly rates and dive packages. No credit cards (unless special arrangements are made in advance). Amenities: Internet; laundry service; lending library; free snorkel equipment. In room: A/C, ceiling fans, coupon book for local hot spots, fridge stocked with groceries and booze.*

→ **Vista del Mar** ★★★ This beach-themed hotel overlooking the San Miguel's shoreline boulevard feels much more expensive than it is. Perhaps that's because rooms have recently been redecorated with seashell mosaics, light wood furniture, new beds, and gauzy white curtains and canopies. The bathrooms have excellent water pressure, the rooms come with balconies, and the air-conditioning and cable TVs in every room complete the illusion of staying in a five-star resort for a fraction of the price. Most importantly, the hotel staff is welcoming to large groups of young travelers and will arrange a special package for you and your friends to stay at this reduced-rate Ritz. *Av. Rafael Melgar 45,*

All-Inclusive Hotels

There are seven all-inclusives in Cozumel, and all of them offer complete packages including airfare, food, and occasionally dive time. See "Basics," p. 33, for info on how to decide if staying at an inclusive resort is right for you. (***Note:*** If you are a serious diver, you'd be better off staying at one of the dive resorts on the island, such as the **Safari Inn** or **Condumel Condo Beach Apartments;** see p. 238 and 239. The quality of the dive instruction, boat trips, gear available, and dive packages will be far superior to what a regular all-inclusive will offer you.)

Rates for these places fluctuate often according to airfare and season, so make sure you check the websites for the most current prices. Following are your options:

→ **Allegro Cozumel** (www.occidentalhotels.com): One of the three Occidental all-inclusives in Cozumel, this one is on Cozumel's best piece of southern white sandy beach. As with the other two Occidental properties, the hutlike squat round buildings with thatched palapa roofs give off a definite tiki-lounge vibe. The chill, rustic charm can be a nice change from the white insulation of the bigger all-inclusive hotels elsewhere on this list.

→ **Grand Cozumel** (www.occidental.com): The Occidental group's newest property on Cozumel, this all-inclusive resort has the same low-key, tropical vibe of the Allegro, with brand new, more artfully decorated quarters. Another advantage of staying here is that you have access to the nearby Allegro's restaurant and beach as well.

→ **Iberostar Cozumel** ★ (www.iberostar.com): Perhaps the best value of all the inclusives, the Iberostar boasts a smaller size, a friendly vibe, and the aforementioned price-cuts. There's also a nice beach next to the lush grounds, although it has more rocks under the water than the two next door. Why not save money by staying here, where you can enjoy the indulgent rooms and food, and then simply walk a little way up the beach to where the ocean floor is softer?

→ **El Cozumeleno** (www.elcozumeleno.com): The biggest all-inclusive in town, this contemporary skyscraper has a giant sparkling pool, as well as tennis courts, golf course, and other activity options on its sweeping grounds. If you really don't want to leave your resort, this one has the most incentives to stay inside its thick white walls.

→ **Melia Cozumel** ★★ (www.meliacozumel.com): I like the Melia because you get all of the services of the bigger El Cozumeleno, without such a big box feel. The beds are soft, the rooms are simple and elegantly decorated with hints of blues and greens, and the beach is long enough for leisurely walks. The Melia is also close enough to town on the north shore of the island that you won't have to muster up too much willpower to leave for a night of dancing or local food.

→ **Reef Club** (www.reefclubcozumel.com): Unhappy reviews of this resort abound, so I don't recommend it. However, because of the bad publicity, prices have dropped significantly, so it may be worth checking out if cash, not comfort, is your main priority.

→ **Costa Club** (www.costaclubcozumel.com): Near many of the popular beach clubs on the island, this is a good option if you want to meet fellow travelers on your trip, or be close to the late night bonfires and impromptu beach parties that Cozumel excels at after dark, while still being able to return to the luxury of a cozy, clean room after the party is over.

between Calles 5 and 7. ☎ 987/872-0545 or 888/309-9988. www.hotelvistadelmar.com. High season $600–$800 double. Ask about special rates for large groups. MC, V. Amenities: Restaurant and bar; office with complimentary computers and other services; 2 small pools with jets; Wi-Fi in lobby. In room: A/C, TV w/cable, fridge, minibar.

SPLURGE

→ **Playa Azul Golf and Beach Resort** ★★ This quiet hotel is perhaps the most relaxing of the island's beachside properties. It's smaller, and service is personal. It's an excellent choice for golfers; guests pay no greens fees, only cart rental. The hotel's small, sandy beach has been restored to its pre-hurricane condition, with new shade palapas and the return of the beach bar. Almost all of the rooms have balconies and ocean views. The units in the original section are all suites—very large, with oversize bathrooms with showers. The new wing has mostly standard rooms that are comfortable and large, decorated with light tropical colors and rattan furniture. The corner rooms are master suites and have large balconies with Jacuzzis overlooking the sea. If you prefer lots of space over having a Jacuzzi, opt for a suite in the original building. Rooms contain a king-size bed or two double beds; suites offer two convertible single sofas in the separate living room. The hotel also offers deep-sea- and fly-fishing trips, and rents a garden house with lovely rooms that's perfect for groups. *Carretera San Juan Km 4. ☎ 987/872-0199 or -0043. www.playa-azul.com. High season $2,300 double, $2,750–$3,250 suite; low season $1,570–$1,700 double, $1,960–$2,900 suite. Discounts and packages sometimes available. AE, MC, V. Amenities: Restaurant; 2 bars; game room; unlimited golf privileges at Cozumel Country Club; laundry service; in-room massage; medium-size outdoor pool; room service until 11pm; spa; tour info; watersports equipment rental. In room: A/C, TV, coffeemaker, hair dryer, safe.*

Eating

No matter if you're pro or con cruise ships, there's no denying that the massive injection of cruise passengers that invade Cozumel every day has left a wealth of edible options in its wake. You can eat better food for cheaper prices, and with a wider variety of choices, than almost anywhere in Mexico. From sweet baked goods, to organic coffee, to cheap seafood, the restaurants here aim to please a wide array of tastes.

In addition to the individual restaurants reviewed below, consider hitting up the loncherías along the **Mercado Municipal** for spicy seafood soup and cheap taco platters, or journey along Calle Rosado Salles, in the center of town, for stands that hawk huevos rancheros and other filling meals for as little as $20.

CHEAP

→ **Camilo's** ★★ SEAFOOD Camilo's slogan is, "The Seafood Difference," and the main difference between Camilo's and the many other seafood joints on the island is that they offer free delivery. This is a big difference indeed if you are sharing a condo with a bunch of buddies and feel like having a cheap seafood feast delivered directly to your door, beer included. If your condo has a grill on the beach (see Condumel, p. 239) you can even have your seafood delivered raw and already marinated. All nine types of ceviche are worth trying, and at Camilo's prices you can afford to taste a few. If you want to have a big order delivered by dinner time, make sure to call well in advance. The restaurant itself is pretty bare bones—another reason to consider delivery. *Off the central Plaza, between Calle 2 and Calle 4 North. ☎ 987/872-6161. Main courses $60–$120. No credit cards. Daily 10am–7pm.*

MTV Best → **Cocos Cozumel** ★★★ CAFE Operated by a Mexican-American couple, Coco's is a sort of home away from home when it comes to breakfast. The menu contains this warning: "Caution: We must warn you that past experience has shown that after just one breakfast at Cocos, most people feel compelled to return every day of their vacation!" The enthusiastic owners aren't exaggerating—the bottomless cups of coffee, fresh fruit, and heaping platters of both Mexican and diner-styled eggs had quite the addictive effect on me. The food is good, fresh, and cheap, but it's the smaller details that seal the deal: In one corner, there is a bookshelf with used books (mostly mysteries and romance novels with a few buried classics) on sale for a dollar each. (I picked up Dennis LeHane's *Gone, Baby, Gone.*) In the other corner, you'll find a variety of emergency toiletries in case you run out of conditioner or the such. *Av. 5 between Calle Adolfo Rosado Salas and Calle 1. ☎ 987/872-0241. Main courses $20–$50. No credit cards. Daily 6am–noon.*

→ **Comida Casera Tonita** YUCATECAN This place serves up home cooking, Yucatecan style. You'll eat right in a lovely couple's dining room, and the menu consists of the most authentic local dishes, plus anything you want deep fried—the fish and chips were fresh and crispy without being greasy. *Calle Rosado Salles 256, between Avs. 10 and 5. ☎ 987/872-0401. Main courses $30–$80. No credit cards. Mon–Sat 10am–8pm.*

MTV Best → **El Moro** ★★★ MEXICAN When heading to El Moro, make sure you head to the *original* location. According to local legend, this restaurant was launched by three brothers, until the younger two brothers branched off to start their own mediocre variations on the original restaurant. Only the oldest brother continued to cook truly amazing food at this, the most beloved restaurant on Cozumel.

This original location is way on the other side of Cozumel, far from the port hood that contains 99% of the island's restaurants. The trip is worth it, if only because you'll get a peek at what life on Cozumel is like for the majority of islanders far from the tourist industry. Of course, the amazing Mexican food and funky atmosphere also prove rewarding. When you arrive at the real El Moro, you'll be greeted by the friendliest waitstaff on the island, and will be seated at one of many plastic orange tables in the center of a giant orange room that also holds an ice cream station, an Internet station, a full bar, and a dance floor where you might see local kids kicking around a soccer ball during the daytime. The walls are lined with relics of cowboys and Indians, exotic (real) stuffed animals, and other eclectic artifacts, including a number of paintings donated by satisfied customers.

None of these quirky diversions matter once your food arrives, though. All of the seafood dishes are sensationally tasty, especially considering that the ingredients used are pretty simple. I had a divine fish and shrimp dish cooked in a packet of aluminum foil *(enpapelado)* with chiles, Mexican cheese, fresh veggies, and local herbs. Judging from the plates I watched come steaming out of the kitchen, you can't go wrong with meat or chicken dishes either. After a scoop of the homemade coconut ice cream with Kahlua sauce, I was ready to paint a masterpiece declaring my dedication to El Moro, too. *75 Bis Norte between Calles 2 and 4. No phone. Main courses $60–$150. MC, V. Daily 1–11pm.*

→ **Jeanie's Waffle House** CAFE For a decadent breakfast with an ocean view, head to Jeanie's. Her waffles are big, golden brown, and come with multiple topping options. Tried and true favorites like strawberries with whipped cream, or bananas with chocolate sauce, will not disappoint. If you're feeling adventurous, I recommend you try one of Jeanie's original waffle recipes; the waffles topped with guava, honey, almonds, and vanilla frozen yogurt were out of this world. If your friend who dragged you here likes waffles but you don't, have no fear—Jeanie makes some quality hash browns and Mexican-style breakfast platters as well. *Av. Rafael Melgar and Calle 11. No phone. Main courses $20–$60. MC, V. Daily 6am–3pm.*

→ **La Choza** ★★ MEXICAN You'd never guess by its modest interior and laid-back prices that La Choza was once chosen as the best restaurant in Cozumel by *Food & Wine* magazine. Specializing in home cooking, this unpretentious restaurant offers some of the best classic Mexican food on the island. The prime time to frequent La Choza is on weekdays between 11am and 3pm, when locals take their siesta break from work. During these hours, La Choza caters to Cozumelenos with its "Comida del Día," which is a special-priced dish served cafeteria style with plenty of accoutrements and side dishes. The afternoon I visited, the main dish was the richest, darkest chicken mole I've ever encountered. (Talk about comfort food—it doesn't get much better than chocolate chicken.) Be prepared to take your own siesta break (aka food coma) after partaking in this tasty local tradition. *Calle Adolfo Rosado Salas 198, at Av. 10. ☎ 987/872-0948. Main courses $40–$70. MC, V. Daily noon–7pm.*

→ **Sushi n' Go** ★★ SUSHI What's cool about Sushi n' Go is that it's not another bland copy of what you could find for less money in the States or Europe. Instead, the owners of this hip restaurant try out creative combinations and add their own local twist to sushi. The rolls include classic sushi stars such as tuna and salmon, but they mix it up by adding indigenous ingredients such as ceviche, avocado, cilantro, chile cream cheese, and even habanero peppers. When I visited, fried tempura rolls (chicken, apple, and shrimp) that oozed hot cream cheese were hands down the most popular order with the late-night crowd filtering in and out of nearby Neptune Disco (p. 246). They also have gourmet meat and veggie subs, as well as salads and rice bowls. *Calle 11 South, across from the Neptune Disco. No phone. Sushi $30–$60, subs $30. No credit cards. Daily 2pm–2am but hours vary.*

→ **Zermatt Bakery & Pastry Shop** ★ BAKERY You can smell the buttery, sugary goodness coming from Zermatt a block before you get to it. Hands down the best bakery on the island, this is *the* place to try coconut cookies, tamarind tarts, and sumptuous guava bread. Almost everything at Zermatt (with the exception of whole cakes and pies) is under a dollar, so you don't have to be shy with sampling. In addition to freshly baked stateside favorites like chocolate donuts and blueberry muffins, you can find pumpkin muffins, caramel croissants, zucchini and banana bread, and flaky ham and cheese pies. *Calle 6, between Av. 5 and 10. No phone. Snacks under $20. No credit cards. Daily noon–7pm.*

DOABLE

→ **Casa Denis** MEXICAN Casa Denis takes pride in being the oldest restaurant in Cozumel, and the menu trumpets this legend by listing the many celebrities—such as Jackie Onassis—who have eaten here. Established in 1945, this local family-run institution sports pictures lining the interior walls that chronicle the life of founder Denis Angulo, who claims to have coined the phrase, "Mi casa es su casa." Whether or not you buy this inflated claim to fame, anyone can appreciate the old-school atmosphere and simple, freshly prepared

Mexican seafood dishes. The red snapper with olive oil and garlic is very good, as is the *sopa de lima* (lime soup with chicken and vegetables). All in all, it's a classic, classy joint—guess that's why Jackie O came here. *Calle 1 South, between Calles 5 and 10.* ☎ *987/872-0067. www.casadenis.com. Main courses $100–$200. MC, V. Daily noon–10pm.*

➔ **Le Chef** BISTRO This little gourmet eatery began as a specialty food store and branched out into a full-fledged French bistro that churns out refreshingly unusual daily specials like Mexican tuna tartare served with toasted flat bread, sea bass carpaccio, and roasted pumpkin and red pepper pizza. The navy blue walls, Art Nouveau French posters, and indie music playing in the background all add to the indie feel of the place. The best part of every dish I sampled (and they were all quite good) was the superb olive oil that was used in everything, whether as salad dressing, dipping sauce, or as garnish for the sandwich bread. You can pick up a bottle, along with some fresh fish, at the store in the entryway of the restaurant if you'd prefer to grill your own meal. *Av. 5, at Calle 5 south.* ☎ *987/878-43291. Main courses $80–$120. MC, V. Daily 9am–10pm.*

➔ **Old Mission Restaurant** MEXICAN The best thing about the Old Mission was the gigantic plate of complimentary guacamole that they brought out with fresh, hot tortilla chips as soon as I sat down. The second best thing was the huge basket of warm garlic bread that I got when my food arrived. Unfortunately, the rest of the meal was mediocre in comparison. I had a typical Mexican meal of fish with garlic and olive oil, but the garlic was burned and crunchy, and the fish was soggy with grease. This seems to be the kind of place where bigger is better, so it may be worth it to come with a bunch of friends and share the $500 seafood platter, which looked pretty good on its way to my neighbors' table and contained enough lobster, shrimp, and fish to fill at least four hungry stomachs (or five with all that free guacamole and garlic bread). *Av. Adolfo Rosado Salas, between Av. Rafael Melgar and Av. 5. No phone. Main courses $90–$200. AE, MC, V. Daily 10am–10pm.*

➔ **Pancho's Backyard** MEXICAN In the courtyard behind Los Cinco Soles (p. 250), Pancho's Backyard is a hidden treasure of healthy, innovative Mexican cuisine. Everything from the tables to the plates were created by the world-class artisans at Cinco Soles, which gives the backyard a garden party feel. The menu boasts healthy variations of old favorites like fajitas and mole enchiladas, which include meat but not saturated oils or lard. Standout dishes include the lobster gazpacho—a steal at $60—and the spaghetti con pollo al tequila, a flavorful combination of thin spaghetti and sliced chicken breast in a cilantro tequila sauce. Vegetarian options, like a savory chiles rellenos stuffed with plantains and walnuts, are also on hand. *Av. Rafael Melgar, between Calle 8 and Calle 10. No phone. Main courses $60–$160. AE, MC, V. Daily 10am–9pm.*

SPLURGE

➔ **Guido's** ★ ITALIAN Though I'd like it more if it was cheaper, Guido's is the undisputed favorite on Cozumel when it comes to true Italian food. Families come for the homey atmosphere and menu that is heavy on homemade pasta and traditional wood-fired pizza. You should come for the pitchers of homemade sangria made with your choice of white or red wine, and thick with fancy liquor and tropical fruit. One more reason to go to Guido's is their *pan de ajo* (garlic bread) made with fresh roasted cloves of garlic spread over fluffy, fresh-baked flour tortillas and drizzled with olive oil. *Av. Rafael Melgar 23,* *between Calles 8 and 6. No phone. Main courses $180. MC, V. Daily 11am–11pm.*

CAFES

➔ **Café Chiapas** CAFE If what you're looking for is good coffee that will also make you feel good about yourself, Café Optima is the place for you. This small storefront specializes in top quality organic free-trade coffee that is grown at high altitudes by people in the region of Chiapas. The flavor and body of the coffees offered will perk up even the toughest of international coffee snobs, while the fact that the coffee was grown locally, and picked by workers given fair wages, will please all the do-gooders reading this. Ground and whole beans are also available for pick-up if you prefer to brew your own. *Calle 2 North 144.* ☎ *987/869-2942. Coffee $10, espresso drinks $30, coffee by the pound $60–$80. No credit cards. Daily 7am–7pm (hours subject to change).*

➔ **Coffeelia** ★★ CAFE Offering much more than just coffee, this pleasant daytime cafe has a good variety of small eats to fill your stomach after a morning dive or swim. In addition to a wide selection of sandwiches, salads, and crepes, the menu lists an impressive variety of local snacks such as *molletes* (thick toast with beans and melted cheese), *calabacitas* (zucchini cups stuffed with grilled vegetables and melted cheese), and fresh tropical fruit with yogurt, honey, and granola. Plus, you can sample pitchers of gourmet iced teas and lemonades with flower essences—a luxurious way to hydrate yourself after a few hours spent below sea level. *Calle 5 South, at Av. 15. No phone. Breakfast and lunch $20–$70, specialty coffees and teas $20–$40. No credit cards. Daily 9am–6pm.*

Partying

Most of the music and dance venues in town are congregated along Avenida Rafael Melgar. On Sunday evenings, all of Cozumel rocks out at the main plaza across from the ferry pier—they come for music, dancing, and delicious local treats. If you're in town, don't miss the chance to join everyone from 70-year-old locals to sunburned cruisers who come to get down to the big brass bands and mariachis.

Since Cozumel has a closer knit party scene than most Mexican resort towns, stopping by one of the chain bars aimed at American tourists here is less lame than on the mainland. In addition to the less touristy options reviewed in full below, you might want to stop by **Carlos n' Charlie's** (Av. Rafael Melgar No. 551; ☎ **987/869-1647**), which is popular with divers winding down after a day in the deep, and nearby **Señor Frog's** (☎ **987/872-0191**), which serves all the gallon margaritas and pizza-size quesadillas you've come to expect from the Carlos Anderson chain.

Then there's **Hard Rock Cafe** (Av. Rafael Melgar, between Av. Juárez and Calle 2; ☎ **987/872-5273**), which has some of the only live bands in town night after night, and **Joe's Lobster House** (Av. Rafael Melgar, across from the pier; ☎ **987/872-3275**), frequented by a cruise ship crowd that's into the all-night reggae and salsa music, as well as the convenient location across from the ferry pier.

See "Heading to the Beach" for info on the island's daytime beach hangs.

BARS & CLUBS

➔ **El Cielo** ★ *Cielo* means "sky" in Spanish, and the lofty name suits this swanky joint's designer martinis, cool blue lighting, and solid glass bar. The lemon drop, orange drop, and lime drop martinis are all the perfect mix of strong and sweet. Have a few of the dirty martinis with blue Bombay Sapphire and you'll really feel on top of the world. *Av. 15, between Calles 2 and 4.* ☎ *987/872-3467.*

→ **Neptune Disco** With laser shows, infused CO2, hot DJs, and hotter bodies on the dance floor, Neptune Disco is the closest you'll get to the mega-clubs of Cancún on this tiny island, without the astronomical covers levied on the mainland. (If you're itching for more after a few nights at Neptune, Playa del Carmen and its legendary clubs are only a short ferry ride away.) After you've gotten your groove on inside the disco, be sure to stop next door at Sushi n' Go (p. 243) for some of their addictive fried Mexican sushi rolls. *Calle 11 South, across from Sushi n' Go.* ☎ *987/872-1537.*

→ **Viva Mexicana** Get your Latin groove on at this dive that serves the cheapest beer in town and plays the hottest Spanish jams all night long. Rowdier than your average salsa club, this local favorite also serves up spicy Mexican finger foods to keep your hips shaking like Shakira till sunrise. *On the same strip as Neptune Disco.* ☎ *987/872-0799.*

Heading to the Beach

Along both the west and east sides of the island you'll see signs advertising beach clubs. A "beach club" in Cozumel can mean just a palapa hut that's open to the public and serves soft drinks, beer, and fried fish. It can also mean a recreational beach with the full gamut of offerings from banana boats to parasailing. They also usually have locker rooms and a pool, and food. The two biggest of these are **Mr. Sancho's** (see below) and **Playa Mía** (☎ **987/872-9030;** www.playamia.com). They get a lot of business from the cruise ships. Quieter versions of beach clubs are **Nachi Cocom** (no phone), **Playa San Francisco** (no phone), and **Playa Palancar** (no phone). All of these beaches are south of Chankanaab Park, and easily visible from the road. Several have swimming pools with beach furniture, a restaurant, and snorkel rental. Nachi Cocom costs $10; the others cost around $5.

Once you get to the end of the island the beach clubs become simple places where you can eat and drink and lay out on the beach for free. **Paradise Beach Club** (see below) is on the southern tip of the island across from Punta Sur nature park, and as you go up the eastern side of the island you pass **Playa Bonita, Chen Río,** and **Punta Morena.** Except on Sundays, when the locals head for the beaches, these places are practically deserted. Most of the east coast is unsafe for swimming because of the surf. The beaches tend to be small and occupy gaps in the rocky coast.

BEACH CLUBS

→ **Mr. Sancho's Beach Club** ★★★ It's always a party on this prime stretch of beach front where you can rent a jet ski or windsurf, than head back on land to drink a piña colada out of a coconut while you sway on a swing at the bar or lounge on one of the soft chairs. As packed and happening as this place always is, the beach is kept remarkably clean and clear, and there is no fee for admission, towels, or chairs. It's generally an awesome setting for a game of pick-up beach volleyball, a sandcastle building contest, rubbing elbows in the swimming-pool-size hot tub, or trying any motorized watersport. I wouldn't recommend snorkeling here, as the rowdy crowd tends to drive the fish out of sight. Locker rooms and showers are available on-site, and there is a tasty seafood restaurant that serves up yummy midday eats including burgers, fries, and, of course, cold beer. *Carretera Sur Km 15.* ☎ *987/876-1629. www.mrsanchos.com.*

→ **Paradise Beach Club** ★★ This quiet little piece of paradise has everything you want and nothing you don't. The long lines of super soft lounge chairs are often empty, giving you a truly relaxing environment to soak up the sun and surf. Admission is $50, but it includes unlimited towels and chairs, as well as kayaking and snorkeling equipment. Calm water and a lack of crowds contribute to perfect conditions for snorkeling, and the noticeably absent jet skis and motorboats are a kayaker's dream. There is a climbing wall and a trampoline out in the waves, as well as a snack bar with a long list of cocktails, sandwiches, and salads. *Carretera Sur Km 15. ☎ 987/871-9010. http://paradise-beach-cozumel.net.*

Sightseeing

➜ **El Cedral** Close to the island's most northern point—and difficult to get to because of damage to already rough roads by Hurricane Wilma—lies the humble ruin of El Cedral. Clustered around it are some other small ruins, poorly preserved remnants of Cozumel's past as a marine trading post. You'll also find the most pristine and undeveloped beaches on this part of the island, but they have strong currents and are best for wading, not swimming. *Playa Sanfrancisco, on the Av. Melgar. ☎ 987/800-2215. Admission $55. Daily 7am–4pm.*

➜ **Museo de la Isla de Cozumel** This museum is like the island of Cozumel itself: small, but packed with unexpected treasures. The biggest highlight is the permanent exhibit featuring indigenous art and an accurate reproduction of a Maya dwelling with a thatched palapa roof. For art buffs, there are always two temporary shows featuring contemporary artists on display. And like many museums in Mexico, the Museo de las Isla Cozumel has a special gallery featuring art by local children. What it has that other museums don't is a lovely steeple cafe with great brunch and some of the best views on the island, overlooking the ocean and the ferry pier. *Av. Rafael Melgar, between calles 4 and 6. ☎ 987/872-1475. Admission $30. Mon–Sat 9am–3pm.*

➜ **San Gervasio** One of the most popular island excursions is to **San Gervasio** (100 B.C.–A.D. 1600). When it comes to Cozumel's Maya ruins, getting there is most of the fun—do it for the mystique and for the trip, not for the size or scale of the ruins. The buildings, though preserved, are crudely made and would not be much of a tourist attraction if they were not the island's principal ruins. More significant than beautiful, this site was once an important ceremonial center where the Maya gathered, coming even from the mainland. Guides charge $20 for a tour for one to six people. A better option is to find a copy of the green booklet *San Gervasio,* sold at local checkout counters and bookstores, and tour the site on your own. *Follow Av. Juárez about 24km/15 miles till you see the San Gervasio sign which points to the gravel road to the ruin. No phone. Admission $50. Daily 9am–6pm.*

Playing Outside

The main reason to come to Cozumel is to play outside, whether you decide to partake in wholesome actives like scuba diving or prefer to dirty dance at one of the bumping beach clubs. Following are some of the less risqué options; see "Partying" and "Heading to the Beach" for the other sort.

PARQUE CHANAKAAB ★

One of the oldest natural parks in Mexico, Chanakaab means "little sea" and refers to Cozumel's enclosed lagoon that is fed by underground tunnels from the ocean. Unfortunately, these tunnels are collapsing, endangering the ecosystem of the lagoon so much that the park's management has forbid any activity in the lagoon since the start of the collapse. (Though there is no proof, locals speculate the system collapsed because of over-exposure

Hyperbaric chambers

Because Cozumel is such a diving hot spot, there are four recompression chambers on the small island. In order to avoid ever having to visit one, follow your instructor's instructions, stay hydrated (don't get wasted the night before a dive—a hangover is just another word for dehydration, which is the number one cause of recompression sickness), and never fly the same day you dive. If you do find yourself with an unfortunate case of the bends, get help as soon as possible. **The Hyperbaric Center of Cozumel** (☎ **987/872-2387**) is on Calle 4 Norte between avenidas 5 and 10. **Buceo Medico Mexicano** (☎ **987/872-2387** or 987/872-1430) is open 24 hours and is on Calle 5 Sur 21-B between Avenida Rafael Melgar and Avenida 5 Sur.

to hoards of crowds from cruise ships.) You can still swim, scuba dive, snorkel, and take part in many other watery activities along the calm beach nearby, though. Chanakaab also boasts a botanical garden with over 350 species of plants from around the world, in addition to 451 indigenous varieties. For animal lovers there is a sea lion sanctuary and an aviary. And if you're into ancient architecture you will learn a lot from the reconstructed ruins here based on the Toltec, Aztec, and Maya archaeological styles.

Dolphin Discovery (☎ **998/849-4757**; www.dolphindiscovery.com) provides dolphin swims at this location, but the spots fill up fast, so you should make reservations well ahead if you want to swim up close and personal with these intelligent mammals. This is also the only place where Dolphin Discovery allows you to swim with sea lions that have been rescued from illegal captivity elsewhere—they're just about the cutest things in the world to have in the water next to you. See p. 230 for more info on Dolphin Discovery.

The park is about 10 minutes south of San Miguel, and a taxi ride from town should cost around $100. Admission is $100. It's open daily from 8am to 5pm. Call ☎ **987/872-0914** for info.

PUNTA SUR ECOLOGICAL RESERVE ★★

If you love nature but not monstrous cruise ship crowds, this underdeveloped ecological reserve is your ticket for encountering nature without the burden of too many bodies obstructing your view of the spectacular array of wildlife. The beaches are wild and almost empty, the snorkeling is divine, and the guides are naturalists with a wealth of interesting information about local flora and fauna to share. Central observation towers allow you to observe crocodiles, egrets, herons, flamingos, and many other species of birds that live around the lagoon.

The park also boasts an old Maya-style lighthouse, **El Caracol,** that makes a high-pitched screech when the wind blows through in just the right way. At the southernmost tip (Punta Celarain) lies another more modern lighthouse which has recently been converted into a museum of navigation. Dazzling views await those with enough oomph to climb the over-100 stairs to the deck at the top that overlooks the sea.

You'll also find a good restaurant in the park, as well as kayak and snorkeling rentals, and guided boat tours of the lagoon. A small souvenir shop, restrooms, and an information center are just inside the entrance. The only downside to this uncut gem is that the reason it has remained so pristine is because it is difficult to get to. If you haven't rented a car, you will need to make arrangements with a taxi driver to come pick you up at a pre-arranged time and pay him the full amount when he lets you off. A round-trip journey will set you back about $400. I recommend making friends and getting a group together to share the cab. Admission to the park itself is $100. Call ☎ **987/872-2940** for info on activity prices. Hours are daily 9am to 5pm. ***Note:*** During the summer months you can participate in a program that permits visitors to assist in observing sea turtles nesting at night. For more info about this program, call ☎ **987/872-2940.**

DIVING ★★★

Diving in Cozumel is as close to perfect as it gets, with its colorful reefs, warm clear water, and sunny climate; it's not surprising that it's the second most popular dive destination in the world. Because of this status, there are an abundant amount of dive shops on the island. I dove and went out on a snorkeling expedition with PADI five-star certified Bill Horn's **Aqua Safari** (Av. Rafael Melgar, at Calle 5; ☎ **987/872-0101;** www.aquasafari.com) and was so impressed by the level of professionalism and friendliness of the entire staff—from the instructors to the women who ran the shop—that I can't imagine recommending anyplace else. Aqua Safari is also the oldest dive shop in all of Mexico, which is why it has its own dock right in the center of town for convenient departures and arrivals on boat trips. Many of the instructors at Aqua Safari have been teaching for over 10 years in Cozumel, and all of them speak excellent English. Aqua Safari offers a complete menu of diving services, from a 1-day intro dive for beginners, to full certification, advanced courses, refresher courses, guided snorkeling tours, fast boat two-tank or three-tank trips, and even night diving.

If you are planning a vacation centered on diving, you may want to consider staying at **Condumel Condo Beach Apartments** (p. 239) or the **Safari Inn** (p. 238), since Aqua Safari offers special package deals for guests at these affiliated hotels.

A scuba dive for beginners costs $700, full certification costs $3,500, and refresher courses cost $600. Call for info on additional courses.

Cozumel has a limitless supply of worthy dive sites, and your dive master will have expert knowledge of where the best sites are for your skill level. Because divers in Cozumel practice drift diving, it is important to go with a dive master until you get the hang of it. A few top destinations include the colorful **Yucab Reef,** which is know for its dazzling formations of colorful coral; the **Palancar Reef,** which draws novices and more advanced divers with its mysterious caves and underwater canyons as well as bright hues of coral and rare fish; the deep **Santa Rosa Wall,** with its towering heights of coral and wealth of wildlife, and the **San Francisco Reef,** which has a wide variety of undersea species within relatively shallower waters.

SNORKELING

You can snorkel in Cozumel from the beach at your hotel or any of the beach clubs, but to get out to the reefs you'll need a boat and a guide who knows where to go. Aqua Safari has the most affordable rates for snorkeling trips in town (at $250), but they only go for the afternoon. If you want to arrange a whole day of snorkeling from a boat, the **Kuzamil Snorkeling Center** (Av. 5 bis 565 Int. 1, between calles 5 Sur and Hidalgo, Colonia Adolfo Lopez Mateos; ☎ **987/872-4637** or 987/872-1028) will hook it up for you and throw in a gourmet picnic lunch on the boat. A full-day trip costs $650 per person; a half-day is $400.

Late Registration

If you plan to go diving in Cozumel, make sure you bring your certification and log book. If you aren't certified, that's okay too—many qualified shops offer a 1-day taster, where you can do a shallow dive with an experienced instructor after practicing the basics. You can see the same incredible array of wildlife at 13m (45 ft.) that you can at 30m (100 ft.), and this is a safe way to do it for the first time.

Most of the dive shops on Cozumel offer 4- or 5-day full certification programs, where you can get certified while diving in real reefs in a short intensive class, rather than taking one of the long certification classes offered in the States. (Why spend every Mon night for 2 months at the bottom of a swimming pool at your local Y if you don't have to?) Don't trust any shop that doesn't ask to see your certification and logbook before taking you out on a boat. I like **Bill's Aqua Safari** (see above); I took part in one of the certification programs there and it was a great experience. Before I even did my first two official dives on the last day, I was able to journey into the ocean and see seahorses, octopuses, stingrays, and electrically colored fish as I got certified by PADI, the international scuba diving association.

That said, certification makes for a great week-long destination trip, as long as you don't try to pack too much fun into your hours above water. If you are looking to party at night, you should do your certification back home and only spend a few days diving, so that you can make sure to be sober the night before. The main cause of recompression sickness, or "the bends," is dehydration (aka hangovers).

Shopping

If you like shopping for silver jewelry, you can spend a great deal of time examining the wares of all the jewelers along Avenida Rafael Melgar.

Don't buy anything made out of coral or any other underwater creature on Cozumel, no matter how exotic or unique. Local laws prohibit harvesting these items, but not making a profit pawning them off on clueless tourists. Do yourself and the ecosystem a favor and choose a handmade silver trinket instead.

For everything else, you can't beat **Cinco Soles** (no phone) the block-size art and craft warehouse with an upscale feel but bargain prices on Avenida Rafael Melgar across the street from the ferry pier.

Playa del Carmen

Playa del Carmen is a rare place in this day and age, a resort town with a distinct personality. Many older Mexicans will tell you that Playa was once a beautiful untouched beach with only one hotel, but that now it's been tainted by developers and partiers. Don't listen to them: Playa has simply grown up. It's decided not to settle for being just another undiscovered sleepy beach town.

This rebellious attitude has offended the town's elders a bit. But Playa del Carmen has the unique distinction of being a resort town built for young people, which makes it perhaps the hippest spot in Mexico. It boasts a party scene that's as crazy as Cancún's but without the hefty cover prices or heaps of tourists. The boutique resorts have been designed with younger guests in

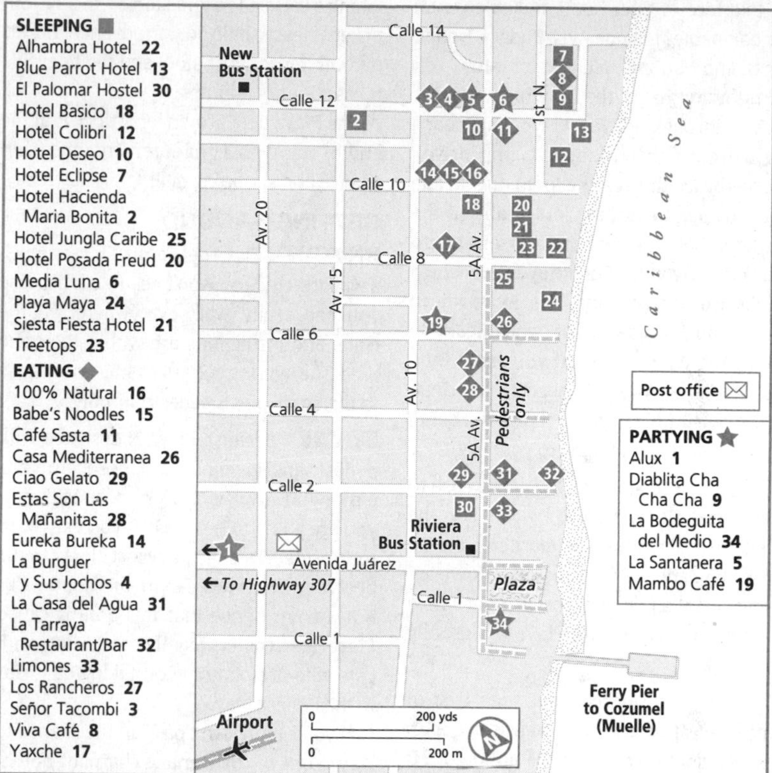

mind—amenities like incense and condoms are often included despite the cheap prices. And, though it doesn't have a gourmet dining scene, Playa boasts some of the best inexpensive seafood and bar food around.

Playa attracts a diverse crowd—its streets are full of jet-setters and backpackers from all around the world—but beautiful people are particularly prevalent. The Pretty Young Things come for the hip parties, hotels, and food, but they also come for the beach scene. A perfect day here involves taking in the sun and the sea air while working your toes into the sand, cooling down with a swim in clear water, strolling aimlessly down the beach, and then using your reserved energy to party until dawn.

Getting There & Getting Around

GETTING INTO TOWN

BY PLANE You can fly directly into Cancún (p. 184) and take a shuttle van directly from the airport. I like **Greenline Shuttle.** They have a booth right as you exit the international terminal, and a ticket costs $90 for a seat in an air-conditioned van; the drive to Playa takes 1 hour. You can also fly into Cozumel and take the passenger ferry here; see "By Ferry" below for info.

BY CAR It makes sense to reserve a car in advance (you'll get cheaper rates if you book weeks before your trip) at the airport in Cancún because all major rental car companies are right there, and you'll save on taxi fare to your hotel. Reliable rental car companies include Avis, Budget, Dollar, Hertz, and National; see p. 51 for info.

Highway 307 is the only highway that passes through Playa. As you approach Playa from Cancún (about a 1-hr. drive), the highway divides. Keep to the inside lanes to permit turning left at any of the traffic lights. The two main arteries into Playa are Avenida Constituyentes, which works well for destinations in northern Playa, and Avenida Juárez, which leads to the town's main square. If you stay in the outside lanes, you will need to continue past Playa until you get to the turnaround, then double back, staying to your right.

BY TAXI It doesn't really make sense to take a taxi all the way to Playa when the Greenline Shuttles (see earlier) are so affordable and easily accessible. However, if you've got a pile of pesos burning a hole in your pocket, a taxi to Playa will usually cost $600.

BY BUS Considering the steep cost of renting a car by day, a first-class bus is an easy, comparatively cheaper option. **ADO** (☎ **998/884-4352**) buses run to just about every destination in Mexico, from urban centers like Mérida, to within walking distance of ruins like Chichén Itzá. A ticket for a 4-hour bus ride (with two movies) to or from Mérida is $200, with most rates for closer locations between $40 and $100.

The ADO bus station in Playa del Carmen is on the corner of Quinta Avenida (5th Avenue) and Avenida Juárez, right before the ferry pier. Taxis are on hand there to take you to your final destination.

BY FERRY **Ultramar** (☎ **987/869-2775**) and **Barcos Mexico** (☎ **987/872-1508** or 987/872-1588) both have passenger ferries that go between Cozumel and Playa del Carmen every hour on the hour between 5am and midnight. If you are counting on taking a certain ferry, make sure to buy your ticket at least a half-hour in advance. Tickets on both ferries cost $100, and the boat ride takes about 45 minutes.

The Playa del Carmen ferry dock is at the end of 5th Avenue, minutes from the main square and shopping mall.

GETTING AROUND

ON FOOT Playa del Carmen is very much a walking city. You won't need a car because you can really walk everywhere; all the clubs and attractions are within the same area. The main street, 5th Avenue, runs close to the beach and is pedestrian-only.

BY CAR Because Playa is designed with pedestrians in mind as opposed to cars, parking in town is a tricky proposition. If you are going to bring a car, you may want to consider staying at a resort closer to the beach or the Playacar in the south. (It's not a coincidence that this area is called Playacar—it caters mainly to travelers with cars who are planning on taking day trips in the Riviera Maya.)

If you simply can't pass up the chance to stay in one of 5th Avenue's charming hotels, there's a big parking lot at Estacionmiento Mexico, on the corner of Avenida Juárez and 10th Avenue. The lot charges a reasonable $12 per hour, or $80 per day, and is open for 24 hours. There's also another 24-hour lot 1 block from the ferry pier, but that one fills up more quickly.

Basics

ORIENTATION

Avenida Juárez is the official main street in town—it stretches from Highway 307 to the main square. The avenues that run parallel from the beach are all multiples of five, with **5th Avenue** being the headquarters for the hippest shops, hotels, and restaurants. Many clubs are 1 block up on **10th Avenue.** On the southern edge of town past the ferry pier and the main mall is the development **Playacar,** which has many resorts that are bigger and have less personality than the hotels on 5th Avenue, but also offer more package options. Staying there could lighten the burden on your budget while still keeping you relatively close to the action on 5th Avenue.

TOURIST INFO & OFFICES

The Tourist Office (☎ **987/873-2804**) is on the corner of Avenida Juárez and 15th Avenue. It's open Monday through Friday 8:30am to 8:30pm and Saturday and Sunday 9am to 5pm.

Recommended Website

- **www.playadelcarmen.com**: *Playa Magazine* is one of Playa del Carmen's best guides, and this online version of the popular magazine has great tips on activities and accommodations, as well as the signature fashion photo spreads that have made the guide so popular.

Playa del Carmen Nuts & Bolts

Banks Because this is a shopping city, ATMs abound throughout downtown. *Casas de cambio* (money exchange houses), which sometimes offer a better exchange rate without the ATM fee, are clustered around the pier, or near the intersection of 5th Avenue and Calle 8.

Emergencies If you are seriously injured, you should take a cab to one of the first-rate emergency hospitals in Cancún. For more minor health issues, **Dr. Jorge Mercado** (☎ **984/873-3908**) is a local doctor with a good reputation who speaks fluent English. His practice is on the corner of Constituyentes and 10th Avenue. After office hours, he takes calls on his cellphone (☎ **044/984-877-7400**).

Internet/Wireless Hot Spots Since Playa del Carmen has so many younger travelers, Internet access is a high priority here. Most hotels along 5th Avenue have Wi-Fi available in the lobby, restaurant, or bar, with at least one computer with access for those who don't think it's wise to cart a laptop along on their vacation. If you're staying at a rare place without Internet, or simply want to add another entry to your e-diary without walking all the way back to your hotel, Internet cafes and stations abound on almost every corner in town. One to try is **La Taberna Internet Café** at Avenida Juárez and 10th Avenue (☎ **987/803-0447** or 987/803-0448). It charges $16 per hour and is open daily 10am to 4am.

Pharmacies There are well-stocked pharmacies all along 5th Avenue, with some of the best selections in discounted prescription medications I've seen. If you have a particular drug you are hoping to stock up on before your return to the States, you may want to comparison shop, as the pharmacies here are very competitive when it comes to pricing. See "Basics," p. 71, for more info on buying prescription drugs in Mexico.

Post Offices The main post office is on Avenida Juárez, between Hotel Playa del Carmen and the *lavanderia,* where you can wash your clothes within view of the ocean.

Telephone Tips The local area code is **984.**

Sleeping

If you stay at a luxury resort in one city during your travels, make it this one. Playa excels at the sort of hotels and resorts that are attractions in their own right. If you're strapped for cash, another option is splitting a room at one of the cheaper hotels in town, such as the Siesta Fiesta, Eclipse, or the cabañas at Hotel Colibri—you'll get a better experience than at the one hostel in town, and for not much more money.

On the stretch of Carretera Playa del Carmen-Tulum between Playa del Carmen and Tulum are the **Xpu-Ha Campgrounds.** The exact location is 81km (50 miles) south of the intersection of Mexican Highway 307 and Mexican Highway 180D near Km 264. There are three different camping areas here with services varying from full hookups for RVs to tent sites. All have restrooms. Though this land has been owned by a Maya family for decades, one section has recently been leased to a cruise ship company, and that's more developed (for better or worse). Prices vary from $50 to $150, depending on the type of site you want.

HOSTELS

➜ **El Palomar Hostel** El Palomar's slogan is, "The best place for backpackers in Playa." This may or may not be true, depending on what you're looking for. The rooms are small and stuffy, with not much to recommend them, although there is nothing particularly repulsive about them either. That said, if your budget is your bottom line, you won't find a cheaper bed, and the hostel does offer all of the services you need as a backpacker—see below for the list. *Av. 5 between Av. Juárez and Calle 2 Norte. ☎ 984/873-0144. www.elpalomarhostel.com. $120 single. No credit cards. Amenities: Breakfast room (with complimentary breakfast); Internet; kitchen; shared bathroom; sheets; telephone (in common area); towels.*

CHEAP

➜ **Hotel Colibri** ★★ *Colibri* means "hummingbird" in Spanish, and when I asked the concierge if it had some other symbolic meaning, he confirmed that the owners of this sweet, sunny hotel, "just really, really like hummingbirds." The hummingbird's cheerful presence can be felt throughout the hotel—unusual bird-themed artwork is omnipresent in the tropical decor (the birds are even carved into the brightly colored headboards). The comfy cabaña rooms, which are set off away from the main hotel on a strip along the beach, don't have air-conditioning, but they are a delightful low-cost option right next to the waves. If you're a diver, this hotel is your best bet in Playa; the Phocea dive shop is a PADI Golden Standard operation that operates right out of the lobby and offers guests their best rates on dive packages, including a rare whale shark tour. *1st Av. Norte between Calle 10 and 12. ☎ 984/803-1090. www.hotel-colibri.com. $250 cabaña, $350–$450 double high season. MC, V. Amenities: Restaurant and bar; dive shop; large pool; Wi-Fi in lobby. In room: A/C, TV w/cable (in some rooms, make sure to request), fridge, minibar.*

➜ **Hotel Eclipse** ★ Hotel Eclipse is a labor of love for the people who own and run it, which is evident by the constant unconventional attention that they give to their guests. The hotel itself is a maze of old and new structures that have been built on top of each other, much in the same way many of the great Maya cities were built in layers to meet the changing demands of ancient civilizations. No matter what your budget is, the Eclipse has got a sweetly decorated room for you, from the doubles with fans all the way up to the two-story penthouses with their own private courtyards and kitchens. Eclipse is more a way of life than a hotel. In fact, the owners (who speak over eight languages) will pretty much go out of their way to arrange pretty much anything you want at a good price, from transportation from the airport to Harley motorcycle tours. Hotel Eclipse is also conveniently a stone's throw away from the beach and Mamita's hoppin' beach club, as well as the delightful Café del Sol, which is way better than your average hotel restaurant and bar. *Av. 1 North, 1a between Av. 12 and 14. ☎ 984/873-0629. www.hoteleclipse.com. $400 basic double, $1,200 penthouse suite. MC, V. Amenities: Restaurant and bar next door; barbecue facilities; free bikes for guests (with reservation); complimentary books; complimentary cocktail parties for guests; free coffee all day; special dive packages; free Internet in office. In room: A/C, cable TV, fans.*

→ **Hotel Posada Freud** If you'd like to be near the rocking scene at the Siesta Fiesta Hotel (see below) but require more sophisticated accommodations, the neighboring Hotel Posada Freud is a good alternative. Although it has minimal amenities, the rooms are charming, and the guests don't seem to mind piggybacking off the Siesta Fiesta Bar and Restaurant for convenient late-night revelry, food, and drink. The airy bedrooms are reminiscent of a New England–style B&B, with their deep blue and sunny yellow painted tiles, hand-carved wooden headboards and furniture, rustic quilts, and lacey white curtains. All bathrooms feature blue mosaic showers. *Av. 5, between calles 8 and 10 North. ☎/fax 984/873-0601. www.posadafreud.com. $550 and up double. MC, V. Amenities: Bar and restaurant (adjacent); fridge; safe. In room: A/C.*

MTV Best → **Siesta Fiesta Hotel** ★★★ The architecture of this hippie hotel works with the trees instead of against them, incorporating natural unfinished branches into its rustic balconies, thatched roofs, and spiral staircases, and the effect is that of a mystical forest full of festive tree dwellers. The bar and restaurant that overflows into the courtyard, with its natural wood tables draped in brightly colored batiked cloths, caters to a liberal, fun-loving crowd. Live music is played every night of the week after dark, when the place gets packed with laid-back revelers. The fishbowl-size piña coladas are divine, as are the dollar cappuccinos in the morning, which compliment the free continental breakfast. The rooms themselves are simple, and may remind you of that house you lived in for a while in college, with some Mexican touches—think a big bed on the floor with indigenous art on the walls, Mexican rugs, and even a dream catcher or two to keep out evil spirits. *Av 5, between calles 8 and 10. ☎ 984/803-1166. www.siestafiestahotel.com. $350 double on ground floor, $450 double on top floor. No credit cards (unless arranged in advance). Amenities: Restaurant and bar with nightly live music; free continental breakfast. In room: A/C.*

→ **Treetops** ★ If you've watched *Survivor* and wished you could be stranded on a beautiful island, your fantasy of living in a do-it-yourself paradise just inched closer to reality. These treehouse-inspired apartments are designed for young travelers partying on a budget. Many of the cute suites have kitchens (though beds are a tad uncomfortable), and instead of a swimming pool, the unconventional resort boosts its own little cenote. You can't beat the hotel's location, just steps away from both the beach and 5th Avenue. This place could charge a lot more, but I guess the owners are just too nice. *Calle 8 s/n. ☎/fax 984/873-0351. www.treetopshotel.com. $400–$800 double, low season $1,000 suite (for 4 people with kitchen), high season $1,500 suite. MC, V. Amenities: Restaurant; bar; cenote (swimmable). In room: A/C, fridge, kitchenette (in some).*

DOABLE

→ **Alhambra Hotel** ★ This clean, whitewashed New Age resort prides itself on being your portal to the healing energy of the sun and sea. Weekend kundalini and hatha yoga classes and daily on-site massage therapists, specializing in Maya aromatherapy treatments using indigenous healing herbs, are available. A rooftop solarium; back courtyard with a small shady pool, waterfall, and Jacuzzi; and beachside restaurant with a vegetarian slant round out the healthy amenities. Despite all of these alluring services, though, the real reason to stay here is the beautiful beachfront, right in the center of downtown. The rooms themselves are simple if spacious, with double beds and a spare futon. *Calle 8 Norte Esquina Zona Federal Maritima (where it meets the beach).* ☎ *984/873-0735. www.alhambra-hotel.net. $750–$850 double. MC, V. Amenities: Restaurant and bar; Internet on computer in lobby; pool; spa; solarium. In room: A/C.*

→ **Hotel Hacienda María Bonita** ★★ *Muy bonita*. This lush, colorful boutique hotel has earned its popularity, so if you want to stay here it's important to reserve well in advance. In addition to the artsy, authentic Mexican decor, complete with flowing fountains, colorful furniture, and vibrant, plentiful plants both inside and out, Hotel Hacienda María Bonita boasts the best swimming pool in downtown Playa, with an ample sunning area. Its ideal location, 1 block away from 5th Avenue and just a few blocks from the beach, combined with its oasis-like atmosphere, attracts a diverse crowd of guests who help make the bar and restaurant

My Maya Massage

While you're in Playa del Carmen, you'll likely stumble upon many opportunities to receive a Maya massage. Here's my verdict on the experience:

I sat in a tent covered with wool blankets (to keep in the steam) in my birthday suit, while steam infused with healing and detoxifying herbs was pumped in through the mesh flap. The steam did feel good for a while, in a Bikram yoga kind of way, but as the minutes ticked by, I realized I was sitting in a puddle of my own sweat and couldn't help but wonder if they cleaned the tent thoroughly between treatments. The massage itself was a relaxing combination of many massage techniques, from hot stone to shiatsu, and the half-hour spent inside the hot tent did relax my muscles. Still, when my masseuse opened the flap and handed me a maraca to shake inside while he chanted outside, I began to wish that I'd simply opted for the usual Swedish treatment. I also could have done without being (lightly) whipped with bundles of spiky herbs (to help with the final detox) and the cream of cacao mask (during which they basically covered my face with melted chocolate). Even though I was assured that chocolate doesn't cause acne, that didn't help assuage my fears that I would wake up covered in zits the next day.

If you still want to get massaged the Maya way, just remember that you should not accept a Maya massage from anyone who offers one for free—you should only receive one in a certified spa setting. This seems like common sense, but you'll be surprised (if you're a girl) how many men who are not certified spa technicians will claim to know the secret massage techniques of the Maya and offer you a private sample for free.

inside a lively place to hang out. *Av. 20 at Norte 215, between calles 10 and 12. No phone. www.haciendamariabonita.com. $600 and up double. MC, V. Amenities: Restaurant and bar; Internet in office suite; large pool; spa; Wi-Fi in lobby. In room: A/C.*

→ **Hotel Jungla Caribe** The pool is the highlight of this highly social hotel, and the lush plants and towering trees that surround it are what put the "jungla" into its name. Since it's in the heart of the party storm on 5th Avenue, the hotel's location can be a deal maker or a deal breaker depending on whether you want to dance all night or actually be able to go to sleep before 1am. (But why would you want to do the former in Playa?) The accommodations are sleek and roomier than most, and they include two double beds—a plus if you want to party all night with a bunch of friends on a budget. *Av. 5 Norte, at Calle 8. ☎/fax 984/873-0650. www.jungla-caribe.com. $700–$900 double. AE, MC, V. Amenities: Restaurant; 2 bars; pool; room service till 11pm; travel agency in hotel. In room: A/C, TV.*

→ **Playa Maya** ★★ This is the cheapest spot to stay on the beach that's still within walking distance from 5th Avenue. You won't get a lot of frills, but you will get all the essentials you need for a relaxing beach vacation. Some luxury rooms have their own plant-filled courtyards with private hot tubs, but even the lowest priced accommodations have breezy balconies with lovely ocean views. *Zona FMT, between calles 6 and 8 Norte (entrance is on the beach). ☎ 984/803-2022. www.playa-maya.com. $900–$1,120 double, $1,120–$1,450 luxury suite (with hot tub). AE, MC, V. Amenities: Restaurant; bar; health club with massage service; Jacuzzi; laundry service; outdoor pool; room service till 7pm; Wi-Fi. In room: A/C, TV, fridge, hair dryer.*

SPLURGE

→ **Blue Parrot Hotel** The Blue Parrot is one of the older trendsetter hotels in Playa, and despite its attractive packaging, staying here almost isn't worth dealing with its snobby attitude and inflated prices. Compared to surrounding hotels on 5th Avenue, the hotel was notably empty during my last visit. That's despite the cool Asian-inspired circular interiors of the rooms, and the designer toiletries made with honey. If you have money to burn and are into having every luxury at your fingertips (the original ocean-side location is right on a prime piece of beachfront, directly next to the Blue Parrot Beach Club), this may be the place for you. Otherwise, there are other places in Playa where the staff members are nicer, the rates are lower, and the atmosphere is more 5th Avenue Playa and less like 5th Avenue New York. *Blue Parrot Beach Club: Calle 12, where it meets the beach. ☎ 984/206-3350. www.blueparrot.com. $1,250 double. AE, MC, V. Amenities: Restaurant and bar; beach club; Internet in office suite; large pool; spa; Wi-Fi in lobby. In room: A/C, TV w/cable, fridge, minibar.*

MTV Best → **Hotel Basico** ★★★ If you saw the name of this hotel and instantly pictured something simple, think again. Imagine instead that one of the most successful hotel developers in Mexico decided to start from scratch and rework the idea of what a hotel should be from the lobby on up. The second hotel from Habita, the creators of the justly popular Hotel Deseo (see below), Hotel Basico is the wilder, brazen younger brother of the two. Everything about this hotel, from the plants growing in the elevator, to the rooms with Mexican women's names (instead of numbers) seems to be an answer to the question, "Why not?" The bathroom boasts a huge rectangular bathtub, big enough to easily fit three average ones, and is lined with expensive toiletries made with fresh Yerba Buena. The bedroom comes with an equally big king-size bed, with a complimentary Polaroid camera chained to it for capturing those special moments. Two small whirlpools (one hot, one cold) are on the roof, which becomes a pulsing dance club at night. Like the Deseo, Basico has incredibly luxurious chariot-like group seating, where you can put up your feet and sit on cushions under a canopy you share with your close friends or new friends you'd like to get closer to. Don't knock it till you've tried it; the whole bar with bed thing is better than it sounds. *Av 5 at Calle 10 Norte. ☎ 984/879-4448. Fax 984/879-4449. www.hotelbasico.com. $1,500–$2,000 double. AE, MC, V. Amenities: Seafood restaurant and bar; Internet in office suite; 2 small pools; free salsa classes; Wi-Fi in lobby. In room: A/C, cable TV, fridge, minibar, cordless phone.*

MTV Best → **Hotel Deseo** ★★ At this impossibly hip, see-and-be-seen hotel, the literal high point is the elevated lounge. A seemingly floating stone stairway leads you above the hustle and bustle of 5th Avenue, to a tranquil islandlike platform pleasantly detached from the commotion below. The mojitos and martinis are the best in Playa (a serious accomplishment) and there is no better way to drink them than lying on one of the canopied beds that surround the pool and overlook downtown Playa. Though it's a great place to enjoy a good book in the daylight hours, I could do without the stagey, ambient music that perpetually plays in the background. Still, the whole scene makes you feel like you're on top of the world, and it is worth checking out the lounge even if you don't splurge on the hotel. As for the actual rooms, the decor throughout is crisp, minimalist, and elegant in contrast to the bombardment of bright colors that rules most Mexican hotels. All of the rooms also have wonderful king-size beds with plush, white comforters and bathrooms with sexy frosted glass showers, and a bathroom cabinet that carries a revised hipster version of the usual basic toiletry kit: earplugs, incense, and condoms. The last two are fun to have, but the earplugs especially come in handy after dark when the lounge becomes one of the most coveted hot spots in the Playa. *Av. 5 at Av 12. ☎ 984/879-3620. Fax 984/879-3621. www.hoteldeseo.com. US$150–US$180 double. MC, V. Amenities: Lounge and bar; Internet; large pool; spa; Wi-Fi in lobby. In room: A/C, fridge, minibar.*

Eating

In many ways, Playa del Carmen has a European vibe, and the relaxed, late-night dining scene is no exception. If you go out for grub at the usual hour, you may find that most restaurants are empty. Most don't kick into high gear until around 10pm, when they morph into barlike scenes. Do what the wise locals do—spend your daytime enjoying the beaches, grab a snack around 5 or 6pm, and cherish the sunset without any distracting tummy rumbling. If you wait until later to eat your dinner, you'll have all the more fuel to burn in the tricked-out clubs, which don't close until at least 4am.

CHEAP

→ **Babe's Noodles** ★ NOODLES Offering much more than just noodles, this funky late-night eatery supports the theory that all types of noodles are delicious, regardless of their country of origin. So while your friend eats the deliciously crispy on the outside, gooey on the inside mac 'n' cheese, you can slurp up a giant bowl of Japanese odon noodle soup, or twirl some first-rate Indian curry noodles onto your fork. The menu covers the map from spaghetti bolognese to Asian-inspired appetizers, featuring Mexican infusions of mango, chiles, and lime. The decor is a fitting synthesis of tiki bar and vintage American pin-up posters. *Calle 10, between Av. 5 and Av. 10. No phone. Main courses $50–$120. No credit cards. Daily noon–2am.*

→ **Eureka Bureka** MEDITERRANEAN This cute cafe specializing in the Mediterranean fast food called *burekas* is just one example of the recent influx of Israelis in Playa del Carmen. The burekas churned out here are pockets of phyllo dough stuffed with a surprising array of meats and veggies, and served with fries, pickles, or side salads. You can choose from cheese and spinach, potato and onion, meat and mushrooms, spicy chicken, or three cheeses, all of which are hot out of the oven and flaky and golden brown in your fingers. *Calle 10, between Av. 5 and Av. 10 No phone. Burekas and salads $20–$30. No credit cards. Daily 9am–10pm.*

→ **La Burguer y Sus Jochos** AMERICAN In the center of most of the late-night action on the Playa, this roadside burger joint keeps the menu simple and the customers, who cluster around the few outside tables or simply scarf their food standing up, satisfied. The minimalist menu consists of three items, plump hot dogs, fat hamburgers, and the much requested but never imitated Ham Hawaiian sandwich, which includes a stack of hot barbecued chipped ham, pineapple, gooey cheese, grilled onions, and salsa on a toasted bun. All are under $30 and come with french fries and unlimited toppings. *Calle 12, between Avs. 5 and 10. No phone. Main courses $30. No credit cards. Daily noon–2am.*

→ **La Tarraya Restaurant/Bar** SEAFOOD Fish is always best when eaten with the sound of waves lapping in the background, and La Tarraya is no exception to this rule. Inside this dilapidated beach shack, local fishermen fry up some of the best fish in town just the way you like it, or the way they like it, which is even better. They can grill it, steam it, sauté it, stuff it, or serve it raw right off the hook with a little lime and hot sauce. *Calle 2 Norte. ☎ 984/873-2040. Main courses $30–$80. No credit cards. Daily 8am–8pm.*

MTV Best → **100% Natural** ★★★ VEGETARIAN Though this popular chain can be found in many of Mexico's resort towns, the original location in Playa del Carmen is far superior to the rest in terms of atmosphere, decor, and food preparation. Well known for their reinterpretation of Mexican cuisine using only the freshest vegetarian ingredients, 100% Natural is the best spot in town for fresh squeezed juices, creative smoothies, salads, soy burgers, fruit dishes, and other colorful celebrations of healthy food. A variety of brown rice and whole wheat spaghetti dishes, unusual salads, and sandwiches (including some free-range meats) are all served with whole wheat bread baked on-site with flour that is ground daily at sunrise. The *nopal* (cactus) salad and the vegetarian tacos are highly recommended. Desserts include whole wheat cookies, carrot spice cake, and cheese pie with amaranth and seasonal fruit sauce. *Av. 5 by Calle 10. No phone. www.100natural.com.mx. Main courses $50–$100. AE, MC, V. Daily 7am–late (hours vary).*

→ **Señor Tacombi Gourmet Tacos** ★★ MEXICAN Conveniently right under the stairs of La Santanera (p. 262), this tricked-out VW bus serves up some of the best tacos to keep your belly full, without emptying your wallet. Serving up excellent chilaquiles, tamales, coffee, cold beer, and satisfying snacks 24 hours a day, it makes for a great pit stop on your way from La Santanera to Mambo Café or vice versa. If your feet are feeling heavy from too much salsa dancing, you can sit at one of the picnic tables under the stars and watch hipsters stroll by as you munch on Mexican treats—all irresistibly priced. *Calle 12 at Av. 10. No phone. www.tacombi.com. Main courses about $100. No credit cards. Daily 24 hr.*

DOABLE

➔ **Casa Mediterannea** ITALIAN I had sworn never again to order spaghetti with meatballs in Mexico, but my waiter convinced me that it would be different in his "casa" and he was right. Come for the freshly made pasta dishes and big, crisp salads and avoid the rest. *Av. 5, between calles 6 and 8. ☎ 984/876-3926. Main courses $80–$150. No credit cards. Daily noon–11pm.*

➔ **Estas Son Las Mañanitas** MEXICAN/ITALIAN If you howl for hot sauce in the best kind of way, look no further than this delightful little cafe with a full hot sauce bar that will knock your flip-flops off. And then there's all the yummy stuff they have to put the sauce on, like salmon skewers, shrimp and steak kabobs, and other grilled treats on sticks. The more elaborate Mexican and Italian entrees also don't disappoint. (Though they don't go quite as well with the mind-blowing sauce selection.) *Av. 5, between calles 4 and 6. ☎ 984/873-0114. Main courses $50–$150. AE, MC, V. Daily noon–2am (sometimes later).*

➔ **Los Rancheros** SEAFOOD/STEAK This gigantic bar and restaurant fills a whole two-story hacienda with its colorful plaid tablecloths, turquoise furniture, and stained-glass globe lanterns. Though it specializes in a wide array of Mexican and Caribbean surf and turf, most of the locals who frequent Los Rancheros come for the turf, and will tell you that this is the place for the best steak in the Playa. All the regular stateside favorites, from filet mignon to porterhouse, come in generous portions. It's a perfect place to try *arranchera* (grilled skirt steak marinated in indigenous herbs), which is often gray, tough, and chewy elsewhere. Many nights a week there is a live mariachi band, and the rotating performers are all talented. *Av. 5, between calles 4 and 6. ☎ 984/873-3430. www.losrancheros.net. Main courses $80–$300. MC, V. Mon–Thurs 10am–9pm and Fri–Sat 10am–11pm.*

➔ **Viva Café** ITALIAN Italian food in Mexico is often overpriced and under spiced, but the Viva Café avoids both of these pitfalls and succeeds in providing good Italian food at the right prices. The lounge, decked out with velvet chairs and polished wooden tables, offers an impressive list of martinis, and often has a live jazz band or saxophone player. To start, the *Polipe e Patate* (steamed octopus with potatoes, parsley, and olive oil) is a surprisingly successful combination of flavors, as is the *Calamari e Zucchini* (fried strips of calamari and zucchini). The *Gnocchi Pomodoro e Basilico* (gnocchi served in a fresh tomato and basil sauce) and the *Risotto al Funghi* (risotto with a delicate porcini mushroom sauce) are both crowd pleasers. Finally, the banana caramel tart with vanilla gelato inspired genuine gasps of pleasure from all who try it. *Calle 12 North at Av 1. North. No phone. www.vivawyndhamresorts.com. Main courses up to $110, martinis $50. MC, V. Daily 1pm–midnight.*

SPLURGE

In addition to the below choices, you should be aware of **Media Luna** (5th Av., between calles 12 and 14; **☎ 984/873-0526**); it's "famous" for fresh seafood with a Mexican twist, but I think it's overrated. The food is average, but the whole scene feels too L.A., not Mexico, for my taste.

➔ **La Casa del Agua** FUSION The menu at this fusion joint boasts both "European" and Mexican cuisine, but I only thought the non-Mexican menu selections were innovative and tasty. Steer clear of the

Mexican dishes, which are overpriced and bland, and you'll do just fine. Lovers of mushrooms, creamy sauces, red meat, seafood, and fresh vegetables combined in unconventional ways will find the most appetizing options. *Av 5 at Calle 2. ☎ 984/803-0232. Main courses $80–$220. AE, MC, V. Daily noon–1am.*

→ **Limones** ★ CONTINENTAL The food and atmosphere at this large outdoor eatery are above par, even if you'll pay for it. Though the restaurant is regularly recommended for expertly grilled steak and seafood, the real reason to come is for the flambéed main courses, including every kind of crepe you can imagine, prepared expertly at your table, and the spiked dessert coffees, which are appropriately soul-warming. This place is also notable for its seclusion—you arrive by traveling down a mosaic path paved with circular bits of broken mirrors, illuminated by lanterns that create quite a romantic effect in the moonlight. *Av 5, before the ferry pier complex. No phone. Main courses $100–$250. MC, V. Daily 6pm–midnight.*

MTV Best → **Yaxche** ★★★ YUCATECAN This restaurant possessed the freshest selection of Yucatecan cuisine I sampled anywhere on the peninsula, with just the right mix of spicy herbs and fresh fruits and vegetables added to the more meaty dishes typical of the cuisine. In fact, if you're a vegetarian, this place has way more options for you than the majority of strictly traditional Yucatecan restaurants. I loved what they did with the indigenous leafy green chaya, which was incorporated into many dishes, such as *poc chuc* (pork with achiote). *Calle 8, between Avs. 5 and 10. ☎ 984/873-2502. Main courses $90–$250. V. Daily noon–11pm.*

CAFES & COFFEE

→ **Café Sasta** ★★★ CAFE Though it may seem an oxymoron to use the words relaxed and coffee in the same sentence, any morning of the week between the hours of 7am and noon, you'll find a relaxed gathering of cheery coffee drinkers populating the round wooden tables in front of Café Sasta. Inside, the walls are painted to resemble the ceiling of an opera house or chapel, with blue skies, delicate clouds, and smiling cherubs. In an age of hyper-energetic and calculated coffee chains, the calm, almost angelic feel of Café Sasta is a precious rarity. *Av. 5 at Calle 12. No phone. Espresso drinks (hot and frozen) $20–$30, pastries $20–$40. No credit cards. Daily 7am–5pm.*

→ **Ciao Gelato** DESSERT If you love gelato or gourmet Italian sorbet, you'll go wild at this place, which produces first-rate flavors and encourages you to sample as many as you like. Both the sorbet and the gelato possess the smooth creamy texture that the Italians are famous for, and are a refreshing sweet treat during a hot day strolling on 5th Avenue. Over 10 types of chocolate gelato, in addition to more luxurious mixtures like amaretto anise, caramel coconut, and the divine dulce de leche, are available. The sorbets feature a wide range of indigenous fruits such as guayaba, pintaya, guava, and Jamaica (hibiscus flower), and are a nice light alternative to the richer gelatos. *Av. 5, between calles 2 and 4. No phone. Small cone $30, large cone $50. No credit cards. Daily 11am–midnight.*

Partying

Playa is truly the place to party in Mexico. The entire city comes alive at night with a beautiful, international crowd that dances to only the best salsa and reggaeton until the sun comes up and they start sipping smoothies again. Clubs here are new, spectacular, and pack personality to spare. Within walking distance from anywhere in downtown, there is a voodoo lounge, a place where you can party inside a real cave, and more than one spot pushing minty fresh mojitos. Following are the best full-fledged bars and clubs in town, but keep in mind that most restaurants listed in the eating section also double as bars that are open late.

➔ **Alux** ★★ If you've always wanted to party like it was the end of the world, this club located in a real system of ancient caves, complete with stalagmites and stalactites hanging overhead and water running underfoot, may be as close as you'll ever get. There are private small caverns and nooks where you can recline on leopard and zebra-print velvet couches, and the oil lamps and votives used to light the place keep it just dark enough to feel like the very real underworld that it is. Because they serve food here as well as liquor, this is more a space for drinking and enjoying the novelty of the surroundings than dancing. However, belly dancers and sometimes even fire performers accompany the live music, all of which complement the simultaneously seedy, sexy vibe. *Av. Juárez, Mz. 12 Lote 13 A, Colonia Ejidal.* ☎ *984/803-2936. www.restaurantalux.com.*

➔ **Diablita Cha Cha Cha** ★ In a town of clubs with crazy themes (see the previous review) what Diablita Cha Cha Cha has going for it is that it isn't trying too hard to attract tourists. It's just a cool club in a hot location with plenty of party energy to spare, and this makes it a favorite hangout for locals and repeat visitors to Playa. The wall-less black palapa (the only black palapa I've ever seen) that serves as a sort of massive umbrella over the whole joint turns this place into a kind of stage once it gets dark—the patrons inside seem to enjoy being watched by people passing by its heavily trafficked corner. The menu includes many tempting Asian-inspired treats and the drinks are strong and sweet. *Calle 12 and Calle 1. No phone.*

➔ **La Bodeguita del Medio** ★★ A sanctuary to salsa music, Cuban cigars, and minty mojitos, this bar and venue for the best live Cuban salsa music in Playa is named after the original Bodeguita in Havana where Ernest Hemingway discovered the magical powers of the mojito. Hemingway loved his Bodeguita so much that he wrote a short story about it entitled "My Mojito in la Bodeguita." The similar minded patrons of La Bodeguita have followed Hemingway's example and tagged their own stories with Sharpies all over the walls, tables, and any other free space they can find. Despite the pictures of famous international celebrities and intellectuals that line the one wall free of ink, the place manages to achieve a comfortably divey vibe. Check the schedule online for a list of the Cuban music legends who may be making an appearance, as well as the frequent offerings of free salsa classes. *Plaza Paseo Del Carmen Local 46.* ☎ *984/803-3950. www.labodeguitadelmedio.com.mx.*

MTV Best ➔ **La Santanera** ★★★ The art of Santeria, or Latin American voodoo, has long been a source of intrigue for those of us looking for answers from the spiritual realm. La Santanera, an awesome club in Playa del Carmen, celebrates the occult with out-of-this-world house music and decor. The upstairs lounge looks like the inside of a very successful psychic's lair—baroque style velvet couches border illuminated round tables, 2m-long (6-ft.) sequined skull masks are arranged in spirals on the high ceiling, and, in the center of the great round ballroom, there is a gigantic, glowing crystal ball. Dried herbs with hidden powers hang from the walls, and inside the decadent, co-ed bathroom stalls, you'll find collections of sacred objects and scripts for spells you can say to do useful things like make your ex-boyfriend impotent, or increase the magnetic powers of parts of your anatomy. The entire 9m (30-ft.) bar is illuminated by crystal, and all of the light shining up from ground level creates an eerie flashlight-under-the-chin effect on the bodies gyrating between glowing orbs. *Calle 12, between avs. 5 and 10. ☎ 984/803-2856. No cover if you enter before midnight, otherwise it varies.*

→ **Mambo Café** ★ There are a few Mambo Cafés in Mexico, but like many other chains, the one in Playa del Carmen is a cut above the rest. There's simply no better place to shake to some salsa. Descending the many flights of stairs to the large underground dance space (there are two stages for live bands) feels like entering one of those glass-walled tunnels under the sea. The decor is retro blue and gold, adorned with subtle hints of waves and foamy ocean bubbles, and accents the live brass bands and sharply dressed musicians nicely. This is an old-school dance club, and as you join the pairs of madly dancing couples, you may feel transported back in time in the best kind of way. Sitting at the glamorously draped tables in the flickering candlelight, I got the feeling that Sinatra and the rest of the rat pack would've been right at home in the posh, old-school surroundings. *Calle 6, between Avs. 5 and 10. ☎ 984/803-2656. www.mambo cafe.com.mx. $40 cover with open bar or pay per drink.*

Heading to the Beach

In my opinion, Playa del Carmen has the best beach on the coast—though it's better for lounging and seeing/being seen than swimming. The beach, which runs parallel to the swinging 5th Avenue, grows and shrinks, from broad and sandy to narrower with rocks, depending on the currents and wind. When this happens, head to the beaches farther outside of town instead; see "Playing Outside" for info.

Note that a strong European influence has made topless sunbathing (nominally against the law in Mexico) a nonchalantly accepted practice on Playa's beaches. If you're not shy, this is your chance to tan without getting any lines.

Playing Outside

Playa del Carmen is an awesome hub to anchor yourself in if you are a lover of outdoor activity. Cozumel and its famous dive sites are a ferry ride away, and Puerto Aventuras, Xcaret, and Xel-Ha, are less than an hour away by car or bus.

For the most outdoor action, simply head out on Highway 307, driving from Playa del Carmen south and stopping in the many towns along the way—you'll encounter beautiful beaches and cabaña hotels, and abundant diving and snorkeling opportunities. The highlights are listed in full under "En Route to Tulum" below.

GOLF & TENNIS If golf is your bag, the **Playacar Golf Club** (☎ **984/873-4990;** www.palace-resorts.com/playacar-golf-club) has an 18-hole **golf course** designed by Robert von Hagge. It's operated by the Palace Resorts hotel chain, which offers golf packages. Greens fees are $1,800 in the morning (including tax and cart) and $1,200 after 2pm; club rental costs $300. The club also has two **tennis** courts, which cost $100 per hour.

HORSEBACK RIDING There are a few places along the highway that offer horseback rides. The best of these, **Rancho Punta Venado,** is just south of Playa past the Calica Pier. This ranch is less touristy than the others, and the owner takes good care of his horses. It has a nice stretch of coast with a sheltered bay and offers kayaking and snorkeling outings. It's best to make arrangements ahead of time and tell them you're a Frommer's/MTV reader, so that they can schedule you on a day when they have fewer customers. You can contact them through e-mail (gabriela@puntavenado.com) or by calling directly to the ranch's cellphone (☎ **044/984-116-3213**); there is a charge for the call. Talk to Gabriela or Francisco; both speak English. You might also try dropping by. The turn-off for the ranch is 2km (1¼ miles) south of the Calica overpass near Km 279.

Hidden Worlds Cenotes

The pros at Best **Hidden Worlds Cenotes** ★★ (☎ **984/877-8535**; www.hiddenworlds.com.mx) have picked such a prime network of underwater caves for their headquarters that the space starred in the IMAX movie *Journey Into Amazing Caves.* Amazing is right. You shouldn't leave this section of the Yucatán without visiting a cenote; these rare, deep, freshwater wells are so beautiful that the Maya quite reasonably believed that they were the portals to the world of the gods. If you're a certified diver, you don't need to obtain cave diving certification to descend into one of these wells with a specialized instructor. I highly recommend it—you'll be amazed at the totally different varieties of plants and wildlife that thrive in these freshwater environments, in addition to prehistoric rock formations and water that's supernaturally clear. If you're not a certified diver, this is one of the calmest and most unusual snorkeling sites you'll ever have. A Jungle snorkel tour is $400. Cenote dives start at $600 with equipment. The shop is located about 1 mile south of Xel Ha (p. 268) on Highway 307.

Shopping

Providing a guide to shopping in Playa del Carmen almost feels like a disservice because half of the fun of shopping here is sauntering along 5th Avenue and scoping out the shops yourself. A number of jet-setting jewelry and clothing stores line the avenue, so you can intercept the trends and be the first to wear them back home. This is also a great place to buy hot bikinis with fashion-forward patterns, brightly colored sundresses in untraditional styles, and anything sexy and white. And even if you don't have a lot of money to burn, it's a great town for window shopping.

Around 9pm the street vendors set up their stalls, so this is the best time to buy handmade jewelry and decorations for a fraction of what they cost in the boutiques. In particular, Playa is known for gold wire and shell jewelry, lanterns made of coconuts, and stamped metal with glass beads. At the end of the avenue by the port is a mall with many popular chain stores like Diesel and Lacoste, with prices that are more affordable than in the U.S.

MinaraliA (Av. 5 at Calle 10; ☎ **984/879-4680**; www.mineralia.net) is a great spot to buy unusual jewelry for your friends and family without breaking the bank. This branch of a small chain stocks beautiful beads made of semi-precious gems (and impressive imitations of them) in an abundance of exotic arrangements. The iridescent shell earrings, long strands of sparkling stones, and big hematite and coral beads here all make great one-of-a-kind souvenirs.

Boutique Shalom and **Boutique Inshala** ★ are two trendy little boutiques managed by the same style-savvy owner, which carry unusual items by well known names for a steal. In addition to the best selection of casual, unconventional dresses I've seen anywhere, the racks are stuffed with hot pants, offbeat shoes, and rock star worthy jewelry and accessories. Boutique Shalom is at 5th Avenue between calles 6 and 8 and Inshala Clothing Calle 8 is between avenues 5 and 10. You can call both at ☎ **984/873-0056.**

The enchanting garden plaza **Jardín de Marieta** ★★, right off 5th Avenue between calles 6 and 8, is a shady place to stop for a coffee and stay to peruse the art galleries that border it on all sides. It's home to a mini artist's colony of sorts, where you can find everything from abstract paintings to a wide variety of wearable (and surprisingly affordable) art. One of the best shops is **La Sandalia,** where you can find hand-painted platform shoes, sandals, and leather boots, as well as some very cool silk-screened tees and patchwork dresses. **Gallery Adriana** has gorgeous stamped leather purses and shoulder bags. Finally, the **Mayan Arts Gallery** has the best selection of Maya jade in Playa, and pays the artists who produce it fairly for their craftsmanship. If you're looking for a contemporary painting in bright colors to hang on your wall, or even just to brighten your day, there are many galleries specializing in hot young painters in this courtyard as well.

Caffeine Fix

Once you're done shopping or browsing the Jardín, stop by **Osteria Pitchu** (no phone), a quaint Italian cafe with rich espresso drinks, homemade pasta, and hearty salads—perfect for a moment of respite while you're admiring the Jardín and all her charms. It sells espresso drinks for about $30 and pasta dishes for $70.

En Route to Tulum

The best way to see most of the Yucatán's heartland is by car. The terrain is flat, there is little traffic once you get away from the cities, and the main highways are in good shape. If you drive at all around this area, you will add at least one new word to your Spanish vocabulary—*topes* (*toh*-pehs), meaning speed bumps. And along with topes you might learn a few new curse words. Topes come in varying shapes and sizes and with varying degrees of warning. Don't let them surprise you.

Off the main highways, the roads are narrow and rough, but hey—you'll be driving a rental car. Rentals are, in fact, a little pricey compared with those in the U.S. (due perhaps to wear and tear?), but some promotional deals are available, especially in low season.

Plenty of buses ply the roads between the major towns and ruins. And plenty of tour buses circulate, too. But buses to the smaller towns and ruins and the haciendas are infrequent or nonexistent. One bus company, **Autobuses del Oriente** (see "Basics," p. 48), controls most of the first-class bus service and does a good job with the major destinations. Second-class buses go to some out-of-the-way places, but they can be slow, stop a lot, and usually aren't air-conditioned. I will only take them when going short distances.

If you don't want to rent a car, a few tour operators take small groups to the following sites, often stopping in Tulum, too; check with your hotel for details. One adventure tour operator to try is **Altournative** (☎ **984/873-2036**).

See the "Getting There & Around" sections throughout this chapter for more tips on traveling around the Yucatán.

Akumal

Driving south on Highway 307 from Playa del Carmen, you'll come to the turnoff for Akumal after 2km (1¼ miles). This is a small, ecologically oriented community built on the shores of two beautiful bays. Akumal has been around long enough that it feels more relaxed than booming places such as Playa and Tulum, and lodging tends to go for less here.

For condo rentals, contact **Info-Akumal** (☎ **800/381-7048** in the U.S.; www.info-akumal.com) or **Akumal Vacations** (☎ **800/448-7137** in the U.S.; www.akumalvacations.com), or **Loco Gringo** (www.locogringo.com).

Both bays here have sandy beaches with rocky or silt bottoms. If you want a real sandy beach, you should drive to Tulum or Xpu-Ha. But if you want to dive, this is the place to do so.

There are three dive shops in town and at least 30 dive sites offshore. The tried and true **Akumal Dive Shop** (☎ **984/875-9032;** www.akumal.com) specializes in cave diving and other kinds of technical diving and will train you to explore Akumal's underwater caverns. If you're more interested in exploring one of the many reef diving sites that this area offers, **Akumal Dive Adventures** (☎ **984/875-9157**) is owned by a friendly American who knows where to find the best dive sites to meet giant sea turtles and other rare animals, and also offers samplers for uncertified divers and full certification courses.

If you want to try out snorkeling in the calm waters of a preserved lagoon park, but can't fathom shelling out the $360 it costs to visit Xel-Ha, **Yal-ku Lagoon** (no phone) is sort of like Xel-Ha's cheaper little sister. Though Yal-Ku doesn't have all the big ticket attractions that Xel-Ha boasts, it does make for a lovely day of sunning, swimming, and snorkeling by the clear water of the peaceful lagoon, and it doesn't have massive crowds. It's open daily from 8am to 5:30pm, and is in the town of Akumal off highway 307. Admission is $60.

Puerto Aventuras

Eight kilometers (5 miles) from Playa del Carmen and 104km (65 miles) from Cancún is the glitzy development of Puerto Aventuras, on Chakalal Bay. It's a condo-marina community with a 9-hole golf course. At the center of the development is a collection of restaurants bordering a dolphin pool. They offer a variety of food—Mexican, Italian, steaks, even a popular pub.

To swim with the dolphins, you must make reservations by contacting **Dolphin Discovery** (☎ **998/849-4757;** www.dolphindiscovery.com)—the same operator that handles the dolphin swims in Isla Mujeres (p. 230). Make reservations well in advance—the surest way is through the link on the website. A 1-hour session costs $1,250. There are shorter programs for less.

This is also one of the best places on the peninusla for boating and deep-sea fishing. I recommend **Captain Rick's Sportfishing Center** (☎ **984/873-5195** or -5387; www.fishYucatan.com). The captain will be happy to combine a fishing trip with some snorkeling, which makes for a leisurely day. Trips start at $900 per person for a half-day tour. The best fishing on this coast is from March to August.

Xcaret

You'll hear locals call the eco–theme park **Xcaret** (pronounced "Eesh-ca-*ret*") (☎ **998/883-3143;** www.xcaret.com) a "Maya Disneyland," which is apt—though it is supposed to be all natural, it has been pre-planned down to its manicured paths, impeccably clean swimming holes, snorkeling lagoons, and scuba diving areas. This pseudo naturalist land also has a butterfly hut, a sea turtle nursery, a bird

The Yucatán's Upper Caribbean Coast

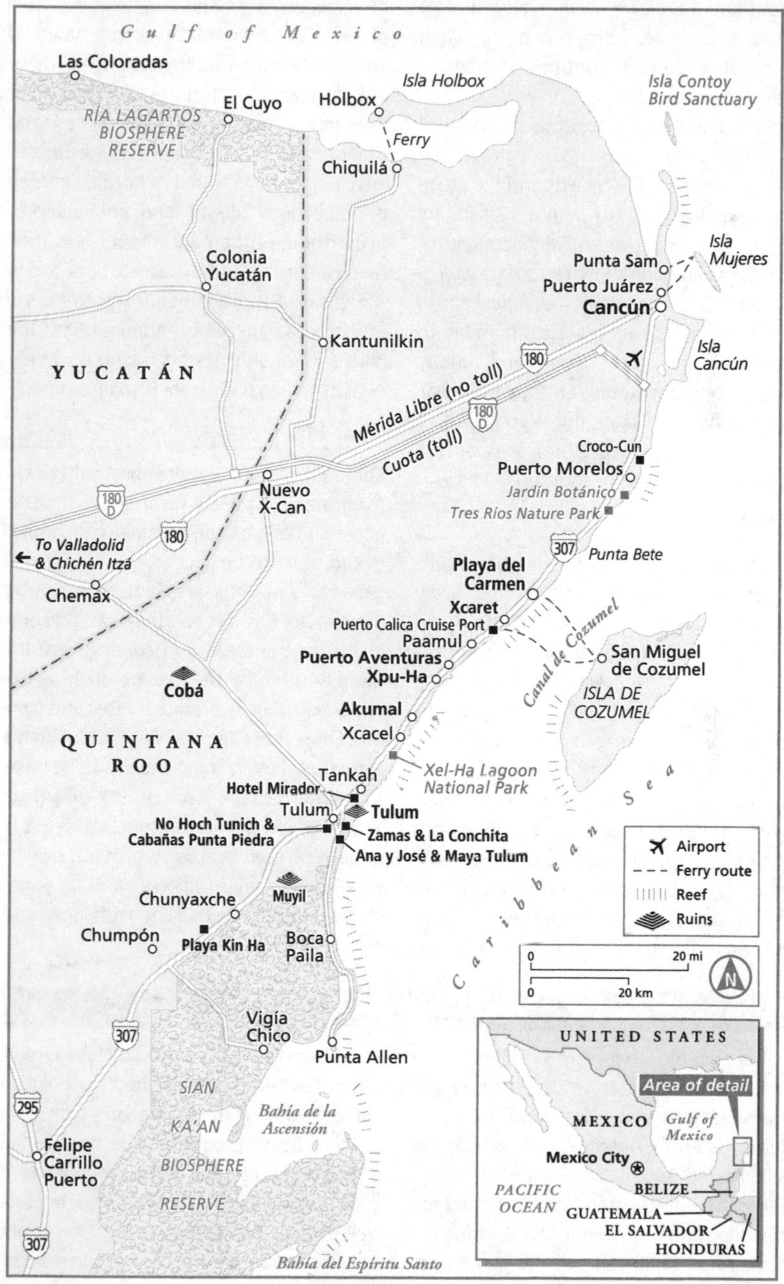

aviary, a botanical garden, a touchable aquarium, a tank for swimming with dolphins, a horseback riding ranch, and much more, all within the confines of a suspiciously bug-free "jungle."

Though there are more authentic natural encounters to be had throughout the Yucatán, without the crowds and the steep price tag, the park is worth a visit for its spectacular fire shows and reenactments of the Maya ball game known as *pok-ta-pok.*

Xcaret is located 10km (6¼ miles) south of Playa del Carmen. It's open Monday to Saturday from 8:30am to 9pm, and Sunday from 8:30pm to 5:30pm. Entrance to basic attractions costs $490, but if you want to snorkel, scuba, swim with dolphins, or ride horses, there are hefty additional fees.

Xel-Ha

Located in a gorgeous freshwater and saltwater lagoon, and only 10 minutes away from the ruins of Tulum, **Xel-Ha** (pronounced "Shell-hah") (☎ **984/875-6000** at the park, 984/873-3588 in Playa; www.xelha.com.mx) offers the perfect end to a morning spent touring the ancient city.

You can do all things active at Xel-Ha: snorkeling, cliff diving, zip lining, rope-swinging into the ocean, swimming with dolphins, jungle biking, and walking on the ocean floor. If you're more interested in chilling out, this place has a river that you can float down, a massage center, an entire island of hammocks, and a number of secluded caves and cenotes which are perfect for some watery rendezvous. If you're an amateur biologist at heart, there are ample opportunities for harmless interaction with giant sea turtles and other exotic wildlife in their protected environments, as well as a botanic garden of indigenous plants, and an apiary of bees. The gigantic park has no less than five restaurants and two snack bars, too.

Signs clearly mark the turnoff to Xel-Ha on the road to Tulum. Admission to the park is $360 on weekdays, $260 on weekends; it's open daily from 8:30am to 5pm.

Xpu-Ha

Three kilometers (2 miles) beyond Puerto Aventuras is **Xpu-Ha** (pronounced "Eesh-poo-*hah*") ★★, a wide bay lined by a broad, beautiful sandy beach.

Lodging options are better in nearby Akumal, so, if you're renting a car, I recommend staying there and coming here for the day to enjoy the beach. Much of the bay is taken up by private houses and condos, but there are a few all-inclusive resorts and even some small hotels. I like **Villas del Caribe Xpu-Ha** (☎ **984/873-2194;** www.xpuhahotel.com; US$55–$75 double; no credit cards), which has beach-side rooms, yoga classes, and a good, cheap seafood restaurant with powerful piña coladas.

Tulum

Tulum pueblo (130km/80 miles from Cancún) is a small town on Highway 307 where it intersects the road to Cobá. Nearby is an incredible beach, which has become the Tulum hotel zone—a collection of about 30 palapa hotels stretching from the Tulum ruins southward, along the Punta Allen Peninsula, all the way to the entrance to the Sian Ka'an Biopreserve. The Tulum ruins are a walled Maya city of the post-Classic age perched on a rocky cliff overlooking the Caribbean.

Tulum beach used to be a destination for backpackers, but the palapa hotels have gone upscale, and the beach now attracts a well-heeled crowd that seeks to get away from the bustle of the big hotels and resorts. The town currently boasts restaurants and

Tulum Ruins

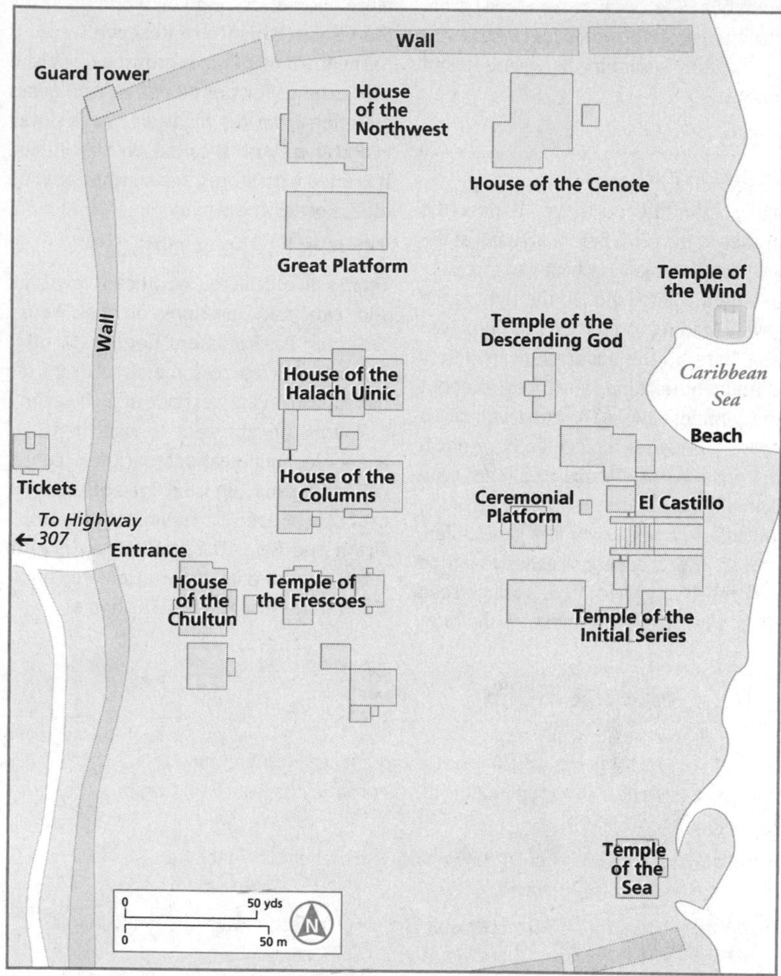

other amenities, such as cybercafes, ATMs, and stores, so you won't feel cut off. And though you can't really party here at night, bumpin' Playa del Carmen is only a half-hour away.

Getting There & Getting Around

BY CAR To visit the Tulum area, get a rental car (see "Basics," p. 51, for rental car companies); it will make everything much easier. Tulum is about an hour and a half south of Cancún and 10 minutes south of Xel-Ha. The most direct route to Tulum is by way of Highway 307, which goes right past the ruins before going into town. See "Orientation" below for more info.

BY BUS **ADO**'s (☎ **998/884-4352**) first-class buses run from Cancún (p. 184) and Playa del Carmen (p. 252) regularly, but buses also run from just about every destination in the Yucatán. A ticket for a 4-hour bus ride (with two movies) from Cancún is $200, with rates for closer locations like Xel-Ha running between $40 and $100.

Basics

ORIENTATION

Coming from the north you'll pass the entrance to the ruins before arriving at the town. You'll come to a highway intersection with a traffic light. To the right is the highway leading to the ruins of Cobá (see "Cobá," later in this chapter); to the left is the Tulum hotel zone, which begins about 2km (1½ miles) away. The road sign reads BOCA PAILA, which is a place halfway down the **Punta Allen Peninsula.** This road eventually goes all the way to the tip of the peninsula and the town of Punta Allen, home to the cheapest, freshest seafood pretty much anywhere. It is a rough road that is slow going for most of the way. Continue along this narrow road for a few more kilometers, and you'll end up at the **Sian Ka'an Biosphere Reserve.**

The town of Tulum is growing quickly. It now extends for 3 or more blocks in either direction from the highway. The highway widens here and is called Avenida Tulum. It is lined with stores, restaurants, and the offices of service providers.

TOURIST INFO & OFFICES

There's no official tourist office in town, but you can ask questions at the **Weary Traveler Backpackers Center** (☎ **984/871-2389**). It's across the street from the bus station on the west side of Highway 307.

You also might want to visit the travel agency/communications/package center called **Savana** (☎ **984/871-2081**) on the east side of Avenida Tulum between calles Orion and Beta. The staff speaks English for the most part and can answer questions about tours and calling home.

THE YUCATÁN PENINSULA

Tulum Nuts & Bolts

Banks **HSBC bank** (☎ **984/871-2201**) is on Avenida Tulum, 2 blocks north from the ADO bus station. It's open Monday through Saturday from 8am to 7pm, with a 24-hour ATM.

Emergencies The **police station** (☎ **984/871-2055**) is in the Delegacion Municipal on Avenida Tulum.

Hospitals **Centro de Salud** (☎ **984/871-2050**) off Highway 307, by the bus station, has a small emergency room that is open daily 8am to 8pm.

Internet/Wireless Hot Spots **Savanna** (☎ **984/871-2050**) is just south of the ADO station and charges $15 per hour of Internet access. It's open daily 9am to 2pm and 4pm to 9pm.

Pharmacies **Canto Farmacia** is on Highway 307, right next to the bus station. It's open daily 8am to 11pm.

Sleeping

If you've rented a car and are planning to take a lot of day trips in the Riviera Maya, I recommend staying at a few different cabañas along the way instead of basing yourself in one resort town nearby. It'll be easier than driving back and forth, and the cabañas in this area offer beach access and charming accommodations for a bit less money.

Note that many cabañas here need to generate their own electricity, so many only offer electricity during peak hours. Even if the place where you choose to stay has regular electricity (call to check), don't expect amenities like TVs, air-conditioning, minifridges, Internet, or phones—for that, you do need to stay in a town like Cancún or Playa del Carmen.

HOSTELS

→ **Weary Traveler Hostel, Café, and Bar** Across the street from the bus station, this hostel is a great place to meet other thrifty backpackers fresh off the road. Since it's in the heart of downtown Tulum, the hostel gives you access to many amenities that cabañas can't offer, like 24-hour Internet access in an on-site cafe (with awesome coffee), a lounge with a TV and VCR, and a shared kitchen with broad tables for group meals. Rather than having one large bunk room, this hostel has many small rooms with a few beds in each, meaning that you and your backpacking buddies could pay for bunks and end up in a private room with your own bathroom. The bunks and bathrooms are kept clean, and each small bunk room has its own bathroom with 24-hour hot water—that means you'll have a better shower situation than many guests at higher priced cabaña resorts. For these reasons, this place fills up fast; make sure to call in advance to reserve a spot. *Av. Tulum, between Avs. Jupiter and Acuariio. ☎ 984/871-2386. www.wearytravelerhostel.com. $100 bunk bed. No credit cards. Amenities: Cafe; complimentary breakfast; Internet; kitchen; laundry; shared bathrooms; sheets; telephone (in common area); towels; TV (common room). In room: A/C (in some rooms), locker.*

CHEAP

→ **Cabañas No Hoch Tunich** These simple cabañas are ideal for beach-loving bargain hunters with a taste for home-cooked Mexican food. Though the decor is spare, the cabañas are clean and have spectacular ocean views. The classic Mexican restaurant and bar serves up freshly made tortillas, ceviches, nopales, and other Maya specialties all day. If you remember to sign up the day before, they'll bring you a full Mexican breakfast to eat on your balcony or the beach. There's even a full-service spa with some interesting indigenous options, including a temazcal purification bath, and free yoga classes every morning for all guests. The electricity ends at 11pm, though, so bring your flashlights. *Carretera Tulum Boca Paila, Municipio Solidaridad. ☎ 987/694-0707. $200 cabañas with shared bathrooms, $500–$750 larger suites with 2 double beds and private bathrooms. No credit cards. Amenities: Restaurant and bar; spa. In room: A/C (in some rooms).*

→ **Cabañas Punta Piedra** ★★ I love this place. They've got bike rentals, a quality dive shop right on-site, free snorkeling gear for guests, dive and snorkeling trips that leave from the beach, and cute, colorful cabañas with good screens to keep out the bugs. Most important, it's likely that you'll meet some cool companions while staying here, as it tends to attract an eclectic mix of dive enthusiasts and international travelers. If you can stand cold showers, you can save 20 bucks on your room—you'll have the option between cabañas with or without hot showers. The electricity lasts till 10pm. *Carretera Tulum-Boca Paila, Municipio Solidaridad. ☎ 984/876-9167. $600–$800 beachfront cabaña with king-size bed and private bathroom, $400–$500 triple cabaña with extra bed and cold shower, $650–$850 upstairs hotel suites with 2 double beds and hot showers. No credit cards. Amenities: Restaurant; dive shop.*

→ **Hotel Mirador** If camping on the beach is your idea of heaven, you can ascend one more level to a minimalist beach bum's Nirvana in these spare cabañas with thatched roofs and sandy floors. If you've got your own blankets, you can even skip the bed and save money by reserving one of the cabañas that only have hammocks. Plus, this hotel is a stone's throw from the ruins of Tulum (you can see them from your window), and 10 minutes from downtown. *Within 500m/1,640 ft. of the ruins, on Hwy. 307. No phone. $200–$250 beachfront cabaña with double bed, $120–$200 garden cabaña with double bed, $100–$150 hammock cabaña. No credit cards. Amenities: Shared bathrooms; sheets; towels.*

DOABLE

→ **Cabañas Ana y José** This funky, opulent resort is situated on a first-class beach and has an awesome swimming pool big enough for some serious laps and spacious rooms decorated with artsy gold-painted suns, moons, and stars. Stone-walled cabañas on the beach have two double beds each and are more than comfortable enough for groups of four. The second-floor oceanview rooms on the main building have thatched palapa roofs and are ideal for catching ocean breezes and romantic sunsets. The homey restaurant here serves up surf-side favorites, and you can call to arrange package deals, including reserving a rental car to meet you at the Cancún airport. *Carretera Punta Ana Km 7 (Apodo. Postal 15). ☎ 998/887-5470. Fax 998/887-5469. www.anayjose.com. $1,000 double. No credit cards. Amenities: Restaurant; Internet in office; package deals and car rental service; 24-hr. hot water and power.*

→ **Playa Kin Ha** This small, ecological resort runs on solar power and consists of only four newly built cabañas on the beach right at the mouth of the Sian Ka'an biological reserve, and about 16 to 24km (10–15 miles) from the Tulum ruins. The light, sunny yellow rooms all have 24-hour power and hot water provided by the solar panels, and new queen-size beds with quality mattresses. The restaurant, perched on the private beach, has a delicious array of healthy, colorful choices, from fresh-squeezed juices and tropical fruit plates, to grilled seafood and surprisingly authentic Italian cuisine. *Off Hwy. 307 right before the entrance to Sian Ka'an. Address of the main hotel: Hotel Kin Ha, Calle Orion Sur Entre Sol y Venus Ote, Tulum. ☎/fax 984/871-2321. $800 double. Amenities: Restaurant; solar power; 24-hr. electricity and hot water.*

→ **Zamas** ★ These simple, comfortable cabañas are made up of separate huts, spaced far enough apart from each other to make you feel like you have your own ocean cottage. Surprisingly, the cabañas on the beach are actually cheaper than the ones in the back jungle area, which should make the beach lovers reading this happy. The open-air seafood restaurant is no exception to the rule that the freshest and most affordable fish is the type you eat right in view of the water; more surprisingly, the restaurant also sells delicious brick-oven pizza. The laid-back Californian owners are friendly and have decorated the cabañas with colorful touches and comfy hammocks that accentuate the homey feel of the huts. *Carrera Punta Allen Km 5. ☎ 415/387-9806 in the U.S. www.zamas.com. $650–$950 beachfront double. No credit cards. Amenities: Restaurant; bar; Internet in office.*

SPLURGE

→ **La Conchita** ★★ These clean, white cottages are arranged in a horseshoe shape on a soft, sandy beach. Each is well-equipped with everything you need for a relaxing vacation, plus artful touches like seashell mosaics above the king-size beds and spiraling iron window frames in all rooms. The screened-in windows keep out the mosquitoes (a luxury in the cabaña scene) and the limited electricity after 10pm gives you an excuse to light the supply of romantic candles you'll be given. The water here is heated by solar power, so you still have hot showers in your private bathroom 24 hours. You have a choice between a beachside cabaña or an upstairs terrace room with balcony; both have palapa rooms. There is a hot complimentary breakfast every morning including filling favorites such as crepes, pancakes, huevos rancheros, and tropical fruit. Many of the guests here told me the lovingly prepared breakfasts were the best part of their stay at La Conchita. But if you feel like venturing out for your meal, a few restaurants are within walking distance. *Carretera Tulum Km 5, Boca Paila, Municipio Solidaridad. ☎ 984/871-2092. $1,100–$1,300 double. No credit cards. Amenities: Complimentary full breakfast; 24-hr. hot water.*

➔ **Las Ranitas** ★ Conveniently located between Tulum and the Sian Ka'an Biosphere, this place is a real escape from the worries of the rest of the world—but it's also very eco-friendly. The spacious cabañas are on an untouched beach where turtles nest, the solar panels and advanced rainwater collection system provide electricity and hot showers 24 hours a day, and the colorful rooms have king and queen-size beds with views of the ocean and the surrounding jungle, which is accessible by soft sandy trails throughout the property. Yoga classes, a swimming pool, a Ping-Pong table, and a restaurant serving up a yummy assortment of Mexican and state-side favorites are also all available on-site. *Carretera Tulum-Boca Paila, Km 9, Tulum. ☎/fax 984/877-8554. www.lasranitas.com. $1,300–$1,500 double. MC, V. Amenities: Restaurant; Ping-Pong table; swimming pool; 24-hr. power; yoga classes.*

MTV Best ➔ **Maya Tulum** ★★★ This cabaña resort is a step above the rest. The walls are thick white plaster, each cabaña comes with a little sitting area, the bathrooms are tiled and have their own private outdoor showers, and as a guest you get an unlimited supply of fresh bottled water. The on-site open-air restaurant boasts chic Mexican decor and an extensive menu of vegetarian and Nuevo Mexican cuisine. The spa is truly luxurious, and special wellness packages are available. Free yoga classes are offered every morning for guests, as are ecotours that conveniently leave right from the hotel. Even more convenient, you can make reservations online ahead of time and pay with a credit card. This hotel's website is particularly stellar, with sample menus, a photo tour, and loads of useful info. *Carretera Boca Paila Km 7. ☎ 984/877-8638. www.mayatulum.com. $US145–$US185 double. MC, V. Amenities: Restaurant and bar; Internet in lobby; spa; 24-hr. electricity.*

Eating

Most of the cabañas and eco-resorts around Tulum include small mom and pop restaurants that are known for churning out fresh seafood and for using indigenous ingredients. The listings below are all in the town of Tulum, but check out the individual reviews in "Sleeping" above for more options.

➔ **Charlies** MEXICAN This art bar and restaurant is a long-standing local favorite, with cuisine that is as adventurous as the mosaics made from smashed wine bottles that cover the walls. Work by local artists is on display inside and outside in the back garden, where you can hear live flamenco music on Sundays while you munch on fried snapper tacos and green enchiladas. The *sopa de lima* (a chicken soup with lime broth and chiles) is particularly divine. *Avs.*

Tulum and Jupiter, across from the bus station. ☎ *984/871-2136. Main courses $50–$100. MC, V. Daily 9am–8pm.*

→ **Taqueria el Mariachi** ★ MEXICAN For classic Mexican food at rock-bottom prices, you can't beat this colorful little diner. I don't recommend the seafood selections, but the fajitas, burritos, and tacos were some of the best I've tasted in Mexico, and they cost a lot less than far inferior versions. If you're a carnivore, get your platters with steak; these guys are justly proud of their *arranchera*, which you can order by itself or as a filling in a taco or burrito. All dishes come with healthy portions of savory rice, beans, cheese, and guacamole. *Corner of Av. Tulum and Orion in downtown Tulum.* ☎ *984/106-2032. Main dishes $30–$80. No credit cards. Daily 9am–8pm.*

→ **Yum Bo'otic Café** ★ HEALTH FOOD Smoothies are a fortifying way to cool down from the inside out after a sweltering tour of the ruins. The icy shakes sold here come in over 20 varieties of fresh tropical fruits, including unusual flavors such as guayaba and pintaya, swirled with old standbys like mango and watermelon and plenty of cooling ice or ice cream. If you want to chew as well as slurp, the owners of this affordable cafe assemble chompworthy sandwiches and tasty desserts, including a justly praised Key lime pie. The menu also has a full list of espresso beverages served with or without ice cream. *Corner of Av. Tulum and Orion, in downtown Tulum. No phone. Smoothies $20–$30, sandwiches $20–$50, espresso drinks $10–$20. No credit cards. Daily 9am–5pm.*

Sightseeing

EXPLORING THE TULUM ARCHAEOLOGICAL SITE

The Tulum ruins lie about a 10 minute walk east of Mex. 207 and are open daily from 8am to 6pm. If you want to avoid the crowds and intense heat, try to show up early. In addition to the ruins, there is a restaurant, a small museum, a bookstore, restrooms, and a ticket booth on-site. Tickets cost $40, parking is $30, and video camera permits are $40. Guides are available at the front and charge $200 for an hour tour in the language of your choice.

If you're taking a bus and considering getting a guide, you should probably visit via one of the many package tour deals to the area, which are cheaper and usually include lunch. Ask the concierge at your hotel for info or check with the Weary Backpackers Center (p. 270).

The most imposing building in Tulum is a large stone structure above the cliff called the **Castillo** (castle). Actually a temple as well as a fortress, it was once covered with stucco and painted. In front of the Castillo are several unrestored palacelike buildings partially covered with stucco. On the **beach** below, where the Maya once came ashore, tourists swim and sunbathe, combining a visit to the ruins with a dip in the Caribbean.

The **Temple of the Frescoes,** directly in front of the Castillo, contains interesting 13th-century wall paintings, though entrance is no longer permitted. Distinctly Maya, they represent the rain god Chaac and Ixchel, the goddess of weaving, women, the moon, and medicine. On the cornice of this temple is a relief of the head of the rain god. If you pause a slight distance from the building, you'll see the eyes, nose, mouth, and chin. In ancient times, the whole city was painted red, and if you squint your eyes, you can still see remnants of red stucco clinging to this building.

Much of what we know of Tulum at the time of the Spanish Conquest comes from the writings of Diego de Landa, third bishop of the Yucatán. He wrote that Tulum was a small city inhabited by about 600 people who lived in platform dwellings along a street and who supervised the trade traffic from Honduras to the Yucatán. Though it was a walled city, most of the inhabitants probably lived outside the walls, leaving the interior for the residences of governors and priests and ceremonial structures. Tulum survived about 70 years after the conquest, when it was finally abandoned. Because of the great number of visitors this site receives, it is no longer possible to climb all of the ruins. In many cases, visitors are asked to remain behind roped-off areas to view them.

EXPLORING THE PUNTA ALLEN PENINSULA

If you've been captured by an adventurous spirit and an excessively sanguine opinion of your rental car's off-road capabilities, you might want to take a trip down the Punta Allen Peninsula, especially if your interests lie in fly-fishing, birding, or simply exploring new country. The far end of the peninsula is only 50km (30 miles) away, but it can be a very slow trip (up to 3 hr., depending on the condition of the road). Not far from the last cabaña hotel is the entrance to the 500,000-hectare (1.3-million-acre) **Sian Ka'an Biosphere Reserve** (see below).

Halfway down the peninsula, at a small bridge, is the **Boca Paila Fishing Lodge** (☎ **998/892-1200;** www.bocapaila.com).

The Sian Ka'an Biosphere Reserve

Down the peninsula a few miles south of the Tulum ruins, you'll pass the guardhouse of the Sian Ka'an Biosphere Reserve. The reserve is a tract of 500,000 hectares (1.3 million acres) set aside in 1986 to preserve tropical forests, savannas, mangroves, coastal and marine habitats, and 110km (68 miles) of coastal reefs. The area is home to jaguars; pumas; ocelots; margays; jaguarundis; spider and howler monkeys; tapirs; white-lipped and collared peccaries; manatees; brocket and white-tailed deer; crocodiles; and green, loggerhead, hawksbill, and leatherback sea turtles. It also protects 366 species of birds—you might catch a glimpse of an ocellated turkey, a great curassow, a brilliantly colored parrot, a toucan or trogon, a white ibis, a roseate spoonbill, a jabiru (or wood stork), a flamingo, or one of 15 species of herons, egrets, and bitterns.

The park has three parts: a "core zone" restricted to research; a "buffer zone," to which visitors and families already living there have restricted use; and a "cooperation zone," which is outside the reserve but vital to its preservation. There are two principal entrances to the biopreserve: one is from the community of Muyil, which is off Highway 307, south of Tulum (you take a boat down canals built by the Maya that connect to the Boca Paila lagoon); the other is from the community of Punta Allen (by jeep down the peninsula which separates the Boca Paila Lagoon from the sea).

Visitors can arrange day trips in Tulum from a few different outfits, whose offices are just a couple of blocks apart and even have similar names. **Sian Ka'an Tours** (☎ **984/871-2363;** siankaan_tours@hotmail.com) is on the west side of Avenida Tulum, next to El Basilico Restaurant, at the corner of Calle Beta. **Community Sian Ka'an Tours** is on the same side of the road, 2 blocks north between calles Orion and Centauro (☎ **984/114-0750;** www.siankaantours.org). The latter is a community organization of Muyil and Punta Allen. Both will pick up customers from any of the area hotels.

David Baird

Not for the general traveler, it specializes in hosting fly-fishers, with weeklong all-inclusive fishing packages.

At this point the peninsula is quite narrow. You can see the Boca Paila lagoon on one side and the sea on the other. Another 25km (15 miles) gets you to the village of Punta Allen.

Punta Allen is a lobstering and fishing village on a palm-studded beach. Isolated and rustic, it's very much the laid-back end of the line. It has a lobster cooperative, a few streets with modest homes, and a lighthouse. The **Cuzan Guesthouse** (☎ **983/834-0292;** www.flyfishmx.com) is a collection of 12 cabins and a restaurant on a nice sandy beach. Cabin rooms rent for between US$30–$90 per night, and the guesthouse accepts cash only. Its main clientele is fly-fishers, and it offers all-inclusive fishing packages. But co-owner Sonia Litvak, a Californian, will rent to anyone curious enough to want to go down there. She also offers snorkeling trips and boat tours.

Cobá

Older than most of Chichén Itzá and much larger than Tulum, Cobá was the dominant city of the eastern Yucatán before A.D. 1000. The site is large and spread out, with thick forest growing between the temple groups. While the ruins here are not as well restored as those at Chichén Itzá or Tulum, something is to be said for the power of seeing the massive structures as they've remained for almost 2,000 years—especially with the shrieks of spider monkeys as background music. In some ways, Cobá's massive, round towering ruins are more impressive than the country's better kept ruins. Most impressive of all is Nohoch Mul (The Great Mound), which is the tallest Maya structure on the Yucatán Peninsula, rising 41m (138 ft.) toward the sky.

Getting There & Getting Around

BY CAR The road to Cobá begins in Tulum and continues for 65km (40 miles). Watch out for both *topes* (speed bumps) and potholes. Close to the village of Cobá you will come to a triangle offering you three choices: Nuevo Xcan, Valladolid, and Cobá. Make sure not to get on the other two roads. The entrance to the ruins is a short distance down the road past some small restaurants and the large lake.

BY BUS Several buses a day leave Tulum and Playa del Carmen for Cobá. A number of companies offer bus tours, but I recommend arranging a first-class bus yourself with **ADO** (☎ **998/884-4352**).

Sleeping & Eating

If nightfall catches you in Cobá, you have limited lodging choices. There is one tourist hotel called **Villas Arqueológicas Cobá**(☎ **55/5203-3086** or 800/258-2633 in the U.S.; $480 double; AE, MC, V) which fronts the lake and is operated by Club Med. Though smaller than its sister hotels in Uxmal and Chichén Itzá, it's the same in style—you'll get modern rooms that are attractive and functional so long as you're not too tall. It has a restaurant that serves all three meals.

Sightseeing

The Maya built many intriguing cities in the Yucatán, but few grander than Cobá (the name means "water stirred by wind"). Much of the 67-sq.-km (26-sq.-mile) site remains unexcavated. A 100km (62-mile) *sacbé* (a pre-Hispanic raised road or causeway) through the jungle linked Cobá to Yaxuná, once an important Maya center 50km (30 miles) south of Chichén Itzá. It's the Maya's longest known sacbé, and at

Cobá Ruins

least 50 shorter ones lead from here. An important city-state, Cobá flourished from A.D. 632 (the oldest carved date found here) until after the rise of Chichén Itzá, around 800. Then Cobá slowly faded in importance and population until it was finally abandoned. Scholars believe Cobá was an important trade link between the Yucatán Caribbean coast and inland cities.

Once at the site, keep your bearings—you can get turned around in the maze of dirt roads in the jungle. As spread out as this city is, renting a bike (which you can do at the entrance for $25) is a good option. Branching off from every labeled path, you'll notice unofficial narrow paths into the jungle, used by locals as shortcuts through the ruins. These are good for birding, but be careful to remember the way back.

Though maps of Cobá show ruins around two lakes, there are really only two excavated groups. The **Grupo Cobá** holds an impressive pyramid, **La Iglesia (the Temple of the Church),** which you'll find if you take the path bearing right after the entrance. Before climbing up, keep in mind that the view is better from El Castillo in the Nohoch Mul group farther back.

From here, return to the main path and turn right. You'll pass a sign pointing right to the ruined ***juego de pelota*** **(ball court),** but the path is obscure.

Continuing straight ahead on this path for 5 to 10 minutes, you'll come to a fork in the road. To the left and right you'll notice jungle-covered, unexcavated pyramids, and at one point, you'll see a raised portion crossing the pathway—this is the visible remains of the sacbé to Yaxuná. Throughout the area, carved stelae stand by pathways or lie forlornly in the jungle underbrush. Although protected by crude thatched roofs, most are weatherworn enough that they're indiscernible.

The left fork leads to the **Nohoch Mul Group,** which contains **El Castillo.** With the exception of Structure 2 in Calakmul, this is the tallest pyramid in the Yucatán (rising even higher than the great El Castillo at Chichén Itzá and the Pyramid of the Magician at Uxmal). Visitors are permitted to climb to the top. From this lofty perch, you can see unexcavated jungle-covered pyramidal structures poking up through the forest canopy all around.

The right fork (more or less straight on) goes to the **Conjunto Las Pinturas.** Here, the main attraction is the **Pyramid of the Painted Lintel,** a small structure with traces of its original bright colors above the door. You can climb up to get a close look.

Admission to the site is $40, parking is $10, and a video camera permit costs $40. The site is open daily from 8am to 5pm, sometimes longer. You can reach the ruins from the bus station by walking south on the town's main street toward the lake, and then turning left on Voz Suave. It's about a 10 minute walk.

Xcalak

If you continue south past Tulum on Highway 307, after about 45 minutes, you will reach the turn off for Majahual and Xcalak. Majahual is mostly a rest stop for cruise ships, so it is a good idea to steer clear of it and continue for another 45 minutes to Xcalek. This town makes a great base for the Southern Yucatán area, which also includes the divers' paradise known as the Chinchorro Reefs, as well as the quaint town of Lago Bacalar.

The beaches in this quiet fishing village (pop. 300) are the most deserted and pristine you'll find on the peninsula. You won't find any parties here, only gorgeous scenery and plenty of peace and quiet, as well as ample opportunities for adventure activities like bird-watching, snorkeling, and butterfly chasing.

Sleeping & Eating

In addition to the below recommendations, check out www.xcalak.com.mx for info on the few other sleeping and eating options in town.

➔ **Costa de Cocos** This delightful bed-and-breakfast is run by an American couple who are happy to help you navigate the wild, wonderful terrain of Xcalak and point you in the right direction of dive shops and other outdoor adventures. I'm not sure what's more impressive, that the whole group of beachfront cabañas runs on wind power 24 hours a day, or that the price of your clean, comfy room also includes three delicious home-cooked meals every day. This place is a local favorite, so make sure to make your reservations as far in advance as possible. *Carretera Majual-Xcalak Km 52. ☎ 983/831-0110. www.costadecocos.com. $750–$900 double. Breakfast included in rates. No credit cards. Amenities: Breakfast room; fast boat; dive master; fly-fishing instructor; tour guide; 24-hr. power.*

➔ **Sin Duda Villas** The name means "Without a Doubt," in Spanish, and there is no doubt that you'll find the treehouse suite at this innovative resort very cool indeed. If you can't afford the suite, the owners have put single beds with pull-out trundle beds in many of the artfully adorned rooms in addition to double beds, so you can easily fit four in a room. The communal kitchen and dining area mean you can stay and dine here while keeping your wallet contents intact. *Xcalak Peninsula, 53km/33 miles south of Majahual, 15km/9⅓ miles north of Costa de Cocos. ☎ 983/831-0006. www.sindudavillas.com. $400–$700 double, $800 treehouse suite. No credit cards. Amenities: Kitchen.*

Playing Outside

CHINCHORRO REEF UNDERWATER NATIONAL PARK

The Chinchorro Reef Underwater National Park is 38km (24 miles) long and 13km (8 miles) wide. The oval reef is as shallow as 1m (3¼ ft.) on its interior and as deep as 900m (2,952 ft.) on its exterior. It lies some 30km (19 miles) offshore of Majahual. Locals claim it's the last virgin reef system in the Caribbean. It's invisible from the ocean side; hence, one of its diving attractions is the **shipwrecks**—at least 30—that decorate the underwater landscape. One is on top of the reef.

The Yucatán's Lower Caribbean Coast

If you're wondering why there have been so many wrecks here, that's because the reef is difficult to detect from the ocean. On the flip side, the reef's concealed nature has protected it from the cruise ships that plague Cozumel, and as a result, you might see more species of giant sea turtles, octopuses, sea horses, and exotic fish than anywhere else in the Yucatán. If you have been diving elsewhere in Mexico, you'll also surely be amazed at the size (as high as 270m/900 ft.) and colorful variety of the coral in these waters.

If you're planning on diving the Chinchorro Reefs, you could stay at a B&B with its own instructor and boat, like Costa de Cocos (see "Sleeping & Eating" earlier in this section). That will save you some serious driving time (and stress, as there is practically nowhere to refill your tank in this area). If your resort doesn't offer dive trips, **Adventuras XTC (☎ 983/931-0461;** www.xcalak.com.mx) is the best fully equipped dive shop in the area.

LAGO BACALAR

Driving south on Highway 307, the town of Bacalar is 1½ hours beyond Felipe Carrillo Puerto, clearly marked by signs. If you're driving north from Chetumal, it takes about a half-hour. Buses going south from

Cancún and Playa del Carmen stop here; see p. 184 and 252 for info.

Lago Bacalar is known as the Lake of the Seven Colors, because, as an unusual body of water that is fed by both the turquoise water of the Caribbean and the crystal blue waters of several underwater cenotes, it takes on all sorts of odd colors. The supernaturally blue yet clear water is mesmerizing to look at and almost too pretty to swim and dive in, though the swimming and diving here are both stellar.

Mérida

As the capital of the state of Yucatán, Mérida is a living, breathing metropolis. More than anywhere else in the Yucatán, partying is distilled to its most potent elements here. Méridianos love nothing more than a party in the plaza or street, and a festive vibe flows through the streets during most weekends, when at least a dozen free stages are set-up along the main roads surrounding the center of downtown. Almost everything imaginable is staged, from local youth ballet performances, to classical music concerts, to singing contests with young Talia and Mana wannabes belting their hearts out over throbbing beats. On Sunday, as everyone shares a collective hangover from 3 days of singing and dancing in the streets, the plaza fills with vendors selling popular snacks like french fries tossed with chopped-up hot dogs and smothered in hot sauce, delicious ice cream, and just about any Mexican food that you can imagine—most of which you can get for under $100.

Often called the gateway to the Maya heartland, Mérida makes a good home base for tourists' daily treks to the ruins of Chichén Itzá, Uxmal, and the many other Maya ruins in the periphery of the city. Once situated in town, most tourists fall unexpectedly in love not just with the nonstop street parties and delicious street food, but with all the great museums, architecture, and skilled artisan shops too.

What is truly memorable about Mérida is that, though it suffers from some of the same congestion problems that plague other colonial cities in Mexico, it hasn't kowtowed to foreign pressure yet. Perhaps its lack of beaches has done Mérida a favor—the hotels and restaurants here are refreshingly naïve about catering to foreign tastes. No matter how long you've been traveling through the Yucatán Peninsula, during your stay in Mérida, you may suddenly be struck with the realization that you have *finally* arrived in Mexico. Not the Mexico of turquoise water, bikinis, and piña coladas, but a more authentic city—one that pulses with the heart and soul of Yucatecan culture.

Getting Into Town

BY PLANE **AeroMexico** (☎ **800/237-6639;** www.aeromexico.com) offers direct service from Miami as well as connecting service via Mexico City and Cancún. **Mexicana** (☎ **998/881-9090** or 800/531-7921 in U.S.; www.mexicana.com.mx) also flies direct from Miami and offers connecting flights from other cities in Mexico City. **Continental** (☎ **999/946-1888;** www.continental.com) provides nonstop flights to and from Houston. Regional carrier **AeroCaribe,** a Mexicana affiliate (☎ **998/884-2000;** www.aerocaribe.com.mx) flies from Cozumel, Cancún, Veracruz, and Villahermosa. **Click** (☎ **800/122-5425;** www.clickmx.com), a Mexican budget airline, provides nonstop service to and from Mexico City and Veracruz.

Mérida

SLEEPING ■
Casa Mexilio 14
Casa San Juan 40
Hobo Hostel 8
Hostal del Peregrino 10
Hostel Zocalo 39
Hotel Caribe 31
Hotel Los Aluxes 9
Hotel Maison Lafitte 12
Hotel Mucuy 20
Hotel Trinidad 17
Hotel Villa Maria 15
Nomadas Hostel 11
0 0.25 mi
0 0.25 km
N
Church
Information
Pedestrian Only
Post Office
UNITED STATES
Gulf of Mexico
MEXICO
Mexico City
Mérida
0 500 mi
0 500 km
Av. Colon
Av. Perez
Paseo de Montejo
Calle 37
Calle 39
Calle 41
Calle 43
Calle 45
Parque Santa Ana
Calle 47
Calle 49
Calle 51
Calle 53
Parque Santa Lucía
Calle 55
Calle 72
Calle 57
Parque Santiago
Calle 68
Calle 66
Calle 70
Calle 59
Parque de la Madre
Parque Hidalgo
Calle 64
Calle 62
Calle 61
Plaza Mayor
Calle 60
Calle 58
Calle 56
Calle 54
Calle 63
Calle 65
Portal de Granos
Mercado Lucas de Gálvez
Calle 67
Bazaar de Artesanías
Parque San Juan
Calle 69
EATING ◆
Alberto's Continental 16
Amaro Restaurant and Bar 24
Café Alameda 19
Cafe La Habana 26
Cafe Los Angeles 34
Eladio's 25
El Hoyo Café 27
El Penoncito 35
Janitzio Jugos, Helados, y Paletas 29
Kantun 7
La Casa de Frida 28
La Casa del Paseo 2
La Reyna de Montejo 4
Portico de Peregrino 22
Villa Maria Restaurant 15
VIPS 3
PARTYING ★
Azul Picante 18
Canta Mexico 5
Concepto 1
El Cielo 1
La Prosperidad 13
La Tratto 1
La Trova 23
Los HeneQuenes 21
Mambo Café 1
SIGHTSEEING ●
Casa de Montejo 38
Catedral de San Ildefonso 33
Museo de Arte Contemporaneo (Museum of Contemporary Art) 36
Museo de la Ciudad 32
Museo Regional de Antropología 6
Palacio de Gobierno 30
Plaza Mayor 37

Aviacsa (☎ **800/006-2000;** www.aviacsa.com.mx) provides nonstop service to and from Villahermosa and Mexico City.

Mérida's **Lic. Manuel Crecencio Rejon International Airport** is on the periphery of the city, about 13km (8 miles) outside of town. Highway 180 runs right by the entrance. At the airport you can rent a car from one of the country's major rental car companies (p. 51) that have booths lined up by the exit. Or outside, you can buy a taxi ticket to the center of town for about $110. See "By Taxi" under "Getting Around" for more info.

BY CAR Highway 180 is the old *carretera federal* (federal highway) between Mérida and Cancún. The trip takes 6 hours, and the road is in good shape; you will pass through many Maya villages. You can slim the drive to Mérida down by taking trusty old Highway 180 only until you reach the autopista, which branches off from 180 at the village of Kantunil, about 64km (40 miles) before you reach Mérida. If you want to avoid paying the $300 toll, stay on 180 and you will get a scenic view of the many small villages and roadside Maya ruins along the way. Highway 180 becomes Calle 65, which will take you straight into the heart of El Centro Historico in downtown Mérida, where most of the hotels are.

If you're driving north from Uxmal, Avenida Izates is your turnoff into the city. The traffic loop, or *periferico,* that surrounds the city, can make you feel like you've missed it—you'll pass signs that imply Mérida is behind you—but keep on going.

BY BUS There are five bus stations in Mérida, two of which offer first-class buses; the other three provide local service to nearby destinations. The larger of the first-class stations, **CAME,** is on Calle 70, between calles 69 and 71 (see "City Layout," below). The ADO bus line and its affiliates operate the station.

The other first-class station is the small **Maya K'iin** used by the bus company **Elite.** It's at Calle 65 no. 548, between calles 68 and 70.

To and from Cancún: You can pick up a bus at the CAME (almost every hr.) or through Elite (five per day). Both bus lines also pick up passengers at the Fiesta Americana Hotel, across from the Hyatt (12 per day). You can buy a ticket in the hotel's shopping arcade at the **Ticket Bus** agency or at the Elite ticket agency. Cancún is 4 hours away; a few buses stop in **Valladolid.** If you're downtown, you can purchase tickets from the agency in Pasaje Picheta, on the main square a couple of doors down from the Palacio de Gobierno.

To and from Chichén Itzá: Three buses per day (2½-hr. trip) depart from the CAME. Also, check out tours operating from the hotels in Mérida if you want to visit for the day.

To and from Playa del Carmen, Tulum, and Chetumal: From the CAME, there are 10 departures per day for Playa del Carmen (5-hr. trip), six for Tulum (6-hr. trip), and eight for Chetumal (7-hr. trip). From Maya K'iin there are three per day to Playa, which stop at the Fiesta Americana.

The main **second-class bus station** is around the corner from the CAME on Calle 69, between calles 68 and 70.

To and from Uxmal: There are four buses per day. (You can also hook up with a tour to Uxmal through most hotels or any travel agent or tour operator in town.) One bus per day combines Uxmal with the other sites to the south (Kabah, Sayil, Labná, and Xlapak—known as the Puuc route) and does the whole round-trip in a day. It stops for 2 hours at Uxmal and 30 minutes at each of the other sites.

GETTING AROUND

ON FOOT Mérida is a great walking city, since it's on a grid, which makes it

I'm Walking Here

For a city full of pedestrians, Mérida has very narrow sidewalks—most are a couple of feet wide—which are elevated almost a foot above the street. This means that if you are walking too slowly, it's likely that someone behind you will give you a gentle (or not so gentle) nudge, which is a locally acceptable way of telling you to either speed up, move aside, or step down into the street and be passed. The first time this happens, you might be startled, but don't take offense—it's a perfectly normal way for locals to move traffic along.

difficult to get lost and encourages exploring. Most attractions are within walking distance of El Centro Historico, so that makes Mérida downright liberating compared to the sprawl of newer resort areas.

BY CAR Parking in Mérida is very expensive, and since it's a great walking city, you may want to skip the car rental for this part of the trip. Hotels offering free parking usually only do so at night, and charge you an arm and leg during the day, so make sure you read the fine print. Also, it's a really bad idea to drive in Mérida when it rains. The streets do not drain and often flood, making accidents likely. If you still insist on putting the pedal to the metal, check out p. 51 in "Basics" for tips on renting cars.

BY BUS City buses are a little tricky to figure out but aren't needed very often because almost everything of interest is within walking distance of the main plaza. Still, it's a bit of a walk from the plaza to the Paseo de Montejo, and you can save yourself some work by taking a bus, minibus, or *colectivo* (Volkswagen minivan) that is heading north on Calle 60. Most of these will take you within a couple of blocks of the Paseo de Montejo. Colectivos run out in several directions from the main plaza along simple routes. They usually line up along the side streets next to the plaza.

BY TAXI Taxis are easy to come by and much cheaper than in the peninsula's resort towns. Two taxi companies to try are **Taximetro** (☎ **999/928-3031**) and **Radio Taxis Group** (☎ **999/982-1171**). But if you are around the main plaza, the Pasco Montejo, or the airport, you never have to worry about calling a cab, as available ones drive by every few minutes.

Basics

ORIENTATION

Downtown Mérida has the standard layout of towns in the Yucatán: Streets running north-south are even numbers; those running east-west are odd numbers. The numbering begins on the north and the east sides of town, so if you're walking on an odd-numbered street and the even numbers of the cross streets are increasing, then you are heading west; likewise, if you are on an even-numbered street and the odd numbers of the cross streets are increasing, you are going south.

Address numbers don't tell you anything about what cross street to look for. This is why addresses almost always list cross streets, usually like this: "Calle 60 no. 549 × 71 y 73." The "×" is a multiplication sign—shorthand for the word *por* (meaning "by")—and *y* means "and." So this place would be on Calle 60 between calles 71 and 73. Outside of the downtown area, the numbering of streets gets a little crazy, so it's important to know the name of the neighborhood where you're going. This is the first thing taxi drivers will ask you.

The town's main square is the busy **Plaza Mayor,** referred to simply as **El Centro.** It's bordered by calles 60, 62, 61, and 63. Calle 60, which runs in front of the cathedral, is an important street to remember; it connects the main square with several smaller plazas, some theaters and churches, and the University of Yucatán, just to the north. Here, too, you'll find a concentration of handicraft shops, restaurants, and hotels. Around Plaza Mayor are the cathedral, the Palacio de Gobierno (state government building), the Ayuntamiento (town hall), and the Palacio Montejo. The plaza always has a crowd, and it's full on Sunday, when it holds a large street fair. (See "Festivals," below.) Within a few blocks are several smaller plazas and the bustling market district.

Mérida's most fashionable district is the broad, tree-lined boulevard **Paseo de Montejo** and its surrounding neighborhood. The Paseo de Montejo parallels Calle 60 and begins 7 blocks north and a little east of the main square. There are a number of trendy restaurants, modern hotels, offices of various banks and airlines, and a few clubs here, but the boulevard is mostly known for its stately mansions built during the boom times of the henequén industry. Near where the Paseo intersects Avenida Colón, you'll find the two fanciest hotels in town: the Hyatt and the Fiesta Americana.

TOURIST INFO & OFFICES

Mérida boasts both city tourism offices and state tourism offices, which have different resources; if you can't get the information you're looking for at one, go to the other. I have better luck with the city's **visitor information office** (☎ **999/942-0000,** ext. 80119), which is on the ground floor of the Ayuntamiento building facing the main square on Calle 62. Look for a glass door under the arcade. Hours are Monday to Saturday from 8am to 8pm and Sunday from 8am to 2pm. Monday through Saturday, at 9:30am, the staff offers visitors a free tour of the area around the main square. The state operates two downtown tourism offices: One is in the **Teatro Peón Contreras,** facing Parque de la Madre (☎ **999/924-9290**); and the other is on the main plaza, in the **Palacio de Gobierno,** immediately to the left as you enter. These offices are open daily from 8am to 9pm. There are also information booths at the airport and the CAME bus station.

Also keep your eye out for the free monthly magazine *Yucatán Today;* it's a good source of information for Mérida and the rest of the region.

Recommended Websites:

- **www.mexonline.com/Yucatan.htm**: A comprehensive list of hotels, rentals, tour companies, and useful background info on the area's surrounding ruins.
- **www.mayaYucatan.com**: This brand-new site by the Ministry of Tourism has the advantage of up-to-date info, and freshly updated lists of services.

Mérida Nuts & Bolts

Banks The mansions along the Paseo de Montejo have virtually all been converted into large banks, and all have ATMs. In the **El Centro,** you can find casas de cambio inside the mall-like tourist center of the Plaza on Calle 60.

Embassies/Consulates A new **U. S. consulate** is at Calle 60 no.338-K, just north of the Hyatt hotel (☎ **999/942-5700).** It can be extremely useful if you've lost your wallet or are in any other kind of a pickle of international proportions. They have a separate window so that you won't have to wait in line for too long and are good at thinking outside the box to solve your most difficult logistical problems. If you need serious help, make sure to get there at 7:30am to get attention before the line forms. The Consulate is open from 7:30am to 1pm. (The Consulate closes the doors at 1pm because it takes from then until 5pm to see all the people already waiting.)

Emergenices Mérida has a special body of police to assist tourists. They patrol the downtown area and the Paseo de Montejo. They wear white shirts bearing the words POLICIA TURISTICA. Their phone number is ☎ **999/925-2555.**

Hospitals The best hospital in town is **Centro Médico de las Américas,** Calle 54 no. 365 between 33-A and Avenida Pérez Ponce. The main phone number is ☎ **999/926-2619;** for emergencies, call ☎ **999/927-3199.** You can also call the **Cruz Roja (Red Cross)** at ☎ **999/924-9813.**

Internet/Wireless Hot Spots **El Hoyo Café** (p. 292) is the best Internet cafe in town, but they only have a few stations. On Calle 61 between calles 62 and 64, you'll find a whole string of places where you can get cheap Internet, make copies, and have other office tasks done quickly.

Pharmacies Farmacia **Yza,** Calle 63 no. 502, between calles 60 and 62 (☎ **999/924-9510**), on the south side of the plaza, is open 24 hours.

Post Office The *correo* is near the market at the corner of calles 65 and 56. A branch office is at the airport. Both are open Monday to Friday from 8am to 7pm, Saturday from 9am to noon.

Telephone Tips The area code in Mérida is 999. If you need to make a long distance call, you'll save a lot of money by going to a cafe with a broadband phone line, like the charming El Hoyo (p. 292) rather than using a pay phone.

THE YUCATÁN PENINSULA

Sleeping

Affordable, beautiful haciendas that have been renovated into hostels, B&Bs, and boutique hotels are the rule rather than the exception in Mérida—this is definitely a place where you should avoid staying in a chain hotel. I also suggest that you skip camping here, since the only place to do so is at my least favorite hostel in town (the Nomades).

Most accommodations are within walking distance from the main plaza, around the intersection of calles 60 and 61.

HOSTELS

→ **Hobo Hostel** ★★★ The best thing about this hostel, other than the rock bottom $70 per bed rate, is that it is brand new. This means that, despite being situated in a 300-year-old mansion, the newly renovated bathrooms and bunk areas are spotless and in excellent condition. Unlike the older hostels in town, which can be dirty and cramped, this place is ideal if you're looking for a lot of space, clean sheets, and hot showers. There are also plenty of amenities on hand, like hammocks, vending machines with real food, a few computers with free Internet access, and a spiffy espresso machine that spits out yummy coffees, cappuccinos, and lattes. The eager-to-please owners are in the process of adding a full kitchen and Wi-Fi. *Calle 60 no. 432, between calles 49 and 47. ☎ 999/928-0880. www.hotelhobo.com.mx. $70 bed. No credit cards. Amenities: Fancy espresso machine; Internet; lockers; shared bathroom; sheets; telephone (in common area); towels; TV w/DVD player (common room); vending machines.*

➔ **Hostal del Peregrino** ★ Before I had the pleasure of visiting this charming little backpacker hotel, I was convinced that the term "hostal" was just a silly euphemism for hostel. Instead, I discovered that Hostal del Peregrine is the definition of a true backpacker spot. Everything from the cheerful periwinkle exterior, to the tiles with creeping roses on the floor in the lobby, to the spacious shared quarters with hardwood floors and beautifully woven Mexican blankets tucked into plump mattresses, sends the strong message that just because you're a backpacker doesn't mean you don't deserve a little bit of loveliness in your life. *Calle 51 no. 488, between calles 54 and 56. ☎ 999/924-5491 or 999/924-3007. www.hostaldelperegrino.com. Starting at $100 bed, $120 with breakfast, starting at $250 private rooms. No credit cards. Amenities: Bar; breakfast room; Internet; kitchen; laundry; lockers; shared bathroom; sheets; telephone (in common area); tours and rental cars available by arrangement; towels; TV (common room). In room: A/C (in some).*

➔ **Hostel Zocalo** Right smack in the center of the main plaza and taking up the entire top floor of an 1800s historic mansion, Hostel Zocalo is by far the oldest and most heavily trafficked hostel in Mérida. It's also a chill place to meet a cool crowd of fellow travelers—the friendly guests lounge on the well-worn couches and hammocks inside, playing guitar, chatting over coffee, and just chilling out. On the other hand, the place could use a thorough cleaning—the wear and tear of years of travelers shows, and the main plaza is never quiet at night. The big balconies overlooking the plaza give you the best seats in the house during the many displays of music and dance that take place in the streets below. *Calle 63 no. 508, between calles 60 and 62. ☎ 999/930-9562. hostel_zocalo@yahoo.com.mx. $80 per bed with breakfast. No credit cards. Amenities: Breakfast room; DVD library; Internet; kitchen; laundry; lockers; shared bathroom; sheets; telephone (in common area); towels; TV (common room).*

➔ **Nomadas Hostel** This popular hostel is run by Hosteling International, and thus possesses the long list of extras you expect from the international organization, if at the cost of less local character and a location farther from the center of downtown than most of the independently owned hostels. Bonuses include a travel agency catering toward backpackers' budgets, a bar and restaurant onsite with live music and free salsa lessons, 24 hour medical service, and a camping area. Because this hostel devotes a significant amount of money to self-promotion and flyers, the main highlight of staying here is the lively international crowd that it consistently draws. *Calle 62 no. 433 at Calle 51. ☎ 999/924-5223. www.nomadastravel.com. Starting at $70 bed with breakfast, starting at $200 private room. No credit cards. Amenities: Restaurant and bar; Internet; kitchen; laundry; shared bathroom; sheets; telephone (in common area); towels; travel agency; TV (common room); 24-hr. medical service. In room: A/C (in some rooms), locker.*

CHEAP

➔ **Casa San Juan** Though I prefer Casa Mexilio (see below), this place has most of the same amenities at a slightly cheaper price, so it's a good option if Mexilio is full. Guest rooms are beautifully decorated, large, and comfortable. Those in the original house have been modernized but maintain a colonial feel, with 7m (23-ft.) ceilings and 45cm-thick (18-in.) walls. The modern rooms in back look out over the rear patio. You can save $200 by skipping the air-conditioning, but since the heat and humidity in Mérida is no joke, it's worth shelling out the extra dinero so that you don't have to wake up soaked in your own sweat. The free continental breakfast is good, but Mexilio's is better. *Calle 62, between calles 69 and 71. ☎ 999/986-2937. www.casasanjuan.com. $300 double without A/C, $600 with A/C. No credit cards. Amenities: Continental breakfast. In room: A/C (in some).*

→ **Hotel Caribe** This three-story colonial-style hotel is great for a couple of reasons: Its location at the back of Plaza Hidalgo is both central and quiet, and it has a nice little pool and sun deck on the rooftop with a view of the cathedral. The rooms are moderately comfortable, though they aren't well lit, and have only small windows facing the central courtyard. Thirteen *clase económica* rooms don't have air-conditioning, but standard rooms do; superior rooms (on the top floor) have been remodeled and have safes, hair dryers, larger windows, and quieter air-conditioning. The rooftop pool and patio provide a stunning view of the town's cathedral, though the swimming area itself is pretty small. The nearby Café Meson, which oozes European charm, makes for a tranquil lunch spot. Another big attraction here is the movie theater next door, which usually shows American blockbusters with Spanish subtitles *Calle 59 no. 500. ☎ 888/903-9512. $450–$600 double. MC, V. Amenities: Restaurant and bar; gym; office suite with complimentary Internet; large pool; spa; Wi-Fi in lobby. In room: A/C (in some), TV w/cable, fridge, minibar.*

→ **Hotel Mucuy** ★ This simple, unpretentious hotel is one of the best values in Mérida. Guest rooms are basic; most contain two twin beds or a queen (with comfortable mattresses) and some simple furniture. But the rest of the hotel makes up for the sparseness of the rooms. The courtyard garden possesses quite possibly the best swimming pool in the city, and the deck comes with enough lounge chairs for sunning around the pool or chatting up the friendly guests. In addition, the owner is a natural born hostess who speaks both English and French, and strives to make guests feel welcome. *Calle 57 no. 481, between calles 56 and 58. ☎ 999/928-5193. Fax 999/923-7801. www.mucuy.com. $220 double with fan, $270 double with A/C. No credit cards. Amenities: Restaurant and bar; gym with classes; office suite with complimentary computers and Internet; large pool; spa; travel desk and agent; Wi-Fi in lobby. In room: A/C, TV w/cable, fridge, minibar.*

DOABLE

MTV Best → **Casa Mexilio** ★★★ Stay at Casa Mexilio and you'll feel like a guest in the house of a hospitable old friend, one who happens to have an artistic eye for interior decorating. The modest owner of this exceptional bed-and-breakfast completely renovated this beautiful 1700s hacienda with his own hands. Today, the building is an impressive maze of secluded, private rooms separated from each other by lush multi-level gardens. Each room is named after a hero of Latin American culture, like Frida Kahlo or Pancho Villa. There is a small, shady pool fashioned to look like a sinkhole in the central courtyard, which you are almost guaranteed to have all to yourself at any time during the day. Finally, the complimentary full breakfasts, which are served in an elegant dining room full of Maya art, are so good, they made me look forward to waking up each morning. *Calle 68 no. 495, between calles 57 and 59 in El Centro. ☎ 999/938-2505. www.casamexilio.com. $750 and under double with breakfast. AE, MC, V. Amenities: Breakfast room; complimentary computers with Internet; free broadband phone calls to the U.S.; pool; Wi-Fi in lobby and in some rooms. In room : A/C.*

→ **Hotel Maison Lafitte** This fancy, French-themed hotel is the perfect alternative to those of you who are still tempted by the Hyatt. It's got all the luxuries you could ever want, but it's also right in the center of the action downtown, and it hires its own live bands on the weekends and sets up tables and chairs where you can drink, munch, and dance late into the night on the historic street right outside your hotel. The food in the restaurant is exceptional, and far less expensive than at an actual Hyatt. *Calle 60, between calles 53 and 55. ☎ 999/923-9159. Fax 999/923-9159. www.maisonlafitte.com.mx. $800–$1,000 double. MC, V. Amenities: Restaurant and bar; full breakfast included; dry cleaning; laundry service; massage; small pool; room service. In room: A/C, TV w/cable, hair dryer, minibar.*

MTV Best → **Hotel Trinidad** ★★★ *Art Nexus,* one of the most influential Latin American art magazines, lists both branches of Hotel Trinidad as contemporary art museums. This is not an exaggeration—both are literally bursting at the seams with art. As you enter the lobby of either place, you'll be greeted by a gaggle of sculptural installations, paintings covering every wall, and full-fledged art galleries, which draw impressive numbers of non-guests. Every space, from the patio around the pool, to the hallways, to the rooms themselves, is filled with funky art objects. If you love art, you should definitely investigate this most unconventional hotel chain. If you don't, you may feel a bit overwhelmed by the hordes of creative clutter. Decor aside, the true strength of the Hotel Trinidad is that they have rooms for every budget, from un-air-conditioned backpacker quarters to luxurious suites. And of course all rooms are arty—with Pollock-inspired, abstract mosaic floors, asymmetrical light fixtures, and other quirky decorations. *Hotel Trinidad: Calle 62 no. 464 at Calle 55. ☎ 999/923-2463. Hotel Trinidad Galleria: Calle 60 at Calle 51. ☎ 999/923-2463. www.hotelestrinidad.com. $350–$2,000 double. Cheaper rates available for "backpacker" accommodations. MC, V. Amenities: Coffee shop; bar; 3 art galleries; office with Internet; pool; Wi-Fi in lobby. In room: A/C (in some), cable TV (in some), fans.*

SPLURGE

→ **Hotel Los Aluxes** ★★★ A large, new luxury hotel that still maintains an authentically local character, Hotel Los Aluxes has got it all. The decor is clean and ocean inspired—tranquil blues and greens rule, accentuated by subtle accents of seashells and light wood. Plus, top quality mattresses and linens make sleeping here a real pleasure. The restaurant and bar are open late and serve a satisfying array of Yucatecan and stateside staples, and the pool in the courtyard is big and a great place for meeting fellow guests.

In case you're wondering 'bout the name, Aluxes are tiny elves in Maya folklore who covertly help farmers look after their crops in difficult times. Farmers in rural Mexican villages still leave small offerings of food outside their doors as a sign of gratitude for help after a good harvest. It's assumed that, if gifts aren't doled out, the farmers will wake up to find their tools stolen and their crops stoned by the unappreciated elves. Feel free to apply this parable toward tipping all of the helpful locals who kindly assist you during your travels here. *Calle 60 no. 444 at Calle 49. ☎ 999/924-2199, toll-free from the U.S. 800/712-8395. Fax 999/923-3858. www.aluxes.com.mx. $1,000 and up double. AE, MC, V. Amenities: Restaurant and bar; gym with classes; office suite with complimentary computers and Internet; large pool; spa; Wi-Fi in lobby. In room: A/C, cable TV, fridge, minibar.*

MTV Best → **Hotel Villa María** ★★★ A crazy combination of a French castle, a Lebanese palace, and a Spanish hacienda, the Hotel Villa María is an attraction in its own right. In a newly restored 17th-century mansion that was for many years a thriving Lebanese restaurant, this luxury hotel somehow manages to successfully combine vintage French art and furniture and a decadent Middle Eastern interior *and* incorporate the remaining touches from the original hacienda without missing a beat. The 11 rooms in the mosque-like central courtyard are filled with canopied beds, antique European furniture, and priceless paintings that are more than a few notches above the usual bland hotel wall hangings. All that, and you can eat well to boot: The central restaurant has fabulous steak and the best french fries in Mexico (p. 291). *Calle 59 no. 553 at Calle 68.* ☎ *999/923-3357. Fax 999/923-7620. www.villamariamerida.com. $1,500 and up double. MC, V. Amenities: Restaurant and bar; Internet in office suite; pool; spa. In room: A/C, TV w/cable (in some).*

Eating

If you want to eat cheap, Mérida is your city. The narrow streets are full of mom and pop restaurants that dish out cheap, home-cooked meals. One of my favorite places for cheap eats is the street stand **El Penoncito** (at the intersection of calles 61 and 52; no phone), which has hot burgers, cheese-steak subs, and Mexican food. Try one of their combos that include a steaming sandwich, soda, and fries for about $50. Local favorite **Café Los Angeles** (Calle 61 between calles 52 and 54; no phone) has fresh Mexican breakfast and lunch platters with drinks included in a sunny cafelike environment, all for under $50.

CHEAP

➔ **Amaro Restaurant and Bar** ★★ YUCATECAN Though this restaurant offers a variety of tasty fish and chicken standbys, the innovative Mexican veggie cuisine is what really stands out. The *papazules* (enchiladas filled with diced hard-boiled eggs smothered in a rich pumpkin seed sauce) and *eggplant meshe* (a dish of thinly sliced eggplant layered with grilled vegetables, cheese, and "kool," a mild white Yucatecan sauce), are all savory and satisfying. Other highlights of the extensive menu include the zucchini cream soup, avocado pizza, and chaya onion pies. Amaro is the best place in town to try Agua de Chaya, a refreshing minty lemonade made with honey and chaya, an indigenous herb that's high in vitamins and iron. There are plenty of alcholohic drinks on offer, too; the lively bar scene kicks into high gear around 10pm and often features live music. *Calle 59 no. 507, between calles 60 and 62.* ☎ *999/928-2451. www.restauranteamaro.com. Main courses $40–$100. AE, MC, V. Daily 11am–2pm.*

➔ **Café Alameda** LEBANESE You may not have expected to stumble upon Mediterranean street food in Mexico, but there's actually a decent Lebanese population in Mérida and it represents itself at this local lunch favorite. The cheap and flavorful food includes a lot of vegetarian standbys that you may be craving if you've been traveling in Mexico for a while, like stellar humus, spinach pies, and tabbouleh salad. Give your belly a break from all those fried beans and tortillas that are offered everywhere else and stop here at least once during your stay. *Calle 58 no. 474, between calles 55 and 57.* ☎ *999/928-3635. Main courses $50. No credit cards. Daily 8am–6pm.*

➔ **Eladio's** ★★ YUCATECAN This is where the locals come to get their Yucatecan food, which means that it's affordable, tasty, and significantly spicier than anywhere else. The standout item on the menu are the *panuchos* (small tortillas fried with beans then smothered in turkey, roasted onions, cheese, and chiles)—the ones I sampled here were the best I've had, ever. You can enjoy a healthy mix of live music, cold beer, and cheap food at one of the tables in the open-air restaurant, or get your goodies to go and picnic right across the street (where you can still hear the music) in the lovely Parque la Majorada. *Calle 59 at Calle 44. ☎ 999/923-1087. Main courses $30–$80. MC, V. Daily noon–10pm.*

→ **La Reyna de Montejo** ★★ DINER This cute outdoor cafe right on the Paseo de Montejo caters to the businessmen and -women who work in the many mansions that have been converted to office buildings and banks along the Paseo. Because it is frequented mainly by working locals as opposed to tourists, you can't get a better bang for your buck in this scenic neighborhood. La Reyna has an entire breakfast menu for under $20, and everything comes with bread, coffee, purified water, beans, and salsa. Yucatecan favorites such as carne asada are served on generous platters with beans, rice, salad, and tortillas for under $40. Tortas, tacos, and burgers are all under 10 pesos, and usually come with a side of french fries. ***An important note:*** The menu and staff completely changes at 4pm with another establishment that shares the kitchen. After 4pm, the price goes up to cater to tourists strolling along the Paseo, and though the name stays the same, it becomes a totally different restaurant with nothing in particular to recommend it. *Paseo Montejo, between calles 39 and 37. No phone. No credit cards. Main courses $40. Mon–Fri 7am–4pm; Sat–Sun 9am–4pm.*

DOABLE

→ **Kantun** ★★ SEAFOOD Though this seafood restaurant has slow service and is significantly off the main drag, it is worth the wait and the trek if you're looking for fresh home-cooked seafood in a genuine family-owned restaurant. Specialties include fish stuffed with a variety of shellfish—a steal for $90. But my favorite dishes were the ceviche accented by fresh crabmeat and cream of oyster soup with over a dozen tender oysters floating in perfect, freshly made cream broth. The dining room is air-conditioned, the furniture comfortable, and the service is every bit as attentive as I'm sure it was when it first opened in 1900. *Calle 45 no. 525, between calles 64 and 66. ☎ 999/923-4493. Main courses $90–$130. No credit cards. Daily noon–8pm.*

MTV Best → **La Casa de Frida** ★★★ MEXICAN If you're a fan of Frida Kahlo or unusual food, don't miss this colorful shrine to the legendary artist, which boasts rare prints and photos of Frida covering its pink and green walls, and menu items that are tasty spins on traditional cuisine. Innovative appetizers include eggplant flan, potato and cheese taquitos, and corn mushroom crepes served with a poblano chile sauce. The main courses include a number of rare local specialties; most notable is the *chile en nogada.* Gabriela's version of this classic dish consists of an ample-size poblano pepper stuffed with ground meat, apples, pears, and plantains, then fried and covered in a rich, creamy pecan sauce. She also offers a meatless version. *Calle 61 no. 526 at Calle 66. ☎ 999/928-2311. www.lacasadefrida.com.mx. Main courses $60–$130. AE, MC, V. Daily noon–11pm (hours vary; call in advance).*

→ **Portico de Peregrino** ★★ MEXICAN What this place has going for it is that it feels classy and elegant but costs the same as a much more modest joint. Portico, which is over 50 years old, has three dining rooms as well as a charming garden, and the decor is reminiscent of a fancy French bistro. The menu, on the other hand, consists of Mexican classics prepared to the highest standards of culinary law. This is a great place to try classics like *pollo pibil* (a half-chicken cooked in bitter orange and achiote marinade and wrapped in banana leaves), *sopa de lima* (chicken soup with lime and vegetables), and *enchiladas de mole* (chicken enchiladas in a thick, spicy chocolate sauce). *Calle 57 no. 501, between calles 60 and 62. No phone. Main courses $70–$140. AE, MC, V. Daily 11am–8pm.*

➔ **VIPS** AMERICAN The motto of this superhero-themed, kid-centric restaurant is "Finding Flavor and Fighting for Justice at VIPS" and doesn't that just scream U.S. novelty restaurant? Sure enough, this restaurant has a very American vibe, from the huge dining room; to the menu with over 50 choices—including big salads full of chicken and fish, specialty sandwich platters, and a long list of desserts; to the restroom speakers which pipe out a constant loop of retro radio shows featuring aliens, submarines, and astronauts. Despite feeling very stateside, the enormous restaurant (it takes up a whole block on the Paseo Montejo) was packed with locals when I visited. That's probably because the food is way better than you'd expect from a hokey place like this, and all portions are huge. *Paseo Montejo at Calle 37. No phone. Main courses $50–$150. AE, MC, V. Daily 9am–9pm.*

SPLURGE

➔ **Alberto's Continental** ★ LEBANESE/MEXICAN This savory spot is great for sharing large portions of kibeh, baba ghanouj, or falafel, right along side local favorites like *pollo pibil*. The sweet, strong, small cups of Turkish coffee served here are just the right pick-me-up, no matter what you order. The decor is nothing glitzy—but the elegant *mudejar*-patterned tile floors and patio area (complete with gurling fountain) help create a romantic mood. *Calle 64 no. 482 at Calle 57. ☎ 999/928-5367. www.albertoscontinental.com. Main courses $80–$200. AE, MC, V. Mon–Sat noon–11pm; Sun noon–8pm.*

➔ **La Casa del Paseo** ★ NUEVO LATINO At this intimate eatery inside one of the city's historic mansions, you can experience food as classy and cultured as the house it's served in. The artichoke mousse makes a great starter, and daily specials like crab and avocado gazpacho, quesadillas made with corn fungus, and *crepes carmel* feature local spices and ingredients combined in artistic ways. *Paseo Montejo no. 465, between Calle 35 and Av. Colon, right next to the American Consulate. ☎ 999/920-0528. Main courses $90–$150. AE, MC, V. Daily noon–10pm (sometimes later).*

MTV Best ➔ **Villa María Restaurant** ★★ FRENCH/BELGIAN Don't expect cheap food. But if you'd like to nibble on the best steak frites this side of Belgium, while soaking in decor fit for the Queen of Sheba, head straight to Villa María inside the hotel of the same name (p. 288). Posh European appetizers like goat cheese tartlets, breaded mushrooms, pumpkin flower ravioli, as well as smashing French onion soup get things started right. For main entrees, I like the succulent roast duck in orange glaze with mashed potatoes, the winning *wiener schnitzel*, and the perfect grilled steak served with french fries. For dessert, I like the hot apple and almond tart served with melted butter, just one of many sugary snacks on offer. The setting, which is like a combination of the Taj Majal and a French 18th-century castle, is in itself sweet. *Calle 59 no. 553 at Colonia Centro. ☎ 999/923-3357. Main courses $80–$240. AE, MC, V. Daily noon–11pm (hours vary).*

CAFES

➔ **Café La Habana** DINER Kind of like a Mexican Denny's, this diner is a comfortable stop for late-night grub, thick shakes, coffee drinks that are both spiked and sobering, and big breakfasts at any hour. Popular platters include *molletes* (fried bread with beans and melted cheese), *chilequiles* (tortilla chips baked in a casserole with beans, meat or chicken, cheese, and green sauce), and eggs made every which way. This is a good, cheap place to taste Mexican desserts such as fried bananas with ice cream or sweet rice with milk. The Michelada, a more macho version of a bloody mary made with beer, hot sauce, spices, and lime, is quite good as well. *Calle 59, between calles 60 and 62. ☎ 999/928-6502. Main courses $20–$80, coffee drinks and shakes $10–$30. No credit cards. Daily 8am–3am (sometimes later).*

MTV Best → **El Hoyo Café** ★★★ CAFE This cafe has a little of everything you want as a traveler. For starters, you can make calls anywhere in the world here from a hand-held wireless phone for a peso a minute. Even better, you can take the wireless to any table you like, and talk to your loved ones while sipping on well-priced designer coffee and tea beverages, sampling one of the many varieties of Belgium waffles that El Hoyo is famous for, or grabbing a sandwich or other quick bite. The atmosphere is arty and open; I sat between an oil painter who was rendering local landscapes on coasters while nibbling on an avocado salad, and a group of girls who were sharing pitchers of infused iced teas and a plate of freshly baked mango bread. Wine and beer are available, as well as single cigarettes for semi-smokers who don't like to commit to a whole pack, and unlimited purified ice water. Since it's conveniently in the heart of downtown and never too crowded, you may find yourself returning to El Hoyo more than once for a midday pick-me-up. It's a good bathroom stop, too; bathrooms feature colorful mosaics and live trees. *Calle 59, between calles 60 and 62. ☎ 999/928-1531. Coffee and tea $10–$20, waffles, snacks, sandwiches, and salads $20–$50. No credit cards. Daily 11am–midnight.*

MTV Best → **Janitzio Jugos, Helados, y Paletas** ★★★ DESSERT After visiting this frozen dessert stand for the fifth time during my stay in Mérida, I began to mourn my return to the comparatively boring such stands in the States. Unlike Americans, who basically are limited to choosing between ice cream, frozen yogurt, sorbet, and some wimpy fruit pops, Méridanos have a broad range of tantalizing frozen treats on offer. At Janitzio, you can try all of them; the shop stocks two huge cases of *paletas*—the equivalent of American popsicles on steroids—which include an incredible assortment of tropical fruit flavors, chocolate chip and chocolate-dipped pops, as well as some surprisingly tasty shockers like avocado, onion, and my absolute favorite, *elote* (sweet creamed corn). The fresh batches of sorbets, ice cream, liquados, and troles all come in equally exotic varieties. Don't be surprised if you end up trying a few of each; they're so cheap, and the thick, wet heat in Mérida is so intense, that you may be tempted to live on Janitzio goods alone. That'd actually be a pretty sweet life. *Janitzio, Calle 62 no. 501, between calles 61 and 63. No phone. Ice cream $20. No credit cards. Daily noon–10pm.*

Partying

Mérida is a city known for its boundless festivities. Though the clubs and bars are top tier, most of the best parties are free and literally take place in the streets. If you visit Mérida, make sure to stay over the weekend, when the best live music and festivities go on. On any given Friday or Saturday night, you can find dozens of stages set up outside with tables, finger foods, and vendors selling cheap beer. See the "Festivals" section on p. 295 for more info.

BARS

➔ **Azul Picante** Bumpin' Azul is all salsa all the time. If you show up early, they offer salsa lessons every night before midnight. The pros on staff can teach you advanced moves guaranteed to get you some action out on the dance floor. (That is, if your new partner can keep up.) They also book a host of live bands, as well as Caribbean theme parties. *Calle 60 no. 484, between calles 55 and 57.* ☎ *999/924-2323.*

➔ **Concepto** This rooftop club and bar features well-known DJs trucked in from around the globe and specialty cocktails with infusions of indigenous fruit juices. The glam couches are comfy, the house music is hot, and the setting with a view of the stars and a covered area for rainy nights is sublime. The dinner food is not recommended, but, hey, this is a bar, not a restaurant. If the munchies do hit you unexpectedly, you'll be safe if you stick to the many varieties of fried Mexican finger foods, which nicely complement the exotic cocktails. *Prolongacion Montejo, between Calle 15 and 17 Col. Mexico.* ☎ *999/948-2469.*

➔ **La Tratto** At night, this hip Italian restaurant morphs into a romantic lounge with warm lighting, slow dance music, and tantalizing Italian snacks to keep you grooving all night long. In addition to the standard set of club cocktails, the bar also stocks a fine selection of wines and a long list of specialty martinis, which are a perfect libation for Mérida's hot nights—they serve their martinis so cold, you can see the frost on the outside of your glass. But be careful, just like the club, the drinks seem super sweet but they pack a real punch. *Prolongacion Montejo no. 479-C, between Calle 17 and Buena Vista.* ☎ *999/927-0434.*

➔ **Los HeneQuenes** ★ Given how competitive the restaurant and bar scene is in Mérida, many places require a gimmick in order to stay ahead. Los HeneQuenes, which offers **free Yucatecan food** with the purchase of beer, has one of the best gimmicks in town. As a result, the large amphitheater-like space (it takes up a whole block), is often packed with crowds drawn by the free food and frequent live bands. The menu changes frequently, but usually includes a good selection of Mexican finger foods like taquitos, quesadillas, panuchos, and tacos. The bar, which is only open during the daylight hours, features unique design elements like a wall constructed out of empty beer bottles—hey, you do have to drink to eat here. *Calle 56 at Calle 57.* ☎ *999/984-5051.*

CLUBS

➔ **Canta Mexico** Get your karaoke on at this club where no one is shy, and the only language spoken is pop music. Follow the example of the locals who love to push their vocal chords to the limit, with a little help from the freely flowing beer and long list of pop hits offered both in Spanish and English. From Shakira and Madonna to Led Zeppelin and Tupac, you'll have lots of options when it comes to channeling your favorite divas and rock idols. This club has one of the best crowds in Mérida—there is no risk of getting booed off the stage, only the possibility of your new fans demanding an encore and bringing tequila shots to the stage to ensure that they get to hear one more round. *Prolongacion Montejo, between calles 41 and 43, in front of Canton Palace.* ☎ *999/928-7005 or 999/928-7004.*

➔ **El Cielo** *Cielo* means "sky" in Spanish, and the inside of this club is painted white to make you feel like you are partying inside a, well, cloud. Cielo also pumps out house music and has an outdoor patio for dancing to keep things heavenly. Because El Cielo caters mostly to locals, the drinks are cheaper here than at many area clubs. *Prolongacion Montejo and Calle 25.* ☎ *999/944-5127.*

Walking Tour

Mérida is over 450 years old, and as such, it has a ton of historically and architecturally interesting buildings worth checking out, from elegant colonial mansions to old haciendas. The buildings' seemingly effortless blend of old and new and formal beauty revitalized by common function (most have been converted into restaurants or shops), makes for a FREE **day of lazy strolling** that just happens to be packed with plenty of blessedly free things to do and see. Following are some not to miss areas to keep in mind when planning your walk around town:

Located in the cube in the center of calles 60, 61, 62, and 63, the **Plaza Mayor** makes a proper starting point for any walking tour around the city. (Note that the name of the Plaza has been officially changed to Plaza de la Independencia, but most locals still refer to it by its original name.) This peaceful park in the center of the city often plays host to live events with free music, performance artists, and art vendors lining up in the grassy park, as well as the streets surrounding it. Even when an event is not happening, the plaza is filled with people taking a moment from their busy day to soak up the sun, read, pick at instruments, or play dominoes on the stone tables lined up on the left side. It's an easy place to strike up a conversation with a local or take a break from walking and put your feet up on one of the white benches that dot the laurel-lined pathways.

Plaza Mayor is home to the town's cathedral, Museo de Arte Contemporaneo, Casa de Montejo, and Palacio del Gobierno, all of which are free (see below), as well as the town hall and city museum. In stark contrast to the severity of the cathedral and Casa Montejo is the light, unimposing **Ayuntamiento** or **Palacio Municipal (town hall).** The exterior dates from the mid–19th century, an era when a tropical aesthetic tinged with romanticism began asserting itself across coastal Latin America. On the second floor, you can see the meeting hall of the city council and enjoy a view of the plaza from the balcony during regular hours (Mon–Fri 9am–5pm). Farther down Calle 61 is the **Museo de la Ciudad (City Museum).** It faces the side of the cathedral and occupies the former church of San Juan de Dios. An exhibit outlining the

THE YUCATÁN PENINSULA

→ **La Prosperidad** This bar features plenty of local wannabe pop stars, who go well with lots of beer on tap and servings of small Mexican snacks, known as *botanas.* It's handy to start your night off here with some jalapeño poppers or chicken tortilla soup mixed with bubblegum sweet pop songs before heading out to a louder club later. *Calle 53 no. 491 at Calle 56.* ☎ *999/924-1407.*

Best → **La Trova** ★★★ Trova music is dreamy bolero music that hails from the Yucatán. Usually sung by a trio of troubadours, and always about love, this music is as sexy today as it was in its heyday 50 years ago, especially in the dark red-lit interior of La Trova, which was recently and rightly awarded the title of "the most romantic place in the Mérida." Though this type of music hails from the 1940s and 1950s, the velvet-voiced performers here make it feel fresh. While you're grooving to the music inside the posh club, you can also try one of the many fine tequilas they have behind the bar, followed by chasers of sangrita, a spicy fresh-squeezed tomato juice that puts V8 to shame. *Calles 60 and 57, in the Hotel Merida Misión.* ☎ *999/938-0657.*

history of Mérida will be of interest to those curious about the city; there is explanatory text in English. Hours are Monday to Friday from 10am to 2pm and 4 to 8pm, Saturday and Sunday from 10am to 2pm. Admission is, of course, free.

Heading north from Plaza Mayor up **Calle 60,** you'll see many of Mérida's old churches and squares. Several stores along Calle 60 sell gold-filigree jewelry, pottery, clothing, and folk art. A stroll along this street leads to the Parque Santa Ana and continues to the fashionable boulevard Paseo de Montejo.

The definition of the perfect path for an evening stroll, the expansive avenue **Paseo de Montejo** that runs north-south starting at Calle 47, 7 blocks north and 2 blocks east of the main square, is lined by grand mansions that were built by the ruling plantation owners in the early 1900s to deliberately show off the wealth of Mérida's finest to visitors. During the revolution, most of that wealth was redistributed, and the majority of the mansions are now home to businesses and banks. Today, this is the fashionable part of town, with many restaurants, trendy dance clubs, and expensive hotels. Of the mansions that survived, the most notable is the **Palacio Cantón,** which houses the **Museo Regional de Antropología** (p. 298).

Walking from the center of downtown and down Paseo de Montejo till you reach the intersection of the Paseo and Avenida Colon will take you past a number of lovely outdoor cafes, dance clubs, and restaurants. The Hyatt and the Fiesta Americana Hotel (both overrated, major splurge hotels), are on that corner, and the complex surrounding the Fiesta Americana is a huge mall catering to visitors with lots of tourist services, shops, and airline offices.

At the end of the Paseo de Montejo, where it meets Calle 34, is a 1956 monument to the motherland, complete with a reflecting pool, which adds a strong Indigenous finish to the colonial walkway. It's a good example of both the neo-Maya style, and the nationalist architectural movements of the mid–20th century.

MTV Best → **Mambo Café** ★★ The Mambo Café in Mérida is my favorite of all the country's Mambos, and they're all pretty wild. Ask any local in any city that has one and you'll be told that the name Mambo Café is synonymous with the sort of night when you wear down the heels of your shoes. This location has live salsa music from Cuba, the Dominican Republic, and other hot zones, and they change the line-up every night, so you can return again and again and never get bored. The stage in Mérida is set up to look like a setting sun—the band plays inside an illuminated orb and the spotlights shine through holes set strategically in the "sun's" shell to make them extend into the club like rays of sunlight. Finally, here's a chance to wear your sunglasses at night. *Calle 21 no. 527, Mezzanine 2.* ☎ *999/987-7533 or 999/987-7534. www.mambocafe.com.mx.*

Sightseeing

FESTIVALS/EVENTS

Though most of the opportunities for dancing in the streets in Mérida are not planned too far in advance, here is a rundown of typical regular weekly festivities:

MONDAY: *Vaquería regional,* traditional music and dancing to celebrate the

Vaquerías feast, was associated originally with the branding of cattle on Yucatecan haciendas. Among the featured performers are dancers with trays of bottles or filled glasses on their heads—a sight to see.

TUESDAY: Mérida has a world-class orchestra, and you can watch them play for free on Tuesday nights, at 9pm in Parque Santiago, Calle 59 at Calle 72. The orchestra often slips out of their classical repertoire, and performs Latin crowd pleasers and big band show stoppers from the jazz age instead.

WEDNESDAY: At 9pm in the Teatro Peón Contreras, Calle 60 at Calle 57, the University of Yucatán Ballet Folklórico presents "Yucatán and Its Roots." Admission is $50. You can see a better show by the same troupe at the Noche Mexicana for free on Saturday night.

THURSDAY: Yucatecan *trova* music (boleros, baladas) and dance are presented at the Serenata in Parque Santa Lucía at 9pm.

FRIDAY: Skip the city's scheduled performances and stroll the streets around the main plaza. You'll be sure to find some rocking parties, and musicians performing more contemporary music.

SATURDAY: Noche Mexicana, at the park at the beginning of Paseo de Montejo, starts at 9pm. It features performers demonstrating traditional Mexican dance and music, from the youth ballet to a group with over 30 indigenous percussion instruments. Great finger foods, ice cream, and cheap beer are on sale. This is also an ideal place to pick up reasonably priced handicrafts at the many stalls that set up a few hours before the show.

SUNDAY: Each Sunday from 9am to 9pm, there's a not-to-be-missed fair called *Mérida en Domingo* (Mérida on Sunday). The main plaza and a section of Calle 60 from El Centro to Parque Santa Lucía close to traffic for over 12 hours from early in the morning to just before dark, in order to fill with people of all ages eating snacks from the booths (you can get a home-cooked meal for about $80) and watching the diverse productions of music and dance. Smaller shows that sometimes involve comedy or edgier themes also take place in many of the smaller plazas around the city, such as the Parque Hidalgo or Parque Santa Lucia.

MAJOR ATTRACTIONS

Archaeological, architectural, and art junkies will all be in heaven in this thriving metropolis where the facades of the past harbor contemporary museums within their interiors, and every attraction is within walking distance and either free or under fifty pesos for admission. (And I haven't even mentioned how close the ruins of Chichén Itzá and Uxmal are.)

Most of Mérida's attractions are within walking distance from the downtown area (see the box above for walking itineraries). To see a larger area of the city, take a popular **bus tour** by **Transportadora Carnaval.** The owner bought a few buses, painted them bright colors, pulled out the windows, raised the roof several inches, and installed wooden benches so that the buses remind you of the folksy buses of coastal Latin America, known as *chivas* in Colombia and Venezuela or as *guaguas* in other places. You can find these buses on the corner of calles 60 and 55 (next to the church of Santa Lucía) at 10am, 1pm, 4pm, and 7pm. The tour costs $70 per person and lasts 2 hours.

FREE → Cathedral de San Ildefonso

★ You'll spot the tall stone cross sticking up from this cathedral many blocks from its location in the main plaza, so it comes in handy with directions. In addition to serving as a great compass in a pinch, San

Ildefonso, built in 1561, is the oldest cathedral in North America. The towering church cost $300,000 (US$2,700) when it was constructed. The people of Mérida are very proud of the fact that local Indian peasants contributed to the cost and provided the raw materials and the labor to build the cathedral—which means that the cathedral, unlike many in Mexico, is not a relic of Spanish colonialism but a testament to the local people.

There are three separate chapels on the inside; look for the one with the small statue of Christ on the altar. This chapel is dedicated to the Christ of the Blisters, and its statue of Jesus is a replica of one that was carved from the holy wood of a tree. (The tree was struck by lightning but did not burn, and later emerged only "blistered but not burnt" from a church fire. The original statue was destroyed when the church was attacked by revolutionary soldiers in 1915.)

You can't miss the wooden "Unity of Christ" at the front of the main room; this is the largest crucifix on the continent, with a body of Christ that stands at over 7.8m (26 ft.), and a cross measuring 12m (40 ft.). Over the small door on the right, there is an interesting painting of the chief of the Xiu people, Ah Kukum Tutul Xiu, in peaceful negotiations with the Spanish colonialists. ***Note:*** Be sure to visit the side chapel, which is hidden and has to be entered from a separate door outside. Inside it, there is a life-size diorama of the last supper and a towering mannequin of Jesus with a crown of thorns on his head and a red velvet cloak. *Calle 60 at Calle 61 on the Plaza Mayor. No phone. Free admission. Mon–Sat 9am–2pm and 4–6pm; Sun 9am–2pm.*

FREE → **Casa del Pueblo** It's a long walk to get to this overlooked memorial to Mexico's revolutionary leaders, but well worth the trip to the other side of the city. The entrance to the building is marked by a 4.5m (15-ft.) sculpture of the socialist organizer Felipe Carrilo Puerto. In the center of the courtyard, you'll find a circle of bronze busts fabricated in differing styles by some of Mexico's most famous sculptors. The subject matter is exclusively leftie, from Mexican revolutionary Emilio Zapata, to former Yucatán governor Victor Manuel Cervera Pacheco (who died in 2004 and still had wreaths of fresh flowers surrounding his statue when I visited years later). Current leftist leaders still have their offices on the second floor of the building. *Calle 35 at Calle 68. No phone. Free admission. No set hours.*

FREE → **Museo de Arte Contemporaneo Ateneo de Yucatán (The Contemporary Art Museum)** ★ Mérida is known internationally for its sculpture collection, and sculpture lovers will find lots to admire at this first-rate museum of contemporary art. Revolutionary artists of all sorts will be pleased with the history of the museum, which was originally the ruling bishop's palace, and was appropriated for the arts as a result of the revolution of 1915. Today, the plaza and outdoor gardens of this large mansion are filled with contemporary sculptures in a variety of media. The eight galleries upstairs strike an impressive balance between permanent and visiting collections, which read like a who's-who of Latin art. Permanent galleries include large collections of works by Fernando Garcia Ponce, Manuel Gonzalez, Miguel A. Alamilla, and Gabriel Ramirez Aznar. The Sala de Historia del Arte (Room of Art History) contains a mind-boggling collection of rare works by Frida Kahlo, Diego Rivera, Goya, and Chagall, though you may be disappointed to learn that they are all just high-quality reproductions placed there for historical reference, and not the real thing. In keeping with a cute tradition practiced at lots of Mexican museums, there's even a gallery of children's artwork. *At the corner of calles 60 and 63. ☎ 999/928-3236. Free admission. Wed–Mon 10am–6pm.*

MTV Best → **Museo Regional de Antropología** ★★★ This museum is a must see for anyone even slightly intrigued by Maya culture. In the renovated mansion "Palace Canton" along the Paseo de Montejo, the beautiful building is full of Maya artifacts, accompanied by clearly written English explanations of Maya agriculture, trade routes, art, astronomy, and other ways in which they were one of the most advanced civilizations on the planet during their reign.

If you've ever been pierced or tattooed, you're sure to find the vividly curated exhibit on Maya body modification fascinating. The glass cases here display beautiful jade and bone earrings that would astonish even professional piercers. Other impressive artifacts include real skulls that have been elongated and flattened to conform to ancient beauty standards, as well as full sets of teeth that are drilled with holes, filled with jade, and sharpened into spikes. The bones, jewelry, and other sacred objects are artfully presented with detailed illustrations that allow you to take in a lot of information without having to try too hard. I found everything in this museum to be 100% interesting, especially after visiting the ruins of Chichén Itzá. *Museo Regional de Anthropologia, Palacio Canton, Paseo de Montejo 485 at Calle 43. ☎/fax 999/923-0557. palacio.canton@inah.gob.mx. Admission $33. Mon–Sat 11am–5pm; Sun noon–3pm.*

FREE → **Palacio de Gobierno Government House)** This massive mint green palace on Calle 61 was appropriated in 1892, but has born witness to historical events since the invasion of the pro-absolutists in 1815. Adorning the walls of the outer courtyard are many murals depicting scenes of Maya and Mexican history and legend by the artist Fernando Castro Pacheco. The walls of the second floor are decorated with a series of more spectacular murals that also speak to these themes. The grand hall, where one can stand in the middle of the graphically painted murals and almost literally absorb the whole narrative of Mexican history, beginning with the exploitation of the Indians and leading up to the revolution, is worth a visit if only because it proves once and for all that a picture can tell a thousand words. *On the north side of the zocalo. No phone. Free admission. Mon–Sat 8am–8pm; Sun 9am–5pm.*

FREE → **Casa de Montejo** When you're walking around the Plaza Mayor, you can't miss the bright orange facade of the early-19th-century Casa de Montejo, with its shocking carvings of conquistadores stepping on the heads of silently screaming Indian chiefs. Though the palacio was built by the imperialist Montejo family for whom the Paseo de Montejo is named, it is fitting that the expressions on the faces of the conquistadores look guilty and confused as opposed to triumphant (perhaps they shouldn't have hired Indians to carve pictures of Indians being conquered). These days, the palace functions as a bank, but the bank managers are happy to let you stroll around the lobby and lush garden in the courtyard during business hours. *Calle 63 in the Plaza Mayor. No phone. Free admission. Mon–Fri 9am–5pm.*

Playing Outside

Mérida is a decidedly urban destination, so other than its parks, there aren't too many adventure options in town. Plenty of outdoorsy road trip options await, though. For a beach escape, go to the port of **Progreso,** Mérida's weekend beach resort. This is

Siesta Time

Meridanos observe the tradition of a midday siesta more religiously than locals in resort towns (it's too hot not to sleep here in the middle of the day). Most businesses and shops are closed from 2pm to 4pm. Take advantage of this and have a relaxing siesta yourself, even if yours is just by the pool.

where Meridanos have their vacation houses and where they come in large numbers in July and August. From Mérida, buses to **Progreso** leave from the bus station at Calle 62 no. 524, between calles 65 and 67, every 15 minutes, starting at 5am. The trip takes almost an hour and costs $30.

Recently, the Yucatán Peninsula has also seen an explosion of companies that organize nature and adventure tours. One well-established outfit with a great track record is **Ecoturismo Yucatán,** Calle 3 no. 235, Col. Pensiones, 97219 Mérida (☎ **999/920-2772;** fax 999/925-9047; www.ecoyuc.com). Alfonso and Roberta Escobedo create itineraries to meet just about any special or general interest. Alfonso has been creating adventure and nature tours for more than a dozen years. Specialties include archaeology, birding, natural history, and kayaking. The company also offers day trips that explore contemporary Maya culture and life in villages in the Yucatán. Package and customized tours are available.

Shopping

Mérida is *the* place to shop in the Yucatán for cheap, locally made, authentic Mexican arts and crafts. The city is known for hammocks, *guayaberas* (lightweight men's shirts worn untucked), and Panama hats. Mérida is also the place to pick up prepared *adobo,* a pastelike mixture of ground *achiote* seeds (annatto), oregano, garlic, masa, and other spices used as a marinade for making dishes such as *cochinita pibil* (pit-baked pork). Simply mix the paste with sour orange to a soupy consistency before applying to the meat. Try it on chicken for *pollo pibil.*

MARKETS

In addition to the many boutiques and craft stores that line Mérida's streets, the city is famous for its old-fashioned open air markets, where you can find everything from fresh fruits and vegetables to handmade silver jewelry for a fraction of what it costs in any old boring store. These markets can be found in many corners of the city, but here is a brief list of some of the best:

Garja Rejon Bazar, on the corner of calles 60 and 65, is often referred to affectionately by locals as "La Plaza Pequena" (The Little Plaza), and it offers the most affordable local clothes, jewelry, and crafts. It's famous for its *maqueches,* or beetle shells enameled and embellished with jewels, then turned into pins or charms—these buggy beauties make great gifts for any eccentric friends back home. **Lucas de Galvez Market,** on calles 56 between 67 and 69, has plenty of crafts, but it's better regarded for its outrageous varieties of local fruits and vegetables, especially chiles. This is also the best place in town to buy sauces and spices, all made from scratch.

The **Maya Handicrafts House** on the corner of calles 60 and 63, has unique crafts that are more than a few notches above the rest. You'll find one of a kind art objects here that you won't find anywhere else, including forged iron, handmade candles, carved wood, art sculpted from recycled paper, and jewelry made by contemporary artists in unusual designs. It's also a hot spot for locally inspired yet contemporary clothing.

BOUTIQUES

→ **Artisanias "Ah Kin Pech"** ★★★ This is my favorite store in town for hammocks, jewelry, and hand painted knickknacks out of many, many stores that sell similar wares. The owner will bargain down to some of the lowest prices in town, and all of the goods are quality and handmade in the Yucatán. I have to admit that the logo—featuring one hammock supporting the weight of a shirtless man sandwiched between two bikini-clad beauties—also helps this store stand out from the rest. *Calle 59 no. 504, between calles 60 and 62.* ☎ *999/930-9871.*

→ **Frida Boutique** The two Frida Boutique stores in town try to capture Frida Kahlo's free spirit with their selection of flirty dresses, trendy jeans, lacey tanks, and plenty of polka-dotted items. Though Frida expressed herself in more traditional Mexican clothes, I think she would approve. Frida was always a fan of sticking one's neck out, and all of the alluring plunging necklines available in this boutique make that task all that easier. *Main store: Calle 62 no. 498, between calles 59 and 63.* ☎ *999/928-5158. Second store: Calle 61 no. 497 Local 1, between calles 58 and 60.* ☎ *999/923-3565.*

→ **Guayaberas Jack** When it comes to linen (a breathable fabric that's essential in humid Mérida), nobody does it better than Guayaberas. The store excels at guayaberas, loose, linen button-downs that run the gamut from formal to casual. Like a Mexican version of Hawaiian shirts, they make a great off-beat addition to any comfort-loving guy's wardrobe. Guayaberas are literally available on every street corner in Mérida, but Guayaberas has the best fabric (not too thin, not too thick) and the most helpful staff. The store also stocks amazing embroidered Mexican dresses for women—compared to the shapeless moo-moos sold on the street, the linen dresses here are more tailored and hip. *Calle 61 no. 500 at Calle 60.* ☎ *999/923-8493. www.guayaberasjack.com.mx.*

→ **Libros Usados Cecilia** ★ Libros Usados Cecilia (Cecilia's Used Books) has a better reading selection than any of the city's new book stores, which mostly stock copies of the *Da Vinci Code* and other Dan Brown novels. Though on the outside this place looks more like a dusty garage than a treasure trove, Cecilia's got more than a few $10 classics and contemporary best-sellers piled inside her street-side junk shop. Plus, Cecilia will trade you a book for a book, or probably even for an old hat if she likes the look of it. She also has an eclectic mix of records, antiques, and other junk shop finds jumbled together for devoted treasure seekers of all sorts. *Calle 61, between calles 62 and 64. No phone.*

→ **Masud** ★ If you hate synthetic fabrics but love sexy dresses, you owe it to yourself to view Roberto Masud's collection. Forget about all your assumptions of linen being about as flattering as a paper bag. Masud stocks gorgeous dresses, from $400 mini-halters that you can wear at a club, to $500 full wedding gowns, all made of 100% linen. The quality of the products is stellar for the price, and the designer's mission seems to be to create comfortable, unusual dresses that complement every woman's curves. All the dresses, skirts, and tops are hand sewn and often incorporate a spray of white or black lace into the design. *Calle 60 no. 496, between calles 59 and 61.* ☎ *999/923-8132. abimeri@sureste.com.*

MTV Best → **Miniaturas** ★★★ This cash-only store is so much fun that you should stop in even if you have no intention of buying anything. On the other hand, if you are looking for cheap, one-of-a-kind souvenirs, this could be your one-stop shop. The politically inclined will smile at all of the miniatures of politicians and CEOs with skulls for faces caught in the act of every type of dirty dealing. From traditional Mexican scenes to barroom brawls, the 3-D cartoons on sale here are smart and often hysterical. I got a bride and groom with skull heads driving a beat-up jeep for my married mechanic friends, some hideously funny male mermaids for my sailing buddies, and one of a chubby Clinton-esque skeleton receiving some "political favors" in the oval office for my protester pals. *Calle 59, between calles 60 and 62. No phone.*

Chichén Itzá

The fabled ruins of Chichén Itzá (no, it doesn't rhyme with "chicken pizza"; the accents are on the last syllables: Chee-*chen* Eet-*zah*) are a World Heritage site and the Yucatán's best-known ancient monuments. They are plenty hyped, but Chichén is truly worth seeing. Walking among these stone platforms, pyramids, and ball courts gives you an appreciation for this ancient civilization that books cannot convey. The city is built on a scale that evokes a sense of wonder: To fill the plazas during one of the mass rituals that occurred here a millennium ago would have required an enormous number of celebrants. Even today, with the mass flow of tourists through these plazas, the ruins feel empty.

When visiting the ruins, keep in mind that much of what is said about the Maya (especially by tour guides, who speak in tones of utter certainty) is merely educated guessing. This much we do know: The area was settled by farmers as far back as the 4th century A.D. The first signs of an urban society appear in the 7th century in the construction of stone temples and palaces in the traditional Puuc Maya style. These buildings can be found in the "Old Chichén" section of the city. Construction continued for a couple hundred years. In the 10th century (the post-Classic era), the city came under the rule of the Itzáes, who arrived from central Mexico by way of the Gulf Coast. They may have been a mix of highland Toltec Indians (the people who built the city of Tula in central Mexico) and lowland Putún Maya, who were a commercial people thriving on trade between the different regions of the area.

In the following centuries the city saw its greatest growth. Most of the grand architecture was built during this age in a style that is clearly Toltec influenced. The new rulers may have been refugees from Tula. There is a mythological story told in pre-Columbian central Mexico about a fight that occurred between the gods Quetzalcoatl and Tezcatlipoca, which resulted in Quetzalcoatl being forced to leave his homeland and venture east. This may be a shorthand account of a civil war in Tula, different religious factions, with the losers fleeing to the Yucatán, where they were welcomed by the local Maya. Over time, the Itzaés adopted more and more the ways of the Maya. Sometime at the end of the 12th century, the city was captured by its rival, the city of Mayapán.

A visit to Chichén Itzá means so much more than learning about history, through. It's also a chance to take in some beautiful and varied wildlife. During my walk through the lush tropical forest surrounding the ruins, I saw about five different species of tropical butterflies; iguanas with colorful skins; exotic birds; and mosquitoes of Jurassic Park–worthy proportions. (Consider yourself officially warned, and bring bug repellent.) Essentially, a trip to Chichén Itzá combines all of the best elements of a museum visit and a nature hike on steroids. Don't expect to be able to climb the ancient walls here, though—that's been deemed unsafe.

Basics

ORIENTATION

The Chichén Itzá site occupies 6.5 sq. km (2½ sq. miles), and it takes most of a day to see all the ruins, which are open daily from 8am to 5pm. Service areas are open from 8am to 10pm. Admission is $100, free for children under age 12. A video camera permit costs $40. Parking is extra. *You can use your ticket to reenter on the same day.* The cost of admission includes the **sound-and-light show,** which is worth seeing since you're being charged for it anyway. The show, held at 7 or 8pm depending on the season, is in Spanish, but headsets are available for rent in several languages. The narrative is okay, but the real reason for seeing the show is the lights, which show off the beautiful geometry of the city. You'll have a very good time if you bring some trusty tequila and a soft blanket to lay-out on the grass, and if you approach the experience with the easy-going attitude you'd bring to any outdoor concert.

The large, modern visitor center, at the main entrance where you pay the admission charge, is beside the parking lot and consists of a museum, an auditorium, a restaurant, a bookstore, and bathrooms. You can see the site on your own or with a licensed guide who speaks English or Spanish. Guides usually wait at the entrance and charge around $450 for one to six people. Although the guides frown on it, there's nothing wrong with approaching a group of people who speak the same language and asking if they want to share a guide. These guides can point out architectural details often missed when visiting on your own. Chichén Itzá has two parts: the central (new) zone, which shows distinct Toltec influence, and the southern (old) zone, with mostly Puuc architecture.

Getting There & Getting Around

BY BUS From Mérida, there are three first-class ADO (p. 282) buses per day that make the 2-hour-long journey. There are also a couple of first-class buses to Cancún and Playa. Otherwise, you can buy a second-class bus ticket to Valladolid and a first-class from there.

From Mérida, Playa del Carmen, and Cancún, there are many tour companies that will transport you from your hotel to Chichén Itzá, along with providing a buffet lunch and a professional tour guide at the ruins. The cost is around $750 from Playa and Cancún, and about $200 less from Mérida. Since a tour of the ruin itself is a hefty $450, it might make sense to take a package tour. It will save you from schlepping to and from bus stations, and if you were going to hire a tour guide at the ruins and buy lunch anyway, it won't cost much more money. Check out www.bestday.com for info on area operators.

BY CAR Chichén Itzá is on old Highway 180 between Mérida and Cancún. The fastest way to get there from either city is to take the *autopista/cuoata* (or toll road). The toll is $80 from Mérida, $200 from Cancún. Once you have exited the autopista, you will turn onto the road leading to the village of Pisté. Once in the village, you'll reach a T junction at Highway 180 and turn left to get to the ruins. The entrance to the ruins is well marked. If you stay on the highway for a few kilometers more, you'll come to the exit for the hotel zone at kilometer marker 121 (before you reach the turn-off, you'll pass the eastern entrance to Mayapán, which is usually closed). Chichén is 1½ hours from Mérida and 2½ hours from Cancún.

Chichén Itzá Ruins

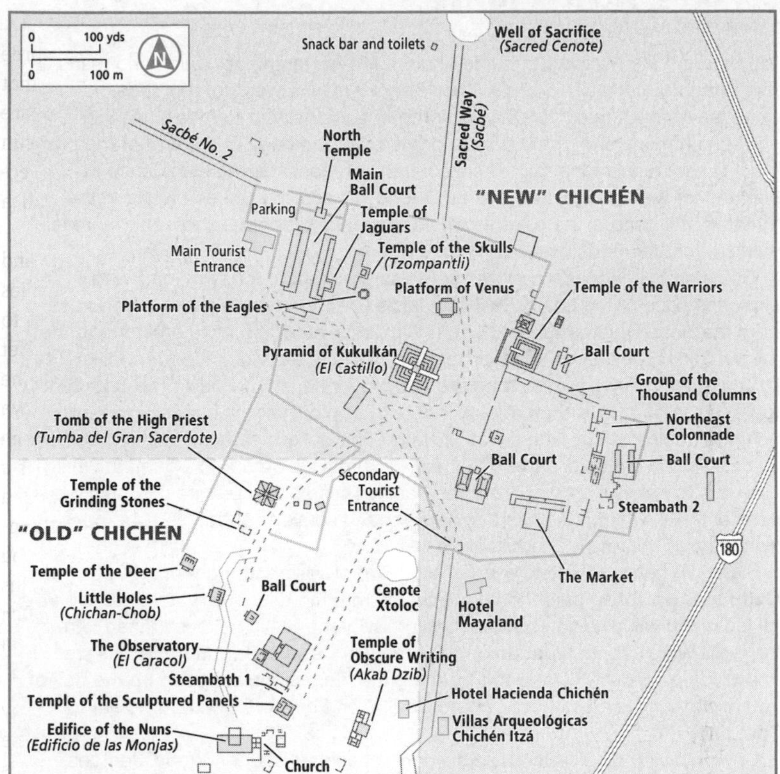

Sleeping

In my opinion, Chichén Itzá is best visited as a day trip. There's little nightlife in the area, so if that's a priority for you, you may want to head back to Cancún or Mérida after a day in the jungle. Also, the huge demand for accommodations near the ruins has driven prices up, so you won't find any rock-bottom deals. That said, if you want to avoid heavy tour bus crowds, you should consider staying in Chichén so that you can explore the ruins early in the morning before the big influx of tourists, or later in the evening after most of the buses have departed. That way, you can also avoid the brutal midday sun.

→ **Hotel Dolores Alba** Two swimming pools make this motel a refreshing value in the humid heat of the jungle. The rooms and beds are large and breezy; if you're with a group, you can fit four in a room with two double beds quite comfortably and conserve your cash. The restaurant is cheaper than most in this tourist saturated small town, and there is free transportation to and fro the ruins to save you time trying to find parking in the packed lots. A small Mexican restaurant on-site offers room service until midnight. To reach the Dolores Alba, head east down Highway 180 (towards Valliodad), and you will see the hotel on your right after about 3km (2 miles). *Carretera Merida, Valliodad Km 122.*

Cenotes: Portals to the Underworld

Itzá means "sacred people" in the ancient Mayan language. *Chich'en* means the "opening of a well," but also the "opening to the world of the gods." Because of this, the city's name is sometimes translated to mean, "At the entrance to the world of the gods," or also, "At the edge of the well of the people." These translations make sense when you consider the prevalence of *cenotes,* or wellsprings, in the area. Due to the scarcity of fresh water in the Yucatán, the cenotes here were considered sacred spots—doors to the underworld where the gods dwelled.

These days, the area's cenotes serve as great spots for swimming and exploring. One of the best is **Ik-Kil,** a large cenote on the highway just across from the Hotel Dolores Alba, 2.5km (1½ miles) east of the main entrance to the ruins. It's deep, with lots of steps leading down to the water's edge. Unlike Dzitnup (see below), these steps are easy to manage. The view from both the top and the bottom is dramatic, with lots of tropical vegetation and curtains of hanging tree roots stretching all the way to the water's surface. Take your swimsuit and enjoy the cold water. The best swimming is before 11:30am, at which time bus tours start arriving from the coast. These bus tours are the main business of Ik-Kil, which also has a restaurant and souvenir shops. Ik-Kil is open from 8am to 5pm daily. Admission is $60.

Eight kilometers (5 miles) west of the town of Valliodad, right off 180, **Cenote Dzitnup** is a cooling place to take a break from the ruin. The water here is crystal clear and will give you new insight into why the Maya believed these refreshing wells were sacred. Just down the road lies **Cenote Sammula,** a less well known dipping spot that's good to hit up if Dzitnip is too crowded on the day of your visit. Admission to both cenotes is $20 and they are open from 7am to 7pm daily.

Cenote diving isn't really possible here; check out Hidden World Centoes (p. 264) to arrange that.

THE YUCATÁN PENINSULA

☎ 985/858-1555. www.doloresalba.com. $500 double. MC, V. Amenities: Restaurant; laundromat; laundry service; outdoor pool; room service until 9pm; tour desk. In room: A/C, TV, safe.

➜ **Villa Archaelogicas Chichén Itzá** ★ Two massive royal poinciana trees tower above the grounds, and bougainvillea drapes the walls of this quiet resort, situated around a large swimming pool. The beds are packed into cozy rooms, which is a deal breaker if you're over 2m (6 ft.) tall (walls border the head and foot of the beds). Most rooms have two beds (usually one double and one single) and comfortably fit three people of moderate to short stature. All rates include continental breakfast, but hungry travelers can upgrade to hot breakfast plus lunch or dinner for $190 a day, or opt for three full meals for $290. *Zona Arqueologica, right before the ruins. ☎ 985/851-0034 or 800/258-2633 in U.S. $900 double. AE, MC, V. Amenities: Restaurants with bar; Internet in lobby; pool; tennis courts; travel agency. In room: A/C.*

Eating

If you come to Chichén on a tour bus, you will probably get a meal ticket to one of the many big buffet restaurants in town that cater to tourists. Most of these offer authentic Yucatecan cuisine mixed with a few familiar options like spaghetti with tomato sauce (always a mistake in Mexico) or burgers. Many also include touristy entertainment featuring traditional dances of the region. Here are a few more intimate options:

➔ **Café Ruinas** DINER The only cafeteria on-site at the ruins, this place is actually not as expensive as you would think, and provides a cooling break from the sweltering temperature outside. A full frozen cocktail menu, plus crowd pleasers like sandwiches, eggs, and popular Yucatecan specialties, make this a very convenient (and wonderfully air-conditioned) spot to refuel and refresh. For those with shallower pockets, a number of stalls are just outside the main cafe that sell frozen treats, iced coffee, shaved fruit ices, and other cooling libations. *Just down the road from Chichén Itzá. No phone. Main courses $50–$150. AE, MC, V. Daily 9am–6pm.*

➔ **Poxil** MEXICAN Poxil is your best bet for cheap dining near the ruins. The menu features simple and well prepared Mexican and Yucatecan classics such as *pollo en escabeche* (chicken in acidic marinade). Right after the west entrance to Piste, this place stays remarkably free of crowds, even at peak lunch hours. *Calle 15 no. 52, Piste. No phone. Main courses $30–$50. No credit cards. Daily 8am–9pm.*

Exploring the Ruins of Chichén Itzá

EL CASTILLO ★★ As you enter from the tourist center, the magnificent 25m (82-ft.) El Castillo pyramid (also called the Pyramid of Kukulkán) will be straight ahead across a large open area. It was built with the Maya calendar in mind. The four stairways leading up to the central platform each have 91 steps, making a total of 364, which when you add the central platform equals the 365 days of the solar year. On either side of each stairway are nine terraces, which makes 18 on each face of the pyramid, equaling the number of months in the Maya solar calendar. On the facing of these terraces are 52 panels (we don't know how they were decorated), which represent the 52-year cycle when both the solar and religious calendars would become realigned. The pyramid's alignment is such that on the **spring** or **fall equinox** (Mar 21 or Sept 21) a curious event occurs. The setting sun casts the shadow of the terraces onto the ramp of the northern stairway. A diamond pattern is formed, suggestive of the geometric designs on some snakes. Slowly it descends into the earth. The effect is more conceptual than visual, and to view it requires being with a large crowd. It's much better to see the ruins on other days when it's less crowded.

El Castillo was built over an earlier structure. A narrow stairway at the western edge of the north staircase leads inside that structure, where there is a sacrificial altar-throne—a red jaguar encrusted with jade. I'd been told that visitors are sometimes allowed inside the inner temple; however the day I visited, the whole area around El Castillo was disappointingly roped off. Even if you can no longer go inside, though, it's still amazing to look at from outside.

JUEGO DE PELOTA (MAIN BALL COURT) Northwest of El Castillo is Chichén's main ball court, the largest and best preserved anywhere, and only one of nine ball courts built in this city. Carved on both walls of the ball court are scenes showing Maya figures dressed as ball players and decked out in heavy protective padding. The carved scene also shows a headless player kneeling with blood shooting from his neck; another player holding the head looks on.

Players on two teams tried to knock a hard rubber ball through one of the two

THE YUCATÁN PENINSULA

stone rings placed high on either wall, using only their elbows, knees, and hips. According to legend, the losing players paid for defeat with their lives. However, some experts say the victors were the only appropriate sacrifices for the gods. One can only guess what the incentive for winning might be in that case. Either way, the game must have been riveting, heightened by the wonderful acoustics of the ball court.

THE NORTH TEMPLE Temples are at both ends of the ball court. The North Temple has sculptured pillars and more sculptures inside, as well as badly ruined murals. The acoustics of the ball court are so good that from the North Temple, a person speaking can be heard clearly at the opposite end, about 135m (443 ft.) away.

TEMPLE OF JAGUARS Near the southeastern corner of the main ball court is a small temple with serpent columns and carved panels showing warriors and jaguars. Up the steps and inside the temple, a mural was found that chronicles a battle in a Maya village.

TZOMPANTLI (TEMPLE OF THE SKULLS) To the right of the ball court is the Temple of the Skulls, an obvious borrowing from the post-Classic cities of central Mexico. Notice the rows of skulls carved into the stone platform. When a sacrificial victim's head was cut off, it was impaled on a pole and displayed in a tidy row with others. Also carved into the stone are pictures of eagles tearing hearts from human victims. The total effect is a horrific (but really cool, like any good horror movie) monument to the bloodiness of warfare.

PLATFORM OF THE EAGLES Next to the Tzompantli, this small platform has reliefs showing eagles and jaguars clutching human hearts in their talons and claws, as well as a human head emerging from the mouth of a serpent. Some historians speculate that the animals are symbols of warriors in the act of sacrificing prisoners.

PLATFORM OF VENUS East of the Tzompantli and north of El Castillo, near the road to the Sacred Cenote, is the Platform of Venus. In Maya and Toltec lore, a feathered monster or a feathered serpent with a human head in its mouth represented Venus. This is also called the tomb of Chaac-Mool because a Chaac-Mool figure was discovered "buried" within the structure.

SACRED CENOTE Follow the dirt road (actually an ancient *sacbé,* or causeway) that heads north from the Platform of Venus; after 5 minutes you'll come to the great natural well that may have given Chichén Itzá (the Well of the Itzáes) its name. Historians believe the well was used for ceremonial purposes—sacrificial victims were thrown in. Anatomical research done early in the 20th century by Ernest A. Hooten showed that bones of both children and adults were found in the well.

Edward Thompson, who was the American consul in Mérida and a Harvard professor, purchased the ruins of Chichén early in the 20th century and explored the cenote with dredges and divers. His explorations exposed a fortune in gold and jade. Most of the riches wound up in Harvard's Peabody Museum of Archaeology and Ethnology—a matter that continues to disconcert Mexican classicists today. Excavations in the 1960s unearthed more treasure, and studies of the recovered objects detail offerings from throughout the Yucatán and even farther away.

TEMPLO DE LOS GUERREROS (TEMPLE OF THE WARRIORS) Due east of El Castillo is one of the most impressive structures at Chichén: the Temple of the Warriors, named for the carvings of warriors marching along its walls. It's also called the Group of the Thousand Columns for the rows of broken pillars that flank it. During a recent restoration, hundreds more of the columns were rescued from the rubble and put in place, setting off the temple more magnificently than ever. A figure of Chaac-Mool sits at the top of the temple, surrounded by impressive columns carved in relief to look like enormous feathered serpents. South of the temple was a square building that archaeologists call **El Mercado (The Market);** a colonnade surrounds its central court. Beyond the temple and the market in the jungle are mounds of rubble, parts of which are being reconstructed.

The main Mérida-Cancún highway once ran straight through the ruins of Chichén, and though it has been diverted, you can still see the great swath it cut. South and west of the old highway's path are more impressive ruined buildings.

TUMBA DEL GRAN SACERDOTE (TOMB OF THE HIGH PRIEST) Past the refreshment stand to the right of the path is the Tomb of the High Priest, which stood atop a natural limestone cave in which skeletons and offerings were found, giving the temple its name.

CASA DE LOS METATES (TEMPLE OF THE GRINDING STONES) This building, the next one on your right, is named after the concave corn-grinding stones the Maya used.

TEMPLO DEL VENADO (TEMPLE OF THE DEER) Past Casa de los Metates is this fairly tall though ruined building. The relief of a stag that gave the temple its name is long gone.

CHICHAN-CHOB (LITTLE HOLES) This next temple has a roof comb with little holes, three masks of the rain god Chaac, three rooms, and a good view of the surrounding structures. It's one of the oldest buildings at Chichén, built in the Puuc style during the late Classic period.

EL CARACOL (OBSERVATORY) Construction of the Observatory, a complex building with a circular tower, was carried out over centuries; the additions and modifications reflected the Maya's careful observation of celestial movements and their need for increasingly exact measurements. Through slits in the tower's walls, astronomers could observe the cardinal directions and the approach of the all-important spring and autumn equinoxes, as well as the summer solstice. The temple's name, which means "snail," comes from a spiral staircase within the structure.

On the east side of El Caracol, a path leads north into the bush to the **Cenote Xtoloc,** a natural limestone well that provided the city's daily water supply. If you see any lizards sunning there, they may well be *xtoloc,* the species for which this cenote is named.

TEMPLO DE LOS TABLEROS (TEMPLE OF PANELS) Just south of El Caracol are the ruins of a *temazcalli* (a steam bath) and the Temple of Panels, named for the carved panels on top. This temple was once covered by a much larger structure, only traces of which remain.

EDIFICIO DE LAS MONJAS (EDIFICE OF THE NUNS) If you've visited the Puuc sites of Kabah, Sayil, Labná, or Xlapak, the enormous nunnery here will remind you of the palaces at those sites. Built in the late Classic period, the new edifice was constructed over an older one. Suspecting that this was so, Le Plongeon, an archaeologist working early in the 20th century, put dynamite between the two and blew away part of the exterior, revealing the older structures within. You can still see the results of Le Plongeon's indelicate exploratory methods.

On the east side of the Edifice of the Nuns is **Anexo Este (annex)** constructed in highly ornate Chenes style with Chaac masks and serpents.

Chicle: The Maya Chewing Gum

In order to stave off dehydration during travel, the ancient Maya molded the sap of the Sapodilla tree into rubbery balls. Chewing these balls of sap, which they called "chicle," helped the Ancient Maya work up enough spit to lessen their thirst until they arrived at their destination point. Long after the end of the Maya civilization, the Maya people continued the tradition of chewing chicle. Modern gum as we know it was born when the Mexican General Antonio Lopez de Santa Ana contacted Thomas Adams, an American inventor, in 1869 with his idea to use chicle as a substitute for rubber. Although that scheme failed, Adams noticed that Santa Ana was chewing a piece of the chicle, and was impressed with the product's superiority to most paraffin-wax chewing gums in the U.S. at that time. Adams created what later became the Chiclet company using Santa Ana's chicle base, and the substance that the Maya had been chewing for thousands of years in the Yucatán became the foundation of the stuff we still pop in our mouths today. Some shops in Piste sell the original recipe of chicle, which looks like chicken jerky and tastes like old shoes. Do yourself a favor and skip that in favor of the modern incarnation.

LA IGLESIA (THE CHURCH) Next to the annex is one of the oldest buildings at Chichén, the Church. Masks of Chaac decorate two upper stories. Look closely, and you'll see other pagan symbols among the crowd of Chaacs: an armadillo, a crab, a snail, and a tortoise. These represent the Maya gods, called *bacah,* whose job it was to hold up the sky.

AKAB DZIB (TEMPLE OF OBSCURE WRITING) Beloved of travel writers, this temple lies east of the Edifice of the Nuns. Above a door in one of the rooms are some Mayan glyphs, which gave the temple its name because the writings have yet to be deciphered. In other rooms, traces of red handprints are still visible. Reconstructed and expanded over the centuries, Akab Dzib may be the oldest building at Chichén.

CHICHEN VIEJO (OLD CHICHEN) For a look at more of Chichén's oldest buildings, constructed well before the time of Toltec influence, follow signs from the Edifice of the Nuns southwest into the bush to Old Chichén, about 1km (1/2 mile) away. Be prepared for this trek with long pants, insect repellent, and a local guide. The attractions here are the **Templo de los Inscripciones Iniciales (Temple of the First Inscriptions),** with the oldest inscriptions discovered at Chichén, and the restored **Templo de los Dinteles (Temple of the Lintels),** a fine Puuc building.

Uxmal

Though Chichén Itzá gets more press, Uxmal is my favorite of all the interior Yucatán's Maya ruins. That's mainly because you can still ascend all the stairs and go inside all of the sacred, secret spaces, unlike at Chichén, where most of the goods have been roped-off to protect them from heavy foot traffic. In other words, a day at Uxmal is much more of an outdoor adventure—you get to climb and touch, instead of just standing back and admiring. Though Uxmal is smaller than

Uxmal Ruins

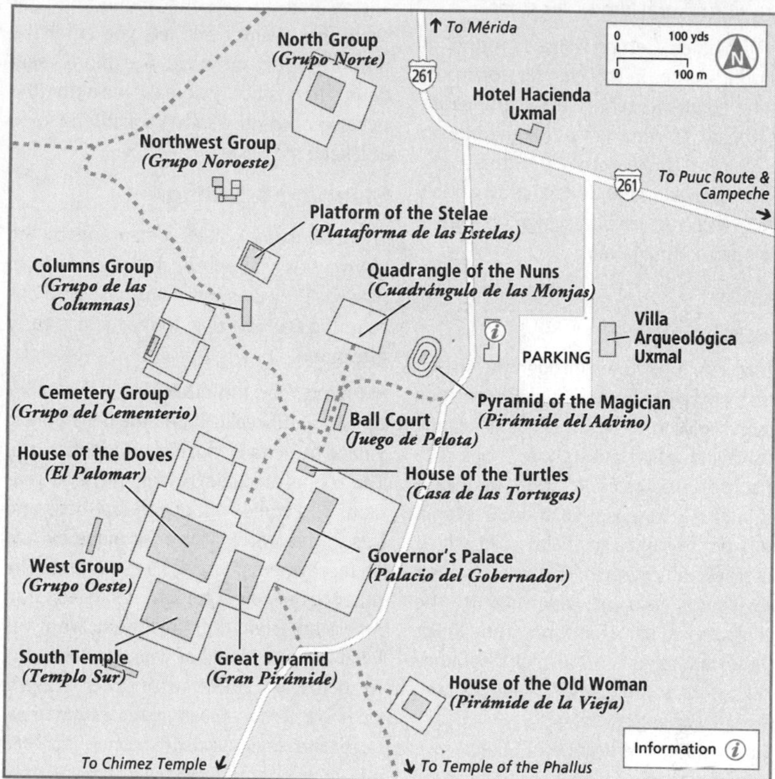

Chichén Itzá, the buildings themselves have much less of a uniform appearance. Unlike other sites in northern Yucatán, such as Chichén Itzá and Mayapán, Uxmal also isn't built on a flat plane. The builders worked into the composition of the ceremonial center an interplay of elevations that adds complexity.

The great building period here took place between A.D. 700 and 1000, when the population probably reached 25,000. After 1000, Uxmal fell under the sway of the Xiú princes (who may have come from central Mexico). In the 1440s, the Xiú conquered Mayapán, and not long afterward the age of the Maya ended with the arrival of the Spanish conquistadors.

Close to Uxmal, four smaller sites—**Sayil, Kabah, Xlapak,** and **Labná**—can be visited in quick succession. With Uxmal, these ruins are collectively known as the **Puuc route.**

Getting There & Getting Around

BY CAR Two routes go to Uxmal, about 80km (50 miles) south of Mérida. The most direct is Highway 261 via Umán and Muna. On the way, you can stop to see Hacienda Yaxcopoil, which is 30km (19 miles) from Mérida. If you have the time and want a more scenic route, try the meandering State Highway 18. This is sometimes referred to as the Convent Route, but all tourism hype aside, it makes for a pleasant drive with several interesting stops.

BY BUS See "Getting There & Around" in "Mérida," earlier in this chapter, for information about bus service between Mérida and Uxmal. To return, wait for the bus on the highway at the entrance to the ruins. To see the sound-and-light show, don't bother with regular buses; sign up with a tour operator in Mérida.

Basics

ORIENTATION

Entrance to the ruins is through the visitor center where you buy your tickets (two per person, hold on to both). It has a restaurant; toilets; a first-aid station; shops selling soft drinks, ice cream, film, batteries, and books; a state-run Casa de Artesanía (crafts house); and a small museum, which isn't very informative. The site is open daily from 8am to 5pm. Admission to the archaeological site is around $100, which includes admission to the nightly sound-and-light show. Bringing in a video camera costs $30. Parking costs $10.

Guides at the entrance of Uxmal give tours in a variety of languages and charge $400 for a single person or a group. The guides frown on unrelated individuals joining a group. They'd rather charge you as a solo visitor, but you can ask other English speakers if they'd like to join you in a tour and split the cost.

Included in the price of admission is a 45-minute **sound-and-light show,** staged each evening at 7pm. It's in Spanish, but headsets are available for rent for listening to the program in several languages. At $25, it's worth it to get the headset—you'll get to hear a tripped out rendition of the great war between the cities of Uxmal, Chichén Itzá, and Mayapan that accompanies all the cool lighting effects.

If you're staying the night in Uxmal, it is possible (and I think preferable) to get to the site late in the day and buy a ticket that allows you to see the sound-and-light show that evening and lets you enter the ruins the next morning to explore them before it gets hot. Just make sure that the ticket vendor knows what you intend to do and keep the ticket.

Sleeping & Eating

There are some palapa restaurants by the highway as you approach the ruins from Mérida. They do a lot of business with bus tours, so the best time to try them is early afternoon.

→ **Flycatcher Inn B&B** This pleasant little bed-and-breakfast is in the neighboring village of Santa Elena, just off Highway 261. The rooms are quiet, attractive, and spacious and come with queen-size beds and lots of decorative ironwork made by one of the owners, Santiago Domínguez. The other owner is Christine Ellingson, an American from the Northwest who has lived in Santa Elena for years and is happy to help her guests with their travels. *Carretera Uxmal–Kabah, 97840 Santa Elena. No phone. www.flycatcherinn.com. $40–$60 double, $70 suite. Rates include breakfast. No credit cards.*

Sightseeing

A TOUR OF THE RUINS

THE PYRAMID OF THE MAGICIAN

As you enter the ruins, note a *chultún,* or cistern, where Uxmal stored its water. Unlike most of the major Maya sites, Uxmal has no cenote to supply fresh water. The city's inhabitants were much more dependent on rainwater, and consequently venerated the rain god Chaac much more than in other places.

Rising in front of you is the Pirámide del Adivino or Pyramid of the Magician. If you've already been to Chichén Itzá, you may be astounded at its height—it's a full 6m (20 ft.) higher than the El Castillo

(p. 305). The name comes from a myth told to John Lloyd Stephens on his visit in the 19th century. It tells the story of a magician-dwarf who reached adulthood in a single day after being hatched from an egg, and who built this pyramid in one night.

Beneath the pyramid are five earlier structures. The pyramid has an oval base and rounded sides. You are looking at the east side. The main face is on the west side. Walk around the left or south side to see the front. The pyramid was designed such that the east side rises less steeply than the west side so that the crowning temples are shifted to the west of the central axis of the building, causing them to loom above the plaza below. The temple doorway's heavy ornamentation, a characteristic of the Chenes style, features 12 stylized masks of what many think to be a representation of the God Chaac.

THE NUNNERY QUADRANGLE From the plaza you're standing in, you want to go to the large Nunnery Quadrangle. Walk out the way you walked into the plaza, turn right, and follow the wall of this long stone building until you get to the building's main door—a corbelled arch that leads into the quadrangle. You'll find yourself in a plaza bordered on each side by stone buildings with elaborate facades. The 16th-century Spanish historian Fray Diego López de Cogullado gave the quadrangle its name when he decided that its layout resembled a Spanish convent.

The quadrangle does have a lot of small rooms, about the size of a nun's cell. You might poke your head into one just to see the shape and size of it, but don't bother trying to explore them all. These rooms were long ago abandoned to the swallows, which are almost always flying above the city. No interior murals or stucco work have been found here—at least, not yet. No, the richness of Uxmal lies in the stonework on its exterior walls.

The Nunnery is a great example of this. The first building your eye latches on to when you enter the plaza is the north building in front of you. It is the tallest, and the view from on top includes all the major buildings of the city, making it useful for the sound-and-light show. The central stairway is bordered by a common element in Puuc architecture, doorways supported by rounded columns. The remnants of the facade on the second level show elements used in the other three buildings and elsewhere throughout the city. There's a crosshatch pattern and a pattern of square curlicues, called a step-and-fret design, and the long-nosed god mask repeated vertically, used often to decorate the corners of buildings—what I call a Chaac stack. Though the facades of these buildings share these common elements and others, their composition varies. On the west building you'll see long feathered serpents intertwined at head and tail. A human head stares out from a serpent's open mouth. I've heard and read a number of interpretations of this motif, repeated elsewhere in Maya art, but they all leave me somewhat in doubt. And that's the trouble with symbols: They are usually the condensed expression of multiple meanings, so any one interpretation could be true, but only partially true.

THE BALL COURT Leaving the Nunnery by the same way you entered, you will see straight ahead a ball court. What would a Maya city be without a ball court? And this one is a particularly good representative of the hundreds found elsewhere in the Maya world. Someone has even installed a replica of one of the stone rings that were the targets for the players, who would make use of their knees, hips, and maybe their arms to strike a solid rubber ball (yes, the Maya knew about natural rubber and extracted latex from a couple of species of rubber trees). The inclined planes on both sides of the court were in play and obviously not an area for spectators, who are thought to have observed the game from atop the two structures.

THE GOVERNOR'S PALACE Continuing in the same direction (south), you come to the large raised plaza on top of which sits the Governor's Palace, running in a north-south direction. This is widely considered to be the most beautiful building in Uxmal, due to the hand-carved decoration covering nearly every inch of its outer walls. The surface area of the raised plaza measures 140m by 170m (459 ft. by 558 ft.), and it is raised about 10m (33 ft.) above the ground—quite a bit of earth-moving. Most of this surface is used as a ceremonial space facing the front (east side) of the palace.

What's great about the Govenor's Palace is that you can walk inside all of the grand chambers here, and really take in the highlights, like the double-headed jaguar throne in the center and a series of Chaac masks covering the building.

THE GREAT PYRAMID Behind the palace, the platform descends in terraces to another plaza with a large pyramid on its south side. This is known as the Great Pyramid. On top is the Temple of the Macaws, for the repeated representation of macaws on the face of the temple, and the ruins of three other temples. The view from the top is wonderful.

THE DOVECOTE This building is remarkable in that roof combs weren't a common feature of temples in the Puuc hills. Each of the combs of the dove's "tail" here feature stucco figures that are sculpted and painted to represent dignitaries who inhabited the city.

Northern Baja

Northern Baja, or Baja Norte, is unlike any other region in Mexico. It lays claim to a striking and bizarre blend of Mexican and American cultures, with the best wine south of California, the freshest seafood on the Pacific coast, and a landscape that's breathtakingly beautiful, but as the world's biggest transportation hub, it's also home to relentless hawkers playing to the thousands of tourists who come for a quick taste of "old Mexico." The land itself is a place of contrasts, too, spanning everything from hot deserts and cool oceans to manicured golf greens and craggy mountains.

For centuries, the only industries here existed to pander to the hunger of gringos. Whatever your weakness might be, you could scratch that itch at one of the bars, porn shops, or gambling casinos in Baja Norte. And to a large degree that's still true. Baja Norte is America's roommate, sleepy and compliant, a place where you can get your prescriptions filled at half the price, no questions asked, or ask that stripper for something a little more "personal," again, with no questions asked.

Tijuana is the biggest destination in Baja Norte. Some say that it could be the biggest city on the West Coast in 30 years if it continues the way it's going. It was once a sleepy village, but when prohibition came, it emerged as sort of a cut-rate Havana, with legalized gambling, prostitution, and all-ages alcohol. In the 1980s and 1990s, it became one of the country's original assembly factory sites. Today, as the city continues to globalize, all bets are off: Though still renowned for its hustling, carnival-like atmosphere, this border town is gradually developing into a more culturally diverse destination.

Baja Norte is far more than Tijuana with its sins and excesses, though. It's also **Ensenada**—more laid-back and provincial but also sweeter in character. Then there's **Rosarito Beach,** another tranquil, if more touristy, resort town. And then south of that is the wild coast of Pacific Mexico, a land of whales and surfers and unbridled beauty.

In some ways Baja Norte is the most welcoming of Mexican regions—it's certainly the most open to tourists—but don't let that make you too comfortable. Here nothing is as you expect, not the party scene, not the surfing, and not the people. Leave your preconceptions at the border and you might just learn to love the region for its complexity.

Best of Northern Baja

- **Best Dive Bar: El Dandy del Sur** is a classic Tijuana dive bar. You won't get much more than some bar stools and some cheap beer, but you also won't get any attitude. Though it's less than 40 years old, it feels like an old favorite because of the welcoming vibe. It's the sort of joint where regulars are hailed as they walk in from the street, but strangers are easily accommodated, too. See p. 328.
- **Best Scene Makers:** The loosely defined and multi-generational alternative art/fashion/music scene known as **MultiKulti** in Tijuana is part attitude, part Zeitgeist reference point. Its home is a burned out cinema off Revolución, and it serves as a playground for everything from raucous punk rock shows to lectures. See p. 328.
- **Best Icon that Lives Up to the Hype:** The distinctive **Centro Cultural Tijuana** is famous for a reason. The soul of Mexico is basically revealed through the performances put on here—the ballet follows Folklorico de Veracruz follows no-name anarchistic punk follows Nayarit classic mariachis. The library and shops and galleries make it destination worthy, even if you can't catch a show. See p. 332.
- **Best Gourmet Grub:** When Marcela Ruiz Chong steps out of her kitchen at her restaurant **El 623** in Ensenada and starts talking about her grandmother teaching her how to blend Asian and Mexican elements, it's captivating. The food is, too. The menu items are so sharp and so full of flavor, that it's hard not to go back for seconds and thirds. See p. 347.
- **Best Cheap Grub:** If you'd prefer a place without linen napkins, then hike your huarache-clad heels down to the center of the tourist zone in Ensenada and look for the street stand **Mariscos La Guerrerense.** Just get there before 3pm if you want a crack at trying some food. This street stand has been an Ensenada landmark for generations—locals and gringos alike line up early for the incredible tostadas and salsas. See p. 346.
- **Best Ride:** You'll have two chances to take part in the **Rosarito-Ensenada Fun Bike Ride,** an 80km (50-mile) ride along the Pacific Coast that's not as hard as it sounds. That's because the event, held in both April and September, has a very partylike vibe—picture already tipsy participants racing to the finish line, where more drinks await. See p. 351.

The Baja Peninsula

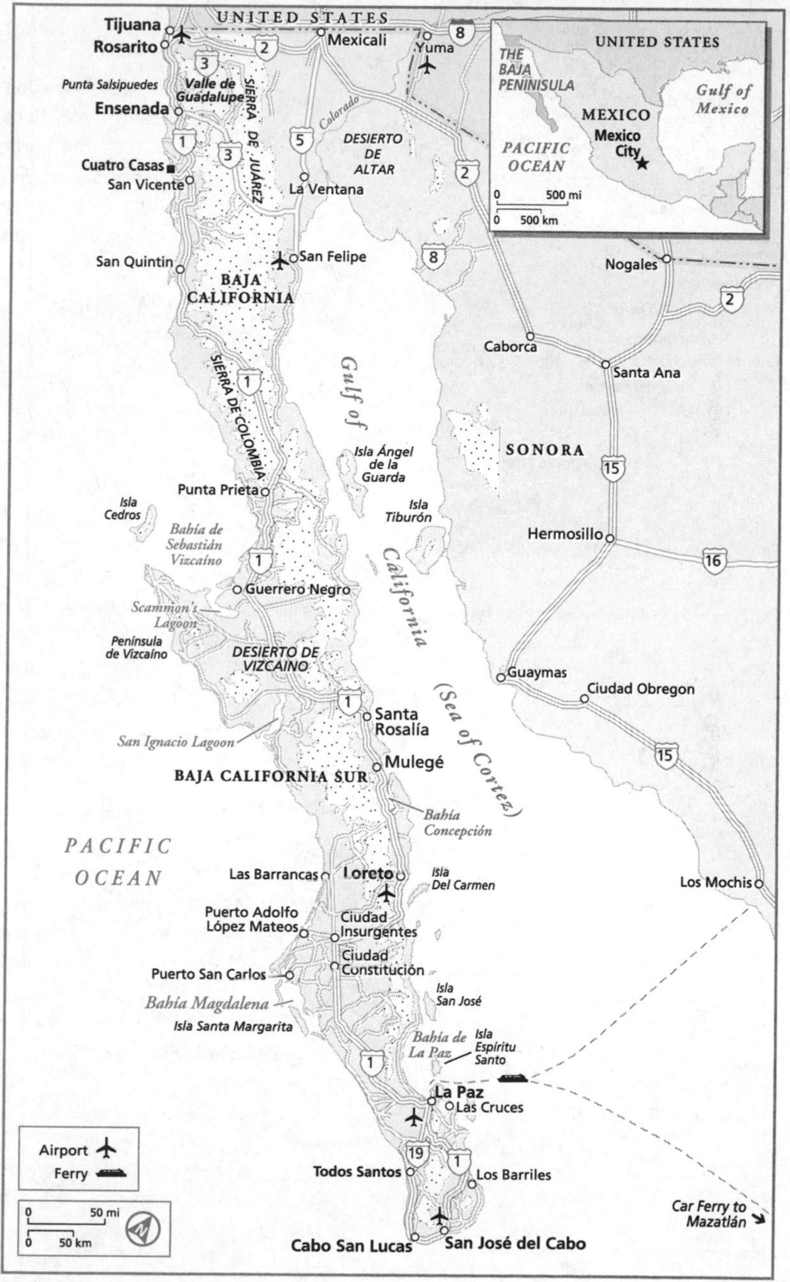

The Upper Baja Peninsula

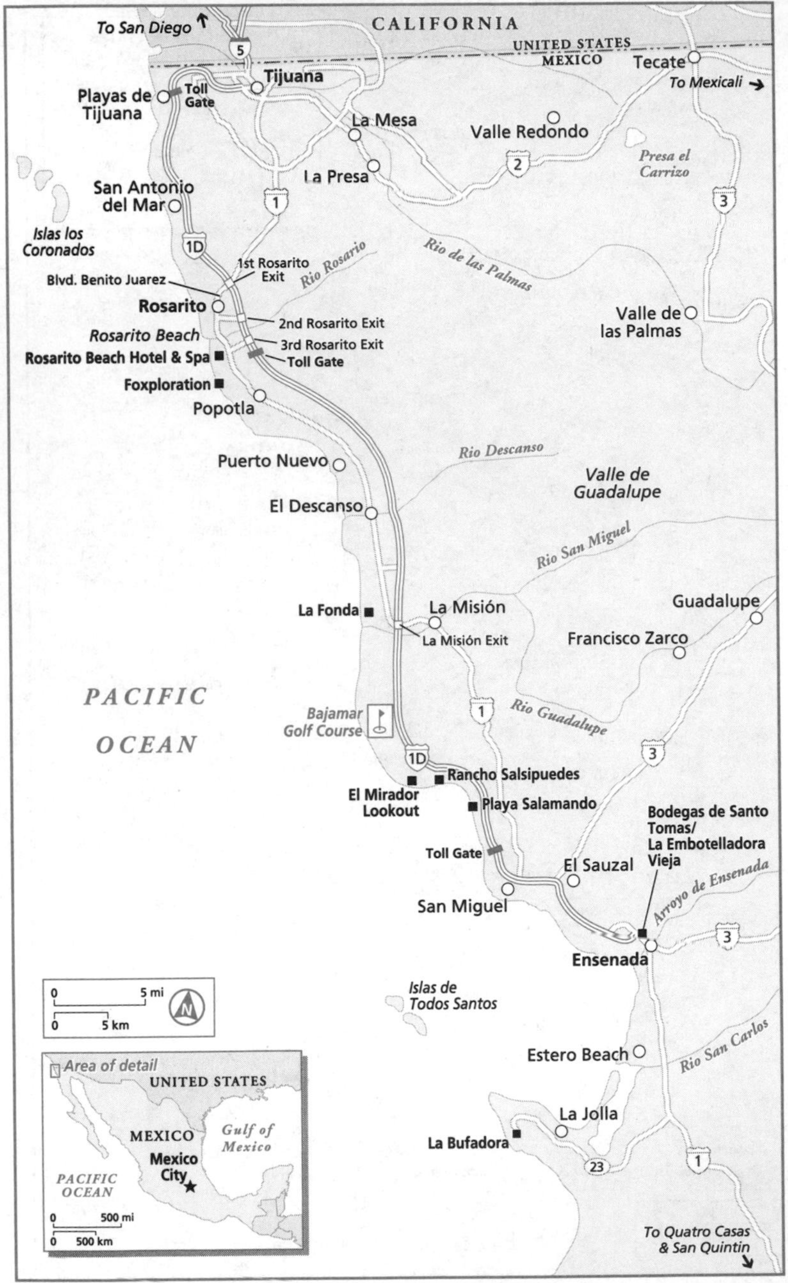

Best Hotel for Wine Lovers: The Valle de Guadalupe wine region, just northeast of Ensenada, is *this close* to becoming a wine destination of Napa-like proportions. The best place to see the vino revolution in action is at **Adobe Guadalupe,** which has comfy rooms to nod off in after all the excellent wine tastings. See p. 356.

Best Alt Scene Openers: While in Ensenada, head first to **Café Café** where owner Guillermo (Memo) Ramierez has established a beachhead for alternative culture in Baja. The staffers will fill you in on what's going on locally. If it's closed, then head to **El Bodegón del Arte,** a club where something happening is always bound to be going on. See p. 348 and 349.

Tijuana

Just 26km (16 miles) from downtown San Diego ("America's Finest City"), Tijuana is the Baja id to San Diego's super-ego. As the busiest border crossing in the world—86.6 million people arrive and 112 million leave each year—it's a place where anything prohibited a few minutes north is not just allowed but for sale at stupidly cheap prices—be it women, drugs, or alcohol. The nonstop partying energy admirably tries to keep up with all the tourists, and to fool them into thinking that a visit here means they've really seen Mexico.

Tijuana is a place where generations of border jumpers congregate for a midnight crossing to the land of the almighty dollar, and where the country's *maquiladoras* (assembly factories) first set up shop, capitalizing on lax environmental and labor laws. As a result, it has become the fastest growing city in Mexico, inching closer to Berlin than Laredo in sensibility. In some ways, it's also the most patient Mexican city, smiling through the tears and desperation. Sixteen percent of its 1.5 million residents have no running water, and one-third are under 15. Yet almost everyone speaks English, and everyone seems happy to cater to tourists.

The music you'll hear on Tijuana's streets speaks volumes about all the city has to offer—on any given day, you'll hear a Sinaloan tambora band hammering away while a mariachi group across the street sings "La Paloma." Basically, Tijuana is sensory overload. The lights are Las Vegas intense, the drinking and dancing nonstop. "Do you want to get drunk?" says the sign in front of Tavo's and Victor's "Last Chance Liquor Store." Like the question needs to be asked. In Tijuana, the drinks are always strong, and reality is always a matter for negotiation.

Yes, it's tacky and there are some important safety issues to keep in mind (see p. 35 for more on that) before traveling here, but you've gotta go to Tijuana. Just don't make it your *only* stop in Mexico.

Getting There & Getting Around

GETTING INTO TOWN

BY PLANE The **International Airport General Abelardo L. Rodriguez (☎ 664/607-8200** or 683-1060; http://tijuana.aeropuertosgap.com.mx), about 8km (5 miles) east of the city, has more than 75 daily national and international flight arrivals. Two new budget airlines fly out, too: **Mexicana's Click** (Diego Rivera 1511; ☎ **664/634-6545;** www.click.com.mx) and **Avolar** (Carretera Al Aeroperto s/n, Otay Mesa; ☎ **800/021-0100;** www.avolar.com.mx) fly from Tijuana to various cities within Mexico for reasonable prices. **AeroMexico, Azteca** (☎ **664/633-9227;** www.aerolineasazteca.com), **Aero California** (☎ **664/684-2100**), and **Aviacsa** (☎ **664/622-5086;** www.aviacsa.com) all have service to Tijuana as well.

From the airport, it's easiest to take a taxi to downtown from the cab stand outside; it costs about $180. A cheaper but more difficult option is to take the bus: **Greyhound** (www.greyhound.com) and **InterCalifornia Bus Service**'s station (☎ 800/443-5343), both service the airport regularly and charge about $55 to downtown Tijuana. You can also try hopping in a *colectivo* (a sort of collective cab) but it's safer to take a cab if you arrive during the night.

BY CAR To drive to Tijuana from the U.S., take I-5 south to the Mexican border at San Ysidro. The drive from downtown San Diego is about a half hour.

If you are driving down the peninsula and into mainland Mexico you must have a **Temporary Importation of Vehicle permit.** You will need your registration, driver's license, and proof of citizenship or passport (as of 2008, though that deadline might be extended; see p. 16 for more info) to obtain one. You'll be able to do this at the border, but check out the Banjercito website in advance at www.banjercito.com for full information. I also strongly recommend that you get **Mexican car insurance** prior to crossing the border. Many drive-through facilities in San Ysidro offer these services.

Note that crossing back over the border can be a nightmare, especially during holiday weekends; regular commuters have taken to lining up and then sleeping in their cars. You can call ☎ **619/690-8999** or 619/671-8999 to find out how long the wait time is to cross north into the U.S.

BY BUS From downtown San Diego (at Union Station), it's quick and easy to take the red **"Tijuana trolley"** bound for San Ysidro. Get off at the last stop (San Ysidro) and follow the signs to walk across the border. It's simple, quick, and inexpensive; the one-way fare is $22. The last trolley leaving for San Ysidro departs downtown around midnight, and the last trolley from San Ysidro to San Diego is at 1am. On Saturday, the trolley runs 24 hours. **The San Diego Transit Bus** 602 or 932 also will drop you at San Ysidro where you can catch a cab across the border.

Bus lines that run through Tijuana include **Estrella de Baja California** (☎ **664/683-5622**), **ABC,** and **Greyhound** (☎ **664/621-2982**). Tijuana has three main bus stations. The main Tijuana bus station is **Central Camionera** near the airport (Calzada Lázaro Cárdenas 15751, Delegacion Mesa de Otay; ☎ **664/621-2982**) and has buses which go anywhere within the state, city, or country. The **Downtown Bus Station** is located at Avenida Madero and 1st (☎ **664/621-2982**). The **San Ysidro station** is near the border (☎ **664/624-9614**). There's also a

Passport Works

Immigration services is located at the border (you can pull over and park as you drive in), at Puerta Mexico within Col. Federal (☎ **664/682-4947;** bcdrbni@inami.gob.mx). Throughout 2007, if you stay less than 72 hours in the border zone you do not need a passport or tourist card; but you will need to bring your passport or get a tourist card at the border crossing Immigration Office if you plan to stay longer, or if you are going south of the checkpoint at San Quintin. However, as of 2008, it's likely that you will need a valid passport to re-enter the U.S., even for day trips. Check travel.state.gov for info.

Tijuana Sleeping & Eating

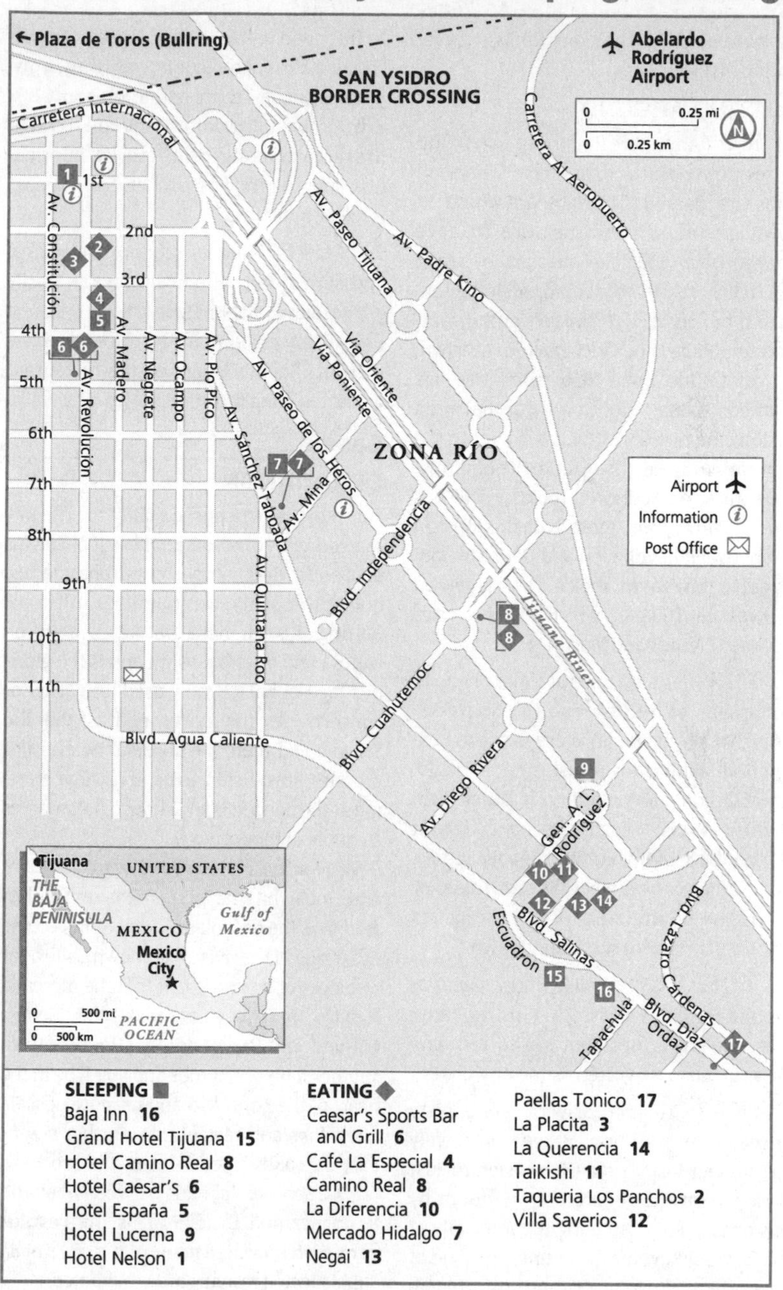

Mexicoach Busticket station (Revolución 1025 between 6th and 7th; ☎ **664/685-1470**) that sells bus tickets for bus travel within Mexico.

GETTING AROUND

BY BUS Anywhere in the city, you'll find buses pretty much across from where all cabs are parked. The fare anywhere in town is around $6.50; be sure to have change (they will take quarters or small U.S. bills). To get to Avenida Revolución, take a bus marked **"Centro"** and disembark on Madero or Constitucion. In town, to get to the **Zona Rio** catch the bus marked "Zona Rio" on 3rd between Revolución and Constitucion. To get to the **Hippodrome** neighborhood, the bull ring, race track, or Auditorio, look for the bus marked "Presa" or "Mesa" which stops on 4th between Revolución and Constitucion. To get to the **Playas,** look for a bus marked "Playas de Tijuana" which stops on 3rd between Héroes and Martinez.

BY TAXI It's easy but not super cheap to get around by **Yellow Cab** (☎ **664/682-4617**), which charge an average $55 to destinations within town (ask first, though). Another comparable option is **Black and Yellow Taxis,** which can be called at ☎ **664/688-0489.** But it's cheaper to take one of the red and white **Super Taxis,** or "libres" (☎ **664/682-8281**); they use meters and only cost about $20 around town.

BY COLECTIVO You'll find *colectivos* around the city's bus stops. Most run anywhere in town for about $10 to $20, and they run almost as often as the city buses.

BY CAR Tijuana drivers are pretty crazy—those who don't drive defensively are indeed lost. It may be easier to just park in a lot and get around on foot or by bus or taxi. (You can park economically at lots around Revolución or underground at Sanborns at Revolución and 8th.) If you insist on driving, see "Basics," p. 49 for some tips.

The good news is that **Green Angels** (Tijuana-Ensenada cuota, ☎ **800/990-3900;** Tijuana-Tecate cuota, ☎ **800/888-0911**) travel up and down the toll roads in this area offering help, tourist information, and roadside assistance. See "Basics," p. 52 for more info.

BY FOOT Tijuana is deceptively large and spread out; although you can easily get around the neighborhood around Revolución on foot. If you are going from there to Puebla Amigo or the restaurant district in Zona Rio, it's a pretty long walk.

Basics

ORIENTATION

For most Americans coming to Tijuana, **Avenida Revolución** is where it all begins and ends. Bars, strip shows, pharmacies, hookers, black velvet paintings, off-track betting. It's all here on Revu, between calles 1 and 9. At the south end is the glorious Jai Alai palace, now used primarily for concerts. At the north end is the Rio Tijuana and then, the border. The avenues crossing Revolución go up in number starting at the border; many change their names a couple of blocks away.

Walk a few blocks east toward the river and you'll hit the plazas (**Plaza Pueblo Amigo** is the best place for nightlife) on the other side of the river. Walk down Calle 9 for 10 blocks or so and you'll find the Mercado Hidalgo and beyond that, the Centro Cultural on Paseo de los Héroes. Walk southeast on Los Héroes and you'll be in the heart of the **Zona Rio** and its more upscale nightclubs and restaurants. Farther southeast and sandwiched between the two areas (off Av. Sanchez Taboada between Abelardo Rodriguez and Escuadron) is the **restaurant district** where many of the city's most sophisticated restaurants are situated.

TOURIST INFO & OFFICES

The main tourist office is at the **Pedestrian Crossing,** 27m (90 ft.) from the San Ysidro border (☎ **664/683-1405**). It's open Monday to Saturday 8am to 5pm and Sunday 8am to 3pm. You can also chat with the knowledgeable and likable agent at the tourist kiosk on Revolución between 3rd and 4th (☎ **664/685-2210;** Mon–Thurs 10am–4pm and Fri–Sun 10am–7pm).

There's another office at the **airport** ("E" baggage claim; ☎ **664/683-8244;** daily 8am–3pm), at the **Centro Cultural Tijuana** (Paseo de los Héroes and Mina, Zona Rio; ☎ **664/687-9600;** www.seetijuana.com; Mon–Fri 8am–8pm, Sat–Sun 9am–6pm), as well as at the shopping center **Viva Tijuana** (Via de la Juventude 8800, #25-23; ☎ **664/973-0430;** Mon–Fri 8am–8pm, Sat–Sun 9am–6pm).

RECOMMENDED WEBSITES

- **www.discoverbajacalifornia.com**: This great site is geared toward the active tourist, with a lot of handy info on the many "routes" you can take to see the peninsula, including the wine route, eco-tourism route, the mission route (which extends from the border to Los Cabos), and walking tours of cities in northern Baja. Although some sections just link you to guide companies, there are also extensive maps and suggestions for ways to do it on your own, such as a guide to "Valle de Gigantes" (a valley near San Felipe known for its giant cardon cacti).
- **www.tijuanaonline.org**: Pretty much a commercial site for tourists, with basic information, tips on border crossings, and links to pages with more info (although many are also tourist oriented).
- **www.tijuana.gob.mx**: This is an official municipal site, with a phone directory of city services and legal and government information (in Spanish). In English, you can find a downloadable tourist legal guide and forms for complaints.

Tijuana Nuts & Bolts

Banks **Banamex Matriz** is at Calle 4th and Constitucion (☎ **664/688-0021**); **Bital** is on Calle 2 at Revolución 129 (☎ **664/633-6400**); and **Bancomer** has a branch at Paseo de los Héroes 10200 (☎ **664/687-9977**). Most banks are open from 8am to 4pm during the week and until 2pm on Saturdays. ATMs dispensing pesos are scattered all around town, but you can use dollars easily almost everywhere. The betting place **Caliente** (Revolución 931 between 3rd and 4th; ☎ **664/633-7300**) has an ATM that dispenses dollars, as does the 24-hour **AM PM** minimart (Av. Revolución at 7th; ☎ **664/685-3997**).

Embassies & Consulates The **U.S. Consular Agency** is open Monday to Friday from 8am to 4pm (Tapacula 96, Col. Hipodromo; ☎ **664/622-7400** or 619/692-2154 in San Diego). The **Canadian Consulate** is open Monday to Friday from 9am to 1pm (German Gedovius 10400-101; ☎ **665/684-0461**). The **Consulate of Great Britain** is open Monday to Friday from 9am to 2pm (Bulevar Salinas 1500, Col. Aviacion; ☎ **664/686-5320**).

Emergencies **Tourist Info** can be dialed through ☎ **078. Red Cross, Fire,** and **Police** all use the emergency number ☎ **066** (like 911 in U.S.). If you have a police emergency, I recommend avoiding contacting the police and getting in touch with the **Tourist Assistance** office at ☎ **664/973-0424** or 664/683-1405.

Hospitals One hospital to try is **Unidad Medica Lation** (Revolución Plaza Madero, Local 18E; ☎ **664/685-5404**). Another option is **Hospital San Luis Rey** (1350 Av. Benito Juárez), which is open 24 hours.

Internet/Wireless Hot Spots There are Internet cafes along every block of Revolución; one to try is **Matrix** (Revolución 619; ☎ **664/685-9949;** $10 per hour; daily 10am–midnight) which has PC repairs, Web design, public telephones, fax, copying, and printing services as well. Another is **WorldNet** (2nd at Revolución; ☎ **664/685-2467;** daily 8am–11pm) which charges $15 per hour. You can find Wi-Fi at the city's five-star hotels, but they may charge a daily fee of $109 even if you are a guest.

Pharmacies **El Fenix** (Revolución 1545-1 at Calle 8; ☎ **664/685-1070**) is open 8am to 10pm Monday to Sunday and accepts credit. There are also numerous pharmacies down Revolución that sell cut-rate drugs to tourists (check what's legal with **The Association of Pharmacies** by calling ☎ **664/685-0170** or 800/025-6580, or visit www.cofepris.gob.mx).

Post Offices Located on Calle 11 at Avenida Negrete, the *correo* is open Monday to Friday from 8am to 5pm. You can buy stamps at the **CANACO** office on Calle 1 at Avenida Revolución.

Safety In 1994, PRI presidential front-runner Luis Donaldo Colosio was murdered here, many say by members of his own party. Political violence has escalated since then—more than 300 people were murdered in Tijuana last year and Mayor Hank Rhon admitted that at least 10 people he personally knows have been kidnapped. Despite this, Rhon recently proclaimed Tijuana to be a safe city for tourists. And he is doing all he can to help—helping to push through a 2005 regulation to have the thousands of sex workers living here tested regularly for STDs and, more questionably, issuing slingshots instead of guns to police members in early 2007 when the police were under investigation. The measures seem to be working, though—crime is plummeting. As long as you take common sense precautions—like not walking around drunk by yourself at night—you should be fine.

Note that if you walk too far north on Revolución you will hit the Zona Norte, a poorer barrio that should be avoided.

Telephone Tips The local area code is 664.

Sleeping

Tijuana boasts many cheap to reasonable hotels that were built in the 1940s—Tijuana's "Golden Age," when film stars flocked here to gamble, drink, and generally act up. Though many are rather shabby now, you can channel their ghosts. If you're staying in hotels of this class, be sure to stick to ones on Avenida Revolución; wander too far off on side streets (or too far north) and you may find yourself in somewhat unsavory and dangerous digs.

Though there aren't any good hostels to mention here, there are more moderate hotels removed from the touristy Revolución that are safe, like the Baja Inn. In addition, there are a few luxury hotels in quirky hoods, including the Camino Real in the Zona Rio and the landmark mirrored towers of the Grand Hotel Tijuana in the Ruta Gastronomica. See below for full reviews.

Remember that hotel rates in Tijuana are subject to a 12% tax; you may also be able to get a discount if you pay in cash.

CHEAP

→ **Hotel Caesar's** Yes, this is where the Caesar salad was invented. My advice: Order a salad and consider staying someplace else. The rooms are basic, simple, and, on the surface, clean. But that's about it. Don't expect charm or amenities. I guess you can't expect much for under $330, but if this is a two-star, I shudder to think what a one-star is like. I only mention it so that you can avoid staying here. *Av. Revolución 1079 (at 5th). ☎ 664/685-1606 or 688-0409. $330–$450 double, $550 master suite. MC, V. Amenities: Telephone in common room; TV (in common area); safe boxes in office. In room: A/C, TV, fans.*

→ **Hotel Nelson** ★ Marilyn Monroe and Rita Hayworth both slept here during the hotel's heyday in the 1950s. Sadly some of the old fashioned touches, like tiled floors, are now long gone. But the rooms are clean and not especially tiny; sheets are clean if thin; and some bathrooms have their original tile. The decor is really secondary here, though. With visitors staying from Japan, Eastern Europe, Germany, and even the Ukraine, the place just feels cool. Rooms on the north side of the hotel can get noisy on the weekends due to live music blaring up from neighbors on Revolución. *Av. Revolución 721. ☎ 664/685-4302. www.hotelnelson.com.mx. $499 single, $500–$521 double, $627 triple (sleep up to 5 in a room and you pay just $100 each). MC, V. Amenities: Bar; restaurant; elevator; wheelchair friendly. In room: TV, safe box in office, telephone.*

DOABLE

→ **Baja Inn** Part of a chain of medium-priced hotels, this is just one of several Baja Inn locations in Tijuana as well as Ensenada. The spot is modeled after a U.S. motel with rooms that are bland if clean and decent sized. Still, there are some Mexican touches, such as quarried stone floors and bright color schemes in the lobby. The newly remodeled space overlooks the country club golf course and a pool and is within walking distance to the U.S. Consulate, should you need it (I hope not). *Tapachula 1 at Bulevar Agua Caliente. ☎ 664/681-7733. www.bajainn.com. $600–$750 double. Amenities: Restaurant-bar; business center; gift shop; Jacuzzi and sauna; laundry service; medical service; pool; tobacco shop; travel agency. In room: A/C, cable TV, heater.*

→ **Hotel España** ★ Location is everything, so try to look past the cement-tiled floors and businesslike vibe here and instead focus on how this place is *right* on Revu. That way, you'll see that España is truly an oasis in the midst of the cheesy sleazy mood of the street below—it's new, grown-up, unassuming, and very fairly priced. Rooms are small but serviceable, with a minimalist decor and balconies—get ready to strut out on one and pity the masses down below. *Av. Revolución 968 (between 3rd and 4th). ☎ 664/685-5100. US$35 single, US$50 double. MC, V. Amenities: Elevator; business center; wheelchair friendly. In room: A/C, TV, hair dryer, telephone.*

→ **Hotel Lucerna** A pretty downstairs lounge and Mexican colonial decor—think wrought iron, heavy wooden furniture, and tiled floors—help to make this a pleasant place to plop your head. It used to be one of the hippest places to stay in TJ but it's beginning to show its age. Thankfully it's still in the Zona Rio, well away from the insanity of Revolución. The older part of the hotel is more charming, the newer five-star section a bit sterile. It gets bonus points for a reasonably priced room service menu and a staff that's notably friendly and helpful. *Av. Paseo de los Héroes 10902. ☎ 664/633-3900. www.hotel-lucerna.com.mx. $850–$1,720 double, $900–$1,850 suite. AE, DC, MC, V. Amenities: Coffee shop; free Internet; outdoor pool; room service. In room: A/C, TV, coffeemaker, hair dryer, iron.*

SPLURGE

→ **Grand Hotel Tijuana** ★ The Grand Hotel isn't just a hotel—it's a veritable landmark in the city. This huge 422-room mirrored twin tower hotel stands out in the skyline from practically anywhere in Tijuana. But it's helpful to keep in mind even if you don't get lost; there are three restaurants, two bars, and all sorts of suites from mini to Governors to Presidential. The Grand Club Rooms on the upper three floors have the best views of Tijuana. It all feels kind of nouveau riche to me, but the location is certainly handy—it's within walking distance to the Zona Gastronomica. *Agua Caliente 4500. ☎ 664/681-7000. www.grandhoteltij.com.mx. From US$140 single/double. AE, MC, V. Amenities: 2 restaurants; lobby bar; business center; fitness center; heated pool; laundry and dry cleaning; 24-hr. room service; sauna; shopping arcade; sports and race book; tennis courts. In room: A/C, TV, dataport, iron, minibar, safe.*

MTV Best → **Hotel Camino Real** ★★ This contemporary chain hotel has 250 rooms, so forget about an intimate personal experience. With service this good, though, you may not care. The lobby bar, while not quite as fabulous as its sisters in other Mexican cities, is still one of the best in town—and it's a magnet for locals, not tourists. It really does rise above the generic hotel bar experience. Even if you don't stay here, come for the bar and to take in the trademark huge lobby, with signature bright splashes of orange and pink walls. *Paseo de los Héroes 10305. ☎ 664/633-4000, or 800/7-CAMINO in the U.S. www.caminoreal.com/tijuana. US$180 single/double. AE, MC, V. Amenities: Bar; restaurant; elevator; laundry service; wheelchair friendly. In room: A/C, TV, fridge, hair dryer, Internet (for additional $110), safe.*

Eating

Once upon a time one had to go all the way to Mexico City's Polanco neighborhood to find high-end cuisine that had the power to both delight and nourish, and Tijuana was known only as the place where the Caesar salad was invented—but that was way back in 1924. In the last decade a very strong, very confident, very local food revolution has taken place in Tijuana. Some describe the new cuisine as Mexi-Med, a blend of Mexican and Mediterranean, but that's not all there is to it. Traditional Mexican cuisine without any nouvelle flourishes is also hot. One big difference between now and decades ago is the quality of the ingredients. Fresh, local, and organic—these are the defining ethics of Tijuana's trend-setting chefs.

That doesn't mean you can only find savory wonders at trendy expensive hot spots in Tijuana. You can also fill your belly for just a few dollars at one of the city's many taco stands—that is, if you can decide which one to try. Some insist on eating at **Carnitas Uruapan** (Bulevar Agua Caliente 12650; ☎ **664/681-6181**) for fabulous grilled thick rich pork. Local Alex Uniga at MultiKulti swears the tacos at **Sonora** stand (Av. Blancarte at Calle 9; no phone) or **El Paisa** (20 Noviembre at Calle 11; no phone) are among the "best on the planet." Then there's always the **Mercado Hidalgo** (Av. Sanchez Taboada at Av. Fco. J. Mina; no phone), which has hundreds of stalls ranging in price and quality.

My favorite taco stand, though, is a bit out of the center of town. MTV Best **Tacos Salceados,** or **La Ermita** ★★, on Av. Ermita Norte 30-A, Fracc. Santa Cruz La Mesa (bus stop Agua Caliente at Ermita; no phone), attracts crowds for such unique creations as a shrimp and strawberry concoction and "quesatacos," which are a cross between quesadillas and tacos, and cheap prices—all menu items are only $15 to $25.

CHEAP

MTV Best → **Cafe La Especial** ★★ MEXICAN Pass down a flight of stairs past tiny stores full of souvenirs, and suddenly you're at the door of La Especial, unchanged (seemingly) in its 55 years. I wouldn't be surprised if the paper curtains, painted wood chairs, flowers, and even the attentive waiters were here on opening day. Why leave, when the food's this good? You can chow down on platters of *carne asada* (grilled marinated beef served with fresh tortillas, beans, and rice), chile rellenos, or tacos, enchiladas, and burritos and cold Mexican beer. Just take it easy on the beer since it's a family place—this is the sort of joint where mariachis play happy birthday to a little Mexican girl and all the waiters join in. *Av. Revolución 718 (between calles 3 and 4). ☎ 664/685-6654. Main courses $50–$160. MC, V. Daily 9am–10pm.*

→ **La Placita** ★★ MEXICAN Come and get your typical Mexican fare, such as platters of steaming grilled fish (prepared on their street-front grill), huge plates of grilled shrimp with beans and rice, and handmade tortillas, all at reasonable prices. The downstairs room has Formica-topped tables with rattan chairs and a marimba band that plays daily. But the best part of dining here is their new rooftop terrace with its fountain, quieter live music, umbrella-topped tables, and view of Avenida Revolución—it's a welcome respite from the craziness below. Locals say the food is better at La Especial but they love the ambience here. *Av. Revolución 961. ☎ 664/688-2704. Main courses $54–$140. MC, V. Fri–Sun 8am–4am; Mon–Thurs 8am–midnight.*

→ **Taqueria Los Panchos** MEXICAN This place looks kind of like a downscale Denny's with its small booths with plastic-topped tables, which line the walls and crowd the middle of the room. Though seafood, giant burritos, and quesadillas are on the menu, I recommend following the crowds and just getting the tacos. The families and tourists who flock here stuff themselves with beef, carne asada, and al pastor tacos. It all makes for a noisy but cheap and pretty darn good meal. *Av. Revolución 892 (at 3rd). ☎ 664/215-4344. $12 per taco. No credit cards. Daily 10:30am–midnight.*

DOABLE

→ **Caesar's Sports Bar and Grill** PUB GRUB On the ground floor of Hotel Caesars (p. 323), this is the place that invented the Caesar salad. Their version is mixed fresh at your table, complete with raw egg yolk whisked into the dressing. The end result is beautiful to witness, tasty to eat, but no doubt bad for your diet. Though there's also typical and standard Mexican fare here, only the Caesar salad is really worth ordering. *Av. Revolution 1071. ☎ 664/638-4562. Main courses $100–$150. MC, V. Daily 24 hr.*

→ **Camino Real** CONTINENTAL On Sundays, locals make the pilgrimage to the famous buffet at the Camino Real Hotel (reviewed above) to stuff themselves with eggs, fruit, fresh breads, champagne, and basically all they can manage to cram into their stomachs. Lunch and dinner here are certainly adequate—but with so many great choices in the nearby Ruta Gastronimica, save it for Sunday brunch. Or come to hang out in the lobby bar, which is pretty happening no matter the day. *Paseo de los Héroes 10305.* ☎ *664/633-4000. Main courses $150–$200. AE, MC, V. Daily 7am–9pm.*

→ **La Diferencia** ★★★ MEXICAN You'll feel like you've settled into a converted hacienda when you nab one of this restaurant's seats, tucked into a space with a curved *boveda* (arched brick) ceiling, thick columns, carved wood, brickwork, and a giant altar smothered in years of candle wax. While the setting is fairly traditional, the food is decidedly unusual, a mix of pre- and post-Columbian food, re-interpreted, such as shredded duck in a crispy tortilla cone (drizzled with tamarind sauce), chicken breast with chipotle cream, tongue tacos, and fried crickets. It's Mexican cuisine that appears familiar but constantly surprises. *Bulevar Sanchez Taboada 10611-A.* ☎ *664/634-3346. Main courses $180. AE, MC, V. Daily noon–1:30am.*

→ **Paellas Tonico** MEXICAN This two-room cafe in an old residential neighborhood, cozily decorated with photos of famous bullfighters, just isn't the same since the owner/chef Tonico passed away. It's still a fave at lunchtime and for take-out; the best bet is the paella, which they haven't messed up . . . yet. *Av. Jalisco 2433 at Col. Cacho.* ☎ *664/684-0941. Main courses $100–$150. MC, V. Mon–Sat 11am–9pm; Sun until 2pm.*

→ **Taikishi** THAI/JAPANESE It's not as hip as Negai (p. 327), but it's certainly cheaper. Specializing in Thai and Japanese food, this modern restaurant has a raised platform where you sit on cushions on the floor adjacent to its front room, which has angular floor to ceiling windows each inset with a giant bamboo. Though the grub consists of more standard fare than you'd find in, say, Little Tokyo in downtown L.A., it's a good option if you've got a hankering for something decidedly not Mexican. The Thai standouts include red or green curry and various types of satay. The best Japanese options are the *yakimeshi* (grilled meats) or noodles. *Sanchez Taboada 10589.* ☎ *664/684-0404. www.estabienrico.com. Main courses $100. AE, MC, V. Mon–Sat noon–11pm; Sun 1–9pm.*

SPLURGE

MTV Best → **La Querencia** ★★★ MEDITERRANEAN Owner-chef Miguel Yagues likes to hunt. This is clear once you see what's on this classy joint's menu—Baja cuisine with an unusual twist. That often means deer, quail, and boar are offered along with more typical seafood, though you'll also get kooky concoctions like manta ray pizza. The main dining room—a mix between a pack rat's warehouse and a lodge—is definitely in keeping with the hunting-friendly menu. Deer heads are mounted over the bar, and they stare glassily at a boar's head and stuffed geese and ducks; the open ceiling is bedecked with old iron cow bells and lanterns, camp coffee pots, and skillets. In contrast, the kitchen is high-tech industrial in tone, both visible and imposing.

There's a very good reason why this place is often cited as the spearhead for Tijuana's surging reputation as a gourmet's wonderland. The level of professionalism in the kitchen isn't surprising, considering that the food here is among the best in Tijuana—changing almost daily depending on what was recently caught. If you can't really afford it, at least stop by for a gourmet taco (the cheapest menu option) and a glass of wine. *Escuadron 201, no. 3110 Local 1-2 (at Sanchez Taboada).* ☎ *664/972-9935, -3340. www.sdro.com/laquerencia/ingles.htm. Tacos $120, main courses $200–$370. AE, MC, V. Mon–Thurs and Sun 1–11pm; Fri–Sat 1pm–midnight.*

→ **Negai** ★ JAPANESE When I visited, this lively hip space next door to La Querencia was full of Gen-Yers singing at the top of their lungs on a Sunday afternoon. I'm sure the sake was responsible, though this place *is* good enough to make you wanna sing. Negai has simple minimalist decor with pale leather banquettes, zebrawood walls, and a sushi bar at the back, where Chef Angel Villegas creates fusion sushi. Try the tuna sashimi dressed with tamarindo and hamachi with Serrano chile, but for God's sake don't dip it in soy! (It's too good for that.) *Escuadron 201, no. 3110-4 (at Sanchez Taboada).* ☎ *664/971-0000. www.negairestaurant.com. Sashimi, sushi rolls $120 and up. AE, MC, V. Mon–Thurs and Sun 1–9pm; Fri–Sat 1–11pm.*

→ **Saverios** ★★★ CONTINENTAL This is the kind of place where high-ranking politicians come to exchange pleasantries while gallery owners and artists sit at the next table nestled under local artists' work, discussing upcoming shows. It's so civilized, it comes with a dress code: no baseball caps, no sandals, no shorts, and no tank-tops. The food also happens to be amazing. Chef Javier Plascencia Huerta displays a definite pride in organic, local food in every dish, from the Albanil-style stuffed eggplant, to the mesquite-roasted oysters, to chiles stuffed with beef, to the mushrooms with huitlacoche. Saverios has the most complete wine list of any restaurant in town (there are 50-something bottles from Valle de Guadalupe), too. *Bulevar Sanchez Taboada (at Escuadron 201).* ☎ *664/686-6502. www.villasaverios.com. Main courses $180–$270. AE, MC, V. Mon–Thurs noon–11pm; Fri–Sat noon–midnight; Sun noon–10pm.*

Partying

Tijuana's nightlife has traditionally been centered around Avenida Revolución, though recently it has moved out to the huge mall-like complexes (complete with outdoor parking) in the Zona Rio. The action on Revolución first took off in the 1980s when L.A. punk bands traveled south of the border to dance in its clubs; in the 1990s, the arrival of rave parties and the inception of the Nortec Collective added a whole new dimension to the scene. Over the years, though, Revolución has remained pretty much the same as it's always been, just with better sound systems and younger strippers.

For most, Revu is a better Vegas—closer, cheaper, and without family-friendly pretenses. Wander down this street on any given night, and you'll spot everyone from Valley kids on dates, to horny jarheads, to slumming conventioneers. But look closely and you'll notice a few other versions of Revu. First, there are the Mexican-friendly dance halls, like Las Pulgas, where Nortena blasts from the speakers and the audience clutch and two-step in oddly graceless moves around the dance floor. Around the corner, just a half-block away, homeless kids and latter-day punks rock at MultiKulti, based in a burned out baroque theater. And at the far south end of Revu, if you're lucky, you'll stumble upon concert-goers taking in a show at the glorious Jai Alai palace (renamed El Foro).

For a true sense of Gen X-Y-Z club-fun, though, you'd better drive past Revu to **Plaza Fiesta,** a square block of bars, clubs, and restaurants in the Zona Rio, kitty-corner to the Culture Center. True, there aren't any Revolución cool dive bars like El Dandy del Sur or dance halls like La Estrella or Blanco y Negro here, but there also aren't relentless lines of shills trying to pull you in for a two-for-one special, "including a lap dance." Or try **Pueblo Amigo,** one of the plazas on the far side of the Rio Tijuana but in Zona Rio, less than 3km (1½ miles) from the border. They don't have addresses within the mall (the mall itself is at Via Oriente 9211, bordered by Av. Paseo Tijuana; ☎ **664/684-2711**) but everyone knows where the clubs are if you just ask; many, like Señor Frog's, also sport signs that are too huge to miss.

BARS

Best → **El Dandy del Sur** ★★★ Tijuana's twist on a standard dive bar, El Dandy has been around since the 1970s but it feels much older than that. It's a low-key jukebox bar, the kind of place where the locals who work in Señor Frog's come when they need a quiet, nontouristy place to unwind. The bartenders are all middle-aged women who plop down bowls of peanuts and popcorn in addition to shilling beer—you won't get any sex come-ons here. Movie star pictures hang on the back wall as if this were some retro Hollywood bar, which it definitely ain't: Tell a local you came here and they'll raise their eyebrows in surprise. The clientele is all ages, from young hipsters to geezers. Despite the name, it's not a gay bar (the dandy in question is the fancy English caricature), although it is gay-friendly. *Calle 6th 2030A. No phone.*

→ **Hookas Café** Around the corner from Mofo and across the way from Señor Frog's, this cafe is named "hookas" for an obvious reason: For $80 you can share a bowl of mango, melon, apple, or other flavored tobacco around a table with your friends. They also serve beer, wine, espresso, and many kinds of tea, and there's live music on weekends. *Pueblo Amigo, Local 9-10.* ☎ *664/975-2505. No cover.*

LIVE MUSIC

→ **El Foro** Housed in the beautiful neoclassical Jai Alai Palace, El Foro stages great live events, ranging from big acts from Mexico to international acts like the Skatalites and the Misfits. There's a big stage on the large standing-room only (first-come, first-served) dance floor. Tiers rise up from there, and include seating and lounges for VIPs. *Av. Revolución 1500 at Calle 8.* ☎ *664/685-8676 or in San Diego 619/734-2333.*

→ **Mofo Bar** This is a decent place to come to chat (well, yell—it's pretty noisy), smoke, drink, catch a band, listen to an alt-rock play list, or watch vintage movies on a big screen behind the stage. The ambience is not as studied as the bigger clubs in town, which suits the scruffy Gen-Yers who pack in here just fine. *Pueblo Amigo.* ☎ *644/688-5426. www.mofobar.com. No cover.*

Best → **MultiKulti** ★★★ The cover ($20–$150 depending on the event) imposed here might make you feel like you're in Berlin instead of Tijuana, but it's worth it. Walk into this ramshackle 1950s baroque theater and you'll feel like you're entering a modern-day coliseum that just happens to be in the middle of a bawdy Mexican border town. Events or concerts are held every weekend, either in the classic but destroyed theater lobby with its arching stairways, or in the main theater, now roofless, which serves as a giant amphitheater. Punk and alt-rock bands pass through fairly regularly, and bands that have played here include **Manu Chao, Molotov, The Misfits,** and **Mad Professor.** Events aren't limited to music, though. Sub-Commandante Marcos spoke here on his "Indigenous Peoples tour" to a crowd of 1,000, and movie stars and directors have been known to drop by. Organizers include Alex Uniga (zugg68@hotmail.com) formerly of **Tijuana No.** *Constitucion at Calle 6. No phone. www.myspace.com/multikulti.*

CLUBS & LOUNGES

Don't bother with the huge Mayan temple–facaded club called **Barak** (Pueblo Amigo; ☎ **664/682-9222** or 607-3566;

Tijuana Partying & Sightseeing

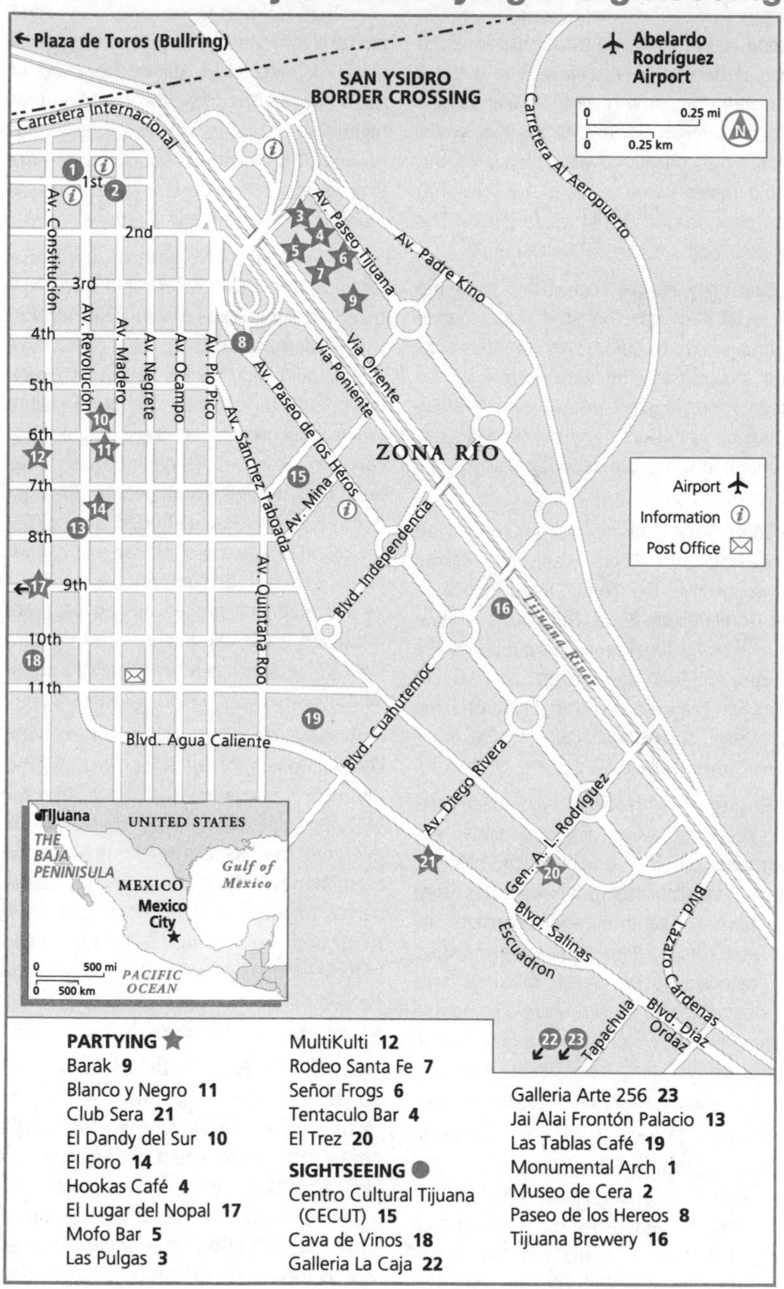

cover $200 for men, $150 for women). The crappy Disneyfied exterior is as fake as the scene inside. If you're into attitude you'll love it here, but otherwise you'll think it's phony and overrated. **Señor Frog's** (Pueblo Amigo; ☎ **664/682-4962;** www.senorfrogs.com; no cover) is also lame, but you'd never know it from the line that stretches around the block to get in. The following options are all much cooler.

➔ **Blanco y Negro** Locals (and some hip tourists) come to this traditional dance hall to groove to Colombian cumbia tracks and live music. The extroverted DJ—he often sports a shirt unbuttoned halfway down his chest, along with some serious bling—knows his old-school music. *Calle 6 no. 2031. No phone.*

➔ **Club Sera** Looking for something a bit more loungey? Then head back across town towards the Zona Gastranomica to the Hotel Corona Plaza. This cool '50s-style lounge books local as well as guest DJs like Deepce and Juan Nunez from L.A., DJ Garth from San Francisco, or Mark E. Quark from San Diego. *Bulevar Agua Caliente 1426, in the Hotel Corona Plaza. Cover $150.*

➔ **El Lugar del Nopal** An art-space cafe, bar, restaurant, and cabaret, El Lugar was instrumental in launching the Nortec movement since the first Nortec DJs often met here. The rambling space consists of a series of rooms where you can see all sorts of performance art, music, or other happenings. Fun salsa lessons are also hosted here regularly, which attract dancers of all levels and classes from across the city. *Cinco de Mayo 1328 at Av. F.* ☎ *664/685-2413.*

➔ **El Trez** El Trez is a trendy nouvelle restaurant with well done minimalist decor threaded throughout, house music blasting, local art hanging on the walls, and an extensive Baja California wine list—what more do you want? Well, maybe it could be cheaper; wine goes for about $65 a glass. Food here (salmon tacos, tempura veggies, pasta) is also somewhat pricey ($115–$150), but excellent. Most dance floor action takes place Thursday through Saturday nights; other nights, you can simply relax on one of the outdoor patio's white-vinyl love seats. *Escuadron 201 at Sanchez Taboada.* ☎ *646/971-0892. No cover.*

➔ **Las Pulgas** ★ A Mexican music disco on steroids, this club is a veritable maze, with three massive rooms of giant dance floors surrounded by full tables and chairs, several smaller side rooms, and bars everywhere—all illuminated by black lights. Videos play on plasma screens but nobody cares; it's like a little city in here, one populated only by *way* drunk people. Since it's not as high class as the Rodeo (see below), the mood is way more intense and chaotic here. (When I arrived on the scene, a woman had just passed out on the floor because I guess she had a little too much fun.) *Revolución 1127 between calles 7 and 8.* ☎ *644/685-9594, or 688-1368. Cover $80.*

➔ **Rodeo de Santa Fe** Norteno and cumbia lovers of all ages flock to this multi-level dance hall just down from the Mofo Bar (see above). On any given night, everyone from middle-aged rancheros and their honeys, to young kids on dates, comes together to dance-hug each other to the oompah rhythm. Yet it's still a rodeo in here—a mechanical bull sits beside the packed dance floor. *Pueblo Amigo Local #9.* ☎ *644/682-4967. Cover $80.*

➔ **Tentaculo Bar** ★★ Down the hill and across the river in the Zona Rio sits this small groovy minimalist space in Pueblo Amigo. It's the city's first pure electronica bar, capitalizing on the booming electronica scene started by Nortec Booker and DJ Wero. As such, it brings in indie bands as well as local and international laptop DJs. When I visited, the place was filled with a

Bet on It

Wanna gamble? Then stop by **Caliente** off-track betting (Revolución 931; ☎ **664/633-7300;** www.caliente.com.mx). This little pocket of Vegas, served up on Revolución, features rows of electronic slots, plasma betting screens, and electronic bingo. After the madness outside on Revu, it almost feels civilized in here.

20-30-something clientele grooving to electro-pop, house, '60s to '80s disco, dance, and Spanish pop and drinking up cheap beers at the long bar. It used to be a male strip bar for women but now sports a vaguely Asian decor, a slightly raised DJ platform, and a large dance floor surrounded by curved white walls. If it feels like it's half finished inside, that's the intent: The roof purposefully looks like it's falling in, and a curved plaster shell hangs over a few simple chairs and tables. Take a few minutes to absorb all the destruction before the music draws you out onto the floor. *Pueblo Amigo (look for the octopus logo out front). No phone. Cover $30 varies by event.*

Performing Arts

If you're interested in checking out some theater, visit www.cecut.gob.mx for event listings (in Spanish only) at the **Centro Cultural Tijuana.** Or head straight to **Teatro de la UABC** (☎ **664/684-0908,** Ticetmovil; 664/681-7084) which has original productions, mostly in Spanish. You can also catch theater performances at **Las Tablas Café** (Union Av. 2191, Col. Marron; **664/684-0386;** www.grupoojo.com; Mon–Sat 10am–10pm) and the **Opera Café** (Calle 7 Col. Libertad; ☎ **664/607-3897**), which is billed as "the ideal place for those who love opera."

If you want to take in some art, you have plenty of options here, too. Local galleries **Galleria La Caja** (Tapachula 1B, Col. Hippodrome) and **Galleria Arte 256** (Merida 256, Fracc. Chapultepec) both represent emerging artists whose work reflects their dialog with the border. **InSITE** ★★ (☎ **619/230-0005;** www.insite05.org) is a public arts organization based in Tijuana and San Diego that sponsors projects that address border cross-cultural issues. They hold events with local artists as well as big names like Roman De Salvo and Sylvia Gruner. The conceptual site-dependent work has been exhibited in as many as 21 different simultaneous venues, from galleries to small parks, throughout the city.

Sightseeing

FESTIVALS/EVENTS

Bi-national Mozart Festival: This festival brings artists from all over the world to perform Mozart. It takes place at the **Centro Cultural Tijuana** (CECUT), Paseo de los Héroes and Mina, Zona Rio. Call ☎ **664/687-9635** or visit www.cecut.gob.mx for info. January to March.

International Dance Festival: CECUT (see above) attracts dancers from across the world to Tijuana. April.

Tijuana Gay Pride Parade: Nearly 400 people marched in the 11th Gay Pride Parade in Tijuana in 2006, cheered on by a crowd of thousands. It was tiny compared to the over 150,000 who turn out for Mexico City's Gay Parade, but for Tijuana it was impressive. The parade takes place in early June (usually the first or second Sat) and goes down Av. Revolución in the midafternoon. Check www.gaymexico.net/tijuana.html for info.

International Seafood Festival: Seafood lovers rejoice at this festival to all things fishy. At Avenida Revolución,

Canirac Tijuana-Tecate. Call ☎ **664/682-8744** for info. July.

Tequila Festival. Break out your shot glasses—this festival gives you a chance to sample all different types of tequila. At Avenida Revolución, Impulsores de Marcas y Productos COTUCO. Call ☎ **664/901-0945** or www.tijuanaonline.org for info. October.

Hispanic American Guitar Festival: An annual jam fest that features guitarists from all over the world. Around Saint Cecilia Square and Plaza Santa Cecilia. Call ☎ **664/685-6671** or e-mail isaacalberto@msn.com for info. November.

MAJOR ATTRACTIONS

If you think there's no culture in TJ, then you haven't been to the MTV Best **Centro Cultural Tijuana** or **CECUT** ★★ (Paseo de los Héroes and Mina Rio Zone; ☎ **664/687-9600,** ext. 9650; www.cecut.gob.mx; daily 9am–9pm; free admission to permanent exhibits). This huge round structure looks somewhat like a nuclear power plant, but houses some amazing art. There's a newly opened pre-Columbian sculpture garden as well as an OMNIMAX theater, a permanent collection of Mexican artifacts, a gallery of visiting exhibits (admission $20 for special events), video rooms, a library, lecture rooms, and a restaurant. The center also includes the **Museum of Mexican Identities,** with a permanent collection of artifacts from pre-Hispanic times through the modern era, and the **Museum of the Californias,** with exhibits that trace the history of the Californias. With so many attractions on-site, it gets about a million visitors a year and world-class billings: Everyone from Lila Downs to Eugenia Leon to the Mariachachi Vargas to Ballet Folklorico de Mexico have performed here. They even host many festivals and special events (see "Festivals," above).

One of the best things about visiting the Cultural Center is that it'll give you a chance to see the more sophisticated Zona Rio. While in this hood, stop to admire the wide, European-style **Paseo de los Hereos.** The boulevard's intersections are gigantic traffic circles, at the center of which stand statuesque monuments to leaders ranging from Aztec Emperor Cuahtemoc to Abraham Lincoln.

One of the first major tourist attractions below the border is also one of the strangest—the downtown **Museo de Cera (Wax Museum),** Calle 1 no. 8281, at the corner of Madero (☎ **664/688-2478**). Featured statues include the eclectic mix of Whoopi Goldberg, Frida Kahlo, Laurel and Hardy, and Bill Clinton, arranged in an exhibit otherwise dominated by figures from Mexican history. If you aren't spooked by the not-so-lifelike figures of Aztec warriors, brown-robed friars, Spanish princes, and 20th-century military leaders (all posed in period dioramas), step into the Chamber of Horrors, where wax werewolves and sinister sadists lurk in the shadows. When the museum is mostly empty, which is most of the time, the dramatically lit Chamber of Horrors can be a little creepy. This side-street freak show is open daily from 10am to 6pm, and admission is $15.

Although the lightning-paced indoor ballgame jai alai (pronounced "*high* ah-*lye*") is no longer played here, it's still worth a visit to the **Jai Alai Palace,** Avenida Revolución at Calle 8 (☎ **664/685-3687,** 664/688-0125, or 619/231-1910 in San Diego), for its exquisite neoclassical architecture. Built in 1925, the building for years was the site of jai alai matches, an ancient Basque tradition incorporating elements of tennis, hockey, and basketball. Now the arena is used for cultural events or occasional boxing matches.

A modern symbol of Tijuana, the **Monumental Arch** (also referred to as the Tijuana or Millennium Arch, or Monumental Clock) was constructed to celebrate the millennium, and has become a source of local debate as to whether it's loved or hated (its modern architecture leaves some with a bad taste in their mouth, as it sits in a historical district). It's at the mouth of Plaza Santa Cecilia, where Calle 1 meets Avenida Revolución.

BEER & WINE TOURS

Want to find out where all that local beer you've been drinking comes from? Then head on over to the **Tijuana Brewery** (Bulevar Fundadores 2951, Col. Juárez; ☎ **664/684-2406** or 664/638-8662; www.tjbeer.com). Guided tours (by prior appointment) demonstrate the beer-making process at the brewery. The family who owns the company has a long tradition of hiring master brewers who worked in breweries in the Czech Republic and brought what they learned back home to Tijuana. Cerveza Tijuana, founded in January 2000, has select distribution in the U.S. Its lager, dark, and light beers are all available to sample in the adjoining European-style pub, where you can also sing your heart out Monday and Tuesday on karaoke nights. There's live music Wednesday through Saturday.

Northern Baja's Valle de Guadalupe produces many fine wines (see the box on p. 356), but you'll need to take a day trip there. While you're in Tijuana, a quick introduction to some of the wines can be had by stopping into **Cava de Vinos** (L.A. Cetto Winer; Av. Cañón Johnson 2108, at Av. Constitución Sur; ☎ **664/685-3031**, ext. 128; lacetto@compuserve.com; Mon–Fri 9am–6pm, Sat 10:30am–5pm). The building's interesting facade—it's shaped like a wine barrel—is made from recycled oak aging barrels. If you're planning a trip to the Guadalupe Valley, though, save your money for there; the wine there is superior to anything stocked at Cava de Vinos.

Playing Outside

Tijuana is definitely not an adventure destination; you'll need to head farther south for outdoorsy options like snorkeling and biking or even for decent, safe beaches. (The main beach here, Las Playitas, is in a very rough neighborhood.) But there are a range of spectator sports to choose from. The best are the **baseball** games at the grand Calimax stadium (Río Eufrates s/n, in the Col. Capistrano neighborhood; ☎ 664/660-9863). Tickets range in price from $100 to $120. Season packages are also available for purchase at the stadium.

The city also has two **Plaza de Toros** for **bullfighting**, one downtown and another out in Playas. The season runs from May through September, on Sunday afternoons. Tickets aren't cheap—they run $545 to $818 for the shaded section—and can be bought either at the bullring or from San Diego's **Five Star Tours** (☎ **619/232-5049** or 664/622-2203). **El Toreo** (☎ **664/686-1510;** www.bullfights.org) is 3km (2 miles) east of downtown on Bulevar Agua Caliente at Avenida Diego Rivera. **Plaza de Toros Monumental,** also called Bullring-by-the-Sea (☎ **664/680-1808;** www.plazamonumental.com), is 10km (6 miles) west of downtown on Highway 1-D (before the first toll station).

It won't cost you anything to watch the dogs run for their lives at the **Caliente Racetrack** (off Bulevar Agua Caliente, 5km/3 miles east of downtown; ☎ **619/231-1910** or 664/682-3110). Admission for **dog racing** is free and races are held daily at 7:45pm, with Tuesday, Saturday, and Sunday matinees at 2pm. This place gets crowded with families—who knows if they are aware that Caliente is the last resort for many greyhounds. (If the greyhounds lose, they get put down rather unceremoniously. Fortunately a pet rescue group in California is adopting as many of the dogs as they can. Visit www.fastfriends.org for info.) You can also bet on slot machines at Caliente; see p. 331.

Shopping

For millions who cross the border into Tijuana every year, shopping is the big draw. While it seems like every place that is not selling alcohol is selling discounted meds, you'll find much more than booze and medicine here. Wander through any market, and you'll spot wares ranging from good-quality low-fire pottery, to finely woven serapes and rebozos, to silver jewelry, to leather products, to piñatas, to black velvet paintings of Tupac, to fake Havana cigars.

ARCADES/MARKETS

Tijuana used to be full of covered arcades like the one in which **Cafe La Especial** (p. 325) still sits, but their numbers are slowly decreasing. Especial is still going strong, though, with a bunch of tourist-friendly goods like T-shirts with stupid sayings on them ("For sale, wife, take over payments") and wrestler masks.

The crafts market **Mercado de Artesanías** ★ (Calle 2 and Av. Negrete; daily 9am–9pm) is almost like an entire city of stuff to buy—the block of vendors crams in that much pottery, clothing, and craft items.

For an authentic middle-class Mexican shopping experience, check out the plazas (shopping centers) like **Plaza Río Tijuana** ★ (Paseo de los Héroes 96 at Av. Independencia, Zona Rio; ☎ **664/684-0402**). In this outdoor plaza, you'll find everything from health shops to bookstores to Sanborns to Dorians and other specialty shops and casual restaurants. **Plaza Agua Caliente** (Bulevar Agua Caliente 4558, Col. Aviación; ☎ **664/681-7777**) is a more upscale shopping center that has many day spas, gyms, and doctors' offices, as well as fine shops and restaurants.

CIGARS

For Cuban cigars (remember that they're not legal to bring across the border, so you better smoke 'em here) check out **La Casa del Habano** (Revolución 1115; ☎ **664/688-3339;** www.lacasadelhabano.com). Sit back in one of their leather chairs and sip an Italian espresso or cappuccino while considering Cohibas and other hand-rolled cigars.

CRAFT STORES

Casa del Angel (Av. Revolución 1026; ☎ **664/685-1044**) sells *alebrijes* (folk art sculptures) from Oaxaca, papier-mâché dolls, and Katrina statues from Guanajuato, mixed in with miniature Virgins of Guadalupe.

A wonderful place for hand-woven tablecloths and runners, *guayaberas* from Mérida, silver jewelry, and tatted lace is **Hand Art** ★★ (Revolución 1040-B between 4th and 5th; ☎ **664/685-2642**). They also have blouses and dresses from all over Mexico, mostly made by hand. A family business since 1955, the store is staffed by folks who will honestly tell you the difference between hand- and machine-made and alpaca and silver.

For decent quality leather, seek out **Shop 12** ★ (Pasaje Condominio, between 5th and 6th; no telephone) where you can find leather handmade bags, wallets, sandals, vests, hats, phone cases, backpacks, and more. The family-owned business has made quality leather goods for 45 years.

Rosarito Beach

Though it's only a 20-minute drive south of Tijuana, Rosarito Beach lacks the same big-city, anything-goes feel. It's true that, during spring break, the whole town becomes a huge wild party. But off season, it's quiet enough to be almost tranquil.

Rosarito Beach saw an explosion of development in the prosperous '80s and has now settled down into its own spirited personality. One reason it became popular is because of its location—it's the first beach resort town south of the border, and party-minded tourists aren't always too discriminating. Expect a very fratty crowd on holiday weekends and during school breaks.

Since the coastal areas in Baja started developing, the amount of American- and Canadian-owned vacation homes here has mushroomed. Unfortunately the building boom, combined with a lack of infrastructure, has resulted in a ton of neon-lit restaurants, strip malls, farmacias, and souvenir shops lining the formerly quaint main drag. Environmentalists and residents fear that, if unchecked, the rapid development could ruin the town's natural beauty. For now, though, Rosarito remains a friendly and still small-enough beach town—certainly worth a visit for its parties, if not its culture.

Getting There & Getting Around

GETTING INTO TOWN

BY PLANE The closest airport is in Tijuana, 29km (18 miles) north. See p. 317 for airport info. It's easiest to drive from the Tijuana airport to Rosarito, though you can take a taxi. See "By Car" and "By Taxi" below for info.

BY CAR Drivers have the option of either taking the coastal toll road (Hwy. 1-D), marked *cuota* (toll road), or the free but slower public road (Hwy. 1), marked *libre* (free) that run between Tijuana and Ensenada. The 29km (18-mile) drive on the *cuota* is beautiful and safer, so I recommend springing for it over the public road.

BY BUS You can take **Mexicoach** (☎ **664/685-1440;** www.gototijuana.com) from the States to Rosarito. Board the bus shuttle service at the Border Station Parking (next to the San Diego Factory Outlet Center) or from the trolley's last stop at the border (see "Getting There & Around," on p. 317), and it will take you to the Tijuana Tourist Terminal, Avenida Revolución, between calles 6 and 7 (☎ **664/685-1470**), where you can continue on to Rosarito. The cost from San Ysidro direct to Rosarito is $120 each way; from the Tijuana Tourist Terminal to Rosarito is $60 each way. It's open daily from 5:30am to 9pm, with departures every 15 to 20 minutes from 8am to 9pm, 365 days per year. Returns to the border leave from the same terminal. Another option is to travel direct from San Diego to Rosarito on **Baja Express** (☎ **619/232-5040,** or 619/230-5049). Pickups can be arranged with 1-day advance scheduling from downtown.

BY TAXI Yellow and white taxis cruise the stretch around the Tijuana-Rosarito-Ensenada corridor until late night. They can take you between towns for about $110.

GETTING AROUND

You can easily get around Rosarito on foot. For distances outside town, your best bet is to take a taxi. You can catch taxis in front of the Rosarito Beach Hotel or Hotel Festival Plaza (Blvd. Benito Juárez 1207-1). You can also get a route taxi to La Misión and Puerto Nuevo for about $100; the *sitio* (taxi stand) is in front of Calle Villa Alamo just east of Bulevar Juárez.

Buses in town, called *calafias,* will shuttle you up and down Juárez for a few pesos all day long; you can flag them down at any corner.

Basics

TOURIST INFO & OFFICES

The **Baja California Tourism Information** office (☎ **800/522-1516** in California, Arizona, or Nevada, 800/225-2786 in the rest of the U.S. and Canada, or 619/298-4105 in San Diego; www.baja.gob.mx) provides tourist advice and makes hotel reservations throughout Baja California. You can also contact the local **Secretaria de Turísmo,** Carretera Libre Tijuana-Ensenada Km 28 (☎ **01-800/025-6288**, or 800/962-2252 in the U.S.; www.rosarito.org). The office is open Monday through Friday from 8am to 8pm, and Saturday and Sunday from 9am to 1pm. Special **tourist aid** service is available by calling ☎ **664/612-0200.**

Sleeping

In addition to the following options, consider **Hotel Sonia** (east side of Bulevar Juárez s/n; ☎ **661/612-1260;** US$20–US$35 double; no credit cards), which is extremely cheap and in the center of the action. If location is most important to you, this is definitely a place you can crawl back to but not necessarily linger in—it's extremely bare bones (but clean). Another cheap alternative is the **Paraiso Ortiz** (Bulevar Benito Juárez s/n, south of Rosarito Beach Hotel; ☎ **661/612-1020;** US$30–US$50; no credit cards) which has old-fashioned cottage-style rooms along a California-style courtyard—some face the ocean.

For true budget digs, you can also try the secluded bare-bone campgrounds at **Rancho Salsipuedes** (Km 88) as well as the funky trailer park (for rent) and fish/surf camp at **Playa Salamando** (Km 94), see below. Just up the road from La Fonda (see below) is **Alisito's Camp** (Km 58, La Misión; ☎ **646/155-1020;** US$17 per car, US$18 per trailer, US$22 per RV, or US$11 day use only; no credit cards), which caters to surfers and car campers. On a big open spot above the beach, there are shared bathrooms and showers and sites with spectacular views and access to the surf break.

Due to the influx of buildings in Baja, prices keep going up, so be sure to ask about the rates listed below before you book.

➔ **Hotel La Fonda** ★★ If you're driving, it's easy to venture a few miles south to this hotel perched on a cliff between the highway and the ocean, with a sandy beach and decent surfing just in front. The whole joint is quirky and cool—no two rustic rooms look alike, and many have decks or patios. Though it's somewhat worn at the edges, the hotel's good location and reasonable prices make it a popular place. (It's at the famous K58 surfing spot, so expect to see lots of surfers.) The moderately priced restaurant (which doesn't take reservations) has wonderful seafood for dinner and their Sunday brunch is justly famous—be prepared to wait. They've also recently opened a pleasant spa that offers massages like "the baja bomb" (sports massage) and the rock buff ("so unique it defies description") for US$60–US$90. If they're full, check out their newly opened second hotel, **Kinda la Fonda,** with rooms that start at only US$75—but minus the fun atmosphere of this location. *Hwy. 1 Km 59. ☎ 646/155-5390. www.lafondamexico.com. US$100–US$150 single/double. No credit cards. In room: TV (in some), fireplaces (in some), kitchenette (in some).*

NORTHERN BAJA

Rosarito Beach

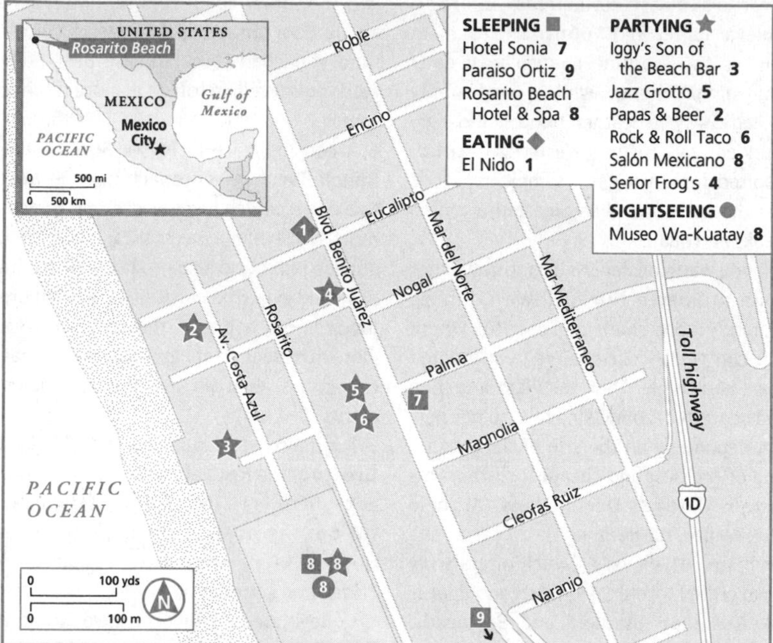

→ **Rosarito Beach Hotel & Spa** ★ Built just after Prohibition by a Belgian architect and Mexican muralist, this beachfront hotel was once a favorite place for Hollywood celebrities and Latin American presidents, but it just ain't the same nowadays. In spite of the glaring nighttime neon and mongo partying, there are still great views of the sea, and the hotel somehow feels cool in a kind of haunted way. The construction throughout is unique and artistic, the furnishings heavy and wooden, and it's on a wide, family-friendly stretch of beach. The newer, air-conditioned units in the tower have pastel color schemes and higher prices. Stay in rooms in the older section with their hand-painted trim and original tile; they may have ceiling fans rather than air-conditioning, but if you have a sea breeze, who cares?

The home of the original owners is now the full-service **Casa Playa Spa,** where you'll pay slightly less than in the U.S. for massages and other treatments. There are two restaurants: the main dining room **(Chabert's Steakhouse)** with way overpriced Continental cuisine; and the less formal Mexican restaurant **Azteca** in the main building. *Bulevar Benito Juárez. ☎ 661/612-0144, or 800/343-8582 in the U.S. www.rosaritobeachhotel.com. US$70–US$140 single/double, US$111–US$175 suite. Packages available. MC, V. Amenities: 2 restaurants; bar; laundry service; playground; 2 outdoor pools; racquetball; spa; tennis; volleyball. In room: A/C (in some), TV, fans (in some).*

Eating

In town, your cheapest bet is to eat at family-run taco and tamale stalls (like **Tacos El Yaqui** or **Tacos Sonora**).

For a grander night out, try one of Rosarito's oldest restaurants, **El Nido** (Bulevar Juárez 67; ☎ **661/612-1430;** main courses $55–$200; no credit cards; daily 8am–11pm). Here, while comfortably tucked away in leather booths and surrounded by rustic, Western frontier-inspired decor, you get to sample generous steakhouse food like mesquite-grilled steaks and quail.

If you want lobster, it's best to go farther south to **Puerto Nuevo** (Hwy. 1, Km 44, 12km/7½ miles south of Rosarito) where you can get a delicious medium lobster, huge handmade flour tortillas, and rice and beans for around $150 to $220 per person depending on the size of the lobster. One of the best and cheapest restaurants there is **Ortega's Ocean View** (Anzuelo 15-A; ☎ **661/112-5322;** no credit cards; call for hours, which vary), which offers truly fresh grilled lobster. Another good spot is the **Rosamar** (Anzuelo and Barracuda; ☎ **661/614-1210;** no credit cards; call for hours, which vary). The lobster here is cheaper than most other places; the place is huge and full of local families instead of tourists, and, though the ambience isn't perfect, there's a good view from upstairs.

Partying

Tons of American kids drive south to Rosarito because they can check out the bars here without being freaked out by safety issues like in Tijuana. That's because Rosarito is less a city and more of a resort—it's the sort of place where, for better or worse, teenagers can let it all hang out and do things they'd never consider doing in their hometowns up north.

The most popular bar in town is **Papas & Beer** (Av. Coronado s/n, a block east of Bulevar Juárez at Eucalipto; ☎ **661/612-0444;** www.papasandbeer.com), though during off season it's deserted like everywhere else in town. Just a block north of the Rosarito Beach Hotel, it's on the beach and the "dress code" reflects that. There are outdoor tables and the bar surrounds a sand volleyball court, in case beer pong gets you revved up for some more athletic games.

A cooler choice is **Iggy's Son of the Beach Bar** ★ (Av. Coronado 11337; ☎ **661/612-0537**), which has a beach bar, restaurant, volleyball, mechanical bull, *and* bungee jump, and also no shortage of cute boys and girls. The music here skews more towards hip-hop and the crowd's a lot more diverse than at Papas; there is a small cover, but keep an eye out for ladies' nights.

For more staid partying, try the **Jazz Grotto** at the Festival Plaza Hotel (☎ **888/295-9669**) or the **Salón Mexicano** (☎ **661/612-0144**) at the Rosarito Beach Hotel (p. 337), which has live music on Friday and Saturday.

College student favorites are **Rock & Roll Taco** (Av. Juárez s/n; ☎ **661/612-2950**), which has theme nights, indoor and outdoor dancing, a pool, and foam dancing (eww); and the ubiquitous **Señor Frog's** (Bulevar Benito Juárez 4358 at Nogal; ☎ **661/612-4375;** www.senorfrogs.com). It's got all the kitschy trappings (like pro-drinking slogans on the walls) and pub grub like nachos that all Señor Frog's have but the magic doesn't work as well here—the scene is fairly dead.

Heading to the Beach

The beach at Rosarito is far more enticing than the cheesy bars, mediocre restaurants, and crowds of pimply valley kids. Stretching for 8km (5 miles) from the north end of town, it's still clean and beautiful, and safe for swimming, though the water is somewhat cold. You'll want to head on to the beaches at Ensenada and its environs for snorkeling and surfing options; see p. 354 for info.

Sightseeing

The Rosarito Beach Hotel (p. 337) is an attraction in itself because of its former status as a preferred hideaway of celebrities. But you'll also want to see the tiny **Museo Wa-Kuatay** (Bulevar Benito Juárez s/n; no phone; free admission; Wed–Mon noon–5pm) that's attached to it. Here, you can tour a photo collection detailing the early history of ranchers, Hollywood celebrities, and political figures in Rosarito. Also on display is a collection of Wakutais Indian (they were the original inhabitants of the area) artifacts.

At the south end of town is the 45-acre **Fox Studios "Foxploration"** (Hwy. 1 Km 32; ☎ **866/369-2252** in the U.S., or 661/614-9444; www.foxploration.com; admission $131; Wed–Fri 9am–4:30pm, Sat–Sun 10am–5:30pm), a blatantly cheesy rip-off of Universal Studios, whose major claim to fame is that it's where *Titanic* was filmed. The "Titanic Expo" is primarily aimed at the *Titanic* freak, a decidedly dwindling demographic. Don't get any ideas that the actual *Titanic* is here, but you can tour the real ship used to film *Master and Commander*. Most interesting is the behind-the-scenes section—with physical explanations that detail just how the "magic" of movie making unfolds. Getting makeup put on by a semi-pro is one of the more popular interactive activities available. There are also costumes, sets, and props from *X-Men, Planet of the Apes, Romeo and Juliet,* and other films.

Playing Outside

Aside from swimming, there aren't really any outdoorsy options in town. If you're itching to do things like biking and kayaking, though, you just have to travel a few more miles south to Ensenada (p. 354).

Shopping

Although the souvenirs are better in Ensenada and Tijuana, Rosarito certainly boasts lots of shops along the dozen blocks of town north of the Rosarito Beach Hotel. Most streets are packed with typical border-town stores—curio shops, cigar and liquor stores, and farmacias. South of the hotel are endless blocks of stores selling furniture. One such reliable but expensive shop is **Casa la Carreta,** Km 29.5, on the old road south of Rosarito (☎ **661/612-0502;** www.casalacarreta.com), which stocks first-rate chests, tables, chairs, headboards, and cabinets.

The **Casa Torres Museum Store** (at the Rosarito Beach Hotel shopping center; ☎ **661/612-1008**) has been around since 1969 selling museum-quality handicrafts from throughout Mexico. You'll find carved wooden masks, beaded Huichol art, Day of the Dead curios, and more here. An adjoining duty-free store sells perfumes, liquors, and cosmetics.

Ensenada

The third largest city in Baja, Enseneda is also the second most-visited port-of-call for major cruise ships in Mexico. But don't let the crowds deter you from visiting: The drive alone here (it's 109km/68 miles south of the border) on the Carretera Tijuana-Ensenada (Hwy.1) is spectacular. And, compared to übertouristy towns in north Baja like Tijuana, Ensenada is quite welcoming—home to the pretty Todos Santos Bay and mountains that are perfect for biking.

Locals rightly assert that Ensenada is, well, *different*. Even though America exerts a significant influence on culture throughout Baja, Ensenada somehow still feels authentically Mexican. Perhaps that's because stricter rules have been enacted here: The tourist board recommends, among other things, that "you can be arrested for disturbing the peace or being a public nuisance, drinking on the streets, fighting, nudity or immoral behavior, possessing, carrying or using forbidden drugs (or weapons)." Get the idea?

On the other hand, there's still a tinge of the Sin City nastiness so commonly encountered in Tijuana here, especially during the annual carnaval season. It's just that any tackiness is diluted by a distinctly more provincial sensibility. Like La Paz in Baja Sur (p. 413), Ensenada is secure in its identity, no matter how many cruise ships are anchored in the bay. That's why I think of Ensenada as the place where the *real* Baja begins, and why I'm sure you will too.

Getting There & Getting Around

GETTING INTO TOWN

BY PLANE Ensenada does not have an airport, but you can fly into the Tijuana airport (p. 317), which is only 110km (68 miles) away. From there, you can rent a car for the 90-minute drive into town; see p. 318 for rental options. Or you can take a bus from the Tijuana airport for about $95 for first class via the carrier **ABC** (☎ **664/178-6680**).

BY CAR You can reach Ensenada via the **Carretera Tijuana-Ensenada** (aka Hwy. 1-D or Old Ensenada Hwy.) outside Playas de Tijuana (watch closely for signs to the right after crossing the border). The *cuota* (toll road) is about $82 and well worth it for the views—even though the *libre* (free) road essentially parallels the toll road the entire way. There are frequent off ramps and turnarounds on the road if you miss a turn, which isn't hard to do since the scenery is truly spectacular. I think it's one of the most gorgeous driving trips in all of Mexico.

Note that the *cuota* from Tijuana is safe because it's regularly patrolled by the highway assistance group the Green Angels (p. 320), recognizable by their green pickups. They offer assistance with flats, breakdowns, or any automotive-related concern, for no charge.

BY BUS If you're coming across the border from the States, head for the Plaza Viva Bus Station in San Diego. The **Autotransportes Baja California** or **ABC** (☎ **664/683-5681**) and **Aragon** (☎ **646/178-8521**) have buses going to Ensenada from there every half-hour, from 6am to 9:30pm. ABC arrives at the Central Terminal in Ensenada (Av. Riveroll at Calle 11) while Aragon arrives at its own terminal on Riveroll at Calle 8. One-way is about $870 and takes almost 2 hours. Round-trip is about $1,850.

GETTING AROUND

Since Ensenada is relatively small, it's quite easy to get around by foot. But here are some other options if you're feeling lazy or want to go a bit farther afield:

BY TAXI Taxis will charge $40 to anywhere within town; $80 to $100 to the outskirts like El Saucel, Lomas, or Estero Beach; or $150 per ride anywhere else. If you're taking what's considered to be a "tour," the price can go up to $400.

Yellow Cabs host many tours in their minivans, which are parked on Miramar at López Mateos (☎ **646/178-3475**). **Taxis Azul y Blanco** have many stands (2nd and Gastélum, ☎ **646/178-3201;** 1st and Ruiz, ☎ **646/178-3202;** 2nd and Miramar, ☎ **646/178-3203**), so they're the most convenient for getting about town.

BY SCOOTER For a fun and alternative way to get around, rent a scooter or four-wheeler at **Chavo's Sports Rentals** (Bulevar Costero at Av. Castillo; ☎ **646/102-5942**).

Ensenada

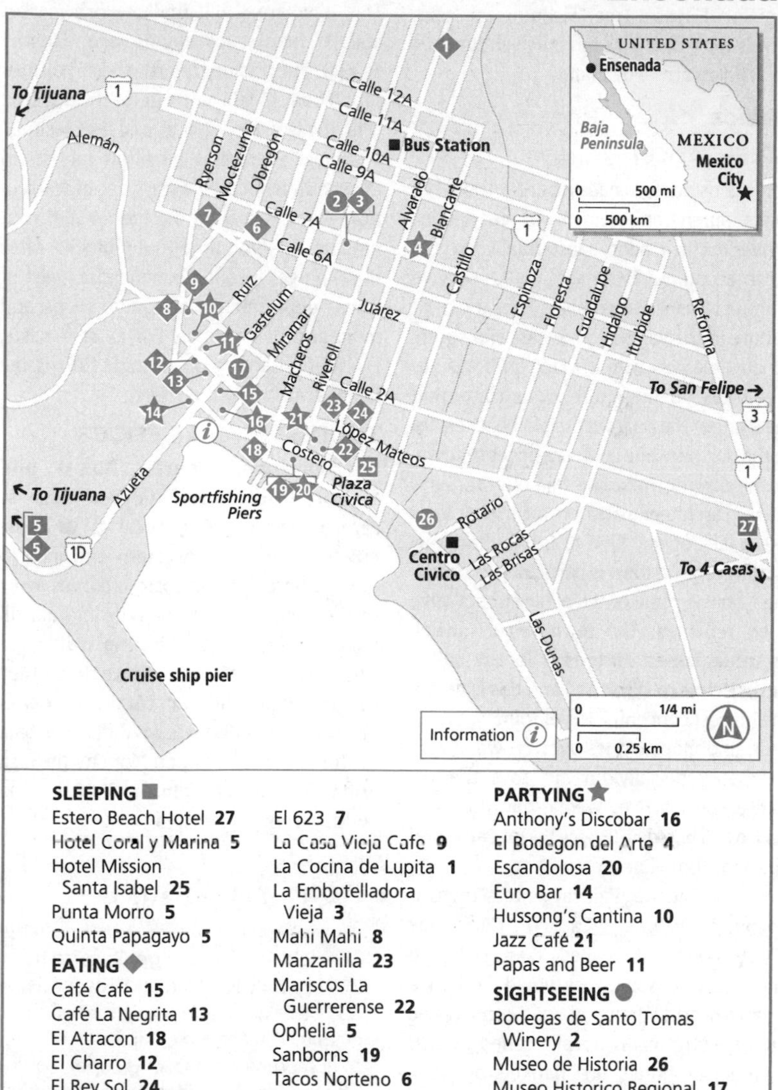

BY BUS The **Main Bus Station** (Riveroll at Calle 11) is served by the long distance bus lines **ABC** and **Aragon;** see earlier for phone info. Buses from here regularly connect to Tijuana and to Cabo San Lucas and Cabo San José for $1,338, $1,373, and $1,498 (depending on the class).

BY BIKE You can rent a bicycle at bike shop **Duran** (Riveroll 542; ☎ 646/174-0160).

BY BOAT Some spots in town, such as the **Coral Hotel** (see "Sleeping," p. 344), have slips where you can pull right up and dock if you arrive by boat.

Basics

ORIENTATION

Some consider Ensenada a border town but that's purely an accident of geography. While tourism adds substantially to the local economy, Ensenada could survive without it thanks to its fishing fleet and agriculture in the valleys to the east and south. Its bustling port with working harbor actually takes up the entire waterfront—that means that the only accessible beaches are at the northern and southern edges of town.

The downtown area is laid out on a grid and the architecture suffers from what feels like a lack of any kind of urban planning. Getting around town is particularly confusing because some of the older streets have been renamed: The town's main street, **Avenida López Mateos** is locally called **Calle Primera (First St.)** and this is where the highest concentration of tourist restaurants and shops are. It's often crowded with tourists, especially on the days the big cruise ships arrive: Wednesday (Carnival cruises), Thursday (Royal Caribbean), and Saturday (both lines).

As the Tijuana highway enters town it becomes **Bulevar Lázaro Cárdenas** (more commonly called **Costero**) and emerges into something you'd find in a bizarro-world version of southern Orange County—strip malls (locally called plazas) with fancy hotels are flanked by strip shows and souvenir shops. Most of the town's shops and restaurants are on these two main streets, between Avenidas Ruiz and Castillo, although there are also new restaurants and tasting rooms on Moctezuma at 6th (see "Eating," p. 345).

The **malecón** runs along the harbor parallel to the Bulevar Costera, from the entrance to town at Gastélum to the river. This is where you'll find the fish market and its many taco stands (see "Eating," p. 345), sportfishing piers where you can rent a boat to take you out for the day (see "Playing Outside," p. 352), and the marina.

Almost everything aimed at tourists in Ensenada is located within a 4-block section going east from the harbor and running north-south for about 6 blocks. After that you get into the commercial heart of town—department stores, auto shops, and mom-and-pop tiendas. For most tourists, Hussong's Cantina on Avenida Ruiz is the farthest east they'll venture.

TOURIST INFO & OFFICES

The **Ensenada Tourist Board and Visitor Information Center** (Bulevar Lázaro Cárdenas 609 Local 5; ☎ **646/178-8578**) is at the western entrance to town, where Bulevar Costero curves away to the right. It's open daily from 9am till dusk. Farther down the strip inside the Hotel Santo Tomás is the **State Secretary of Tourism** (Bulevar Lázaro Cárdenas 1477; ☎ **646/178-2411;** www.discoverbajacalifornia.com). It's open Monday through Friday from 9am to 7pm and Saturday and Sunday from 9am to 5pm.

Read All about It

The right-leaning ***Gringo Gazette*** has local (mostly Rosarito and Ensenada) and state news and a calendar of events. You can pick it up for free at numerous stores along López Mateos. You'll also find the free ***Fish Rap*** (www.thelog.com), with detailed reports and information about sportfishing throughout Baja. **Sanborn's** in the Plaza Marina has a small selection of English books, maps, and magazines, as does **Libros Libros** (see "Shopping," p. 355).

RECOMMENDED WEBSITES

- **www.discoverbajacalifornia.com**: The Ensenada Tourist Board and Visitor Information Center's site has a wealth of information, including especially good details on the mission trail.
- **www.ensenada.com**: A more generic destination site with links to hotels, clubs, bars, and outfitters.
- **www.ensenadagazette.com**: A handy site for events, concerts, and general listings in Ensenada.
- **www.worldtalkradio.com/show.asp?sid=126:** The site for Baja Talk Radio, an Internet radio show that is all about Baja.

Ensenada Nuts & Bolts

Banks There are ATMs scattered all around town, especially along Costero and in the tourist plazas (Plaza Marina, Bulevar Costero). A **Banorte Bank** is on the corner of Gastélum and Calle 4 (☎ **646/174-0305**) and a **Banamex** is at Ryerson #279 (☎ **646/176-0438**).

Embassies The **U.S. Consular Agency** is in Tijuana (p. 321), but the local 24-hour hot line is ☎ **646/692-2154.**

Emergencies For the **Red Cross,** dial direct ☎ **066,** or ☎ **646/174-4545** or -4585; for **police** dial direct ☎ **060** or ☎ **646/176-43453;** to report a **fire** dial direct ☎ **068** or ☎ **646/177-1325.**

Hospitals For emergency care, two of the best hospitals in town are **Del Carmen Hospital** (Obregon at Calle 11; ☎ **646/178-3477**) and **Isstecali Hospital** (Las Duna at Las Rocas; ☎ **646/176-4261**).

Internet Cafes/Wireless Hot Spots There are Internet cafes all over Ensenada, including **Equinoxio** (Bulevar Costero 267; ☎ **646/174-0455;** Mon–Sat 9am–10pm, Sun 10am–10pm), which in addition to Internet service ($20 per hour) can fix or maintain your laptop, print, and serve you coffee while you're at it. Wi-Fi here or on their outside terrace is free. You can also go online at **Net Café La Weba** (Centro de Art 37; ☎ **646/175-9570;** Mon–Sat 8am–9pm, Sun 9am–8pm) for $10 per hour.

Laundry There are laundromats all over town that charge by the kilo, but one I like is **Lava Matica** (Calle Riveroll at 4th; no phone; $30 a load).

Pharmacies **Farmacia el Sol** (Bulevar Costero 678 Local 411; ☎ **646/178-1168**) is open from 8am to 11pm daily and boasts an on-site pharmacist. Their branch on Calle Com. Limon (☎ **646/176-3775**) has 24-hour delivery.

Safety Ensenada is fairly safe, but there are neighborhoods to avoid. Wander just a half block off the main strip Calle Premiera, for instance, and you'll stumble upon the red light district. Beware of parking at night around Gastélum or Miramar between 1st and 2nd since this is also the red light district and it can get rough. A handful of brothels (masquerading as strip shows) are sprinkled around here, which advertise "girls, show for men." Accompanying them are meth freaks and assorted other all-night lost souls who wander the back streets. Also avoid Calle Secundo and the alley behind the Cosmos Club.

Telephone Tips The local area code is **646.** There's a branch of mobile phone store **Movistar** at Bulevar Costero 678-5 (☎ **646/174-0470** or -0418) where you can get a cellphone for $200—that includes 50 free minutes. There's also a **Telcel** office next to **AeroMexico** (Bulevar Lázaro Cárdenas 656, Plaza Marina; ☎ **646/178-1623** or -1653).

Sleeping

Ensenada is far enough away yet close enough to the U.S. border that an overnight trip from San Diego is totally feasible. (Or you can easily visit it as a day trip from Rosarito or Tijuana.) But if you decide to stay in town, there are lots of accommodation options. **Zona Playitas,** the area fronting the beaches just north of Ensenada (about a 5-min. drive), boasts several moderately priced motel or condo-style hotels (running about US$30–US$50 a night); I list the best below.

Cheaper hotels are found in town on López Mateos (Calle Primera); most of them are older and you get what you pay for—so-so water pressure, hard beds, and a Lysol stench. As with most spots in north Baja, because of the number of cheap hotel rooms, there really aren't great hostels to mention in town. (There are a couple of great hostels south of town, though; see "Road Trip: Quatro Casas," p. 358.)

Camping on the beaches in town isn't an option because they're not safe enough. Camping farther south is fairly safe (the hostels listed on p. 358 offer camping on their property) but do so at your own risk.

CHEAP

MTV Best → **Hotel Mission Santa Isabel** ★★ Designed and built by French engineer Gaston Flourie, who first came to Baja in 1924, La Mission has been one of the best cheap hotels in town for more than 60 years. Flourie was an amateur archaeologist, and was particularly interested in uncovering info on the lost Misión de Santa Isabel, one of the first Franciscan outposts here. Out of that obsession emerged this hotel, built in the mission style. Its attractive thick walls, tiled floors, arches, and heavy wooden doors are reminders of the Spanish-style design from the days of the Jesuit pioneers. The rooms themselves are clean and good sized, and there's an outdoor barbecue area near the pool. *Bulevar Lázaro Cárdenas 1119. ☎ 646/178-3345. missionsantaisabel@yahoo.com. $450–$750 single, $860–$950 double, $1,000–$1,250 junior suite. AE, MC, V. Amenities: Bar; restaurant; barbecue area; pool. In room: TV, fridge (in the junior suites), heater.*

DOABLE

→ **Estero Beach Hotel** The 10km (6-mile) trip south of the centro to stay at the Estero is definitely worth it, since it's a great outdoorsy alternative to the downtown hotels. It's set on a bay and protected lagoon that's good for swimming and sailing. There's also horseback riding, volleyball, tennis, and a game room with Ping-Pong and a pool table. The place has been here awhile so the cottages and rooms are a bit frayed at the edges, but they're clean and quiet (except for the occasional screaming kid roaming down the halls). *Estero Beach, at the end of Bulevar José María Morelos, off Hwy. 1, right after the military airfield. ☎ 646/176-6225. www.hotelesterobeach.com. US$75–US$156 double. MC, V. Amenities: Restaurant; game room; Jacuzzis; pool; shop; tennis court; volleyball court. In room: TV.*

→ **Quintas Papagayo Resort** This cool if somewhat funky hotel/motel was built in

NORTHERN BAJA

1935 and it could stand to be updated a bit. The look throughout is very 1950s Mexico—individual bungalows come with their own carports and little backyards complete with picnic tables. All of the (spacious) rooms also boast Saltillo tiled floors, plastered adobe walls, retro rattan furniture, and plaid drapes. It fills up during the Baja 1000 (see p. 351 for info) months in advance, probably because there's plenty of parking space for all the dune buggies on hand. Rooms with ocean views are more expensive, but the views overlooking the marina and fronting a paved walkway along the cliff might make the price difference worthwhile. *Carretera Tijuana-Ensenada Km 108. ☎ 646/174-4575. www.hussongs.com.mx. US$62–US$84 double, US$122–US$152 suite. MC, V. Amenities: Bar/restaurant. In room: A/C, TV, fridge, heater, kitchen (in some).*

SPLURGE

→ **Coral Hotel & Marina** ★ Cruise on up in your big boat and tie it to the marina that fronts this hotel. Don't have a big boat? Then at least come by to peek at all the sailing-inclined folks staying here on company vacation; it's slightly surreal to see all the boats parked like cars directly in front of the lobby. It's not all about boating here, though. A fitness center, spa, and tennis and volleyball courts are also on hand. The rooms are clean and spacious, if not super exciting—you won't get more than Ramada-style rooms here. *Carretera Tijuana-Ensenada Km 103. ☎ 646/175-0000, or 800/862-9020 in the U.S. www.hotelcoral.com. US$150 standard double suite, US$165 junior suite, US$250 deluxe suite. Mid-week and fall/winter packages available. MC, V. Amenities: Bar; restaurant; fitness center; pool; spa; store; tennis courts; volleyball court. In room: TV, hair dryer, safe.*

→ **Punta Morro** ★★ Right on the rocky point of Ensenada's harbor, the Morro fronts the best open stretch of natural ocean you'll see for miles. Though it's not really a swimming beach, they've got a pool and Jacuzzi and stunning views to make up for it. The property is made up of individual apartments, including studios and one- to three-bedroom suites that all have ocean views. None have kitchens, but there's a decent restaurant on-site, and the sleeping space is still a good value if there are several of you. The owners aren't really interested in hosting teenagers or frat boys; it's more of a low-key place to come and relax. *Carretera Tijuana-Ensenada Km 106. ☎ 646/178-3507 or 800/526-6676 in U.S. www.punta-morro.com. US$145 single/double, US$350 3-bedroom suite. Rates include continental breakfast. AE, MC, V. Amenities: Bar/restaurant; breakfast room; laundry service; wheelchair friendly; Wi-Fi. In room: TV, fridge, hair dryer, telephone.*

Eating

Thanks to its distance from the tawdry glitz of Tijuana and its proximity to the emerging Valle de Guadalupe (see the box on p. 356), Ensenada has developed into a bit of a culinary destination. Smaller high-end haute cuisine restaurants are springing up all over, dishing out Mexi-Med dishes that have justly drawn the attention of food writers from around the world. Yet one gets the impression that all Ensenada chefs—whether at street stands or working over stainless steel Viking ranges—are cooking for the joy of food, *not* to impress foodie snobs. The town is that laid-back.

The place to begin any culinary tour here is on the walking street that leads past the fish market by the pier. It doesn't get any fresher (or smellier) than this. Just 15m (50 ft.) away is Mercado Negro, the local black market. These stalls specialize in tempura-style fish tacos (according to legend, they were invented here, after a Japanese sailor hooked up with a local woman), while on the Calle Primera a bit farther north you'll find everything from classic Mexican old-school enchiladas and chiles rellenos to amazing street ceviche tostadas.

CHEAP

→ **El Atracon** MEXICAN The first taco stand on the pedestrian street running past the marina and past the main fish market, this place makes good fish tacos in the tempura batter style unique to Ensenada. They bring out big bowls of chile sauce, and you can choose between one that's blistering hot with lots of seeds, slightly milder green salsa, and salsa cruda that's almost palatable. Other taco condiments include limes, a big bowl of "pura mayonessa," creamy guacamole, and cabbage. Don't eat the cabbage—it isn't purified. Now that I think of it, nothing else here is exactly sparkling clean, from their bathrooms to the kitchen. But who cares when you can get seafood soup for about $90 and ceviche tostadas for $80? *Callejon Miramar 1, at Mercado Pescado. No phone. Nothing over $100. No credit cards. Mon–Sat 8am–9pm; Sun 8am–6pm.*

→ **El Charro** MEXICAN This place has been here forever, well, 50 years to be exact. Originally the spot was tucked away across the street in a wood cabin—it was a funky Ensenada landmark that set the tone for the food and service. Sadly some of that has changed now that they've moved across the street and gone all upscale and hygienic. Their specialty is the roasted chicken, which you can see rotating on big spits through the front window, next to the woman patting out tortillas. The hacienda-style furniture and wide circular staircase in the center of the room evoke another time, and another country. The big tables full of crowds of folks off cruise ships, sucking on chicken bones and wiping the grease on their Hawaiian shirts, however, slightly spoil the effect. *López Mateos 454. ☎ 646/135-1346 or 178-2114. Main courses $70–$100. AE, MC, V. Daily 9am–11pm; until midnight on weekends.*

→ **La Cocina de Lupita** ★ MEXICAN There were literally nine delivery trucks parked in front the morning I came here, a testament to the huge steaming platters of food served inside. Here you can get real guacamole, hard to find in this tourist town, accompanied by *huevos albanil* (eggs poached in red sauce), *nopal* (eggs scrambled with cactus), *rajas* (eggs scrambled with green chile), or any other style you want, as well as big bowls of menudo or pozole, and even pancakes. Everything comes with beans and slivers of fresh cheese, tortillas, searing red chipotle sauce, and *café de la olla* (cinnamon flavored and strong) too—yum. You'll have to work hard to spend more than $50. Since it's down the street from the Duran bike store, you can stop to pick up some sandwiches on your way for a bike ride. *Riveroll 1424-4. ☎ 646/175-3477. Nothing over $60. No credit cards. Mon–Sat 8am–8pm.*

MTV Best → **Mariscos La Guerrerense** ★★★ SEAFOOD This seafood cart has about the best ceviche I've ever eaten. Thirteen types are on offer, including shrimp, octopus, clam, and sea urchin, all served on small crunchy tortillas. The owners Sabina Bandera and Eduard Oviedo have parked their cart on this corner since 1960 and run one of the few places that keep their fish on ice. (Get here before 3pm, not only because the fish will be freshest then, but because they run out early in the afternoon.) Sabina also makes fabulous sauces, including a *chile de mi jardín* (olive oil with lots of chunks of fried garlic and chile), *guacachile* (guacamole with chile), and *chile de la suegra* (chile from her home state of Guerrero). The couple managed to put their daughter through university with proceeds from this cart, even though nothing is over $100. *Av. López Mateos at Av. Alvarado. ☎ 646/174-2114. Main courses under $100. No credit cards. Daily 8am–6pm.*

→**Tacos Norteno** MEXICAN Look for the locals hunkering down on the street and wolfing down hot carne asada tacos and you'll find this stand right nearby. It's no wonder it's popular—this is one of the best spots for meat in Ensenada. *Calle Obregon at 6th. No phone. Main courses $20. Daily 10am–2am.*

DOABLE

MTV Best → **El 623** ★★★ MEXICAN This is the best and hippest restaurant in town—it's a place for those that appreciate really good food. Local chef Marcela Ruiz Chong has worked with Valle de Guadalupe winemaker Hugo D'Acosta since the 1990s. Her menu of Mexican items, given a Mediterranean and Japanese twist, boasts a mouthful of surprises. Though she learned how to cook from her grandmother, I'm willing to bet that granny never dished up de-boned quail like Marcela. She mixes ingredients and flavors that startle the palate in the most agreeable yet radical ways—dishes manage to be sour and sweet and biting and soft, all at once. Eating here is so shocking and endlessly enticing, I felt like I was tasting nouvelle cuisine for the first time.

Even better, it's all organic: Nothing that comes to your plate will have been through a processing plant, from the lamb to the lobster to the quail. Another bonus: They have the best Valle de Guadalupe wines, available by the glass or bottle, at good prices. The service is first-rate, too; the attentive, black-clad waiters provide a stark counterpoint to the white walls, polished wood floors, and the overall minimalist décor of the interior space. Outdoors there's a more casual deck space, under a huge pepper tree surrounded by big stones. *Moctezuma 623. ☎ 646/156-5030. 623rest@prodigy.net.mx. Main courses $135–$275. MC, V. Daily 6–11pm.*

→**Mahi Mahi** SEAFOOD In an old rambling wooden building on a hill overlooking Ensenada, this restaurant somehow churns out seafood that's worthy of fancier digs. It's one of the most popular moderately priced fish restaurants in Ensenada for two very good reasons—the fish is fresh and the prices are fair. Tasty options include Sinaloan-style fish marinated in chile and lemon shrimp; fish filets in almond sauce, chipotle, and cilantro sauce; and Italian octopus in garlic. *Paseo Hidalgo 33. ☎ 646/178-3494. Main courses $100–$300. MC, V. Sun–Thurs noon–10pm; Fri–Sat noon–11pm.*

→**Manzanilla** ★ SEAFOOD Grab a seat at the curved wooden bar at the front of this contemporary meets '70s designed seafood restaurant, and you'll instantly feel cool. Sample some food, and you'll feel even cooler—the dishes here showcase the new Mexican style cuisine that's all the rage in Ensenada, a blend of Euro bistro and mesquite flavors that manages to be sophisticated, unique, and trendy. *Saveur Magazine* gave this place a rave in 2004, complimenting them on their rice and pasta dishes. I personally love the fresh abalone, and think the chef, Benito Molina, has done things with poblano chiles that should be outlawed, they're so good. Bonus: Their bar is stocked with boutique tequilas and Baja vintners. Folks day-trip all the way from San Diego just to eat here, so make reservations, especially on the weekends and during tourist seasons. *Av. Riveroll 122. ☎ 626/175-7073. Main courses about $200. MC, V. Wed–Sat 1pm–midnight.*

MTV Best →**Ophelia** ★ SEAFOOD This little restaurant lounge just north of the centro in the neighborhood of El Sauzal is one of the major forces behind Baja's changing culinary scene. After spending 10 years in various Mexico City restaurants, chef Rosende Ramos moved back to his hometown to open up this spot, where he cooks Baja style and surfs right out the front door at the San Miguel break. It's a modern minimalist space, where hipsters rub elbows with olive oil and wine merchants.

Come here for a chance to sample new Baja cuisine at a reasonable price, in cool, comfortable surroundings. The food manages to be both unique and tasty: The mini-tostadas with seared tuna and fried garlic slivers are crunchy, savory, and tangy; the crab ravioli come drenched in a tasty mushroom-*pilloncillo* (sugar cone) reduction sauce. *Carretera Tijuana-Ensenada Km 103, #7165A, El Sauzal. ☎ 646/175-8365. Tapas $60–$100; pasta $80–$120. MC, V. Mon–Thurs 1–9:30pm; Fri–Sat 1–11:30pm.*

→ **Sanborn's** DINER This venerable country-wide restaurant/store chain is Mexico's answer to Denny's. Put aside the definite camp factor, though, and all you're left with is another sterile plaza restaurant, which dishes out bland pastas, salads, pancakes, Americano coffee, and other essentially tasteless fare. A stop here could be a good cure for homesickness, but that's about it. But they do have a small selection of English books (see "Shopping," p. 355) that are worthy of browsing. *Plaza Marina, Bulevar Costero 626, Local 2. ☎ 646/174-0971. Breakfast $40–$80; main courses $80–$116. AE, MC, V. Daily 7am–11pm.*

SPLURGE

→ **El Rey Sol** ★ FRENCH This long-standing Ensenada landmark has been in town more than half a century and has won five-star diamond awards in the last 3 years. If you're in the mood for something decidedly not Mexican, it's a trip to come here and absorb the old-fashioned atmosphere, which practically drips from the wrought-iron chandeliers and heavy velvet curtains. Everything on the menu (including the wine list) is old-school French, so brace yourself for heavy sauces that tend to smother the food. Meat eaters will love the Sonoran beef and the chateaubriand—ask for the sauce on the side, $500 (for two). There's an outdoor dining area, but when you're paying so much, you should really take advantage of the quiet and comfy interior dining room. *Primera 10001 (at Blancarte), Centro, by the Motel Casa del Sol. ☎ 646/178-1601. www.elreysol.com. Main courses $100–$500. MC, V. Daily 8–10am and 7:30–10pm.*

→ **La Embotelladora Vieja** ★★ MEXICAN/MEDITERRANEAN Across the street from the Santo Tomás winery, this historic building was once part of the winery but now houses several gallery spaces and a small restaurant in the back. Once one of the best restaurants in town, it's been somewhat eclipsed by all the new haute gourmet Mexi-Med places popping up. You can still get good steak, fish, and curry but the atmosphere is now the biggest draw. You'll really feel like you're escaping the tourist strip if you come here, and the gallery spaces—where the smell of wine will remind you immediately that the space was once used to store vats—function almost as postmodern works of art. Not shockingly, the wine list is good but slanted towards Santo Tomás wines. I recommend sampling the abalone ceviche or the quail in sauvignon blanc sauce, and choosing a wine around that. *Av. Miramar 666 at Calle 7. ☎ 646/174-0807. Main courses $40–$350. MC, V. Daily 10am–3pm and 5–10pm.*

CAFES

MTV Best → **Café Café** ★ ESPRESSO This was the first espresso bar in town, opened by the visionary owner Guillermo (Memo) Ramierez—a fan of espresso but also a scene-maker, who's brought bands like Sublime and Manu Chao and jazz trios to play in his small space. The cafe is also a supporter of local artists; the long narrow space is filled with original art and reproductions. Plus, it's cheap—you can get espresso shots for just $12 and beer is on hand for $30 a bottle. *Av. López Mateos 496-2.* ☎ *646/178-3271. www.bajabargains.com. Coffee $12 and under. Mon–Thurs 10am–9pm; Fri–Sat 10am–11pm; Sun 10am–6pm.*

➔ **Café La Negrita** COFFEES/DESSERTS This cafe boasts a great location in a hip area right down the street from Hussong's (see below), along with a groovy interior. Try their flavored coffees (avellana, amaretto, Irish cream, or vanilla). Chai, teas, or smoothies range in price from $10 to $30 each. *Calle Gastélum 61. No phone. www.cafe lanegrita.com. Coffee and other drinks $10–$30. No credit cards. Daily 7am–9pm.*

➔ **La Casa Vieja** CAFE Tourists and locals alike come to La Casa to enjoy delicious coffee and homemade cakes in the oldest house in Ensenada. The wood-frame historical landmark was shipped down for use by a Presbyterian missionary family in 1888. Today, you can sip your coffee while checking out the 1900s-era photos of the family, which the owner, Ana María Orta Inzunza, found in the attic. She and her brothers and sisters were all born here, and her 90-year-old mother still lives on the property. Clearly, they knew they have a good thing going. *Obregon 110.* ☎ *646/175-7320. lacasaantiguacafe@hotmail. com. Coffee and other drinks $10–$30. Daily 8am–11pm.*

Partying

This ain't Tijuana, so the good news is that you won't be besieged by shills trying to rope you in for donkey shows and such. On the flip side, it's so much quieter here, the sidewalks are almost empty by midnight. Most local nightlife centers around Ensenadians cruising around in their cars, reggaeton blasting from their stereos; if that doesn't do it for you, read on for some other options.

BARS

MTV Best ➔ **El Bodegón del Arte** ★★ Desperate for a sense of Ensenada's anti-cruise ethos? Then come to this warehouse-like space—one of local scene-maker Memo's faves. The "kitchen" in the center is actually a couple of mismatched stoves that look like they were just hauled in from the second-hand shop. The service is charmingly irregular—you may not get your tacos or burritos or even your flash-fried shrimp in garlic sauce on time, but on the other hand, they may also forget to charge you for your drinks. The zero attitude, good food, live music, and strong drinks help create an underground feel. This is truly a place for intellectuals, bohos, locals, and expats, not cruise-shippers. It's not a restaurant or a bar or a club or a clubhouse—but an appealing combination of all four. *Calle Siete 950, at Blancarte.* ☎ *646/156-5223.*

➔ **Hussong's Cantina** ★ Any visit to Ensenada requires a visit to Hussong's, The place where the margarita was born. This is the oldest bar in Baja, dating from 1892, and little has changed in the last 115 years. The bar is long, the drinks strong, the floors covered in sawdust, and the lights too bright for the surrounding chaos. The margarita is the drink to get here, of course, in honor of bartender Don Carlos Orozco who, in 1941, mixed equal parts tequila, Damiana (instead of Cointreaun as is now used), and lime, and served it on ice in a glass laced with salt. The drink was made for the daughter of the local German ambassador to Mexico, probably because the founder, Johann Hussong, was born in Germany. It's not as wild as Papas and Beer across the street but it's far more popular among locals. *Av. Ruiz 113, near Av. López Mateos.* ☎ *646/178-3210. www.cantinahussongs.com.*

→ **Papas and Beer** If you need to be hung upside down while some stranger pumps cheap tequila down your gullet, come by here. There's another of these up in Rosarito Beach (p. 338) but this one is the original, now almost 25 years old. It's a cruise ship favorite and right across the street from Hussong's, so on Saturday nights (when the boats are in), it gets truly bizarre. *Av. Ruiz 102, at Av. López Mateos. ☎ 646/174-0145. www.papasandbeer.com.*

CLUBS

→ **Anthony's Discobar** Look for the giant funky gorilla head outside, along with a painted monkey saying *"Los borrachos somos gente decente"* ("We drunks are decent people") and you'll be at Anthony's. Get past that, and your reward will be an old-style bar, festooned in tinsel year-round, with tables surrounding a tiny dance floor with a stripper's pole in the center. (No, there are no strippers here but you are welcome to take off your clothes if you get a little warm.) The bar is mostly full of Americans sucking down the $15 beers and two-for-one margaritas. There's live music every night with a pretty mediocre cover band and DJs at other times playing reggaeton, banda, and disco. *Miramar 697 at Bulevar Costero. ☎ 626/178-1795.*

→ **Euro Bar** ★ For something a little different, try the Euro Bar, which oozes a discernible European feel via its Spanish owner. This very boho space lies just off Calle 1 and is comprised of twin drinking areas and a dance area behind wooden jail-like bars in the center space. One side, where there's a space for sitting and chatting, looks like a cantina—with the sort of scruffy wood tables and hard leather-backed chairs you'd expect to find in a Barcelona dive. The adjoining area is better for dancing. Throughout the space, stuffed bull heads on the walls and murals of bullfighters pay homage to España. There's bar food and cheap drinks (nothing is over $40). A hip punkish crowd makes this a cool hangout most of the week, though on Wednesday, the crowd changes when live jazz comes in (9pm–midnight). This being a Spanish joint, there's also live flamenco sometimes. *Ruiz 13. ☎ 626/175-7214. No cover.*

GAY NIGHTLIFE

Jazz Café (Calle Primera #688 and Costero #277; ☎ **646/178-1643;** www.jazzcafe.com.mx) is a gay hangout that has lost some of the cachet it once had back when the retired members of the Cockettes used to drop by. It was once a very forward-looking coffee-clubhouse for the closeted of Ensenada but now that the gay nightlife scene is expanding, it's feeling slightly old and tired. It's still a nice place to pop in for a drink while you study the tourists stumbling down Calle Primera.

A more happening scene is going on at **Escandalosa** (Plaza Marina, Costero 656, up the stairs from Sanborn's; no phone), a disco in a mall next to a babysitting place . . . that still manages to swing nightly until 2am. **Coyote Club** (Bulevar Costero 1000, at Av. Diamante; ☎ **646/147-3691**) is a popular dance club with a low-key mood. It's closed Monday to Tuesday but open until 3am during the rest of the week. Finally, there's a lively bath scene going on at **Baños Floresta** (Calle Segunda 1357; no phone) but it's on shady Calle Segunda, so be cautious if you visit there.

Sightseeing

FESTIVALS/EVENTS

Carnaval ★: Ensenada gets the party started weeks earlier than other towns in Mexico (except Mazatlán) with special pre-carnaval events. School programs, historical overviews, and of course costumed parades, live music, and dancing in the streets are all on the bill. A miniversion of what happens in Rio, Carnival in Ensenada is easily the most important street party in town, all over town. The 3 days preceding Ash Wednesday, in February or March.

Rosarito-Ensenada Fun Bike Ride ★★★: A real blow-out, with thousands of riders from the U.S. coming down to compete in the 80km (50 miles) ride along the *libre* road from Rosarito to Ensenada. The finish line party at the end is infamous for being a real good time. The **fall edition** of the ride takes place in September. Visit www.rosaritoensenada.com for details. **Spring edition** in April.

Newport to Ensenada International Yacht Race: Now in its 50th year, this is the largest international yachting regatta in the world and brings a whole new crew of sailors to town. E-mail Nosa1@juno.com for info. April.

Fiesta La Misión: A rodeo and country-style festival celebrating the rich cultural and mission history in La Misión valley just north of Ensenada. May.

Baja 500: A certifiably insane race from Ensenada to Ensenada, a loop route that brings off-road maniacs down to Ensenada for a crazy ride in cars, trucks, motorcycles, and ATVs over some of the harshest terrain in Baja Norte. It's the baby version of the **Baja 1000** that takes place in November. June.

Estero Beach Volleyball Tournament: This volleyball event brings hundreds of international players to the Estero Beach Resort. Visit www.esterobeach.com for info. June.

Fiestas de la Vendimia ★★: Held in early August, this 2-week festival brings together all the wineries and restaurants in the Valle de Guadalupe for a series of samplings of new wines and cheeses. This movable feast is unique and well worth planning a trip around. In 5 years you won't be able to buy a ticket. Now it's still off the grid. August.

Ensenada International Seafood Fair and Baja International Chili Cook-off & Fiesta: Local chefs from both sides of the border compete in a cook-off at the International Seafood and Chili Cook-offs. The events take place at various restaurants that are members of the Chamber of Restaurants. Call ☎ **646/174-0448** for info or e-mail canirace@prodigy.net.mx. September.

Baja 1000 ★★: It's called "the most famous off-road race in the world" and it's hard to argue with that. Now in its 50th year, this Ensenada to La Paz race was called "a 24-hour plane crash" by two-time winner Parnelli Jones. No sleep, no limits, no pavement. It's very Baja in tone. Call ☎ **818/225-8402** or visit www.score-international.com for info. Starts second week of November and continues for 6 days.

TOURS

To get the lay of the land, consider a guided walking tour of downtown Ensenada with **Jatay Tours** (☎ **646/172-2246** or 107-4373). Depending on how much time you have—they'll tailor it to your needs—you'll get a nice overview of bars like Hussong's, the attractions along the marina-harbor, and the boutiques and stores in the downtown area.

MAJOR ATTRACTIONS

The Bodega Santo Tomás (Miramar 666; ☎ **646/178-2509;** www.santo-tomas.com; admission $20; daily 11am, 1pm, and 3pm) is the oldest winery on the peninsula and is located in a landmark building dating from the early 1900s. The interesting 45-minute tour here shows the old-fashioned methods for distilling grapes as first grown by Dominican monks in 1791. After checking out the aging rooms, you'll be invited to a wine tasting. Be sure to check out the

La Bufadora

La Bufadora is a natural sea spout in the rocks, located 45 minutes south of Ensenada. Literally translated as "buffalo snort," the sound made at this site is caused when a wave is forced upward through the rock, creating a geyser that grunts loudly. The less scientific explanation has it that a whale calf traveling north with his mother from San Ignacio Lagoon was caught in the rock and the sound is the animal grunting and calling for its mother.

To get here, drive on Highway 1, the Transpeninsular road south, and about 30 minutes out of town look for the large La Bufadora sign on the right. Or take the blue bus marked Bufadora for about $10. On your return to town, look for a Centro El Sauzal bus heading on Highway 1 back to Ensenada.

galleries, bookstore, and cafe at La Esquina de Bodegas—once part of the Santo Tomás complex—as well as the neighboring restaurant La Embotelladora Vieja (see "Eating," p. 345).

Other attractions worthy of note are the **Museo de Historia** (at the corner of Riviera del Pacífico at Bulevar Costero; ☎ **664/177-0594;** $10; daily 9:30am–2pm and 3–5pm) with exhibits on Baja Californian culture and the **Museo Historico Regional** (Gastélum 224 near Paseo Calle Primera; ☎ **664/178-2531;** free admission; Tues–Sun 10am–5pm), which has detailed displays on Meso-America culture. Finally, it's worth a visit to the **"Caracol" Museo De Ciencias** (Obregon 1463; ☎ **664/178-7192;** $20; Tues–Fri 9am–5pm, Sat–Sun noon–5pm), a weird little science museum with funky but heartfelt exhibitions on everything from marine biology to paleontology.

Playing Outside

For general adventure tours in the region, contact **Expediciones de Turismo Ecológico y de Aventura,** Bulevar Costero 1094–14, Centro (☎ **646/178-3704;** www.mexonline.com/ecotur.htm), which runs hiking, mountain bike, ATV, and other adventure tours around the area.

BIKING

If you like to bike, try to time your visit to Ensenada around the two versions of the MTV Best **Rosarito-Ensenada Fun Bike Ride** ★★★ (p. 351), one in late April and the second in late September. In 2005, this drunken pedal down the free road from Rosarito to Ensenada was called one of the top three International Cycling Events of the year, following the Tour de France and the Giro d'Italia. It's mind-numbing to think of the hardscrabble Fun Ride—begun in 1980—in this company but that's the Internet for you. It begins in downtown Rosarito in front of the Rosarito Beach Hotel, going south fairly level for about 32km (20 miles) until you hit El Tigre, a 3.2km (2-mile) climb that starts to thin the pack. At the top of the hill there's a fantastic view of the coast south and west, which makes for a pleasant breather before the descent into Ensenada. Sober cyclists can do it in just over 2 hours. More tipsy riders take two to three times that. Up to 10,000 people take part in the ride, which results in lots of accidents—so wear a helmet, watch out for idiots, and ride defensively.

Other times of the year, great mountain biking can be had up the **Cañon Dona Petra.** Just ride straight east of Calle Ruiz, which dead ends in the foothills. There are many routes all over the area, including a steep technical one that goes to the top. Hook up with other cyclists in front of **Ivan Jimenez** (see "Shopping," p. 355) or **Duran Bike Shop** (p. 342) on Sunday mornings for the ride out to the Cañon (first stop for a dynamite breakfast at La Cocina de Lupita, p. 346). Roberto Garcia at Jimenez also recommends riding around **el Parral** in San Antonio de las Minas (Valle de Guadalupe), which has the most complete and least public route in the area, as well as farther south outside of Camalu.

FISHING

If you like to fish, then you can't come to Ensenada without taking at least a half-day trip bottom fishing. The fish here are close to shore and are smart enough to make your trip challenging but plentiful enough to make it satisfying. If you go out in late summer when the yellowfin tuna are running, prepare for a real upper body workout as you haul fish endlessly into the boat. An in-shore trip takes place from 7am to 3pm but if you're serious you'll head out to Santo Tomás reef for a 5am or (better yet) 2am departure for a long range trip. Check out www.ensenada-sportfishing.com for reports from various boats.

Arnulfo Lozano (☎ **646/118-2699**) can take you out to catch bonita, yellowtail, red snapper, ling cod, sea bass, halibut, or marlin (in your dreams). His trips are just 2 hours out and back, and involve trolling as you go, which isn't really reasonable in my opinion. Better yet, spring for the tour that costs $3,270 for 8 hours (which includes tackle and bait, and up to five passengers), and do some real fishing.

Another option is **Boogie's Fishing and Tackle** (Bulevar Costero 609-15; ☎ **646/178-8779;** boggeano@telnor.net), a full service tackle shop that does reel repair, rod wrapping, and offers "free fishing advice" in English. And of course Boogie can set up charters for you.

The cheapest (and most satisfying) way to fish out here is to get together a group of friends. **Gordo's Sport Fishing** (in the Marina; ☎ **949/678-1187;** www.gordossportfishing.com/index.html) has boats that can handle groups of 5 to 40, which rent for $4,360 to $27,250. The latter price is for an all-night trip. If you don't have any friends, it'll cost you $1,526 per person (the boat departs 1am) for a full day of searching for tuna, albacore, dorado, and yellowtail.

If you get seasick (or are just cheap) consider **Playa Salamando** ★ (Playa Salamando Km 94; if coming from Ensenada, use Sal Si Puedes off ramp, 5km/3 miles north; ☎ **619/857-9242;** gsaldamando@cox.net; US$15 camp site; no credit cards),

Diving with Sharks

Ever wanted to dive with the great whites? Well, now's your chance to experience this life-changing thrill. You can go out with **Shark Divers** (☎ **888/405-3268** or 415/404-6144; www.sharkdiver.com) to the rugged **Isla Guadalupe** 241km (150 miles) off the mid-coast of Baja. This San Diego–based company hosts 5 day-long tours on the fully equipped yacht with shark expert guide Pat Douglas. He puts you in a full wet suit, straps a hookah breathing system over your face, and submerges you in a 9.3 sq. m (100 sq. ft.) shark cage that will resist even the hammering of a giant female great white.

Nobody knows why this remote rock in the middle of the ocean attracts great whites but it does. Though I can't guarantee that you'll see one, the odds are good—on a November trip to the island, more than 16 different females came by to sniff at the human meat behind the bars. You cannot get any closer to a great white and live to tell the story. Before going through with this, though, check out "Basics," p. 59 for some info on the environmental implications of shark diving.

a wonderful and inexpensive fishing camp just north of Ensenada. It's 100% old Baja in every way. You can rent a funky weathered trailer for $300 to $400 a night or get yourself a camping site for $150.

Salamando is one of the most spectacular, quiet coves along the coast. It's rustic and funky but highly recommended, especially if you're a hardcore shore fisherman or surfer. There are five trailers for rent and the camping sites all have covered tables for cleaning fish, a large plastic barrel for the guts, separate men's and women's showers, wood for sale (at $5) and no electricity (just kerosene lamps). There is a small store on site that sells soft drinks and water but plan on bringing in all other supplies. If you're planning to stay in a trailer, bring your own sheets.

PARKS

Ideal for a day-long picnic, hike, or mountain bike ride, the **Parque Nacional Constitucion de 1857** sits on top of the Sierra de Juárez Mountain Range with a large lake in its center. Despite being in the middle of an often barren peninsula, the 1,200m-high (3,936-ft.) park is covered in places with pine forests. There is a 10km (6-mile) developed trail around the perimeter of the lake, but otherwise there are no developed trails, just donkey or cow paths. To get to the park, take Highway 3 south from Ensenada and exit at the graded dirt access road at Km 55. The park entrance road (35km/22 miles to the park entrance) is gravel and generally well maintained, but can be really rough after a rainy year. If the entrance is staffed, you'll be asked for a modest entrance fee.

NORTHERN BAJA

The **Parque Nacional Sierra San Pedro Máritir,** 67km (42 miles) east of the town of Colonet, encompasses the highest mountains on the peninsula in a 71,136-hectare (177,840-acre) park filled with alpine meadows, four creeks, and rugged granite peaks. There are cow trails rather than official trails and the park is so isolated that a visit here is done at your own risk. There is no emergency support and there's no cellphone coverage, so if you get lost, you're on your own. If you feel comfortable navigating with a compass, though, the hiking can be truly remarkable, especially the overnight climb up to the Picacho del Diablo peak.

You'll have to rent a car to get to Sierra San Pedro. Fill up with gas in Colonet—there is no more until you exit this way again—and reset your trip odometer at the turnoff. In between, it's entirely possible to put on a gas-guzzling 242km (150 miles) of rugged driving. It's 76km (47 miles) to the park entrance.

SCUBA DIVING & SNORKELING

La Bufadora (p. 352) is a great dive spot with wonderful sea life. Once underwater, you'll zoom through lovely kelp beds and rugged rock formations covered in strawberry anemones. You may also spot spiny lobsters and numerous large fish. It's possible to swim right over to the blowhole, but use extreme caution in this area—you don't want to end up like that mythical whale calf.

Dale's La Bufadora Dive Shop (☎ **646/154-2092**) is on shore at the best entry point. The staff will set you up with fills for air tanks, as well as dole out advice.

SEA KAYAKING

The rocky coastline of Punta la Banda is a favorite first trip for beginning ocean kayakers due to its several secluded beaches, sea caves, and terrific scenery. Many kayakers use La Bufadora as a launching point to head out to the Todos Santos Islands. It's about 11km (7 miles) from La Bufadora to the southern and larger of the two islands. The first 4.8km (3 miles) follow a rocky coast to the tip of Punta la Banda. From here you'll need to size up the wind, the waves, and the fog. If the coast is clear, take a compass and begin the 6km (4-mile) open-water crossing. Bring water and camping gear to spend a night on the pristine island. **Dale's La Bufadora Dive Shop** (see above) has kayak rentals and is open weekends or by prior reservation. **Expediciones de Turismo Ecológico y de Aventura,** Bulevar Costero 1094–14, Centro (☎ **646/178-3704;** www.mexonline.com/ecotur.htm), offers guided kayak trips, including a full kayak expedition through the Bay of Los Angeles.

SURFING

Only the best and boldest surfers challenge the waves off Islas de Todos Santos, two islands about 19km (12 miles) west of Ensenada, considered to be some of the best surf on the coast. Waves can reach 9m (30 ft.) in winter, and surfers must hire a panga to take them out. You'll find gentler but still challenging waves at San Miguel and Salsipuedes. For local surf reports and gear rental, visit the **San Miguel Surf Shop,** Avenida López Mateos at Calle Ruiz, Centro (☎ **646/178-1007**), the most popular local surf shop

WHALE-WATCHING

Guided **whale-watching** tours are held in Todos Santos Bay December through March, while pregnant females migrate from the Arctic to San Ignacio Lagoon south where they'll spend the winter. Check with **Sergio's** (northern end of malecon, next to marina; ☎ **646/178-2185** or 800/336-5454 in U.S.; www.sergios-sportfishing.com) for info.

Shopping

Ensenada's equivalent of Tijuana's Avenida Revolución is crowded Avenida López Mateos, which runs roughly parallel to Bulevar Lázaro Cárdenas (Costero); the highest concentration of shops and restaurants is between avenidas Ruiz and Castillo. Beggars fill this street, and sellers are less likely to bargain here than in Tijuana—they're used to gullible cruise-ship buyers in Ensenada. However, compared to Tijuana, there is more authentic Mexican art- and craftwork on offer—many traditional pieces are imported from the surrounding rural states and villages.

Note that regular shopping hours here are as elsewhere in Mexico, except most stores don't close midday.

ARTS & CRAFT STORES

For local art, check out **Café Café** ★ (see "Eating," p. 345) which carries whimsical surreal ceramics made by artisans who were trained by superstar artist Sergio Bustamante. Pieces range from $44 to $164, and include contemporary metal sculptures that are great for outdoor garden use. This is also one of the few places where you can get reproductions of work by Remedios Varo, the artist who was part of the surrealist inner circle with Leonora Carrington in Paris. Also on sale are contemporary Huichol woven framed carpet "paintings" by local Juan Silva ($3,270), who learned the art from his mother when he grew up in the mountains north of Guadalajara.

Art & Stuff (Carretera Tijuana-Ensenada Km 103, El Sauzal; ☎ **646/175-8859** or 949/202-5321 in U.S.; www.ensenada.com; closed Tues) is a small gallery that has been in Ensenada for 14 years, and specializes in local Baja artists. It sells mainly outsider art—anything rough and quirky, primitive and folkish. Though the store also stocks the sort of Oaxacan and Huichol art you'll find elsewhere in Mexico, it's the local stuff that's unusual and most worthy of purchase.

For cool T-shirts, jewelry, deconstructed layered skirts ($150–$200), and woven

Ruta del Vino

It's taken a few centuries, but Baja California wines are finally getting the respect they deserve, thanks in large part to the efforts of a handful of foreign and local vintners spearheaded by Hugo D'Acosta, an agronomist who studied oenology at the University of Montpelier and is recognized as one of Mexico's top winemakers and consultants. D'Acosta came to Valle de Guadalupe, 11km (7 miles) northeast from Ensenada, to work as the winemaker and manager for the giant Bodegas Santo Tomás organization. He worked there for a few years, learning what to do and not to do when he set out to establish his own winery (Casa de Piedra), along with an informal winemaking school for locals. His philosophy, basically, is that the best wines are created on the vine, not in the vat, and are best achieved by stressing the plant and pruning it aggressively, which results in a smaller, high quality yield.

Clearly the approach has worked. Now the 20 Valle de Guadalupe wineries (not including some smaller artisan/home-based operations) are shipping their product worldwide at premium prices and winning prestigious competitions. What makes the wines of Guadalupe different is a peppery background that is especially noticeable in some of the whites. The valley is about 23km (14 miles) long and just 8km (5 miles) wide, and though arid, it's cooled by sea breezes that come over the hills from Ensenada, creating a micro-climate that wine makers adore.

Besides wine, the area also produces great olives (and oil), artisan cheeses, sausages, and chorizo. But if it sounds like a baby Napa, forget it. There are a few boutique hotels, one high-end restaurant, and the Baja government has plopped "Ruta de Vino" signage all along Highway 3, but you won't find any delis selling picnic lunches or any crowds. It's still an emerging scene where the emphasis is less on marketing and more on producing the best wines possible. Here are reviews for the best of the best:

MTV Best **Adobe Guadalupe** ★★★ This is one of the best boutique wineries in the valley but it also functions as a B&B. The combination of hotel/winery/restaurant is elegantly done, with rooms lining the interior courtyard. You won't

zipper sweaters by Naco ($200–$350), stop by the **Royal House** (Gastélum 55 at Ruiz; ☎ **646/178-3881**). Here owner Suzanna Rodriguez tends shop while her twin sister, designer Cynthia Rodriguez, also sells deconstructed urban "hip shaker" clothes out of her backroom workshop. **Todos a 180 Pesos** (Plaza Marina, Costera 656; no phone) was having a 50% off sale when I stopped by, which meant everything in the store cost about $100 each: from cool Japanese-looking duffle bags, to great Bijoux/Terner watches, to silver jewelry.

When it comes to mission-style furniture, **Muebles la Mission Furniture** (Carretera Tijuana-Ensenada Km 103; ☎ **646/174-7556;** www.furniture-mexican.com) has great antique chests from Guadalajara ($1,500–$1,700), hacienda-style beds for $1,700, and handmade appliquéd handbags for $218. Better yet, they can knock off a wooden replica of just about anything you want. Just send them a photo by e-mail. They're in the up-and-coming neighborhood of El Sauzal (next to Art & Stuff).

get any TVs or phones in the rooms, which is just the way it should be: It's restful, tasteful, and just about perfect in every way. The beds are way comfortable, the ceilings 4.8m (16 ft.) high, and everywhere you look there are beautiful vineyards. It's designed for the heat, so the fan, tiled floors, and thick walls keep it nice and cool. The interior courtyard has a fountain that is framed by a rolling series of arches that also bring in breezes. High tea, horseback riding, and massages are offered at an extra charge, but you may come just for a wine tasting ($50 per person) or dinner ($600 per person, including a horseback ride) by reservation. *Hwy. 1-D, Km 77.5, El Porvenir, Valle de Guadalupe.* ☎ ***646/155-2094*** *or in U.S. 649/631-3098. www.adobeguadalupe.com. US$168 double. Rates include breakfast and wine tasting for 2. DISC, MC, V. Amenities: Dining room; library/TV room; living room; heated swimming pool and Jacuzzi. In room: A/C, fans, heater.*

MTV Best **Laja** ★★★ NOUVELLE MEXICAN Everyone in Valle de Guadalupe cites Laja as being the best restaurant in the valley, if not all of Baja. It was founded by Chef Jair Tellez, a native of Tijuana who trained with Daniel Boulud at Daniel Restaurant in New York and then spent a year at the Four Seasons in Mexico City. Tellez and his wife, Laura Reinert, conceived the place as a French country-style inn where the chef dictates the best menu for the day. The fixed-price menu offers anywhere from four to eight courses, so it can easily take 4 hours to plow through the entire experience—but really, who would want to treat caramelized lemon peel scallops like fast food? Reservations are a must, as is proper attire—no flip-flops or T-shirts, please. The dining room is all Chiapas hardwood floors and heavy beamed ceilings, properly serious and sedate for the culinary feats that are dished out. The emphasis here is primarily on organic produce and local wines, which means it's the most Chez Panisse–like experience you'll find outside of Berkeley. *Hwy. 3 Km 83, Valle de Guadalupe.* ☎ ***626/155-2556.*** *www.lajamexico.com. 6-course tasting menu $460. MC, V. Thurs 1:30–5pm; Fri–Sat 1:30–10pm; Sun 1:30–8pm.*

RECORD STORES

Sanborn's in the Plaza Marina (see "Eating," p. 345) has a small selection of English books and magazines, as well as a larger one in Spanish. They also stock CDs, DVDs, and, more oddly, Magic Bras. **Libros Libros** (Calle Primera 277; ☎ **646/178-4884**) has maps, a very small selection of books in English, as well as CDs, VHS tapes, and a large kids and educational selection of texts.

Sonido Musical (Av. Ruiz 579; ☎ **646/175-7393**) has five branches around town and sells mostly Mexican pop, rock en Español (Mana, El Tri), alt en Español (Café Tacuba), and reggaeton, as well as Norteno, banda, ranchero salsa, and cumbia music. Along the wall of karaoke tapes, you're also sure to find old Celia Cruz CDs and other music by Latin heart-throbs of the past and present.

SPORTS STORES

If you need stuff to maintain your boat or scuba gear, including dive knives and wet suits, a visit to **Agencia Arjona** (Bulevar Tte. Azueta 106; ☎ **646/178-3101**) should do the trick.

San Miguel Surf (López Mateos 529 at Gastélum; ☎ **646/178-1007;** www.sanmiguel.com) sells boards made by the famous local shaper Eduardo Echegaray, who's been making boards since the '70s. You can also rent boards for $250 a day, as well as fins and wet suits. New boards sell from $4,142 to $21,800, depending on the size. Other surf gear (that is, wax, leashes, T-shirts) is for sale as well.

At **Ivan Jimenez** (Riveroll 1358; ☎ **646/178-6834,** cell 117-0094; ivan-jimenez@hotmail.com), friendly Roberto Garcia can fix your bike or sell you a new one. If you need repair on a road bike, it may take a special order, so be sure to bring extra spokes along. Roberto can also steer you to great rides (see "Playing Outside," p. 352).

Bike shop **Duran** (p. 342) is the largest in town and sells mountain bikes in addition to renting them.

WINE STORES

Great local wine can be bought all over town but the best one-stop shop is **La Contra Wineshop** (Moctezuma 623 at 6th; ☎ **646/156-5030**) on the first floor of the groovy '50s-style restaurant El 623 (see "Eating," p. 345). Hugo d'Acosta's wine, as well as that of other family-owned wineries in the Valle de Guadalupe, is sold at good prices, ranging from $100 to $1,700. The store also carries Liquor de Naranja or Limon in beautiful hand-blown glass bottles, Baja olive oil, and boutique mescal from Acosta's plant in Oaxaca. The presentation and design of the shop is wonderful, with slanting iron shelves resting atop stone footings and glass-topped counters lying on old mattress springs. **The Bodega Santo Tomás** (Miramar 666; ☎ **646/178-2509;** www.santo-tomas.com) is the oldest winery on the peninsula and is in a landmark building dating from the early 1900s. In addition to selling wine, they host tours and wine tastings daily at 11am, 1pm, and 3pm for $20.

Road Trip: Quatro Casas

Driving south out of Ensenada, the first 12km ($7^1/_2$ miles) are a complete mishmash of *yonques* (auto junkyards), liquor stores, tacky furniture, birria stands, and small shops. Let's not forget the Hotel Joker, a theme hotel which looks like it's straight out of a slasher movie. Slow down, check out the bizarre Fantasyland-meets-miniature golf architecture, and keep going.

Soon the four lanes narrow to two, the shoulder of the road vanishes, and all the outlying colonias of Ensenada fade away as the road opens out to a spectacular valley winding through stunningly beautiful, if barren, mountains. Expect your speed to decrease as trucks and buses slow you down. Just be patient. At kilometer 141, look for the National Observatory sign, turn right before it, and take the rutted dirt road 13km (8 miles) towards the beach. Bear right when possible until the ocean is visible—you'll run into the town of Quatro Casas.

The best place to stay in town is **Quatro Casas Surf Hostel** (no address; ☎ **616/165-0010;** US$15–US$40 double, US$300 suite; no credit cards), right on the edge of the cliff over the water. It's a two-story building with a small restaurant, board rentals, and a kidney-shaped skate pool designed by Tony Alva of the Dogtown crew. There are also bikes, wet suits, fishing tackle, hookah diving, kayaks ($273), and pangas for rent. Costs run from US$15 for a bunk to US$300 for a "penthouse" that can hold seven people.

The busiest time here is summer when the south swell is pumping. But just because it's Mexico, don't expect the water to be warm then. It's usually colder than in San Diego, hundreds of miles north. You'll want a full wet suit with booties.

There are lots of breaks here, one of the most famous being Shipwrecks (aka Freighters), a fast left point break. Apparently a huge LNG terminal is going in just north of here, so go now before the area gets too crowded.

Los Cabos & Southern Baja

It doesn't take long to realize that the character of Los Cabos—made up of Cabo San Lucas and San José del Cabo—is bipolar. The Two Capes, Los Cabos, are spoken of as one, connected by the four-lane 33km (20-mile) Corridor, but they could not be more different. Cabo San Lucas, with its never-closed bars, strip shows, and dope/fake silver jewelry sellers wandering the playas, is the manic, shooters-inhaling child; San José, with its cobblestone streets, historical center, and a main square with a sweet little wrought-iron gazebo, is the responsible, Mass-attending grown-up.

Despite their differences, both Cabos share one thing in common—they're expensive. Everyone here likes to say that everything costs so much because Baja is an island. And until the 1973 completion of the 1,610km (1,000-mile) Transpeninsular Highway 1, linking Los Cabos with the California border, Baja was indeed as isolated as an island. But today the area seems far from removed—when I visited, crowds gathered around a day-tripper being hung upside down from the Giggling Marlin's tequila harness by the marina in Cabo, and a bunch of folks browsed a large book fair going on in San José's main square.

Books vs. tequila shots? That pretty much sums up San José vs. Cabo. Recent gentrification is slowly turning San José into less of a provincial Mexican town, though, and more of a cosmopolitan resort community. As a result, San José stands out as a good base in the area—stay in one of its increasingly plush resorts, and you'll be perfectly situated to go up The Corridor for partying and down the Cape for outdoor fun.

As for the rest of southern Baja, development has spread all around, to the East Cape and up the coast toward Cabo Pulmo. Yes, there are still miles of undeveloped desert meeting the sea and things are cheaper here than in Los Cabos, but the region as a whole is attracting more tourists. Most come for **Todos Santos,** an artistic community on the Pacific side of the coastal curve (just north of the tip) that draws travelers who find that Cabo has outgrown them and **La Paz,** the capital of Baja Sur and an easygoing maritime port.

Best of Southern Baja

- **Best Reason to Stay in San José: Casa Natalia** is the kind of place that's popping up more and more frequently in Mexico—a privately owned and run boutique hotel that is both modern and minimalist and Mexican and international. The affordable food is European/Mexican fusion and the warm vibe is absolutely pitch perfect. See p. 371.
- **Best "I Need a Taco Right Now" Spots:** There's no need to fight. Both **Guacamayas Taqueria** and rival **Hangman's** are winners. They're also two more reasons to stay in San José. Guacamaya gets props for its tortillas—handmade, thank you—while Hangman's gets the nod for its eye-candy pack-rat decor. See p. 373 and p. 373.
- **Best Gifts That Don't Scream Baja:** The **Galería de Ida** stocks amazing things that obviously won't fit into your suitcase—contemporary metal sculptures, paintings, bronzes, and huge cool stone sculptures. If shipping isn't possible, then **Veryka** is your place—it stocks such amazing clothes, you'll want to layer up. See p. 380 and p. 380.
- **Best Hotel for Clubbing:** Right across the street from Cabo Wabo in Cabo is the **Hotel Mar de Cortez,** a slightly funky but cheap fisherman's hotel. It's the kind of place that Cabo and San José have a lot of—not too glamorous but totally friendly and serviceable hotels. Here, though, you can rock out at Cabo Wabo till you can't stand anymore and at least your bed won't be far away. See p. 394.
- **Best Food within 1,000 Miles:** Food like you find at the **French Riviera** in Cabo doesn't come into your life very often. From the lobster to the braised dorado to the stuffed miniveggies, this is French/Mexican fusion food that brings a whole new definition to "resort fare." Yes you may drop a couple of hundred for a 4-hour foodie's fantasy made real—but trust me. It's worth it. See p. 386.
- **Best Overall Club:** God knows that Cabo is full of clubs, but the old standby **El Squid Roe** gets the nod for its end-of-the-world carefree spirit, strong but cheap drinks, and killer soundtracks. It's large, crowded, and noisy, but it's one helluva party. See p. 403.
- **Best Waking Dream:** The **Hotel Posada Yeneka** is not the kind of place you find in most beach towns. Indeed, it's a very odd and surprising place for anywhere on earth. Even if you don't stay here, it's worth a visit to see the odd display of knickknacks hanging about, from bones to bits of bikes to tons of stuffed animals. That said, though, you *should* stay here—it's supremely comfortable. See p. 419.
- **Best Restaurant Experience:** Like the French Riviera in Cabo or the Café Santa Fe in Todos Santos, **El Madero** in La Paz is a place that has raised the standards for inventive cooking. Its Italian-Mexican menu gracefully balances local

and foreign influences on seafood. Plus the prices are really reasonable and you won't get any attitude or a line out the door. See p. 422.

- **Best Nowhere Near Ireland Pub:** Give the owner of the **Isolde Tower Irish Pub** in La Paz some props. He's managed to make a scene happen in a town that rolls up its streets around 10pm. This decidedly un-Mexican bar (think pints and darts) is simply the best place to go in town to listen to visiting DJs, check out the art scene, and soak in an alternative vibe. See p. 424.
- **Best Crash Course Experience:** It doesn't matter if you came to Todos Santos for the waves or the artists or just the laid-back sensibility of the place. Whatever your motivation, a couple of nights at **Casa Bentley** will give you an entirely new understanding not only of this unique bit of Baja geography but also the pleasure of cold stone walls when it's blistering outside. If you want to get an idea of how perfect Todos Santos life can be, come by Bentley's. See p. 435.

San José del Cabo

Originally founded in 1730 by Jesuit missionaries, San José is a cozy Mexican town on the cusp of genuine sophistication, home to great hotels, from elegant secluded B&Bs to a clothing-optional resort on the edge of town (p. 371), and great food, from a gourmet restaurant headed up by a Master Chef (one of only six in Mexico) to some of the best taquerias around.

While Cabo gets the cruise ship crowds and San José the spring-breakers, San José retains its small-town ambience even as new galleries open up and development continues, tumorlike, in the Zona Hotelera. Though not as exclusive as the monstrosities along The Corridor, these new resorts are cutting off access to the beach, a very contentious local issue. And while San José locals roll their eyes when Cabo is mentioned, remarking how much they hate the place, it's obvious that they are not immune to making the same mistakes. The construction of a controversial marina, for instance, is wreaking environmental havoc; where once there were about 250 species of birds in the area, now there are just 50.

At least for now, though, San José is still well worth a visit. In addition to its great hotels and food, the town boasts a laid-back sensibility that is charming yet refined—adjectives that simply don't apply to party hardy Cabo. Local bar patrons are eager to raise a glass of cerveza with visitors, or point you towards one of the many outdoor options within just a few miles away—kayaking, biking, and snorkeling are just three of the many highlights. Simply put, San José is a great base for the area; it's the best choice for those who want to enjoy the paradoxical landscape of northern Baja but still feel like they're actually *in* Mexico.

Getting There & Getting Around

GETTING INTO TOWN

BY PLANE **The San José del Cabo International Airport** (airport code SJD; ☎ **624/146-5111**) that serves both Cabos and the connecting Corridor is 48km (30 miles) northeast of Cabo San Lucas. Although very small, it has separate terminals for national and international flights, so be careful to ask for the correct terminal when you return.

AeroMexico (☎ **800/237-6639** in the U.S., 01-800/021-4000 in Mexico;

The Lower Baja Peninsula

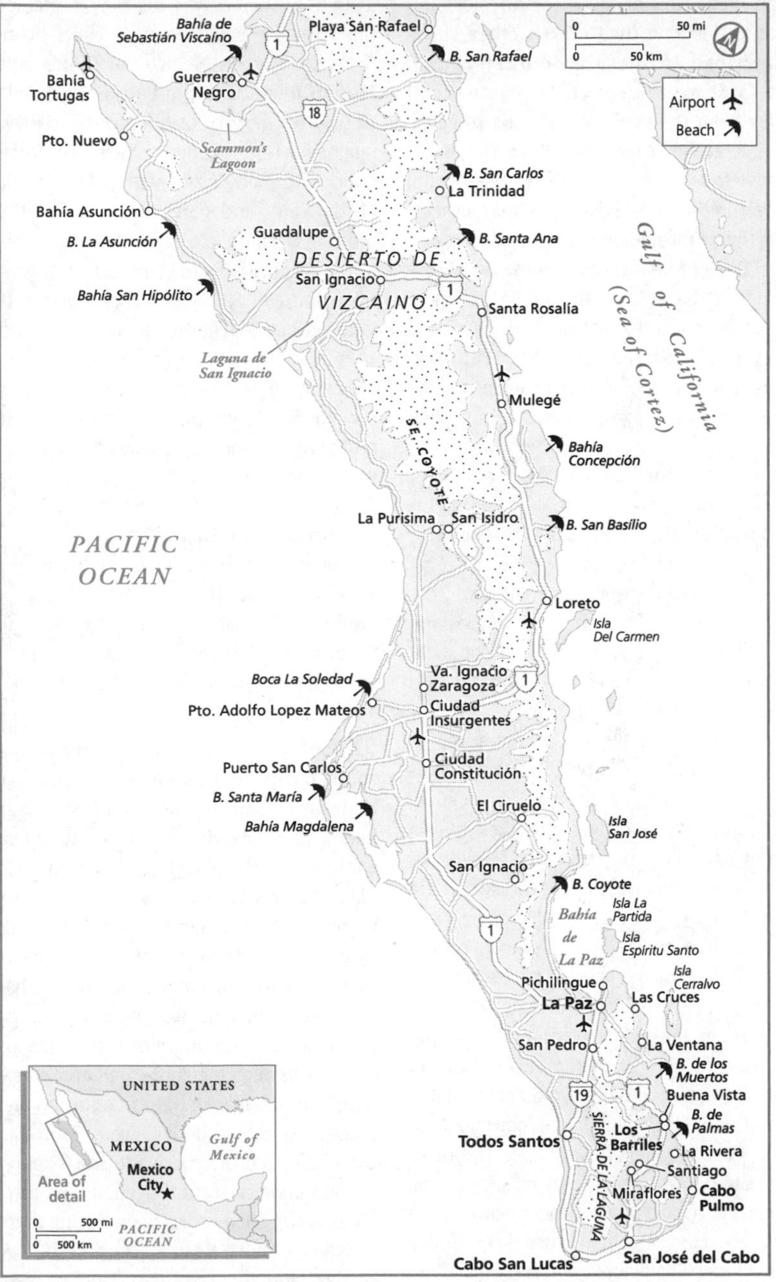

www.aeromexico.com), flies nonstop from San Diego, Ontario, and Los Angeles, and has connecting flights from other cities; **American Airlines** (☎ **800/223-5436** in the U.S. or 624/146-5300; www.aa.com) flies from Dallas/Ft. Worth, Los Angeles, and Chicago; **America West** (☎ **800/327-7810** in the U.S. or 624/146-5380; www.americawest.com) operates connecting flights through Phoenix, Las Vegas, and San Diego; **Alaska Airlines** (☎ **800/252-7522** in the U.S. or 624/146-5100; www.alaskaair.com) flies from Los Angeles, San Diego, Seattle, and San Francisco; **Continental** (☎ **800/537-9222** in the U.S. or 624/146-5040; www.continental.com) flies from Houston and Newark; **Delta** (☎ **800/221-1212** in the U.S. or 624/146-5003; www.delta.com) has flights from Atlanta and Salt Lake City; **Frontier** (☎ **800/432-1359** in the U.S. or 624/146-5421; www.frontierairlines.com) has direct service from Denver; **Mexicana** (☎ **800/531-7921** in the U.S. or 624/146-5001; www.mexicana.com) has direct or connecting flights from Denver, Guadalajara, Los Angeles, Sacramento, Las Vegas, and Mexico City; **United Airlines** (☎ **800/538-2929** in the U.S. or 624/146-5433; www.united.com) flies direct from both San Francisco and Denver. At the time of this writing, **Aero California** (☎ **800/237-6225** in the U.S. or 624/143-3700) was grounded and their local offices closed, but you might want to check to see if they're back up and running.

Airlines that serve destinations within Mexico to Cabo include: **Aereo Calafia** (☎ **624/143-4302;** www.aereocalafia.com) with daily flights to-from Mazatlán and Puerto Vallarta (they operate out of the **Cabo San Lucas Airport;** see p. 366); **AeroPacifico** (☎ **624/105-0908**) which serves Los Mochis; **Interjet** (Mega Comercial Mexicana, Bulevar Mauricio Castro 4650, Zona Hotelera; ☎ **01-800/011-2345** in Mexico or 555/102-5555 in Mexico City; www.interjet.com.mx) which connects to cities in Mexico via Toluca; and **MagniCharters** (Plaza Patria, Highway 1; ☎ **624/105-2535** or 01-800/201-1404; www.magnicharters.com.mx) which connects Cabo with many cities within Mexico via Mexico City and connects with the U.S. only via Orlando.

The airport is 13km (8 miles) northwest of downtown San José. Once outside it, you can buy a ticket for a taxi or a *colectivo* (minibus), which up to four passengers may share. Colectivo fares run about $90 for up to eight passengers to San José and $140 to Cabo San Lucas from the airport. A private taxi will charge you $2,400 to La Paz, $400 to San José del Cabo, or $900 to Cabo San Lucas.

Timeshare resorts have booths in the airport's arrival/baggage area. The promoters hook visitors with a free ride to their hotel in return for listening to their sales presentation (see the box on timeshares, p. 404).

BY CAR From La Paz, take Highway 1 south; the drive takes 3 to 4 hours. Or take Highway 1 south just past the village of San Pedro, then take Highway 19 south (a less winding road) through Todos Santos to Cabo San Lucas, where you can pick up Highway 1 east to San José del Cabo. This route has spectacular views of the ocean; the east one is more mountainous and has more stops along the way; both are around the same distance (more or less 182km/113 miles). Although the route via Cabo seems longer, the road is in better condition and takes only 2 to 3 hours. From Cabo San Lucas, it's a half-hour drive to San José.

The major car-rental agencies all have counters at the airport, open during flight arrivals. **Avis** (☎ **800/331-1212** in the U.S. or 624/146-0201; www.avis.com) is open

San José del Cabo

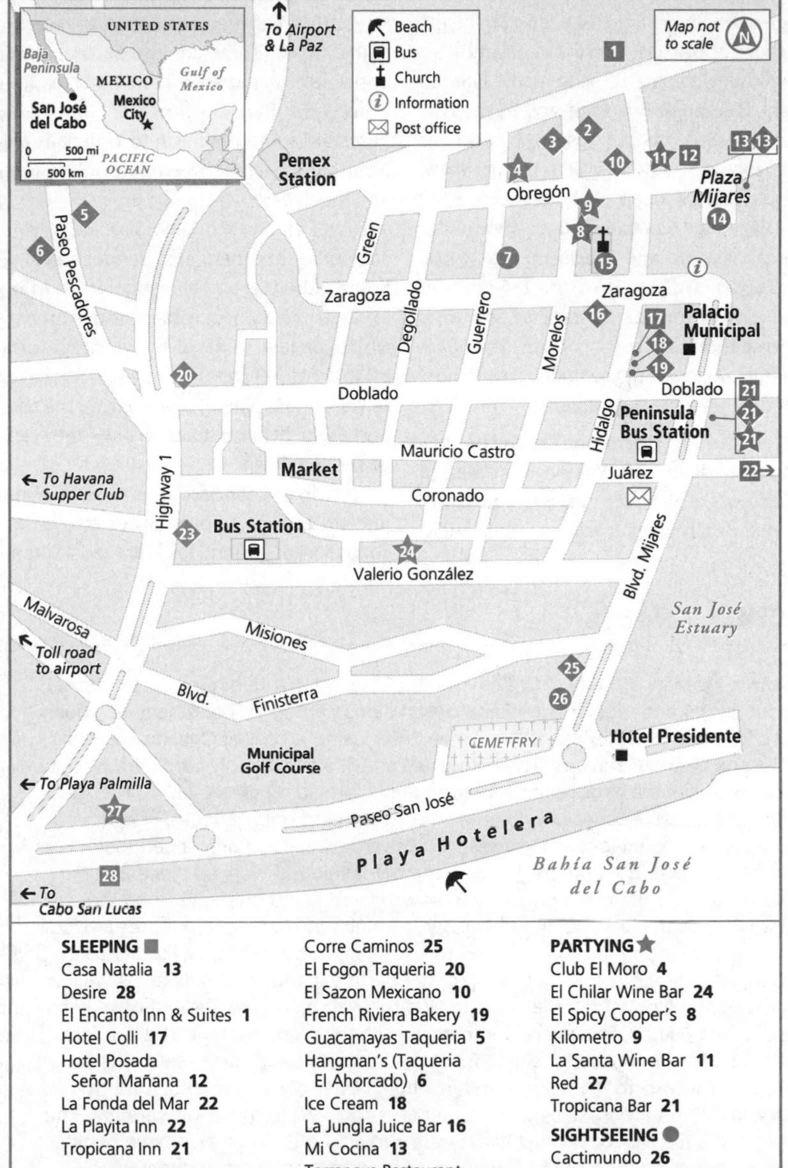

SLEEPING ■
Casa Natalia **13**
Desire **28**
El Encanto Inn & Suites **1**
Hotel Colli **17**
Hotel Posada Señor Mañana **12**
La Fonda del Mar **22**
La Playita Inn **22**
Tropicana Inn **21**

EATING ◆
Baan Thai **3**
Buzzard's Bar and Grill **22**
Café Vanilla **23**
Corre Caminos **25**
El Fogon Taqueria **20**
El Sazon Mexicano **10**
French Riviera Bakery **19**
Guacamayas Taqueria **5**
Hangman's (Taqueria El Ahorcado) **6**
Ice Cream **18**
La Jungla Juice Bar **16**
Mi Cocina **13**
Terranova Restaurant & Bar **15**
Tropicana Bar and Grill **21**
Voila Bistro **2**

PARTYING ★
Club El Moro **4**
El Chilar Wine Bar **24**
El Spicy Cooper's **8**
Kilometro **9**
La Santa Wine Bar **11**
Red **27**
Tropicana Bar **21**

SIGHTSEEING ●
Cactimundo **26**
Galeria de Ida Victoria **7**
Iglesia San Jose **15**
Plaza Mijares **14**

Monday to Saturday 7am to 9pm, and Sunday 6am to 9pm; **Budget** (☎ **800/527-0700** in the U.S., 624/146-5333 at the airport, or 624/143-4190 in Cabo San Lucas; www.budget.com) is open daily 8am to 6pm; **Hertz** (☎ **800/654-3131** in the U.S., 624/146-1803 in San José del Cabo, or 624/105-1428 in Cabo San Lucas; www.hertz.com) is open daily 8am to 8pm; **Dollar** (☎ **624/146-5060;** www.dollarloscabos.com) and **National** (☎ **800/328-4567** in the U.S., 624/146-5022 at the airport, or 624/142-2424 in San José; www.nationalcar.com) is open daily 8am to 8pm. Also see p. 392 under "Los Cabos" for info. on local companies.

BY BUS The **Terminal de Autobuses (bus station),** on Valerio González, a block east of Highway 1 (☎ **624/142-1100**), is open daily from 5:30am to 8pm. Here you can catch **Flecha Verde** and **Aguila Autotransportes** (☎ **624/142-1100**) which run hourly between Los Cabos as well as points north. There are also second-class buses for La Paz and points north; the **Peninsula Bus Station** for first-class buses to La Paz and north to Tijuana is on Mauricio Castro between Bulevar Mijares and Hidalgo.

To get to and fro Cabo San Lucas, you can take another bus service, called **Suburcabo** (big and blue tour buses) from M. Castro (Hwy. 1, across from the Tourist Office, or just south of the glorietta turn off to the Hotel Zone) for just $20. You have to walk about 2km (1¼ miles) from the airport to the highway to catch one—they can be flagged down.

The trip to Cabo San Lucas takes 40 minutes; to La Paz, 3 hours. Buses also go to Todos Santos; the trip takes around 3 hours.

Cheap Seats

Aereo Calafia is the only Cabos-based airline, a mixture of air taxi, air charter, tour guide, and regular scheduled destinations carrier. The company has been working out of Cabo San Lucas since 1993, using a fleet of Cessna 206 and Cessna Grand Caravans. The planes are small, and can only carry a dozen passengers, but the experience is unforgettable, providing views you'll never get anywhere else—especially if you ask to sit in the co-pilot's seat. There are no beverages, no snacks, no movies, no stewardesses, and only a perfunctory safety speech. But you do get to fly the old-fashioned way, up close and personal, and it's really the only way to move quickly (and cheaply) along the Pacific Coast. Note that the planes fly low since the cabins aren't pressurized.

The carrier connects Los Cabos to Mazatlán, Los Mochis, La Paz, Ciudad Constitucion, Loreto, Ciudad Obregón, Puerto Vallarta, and Culican as well as connecting flights from Mazatlán to Puerto Vallarta. Tickets sell out quickly so book in advance. Prices are competitive with the giant carriers. The sea ferry from La Paz to Mazatlán takes 22 hours and costs $209 for a seat in the salon; $415 for a two- to four-person cabin without bathroom; and $622 for a two-person with a bathroom cabin. It will cost about $3,270 to transport your car. The one-flight from Cabo to Mazatlán costs about $1,635. They also have package tourism trips to the Copper Canyon and the whale spawning waters of Magdalena Bay. The Aereo Calafia flies out of the dirt runway known (somewhat vaingloriously) as the Cabo San Lucas Airport. Bulevar Marina, local A-4, Hotel Plaza Las Glorias, Cabo San Lucas. Call ☎ **624/143-4302** or visit www.aereocalafia.com.mx/index_en.php for info.

GETTING AROUND

BY FOOT Downtown San José is small; you can walk almost anywhere in the centro. It's 5 long blocks from the centro to the beach, though, so take a taxi.

BY BIKE Biking may be the best way to get around long distances since the town is often choked with traffic and parking is often a nightmare. You can rent bikes at the **Hotel Presidente** (p. 378) and the **Vasquez** bike shop (Bulevar M. Castro in the Colonia Cinco de Febrero; no phone).

BY BUS There is no local bus service between downtown and the beach. You can catch the city bus, or *urbanos*, on the corner of Hidalgo and Benito Juárez next to Telmex for destinations around town or out to the Colonias for a mere $6.

TAXIS Taxis in town charge about $50 for a ride around town. Always establish the fare before you get in. Wave one down in the street, call one at (☎ **624/142-0580**), or have your hotel call one for you. Many often wait outside hotels on The Corridor.

Basics

ORIENTATION

Highway 1, connecting the airport to Cabo San Lucas, skirts San José and at this section the road is also called **Bulevar Mauricio Castro** or more commonly, the **Carretera Transpeninsular.** San José del Cabo consists of **downtown,** with sophisticated inns and traditional budget hotels, and the **Zona Hotelera** (hotel zone) along the beach. **Zaragoza** is the main street leading from the Carretera Transpeninsular into the north end of town; **Paseo San José** runs parallel to the beach and is the principal boulevard of the hotel zone a couple of miles south. The mile-long **Bulevar Mijares** connects the two areas, and is where many of the shops and restaurants catering to tourists are located. The revitalized **Old Town** is roughly the 8-block area behind the main square running down Obregón to Guerrero.

TOURIST INFO & OFFICES

The Municipal Tourist Information Office (☎/fax **624/142-3310,** or 624/142-9628) is downstairs in the Plaza San José on Highway 1 (Carretera Transpeninsular) between Valerio Gonzalez and 5 de Mayo. It offers maps, free local publications, and other basic information about the area. It's open Monday through Friday from 8am to 3pm.

Before your trip, you can contact the **Los Cabos Tourism Board** (☎ **866/567-2226** in the U.S. or 624/143-4777; www.visitloscabos.org). You might also want to check out ***The Baja Survivor's Guide*** (edited by Lee Moore, Todos Santos Press), a 220-page spiral-bound booklet of opinions, advice, jokes, and commentary about how to live happily in Baja Sur.

RECOMMENDED WEBSITE

- **www.loscabosguide.com/links.htm:** Features links to all things Cabo, including rentals and the local paper *Gringo Gazette's* online site.

San José del Cabo Nuts & Bolts

American Express An Amex office is located in the Plaza La Misión L-1B, Bulevar Mijares at Paseo Finisterra (☎ **624/142-1343** or -1306). It's open Monday to Friday from 9am to 6pm and Saturday 9am to 1pm.

Banks Banks here exchange currency during business hours, which are generally Monday through Friday from 8:30am to 4pm, and Saturday from 10am to 2pm. **HSBC** (Francisco Madero 1290 at Cinco de Mayo; ☎ **624/142-2289**) stays open until 7pm. There are several major banks on Zaragoza between Morelos and Degollado, including **Bancomer** (☎ **624/130-7064**).

Embassies The **Consular Agency of the USA** is on Bulevar Marina, Local C-4, Plaza Nautica, Cabo San Lucas (☎ **624/143-3566,** emergency ☎ **001/619/692-2154;** usconsulcabo@yahoo.com). The consul is Michael J. Houston, and his office is open Monday to Friday 9am to 2pm. The **Canadian Consulate** can be reached at San José del Cabo Plaza José Green, Local 9, Bulevar Mijares s/n (☎ **624/142-4333**).

Emergencies If you have a general emergency, dial ☎ **066,** or the local police number at City Hall (☎ **624/142-0361**). If you have a problem with the police, be sure to get their name and badge number and report it to the tourist office; see above. The Fire Department is at ☎ **624/142-2466** and Red Cross is at ☎ **624/142-0316.**

Hospitals The public hospital, **Hospital General,** is at Retorno Atunero s/n, Col. Chamizal (☎ **624/142-0013**). A better, private, and therefore more expensive hospital is the **Medica los Cabos** (Zaragoza 148 at Green; ☎ **624/142-2770**). They are open 24/7, most insurance policies are accepted, and the staff is bilingual and linked to American hospitals and air ambulance service. They also make hotel and office calls.

Blue Net Medical Group also offers 24-hour emergency medical service (Plaza La Misión L-3, Bulevar Mijares at Paseo Finisterra; ☎ **624/142-3511,** or -5511; Mon–Sat 8am–7pm). On-staff physicians Dr. Jose Ramon Garcia Vinay (☎ **044/624-122-1484**) or Dr. Raul Rivas Maldonado (☎ **044/624-147-7412**) both speak English and are emergency care physicians.

Internet Cafes & Wireless Hot Spots **Trazzo Internet,** on the corner of Zaragoza and Morelos, 1 block from the central plaza (☎ **624/142-0303;** www.trazzo digital.com) is open Monday through Friday from 8am to 9pm, and Saturday from 9am to 7pm. They charge $25 for 30 minutes or less of high-speed access. **Ciber Spacio** (Valerio Gonzalez at Mijares, inside Plaza del Arbol; ☎ **624/142-2884**) is open daily 8am to 9pm, and charges $20 for an hour to use one of their nine high-speed computers. Plus, there's a nice bonus—air-conditioning.

Alternately, check out **Corre Caminos** (Plaza Misión Local A-1, Bulevar Mijares s/n at Paseo Finisterra; ☎ **624/142-3510** or -3514) where you can sit all day with your laptop for $20 while eating homemade pastries and drinking espresso; or log on with their computers for $1 per minute (20-min. regular). The comfortable **Café Vanilla** (see "Eating," p. 375) above the Tourist Office charges roughly the same to go online with their computers; they don't charge anything for Wi-Fi if you sip one of their coffees while you're googling.

Laundry **ECO Lavanderia** (Morelos s/n, at Obregón, Old Town) is one of many laundries all around town. A load runs $18 to wash and $18 to dry; dry cleaning is also $18, and pressing is $9 per piece. Or try **Cabomatic** (Bulevar Mijares s/n at Paseo Finisterra, Plaza La Misión L-6; ☎ **624/142-2933**), which will do a load of laundry for $37, including washing, soap, drying, and folding; ironing is $15 per piece.

Pharmacies **Farmacia ISSSTE,** Carretera Transpeninsular Km 34, Plaza California Local 7 (☎ **624/142-2645**), is open daily from 8am to 8pm.

Post Offices The *correo* (Bulevar Mijares 1924, at Valerio González; ☎ **624/142-0911**) is open Monday through Friday from 8am to 6pm, Saturday from 9am to noon. Other mail service includes **Mailbox Etc.** (Plaza Las Palmas #15 in San José; ☎ **624/142-4355**), which can ship with UPS.

Safety San José is a small town and probably much safer than most American cities, but use common sense and don't do anything here you wouldn't do at home. As elsewhere in Mexico, don't carry valuables; don't walk in unlit areas at night; and don't drive to rural areas after dark. Also use caution driving between the two Cabos late at night.

Telephone Tips The local telephone area code is **624.**

Sleeping

Due to the booming tourism in Los Cabos, everything here tends to be way overpriced. Hostels are either non-existent or are so funky I'd recommend crashing on the beach over staying in one (except you'd probably get hassled by security guards). San José's budget hotels are in the $450 to $650 a day range, and it's best to call ahead or reserve online unless it's low season (then you can try to bargain). Fairly recently, smaller inns or bed-and-breakfasts have started opening up, and they're a good option if you're angling for more stylish accommodations in town. Properties in the beachside hotel zone (see "The Corridor," p. 382) may offer package deals that bring room rates down to the moderate range, especially during summer months.

CHEAP

➜ **Hotel Colli** ★ This 30-year-old small hotel is almost too good to be true. It's clean, cheap, safe, and centrally located. Best of all, it's right next door to the French Riviera Bakery (see "Eating," p. 374), so good eats are close by. But because it is so cheap, expect minimal amenities: There's nada in the rooms except for a TV, chair, bed, and dresser. Fishermen have been coming here for years, though, so the hotel at least has large freezers for the guests for storing their catch (or for the non fishermen reading this, their beer). *Calle Hidalgo between Zaragoza and Doblado.* ☎ *624/142-0725. $190 double. No credit cards. Amenities: A/C; fan; shared bathrooms; TV; purified water. In room: TV, safe.*

➜ **Hotel Posada Señor Mañana** ★ This is a backpackers' heaven even though it's not totally cheap. But for a little more money than a hostel, you get a great location just off the main plaza and access to outdoor sitting areas under pretty palapas. Unfortunately you may want to hang outside because the rooms aren't too appealing—most come with concrete floors, painted metal doors, and sub par ventilation. They're certainly clean, though. The rooms on the bottom floor have queen-size beds and new tiled floors, but the best room overlooks the estuary and boasts a mid-century design feel. It's in a separate building in the back of the property.

Since the place sprawls out over many levels, that means it's great for big groups. There's a large Baja-style kitchen with two stoves, a long counter, and several tables, though you may not need it; the room price even includes a coupon for breakfast at **El Sazon** just down the street (see

"Eating," p. 372). *Calle Obregón 1 behind the main square.* ☎ *624/142-0462. www.srmanana.com. $700–$750 double. No credit cards. Amenities: Communal kitchen; small pool. In room: A/C (in some), TV, fan.*

DOABLE

→ **La Fonda del Mar** ★★ This place is a wonderful choice if you're looking for a sense of Baja Sur before the madness began—it's a good alternative to the big resorts on the beach. It's possible to have a real "get away from it all" experience here, even though San José is just 15 minutes away. There are four plastered-brick casitas with palapa roofs and wide shuttered windows in a cluster just off the beach. The large bungalow-style rooms with palapa roofs are clean, with tiled floors and brightly painted walls. Yes, the rooms are lacking in amenities—you won't get your MTV here—but with good surfing at La Bocana, Shipwrecks, and Nine Palms so close, why'd you want to hole up in your room anyways? Be warned that you'll have to use water and electricity carefully, as the whole place runs on solar panels. *Old East Cape Rd. 23400, go towards La Playa, bear left at the first 3 gloriettas and right at the 4th, follow signs to El Encanto.* ☎*/fax 624/142-1916, 909/303-3918 in the U.S. www.buzzardsbar.com. US$100 double. Includes breakfast. No credit cards. Amenities: Bar; restaurant. In room: Fans, safe.*

→ **El Encanto Inn & Suites** ★★ On a quiet street in the historic downtown district, this once minimalist inn has expanded into a luxurious spot with larger rooms called "suites" facing either the garden or the pool (prices for poolside rooms are slightly higher). You enter down a long, lovely walk with an arched brick, or *boveda,* roof, through the original inn area—smaller and somewhat claustrophobic, since it faces a high wall with a narrow strip of garden. The rooms are clean and comfortable if somewhat motel-esque in feel. *Morelos at corner of Comonfort (suites) and Morelos 133 (kitty-corner to the Suites, between Obregón and Comonfort).* ☎ *624/142-0388 or 210/858-6649. www.elencantoinn.com. US$79 double, US$105–US$175 suite, US$133 poolside suite. MC, V. Amenities: Restaurant; bar; bike rental; laundry service; pool. In room: A/C, TV, coffeemaker, fans, fridge (in some), Internet.*

→ **La Playita Inn** An alternative spot that's slightly east of town, this 10-year-old Baja-style two-story motel is built around a newly renovated swimming pool and faces the beach. Unfortunately, it's also a stone's throw away from the marina that's under construction, which (temporarily) brings with it a ton of dust and noise. Nonetheless, if you gather together enough people to get the penthouse upstairs at the back—it has a terrific view and is quieter—the price is hard to beat. The other hotel rooms here are roomy if not special, kind of in the style of a typical U.S. motel.

All the construction doesn't only equal bad news—a malecón will soon link the hotel to town. In the meantime, the on-site bar and nearby restaurant, along with the very helpful and friendly manager, should help put most construction woes at bay. *Pueblo la Playa s/n .* ☎*/fax 624/142-4166. www.laplayitahotel.com. $800 double plus 13% tax. Includes coffee. No credit cards. Amenities: Restaurant; bar; outdoor pool. In room: A/C, TV, kitchen (in some).*

→ **Tropicana Inn** ★★ First things first: The Tropicana is not on the beach. But if a pool and a pleasant Colonial-decorated room are all you need, then by all means consider this place. They've got 40 rooms, so it's not so big you'll get lost, and the space boasts a nice stone courtyard and hand-painted-tile murals. Some of the suites have Jacuzzis. My favorite was the "Troje

Suite," which has a mosquito net–covered bed in a traditional Sinaloan-style wooden house with a palapa roof. *Bulevar Mijares 30. ☎ 624/142-1580. www.tropicanacabo.com. US$80 double. Includes continental breakfast. AE, MC, V. Amenities: Restaurant/bar; swim-up bar; Internet; laundry service; small outdoor pool; limited room service; shuttle to beach. In room: A/C, TV, coffeemaker, fans, hair dryer, minibar, Wi-Fi.*

SPLURGE

MTV Best → **Casa Natalia** ★★★ Throughout Mexico's resort cities and towns, there are little pockets of good taste that manage to filter out the party-till-you-puke mentality and the endless catcalls of the timeshare sharks. These places manage to remind you that you're in a foreign country yet provide an experience that is modern, exquisitely comfortable, and sensually satisfying. Casa Natalia is such a place. Somehow, it melds the comfortable and the exotic—think high-end amenities coupled with a traditional Mexican spirit. It's located right off the tiny main square of San José, next to the church, in a renovated historic home. The architecture is modular and minimalist, with small square windows

All Clothes Barred

It's so hot. I think I'll just slip off my top . . . Oh that's MUCH better . . .

If this sounds like your idea of a dream vacation, then **Desire** is the place for you. This new "erotic resort" right on the edge of San José is an all-inclusive, couples only, adults only, clothing-optional playground. How adult? Well they sell dildos and Viagra in the gift store. It's for "open-minded" people and, no you don't need to be a swinger to enjoy it. Or a voyeur. Or an exhibitionist. But it sure helps at this nonstop flesh-fest. Set in a former Fiesta Americana hotel, the three-story 133-room U-shaped complex is clustered around the pool with a swim-up bar topped by a palapa roof. On another rooftop, overlooking the sands, an infinity Jacuzzi is centered around another bar, ringed with broad lawn chairs. Around the main pool are two rows of mattresses, a Nikki Beach–like (p. 405) set-up—only here everybody is nude or nearly so.

This is the only clothing-optional resort in Baja Sur, a sister of a successful 4-year-old facility in Cancún. The staff is dressed and clothes must be worn in the restaurants, but beyond that, there's nary a sleeve in sight. Somewhere between a nudie romantic getaway and a swingers' wet dream, Desire is jammed with cheesy unsubtle reminders about s-e-x: busty nude torso sculptures and salacious large modern art renditions adorn the hallways. Down around the pool, it's mainly Americans and Mexicans of all ages, all physiques and forms, with visible tans lines anywhere, and more than a few reminders that not everyone is circumcised. It's all there for the world to admire: wrinkles, scars, stretch marks, implants, tattoos, and nipple rings.

As much as Baja may feel like southern California, this is still conservative Mexico and one wonders just how long this Desire will last. For now, they've found a tumescent niche market that is starting to swell—it books up quickly with guests coming to seek their happy endings for 5 to 6 days. It's located at Bulevar Malecón San José s/n, behind the Mega mall, Zona Hotelera. Call ☎ **998/848-7930,** from the U.S. 888/201-7551, for info. Rooms start at US$175, per person all inclusive (food/drink); if booked in advance, the price includes a fifth night for free; all come with a slew of amenities, from Viagra to volleyballs.

that allow for wonderful cross breezes and light. The subtle gray and white tiles are offset by blue and white Talavera pots and glass balls on pewter shells that line the long pool area, shaded by bougainvillea, palm, and bamboo. The beds are massive and comfortable and the rooms have private patios where you can hang your hammock for an afternoon snooze. If you get hungry, just head down to the Mi Cocina (p. 375) kitchen—one of the best in San José. *Bulevar Mijares 4, at the far end of the main plaza. ☎ 624/142-5100 or 888/277-3814 in the U.S., 866/826-1170 in Canada. www.casanatalia.com. US$220–US$295 double (seasonal), US$350–US$475 spa suite. Includes breakfast. AE, MC, V. Amenities: Gourmet restaurant; bar; laundry service; massage; heated outdoor pool w/waterfall and swim-up bar; room service. In room: A/C, TV, bathrobes, DVDs, fans, hair dryer, Internet, private terraces/patios, safe.*

Eating

As all over Baja California Sur, there aren't many budget eating options in San José other than taco stands (fortunately, some of those are absolutely amazing). You will find lots of places that are simply overpriced and provide less-than-special food. But at least once on your trip, try to seek out some incredible gourmet or haute cuisine places that, despite their prohibitively high prices, actually come closer to giving you your money's worth. See these options under the "Splurge" section below.

No matter your budget, expect to pay around $100 for breakfast and more for lunch. What I often do is eat a large breakfast—frittatas (called Mexican omelets), huevos rancheros or *divorciados* (eggs in red and green sauces), and consume everything that comes with it: beans, fruit, salsa, and lots of tortillas. This can sustain you until early afternoon. Then have a comida corrida and forget about dinner (or grab some great cheap tacos, at the several great stands that stay open until early morning).

CHEAP

→ **El Fogon Taqueria** MEXICAN Within walking distance from the centro, this taqueria jumps at night with couples on dates, families, and pub crawlers getting grounded. They serve piping hot and delicious meaty tacos for just $10 each until 4am, the highlight being the *vampire*, a cheese and beef concoction in a crispy tortilla shell that somehow manages not to be greasy. If you want vegetarian tacos, this is not the place for you. Like other local taco places, they'll bring you a plate of grilled onions, jalapeños, raw cucumbers, and bowls of fiery salsa to accompany your pick. The ambience is about what you'd expect: plastic tables set up under TVs blasting soccer games. And as you chow down, you likely won't see a tourist in sight. *Calle Manuel Doblado at Calle Centrica. No phone. Tacos $10–$12. No credit cards. Daily 6pm–late.*

→ **El Sazon Mexicano** ★ MEXICAN The locals call it "Mama's Café" and, like a surrogate momma, this place dishes out huge breakfasts and lunch to regulars, only on weekends. A typical comida corrida consists of soup of the day, rice, beans, and a main course like chicken in green sauce, tacos, and pork. The food is cooked behind a counter in front of you, while you sit at plastic tables on the '50s concrete tiled floor. The chief cook and bottle washer, Lupe, is the aunt of Eduardo at the Jewelry Factory so if you're staying at **Señor Mañana** (p. 369), you'll get a coupon for breakfast here. A local expat couple told me they eat here every single weekend—that seems like a definitely reasonable, if somewhat fattening, habit. *Alvaro Obregón s/n, corner Calle Hidalgo. ☎ 624/108-2712. Nothing over $65. No credit cards. Sat–Sun 9–11am and 1–3:30pm.*

Best → **Guacamayas Taqueria** ★★★ MEXICAN Locals argue over which is better, Guacamayas or Hangman's, and I'm the first to give the nod to the latter for overall coolness. That said, I honestly do think Guacamayas' huitlacoche quesadilla is about the best thing I've ever bitten into. The thick corn tortillas here are warmed to just the right degree of crispiness and can then be filled with a slew of vegetarian choices, like flor de calabaza, nopales, or potato. Slather on one of the many unique salsas or garnish with the fire-grilled onions or raw cucumbers and you've got just about the best thing ever for a measly $10 a pop. You can also get all kinds of beef or pork—the *al pastor* (meat layered with onions and roasted vertically on a spit) here is topped with a big chunk of pineapple, which the cook expertly slices along with your meat. They've just opened a branch in Cabo, so they're bound to win the fight for the most authentic and highest quality taco there, too. My only caveat is that it's in an open palapa and can be chilly on winter nights, so wear layers. *Calle Marinos s/n, at Paseo Pescadores, Colonia El Chamizal.* ☎ *044/624/109-5473. Main courses $10–$20. No credit cards. Daily 6pm–late.*

Best → **"Hangman's" (Taqueria El Ahorcado)** ★★ MEXICAN Some in town will argue that Hangman's is simply the best. I disagree—though stellar, the tortillas are slightly smaller here than at Guacamayas and not handmade. Still, the atmosphere more than makes up for it. The roof is a tarp stretched taut, the walls are made of dried sticks, twigs, and vines, and every imaginable kind of stuff hangs from the ceiling, perched or stuffed on shelves improvised from sewing machines or whatever. Over to the side are some plastic carousel horses, wrapped with Christmas lights, and surfboards hang from the trees in the courtyard. And, as if in homage to the stunning surroundings, an elderly man in a checked suit and Vegas-style tinted glasses sits elevated behind an ancient electronic organ smoothly segueing from one '40s or '50s lounge nugget into another.

Though not as amazing as the visuals, the tacos here do hold up. During certain times of year, you can get a taco with big chunks of white turkey meat swimming in a flor de calabaza cream sauce, which puts the turkey sandwich at Caffee Todos Santos (at 10 times the cost) to shame. Their tacos al pastor and carne asada arrive hot and yummy off the grill. Supplemented with frijoles charros, they're hard to beat—although I could have done without the chopped up hot dog in the beans, thank you. Great service and a lively crowd of families, surfers, and daters make this place really hop. It's a bit hard to find, so keep your eyes peeled for the surfboard on the corner with "Hangmans" painted on it. *Paseo Pescadores and Marinos, Colonia El Chamizal.* ☎ *624/148-2437. Tacos, quesadillas $10–$20. No credit cards. Daily 6pm–3 or 4am.*

DOABLE

→ **Buzzards Bar and Grill** MEXICAN This B&B (see "Sleeping," p. 383) is very much an eating destination too, especially for their Sunday brunch. For $60 you can stuff yourself sick with their "mexi-stack" (ham and cheese grilled between tortillas and topped with fried eggs, cheese, salsa, and avocado), eggs Benedict, other typical Mexican breakfast eggs, and pancakes. For lunch, they've got pretty good organic salads, burgers and fries, enchiladas, and taco salad. Also look for their dinner specials: on Mondays, the menu includes coconut shrimp, burritos, enchiladas, and $20 beers. It's popular with old-timers commuting on ATVs, surfers, and the growing mob of realtors hyping the exploding development creeping up the coast to

Zacatillos. Sadly the old-school Baja ambience—think surfboards suspended under a palapa—may not be around much longer if those realtors have their way. *Old East Cape Rd. 23400, turn off Mijares towards La Playa, bear left at the first 3 gloriettas and right at the 4th, follow signs to El Encanto. ☎ 909/303-3918 in the U.S. www.buzzardsbar.com. Main courses $60–$120. No credit cards. Mon–Sat 8am–8:30pm; Sun 9am–2:30pm.*

➔**French Riviera Bakery** ★★ BISTRO If you've been craving something buttery and flakey, flavored with sweet creams and fruits, you have to come to this San José outlet of the highly respected French Rivera Restaurant in Cabo. It's not exactly cheap, but OMG is it good. This is French baking like you haven't had since you were last in the Loire Valley. The bakery is located in a classic historic building with a large window where you can watch the pastry chefs at work while you sip your espresso and wonder if you can handle just one more strawberry tart. Get the bread and roll basket to sample the variety. They also have great spinach/mushroom/cheese crepes, shrimp steaks, sandwiches (topped with the best organic produce in the area). Because they sell fabulous baguettes and other breads, it's a good place to get fixins for a beach picnic, too. *Manuel Doblado s/n, at Hidalgo. ☎ 624/142-3350. www.frenchrivieraloscabos.com. Breakfast $40–$120; dinner $70–$230. MC, V. Daily 7am–11pm.*

➔**Terranova Restaurant & Bar** MEXICAN This reasonable place on the first floor of the Terranova hotel is best visited during breakfast—when locals come to hit up the large and relatively affordable spread. In addition to standard huevos rancheros, the menu includes chilaquiles that are tasty and reasonable (if nothing special). There's also typical Mexican antijitos for lunch and dinner done "Baja ranch style." The vibe is decidedly informal, with a TV blasting in the main inside room and musicians on the outside terrace. *Degollado s/n, off Zaragoza. ☎ 624/142-0534. www.hterranova.com.mx Main courses $100–$150. MC, V. Daily 7am–10pm.*

➔**Tropicana Bar and Grill** CONTINENTAL The Tropicana is all about its alfresco sidewalk dining during the daytime. That's because it's on Bulevar Mijares and you can watch all the passing traffic as people come and go from the plaza. For evening dining, the garden area with its candles and murals is the best choice, though you can stay inside if you want to take advantage of the live music and satellite TV. The end result of all these seating arrangements? There's a little bit of everything for everybody. That's just like the popular if not outstanding menu, which includes steaks, fajitas, shrimp, and paella (on Sun). *Bulevar Mijares 30, 1 block south of the Plaza Mijares. ☎ 624/142-1580 www.tropicanacabo.com/bar. Breakfast $40–$60; main courses $100–$200. AE, MC, V. Daily 8am–midnight.*

SPLURGE

➔**Baan Thai** ★★ THAI Set in one of San José's lovely historic buildings and decorated with giant bamboo as well as sculptures imported from Indonesia and Asia, this Thai restaurant has many traditional dishes such as Pad Thai, green papaya salad, and chile garlic shrimp, but it also moves beyond that to blend in a taste of Mexico. More unique menu items include blue crab stir-fried with chile, garlic, and tomatoes; mild chiles stuffed with smoked marlin and served with a soy-ginger dipping sauce; and seared steak tossed with mangoes, green apples, and chiles. Judging from the crowd, locals seem to love the food as much as tourists. *Morelos s/n, at Obregón. ☎ 624/142-3344. Main courses $150–$280. MC, V. Mon–Sat noon–10:30pm.*

MTV Best → **Mi Cocina** ★★★ NUEVO LATINO Located in the stunning boutique hotel Casa Natalia (p. 371), this restaurant is one of the best reasons to stay in San José instead of Cabo. The patio setting is elegant without being intimidating—you'll dine on classic Villeroy & Boch china on limestone-lava tables, surrounded by towering palms, exposed brick walls, and four cascading waterfalls that feed into the pool. Chef Loïc Tenoux brings an inventive and always creative approach to his very distinctive blend of Mexican/European fusion, from the baby clams with a cilantro sauce, to the chile poblano stuffed with crispy lamb and Oaxaca cheese, to the Provençal-style risotto with sautéed fish and roasted tomato. Nothing on the menu is undeserving of sampling. But save room for dessert. The crème brûlée and chocolate cake are both exquisite. There's also a full service bar with a long wine list, single malt scotches, premium tequilas, and signature martinis. You will *not* have a bad meal here, I guarantee it. *Bulevar Mijares, in Casa Natalia Hotel.* ☎ *624/142-5100. www.casanatalia.com/dining.cfm. Main courses $150–$320. AE, MC, V. Daily 6:30–10pm (hotel guests only 6:30am–6pm).*

→ **Voila** ★ NOUVELLE MEXICAN-EURO Chef Roberto Valle Hernandez, winner of a best local caterer award, serves Mexican cuisine fused with French and Asian twists. His restaurant is done up in a sort of contemporary-industrial Baja style, with original adobe walls in the dining room that date from back when it was a cantina in 1860. The outside restaurant design is pleasant, if a bit of a knock-off of Mi Cocina's landscaping. Try the huitlacoche ravioli, crusted camembert salad, "World Famous Lobster Burrito," or duck, lobster, or chicken salad with locally grown organic produce. Main plates include scallops, filet mignon, lobster, halibut, and a New Zealand rack of lamb with manchego cheese, avocado, cabbage, and mango chipotle salsa. The space hosts a Thursday night art walk (p. 380) and displays local artists' work, including pottery, in the Mata Ortiz genre. *Plaza Paulina, Morelos at Comonfort.* ☎ *624/130-7569. www.voila-events.com. Main courses $150–$320. MC, V. Mon–Sat noon–10pm and Sun 3–10pm.*

CAFES

In a clean, modern, and open space upstairs from the Tourist Office, the **Café Vanilla** (Plaza San José Local 3&4, Hwy. 1; ☎ **624/307-7778;** Mon–Sat 8:30am–10:30pm) sells pastrami, roast beef and veggie sandwiches, espresso and other coffee drinks, smoothies, and English and Spanish magazines, all while a rock and reggae playlist blasts in the background. You can pay to go online here, or get free Wi-Fi if you buy a cup of coffee.

For ice cream, the best in San José is probably at the aptly named **Ice Cream** (next door to the French Bistro, Hidalgo s/n, at Doblado; ☎ **624/142-3350,** daily 9am–9pm), which has homemade gelato and ice cream and is also run by the Bistro's chef. **La Jungla Juice Bar** (Zaragoza s/n; ☎ **624/142-3838;** Mon–Sat 8am–7pm) has all-natural papaya, carrot, and other fruit and veggie juices or milk shakes. Try the "vampire," which is a dark red beet, orange, carrot, and apple concoction (just don't be too alarmed at the color of your pee afterwards).

Partying

Yes, serious partiers usually head down the coast to Cabo, but that just means there are more *refined* options here in San José. For starters, you can actually soak in some culture while you party here. Check out the **Art Walk** in San José's historical district on Thursday early evenings (see "Shopping," p. 380), based out of the **Voila**

Bistro. And don't fret that seeing art will curtail your drinking—this is small-town San José, after all, so the walk won't take *that* long.

A great source for what's going on in town is ***Noche Magazine*** (www.nochemexico.com), which you can pick up free around town. The irrepressible co-publisher Anastasia Lee Snider makes the club rounds regularly. Check out the funky nightlife photos online to get a feel for what's going on and to get a feel for what you need to do to be included.

Most bars and clubs in San José close at 1am during the week, or 2am on the weekends and many are closed Sundays. Most of the bars are scattered around the art district, along Mijares, or around the Zona Hotelera.

Note that there isn't really a gay nightlife scene here or in the rest of south Baja; for that, you should head farther south to Puerto Vallarta.

BARS

In the centro historico is **La Santa Wine Bar** (Alvaro Obregón 1732, at Hidalgo; ☎ **624/142-6767,** 355-3272; www.lasanta.com.mx), a restaurant/bar housed in a centuries-old building. The bar area fronts the original rough hewn stone wall but there's more intimate and romantic seating in back. Touches like old palm tree vigas set against oxblood red walls and a polished concrete floor help create a hip vibe. The selection of wines, while extensive, isn't stellar (there isn't a comprehensive Valle de Guadalupe selection, unfortunately), and you'll need to be prepared to drop a few pesos ($70 for a glass of wine). But the zillion kinds of tequila available to order make up for it.

Looking for something hotter and less sophisticated? Try **El Spicy Cooper's** ★ (Morelos at Obregón; ☎ **624/156-8717**) which is just down the street from La Santa. Owner Caesar greets every guest with a sincere "welcome home" when you walk in the door of this old New Orleans–style building in the centro historico. The ambience here is warm, a mixture of South American/Cuban style with a dash of Italy. There's a pool table, humidor, good wine list, and live music Thursdays to Saturdays, which brings in everything from blues bands to bongo players to karaoke singers. Next door is **Kilometro** (Morelos at Obregón, in the Art District; ☎ **624/156-8717**), a hot bar that has everything from unplugged Sessions, to Retro Night with live '70s, '80s, and '90s music.

Club El Moro (Obregón and Guerrero; ☎ **624/142-4647**), also right around the corner, is run by Dana, a former schoolteacher turned bar owner. She's redheaded, gregarious, and, well, stacked. She seems to employ only studly guys in cut off sleeved T-shirts. And why not? The soundtrack rocks but the entertainment is casual—you'll get pool, and table games like chess, backgammon, and dominoes. Set in a renovated brick building, the bar boasts comfortable seating around fire pits, too.

Great as El Moro is, **El Chilar** ★★ (Benito Juárez 1490, corner with Morelos; ☎ **624/142-2544** or 146-9798) has pretty much replaced it as the locals' wine bar/restaurant of choice. It's a small, totally charming, intimate "rustic" space, and part of the popular restaurant of the same name. Inspired by the use of chiles, Oaxacan Chefs Armando Montano and Casiano Reyes create dishes here like shrimp in a roasted garlic and guajillo chile sauce or grilled tortilla and salmon Napoleon, accompanied by a mango pico de gallo. Although the menu at the restaurant regularly changes, the full bar, with its great wine selection, remains constant.

Two other spots to include on your bar crawl include **Casa Natalia** (p. 371) and **Tropicana** (p. 370). The former, set above their lovely terrace restaurant in a minimalist-meets-Mexican designed space, caters to sophisticates. The latter is popular, with a more casual, old-school Baja-rowdy crowd that expects sports TV (on plasma screens), a Mexican/Cuban playlist, and the ubiquitous live mariachi band.

CLUBS

Down in the Hotel Zone, new places are sprouting up including **Red** ★ (Malecón San José, Hotel Zone, across from Desire; ☎ **624/143-5644**). Locals insist it's the hottest place in town, but the night I was there, it was totally dead. Still, I can imagine that on a weekend during high season, it could get packed with tourists from the neighboring hotels. Its architecture is high-tech and the decor industrial, with a lot of, well, red everywhere, and an accompanying thumping house soundtrack. There are black and white comfy loungey leather chairs and sofas clustered around low tables, as well as an open fire pit outside with a view of the sea. The drinks are overpriced, but the joint is welcoming enough to help you forget.

Though it's on the way to Cabo, the MTV Best **Havana Super Club** ★★ (Km 29 Hwy. 1, Costa Azul; ☎ **624/142-2603;** no cover; daily 6pm–1am; closed Aug through mid-Nov) is still considered part of San José. In addition to delicious food and drinks, there's a great mixed crowd consisting of high rollers who come down from Palmilla to rub shoulders with surfers. The palapa-roofed club is set above the highway overlooking the sea and, while it's not exactly cheap, it does boast a great Havana beach shack feel. It's a great place to come just to dance—it books first-rate live salsa and other bands regularly on weekends.

Heading to the Beach

The **Playa Hotelera** fronts the Hotel Zone, and is great for walking, fishing, and beach volleyball. It's a steep beach and the shore break can make it difficult to get out of the shallows. There also can be strong cross-currents here and people drown every year, so don't be tempted to take a dip unless you are very comfortable in the ocean. Farther along the same stretch you'll find beach volleyball at **Playa Las Palmas,** which has palapas and is accessed below Plaza Garuffi and Caracol (at Viva condos)—look for the nets strung in the sand.

Near the Presidente Inter-Continental Hotel is the Don Manuel Orantes sea turtle camp, a miniature golf course, and a children's play park. Keep going and you'll hit the **San José estuary,** a protected eco reserve. A malecón connecting this beach to the beaches at the next community of **La Playita** is promised but who knows what that will do to the estuary?

See "Playing Outside" below for info on the best beaches for swimming. For a list of other nearby beaches worth exploring see "Heading to the Beach" under Cabo San Lucas later in this chapter.

Sightseeing

FESTIVALS/EVENTS

San José del Cabo celebrates the feast of its patron saint on March 19. June 19 is the festival of the patron saint of **San Bartolo,** a village 100km (62 miles) north. July 25 is the festival of the patron saint of **Santiago,** a village 55km (34 miles) north. These festivals usually feature music, dancing, feasting, horse races, and, more unusually, cockfights.

MAJOR ATTRACTIONS

Although the two Cabos now seem like two sides of the same coin, it wasn't always that way. Since San José del Cabo was settled in the 1700s by the first missionaries to the area, it became the more established city at first. It wasn't until hotel resorts starting going up fairly recently that neighboring Cabo developed into more than just a fishing village. And even though Cabo is the more popular destination today, San José still gets funneled most of the money for the two capes because it's the county seat of Los Cabos. One look at the roads proves which town is wealthier: Most of the roads in San José are paved, while you'll still find sandy dirt roads connecting the main roads in Cabo.

Perhaps because it's more loaded, San José's cultural sites are also superior to those in Cabo. The **Plaza Mijares,** the main plaza in San José, north of where Zarazoga curves into Mijares, is where most of the sightseeing action takes place. The plaza is named after José Antonio Mijares, a local boy who did well as a soldier. Take time to hang out here to get a feel for the town (you may even want to stay at a nearby hotel rather than one on the beach). On the west side of the plaza, be sure to check out the **Iglesia San José** and its mosaic tiles, which depict the first missionaries meeting their end at the hands of the hostile Indios. Gory but fascinating stuff.

A trip to **Cactimundo** (Bulevar Mijares near the turnoff to Las Plazas; ☎ **624/146-9191**), a groomed garden with over 850 species of cacti from Baja as well as the mainland, is a must. Founded by Pablo Gonzalez Carbonell and Josef Schrott over a decade ago, the garden conserves, promotes, and reproduces the versatile prickly plants. You'll come away with the knowledge that cacti aren't just impossible to kill—they also provide shelter for nesting wildlife and food and medicine for humans.

Playing Outside

For more on outdoor activities in the area, see "Playing Outside," p. 407, in the Cabo San Lucas section.

BIKING You can rent bicycles to explore the city at the **Hotel Presidente** (Bulevar Mijares at Paseo San José, Hotel Zone; ☎ **624/142-9229**), which is also the best way to get to the estuary (and the volleyball sand courts on the beach there).

FISHING To arrange a fishing expedition, simply venture to where the new marina is under construction (La Playita) and visit the fishing co-op **La Playa Sport Fishing** (Tomas Cantor; ☎ **624/148-0469** or 044/624/118-1496). They can set up a regular package for $2,398 for six out to the Gordo Bank or $2,998 for the faster SuperPanga.

GOLF **The Mayan Palace Golf Los Cabos** (1 Paseo Finisterra; ☎ **624/142-0901**) here is historical in the sense that it was the first golf course in southern Baja. Though now overshadowed by the score of luxury courses on The Corridor, it's still a fun and affordable 9-hole course. With greens fees costing $640 for 9-holes, this place has the lowest prices in the area. That means it's a good option if you're not very serious about the sport but want to give it a go.

SEA KAYAKING Fully guided, ecologically oriented **ocean kayak tours** are available through **Baja's Moto Rent** (☎ **624/143-2050**), **Cabo Expeditions** (☎ **624/143-2700**), and **Aqua Deportes** (☎ **624/143-0117**). Most ocean kayaking tours depart from Cabo San Lucas.

SNORKELING/DIVING **Gray Line Los Cabos** (☎ **624/146-9410;** www.graylineloscabos.com) and **Amigos del Mar** in Cabo San Lucas (☎ **800/344-3349**

in the U.S. or 624/143-0505; www.amigosdelmar.com) arrange snorkeling and diving trips starting at $500 per person. Among the area's best dive sites are **Cabo Pulmo** and **Gordo Banks.** Cabo Pulmo has seven sites geared for divers of all experience levels, so it never feels crowded. It also offers the possibility to snorkel with sea lions, depending on the currents and the animals' behavior. Gordo Banks is an advanced dive site where you can see whale sharks and hammerhead sharks. It's a deep dive—27 to 30m (89–98 ft.)—with limited visibility (9–12m/30–39 ft.). Most dives are drift dives, and wet suits are highly recommended.

SURFING **Playa Costa Azul,** at Km 29 on Carretera Transpeninsular just south of San José, is the most popular surfing beach in the area. A few bungalows are available for rent, or surfers can camp on the beach.

If the heart of San José surf culture is Costa Azul, then the MTV Best **Costa Azul Surf Shop** ★★ (Costa Azul Plaza, No. 8, Km 28; ☎ **624/142-2771;** www.costa-azul.com.mx) is the nerve center. In addition to renting good quality surfboards ($218 per day), body boards ($164 per day), snorkeling equipment ($164 per day), and skim boards ($109 per day), they have awesome teachers who will take you wherever the surf is breaking and get you up on that board without making you feel totally stupid. The staffers also are really fun to hang out with, especially when you go out for tacos and beer at the end of the day. They'll haul along umbrellas, coolers of drinks, snacks, rash guards, whatever you need. The owner, Alejandro Olea, is a famous board shaper and surfer in his own right. Drop by their cool shop for board shorts and T-shirts that actually fit (you get a free T-shirt with a half-day lesson) or information about local conditions.

When summer hurricanes spin off the southern end of the peninsula, they send huge surf northward to beaches like Zipper's, Punta Gorda, and Old Man's. Surfers have compared **Zipper's** ★★ (near the Brisa del Mar Trailer Park and the Costa Azul Surf Shop outside San José del Cabo; see p. 387 for info) with places like Pipeline, on the north shore of Oahu. That may be a bit of an exaggeration, but there are great waves nonetheless.

SWIMMING The ultimate irony of visiting San José is that you're surrounded by gorgeous beaches in perfect weather and yet you can't go in the water, since swimming is not recommended in the Bahia San José del Cabo (the beaches fronting the Zona Hotelera) due to currents. It's safe to swim and snorkel (with caution) at beaches up the East Cape, though, like **La Playita** and **Cabo Pulmo** (see "Road Trips," p. 430) where the currents aren't usually as strong.

TENNIS You can play tennis at the two courts of the **Club Campo de Golf San José,** Paseo Finisterra 1 (☎ **624/142-0905**), for $130 an hour during the day, $220 an hour at night. Club guests can also use the swimming pool.

Shopping

For authentic and fun shopping in San José, head to **Old Town** behind the main square (off Obregón, bordered roughly by the Main Square and Guerrero), which has grown up lately due not only to the influence of the sophisticated **Casa Natalia** (see "Sleeping," p. 371) but also to an influx of galleries. Wander this area for a bit and you'll find no shortage of cute boutiques, sophisticated folk art shops, and trendy wine bars. In addition to the main plaza, shops are also clustered up and down **Bulevar Mijares** and **Zaragoza,** San José's main streets.

Most shops are open 9am to 10pm daily with shorter hours on Sunday; a few may still close for the traditional lunch siesta from 2 to 4pm. Most galleries are open Monday to Saturday from 10am to 7pm. As in other parts of small-town Mexico, many of the shops don't have street numbers (s/n indicates "sin numero," or without number) so cross streets are indicated here.

ART GALLERIES

For a quick overview of the galleries in town, take the **Art Walk** held on Thursdays from 5 to 9pm that starts at **Voila** (Plaza Paulina, see "Eating," p. 375). Join in, and you can check out the town's galleries *and* drink wine. Best of all, it's free.

There are currently 15 galleries in the roughly 6-block area that makes up Old Town. But perhaps the best gallery in town is the MTV Best **Galería de Ida Victoria** ★★★ (Vicente Guerrero 1128, between Obregón and Zaragoza; ☎ **624/142-5772;** www.idavictoriaarts.com). Built on the foundations of a historical building, the owners Ida Victoria Gustavson and Pete Signorelli had architects design this space to feature 5m-high (16-ft.) ceilings, and so are able to exhibit large works by internationally known artists. They sell contemporary metal sculptures, paintings, bronzes, and huge cool stone sculptures, and represent artists like Lucian Hispano, New Yorker Andres Garcia, and many others. Ida Victoria Gustavson is the curator; partner Pete Signorelli also does custom archival conservation framing for high-end fine art and heirlooms. If you do find something you like that obviously won't fit into your suitcase, they do ship.

Other notable galleries include **Arte, Arte** (Plaza Paulina, Morelos at Comonfort; ☎ **624/142-3566;** www.juliangarciaf.com) with sculpture and steel installations by Julian Garcia; **Dona Pitaya** (Alvaro Obregón 8, between Morelos and Hidalgo; ☎ **624/142-6550**), which has high quality Huichol art; and **Arenas Art Gallery** (Alvaro Obregón, between Morelos and Hidalgo; ☎ **624/142-4969**), which features beautiful geometric designed ceramics by Mata Ortiz potters.

BOOKSTORES

Although slightly out of the center at the edge of the Hotel Zone, it's worth the trip to the small English bookstore, MTV Best **Spiderweb Internet and Baja Book Center** ★★ (Carretera Transpeninsular Km 30, Plaza los Portales 102, adjacent to **Mega;** ☎ **624/105-2048;** bajabook_center@yahoo.com.mx; Mon–Sat 9am–6pm) run by expat August Schultz, a man who really loves books. He's amassed a large selection—compared to other bookstores in Mexico anyway—of new and used books on Baja as well as cookbooks, adventure, fiction, travel, and pulp fiction novels. You can trade books here, too and since many vacationers do so, there is a fairly current supply at a third of what you'd pay at a bookstore in el Norte. There are even a couple of computers available that offer online access for $10 for 15 minutes.

CLOTHES & CRAFTS

For high quality folk art and textiles, bags, and hats, head to MTV Best **Veryka** ★★ (Bulevar Mijares 418, at the east end of the main plaza; ☎ **624/142-0575;** sabinamacouzet@hotmail.com) to browse its marvelous merchandise. A branch of a shop that was formerly in San Miguel de Allende, it's rather expensive, but the selection of crafts here is so high quality—featuring some of the best artisans or craftspeople in the country—that the cost makes sense. Here's your chance to buy cactus fiber woven bags from Chiapas; textiles from Guatemala, Oaxaca, and Chiapas; beautiful glass beaded Huichol handbags; amazing folk art pieces; white thickly embroidered blouses; fine Oaxacan rebozos; finely woven Ecuadorean straw hats; art books; and much, much more.

A few doors down, **Necri** (Bulevar Mijares 16, Plaza Mijares; ☎ **624/130-7500**) has Majolica and Talavera pottery, including vases and full sets of dishes made in a tin-enameled style; pewter from the state of Mexico; as well as their own brand of hot sauce, Cabo Heat. They also have a branch in Cabo San Lucas.

ADD (Arte, Diseño y Decoración) (Zaragoza at Hidalgo; ☎ **624/142-2777**) sells creative home accessories, fine arts and crafts, pewter, and authentic Talavera ceramics. **Mexicanissimo** (Zaragoza 4, at Mijares; ☎ **624/142-3090**) has folk art, including embroidered blouses from Chiapas, Huichol bracelets from Nayarit, jewelry from Taxco, serapes, miniatures, English design and art books, and local low fire clay *(barro)* pots.

For a much funkier look, check out **Punk Latino** (Doblado s/n, at Hidalgo; ☎ **624/142-0626;** gibellef@hotmail.com), which carries fake furry pink bags and wraps, stilettos, sequined belts, and tiered skirts with black lace. Everything on sale here is hip and quirky, if not the best quality (but hey, the prices are good).

If you're hunting for beach gear, then visit **Big Tony** (Zaragosa s/n, at Mijares; no telephone), which sells everything you need for fun in the sun—including sandals, swim trunks, surf wax, boogie boards, snorkels, fins, and masks. They also have a branch at Costa Azul and in San Lucas.

JEWELRY

There are a zillion jewelry stores clustered around the main square; one notable one is **Tony's** (east end of Main Square, Bulevar Mijares s/n; ☎ **624/142-1827**), which has silver from Taxco, and exchanges wares between those silversmiths and Navajos in Arizona as well as Thai smiths. It's staffed by friendly and honest clerks who will show you how to distinguish silver from alpaca (which they also carry) and amber from resin (if you can't wait to find out, see "Basics," p. 392). In addition to contemporary necklaces with amber from Russia or Chiapas, the store stocks Huichol art and Native American turquoise jewelry.

Another good jewelry shop to check out is **The Jewelry Factory** (Bulevar Mijares 5; www.loscabosdirectory.com), which is owned by a large local family and has a workshop in the back of the store where clerks can fashion a piece of jewelry according to whatever design you want. Son Eduardo and his father helped design the store in what is a historical 300-year-old former library building. They specialize in opals, but sell lots of other jewels, too.

Mexican Fire Opal Jewelry Factory, (Bulevar Mijares 5, north end of plaza; ☎ **624/142-4160;** www.theopalhouse.com) sells Mexican fire opals which are distinct from their Australian cousins because of the quantity of copper that is infused in the stone during its volcanic creation. The opals here come from a mine near Queretaro and aren't cheap, ranging in price from $545 to $109,000. They have silver, platinum, or gold backings and the jewelers are GIA-trained.

SAX ★★ (Mijares 2; ☎ **624/142-6053;** www.saxstyle.com) next to Casa Natalia is one of the best places in town to buy truly unique cool jewelry (as well as clothes). Its sophisticated contemporary jewelry is designed by owner Susanna Buena—I love her chunky bracelets made of Talavera tile pieces. You'll also find lots of little unique modern bags and great hats on sale, and they can fashion a piece according to your own design in 24 hours.

MARKETS & MEGASTORES

A municipal **market** on Mauricio Castro and Green sells food and things for everyday life (toilet paper, batteries) from 8am to 5pm Monday to Saturdays. An organic market, held on Saturdays from 9am to

Smoke 'Em If You've Got 'Em

It's not illegal to smoke Cuban cigars in San José, and the town definitely takes advantage of this fact. Among the many cigars shops in town are:

- **Los Amigos Smokeshop and Cigar Bar** (Calle Manuel-Doblado and Morelos; ☎ **624/142-1138**), which sells fine Cuban cigars and cigarettes, as well as Veracruz cigars and a range of smoking accessories, including humidors and cutters. Also available are private lockers, a bar with an excellent selection of single malts and California wines, Wednesday evening cigar tastings, and a VIP club for frequent visitors.
- **La Habanera** (Mijares 10, Main Plaza; ☎ **624/105-2612**). Another cigar shop that carries Cuban cigars as well as a selection of Yucatecan hammocks, woven bags, serapes, and Oaxacan rugs.
- **Fidel's Cigar Shop** (Bulevar Mijares 33B, Centro; ☎ **624/142-6162**), a small comfortable place that sells Montecristos, Edmundo, Cohiba Siglo 6, and many other types of cigars from their humidor in back.

Finally, for fans of plain old cigarettes, there's a branch of **Cabo Wabo** (Mijares 16-2, at Zaragoza; ☎ **624/142-2223**) in town where you can pick up regular smokes and can choose between over 40 types of tequila, including one by Van Halen's own Sammy Hagar. You can also pick up typical souvenir junk like keychain shot glasses (handy for all that tequila), T-shirts, and baseball caps.

1pm, takes place at the **Tropicana Jockey Club** on Morelos, slightly out of the center, between the estuary and San José Arroyo.

At the time of this writing, three new "box" grocery stores had opened within a few months of each other in Los Cabos, including **Mega** (Carretera Transpeninsular Km 30, San José), **C.C.C.**, and **Soriana** (Hwy. 19 just north of Reforma "outbelt", Cabo San Lucas), and **Costco** (Carretera 1, Km 4.5). The local **Arambullo Supermarket** chain, which many locals once resented for its price gouging, is now all but closed down, except in Cabo where its location is convenient enough to continue drawing customers.

The Corridor

The narrow four-lane blacktop 32km (20-mile) stretch between the two Cabos is called "The Corridor." Once a dirt road that took 4 hours to traverse, it now takes about half an hour and is pimpled with expensive luxury hotels and golf courses. But even if you find that it's too pricey to stay at one of the resorts here, it's worth hitting up the beaches and restaurants in the area. You can easily do so on a day trip from San José or Los Cabos.

Getting There & Getting Around

If you plan to explore southern Baja while staying at a Corridor hotel, get a rental car for at least 1 or 2 days. But keep in mind that there are accidents daily, so watch your speed and drive with caution. People drive this stretch of highway as if it were the freeway, but with many blind curves, a lack of shoulders, sudden turnarounds, and turnoffs to hotels and strip malls appearing without warning, it can be quite dangerous (especially at night). It helps to orient yourself before you actually start driving; also see the driving tips in "Basics" on p. 49.

See p. 390 for info on getting to The Corridor from San José or Cabo via bus or taxi.

Basics

For visitor info, see p. 367 in San José or p. 392 in Cabo.

The five major resort areas here are **Palmilla** (at Carretera Transpeninsular Km 27.5, home to the One&Only hotel), **Querencia, Cabo Real** (Querencia and Cabo Real are both roughly between Km 18 and 24, and are home to Case del Mar and Las Ventanas resorts), and **Cabo del Sol** and **Punta Ballena** (both at Carretera Transpeninsular Km 7 and home to the resort Esperanza). Each is a self-contained community with golf courses, elegant hotels, and million-dollar homes (or the promise of them).

Sleeping

First things first—it can be very expensive to stay here. There aren't any hostels or campgrounds along The Corridor, and there are very few cheap hotels. Resorts such as movie star hangout La Palmilla can run as high as $5,000 a night. Cheaper options are available if you look, though. Several hotels offer package deals that significantly lower the nightly rate; ask your travel agent for information.

Address Tip

Note that the kilometer numbers listed in directions throughout this chapter reflect the distance starting from Cabo San Lucas; the number increases the closer the address gets toward San José del Cabo.

More reasonably priced hotels here include the classic '60s architectural style **Hotel Twin Dolphin** (Carretera Km 12; ☎ **800/421-8925;** www.twindolphin.com; $270 and up double; MC, V), in a wonderful location near Bahia Santa María. Go soon, cause it may be torn down for a new development. Also recommended is the **Cabo Surf Hotel** (Km 28, Playa Acapulquito; ☎ **624/142-2666;** $241 and up double; MC, V; www.cabosurfhotel.com), which caters to surfers because it's, duh, on a prime surfing beach.

➔ **The Casa del Mar Golf Resort & Spa** ★★★ This hotel may be one of the best values along The Corridor, but that doesn't mean it's cheap. The main building, which houses the main restaurant, bar, and a pool with swim-up bar, is modeled after Mexican hacienda-style homes (hence the big archways) and is quite lovely. By all means ask to stay in this building, where heavy colonial furniture and modern sculpture complements the cool and modern rooms. The outlying buildings are much more motel-like in style; although the large suites have wooden doors and curved ceilings, rattan furniture, wrought iron headboards, and so on, they're simply more generic.

All of the rooms have balconies with ocean views, and each three-floor "unit" of 24 suites has its own heated pool surrounded by flowering gardens leading out to the sand and sea. There are palapa beach club/spa areas on the beach. If you're in an outlying building, you can call the front desk and they'll drive you around in golf carts. To actually swim you need to walk 10 minutes down the amazingly beautiful beach to the Hilton's man-made small "harbor." Along the way, check out Las Ventanas (their hammock-slung palapas come complete with flags you can put up if you want to take a nap and be awakened

The Two Cabos & The Corridor

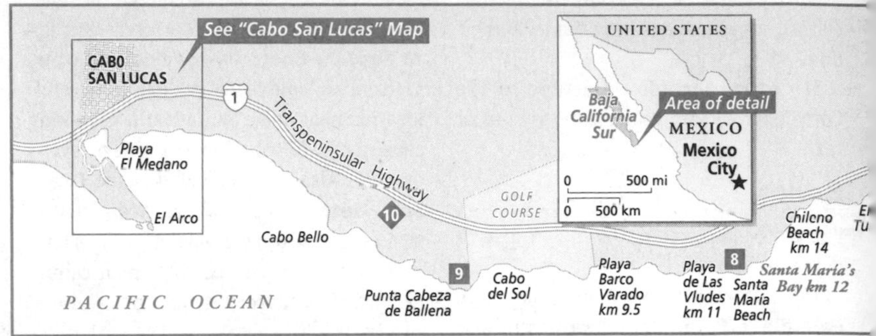

by a staff member) and Cabo Real's beach spas and dining areas.

There are fire pits at night where you and that special someone can imbibe. But in general the vibe is quiet and private—if you're a party animal, don't stay here. And if you aren't staying here, you are still welcome at the restaurant or bar, as well as at the on-site spa and nearby golf facilities. There's very little signage on the highway here, so keep your eyes peeled for Hilton or Cabo Real "Zona Hotelera" signs to find your way. *Km 19.5 on Hwy. 1. ☎ 888/227-9621 in the U.S., or 624/144-0030 www.casadelmarmexico.com. US$290–US$495 double, US$340–US$500 suite. Ask about promotions and discount rates. AE, MC, V. Amenities: Restaurants; lobby bar; beach club (adults only) w/outdoor pool, hot tub, pool bar, open-air restaurant; dry cleaning; privileges at Cabo Real and El Dorado golf clubs; Internet; laundry service; in-room massage; 6 other outdoor pools (2 w/whirlpools and swim-up bars); room service; full-service spa; 2 lighted tennis courts; tour desk; small workout room. In room: A/C, TV, bathrobes, hair dryer, Jacuzzi, minibar, safe.*

➔ **Esperanza** ★★ Although this relatively new luxury resort along Cabo's over-the-top Corridor sits on a bluff overlooking two small, rocky coves, the absence of a real beach (though they are still sandy) doesn't seem to matter much to its guests—the hotel more than makes up for it in terms of pampering services and stylish details. Created by the famed Auberge Resorts group, the architecture of this hotel is similar in style to that of Careyes, on Mexico's Pacific Coast, meaning it's dramatic, elegant, and comfortable. The casitas and villas are spread across 6.8 hectares (17 acres), designed to resemble a Mexican village, and are connected to the resort facilities by stone footpaths. The top-floor suites have handmade palapa ceilings and a private outdoor whirlpool spa. All rooms are exceptionally spacious, with woven wicker and tropical wood furnishings, original art, rugs, and fabrics in muted colors with jeweled-tone color accents, and Frette linens gracing the extra-comfortable feather beds. Terraces are large, extending the living area to the outdoors, and all have hammocks and views of the Sea of Cortez. The oversize bathrooms have separate tub and showers with dual showerheads. *Carretera Transpeninsular Km 7, at Punta Ballena, 23140 Cabo San Lucas, B.C.S. ☎ 866/311-2226 in the U.S. or 624/145-6400. www.esperanzaresort.com. High season US$575–US$925 double, US$775–US$1,050 beachfront suite, US$3,500–US$5,000 villas; low season US$375–US$650 double, US$500–US$775 beachfront suite, US$2,000–US$3,000 villas. AE,*

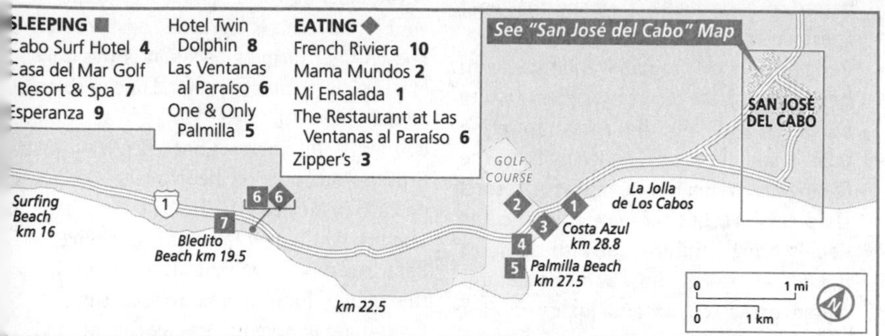

MC, V. Amenities: Oceanfront restaurant; bar; private beach w/club; dry cleaning; fitness center; golf privileges; laundry; gourmet market; in-room massage; infinity swimming pool; 24-hr. room service; deluxe European full-service spa; concierge w/tour services. In room: A/C, plasma TV w/DVD, hair dryer, high-speed Internet access, safe, stereo.

Best → **Las Ventanas al Paraíso** ★★ Las Ventanas is known for its luxury accommodations and attention to detail. The architecture, with adobe structures and rough-hewn wood accents, provides a soothing complement to the desert landscape. The only color comes from the dazzling *ventanas* (windows) of pebbled rainbow glass handmade by regional artisans. Richly furnished, Mediterranean-style rooms are large (starting at 93 sq. m/1,000 sq. ft.) and appointed with every conceivable amenity, from wood-burning fireplaces to computerized telescopes for star- or whale-gazing. Rooms contain satellite TVs with VCRs, stereos with CD players, and dual-line cordless phones. Sizable whirlpool tubs can have views of the rest of your room or the ocean, or may be closed off for privacy. Larger suites offer extras like rooftop terraces, sunken whirlpools on a private patio, or a personal pool. The spa is among the best in Mexico. With a staff that outnumbers guests by four to one, this is the place for those who want (and can afford) to be seriously spoiled. It even has special packages for pampered pets that can't be left behind. *Carretera Transpeninsular Km 19.5, 23410 San José del Cabo, B.C.S. ☎ 888/525-0483 in the U.S. or 624/144-0300. www.lasventanas.com. High season US$600 garden-view double, US$800 oceanview double, US$950 split-level oceanview suite w/rooftop terrace, US$1,150 split-level oceanfront suite w/rooftop terrace, luxury suites (1 and 3 bedrooms) US$2,600–US$4,500; summer US$450 garden-view double, US$550 oceanview double, US$675 split-level oceanview suite w/rooftop terrace, US$900 split-level oceanfront suite w/rooftop terrace, US$1,800–US$3,800 luxury suites (1 and 3 bedrooms). Spa and golf packages and inclusive meal plans available. AE, DC, MC, V. Amenities: Oceanview restaurant; seaside grill; terrace bar w/live music; fresh-juice bar; car rental; dry cleaning; access to adjoining championship Cabo Real golf course; Internet; laundry; pet packages, including treats and massages; 24-hr. room service; shuttle services; deluxe European spa w/complete treatment and exercise facilities; sportfishing and luxury yachts available; tour services; watersports. In room: A/C, TV, hair dryer, iron, minibar, safe.*

Best → **One&Only Palmilla** ★★★ The One&Only Palmilla is the grande dame of Los Cabos resorts, and a complete renovation in 2003 made it among the most spectacular resort hotels anywhere. Perched on a cliff top above the sea (with beach access), the resort is a series of white buildings with red-tile roofs, towering palms, and flowering bougainvillea. The feeling here remains one of classic resort-style comfort, but the new sophisticated details bring it up-to-date with the most modern of resorts. The new decor features muted desert colors and luxury fabrics, with special extras such as flatscreen TVs with DVD/CD players and Bose surround-sound systems. Bathrooms feature inlaid-stone rain showers and sculpted tubs. Ample private balconies or terraces have extra-comfortable, overstuffed chairs, and each room also has a separate sitting area. Guests receive twice-daily maid service, a personal butler, and an aromatherapy menu—to ensure you leave completely relaxed and rejuvenated. *Carretera Transpeninsular Km 7.5, 23400 San José del Cabo, B.C.S. ☎ 800/637-2226 in the U.S. or 624/146-7000. www.oneandonlypalmilla.com. High season US$475 double, US$775–US$1,600 suites and villas; low season US$325 double, US$575–US$1,300 suites and villas. AE, MC, V. Amenities: 2 restaurants; terrace bar; pool bar; car rental; dry cleaning; championship Palmilla golf course; Internet; laundry; 24-hr. room service; shuttle services; deluxe European spa w/complete treatment and exercise facilities; sportfishing; tour services; watersports; yoga garden. In room: A/C, TV, hair dryer, iron, minibar, safe.*

Eating

Most of the restaurants in The Corridor between the two Cabos are attached to the hotels and so are expensive; look in the strip malls along the Carretera Transpeninsular for more reasonable eating choices.

MTV Best → **French Riviera** ★★★ FRENCH Along this stretch of beach by the Carretera Transpeninsula, there are any number of world-class places to spend your money. This is one of the best. Master French Chef Jacques Chrétien is the only Master Chef in all of Baja (and one of six in all of Mexico). He's worked at Tour d'Argent in Paris, Chez Bruneau in Brussels, and opened the five-star Maxim's de Paris in Mexico City. Then he came here and brought a new level of fine dining to Baja. You'd pay five times the amount for this quality food in New York or London. Everything is organic, freshly caught, and paired with wines if you desire. Consider the choices: roasted black angus filet mignon, roasted lobster on a bed of baby greens with a truffle vinaigrette, braised dorado with stuffed miniveggies, and ravioli with Nicoise olive "jus." It just goes on and on and on, each one better than the last—if that's possible.

This is food nobody deserves unless they've been very, very good (or are having their last meal). You could go crazy trying to make up your mind about what to choose from the menu so I suggest you go for the tasting menus (vegetarian, seasonal, or master chef). They're not cheap—the master chef's, with a wine pairing, is $1,900 per person—but as most reviews put it, the experience is "transcendental." There are 294 wines on the 14-page wine list, the biggest and best in all of Los Cabos outside of a hotel. The presentation is choreographed, with plates deposited simultaneously around the table, and the service, as you'd expect, is perfectly attentive without being obtrusive. Who's eaten here? Orlando Bloom, Jennifer Anniston, Bono, and Will Smith, to name a few. And you should too. Life is too short. *Carretera Transpeninsula Km 6.3, Cabo San Lucas. ☎ 624/104-3125. www.frenchrivieraloscabos.com. Main courses $395–$595. AE, MC, V. Bar service 10am–11pm; lunch noon–4pm; dinner 5:30–11pm.*

→ **Mama Mundos** ★★ HEALTH FOOD Finally! This cool little place nearby the Costa Azul Surf Shop meets a huge need for fresh organic health food. Make up for eating all those huevos rancheros with a shot of fresh wheat germ ground on the spot or spirulina energy balls. Or try the homemade granola, liquados with homemade almond milk, fruit, and wild local honey, or fresh-squeezed juice smoothies. They've also got reasonably priced veggie burgers and tacos, smoked tuna or tofu tostadas, and sandwiches on whole wheat bread and soy ginger or Thai peanut dressings, organic tofu, and heaps of veggies. If you've gotta have your breakfast egg fix, get 'em with vegetarian chorizo at least. *Carretera Transpeninsular Km 28, Costa Azul Plaza. ☎ 624/172-6171. caboamy@yahoo.com. Nothing over $60. No credit cards. Daily 8am–4pm.*

→ **Mi Ensalada** HEALTH FOOD Tucked as it is into a mini mall just off the highway on the ocean side between Los Cabos, this restaurant is a bit noisy. If you're craving something green, though, it's well worth the racket. All salads here are made with local organic greens; try the delicious strawberry and goat cheese salad or the house salad with avocado, corn, and veggies with chipotle dressing. Veggie, turkey, cheese burgers, pastas, and burritos are also on hand. It's even a good breakfast place—dishing up waffles, fruit, yogurt, and chilaquiles that are rich and savory, if somewhat heavy (topped with two fried eggs). No matter what you choose to eat, you'll get a nice breeze (under the ubiquitous palapa of course), with a bit of an ocean view through the Condos El Zalote. *Carretera Transpeninsualr Km 29.5, El Zalate Plaza. ☎ 624/119-8869 or 142-4956. Breakfast $40–$60, salads $70–$85. MC, V. Daily 7:30am–10pm.*

→ **The Restaurant at Las Ventanas al Paraíso** ★★★ NUEVO LATINO If you want to experience how the better half lives, a visit to Las Ventanas will do the trick. If you can't afford to eat here, at least come by for a cocktail in The Lounge, the casually elegant bar area overlooking the hotel's stunning pool. But if you actually do eat here, you'll get a sense of the Las Ventanas signature service—for example, napkins that match the color you're wearing. First courses may include steamed Ensenada mussels, served in coconut milk with a hint of chile árbol and a dash of tequila; or a stone crab salad with baby watercress, mango, phyllo, and sweet mustard sauce. The constantly changing menu of main courses generally includes an ample selection of seafood, including lobster, creatively presented, but their grilled rack of lamb with garlic potatoes is as good as you'll find anywhere. Especially recommended are the chef's gourmet variations on traditional Mexican cuisine—such as the suckling pig enchilada in chile ancho sauce, a grilled New York steak in a tequila-infused red wine sauce served with spicy nopal cactus paddle, or the chocolate tamale with guanábana sorbet. Note that reservations are required. *At Las Ventanas al Paraíso, Km 19.5 on Hwy. 1. ☎ 624/144-2800. www.lasventanas.com. Main courses $380–$600. AE, MC, V. Daily 5–11pm.*

→ **Zipper's** PUB GRUB Just east of Costa Azul, this casual hangout owned by American expats Mike Posey and Tony Magdaleno, is popular with gringos in search of American food. While sitting on a bluff above the surf break (see "Playing Outside," under Cabo San Lucas) of the same name, you can indulge your homesickness for burgers, spicy curly fries, steaks, beer-battered shrimp, deli sandwiches, and sports TV. *Playa Costa Azul, Transpeninsular Hwy., Km 28.5. No phone. Burgers and sandwiches $70–$100; main courses $70–$180. MC, V. Daily 11am–11pm.*

The Los Cabos Spa Experience

Golfers flock to Los Cabos because of the diversity of course options available, and spa enthusiasts are right behind them. Claiming the distinction of having the most world-class luxury spas in all of Mexico, Los Cabos resorts seem to be having an unstated competition to see who can create the most intriguing spa menu. While most spas offer traditional European therapies, the trend here is to emphasize an authentic Mexican experience through signature treatments that incorporate indigenous ingredients found on the Baja peninsula. These include aloe, clay, tropical fruits, and desert flowers and herbs like damiana, sage, and plumeria, used for their detoxifying and healing properties. Added to this is the mystical wisdom of ancient indigenous cultures, which incorporate elements such as quartz crystals and shamanic rituals into certain therapies.

One of the original Los Cabos resorts to offer spa services was **Casa del Mar** (p. 383), and it still offers impressive services in a bright, airy atmosphere. Its Sueños del Mar Spa offers guests a mix of salon services, massages, and wraps. Specialties include the Tropical Exfoliation, which uses a combination of fine-milled coffee beans and dried coconut to soften skin, and the Chocolate and Mint Escape, which literally massages the body in chocolate and mint. (Ground cacao beans were an Aztec currency, and the source of a highly prized beverage consumed by ancient nobility.)

Just the entry to the spa at **Esperanza** (p. 384) is an exercise in relaxation—you follow a garden path illuminated by candles to the natural stone reception area. Before your treatment, enjoy the Pasaje de Aqua (water passage), which includes a visit to a seaside grotto environment with a mineral-rich pool, steam caves, and a cool, cascading waterfall. Each of the seven private treatment rooms comes with a private garden and an outdoor shower and soaking pool. Signature treatments here include the Grated Coconut and Lime Body Exfoliation and the Hibiscus Antioxidant Flower Bath. The Couple's Clay Bake

Heading to the Beach

Because many of The Corridor area resorts have exclusive beach access, many of the swimming beaches have been effectively cut off. What's left open to public access are the beaches at **Chileno Bay** or **Bahia Santa María** (see "Beaches Outside the Center" under Cabo San Lucas; p. 405).

Playing Outside

Many of the resorts mentioned under "Sleeping" have first-class golf courses and boating options. If you're not staying at one, there are lots of surfing, fishing, and other outdoor options available to you throughout southern Baja. See "Playing Outside" under San José del Cabo and Cabo San Lucas for specific info.

Shopping

The **Costa Azul Surf Shop** (Carretera Transpeninsular, Km 28; ☎ **624/142-2771;** Suburcabo bus stop Costa Azul) sells and rents boogie boards, surf boards, skim boards, snorkel gear, rash guards, tees, board shorts (ones that actually fit!), sandals, and surf leashes. You can also get your board repaired here, rent boards, or take surf lessons.

starts with a Damiana liquor-based beverage, made with the damiana herb (which grows wild in Baja, and is considered an aphrodisiac). A warm bath and clay body mask are followed by a massage with desert sage oil. The most intriguing treatment, however, may be the Corona Beer Face-Lift—they claim this popular beverage tightens skin and refines the pores.

Las Ventanas al Paraíso (p. 384) raised the bar of the spa experience when it opened in 1997, but you won't find it resting on its laurels—a recent expansion doubled the spa's size. Private outdoor Jacuzzis, cold plunge pools, and relaxation areas prepare you for your treatment, which may be a Desert Healer Anti-Oxidant wrap, using sage, elephant tree bark, eucalyptus, and chaparral, or perhaps a Nopal Anti-Cellulite and Detox Wrap. This treatment uses locally grown *nopal* (cactus paddles) to help transfer fluids from the tissue to the bloodstream. A body scrub of grape seeds, papaya, and pineapple, followed by a body mask of green tea, ginger root, and seaweed, is also a favorite. The Spa also has several treatments that employ quartz crystals, minerals, and stones.

During its recent renovation, the **One&Only Palmilla** (p. 385) spared no expense in launching its new 2,044-sq.-m (22,000-sq.-ft.) Mandara Spa, which comprises 13 indoor and outdoor spa villas, some with rain showers, daybeds, and whirlpool baths. Indulgent treatments include the Aztec Aromatic Ritual, a body wrap that uses spices such as clove, cinnamon, and ginger, followed by a massage with rosemary and pine essential oils.

Impressive spa facilities can also be found at the **Marquis Los Cabos Beach** (☎ **624/144-2000;** www.marquisloscabos.com), the **Hilton Los Cabos Beach & Golf Resort** (☎ **624/145-6500;** www.hiltonloscabos.com), the **Sheraton Hacienda del Mar** (☎ **624/145-8000;** www.sheratonhaciendadelmar.com), the **Pueblo Bonito Rose Resort** (☎ **624/142-9898;** www.pueblobonito.com), and numerous other spots in the Los Cabos area.

Cabo San Lucas

"What you do in Cabo, stays in Cabo." Well, you can always hope.

Cabo San Lucas is Mexico's most elite resort destination. The hundreds of luxury hotel rooms here and along The Corridor have transformed the very essence of this old fishing outpost, once praised for its rustic nature in Steinbeck's *The Log from the Sea of Cortez.*

These days, Cabo is anything but rustic. Every couple of days, cruise ships magically appear overnight, towering minicities at anchor in the bay, discharging their passengers upon the streets in waves of tropical prints. Nobody seems to mind. Cabo is a town of transients, for transients, and created by transients. In that sense, the appropriation of the Las Vegas slogan "What happens in Cabo stays in Cabo" is apt. Like Vegas, Cabo is a place for letting your inhibitions out, for doing things you'd never dream of doing anywhere else. At Slim's Elbow Room, I'm assured that if I just take a sip of one of their 43 tequilas, within minutes I will be dancing on the bar topless. The barmaid tells me it does get crazy in the 6×3m (20×10-ft.) space. She just smiles and shrugs. What you do in Cabo . . .

Maybe that cavalier attitude is what draws the celebrities. This is the kind of place where nobody really cares if you're famous, only if you're interested in a time-share opportunity. Spielberg has a home here as do the Chili Peppers, John Travolta, and Tom Cruise. Gwyneth Paltrow can walk around the streets here and no one will bother her. Sammy Hagar is another matter. He's a huge force in the community, partially because of the success of his bar Cabo Wabo (p. 403).

The marina here is one of the five richest in the world, the $4-million marlin sportfishing prize the biggest in the world, and realtors say Cabo is the best investment destination in the world, higher per square foot than anywhere else in Mexico.

Not bad for a former fishing village. Once legendary for the big-game fish that lurk beneath the deep blue sea, Cabo San Lucas now draws more people for its nearby fairways and its raucous nightlife. Travelers here can not only enjoy a growing roster of adventure-oriented activities, they can also rest assured that playtime doesn't end when the sun goes down.

Getting There & Getting Around

GETTING INTO TOWN

BY PLANE The San José del Cabo airport (p. 362), approximately 32km (19 miles) away, serves the entire south Cape including Cabo San Lucas.

Aereo Calafia (☎ **624/143-4302,** see box on p. 366) lands at the airstrip in San Lucas (Colonia Lomas del Sol, 1.8km/1 mile from turnoff at Bordo) and services other cities within Mexico. **Alaska Airlines** (☎ **624/146-5100**); and **Mexicana** (☎ **624/143-5352**) also have offices in Cabo San Lucas.

At the San José airport, you can buy a ticket for a colectivo from the authorized transportation booth inside the building for about $130. Or up to four people can share a private taxi, which costs between $654 to $872 (you may be charged more for extra people); taxi and colectivo rides take about 45 minutes.

See p. 362 under San José "Getting into Town" for rental car info for the airport.

BY CAR From La Paz, the best driving route is Highway 1 south past the village of San Pedro, then Highway 19 south through Todos Santos to Cabo San Lucas, a 2- to 3-hour drive. From San José, it's about 30 to 45 minutes on the four-lane highway, about an hour from the airport north of San José by toll road, and a bit longer on the free road which passes through the outskirts of town.

BY BUS The **Bus Terminal** (☎ **624/143-5020**) is on Héroes at Morelos; it is open daily from 6am to 10pm. Buses leave for La Paz every 2 hours starting at 7:15am, with the last departure at 9:15pm, and leave for San José every hour daily between 6:30am and 8:30pm

If you're traveling to and from San José, take the more convenient and economical **Suburcabos** public bus service. See p. 392 under San José for more info. **Interbaja** (green buses) also shuttles between the towns and as far north as the town of Santa Anita, north of the airport, for just $25.

GETTING AROUND

BY FOOT The center of town, where most of the hotels and restaurants listed here are located, is very walkable. Especially during high season when the whole center is completely clogged with traffic, you really don't need to rent a car unless you are staying in The Corridor.

BY BUS The short white and green buses in town are colectivos (also called *peseras*). They are marked with their destination on

Cabo San Lucas

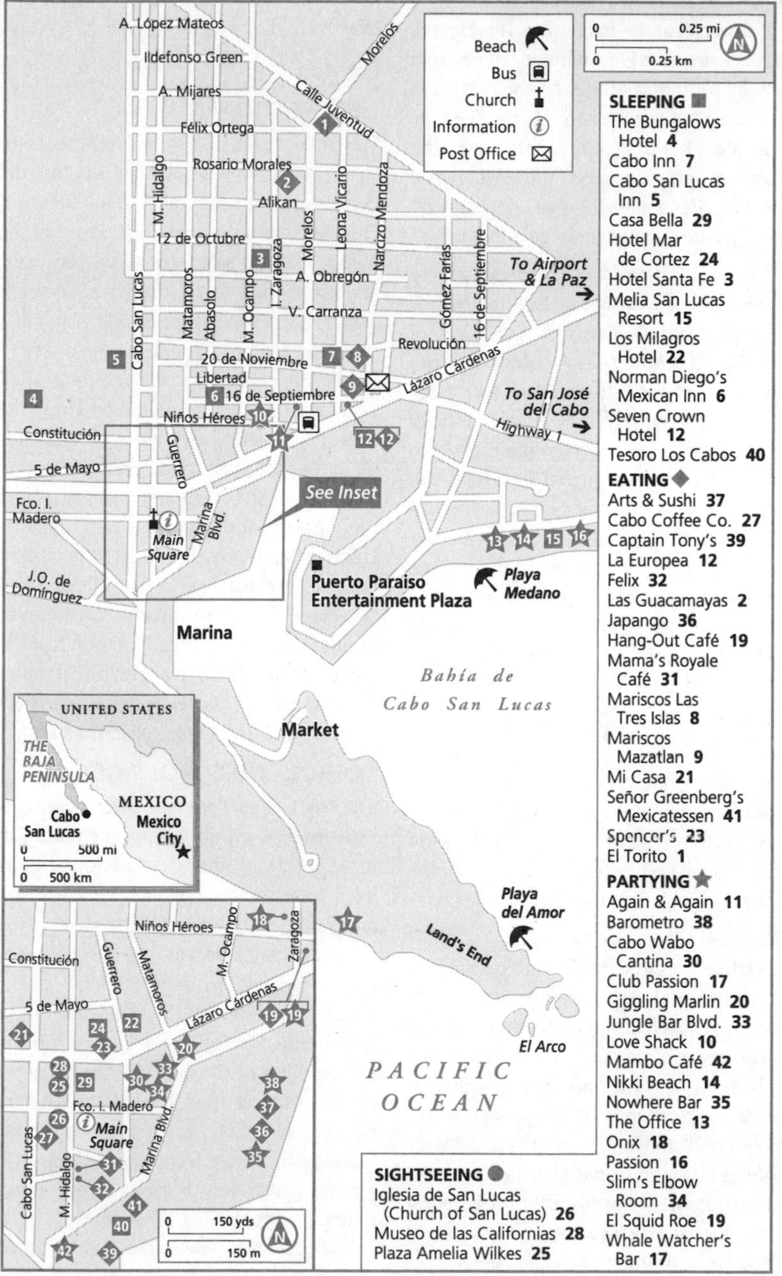

the front, are easy to catch at most street corners in the centro, and are cheap.

Suburcabos or **Interbaja Buses** (see earlier) run every 20 minutes daily from 6:30am to 11pm, and are the cheapest way to shuttle between towns. There are stops near most beach access points along The Corridor (let your driver know when you get on). Have pesos (small change) on hand, as they don't take large bills.

BY BOAT There are water taxis from the Marina to Medano Beach (see below) for $40 each way; they leave from the far end of the Marina (**Cabo Zaida's Glass Bottom Boat,** Plaza Las Glorias dock; ☎ **624/143-1306** or 147-7657; cabozaidas_connie@hotmail.com) every hour on the hour from 9am to 5pm. You can travel for free if you have a wristband from certain hotels like the Tesoro. You can also catch a glass-bottom water taxi to go out to see the Arch or Playa Amor, for example, for about $100 per person to take you there, drop you off, and pick you up later. You can negotiate snorkeling stops in between.

BY TAXI Taxis are easy to find in town but are expensive, costing at the minimum $50 in town; hotels often post a list of how much you should expect to pay. Taxis running between the two capes can run $500 to $600; a taxi between Cabo and The Corridor hotels usually costs $150 to $250.

BY CAR There are **car-rental** specials advertised around town, but be sure to check the total price carefully after insurance and taxes are added. Rates can run between $500 and $750 per day plus tax, plus extra for insurance. One good local rental car company that will pick you up at the airport and deliver your car to your hotel (saving you time and hassle at the airport) is **All Over Baja** (Plaza Catedral Local 10; ☎ **624/146-9154;** www.alloverbaja.com). Another reliable agency is **Advantage Rent-A-Car** (☎ **624/143-0909;** ☎/fax 624/143-0466), on Lázaro Cárdenas between Leona Vicario and Morelos.

Basics

ORIENTATION

This small town (183km/113 miles south of La Paz; 33km/20 miles west of San José del Cabo; 1,792km/1,111 miles southeast of Tijuana) spreads out north and west of the harbor of **Cabo San Lucas Bay.** Because it faces south and east to the Sea of Cortez, it can be somewhat disorienting. You can't really see the sun set unless you go over to the Pacific side. The town also feels small because the center is clustered along the waterfront marina, even though it spreads up to the mountains and desert.

The main street leading into town from the airport and San José del Cabo is **Lázaro Cárdenas.** As it nears the harbor, **Bulevar Marina** branches off from it and becomes the main artery that curves around the waterfront. Much of town is centered along this main strip. The tip at the end of the curve of the bay, visible from around town, is called **Land's End.**

TOURIST INFO & OFFICES

The **Los Cabos Tourism Office** (☎ **624/146-9628**) is in San José, in the Plaza San José, Locales 3 and 4, and is open daily from 8am to 3pm. The tourist kiosks on many corners of town in Cabo are actually timeshare sales booths, but the salespeople can help you with simple questions.

The **Secretaria de Turismo Baja California Sur** office in Cabo is on the second floor of the Cabo Maritime Center on the Marina (just behind Las Glorias water taxi) and is supposedly open Monday to Friday from 9am to 6pm—on several trips that I took during those hours, no one was in the office.

The English-language ***Los Cabos Guide, Los Cabos News, Cabo Life,*** and

Baja Sun, as well as the ***Gringo Gazette*** are distributed free at most hotels and shops, and have up-to-date information on new restaurants and clubs.

Recommended Websites

- **www.MexPacific.com**: This site was given the "Lenta de Plata Award" for the best travel website by the Mexican Secretariat of Tourism (SECTUR). It has informative travel articles as well as an eco-adventure guide to Los Cabos. They also publish an informative English guide quarterly focusing on nature as well as tourism.
- **www.allaboutcabo.com**: It's pretty much what it says—all about Cabo.
- **www.visitloscabos.org**: Visit Los Cabos is a comprehensive site with good descriptions and basic guidance about the most worthwhile places in town.

Cabo San Lucas Nuts & Bolts

Banks There are several banks around the intersection of Lázaro Cárdenas and Zaragoza, including **Serfin** (Super Plaza Aramburo s/n; ☎ **624/143-0991**), which is open Monday to Friday from 9am to 4pm, Saturday 10am to 2pm, and offers money changing services and an ATM.

Embassies Consul Mike Houstan can be reached at ☎ **624/123-3566.** The consulate office is located in the Plaza Nautical, Suite C-1, Bulevar Marina, Cabo San Lucas.

Emergencies The police department can be reached at ☎ **624/143-3977,** the fire department at ☎ **624/143-3577,** and the Red Cross at ☎ **624/143-3300.**

Hospitals **Baja Médico** (Camino de la Plaza s/n, corner Pedegral; ☎ **624/143-0127** or -7777) has a 24-hour walk-in clinic, and provides air ambulance services. **Amerimed** (☎ **624/143-9671**) is a 24-hour, American-standardized clinic with bilingual physicians, and accepts major credit cards. Most of the larger hotels in town have a doctor on call.

Internet/Wireless Hot Spots Rates for Internet access here are outrageous, but the farther you walk from the center, the cheaper the rates get. **Cabo Mail** (Super Plaza Arambura, Local 1; ☎ **624/143-7798;** www.cabomail.com) charges $10 for 10 minutes, $20 for 10 minute calls to the U.S., and you can sit in cute blue and yellow leather booths and use their webcam for free. It's open daily 9am to 7pm. **Onda net Café & Bar,** Lázaro Cárdenas 7, Edificio Posada, across from the Pemex gas station (☎ **624/143-5390**), charges $50 for 15 minutes, $70 for 30 minutes, or $85 for an hour. It's open Monday through Saturday from 8am to 11pm.

Laundry There are laundries all over town; one to try is **Lavanderia San Lucas** (Leona Vicario at the corner of 20 Noviembre; ☎ **624/143-11356**) which charges $50 a load (about 15 lb.) and also has a dry-cleaning service.

Pharmacies A drugstore with a wide selection of toiletries as well as medicine is **Farmacia Aramburo** (Super Plaza Aramburo, on Lázaro Cárdenas at Zaragoza; ☎ **624/143-1489**). It's open Monday through Friday from 7am to 11pm, and accepts MasterCard and Visa. As with Internet cafes, drugstores get cheaper the farther you venture from the water. **Farma Express** is one such cheaper alternative (Leona Vicario just above 20 de Noviembre, Local 1; ☎ **624/143-9333** or -6182). Plus, it has a delivery service, is open 24 hours, 7 days a week, and the owner speaks English.

Post Offices The *correo* is at Lázaro Cárdenas between Medano and Gomez Farías (☎ **624/143-0048**), on the highway to San José del Cabo, east of the bar El Squid Roe. It's open Monday through Friday from 9am to 5pm, Saturday from 9am to 3pm.

Safety Cabo is generally safe, but that doesn't mean you can act badly. Behave yourself and follow basic rules of safety and you'll have a blast. See "Playing Outside," p. 407, for info on beach safety.

Telephone Tips The telephone area code here is **624.**

Sleeping

Cabo San Lucas has a dearth of cheap hotel rooms. If you're a backpacker, there are a couple of reasonable alternatives, but for hostel rates, there's not much besides surf camps (see info on Pescadero, p. 433) out of town. The number of small inns and B&Bs is growing, but they're still an anomaly in this spring break, timeshare package-oriented resort town. Your cheapest, most comfortable option might be to stay at one of San José's budget hotels. Most of the larger hotels in Cabo are well maintained and offer packages through travel agents, though, so ask around.

CHEAP

→ **Cabo Inn** ★★ This bright and cute budget hotel on a semi-quiet street has three stories with wide walkways centered around a patio and garden area. It's really pretty at night, when the lights strung between trees in the garden light up, and by day it's clean and comfortable if somewhat spartan. The small rooms have tiled floors, fans, rustic furniture, and are made to seem more spacious by placing tables and chairs on the *"balconcitos"* outside. There are two "penthouse suites," which are completely open air (under a palapa) with mosquito netted beds, stick-walled showers, and private terraces with tables and chairs. The larger more expensive "suite" also has a Jacuzzi. A lively restaurant next door will deliver pitchers of margaritas and dinner to your room. *20 de Noviembre and Leona Vicario. ☎/fax 624/ 143-0819 or 619/819-2727 in U.S. www.caboinn hotel.com. $220 single, $500–$650 double, $790 triple, $800–$1,350 rooftop suites. MC, V. Amenities: Kitchen; small rooftop pool and sunning area; communal TV and barbecue; Wi-Fi. In room: A/C, fridge, Internet, safe in office.*

MTV Best → **Hotel Mar de Cortez** ★★ Kitty-corner to Cabo Wabo (p. 394), this sometimes fisherman's hotel packs in rock 'n' rollers when Sammy's in town. Reminiscent of the old Tropicana Motel in West Hollywood during its punk heyday, the colonial-style block hotel forms a U around a '50s-style pool bordered with a smattering of banana trees and birds of paradise. Each room has two full-size beds, tiled floors, clean (if thin and coarse) sheets, and overall, the rooms are in good condition considering how much partying gets done here. It's such a good value, you even get a desk and chair in the room and tables and plastic chairs on the little balconcies leading to the rooms. Bonus: In the lobby area, you'll find **Spencer's** restaurant (see "Eating," p. 397), which has good cheap breakfasts, and lets you bring in whatever fish you catch to be cooked.

Lázaro Cárdenas at Guerrero. ☎ 624/143-0232, -0034. www.mardecortez.com. $650 double. MC, V. Amenities: Restaurant; bar; fax; travel desk. In room: A/C, fans, fridge (for rent), safe in office.

→ **Norman Diego's Mexican Inn** ★ Three blocks up from the marina, Norman's is somewhat difficult to find but worth the time. For your efforts, you'll get to stay in a really cute, if a bit overpriced, spot that caters to North American and European travelers of all ages. Its nine colorfully painted, clean, and sweetly decorated rooms are arranged around a central patio and outside dining area. Although continental breakfast is included, for $50 you can get a full breakfast cooked and served under their palapa. *Septiembre 16th s/n, between Matamoros and Abasolo (Note: Abasolo isn't a through street). ☎ 624/143-4987. www.themexicaninn.com. $650 double for 1 bed, $750 for 2 beds. Includes continental breakfast. AE, DISC, MC, V. Amenities: Breakfast room; laundry; lock-box; travel desk; wheelchair friendly. In room: A/C, TV, DVD.*

DOABLE

→ **The Bungalows Hotel** ★★ You'll feel like you're crashing at your neighbor's pad when you stay in this two-story unit or in one of the several cottages clustered around a blue mosaic-tiled saltwater pool. It's that comfy. The entire unit is a veritable oasis, with lush gardens and banana trees scattered throughout, even though it's just 5 blocks from downtown Cabo. The affable manager Junior will do everything he can to make sure you're comfortable. If you're lucky, this may include a home-cooked dinner. (His cooking is good, so be nice to him.) There's an extensive VCR collection and microwave popcorn you can make in your room. Breakfast (which changes daily and can include eggs, waffles, and smoothies) is served outside around a fountain adjacent to the pool. The bungalows themselves have nice small kitchenettes with shutters that open out to palapa-roofed terraces. All beds are comfy with good linen and mosquito nets, and rooms are nicely decorated and furnished. Some have extra rooms with fold-out beds. *Miguel Av. Herrera s/n, in front of Lienzo Charro. ☎/fax 624/143-5035 or -0585. www.cabobungalows.com. $1,050 double, $1,650 suite, $200 extra person. Rates include full breakfast. MC, V. Amenities: Breakfast room; Internet; massages (upon request); outdoor pool; tour desk; Wi-Fi. In room: A/C, TV/VCR, coffeemaker, fridge, kitchenette, kitchens (in some rooms).*

MTV Best → **Los Milagros Hotel** ★★ You can't beat staying in the middle of downtown Cabo San Lucas, sitting on a banquette under an umbrella on the upstairs terrace abutting a rock garden (part of a neighboring park), watching hummingbirds and butterflies in the bougainvillea, and wallowing in the quiet. And that's what I got here, mainly—I also heard what sounded like a sheet rock drum followed by whooping-inebriated-joy from God-knows-which club at 3am, but that's a small price to pay for being so close to the party. This lovely small hotel, run by co-owners Sandra Scandiber and Ricardo Rode, is the perfect convenient retreat in downtown Cabo, just 1½ blocks from Squid Roe, the Giggling Marlin, Cabo Wabo, and the marina. It's simply furnished, with bold Mexican touches added in the tile work and dashes of color from the plants on the patio and terrace. Delightful touches include boveda ceilings in some rooms, quality linen, wrought iron headboards, Saltillo tiled floors, and handmade Guadalajaran furniture. *Matamoros 116. ☎/fax 624/143-4566 and 718/928-6647 in U.S. www.losmilagros.com.mx. $800 double, $900 kitchenettes, $1,150 master suite on the 3rd floor. No credit cards, but they take Pay Pal or personal checks. Amenities: Small outdoor pool; Wi-Fi on patios. In room:*

A/C, cable TV, kitchenettes (in some rooms), telephone.

SPLURGE

The big splurges in this area are the US$1,000 rooms in resorts along The Corridor (p. 383); those listed below are somewhat more "doable" splurges.

→ **Cabo San Lucas Inn** It won't be long before this place gets snapped up for a future reality TV show. The amazing views of the city and ocean and plush digs simply scream made-for-TV. Not to be confused with the Cabo Inn, this B&B built on two stories on the hill above the old part of town has Mexican designed rooms with wrought iron headboards, "comfort bedding," good quality linens, Saltillo tiled floors, and private terraces or balconies. Two rooms have palapas roofs. There's also a shared outdoor heated pool, Jacuzzi, barbecue and kitchen area, shaded area for hanging hammocks, a small library, and a giant communal TV. Ask about discounts and, if you're with five of your closest friends, know that some rooms can fit that many comfortably. *Cabo San Lucas Bulevar, between Revolución and Liberdad (just up the dirt road).* ☎ *624/143-5200 or in the U.S. 541/306-6570. www.thecabosanlucasinn.com. US$300 double. Shuttle service to/from airport for US$15 per person. AE, DISC, MC, V. Amenities: Breakfast area; laundry service; communal TV; wheelchair friendly. In room: A/C, fans, hair dryer, Wi-Fi.*

→ **Melia San Lucas Resort** This is one of the most sophisticated places in town, but that doesn't mean it's stuffy—it's also one of Cabos' biggest party hotels. It's somewhat more removed from the main action but that's actually a good thing—it's on Medano Beach, where you can safely swim. Their club **Passion** (see "Partying," p. 401) swings at night, and *the* place to be seen here during the day is at the **Nikki Beach** beach club (see "Partying," p. 401). It's a beautiful, hip, and sexy setting where you can toss back a few (if you can afford beer at $55 a pop), while ogling bathing beauties swimming up to the poolside bar. The hotel itself boasts a hugely high-ceilinged lobby that promises so much; the rooms themselves don't really deliver, instead falling into the nicely comfortable generic hotel style that's so popular in town. *Medano Beach.* ☎ *877/694-4134. www.meliacabosanlucas.com. US$270–US$1,145 double and up. MC, V. Amenities: 2 restaurants; 2 bars; pool bar; car rental; minimarket; spa; tobacco shop; Wi-Fi. In room: A/C, TV, hair dryer, iron, Jacuzzi (in some), safe.*

→ **Tesoro Los Cabos** ★ Looking to partee? Come here. If you want a good night's sleep, look elsewhere. During the day, reggae and rock serenades the sunbathers and frat boys out playing loud games of volleyball; when evening comes, guests at this all-inclusive hotel screech "I Love Rock and Roll" karaoke at the top of their lungs into the small hours. A fun if not exactly luxurious hotel, the spot boasts New Mexico–style rooms that are clean and serviceable, though the beds could be softer. If you want something slightly less frenetic, ask for one of the bigger rooms with a marina view—they're farther from the rowdy pool area. The hotel boasts a great central location, but also offers free water taxis to Medano Beach. The all-inclusive plan isn't necessarily the best if you want to try the food around town; it's typical hotel buffet style here, with a 24-hour snack bar where you can load up for free. ***Tip:*** Get the short order cook to make you something fresh on the grill rather than getting food that's been sitting out all day. *Marina Bulevar, Lots 9, 10.* ☎ *624/143-1220 or -9300. www.tesororesorts.com. $1,800 all-inclusive double; can upgrade for $50 more per day. Check for packages. MC, V. Amenities: 2 restaurants; 24-hr. snack bar; 3 bars and lounges; Internet kiosk; Jacuzzi; minimart;*

pool; spa and fitness center. In room: A/C, TV, fans, minibar, safe.

Eating

Wonderful high-end restaurants, especially at the marina, the Plaza Bonita, or along The Corridor, abound here. Unlike other parts of Mexico, though, it's difficult to eat well on a budget. Yes, there are several excellent cheap taco places and the farther you get from the marina and Lázaro Cárdenas, the more affordable become the restaurants. But in between you can expect to pay $110 to $170 at the majority of mid-range places for breakfast, $130 to $220 for lunch, and $160 to $430 for dinner.

Hidalgo, running up from the marina, has become a kind of restaurant row; so you'll want to head there to check out some restaurants. Stroll around the main plaza, and you'll find more options.

CHEAP

→ **Las Guacamayas** ★★ MEXICAN One of the best late-night taco joints in the city, period. This is a new "branch" (the sister store is in San José, see "Eating" under San José, p. 372), but with the same menu as the original. While tucked away on the second floor under a palapa and grapefruit trees, you can eat like a king (or queen) for under $50. Thick corn tortillas are grilled almost to a crisp and wrapped around glorious fillings of exotic huitlacoche, nopales, or *rajas* quesadillas. They also include more typical menu items like al pastor, carne asada, and so on, and serve charro style beans, and *papas rellenas.* Grilled jalapeños, onions, and a variety of salsas and fresh peeled cucumbers come with every meal. *Morelos at corner of Alikan. ☎ 044/624-109-5473. Main courses $20. No credit cards. Daily 6pm–2am.*

MTV Best → **Mariscos Las Tres Islas** ★★ MEXICAN Las Guacamayas does most tacos right, but when it comes to fish tacos, nothing beats the ones here. They're simply the best and most reasonably priced ones in town. But come see for yourself: On the dirt end of Revolución, half under a tarp and half under a palapa, you can sit at plastic tables set on a con-

To Market

For everthing you need to picnic at the beach (or for timeshare kitchen supplies), head to **La Europea** for ham and cheese baguettes ($55–$85), pastrami, and squid and green salads. The chain has a huge store inside Plaza Puerto Paraiso Local 3913 (☎ **624/105-1818**). They also stock booze, including an extensive supply of wine from North Baja, Napa, and Chile, and a large variety of the harder stuff such as boutique tequilas. Or try **Señor Greenberg's Mexicatessen** (Plaza Nautica, Bulevar Marina; ☎ **624/143-7808**), which has pastrami, bagels, cheesecake, and other picnic-fixings. Both markets are generally open daily 10am to 8pm.

Although it's been accused of having a stranglehold on local politics, the **Supermercado Aramburo** (Super Plaza Aramburo, on Lázaro Cárdenas at Zaragoza; ☎ **624/143-1489;** open daily 6am–midnight), has a decent if expensive selection of food. And the coffee bar in front rocks. For just $40 you can get a giant cup of gut-wrenching coffee; stop by to fill up your thermos on the way out of town (they close at 11pm). Other new box stores in town include **Costco** (Carretera 1, Km 4), **C.C.C.,** and **Soriana** (next to each other on Hwy. 19 just past El Bordo),and **CeCeCe** (the cheapest) on the way out of town toward Todos Santos.

crete floor surrounded by gravel, or better yet at the "counter" in front of the coolers where the fish is prepared. Then take a seat and chow down with the mostly Mexican young men and couples who come here—you can thank me later.

If you're crazy enough to try something other than the fish tacos, know that anything involving seafood will be delicious, from the shrimp ceviche that sits on a bed of fresh (peeled) cucumbers and is covered in a variety of sauces (the *aguachile* is dynamite) to seasonal fish ceviche tostados or *sierra* (shredded carrots with fish) style tostadas for $20. The yummy shrimp ceviche plate for $60 will completely fill you up. The most expensive thing on the menu, *camarones imperial* (a brochette of fish wrapped in bacon), with rice and salad, is just $130. *Revolución at Narcisco Mendoz. ☎ 624/143-3247. Main courses under $75. No credit cards. Daily 10am–7:30pm.*

→ **Spencer's** ★ DINER Lunch and dinner here are nothing special, but this restaurant inside the Hotel Mar de Cortez (see above) has, hands down, the cheapest, best breakfast in town. You'll get two eggs, roasted potatoes, fruit, and toast for just $25. Other cheap hangover grub includes vegetarian specials, French toast stuffed with cream cheese and covered in a flambéed peach sauce, omelets, and smoothies. The decor was probably modern in the '70s but it's worn at the edges now—though in a comfortable only-in-Baja sort of way. With posters of Los Tigres del Norte on the walls, Mexican talk radio blasting, fishermen talking fish and surfers talking waves, this is the real deal. You can sit inside on brightly painted (if slightly uncomfortable) Michoacan chairs, or outside adjacent to the hotel's bar. *Calle Lázaro Cárdenas between Matamoros and Guerrero, inside the Hotel Mar de Cortez. ☎ 624/143-5410. Breakfast $25–$100, lunch/dinner $100–$150. MC, V. Daily 7am–10pm; closes Tues at 2:30pm.*

DOABLE

→ **Captain Tony's** CONTINENTAL More authentic than many places in town, this pleasant marina palapa-covered restaurant only fills up with tourists when the cruise boats dock. Otherwise, it works double shifts: Fishermen come for breakfast early in the morning, while non-working locals swing by later on to sample their decent thin-crust pizza and calzones baked in a wood-fired oven. If neither of those appeal to you, they also serve typical Mexican snack food, jumbo shrimp tacos, egg wraps, and a good Greek salad served with hot focaccia bread. Drinks are good, too; the Cadillac margarita (made with Diamana liquor) is a killer. *Plaza Las Glorias Dock, Marina (kitty-corner to Tesoro Hotel). ☎ 624/143-6797. Main courses $85–$300. MC, V. Daily 4am–6pm.*

→ **El Torito** ★★ SEAFOOD This Mazatlán-style seafood joint is a bit hard to find but well worth the search. Because of its remoteness, you'll never see a timesharer or cruise-shipper here but rather locals, surfers, and others in-the-know. The food's also good—it's slightly cheaper and tastier than the also recommended Mariscos Mazatlán (see below). The waiters are fast to the point of being brusque, but you'll appreciate getting menu items like fresh ceviche tostadas and various styles of grilled fish filets quickly. The barnlike decor suits the service: Chairs are set up under a tin pan roof with wood tables on a concrete floor, and a crew of Mazatlán musicians dressed in red polka-dot shirts work the room, hauling their tambora drum, accordion, sax, and bass and every so often going at it, full tilt. Oh yeah, man! They may close a bit early, so don't be late. *Narcisco Mendoza s/n, between I. Green and Felix Ortega. ☎ 624/125-0435 or 144-4682. Main courses $100–$130. No credit cards. Daily 10am–7pm.*

→ **Hang-Out Café** CAFE Walk through the Onix (see "Partying," p. 401) or follow the lit candles up from Ninoes Héroes to find this small cafe. The multiple connecting rooms function to help people move around without ever feeling the need to split. (There's even a promise of a swingers' club upstairs, for the truly mobile.) The cool hostesses will help you get grounded by helping you choose between diverse menu items like burgers made from real Angus beef, feta and pine nut salad, portobello pasta, or an individual pizza. A martini menu includes exotic flavors like chocolate. *Ninoes Héroes s/n, at Zaragoza. ☎ 624/172-0308. www.cabohangout.com. Main courses $100–$150. MC, V. Daily 5pm–late.*

→ **Japango** JAPANESE Run by a chef trained at the local award-winning Nick San restaurant, Japango dishes up great quality sushi and sashimi in a lively locale, right on the marina and next to Nowhere Bar (they are all hooked together). Though it's a bit pricey (individual sushi is $40 for two pieces; a sashimi plate is $240; tempura is $200), it's still cheaper than Nick San and much more fun. Grab a seat at the bar, and you can see the catch of the day up close and personal. There's a $36 all-you-can-eat special from 5 to 8pm. *Plaza Bonita, Bulevar Marina 19. ☎ 624/143-4493 or -4419. Main courses about $700. No credit cards. Daily noon–2am.*

→ **Mama's Royale Café** MEXICAN This restaurant space is home to Felix (p. 400) restaurant during dinner, but chef Spencer Moore from San Francisco opened it under a different name during breakfast hours to distinguish between the divergent menus. The extensive menu includes French toast as well as a million kinds of typical and not-so-typical Mexican egg dishes. Try their excellent eggs scrambled with nopales, Mexican-style omelets (frittatas), *huevos charros*, or chilaquiles. All of the main plates are huge, but if you're *really* hungry, you'll be most sated by the eggs Benedict on crab cakes, hollandaise crepes, or chicken enchiladas topped with two fried eggs. The service is great, and the dining room is large, colorfully decorated, with generous windows opening to the street and patio. *Hidalgo s/n, between Zapata and Madero. ☎ 624/143-4290. Main courses $100–$150. MC, V. Daily 7:30am–2pm.*

→ **Mariscos Mazatlán** ★ SEAFOOD Every local in town tells me that this is *the* place to go for seafood. The grilled fish filets and Mojo de Ajo are good if somewhat greasy; huge shrimp cocktails, giant molcajetes full of deep batter-fried shrimp or seafood, and breaded fried fish are more solid standouts. Housed as it is in a warehouse-themed building, the restaurant is large and boisterous, with a tin roof and giant adverts painted above the food counters. Large parties of friends and couples alike come here not only to eat, but to sing at top volume along with the strolling Musicos. It's a fun and lively experience and not a bad value, considering the huge portions—two can easily share the giant *molcajete* that is jam-packed with seafood. *Narcisco Mendoza, corner 16 de Septiembre. ☎ 624/143-8565. Main courses $75–$138. AE, MC, V. Daily 11am–10pm.*

SPLURGE

→ **Arts & Sushi** JAPANESE More than once while in town I heard the joke "You know what we call sushi in Baja? Bait." Well, that's not the case at this restaurant, where the prices aren't so funny but the presentation and selection is almost worth the money. Chef Jacques Chrétien from the French Riviera (p. 386) loves this place, which is recommendation enough for me. It's set inside an art gallery, but if you find that sitting inside an art gallery eating food that *looks* like art can be somewhat surreal, just run with it. A mixed plate of sushi is $160; sushi at the bar cost $45 to $60 per pair; there's also lobster *teppanyaki* for $320. You can request a "tasting" of the best of the day, but be prepared to pay for it. Dessert is just as decadent—their huge chocolate cake functions just as well as an installation piece as food. In case you're looking to buy vs. eat the art, just ask for the seller Luis Rionda. *Plaza Bonita, Bulevar Marina next to the boat ramp. ☎ 624/144-4554. Main courses $180–$320. AE, MC, V. Daily 11am–10pm.*

➔ **Felix** MEXICAN FUSION On restaurant row in the same location as Mama's Royale Café (see earlier in this section), this place completely changes its name and menu for dinner. The outdoor patio with walls made from the plant arco de palo is colorful and romantically lit at night; the main room looks out through bougainvillea to passersby. They serve 30 salsas; try them with *mancha manteles* (a sauce of herbs, spices, fruit, and nuts that goes well with anything from chicken to iguana), fajitas, mole, pollo en *pipian* (pumpkin sauce), *barbacoa de Borrego* (barbecued lamb), chipotle shrimp—all part of what they call "Mexican fusion and seafood." *Hidalgo s/n, between Zapata and Madero. ☎ 624/143-4290. www.felixcabosanlucas.com. Main courses up to $195. MC, V. Mon–Sat 5–10pm.*

➔ **Mi Casa** MEXICAN This lively and popular restaurant off the main square has traditional Mexican food that feels more like something you'd get in Southern California than Mexico. Ditto the decor—diners sit fronting a patio on tiers rising up under a palapa to a second upscale-quaint patio. Mexican murals painted of "old school" Mexico on the walls, and crosses and retablos in the bar areas attempt to create a "mi casa" feel. Unfortunately, the food is overpriced and only a bit better than mediocre. Chipotle beef or typical seafood is $200, with a seafood platter for two at $440. It's done up quite romantically at night, so down enough margaritas—the two bars serve *giant* ones—and you'll likely forget about the food. *Calle Cabo San Lucas, at Madero. ☎ 624/143-1933. www.micasa.name. Main courses $180–$250. MC. Daily 5:30–10:30pm.*

Mens' Clubs

There's a changing selection of strip clubs to choose from in Cabo, but the mainstays include **Mermaid's,** corner of Lázaro Cárdenas and Vicente Guerrero (☎ **624/143-5370;** www.loscabosnights.com/mermaids.htm), which offers its patrons their choice of topless stage shows or private dances. Admission is $50 for the general show or $200 for the private dances. It's open nightly from 7pm to 3am. Another popular option is **Twenty/20 Showgirls,** Lázaro Cárdenas at Francisco Villa (☎ **624/143-5380**), also with a bevy of beauties to entertain you with their dancing skills on any one of the numerous stages. It's the largest of these clubs in Cabo. In addition to a topless cabaret show, it offers topless lap dances as well as televised sports, pool tables, and food service. It's open from 8:30pm to 3am, closed Tuesdays.

CAFES

➔ **Cabo Coffee Co.** ★★ CAFE Word is out that Cabo Coffee sells some of the best coffee in town—a line forms out the door every morning. Maybe the popularity is owed to the fact that you can get "real" (as in ground) decaf here. They also make milk shakes with real ice cream, not cornstarch, Ghirardelli frappe, and other cold coffee drinks. And the caffeinated fresh roasted coffee and espresso drinks are simply damn good. Internet access is even available for $25 per half-hour. *Hidalgo s/n, at Madero (on the main square).* ☎ *624/105-1130. www.cabocoffee.com. Snacks and beverages $20. No credit cards. Daily 6am–10pm. Also on Marina Bulevar by the Giggling Marlin.* ☎ *624/143-0954.*

Partying

Partying is what Cabo is all about. Wander down Bulevar Marina or Cárdenas where many of the main bars and clubs are located and you'll encounter wall-to-wall tourists sitting at tables staring blankly ahead, glassy-eyed and wasted. And that's only at 10am. The per capita of bars per square block is . . . well, a lot. You can even walk down the street with a beer in one hand (although this is technically not legal throughout the country, laws are a bit more lax here). Speaking of not legal: Wander the beach or Marina and you're bound to be offered pot, 'shrooms, whatever you want. Abide by the laws (see "Basics," p. 43) and you'll be okay.

Since Cabo excels at getting people loaded, those who are rationing their brain cells know there's an art to achieving the perfect Cabo Wobble—knowing which places to go to hang out *before* you get too drunk, and those to gravitate to when you're ready for a massive public humiliation. **El Squid Roe** and the **Giggling Marlin** would definitely fit in the latter category—they're places where you can: 1) String up your mate by their ankles and pour tequila down their gullet, 2) Flash your breasts or butt, and 3) Lick Jello off a stranger's sweaty stomach. Or all three. The **Onix** is a good place to start—and end—your evening when you want to settle it all down with some house music in a loungey atmosphere.

Locals say to shop around and find which bar or club features ladies' night because where the girls are, the boys follow—such places are usually packed with owners of both chromosomes. **Love Shack** on Wednesday nights, for example, is the most happening place in town. You can also find an *hora alegre* (happy hour) somewhere in town between noon and 7pm.

Since Cabo actually faces south, for prime **sunset viewing,** head over to Land's End, where the two seas meet. At **Whale Watcher's Bar,** in the Hotel Finisterra (☎ **624/143-3333;** daily from 10am–11pm), there's a fabulous view of the sunset. The high terrace offers vistas of the beach, as well as glimpses of whales from January to March. Mariachi bands play on Friday from 6:30 to 9pm.

Note that some larger hotels here have weekly Fiesta Nights, Italian Nights, and other buffet-plus-entertainment theme nights that can be fun as well as a good buy. Check travel agencies and the following hotels: the **Solmar Suites** (☎ **624/143-3535**), the **Finisterra** (☎ **624/143-3333**), and the **Hotel Meliá Cabo San Lucas** (☎ **624/143-4444**). Prices range from $220 (not including drinks, tax, and tips) to $350 (which covers everything, including an open bar with national drinks).

There's a **limousine service** (☎ **044/624-155-3103;** www.CaboLimoCompany.com) that will take you from your hotel around to the bars in town so that you can drink and not worry about where you are. Even if you're not drinking, it gets so crowded in town during high season that you're better off walking or taking a cab or water taxi instead of driving.

BARS

➔ **Barometro** ★★ This extremely cool space on the marina marks the boundary between the town's two malls—cross the boat ramp dividing them and suddenly the pavement changes to polished red concrete and the vendors disappear along with the timeshare salesmen. The bar screens trippy nature films (among other trippy films) on a 7.5m (25-ft.) expanse of wall outside. White leather sofa-stools and low tables line either side of the malecón, warmed by outdoor heaters. It's lovely to sit here sipping some (over-priced) wine with the electronica/alt-rock soundtrack playing unobtrusively in the background. There's no happy hour but I recommend splurging and stopping for at least one drink. *Plaza Bonita, on the Marina.* ☎ *624/143-1466.*

→ **Jungle Bar** The driving rock bass line of music blaring out of this locals' bar set inside the Plaza Mariachi attracts tourists later in the night. A black light casts a kind of skuzzy glow on the fluorescent jungle motif on the walls, tables, and banged up sofas, but that's all part of the casual charm. It's worth a visit if only to chat up the ebullient owner/bartender, Antonio La Ruso. He's quick to point out the "take any bartender for only $700 a night" sign hanging up, and insists the people manning the bar stalls during the day are his friends and live at the bar, too. *Bulevar Marina Cabo s/n, Plaza Mariachi.* ☎ *624/147-3130.*

→ **Love Shack** ★★ Ladies night, oh what a night. This is the place to be on Wednesday, when it's packed with a bevy of beautiful local girls. Two-for-one happy "hour" goes all day, from 11am to 7pm. (Why don't they just call it Happy Drunk Day?) There's a pool table and large windows opening out to the street. The TVs have music videos playing instead of sports, and surfboards adorn the walls. But the real attraction is the stunningly beautiful girls sprawled in the leather booths, sipping well drinks. The playlist covers everything from rock to hip-hop to reggae to dance music. *Morelos s/n, between Ninos Héroes and Lázaro Cárdenas.* ☎ *624/145-5010.*

→ **Nowhere Bar** Right on the marina, this is a cool, understated place where hip locals come to see their friends. Visitors like the Playboy girls always seem to end up here, too, when they come to town (perhaps that's why Lance Armstrong has also been sighted here). It's next door to Japango (p. 399), so you can get excellent sushi while knocking down the two-for-one cocktails during happy hour. Stools are set around high tables right up to the marina walkway, while the bar is set back and a level up with four TVs and '70s and '80s rock blasting (not too loudly—people do come here to talk). Ladies' Night is Tuesday, and it's packed since women drink free (!) from 8 to 10pm. *Plaza Bonita, Bulevar Marina 17.* ☎ *624/143-4493 or -4419. www.nowherebar.com.*

→ **Onix** Add this to the growing list (Nowhere Bar, Barometro) of super cool and loungey bars in town that somehow manage not to be stuck up. You can wear whatever you like, sit on sofas on the front porch, and watch the whole drunken parade that is Cabo pass by. Attached to the Hang-Out Café (see "Eating," p. 397), the Onix plays everything from house soundtracks to alt music by the Killers (on Thurs); there are live bands and re-mixed salsa on the weekends. *Zaragoza at Ninoes Héroes.* ☎ *624/143-8999. rsvp@onixclub.com. Mon and Wed–Sun 5pm–early morning.*

MTV Best → **Slim's Elbow Room** ★ It bills itself as the "world's smallest bar" but, even so, they manage to pack in everything from spring-breakers primed to flash you to Wyoming fishermen on vacation. The laconic female bartenders say *nothing* really fazes them anymore. They sell nothing here but beer and 45 kinds of tequila, a combination of which is supposed to magically lift your blouse and unclip your bra. The funky decor is tiki bar meets fishing bar and everything—from the walls, to the floors, to the ceiling fan—is plastered with dollar bills. The music is pretty much Jimmy Buffet country with Bob Marley and the Gypsy Kings thrown in. *Bulevar Marina, Plaza Mariachi Local 1. No phone.*

CLUBS

MTV Best → **El Squid Roe** ★★ Although some locals say Squid Roe was happening a few years ago but no longer, I'd argue that there's still some life in its tentacles. On a cold night in early December, it was the only place I visited with any kind of a crowd inside (including Cabo Wabo, see below). And the crowd was *on fire*—singing, dancing, working the catwalks, and sucking Jello shots. Part of the appeal here are the regular DJs, Farid and Ivan, who are geniuses when it comes to spinning. They play house, electro, and hip-hop. Then there's the basic ethos of burned-out brain cells, proclaimed by the signage on the walls: "How can I be so thirsty when I drank so much last night?"

As one of Carlos Anderson's creations (he's the man behind Señor Frog's, Carlos 'n Charlie's, the Shrimp Factory, and so on), El Squid Roe has relentless eye-candy and over-the-top anything-goes ambience (the decor is House of Blues meets trailer park trash) down to a science. The frenzied partying takes place in a big shedlike structure, with bleachers up top on the second floor. It's truly a warehouse, except the main products manufactured here are out-of-body experiences fueled by alcohol. As such, it brings in 80% tourists (except for Saturdays when locals come), as well as celebrities like Christina Aguilera—she had her pussy-posse post-bachelorette party here.

Wear pants since you may end up dancing on tables and you don't want your skirt action appearing on some website in a few weeks. That said, this is the kind of place where women flash body parts casually. There's a patio out back when it gets too packed inside, which happens often. *Bulevar Marina, opposite Plaza Bonita.* ☎ *624/143-0655. www.elsquidroe.com. Daily noon–4am.*

→ **Giggling Marlin** Proud to call itself the spot where the upside-down harness hang was first made popular, the Giggling Marlin is not for the shy at heart—lots of bare breasts (and other things) are exposed here. When it started in 1984, it was the first bar in Cabo. Today, nearly all of the patrons are tourists who come not only for the harness hang, but also for a live chicken toss that you have to see to understand. Yes, this place loves its gimmicks—if you can drink four of their signature drink, Skip And Go Naked, you get to write your name on the wall. Be warned that the drink is a blend of vodka, rum, and amaretto and at $70 it isn't cheap. The playlist is generic rock, pop, and oldies. In general, it all pales in comparison to Squid Roe, though the baristas are friendly and, like Roe, it's very much an all-ages kind of place. They also dish out food, most notably The Mother Of All Burgers (it weighs 3 lb. and feeds at least three people) and the Burrito Of All Burritos (equally gigantic). *Bulevar Marina at Matamoros, s/n.* ☎ *624/143-0606. www.gigglingmarlin.com. Daily 8am–2am.*

LIVE MUSIC

→ **Again & Again** This is *the* place to visit, well, again and again if you like banda music, or if you're just banda-curious. It's a wonderful locals' dance hall, well lit and full of couples all dancing wildly before a live band. If you want to appreciate this Mazatlán-inspired genre of music, you simply have to hear it played live. *Bulevar Lázaro Cárdenas s/n, down the street from Squid Roe.* ☎ *624/143-1795.*

→ **Cabo Wabo Cantina** ★ Co-owned by former Van Halen frontman Sammy Hagar, this spot is part concert hall, part restaurant, and part club (it's also one of the few large clubs in Cabo that is air-conditioned). Since it boasts one of the best sound systems in town for live music, it packs in huge crowds—but the kind of people who go nuts when old John Cougar Mellencamp songs are played. When it's rumored that Sammy himself is going to play, people camp out the night before. It was voted #1 Bar in the *Gringo Gazette's* 2006 Readers Choice poll, but the food's pretty decent, too: The restaurant churns out food until 11pm and the taco stand keeps cranking till 4am. *Vicente Guerrero at Lázaro Cárdenas.* ☎ *624/143-1188. www.cabowabo.com.*

→ **Mambo Café** If you're looking for a place to take your honey and dance close and get all sweaty, come to this recent addition to the Cabo nightlife scene. Opened in December 2004, it's part of a chain of bars around Mexico. It features a Caribbean concept club with a marine tropical ambience and a slate of contemporary Latin music, mainly salsa, merengue, and pop. Live music is also featured on the weekends. There's a great hardwood dance floor, a veritable jungle of fake foliage hanging from the ceiling, a bone-shaking sound system, and water streaming down the curved window that looks out onto the parking lot. The disco balls and dim lighting lend to the party atmosphere and the comfy bamboo furniture means you don't have to dance if you prefer to just sit and watch. Drinks are pricey—$50 for a glass of just-above-vinegar wine—but if you stick to beer ($37) you'll be okay. Ladies drink free from 9 to 11pm on Thursdays, but people swear this place really swings on Friday

Sharing My Time with Only You

Everywhere you go in Cabo San Lucas (and other spots in Mexico), you'll be accosted by timeshare salespeople. Everyone from the guy at the rental car agency, to the folks staffing the "tourist info" booths on the corners, to the friendly travel desk "agent" in your hotel may try to rope you into just "checking out" a club/resort for "75 minutes" for a "gift."

Instead of getting mad or irritated, why not get even? Don't settle for a crummy free massage or T-shirt or boat ride, go for the cash, muchachos! The guy on the street who ropes you in gets about $2,180 for each person he brings in. And you can get $2,180 off the price of your rental car or $2,180 to $4,360 just for sitting and listening to the spiel.

Be warned, though: The spiel seldom lasts 75 minutes but more commonly takes 2 to 4 hours. If you're prepared to spend that much time, here are some hints that might help you get the cash: They are looking for single women—ladies take off your rings and *don't* say "I gotta call my husband" or you'll get the boot—or couples with incomes of $40K plus. Don't ever tell them that you have a prior appointment or that you want to leave or it could disqualify you immediately, even after you've already suffered through 2 hours. Just hold your tongue and endure. How to get out faster? Tell them you're at a cheap hotel, don't vacation often, or want to travel someplace that may not have share-resorts. Don't ask too many questions and don't show too much interest. If they can't make the numbers work and decide you may fall into the percentile that really won't buy, they'll let you go. Most importantly, don't be intimidated. Some of the deals really are so good (especially for big groups) that you may just get yourself a new place at the beach.

nights. *Bulevar Marina Local 9–10, next to the Costa Real Cabo Resort. ☎ 624/143-1484. www.mambocafe.com.mx. Cover varies with the night.*

DAYTIME HANGS

➔ **Nikki Beach** ★★ This haven of the hip hails from South Beach, Miami, and St. Tropez, and brought its ultra-cool vibe to the Meliá San Lucas resort beachfront in March 2005. It's a very white scene here: The waiters are dressed in white, the signature lounge beds and umbrellas are white, and they put on a "White Party" every week that seems kind of superfluous if you ask me. The setting is great, however, overlooking Cabo's best swimming beach. Even better, you don't have to stay at the hotel just to hang out. The waiters have tongue studs and attitude but the service is adequate. The music is the latest in electronic, house, and chill, with visiting DJs playing on weekend nights; you can always go inside and check out the scene at Passion at night (Wed–Fri starting at 8pm). Sundays are all about the signature beach brunch. It's a great choice for catching rays during the day, and to escape the endless jewelry/dope salesmen working the sands. *On Playa El Medano at the Meliá San Lucas. ☎ 624/145-7800. www.nikkibeach.com.*

➔ **The Office** Just down the beach from Nikki's is The Office, which is more casual (you definitely don't have to worry about a dress code here). You can sit at the white wrought-iron chairs all day nursing drinks and count your blessings that this is your current office. *Playa Medano, down a bit from Nikki's. ☎ 624/143-3464. www.theoffice onthebeach.com.*

Heading to the Beach

CABO BEACHES

The main beach in Cabo San Lucas, **Playa El Medano** ★, is a busy one, full of swimmers, families, jet-skiers, all day happy hour imbibers, and vendors. It's the safest for swimming, and is where clubs like **Nikki Beach** (see "Partying," p. 401) have tables (or in some cases, beds) set up so that you can lounge there all day for the price of a beer or six. You can get here by water taxi or simply walk around the marina and turn left at the channel entrance.

Swimming Safety

Before swimming in the open water, *check if conditions are safe.* Undertows and large waves are common. **Medano Beach,** close to the marina and town, is the principal beach that's safe for swimming. The Hotel Meliá Cabo San Lucas, on Medano Beach, has a roped-off swimming area to protect swimmers from personal watercraft and boats. Colored flags to signal swimming safety aren't generally found in Cabo, and neither are lifeguards.

A favorite beach for watching sunsets (or whales) is **Playa Solmar,** within walking distance from downtown. It runs from the rocks of Land's End to the base of El Pedregal on the Pacific (access at the end of Av. Solmar off Bulevar Marina). **Playa Amor** is at the tip of the curve of the bay, reached only by water taxi (see "Getting Around," above) or a swim/hike along the shore (or over the rocky crest) and has no amenities, so be sure to take sunscreen, water, and food if you plan to stay awhile. The beach on the Pacific side (Solmar) is called **Playa Divorciado** by locals, since it's less idyllic than Amor—swimming here is unsafe.

BEACHES OUTSIDE THE CENTER

For a more secluded beach experience, head to the beaches on The Corridor off

Carreterra Transpensinsular by bus (take a Suburcabo; see "Getting Around," p. 390) or rental car. There are no facilities and no lifeguards at most of these beaches, so be sure to bring water, hats, and sun block and swim with caution.

Playa Barco Varado (Km 10, access on the southwest side of the Sheraton Hacienda) has great tidal pools and swimming areas. **Playa Las Viudas** (Km 12.5, access on the southwest side of the Twin Dolphin Hotel) is a more secluded choice, and boasts interesting rock outcroppings and tidal pools.

The protected marine sanctuary **The Bahia Santa María** ★★ (Km 14) is your best choice in the area for snorkeling and swimming over live coral heads—you'll spot gorgonians (sea fans) on the underwater rock walls and a profusion of tropical reef fish. It's best in the morning before the booze cruises arrive. (If you don't mind that sort of thing, you can get a booze cruise snorkel tour from the marina in Cabo; see p. 407 for info.)

A calmer bet is the next beach down at **Bahia Chileno** ★★ (Km 14.5, it's not well marked, so be careful or you'll see the parking sign after you've passed the exit). It's also best explored in the morning before the wind kicks up and the booze cruisers arrive. Tucked away inside a beautiful cove with pebbly sand, the beach itself is rather small—certain parts are strangely off limits. I attempted to walk over the headland to see Santa María and the view of the coast but was thwarted by a security guard, who told me it was "private property."

Playa Bledito (Km 19.5, accessed through the Hilton and Cabo Real Hotels) has a breakwater that forms a small manmade cove called Tequila Cove. The beach itself is spectacularly beautiful, flat above with rolling dunes to the water, but, except for Tequila Cove, it's not good for swimming. If you're staying at the Casa del Mar, it's about a 10- to 15-minute walk to Tequila Cove—past all the guests at the exclusive resorts getting massages.

Bahia Palmilla (Km 27, Palmilla exit) is the longest swimming beach in The Corridor, but it's one of the hardest to access since it's such a long walk from the highway. Fronted by the Palmilla resort and fabulous homes, it's a good place to drive to for kayaking since parking is nearby. It's also been a fishing camp for years and you can rent a panga or charter boat nearby. There's good swimming on calm days.

If you want to surf, head straight to **Playa Acapulquito** (Km 27.75, at the Cabo Surf Hotel), where you'll find the famous surf break Old Man's. You can rent surf, boogie, or skim boards and get surf lessons at **Costa Azul** (see "Playing Outside," p. 407).

You might also want to check out the Acapulquito-adjacent **Playa Costa Azul** (Km 28 via Costa Azul bridge), home of Zipper's and La Roca surf breaks, which are really for intermediate or experienced surfers—they're fast and can be dangerous for beginners. Besides Zipper's restaurant (see "Eating," p. 397) the area also boasts a minimart and a beach bar with sand volleyball at the Brisa del Mar Trailer Park.

Sightseeing

FESTIVALS/EVENTS

Cabo San Lucas celebrates many of the national festivals of Mexico such as Independence Day and Semana Santa (see "Basics," p. 21) but it isn't necessarily the best place to do so. Unique to the town is **St. Luke's (Lucas) Day,** Cabo San Lucas's patron saint's day, which is celebrated on October 18 with music and dancing in the streets as well as special events that vary from year to year.

Cabo often hosts an annual jazz festival in December, **The Cabo Jazz Escape,** at various venues around town, although it was cancelled in 2006. Contact the Cabo Jazz Festival Foundation (www.loscabos guide.com/cabojazzescape) for info.

MAJOR ATTRACTIONS

Culture vultures be warned: Cabo was a fishing village not too long ago and its rush to become all things to all tourists did not include much in the way of historical/cultural attractions. There are a few, but not many. Most sites are arranged around the main plaza. Many of the historical buildings on the streets surrounding this plaza have been renovated to house restaurants and shops, giving this neighborhood the most authentic Mexican feel in town. (Which isn't saying much, unfortunately.)

The Spanish missionary Nicolás Tamaral established the stone **Iglesia de San Lucas (Church of San Lucas;** no phone; free admission; hours vary) on Calle Cabo San Lucas in 1730, close to the Plaza Amelia Wilkes (commonly referred to as Plaza San Lucas). A large bell in a stone archway commemorates the completion of the church in 1746. The Pericúe Indians eventually killed the priest. Rebuilt in 1950 and remodeled in 1980, the Iglesia is not a beautiful colonial church, but instead a sweet simple edifice with wood benches and concrete swirled tiles.

At the other end of the Plaza is the small, but charming **Museo de las Californias** (Av. Hidalgo s/n; ☎ **624/143-0187;** admission $10; Tues–Sat 8am–3pm). The museum currently has exhibits on Baja Sur's fossils and indigenous communities but it is being enlarged to contain more. In front of the museum is a complete whale skeleton—it's worth a stop here if only to check that out.

Perhaps the most famous attraction nearby Cabo San Lucas is **El Arco** (Rock's Arch) ★★, the spectacular natural rock formation at the tip of Land's End. Approaching it by water simply shouldn't be missed—it's visible from all over the Cape. You can get there by glass-bottom boat or kayak; see "Playing Outside" for details.

Playing Outside

BIKING

A great way to go out mountain bike riding here is with authorized dealer Jorge Parra of **JP Bicycles** (Prolongacion Morelos s/n, between Diag. Morelos and Zaragoza; ☎ **624/105-1858** or 624/129-2494; www.clubcactusbike.org; for info in English contact Mario at patonet2@yahoo.com). Serious riders should bring their own shoes and clipless pedals, and if you're bringing your own bike, use a wide 2.7 front tire, slimmed. Otherwise you can rent a bike from Jorge for $250 and go out for free with the **Cactus Bike Club** just for the fun of it. Bikers in this club meet up at 6am for a 2-hour climb up the hills above Cabo and a screaming downhill back to town. You'll ride with locals ranging from waiters to computer techies, but everyone's a bike enthusiast.

Feeling strong? Ask JP Bicycles to take you on the **Los Naranjos** trek from the Sea of Cortez to the Pacific. This single track ride is 72km (45 miles) with an elevation gain of 600m (2,000 ft.)—in other words, it's tough. There's also an annual organized 80km (50 miles) road ride (police escorted) from Todos Santos to La Paz to Todos Santos. E-mail Mario for more information.

BOAT TOURS

There are a variety of water-based trips available at the marina, including the ubiquitous booze cruises to Los Arcos or other beaches. From the "pirate" ship **The Buccaneer Queen** (Marina at Hotel Hacienda; ☎ **624/144-4217**) to the "jungle" ship **Jungle Cruise** (at Hotel Tesoro; ☎ **624/143-8150;** www.cabobooze-cruise.com/). The latter is a *very* party-centered boat, so expect to hear reggae, top 40, and classic '60s and '70s rock blasting if you go out on their tri- or catamaran. Most trips include a continental breakfast and full lunch; others are all you can drink if you pay a little more cash. Many of these trips include snorkeling; among the beaches visited are Playa de Amor, Santa María, Chileno, and Barco Varado. Snorkeling gear alone rents for around $109 to $164. Without the add ons, most trips cost $709 for a sunset trip around the Arch rock formation, or $436 for morning trips.

Glass-bottom boats leave from the town marina daily every 45 minutes between 9am and 4pm. They cost $140 for a 1-hour tour to the Arch (p. 407). Make sure you understand which boat will pick you up—it's usually a smaller one run by the same company that ferries people back at regular intervals. If you don't get in the right boat, you may end up paying an additional $100 to the operator. One operator to try is **Cabo Zaida's Glass Bottom Boat** at Plaza Las Glorias dock (☎ **624/143-1306** or 147-7657; cabozaidas_connie@hotmail.com).

DIVING

You can dive with octopus, tropical fish, schools of barracuda, tuna, shar, manta ray, and turtles at the nearby **Neptune's Finger.** With descents to 30m (100 ft.), this is where the largest of two famous sand falls begins. Other dives here are at **the Point** (Land's End) and **La Anegada,** whose canyon walls are covered in sea fans—it's also great for night diving. Farther away, there's excellent diving in **Cabo Pulmo** (see "Road Trips," p. 430), now declared a national marine park, and **The Gordo Banks,** a 7-hour trip by boat for experienced divers only, due to currents and its depth.

One company to try for scuba diving is **Amigos del Mar** (Marina, near the Solmar hotel; ☎ **800/344-3349** or 310/459-9861 in the U.S.; www.amigosdelmar.com). Prices in general start at $491 for a one-tank dive, $763 for two tanks; trips to the coral outcropping at Cabo Pulmo start at $1,417. You'll need a wet suit for winter dives. A 5-hour resort course is available for $1,090, and open-water certification costs around $4,905.

FISHING

Sportfishing ★★★ in Cabo is world-class. From June through November, you'll reel in sailfish and wahoo; yellowfin tuna comes May through December; yellowtail from January through April; black and blue marlin from July through December. Striped marlin are prevalent year-round but especially in late September through November; and then again in spring starting in late March.

The 25-year-old **AutoExotica-Bisbee's Black & Blue Marlin Jackpot Tournament** (www.bisbees.com) has one of the biggest purses in the world ($4 million) for a reason. Although hooking a 100-pound marlin is supposedly routine, catch and release is widely promoted in order to keep the fish population up (one is allowed per boat; but you can get a replica made out of fiberglass from a photograph of the fish). Cabo also hosts the newer **Los Cabos Billfish Tournament** (www.loscabosbillfishtournament.com), which again requires that teams release fish. Both tournaments are held in October and anyone can enter.

Most fishing outings can be arranged through a travel agency, but if you're serious about fishing go with an outfitter like **Pisces** (Cabo Maritime Center Marina 8-6, Suite 1-D; ☎ **624/143-1288** or 619/819-7983 from the U.S.; www.piscessportfishing.com). They have a fleet of boats that charge everything from $9,265 for an 11m (35-ft). high-speed six-passenger yacht to $54,500 for their 24m (80-ft.) luxury

Tee Time

If you have the time, money, and inclination to tee off, you'll have lots of world-class golf courses to choose from in Cabo and The Corridor. The master plan for Los Cabos golf calls for a future total of 207 holes, but they're all expensive.

One of the best is the 27-hole course at the **Palmilla Golf Club,** at the One&Only Palmilla resort (☎ **800/386-2465** in the U.S., or 624/144-5250; daily 7am–7pm). It was the first Jack Nicklaus Signature layout in Mexico, on 360 hectares (900 acres) of dramatic oceanfront desert. The course offers your choice of two back-9 options, with high-season greens fees of $2,150 (lower after 1pm), and low-season greens fees running between $1,300 and $2,100. Guests at some hotels pay discounted rates.

The lowest greens fees in the area are at the public 9-hole **Mayan Palace Golf Los Cabos** (p. 378).

Several specialty tour operators offer golf packages to Los Cabos, which include accommodations, greens fees, and other amenities. These include **Best Golf** (☎ **888/817-4653** in the U.S.); **Golf Adventures** (☎ **800/841-6570** in the U.S.; www.golfadventures.com); and **Sportours** (☎ **888/465-3639** in the U.S.; www.sportours.com).

"Ocean Alexander." That includes tax, fuel, tackle, crew, licenses, beverages, breakfast, and lunch. Prices vary depending on the package and length of time you're out (1-week charters are also offered). Many larger hotels, like the **Solmar Suites** (Av. Solmar 1; ☎ **624/143-3535**), also have their own fleets.

You can also make your own fishing arrangements directly at the marina in San José. See p. 378 for info.

HORSEBACK RIDING

Get on the saddle with **Cuadra San Francisco** (Km 19.5 across from Casa del Mar; ☎ **044/624-141-6036** or 144-0160; www.loscabos.com; $436 hourly for trail rides; $818 for lessons), a horseback riding company with expert trainers. Run by classical *charro* (Mexican cowboy) Francisco Barrena and his son Valente, Cuadra is a company for people who *really* appreciate horses. The company teaches all the equestrian disciplines including dressage and polo. Be sure to tell them if you want to go faster (or slower); two guides accompany you on trail rides, so levels can be mixed. You can ride up an arroyo through 800-year-old cactus or gallop along the beach; the beautiful and responsive horses pretty much make it an excellent experience.

A cheaper alternative can be had through **Rancho Collins** (across from the Hotel Club Las Cascadas, Medano Beach; ☎ **624/143-3652,** cell 044/624-122-0774). They charge around $327 per person per hour (beach), or $654 per person for a 2-hour ride through the desert and along the beach.

RACE CAR DRIVING

MTV Best **Wide Open Baja Racing Experience** ★★ (☎ **888/788-2252** in the U.S. or 624/143-4170; office in Plaza Nautica; www.wideopencabo.com) gives you the chance to drive actual Chenowth Magnum race cars at their 600-hectare (1,482-acre) racing ranch on the Pacific Coast. It's a real taste of the peninsula, complete with mondo twists, turns, bumps, and sand washes.

Session times for the **test drive** are at 10am and 1:30pm. A fee of $2,725 includes shuttle transportation from downtown Cabo to the ranch, driver orientation, and safety equipment; private group rates are available as well. They also have multi-day tours where you can drive race vehicles through Cabo, Ensenada, or the entire Baja peninsula.

SKY DIVING

One sky diver I know with 3,000+ dives under his belt says Cabo San Lucas is the most beautiful place he's ever jumped, no question. According to him, it's "like jumping into a picture postcard." **Sky Dive El Sol** ★★ (Playa Medano side of Hotel Cascadas; ☎ **624/129-7173;** www.skydiveelsol.com) will take you up in a twin-engine plane from the airstrip outside Cabo. Never dove before? No problem. They'll harness you to one of their USPA licensed and certified instructors, so you can experience in tandem the rush of free fall at 3,900m (13,000 ft.). It's completely safe, as all instructors must go through the same training as they would in the states, and be certified from the FAA. For $2,398 you'll experience a minute of free fall and 5 minutes of parachute gliding 4km (2½ miles) above Land's End. If you're lucky, you'll get to see whales and whatever else is down there while high up above. For an extra $100, they'll make you a video of your dive.

SNORKELING

If you brought your own snorkel gear, consider renting a kayak or panga at the marina or Medano Beach, or taking a bus to the various beaches in The Corridor described in the "Heading to the Beach" section. To rent snorkeling and other beach gear at Medano, try **JT Watersports** (Melia Cabo Real Resort; ☎ **624/144-4066**). Or you can check with any of the boat tours mentioned earlier to arrange a guided snorkeling tour.

SURFING

Unlike other parts of the world, surfing is really good in Los Cabos in the summer (Mar–Nov along Corridor beaches) when the swells generated by hurricanes south steam up the coast. Typically the area gets three big swells from Hawaii around Christmas and then a couple more in March. Then it can get 7.5m (25-ft.) high, big gun waves. You can find good surfing from March through November all along the beaches west of Cabo, and **Playa Chileno,** near the Cabo San Lucas Hotel east of town, has a famous right break. Other good surfing beaches along The Corridor are **Acapulquito, El Tule,** and **La Bocana.** ***Warning:*** Several accidents have involved visiting surfers who are not familiar with the rocky break, so surf with care!

Also see "Surfing" in "San José del Cabo," earlier in this chapter, for details on nearby Playa Costa Azul and Zipper's.

Matteo and Veronica Brooks (☎ **624/117-3817;** www.buenaondasurfphotography.com) who teach surfing here can also make you a DVD and a photo disk of your adventure—they specialize in surf videography and photography. If it's not breaking locally, they'll even take you up the Pacific Coast an hour or two to **Los Cerritos** beach at Pescadero (see Todos Santos under "Road Trips," p. 430).

You can also take **windsurfing** lessons at Medano Beach, although **Los Barriles** on the East Cape is really the place to go if you're serious about that sport (see "Road Trips," p. 430).

SWIMMING

As the main beach in Cabo, **Medano Beach** is pretty much a zoo populated with sun burnt tourists, vendors selling everything from pot to fake silver to Chiclets, to timeshare salespeople doing their hustle. It's the place to see and be seen, but you *can* escape the frenetic activity by swimming. If you want a more tranquil place to swim, go to Chileno or Santa María in The Corridor. See "Heading to the Beach" for info.

WHALE-WATCHING

Between January and March, **whale-watching** is one of the most popular local tours around. The agency **Gray Line Los Cabos** (☎ **624/146-9410;** www.graylineloscabos.com) works with many different companies and can tell you what's available out there. The tours ($1,908 per person) take place in Magdalena Bay, about 2 hours north.

Shopping

San José is better than Cabo when it comes to higher quality items, but if you're after a lowest-common-denominator T-shirt, Cabo San Lucas can't be topped. Many touristy souvenir shops are on or within a block or two of **Boulevard Marina** (Lázaro Cárdenas) and the **Plaza.** The main shopping drag for locals is along **Morelos**—there you can find things like huaraches and huipils. Morelos is also where you'll find cheap Internet cafes, pharmacies, and local merchants whose clients are locals, not cruise ship passengers.

CLOTHES & SOUVENIERS

Dying to tell those viewing your chest—"It's all about me," or "Who are these people and why am I naked?" You can get all sorts of cheesy tees at **Die Trying** (Bulevar Marina s/n, Plaza Mariachi Local 7; ☎ **624/143-5021**). Tees are also available at **Huacheria Ber & Ber** (Morelos Local 2, corner Carraraza; ☎ **624/156-8360**) but you'll also get a surprisingly good selection of shoes—from old school un-dyed leather sandals with tire rubber

Kayaking the Sea of Cortez

The Sea of Cortez is considered one of the world's richest and most diverse marine ecosystems. Even Jacques Costeau was astounded not only by the diversity of life here, but by natural phenomena like the "sand falls" near El Arco where sand "falls" continuously over an underwater reef. No one has been able to understand the source or cause. The water is bathtub warm and the canyon drop-off falls more than 36m (120 ft.) down, a few minutes from the beach.

The Sea of Cortez's diving and snorkeling, as well as its surfing, are stellar—but I love to kayak here best. I recommend arranging an adventure tour through either **Baja Wild** (Plaza Costa Azul, Hwy. 1 Km 29.5; ☎ **624/172-6300**) or **Costa Azul** (Plaza Costa Azul, Hwy. 1 Km 29.5; ☎ **624/142-2771**). I prefer the knowledgeable guides from Baja Wild, who will give you a quick kayaking lesson and then take you out to the best snorkeling spots via kayak or panga—about 15 minutes of paddling away. Most trips leave early to avoid the zillions of kayaking tourists who disembark later when there are cruise ships in port; operators should provide the kayaks, snorkel gear, snacks, and even beach umbrellas.

One typical kayaking trip goes from the Marina around the El Arco (see "Sightseeing"; p. 406) to Land's End. I highly recommend approaching El Arco this way to get a first glimpse of the Pacific through La Ventana, a natural window carved by the sea through the limestone cliffs. Then you can stop to snorkel around Pelican Rock—in my opinion, it blew the hell out of other local snorkeling areas in terms of beauty and sheer volume of fish. It's a prime dive spot as well, with depths to 24m (80 ft.). Huge fish can be spotted sleeping on the bottom; sometimes manta rays even pass by.

soles for $140 to well-made woven topped clogs for $340.

Stevie Nicks would love **Magic of the Moon** (Hidalgo s/n, between Zapata and Lázaro Cárdenas; ☎ **624/143-3161;** www.magicofthemoon.com). The racks are filled with "over 100 original styles" of clothes, including hippy-gypsy chiffony layered skirts and ruffled blouses and evening wear. Everything is made by a local designer and, though rather pricey, totally unique.

FOLK ART

Several options for good folk art from the mainland are slowly making their way here. The new **Colores de Mexico** ★★ (Av. Cabo San Lucas, at the main plaza; ☎ **624/143-3559**) has crafts from all over Mexico including jewelry from Taxco, drums from the Tarahumaura of the Copper Canyon, full sets of Puebla Talavera dishes, recycled and outsider art, as well as fine art and local crafts. Owner Manuela Trasvina's goal is to promote local crafts; she and her husband Gerardo also plan to host fine art exhibitions.

Another new shop with contemporary and traditional Mexican art and crafts is **Osuna's** ★ (Zaragoza s/n, in front of Plaza Aramburu between Ninos Héroes and Lázaro Cárdenas; ☎ **624/143-2008**), which has objects from Guerrero, Oaxaca, Mexico State, Morelos, and San Luis Potosi, including rebozos, jewelry, Michoacan tablecloths, contemporary pewter trays and iron sculptures, iron vases, and gorgeous contemporary shell bracelets from Acapulco. Like its branch in San José (p. 381), **Necri** (Bulevar Marina; ☎ **624/143-0283**) has fine home accessories and Mexican handicrafts, with an extensive selection of pewter and Talavera.

MISCELLANEOUS SHOPS

J & J Habanos (Madero between Bulevar Marina and Guerrero; ☎ **624/143-6160** or -3839) is Cabo's largest cigar shop, with premium Cuban and fine Mexican cigars and a walk-in humidor.

You can get economical and custom ordered candles in the funky shop **Velas** downstairs from Guacamaya's Tacos (Morelos s/n, at Alikan; ☎ **624/143-1553** or -1768). Everything from votives ($4) to huge rainbow colored columns ($150) can be made right on the spot.

Gamaleon Tatoo and Body Percing (Matamors at Lázaro Cárdenas, Local #1; ☎ **044/624-132-3262;** $50–$70 per hr.) does original custom work and cover-ups in a clean, sterile environment. The owner Roberto explains that he's busy in the morning when the cruise ships come in, but he won't work on drunks because he's "not patient" with them. At presstime, Gary Hart (Pink's husband and creator of *Inked*) was about to open a *huge* branch of his tattoo shop, **Hart and Huntington** (www.hartandhuntington.com) next door to Squid Roe—that will probably blast everyone else out of the water.

SHOPPING CENTERS

High-end shops are clustered in the **Plaza Puerto Paraíso** (Av. Lázaro Cárdenas and Cabo Bello, Colonia Medano, Marina-side between the Plaza Bonita Mall and Marina Fiesta Resort; ☎ **624/144-3000;** www.puertoparaiso.com). Spread out over three levels, with parking and movie theaters, the stores here include a **Harley Davidson** store, boutiques with some upscale designer-ware (**Azul Swimwear** carries Dolce Gabbana and Ralph Lauren swimwear), and lots more stuff you can't afford. Around the mall along the marina, you'll find good bars (**Barometro** and **Nowhere Bar,** see "Partying" earlier) and restaurants like **Arts & Sushi** and **Japango** (see "Eating" earlier), as well as the local branch of the wine shop **Europea** (☎ **624/145-8760**).

The Plaza Bonita Shopping Center (Cabo San Lucas, Bulevar Marina at Cárdenas) is an older shopping center on the edge of the Cabo San Lucas marina, and has restaurants as well as shops. Most shops in the plaza, including a branch of the boutique **Veryka** (☎ **624/105-1855;** L-34C; see p. 380) and a branch of sportswear boutique **Dos Lunas** (☎ **624/143-1969**) are open daily from 9am to 9pm.

La Paz

La Paz has a character unlike any other city in Baja, or Mexico, for that matter. Although it's only a day's sail across the Sea of Cortez to the mainland or a long day's drive to the border, you'll feel a sense of being cut off from the entire world. The sea and the desert truly define life here—acting as natural barriers from outside distractions.

Yet the town boasts an intellectual flavor one doesn't find elsewhere in Baja Sur, a result possibly of the eight universities in the city and its role as the state capital. And though it's not as popular as San José or Cabo San Lucas, that's actually a good thing. When you go out to eat you won't be surrounded by tourists but by regular Mexicans living a life that isn't necessarily dependent upon yours.

La Paz is also relatively small—it's made up of about 200,000 Pacenos—but with a very long history. Cortez landed here in 1535 and 200 years later the Jesuit missionaries arrived to set up a mission and put the locals to work diving for pearls. For more than a century the pearling industry (and fishing) defined the town's identity, until the 1930s when a disease destroyed the oyster beds. It took the building of the Transpeninsular highway in 1973 to revive the city's fortunes and it, along with the designation of La Paz as a duty-free port, helped to bring growth back to the area.

These days, La Paz is ideal for anyone nostalgic for Los Cabos the way it used to be, before development and burgeoning crowds. From accommodations to taxis, it's also one of Mexico's most outstanding beach-vacation values.

Getting There & Getting Around

GETTING INTO TOWN

BY PLANE The **Aeropuerto de la Paz "Gral Manuel Marquez de Leon"** is located on the Carretera Transpeninsular Km 13 (☎ **612/124-6625**) and is 18km (11 miles) northwest of town along the highway to Ciudad Constitución and Tijuana. **AeroMexico** (☎ **800/237-6639** in the U.S. or 612/122-0091) connects through Tucson and Los Angeles in the United States, and flies from Mexico City and other points within Mexico. At press time, **Aero California** (☎ **800/237-6225** in the U.S., or 612/125-1023) was grounded and their offices were closed in La Paz, although they were still booking future flights; call to see if they're back up and running. **Alaska** (☎ **800/252-7522**) and **Continental** (☎ **800/525-0280**) have flights from the States, and **Aereo Calafia** (☎ **624/143-4302;** www.aereocalafia.com) services various small towns along Baja and connects to Mazatlán on the mainland.

Budget airline **Avolar** (☎ **800/328-6527** in U.S.; www.avolar.com.mx) runs cheap flights between Tijuana and Guadalajara to La Paz, but be warned that booking a flight online can be frustrating (the carrier is still fairly new and so is working out some kinks).

You can reach town via airport **colectivos,** which cost around $150 to town; you may have to wait until they fill them up with passengers because it's cheaper when more trips are taken. Or you can buy a ticket at the kiosk for **taxi** service; it's $275 from the airport to town but only $150 from town to the airport.

Another option is the **Baja Shuttle** (☎ **612/122-1826** or -7010; www.clubcantamar.com/bajashuttle) which costs $273 per person round-trip to the La Paz airport, or $75 per person round-trip to the San José del Cabo airport (two person minimum).

BY CAR The best way to drive from San José del Cabo to La Paz is to take Highway 1 north. It's slightly longer (2–3 hr.), but a more scenic route, which passes through valleys of cordon cacti, over mountain passes, and down through valleys that are a green oasis of palm and banana trees after the harsh desert. The road is very curvy in many places and you'll need to be mindful of *topes* (speed bumps), especially on the outskirts of Los Barriles. By taking this road, you'll also pass the turnoff to Cabo Pulmo, La Ventana, and Los Barriles (see "Road Trips," p. 430).

For a flatter and faster route, head south and east along Highway 1 to Cabo San Lucas, then Highway 19 north through Todos Santos. A little before San Pedro, Highway 19 rejoins Highway 1 and runs north into La Paz; the trip takes about 2 hours. From San José del Cabo either way is almost equidistant; the west route may be a bit faster.

Most major rental car agencies have booths inside the airport. **Budget**'s local number is ☎ **612/124-6433** or 122-7655; you can contact **Avis** at ☎ **612/122-2651, Alamo** at ☎ **612/122-6262, Thrifty** at ☎ **612/124-6365, Dollar** at ☎ **612/122-6060,** and **National** at ☎ **612/122-4747.** As elsewhere it is cheaper to book online in the states, although in town many car rental places have deals that include tax and insurance.

BY BUS The new bus station **Central Camionera** (on the malecón at Obregón and Cinco de Mayo and Independicia; ☎ **612/122-7898**) is open daily from 6am to 10pm. A great improvement over the old station, it is quite clean and comfortable. There's even a Superway minimart here where you can get drinks and snacks and go online. The station is about 25 blocks southwest of downtown and taxis line up in front regularly.

From the Camionera station, you can travel north to Tijuana on the **ABC** (☎ **664/683-5681)** and **Aguila lines** (☎ **612/122-7898,** ext 126), to San José each hour on the hour (3 hr.); or to Cabo San Lucas every hour on the half-hour (2½ hr.) for $171. The fares to Tijuana, Mexicali, and Tecate are $1,338, $1,373, and $1,498 respectively and seven departures leave daily for the 24-hour trip to the border.

Another option is the new **Peninsula line,** a first-class bus which goes directly to the two Cabos. When you buy a ticket, you can use their Internet terminals at the bus station for free. It departs every 2 hours after 6:30am and takes 2 hours to Cabo San Lucas (for $193), or you can continue on for another half-hour to San José del Cabo (for $232). They also offer 7-hour tours to Todos Santos leaving daily at 10:30am for $500, which includes round-trip transportation, a guide, and a drink at the Hotel California.

The Camionera station doesn't offer bus routes to the north. All routes north and south, as well as buses to Pichilingue ($20), the ferry pier, and to close outlying beaches, are available through the **Transportes Aguila station,** sometimes called the beach bus terminal, on the malecón at Alvaro Obregón and Cinco de Mayo (☎ **612/122-7898**).

BY FERRY **Baja Ferries** makes the 10-hour crossing from La Paz to Topolobampo

La Paz Area

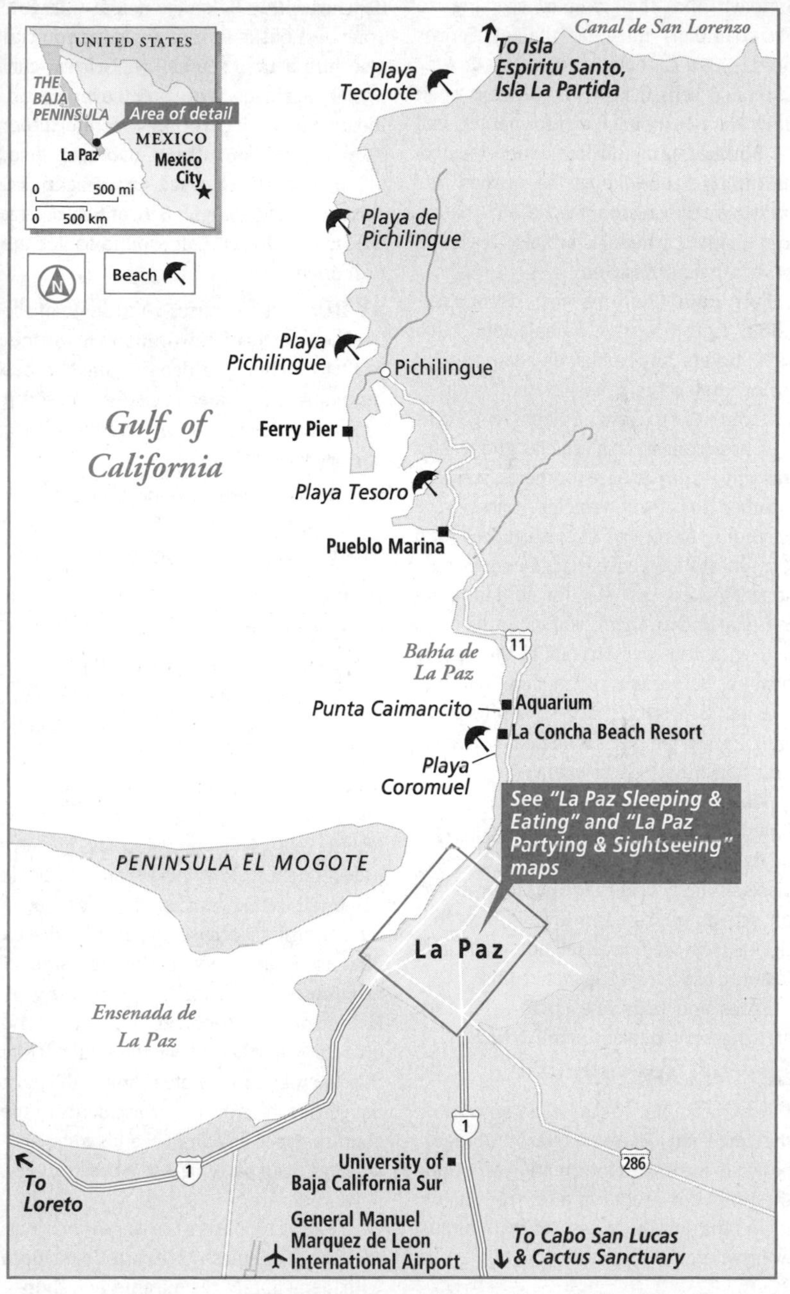
Canal de San Lorenzo
To Isla Espiritu Santo, Isla La Partida
Playa Tecolote
UNITED STATES
THE BAJA PENINSULA
Area of detail
MEXICO
La Paz
Mexico City
0 500 mi
0 500 km
N
Beach
Playa de Pichilingue
Playa Pichilingue
Pichilingue
Gulf of California
Ferry Pier
Playa Tesoro
Pueblo Marina
11
Bahía de La Paz
Punta Caimancito
Aquarium
La Concha Beach Resort
Playa Coromuel
See "La Paz Sleeping & Eating" and "La Paz Partying & Sightseeing" maps
PENINSULA EL MOGOTE
La Paz
Ensenada de La Paz
1
286
To Loreto
University of Baja California Sur
General Manuel Marquez de Leon International Airport
To Cabo San Lucas & Cactus Sanctuary

(the port for Los Mochis), daily except Sunday, and the 17-hour crossing to Mazatlán daily. In La Paz, the Baja Ferries office (I. La Catolica y Navarro; ☎ **612/125-7443**) sells tickets. The office is open daily 8am to 6pm. For information, call ☎ **800/122-1414** toll-free within Mexico, or 612/123-0208—though be warned, it's hard to get through to someone. Information and updated schedules are also available at www.bajaferries.com.

Fun Baja (Reforma 395; ☎ **612/121-5884,** 125-2366; www.funbaja.com), also sells tickets but unlike the Baja Ferries office, they actually answer their phones. Their ferries can carry 1,000 passengers, as well as accommodate vehicles and trucks. Passengers pay one fee for themselves and another for their vehicles—prices vary according to the car size. A car less than 5.5m (18 ft.) long costs $120. One-way passenger tickets cost $65; for an additional fee (starting at $500), you can also get a bed in a four-person cabin. The ferries boast a restaurant, coffee shop, bar, and live bands. Disabled access is offered as well. Passengers are requested to arrive 3 hours prior to departure time.

Viajes Los Delfines (Cabo San Lucas, Bulevar Marina across from Burger King; ☎ **624/142-0752**) is a travel agency which also sells ferry tickets and has information on schedules. You can always buy your tickets from the ferry itself but it'll be a lot faster to use a travel agent like this.

Buses and taxis line up to meet each arriving ferry to take you into town.

GETTING AROUND

ON FOOT Most of La Paz is centered on the malecón (Paseo Alvaro Obregón) between the tourist information office and the Hotel Los Arcos, up a few blocks into town. That makes it easy to walk almost everywhere.

BY CAR If you want to visit the many beaches within 80km (50 miles) of La Paz, your best bet is to rent a car (or you can also hire a taxi, see below). Several car-rental agencies are on the malecón, including **Thrifty** (Obregón at Lerdo; ☎ **612/125-9696**), **Hertz** (Obregón 2130, at Allende; ☎ **612/122-5300**), and **BC Autorentals** (Obregón 826, at Salvatierra; ☎ **612/125-7662**). Call around to get the best price.

BY BUS Public buses go to some of the beaches north of town. **Buses** ($18 one-way) to Pichilingue depart from the bus terminal on the malecón (see above) seven times a day from 8am to 5pm. Trips are $20 one-way within town.

BY TAXI **Taxis** around town charge about $40, and they meet each ferry (charging about $80 to downtown La Paz).

Basics

ORIENTATION

Although La Paz has grown well inland from the **malecón** (Paseo Alvaro Obregón), the older, more authentic, and friendly downtown area a few blocks up from the waterfront is the only real place to hang. The main plaza, **Plaza Constitucion,** or Jardín Velazco, is bounded by Madero, Independencia, Revolución, and Cinco de Mayo. Orienting yourself here can be a bit confusing because the **Bahia de La Paz** itself faces north; the **beaches** of **Coromuel, Tesoro, Pichilingue, Balandra,** and **Tecolote** actually extend on a curve northeast from the center. (Note that the road to Tecolote is one of the most dangerous in terms of car accidents in the country, especially on weekends when people have been partying at the beach all day. Drive with care.)

La Paz also boasts several new marinas, including the splashy **Marina Costa Baja** with many hotels, restaurants, and shops.

TOURIST INFO & OFFICES

The visitor information office is on Alvaro Obregón at the intersection of Calle 16 de Septiembre (☎ **612/122-5939;** turismo@correo.gbcs.gob.mx). It's open Monday through Friday from 8am to 10pm, Saturday and Sunday noon to midnight; the staff is bilingual and has information on all of Baja Sur.

More difficult to find and perhaps not as helpful is the office of the **Secretary of Tourism** (Carretera al Norte Km 5.5, Edificio Fidepaz, Col. Fidepaz; ☎ **612/124-0100**); it's open daily from 8am to 3pm. There's also a tourist information kiosk on the malecón, open daily from 8am to 8pm, as well as the **"White Tourist Police"** (Policia Turistica, see "Emergencies," below) at the skateboarder's park Cuahetomoc.

RECOMMENDED WEBSITES

- **www.vivalapaz.com**: The official website of the La Paz Tourism Board.
- **www.clubcruceros.org/Services.html**: Visit this site for a handy listing of phone numbers relating to many services in town.

La Paz Nuts & Bolts

Banks Banks generally exchange currency during normal business hours: Monday through Friday from 9am to 6pm, and Saturday from 10am to 2pm. **Banamex** has several branches including one downtown on the corner of Isabel La Catolica and Bravo (☎ **612/122-4560**); there is a branch of **Banorte** on Ignacio Allende 2125 (☎ **612/122-3855**); and a **Grupo Scotiabank** at Av. Esquerro 15 (☎ **612/122-2656**). ATMs are everywhere downtown, though.

Embassies See p. 368 under San José del Cabo for info on nearby embassies and consulates.

Emergencies Dial ☎ **066** for general emergency assistance. **The Policia Turistica** (Paseo Alvaro Obregón between Rosales and Bravo, at the Parque Cuahutemoc; ☎ **612/122-5939,** daily 8am–10pm) not only offers tourist advice but is also available for tourist emergencies or complaints. Tourist police (dressed in white) patrol the area surrounding the malecón on foot and bike, as well.

Hospitals The city's general hospital is the **Hospital Juan María de Salvatierra,** Nicolás Bravo 1010, Col. Centro (☎ **612/122-1497**). A better if slightly expensive hospital that caters to foreigners is the **Hospital Especialidades Médicas,** in Fidepaz (☎ **612/124-0400**). One of the best hospitals here is the **Hospital Militar,** on Revolución between Salvatierra and Torre Iglesias (☎ **612/122-3466**); although it has a third-world touch, it is economical and has excellent doctors, some of whom speak English.

Internet/Wireless Hot Spots **Don Tomas Cyber Café** (Alvaro Obregón 229, at Constitución; ☎ **612/128-5508**) has good wireless and Internet access for laptops ($15 per hr.), VoIP international calling, translation services, and a cafe and bar. **BajaNet** (Madero 430; ☎ **612/125-9380**), charges $1 per minute, with a $10 minimum charge. The **Omni Services Internet Café,** on the malecón (Alvaro Obregón 460-C; ☎ **612/123-4888**), has hookups for laptops, color printers, copy, fax, and VoIP phone services to the U.S. and Canada for $3 per minute. Most Internet spots are open Monday through Saturday from 8am to 10pm, and Sunday 9am to 9pm.

There are Wi-Fi connections around town, too, at coffee houses and at many hotels.

Laundry There are many laundromats in town; most charge $18 to wash, another $18 to dry, plus something nominal for soap and folding. One to try is **Lavanderia Vijando** (Aquiles Serdan at Cinco de Mayo, Centro; no phone), which is just around the corner from the Angel Azul (see "Sleeping," below).

Pharmacies Once one of the largest pharmacies in town, the **Farmacia Baja California** (corner of Independencia and Madero; ☎ **612/122-0240** or 123-4408) now focuses on selling cheap Chinese goods, with just a small counter allotted for selling drugs. A more comprehensive pharmacy is **Farmorama** (16 de Septiembre 806; ☎ **612/122-4920** or -5280) which offers 20% to 50% off medicine.

Post Office The *correo*, 3 blocks inland at Constitución and Revolución de 1910 (☎ **612/122-0388**), is open Monday through Friday from 8am to 3pm, and Saturday from 9am to 1pm.

Safety La Paz is much safer than Los Cabos probably due to the fact that it's less touristy, and more traditional. Take the same precautions you'd take anywhere else and use common sense and you'll stay perfectly safe.

Telephone Tips The telephone area code here is **612.**

Sleeping

Although hotels here are generally much less expensive than in Los Cabos, there are only a couple of hostels and not much else in terms of budget options. Since La Paz is a working Mexican city, not a resort dependent on tourism, the hotels cater mainly to businessmen. That means that you can stay in the center of town and not be surrounded by tourists. It also makes available spots like the wonderful Angel Azul B&B, where you can stay in style, but affordably—especially if you're traveling with someone else and can share a room.

Sleeping alternatives exist outside the center along the beaches, too. You can camp on beaches north of town toward Pichilingue, and there are nearby RV facilities (p. 434). I recommend staying in the town center to really get a sense of La Paz's unique character, though.

HOSTELS

→ **Hosteria del Convento** Missionaries once lived in this area, hence the name of this hotel. And while you won't have to live like a monk here, the party scene at the Convento is quieter than at it sister hotel the Pension California, right across the street. It's also a step down in quality. There's not really a courtyard to hang in, just an outdoor communal kitchen. The rooms are bare-bones but fairly clean, without windows but with a fan. Assorted backpackers stay here, but the real backpacker scene in town is at the Pension. *Madero 85, at Degollado. ☎ 612/122-3508. pensioncalifornia@prodigy.net.mx. $200 double, $250 triple, up to $400 for a room of 6. Monthly rates also available. No credit cards. Amenities: Kitchen; sheets; communal TV. In room: Bathroom, fans.*

→ **Pension California** This hostel has a reputation for renting rooms by the hour,

La Paz Sleeping & Eating

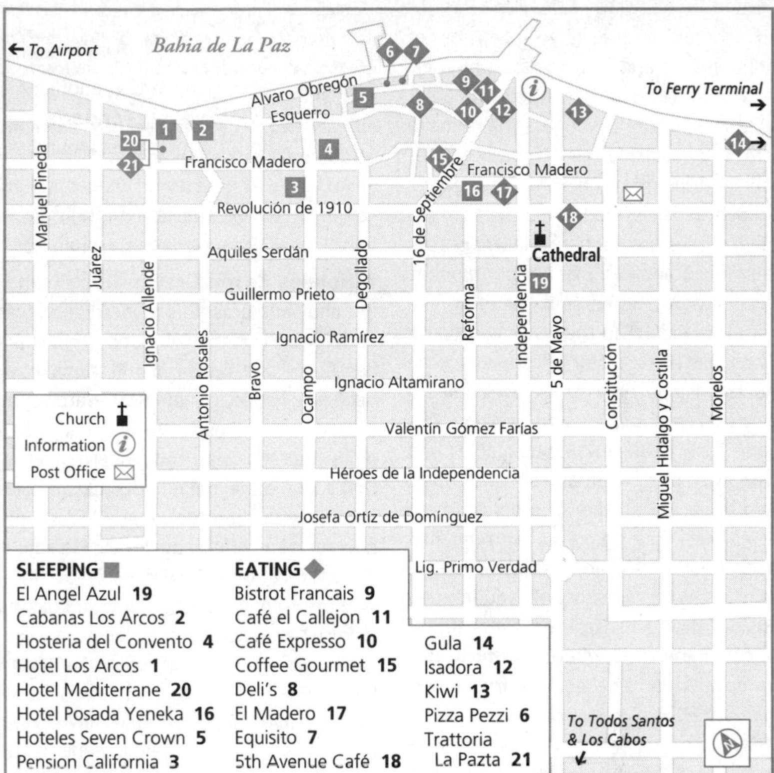

which means you may be woken up by a couple loudly having sex next door. But don't think about peeking—rooms are private (secured by a padlock from the *outside*—yikes); they don't have windows but rather slatted wooden windows above the doors. It can get *muy caliente* here during the summer, and the rooms are pretty funky, with clean if somewhat holey sheets. But, the price is right, and the atmosphere fun. The building that houses the hostel was built at the end of the 1800s; the wood has now been painted bright yellow and there's a huge stuffed turtle as well as whale jawbones and other scary objects hanging from the walls. Most important, someone interesting is always hanging around the communal kitchen (which boasts a Coke machine, hot water when you're lucky, and purified drinking water) or on one of the battered sofas. Backpackers, hippies, Europeans, Mexican families, and market vendors all stay here. *Degollado 209, between Madero and Revolución. ☎ 612/122-2896. pensioncalifornia@prodigy.net.mx. $220 double, $280 triple. No credit cards. Amenities: Internet; kitchen; shared bathrooms; shared fridge; sheets; travel info; communal TV. In room: Fans.*

CHEAP

MTV Best → **Hotel Posada Yeneka** ★★ This has got to be the strangest hotel I've ever set foot in. The original owner was a collector of all sorts of oddities, and the outdoor hallways of the two-story 16-room hotel feature large portraits of Benito Juárez and other revolutionaries; every other centimeter is filled with bicycle frames, whale jawbones, chairs made from keys, outsider art, Indian figures made of dried meat, varnished twig doors, prospector tools, and other iron wares hanging from the ceiling. The owner especially loved animals, like his pet monkey Pancho—now stuffed and manning the seat of a Model T in the inner courtyard. Saying this place is still pet friendly is an understatement—guests are welcome to bring snakes, dogs, cats, and monkeys. The rooms are relatively comfortable and clean, with fresh paint and concrete tiles. Then there are all the little perks: There are 50 bikes here that you can rent (just check their condition first), and they'll greet you with two shots of tequila upon arrival. Coffee is also free in the morning in the communal area, where you might just stay up all night using their Wi-Fi. *Francisco Madero 1520, at 6 de Septiembre. ☎ 612/112-5468. ynkmacias@prodigy.net.mx. $392 double. No credit cards. Amenities: Bar; bike rental; Wi-Fi. In room: A/C, TV, fans, safe.*

DOABLE

→ **Cabañas Los Arcos** ★★ The Hotel Los Arcos' sister property, this place maintains a certain mid-century Baja-style charm with its "bungalow" rooms (ask for those in front, not the back building, if you want to have the vintage experience). Those rooms have laja stone walls going up to a high slanted beamed wood ceiling, non-working fireplaces, old tiled floors and newly tiled bathrooms, and porches with rocking chairs that open out onto the lush gardens surrounding the pool. I guarantee that you'll want to take advantage of both the gardens and the patio—a lovely breeze usually blows through the area, since it's just a quarter of a block from the malecón. *Mutalismo s/n, between Bravo and Rosales, next door to Hotel Los Arcos. ☎ 612/122-2744, ext. 646 or 800/347-2252 in U.S.. www.losarcos.com. $110–$120 cabaña, $800–$1,020 double, tax included. AE, MC, V. Amenities: Cafeteria; restaurant; bar (all next door at the Hotel Los Arcos); info desk (next door); Internet; laundry service; pool; room service; sauna (next door). In room: A/C, TV, fridge, hair dryer, iron, safe.*

→ **Hoteles Seven Crown** Like its branch in Cabo San Lucas, this modern hotel was built for business travelers, but its upstairs bar **C.I.P.** and restaurant **El Aura** have become hangouts of sorts—attracting everyone from young Mexican couples to older tourists. Clean and modern in a way that's not quite pulled together, it tries harder with "International Clocks" and faux metal furniture; the hotel also enjoys a great location on the malecón. In addition to seven oceanfront suites, it boasts a terrace bar and a gym with Jacuzzi. *Bulevar Alvaro Obregón s/n, at Lerdo de Tejado. ☎ 612/128-7787. www.sevencrownhotels.com. US$112 double. MC, V. Amenities: Restaurant; bar; business center; gym; Internet; travel agency. In room: A/C, TV, coffeemaker, hair dryer.*

→ **Hotel Los Arcos** Built in the 1950s in a neo-colonial style, this three-story hotel at the end of the malecón was remodeled in the 1990s but it would have been cooler if they left it mid-century modern like its sister Cabañas Los Arcos (see above). Now it's built around a central courtyard but also has rooms with ocean views (ask for numbers 201–210, or 301–310). Though Los Arcos is pretty functional in its furnishings and amenities, the hotel's rambling nooks and crannies are filled with fountains, plants, and even rocking chairs that lend lots of old-fashioned charm. Most of the rooms and suites come with two double beds. Each has a balcony overlooking the pool in the inner courtyard or the waterfront. The restaurant is worth a visit for dinner. *Av. Alvaro Obregón 498, between Rosales and Allende. ☎ 800/347-2252 in the U.S., 612/122-2744. www.losarcos.com. $1,000 double, $1,100 suite, special rates $800 for locals. AE, DC, DISC, MC, V. Amenities: Cafeteria; restaurant; bar w/live music; gift shop; Internet; laundry service; Ping-Pong; 2 outdoor pools (1 heated); room service; sauna. In room: A/C, TV, hair dryer, minibar.*

→ **Hotel Mediterrane** ★ The name does not lie—this white-washed hotel with blue accents, stuccoed in a Greek style, really makes you feel transported to the Mediterranean. With its white-tile floors, modern art, serape bedspreads, and *equipale* (Mexican leather) furniture, the hotel appeals to travelers of all ages and types—it's definitely a gay-friendly place. Although the rooms are rather closed in, the fact that they all face an interior courtyard and have large windows helps maintain an open ambience. Ask for the second floor rooms, some of which have bay views; the "Mikonos" has a large boveda ceiling and great ventilation. Its location is great—just a block from the malecón. The adjacent La Pazta restaurant (see "Eating," below) is one of La Paz's best. Rates include use of kayaks and bicycles for exploring the town. *Allende 36, between Madero and Obregón. ☎/fax 612/125-1195. www.hotelmed.com. $716 single, $782 double, $109 extra person. Includes kayaks. Weekly discounts available. AE, MC, V. Amenities: Restaurants; cafe; bar; breakfast; Internet; laundry service. In room: A/C, TV/VCR, fridge, Wi-Fi.*

SPLURGE

MTV Best → **Angel Azul** ★★ Now's your chance to see the inside of a courthouse, without having to go to jail. Swiss owner Esther Ammann created this lovely and charming B&B in the 140-year-old historical landmark that was once the Federal Courthouse. The former ruin is now fully restored (under the guidance of the National Historic Institute), and charmingly styled with quirky tiles, colors derived from a historical palette, and a great cactus garden (all cacti are numbered and identified for your personal elucidation). You can breakfast either in the courtyard or inside the bar/lobby area—either way, the breakfasts are large and delicious, and fueled by Italian Lavazza coffee.

All in all, it's quiet and civilized but a great meeting spot—not surprising, since Esther knows everybody in town. The location, just a few blocks from the main square, also means it's *this close* to the city's best restaurants and clubs. *Independencia 518, at Prieto. ☎ 612/125-5130. www.elangelazul.com. US$145 double. Includes full breakfast. MC, V. Amentities: Bar; breakfast room; Wi-Fi in lobby/garden. In room: A/C, fans.*

Eating

For the longest time, the restaurants in La Paz were adequate but not outstanding. Fortunately, the general gourmet trend that has swept Baja in the past few years is having its way here as well—fine dining is now a real possibility. Seafood (surprise surprise) is still the biggest draw here but recently the town has attracted French and Italian restaurants, as well as good Chinese spots. There are even a few vegetarian restaurants, a rarity in Mexico.

Though all restaurants here are much cheaper than those in Los Cabos (or Todos Santos), the restaurants along the malecón tend to be more expensive than those a few blocks inland.

CHEAP

→ **Café de Callejon** MEXICAN Nothing tops a *hurache* to start the day off right—and no I don't mean the shoe. This place excels at the thick foot-long corn sopes, which you can order with your favorite topping, from beef to nopal and bean. They also dish out seafood and more typical Mexican dishes, and an Internet cafe is tucked away inside. *Callejon La Paz 51, at Alvaro Obregón. ☎ 612/125-4006. Main courses $70–$100. MC, V. Daily 8am–7pm.*

➔ **Isadora** MEXICAN Gourmet seafood tacos and Mexican combo plates, with great salsas, are served at this simple place. You'll dine in a courtyard under a ceba tree, next to a nice little gallery featuring local artists' work. *16 de Septiembre, at Alvaro Obregón 8. ☎ 612/123-3000. Main courses $60–$100. No credit cards. Mon–Sat 8am–3pm; Sun 8am–1pm.*

➔ **Kiwi** CONTINENTAL Grab a spot at this restaurant on the malecón and soak in the great view of the Sea of Cortes and the ships at anchor in the bay. Then try one of the tasty and filling menu items, from chicken in peanut sauce, to garlic fillet, to tampiquena steak, to a simple burger. They also have a typical variety of Mexican egg-based breakfasts that come with beans and tortillas, salsas, and coffee. Overall, this is a great spot for savoring your food while doing some serious people-watching. *Alvaro Obregón, between 5 de Mayo and Constitucion. ☎ 612/123-3282. Main courses $50–$100. AE, DISC, MC, V. Daily 7am–10pm.*

➔ **Pizza Pezzi** ITALIAN This Italian-owned joint on the malecón makes the best and most authentic pizza in town. Small and narrow, there's a counter at one end and tables on the malecón. Red and white is the basic decor and the chairs and tables outside give you a nice alfresco experience (despite the traffic). Best of all, you can get pizza by the slice (hard to come by in Mexico)! The thin crust is exquisite. Toppings include the usual, nothing outstanding. The only drawback is that they're not open for lunch. *Alvaro Obregón, between Lerdo de Tejada and Cabezud. ☎ 044/612-140-2588. Nothing over $80. No credit cards. Daily 6–11pm.*

DOABLE

➔ **Bistro Francais and Dolce Vita** FUSION Housed in a 160-year-old house and formerly a grain storehouse, this restaurant is sectioned into one French and one Italian half. The Italian menu sticks pretty much to pasta and pizza (and is rather mediocre), but the French menu is quite extensive, reasonably priced, with hearty simple fare including various types of partridge, rabbit, and two whole menu pages devoted to seafood. Perhaps it's too extensive; not every dish here is wonderful, even though the ambience is. You will consistently get huge plates of food and decent red wine. The house forms a U around a garden filled with tables and the ambience is pure 19th-century Mexico—it's all very Zorro-esque. Exposed brick, high ceilings, palm vigas, distressed wooden lattices, and an acoustic guitar player (sometimes supplemented by a flutist or an unfortunate drum machine) add to the romantic feel of the place. *Esquerro 10, at 16 de Septiembre. ☎ 612/125-6080 (Bistro Francais) 106-7009 (Dolce Vita). Main courses $80–$240 (most in the lower range). MC, V. Daily 1–10pm; closed Sun in Sept.*

MTV Best ➔ **El Madero** ★★★ ITALIAN One more reason I'm thinking of moving to La Paz is the food at Madero. This unassuming restaurant just off the main plaza delivers one of the best meals for the price I've ever had. Porro and her husband Roberto Meloni from Rome have done everything just right. With its big bronze doors and pool table, the front room, modern and relatively chic, is somewhat misleading. Walk past to the Mediterranean-Mexican-beachy back room, "El Patio Grill," and you can watch the wonderful chefs cook behind a counter. Of all the creations they whip up, be sure to try the carpaccio de pescador and filete de pescado guajillo—and end your meal with the divine tiramisu. *Calle Madero 93, between Independencia and 16 de Septiembre. ☎ 044/612-137-5786. barmadero@hotmail.com. Main courses $90–$130; pastas $70–$100. No credit cards. Daily 5–11pm.*

➔ **La Pazta** ★ ITALIAN/SWISS Go back to the future at this gay-friendly restaurant adjoining the Hotel Mediterrane (p. 421)—with its black tubular furniture, black and white checked floor, and walls literally broken into huge holes to expose bricks, it's lost in an '80s time warp. The food fortunately proves to be more timeless—the ravioli verde and extensive wine list featuring Baja (and Chilean) wines, salmon in white wine sauce fettuccini, and homemade pasta with squid are all great. All their pasta, bread, and cakes are homemade, and they have fresh seafood and calamari as well as homemade lasagna. Pizza and calzone baked in a wood-fired oven are also on the menu. *Allende 36. ☎ 612/125-1195. www.hotelmed.com. Main courses $80–$165. AE, MC, V. Wed–Mon 3–11pm.*

SPLURGE

➔ **Gula** ★ FUSION Set on the new marina out toward the beaches northeast of downtown, this is a beautiful spot to enjoy gourmet food with an Arab, Asian, and Mexican inspired slant. Try the octopus salad, or the unique fish in epazote sauce—both are to die for. Also on the menu is Thai stir-fry; salmon stuffed and wrapped with spinach; tacos in pumpkin seed and poblano chile sauce; and Indian curries. With whatever you order, you'll get steaming hot baskets of Arab flat bread, set in front of you with herb-flavored dipping oil. *Pueblo Marina Local 43, at Marina Costa Baja. ☎ 612/106-7001. jconstant@prodigy.net.mx. Main courses $180–$230. MC, V. Tues–Sat 7am–11pm.*

CAFES

Ten years ago, you could hardly find a decent cup of Nescafe in town, but now a mind-boggling array of coffee houses are on offer. **Equisito** (Obregón s/n; ☎ **612/128-5999;** no credit cards; Sun–Fri 6:30–11pm, Fri–Sat 6:30pm–midnight) has a wonderful array of cakes and cookies in addition to espresso and coffee drinks—they even sell Slim-Fast shakes to compensate for all the cookies you'll be tempted to eat. It's a happening local date spot, and since it's on the malecón, you can sit out front and accomplish some serious people-watching while also using their Wi-Fi.

A couple of blocks up from the malecón, the **Coffee Gourmet** (Esquerro, at 16 de Septiembre; ☎ **612/122-6037;** no credit cards; daily 8am–11pm) is also jumping with many muchachas and their dates who come to listen to a mix of cumbia, salsa, Indian, and Chinese music while drinking espresso, munching pastries and cookies, and going online or hanging on the low white sofas off to one side of the exposed brick space. Among the appetizing snacks on offer are four kinds of macaroons and pieces of streudel as big as your head—nothing is over $40.

Around the corner is the more gringo-friendly **Deli's** (Esquerro, at Calle la Paz s/n; ☎ **612/125-9909;** daily 7am–11pm; no credit cards) which serves beer in addition to coffee and is good for people-watching. The pastries, baguettes, and other breakfast items are somewhat sadder-looking here, though.

For a more sophisticated spot, head to **Café Expresso** (Av. Obregón, and 16 de Septiembre; ☎ **612/123-4373;** no credit cards; Tues–Sun 6pm–4am), which serves espresso coffee drinks and French and Austrian pastries in addition to more standard fare. You'll dine at marble-topped bistro tables, with jazz playing in the background.

The biggest Starbucks rip-off in La Paz has to be **5th Avenida Café** (Absalo, at Encinas, on the main square; no phone; no credit cards; daily 7am–11pm), which has knocked off the Starbucks logo as well as the types of drinks (they serve frappucinos, in addition to other cold and hot coffee drinks). If you want something more authentic, you should visit any of the above cafes instead.

Partying

Although the partying scene here is more low key than in Los Cabos, it also feels more real and less sleazy. One gets the impression, for instance, that the local university girls and guys may actually be interested in *you* rather than just hooking up with a gringo.

Most clubs have live music on weekends and, while most of the clubs and bars are centered on the malecón, they tend to be commercial places. More cutting-edge alternatives exist a few blocks up in the centro. Still, it's hard to beat strolling the malecón and taking in the wall-to-wall open-air bars and clubs on a weekend night, each with their own live band playing everything from ranchera to brass marching music, and competing with kids crusing by, blaring rap and reggaeton from their souped-up pick-ups.

BARS

Run by native son Hector Majaica, who was bred in Sinaloa and London, the Best **Isolde Tower Irish Pub** (Belizario Dominguez Loc. 10, at Independencia; ☎ **612/123-3281;** latorreisolda@dublin.ie) enjoys an ideal location in downtown La Paz, and it takes advantage of that fact with huge plate glass windows that overlook the main square. According to Hector, there are more Irish pubs in the world than there are McDonald's, and he clearly wants Baja to play a part in that accomplishment. In order to bring a bit of Ireland to Mexico, his bar serves Guinness and Bass, as well as local beer, on tap. And the vibe is certainly welcoming—you can sit in leather club chairs and watch La Paz go by, play a game of darts, or make friends with university kids who hang here. Hector has grand plans for a cool upstairs disco, **Abalon Urban,** which opens in the summer of 2007 and will hold 1,000 revelers and feature live music or local DJs. It'll charge a cover of $50 to $200 depending on the act.

Fine art by local artists hangs on the walls of the upstairs space **Indigo** (Independencia s/n; ☎ **612/165-6161**), and that's the draw. This new "cocina-arte-bar" hosts art openings where you can eat while overlooking the street. If you need to smoke after eating, journey a couple of doors down to the **Hookah Bar** (Independencia s/n, 1/2 block from the main square; no phone) where you can share a bowl of mocha, guava, mango, or pear tobacco with your friends.

Casa de la Villa (enter through La Pitabaya, Obregón s/n, at 16 Septiembre; no phone) is an upstairs bar at palm tree level, which means it overlooks the ocean and maintains its distance from the craziness down on the street. It's essentially an outdoor tropical veranda, pulled into the modern age by Pussy Cat Dolls music blaring from the sound system and Madonna vogueing on TV screens. Downstairs, the more traditional **La Pitahaya** (Alvero Obregón, at 16 de Septiembre; ☎ **612/127-0170**) has a live guitarist playing to a drum machine, while the working-class clientele amuse themselves by drinking and watching soccer on TV.

Just off the malecón and down a long hallway, **La Misión** (Esquero 1520; no phone; barmision@yahoo.com) is a working-class bar with a huge "Enterprise" jukebox blaring rock en español, banda, norteña,

LOS CABOS & SOUTHERN BAJA

La Paz Partying & Sightseeing

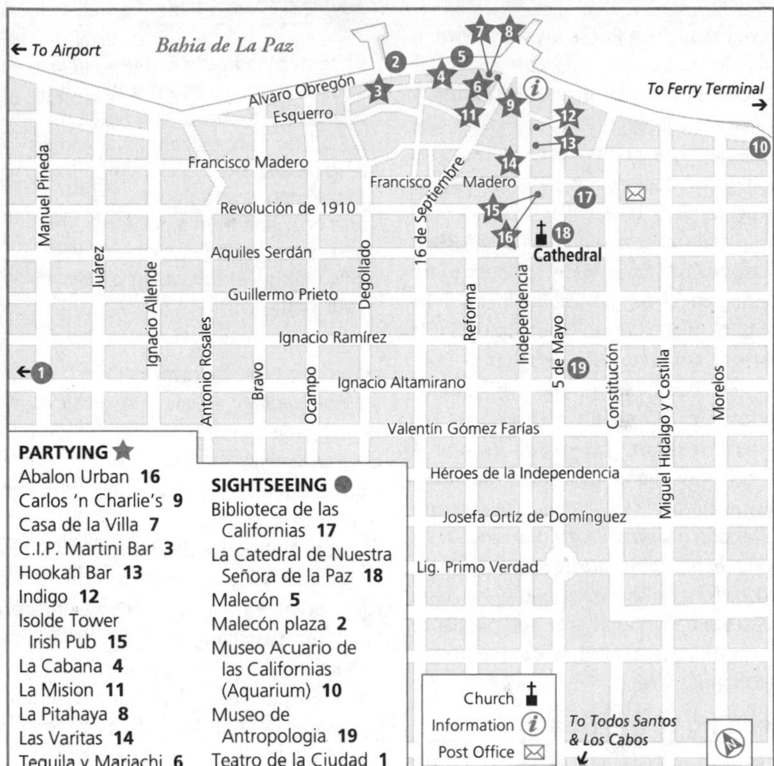

reggaeton, and cumbia. It's super noisy, the beers are cheap, and guys in cowboy hats play pool in the back while three TVs tuned to sports attract their own fans.

For a more upscale experience, check out the **C.I.P. Martini Bar** upstairs at the Hoteles Seven Crown (Bulevar Alvaro Obregón s/n, at Lerdo de Tejado; ☎ **612/128-7787**). Much calmer than the scene downstairs, it's a relatively hip place to hang out—locals come here for special events like bachelor parties.

CLUBS

When you're hunting for a club, I recommend just sitting on a bench on the **malecón,** listening to the cacophony pouring out of the 2 blocks of clubs there, and picking the spot that sounds most happening on that night. Or check, 'em all out if you want to be thorough.

The place to be on Friday is Best **Las Varitas** ★★ (Independencia and Domínguez; ☎ **612/125-2025**) because this is where and when the local ladies completely rock out to live cumbia, rock en español, ranchero, and salsa. Looking for a cheering gyrating mass of women singing along to hits? Look no further. Reminiscent of the Whisky in L.A., the club boasts an elevated stage and dance floor, loft space seating, and tables at angles to the stage. It stays open until 3 or 4am, and the cover starts at $55 and inches up depending on the act; it's ladies' night on Friday.

Even though La Paz is a young town, it still feels traditionally Mexican, and this is reflected in many of its clubs. **Tequila y Mariachi** (Obregón s/n, opposite the whale statue; no phone) features a norteña band in white cowboy hats serenading young couples, blue collar workers, and university students out for a night. Next door a cowbell rings wildly, in order to try shutting up the worst karaoke singers at **La Cabaña** nightclub in the Hotel Perla (Obregón s/n; ☎ **612/122-0777**).

A few doors down, the old standby **Carlos 'n Charlie's** (Orbregon s/n (malecón); ☎ **612/122-9290**) features a full-on brass band that plays outside—making this place feel almost like a grown-up version of Señor Frog's. But since it's a local's hang, there are few gringos here and no one misbehaves badly (no bare breasts or belly shots here). You can dance to everything from hard rock to rap to rock en Español.

Culture Vulture

El Teatro de la Ciudad (Av. Navarro 700; ☎ **612/125-0486**) is the city's main cultural center and hosts musical performances from local and visiting artists, small ballet companies, experimental and popular theater, and now and then a classical concert or symphony. Call to get specific info on what's going on during your visit.

Heading to the Beach

Although the malecón's beach is convenient, locals don't swim here and neither should you. (Like in San José, the sewage plant is just a bit overtaxed.) Instead, head northeast for 10 to 45 minutes to find beautiful beaches with clear, turquoise water. **El Mogote,** on the far side of the bay, is now being developed as a huge resort with just one problem: It's being built on sand. **Ballandra Bay** also has a new project slated, so visit now before it swarms with tourists.

Playa Caimancita by the La Concha Beach Resort (Pichilingue Hwy. at Km 5.5) is a good place to swim laps; non-guests may use the hotel restaurant and bar and rent equipment for snorkeling, diving, skiing, and sailing. **Playa Pichilingue** (Km 10) used to have oysters with black pearls, but in the '40s a disease ravaged them (and the local economy). Locals still picnic here, though; you can bring oysters to eat and have a beer under beach palapas, while watching the ferries and fishing boats at sea.

Playa Balandra (Pichilingue Hwy. Km 21) is actually several small coves around a rocky point; you can seek out a calm area good for swimming and there's decent snorkeling (bring your own gear). There are a few palapas and camping is permitted but aside from fire pits, there are no amenities.

You'll have to trek a bit farther to get to **Playa el Tecolote** (Km 24) but you'll get to experience an old-style Mexico beach. Families picnic, older women go in the water in dresses, and kids go nuts splashing about. You can rent beach chairs, umbrellas, kayaks, or lanchas; there are palapa restaurants with fresh seafood. Camping is also permitted here.

Sightseeing

FESTIVALS/EVENTS

February features the biggest and best **carnaval,** or Mardi Gras, in Baja, as well as a month-long **Festival of the Gray Whale** (starting in Feb or Mar). On May 3, **La Fiesta de La Paz** (Celebration of Peace) celebrates the city's founding by

Cortez in 1535, and features artisan exhibitions from throughout southern Baja. The annual **marlin-fishing tournament** is in August, with other fishing tournaments in September and November. And on November 1 and 2, the Days of the Dead, altars are on display at the Anthropology Museum. For more events, check www.bajaevents.com.

MAJOR ATTRACTIONS

One of La Paz's main attractions is its **malecón** ★, which borders Paseo Alvaro Obregón along the waterfront. Sitting on one of the benches and gazing at the sea or turning the other way to watch life in La Paz pass by is an attraction in its own right. In **Malecón Plaza,** centered around a two-story white gazebo, you can watch everyone from skateboarders, couples, cruisers, and mothers with their kids. Or amble into one of the cafes here for coffee, or a beer at a club or restaurant, and watch the action unfold from there.

Although Cortez first named the Bay here "Santa Cruz" when he landed in May 3, 1535, the first Spanish Jesuit priest in 1683 decided Nuestra Señora de la Paz (Our Lady of Peace) worked better. And so the permanent mission of La Paz was set up here in 1720, by Jaime Bravo, another Jesuit. The imposing downtown church, **La Catedral de Nuestra Señora de la Paz** (Calle Juárez, off the main plaza, between Cinco de Mayo and Independencia; no phone; free admission; no fixed hours), built in 1860, stands on the site of the original mission.

The Museo de Antropologia (Altamirano and Cinco de Mayo; ☎/fax **612/122-0162,** or 125-6424; free admission; daily 9am–6pm) is worth a visit to see re-created Indian villages surrounded by large, if faded, color photos of Baja's prehistoric cave paintings. Here you can see copies of Cortez's journals of his impressions on first arriving in La Paz as well exhibits of geological history of the peninsula and fossils (all in Spanish).

Day Trip

The 50-hectare (124-acre) **Cactus Sanctuary** (Ejido El Rosario; ☎ **612/124-0245;** hnolasco@cibnor.mx; free admission; no fixed hours) has self-guided tours along the 1,000m (3,280 ft.) of pathways winding their way through the natural reserve. I highly recommend coming here to educate yourself about the desert and its flora and fauna; you will spot a lot of wildlife that lives in this ecosystem. It's 45 minutes south of La Paz; take Highway 1 toward El Triunfo and then drive 10 minutes inland on a dirt road.

Also worth a visit is the **Biblioteca de las Californias** (Av. Madero, at 5 de Mayo; ☎ **612/122-0162;** free admission; Mon–Fri 9am–6pm), which has been tucked into a section of a building now mainly used as a children's cultural center. It has a wonderful collection of historical documents about the history of Baja California in which it specializes.

The Museo Acuario de las Californias (Aquarium) (Pichilingue, Km 7; ☎ **612/121-5872;** admission $50; daily 10am–2pm) has ponds and waterfalls outside, and inside are aquariums displaying corals, lobsters, seahorses, and other species from the Sea of Cortez. Go, they need your support.

Playing Outside

La Paz made its name originally as a sportfishing center 50 years ago, but now the outdoor activities are as varied as the fish that call the Sea of Cortez home. There's a reason why La Paz is considered the outdoors mecca for Baja California. Down around the East Cape is amazing windsurfing and kite surfing—the best in the world, some people say, especially around the islands. Within an hour you can either catch a record-breaking dorado or explore a wreck on the most famous seamount in Baja. And for all these activities, the prices are far more reasonable than on the other side of the peninsula.

One of the primary attractions in La Paz is Isla Espíritu Santo, which is actually a group of islands: Espiritu Santo, Isla Partida, and the Los Islotes, home of Baja's largest sea-lion colony.

DIVING

Grupo Fun Baja ★ (Reforma 395; ☎ **612/121-5884** or 125-2366; www.funbaja.com) is an excellent source for diving excursions (diving is the company's specialty, but they also do kite surfing). Run by a local who speaks Spanish, English, and Japanese, the company's guides and instructors are all PADI-SSI certified and their tours adhere to a ratio of one instructor to four divers. That's a good thing since diving in the Sea of Cortez can be tricky due to its strong currents. The visibility can be 30m (100 ft.) or more, although around some dive sites it can be cut in half due to the rich phytoplankton in the area. They offer deep dives, drift dives, night dives, as well as certification courses ($4,905, takes 4 days). May through November is when you're likely to see whale sharks and giant manta rays. Basic costs start at $1,417 for a two-tank dive.

Azul Tours (Paseo Alvaro Obregón 774; ☎ **612/122-4427;** azultours@gmail.com) is a smaller, new, and friendly outfit that also offers all-day diving tours to the Isla ($491) as well as kayaking.

DeSea Baja (Marina Palmira L3, Carretera a Pichilingue Km 2.5; ☎ **612/121-5100;** www.deseabaja.com) has regular scuba diving ($1,581 for three-tank dives including equipment; $1,853 includes a resort dive course) as well as unique courses in **free diving** (call for prices). Internationally experienced free-dive instructors Aharon and María Teresa Solomon will show you how to go down really, really deep without a tank, using yoga-based breathing exercises and mental control. Beginning through advanced instruction is available, as is spear-fishing instruction. In addition, they have private boats with guides for underwater photo or video diving, and you can hire a private dive master or instructor for yachts or charters.

KAYAKING

BOA (Baja Outdoor Adventures) ★★★ is next to Moyeyos Restaurant (after Hotel El Moro, Carretera A Pichilingue, s/n; ☎ **612/125-5636;** www.kayakinbaja.com) and offers a wide variety of kayaking-camping tours. They have 4- to 10-day trips to Espiritu Santo (starting at $4,578), as well as coast hugging kayaking explorations down from Loreto. On the Espiritu Santo trips, you only kayak a few hours a day, moving from beach to beach as you work your way around the island. Late spring can be very windy and summer is way hot, so you might as well go from January to March—it's whale-watching season and is also the best time for viewing cetaceans. All trips are motorboat supported.

MOUNTAIN BIKING

Katun (at BOA—see above; ☎ **044/612-348-7758;** www.katuntours.com) is a mountain bike outfitter that has a wonderful 2-week trip, called the Sierra de la Laguna Loop ($21,582), that takes you south from La Paz along the coast and over to the Pacific side. They also have single day ($654) trips north from La Paz and down around Los Barriles where there's 64-plus km (40-plus miles) of single track. ***Be warned:*** Some are very technical and you'll want to bring your own shoes and pedals (if you use a unique system).

SPORTFISHING ★★

Since the Sea of Cortez around La Paz is home to more than 850 species of fish, sportfishing here is awesome. You can rent a panga ($1,363 for three) or go farther out in a super panga ($1,962 for two); they have awnings for shade and comfortable seats. Larger cruisers with bathrooms start at $2,616.

Local hotels and tour agencies arrange sportfishing trips; one good one is the **Mosquito Fleet** at La Concha Hotel (☎ **612/121-6120,** -6123), which has cabin cruisers ($5,995 for four) and super pangas ($2,398 for two). Another good guide, David Jones of **The Fishermen's Fleet** (☎ **612/122-1313;** www.fishermensfleet.com) also has a fleet of panga and super pangas. Try to contact him before you come since his tours book up quickly. David is a *fisherman*'s fisherman, and he's also bilingual, so he's worth the trouble. The average price charged is $225 per boat.

Shopping

Despite its long history, La Paz has little in the way of folk art or other treasures from mainland Mexico—the few options are noted below. And because it is not primarily a tourist town, you won't find the usual overload of souvenir shops and cheesy bric-a-brac.

The city's **downtown** commercial area is clustered behind the Hotel Perla, between 16 de Septiembre and Degollado. This area is home to scores of small shops, some tacky, but others quite upscale. There's also a very small but authentic **Chinatown,** dating from the time when Chinese laborers were brought to settle in Baja. Serdán from Degollado south is home to dozens of food sellers of dried spices, piñatas, and candy. Stores carrying crafts, folk art, clothing, and handmade furniture and accessories lie mostly along the **malecón** (Paseo Obregón) or within 1 or 2 blocks going inland.

The **central plaza** boasts an abundance of stores selling **electronic equipment,** including stereos, cameras, and televisions. This is partially a holdout from La Paz's history as a duty-free port and because it's also the primary entrance for electronic imports to Mexico from the Far East. The area therefore offers some of the best prices in Baja and mainland Mexico.

The **municipal market,** at Revolución and Degollado, has little of interest to visitors. The major department store here is **Dorian's** (16 de Septiembre, between Esquerro and 21 de Agosto; ☎ **612/122-8014**)—hit it up only if you've forgotten essentials (socks and other mundane matters).

CRAFTS

At the far end of the malecón, **the Casa del Artesan Sud Californiano** (Obregón at N. Bravo, Parque Chauhtemoc; ☎ **612/128-8707;** pintapqco@hotmail.com) brings together an association of local artisans who come to this large store to sell their regional crafts. You'll find simple shell mobiles, clay pots with woven tops, rough spun cotton women's and children's clothes, and some wonderful regional costumes. Proceeds go straight to the artists.

For a good selection of folk art, **Antigua California** (Paseo Alvaro Obregón 220, at Arreola; ☎ **612/125-5230**) is a good bet, with work from all over Mexico. **Artesanías Cuauhtémoc (The Weaver)** (Abasolo 3315, between Jalisco and Nayarit; ☎ **612/122-4575**) has beautiful hand-woven tablecloths, place mats, rugs, and other textiles. The weaver is Fortunato Silva, who makes his textured cotton textiles from yarn he spins and dyes himself.

Out at the marina, there are many more upscale, tasteful shops like **WorlDeckor** (Pueblo Marinero, L-33, Marina CostaBaja;

☎ **612/106-7010,** www.worldeckor.com), which sells stuff for interiors including art from India, Mexico, and Africa.

ELECTRONICS & MUSIC

You can get CDs, DVDs, and record players at **Dragma Records** (16 de Septiembre 202; ☎ **612/157-6870**).

Odisea Centro (Independencia 508; ☎ **612/125-1800**) is a game store selling Play Station, Nintendo, Xbox, and other games and accessories in the electronics district.

SPORTING GOODS

If you're into off-roading, check out **Chic** (Madero 1428; ☎ **612/122-7702;** chicracing@prodigy.net.mx) for motorcycle helmets, pants, jerseys, body armor, gloves, and boots. **Oceanus** (16 de Septiembre 127, between Madero and Revolución; ☎ **612/143-3929**) has surf gear, while **4Street** (Zaragoza at Artesaniios 40; ☎ **612/122-0505**) sells skateboarding clothes and boards.

Road Trips: Los Barriles, Cabo Pulmo & Todos Santos

Los Barriles

Heading around the East Cape towards Los Cabos, the first major hot spot you'll get to is Los Barriles (62km/38 miles south of La Paz), a small town bordered by even smaller villages that is famous for its winds. Enthusiasts say it is the best place in Mexico for windsurfing and kite surfing. Indeed, the winds here are consistent and strong—18 to 30 knots all winter long. The winter El Nortes winds can be cool, so wearing a wet suit is advised. And because of the wind and choppy waves, this is not a place for beginners. Vela Windsurf has an outlet here, the **Baja Vela Highwind Center** (☎ **800/223-5443;** www.bajaquest.com/bajasports/velabaja), which offers lessons and rentals and can arrange package tours with hotels in the area.

When it comes time to grab some grub in Los Barriles, check out the Plaza del Pueblo, a little minimall where you'll find a sports bar at **Buzzards Bay** (Local 21, Plaza del Pueblo, Entrada los Barriles; ☎ **624/145-4102**), with $20 beer, half-pound burgers for $45, and happy hour specials daily from 4 to 7pm. It's popular both with locals and tourists.

Cabo Pulmo

A half-hour drive southwest down a dirt road (The Old Coast Road) is Cabo Pulmo, a tiny village halfway to San José del Cabo. It's seen a lot of development over the past few years but in 2006, Hurricane John—the biggest storm in the history of the pueblo—came through and trashed the place.

Despite a newish community of gringo homes that's developing on the beach, Cabo Pulmo still feels like what it has always been—a wind-blown speck of nothing in the middle of nowhere. It's literally off the radar: This place is so small, there are no addresses, and there are only two *caseta* (public) phones in town. (Rumor has it, however, that they'll be getting a cellphone tower soon, so that may change.)

Perhaps because the sense of remove is so unparalleled, the diving and fishing here are outstanding. Whales pass by close off shore and the continent's farthest northern bit of living coral is within snorkeling distance from the beach. Thanks to the efforts of a local dive master, the reefs and sea extending north and south from here are now a Federal Marine Reserve, so fishing of any kind is prohibited.

SLEEPING

For such a small village, the number of lodging possibilities here is surprisingly large. Your most comfortable option is to rent one of the three homes from **Villa & Casa del Mar** (Domicilio Conocido; ☎ **208/726-4455** in U.S.; www.bajaparadise.com; US$135–US$500 per house; MC, V). Two of the houses are large enough for four to five; the front one is the most luxurious with ocean views, a huge living room and kitchen, as well as well-appointed bedrooms. Casa Nido is behind the Villa and is smaller but has a decently equipped kitchen, rooftop views of the sea and its own private yard with hammocks looking out on a beach path. There's an entirely separate upstairs area, so five could fit here. Rates range depending on the season, and include beach equipment like snorkel gear and kayaks.

Another choice is **Cabo Pulmo Beach Resort** (Domicilio conocido; ☎ **624/141-0244,** 888/99-PULMO in U.S.; www.cabopulmo.com; US$49–US$199; MC, V), which has everything from a beachfront house that sleeps eight (US$199) to casitas that sleep four (US$49). Some have air-conditioning (you will be charged more for it), and all have kitchens. They swear telephone service and Wi-Fi are coming. The bungalows are built across a sprawling and pleasant 8-square block compound that winds from the main dirt road down to the beach bordered by sandy paths; the pleasant garden has been a subject of some controversy here since water is at such a premium.

Nancy's Restaurant (Domicilio conocido; ☎ **617/524-4440;** no credit cards) has a couple of very rustic if historic thatched roof adobe casitas to rent out back; they may be the oldest buildings in town. Rooms come with expensive percale sheets swathed in a mosquito net but no screens, and they feature concrete floors and peeling paint. For US$50 you get your own bath and a private patio; for US$40 you get a room with a shared bathroom. There's no electricity so there's no TV, phone, or air-conditioning.

You can pretty much stop at any unoccupied stretch of beach up or down the coast of the East Bay and camp; remember it can get very rough and windy here, and there aren't many places to buy supplies, so come prepared.

EATING

Be warned: If you're coming to Cabo Pulmo for more than a few days, you'll want to stock up on groceries back in either La Paz or Los Cabos. And bring cash since nobody but Cabo Pulmo Beach Resort uses credit cards. There are tiendas in El Rubio, about 40km (25 miles) away, back on the paved road, but they are limited. Usually you'll find nothing for sale but tired-looking produce, eggs, stale cereal, and boxed milk—if you're lucky.

Nancy's ★★ (Domicilio conocido; ☎ **617/524-4440;** $80–$200; no credit cards; Mon–Tues and Thurs–Sun 8am–10pm) was closed during my visit—she'd run out of gas and was out looking for parts to fix her stove. Nancy, who came here 13 years ago because of her daughter and wound up staying, is simply that sort of can-do gal. Her heavenly food is definitely the best in town, with shrimp tacos, chile rellenos with shrimp, or lobster enchiladas, and lots of veggies and salads on the menu. Her homemade desserts include mango and banana flambé, cakes, pies, and flan. If you want it and it's available, she'll cook it. She can also do picnics, and has sit down meals inside at night by the large stone fireplace, or outside on the patio under a palapa. Most meals run about $100 to $150.

The only restaurant on the beach is **La Palapa** ★★ (Domicilio conocido; no phone; no credit cards; Tues–Sun noon–9pm). It's run by María de los Angeles (who everybody just calls Angeles), who cooks up delicious fare including (of course) fresh grilled fish dinners, grilled chicken, and carne asada (for $75–$125). For lunch, try the fish tacos or shrimp fajitas ($55–$100). The $20 beer is a bargain in this neck of the woods, where even getting ice can be a struggle. Just eating under the palapa on the beach by candlelight after a full day of snorkeling is hard to beat, though.

All of the Cabo Pulmo Beach Resort (see above) rooms are located behind the **Coral Reef Restaurant** (☎ **624/141-0244;** no credit cards; Tues–Sun 8:30am–9pm). On the second floor of a cement block building, it's clean and decent if not romantic; and there's a great breeze and views of the sea a block away. Figure on spending $100 to $140 for typical Mexican snack type food and fish entrees here.

It's hard to avoid **Los Caballeros** (next to Nancy's; $50–$100 main courses; no credit cards; Tues–Sun 9am–8pm) if you're here for any length of time. Even though the standard Mexican food is wretched, you'll want to come here to drink and meet the locals, sit under the cane roof, and study the old B&W photos of Mexican rodeos.

PLAYING OUTSIDE

The snorkeling, diving, and kayaking here are the main reasons to visit. There are eight reefs that run more-or-less parallel to the beach, creating a miniecosystem that provides a home for countless species of fish. And since there's almost no undertow, the beach here is safe even though it's exposed to the open ocean. You could actually dive directly from the beach, but if you want to go deeper, head to **El Bajo** (90 min. away) where you might see hammerheads or turtles. Or take a trip to **Los Moros,** or Shipwrecks, 40 minutes out, where there are a pair of wrecks to explore. See www.bajadiving.com/divesites_pulmo.html for a more detailed description of the dives available here.

You can arrange to dive through either **Pepe's Dive Center** (inside the palapa structure as you come into town from the northeast; no phone), for $927 for a two-tank dive, or $709 if you have your own BCS and regulator. They leave from the beach around 9am and return by 1pm. Pepe's also rents kayaks for $436 a day, and snorkel gear for $164. **Cabo Pulmo Divers** (at the south end of the village in a pink building; no phone; www.cabopulmodivers.com) has beach dives starting at $382 and two-tank dives starting at $709. It's run by members of the Castro family who have been here since 1900 and know this area like nobody else.

Todos Santos

Midway between La Paz and Cabo San Lucas is the art/surfing colony of Todos Santos. Once a charming little village, made slightly run-down after the collapse of the sugar cane industry in 1950, it's managed to retain a certain idiosyncratic, if slightly inbred, persona. For years, its only claim to fame was the wonderful Café Santa Fe (p. 436), one of the best Italian eateries in Baja Sur; people drive up from Los Cabos, an hour away, just to eat here (though not quite as much as they used to). Surfers have also come down from California for years, drawn by the variety of breaks that line the coast nearby.

Following the paving of the La Paz road in 1980, expat artists began to arrive, drawn by the beautiful light, the cheap rentals, and the warm winters and cool summers. And slowly Todos Santos began to blossom, first with a bookstore, then a cafe, then a gallery or two, and then an organic farm started up outside town.

Todos Santos

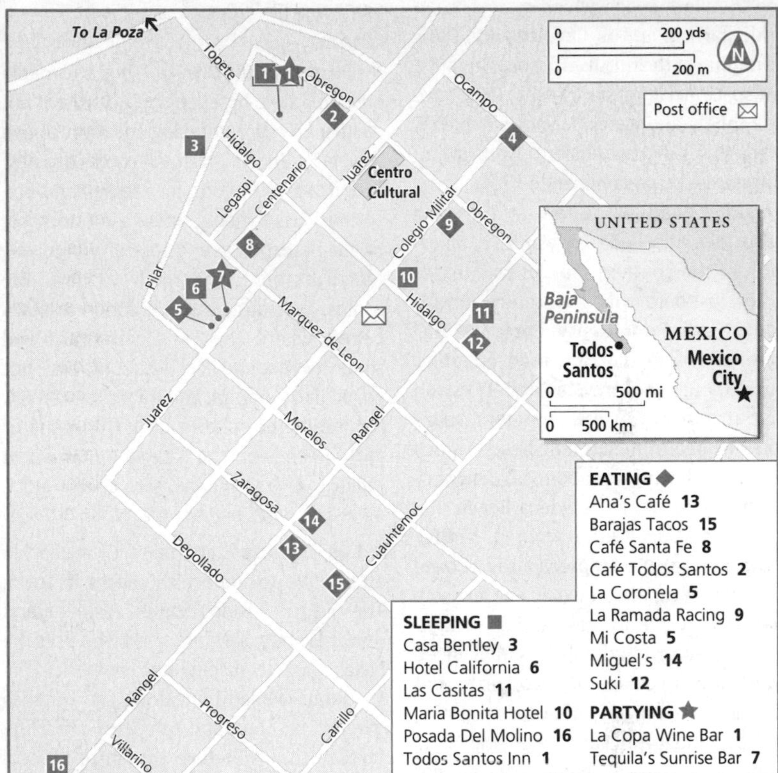

During this period, it seemed the place represented the best of all worlds—with slow growth, a low-rent economy, and a faithful if small stream of regular visitors.

Then, the town was "discovered" and almost overnight the character changed. Prices went way up, real estate offices opened, and, finally, the kiss of death—it was declared a Pueblo Magico by the federal government. Travel writers breezed through and wrote up raves about the charming little village just up the coast but light years away, culturally, from Los Cabos.

Today, million-dollar homes are going in and a major resort is planned for the Cerritos beach, just outside town. That doesn't mean that Todos Santos isn't still a haven for the disaffected, artist wannabes, or gypsy surfers living out of their vans, but the off-the-radar character isn't *quite* the same as it used to be.

Check out http://elcalendario.wordpress.com, the Todos Santos blog, to get an idea of the current sensibility in town.

SLEEPING

The sleeping choices are somewhat limited in Todos Santos. But in addition to the hotels listed below, there are some cheap alternatives to be had.

You can try camping at Pescadero Beach or any of the other deserted beaches north or south of town but do so at your own risk; there are also no facilities. A better option is Los Cerritos Beach, a wide, 8km-long (5-miles) beach which curves westward, starting at **Los Cerritos RV Park** (no phone) at the north end. You can rent a tent space here for $10 a night. They have flush toilets and water but not much else. Although it's a great place to walk, swimming here is not recommended.

Another good camp site is at Playa San Pedro (aka San Pedrito), 7km (4⅓ miles) south of the southern outskirts of Todos Santos, just before the signs and entrance road to **San Pedrito RV Park** (☎ **114/125-0170**). Note that the road is rather rough, though motorcycles and ATVs can drive it easily. You can rent tent space along the beautiful half-mile beach (which is great for surfing) for about $10 a night.

Just inland from Pescadero Beach, the **Pescadero Surf Camp** (Hwy. 19 Km 64; ☎ **612/130-3032;** www.pescaderosurf.com) is run by an American expat and his son. It's a great place to crash either in their larger palapa-roofed cabañas that sleep six, the private palapas (US$40), or to rent a tent for $10 a night. There's a swimming pool, bar, and lots of surfers hanging in the main palapa tossing back cervezas and bragging about the best breaks. They also rent boards, boogie boards, and have surf lessons and will take you to wherever it's breaking.

Teampaty (www.todossantos.cc/ecosurfcamp.html) is a women's only surf camp which sets up for 5-day sessions several times a year on Cerritos Beach. You can stay in their cabañas for US$40 a night and wake up to a hot breakfast, yoga, and then surf, baby, surf. The cabañas sleep two to four and include bathroom and solar heated showers. You'll be taught by 11-year resident Paty Baum who "is dedicated to promoting surfing for women, saving endangered sea turtles, and to the appreciation of Mexico, her incredible beauty and her wonderful people." See the website for schedules and more information.

Cheap

→ **Hotel María Bonita** This affordable business-style hotel enjoys a central if not particularly breathtaking location above the María Bonita Plaza. All rooms are new and clean, with good mattresses and box springs, crisp sheets, white tile floors, big bright bathrooms, and lots of windows—although there isn't really a view. The rooms look out onto the concrete plaza below, where there's a restaurant and some lawyers and accountant offices—not particularly *bonita.* You might as well ask for the larger suite in back (room #12 or #10), which is quieter. *Colegio Militar s/n, at Hidalgo. ☎ 612/145-0850. $600 double. MC, V. Amenities: Wi-Fi. In room: A/C, TV.*

→ **Las Casitas** A charming if ramshackle alternative to the pricier places in town. The old-time Todos Santos resident and owner Wendy is a glass artist who uses the hotel space to display her art works. The six adobe-walled bungalows she watches over at her bed-and-breakfast are clustered within a mature garden of mango, banana, palm, and hibiscus trees and some feature bay windows and palapas tied with yucca string. Surfers, families, and singles all come back for the idiosyncratic sensibility of the place. The share one, share alike breakfast, which Wendy boasts is one of the best in town, says it all. "If we shared food, there'd be peace on this planet" is her motto. Considering how good it is—you'll get everything from Las Casitas blended coffee to filling egg dishes—she just may be right. *Rangle s/n, between Obregón and Hidalgo. ☎ 612/145-0255. www.lascasitasbandb.com. US$55–US$90 double. Includes breakfast. No credit cards. Amenities: Breakfast room; Wi-Fi.*

Doable

Best → **Casa Bentley** ★★ This spot is basically three homes on a .8-hectare (2-acre) lot that are now one split-level rambling unit. The owner, professor of geology Bob Bentley, has called Todos Santos home for more than 20 years and has incorporated much of his love for rocks into the design of this very unusual, comfortable, and spectacular boutique hotel, modeled after a Portuguese castle. The private suites have patios and the rooms are large, with rock walls, high ceilings, views of the surrounding garden, Saltillo tiled floors, books for guests to read, arched doorways, and heavy wide wooden beds. Words don't do it justice—this is a remarkable place. *Calle del Pilar 38. ☎ 612/145-0276. www.casabentleybaja.com. US$80–US$250 double depending on length of stay and season. MC, V. Amenities: Outdoor kitchen; 300-count Egyptian linens; a large heated pool with waterfalls; Wi-Fi.*

→ **Hotel California** ★★★ A fabulous little hotel built in a renovated 19th-century building on the main street of town, the Hotel California has *no* connection to the Eagles song of the same name. Now that that's out of the way, you can focus on the important matters. With deep dark hued walls, hand-blown colored glass chandeliers, antiqued carved heavy wood, and Moorish accents, the place feels like a swanky L.A. joint crossed with old-school Todos Santos ambience. It used to be a rundown surfers hotel but has been upgraded and redecorated, mainly by the late owner John Stewart and his wife Debbie. He was a talented designer and lighting expert, with a great sense of color, and his legacy lives on in the hotel's wonderful balance of color and light. Although the rooms on the street can be noisy, those looking out southwest over the restaurant patio below aren't *and* they have large terraces and an ocean view. On occasional weekends, there's live music in the courtyard off the bar below, but that stops around 11pm. *Calle Juárez, corner of Morelos. ☎ 612/145-0525 or -0522. info@hotelcaliforniabaja.com. US$95–US$220 depending on season. MC, V. Amenities: Laundry service; small pool; terraces. In room: A/C, fans, Internet (in some rooms).*

→ **Posada del Molino** The Posada is a former trailer park that has been remodeled according to the one-story brick "colonial" style of the town. Built around the ruins of the 100-year-old sugar mill's chimney, the spacious and well-ventilated rooms in the redbrick front section look out onto a large, lovely pool. The larger rooms have more of a full kitchen and a bigger living room, but the smaller rooms are still quite big and are a better value if you can share one (and cook at the outside barbecue). Run by Alice Corado and her two surfer sons, the place attracts Europeans in summer, and surfers, artists, and retirees the rest of the time. *Rangel, between Villarino and O. Verduzco. ☎ 612/145-0233. US$90 double, US$120 suite. 7th night is free. MC, V. Amenities: Beach mats and towels; CD players; Internet; library. In room: A/C, TV, fridge.*

Splurge

→ **The Todos Santos Inn** ★★★ Come and get it, if you can afford it. In a remodeled historic house, the Todos Santos is a quiet, beautiful, and elegant place to stay but the prices reflect that. The newly remodeled Inn was once a sugar baron's hacienda and has also been a general store, cantina, and school. The rooms have windows opening to the street on one side and to the lush garden on the other. The walls are thick, the ceilings high, and the linens luxurious. The bathrooms are all Talavera tiled and there's tasteful antique furniture scattered throughout. Lower rooms and suites look out onto the pool.

Calle Legaspi 33, between Topete and Obregón. ☎ 612/145-0040. www.todossantosinn.com. Closed Sept. US$185 double. No credit cards. In room: A/C.

EATING

Sick of Mexican food? **Suki's** (Hidalgo, between Rangel and Cuauhtemoc; ☎ **612/145-0619;** main courses $100–$120; no credit cards; Tues–Sat 5–9pm) has delicious Asian fusion served under guava, banana, papaya, and mango trees and at small tables connected by paved pathways flowing down a hillside. Owners Suki and Matt Knoke traded their pick-up truck for this spot in the residential section of town, and Todos Santos is all the better for it. A Korean immigrant, Suki stirs up everything from coconut curry soup to pad Thai to vegan dishes with the help of husband Matt. The only bad thing about Suki's is that it's only around during winter months.

Part of the Hotel California, the excellent if pricey Best **La Coronela Restaurant and Bar** ★★ (Hotel California, Calle Juárez; main courses $70–$220; MC, V; daily 7am–11pm) sprawls out onto a back patio abutting the hotel. Executive chef Dany Lamote serves up "nouvelle fusion" dishes like duck breast with wild honey and saffron glaze, salmon on rosemary skewers, and seafood burritos. There are also great breakfasts like the Brie and asparagus omelet or chicken frittata and fresh homemade cinnamon rolls or fruit turnovers, and for lunch you'll find salads, pasta, and steak burgers. At night, this is about the hottest spot around, with live guitar, jazz, and blues (on Sat). It's the closest thing to a singles bar you'll find in town.

Probably the best place to eat (and sometimes party) in town, Best **The Café Santa Fe** ★★★ (Calle Centenario 4; ☎ **612/145-0340;** main courses $180–$440; MC, V; Wed–Mon noon–11pm, closed part of Sept. and Oct.) put Todos Santos on the boho-art colony map nearly 20 years ago when chef Ezio Colombo emigrated from North Italy and started the restaurant with his Asian-American wife Paula. This is where modern Todos Santos got reborn, and began to draw day-trippers from Los Cabos and La Paz. Sit in the enclosed dining room or the palapa covered courtyard, surrounded by the garden, and indulge in their fantastic capriccio de tuna, amazing lobster ravioli (minimalist yet succulent), fresh mixed organic salad, and flan or tiramisu for dessert. There's also killer pizza and calzones for $150 to $250, though anything you order here will equal a perfect meal.

At the other end of the spectrum, **Caffé Todos Santos** (Centenario 33, across from the Todos Santos Inn; ☎ **612/145-0300;** main courses $100–$120; no credit cards; Tues–Sun 7am–9pm) used to be a favorite brunch and lunch place but prices are escalating and quality is declining. A turkey sandwich for $120!? No sandwich should cost that much, especially since instead of a nice juicy breast, I got somewhat shredded dark meat. Add to that surly waitresses and you gotta wonder why the place is still full of tourists.

On the Degollado (the main hwy. to Los Cabos) at Rangel, **Ana's Café** (☎ **612/145-0824;** main courses $30–$45; no credit cards; daily 8am–8pm) boasts a small curved counter open to the street where Ana cooks the cheapest, tastiest, and biggest breakfast in town. In addition to chilaquiles verdes and huevos rancheros, she can whip you up hot cakes, enchiladas verdes, chili rellenos, and more for lunch.

Meanwhile across the street **Miguel's** (corner Degollado and Rangel; ☎ **612/145-0735;** main courses $50; no credit cards; Thurs–Tues 8am–9pm) has the best chile rellenos in town. The recipes, cooked by the local chef, are different from those you may have tried elsewhere in Mexico. Yet everything, from the regular cheese rellenos to the lobster rellenos, somehow tastes like Grandma's, probably because many of these recipes were passed down from generations ago. The floor is sand, the roof palm, the walls sticks, and it's a bit noisy since it's close to the highway, but it's still charming.

The best tacos in town are at **Barajas Tacos** (corner of Cuauhtemoc; no phone; nothing over $70; no credit cards; Tues–Sun 8am–9pm), where you can belly up to the bar to eat elbow to elbow with locals, truck drivers, and a smattering of tourists. Everyone slathers on their choice of many salsas on fish, carne asada, papas, and shrimp tacos. Don't forget the grilled jalapeños and fresh peeled cucumber slices that seem to be a fixture at Baja taco stands; or their special coleslaw or guacamole. Fish is served 8am to 6pm and meat after 6pm daily.

You can eat family style a few blocks up and in from the highway at **La Ramada Racing** (Colegio Militar, corner of Obregón; no phone; nothing over $70; no credit cards; Tues–Sun 11am–3:30pm). The restaurant is actually set on the porch of a home where the mother cooks delicious and reasonable fish filets (served mojo de ajo or grilled) and Mexican plates daily. Big chunks of garlic float in the buttery mojo de ajo sauce; empapelado style fish comes steamed with chiles, onions, and tomatoes; and huevos *todosantenos* are cooked with rajas, onions, and cheese. You can even get fries and hamburgers for just $25.

Just up the street, twin brothers Jose and Ricardo Marco Salgada cook up yummy and cheap seafood at **Mi Costa** (Colegio Militar s/n, corner M. Ocampo; ☎ **612/156-9932;** main courses $25–$170; no credit cards; Mon–Fri 11am–7pm; Sat–Sun noon–7pm), a sand-floor palapa-roofed joint. You can get ceviche tacos for $25; snail, octopus, clam, shrimp, scallop, oyster, or giant mixed seafood cocktails for $85; and standard fish filets for $100 to $170. For that last price you get *huge* portions with two to three filets, so take a friend and split it.

PARTYING

On the upper level of the Hotel California (p. 435) is the **Tequila Bar,** complete with red and black settees and a huge selection of tequilas, including their own boutique label, "Hotel California."

Giving the Tequila Bar a run for its money is **La Copa** (Legaspi 33; ☎ **612/145-0040**), the small wine bar on the lower level of the Todos Santos Inn. Gallery Todos Santos owner Michael Cope is opening a small restaurant serving yummy tapas and Asian crossover hors d'oeuvres 3 nights a week (Tues, Fri, and Sat) to go with the wine and dynamite margaritas at the bar. As a *wine* bar, however, they could have more local wines; that said, the list of 22 wines has good selections from New Zealand, Chile, and Napa. Arranged outside around a fountain, and nestled in the hotel's lush gardens, it's a quiet, cool, sophisticated, and civilized space, with a heavy wood bar set against an ancient (looking) stone wall. You pay for the ambience, though (wines are $60–$90 per glass). The gay-friendly crowd is made up of people staying at the inn or local expats meeting up with friends.

SIGHTSEEING

During the **Festival Fundador** (Oct 10–14), which celebrates the founding of the town in 1723, streets around the main plaza fill with food, games, and wandering troubadours. Many of the town's shops and some restaurants close from the end of September through the festival. The Arts Festival, held in February, seems to be gaining importance, with film festivals, dance and music performances, and more.

Todos Santos is going to need more than a sprinkling of pixie dust to make it a Pueblo Magico. If you don't believe me, just drop by the only museum in town, the **Centro Cultural** (Benito Juárez at Obregón; ☎ **612/145-0021;** free admission; Mon–Fri 8am–7pm; Sat–Sun 10am–2pm). The portales around the center courtyard actually house the museum, and the collection itself looks like it could have been collected at flea markets. The most notable thing here is the collection of historical photographs of families that settled the town.

PLAYING OUTSIDE

Todos Santos is all about surfing. Sure, there are other outdoor options nearby (see p. 378 under San José and p. 407 under Cabo San Lucas), but you should really spend as much time on your board as possible while here.

The first decent (and easy and accessible) break is at **Los Cerritos,** about 19km (12 miles) south of town. Cerritos is an easy right point break, a long board newbies kind of place that's low-key and very friendly. North of Todos Santos there are breaks all the way up the coast, most notably the closest break to town, a very fast board-breaking right that is not suggested for wishy washy surfers.

A couple of hundred kilometers up the coast is **Scorpion Bay** at San Juanico, one of the 10 best surfing spots in the world. It has a whopping seven fabulous right breaks. It's hard to get to, at the end of an axle-busting dirt road about 161km (100 miles) south of San Ignacio. Up at the northern border of Baja Sur, **Punta Abreojos** is 97km (60 miles) southeast of Highway 1 from Guerrero Negro. It's very sandy, and often very windy, but on the right swell you can get 273m (895-ft.) rights, especially in the afternoon when the wind blows offshore. Watch out for sea urchins in the rocks.

You can rent boards and other gear at the Costa Azul shop in town; see "Shopping" below for info.

SHOPPING

Small though it is, Todos Santos is a great place to shop, especially for art. One of the oldest galleries in town, run by talented artist Michael Cope and his wife Pat, the **Galería de Todos Santos** (corner of Topete and Legaspi; ☎ **612/145-0500;** mplcope@yahoo.com), has work by local as well as international artists. **The Annex** (Centario s/n, at Hidalgo; no phone) is a branch of the Galería de Todos Santos that has figurative abstract work. And the **Galería Charles Stewart** (Obregón and Centenario; ☎ **612/145-0265**) can't be missed. Once inside this eccentric "original Todos Santos artist's" home, you can view his work amidst his charming collection of, well, other stuff.

If you still haven't had your fill of art, head over to **Las Casitas** (see "Sleeping," above) to see Wendy Faith's glass art, or to the **Galería Santa Fe** (Centenario, at the Plaza; ☎ **612/145-0340**) to glimpse an eclectic collection of Mexican folk art and artesanía.

There are several typical souvenir places along Colegio Militar, as well as a branch of the **Costa Azul Surf Shop** (Colegio Militar s/n, at Hidalgo across from the Hotel California; no phone; info@costa-azul.com.mx) where you can buy swimwear and board wax, or rent surf equipment.

A great shop to browse is the **Santa Fe Deli** (Calle Centario, between Hidalgo and M. Marcas de Leon; ☎ **612/145-0301**) run by Paula Colombo of the Café Santa Fe. The deli is behind the boutique, which carries home decor, including woven twig lampshades and recycled tin laminated folk art frames from Nepal, and much more. The deli in back is a great place to grab enchiladas, sandwiches, fresh orange juice, and espressos for a picnic lunch.

If you need a pharmacy while in town, try the **Farmacia Misión de Pilar** (Plaza María Bonita, Colegio Militar; ☎ **612/145-0114**).

El Tecolote Libros (corner of Hidalgo and Juárez; ☎ **612/145-0295**) has a small but great (if pricey) selection of books about Mexico in English. There are also new and used Latin American literature, poetry, children's books, and fiction, as well as maps, magazines, cards, and art supplies.

Puerto Vallarta

Excuse me for being opinionated, but I think Puerto Vallarta is the most complex and diverse of all of Mexico's beach resort cities, offering a paradoxical innocence and sophistication that is, quite honestly, irresistible. Vallarta, as locals call it, is that rare fully functional place that manages to stay in tune with its spectacular natural setting and ecstasy-inducing partying scene. Jaded old Mexico hands may scoff at the planeloads of pasty-white tourists who extrude from the airport every day and Euro-trash backpackers may complain of the fact that you can get busted for the smell of pot on your breath. On the other hand, the police are out in force to keep you safe from scams and assaults—not exactly a bad thing. And compared to more developed resorts in the country, Puerto Vallarta is still a 20-something fresh young thing, blooming with promise despite increasing numbers of tourists.

The Aztecs, who went on to dominate and define Mexico just prior to the arrival of the Spanish, originated from just up the coast in Nayarit. While civilizations rose and fell elsewhere, though, Vallarta, protected by the wide Bay of Banderas, saw little activity for hundreds of years. It took Hollywood, personified by director John Huston and an all-star cast of horny actors at the peak of their notoriety (see p. 468 for info), for Vallarta to finally be discovered.

Vallarta was named friendliest city in Mexico by *Condé Nast Traveler* a few years ago, a recognition that everyone seems to know about, even the guy at the taco stand slicing off your al pastor. It's also known as the "most wired resort in Mexico" which makes it geek friendly. And it's the most gay-friendly resort in Mexico, hands down. If Puerto Vallarta lacks Oaxaca's Hippie Trail background, that's simply an oversight. Once here you have access to an ocean that is used by whales to birth their young, an expat culture that is seamlessly blended with the locals', cutting-edge world-class restaurants, so many hotel rooms that you can always find a deal, locally regulated potable water, and the best street stand fish tacos on the planet.

Don't be distracted by the timeshare sharks, the depressing beehive monstrosities of the Hotel Zone, the packs of gringo drunks stumbling down the malecón, or the presence of all the corporate evil-doers you came to Mexico to escape. Literally minutes out of town there are beaches where you can swim with giant manta rays and imagine Ava Gardner cha-cha dancing on the sand in the moonlight with her beach boys. Endless promise is here, from the 37km (23 miles) of still pristine beach, the safest and cleanest of any resort city in Mexico, to the miles of mountain bike trails, to the nightclubs that operate until dawn, to the cheap and easy transportation, to a climate and lifestyle that is relentlessly forgiving.

Simply put, I think Puerto Vallarta represents the best of Mexico. Maybe it's because I'm from California and Vallarta reminds me of the Pacific Ocean towns of my youth—uncluttered, clean, relatively undeveloped, and still wild enough to be exciting but explored enough to be comfortable. But I also think *anyone* can see that it's friendly, cheap, and incredibly alive.

Best of Puerto Vallarta

- **Best Hotel:** The **Hotel Premier** is not cheap but that keeps out the riff-raff, thank you. It's super convenient to El Centro but on a dead-end street at the beach so it's quiet. And it's an understated but elegant place—a true island of mature civility and high-end art, marked by a spa that's one of the best in PV. An afternoon spent here is like a vacation within a vacation. See p. 456.
- **Best Thing to Put in Your Mouth upon Arrival:** Once you land at the PV airport run, don't walk, to the **El Tacón del Marlín** restaurant that's on-site. They have another outlet in town but if you like quality burritos, you won't want to wait. Their marlin burrito is kind of like Puerto Vallarta—amazing, substantial, and wild. See p. 457.
- **Best Reason to Be Vegetarian:** The ever-popular **Planeta Vegetariano** is the kind of place people come to repeatedly, even though you can find vegetarian fare all over Vallarta. But here, it's the star of the show—platter upon platter of tasty fresh vegetarian and vegan choices are on hand. And did I mention it's all you can eat? See p. 458.
- **Best Place to Go Wild:** The animal-themed club **Zoo** is not for the shy at heart. But if you feel like dancing crazy to some throbbing beats, while surrounded by some hallucinatory wildlife decor, you'll feel right at home. See p. 464.
- **Best Peyote Pop Art:** The value of a co-op like **Peyote People** goes beyond just the depth of the selection on the shelves. Not only can you buy jewelry, art, and masks done in distinctive tribal designs—Huichol, Yaqui, Huave, and Tarahumara—but all are Fair Trade goods, which means you pay a top price directly to the maker. It's ethical tourist shopping at its best. See p. 475.
- **Best Karmic Work:** The Olive Ridley sea turtle is the unofficial mascot along this coast. Even as their eggs are being poached and slaughtered, local efforts

to protect them are gaining serious steam. You can be a part of this effort by harvesting freshly laid eggs with the volunteers of **Grupo Ecológico de la Costa Verde.** It's a 40-day-long process, but your time will be very well spent. See p. 486.

Getting There & Getting Around

Getting Into Town

BY PLANE Aero California, AeroMexico, Alaska, America West, American, Continental, Delta, Frontier, Mexicana, Northwest, United, and US Airways all make nonstop flights to Puerto Vallarta from U.S. hubs. There are nonstop flights within Mexico from Mexico City, Guadalajara, Leon, Cancún, and San José del Cabo (Cabo San Lucas) via Aerolineas Mesoamericanas, AeroLitoral, Aeromar, Aviacsa, Lineas Aereas, and Magnicharters. For phone numbers and websites, see the "Basics" chapter, p. 10.

Puerto Vallarta's **Gustavo Díaz Ordaz International Airport** (airport code PVR; ☎ **322/221-1325**) receives more than 450 flights a week. The airport is about 10km (6¼ miles) north of the city on Highway 200 as it heads towards Nayarit. Outside Customs you'll encounter crowds of porters, taxi drivers, timeshare shills—everyone calling out and trying to catch your eye. If you have a lot of gear, it's perfectly safe to immediately get a porter who can help you make your way to the rental desk or taxi kiosk or *casa de cambio* (money exchange office) and ensure that no one waltzes off with your bags full of scuba gear.

As is the case with all international airports in Mexico, the airport taxi is an inescapable evil. They cost more than normal cabs ($80–$220) but I recommend ponying up the extra cash for the convenience. You can find a city cab under the pedestrian overpass on the south side of the airport but that means hauling your bags and yourself out of the airport, up the steps and down the steps. And then you're on the access road that goes north so the cab will have to make a U-turn. It's doable but annoying.

Airport taxi rates are set by zone, ranging from $110 to the Hotel Zone to $200 to the Old Town. There are VIP pickups also available from www.puertovallartatours.net/airport-transfers.htm, for $109 to $196, depending on your destination.

Buses (labeled "Centro" or "Olas Altas") run into town from the airport and cost approximately $8 one-way, so that's one other option for getting into town. Buses operate from 7am to 11pm and make stops regularly.

BY BUS The bus station, **Central Camionera de Puerto Vallarta** (visit www.costalegre.ca/Busing_PV.htm for a map of the station) is 1.5km (1 mile) north of the airport and about 11km (7 miles) from downtown. It has overnight guarded parking and baggage storage. Most major first-class bus lines such as **ETN** (☎ **322/290-0996**), **Premiera Plus** (☎ **322/290-0715**), **Futura** (☎ **322/290-1001**), and **Pacifico** (☎ **322/290-0996**) stop here from Mazatlán, Manzanillo, Guadalajara, and Mexico City for $130 to $800 depending on the trip distance.

BY CAR The coastal **Highway 200** is the only choice from Mazatlán (6 hr. north) or Manzanillo (4 hr. south). Highway 15 from Guadalajara through Tepic takes 6 hours. Bypassing Tepic will save you 2 hours; go on Highway 15A from Chapalilla to Compostela, and then continue south on Highway 200 to Puerto Vallarta. The road is narrow, winding, and two-lane, which means you might get stuck behind a bus or truck; be patient and go slow.

All the car rental agencies have counters at the airport and their parking lots rest on Highway 200 heading north, away from downtown PV. A shuttle will take you from the airport to the office where you'll fill out the necessary paperwork. Here are phone numbers for all options: **Advantage** (☎ 322/321-1809); **Budget** (☎ 322/321-2980); **Hertz** (☎ 322/322-2980); **Alamo** (☎ 322/324-1071); **Thrifty** (☎ 322/324-9280); **National** (☎ 322/322-0515); **Avis** (☎ 322/321-1112); and **Dollar** (☎ 322/323-1354). Call around and get the best price, but Dollar is my preferred rental choice here after having bad experiences with the others.

Once you have your car, you'll soon discover you're facing the wrong way for getting into town. Take note of the access road that the car rental office is on. It parallels the fast moving Highway 200 going north. You need to make a U turn to head south again and to do so, it's easiest to go north, in the right lane and turn off at the first stop light. Make a U turn here and wait for the light to allow you to cross the highway and then go south. There is a left hand turn light also on Highway 200, but it's short and a headache to use. Trust me on this. See "Basics," p. 49, for more driving tips.

Getting Around

BY BUS Taking the bus is the easiest, cheapest (just $4.50 a ride, so have small change), and most convenient way to get around Vallarta. Buses generally run from 6am to 11pm, and it's rare to wait more than a few minutes for one.

To see city bus routes, go to **www.todopuertovallarta.homestead.com**, but you really don't need to pay much attention if you're staying within the Hotel Zone–Old Town stretch. The destination of the bus will be written on the front: Just watch for the Tunel bus since it will *not* go past the malecón. Buses that have "Centro" over the windshield go past El Centro and on to Old Town. Buses to the airport say "Ixtapa," "Juntas," or "Las Palmas." Buses going south to Mismaloya or Boca de Tomatlán depart from Calle Constitucion and Basilio de Badillo in Old Town and will be marked accordingly. ***Note:*** The marina is covered by only one bus line.

BY FOOT After taking the bus, most people just hoof it around Vallarta. You'll want to walk especially if you're staying in El Centro or Old Town; this part of town is so condensed, you really don't need a car.

BY TAXI Taxis are abundant and easy to flag down on the street. From the Marina to Los Muertos, a ride will cost about $80 at most. Anywhere within El Centro to Old Town will be about $40. Always confirm the price before you get in, of course. If you're heading farther south, to Mismaloya, for example, it could be $100, to Boca de Tomatlán $120. Going north, from El Centro to the Marina is $50, to the airport is $80, and to Nuevo Vallarta is $150. A large van (capacity 14 people) will cost about $350 an hour. You can also rent a cab by the hour, usually for about $150. Some locals warn against being talked into going to a different restaurant by the cab driver (although that's never happened to me), but at least now you know there's a small risk.

BY CAR Driving isn't the best option for getting around PV—the layout is confusing and parking on streets can be a nightmare (except in Old Town). Most of the streets are one-way. There are two very convenient secure covered public parking garages in town, though. The first is at the Plaza Parque Hidalgo at the corner of Argentina and Avenida Mexico, on the left, a block before the malecón begins. The second is a multi-level affair that you'll spot just before you cross over the Isle Cuale into Old Town on Morelos. Both charge about $6 an hour.

BY WATER TAXI The water taxis for Las Animas, Quimixto, and Yelapa leave from Los Muertos beach in Old Town (next to the Hotel Marsol) hourly from 9am until 6pm and cost $100, pier to pier. There are also taxis from Boca de Tomatlán for about $65 but with the cost of a bus ($20) or a cab ($120) from Old Town to Boca, you're really just saving time on the water, not money.

Basics

Orientation

Puerto Vallarta is laid out in a grid along Banderas Bay. It's just over a half-dozen blocks deep in El Centro and twice that in Old Town. It shouldn't be that confusing to get around but I managed to misplace my rental car three times in 10 days. Maybe it's because almost nobody local uses street names when giving directions, instead referencing various landmarks like Señor Frog's or the Holiday Inn. Maybe it's because Old Town is alternately known as the Romantic Zone (a marketing name), South Side, Olas Altas (a street name), and Los Muertos (a beach name). Or maybe it's because the street names of even the major arteries change without warning. You could be driving in a fairly direct line from the airport to Old Town only to find yourself first on Avenida Las Palmas, then Avenida Francisco Medina Ascencio, then Avenida Mexico, then Paseo Diaz Ordaz, and finally Isla Vallarta.

Or maybe it's just the fact that two-for-one happy hours last all night long.

The basic flow of the town runs from the marina in the north to Old Town in the south. People sometimes say North Side and South Side to indicate the demarcation formed by El Centro, in the center. Moving southward you first pass the marina where the cruise ships dock, then almost seamlessly move to the Hotel Zone where all the humongous hotel complexes are located. After a few minutes you enter El Centro, the commercial heart of the city and where all the municipal offices are located. Here is where the malecón begins, on the ocean side of the Paseo Diaz Ordaz. The malecón continues along the water while Paseo Diaz jogs eastward and goes over Isla Cuale, the little island in the middle of the Rio Cuale that separates El Centro from Old Town. The neighborhoods here are the oldest parts of Vallarta—hence the Old Town designation.

The usefulness of the mental map I've provided above is contingent upon you taking a "direct line." Locals going from the marina area to Old Town usually entirely bypass the traffic crawl of the Hotel Zone/El Centro/malecón stretch by taking the Libramiento ring road that goes through the tunnels to meet Highway 200 in Old Town.

For simplicity's sake, let's forget about **Nuevo Vallarta,** across the Rio Ameca in the state of Nayarit. This blatantly cheesy attempt by developers to capitalize on their famous neighbor to the south is not worthy of consideration when you're trying to figure out what's where. You can certainly stay at one of the all-inclusive resorts here, but that means you'll have to pay to cab it to any action outside your hotel.

The northern **Hotel Zone** and the **marina** are where tourism has been writ large—the ginormous beehive hotel complexes here are just land-based versions of the equally huge cruise ships that dock in the marina. **Old Town** in the south is where Puerto Vallarta began and in many ways, is still the soul of the city. It's hipper, younger, and cheaper than other hoods. Its cobblestone streets are lined with decent affordable restaurants and the bars specialize in martinis. It's also the heart of gay PV.

In some ways, **El Centro** is a blend of both the marina and Old Town extremes. You'll get the sense of a working, living city here, with all its attendant options—cheap American fast-food spots are interspersed with high-end restaurants, art galleries, and Huichol crafts stores. You can shop, go wine tasting, have some fascinating conversations with the timeshare shills, go online 24/7, eat some of the best (and worst) food in Vallarta, and still have time to get into a fight with a gringo drunk.

The **malecón,** running along much of the coast, is the most common reference point in Vallarta, where everyone ends up at some point: sad, happy, lost, angry, desperate, hungry, and, of course, drunk. Go there at least once to take in all the emotions.

Bucerías, a small beachside village of cobblestone streets, villas, and small hotels, is farther north along Banderas Bay, 30km (19 miles) beyond the airport. Past Bucerías, following the curved coastline of Banderas Bay to the end of the road is **Punta Mita.** Once a rustic fishing village, it has been artfully developed as a luxury destination. In the works are a total of four exclusive luxury boutique resorts, private villas, and three golf courses. The site of an ancient celestial observatory, it is an exquisite setting, with white-sand beaches and clear waters. The northern shore of Banderas Bay is emerging as the area's most exclusive address for luxury villas and accommodations.

In the other direction from downtown is the southern coastal highway, home to more luxury hotels. Immediately south of town lies the exclusive residential and rental district of **Conchas Chinas.** Ten kilometers (6 miles) south, on **Playa Mismaloya** (where *Night of the Iguana* was filmed), lies the Barceló La Jolla de Mismaloya resort. There's no road on the southern shoreline of Banderas Bay, but three small coastal villages are popular attractions for visitors to Puerto Vallarta: **Las Animas, Quimixto,** and **Yelapa,** all accessible only by boat. The tiny, pristine cove of **Caletas,** site of John Huston's former home, is a popular day- or nighttime excursion

Tourist Info & Offices

The Municipal Tourism Board (☎ **322/223-2500;** Mon–Fri 8am–4pm) is at the corner of the Presidencia Municipal building on the southwestern corner of the Plaza Principal at Juárez and Independencia. They've got scads of brochures and a few serviceable maps and usually have an English speaker on hand. For more serious problems the tourist **police** office is right next door. **The Jalisco State Tourism Office** is in the Marina (Plaza Marina L144; ☎ **322/221-2676;** Mon–Fri 9am–5pm) and has info about Vallarta as well as Guadalajara, Careyes, Chamela, Tequila, Barra de Navidad, Tlaquepaque, Ajijic, and other Jalisco hot spots.

Vallarta Today (☎ **322/225-3323** or 224-2829; www.vallartatoday.com) is the city's only daily English language newspaper. It's not really a newspaper per se but mixes up a blend of local party pictures, recycled restaurant reviews, local artist profiles, a smattering of Mexico/international news from AP/Reuters, local gossip, tourist maps, and a calendar of local goings-on.

Vallarta Tribune (☎ **322/223-0585;** www.vallartatribune.com) publishes weekly and calls itself "Vallarta Bay's Most Comprehensive English Language Newspaper." Like *Vallarta Today,* it has restaurant reviews, activities, fashion, arts, real estate, maps, and more. They also have translations of local news from www.noticiaspv.com along with a very complete directory of non-profit charities.

Bay Vallarta (☎ **322/223-1127;** www. bayvallarta.com) is a bilingual twice-monthly that functions much like a local *Time Out,* which means it contains the most up-to-date listings for workshops, clubs, movies, bars, home delivery services, and restaurants. Of the three publications listed here, it's the most useful for the casual tourist.

Recommended Websites

- **www.virtualvallarta.com**: Probably the first website you'll want to check out if you've never been here and want to check up on news, reviews, and advice.
- **www.puerto-vallarta.com**: The city's official website.
- **http://vallartafish.8m.com**: A very comprehensive guide to all things fishy in Vallarta's waters.
- **www.discoveryvallarta.com/guide.html**: Queens, queers 'n' dykes, and other gay lifestyle picks in town.
- ***www.vallartascene.com/pvforum/phpBB2/index.php**: An essential place for tourists to ask questions and get answers from locals.
- **www.pvmirror.com**: A very current site that covers everything Vallarta related, without bias or overt commercial hype.
- **www.puertovallarta.net:** The closest thing to a yellow pages for tourism in PV.

Puerto Vallarta Nuts & Bolts

American Express The local Amex office has typical travel agency services, money exchange, and traveler's checks (Morelos 660, corner of Abasolo; ☎ **322/223-2955** or toll free in Mexico 01-800/504-0400). It's open Monday to Friday 9am to 6pm and Saturday 9am to 1pm.

Banks Banks are found throughout downtown, especially in El Centro. Here are some of the most convenient spots: **Banamex,** corner of Juárez and Zaragoza (☎ **322/222-5377**); **Bancomer,** corner of Juárez and Mina (☎ **322/222-1919**); **Banorte,** Olas Altas 246 (☎ **322/223-0484**); **Bital,** corner of Libertad and Miramar (☎ **322/222-0227**); **Scotia Bank,** Juárez 403 (☎ **322/223-1224**); **Santander Serfin,** Av. Mexico 1326 (☎ **322/222-6120**). The Plaza Genovesa and neighboring Plaza Caracol, in the Hotel Zone, have branches of Banamex, Bancomer, and Santander Serfin. Banks are open Monday through Friday from 9am to 5pm, and until 2pm on Saturday. The Bital bank at the airport (☎ **322/221-2061**) is open Monday to Saturday from 8am to 7pm.

You'll find ATMs all over the place, especially around the malecón in the little shopping arcades. Currency exchange hours in banks are 9am to 1pm. There are *casas de cambio* (money exchange houses) all along Avenida Mexico.

Embassies & Consulates The **U.S. Consular Agency** is at Paradise Plaza, Paseo de los Cocoteros, Local #14, Int. #17 (☎ **322/222-0069;** fax 322/223-0074; http://guadalajara.usconsulate.gov/Vallarta.htm). It's open to the public Monday through Friday, from 8:30am to 12:30pm, except for U.S. and Mexican holidays, and it's closed on the third Wednesday of every month for in-service training. Consular Agent Kelly Trainor provides emergency services to U.S. Citizens residing in or visiting the area.

They also provide notary service and receive applications for U.S. passports and Consular Reports of Birth Abroad (CRBAs), which are forwarded to the United States. For consular emergency issues, call the Duty Officer at the U.S. Consulate General in Guadalajara (☎ **333/268-2145**). **The Canadian Consulate** is at Av. Francisco Media Ascencio 1951 (☎ **322/293-0099;** Mon–Fri 9am-3pm).

Emergencies Tourists with complaints about anything from rip-off taxi cabs to the ubiquitous timeshare sharks should contact the consumer protection office **PROFECO** (☎ **322/225-0000;** Mon–Fri 8:30am–3:30pm). Just to add salt to the wound, though, it's likely nobody will speak English when you call.

Other useful numbers include: **Police emergency** (☎ **060**); **local police** (☎ **322/290-0513** or -0512); **intensive care ambulance** (☎ **322/225-0386;** note: English-speaking assistance is not always available at this number).

Hospitals If you need medical aid, then you're in luck, sort of. Vallarta is full of hospital facilities that rival anything in the U.S. (and are better than what I can get via my local Blue Cross). For 24-hour service, there's **Ameri-Med Urgent Care** (Av. Francisco Medina Ascencio at Plaza Neptuno, D-1; ☎ **322/221-0023;** www.ameri med-hospitals.com). Down in Old Town there's **C.M.Q.** (Basilio Badillo 305; ☎ **322/223-1919**). Finally, **Hospital Medasist** (Manuel M. Dieguez 2360; ☎ **322/223-0444**) has complete medical assistance with English-speaking doctors and accepts most insurance plans.

Internet Cafes/Wireless Hot Spots **Aquarius Internet** (Juárez 523; ☎ **322/282-1168**) has to be the absolutely best net deal anywhere in PV. They're open 24 hours, 364 days a year, except Christmas, and have 48 terminals with Skype, USB hookups, and cameras—all for $200 for 2 hours, plus there's air-conditioning. It just gets cheaper if you buy more time. There are loads of other Net cafes scattered around town, but after the Aquarius the best is **Café@com** (Ola Altas 250; ☎/fax **322/222-0092**), which charges $20 for 30 minutes of DSL and is open from 8am to 2am, daily. It offers full bar service, Skype, and free Wi-Fi for 30 minutes (with a beer order). A less intoxicating option is just a few blocks down: **CyberSmoothie** (Rodolfo Gomez 111; ☎ **044/322-294-2565**) offers salads, smoothies, and massages in addition to DSL.

Laundry There are laundry services all over Vallarta and all charge by the kilo. Generally it'll take about 3 hours for a load to be washed, dried, and folded. Laundromats are generally open 8am to 7pm, until 5pm on Saturday, and are closed on Sunday.

Pharmacies **CMQ Farmacia** (Basilio Badillo 365; ☎ **322/222-1330**), is open 24 hours and makes free deliveries to hotels between 11am and 10pm with a minimum purchase of $200. **Farmacias Guadalajara** (Emiliano Zapata 232, Old Town; ☎ **322/224-1811**) is also open 24 hours.

Post Office The main post office is at Mina 188 (☎ **322/222-1888**). It's open Monday to Friday from 9am to 6pm, Saturday from 9am to 1pm.

Safety Puerto Vallarta is a very safe place. There are five police forces, one of which is solely dedicated to tourist complaints. And one of the first things that criminals learn is that if you mess with a tourist in any way, you'll go to jail. No questions asked. The Tourist Police are easily identifiable in their white safari uniforms and white hats. They'll give directions, offer advice, and basically serve as your advocate in any street-side disagreement.

If you ever have an occasion to deal with the cops it'll likely have to do with either dope or alcohol. Don't even consider buying drugs from anyone who approaches you—and they will—especially in Sayulita or Yelapa; the cops are vigilant about busting users. See "Basics," p. 41, for more info.

Telephone Tips If you want to use your cellphone within Vallarta (and didn't set it up with your mobile company before leaving; see "Basics," p. 46), go to the **Tercel** distributor across the street from the Sheraton (Av. Las Palmas 614) where you can buy a local SIM card for $400 and also purchase minutes. You can buy new card minutes at any pharmacy in town.

The telephone area code here is 322.

Water PV water has been certified as being fit for human consumption. That means that the water is clean and drinkable once it comes out of the water plant. Unfortunately, then it goes through questionable pipes, so my advice is to buy bottled water. Just about any restaurant you'll encounter will offer purified water and, of course, bottled water is available everywhere.

Sleeping

Vallarta has more than 33,000 hotel rooms—and more are being built every day—so there are plenty of choices, from the humungous beehive complexes in the Hotel Zone to sweet little four-room B&Bs in Old Town.

If you're without a car and just want to hit the town's bars and clubs, your best bet is to stay in **Old Town** where everything is within stumbling/crawling distance, be it the beach, Net cafes, coffee shops, clubs, or pangas. True, there's no Burger King or McDonald's or high-end restaurants (outside of Maximillian's at Playa Los Arcos) in this hood, but there's far less traffic and you don't have to navigate the tourist lemmings on the malecón. The vibe here is young, gay, and sophisticated without being moneyed. Old Town feels more like a neighborhood and less like a Disneyland version of tropical Mexico, which is what you get in so many parts of El Centro and around the marina. And really, if you *must* have a 31 Flavors ice cream or the obligatory stroll on the malecón, it's just a 15-minute walk into El Centro from Old Town.

Those who have their hearts set on a sparkling beach experience punctuated by a swim-up bar should consider the **Hotel Zone** at the other end of Vallarta. The beaches here have the same bathtublike quality one finds all along Banderas Bay. In the Hotel Zone, however, the water and the sands are perceptibly cleaner than at the southern end. The strolling beach vendors hawking jewelry and sarongs and hair-plaiting services are more numerous up here but, remember, the swim-up bar is just a few short feet away. While the name implies variety, the Hotel Zone is depressingly similar in tone—think mammoth high-rises with hundreds of rooms, warrens of blasting air-conditioners, and elevators filled with chattering tour groups.

Downtown Puerto Vallarta Sleeping & Eating

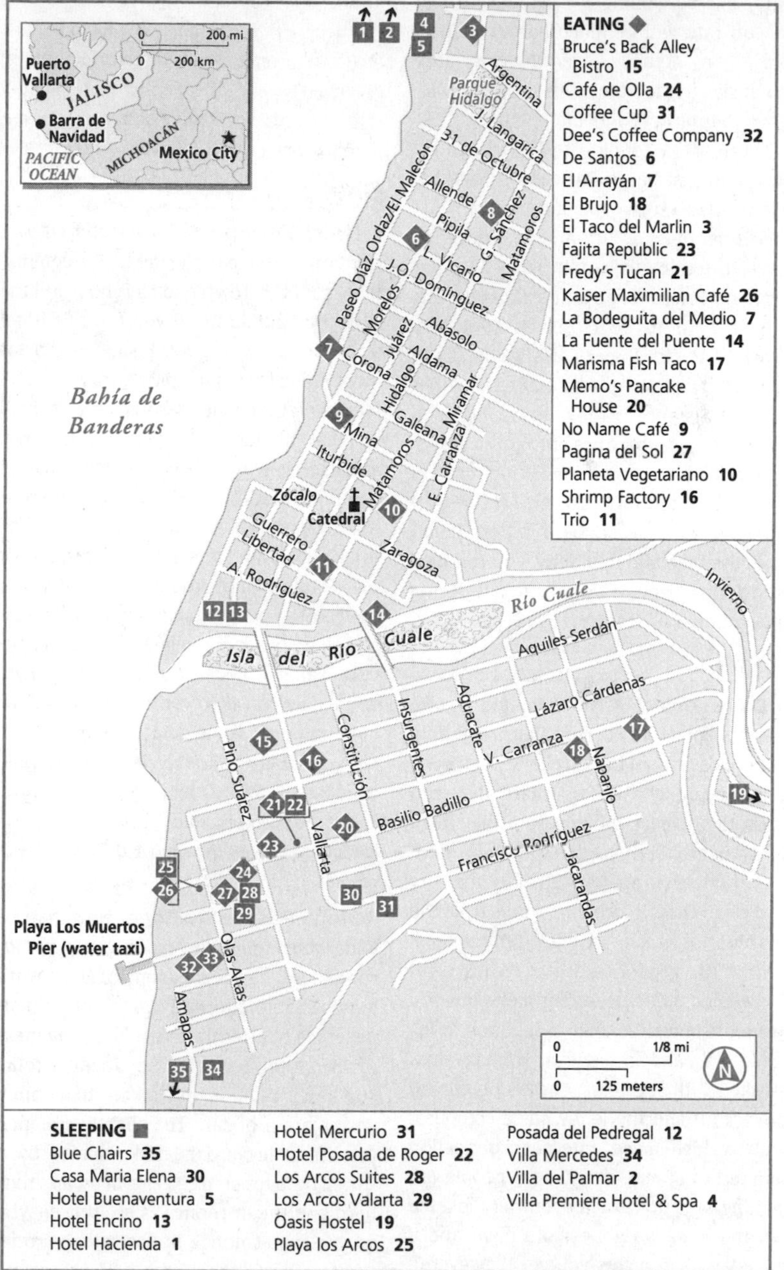

There are literally scores of possibilities here, but bargaining for a reduced low-season rate will be much harder than in Old Town. Actually, *everything* is more expensive in the Hotel Zone, from cappuccinos to Internet connection to taxis.

There are a couple of RV parks in PV but your best bet is **Rancho 3 Portales** (☎ **322/222-1213;** www.3portales.com) just this side of the Rio Ameca bridge to Nayarit. It's low-key, and perfect for car camping. Prices vary by the size of your rig. If you want to be closer to town, try **Trailer Park Puerto Vallarta** (Calle Francia 143; ☎ **322/224-2828**) within walking distance of downtown PV. Book ahead because there are only 49 spaces.

Prices quoted below are for high season rates. During low season (May–Oct) expect to pay at least one-third less. If you have the time and flexibility, you can bargain for an even more drastic cut during the nadir of low season (Aug–Sept).

Hostels

→ **Oasis Hostel** ★ An estimated 50,000 tourists flood into Puerto Vallarta a month, but only a few are backpackers looking for a European-style hostel where they can stash their sleeping bag before they head to the beach. Perhaps that's because there is only one good hostel in all of PV, the cozy and clean Oasis. More than a mile from the Los Muertos beach, it's small—only 20 bunk beds in two gender separated rooms, eight for women and a dozen for men—but you get extra amenities like a laundry room, cable TV, and a central kitchen area stocked with $25 beers. There's no curfew or lockout and the lobby has a computer with a high-speed Internet connection (limited to 15 min. at a time if people are waiting). It's not exactly centrally located but the price is right—$130 a night and if you stay for 6 nights you get the seventh free. Plus, the rates include a Continental breakfast. *222 Libramiento.* ☎ *322/222-2636. http://oasishostel.com. $130 per bed, with a $50 deposit for keys and bedding. Breakfast included in rates. No credit cards. Amenities: Breakfast room; Internet; kitchen; laundry room; security box; shared bathrooms; sheets; TV (in common room). In room: Lockers.*

Cheap

→ **Hotel Encino** ★★ The location alone, right on the edge of the Rio Cuale, equidistant from Old Town and El Centro and the malecón, should make you put this hotel on your radar. Yet the Encino has a lot more going for it, including a cozy intimate feel, even though its 75 rooms aren't small by local standards. The decor is also pleasantly retro, with old-school *alegré* (cheer) complimented by bright pink/purple pastels against white stucco, red tile roofs, brick arches, and tiled kitchenettes. Even if the Hotel Encino's rooms are a bit worn, the rooftop pool is fabulous and offers an amazing 360-degree view of all of downtown Vallarta. Because you are downtown, you'll need to ask for a room in the back or high up to get some quiet time. *Juárez 122.* ☎ *322/222-0051. www.hotelencino.com. $662 double. AE, MC, V. Amenities: Restaurant; sports bar; coffee shop; beauty salon; car rental; gym; pool. In room: A/C, TV, safe, telephone.*

→ **Hotel Posada de Roger** Now that the venerable Molino de Agua is gone, this 47-room hotel has become one of Old Town's most reliable alternatives, the place people come to after they've fled the madness of the Hotel Zone. It's nominally a four-star but I recommend taking that rating with a grain of salt. The slightly cramped interior courtyard is dark, shaded by a towering pepper tree. The beds are rock hard and the in-room TVs are tiny, maybe so you won't notice how small the room itself is. To add to this, the staff is surly and

Puerto Vallarta: Hotel Zone & Beaches

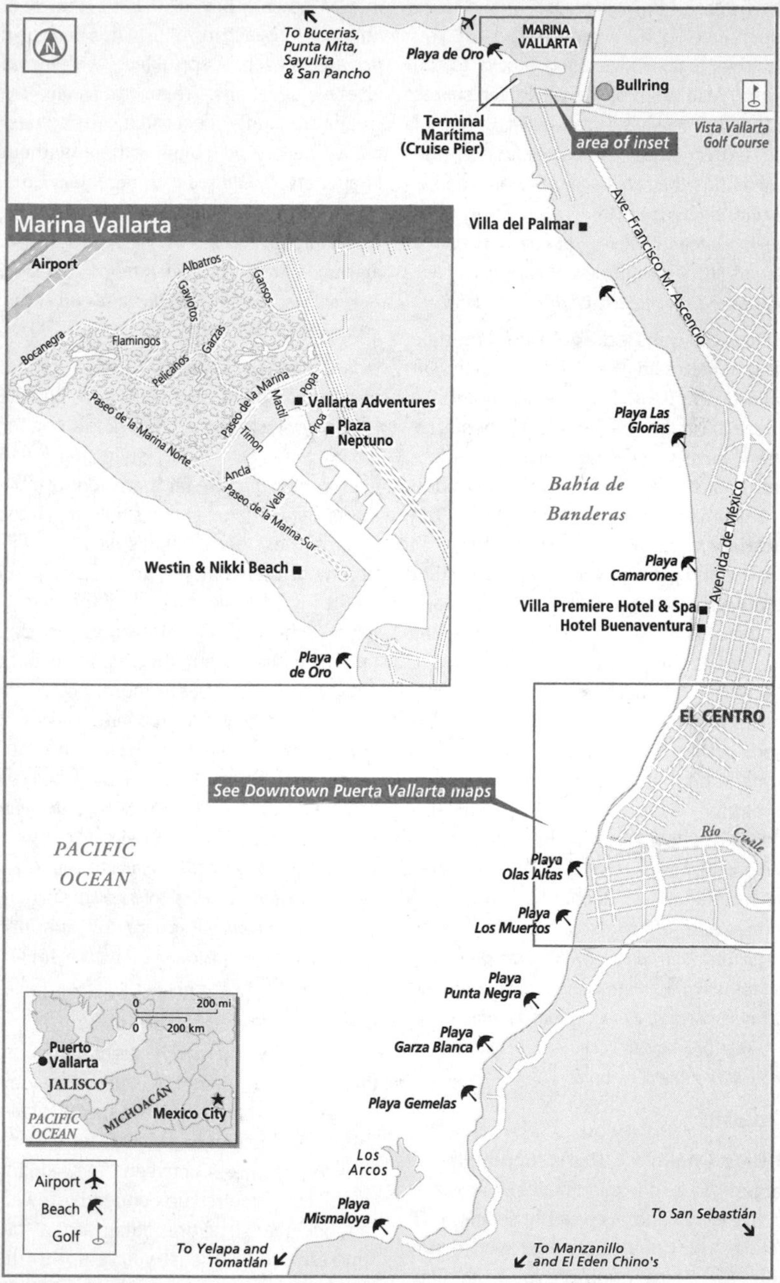

bars cover the windows. So why do people come here? Maybe because of the large upper level pool, a great option if you don't want to trudge the 3 blocks to the beach. Also the Posada de Roger shares space with Fredy's Tucan (p. 458), one of the better places for breakfast in Old Town. Plus the rates are quite affordable. *Basilio Badillo 237.* ☎ *322/222-0836. www.hotelposadaderoger.com. US$50–US$60 double. DC, MC, V. Amenities: Community kitchen; pool; safe. In room: A/C, TV, fans, telephone.*

→ **Posada del Pedregal** One long-time local I met said that after 30 years in Vallarta, this is still his preferred hotel. Try to see past the inadequate kitchenettes, which have only a two-burner hot-plate and a minifridge, and cement floors and walls, and you might understand why. The location, right on the lower end of El Centro, and just a few minutes walk either to the malecón or to Old Town's clubs and restaurants, helps a lot. (And though the flea market is right across the street, there's zero traffic, which means rumbling buses or hoards of serenading drunks won't wake you up at 4am.) The rooftop bar and pool, as well as the adequate, if somewhat spartan, rooms, help too. Finally, the low-key vibe, best sampled in the quiet interior courtyard, almost makes up for the sterile decor. They've got 28 rooms and offer discounts for groups. *Augustine Rodriguez 267.* ☎ *322/222-0604. hotelpedregal@hotmail.com. $550 double. MC, V. Amenities: Bar; elevator; rooftop pool; security safe in lobby. In room: A/C, TV, minifridge, some with 2-burner ranges.*

Doable

→ **Blue Chairs** ★★ This is supposedly the largest gay and lesbian beachfront resort in the world and it certainly seems it. Of course, you don't have to be gay to stay here—the casual atmosphere of the place is a draw all in itself. There are rooftop drag shows, and it's close to the best clubs in Old Town. They also have the most famous gay beach in Vallarta (it's their own private beach), sprinkled with—what else?—blue chairs. Their 40 rooms are clean, tastefully decorated, with super comfy beds, and come with or without kitchenettes. *Malecón 4 (at Almendro).* ☎ *322/222 2176 or 866/514-7969 in U.S. www.bluechairs.com. From US$99 double. MC, V. Amenities: Hot tub on roof; Internet; tour desk. In room: A/C, TV, fans, kitchenettes (in some), memory-foam mattresses.*

→ **Casa María Elena** ★★ There are lots of accommodations in Old Town, but the four-story Casa María Elena gets a nod for having a pleasant family-style charm and eight rooms that are far more comfortable than the cell-like choices at Los Arcos Vallarta, next door. There's no air-conditioning or pool, but you do get free Wi-Fi on the lower levels and each of the "suites" has a kitchen. The cheapest rooms are certainly functional but the casitas in back (which run about US$20 more) are worth the extra money. The top one looks out over the small courtyard, has great ventilation, and boasts lovely arched boveda ceilings. *Francisca Rodríguez 163.* ☎ *322/222-0113. www.casamaelena.com. US$75 for 2 people, extra person US$10 more. Discounts for weeklong stays, 3 hr. of free cooking or language classes from the owner. MC, V. Amenities: Wi-Fi. In room: TV, basic stove top, fans, fridge.*

→ **Hotel Buenaventura** Next door to the Hotel Premier (see below) is its sister facility, the much larger 236-room Buenaventura. Some of the rooms are massive and the gardens are spectacular—tall mature palms and delightful curving walkways snake between the linking pools. True, you're surrounded by towering beehive structures that are a tad repressive, but at least you're not in the Hotel Zone where your only choices are monstrous behemoths. This is very much a family-friendly hotel, but you can take advantage of that with the wide assortment of water toys available: paddle boats, boogie boards, kayaks, snorkeling gear. If you're thinking of going deeper, you can also get a free introductory scuba lesson in the pool. Props to the Buenaventura, too, for having two rooms for handicapped guests (on the first floor). *Avenida Mexico 1301. ☎ 322/226-7000, or 888/859-9439 in U.S.. http://hotelbuenaventura.com.mx. From US$129 double. AE, DC, MC, V. Amenities: Restaurants; bars; car rental; gift shop; gym; Internet; laundry/dry cleaning; pools; safe; spa. In room: A/C, TV, fridge, hair dryer, iron and ironing board, telephone.*

➜ **Hotel Hacienda** This 155-room hotel is 20 years old, built around the shell of the Hacienda del Lobo which dates from 1895. While the hotel has gotten mixed reviews due to its hard beds, I found its faux-Colonial style, evident in the stone work and *teja* (tile) roofs, charming enough to make up for it. Unlike other hotels in town, it's very Mexican in tone, from its decor to the temazcal sweat lodge in the pool/garden courtyard. And though the spa can't compete with that of the Premier (see below), it's certainly worth a look. It's on a mini-island, surrounded by a "river" of gurgling water that somehow soothes while you get pummeled, stroked, and rubbed. The chocolate scrubs and wine wraps here are almost enough to make you forget the over-priced Internet connection ($20 for 15 min. . . . are they kidding?). The Hacienda is *not* on the beach but there's a shuttle and the pool is large, and surrounded by palm tree and bamboo landscaping. The hotel's also convenient to the airport. *Bulevar Francisco Medina Ascencio 2699. ☎ 322/222-2692. US$96 double. AE, MC, V. Amenities: 3 restaurants; boutique; Jacuzzi; laundry service; pool; 24-hr. room service; spa. In room: A/C, TV, telephone.*

➜ **Hotel Mercurio** ★ This is a gay-friendly budget option with 28 rooms, ranging from singles (which will accommodate two) to king size. All have wonderfully firm mattresses, tile floors, and good linens. The bathrooms are small but doable. There's a small pool where skinny-dipping is allowed and the vibe is very relaxed and attitude free. The staff here is very welcoming and helpful. Maybe they're in a good mood because the hotel is right in the heart of Old Town, just a few steps from Olas Altas and all the clubs and bars and restaurants. *Francisca Rodriguez 168. ☎ 322/222-4793. www.hotel-mercurio.com. US$60–US$85 double. Includes all-you-can-eat buffet breakfast, 2 free drinks when you arrive. MC, V. Amenities: Breakfast nook; laundry service; massage services; pool; towel service; Wi-Fi. In room: A/C, TV, fans, fridge, kitchenettes (in some), safe.*

➜ **Playa Los Arcos** Playa is actually part of a three-facility complex that exemplifies both the best and worst of the weathered cobblestone street hood. The original building, the 42-room **Los Arcos Vallarta,** is on a cul-de-sac off Olas Altas. It's claustrophobic, reeks of mold, and security fascists roam the walkways, peering into your room to see if you have an unregistered guest (that is, date). Then there's **Los Arcos Suites,** opposite the original hotel. There are 44 "suites" available here, all with kitchenettes that are just barely adequate for making breakfast. The set up is essentially condo-style with a sad attempt at decor—from tile details and stripes on the floor, to in-room plants, to ornate headboards on the king-size beds.

Playa los Arcos is easily the best option of the three. If you're not a guest, you can still sneak in and use their small pool—they probably won't throw you out if you buy a few beers. But if you've got the budget, you might as well stay at the Playa. In addition to its pool, it boasts restaurants,

Two Very Different Out of Town Hotels

One risk of visiting Vallarta in summer is that you may find your vacation upset by the arrival of a Pacific hurricane sweeping up the coast from the south. When a storm comes too close, the government decrees that all boats must stay off the bay, which means that everyone is trapped *in situ* until the all-clear is announced. I was at **Majahuitas** resort ★★★ when Hurricane John swooped into town, forcing me to delay my departure by a few days. I couldn't believe my luck.

Majahuitas is a throwback to another time, a solar-powered miniresort of eight buildings scattered along a pristine little bay about 150m (500 ft.) across, on the cusp of the Cabo Corrientes at the south end of Banderas Bay, about 10 minutes from Yelapa. In summer, Ridley turtles waddle up onto the sand to lay their eggs and in winter whales give birth offshore. All year round a giant manta ray named Manny works the shallows, occasionally swooping out of the water in high graceful arcs. Majahuitas is powered primarily by solar electricity and there are no phones, no TV, no cars, no mechanical sounds of any kind except for the outboards of passing water taxis. There are eight buildings, only one of which has what you'd call real windows. The rest are semi-enclosed affairs with open decks that bring the outdoors right into your bedroom. (Thankfully Majahuitas is also largely bug free despite the proximity of the jungle.) There are two dozen fruit trees scattered around the property—banana, papaya, plum, mango—the raw material for the very reliable haute cuisine that the Majahuitas chefs dish up. There's also a small gift shop, a rudimentary gym, kayaks, and a candle-making facility—they use *lots* of candles, more than 100 each night light pathways in the sand to the various buildings. The resort used to be a private home but was turned into an all-inclusive hotel in 1996, but the feeling that you're staying with a large extended family of locals remains.

The coasts of Jalisco and Nayarit are changing rapidly but here at Majahuitas, it's still so wonderfully last century. It's the sort of place that guests describe as "magical" but that over-used adjective doesn't do it justice. It's a paradoxical mix of rustic and high-end—"barefoot with linens" says part-owner (and long-time PV resident) Margot Simms almost apologetically. It's an approach that is repeated at other PV area resorts but here the package feels totally natural, not simply a background set for a *Vogue* fashion shoot. What makes Majahuitas work is the people—a highly attentive friendly staff, four chefs who turn out one inventive fresh meal after another—and a true sense of getting away from it all that is beyond seductive. They can only handle 29 guests at a time and are booked up far in advance, mostly with repeats who stay a week or more in order to truly reconnect with nature and life. You can take a panga from Boca de Tomatlán in about 20 minutes. There's no address, but you can call ☎ **322/293-4506** or 800/728-7098 in the U.S. for info or visit

a bar, and a great location right on the beach. Its standard rooms are small but well decorated and clean. *Olas Altas 380. ☎ 322/222-0583, 226-7100 or 800/648-2403 in U.S. www.playalosarcos.com. US$74–US$100 double. AE, DC, MC, V. Amenities: Bar; 2 restaurants; Jacuzzi; laundry service; pool; room service. In room: A/C, TV, hair dryer, kitchenettes (in some), safe.*

www.mexicoboutiquehotels.com/majahuitas. Rates are US$250 to US$375 for double occupancy including all meals, and are based on a 4-night stay. MasterCard and Visa are accepted.

Although only 10 minutes away by water taxi, the neighboring coastal village of **Yelapa** couldn't be more different from Majahuitas. After decades of being a favorite day-trippers' excursion from Vallarta, adored for its laid-back hippie sensibility, Yelapa has entered into a difficult period. The 2,000 Yelapa residents are learning to enjoy the basics of progress: public telephones, electricity, Net cafes, and (soon) potable water. Unfortunately, they're also getting some of the less enjoyable aspects of modern life: drug abusers and assaults. It's uneasy in paradise after dark, but maybe it was inevitable. There used to be just one boat coming here a day—now the pangas from Los Muertos leave every hour, starting at 9am. And that doesn't include the party boats, booze cruises, divers, and Boca de Tomatlán taxis. Every day hoards of tourists arrive, the thump of the boats' disco echoing across the water far in advance. The day-trippers clog the narrow walkways, swarming up to the waterfall, down to the beach, plucking up bottles of *raicilla,* a zillion-proof bootleg alcohol. And then in the late afternoon, they reboard and vanish like a cloud of locusts blown away by the evening breezes.

Only after the boats leave for the day can you get a sense of Yelapa's somewhat damaged charm. Then the fishermen return, hauling their boats up on the beach, cleaning the day's catch; and the kids amble back from the primary school and head off into the jungle to play. After you've seen the waterfall, what else is there to do here? Plenty. There are lots of classes in Yelapa—take your pick between yoga, meditation, birding, filmmaking, writing, pottery, Spanish, massage, and painting—although most of the people I met just swam and drank. There are also far more choices for sleeping here than you'd think, most in the $350 to $1,200 range, but my favorite is the oldest and most convenient: **Hotel Lagunita** ★ (no address; ☎ **322/209-5056;** www.hotel-lagunita.com). It's right on the main beach—the only beach—perched on the eastern edge of the rocks, and even has its own dock. Some of the 32 rooms are pretty funky—there's no air-conditioning, bush-pole bars stand in for security, and there are lumpy beds and very minimal decor—but the location is primo and there's a very delightful ocean-side pool that is hard to beat. And the prices, US$60 to US$125, are mid-range. For food there are also lots of possibilities but again, if you're here just briefly, go with the oldest: **The Yacht Club** by the beach (no address; no phone; daily 11am to whenever). They're closed all summer, June to October, but when they're open they're *wide* open. Along with an "international" menu that includes everything from sushi to mole, and with menu items only costing US$25 for two, you'll get to work out to live reggae/world music on the open air dance floor.

MTV Best → **Villa del Palmar** ★★ This place offers a pleasant respite in the Land of the Giant hotels. It feels smaller than most of its neighbors, even though there are seven buildings with 425 rooms—all of them suites with cooking facilities. It helps that it's on 3.2 tropically landscaped hectares (8 acres)—there's plenty of room for the spa and fitness center, three pools, three tennis courts, and a basketball court (!). It even sits on a 100m (328-ft.) beach that is predictably populated with palapas, lounge chairs, strolling vendors, and guests passed out on the sand, working on a third-degree burn while they sleep. And they've got shuffleboard, boccie ball, volleyball, a water slide, and best of all, *four* bars! That means you can swim up to order that eye-opener and then plan the night's damage at three of Vallarta's most exclusive adult clubs—J&B, Christine's, and Nikki Beach—all of which are in the hood. One word of warning: You may get asked if you want a "Gold Card," which will give you a 15% discount off all the hotel's facilities. It ain't free. You'll have to sit through a 3-hour timeshare harangue to earn your gold and I have a feeling your time might be worth more than that. *Bulevar Francisco Ascencio Km 2.5. ☎ 322/222-0635. US$92–US$178 double. www.villadelpalmarvallarta.com. AE, DISC, MC, V. Amenities: Restaurants; sports bar; basketball court; laundry service; pools; security boxes; spa and fitness center; tennis court. In room: A/C, blender, coffeemaker, cooking utensils, fans, large fridge, hair dryer, iron/ironing board, kitchenette with 2 burners, microwave, safe, toaster.*

➔ **Villa Mercedes** This small 12-room facility is a cozy place to stay, so partiers should look elsewhere. Built in a family home in 1959 but renovated 7 years ago, it's still considered one of the oldest buildings by Playa de Los Muertos. It has thick walls, a small palapa near the pool, and is on one of the quieter streets in the historic hood. Basically, you'll get the feeling that you're staying in a small private home, even though you're right in the heart of Old Town. *Amapas 175. ☎ 322/222-2148. www.villamercedes.com.mx. US$84 double. Rates include continental breakfast. MC, V. Amenities: Pool; Wi-Fi. In room: A/C, TV, coffeemaker, fans, kitchenette, phone.*

Splurge

In addition to the Hotel Premier, you might consider a stay at the **Westin Resort & Spa** in Marina Vallarta (Paseo de la Marina, Sur 205; ☎ **800/228-3000** in the U.S., or 322/226-1100; www.starwoodhotels.com/westin), which offers doubles ranging from US$255 to US$599 in high season. Stunning architecture and vibrant colors are the hallmark of this award-winning property, and the fitness center is one of the most modern, well-equipped facilities in Vallarta, with regularly scheduled spinning and yoga classes. Plus, Nikki Beach (see p. 464 in "Partying") is right nearby.

MTV Best ➔ **Villa Premiere Hotel & Spa** ★★★ When you're feeling like you'd like a genuine adult experience (hey, sometimes dorm living just doesn't cut it), head to this delightful, adults-only hotel. It's sequestered on a quiet dead-end street that fronts the beach at the northern edge of El Centro. From here you can walk just about anywhere—or catch a bus easily down to Old Town. The 40 rooms are wonderful, with tiled floors, ginormous beds, digital TVs, Wi-Fi throughout (although it's not free), and 300-count thread linens. The overall decor is a tasteful mix of minimalism and high-end art, everything tempered by the soft dulcet tones of the staff, and the gurgling of the fountain out by the pool.

It's all so wonderfully soothing that you might never want to set foot out into the jarring reality of the city beyond. There are very few hotels in Vallarta that combine this blend of boutique intimacy, high-end service, convenience, and New Age sensibility (in a *good* way). Check out the second floor honeymoon suites that have balcony Jacuzzis, palapa roofs, and all the privacy you'd want while still having an indoor-outdoor tropical bonding experience. The icing on this very scrumptious cake is the spa. It's good beyond all description: two floors of meditative tranquility feature everything from facials and milk wraps, to coconut scrubs, to papaya hydrotherapy. *San Salvador 117 (at Av. Mexico).* ☎ *322/226-7040. www.premiereonline.com. mx. US$135–US$375 double. Amenities: Bar; 3 restaurants; cigar room; fitness center; laundry service; 2 pools; spa; Wi-Fi. In room: A/C, TV, coffeemaker, hair dryer, Jacuzzi, minibar, robes, safe.*

Eating

Puerto Vallarta has the most exceptional dining scene of any resort town in Mexico. It excels at cheap food, too. For $40—less than a Happy Meal—you can get a half dozen dishes, soup, and a big jug of the day's fruit-water at any of the town's many comida corrida spots. (Speaking of Happy Meals, Vallarta has more American junk food outlets than an L.A. strip mall, but why bother with them when such good Mexican fast food is on hand?) Equally filling and cheap are the scores of street stands that set up shop (usually during the day but some open as late as 4am) throughout town. The most popular stands are near the corners of Constitucion and Cardenas and Caranza and Madero.

If you're in the mood for fancier stuff, know that Vallarta hosts a 2-week-long gourmet dining festival each November. And with over 250 gourmet restaurants that serve cuisines from around the world, you're bound to find something to sate your inner foodie.

In addition to the following listings, you might also check out some of the hotel or bar restaurants in town, like the one at Nikki Beach (p. 464), as well as De Santos (p. 463).

Cheap

→ **El Brujo** SEAFOOD Although it's not easy to find, El Brujo (aka "The Wizard") is worth the effort. The homemade tortillas, chart-topping tortilla soup, and ribs and fish are bound to make you happy—especially since almost nothing is over $100. The decor is about what you'd expect for such a cheap joint: oilcloth covered tables and plastic chairs. It's a locals' fave for a reason, though, so you should expect to wait for a table. *Venustiano Carranza 510 (at Naranjo). No phone. Main entrees $80. No credit cards. Tues–Sun 1–9:30pm.*

MTV Best → **El Tacón del Marlín** ★★★ SEAFOOD My first encounter with a marlin burrito was at El Tacón's airport outlet 5 years ago. It was my last meal before leaving Vallarta and was a better memory than all the snorkeling, massages, or spectacular sunsets combined. So when I stumbled on their El Centro location, I was in heaven. No more stupid trips to the airport just to satisfy my hunger. If you've ever been addicted to inexplicably savory fast food, you'll know what I mean. Their huge burrito comes seared on a hot grill and stuffed with shredded strips of gloriously smoked fish, wonderfully counter-balanced with a slightly sweet-sour mayo dressing. It also comes with a little plastic cup of diced jicama, dressed in mayo but with a sprinkle of cayenne and lime, and manages to be totally filling, cheap, delicious, and exotic, all at once.

There's zero ambience, unless if you like plastic chairs, unadorned metal tables, and plastic ware, but who cares. Besides a selection of old black-and-white photos of Puerto Vallarta pre–*Night of the Iguana* days, the restaurant has pictures on the walls of pirates with lines through them, a plea to avoid any imitators. They shouldn't worry. Once you have a Tacón marlin burrito, nothing else comes close. On my last visit, a busker stumbled in with a boombox and did a wonderful version of "Sea of Love." I gave him $20 and the grill chef gave him a burrito, and I think he was happier with the burrito. Enough said. *Perú 1229 (across from Pemex station). No phone. Everything under $60. No credit cards. Tues–Sun noon–10pm.*

→ **Fredy's Tucan** DINER Freddy's is open until 2:30pm but don't get any ideas about ordering lunch—everyone comes here for breakfast. Over its 25 years of existence, the restaurant has learned to perfect this most basic meal. Nothing is over $60, from eggs Benedict to shrimp Florentine to huevos albanil. Best of all, the coffee ($12) is a bottomless cup. The decor is a little jarring for anyone nursing early morning hangovers (there's a little too much orange on the walls) but the seats are comfy and the service is fast and friendly. *Basilo Badillo 245. ☎ 322/223-0778. www.fredystucan.com. Nothing over $60. No credit cards. Daily 8am–2:30pm.*

→ **Marisma Fish Taco** ★★ SEAFOOD It took me a good hour to find this stand off Basilio Badillo (right before the Little Tunnel, coming from Old Town) but the search was totally worth it. Every local I talked to about taco stands mentioned Marisma as one of the best. The fish (and shrimp) are battered and deep-fried and they also have smoked marlin, ceviche, and a half dozen great homemade salsas. Diners sit under a huge ficus tree at one of the stainless steel stands on a quiet street far from the traffic on Basilio Badillo, sipping guava agua frescas while wolfing down tacos at $10 a pop. I managed to consume four, they were so good. *Naranjo 320 (between Basilio Badillo and Venustiano Carranza). ☎ 322/222-1395. Nothing over $20. No credit cards. Tues–Sun 9am–5pm.*

MTV Best → **Planeta Vegetariano** ★★ VEGETARIAN Perched on a narrow walkway at the end of a cul-de-sac near Our Lady of Guadalupe Church, this tiny 10-table hideaway offers one of the best deals in town. The all-you-can-eat buffet style set-up features a huge assortment of changing menu items. You can stuff yourself silly, without worrying about your conscious, on some of the best fruit-veggie-soy choices anywhere in Vallarta including: cream of cauliflower soup, soy enchiladas, banana lasagna, falafel in tomato sauce, and cactus and mango salad. As the name suggests, it's vegetarian, but since it's not vegan, milk products are used in some dishes. The vibe is very casual and easygoing. The walls are adorned in fabulously colorful dioramas of parrots and other tropical birds and while you're eating, you can page through copies of *Shambala Sun, Yoga Journal,* and other enlightened reading material. It's easy to miss, though: Look for the yellow sign on the walkway out front saying "65 Pesos All You Can Eat." *Iturbide 270 (at Hidalgo, up sidewalk steps). ☎ 322/222-3073. www.planetavegetariano.com. Nothing over $65. No credit cards. Daily 8am–10pm.*

Doable

→ **Café de Olla** ★ MEXICAN The sidewalk grill of this venerable Old Town landmark really attracts crowds—needless to say, during high season the lines go down the block. Once you've made your way inside, though, you'll find the food isn't spectacular, just simple reliable Mexican fare. Standards like tacos and burritos are all faithfully reproduced without many inspirational twists. If you want something a little more *real,* try one of the taco stands just down the street. The back room is the place to sit, so grab a seat there under the chugging air-conditioner and next to the trees going through the ceiling. *Basilio Badillo 168. ☎ 322/223-1626, 222-0087. Main courses $40–$165. No credit cards. Wed–Mon 9am–11pm. Closed Sept 15–Oct 15.*

➔ **Fajita Republic** TEX-MEX Folks come to this republic of fajitas for the sizzling fajitas but this restaurant also cooks a mean barbecue chicken, fish Oaxacan, molcajetes, and, according to a former bouncer at Señor Frog's, cheeseburgers that are the best in town. The mango margaritas are outstanding, too. But being a purist—or just unimaginative—I got the chicken fajitas. The guy at the table next to me got the *fajitas presidente:* Angus beef flambéed at the table with tequila. I could practically hear the skin of his mouth blistering as he shoveled in the hot 'n' greasy dish, and I'm sure he felt the same when mine arrived. Whatever, it was good. The setting is wonderfully Old Town in ambience—you'll dine on a patio, sheltered by a palapa and mango and palm trees. As twilight sets, the scene is dimly lit by woven twig basket lamps that barely cast a glow on the passing drunks and sad-eyed waifs selling Chiclets. *Basilio Badillo 201 (at Pino Suárez).* ☎ *322/222-3131. www.fajitarepublic.com. Main courses $74–$128. MC, V. Daily 5pm–midnight.*

➔ **La Bodeguita del Medio** CUBAN The original version of this local fave opened in 1942 in Havana. For 7 years now, this particular malecón outpost has been dishing out their great Cuban and Creole cuisine to some very lucky Puerto Vallartans. The rice cooked in beer is crazy good, and the shrimp flavored with tamarind and pork are positively revolutionary. But I'd avoid the mystery meat selection in the Cubano mixto appetizer sampler—it should remain a mystery—and the shrimp in orange sauce, which was a little too buttery and sweet. Whatever you order, wash it all down with killer rum mojitos and you'll be ready to scrawl your name on the walls, columns, stairs, and furniture like a zillion other visitors have done. Great Cuban music is played nightly (except Mon) and the restaurant is—surprise, surprise—cigar-friendly. *Paseo Díaz Ordaz 858.* ☎ *322/223-1585. Main courses $55–$220. AE, MC, V. Sun–Wed 8am–1am; Thurs–Sat 8am–2am.*

➔ **La Fuente del Puente** MEXICAN La Fuente is all about the view and people-watching. True, the food ain't bad—the pumpkin crab empanadas, fresh fruit crepes, Tarrascan soup, and filet mignon all deserve raves. Bonus: You even get a free margarita with your entree. But the open-air setting on the Insurgentes bridge at Rio Cuale is what makes this place really wonderful. It's a romantic setting, ideal for getting acquainted with that stranger you hooked up with last night. *Insurgentes 107 (at Rio Cuale).* ☎ *322/222-1141, -2987. Main courses $100–$200. AE, MC, V. Daily 8am–11pm.*

➔ **No Name Café** PUB FARE This long established sports bar boasts a dozen screens of every medium—analog, flatscreen, plasma—each one playing a different sport. Over the bar, football shares space with baseball, while in the main room soccer, hockey, and NASCAR compete for your attention. Personally, I gravitated toward the little black-and-white TV in the corner playing old boxing clips. But make no mistake. Competitive drinking is the real game here, and unless you've been in training, don't even consider joining in. There's enough going on, though, that you can discreetly order a beer and watch from the sidelines while the pros show you how it's done. Or sample some grub; the Q'ed baby back ribs are the most popular item on the menu, but I liked the deep-fried onion rings and heart-stopping sirloin burger. Forget the cases of sports memorabilia on display—the one thing that unites the crowd here is when the bartender pushes a buzzer and flashing red light that reads "Didn't wash hands!" when certain guys come out of the bathroom. Consider yourself warned. *Morelos 460 (at Mina). ☎ 322/223-2508, 322/222-6019. Barbecue $139–$239, pizzas $129–$229. AE, MC, V. Daily 8am–10pm; until 12:30am on weekends.*

➔ **Shrimp Factory** ★★ SEAFOOD Need to put on some weight? Then load up at the Factory, where gluttony is a prized characteristic. It's an all-you-can-eat sort of place, with shrimp prepared in a variety of styles from *ojo de ajo* (garlic) to deep-fried beer-battered, grilled, ranchero, and coconut. (You peel the shrimp yourself, which makes for a very messy but fun meal.) You also get lobster, fish, and chicken, all delivered quickly and without any raised eyebrows—even when you demand your sixth plate of tasty beer-battered whatevers. The signature drink is a very generous Margarita Gold with mango. Bonus: There are high windows that look out on the sidewalks of Old Town so that everyone passing can see how much you're eating. *Ignacio L. Vallarta 237. ☎ 322/222-2365. www.theshrimpfactory.com.mx. Main courses $200. AE, MC, V. Mon–Sat 11am–11pm.*

Splurge

➔ **Bruce's Back Alley Bistro** ★ STEAK The Back Alley is dark and cozy, befitting the name, but owner Bruce was a tad cranky when I dropped by. Maybe he's getting too much protein: steaks, chops, ribs, and lamb are all on the menu here. The signature dish is steak, hand cut from the cow and then hand cut again at your table—it's a wonderful cycle of butchery that melts in your mouth. I was most intrigued by the Bag of Bones, though: ribs, braised for 4 hours in a sweet tangy sauce of honey and pomegranate, and then delivered to your table in the bag. Vegetarians can order roasted veggies off the menu, but I doubt they'll feel comfortable: This is the sort of place where you use your fingers to gnaw away at bone. Bruce uses the same steaks as Brooklyn's Peter Luger Steakhouse, a venerated Brooklyn restaurant. But here the steaks are only $280—try getting a glass of water for that in Brooklyn. *Francisco Madero 225. ☎ 322/223-3560. www.brucesbackalleybistro.com. Main courses start at $280 and can reach double that for more beef. MC, V. Mon–Sat 5pm–midnight.*

MTV Best ➔ **El Arrayán** ★★★ MEXICAN Arrayán was voted "Best Mexican Restaurant" and "Best Moderately Priced Restaurant" in 2005 in a virtual Vallarta readers poll for very good reason. It's hard to rave more about this traditional/gourmet hideaway, marked by a Jaliscan tree, or Arrayán, in the main dining area. The walls are covered in tasteful Huichol art but it's the dishes that really shine. Home-cooked items include pozole and pork *pibil* (with Habernero chiles), mole with hazelnuts, a fabulous pork leg, and even grasshoppers (yum!). The prices are reasonable considering the quality of the food. Beef mole is $160, fish filet *achiote* is $150, and crab chile rellenos is $210. And by no means ignore the flan, at $50; it's the best in PV. *Allende 344. ☎ 322/222-7195. http://elarrayan.com.mx. Main courses $130–$250. MC, V. Mon and Wed–Sun 6pm–10pm. Closed all of Aug.*

➔ **Trío** ★★★ INTERNATIONAL You won't find better food anywhere in Vallarta, but it's upscale haute cuisine best served to those who never have to check the price of an entree. Trio is where other Vallarta chefs come to enjoy a meal they don't (or can't) make themselves. Throw in a Five Star Diamond award from the prestigious American Academy of Hospitality Science and you're in for a meal that is literally worth every centavo. Unique, delicate, startling, succulent, savory—any one of these adjectives fits the world-class food, worthy of New York, Paris, San Francisco, and Rome but at a fifth of the price. I had the calamari (marinated with cilantro-ginger, avocado, and a smoked tomato/jalapeño salsa), which I followed up with the sea bass, crusted with mushrooms and served on spinach with a red wine butter compote. You can't go wrong with any of the dishes, though, or with anything on the six-page wine list. The owners claim they're going for a Southern European feel, but the Tiffany-styled windows, mahogany bar, alfresco decorated walls, and rooftop garden dining area make for a unique vibe that's part southern European and part Mexican. *Guerrero 264. ☎ 322/222-2196. www.triopv.com. Main courses $85–$300. AE, MC, V. Daily 6–11:30pm.*

Cafes

➜ **Coffee Cup** COFFEE SHOP Their breakfast burrito is tasty but I came here for the pastrami sandwich—not the sort of thing you'd expect at a hole-in-the-wall coffee shop. Pastries, brioche, croissants, and smoothies round out the sweet offerings—you might want to grab one before heading to the Internet cafe across the street. *Rodolfo Gomez 146A. ☎ 322/222-8584. Main courses $35. No credit cards. Mon–Sat 7am–10pm; Sun 8am–noon.*

➜ **Dee's Coffee Company** ★★ COFFEE SHOP While the Coffee Cup up the block has its fans, Dee's gets my vote for having the best coffee, pastries, and breakfast bagels in town. Owner Dee Rindt has been running her shop for about 5 years, during which time she's made a name for herself as having some of the best baked goods in Old Town. She has a French baker do her croissants, but the pies, cakes, scones, and brownies are all made from her own recipes. You can sit alfresco out front or in the lounge area in the back where there's a lending library. While you wait for your cinnamon roll to be heated up, you can even check your e-mail on the free Internet connection. *Rodrigo Gómez 120 (at Amapas). ☎ 322/222-1197. Most items under $60. No credit cards. Daily 7am–10pm.*

➜ **Kaiser Maximillian Café** COFFEE SHOP/DESSERT Part of the Café Kaiser Maximillian restaurant, the Kaiser Café has coffee drinks with brandy and Kahlua, frappes, Linzer tortes, tiramisu, or a Honeymooner's Delight—a giant ice cream sundae for two, topped with tropical fruit. I recommend snagging sidewalk seating at the cafe instead of partaking in the slightly funeral mood inside the restaurant proper. It's Old Town's classiest restaurant, but an odd fit for the boho neighborhood. How does duck foie gras sound, or escargot in puff pastry? You get the idea—it's very European, elegantly prepared down to the white tablecloths, and as prim and proper as a library. I'll take my coffee without all the fuss, thanks. *Olas Altas 380. ☎ 322/223-0760. http://kaisermaximilian.com. Main courses $250–$350. AE, MC, V. Mon–Sat 6–11pm; the adjoining cafe is open 8am–midnight.*

➜ **Memo's Pancake House** CAFE I admit it. I was seduced by the name as well as the nice setting—open to the sidewalk in Old Town and done up classier than one might expect from a pancake house. Aside from pancakes (or hot cakes, as they're known locally), this place serves up good eggs and blintzes, as well as coffee. But avoid the waffles: I ordered an orange syrup waffle and got something that tasted oddly like cardboard, except it was just a little warmer. *Basilio Badillo 289. ☎ 322/222-6272. No credit cards. Main courses US$15. Daily 8am–2pm.*

➜ **Pagina del Sol** ★★ COFFEE SHOP At some point, you'll want to grab a seat on the sidewalk of this cafe that's right in the center of Old Town. It's that good a spot to order an espresso and try to figure out what you're going to do during the day. They have decent pastries, sandwiches,

"Beck's Best" ★★

Gary Beck is a writer who divides his time between San Francisco and Puerto Vallarta. He's been coming here for the last 27 years and has spent more than 20 years in the restaurant business. While you can find restaurant reviews in every guidebook, magazine, or local tourist rag, MTV Best **"Beck's Best"** is a unique publication, offering very up-to-date reviews and listings of just about every eatery worth noting in PV, even tiny street stands that only operate during the day. If eating is your primary vacation activity, this is an essential read. You can get a copy ($240) before you go from www.cafepress.com/vallartaguide or www.lulu.com/content/132501. Copies are also for sale locally at **The Book Store** (V. Carranza 334A), **Bruce's Back Alley Bistro** (Francisco Madero 225), **El Arrayán** (Allende 344), **¡Chili's!** (Púlpito 122), and the **Mama Dolores Diner** (Olas Altas 534B).

and a very nice used book library, too. For insider info on moving sales, sublets, classes, and more, check out the bulletin boards here. *Olas Altas 299.* ☎ *322/222-3608. Coffee $10; pastries $30. No credit cards. Daily 7am–midnight.*

Partying

Jalisco, the state that Puerto Vallarta calls home, lays claim to tequila, both the town and the drink. So, yes, it's the drink of choice in PV, be it mixed, straight, sipped, Jello-ed, slurped, or chugged. I never saw anyone snort any, but maybe I didn't go to the right places.

Like the drink of choice, the club scene in PV is intense, an often all-night affair that doesn't get interesting until at least midnight. There are more sedate possibilities where the booze stops flowing at 2am for those who have an early flight out, but for the rest of you, pick up a copy of the free bi-weekly *Bay Vallarta*. This local version of *Time Out* contains a very current and complete listing of the nearly 90 bars and clubs that you're likely to stumble into. And of course I list the best below.

Bars & Lounges

My favorite bar in terms of low-key sensibility is Old Town's **Andale** ★ (Olas Altas 425; ☎ **322/223-1054;** www.andales.com) right in the center of Olas Altas. The bar on the ground floor is open to the sidewalk and the passing pedestrian traffic is pretty much endless—and entertaining. The mood is loose and casual, making it an ideal place to stop for an afternoon beer . . . or a late night beer. Local expats and first-timers blend pretty seamlessly, as do the gay and straight and the old and young. The restaurant on the second floor is popular, especially for breakfasts, even in rainy season. It's on the second floor and worth a meal, not for the food as much as the view over Olas Altas and the stream of humanity below. There's also a newish three-story hotel—closed for renovations when I was there, on the third floor. I can imagine staying in the hotel would be noisy, but maybe that's not a problem for you. And really, what could be more convenient than being able to crawl from the bar to the elevator to your room?

Next up is **Hilo** ★ (Paseo Diaz Ordaz 588; ☎ **322/223-5361**), on the malecón, which is hugely popular both with locals and tourists. It's on the small side but there are

Downtown Puerto Vallarta Partying & Sightseeing

two levels, so be sure to slip the waiter a tip and ask for a table upstairs where it's cooler and there's a great view. Although it's said to be gay-owned, it's very much a mixed crowd. The crowd ranges from folks in their 20s to 40s, and there's zero attitude, no dress code, and no dance floor (although dancing on the bar is not just allowed but actively encouraged). They have name DJs and a largely techno ethos—although that may change depending on the night.

The restaurant/bar **De Santos** ★ (Morelos 771; ☎ **322/223-3052;** www.desantos.com.mx) is partly owned by Alejandro Gonzalez, the drummer for superstar band Mana. Consequently, the DJs here are the cream of the crop. Though the food is very good (if a little pricey), many people come just for drinks—either in the disco with its palm trees, belly dancers, and high-powered sound system or in the Sky Bar on the roof. The latter is the place to come if you're with a date. It's lounge-perfect, with comfy sofas and, as the name promises, a view that opens to the sky. Like Christine's and Nikki Beach, this is a place to dress up and act cosmopolitan.

No Name Café (see "Eating," p. 457) is the best known sports bar in Vallarta but a more low-key outlet exists down in Old Town at **Steve's Sports Bar** (286 Basilio

Badillo; ☎ **322/222-0256**). It's cozy without being small. All the action is centered around the curved wooden bar, with all eyes on the eight TVs hanging from the ceiling. It's *very* American, with American flags, a giant Budweiser sign, a Ground Zero memento, NASCAR signage, and a pair of Muhammad Ali's boxing gloves on display. There's free Wi-Fi here also, if you don't have enough screens to look at already.

Clubs

For a 180-degree change in mood, ambience, and clientele, drop by **Christine's** (Avenida Francisco Medina Ascencio s/n, next to the NH Krystal Hotel; ☎ **322/226-0700;** www.christineclubpv.com; cover $200 for men, $100 for women, plus another $50–$100 for getting seated soon). This trendy hangout is up in the Hotel Zone and is the home of house music in Vallarta. Name DJs from Miami and New York pop in regularly. It's a silly shell of a bar where the lasers dance through clouds of dry ice, flickering over the gyrating shoulders of the rich and famous along with the thin and young. If you don't fit that mold, don't bother coming.

At the marina is the PV outlet for **Nikki Beach** ★★ (Paseo de la Marina Sur 205, inside the Hotel Westin Regina, Marina; ☎ **322/226-1150;** www.nikkibeach.com/pv/findUs.asp). It's part of a country-wide chain of uber-cool hipster hangouts, and a *para tirar rostro* (see and be seen) sort of place. Technically, it's a restaurant but it's the bar that people come for—that and the signature white-draped beds-on-the-beach. Drinks are way expensive, but service is decent. The music is the latest in electronic, house, and chill, with visiting DJs often playing on weekend nights.

Right on the malecón are a series of clubs, starting with the so-last-century **Hard Rock Cafe.** Don't bother. It's boring, stupid, over-priced, and empty. I won't even give you the address. Instead drift down a half block to the MTV Best **Zoo** ★★★ (630 Paseo Diaz Ordaz; ☎ **323/222-4945;** www.zoobardance.com). This is on everyone's list as one of the best places to get wild and crazy without having to set foot into Señor Frog's. They've got a dancing cage, a galloping rhino painting coming out of one wall like a bad hallucination, and a leopard-skin/zebra-stripe motif going on. Who cares if the dance floor is tiny? Have a Gorilla (banana-rum-coconut cream-Kaluha), settle down at a banquette, and get ready to let your inner animal loose. After hours, the line stretches down the block and up the next street. Since only 350 people can get in here on any evening, arrive early.

Almost right next door is **Mogambo** (Paseo Diaz Ordaz 644; ☎ **322/222-3476;** www.mogambo-vallarta.com). Try to forgive it for having a badly defined African motif. With pool tables, it's slightly—ever so slightly—more adult than the Zoo. Covers vary but can be as much as $250 for men on a popular night. Drinks, however, are two-for-one all night, so come early to get your liver's worth. ***Warning:*** Supposedly this is a Ricky Martin hang out (although it's *not* a gay club . . . go figure).

Late Night Bites

When it's late and that last margarita isn't sitting too easily, crawl your way into El Centro and stop off at **Pizza Metro** (Morelos 685; no phone; no credit cards; Mon–Sat noon–4 am) for a much needed greasy anchor. This late-night restaurant sells $20 pizza by the slice, has only a half-dozen stools, and frankly, it offers pizza that's not very good. But when it's late and you're hungry, you probably aren't looking for gourmet—just something to settle your queasy gut, quickly and cheaply.

They're Here, They're Queer & They're Going Whale-Watching

PV is the most comfortable resort city in Mexico for the GLBT gang and while it's not quite the Castro District in San Fran, it's fairly common to see same-sex couples holding hands in public, something very rare in the rest of Mexico. Some things to keep in mind are that Old Town is the heart of gay Vallarta and *ambiente* is local slang for gay, so much nicer than *maricon*, thank you. There's a spiffy *Gay Guide to Vallarta* (☎ **322/222-7980;** www.gayguidevallarta.com) that comes out monthly, and the town boasts 16 gay bars at last count and a dozen hotels or B&Bs that are gay-friendly. There's Gay Bingo night on the roof of the Blue Chairs (p. 452), gay fishing tours, gay horseback tours, gay booze cruises, gay ecotours, gay tequila tastings, a gay wilderness park, gay happy hours, gay cooking clubs, gay auto repair shops, gay laundromats, gay cybercafes and, yes, gay whale-watching tours. Basically, if the straight world does it, there's a gay equivalent to be had here. Check out the gay bar and club listings earlier or visit www.doinitright.com for more info.

Gay Nightlife

Tired of margaritas? Then think about having a martini at the **Kit Kat Club** (120 Pulpito; ☎ **322/223-0093**) and **Garbo** ★★ (Pulpito 142; ☎ **322/229-7309**), two faves that are both on the same block in Old Town, both Art Deco in tone, both popular with the gay crowd, both with extensive martini menus. The Kit Kat is more loungey, with Jetsons-style signage, a large plate-glass front, and way comfy banquettes and chairs. It's also got a New York vibe—think live jazz and snooty waiters and more of a mixed crowd. For $80 you can get two-for-one martinis—all night long. Just up the block, Garbo is a lot more fun, gayer, and less stuffy. There's a piano in the back and, again, live jazz. Around the corner is **Sama** (Olas Alyas 510; ☎ **322/223-3182**), also a martini bar but smaller and more minimalist in tone than Garbo or the Kit Kat. The sidewalk seating here is a welcome relief since there's not much room inside.

Blue Chairs, the beach bar at the hotel (p. 452), is another popular gay hangout spot, as is **Club Paco Paco** (Ignacio L. Vallarta 278; ☎ **322/222-7667;** www.club-pacopaco.com), which stages a spectacular transvestite show on sporadic nights.

Live Music

In addition to great Cuban food (p. 459), **La Bodeguita del Medio** ★ (858 Paseo Diaz Ordaz; ☎ **322/223-1585;** cover $10–$20) boasts live traditional Cuban music, with boleros and rumbas nightly. The small dance floor here fills up pretty quickly.

If you don't have your salsa steps quite down, maybe first pay a visit to **J&B Salsa Club** (Av. Francisco Medina Ascencio Km 2.5; ☎ **322/224-4616;** cover $120). This is strictly a Latin-based club, with salsa, meringue, and samba typically on the roster. Live bands usually play on the weekends and locals love it as a place to come to practice their steps. At 8pm, before the club opens officially, lessons are available. It's got a sophisticated feel, plenty of room, a low stage, a huge dance floor, black lights, and portraits of Elvis and Marilyn Monroe on the wall coming in.

I'm not a fan of **Señor Frog's** (218 Venustiano Carranza; ☎ **322/222-5177**), but I'm willing to see its appeal. The drinks are over-size, you get five beers for $18, and the place is in full party mode. It's three stories of mayhem, an endless spring break that stretches year-round. The bar is huge and all the tequila and disco lights produce a psychedelic effect. It's a cartoon world here—literally, there's a big plastic cow suspended from the ceiling and various cartoon ninja frogs on the walls. For the competitive folks reading this, there are thong contests, wet T-shirt contests, wet boxer contests. One sign that's posted says it all: "Men—no shirt no service. Women no shirt, free drinks."

Heading to the Beach

From the first settlers from Asia to American gunboat runners, to factory fishers, and now to cruise ship passengers, the waters of Banderas Bay and points north have seen it all. Considering how much Vallarta has grown in the last 50 years, it's amazing that the ocean here is still relatively clean and the sands litter-free. Vallarta sits astride a 41km (26-mile) wide, largely clean, featureless stretch of white-gold sand. The water is bathtub warm, and the shore break forgiving, with few riptides, even though it's marked by a very rapid drop off. The Bay itself is very deep, more than 900m (3,000 ft.) in places.

The only blemish on this pretty picture is the fact that, after heavy rain, the rivers send a muddy runoff into the bay, turning the normally deep blue waters a murky brown. After a rain, one should avoid the following beaches according to a recent report from the Clean Beaches Commission: Quimixto, Las Animas, Rio Cuale, Boca de Tomatlán, Mismaloya, and Los Muertos. All registered unacceptable levels of bacteria. If you see a sign reading *"no es apta para uso recreativo"* ("not apt for recreational use") that means it's time to stay in the hotel pool.

Depending on the conditions, most of Puerto Vallarta's beaches are safe for bathing but not great for more active watersports. There are no waves to speak of and the underwater scenery is relatively devoid of fish (except for pods of coastal dolphins).

Beach Orientation

IN TOWN At the southern end of the malecón is PV's most popular beach: **Los Muertos,** in Old Town. It's got the most idiosyncratic old-school feel to it, with Mexican families, honeymooners, and drag queens all working on their tans next to each other. Ironically this is also the beach with the most constant whiff of gasoline in the water—caused by the pangas departing for Yelapa from the Los Muertos pier. If a hurricane is blowing in from the south, Los Muertos is about the only beach around for decent boogie boarding. Surfers have to either make the long trek south down Highway 200 to the Costa Alegre or north to Nayarit state, about 40 minutes away to the first reliable break just below Punta de Mita. See the "Playing Outside" section that follows for more info.

The **Hotel Zone** is also known for its broad, smooth beaches, accessible primarily through the hotel lobbies. Moving south from the airport is the **Marina Vallarta** beach, sometimes rocky in low tides but essentially a flat line punctuated by a series of short breakwaters. From the southern tip of Marina to the malecón, the beaches are **De Oro, Los Tules, Las Glorias,** and **Camarones.** They have names but there's no real demarcation between them since they are still pretty nondescript, flat, with just a few curvy sections. Starting at the malecón, the water becomes noticeably dirtier and the rocks and breakwaters of these beaches aren't even appealing for a quick dip.

SOUTH-OF-TOWN **Playa Mismaloya** is in a beautiful sheltered cove about 10km (6 miles) south of town along Highway 200. The water is clear and beautiful, ideal for snorkeling off the beach. Entrance to the public beach is just to the left of the **Barceló La Jolla de Mismaloya** (☎ **322/226-0600**). The movie *Night of the Iguana* was filmed at Mismaloya, and the resort has a restaurant on the restored film set—**La Noche de la Iguana Set Restaurant,** open daily from noon to 11pm. The movie runs continuously in a room below the restaurant, and still photos from the filming hang in the restaurant. It's accessible by land on the point framing the south side of the cove. Just below the restaurant is **John Huston's Bar & Grill,** serving drinks and light snacks daily from 11am to 6pm.

The beach at **Boca de Tomatlán,** just down the road, has numerous palapa restaurants where you can relax for the day—buy some drinks, snacks, or lunch, and you can enjoy their chairs and palapa shade.

Both Mismaloya and Tomatlán beaches are accessible by public buses, which depart from the corner of Basilio Badillo and Insurgentes every 15 minutes from 5:30am to 10pm and cost just $5.

Las Animas, Quimixto, and **Yelapa** beaches offer a true sense of seclusion; they are accessible only by boat (see "Getting Around," above, for information about water-taxi service). They are larger than Mismaloya, offer intriguing hikes to jungle waterfalls, and are similarly set up, with restaurants fronting a wide beach. Overnight stays are available at Yelapa (see the "Two Very Different Out of Town Hotels" box earlier in this chapter).

Sightseeing

Festivals/Events

Cultural Festival: Based in **El Pitillal,** across from the Marina, this festival features rides and exhibits, food and shopping stalls, and bands. In the second half of the month, the festival brings theater, concerts, mariachi band competitions, parades, and art shows to locations throughout the city. It culminates on May 31 with the city's anniversary celebration.

Charro Day: This day is a reminder of Jalisco's deep cowboy culture. A parade starts at 10am and winds through downtown with men and women atop beautiful horses that are totally outshined by the charro outfits the riders are wearing. There are also performances of calf roping, dancing, dressage, and bullfighting at charro rings set up around the city. September 14.

International Half Marathon: A 13-mile run for locals and international runners takes place during the first week of November. Visit www.maratonvallarta.com for info. Early November.

Festival Gourmet International: For the past dozen years, this festival has brought out the best of the city's restaurants for 10 days of classes, usually starting the second week of November. Included are demonstrations, special dinners, and cheese and wine tastings. The chefs from two dozen of the city's most reliably inventive and respected restaurants—joined by a sprinkling of international name guests—sharpen their blades to produce the sort of amazing palate-pleasers you'll never be able to reproduce at home. And why should you? It doesn't get any better than this. Visit www.festivalgourmet.com/index.html for info. Mid-November.

International Sailfish and Marlin Tournament: Also in mid-November is the annual sailfish and marlin tournament, now in its 52nd year. It's hosted by the Puerto Vallarta Fishing Club (www.fishvallarta.com) and lasts for 4 days. Registration is not cheap ($14,715), but the prizes aren't petty change either. Be the first to catch a sailfish of more than 65kg (143 lb.) or a marlin of more than 300kg (660 lb.) and you'll take home $109,000. There are also prizes for mahimahi and tuna. Mid-November.

Vallarta Film Festival: This film festival is only 3 years old and is hardly cutting edge—some of the featured films are already out on DVD by the time the festival rolls around. The Latin American film selections are good and the short film section is always interesting, though. Visit www.vallartafilmfestival.com for info. Late November and into early December.

Nuestra Señora de Guadalupe: The Madonna's birthday falls on December 12, and Puerto Vallarta's main church is the focal point for local festivities on this day. The church's main tower boasts an elaborate crown, said to have been copied from a tiara once worn by a mistress of Emperor Maximilian. (Only in Vallarta would a church be topped with the jewelry of a dictator's mistress.) The first 2 weeks of December are marked by parades and festivities all around Vallarta, most starting near the main church. Early December.

Major Attractions

Looking for a peek at celebrity? Then visit Liz Taylor's former home, now **Casa Kimberly** (Zaragoza 446; ☎ **322/222-1336;** free admission; Mon–Fri 9am–6pm) where you can finger fading newspaper clippings in the not-at-all ironic Liz Taylor/Richard Burton museum.

Now that we've gotten that out of the way (and you've posed for your picture under the pink "love bridge" that arches over Zaragoza), it's time to hit another Vallarta landmark: the **malecón** ★★★. This is the most obvious sightseeing landmark in Vallarta, a pedestrian walkway marked by a series of statues that are alternately cheesy and tasteful, stretching from Calle 31 de Octubre to the Los Arcos outdoor amphitheater. Even though it's an uber-touristy experience, you can't come here and *not* walk the half-mile malecón—or weave your way around its clowns, buskers, vendors, and Huichol pole-flyers—if for no

Living Movie Set

No guidebook to PV is complete without making at least a passing reference to the movie set that made a city, *The Night of the Iguana.* This 1964 film, directed by John Huston, was a primary catalyst for the modern development of Puerto Vallarta. The film was primarily shot at La Jolla de Mismaloya (see p. 467 under "Beach Orientation") but it was in Vallarta, up in Gringo Gulch, where all the gossipy off-screen activity took place. The themes of the Tennessee Williams play were adultery, underage sex, alcoholism, lost faith, and shattered morals—decades later the echoes continue to reverberate on the cobblestones of Old Town and beyond. At the entrance to the island, for instance, you'll encounter Vallarta's godfather, a statue of John Huston, sitting in a director's chair, with a quote from his eulogy to Humphrey Bogart on the plaque.

other reason then to admire the wide-ranging outdoor sculpture garden.

Among other sites you shouldn't miss is the **municipal building** on the main square (next to the tourism office), which has a large Manuel Lepe mural inside in its stairwell. Nearby, right up Independencia, sits the picturesque **Parish of Nuestra Señora de Guadalupe church,** Hidalgo 370 (☎ **322/222-1326**). Services in English are held each Saturday at 5pm, and Sunday at 10am. Regular hours are Monday through Saturday from 7:30am to 8:30pm, Sunday from 6:30am to 8:30pm. Note that entrance is restricted to those properly attired—no shorts or sleeveless shirts allowed. Three blocks south of the church, head east on Libertad, lined with small shops and pretty upper windows, to the **municipal market** by the river.

After exploring the market, cross the bridge to the island in the river; sometimes a painter is at work on its banks. Walk down the center of the island toward the sea, and you'll come to the tiny **Museo Rio Cuale** (seaward end of island; no phone; free admission; Mon–Sat 10am–5pm), which has a small but impressive permanent collection of pre-Columbian figurines. Nearby is the **Centro Cultural Cuale** on the east end of the island (☎ **322/223-0095;** Mon–Sat 10am–2pm), where if you feel like a little aesthetic education, you can take music, dance, photography, acting, sculpture, painting, and drawing classes.

You can cover the entire Isla del Rio Cuale in 15 minutes if you just want to march through, but a leisurely stroll is the way to do it. You'll want to park on one of the benches or secluded places along the riverbank to really soak it all in; joining you will be couples and lovers and mothers with kids, all relaxing under the fig trees covered in vines.

MTV Best **The Botanical Gardens of Puerto Vallarta** ★★ (☎ **322/105-7217;** http://vallartabotanicalgardensac.org; free to members, $50 for non-members; daily 10am–6pm) are located on 9.6 hectares (24 acres) of jungle land south of Old Town at Km 24 on the Carretera de Barra de Navidad, between Vallarta and El Tuito, 3km (2 miles) past Chico's Paradise. If you're coming by bus, the El Tuito bus stops at the entrance to the gardens. Although relatively new, the gardens have quickly become a favorite with birders, botanists, and orchid freaks. Bob Price, the founder and curator, came to Vallarta a few years ago and, being an orchid collector himself, he decided to start propagating plants to sell to local gardeners. This basic concept quickly expanded to establishing a full-on botanical garden dedicated to tropical flora. There are jungle trails that wander though the 11,000 plants (more than 3,000 species) scattered around the property, including ferns, bougainvillea, morning glories, orchids, and 6,000 blue agaves (the cactus used in making tequila). There's also a restaurant as well as a tequila tasting room, a full bar, and a lovely porch on which visitors can watch birds swooping down over the nearby Los Horcones river (where you can swim on a hot day). If you visit, just wear closed-toe shoes and bring both insect repellant and warmer clothes, since this is in the foothills of the Sierra Madre and it will be cooler than at the beach.

You don't have to go to the town of Tequila to see the distillation process in action. **Tequila Porfidio** ★★ is just 20 minutes north (on the Vallarta-Tepic Highway 200, 12km/7½ miles north of town; ☎ **322/221-2543**). They have tours that show the entire process from the crushing of the agave hearts to the stills that produce the precious fluid, drop by drop. The 1-hour tours take place Monday to Friday 9am to 5pm, and cost $109 (which includes tastings).

Playing Outside

Fishing

Vallarta has never gotten the fishing rep it deserves but maybe that's a blessing in disguise. As a result, the waters of Banderas Bay are still full of marlin, tuna, mahimahi, and roosterfish and, though the fall International Sailfish tournament is 50 years old (and world famous), catch-and-release is the norm rather than the exception. A half-day chartered boat—with six passengers—will start at $2,180 and go up from there. The best year-round locations are La Corbeteñia and El Banco, 63km and 80km (39 and 50 miles) out respectively. Any deep-sea fisherman worth the weight of his tall tales will plan on at least a 10- to 12-hour charter—anything shorter is a waste of everyone's time. Most charters leave at 7am and start to return in the early afternoon, depending on the catch, and most leave either from the north end of the malecón or the Marina Vallarta docks. ***Note:*** You *will* need a Mexican fishing license ($142, good for 1 day).

One charter to try is **Felipe's Fleet** (☎ **322/221-5402,** 044/322-888-5161; http://vallartafish.8m.com), which has everything from 6.6m (22-ft.) pangas to an 11m (38-ft.) Luhrs.

Golf

Puerto Vallarta is an increasingly popular golf destination; five courses have opened in the past 5 years, bringing the total in the region to nine. One of the best is the breathtaking Jack Nicklaus Signature course at the **Four Seasons Punta Mita** ★ (☎ **329/291-6000**), but it's open only to guests of the Four Seasons resort or to members of other golf clubs with a letter of introduction from their pro. A more practical option is the town's other Jack Nicklaus course at the **Vista Vallarta Golf Club** (☎ **322/290-0030**), along with one designed by Tom Weiskopf. These courses were the site of the 2002 PGA World Cup Golf Championships. It's in the foothills of the Sierra Madre, behind the bullring in Puerto Vallarta. A round costs $167 per person. Cart fee is an extra $43, with club rentals available for $45 per set/per round.

Horseback Riding

There's really no more enjoyable way to explore the Sierra Madre foothills than on top of one of **Rancho Palma Real's** palominos. Rancho Palma Real (Carretera Vallarta, Tepic 4766; ☎ **322/321-2120**) is on the road to San Sebastian but they will pick you up at your hotel for the hour drive into the Sierra. The staff is bilingual and will match you up to a suitable mount. The 4-hour horseback ride ($567) starts at the nearby La Palmas pueblo and then proceeds into a nature reserve along the San Sebastian River. A visit here is also a great **bird-watching** opportunity.

Mountain Biking

Puerto Vallarta, unlike many tropical beach resorts, is cool enough most of the year for some serious off-road fat tire fun. The worst time to bike is during the summer, when rain turns the tracks into rutted mud and the humidity is unpleasantly dense. But the rest of the year—late September to early June—the mountain biking is outstanding. Between November and March, rides into the Sierra Madre might even take you up in the frost zone.

Bike Mex ★★ (Guerrero 361; ☎ **322/323-1680**) has Kona hard tail front-suspended bikes and the most active off-road bikers in the Bay, the ones who build the trails you'll ride on. Don't believe me? Check out the sidewalk out front where there are pieces of shattered bike parts

If You Prefer to Watch

Bullfights are held December through April beginning at 5pm on Wednesday at the La Paloma bullring, across the highway from the town pier. Travel agencies can arrange tickets, which cost around $250. See "Basics," on p. 10 for more info on the sport.

embedded into the cement. Serious riders should bring their own pedals and shoes. The groups are small and Bike Mex will supply gloves and helmets. While there are short half-day trips in and around the foothills, the 53km (33-mile) overland route to Yelapa from Chacala will earn you true bragging rights. The route boasts 900m (3,000-ft.) climbs, tricky technical sections, jungle roots, and a blissful descent into Yelapa's bay. And unlike the day-trippers who come in by boat, you'll have really worked for a beer on the beach before you catch a panga back to Vallarta. Trips start from the Bike-Mex shop at 7am and cost $750.

Just up the hill is another bike outfitter, **Eco-Ride** (Calle Miramar 382; ☎ **322/222-7912;** www.ecoridemex.com). They have the Las Agujas downhill course, a full-suspension track, as well as the 5-hour San Pedro advanced ride that takes you up a 960m (3,200-ft.) climb past small pueblitos in the Sierra Madre, followed by an amazing downhill return to Vallarta. The less ambitious might try the Vallejo ride, an easy 3-hour, 11km (7-mile) ride along the Vallejo River (bring a bathing suit) with a fun return descent back to town. Or, for $250 a day, simply rent a bike and explore on your own.

Parasailing

Parasailing and other watersports are available at many beaches along the Bay of Banderas. The most popular spot is at Los Muertos Beach. WaveRunners, banana boats, and parasailing are available by the hour, half-day, or full day. Be forewarned, however, that the swiftly shifting winds in Banderas Bay can make this a dangerous proposition. Fly at your own risk!

Sailing

Vallarta Adventures (☎ **866/256-2739** in the U.S., or 322/297-1212, ext. 3; www.vallarta-adventures.com) offers two beautiful sailboats for charter or small-group sails (up to 12 people). Daytime sailing charters are priced at $800 per person, and sunset sails are $600 per person. Included in your charter are top notch food and beverages. The operator's boats tend to sail out farther than most—many other sailing charters prefer to motor around the bay.

Scuba Diving

Oddly, Vallarta gets mediocre ratings by some hard-core scuba divers, but maybe that's because of the crowds and the fairly accessible locations. The closest dive spot, **Los Arcos,** is also one of the most spectacular. There will be snorkelers and swimmers on the surface, but divers with the proper training and plenty of air can go deep . . . way deep. The Devils Wall here extends all the way to the continental shelf, more than 540m (1,800 ft.). At Los Arcos, odds are good that you'll spot giant manta rays, eagle rays, Ridley turtles, puffer fish, and moray eels among other sea creatures.

Chico's Dive Shop (Diaz Ordaz 772; ☎ **322/222-1895;** www.chicos-diveshop.com) is one of the oldest and most respected local dive shops in town, and it should be your first choice for a diving expedition. They have PADI and NAUI instructors, offer all levels of certifications, and certainly have experience—they've been in Vallarta for nearly 40 years. Their rental gear is updated annually and they have underwater cameras (video and still) available. They offer dive packages to Los Arcos ($650 for one dive, $985 for two dives, departures at 9am or 2pm, for 4 hr.), as well as Majahuitas, the Marietas, and El Morro.

Another possibility is **Scuba Ocean Quest Dive Shop** (Lazaro Cardenas 230; ☎ **322/223-4103;** www.oceanquestmexico.com). They limit their groups to six divers, led by a PADI Dive Master and a Dive Instructor. Besides the sites listed under Chicos, they also do a night dive ($818, departure at 7pm, 3 hr.) to Los Arcos where you'll see octopus and other nighttime reef feeders. And they do a trip to La Corbetna, a small island 56km (35 miles) out (meaning a nearly 3-hr. boat trip). Because of the distance, you won't see any cattle boats out there, which might improve your chances of seeing giant mantas, sharks, zillions of fish, and Ridley sea turtles. You get two dives for $1,417 (departure is at 7am, for 10 hr.).

Snorkeling

If you want to snorkel, you'll need to travel by boat or drive to the protected bays to the south where the water is cleaner. The best in terms of swimming, photo ops, and dining choices is Mismaloya (where you can see the remains of *The Night of the Iguana* movie set). From here, you can then hire a panga for the short trip to the excellent offshore snorkeling/diving at **Los Arcos.** This eco-preserve, under government protection, is simply the best close-in snorkeling spot around. You're bound to see parrotfish, angel fish, croakers, cornet fish, and more, drifting and feeding on the seaweed and algae on the Los Arcos rocks. Other alternatives are the snorkeling choices along the edge of **Cabo Corientes,** the southern tip of the bay. Catch a bus (or a cab) from Basilio Badillo and Constitución in Old Town and ask to stop at Los Gatos, Los Venados, Punta Negra, or Gemales beach. They're all within a 15-minute (or less) ride and can be reached from the road.

Any of the diving operators listed above do snorkeling trips, too.

Tennis

Many hotels in Puerto Vallarta offer excellent tennis facilities; they often have clay courts. The full-service **Canto del Sol Tennis Club** (☎ **322/224-0123;** www.cantodelsol.com) is at the Canto del Sol hotel in the Hotel Zone. It offers indoor and outdoor courts (including a clay court), full pro shop, lessons, clinics, and partner matches.

Tours

DOLPHIN-WATCHING TOURS

Vallarta Adventures (see "sailing") is the one name you'll see everywhere on your trip here. It's on billboards, on the sides of trucks, and prominently displayed in every guidebook and tourist magazine. That's because they are the biggest and most established name in eco-tourism in Vallarta, with a dizzying assortment of outdoor possibilities. However, they're best known for their dolphin encounters in special swim facilities—which I'm not convinced are eco-friendly enough (see "Basics," p. 58, for more info). They have the broadest schedule and the best connection to most hotels, though, so you might want to consider using them.

If you want to do something less questionable, consider a swim in the ocean with *wild* dolphins. There's no guarantee that you'll actually spend quality time with a local pod, but going with a reliable guide like Alfredo Herrera from **Discover Pacific Tours** (☎ **044/322-142-6296;** www.discoverpacifictours.com; 4-hr. $818) will increase your chances. He and his crew know all the coastal dolphins that call Banderas Bay home and he'll take you out along their routes, and do so in a way that won't disturb their natural environment.

Another choice for swimming with wild marine mammals is **The Whale Watching Center of Puerto Vallarta** (Guerrero 339, El Centro; ☎ **866/422-9972;** www.vallartawhales.com/delfins.html; 4 hr. $600).

ECOTOURS

Open Air Expeditions (☎/fax **322/222-3310;** www.vallartawhales.com) offers nature-oriented trips, including birding and ocean kayaking in Punta Mita. **Ecotours de México,** Ignacio L. Vallarta 243 (☎/fax **322/222-6606**), has eco-oriented tours, including seasonal (Aug–Dec) trips to a turtle preservation camp where you can witness hatching baby Olive Ridley turtles.

WHALE-WATCHING TOURS

First, a note about whale-watching in general: The humpback whales that migrate to PV annually are an endangered species and visitors can help them survive by not patronizing tour boat operators that don't comply with Mexican regulations. All currently approved guide boats fly a distinctive red flag. If the flag is old and tattered, obviously last season's, it's not current. Check out www.puertovallartawhalewatching.com/html/approved_vessel listing.html to get a listing of up-to-date tour guide vessels.

ZIP LINE TOURS

Want to get high? There are a half dozen canopy tours in Puerto Vallarta and they all promise the same thing—an exhilarating gravity-free swoop on a taut wire strung between two trees high above the ground. The best choice is MTV Best **Los Veranos** ★★ (☎ **322/223-0504;** www.puertovallartatours.net/las-juntas-y-veranos-canopy-tour.htm; $800; departures daily on the hour from 9am–2pm from Old Town, Nuevo Vallarta shuttles 10am–noon, Tues and Thurs). Los Veranos is about 40 minutes south of PV on the Barra de Navidad, Highway 200, within the Los Veranos Nature Preserve. There are 15 lines that crisscross over a 2-mile track, sometimes 150m (500 ft.) high. They start you off gradually until you get used to the system of braking, but soon you'll be zipping along on the steel cables at 30 MPH over coffee trees, orchids, vanilla vines, philodendron, and termite nests. The last cable track spits you out at a palapa right next to the Orquidias River, where you unfasten your harness and are confronted with something even more challenging—more than 80 different tequilas to sample.

After drinking and zipping, you can visit Pancho's Jungle Restaurant, perched on a river bank where you can jump in to wash off the bugs and fear-induced sweat. The whole tour takes 4 hours (which includes the 30-min. drive from PV). You'll meet at the Conchas Chinas Pemex gas station on the highway to Mismaloya in Old Town. Reservations are a must. Wear shorts, tie back your hair, and bring a money belt if your camera doesn't have a strap, and you'll be ready to zip.

Shopping

There are a few key shopping areas: central downtown, the marina malecón, the popular mercados, and on the beach—where the merchandise comes to you. Some of the more attractive shops are 1 to 2 blocks in **back of the malecón.** Start at the intersection of Corona and Morelos streets—interesting shops spread out in all directions from here. **Marina Vallarta** has two shopping plazas, Plaza Marina and Neptuno Plaza, on the main highway from the airport into town, which offer a limited selection of shops, with Plaza Neptuno primarily featuring home decor shops. Although still home to a few interesting shops, the marina malecón is dominated by real estate companies, timeshare vendors, restaurants, and boating services.

In addition to "Top 10 Must-Have Souvenirs," keep in mind that PV has the best selection of Huichol art in Mexico. Descendants of the Aztec, the Huichol are one of the last remaining indigenous cultures in the world that has remained true to its ancient traditions, customs, language, and habitat. The Huichol live in adobe structures in the high Sierras (at an elevation of 1,400m/4,592 ft.) north and east of Puerto Vallarta. Due to the decreasing fertility (and therefore productivity) of the land surrounding their villages, they have come to depend more on the sale of their artwork for sustenance.

You'll see Huichol handiwork everywhere in town. It's a serious business—you'll spot everything from Huichol masks, to bowls, to beaded figurines. (I've yet to see a beaded Bart Simpson but I would not be surprised if one popped up—and you bet I'd buy it.) Colorful, symbolic yarn "paintings," inspired by visions experienced during spiritual ceremonies, are probably the most famous forms of Huichol art, though. In the ceremonies, artists ingest peyote, a hallucinogenic cactus, which induces brightly colored visions; these are considered messages from their ancestors. The visions' symbolic and mythological imagery influences the art. See "Art Galleries" below for recommendations on the best places to buy art.

Art Galleries

Outside of D.F., there is probably no other Mexican city where the gallery scene is quite so developed and supported by both local and international talent. The quality of fine art on display (and for sale) in Vallarta is remarkably rich, diverse, and, unfortunately, on the pricey side. But don't forget: Art is a duty-free purchase, as well as a guilt-free one—you'll be adding to the wealth and treasure of not only your apartment but the country as a whole through your purchase.

From late October to late April, many of the 30-plus galleries in Vallarta participate in unguided free **Art Walks** every Wednesday night from 6pm to 10pm. I can't recommend this highly enough. It's the

Top 10 Must-Have Souvenirs

- A high-quality minibottle of vanilla (such as *vanilla tecul*) from any deli and some liquor stores
- A Bimbo soccer shirt, available at any flea market
- A Mexican wrestler's mask, also at any flea market
- A Presidente cigar from the Cigar Factory
- A string crocheted bracelet from a beach vendor
- A 190ml bottle of *salsa huichol* (any grocery store)
- A Zapatista doll from Peyote People
- A stuffed frog from the municipal mercado on Isla Cuale
- A keychain with the image of the Virgin on it from the street vendors in front of the main Señora de Guadalupe Church
- A bottle of tequila *porfido plata* purchased at the distiller

perfect way to mingle with interesting locals, sip some free alcohol, and see some very good art. If you can't make the art walks, you can attempt to re-create them on your own by stopping at the following spots:

At the **Huichol Collection Gallery** (Paseo Díaz Ordaz 732; ☎ **322/223-0661**) you'll be able to watch a genuine Huichol Indian artisan working at his art despite the endless parade of gringos. When I visited, the artisan was assembling a 1.2m-long (4-ft.) tiger with an iguana perched on it that would take 5 months to finish and sell for about $2,500. Note that this is a timeshare location, so don't be surprised if you're hit with a pitch for a "free" breakfast and property tour when you visit.

For a more respectable shopping experience, head to MTV Best **Peyote People** ★★ (Juárez 222; ☎ **322/222-2302;** www.peyotepeople.com). This co-op carries the finest arts and crafts of the Huichol, Tarahumara, Yaqui, Mayo, and Oaxacan Huave Indians. The stock of pots, carvings, masks, Zapatista dolls, Katrina figures, and jewelry is unique, museum-like in quality, and very reasonably priced, despite being Fair Trade certified. If you shop nowhere else in Vallarta, come here. You won't be disappointed when you get home and unpack your purchases. This is once-in-a-lifetime souvenir shopping and, while the stuff on sale isn't as cheap as a Señor Frog's "Drinking Team" T-shirt, it's far classier.

There's a noticeable scarcity of public museums in Vallarta, maybe because the culture of the town is dedicated to tourism and commerce. No matter. Who needs a stinkin' museum when you have places like **Galería Indígena** ★ (Juárez 270; ☎ **322/223-0800;** www.galeriaindigena.com)? They've got 16 showrooms of museum-quality folk art and crafts from all over Mexico but here you don't have to be quiet—you can touch the art and even buy it at very reasonable prices. Try doing that in a museum. They sell Uruapan lacquer boxes, Oaxacan wooden animals, Huichol jewelry, Zapotecan Day of the Dead figures, Michoacan Katrina dolls, Tarascan ceramics, as well as the largest collection of one-of-a-kind handmade masks I've ever seen in a folk art store. They also carry a limited selection of fine art as well, including stuff by Guerrero artist Nicolas de Jesus.

Another fine (although smaller) folk crafts outlet is **Alfarería Tlaquepaque** (Av. Mexico 1100; ☎ **322/223-2121**). They specialize in ceramics from Puebla, Michocan, and Guanajuato and have been a PV landmark for more than 50 years. Most of the wares are low-fire stuff but they also have some unusual pastel glass concoctions (vases and bottles) from Jalisco.

Finally, if you really want to drop a bundle to decorate your condo, drop by **Banderas Bay Trading Company** (Lázaro Cárdenas 263; ☎ **322/223-4352;** Constitución 319A; ☎ **322/223-9871**). They have the sort of high-end Mexican interiors that make it into *Architectural Digest* spreads: religious collectibles, antique wooden doors, cantera stone carvings, and lamps.

It's not every collector who can turn the decor of a pizza parlor into the basis for a hugely successful art gallery, but that's what happened at **Galería Dante** (Basilio Badillo 269; ☎ **322/222-2477**), which is currently Vallarta's largest art gallery, offering more than 186 sq. m (2,000 sq. ft.) of covered space and another 372 sq. m (4,000 sq. ft.) dedicated to a sculpture garden. Owners Claire and Joe Guarniere started off with a successful restaurant, Pizza Joe, which during its 8-year run attracted as many people for its decor as its pies. As more and more patrons started asking to buy the restaurant's decorations—collected on numerous European art tours—the owners switched careers.

The space now features more than 50 internationally known artists, including Jonás Gutiérrez, Francisco Quintero, and Víctor Manuel Villarreal. Prices range from $55 to $545,000.

Galería Uno ★ (Morelos 561; ☎ **322/222-0908;** www.mexonline.com/galeriauno.htm) is the oldest and most respected gallery in Vallarta and carries more than 30 different artists from Mexico and North and South America. Owners Jan Lavender and Martina Goldberg change the featured exhibition every few weeks. The overall collection is comprised mostly of paintings, prints, and sculpture. It's a great place for an opening, right in the heart of Old Town and in a wonderfully laid-out space that allows for easy meandering from room to room. Among the stars are Lee Chapman, João Rodriguez, and Melvinita Hooper.

Finally, one gallery that even non-art fans will enjoy is the **Galería de Ollas** (Morelos 101, 3B; ☎ **322/223-1045**) dedicated to the potters of the village of Mata Ortiz. This tiny pueblito in the dusty badlands of Chihuahua is famous throughout the world for the quality and distinctive style of its wood carvings and pottery. It's commonly said that Mata Ortiz pottery is art, not craft, and that it moves beyond pre-Hispanic imitations to create fine art works. The style melds Southwest Navaho and Zuni with elliptical shapes and forms, merging the past with the future in ways that have to be seen to be appreciated.

Really Catty

For themed art, drop by **La Casa de los Gatos** (Basilio Badillo 220; ☎ **322/222-3076**) where it's all cats, all the time. Owner Eloise Sosa Sánchez has crocheted hats, Huichol beadwork, Oaxacan statues, miniature Calaveras, and assorted Day of the Dead artifacts and lots and lots of cats, both actual and artistic. She rescued one large street cat a few years ago. It gave birth to a litter and now Eloise is the reluctant caretaker to more than 60 felines, some of whom hang out in the store like timeshare shills, waiting for a ready stroking hand or a handout. There's a big bottle in the front for donations to the kitties' food bill, pasted with a hand-lettered sign that says "I'm crazy." Like we didn't know. But it's a *good* sort of nutty.

Cigar Shops

Okay, you're in Vallarta and the tropical sensibility and endless happy hour mentality means there are no recriminations. Get that tattoo, make that a double margarita, smoke 'em if you've got 'em—whatever, you'll live forever. Now that we've established that, let's pop into the **Cigar Factory** (Libertade 100-3; ☎ **322/222-0300;** www.vallartacigarfactory.com) for some nice Communist-grown stogies that will add a new dimension to your lung capacity. You'll see "Cuban cigars" advertised all around Vallarta, even in tiny local tiendas, but don't be fooled. You're more often than not getting funky counterfeits that have none of the verve and essence of the real deal. You want that genuine Cuban flavor, you come here. They have the rolling forms, a humidor room, a lovely wall of pictures of Fidel puffing away, air-conditioning, plasma screens, a bar, and the freshest nicotine delivery systems in town, priced from $25 to $150. Clip the end, fire up the tip, and *suck*.

Clothing & Craft Stores

On 1 short block of Basilo Badillo in Old Town, you'll be able to troll past all kinds of lovely artifacts that will take up too much room in your luggage—a veritable

World of Whatever. **Mundo de Azulejos** (Carranza 374; ☎ **322/222-2675;** www.talavera-tile.com), is, as the name translates a "World of Tiles." It goes on forever, a garish eye-candy extravaganza of low-fire tile work—tabletops, bathrooms, and kitchen sinks. **Mundo de Pewter** (Carranza 358; ☎ **322/222-8503**) on the other hand, is all about pewter (bowls, candle sticks, boxes, and gee-gaws). Finally, just around the corner is **Mundo de Cristal** (Insurgentes 333; ☎ **322/222-4157**). This is the only place in PV where you can see someone blowing something into a glass instead of inhaling something out of one. Jalisco is famous for its glasswork and this glass-blowing factory/outlet has almost-wholesale prices and a wonderful variety of glasses, objets d'art, decanters, pitchers, and vases.

Farther down the street, **Marsar** ★★ (Carranza 375; ☎ **322/222-6548**) stocks nothing but lovely huge copper products, primarily from the Michoacan crafts village of Santa Clara de Cobre. It may sound like the sort of thing you'd never shop for on your 1-week tropical getaway, but making room for a 24-piece tiled mosaic of the Virgin or an insanely large hammered copper fruit bowl makes for a vacation memory that lasts far longer than a tan. And you'll never find prices this great again.

Maybe you want something a little easier to pack, though? **Indigo Textiles** (Basilio Badillo 241; ☎ **322/223-0107;** www.indigotextiles.com) has a wonderful selection of handmade fabrics from Mexico, Guatemala, and India. Pillow covers, bedspreads, and mosquito nets are all on sale, ranging in price from $150 to $2,400.

The little hole-in-the-wall **Fabiola Huaracheria** (Ignacio L. Vallarta 145, Old Town; ☎ **322/222-9154**) makes custom huaraches (2 to 3 days required) fairly cheaply ($218–$545, depending on style). They've been in the business for more than 50 years and have an enormous supply of ready-mades if you don't have the time for the fitting process.

Jewelry Stores

Mexican fire opals were used by the Aztecs to adorn their most sacred objects and at **The Opal Mine** (Paseo Díaz Ordaz 528; ☎ **322/222-9410**) you can get something for *your* most sacred object—your body. Prices are good and the opals are stunning, plus the store itself, on the malecón, is truly bizarre: a somewhat cheesy blend of a jewelry store, museum, and Disneyland set—complete with faux-cave walls, a miniriver, mining cars, and statues of miners with jackhammers. There's a plasma screen documentary showing how opals are mined but really, who cares? Just slap down your card and get your babe or guy some baubles. It'll return to you 10-fold.

Speaking of glittery body art, you'll see silver jewelry for sale everywhere in Vallarta—from vendors on the beach, to timeshare storefronts, to coffee shops. Yes, it may look shiny, but it's usually alpaca and that shine won't last. For the real deal, head to established jewelry shops, which sell their products based on the weight as well as the complexity of the design. **Alberto's** ★ (Juárez 185; ☎ **322/222-8317;** www.albertos.com.mx) has been in the silver business since 1930 and is one of the town's best. The family is now in its third generation of making silver for Vallarta customers, attracting repeat customers thanks to their uniquely organic designs.

Markets

Puerto Vallarta's **municipal market** is just north of the Río Cuale, where Libertad and Av. Rodríguez meet. The mercado sells clothes, jewelry, serapes, shawls, leather accessories and suitcases, papier-mâché parrots, stuffed frogs and armadillos, and, of course, T-shirts. Be sure to comparison-shop, and definitely bargain before buying. The market is open daily from 9am to 7pm. Upstairs, a **food market** serves inexpensive Mexican meals—for more adventurous diners, it's probably the best value and most authentic dining experience in Vallarta. An **outdoor market** is along Río Cuale Island, between the two bridges. Stalls there sell crafts, gifts, folk art, and clothing.

Fairly new to downtown is the **Small Vallarta** (☎ **322/222-7530**) on Paseo Díaz Ordaz 928, on the eastern side, just before the start of the malecón. It is a "small mall" featuring tourist-friendly shops and dining options, including Carl's Jr.'s burgers, Häagen-Dazs ice cream, a Swatch watch shop, an El Mundo de Tequila, and a Diamonds International jewelry store.

Doing It Safely

Best **The Condom House Condonerío** (Malecón 164; ☎ **044/322-126-7722**) touts itself as the first condom store in PV (and probably the only one, I'll bet). Owner Lolita Velasco carries everything from scented and flavored skins to textured, ribbed, smooth, thin, and female specific. The stock—singles for $6, packages for $88—comes from Japan, Germany, the U.S., and parts of Mexico. It also sells massage oils, water-based and oil-based lubricants, souvenirs, latex gloves, and doles out HIV information. It's just down the street from Blue Chairs (p. 452), because location is everything.

Record Shops

If you're reading this book because of its MTV title, then you'll certainly want to drop into **Sonido Rana Record Store** (Madero 325 and 331; ☎ **322/222-4176**) to browse its huge selection of Latin, world, dance, trance, lounge, and much more music. The jazz collection is so large, it has its own room. If you'd rather make your own music than listen to someone else's, stop by **Galería Tajin** (Ignacio Vallarta 335-B; ☎ **322/222-5558**) where you'll find musical instruments from pre-historic times and Latin America-like guitars, flutes, and drums.

Sports Shops

Coral Surf & Skate Shop (Insurgentes 322; ☎ **322/222-7785**) is a well-stocked surf and beachwear shop just a few blocks from the Los Muertos beach. They've got surfboards, skateboards, body boards, name brand board shorts, bikinis, rash guards, and sandals. The prices aren't cheap—about what you'd pay in the U.S.—but the selection is good and the staff surprisingly helpful.

Road Trips: Central Pacific Coast

Punta de Mita used to be a wonderful little fishing village, with a scrubby coastal landscape, dotted with little private coves and dirt trails. Then the Four Seasons moved in, building a world-class golf course (p. 470) and installing watchtowers in the hills, effectively shutting off access to the coast here from the south. Needless to say, unless you're living really large, you don't want to even bother turning off to Punta de Mita now. Surfers may want to check out the breaks around the point, but only if you're comfortable with crowds. Everyone else should just keep motoring on to **Sayulita,** 35km (22 miles) north of the airport.

The Central Pacific Coast

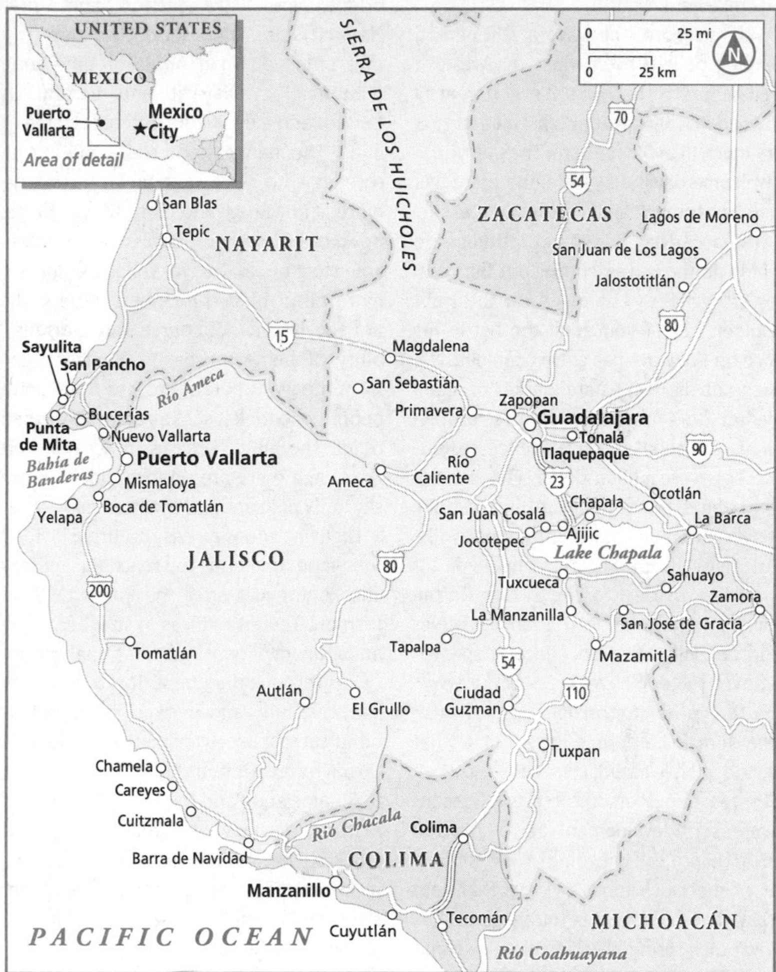

Sayulita

As recently as 10 years ago, Sayulita was a sleepy little fishing village whose most notable asset was a forgiving reef break that wrapped around Punto Sayulita, depositing an easy (and fun) wave that was reliable, large enough to handle a crowd of surfers, and similar in both speed and ease to Malibu's breaks. California surfers discovered Sayulita back in the '80s and as a result a few hammock hotels sprang up on the beach facing the break. It was hard then not to be seduced by Sayulita's charm, which consisted of no paved roads, dogs sleeping in the sandy streets, a cozy little main square, and a half-dozen almost adequate restaurants, mostly down on the sand or a few steps away. Best of all was the fact that you could rent a hammock at one of the beach-front palapas for just a few dollars a day.

Well, no more. The wave is still here, a pumping delight even when the western swell is pretty flat. But it's gotten way crowded and a locals-only surf mentality is very much in evidence here. The everyone-is-welcome days of El Tigre, the first local surfing champion, are gone. Now local kids with bleached hair and snarky attitudes are ripping up the waves, cutting out the newbies struggling to stand up on the right shoulder. And if you think the battle for space on the wave has gotten competitive, check out the real estate market on land. Sayulita now has Internet cafes, professional surf shops, even a French restaurant. There are million-dollar homes in the hills behind town going up and swanky interior stores are starting to appear, like pilot fish clinging to the underside of a whale's jaw, eager for any scraps. On the other hand, you can rent a fabulous five-bedroom villa with pool/Jacuzzi/spa for just over $98,000 a week. Check out www.move2sayulita.com/properties/rentals/prices.htm for a depressing look at what else is available in that price range.

To top things off, the biggest Cancún-style resort development in 20 years, a FONATUR project, got going in late 2006—a sign of enormous things to come. That's not to say that the appeal is totally gone. Just avoid the spring-break/Easter/Christmas hoards. The best times to visit are the dead zone in-between seasons of August to November, April to June.

And no matter where you're staying, bring cash. There are no ATMs in Sayulita, no banks, and almost nobody takes credit cards.

GETTING THERE & GETTING AROUND

BY CAR When you drive north from Puerto Vallarta on Highway 200, passing the airport and crossing the Rio Ameca bridge, you leave **Jalisco** and enter **Nayarit** state. It's a short 20-minute trip that puts you in a different time zone (Mountain in Nayarit and Central in Jalisco) and a decidedly different frame of mind. The madness and traffic of Vallarta recedes into your rear view mirror—no more Señor Frog's, no more Burger Kings, no more timeshare harassment (unless you stop off in Nuevo Vallarta), and no more all-night two-for-one shooters. It's not tourist-free, of course, but the sensibility of being in coastal Mexico, away from the giant hotels, endless traffic, and people who look just like you, is a welcome relief. The jungle presses in here and on the beach there are no paragliders in the sky, only pelicans and frigate birds.

Highway 200 is an easy-to-drive divided four-lane road until you reach the military checkpoint just after the Punta de Mita turn off. Then it reduces in size, becoming an undivided two lane that snakes and twists through the jungle. It is a *very* busy highway, hilly and marked by numerous blind curves. Because it is the main artery through Nayarit's coastal strip running up to Sinaloa state and then onto Sonora and Arizona, it's inevitable that you will get stuck behind buses, trucks, and wheezing pick-ups and passenger cars. Drive defensively and carefully and you'll be okay. See p. 49 in "Basics" for driving tips.

BY TAXI To get to Sayulita without renting a car, you can take a taxi from the airport or downtown Vallarta, for about $654 to the Sayulita town plaza. You can also take a taxi back to Vallarta, although you'll need to book the night before.

BY BUS You can get a bus (for about $20) to Sayulita directly from the airport by crossing over the pedestrian bridge and waiting for a bus to Compostela or Sayulita—the destination is written clearly above the front windshield. You will see these buses as you wait at the bus stop at the bottom of the stairs.

Within Vallarta you can also catch the Compostela bus in front of the Sheraton in the Hotel Zone. The bus will drop you off at the Sayulita turnoff on Highway 200, leaving you to fend for yourself for the roughly 3km (2-mile) walk into town. Cabs come along fairly often if you don't want to walk, though.

Getting back to Puerto Vallarta from Sayulita is easier. The bus to Vallarta leaves from the main square hourly, starting at 6am with the last one leaving at 5:30pm. It will drop you off at the airport or at the Sheraton (again for $20). From there you can just grab a city bus or taxi into El Centro or Old Town.

See p. 443 under "Getting Around" Puerto Vallarta for more details.

SAYULITA BASICS

RECOMMENDED WEBSITES

- **www.sayulita-mexico.com**: The primary forum/message board for all things Sayulita. Here you'll find hotel/restaurant reviews and surfing advice, and read locals sounding off about how their little paradise is being ruined.
- **www.sayulita.com**: A more commercial site but updated consistently and with rentals, surf reports; also another forum/message board.
- **www.sayulita.to/My_Homepage_Files/Page16.html**: A very handy list of local restaurants.
- **www.sayulitalife.com**: The official website of the town.

SLEEPING

For nostalgic folks out there, **Papa's Palapas** is the place to come (Playa Principal s/n; ☎ **329/291-3076** or 800/899-4167 in U.S.; www.sayulita.com/papaspalapas.html; US$40 and up double; no credit cards). This was once *the* place to hang a hammock back in the good old days—it's right opposite the break and the main beach, and so it's ideal for those determined to be the first in the water. The original hammock rooms are still here, basically simple concrete block shells with open balconies covered by palapa style fronds. Now, however, they rent for US$50 a night while the top floor penthouse is five times that. There are fans but no air-conditioning in all rooms.

Also on the budget end is **Hotel Sayulita** (Delfines 1; no phone; US$40 and up double; no credit cards). When there's no room anyplace else and immediate beach access is an issue, this slightly funky bare-bones place might work. The owner is a very cranky elderly gentleman who owns the hardware store next door. Like most things in Sayulita, it's cash only, doesn't take reservations, and complaining about the Lysol smell will just get you tossed out. You'll get cement floors, cracks in the walls, and a dank environment—but what do you want for $400 a night (or less in off season)? Just stay out of the back rooms where there's no breeze, and you'll be fine. There's no air-conditioning but there are fans, and the geckos on hand keep the bugs down.

A bit farther up the food chain is **Bungalows Aurinko** ★ (Calle Marlin s/n; ☎ **329/291-3150;** www.sayulita-vacations.com; US$78 and up double; no credit cards). It's just barely off the main square and is notable for its pretty entrance, a reflection of its Finnish connections—*aurinko* means "sun" in Finnish. Though it's reasonably priced, as everywhere, expect to pay a premium during holidays—usually about an additional US$12. Some rooms have air-conditioning, but most just have fans. Kitchens are outside and bedrooms are enclosed. It's clean and well maintained, with palapa roofs, curved cement walls painted a pleasing vermillion, and if you opt for the

Surf's Up

Surfing is what Sayulita is all about—in the 2006 Nayarit state competition, the top three winners were Sayulita locals. The main surfing break off the Playa Principal is a classic long board right, forgiving enough for newbies to be able to get on the shoulder without too much effort. Short board enthusiasts will have more fun up the beach north in front of the campgrounds. Sadly, the break at Sayulita has gotten lots of press, which has brought crowds. If you already know how to grab a rail, then consider hiring a taxi or a panga to take you to less crowded spots to the north or south. Heading south around the Punta de Mita cape, ask about checking out Burros, La Lancha, or El Faro, all reached by car or panga. If you cab it, it'll cost about $436 if you want the driver to hang out. The breaks at Pasquero and Pasquerito are a 45-minute walk south from the main beach. Heading north from Sayulita are San Pancho (often closed out), Chacala (accessible only by boat), Santa Cruz, and San Blas's famous Stoners break (about an hr. by car).

You can rent boards at the surf shops **Luna Azul** (Marlin 4; ☎ **329/291-2009;** 111.lunazulsurf.com) and **Sininen** (Calle Delfin s/n; ☎ **329/291-3186**). The latter is the best outfitted surf shop in town, hands down—maybe because the son of the owner has won the nationals twice. They have rental boards ($200 for the day, $300 for 24 hr., $1,500 for the week), new boards ($8,400 for short boards, $7,400 for long boards), rash guards ($500), Sex Wax ($20), a quiver of used boards (under $4,000), and lessons ($300 for group lessons, $400 for individual lessons).

El Tigre (☎ **329/291-3267**) has surf lessons also; look for their tent on the beach. After running into a newbie on the shoulder, **Ding Batz Surfboard Repair** (José Mariscal 5; ☎ **329/291-3002**) is the place to go. And if you want to hang with the locals once the sun is down, go to **El Tigre's** restaurant above the surfing champ's surf shop, on the main plaza, to tell lies and settle scores.

penthouse (US$108 nightly) then you'll get a lovely breeze and a great balcony view. Bonus: There's a good lending library.

Also close to the main square are the **Luna Mar** bungalows (José Mariscal 5; ☎ **329/291-3002;** www.surfingsayulita.com; US$55 and up double; no credit cards). They're simple, clean, and in a good price range; the more expensive rooms come with air-conditioning, which you won't really need except in mid-summer. All come with minifridges and fans. It's a three-story five-room newish structure with Wi-Fi and tiled floors. All the other details are pretty unremarkable.

The 50-unit **Villa Amor** ★★ (Playa los Muertos s/n; ☎ **329/291-3010,** 619/822-2731 in U.S.; www.villaamor.com; $US85 double; no credit cards) imparts a villa feel thanks to the setting—clinging to a hill that overlooks the break—and is now one of the "old" reliables of Sayulita even though it's light years beyond what Sayulita once was. It's on the south end of the beach, down a rutted narrow dirt road next to the water's edge. The standard rooms are tasteful, open air, and designed with nice little touches that somehow make it feel slightly more luxurious than it actually is. The bathrooms aren't fully enclosed—you'll simply get a wall that doesn't quite meet the ceiling. There are coffeemakers and fridges in the rooms but the nicest bonus is the small personal plunge pool. They also have a restaurant and lots of toys—bikes, boogie boards, and surfboards are included in the rental. ***Note:*** If you're making a reservation online you'll need to pay in full 1 week before you arrive.

EATING

Sayulita has far more restaurants than one might expect a small beach town to have—more than three dozen at last count. Everything from high-end French food to Thai to sushi to handmade ice cream is on offer. It's like a miniversion of Vallarta, all crammed into a few square blocks. Following are some of the most popular options.

El Costeño (Playa Principal s/n; no phone; main courses $200; no credit cards; daily 9am–way late) is the beach palapa of choice for many locals. It was the first restaurant on the sand but the service sucks and the food is barely adequate. It's all about location, right in front of Papa's Palapas and with the best view of the main break. Come here for drinks and something very simple and you'll do just fine.

For a substantially better meal at a real table on a real floor, check out **Don Pedro's** (Marlin 2, on the beachfront; ☎ **329/291-3090;** main courses $125–165; MC, V; daily 8am–11pm). They have wood-fired pizza, grilled ahi tuna, decent breakfasts, TVs, a full bar, and a great view of all the surfing. Prices aren't cheap—you'll pay $125 for a pizza—but at least they take credit.

At the other end of the price range is **Sayulita Fish Taco** (Calle José Mariscol s/n, behind the main square; ☎ **329/291-3271;** www.sayulitafishtaco.com/index.html; main courses $100; no credit cards; daily 10am–11pm). This is easily the best restaurant in all of Sayulita, and the sort of rare restaurant that is equally popular with tourists and locals. Mark Alberto and his wife Dora have taken a simple idea—the Baja fresh soft fish taco with cabbage—and brought it to a whole new level. The shrimp and fish tacos (with a sweet/tangy pineapple-garlic sauce), kilo burritos, fajitas, and open flame broiled whole fish are all divine.

For even cheaper tacos ($6 each) try the **stand** under the white tarp near the bridge which is open roughly Monday to Saturday 7pm to 2am. Another cheap spot is **Choco Banana** (14 Calle Delfin, on the main plaza; no phone; main courses $200; no credit cards; daily 8am–11pm). This is one of the original pioneers in Sayulita and thankfully has not been priced out of the market, yet. Its breakfasts and lunches are excellent—especially the handmade veggie burgers. But their signature item is the espresso/milk/chocolate/frozen banana shake. I like to get two at once—one to inhale and the second to sip. The space also functions as a local clearing house for gossip. At some point everybody in town drops by.

Finally, a big shout-out should go to **Café Tratoria** (across from the main church; ☎ **329/291-3206;** main courses $75–$155; no credit cards; daily 5–11pm). Owner Leonardo Dalla is from Venice, Italy, and the food reflects his passion for his homeland. I love their grilled calamari almost as much as I do the wood-fired pizza.

PLAYING OUTSIDE

See the "Surf's Up" box for info on surfing in Sayulita. If the swell is too big or too small, consider taking a canopy tour instead. **Canopy Sayulita** (Manuel Rodríguez Sanchéz 14; ☎ **329/291-3112;** www.michaparrita.com) has a three-bridge, 10-line course—one of them a heart-stopping quarter-mile long. It's a 90-minute joy ride ($491) up on Monkey Mountain, just a few minutes south on the Punta de Mita libramiento.

If canopy touring isn't your thing, **Rancho Mi Chaparitta** (Sanchez, across from the baseball field; ☎ **329/291-3112;**

e-mail rmichaparrita@hotmail.com) has 1- to 4-hour horseback riding tours, fishing excursions, and ATV rentals.

SHOPPING

Another sign that Sayulita lies somewhere between gritty surf town and high-end resort is the gallery **La Hamaca** (Revolución 110; ☎ **329/291-3039**). It reminds me of a Vallarta gallery-crafts store with its Katrina dolls, Huichol statues, Milagro crosses, Uruapan lacquerware, Michoacan masks, and, of course, hammocks on sale. The last item is what the store is named for; their line is Mayan and made out of synthetic thread—preferable because it doesn't rot. They're not cheap, at $1,090 for a king-size version, but they're quality.

The **Librería Sayulita Bookstore** (Miramar 17A; ☎ **329/291-3382**) has a little bit of everything. In addition to new and used books in Spanish and English, it offers Spanish classes and doles out caffeine via its coffee shop. It's a good place to get nature and art books, guidebooks, Sayulita-specific maps, and more.

San Pancho

Just 10 minutes up the coast from Sayulita is San Francisco, known commonly as San Pancho. Although right next door to Sayulita, San Pancho is radically different in mood, partially because of the currents offshore. Unlike Sayulita, San Pancho's ocean is unprotected and the rips and shore break can be dangerous. Every year a couple of people drown here. "Over in Sayulita they have excellent surfing so they get all the neon and traffic and screaming and yelling drunks," a local told me. "San Pancho is left alone. That's the way most of us like it." There are breaks at both ends of the main beach, but they're short board fast. While Sayulita is a sort of party central, San Pancho is where quieter folks and American expats head—160 homes have been built for gringos in the last year. And although Sayulita is busy even in mid-summer, in August things basically shut down in San Pancho. The biggest annual event here is the regular sunset turtle hatchling release (see the "Tortuga Turtles" box on p. 486), which pretty much sums up the general mood of the place.

SLEEPING

Bungalows Lydia (☎ **311/258-4337;** www.bungalowslydia.com; US$80–US$150 a night double with 3-night minimum; no credit cards) is on the jungle beach road about 3km (2 miles) north of the center of San Pancho. You'll need a map to find it, but once there, out on a deserted point with two private coves, you'll reach a version of the coast that is surreal, with overwhelming sunsets, whales resting a few hundred feet offshore, and pelicans drifting endlessly past the cliffs right at eye level. Owner María Esther Cisneros and her sister inherited the property from their father and have slowly added rooms to the two-story building perched right on the edge of the rocks. The combination of vistas and privacy like this is rare anywhere, but here it's mind-numbingly impressive. There's a common area with a barbecue, chairs, and tables and hammocks hanging under a palapa on the point. Rooms have fridges, coffeemakers, king-size beds, and an outdoor kitchen. There are no shops or restaurants within walking distance, so plan on stocking up for *all* essentials in San Pancho beforehand.

The 25-room **Costa Azul** (Amapas at Palmas; ☎ **949/498-3223** or 800/365-7613 in U.S.; www.costaazulresidenceclub.com; US$136 double; AE, DISC, MC, V) is an "adventure resort" right on the edge of San Pancho. It's not cheap, but dedicated surfers flock here consistently, drawn by the various packages that include all drinks, food, and daily panga rides to secluded breaks. For divers and snorkelers, Costa Azul is the closest you can get to the Marietta Islands for scuba tours. Staying here puts the Mariettas only a 90-minute trip away, not the full day excursion it takes to come from Vallarta. There's also a nice pool, a spa, a decent restaurant, kayaks, and fishing available.

A couple of other choices right in the tiny sandy heart of San Pancho are **Roberto's Bungalows** (America Latina 777; ☎ **311/258-4375** or 971/239-4120 in U.S; www.robertosbungalows.com; US$75 double). There are only five one-bedroom places, but four of them have outdoor kitchens with fridges, microwaves, toasters, coffeemakers, and blenders. All are nicely decorated, well built, and comfortable, plus you get a pool and no TVs. Best of all, owner Roberto is very welcoming and laid back.

Just around the corner is **Hotel Cielo Rojo** (Calle Asia 6; ☎ **311/258-4155;** http://hotelcielorojo.com; $350 double; MC, V). The very clean and simple (but slightly small) rooms here have king-size beds, but have no air-conditioning (although they claim it's on the way). Still, there's free Wi-Fi and the rates include breakfast. There's also a nice gourmet Mexican restaurant, Cena Azul, located in the courtyard. The rooms look over the pool and the decor is folky (with tin lamps, mosaics, and tiled floors).

EATING

San Pancho boasts one of the best small delis you're likely to find anywhere along this coast, **Don Chuey's Wine and Deli** (Av. Tercer Munco 85; no phone) which is the only visible indication of the very pricey homes hidden in the jungle. It stocks Starbucks drinks, imported wines, local mango chutney, peanut oil, gourmet mustards, boutique vanillas, premium tequilas, Japanese sesame oil, Thai fish sauce, sun-dried tomatoes, Adelles sausages, and Brie and other cheeses, as well as fixings for sandwiches. It's like something you might find in Napa instead of on a rutted dirt road in a sleepy beach town in Nayarit.

For something a little more affordable, try **Gino's Pizza,** 2 blocks east (Tercer Mundo s/n; ☎ **311/258-4049**). It's a tiny hole-in-the-wall joint with very decent pepperoni pizzas ($60 for a medium, no smalls) and they're likely to be closed when everything else is open, and open when everything else is closed.

Across the street and west slightly is **Lavanderia America** ($45 for 3 kilos), next door to **Café Internet** (Av. Tercer Mundo 90) where you can get an espresso for $20 and a half-hour high-speed connection for the same price.

PLAYING OUTSIDE

For outdoor excursions, especially surfing, check out Costa Azul. (No, it's not necessary to be a guest to surf with them; see earlier for info). They have surf trips by covered panga ($400), leaving daily at 7am and returning by 2pm (depending on the conditions). They also offer horseback trips into the jungle, guided snorkel/kayak trips ($300), surfing lessons ($400 for one-on-one instruction), trips to the Mariettas ($450), whale-watching ($400), and, of course, surfboard rentals ($200, tri-fins, with leashes).

Another source for panga rentals, etc. is the **San Pancho Surf Shop** (Av. Tercer Mundo 28; ☎ **311/258-4212**).

Despite the rips, it's possible to surf on your own off the beach at San Pancho, mainly a short board shore break down at the southern end at President's Point. Otherwise plan on going to Chacala, which is right up the coast and accessible only by boat. This is a year-round north and south swell left.

Tortuga Turtles ★★★

Every summer, the beaches of Mexico become the nesting grounds for the Olive Ridley sea turtle, an endangered species that is also considered a delicacy (and aphrodisiac) by many coastal Mexicans. Because there have been numerous efforts to save the turtles by ecological groups both in Mexico and from abroad, remarkably the tide seems to be turning for these giant reptiles. While there are conservation groups all along the coast, in San Pancho the MTV Best **Grupo Ecológico de la Costa Verde** ★★ is one that actively invites and supports volunteers for 10-week stays. Grupo Ecólogico de la Costa Verde (America Latina #102, San Francisco, Nayarit; ☎ **311/258-4100;** www.project-tortuga.org) has been around since 1992 but local expat volunteers were involved in turtle rescue projects before that. In the last 15 years, they've released more than 280,000 hatchlings, building the nesting population from a low of 70 to the current number of more than 650. The work is entirely volunteer-based, reaching a peak of activity in August to September when waves of Olive Ridleys (and the occasional Leatherback) waddle up the sands to lay their eggs. It's nighttime work, starting at 9pm and finishing up as dawn breaks. Volunteers roam the beaches of San Pancho, scaring off poachers and collecting eggs to be transported to a nearby incubation facility. The organization operates with no government funding, supporting themselves by selling T-shirts as well as by publishing the only telephone directory of San Pancho's burgeoning expat population. If you're in town on a Thursday, drop by for their free slide show. Volunteers are always needed for the peak of the summer nesting period. Your only expense will be contributing to your lodging—considering that you'll get a 10-week understanding of coastal Mexican life in exchange, it's a real bargain.

San Sebastian

San Sebastian del Oeste and the highlands of the Sierra Madre used to be accessible only after an all-day butt-crunching bus ride coming up from the south or by small plane from Vallarta. Now San Sebastian is just a few short hours from Puerto Vallarta thanks to a recently completed road (and the stunning El Progresso bridge over the Rio Sebastian river). It's an easy ride, free of buses and trucks, and only the last 10km (6 miles) from the turn off are slightly troublesome. Along the way, you'll pass farmers coming back from their fields, kids on bikes, market women trudging slowly past young corn, and agave plantings.

Entering the town's main square is like going back in time to the 19th century—San Sebastian is a place truly worthy of the Pueblo Magico designation recently bestowed on it by the federal government. With a 500-year-old history, only 600 inhabitants, and an altitude of 1,350m (4,500 ft.), it's light years away from a Vallarta frame of mind. There's a sweet little main plaza bordered by roses, a filigreed wrought iron fence, a main church dedicated to San Sebastian, and a few low-key hotels and restaurants. You won't find any touristy ventures of any kind. The shops and facilities seem to be geared entirely for the people who live here.

For Internet access, you can try to go online at the community center, across the square, but the service is dial up and totally unreliable—another plus, in my opinion.

For more info on the town, visit www.sayulitalife.com.

SLEEPING

There are only a few places to stay in San Sebastian but the prices are right. My choice was the **Hotel Pabellon** (Lopes Mateo 55; ☎ **322/297-0200;** $200–$250 double; no credit cards) which, as the name suggests, is on the pavilion, or central square. The 11-room hotel was part of an old hacienda and boasts thick Colonial-style walls, high ceilings, king-size beds, a writing desk, and a wonderful inner courtyard with mature citrus trees, olive trees, giant ferns, and benches.

The **Hotel del Puente** (Lerdo de Tejada 3; ☎ **322/297-2834;** $150 double; no credit cards) is a cheaper option. The hotel is located in a former hacienda, on the east side of the main square. There are only seven rooms—clean, nicely decorated, and with private baths—and the inner courtyard and proximity to all things San Sebastian make it a very viable choice. It renovates often, though, so check in advance to make sure it's not closed.

Film buffs will want to check out the local landmark **Hacienda Jalisco** ★ (on the Las Palmas road at Km 55; ☎ **322/223-1695;** www.haciendajalisco.com; US$80 double; no credit cards). Owner Bud Accord has been here for decades and his Hollywood connections—going back to *Night of the Iguana* days—makes a stay here historical on many levels. The rates include breakfast and dinner, but you must book at least a week in advance. The 7-hectare (17-acre) ranch is anchored around a hacienda built 170 years ago as a facility to hold the silver and gold of San Sebastian before it was shipped out from Puerto Vallarta on the way to Spain. The main house has foot-thick walls, wooden shutters, high ceilings, and elegantly painted trompe l'oeil walls. Each of the 10 rooms has antiques and fireplaces but no electricity and obviously no TV or Internet, but the remodeled tiled bathrooms have skylights and good water pressure. Behind the original building are the ruins of a hydroelectrical plant, caved-in ovens used for smelting, now overgrown with ferns, and the detritus of the original hacienda.

EATING

There are a few restaurants in town but the best is **Lupita's** (on the Las Palmas rd. towards Puerto Vallarta; no phone; main courses $60–$80; no credit cards; daily 9am–9pm), which boasts a standard Mexican menu of tacos, burritos, sopes, caldos, and salsas. All the food is reliably good, from breakfast to dinner. The coffee, grown locally, is especially tasty.

On the main square there's also **El Fortin** (Cuahetmoc 40; no phone; main courses $48–$88; no credit cards) which has simple but tasty pastas, chicken dishes, and soups. The space includes a gallery and cafe where you can get drinks like freshly roasted coffee and even jewelry—all locally produced.

SIGHTSEEING

I can't stress enough that San Sebastian is slow, peaceful, and not tourist oriented. In keeping with that, there's not much to do here other than mountain bike and pay a visit to the local mines, called **La Quiteria** (8km/5 miles outside town; no phone; free admission; no set hours). This mine closed down in the 1930s and everything of possible use was quickly looted by locals. Still, a peek at the abandoned remains is a worthwhile education. Massive mountains of tailings from the diggings, abandoned machinery, and Industrial Age garbage litter the entrance into the earth. There are also trails on site that lead to Los Reyes, a nearby town that's even older than San Sebastian, but the hills are full of marijuana plantings and I don't suggest you go wandering off around there by yourself.

SHOPPING

At **Arte y Plateria** (Alcald 3; ☎ **322/297-2857**) Imelda Gutierrez and her husband, Jesus Gutierrez Castelanos, make very affordable delicate silver jewelry from local ore. They also have a half-dozen mountain bikes for rent ($50 per hr.) as well as *ponche,* a fruit-flavored alcohol that is a specialty of the area—the apple and peach are especially tasty.

Mazatlán

Mazatlán was a port and fishing center long before it became a spring break hot spot back in the 1960s. And it's still a fishing town, processing more than 40 tons of shrimp a year, while remaining Mexico's busiest harbor—it's the largest facility between Panama and Los Angeles. Its status as a tourist spot is more volatile. Even though surfers and snowbirds looking for a tropical getaway within easy driving distance from the U.S. have always come here, since the early 1970s, Mazatlán has been overshadowed by the tourism explosions of relatively nearby Cabo San Lucas and Puerto Vallarta and the development of Cancún and Ixtapa and Zihuatanejo farther south. The downward trend has been reversed by the gradual expansion of the Zona Dorada stretch of high-rise hotels at the northern end of the peninsula over the last 40 years—even now, though, there are almost no major international chain hotels. That's ironically a good thing as Mazatlán currently boasts far more independent locally owned accommodations than other Mexican resort cities. As a result, you'll get cheaper prices but won't sacrifice on service.

In the last 5 years, Mazatlán has undergone two more explosive changes. The arrival of the new marina complex at the northern end of the Zona Dorada has been accompanied by a rash of high-rise condos, while at the other end of town, the Centro Historico is emerging, phoenixlike, after decades of neglect. The latter development, led by both proud locals and pioneering foreigners, is very promising for Mazatlán's future. Four hundred seventy-nine buildings now dot the 180-block district, most of which were built in the 19th century and are now designated as historical landmarks. The Centro Historico is the antithesis of the Zona Dorada, notable for its narrow streets (built wide enough for horses but not trucks) and wonderful 19th-century buildings with thick walls, high ceilings, and neoclassical touches. It's the perfect environment for all the gourmet restaurants, boutique hotels, B&Bs, and art galleries that are developing there, and serves as a nice counter-point to Mazatlán's traditional spring break focus.

Thankfully, change hasn't ruined things yet, and the old-school Mazatlán approach that made this place hot back in the '60s is still going strong. Just ask any local, called Mazatlecos or *pata salada* (salty feet), and they'll be quick to cite three simple things—their beer, music, and baseball—as the main reasons for visiting. Indeed, the local Pacifico Brewery produces the Pilsner-style brew pacifico cerveza that has achieved worldwide fame. It's the perfect liquid for the climate, particularly when you're enjoying another local specialty: *banda tambora,* a variation of Bavarian music that is infectiously danceable. Finally, Los Venados, the baseball team that dominates local sports, has helped make Mazatlán that rare Mexican city where baseball is far more popular than soccer. The love of the game here is practically as infectious as the town's golden beaches and refreshingly simple vibe.

Best of Mazatlán

- **Best Six Degrees of Separation from Herman Melville:** Want to lay your claim to *Moby Dick*'s creator? The **Melville Boutique Hotel** in the Centro Historico of Mazatlán is so named in homage to a visit Melville made here back in the 1840s. The place exudes the charm of Mazatlán's classic era, at the turn of the last century; it's Pacific colonial in style, with high ceilings and thick walls. Like so many of Mexico's beach resorts, though, it's stuffed with amenities like Wi-Fi and cushy beds so you can get a dose of history without missing out on modern comforts. See p. 496.
- **Best Second Act Restaurant:** The resurgence of Mazatlán over the last decade or so is in many ways inspirational. And you can't get a better idea and appreciation of how some things change while some things stay the same than in Mazatlán's Centro Historico hood, with a visit to the amazing restaurant **Pedro Y Lola's.** Inside this renovated historic salon, you'll find some of the best new spins on Mexican cuisine in the country. See p. 501.
- **Best Hands-on-Body Experience: Bathhouse Indigo** has the best out of body experience you can rent by the hour, no doubt about it. Their massages are the perfect remedy for bruised and tired bodies fresh from the surf. And along with each one comes a soak in a Japanese-style *ofuro,* a precursor to the hot tub, and some choice local's advice about where the best breaks can be had. Founded and run by a woman surfer—and third-generation Mazatlateco—this spa is truly the sensual soul Mazatlán. See p. 510.
- **Best Nonstop Party: Carnaval** here is a serious business—Mazatlán's festivities are the biggest in Mexico. Expect weeks of pre-Lenten festivities that pit one outrageously dressed celebrant against another, and equally outrageous dancing and drinking. See p. 501.
- **Best Excuse for Lacing Up Your Sneaks:** Mazatlán's malecón is the

second longest in the world, and its 22km (14 miles) provide ample opportunities for in-line skating, jogging, or cycling. You might want to simply walk it, though, to soak in the amazing view and tons of art works lining it. See p. 505.

Getting There & Getting Around

Getting into Town

BY AIR **Mexicana** (☎ **800/531-7921;** www.mexicana.com) has the most direct flights to Mazatlán from cities in Mexico and the U.S. **AeroMexico** (☎ **800/237-6639;** www.aeromexico.com) connects flights via Mexico City and Hermosillo. From the West Coast, **Alaska Airlines** (☎ **800/252-7522;** www.alaskaair.com) and **Aero California** (☎ **1-800-AERO-CAL;** www.aerocalifornia.com) fly direct. If you're coming from Baja or somewhere else on the west coast, then **Aero Calafia** is the way to go (see box p. 366 in the Cabo section).

Mazatlán's **General Rafael Buelna Airport** (airport code MZT; ☎ **669/982-2177**) is about 20km (12 miles) south of the city on Highway 15. To get into town, you can take a fixed-price van (about $50 one-way) lined up outside or one of the official yellow airport taxis ($160 one-way, get a ticket from the kiosk near baggage claim).

BY BUS **Elite** (☎ **669/981-3811**), **Transportes del Norte** (☎ **669/981-2335**), **Transportes del Pacifico** ☎ **669/982-0577**), and **Estrellas del Pacifico** (☎ **669/984-2817**) all service Mazatlán from other parts of Mexico. The most reliable (and cleanest) carrier is Elite, though, which departs on the hour. So many bus lines service Mazatlán that you can find a departure almost anywhere within 45 minutes, starting from 5am.

The **Central de Autobuses** (main bus terminal; ☎ **669/982-8351**) is at Río Tamazula and Chachalacas. To get there from Avenida del Mar, walk 3 blocks inland on Río Tamazula; the station is on your right. Taxis line up in front of the bus station and run downtown for about $35, or you can take any of the red "Centro" or "Mercado" buses into downtown; see "By Bus" under "Getting Around" for info.

BY CAR To reach Mazatlán from the United States, take International Highway 15 from Nogales, Arizona, to Culiacán. At Culiacán, change to the four-lane tollway—it costs about $400 but is the only road considered safe and in drivable condition. On the tollway, total trip time from the United States to Mazatlán is about 10 hours. Consider an overnight stop, because driving at night in Mexico can be dangerous. From Puerto Vallarta, the 560km (350-mile) drive is not easy—the road winds through the mountains, but is in generally good condition. Take Highway 200 north to Las Varas. There it becomes four-lane Highway 68; follow that until you see a detour for Highway 15. Take 15 north to Mazatlán.

Europcar (☎ **669/989-0525**), **Alamo** (☎ **800/327-9633**), **Thrifty** (☎ **800/847-4389**), and **Hertz** (☎ **800/654-3131**) all have offices at the airport.

BY BOAT The ferry from La Paz to Mazatlán (the docks are south of the center) takes almost 18 hours and is far from comfortable—even if you have a cabin ($193, about three times the standard "salon" fare of $64). It leaves La Paz at 3pm and gets in at 9am the next day, God willing. One of the rules of passage is that no pregnant women are allowed. Hmmm. Could the ride be bumpy?

If you're masochistic enough to still want to take the ferry, don't bother trying to phone the ferry office to book ahead—they rarely answer. Instead, check out www.bajaferries.com/modules/content/index.php?id=2&sel_lang=English for timetables and specific pricing info.

Getting Around

BY BIKE Biking is my first choice for getting around Mazatlán even though the downtown traffic can be a bit much. That said, the city's terrain is level and the malecón here is wide and perfect for biking. **Kelly's Bicycle Shop** (Av. Cameron Sabalo 204, Zona Dorada; ☎ **699/914-1187;** www.kellys-bikes.com) is fairly central and has decent mountain bikes for $150 a day.

BY BUS After biking, the cheapest way to get around Mazatlán is on one of the city's four bus lines. **Sabalo Distrito** goes down the malecón into downtown; **Sabalo Cocos** goes past Gigante, Sharp's Hospital, and then on to downtown. Sabalo buses can be new green buses (with air-conditioning), costing $8, or white or yellow buses, (no air-conditioning) costing $4.50. Both run roughly from 6am until 10:30pm. **Cerritos Juárez** buses run from the Costa Bonita Resort to La Gran Plaza Mall via the Golden Zone, 5:40am to 8:30pm, for $5.50; **Toreo** buses also start at Costa Bonita Resort but go past the aquarium, the baseball stadium, and the central market and downtown; they run from 5:30am to 8:30pm and cost $5.50.

BY *PULMONIA* *Pulmonias* are open-aired souped-up **golf carts** and are simply a very Mazatlán way to get around. (They got their name because locals say that riding in one during winter could give you pneumonia.) Some drivers have pumped up the experience with bone-rattling sound systems. Don't expect seat belts or meters. Tourists love them but they are expensive, so be sure to confirm the price before you set off. The cost varies from $40 to $80 to go to the Centro Historico from Zona Dorada depending on the time of day (and on the operator's discretion). There's no *pulmonia* number to call; just hold out your hand while downtown and one will stop within a few seconds.

BY *AURIGAS* These red pickup trucks can carry eight passengers, for about $50 for the trip from Centro Historico to Zona Dorada. Call ☎ **669/981-3535** to arrange a drive in one.

BY SCOOTER In the Zona Dorada, you'll see a number of places that rent scooters. **Mania of Mazatlán** (Av. Camaron Sabalo 1102; ☎ **669/983-2196;** www.mazinfo.com/scooters/index.htm) is one of the best. Prices run about $100 an hour, $180 for 2 hours, and $650 for all day, plus gas. It's a fairly easy way to get around but not that cheap or safe, considering all the traffic.

BY TAXI Taxis in town aren't metered but are sometimes cheaper than *pulmonias* since a ride in one entails less price gouging. A taxi ride from Zona Dorada to Centro Historico runs $50 to $80. Call ☎ **669/985-2828,** or 669/981-5017 for service.

BY CAR You really don't need to have a car while in Mazatlán since public transportation is quick and plentiful; plus, parking can be a nightmare.

Basics

Orientation

Known as "The Pearl of the Pacific," Mazatlán is situated on a nearly 21km (13-mile) peninsula that runs north-south. It is basically broken up into a few distinct districts:

The **Zona Dorada** (Golden Zone) begins where Avenida del Mar intersects Avenida

Rafael Buelna and becomes Avenida Camarón Sábalo, which leads north through the abundant hotels and fast-food restaurants of the tourist zone. From here, the resort hotels, including the huge El Cid resort complex, spread northward along and beyond **Playa Sábalo.** The **Marina Mazatlán** development has changed the landscape north of the Zona Dorada considerably; hotels, condo complexes, and private residences rise around the new marina. This area north of the Marina El Cid is increasingly known as Nuevo Mazatlán. North of here is **Los Cerritos (Little Hills),** the northern limit of Mazatlán.

About 6km (4 miles) north of downtown lies the Sábalo traffic circle near the **Punta Camarón,** a rocky outcropping over the water.

In south Mazatlán is the **Centro Historico** (Historic Center), also known as **Old Town** or **Olas Altas,** after the closest beach. It is next to **El Centro,** the downtown area where the main market, church, and businesses are located.

The Centro Historico and Zona Dorada are like two ends of a dumbbell, linked by Avenida del Mar, which parallels the landmark 27km (17-mile) **malecón** boardwalk that starts at the Fiestaland complex (at the southern end of the Zona Dorada) and runs down to Olas Altas.

Tourist Info & Offices

The Sinaloa State Tourism Office (☎ **669/916-5160;** fondomixto@red2000.com.mx; open Mon–Fri 9am–6pm) is on the fourth floor of the Banrural Building, on the corner of Avenida Camaron Salo and Tiburon, Zona Dorada.

MTV Habla Español

Centro de Idiomas de Mazatlán, S.C. is located downtown, near the Cathedral, Callejón Aurora 203 Poniente (☎ **669/985-5606**). They have both group and individual instruction as well as home-stay possibilities. **English/Spanish For All** (Eloy Cavalos 149; ☎ **669/986-2471**) has an intensive 100-hour, 5-week course as well as home stays and field trips.

To hear some Mazatlán culture, tune in to either 89.7fm or 100.3fm, which plays banda, rock en Español, world, and dance music.

Recommended Websites

- **www.mazinfo.com**: A very complete, and consistently updated, general site about Mazatlán.
- **www.maztravel.com**: More advice about traveling to Mazatlán, including discount coupons and cruise ship info.
- **www.mazatlan.com.mx**: Maps, sports, and cultural, ecological, and tour info.
- **www.pacificpearl.com**: The site for Mazatlán's best free English language tourist publication, a monthly publication that is available all along the Golden Zone. It has news, maps, essential phone numbers, event calendars, classified ads, real estate info, fishing reports, and discount coupons.
- **www.mazatlaninteractivo.com.mx/new/en/**: The site for a tabloid monthly that you're likely to see around town.

Mazatlán Nuts & Bolts

American Express There's an American Express at Av. Camaron Sabalo 500, Zona Dorada (☎ **669/913-0600**). It's just south of the El Cid Mega Resort, on the beach side of the street. Hours are Monday to Friday, 9am to 6pm, and Saturday 9am to 1pm.

Banks **Banamex** is at Camaron Sabalo 424, Zona Dorada (☎ **669/913-8301**); it's also at the corner of Benito Juárez and Angel Flores, Centro (☎ **669/982-7665**). Banking hours are Monday to Friday, from 9am to 6pm. There are also ATMs all along the Zona Dorada.

Emergencies The best hospital in town is **Sharp Hospital,** Avenida Rafael Buelna and Las Cruces s/n (☎ **669/986-5676**). The runner up is **Balboa Hospital** (☎ **669/916-7933**), which has bilingual doctors, emergency services, and pre-approved traveler's insurance. The local **police** number is ☎ **669/914-8444.** Call ☎ **060** for any emergency and to report a traffic problem, call ☎ **669/983-2616.**

Internet/Wireless Hot Spots There aren't a lot of Internet cafes in Mazatlán but if you're in the Zona Dorada, you should be able to stumble upon one (or go to a coffee shop inside a hotel—most have Wi-Fi). If you can, try to seek out **Internet Cyber Café** across the street from the Costa de Oro hotel (Av. Camaron Sabalo 610; ☎ **669/913-2847**), it's open daily 8:30am to 10:30pm. Or try **Cyber Café** (Av. Camaron Sabalo 204; ☎ **669/913-2847**), next to Dominos Pizza; it's open daily 9am to 10pm. Costs vary from $15 to $20 for 30 minutes.

Laundry **Glemnsa Lavanderia & Tintoreria,** across from the Hotel Royal Villa (Calzada Cammaron Sabalo 1670s; ☎ **669/913-5555**), is open daily 7am to 9pm, and it charges $14 a load. They also have dry cleaning and service local hotels.

Pharmacies There are many pharmacies all along the Zona Dorada. **Farmacias Hidalgo** (German Evers at Hidalgo s/n; ☎ **669/985-4545**) is open 24 hours and makes home/hotel deliveries. Other 24-hour English spoken pharmacies include **Farmacia Belmar** (☎ **669/914-3199**), **Farmacia Dorada** (☎ **669/916-5741**), and **Farmacia Moderna** (☎ **669/916-5233**).

Post Offices The main post office is at Avenida Benito Juárez at Calle 21 de Marzo (☎ **669/981-2121**); it's open Monday to Friday from 8am to 5pm, and Saturday 9am to noon.

Safety Mazatlán is very popular with older snowbirds and people on fixed incomes for two reasons: It's cheap and it's very safe. As a family-oriented town that doesn't depend 100% on tourism, it simply does not have a major drug presence. Frankly, your greatest danger in Mazatlán stems from venturing into the water during high waves or jellyfish season. That said, as in all beach resort towns, the typical advice applies to having a safe time: Don't wander back streets away from the main drag, drunk; don't wander the unlit beach at night, drunk; don't accept rides from strangers, drunk.

Telephone Tips The local area code is **669.** Also be warned: Do *not* use the pay phones scattered throughout town that promise calls to the U.S. or Canada using just your credit card. The costs are insane. Buy a phone card from a pharmacy and use the Telmex public phones instead.

Sleeping

Without a doubt, Mazatlán is one of the cheapest resort cities in Mexico, and a shoppers' paradise when it comes to lodging. Cruising up Avenida del Mar along the malecón, you will see many places advertising rooms for around $500 a night and even less in low season. Stop and bargain and you'll get a room for one-third less.

As you might expect, staying in the Zona Dorada is the most expensive option. The farther south you go along Avenida del Mar, the cheaper it gets. Surprisingly the very sweet, well-appointed boutique hotels in the Centro Historico are affordable. Things will be changing soon, however. About 500 new hotel rooms are slated to open in 2007, including a new five-star Crown Plaza.

There are unfortunately no hostels in Mazatlán but with some very cheap hotel rates available and since bargaining is always possible, who needs 'em?

Cheap

→ **Hotel Playa Victoria** Right smack in the middle of the malecón is this very affordable, very ugly, but very clean low-rise. The traffic out front may drive you mad but that may be softened by the fact that you'll be staying in a suite, not just a basic bedroom. That means you get access to a basic but adequate kitchen and TV that you can turn up to ignore the cars down below. The rooms are outfitted with plastic chairs and such—barely a step above dorm room furniture—and the ugly pastels with little flourishes like stenciling on the block walls makes for a forgettable color scheme. And the bed? Well, you get what you pay for. The balconies with iron railings, which extend out to great views, make the whole experience bearable, though. *Av. del Mar 721. ☎ 669/981-5226. $354 double. MC, V. Amenities: Elevator. In room: A/C, TV, kitchen.*

→ **Hotel Posada la Misión** Gringo visitors have been coming back to this sweet, quiet, and cheap place for years and for good reason. Tucked away at the north end of the Zona Dorada, this long-time favorite hotel has survived the onslaught of the giant resorts because it is reasonably priced, clean, safe, and right in the heart of the Zona Dorada. Still, you don't get many amenities and the rooms themselves are spartan, with heavy uncomfortable furniture. Some rooms have very bare-bones kitchenettes, lacking coffee makers and other amenities, but that's fine with the long-time residents—some of whom come and stay for 6 months. *Av. Camaron Sabalo 2100. ☎ 669/913-24444. posada_la_mision@hotmail.com. $300 double. 2 free days for 5-day stays. MC, V. Amenities: Internet cafe; laundry; pool. In room: A/C (in 10 out of 90 rooms), TV, kitchenettes (in some).*

Doable

→ **Casa de las Leyendas** This spacious B&B, which helped to contribute to Centro Historico's renaissance, is housed in a building that was a storage warehouse for gold bullion in the 1800s—legend has it that gold is still buried under the courtyard. Today, the hotel is full of the sort of rewarding amenities that'll make you feel like you're living the 19th-century good life. The six rooms are spacious, with high ceilings, loaded with classic 19th century antiques, big windows for ventilation, and dark wood and ceramic touches throughout. Perks include yoga classes twice a week; a hot breakfast (included in the rates) that should hold you the entire day; and a big library and a common entertainment area with a large screen LCD TV and a big selection of DVDs. There's even an honor bar—it's that friendly of a place—and the view from the rooftop terrace is

MAZATLÁN

spectacular, offering picture-postcard sunsets over the Pacific. *Venustiano Carranza 2 & 4. ☎ 669/981-6180 or 602/445-6192 in U.S. www.casadeleyendas.com. US$79–US$85 double. MC, V. Amenities: Common use computer; free calls to the U.S.; free laundry service; small wading pool; Wi-Fi. In room: A/C, coffeemaker, fans, fridge, hair dryer, purified water, safe.*

MTV Best → **El Loro de Oro Inn** ★★★ The location, a half-block from the Plaza Machado and its restaurants and cafes, and attention to detail (free Internet, always-on hot water, totally new appliances in the kitchenettes) all help to make the El Loro the best choice if you want to stay downtown. It's small, only four studios and two suites, but that just enhances the casual atmosphere created by owners Tony and Lucy. The hotel is anchored around a tiny but charming central tropical courtyard with a swimming pool and an area for lounging. A major bonus of staying here is the proximity to Te Amo Lucy's Taqueria y Mas restaurant, which is part of the Inn (see "Eating," p. 498). *Constitución 622. ☎ 669/982-8996 or 714/369-8205 in U.S. US$99 double. MC, V. Amenities: Restaurant; pool. In room: A/C, TV, fan, Internet, kitchenettes/kitchens, purified water.*

→ **Hotel La Siesta** La Siesta hangs a plaque with a quote from Jack Kerouac's *On the Road:* "The people that interest me the most are the crazies." But you'd be far from crazy to stay at this place, located at the edge of the Centro Historico, overlooking the malecón and right next to the original Shrimp Bucket (which functions as its in-house restaurant). Built in 1952, it's showing its age a bit with uneven tiles and a slightly musty odor, but the location is nice. There are 58 rooms, so there are plenty of choices; just note that the rooms in the back are vaguely dark and musty. All of the rooms are simply furnished: one chair, one table, decent beds. I'd try for one of the oceanfront rooms, since they boast a full-size balcony—a very nice perk if the traffic doesn't bother you. *Olas Altas 11 Sur. ☎ 669/981-2640. www.lasiesta.com.mx. $472–$1,000 for oceanview double, $413–$850 no view. AE, MC, V. Amenities: Restaurant; bar; business services (free computer use); car rental; laundry service; pool. In room: A/C, TV, phone, Wi-Fi.*

MTV Best → **The Melville Boutique Hotel** ★★★ All the 20 suites here are named after artists, poets, and writers—in keeping with the creative vision of owner Alfredo Rubio, the primary force behind the renovation of the Centro Historico. As for the hotel's own literary name, it's in honor of Herman Melville's stay back in the spring of 1843. Since that historic visit, the building has served as the city's first post office in the 1870s and then became a Carmelite convent near the turn of the 20th century. Today the Melville, heavy with tasteful antiques, probably gets some decent action within the confines of its massive colonial-era walls and 6m-high (20-ft.) ceilings—especially with rooms devoted to the likes of Anaïs Nin. Each room is decorated slightly differently, but my favorite was the Nin, which has a custom-made wrought iron bed frame that curls and swoops around a sexy red lace curtain. In addition to kitchenettes in most rooms, there's a pleasant interior courtyard—a perfect spot to finally read your copy of *Moby Dick. Constitucion 99. ☎ 669/982-8474. www.themelville.com. US$80–US$100 double. AE, MC, V. Amenities: Laundry; library; wheelchair friendly. In room: A/C, TV, kitchenettes, purified water, telephone, Wi-Fi.*

Splurge

→ **El Cid Marina Beach Hotel** ★★ There are two El Cids in town, El Cid Mega and El Cid Marina. The Mega is truly mega, a

Mazatlán Sleeping & Eating

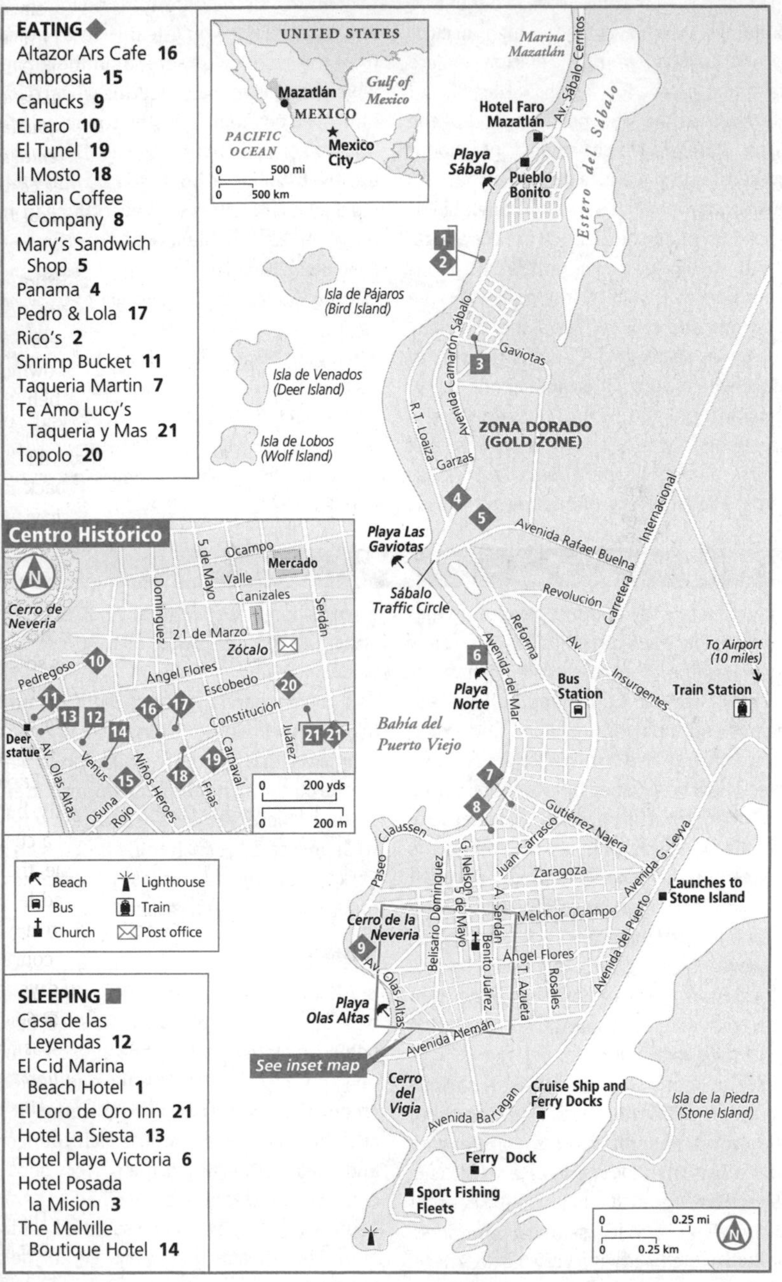

minicity of a sort. Its northern neighbor, the Marina, is also huge, spread out over 11 buildings, some seven stories high, all clustered around a new marina where yachters come for berths. The El Cid Marina is at the very northern end of the Zona Dorada, which means just about everything you want to do in Mazatlán is a bus or *pulmonia* ride away. Though El Cid offers free shuttle service to the Mega, about 10 blocks down, you're still miles from Centro Historico, the aquarium, the malecón, and el Faro. For some, that may not be an issue since El Cid is the sort of place where you can do just about everything without setting foot outside. On-site are pools, swim-up bars, a nearby golf course, a fleet of fishing boats, and restaurants. The hotel's grounds are so spread out that electric cart trams are on hand to take guests to the outermost buildings. If you're a yachter you'll feel right at home from the second you set foot in the lobby, which has a giant ship steering wheel doubling as a chandelier, to the rooms, which boast a general nautical theme. The rooms are even big as a boat, some with well-stocked kitchenettes with everything from microwaves to blenders. *Av. Camarón Sábalo s/n, between Av. Rodolfo T. Loaiza and Circuito Campeador.* ☎ *669/913-3333. www.elcid.com. US$116 double. AE, DISC, MC, V. Amenities: Restaurant; bar; laundry service; luggage storage; pools; wheelchair friendly; Wi-Fi; yacht slips. In room: A/C, TV, balcony, blender, coffeemaker, fans, hair dryer, kitchenettes (in some rooms), microwave, security box, telephone.*

Eating

Unfortunately the gourmet revolution that has hit other Mexican cities has been slow to arrive here. There are a few bright spots such as **Pedro Y Lola's** and **Topolo** (see below) and thankfully you can find excellent coffee all over town. Generally, however, you'll be satisfied but rarely surprised while dining out in Mazatlán. The prices are usually quite reasonable—no complaints there—but the next generation of great local chefs has not yet surfaced. Based on what's happening in the Centro Historico, however, it won't be long. Within a few blocks walk you can get everything from fish tacos to great espresso to vegetarian to upscale gourmet food.

For now, it's safe to stick with shrimp. Mazatlán calls itself the shrimp capital of the world and it's hard to argue with that. Visit the **Mercado Central** (see "Shopping," p. 510), and you'll see that shrimp—be it fried, sautéed, shredded, boiled, or steamed—is a very big deal here. But also keep in mind that because the town is in an agricultural and ranching state, there's also plenty of good beef on hand.

If you're searching for cheap eats, stop in one of the many loncherías (small establishments that are only open for lunch) scattered throughout the downtown area. At any of these, you can get a *torta* (a sandwich on a small French roll) stuffed with a variety of meats, cheeses, tomatoes, onions, and chiles for around $20.

Cheap

➔ **Altazor Ars Café** BISTRO This was one of the original cafes on Machado, helped in large part by the presence of neighboring Pablo Y Lola's, the undisputed cream of the culinary crop in Mazatlán. It's as smart as its neighbor but much younger and cheaper—making it the perfect bookend for this section of Machado Plaza. There's good coffee—some say the best in Mazatlán—cheap (and very good) deli sandwiches, tasty bagels and lox, and adequate reasonably priced dinner offerings (cordon bleu chicken, steak, and, of course, shrimp). Everyone who talks about the cafe calls it "bohemian," which I guess it is. If you want to hook up with the local art scene, come here and strike up a conversation with any of the moody disaffected types nursing a coffee while chain smoking their cigarettes right down to the filters. The best seats are out on the sidewalk under the umbrellas—grab one, as well as one of the chess boards on hand, and make yourself comfortable. On weekends, there's live music. *Plaza Machado s/n. ☎ 669/981-5559. Main courses $100. No credit cards. Fri–Sat 9am–1am; Sun–Thurs 9am–11pm.*

➜ **Ambrosia** VEGETARIAN Hungry for tofu? Then come down to Mazatlán's one-and-only vegetarian restaurant, in the Centro Historico. The pastas are totally satisfying, the salads are wonderful, the soups are savory, and the comida corrida is really one of the best deals in town. I didn't like the beet soup but, then again, I'm normally not a fan of beets. No matter what you end up eating, just be sure to order the lemonade—it's killer. *Sixto Osuna s/n. ☎ 669/985-0333. Main courses under $100. No credit cards. Daily 11am–11pm.*

➜ **El Tunel** MEXICAN Located across from the historic Angela Peralta Theater, this small but significant place dishes up the best home-style Mexican eats in town. Their pozole gets raves, as do the gorditas and *polla a la paza* (essentially grilled chicken). Their *horchata* (rice beverage) is also quite satisfying. You'd be hard-pressed to spend more than $100 on anything here. *Calle Carnaval 1207, at Plaza Machado. ☎ 669/698-26905. Main courses under $100. No credit cards. Mon–Tues and Wed–Sun around 6pm–late.*

➜ **Mary's Sandwich Shop** GRILL Locals insist that this place has the best hamburgers in Mazatlán but I can't imagine why you'd come here and eat American. The whole experience is pretty fast-food-like—you sit outside on red plastic chairs at plastic tables under red umbrellas. At least it's better than going to Burger King (which is just down the street), and it's cheap and filling. There are two locations for your dining pleasure, both on Camarón Sábalo. The first is behind Rico's Coffee Shop (across from The Inn at Mazatlán) and the second across from Pueblo Bonito Mazatlán. *Camaron Sabalo s/n, between Av. Rodolfo T. Loaiza and Circuito Campeador. ☎ 669/913-0090. Main courses under $100. No credit cards. Daily 10am–10pm.*

➜ **Panama** BAKERY The main reason to come here is for the bakery, which churns out downright excellent pastries and breads. When it comes to the main entrees, baked goods still stand out—the Huevos Bravos (essentially eggs Benedict with a pork loin for extra pep) come on top of great bread, but the heavy cheese topping is heart-stoppingly thick. There are Panama bakery outlets all over town so if you just need a quick pick-me-up, you can drop into one easily. The decor at all locations is a mix of Parisian meets Mexican; I've listed the best located one here. *Calle Camaron Sabalo s/n, between Juárez and Carrasco. ☎ 669/913-6977. Main courses under $100. MC, V. Daily 7am–11pm.*

➜ **Taqueria Martin** TACOS Their beans are cooked *de la olla* style (in the pot), they grill their green onions, and best of all, they're open until 4am. All three are reasons why this place, about 3 blocks east from the Fisherman's Monument on the malecón, is where the city's *pulmonia* and taxi cab drivers come when they need to fill up in the wee hours. There are no surprises here—you'll get al pastor, carne asada, quesadillas—but at 4am, your stomach isn't necessarily ready for something startling, no? Plus, the beans are amazing *and* free. *Gutrerrez Najera 302. ☎ 669/981-0126. Main courses under $50. No credit cards. Daily 6pm–4am.*

Doable

→ **Canucks** PUB FARE This is more a locals' hangout than a culinary destination (the food isn't that amazing, honestly). Yet the atmosphere is fun enough to take your mind off the mediocre quality of what's on your plate, and the prices are okay. (If you've got Canadian money on Mon and Tues, you'll get a discount.) Live music and comics, pool, darts, and TV dominate the scene. Basically, it's the Señor Frog's approach to fine dining. Every Friday at 4pm, this is also the meeting place of choice for a large group of foreigners and Mexicans, called "What's Up Amigos." Everyone is welcome to join this social gathering, so if you visit at this time, come prepared to break out your *"Que paso?" Paseo Claussen 259. ☎ 669/981-5916. www.canucksinmaz.com. Main course $150. MC, V. Daily 1–11pm.*

→ **Shrimp Bucket** SEAFOOD No doubt you'll be tempted to stop in at this legendary Mazatlán landmark since it's where Carlos Anderson started out building his mega-chain of restaurant-bars-entertainment centers (Señor Frog's and so on), but do so only for historical perspective. True, it's air-conditioned and there's Wi-Fi on the patio, but it's probably going to be full of fools fresh off the cruise ship. Go ahead, have a bucket, but if it's bland and overpriced, don't blame me. *Av. Olas Altas 11-126 Sur, inside the Hotel La Siesta. ☎ 669/981-6350. Main courses $100. AE, MC, V. Sun–Thurs 6:30am–11pm; Fri–Sat until 3am.*

→ **Te Amo Lucy's Taqueria y Mas** ★ MEXICAN You can spot this little sweet taqueria by the sign out front with a red heart and the words "Te amo Lucy." Lucy is owner Tony's wife and she's the one who dishes up mole according to her grandmother's recipes, as well as tacos, huge breakfasts, pozole, and a Wednesday night comida corrida ($99) of pan-fried steak, mashed potatoes, and nopales salad. The dining is practically alfresco, since the restaurant is located on a side courtyard of the Loro de Oro Inn (see "Sleeping," p. 495). *Constitucion 622. ☎ 669/982-8996. Main courses $100. No credit cards. Daily 8am–1pm and 5–11pm.*

→ **Topolo** ★★ MEXICAN Props to owner Manolo Cardona for developing a very civilized alternative to the bland overpriced "Mexican" food one finds up in Zona Dorada—though it's just a block off the Plaza Machado, this place is moderately priced. It's accurately billed as "contemporary Pre Hispanic"; there are grasshoppers on the menu and huitlacoche is used in several dishes. Often the menu veers off track, though; consider the chicken breast stuffed with ham and topped with a plum sauce. Please. I did like the *camarones en coco*, sweet and sour coconut shrimp that was certainly way better than the slop one gets at the Shrimp Bucket. But this is Mazatlán, and *everyone* here knows shrimp. The decor in this converted 19th-century home, however, is stunningly seductive—the red-white-black color scheme is highlighted by a curvy bar. It all feels very grown up. *Constitucion 629, corner Juárez. ☎ 669/136-0660. www.topolomaz.com. Main courses $200. MC, V. Mon–Sat noon–11pm.*

Splurge

→ **Il Mosto** ★ ITALIAN This Italian joint right on the plaza of the Centro Historico is one of the longstanding restaurants that has helped make this part of town a tourist destination. The waiters are a little stuffy but the homemade olive bread and the appetizers more than make up for their undeserved snooty 'tude. Their fish soups and fried octopus are wonderful and could make a meal by themselves. If you're just sick of fish, then try the black burro—a thick steak with a crunchy burned butter crust. They also get high marks for a very good wine list. *Sixtosuna 510. ☎ 669/985-4366. Main courses $140. MC, V. Daily noon–midnight.*

MTV Best → **Pedro & Lola's** ★★★ MEXICAN Alfredo Rubio, the man everyone says is responsible for the Centro Historico's revitalization, managed to turn a fading 1890s building on Machado Square into its current incarnation as one of Mazatlán's most popular restaurants. It was formerly a major salon/artistic hangout for decades, and its name is in homage to Mexican superstars Pedro Infante and Lola Beltrane who frequented the salon long ago. Today, an artistic vibe is threaded into the decor, which is blue and white with high arched doors that lead out to the sidewalk. On the walls hang modern art paintings and portraits of musicians, and the main room is focused around a small stage where Jock, a 70-something session man, plays solo saxophonist renditions of any tune you toss out. Then there's the food; the menu is one of the best in town—it includes garlic shrimp, *machaca* (dried beef cooked with peppers and eggs), and garlic octopus in guajillo pepper, wine, and lemon. I personally loved the almond fish (in a guajillo chile sauce over fettuccini), though. The alfresco dining on the sidewalk is great for people-watching. *Carnaval 1303 at Constitucion, Plaza Machado. ☎ 669/982-2589. www.restaurantpedroylola.com. Main courses $80–$155. AE, MC, V. Daily 6pm–2am.*

Cafes

Caffeine centros are all over Mazatlán, which is probably not a surprise, considering the town's long European history and its status as a major port. You can find very good coffee at a lot of places but three stand out: the **Italian Coffee Company** (Av. del Mar 1020; ☎ **669/992-0100**) about midway down the malecón, is the first that catches the eye. It's a cozy date-friendly coffee shop, popular with local kids, and open 8am to 11pm daily. They have everything from two dozen different coffee choices to great hot chocolate, paninis, pastries, croissants, and even free Wi-Fi. Farther north in the Zona Dorada is **Rico's,** inside the El Cid Mega (Av. Camarón Sábalo s/n, between Av. Rodolfo T. Loaiza and Circuito Campeador; no phone). The pastries are fab but it's the Granita coffee, from Veracruz, Chiapas, and Oaxaca, that will get your blood pumping. But my absolute favorite cafe is **El Faro,** a tiny stall in Centro Historico (corner of Mariano Escobedo and Heriberto Frias s/n; no phone) where the lone woman barista makes great cappuccinos. It's right on the corner of a building and can't be more than 3 by 1.5m (10 by 5 ft.). She has a very loyal following of local customers, despite the small space. The stand is only open in the daytime, closing around 7pm.

MAZATLÁN

Partying

In the 1960s, Mazatlán was *the* prime party town in Mexico—without it, we wouldn't have spring break madness as we know it today. Though it's been eclipsed by other Mexican beach resorts over the years, spring break is still a huge presence here. It gets going with MTV Best **carnaval** ★★★, the pre-Lenten submission to all things carnal. It's not quite Rio, but don't let that stop you: Mazatlán's hundred-year tradition of bacchanalia and bad behavior is truly a city-wide event, stretching all along the malecón. After New Orleans and Rio, Mazatlán's carnaval is the world's biggest pre-Lent celebration, attracting a half-million annually. It gets going in mid-February and goes on for weeks—meaning you'll have no shortage of parades, concerts, and fiestas to frequent. And the rest of the year is just a replay of this mania—picture a year-round onslaught of Jello vodka shots and bass-heavy house music.

These days, Mazatlán's nightlife scene is primarily centered around the Zona Dorada-malecón. While the **Valentino's** (Fiestaland) complex gets a lot of well-deserved attention, you can't forget that down the malecón is the **original Señor Frog's,** a landmark that sadly will be moving from its long-time home in 2007.

Bars

→ **Joe's Oyster Bar** A perennial favorite, mainly for its live music and laid-back ambience, this bar is on the sand, under a palapa, and boasts daily two-for-one beer specials. The first special is from 4pm to 7pm (when the pre-club drinking begins) and then it kicks in later at 8pm to midnight. It's open until 2am. *Inside the Los Sabalos Hotel, Av. Rodolfo Loaiza 100.* ☎ *669/983-5333.*

→ **Señor Frog's** ★★ If you go into only one Señor Frog's (you'll practically trip over them in Mexico), make it this one. That's because this location is where the chain and concept all began, over 30 years ago. Unfortunately, everyone seems to know it: On any weekday morning, you'll find cruise ship passengers dancing in a conga line around the room, bedecked in balloon hats, and drinking from 46cm-high (18-in.) "yard" glasses.

Despite the touristy crowds, though, this Señor Frog's somehow manages to be a major locals' hangout, especially on weekends. I dare you to leave without getting drunk on a weekend—you'll have to resist the temptations of one very convincing Jello shot man, waitresses carrying tequila bottles and shot glasses in their bandolier belts, who scan the room for victims, and giant ice-filled buckets of beer on every table.

In the beginning, the idea here was simple: all you can drink and eat for $4. Though Señor Frog's now has a sound system that rocks—playing house, reggae, and Nortec tunes—along with all the fancy drinking mechanisms, it's still a fairly fun, inexpensive trip to oblivion.

It's worth repeating that this place is planning on moving to the new classier marina area, north of the Zona Dorada in 2007, which might mean a certain loss of mood. You may not care after your third Jello shot, though. *Av. del Mar 882.* ☎ *669/982-1925. www.senorfrogs.com.*

Clubs

Without a doubt, the **Fiestaland Complex** (intersection of Camaron Sabalo at Rafael Buelna; ☎ **669/984-1666** for all clubs) is the heart of Mazatlán's club-land. The location is perfect, right at the end of the Zona Dorada and the start of the malecón. Six clubs make up the venue but **Valentino's** is the centerpiece, a ginormous Moorish-looking ice-cream castle plopped on the edge of the rocks right above the ocean. The laser shows here are a big draw, along with the pool tables, foam parties (every Thurs), and massive sound system.

Recently, though, Valentino's has been overshadowed somewhat by its twice as large 2,000-capacity downstairs neighbor, MTV Best **Bora Bora** ★★. This open-air space seems to have done everything right in creating an unlike-any-other-club ambience. After you walk down the covered walkway entrance, leaving the endless grind of the traffic from the Camaron Sabalo intersection behind, you'll find yourself in a space that is open to the sky and framed by curved stairways and

Mazatlán Partying & Sightseeing

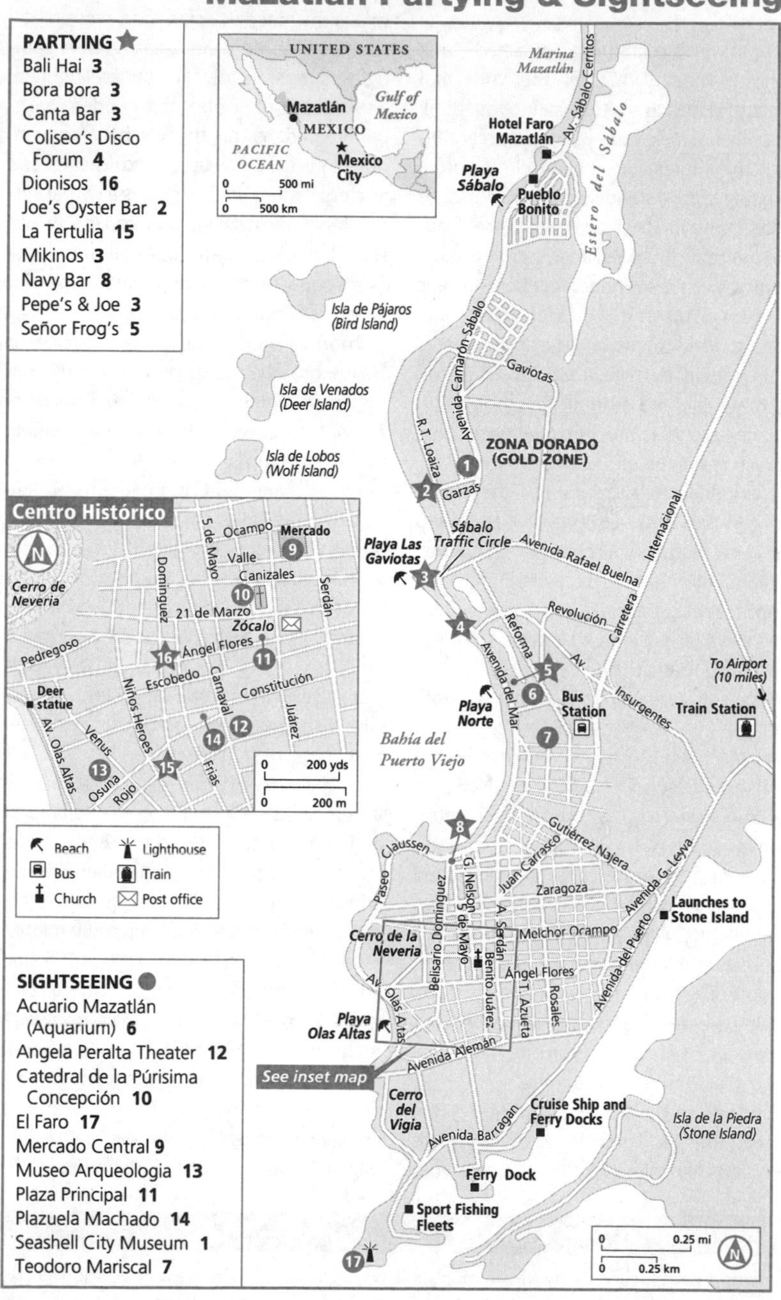

platforms that rise above the dance floor. The effect is somewhere between a Klingon war-bird and a half-finished Frank Gehry project. Don't let the volleyball court and beach setting make you think this place is relaxed—you won't blend in with the sophisticated clientele if you're sporting sloppy sandals, soiled shorts, or 2-day stubble. There are two dance areas and the soundtrack—trance, hip-hop, electronica, even some banda tambora—keeps the crowd moving. And, for those who need a little sit down, there are picnic tables down by the water. Covers range between $55 and $109, although for $218 you can drink as much as you want from 8pm to midnight.

Next door to Bora Bora is the often-ignored **Bali Hai,** a sports bar; **Pepe's & Joe,** a restaurant/microbrewery; **Mikinos,** a piano bar that offers something a bit more sedate than its way pumped-up neighbors (and no cover); and last, but not least, the **Canta Bar,** a karaoke place where you can sing your heart out until 4am.

Just a block down Avenida del Mar is **Coliseo's Disco Forum** (Av. del Mar 406; ☎ **669/990-1199**), a 2,500-person monstrosity that is the home of Mazatlán's electronica DJs as well as a major live band venue. It's round (like a coliseum) and insanely popular. Get here soon after they open at 10pm on the weekends if you want a table. They do have two-for-one drinks during the week but on the weekends, your $109 cover will only get you one free drink. After that, you're on your own.

Outside of the Golden Zone, you'll find places like **La Tertulia** ★ (Casa de los Forcados Mazatlecos, Belisario Domínguez 1414; no phone). This very old-school cantina is the place to come for a sense of the soul of Mazatlán. It's dedicated to bullfighters, specifically Portuguese fighters, and consists of nothing but wooden chairs, punctuated by a few open-barred windows onto the street and bull heads and posters on the walls. It's a manly bar, for manly men, with the prices of drinks scrawled in colored chalk on the metal doors out front. Take that earring out before you come in here bub. . . .

Another major downtown space is **Dionisos**—aka the House of Funk ★★ (Belisario Dominguez 1406; ☎ **669/985-0333**). It's in a great neoclassical building in the heart of the Centro Historico, and is open until midnight during the week, and 2am on the weekends. If you're in the mood for a low-key environment, with electro clash, Brazilusion, rave, and psychedelic tunes, come here. This is a gay-friendly place with some of the best music and DJs you'll find in Mazatlán. They were just putting in a sushi bar when I visited, which should go well with the martinis—they're the best in town.

If you're ready for something that is totally sleazy and scary, grab a *pulmonia* and head south to the **Navy Bar** (Av. del Mar 5500; no phone). It's a big empty warehouse kind of place where the drinks are cheap, the DJ snarls, lining up some rock en Español, followed by some electronica, and you can get "anything you want"—or so I was told by a charming bum out front with no front teeth. And we're not talking about silver jewelry or T-shirts with funny sayings on them. The bar's just-above-Skid-Row ambience, though, might have a certain appeal if you're tired of touristy glitz.

Heading to the Beach

Mazatlán is that rare town where most of the beaches are easily accessible and the water is largely clean everywhere. The city beaches, running north to south, are

Playa Gaviotas, running from the Hotel Playa Mazatlán up to the El Cid Mega Resort; **Playa Sabalo** ★, in the Golden Zone, north of Valentino's and probably the most popular beach in town; **Punta Camaron,** south of Valentino's, popular with surfers; **Playa Marlin,** along Avenida del Mar and notable for palapa restaurants on the sand and a great boogie boarding beach; **Playa Norte,** popular with soccer players; **Olas Altas,** in Old Town and marking the southern start of the malecón—it's sometimes less-than-clean and with a rough shore break; and **Playa Los Pinos,** where local fishermen pull their pangas up on the sand and sell their catch from their boats. As a result, it's *not* clean or suitable for swimming; still, it's known for good waves.

Off shore there are the three islands that define the coast here: **Lobos** (Wolf), **Venados** (Deer), and **Parajos** (Bird). Of the three, **Venados** is the only one open to visitors, and it's a fairly popular diving and snorkeling site. If you decide to visit the island, bring your own food and drinks since there are no facilities. You can get to Venados via catamaran boats, which depart from the Agua Sports Center at El Cid Resort in Zona Dorada; the cost is about $100 round-trip and boats leave daily at 10am, noon, and 2pm.

Green Means Go

Mazatlán lifeguards have instituted a flag system to advise bathers of the water conditions here. Green = calm, Red = danger, White = jellyfish (usually in June), Orange and Yellow = caution due to sting rays.

Farther south there is **Isla de la Piedra** (Stone Island), which is not really an island but rather the tip of a long peninsula. It's notable for miles of deserted beaches sprinkled with palapa restaurants. To get there from the center of town, board a Circunvalación or Playa Sur bus from the north side of the Plaza Principal for the ride to the boat landing, Embarcadero–Isla de la Piedra. Small motorboats make the 5-minute trip to the island every 15 minutes or so from 7am to 6pm for a modest price of about $20.

Sightseeing

Festivals/Events

See "Partying," p. 501, for info on Mazatlán's biggest festival, carnaval.

On the weekend of the first Sunday in October, **Rosario,** a small town 45 minutes south on Highway 15, holds a **festival honoring Our Lady of the Rosary.** Games, music, dances, processions, and festive foods mark the event. From May 1 to May 10, Rosario holds its **Spring Festival.**

In mid-October, the village of **Escuinapa,** south of Rosario on Highway 15, holds a **Mango Festival.**

For more information on area festivals and events, call the State Tourism Office at ☎ **669/981-8886.**

Main Attractions

The best tour operator here is **Pronatours** (☎ **669/916-7720;** www.elcid.com.mx). In addition to a 3-hour city tour, they offer tours to many interesting villages nearby, as well as to the Pacifico Brewery that churns out the pacifico cerveza you'll probably enjoy a lot of during your visit.

Mazatlán's MTV Best **malecón** ★★ is one of the city's premier attractions, and rightly so. It is the second longest in the world, stretching 22km (14 miles) from the Valentino's complex (aka Fiestaland) all the way down to Olas Altas beach, in the historic district. It's broad enough for in-line skating, jogging, or cycling, and it allows for easy access to the beach. It's also where Mazatlán's character reveals itself through some pretty amazing public art. Among the statues and art works scattered along its length are a full-size bronzed *pulmonia;* an original 1900, 6,000-plus-gallon Pacifico beer vat; the Fisherman's Monument (which includes a representation of El Faro, the lighthouse); a statue of a school of dolphins . . . you get the idea.

One particular statue worthy of a viewing is the one dedicated to **Don Cruz Lizarraga,** at the intersection of Avenida de los Deportes and Rio Fuerte. Cruz was the founder of the 16-member Banda El Recodo group, which is now in its second generation cranking out the polka-fied banda tambora style of music, a distinctive mix of four clarinets, three trumpets, a tuba, three trombones, and a tambora (similar to a large marching snare drum).

After you're done checking out the statue, drop into the **Acuario Mazatlán** ★★, right across the street (Av. de los Deportes 111; ☎ **669/981-7815;** www.acuariomazatlan.gob.mx). This is the best aquarium in Mexico, with about 250 species of fish. They have seal shows (for $20 you can get a kiss from a sea lion here), diving exhibitions, a shark tank, crocodiles, and a "bird theater." The cost is $50 for adults and the hours are daily 9am to 6pm.

Before leaving the aquarium, try to stop in and buy something from the gift shop, **El Planeta Azul.** It supports the facility's rehabilitation center for pelicans, birds of prey, parrots, and ducks.

No visit to Mazatlán is complete without a trip to **El Faro** ★, the world's tallest operating lighthouse (now that the one in Gibraltar has been shut down). It's perched on top of the 154m-high (515-ft.) Cerro del Creston hill that overlooks the harbor and makes for a brisk half-hour climb up to the top. And, of course, if you're attempting to climb El Faro in the middle of August, bring an umbrella and plenty of water. The 1500-watt halogen light inside is visible for more than 48 nautical miles out, but it's cool to check out up close.

The **Plaza Machado** was Mazatlán's original central plaza and today is the heart of the Centro Historico. It also functions as a patch of quiet in the bustling center—it's surrounded by landmarks new and old, from the Peralta Theater, to new restaurants and cafes, to art galleries. The streets are narrow here, so traffic is minimal, which makes the plaza one of the best places in Mazatlán to spend a peaceful afternoon.

Two blocks south of the central plaza, the **Angela Peralta Theater** ★ (Carnival 1024; ☎ **669/982-4446;** www.teatroangelaperalta.com) is the city's main cultural attraction. The theater was built in the 1870s and was named after opera diva Angela Peralta following her visit to Mazatlán. The entire town turned out to escort her to her hotel, where she then gave an impromptu performance from the balcony. Sadly, that was to be her last performance. She fell victim to yellow fever during her boat trip over, and she died without ever setting foot inside the theater. The Peralta has gone through a number of incarnations, playing host to vaudeville, movies, boxing matches, and even cars (during its ignominious parking garage period). In the mid-1970s, a hurricane trashed it and it was left abandoned for more than a decade until a 5-year restoration was finished in 1992, setting the stage (so to speak) for the gradual gentrification of the Centro Historico. It is one of the few remaining 19th-century opera houses in Mexico that still functions as a theater, exhibition space, gallery, and concert hall. When I visited during the first few weeks of March, for example, there were a local artists exhibition, an author's reading, a ragtime band performance, a contemporary dance, a Flamenco dance performance, and a solo Cuban music show on offer. Shows begin anywhere from 6 to 10pm, depending, with tickets ranging from $350 to free. Check the events schedule on the local website www.pacificpearl.com for details.

One and a half blocks from Paseo Olas Altas is the **Museo de Arqueologia** (Sixto de Osuna 76; ☎ **669/985-3502**). The museum is small but offers a very complete look at Sinaloan pre-Hispanic history. Displays are devoted to petroglyphs, figurines, and unique Sinaloan red/black glazed pottery. It's open Tuesday to Sunday from 10am to 1pm and 4pm to 7pm, and admission is free.

The **Plaza Principal,** also called Plaza Revolución, is the heart of the city, filled with vendors, shoeshine stands, and people of all ages out for a stroll. At its center is a Victorian-style, wrought-iron bandstand with a diner-type restaurant underneath. No matter what your religious beliefs are, a visit to the city's main church, the **Catedral de la Purísima Concepción** (Cinco de Marzo at Juárez; no phone) here is a rewarding experience. The cathedral, finished in 1899, is jaw-droppingly beautiful, a mish-mash of styles that reflects centuries of religious architecture: Moorish, Roman, Doric, Gothic, neoclassical, baroque. There are even stars of David in the upper stained glass windows, a nod to Jesus, the King of the Jews. Massive chandeliers hang over the nave and marble and gold cover almost everything. The cathedral is open daily from 6am to 1pm, and 4pm to 8pm and there's no fee to visit it.

Finally, are you looking for Pink-mouth Murex to complement your Umbilica Ovula? Or just confused? Then it's time for a visit to the **Seashell City Museum** (Av. Playa Gaviotas 407; ☎ **669/913-1301;** www.seashellcitymuseum.com). Reportedly the only sea shell museum in Mexico, at first glance this place seems more like a store than a museum. Wind chimes, shell jewelry, and, of course, shells of every color, size, and shape are for sale. But venture upstairs and you'll see the rarest display-only items in the free museum. The museum is open daily 9am to 7pm.

Playing Outside

Biking

Mazatlán is a biker's paradise many mountain bike paths dot the foothills just northeast of town. I recommend going with a guide, however, because you won't be able to find the trails by yourself—at least not the first time. **Kelly's Bicycle Shop** (Av. Cameron Sabalo 204; ☎ **699/914-1187;** www.kellys-bikes.com) is the best bike rental space in the Golden Zone and they book tours. Besides selling pedals, shoes, tubes, tires, and everything else you'd expect from a full-service bike store, Kelly's rents mountain bikes ($150 a day) that are perfect for spinning down the malecón to the Centro Historico. Owner Fernando Kelly is even the only certified bike mechanic in Mazatlán, so you can rest assured that whatever bike you rent there will work fine.

Among the mountain bike tours on offer at Kelly's are **Piedras Blancas,** the 2000 World Cup mountain bike route, a short 8.5km (5 ¼-mile) 3-hour trip over very technical terrain with tight turns, switchbacks, and short climbs, for $450, and the easier **Eco Ride Tour,** a 20km (12-mile) ride over single track and dirt roads, and into the jungle through some very dense foliage.

Note that it gets *hot* in Mazatlán, so it's best to plan any biking excursions for the morning.

Fishing

Sport fishing was the first major tourist sport in Mazatlán and with good reason. The town is right at the mouth of the Sea of Cortez and the fishing off Mazatlán is some of the best you'll find anywhere along the coast of Mexico. Within 24km (15 miles) you'll find marlin and sailfish (catch and release only, please) from May to November, as well as tuna, yellowfin, dorado, and mako shark. And the **Billfish Classic,** which boasts a half-million-dollar prize, takes place in the second week of November here. The biggest fish caught at this contest? A 431kg (950-lb.) blue marlin that took 4 hours to land.

Check with Geronimo Cevallos, the manager of the **Aries fleet** at the El Cid Marina complex to arrange your own fishing trip (El Cid Marina, Camarón Sábalo s/n; ☎ **669/916-3468;** www.elcid.com). It's relatively cheap ($240–$650), and you can leave with them at 7am and return by 3pm with enough fish for the entire year. They'll even clean and freeze your catches for you.

Golf

Golf hasn't moved onto the landscape in Mazatlán quite the same way it has in Cabo San Lucas or Puerto Vallarta but it does have a presence. The **El Cid Mega Resort** recently added a Le Trevino designed 9-hole to their 18-hole 5,889m (96,472-yard) PGA-rated par 72 course (☎ **888/733-7308;** www.elcid.com/mexico_golf_resorts.html). Supposedly tee times happen every 8 minutes, starting at 7am until 5:30pm. (Last tee time is 3:30 pm.)

There's another waterfront course near Stone Island at **Estrella del Mar** (☎ **800/PAR-GOLF;** www.estrelladelmar.com/Golf.htm). It's an 18-hole designed by Robert Trent Jones and close to the airport, and costs about $1,090 for a round (which includes transportation from Zona Dorada). Since it's about 45-minutes to the Hotel Zone, the links are thankfully empty.

Sailing & Snorkeling

The **Kolonahe Sailing Adventure** departs for Isla de Venados (Deer Island) Tuesday through Sunday from Marina El Cid. Reserve through any travel agent or through El Cid directly (see above). This excursion sails aboard a 15m (50-ft.) trimaran to the island, where guests enjoy a picnic lunch and beverages, plus the use of snorkel equipment (as well as kayaks and canoes) for a cost of $350 per person. Departure is at 9:15am, with the boat returning at 3:30pm.

Spectator Sports

If you're in Mazatlán during the fall, by all means consider taking in a ball game at **Teodoro Mariscal** stadium (Bulevar Justo Sierra; ☎ **669/981-1710;** www.venadosdemazatlan.com) where **Los Venados** play. Regular season runs from October to December and the ticket prices are very affordable, ranging from $25 for the bleacher seats to $95 for box seats at field-level. The team has won back-to-back league championships and games are a high-energy affair, complete with chanting, singing, and dancing in the stands.

For a decidedly bloodier afternoon, from December to April **bullfights** take place every Sunday at the Plaza de Toros Monumental at Calzada Rafael Buenla (☎ **669/993-3598;** ticket prices range from $120–$300).

Rodeos, or *charreadas,* take place at the Lienzo Charro (bullring) of the Asociación de Charros de Mazatlán (☎ **669/986-3510**) on Saturday or Sunday beginning at 4pm. Tickets (around $45) are available through local travel agents and hotel concierge desks, which will have the current schedule.

Definitely try to check out **Divers' Point** ★★ at Playa Olas Altas before leaving town—it boasts four-story high platforms for divers to leap from into the shallows below. A semi-circular plaza with statues on the rocks over the sea, it's ideal for souvenir photos. Follow the malecón to the esplanade and look for the mermaid station to find the diving spot. The divers perform sporadically during the day as tour buses arrive near their perch, usually around lunchtime. It's free to watch, though the divers might ask for donations.

Surfing

April through October is the main surfing season here, because that's when southern swells develop that are reliably in the 1 to 2m (3¼–6½ ft.) range. There are decent **surfing** breaks all along the city's beaches, all of them easily accessible from the malecón. Most are short board fast and left breaks, although there is one lovely right break at **Valentinos,** called Jacaranda's. Locals also call it Lupe's Point after a woman who used to sell tacos to the surfers there. It's on the Fiestaland point and has a nice left called El Camaron just south of it.

During the winter, surfers head for **Playa Brujas,** next to Punta Cerritos on the northern edge of the city. In the spring and summer, the action is all up north, especially around Las Barras De Piaxtla, about 90 minutes away.

The San Diego–based **Sinaloa Surf School** (☎ **619/316-5498** in the U.S.; www.sinaloasurfschool.com) has a surf camp in Las Barras with all-inclusive stays—4 days cost $7,739, 7 days cost $11,445. Closer in, about 30 minutes north, the small village of Marmol, home to an abandoned cement factory, is another popular surf spot. It rarely gets crowded and, since the locals aren't territorial, plenty of waves can be had for everyone. I recommend that you bring something to leave the locals of this poor hamlet—clothes, batteries, whatever.

For rentals and information about the area beaches, stop by the **Mazatlán Surf Center** (Av. Camaron Sabalo 500; ☎ **669/913-1821;** www.mazatlansurfcenter.com). This is one of the few full-service surf shops in Mazatlán and it's noted for its teachers, who lead both private ($500) or group ($300) lessons. They also have boards for rent ($218 daily, $1,090 weekly) as well as a small selection of new boards ($5,450 for a short board), wax, leashes, and clothes. It's open from 9am to 9pm daily.

Note that to find many of the surf spots on this coast, it's best to have a four-wheel-drive vehicle. See p. 491 under "Getting into Town," for info on renting one.

Watersports

Among the best places to rent watersports equipment, from snorkeling gear to kayaks, are the **Aqua Sport Center** at the El Cid resort (☎ **669/913-3333;** www.mazatlan-aquasports.com) and the Ocean **Sport Center** at the Hotel Faro Mazatlán (☎ **669/913-1111**).

Whale-Watching

For years, many locals maintained that there were no whales off Mazatlán but in 2006 a new research organization started up, disproving this myth. **Onca Explorations** (Av. del Mar 1022-1; ☎ **619/116-0301;** www.oncaexplorations.com) is Mazatlán's only whale-watching company and while it's open to tourists, the emphasis here is on research rather than recreation. Whale watching generally is a fairly passive experience, but Onca founder/oceanographer Oscar Guzon Zatarain, has a different vision. He set up Onca to enlist the help of interested tourists to aid in collecting research regarding local whale populations. From

Spa Day

After a day in the sun, you might need to give your body a treat. The best way to do so is a visit to the spa at Best **Bathhouse Indigo** ★★ (5 de Mayo 109, between Morelos and Zaragoza, in front of Zaragoza Park; ☎ **669/981-5173,** cell 044/669-123-9023; www.indigoesvida.com). This spa was founded and run by surfer Roberta Lopez, who not only will work out your surfing-induced kinks but will also give you advice about where to go for some choice waves. She's a Mazatlán local who set up her spa in a wonderful 100-year-old neoclassical building on the edge of the Centro Historico—it was formerly the home of her grandmother. It's not the sort of place you expect to find in Mazatlán. On hand are a water massage bed, a sauna, and a Japanese-ofuro room that handles five people at a time. Yoga and pilates classes (with surfers' yoga a specialty), as well as tango and salsa classes, are offered regularly. Everything is by appointment only, and men and women visit on separate days (although couples can book appointments together). The spa is open 9am to 6pm daily, followed by yoga and dance classes. Prices range from $230 (foot massage) to $850 (four hand massage); yoga classes start at $75 for a group class. The best deal is the #2 package, which includes the bathhouse, sauna, Jacuzzi, 1-hour massage, and exfoliation for $1,200.

December through March humpbacks, fin whales, Bryde's, and occasionally orcas work the waters offshore, moving in and out of the Sea of Cortez. The 5-hour trip ($89, maximum six passengers) is on a 7m (22-ft.) Mako and passengers help take notes of fluke markings and pod and mating behavior. Onca is focused primarily on humpbacks and collects basic information regarding populations and the impact of drift nets, while observing courtship behavior. They also do dolphin research, primarily with bottlenose and spotted dolphins.

Shopping

Most of Mazatlán's shopping can be had in the **Zona Dorada,** but there you'll find mainly typical souvenirs and tourist-related gear—think sombreros, T-shirts, leather goods, and serapes. The **Centro Historico** is the place to go for the best variety of fine arts and crafts. The selection may not be as varied as what's on offer down the coast at Puerto Vallarta (where there seems to be a Huichol store on every block) but it's also mellower—you can hit all the best shops here in an afternoon.

As in most large towns in Mexico, shops are open until 8 or 9pm during the week, closing in the early afternoon on Sundays. Saturday is the busiest market day.

Craft & Clothing Boutiques

Nidart (Libertad 45; ☎ **669/981-0002;** www.nidart.com) is famous for its masks—which are kinda creepy if you ask me, made out of leather and looking just a little too lifelike for my tastes. Still, this art store in a 19th-century building next to the Angela Peralta Theater is unlike any other gallery/crafts store you're going to find in Mazatlán. They've been here for more than 15 years, which makes them one of the pioneering forces behind the revitalization of old Mazatlán, as well as a center for local artists who otherwise would have no other outlet for their work. In addition to handmade leather masks, they excel at miniatures, clay figurines, children's toys, clothes, and jewelry.

Ganadava Bazar (Constitucion 616; ☎ **669/136-0665**) is named after a Hindu musical angel and it doesn't take but a few minutes to see why. Next to El Loro de Oro Inn (p. 496), this small shop sells Day of the Dead artifacts, Oaxacan pottery, Huichol art, and Taxco silver, but it's the very large collection of ethnic musical instruments that catches the eye (and ear). The wares come from all over the world, and range from flutes, to pipes, to ocarinas, to rain sticks. Prices are fair and much cheaper than Drum City—you are in Mazatlán, after all. Know a percussionist you're shopping for? Come here.

Casa Etnika (Sixto Osuna 50; ☎ **669/136-0139**) is a family-owned place with ethnic goods from all over Mexico (as the name implies). The store also stocks lots of fine art, maps, nature books, guidebooks, and jewelry. The goods are different than you're likely to find at most arts and crafts stores—high in quality and slightly pricey. It's tucked inside one of the oldest buildings in the area, built in 1865 when the French occupied Mazatlán.

Casa Antigua (Mariano Escobedo 206; ☎ **669/982-5236**) is primarily an arts and crafts store, though the wares are arranged in a slightly stuffy museum-like way. (The store's in the former home of the city's first bishop, so maybe that's why.) It's one of the oldest such stores in town and has fair prices for items from Sinaloa, Jalisco, Oaxaca, and Michoacan. Good Day of the Dead mementoes, jewelry, pottery, and papier-mâché items are all stocked.

If you're sweating through your jeans and really need some new clothes to help you blend in, stop by **Manta Maya** (Av. Camaron Sabalo 610; ☎ **669/913-2265**), a wonderful little boutique in the Zona Dorada. The store sells finely made Maya guayaberas, pants, shorts, dresses, and skirts. Most everything is very reasonably priced, slightly dressy, and all cotton—much better for this climate than those Levi's you brought with you.

It's always hard finding affordable English books in Mexico, and Mazatlán is no different. You'll have to search a bit for the **Mazatlán Book & Coffee Company** (Camaron Sabalo 610, Plaza Galerías, Suite 11; ☎ **669/916-7899**; mazbook@prodigy.net.mx) but once you find it, you'll be in heaven. Owner David Bodwell has amassed a huge selection of used and new books, maps, and guidebooks here. He can also offer a wealth of information about life in Mazatlán and can set you up for a massage (non-sexual, sorry) with a local masseuse.

Markets & Malls

Just 2 blocks behind the cathedral is the **Mercado Central** ★★, downtown's covered central market, open from 6am to 7pm. It's a square block of stalls and jammed aisles, bordered by the streets of Juárez, Ocampo, Serdan, and Leandro Valle. The market was built at the turn of the century and is an art nouveau delight, notable for its iron latticework roof. Here you'll find everything from shoes to serapes, tamales to tomatoes, and pottery to powdered rattlesnake (said to be good for boosting your immune system). It goes on and on, so come prepared to spend some time. It opens at 6am and runs until 7pm (or later at some stalls).

If you're looking to do one-stop shopping, head to **La Gran Plaza** (at the corner of Reforma and Apollo; ☎ **669/986-3838**). It's Mazatlán's biggest mall, next door to a Sam's Club, with more than 120 stores including a mega superstore, bookstores, a three-screen theater, and international food court. This is as close to one-stop shopping as you're likely to find in Mazatlán. And yes, for you junkies looking for 36 rolls of toilet paper for $4.25, your U.S. Sam's Club membership is valid here. From the Zona Dorada, take the Cerritos Juárez bus going south; from Centro Historico take buses marked Play Sur (going north) or buses marked GP (Gran Plaza).

Road Trips: El Quelite, Las Labradas & Cosala

El Quelite, 29km (18 miles) northeast of Mazatlán, off Highway 15, is almost a little *too* postcard-perfect. The houses are all painted in contrasting pastels, and the cobblestones are so clean and regular they look like they've been varnished. And you enter the town by passing through a soaring colonial-style yellow archway on the main road that proclaims "Welcome to Quelite."

Clearly, the town's 3,500 residents know the appeal of the town is its living museum atmosphere and they have worked hard to maintain the illusion. This isn't some Disney version of rancho life, however. On December 12, the Virgin's birthday, the town swells with locals from the surrounding countryside for dancing and music in front of the 123-year-old church. And though the town is ostensibly an agricultural pueblito, in recent years it's also become a place for Mazatlán locals to escape from the coast for a few days of campo life. They come out for the various tourist attractions like *charreria* rodeo-style roping and horsemanship; Mexico's largest fighting rooster farm; or the regular demonstration of *ulama*—the pre-Hispanic basketball/soccer game where the winners were executed.

For day-trippers, the biggest draw, however, is the food at **El Mason de los Laureanos** (Frco Bernal 1, El Quelite; ☎ **669/965-4143;** ruralosuna@hotmail.com; main courses $100; no credit cards), the home of the town's most prominent citizen (and tourism booster) Dr. Marcos Osuna. Its old style ranchero food is reminiscent of El Quelite's 17th-century heritage—menu items include broiled quail, pigs' feet, tongue, carne asada, and local cheeses. The setting is wonderful, in a semi-enclosed veranda with gourds hanging from the ceiling and an Amapas tree in the courtyard. The urinal in the "bathroom" is a hollowed out tree trunk, the spigots for the basin are made of old keys. They even have three rooms for rent—for about $50 each, which includes breakfast. (If these are full, ask about one of the homes off the main square kept empty for tourists—a three bedroom costs about $70.)

Back on Highway 15, head north again for the road to La Noria. A few miles before La Noria is the **Los Osuna Tequileria** (no phone), a 19th-century facility that makes tequila with a combination of old and new techniques. It's one of the few remaining tequila factories still open in this Sinaloa region after the government forced many to close. At one time Sinaloa was the largest producer of tequila after Jalisco. Los Osuna is both a producer of very good double-distilled tequila as well as a great place to come for a picnic beneath the towering 200-year-old Guanacaste tree in front of the tasting bar. You can also take an informative tour of the open-air factory—just be careful not to fall into the 60m-deep (20-ft.) ovens in the ground where the massive "pinos"—hearts of agave—sit smoldering in the first process of fermentation. Plus, you can't buy the brand anywhere but here (it runs about $300 for a bottle). Just don't look for the word "tequila" on the label: That designation is only allowed for Jalisco-made spirit, though, in my opinion, it doesn't get any smoother than the stuff here. The factory is about an hour's drive from Mazatlán. It's open Monday to Saturday 8am to 5pm, and charges $25 for the tasting/tour.

Out on the coast, about 45 minutes north of Mazatlán on Highway 211, is a beach called **Las Labradas** where the main attraction isn't the water or the waves—although it's just south of a surf camp at Las Brujas. Rather, it's the stones on the beach, some 500 of which bear 1,500- to 2,000-year-old petroglyphs of suns, comets, swirls, faces, animals, and even genitals. The carvings in the lava rocks are right on the edge of the beach and Mexican archaeologists think they are Toltec in origin. (Although some claim the rock carvings are more than 3,000 years old, or pre-Toltec.) Take your time here. The longer you sit observing and the more the sun moves across the sky, the more apparent become the designs. At presstime, there was no cost to check out the stones but a small entrance fee had been proposed.

Before leaving the area, you might want to visit one additional attraction: **Las Labradas** sits inside a 40,000-hectare (100,000-acre) reserve that's popular with birders. To get there, look for the exit to Barras de Piaxtla, about 75km (47 miles) from Mazatlán and ask in the village for the dirt road to Las Labradas.

About 2 hours northeast of Mazatlán, 900m (3,000 ft.) up in the Sierra Occidental, is **Cosala,** considered to be one of the most beautiful colonial towns of Sinaloa. Indeed the name, Cosala, means "place of the beautiful landscape" in the native Cahita language. Like El Quelite, this town is perfectly preserved, boasting relics from its wealthy past as a mining center and some of the best neo-colonial architecture in the state. The Spanish arrived here in 1531, setting up a town 30 years later after discovering rich veins of silver and gold. The missionaries weren't far behind, and put their mark on it by calling the pueblo "The Royal Mines of our Lady of the Eleven Thousand Virgins of Cosala." The mines here hit their first bonanza in 1816, churning out silver and gold for more than a century, and there are still working mines in the area. Now tourism is poised to become the next bonanza following federal designation of Cosala as a Pueblo Magico, one of two dozen historic towns in the nation. To get here, take Highway 40 to Culiacan to the Cosala turnoff (106km/66 miles from Mazatlán). From there it's another 90 minutes on a narrow paved road into the mountains.

A fancy new B&B was going up in Cosala when I was there but the place I stayed, **Hotel Real del Conde** (Rosales 6, Centro Historico, Cosala; ☎ **696/965-0006;** $590 double; no credit cards) was very adequate. It's comfy, if small, with tiled floors, air-conditioning, a glassed-in shower, fake marble, and thick colonial-style walls that do nothing to dampen the laughter and chatter from the bar area downstairs. There are a half-dozen other hotels in town, mostly on the level of the **Hotel Ray 4 Hermanos** (Arteaga s/n, Colonia Centro; ☎ **696/965-0303;** $300 double; no credit cards), which is clean if *very* basic, with no phone, parking, Internet, or charm.

The restaurants here are also hit or miss, mainly *cenadurias*—restaurants run by housewifes for a few hours a day, usually late afternoon until evening—for tacos and gorditas. One of the better regular restaurants is **El Pueblito,** just off the main square (Rosales s/n, Centro Historico; ☎ **696/965-1039;** main courses under $70; no credit cards; daily 8am–10pm) where the most expensive thing on the menu is tampequeno steak and there's a wonderful view of the mountains from the outside dining area. On the main plaza the **Restaurant Meredero** (Arteaga 5, Centro Historico; ☎ **696/965-0236;** main courses under $120; no credit cards; Thurs–Sun 9am–11pm) has pictures of Pancho Villa and other revolutionaries on the wall as well as a mammoth 122cm (48-in.) plasma screen. Here the steak again is the most expensive thing on the menu. There's a basin in the dining room for washing your hands before you eat—a very old Mexico touch.

Cosala is still adjusting to its new identity as a tourist destination, so don't be surprised if kids wander up and stare if you're a stranger. That it's not yet ready for prime time is a good thing in many ways, though—it retains an innocence that has vanished in other parts of Mexico. There are a few mines still open to visit and one optimistic entrepreneur has set up a *tirasol* with four zip lines and three canopy platforms out on the road to El Rodeo (about 30 min. away). The biggest outdoor attraction in the area is the legendary fishing at El Salto lake, stocked with some of the biggest largemouth bass found anywhere in Mexico. Hikers will also appreciate the Vado Hondo waterfall, just outside town, and the Gruta cave, known for its huge stalactites.

It's easiest to reach all of the above attractions around Mazatlán by car, but you can take a bus to Cosala from the station in Mazatlán (p. 491). You can also arrange to visit on an organized tour; check with Pronatours (see "Sightseeing," p. 505) for options.

Acapulco

While it will always reserve its place in history as Mexico's first world-class vacation spot, the essence of Hollywood cool in the 1950s and 1960s, Acapulco is currently experiencing an identity crisis in which it must decide whether to cling to its glorious past or evolve into something still undefined yet decidedly different.

Pessimists might view Acapulco as a has-been, an over-the-hill dowager that had her 15 minutes in the spotlight years ago (and a scrapbook of faded reviews to show for it), but that was then. The light is too harsh for a close-up now and no amount of stucco pancake makeup will cover the cracks and wrinkles as the former glory is enveloped by the dirty, seedy side of unchecked tourism development: poverty, crime, and disregard for a delicate ecosystem. Optimists might see Acapulco as undergoing a transition, perhaps a renaissance, in which it will emerge to reclaim its reputation as one of the hottest Mexican beach resorts of all time.

I side with the pessimists but don't dismiss the optimists—what Acapulco lacks in local culture it makes up in tourist-pleasing entertainment and activities. The town is beautifully situated on a natural South Pacific port where the average annual temperature is 80°F (27°C). If you come here, you'll get your spring break tan, that's for sure. But Acapulco is like a painting of the Mona Lisa with a mustache painted over it: Panoramic views of the ocean and sunset are ubiquitous, yet so are the noxious fumes and annoying drone from jet skis that shatter the serenity of the scene. The white sandy beaches stretch for 6.4km (4 miles) but are littered with garbage and God-knows-what, and, despite the litter, they quickly become overcrowded. It's a city without a soul, with a skyline lacking any beautiful architecture, just hotel after hotel built to accommodate more and more tourists—and yet, there they are, ready to party with you.

The 4.8×3.2km-wide (3×2-mile) bay framed by the Sierra Madre del Sur Mountains (to the north, curving around to the southern cape) is still home to families of sea turtles and large game fish like swordfish and marlins. Snorkeling and scuba diving provide perfect opportunities for you to catch a glimpse of some beautiful, colorful fish while that unforgettable view of Acapulco Bay is available from hundreds of different vantage points (a popular one being the upside-down view while attached to a bungee chord). Despite its need for a tune-up, Acapulco creates a contagious sense of adventure that becomes especially infectious during the debauched spring break season when the town is bursting at the seams with suntanned tourists both night and day. Young people still flock here to enjoy both the nightlife and the watersports, and after 1 night here, you'll see that it doesn't disappoint.

It might no longer be the most glamorous Mexican beach resort, but one thing Acapulco does right is nightlife. New chic establishments are starting to open up and Mexicans from neighboring towns still pour in to enjoy Acapulco's famous nightclubs. Acapulco is also trying to adapt to a completely new kind of traveler—no longer the Hollywood hotshot but generations X and Y. Clean-up efforts in the Bay are underway and new hotels are being built, with the optimistic anticipation that Acapulco will reclaim its reputation as one of the top beach resorts in the world. We can either help it along, or watch as it fades away. As a strapping Elvis sang in *Fun in Acapulco* in 1963:

"Where romance blooms, and love is in the air

So kiss me tender, love me true

Darling, feel this magic too

Don't say no, you can't say no, in Acapulco."

The King's words still hold true. Like many celebrities Acapulco has been famous, turned to the bottle, checked into rehab, and now she's just coming out with a new outlook on life. Everyone is just waiting to see if she can pull off the comeback.

Best of Acapulco & Taxco

- **The Best Place for a Pre-Hangover, Late-Night Meal: Taco & Beer**—the name says it all. After a night of partying, is there any better way to top it off than with a greasy taco and an ice cold beer? See p. 534.
- **Best Place to View the Sunset:** If you have a chance to get away from the main section of town, make your way out to **Pie de la Cuesta** beach for an unforgettable view, accompanied by a tropical drink. See p. 536.
- **Best Place to (Actually) Sleep for Cheap: California Inn** costs less than some of the town's hostels and has quiet rules in effect after 10pm. Plus, the cozy rooms come with a rocking chair so you can rock yourself right to bed. See p. 524.
- **Best Natural Wonder:** The enormous cave **Las Grutas de Cacahuamilpa** in Taxco is full of crazy natural rock formations that should make you gaze in wonder and amazement while laughing at the uncanny resemblances the rocks have to different objects and famous people/places. Batman's "Batcave" has nothing on this place. See p. 551.

- **Best Place to Eat Every Meal:** Breakfast, lunch, and dinner—they're all amazing at **Café Sasha** in Taxco. Sasha is the sort of place that you just never want to leave—if only they had couches, I know I wouldn't. See p. 545.

Getting There & Getting Around

Getting into Town

BY PLANE Several airlines offer service to Acapulco's **Juan N. Álvarez International Airport,** Bulevar de las Naciones (☎ **744/435-2060**), including **AeroMexico** (☎ **800/237-6639;** www.aeromexico.com), **American** (☎ **800/433-7300;** www.aa.com), **Continental** (☎ **800/231-0856;** www.continental.com), **Mexicana** (☎ **800/531-2921;** www.mexicana.com), **America West** (☎ **800/235-9292;** www.americawest.com), and **Delta** (☎ **800/221-1212;** www.delta.com). Budget airlines Interjet, Viva Aerobus, and Aerolitoral offer air service from other towns into Mexico, see "Basics," p. 10 for information. If you're flying from the U.S., you will most likely have to transfer flights in Mexico City through the Benito Juárez International Airport (airport code: MEX). Acapulco's International Airport (airport code: ACA) is 22km (14 miles) southeast of town.

Authorized taxis are the best way to get to your hotel but could cost anywhere from $300 to $500. Rental car agencies are available, as are colectivos, or group taxis that you can buy tickets for at the **Transportes Terrestres** desk in the front of the airport. The colectivos are considerably cheaper than cabs, at around $100.

BY BUS There are several main bus stations in Acapulco. The **Ejido/Central Camionera station,** Ejido 47, located near Old Acapulco, serves more bus lines and routes than the other Acapulco bus stations (like the Estrella de Oro terminal at Av. Cuauhtemoc that only offers bus service on Estrella de Oro buses). **Turistar, Estrella de Oro,** and **Estrella Blanca** buses leave from this station with almost hourly service to Mexico City and Zihuatanejo.

You can also book a flight directly to Mexico City and then take a bus from the **Estación Central del Sur** (p. 82) to Acapulco. The buses are surprisingly comfortable and affordable. Prices range according to the class you choose to travel, with one-way tickets to/from Mexico City ranging from $300 to $450, to/from Ixtapa/Zihuatanejo for around $150 and to/from Taxco for $120.

BY CAR To get from Mexico City to Acapulco, take the toll-free Highway 95D South (6 hr.). The alternative is Highway 95 (3½ hr.), which is faster but will cost you a frightening $500 one-way in tolls. Highway 95D South is a beautiful ride, so a few extra hours aren't so bad.

Getting Around

BY CAR I don't recommend driving in Acapulco. Parking is difficult to find, and you'll find yourself pushed around by the taxi drivers swarming the place; a car could become more of a hassle than a luxury. Most major rental car agencies, including **Avis** (☎ **744/466-9174**), **Budget** (☎ **744/466-9003**), **Hertz** (☎ **744/466-9172**), and **Saad** (☎ **744/466-9179**) are available at the Acapulco International Airport. There is also a **Hertz** (open Mon–Sat 8am– 7pm, Sun 9am–5pm) along the Costera, at Costera Miguel Alemán, No. 137, on the corner of Gonzalo Sandoval beneath the Monaco Hotel (☎ **744/485-8947**).

BY BUS Getting around by bus is easy and cheap. White and blue buses travel along the popular stretch of hotels, shops, and restaurants lining the Costera Miguel Alemán, the main street that brings you from Old Acapulco all the way through to the expensive Diamante region of town. Bus stops are sometimes ambiguous and unmarked; watch for groups standing on a street corner. Normally they are marked with a flagpole-like bus sign. Buses cost between $3 and $5.50, depending on how old they are and whether or not they have air-conditioning. Look for the buses that say "Zócalo" on the front windshield and have "Costera" written on the side of them in blue writing. But be careful. Although most buses are relatively safe, many robberies have been known to happen in the back of the bus. Sit near the bus driver in the front whenever possible.

BY FOOT Getting around by foot in Acapulco is doable if you stick to the Condesa Beach area and Old Acapulco sections of town. At 29 sq. km (11 sq. miles) with a 6km-long (4-miles) Bay, there is definitely a lot of ground to cover, especially if you include the hills and pedestrian-*unfriendly* Diamante region of town. There is plenty of sidewalk space along the Costera Miguel Alemán, and chances are there will be many restaurants and beach activities within walking distance from your hotel/hostel.

Basics

Orientation

Acapulco stretches for about 6 km (4 miles) around the sweeping (4.8×3.2km-wide) Acapulco Bay. The city wraps itself around the water, making attractive views of the bay attainable from almost every angle. Simply use the ocean as a point of reference whenever possible.

When you first arrive in Acapulco, whether you're coming from the airport or the main highway, the first thing you'll notice is the amazing view of Acapulco Bay and the famous row of high-rise hotels that marks the center of the Acapulco coastline. There are three main "neighborhoods" of Acapulco: **Old Acapulco (Acapulco Viejo)** located on the western end of the Bay, the **Hotel Zone (Zona Hotelera)** located in the center of the Bay following the main boulevard, and the **Diamante (Diamond)** section of town located at the southern end of the Bay, closest to the airport.

Old Acapulco is located on the northwestern end of the Bay. Speckled around the central zócalo, there are tons of cheap restaurants, hostel-priced hotels, and local stores. Many of the day cruises and fishing excursions leave from nearby Terminal Maritima pier. Local public buses can also be found here that take you to Pie de la Cuesta or Coyuca Lagoon, and up and down the Costera Miguel Alemán.

Old Acapulco is mainly flat, with a slightly disheveled grid layout formed by small side streets and crowded avenues that make it very pedestrian-friendly. At the heart of Old Acapulco is the central square, called the zócalo, which is a great place to sit in the shade next to shoe-shiners and beauty-school students. Many of the oldest and most famous hotels are located in this area, where the Hollywood elite used to vacation and film movies. The best thing you can do here is walk around, have a couple of meals, and get a feel for the local culture; the nightlife is tame and simple, with few clubs or major bars that cater to the tourist population. Your best bet is to stick to the Hotel Zone and Diamante neighborhoods for any late-night bumping and grinding.

If you've ever seen a picture of the Acapulco skyline, you probably have a mental image of the **Hotel Zone.** If not, imagine building after building lined up

Acapulco's Deadly Drug Trade

While Acapulco might feel like a safe place, the police officers and soldiers who ride trucks through town carrying gigantic machine guns are a reminder of the potential threats that they and you face. In early 2007, a series of drug-related crimes resulted in several beheadings. A few of the severed heads were discovered on the beaches by tourists—not the sort of souvenir they'd anticipated, no doubt. At times the victims have been police officers who refused to let drug traffickers past certain checkpoints. In one case, stray bullets hit two Canadian tourists lounging in a hotel lobby. Despite the number of beheadings that have occurred—some attributed to a clash between rival Gulf and Sinaloa drug cartels—Acapulco's Mayor, Félix Salgado Macedonio, assures visitors that the violence is 100% drug-related and that tourists are perfectly safe. He's increased police presence in town and on the beaches to ensure safety.

Drug activity here isn't especially prevalent, as Acapulco is more of a trafficker's transit stop on the way to el Norte. Still, you may be approached by locals trying to sell cheap marijuana or coke; given the crimes in the area, we suggest you follow the old public service announcement advice and "Just Say No."

side by side for over a mile—some colorful, some in shades of white and grey—beaming into the sunny sky while the golden sandy beaches sprawl out from beneath them, with sunbathers scattered conspicuously along the shore. Between the cars, people, and watersports, everything is in constant motion. The high-rise hotels range in price and personality along the main stretch of sand surrounding Condesa Beach, which attracts the biggest crowds of young people. If you are somewhere within the **Hotel Zone,** you will be able to enjoy any watersport, sip any tropical drink at any time of day, and constantly have your feet in the sand. This is the party section of town, both day and night.

Finally, there's the aptly named **Diamante** section of town at the southern end of the Bay that rises into the hillside. Located only about a mile or so away from the Hotel Zone, this is where the hottest clubs, fanciest hotels, and chicest restaurants can be found. It is also where the dirty, crowded, loud Avenida Costera Miguel Alemán turns into the Carretera Escénica (scenic highway) and the flat expanse of the Costera highway that serves as the main road in the Hotel Zone begins to wind into the Diamante hillside. Almost every spot you'll visit here will give you an incredible view overlooking the Bay. Its only downside is that it's not very pedestrian friendly.

See "Heading to the Beach" later in this chapter for info on Acapulco's beaches.

Tourist Info & Offices

You'll find the **State of Guerrero Tourism Office** in the **Procuraduría del Turista** at the Acapulco International Center on Avenida Costera Miguel Alemán (☎ **744/484-4416;** or fax 744/484-4583). It is located on street level in the front area of the Convention Center of Acapulco at Av. Costera Miguel Alemán no. 4455, which is found at the end of a long, unnamed walkway with fountains and white flag-like awnings.

Another place you can get information and perhaps friendlier assistance is the **Oficina de Convenciones y Visitantes,** which is in front of the Convention Center on the Costera Miguel Alemán at Av. Costera Miguel Alemán no. 38-A, Fracc. Costa Azúl, (☎ **744/484-8555**).

Acapulco Nuts & Bolts

Banks Banks are extremely easy to find, but here are a couple to start you off: **Banamex** (Av. Costera Miguel Alemán 38-A; ☎ **744/484-3381**) and **Bancomer** (Av. Costera Miguel Alemán at Calle Laurel, by the Golf and Tennis Club; ☎ **744/484-8055**).

Embassies & Consulates The **United States** has an agent at the Hotel Club del Sol, Costera Alemán at Reyes Católicos (☎ **744/481-1699** or 469-0556), across from the Hotel Acapulco Plaza, open Monday through Friday from 10am to 2pm. The **Canadian** office is at the Centro Comercial Marbella, Local 23 (☎ **744/484-1305** or 01-800/706-2900 within Mexico), open Monday through Friday from 9am to 5pm. The **United Kingdom** office is at the Las Brisas Hotel on Carretera Escénica near the airport (☎ **744/481-2533** or 484-1735).

Emergencies In an emergency, dial ☎ **065** or **744/485-0490** for the **Tourist Police,** which will connect you with an English-speaking police officer specifically on duty to help tourists.

Internet/Wireless Hot Spots You can access the Internet at **@canet** (Costera Alemán 1632 Int. La Gran Plaza, Local D-1, lower floor; ☎ **744/486-8182**). Internet is open daily from 10:30am to 9pm. Another place is **@qua** (Av. Costera Miguel Alemán #78 L-5, Fracc. Club Deportivo; ☎ **744/481-3555**), which is air-conditioned. Internet generally costs $20 an hour at both places.

Laundry To have your clothes washed, dried, and folded within 2 hours ($75), go to **Wash & Wear,** located in front of Hotel Calinda (Av. Costera Miguel Alemán No. 1260, by the golf and tennis club right next to **@qua**), open Monday through Friday from 9am to 9pm (☎ **744/484-9365**). If you're in the Old Acapulco section of town, try **Lavanderia Lavadin** (corner of José María Iglesias y La Paz; ☎ **744/482-2890**). It's open Monday through Saturday, 8am to 10pm and can get your clothes back to you dry and folded by the end of the day for $14 per kilo.

Luggage Storage You can store your luggage at **K3 Hostel** (p.521) for free if you stay there or for $50 a day if you're not a guest.

Pharmacy The large drugstore **Farmacia Daisy** (Francia 49; ☎ **744/484-7664**) is across from the Convention Center, but it is easy to find a pharmacy along the Costera if you need one. **Botica Acapulco** (Jesús Carranza 3, just off the zócalo; ☎ **744/483-8429**) is open 24 hours and dates back to 1858.

Safety Avoid the beach at night, and avoid drug pushers (see the box "Acapulco's Deadly Drug Trade," above). Observe tide warning flags on the beaches, and don't swim if they're black or red; be especially careful of Condesa beach's dangerous rip tide. In addition, avoid wearing expensive jewelry, flaunting money in general, or carrying a lot of cash on you. If you have a robbery or crime to report, your best bet is to report it to the embassy and not the local police, who may find it more entertaining to mock a gringo than do their job. And always remember: Public drunkenness makes anyone a bigger target for crime.

Tipping Most people providing services expect a 10% tip, and there is no need to give more unless you want to. But keep in mind that tips are a large portion of most waiters' income, so a tip is important. Tipping cab drivers is optional. In hotels, generally tip the bellboy $10 a bag.

Sleeping

Take one look at Acapulco's skyline, dotted with hotels, and you'll have a sense of how many accommodations options there are. As one of the biggest tourist destinations in Mexico, Acapulco has around 250 hotels that range in price, personality, and location. For cheap, no-fuss sleeping accommodations there are dozens of small hostel-priced hotels located right around the zócalo in Old Acapulco. If you came with the intention of spending all day on the beach and all night at a bar, then consider the hotels along Playa Condesa, where both beach and booze are close. If you want some distance from the somewhat loud and rowdy Acapulco nightlife and you're not afraid to blow a couple extra bucks, there is always the expensive Diamante region of town. But unless your Super Sweet Sixteen party-throwing parents are funding this trip, that's unlikely.

Hostels

→ **Kingdom Hostel** ★ Kingdom Hostel is located relatively far away from the action of Acapulco, a brief walk away from Playa Marqués, but that's a small price to pay to stay at one of the cleanest, most luxurious hostels in the area. The rooms are immaculate, with new and comfortable beds, and some even have their own private bathrooms. All have air-conditioning and TVs, along with real blankets and windows that open. A circular TV lounge, snack shop, soccer field, and swimming pool are also available. Depending on how adventurous you're feeling, the hostel's location outside the center might be a good thing—unlike the tourist strip in the Hotel Zone, this is a part of town where locals actually *live*. That means you should be careful when venturing into the neighborhood beyond the Kingdom walls. *Carretera a Puerto Marquez #104, just off the corner of Glorieta de Puerto Marquez; enter a gated area to get to the hostel. ☎ 744/466-3736. www.kingdomhostel.com. $200 beds. Rates include breakfast. MC, V. Amenities: Bar; snack bar; fax; Internet; luggage storage; pets allowed; pool; security lockers; telephone; towels; travel desk; Wi-Fi. In room: A/C, TV.*

→ **K3 Hostel** ★★ You couldn't be more in the middle of the action than at K3. It's smack in the center of Acapulco's most touristy strip, which means the famous Condesa Beach bars are lined up right outside your door. Almost everything you need to make an Acapulco vacation complete (laundromats, Internet, restaurants, watersports, shopping, convenience stores, and banks) is within walking distance. Each bathroom has a toilet, shower (with one-temperature for water), and sink. Most of the rooms have two bunk bed units and sleep four, but good luck moving around at the same time in the tiny rooms. In order to avoid overcrowded rooms, I recommend

Acapulco Sleeping, Eating & Partying

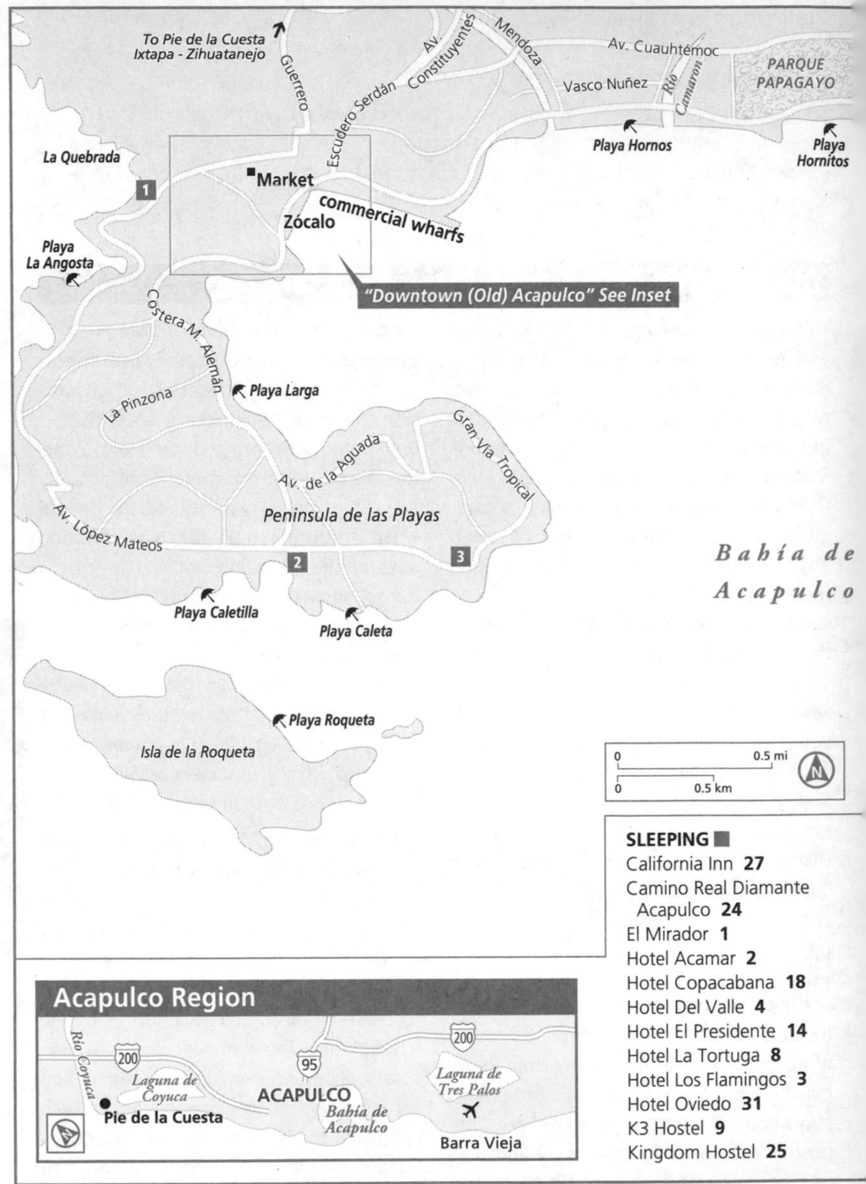

SLEEPING ■
California Inn 27
Camino Real Diamante Acapulco 24
El Mirador 1
Hotel Acamar 2
Hotel Copacabana 18
Hotel Del Valle 4
Hotel El Presidente 14
Hotel La Tortuga 8
Hotel Los Flamingos 3
Hotel Oviedo 31
K3 Hostel 9
Kingdom Hostel 25

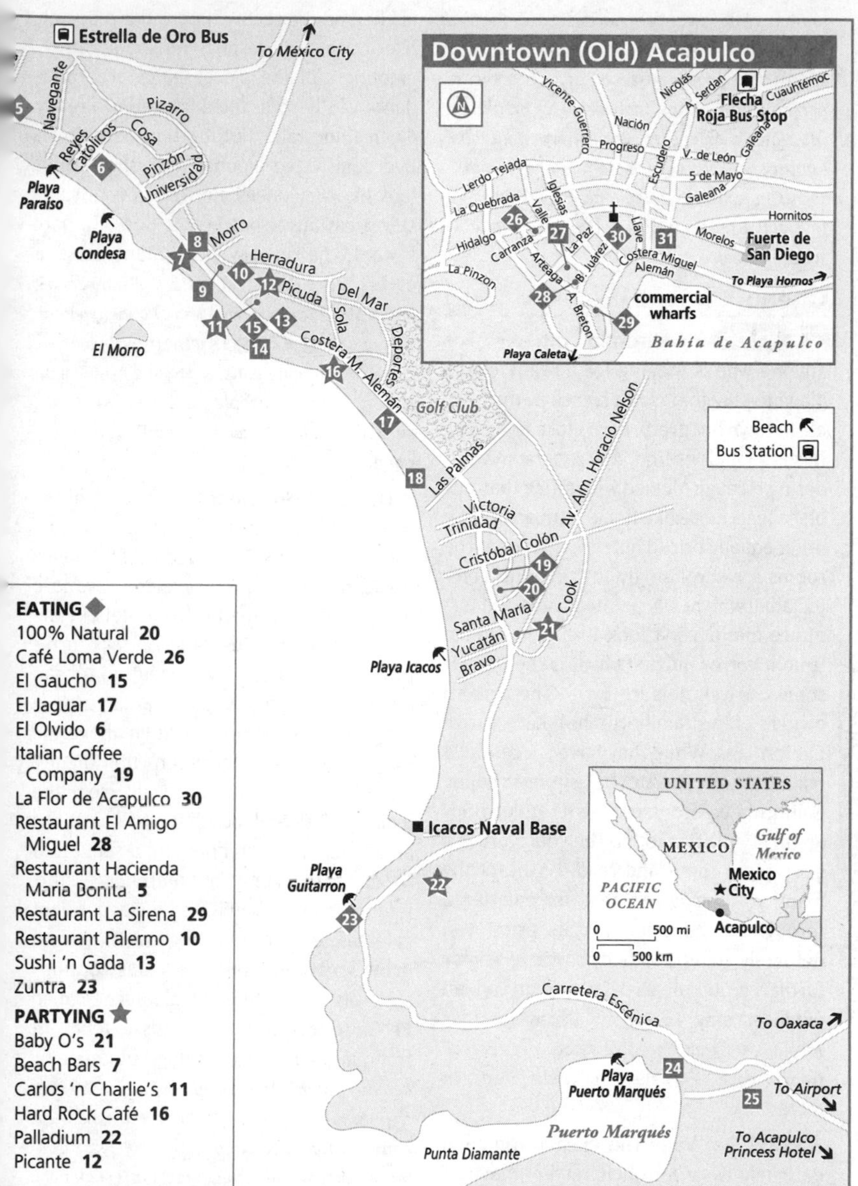
Downtown (Old) Acapulco
Estrella de Oro Bus
To México City
Navegante
Pizarro
Reyes Católicos
Cosa
Pinzón
Universidad
Playa Paraíso
Playa Condesa
Morro
Herradura
Picuda
Del Mar
Sola
Deportes
Costera M. Alemán
El Morro
Golf Club
Las Palmas
Av. Alm. Horacio Nelson
Victoria
Trinidad
Cristóbal Colón
Santa María
Cook
Yucatán
Bravo
Playa Icacos
Icacos Naval Base
Playa Guitarron
Carretera Escénica
To Oaxaca
Playa Puerto Marqués
Puerto Marqués
Punta Diamante
To Airport
To Acapulco Princess Hotel
Vicente Guerrero
Nicolás
A. Serdan
Flecha Roja Bus Stop
Cuauhtémoc
Nación
Progreso
Escudero
V. de León
Galeana
5 de Mayo
Lerdo Tejada
La Quebrada
Iglesias
Valle
Hidalgo
Carranza
La Paz
Llave
Hornitos
Morelos
Fuerte de San Diego
La Pinzon
Arteaga
B. Juárez
Costera Miguel Alemán
To Playa Hornos
A. Breton
commercial wharfs
Playa Caleta
Bahía de Acapulco
Beach
Bus Station
UNITED STATES
MEXICO
Gulf of Mexico
PACIFIC OCEAN
Mexico City
Acapulco
0 500 mi
0 500 km
EATING
100% Natural 20
Café Loma Verde 26
El Gaucho 15
El Jaguar 17
El Olvido 6
Italian Coffee Company 19
La Flor de Acapulco 30
Restaurant El Amigo Miguel 28
Restaurant Hacienda Maria Bonita 5
Restaurant La Sirena 29
Restaurant Palermo 10
Sushi 'n Gada 13
Zuntra 23
PARTYING
Baby O's 21
Beach Bars 7
Carlos 'n Charlie's 11
Hard Rock Café 16
Palladium 22
Picante 12

avoiding the high seasons when this place teams with sweaty tourists. *Av. Costera Miguel Alemán #116, Playa Condesa. ☎ 744/ 481-3111 or -3113. $175–$200 single bed in 1–4 person dorm. Rates include light breakfast. DISC, MC, V. Amenities: Bar; Internet; kitchen; laundry service; luggage storage; shared bathrooms in hallways; telephone; towels ($10); TV. In room: A/C, sheets, locker ($25 lock available for purchase).*

Cheap

Best → **California Inn** ★★ For anyone who is looking for a really cheap place to stay that is not smack in the middle of town but pretty darn close to it, then this is a fabulous find. Any American wandering through Mexico will notice that this place feels more like home than any of the other equally priced hotels in the area. The rooms are surprisingly inviting and comfortable, with newly painted walls and furniture that doesn't look like it was taken from a horror movie (which is the case at some cheap hotels in town). The current owners of this family-run hotel are native Californians. While they have successfully managed to create a sunny, happy California-environment, strict quiet-rules are in effect after 10pm. The courtyard is a good place to sit and read in one of the many rocking chairs that are scattered throughout the place. For its price, you definitely get your money's worth; ask for further group deals if you plan on an extended stay. *La Paz #12, Centro near the zócalo. ☎ 744/482-2893. $100 per person (rooms have 1–5 beds). No credit cards. In room: Fans.*

→ **Hotel Del Valle** This cheap little hotel definitely has a lot of character—maybe a little too much character (I swear I detected a ghost or two). Stay here for the location only, which is across the street from **Parque Papagayo** and 30 seconds off the main road, so you're near the beach, the restaurants, and the buses. A shared kitchen on the second floor adds a hostel-like touch, and despite the spooky near-emptiness of the place, maids are abundant—you'll spot them cleaning already clean floors and fluffing unused pillows. Bedrooms have wooden furnishings that look like they once belonged to your spinster great aunt—but hey, it does the job. I would never stay here alone. *Costera Miguel Alemán and Gonzálo G Espinoza #8, Fracc. Magallanes, across from Papagayo Park. ☎ 744/485-8336 or -8388. www.travelbymexico.com/guer/hoteldelvalle. $500 for 2 people with A/C, $400 for 2 people with fan. No credit cards. Amenities: Pool. In room: TV, fan or A/C, phone.*

→ **Hotel El Presidente** ★★ This hotel, which is in the hotel district but not surrounded by bars, is a solid find for neat-freaks and high-class travelers. It's more modern looking than other hotels in the area, with clean lines and no-fuss furniture. The rooms have beautiful ocean views and position sophisticated guests—who seem a solid notch or two above the average spring-breaker on the dignity meter—only a 10-minute walk from the main spring break beach (Condesa). It has an attractive, clean pool and a section of beach reserved only for hotel guests, a rarity in Acapulco. You'll find a clean, bright cafe/cafeteria called **Bugambilias** with many fresh and tasty breakfast options and an Argentine steakhouse called **El Gaucho.** This hotel adds a touch of tranquillity to an anything-but-Zen city. *Costera Miguel Alemán no. 8 and 9. ☎ 800/ 090-1800 or 744/484-1700. Fax ext. 156. www.elpresidenteacapulco.com.mx. $785–$984 double. AE, MC, V. Amenities: Beach; Internet; pool; room service; safe; salon; 24-hr. doctor; Wi-Fi. In room: A/C, TV w/cable.*

→ **Hotel La Tortuga** ★ Located directly across the street from the long row of beach bars that plays host to spring break debauchery, La Tortuga provides an affordable, yet slightly drab room in which a small group of friends can nurse pounding, tropical hangovers. The hotel is slightly rundown, though the inner courtyard's long vines add a nice touch of green to the breakfast buffet. Guests must be able to sleep through the loud, thumping music that becomes the La Tortuga guests' drunken lullaby. Sensitive sleepers should ask for a room in the back of the hotel where windows face away from the beach bars. La Tortuga welcomes large groups and people of all ages, but this place is best for people who plan on spending a lot of time at the beach or beach bars rather than those willing to spend a lot of money for luxury. *Costera Miguel Alemán no. 132, Fracc. Farallon. ☎ 800/710-9900 or 744/484-8889. Fax 744/484-7385 or -6079. $700–$1,200 double. Rates may include breakfast buffet. MC, V.*

➔ **Hotel Los Flamingos** ★★★ Perched in an appropriately junglelike pocket of Old Acapulco at the top of a hill overlooking the water, Hotel Los Flamingos makes you feel like you're on the set of *Tarzan*—which you are, as the original film was shot here. (Unfortunately, handsome toned men in loincloths no longer prance through the tree-covered verandas.) Built in the '30s and popular with the Hollywood crowd in the '50s, the hotel features a Hollywood Hall of Fame near the concierge, with pictures of former guests Johnny Weissmuller, Cary Grant, and John Wayne, among others. Deep magenta walls contrast nicely with the lush surroundings and a gorgeous ocean backdrop adds romance and tranquility. The highlight of the dimly lit rooms is the ocean-side balconies, complete with bright-colored hammocks and cushioned chairs. Air-conditioning is available, but the ocean breeze (the freshest smelling in Acapulco) is sufficient. Even if you don't stay here, stop by on a Thursday between 3pm and 6pm for one of their pozole parties. *Av. López Mateos s/n, Apdo. Post no. 70. ☎ 744/482-0690 or -0691 or -0692. Fax 744/483-9806. $600–$850 double. AE, MC, V. Amenities: Restaurant; bar; book exchange; car rental; pool; room service. In room: TV, fans, fridge, phone.*

➔ **Hotel Oviedo** ★ This place is around 70 years old, but it doesn't look a day over 50. This seven-story hotel can be found in an old building a block or so away from the zócalo and famous church, Nuestra Señora de Soledad, in Old Acapulco. The rooms are basic, with air-conditioning, closets, and a desk that seems much newer than the hotel. It's nothing special, but the place is cheap and has a bit more history than some of the other joints in town. Internet cafes, banks, and a major department store are all downstairs, as are many cheap restaurants. Plus, the building has an elevator—a rarity in this part of town and a great alternative to lugging backpacks up stairs. *Av. Costera Miguel Alemán 207, Col. Centro. ☎ 744/482-1511. Fax 744/482-1512. $250 per person with A/C, TV w/cable, and hot water; $150–$300 for room with ceiling fan, TV (no cable), no hot water. No credit cards.*

Doable

➔ **El Mirador Acapulco** ★★★ Located on the edge of a cliff at La Quebrada, home to the famous Acapulco cliff-divers, this hotel offers just about the best ocean view available, but it's still completely accessible to Old Acapulco. But be forewarned: There are a lot of stairs at El Mirador since it's built on a cliff. Both the views and the rooms (which are simple but clean) are beautiful, but look elsewhere for any bar or beach action. A unique alternative to the inconspicuous swimming pool is the rocky saltwater "pool," which allows swimming in a closed off section of the ocean.

Even if spending the night here is not on the agenda, make sure to reserve one night for dinner at its famous restaurant, **La Perla,** where one can watch the cliff-diver action in the evening from the best seats in town. (Just remember, the restaurant isn't known for its food.) *Plazoleta La Quebrada no. 74, Col. La Mira. ☎ 800/021-7557 or 744/483-1221. Fax 744/483-8800 or 482-4564. $850 1–2 people, $1,200 4 people. Rates include breakfast. AE, MC, V. Amenities: Restaurant; bar; jewelry store; luggage storage; money exchange; 3 pools (one is freshwater); travel agency; 24-hr. doctor. In room: A/C, TV w/cable, safety deposit box.*

➔ **Hotel Acamar** ★★ Situated directly on an uncluttered spot of beach, Acamar has everything, *and* it's affordable. As a result, it's perfect for groups of friends who want a resort feeling without the resort prices. The hotel overlooks **Caleta Beach,** one of the most popular beaches in Acapulco. From the hotel lobby, guests can wander out to a small but inviting pool, and then walk straight onto the beach—a rare luxury here. Rooms look a little more expensive than they are, with fancy touches throughout—for instance, your towels come folded on the bed in their signature style, portraying two swans kissing in the shape of a heart. Cheesy but effective. Another perk: Many rooms have terrace kitchenettes. *Av. Costera Miguel Alemán no. 26, Fracc. Las Playas. ☎ 800/719-3684 or 744/482-0570 ext. 73. Fax 744/482-2119. www.acamaracapulco.com. $730 double, $915 up to 4 people. DISC, MC, V. Amenities: Restaurant; snack bar; beach; Internet; laundry service; minisupermarket; money exchange; pharmacy; pool; 24-hr. doctor. In room: A/C, TV, kitchenette (for extra charge), phone, safe.*

➔ **Hotel Copacabana** ★★ This is one of the best places around for nonstop beach action in a party atmosphere, with an excellent view of the bay (but at some distance from main Acapulco highway). Joining the other high-rise hotels around the bay, this one is 18 stories high and feels like a bustling metropolis of international vacationers. This hotel is itching to deliver a fabulous time, and organized social activities and free beer and wine at lunch assure that nobody gets bored and most people get drunk. The rooms are simple and the bathrooms are a little run-down and sad, but the Jacuzzis, pools, and beach chairs outside are all a person really needs. A 24-hour Internet cafe and coffee shop called K'Ffe Zucco are located in a frantic lobby that resembles Grand Central Station at rush hour. Unlike some hotels that provide an oasis for beach-naps and romantic poolside cuddling, this one will pull you in and throw you into the big game; be ready. *Tabachines no. 2, Fracc. Club Deportivo. ☎ 800/562-0197 or 744/484-3260 ext. 61. Fax 744/484-6268. www.hotelcopacabana.com. $90–$220 single/double. AE, MC, V. Amenities: 2 restaurants; 4 bars; boutiques; business center; drugstore; gym; Internet cafe; Jacuzzi; laundry service; pool; room service; travel agency; 24-hr. doctor. In room: A/C, TV w/cable, hair dryer, safety deposit box.*

Splurge

➔ **Camino Real Diamante Acapulco** ★★★ Nestled in the hillside of Puerto Marqués just off the Carretera Escénica, this beautiful hotel possesses one of the only privately owned beaches in Acapulco; come here for a luxurious and relaxing getaway that will mostly keep you from the nightlife and old Acapulco. While couples and 20-somethings frequently vacation here, it is mostly a family resort where parents can enjoy a relaxing, upscale vacation in a party-city without having to worry about their children witnessing a wet T-shirt contest or booze cruise. The scene is calm and classy, with the occasional screech of a child (or monkey) outdoors. Rooms are very spacious and bright, with marble tiles, yellow and blue bed spreads, and semi-private terraces that overlook the water and pool area. Upon arrival, you'll immediately know you're on vacation when you receive a complimentary "welcome" drink, which is welcome indeed after the somewhat arduous hike from the highway. *Carretera Escénica Km 14, Baja Catita s/n Pibhilingue. ☎ 744/435-1010. Fax 744/435-1020. www.caminoreal.com/acapulco. $1,199–$2,200 double. AE, MC, V. Amenities: 2 restaurants; lobby bar; concierge; gym; health club; laundry service; 3 pools (1 for children); 24-hr. room service; salon; shopping arcade; spa; tennis court; tour desk; travel agency desk; watersports equipment rentals. In room: A/C, TV w/cable, dataport, hair dryer, iron, minibar, safe-deposit box.*

Eating

It doesn't take a rocket scientist to observe that people eat a lot of fish in Mexico. This is doubly true in beach resorts such as Acapulco, where you can rest assured that the fish you'll be eating is about as fresh as it gets. Sure, there is always chicken and beef to break the cycle, but in Mexico it's all about the fish. And, except for the town's slightly upscale restaurants, there aren't many salads to write home about (100% Natural is one big exception to that rule).

Even if you're on a tight budget, it's worth splurging on a fancy meal here one night. Try one of the swanky restaurants (such as Zuntra and Baikal) that hug the cliff-side of the Diamante neighborhood (along the Carretera Escénica). These restaurants promise innovative menus, upscale service, and the quintessential sunset. A few top restaurants are also folded into the busier Condesa Beach area, such as El Olvido, but, generally speaking, the closer you are to the sand on the beach, the more casual the restaurant.

Super Gigante is a massive supermarket located around the corner from Hotel Copacabana and south of Hotel Elcano. Whether you're buying alcohol (to make a round of drinks in your own room before you go out), large water jugs, cereal bars, or fruit, you can save on meals by making them yourself whenever possible.

Cheap

→ **La Flor de Acapulco** ★ MEXICAN If you find yourself standing directly in the center of the zócalo in Old Acapulco with hunger pangs and no idea where to satisfy your empty stomach, here's a tip: Look west. On the second floor, you should see this joint, which first opened in 1939. They serve a variety of fresh juices, as well as good ol' spaghetti with meat sauce, fried fish, and—on the slightly heavier side—a decent slab of steak. Sit on the balcony overlooking the zócalo and pity all the people dining below who have to fend off jewelry salesmen while they eat. *Plaza Alvarez, zócalo, Acapulco. Main courses $40–$150. No credit cards. Daily noon–11pm.*

→ **100% Natural** ★★ MEXICAN/VEGETARIAN Healthy, affordable, and tasty, 100% Natural offers something different from most of the strictly Mexican-fairing menus in town. This chain can be found all over Acapulco, but this is the best: the high, palapa roof restaurant boasts an upbeat atmosphere and a mixture of young health-conscious Mexicans and tourists alike. The menu includes bakery items (croissants and chocolate almond muffins) and desserts (cookies, pies) as well as salads, soups, pastas, burgers (including soy burgers), and traditional Mexican dishes (quesadillas, enchiladas, tacos, and so on). Be sure to order one of their fantastically fruity juices like the Conga, made from melon, watermelon, papaya, plantain, and guayaba (it costs $29 for an enormous "small.") The food and drinks are so tasty and uncomplicated, I guarantee you'll leave 100% satisfied. ***Note:*** Speaking of percentages, look for 10% discounts in tourism brochures. *Av. Costera Miguel Alemán no. 3126, Fracc. Costa Azul. ☎ 744/484-8440. www.100natural.com.mx. Main courses $50–$115. Daily 7am–11pm.*

→ **Restaurant El Amigo Miguel** ★★ SEAFOOD Located on a pointy corner block a few blocks away from the zócalo, this is the go-to place for reliably good seafood in the area. The fish is completely fresh and deliciously prepared in a number of different styles (including fried, breaded, or in the popular Veracruz-style with peppers, tomatoes, and capers). The drunken shrimp *(camarones borrachos)* are also tasty, sautéed in a sauce of ketchup, beer, applesauce, mustard, and pieces of fresh bacon (that somehow work very well together). Service is extremely fast, so there is barely a chance to enjoy the fresh-baked bread before the actual meal arrives. The completely open dining area has turquoise and white tablecloths, shiny wood chairs, and random maritime details that make you feel like you're on the very boat in which your meal was caught. *Benito Juárez no. 31, Col. Centro, Old Acapulco, walking distance from zócalo. ☎ 744/483-6981. AE, DISC, MC, V. Main courses $40–$95. Daily 10am–9pm.*

→ **Restaurante Hacienda María Bonita** ★★ MEXICAN It looks like just another unremarkable Mexican restaurant on the Costera Hotel Zone strip, but think again. The chicken tacos were the best I have ever eaten in my life. There's no mystery-meat whatsoever: inside the crunchy fried tortillas here, you'll find delicious, golden fried chicken. Cover those beauties with black bean sauce, throw on some homemade guacamole, cheese, and a dollop of María Bonita magic and you've got yourself a winner. It'd be worth staying at the tacky-looking hotel in the back just to eat those tacos every day. But consider bringing earplugs; even though mariachi music blasts from nearby speakers, it still doesn't drown out the traffic sounds outside. *Attached to Hotel María Eugenia at Costera Miguel Alemán no. 176, 200m/656 ft. from the Galerías Diana. ☎ 744/481-2989. www.haciendamariaeugenia.com.mx. Main courses $35–$150. AE, DISC, MC, V. Daily 8am–midnight.*

→ **Restaurant La Sirena** ★ SEAFOOD/MEXICAN For a quick bite that's easy to find and doesn't pull out any bells or whistles, this is a safe choice. The menu has your basic Mexican dishes, with an assortment of fish options, but I recommend the *chalupas*, which are small, crunchy tortilla cups with lettuce, salsa, and salty chicken meat inside, sprinkled with cheese. There are many restaurants like this in Old Acapulco, but La Sirena's off-center location (tucked away on a side street) means most clients are locals and friends of the owners, not tourists. The atmosphere is cheery and calm, and despite the American music, you feel like you're really in Mexico—that's a good thing. *Teniente José Azueta no. 5, Col. Centro. ☎ 744/482-0647. Main courses $25–$95. No credit cards. Daily 9am–8pm.*

→ **Restaurant Palermo** ★ MEXICAN If you tell the housekeeper in K3 Hostel that you're hungry, she'll quickly call her friend, a friendly and talkative old man, to pick you up downstairs, at which point he'll lead you around the corner from the hostel, up some stairs to his delightful, hidden restaurant. When I got there, he said (in English) "Welcome to my restaurant. You are home." Indeed, this gardenlike place makes you feel like you're sitting on the porch of your grandma's house, complete with a TV blasting a Mexican comedy show that causes all the waiters to break down in laughter. Here you'll find everything from pre-fixed breakfasts to fish and your usual Mexican fair, including fried or breaded red snapper, chicken or fish tacos, and seafood soup, which can be found all over Acapulco. The homemade food is surprisingly good, with just the right touch of comfort. *Plaza Condesa across the street from Fiesta Americana (up the stairs to the right of K3 Hostel).* ☎ *744/484-1617. Main courses $40–$45. No credit cards. Daily 8am–10pm.*

→ **Sushi 'N Gada** ★ JAPANESE You can easily walk right by this place if you're not paying attention, but if you're in the mood for something besides Mexican, it's worth stopping in. There's nothing fancy here, just simple, typical Japanese dishes and sushi rolls in a no-fuss environment with five small tables lit by five white paper lanterns. Inside it is surprisingly quiet and peaceful, given its location in such a busy and boisterous part of Acapulco. You might even forget that you're in Acapulco while you're there, which could be a good thing. Just know that there is no English menu, so you might want to remember the Japanese words for your favorite dishes. *Costera Miguel Alemán, next to Carlos 'n Charlie's.* ☎ *744/484-5700. Pre-fixe combos $63–$100 (with a drink), sushi $20–$75 per roll. No credit cards. Tues–Sun noon–11pm.*

Doable

→ **El Gaucho** ★★ ARGENTINE/STEAKHOUSE If you're sick of fish and want a nice slab of juicy meat, plan a meal at El Gaucho. Here, the decor feels authentically Argentinian but the quality of the meat—what Argentine cuisine is most famous for—will remind you that you're still in Mexico. Nevertheless, this is still probably the best meat you'll find in Acapulco. Dab on some of the delicious, spicy chimichurri sauce that comes with fresh bread if you want to add some kick to the meat. An authentic *asado* grill (used for slow cooking) is encased in a glass room at one end of the restaurant, and old gaucho horse and cattle equipment hangs on one wall. Service is friendly, and the wine list is extensive and well-balanced. *Costera Miguel Alemán, Hotel El Presidente.* ☎ *744/484-1700. Main courses $126–$250. AE, MC, V. Daily 5–11:30pm.*

→ **El Jaguar** ★ SOUTHERN MEXICAN This restaurant is one of your only options for decent food in this particular area of the Costera Highway. You'll find an authentic Guerrero menu, though the decor may as well have been designed by Disney, with its bright colors, festive mariachi soundtrack, fake flowers, and even a gift shop in the back. Unusual dishes include fried pigeons and pigs' feet. I'd go with the curried shrimp or *huachinango* (red snapper) instead. Enjoy the complimentary coconut treat that comes with the check. The food definitely has a spicy kick; don't believe the waitress when she says something isn't spicy at all, or *"no pica."* It's all spicy here. *Av. Costera Miguel Alemán #79, Fracc. Club Deportivo, across the street from the golf club.* ☎ *744/481-4099. Main courses $25–$170. DISC, MC, V. Tues–Sun 8am–10pm.*

Splurge

→ **El Olvido** ★★★ INTERNATIONAL FUSION *Olvidar* is the Spanish verb for "forget," which here may mean "try to forget you're in a shopping mall area." This restaurant more or less succeeds at doing just that—it doesn't hurt that the mall it's in just happens to be located right next to the ocean overlooking gorgeous Acapulco Bay. The menu asserts that the restaurant has a contemporary take on classically rooted dishes, and that's also true. Try the spinach salad, with goat cheese, pecans, glazed pears, and hibiscus vinaigrette. The shrimp with coconut and ginger sauce, adorned with avocado and mango slices, is also delicious. For something different, try the green apple ravioli dessert. Add together the food, the excellent service, the relaxing, pastel-hued décor, and the soothing music and you get a memorable, if pricey, dinner here. There's technically no dress code, but most people dress up for this one. *Plaza Marbella, Av. Costera Miguel Alemán.* ☎ *744/481-0203 or -0214 or -0240. Fax 744/421-0256. www.elolvido.com.mx. Main courses $145–$380. AE, MC, V. Daily 5–11:30pm.*

➔ **Zuntra** ★★★ FUSION This restaurant has it all: impeccable service from start to finish; an innovative menu (chorizo-infused bread with pepper flavored butter and shrimp with mango, cooked with tequila and green chiles); and an amazing view. Its location up in the Diamante hills happily takes diners away from the grimy streets. The decor is simple and chic, with white tablecloths that contrast against jet-black chairs, a large mask sculpture in the back of the room, and paintings on the walls of identical swirls of black, white and brown. The New Age samba music in the background gives the restaurant an edge, and keeps it from feeling too romantic. The simplicity of the decor cleverly keeps the focus of the restaurant on the stunning view of a glittering Acapulco Bay. This is a great place for a not-too-sappy romantic dinner, but a date is not required to leave happy. For a swanky upgrade, sip a cocktail while sitting on one of the white benches with ruby-colored pillows at the posh lounge upstairs. For those who decide to lounge it, dress the part and pretend you're unfazed by the incredible view in order to fit in with the crowd. *Carretera Escenica s/n local 1-2, Marina Brisas.* ☎ *744/446-5601. Fax 744/446-5602. www.zuntra.com.mx. Main courses $140–$400. AE, MC, V. Tues–Sun 7:30pm–2am. Deck lounge Thurs–Sun 9pm–4am (and daily during high season).*

Cafes & Tearooms

MTV Best ➔ **Café Loma Verde** ★★★ CAFE This adorable little cafe smells of fresh coffee and fruit, and feels untouched by tourism—a rare find in Acapulco. The small, homey space consists of tables with stools creatively draped in different colored fabrics and photos of coffee plantations dotting the walls. The menu is full of coffee concoctions, including a coffee with tequila and an iced vanilla cappuccino that's as deliciously frothy as a milkshake. *Hidalgo 13, Local 8, Col. Centro.* ☎ *744/482-3565. cafelomaverde@hotmail.com. Nothing over $60. No credit cards. Daily 9am–9pm.*

➔ **Italian Coffee Company** ★ CAFE Though it's not a Starbucks, it might as well be. You won't get a chance to interact with locals like at Café Loma, and the whole vibe is more manufactured. But it's certainly comfortable—inside this air-conditioned cafe you can sip your favorite coffee drink while reading from one of the magazines or newspapers available in the back. In addition to coffee, you can snack on paninis, croissants, or cakes. Non-coffee lovers can try the jungle berries or piña colada–flavored teas. The two street-side walls are comprised completely of glass, making this a great place to take a break, re-caffeinate, and people-watch. *Costera Miguel Alemán no. 34, Colonia Costa Sur, across the street from the Procuraría de Turista.* ☎ *744/484-4994. www.italiancoffee.com. Nothing over $60. No credit cards. Daily 8am–midnight.*

Partying

Acapulco may have had its heyday in the '50s, but it still knows how to party. In fact, many people come to Acapulco specifically for its nightlife, which is so raging, it seems to never stop. Between the assortment of hip telenovela-star-populated hot clubs to the always fun beach bars that encourage naughty behavior (don't worry, nobody will tell on you), there are many places to party all night, make lots of mistakes, and forget it all by the morning. Pack your Advil.

The party scene basically breaks into two categories. First, there are the obvious beach bars and the Señor Frog's on or around Condesa Beach, where the party atmosphere begins at noon and continues through the night and into the morning. These bars are easy to find and have a more laid-back atmosphere. Second, there are the hot clubs like Palladium, Baby O's, and Alberije, which can be found in the hills of the Diamante area. Here you must dress to impress and wait in line, but you're rewarded with an incredible all-night party that lasts until the sun comes up. This is the real deal. Acapulco owes its renaissance to these clubs that transport the town back to its *Tarzan* heyday.

At the clubs, be prepared to hear a lot of old '80s songs remixed with techno or Spanish beats, with some salsa, reggaeton, and occasional American Top 40 hits thrown in. And at both bars and clubs, expect to find crowds that are a healthy mix of Mexicans and tourists.

Clubs

→ **Baby O's** ★★ Known for its cavernous appearance, Baby O's is one of the biggest It-clubs in town. Despite its dark and mysterious atmosphere, this club is very easy to find: Don't be surprised if a limo full of telenovela stars waltzes in through a small cloud of paparazzi and local news cameramen. Once inside, the sexy lighting and cavelike decorations should inspire some animalistic dancing to techno and Top 40 beats. People come from all over the world to dance here, so plan on spending a lot of time and money to impress. *Costera Alemán 22. ☎ 744/484-7474 or 481-1035. www.babyo.com.mx. Cover $50–$350.*

→ **Carlos 'n Charlie's** ★★ Just 1 block from K3 Hostel and a couple blocks south of the beach bars, this relative of Señor Frog's is a tourist-filled spot to jump-start a night on the town. If you need to act fast, yard-glass drinks are there to help. Want a challenge? Try the African Bull yard-glass after a day at the beach, which boasts seven different types of rum, among other things. The menu includes a set of rules, including: *Don't laugh, don't chew with your mouth full,* and, finally, *there are no rules.* The last one seems to apply best, though things stay under control; this bar is like a frat party that people actually remember going to. *Costera Miguel Alemán no. 112, Club Deportivo. ☎ 744/484-0039. www.carlosandcharlies.com/acapulco/index.htm. Food $90–$210.*

MTV Best → **Palladium** ★★★ If you come to Acapulco for the nightlife experience, your trip is not complete without a long night of inappropriate dancing at the super-trendy Palladium. This club sits on a hill in the expensive Diamante section of town with a whole side of the club functioning as one enormous window overlooking the glittering bay. It's a view you shouldn't miss, so try not to arrive completely smashed. Dress to impress, or you may not get in. While cover charges can reach up to $300 for the night, there is an open bar once you get inside. If you want to sit and take in the view, VIP couches

Acapulco Sightseeing & Playing Outside

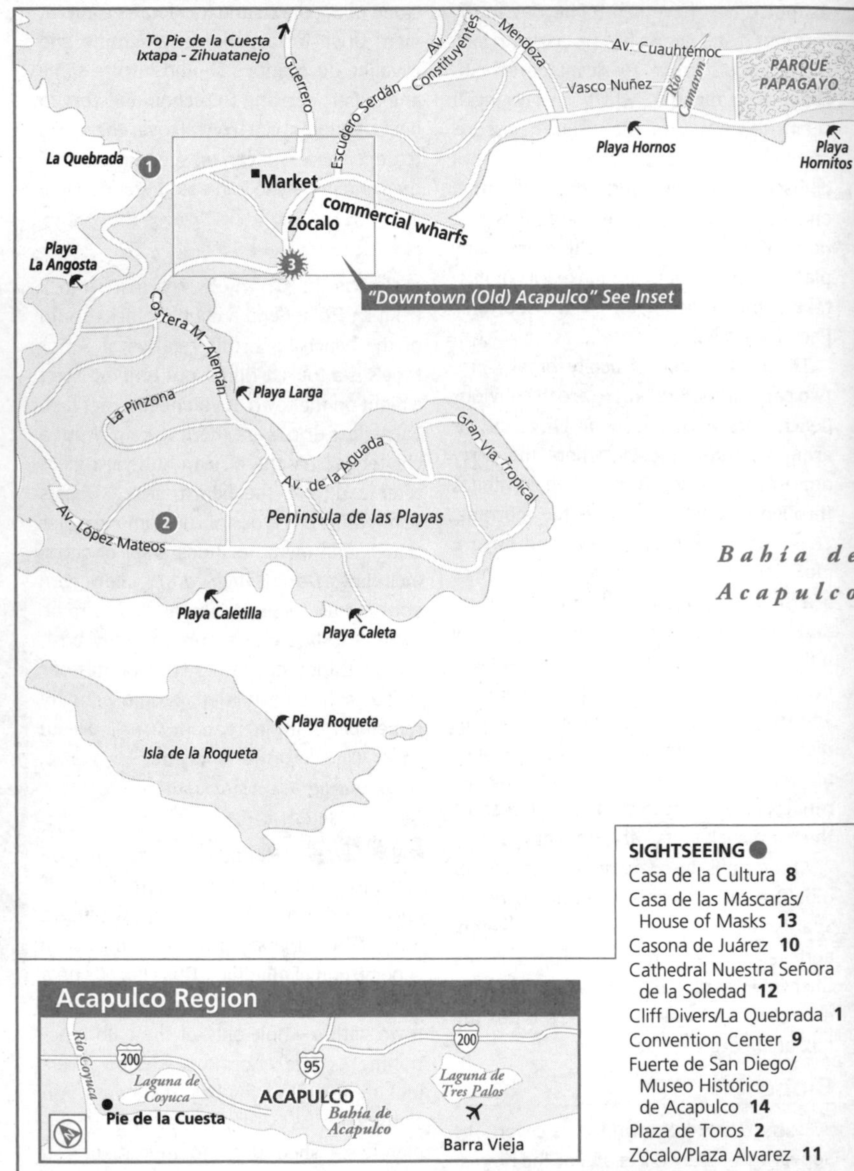

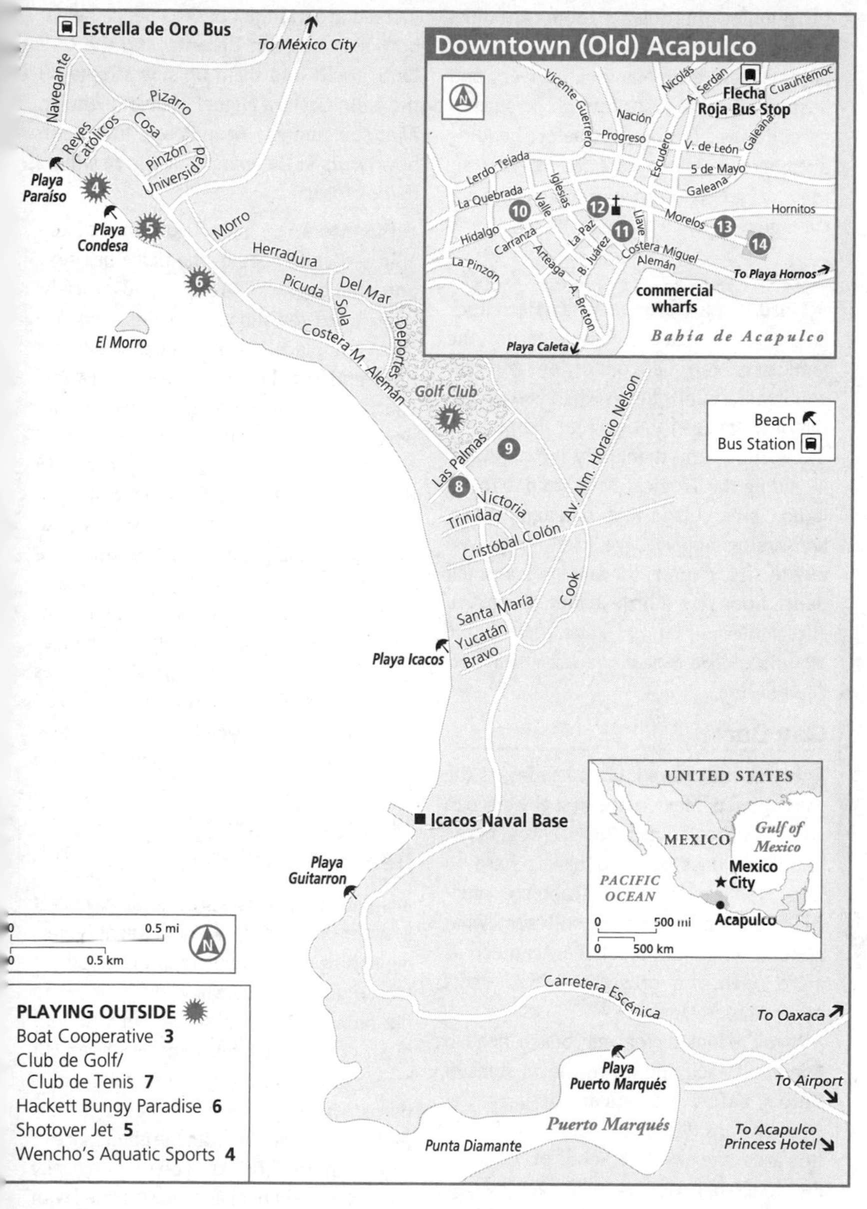

Estrella de Oro Bus
To México City
Downtown (Old) Acapulco
Vicente Guerrero
Nicolás
A. Serdan
Flecha Roja Bus Stop
Cuauhtémoc
Nación
Progreso
Escudero
V. de León
Galeana
5 de Mayo
Galeana
Lerdo Tejada
La Quebrada
Iglesias
Valle
Hidalgo
Carranza
La Paz
Llave
Morelos
Hornitos
Arteaga
B. Juárez
Costera Miguel Alemán
La Pinzon
A. Breton
commercial wharfs
To Playa Hornos
Playa Caleta
Bahía de Acapulco
Navegante
Reyes Católicos
Pizarro
Cosa
Pinzón
Universidad
Playa Paraíso
Playa Condesa
Morro
Herradura
Picuda
Del Mar
Sola
Deportes
Costera M. Aleman
El Morro
Golf Club
Beach
Bus Station
Horacio Nelson
Av. Alm.
Las Palmas
Victoria
Trinidad
Cristóbal Colón
Cook
Santa María
Yucatán
Bravo
Playa Icacos
UNITED STATES
Gulf of Mexico
MEXICO
Mexico City
PACIFIC OCEAN
Acapulco
500 mi
500 km
Icacos Naval Base
Playa Guitarron
0.5 mi
0.5 km
Carretera Escénica
To Oaxaca
Playa Puerto Marqués
To Airport
Puerto Marqués
Punta Diamante
To Acapulco Princess Hotel
PLAYING OUTSIDE
Boat Cooperative 3
Club de Golf/ Club de Tenis 7
Hackett Bungy Paradise 6
Shotover Jet 5
Wencho's Aquatic Sports 4

facing the windows overlook the club, with its cylindrical stages and flatscreen TVs surrounding the pulsing room. Although only accessible by taxi, you won't want to be anywhere else. Many cab drivers and hostels offer $30 discounts, so be sure to try and snag a few of those before heading over here. *Carretera Escénica. ☎ 744/481-0330 or 446-5483. www.palladium.com.mx. Cover $100–$350.*

Bars

➔ **Hard Rock Cafe** Entering a Hard Rock Cafe while abroad is a guilty pleasure; the familiarity can be comforting and yet you'll feel a pang of guilt when you realize the only Mexican thing about the place is the waiters—and thankfully the cocktails, including the Tropical Rock (rum, banana liquor, piña colada mix, pineapple juice, and melon liquor). Live music is played nightly from 10pm to 2am and a small dance floor sees a little action. *Av. Casiera Miguel Aleman no. 37, Fracc. Costa Azul. ☎ 527/484-6680. www.hardrock.com/acapulco. Cocktails $79.*

Gay Bars

Acapulco may have had its heyday as the gay capital of Mexico (the first gay disco in all of Mexico, "Sans Souci," was here), but these days, a good bar is hard to find. Homosexuality in Acapulco, especially among women, is still somewhat underground. Still, most see Acapulco as more open and progressive than most other cities in Mexico.

If you're looking for a gay beach, head to Condesa Beach and down the 72 steps of **Beto's Safari Restaurant** to arrive at what is considered "gay Condesa Beach" (towards the western end of Condesa Beach). **Fish-R-Us** (p. 539) is a gay-owned, gay-friendly yacht company with fishing and scuba-diving tours.

There are a few gay bars, such as **Demas, Savage,** and **Relax** that are all located around the Condesa Beach neighborhood, between **Picante** and the Golf Club. You'll find them on side streets off the main Costera Miguel Alemán highway. That sums up gay Acapulco: A little rainbow exists in the margins if you're willing to look for it.

➔ **Picante** ★ This "spicy" club is more like a mild red chile pepper; the place has sexy potential but lacks strong crowds. Luckily, it just takes you and your friends to change that. This place has a medium-size dance floor and circular two-person tables and couches that invite you to flirt with someone nearby. Still, the first thing you'll notice will probably be the bar with a male dancer prancing around in a black Speedo. There are daily stripper shows between midnight and 4am; transvestite shows are on Fridays and Saturdays at 2:30am. Picante provides a sassy and fun environment for the small but growing gay population of Acapulco, and of course it welcomes any visitors. Give this place some love. *Privada de Piedra Picuda #16, down side street off of Costera Miguel Alemán that is to the right of Carlos 'n Charlie's. ☎ 744/484-2342. $50 cover plus 1 drink minimum.*

Beach Bar Crawls

Acapulco's beach bars are a great way to get a night started or keep a night going, depending on what you're in the mood for. Most of the beach bars have direct access to the popular Condesa Beach, but you definitely don't want to be on the beach at night (especially when drunk) for safety purposes. The constant ocean breeze is wonderful, but combined with the abundance of tequila-infused drinks, you're practically guaranteed a hangover. Since it's lined with several bars, as well as a great place for late-night tacos, MTV Best **Taco & Beer** ★★,

(Costera Miguel Alemán; no phone) and a crepes and churros stand, I recommend walking up and down the strip before choosing your plan of attack. Each bar offers something slightly different, but they all want to get you drunk. Let us move from the southern end to the northern end of the bars (that would be from left to right when facing the water).

For a sports bar with as many females as males, try **Mangoes** (Costera Miguel Alemán; ☎ 744/446-5736). For the experience of sailing on a pirate ship with talkative Mexicans wearing bandanas and the occasional eye-patch (minus the actual ship), have a couple beers at the pirate-themed **Barbaroja** (Costera Miguel Alemán; ☎ 744/84-5932), where the music volume is low enough that people can have interesting conversations with their friends, though that all changes during their spring break Mardi Gras party. As the drinks keep coming, enjoy a perfect view of crazy bungee jumpers (or be inspired to jump yourself) at **Paradise** (Costera Miguel Alemán; ☎ 744/484-5988) where kids come with their thirsty parents and play with large colorful balloons early on, but after their bedtime, the music gets louder and the real party begins.

Bombay (Costera Miguel Alemán; no phone) has a large circular bar and high ceilings, but not as much action as some of the other bars nearby. Finish the evening off at **Disco Beach** (Costera Miguel Alemán; ☎ 744/484-8230), where there is plenty of dancing all night right beside the ocean and it is easy to engage in the messy spectacle of a foam party once a week.

Many of these beach bars have ladies' nights or two-for-one drink deals for $60, so try avoiding the nights with cover charges (although it won't be as easy to avoid the mornings with hangovers).

Heading to the Beach

Here's a quick snapshot of what you'll find at each beach, going from west to east around Acapulco Bay.

Playa la Angosta is very small and often empty. Located near **La Quebrada** (where the cliff-divers perform), it is known for good snorkeling but there is no real need to visit unless you prefer semi-desolate beaches for privacy.

Near Old Acapulco are the sister-beaches, **Caleta** and **Caletilla.** The two small beaches are divided by a pier that leads to the uninspiring, small **Mágico Mundo Marino.** These were both favored by the Hollywood crowd because of the calm waters and proximity to the old section of town. **Caleta** is slightly bigger than **Caletilla** but both are popular with locals. At Caleta and Caletilla, people can rent beach chairs, partake in watersports activities, or eat at one of the many restaurants lining the beach. These beaches are very pretty, but tend to get crowded and loud. From here, people can visit **Roqueta Island,** a great place to chill, snorkel, and visit a lighthouse, with a great view of Acapulco (pay $30 for a round-trip ferry ride that leaves from the pier every 10 minutes).

Hornos, Hornitos, and **Paraíso** beaches tend to blend together a bit, but all have plenty of sand and shore to play in, along with a huge array of watersports and beach activities. Many restaurants and some bars line these beaches, so expect to hear loud music and smell food or exhaust while there.

Next up is **Condessa Beach,** probably the most crowded, but definitely one of the most fun beaches in town. It is bursting with activities and hosts the famous beach

Arts & Culture in Acapulco

Acapulco is not the most culturally rich Mexican city, but it does have one or two cultural centers that strive to keep the city from becoming one big tourist attraction. In addition to the **Convention Center** (p. 520), you'll find the FREE → **Casa de la Cultura** ★★ (Costera Miguel Alemán, across from Convention/Visitor Center in Fracc. Costa Azul; ☎ **744/484-6626**). Literally "The House of Culture," this government-owned cultural center Is really an assortment of small buildings. For 18 years, this place has been providing the somewhat culturally starved city of Acapulco with a healthy dose of art displays (often by local artists), book readings, dance/music/theater performances, film festivals, and language classes. It is open to everyone 365 days of the year and almost every exhibit is free. Exhibits in the art gallery rotate every 2 weeks, and there are three small classrooms, an Internet cafe, a library, and both an outdoor and indoor auditorium. For anyone who plans to be in the area for an extended period of time, consider coming here for painting, writing, or language classes—you can sign up on-site.

bars you'll find in between the popular hotels. Condesa beach is extremely active both day and night (though you should avoid beaches here at night; see "Acapulco's Deadly Drug Trade," p. 519). Unfortunately, like most of the beaches in Acapulco, this one can be pretty dirty. The Bay is cleaned every morning, but don't be surprised if you come up for air with a plastic bag in your hair. Also, be careful of the dangerous rip-tide that looks harmless from the sand but is extremely powerful and somewhat dangerous just 3m (10 ft.) into the water. Remember that there are no lifeguards around.

Playa Puerto Marqués is another beautiful beach for swimming, but it is harder to get to than some of the area's other beaches. The beach here is surrounded by tropical vegetation and the waves are gentle.

Just past Playa Puerto Marqués lies **Revolcadero Beach,** where some of the nicest hotels in Acapulco enjoy the expansive shoreline and surfer-friendly waves. Beware of a strong undertow, and the occasional inexperienced horseback rider. This is one of the most beautiful beaches in Acapulco.

Located just outside of the hustle and bustle of Acapulco are a few other beaches worth checking out: the most famous is MTV Best **Pie de la Cuesta** (located 13km/ 8 miles outside of downtown), known for having the absolute best sunsets. You'll find plenty of restaurants offering *coco locos* (coconut drinks) at this beach, plus some really good horseback riding, but it's too dangerous for swimming. The best way to get here is by car, but buses leave from the Sanborn's near the zócalo in Old Acapulco every 10 minutes, just check on when the last one comes back. Taxis can also get you here, but they charge anywhere from $200 to $400.

Sightseeing

There is a lot to see and do in Acapulco aside from partying and being a beach bum. Here are a few culturally enriching experiences that would make mom and dad proud.

Festivals/Events

The two biggest festivities in this town are 1) spring break, and 2) Semana Santa. Other than that, count on a bunch of fishing competitions and events on a smaller scale.

Semana Santa: Although predominantly a religious festival, this week is also tons of fun, with parades and parties galore. The week before Easter, March.

Spring Break: Thanks to thousands of spring-breakers who flock to the Bay, Acapulco becomes one big party, day and night. They even host their own **Mardi Gras** party. Late February through early April.

Acapulco Boat Show: Considered the most important nautical event in Mexico, some of the biggest names in sport-fishing gather for this annual show at the Acapulco Yacht Club. May 5 to 8. Visit www.istc.org/sisp/index.htm?fx=event&event_id=93776.

Museums & Galleries

MTV Best → **Casa de las Máscaras (House of Masks)** ★★★ This museum gets points for quirkiness. When you step into this small, privately owned house of over 1,000 masks, the tribal drumming music may tempt you to don a mask and do a dance. This place is that funky and cool, with crazy ritual and decorative masks from all over the world, including an especially good collection of traditional local masks used for religious and non-religious purposes. The masks are colorful and at times spooky, with snazzy surprises in the details. The collection can be found less than a 5-minute walk down the street from the main entrance to the Fuerte de San Diego. *On the Cultural Corridor next to the Fort of San Diego.* ☎ *744-486-5577. Free admission (donations welcome). Daily 10am–4pm.*

FREE → **Casona de Juárez** ★★ This gallery in Old Acapulco displays beautiful artwork from local artists and also doubles as a venue for poetry readings and theater displays. The building itself is a beautiful old structure that is almost as interesting as the art itself. Artists from all over the world are displayed, from painters to sculptures to photographers. Exhibits tend

Free & Easy

- Thank God, **the beach** (see "Heading to the Beach" earlier for options) doesn't cost a damn thing. For those who don't need to parasail, jet ski, scuba dive, or snorkel, there's always good old-fashioned sand and ocean to keep a vacation simple, relaxing, and cheap.
- **Old Acapulco,** the area around the **zócalo** (p. 518), is definitely worth an afternoon trip. People come here to wander the streets or sit in the shady, tree-filled zócalo while they take in a healthy dose of local Acapulco culture. While in the area, pay a quick visit to the **Cathedral of Our Lady of Solitude,** an interesting blue and gold, Byzantine-style church.
- The **Fort of San Diego/Museum of Acapulco** (p. 538) is free on Sundays. Just down the street is the **House of Masks** (p. 537), which is always free.
- Don't forget that most events at the **House of Culture** (p. 536) are free.
- Take a quick trip to the free **House of Dolores Olmeda** to see where Diego Rivera lived his final days. One of his final works is a long mosaic of a serpentlike creature that spreads across the entrance to the house. It's located at Inalámbrica #6 Cerro de la Pinzona.

to run on a 1- to 2-month rotation and the gallery is booked through 2007 already. This seems like one of the few areas where serious artists (both plastic and written) can gather, share, and appreciate each other's art. Seeing as it's completely free, you might as well swing by and grab a treat from the bakery a few doors down afterwards. Ask them about the 2-day "written word fair" they host every year. *Calle Hornitos no. 7, Col. Centro. ☎/fax 744/440-7140 ext. 4731. dircultaca@yahoo.com.mx. Free admission. Daily 8am–7pm.*

MTV Best → **Cliff Divers at La Quebrada** ★★★ One of the must-see spectacles of Acapulco. Every night at 7:30, 8:30, 9:30, and 10:30pm, professional cliff-divers march down a staircase by El Mirador hotel, holding torches that light their way. One by one, they launch themselves into a dangerously shallow channel, planning their dives according to when the waves have filled the channel with enough water to complete the task. The divers make it look easy, but it's actually a very dangerous stunt and definitely worth watching. You can watch from a public viewing area for about $30 or eat at the famous **La Perla** restaurant (p. 526), where the food isn't as good as the view and you pay a lot more. *Plaza Las Glorias/El Mirador. Public viewing area costs around $30.*

→ **Fuerte de San Diego/Museo Histórico de Acapulco** ★★ Built in 1616 to protect the town from the onslaught of pirate attacks, this star-shaped fort now houses the Historical Museum of Acapulco, which is definitely worth checking out, especially on a Sunday when it's free. Exhibits offer visitors a glimpse into the history of Acapulco without overburdening them with information. Hopefully you'll already know that Acapulco wasn't always a big beach resort town but, if not, a visit here will teach you that the town has a very rich history. For instance, it served as an important port during the 17th century for trade between the Americas and the Philippines. A parklike area near the entrance is a great place to picnic or just sit in the sun or shade with a beautiful view (although watch out for public displays of affection nearby). Go to the top of the fort by the canons for a great 360-degree view of Acapulco. *Off of the Costera Miguel Alemán on the corner of Morelos and Hornitos. ☎ 744/482-3828 or -1114. Admission $33 (plus $30 to use camera); free for students with ID; free on Sun. Tues–Sun 9:30am–6:30pm.*

ACAPULCO

Playing Outside

People come to Acapulco for a number of different reasons but most of them revolve around being outside, from lying on the beach drinking piña coladas, to blasting through the ocean on a jet ski, to strolling through the sand on horseback. Rest assured the playing outside never stops.

Booze Cruises

If you are one of the many people who think combining booze with a cruise is a good idea, then consider one of the many **booze cruises** that take off from right next to the boat cooperative. Trips can cost from $200 to $500 (or even more) and range in duration and quality. But be careful, the "cruise" is by no means a walk in the park. Combining alcohol with a boat can be either really fun or really nauseating. For many, it is the latter. But taking one of these cruises does offer a great view of all of Acapulco Bay for those who can stomach the trip.

Bungee Jumping

For anyone who ends up by the beach bars, it is hard to ignore the giant bungee tower that overlooks the chaos of the Hotel Zone's nightlife. Contrary to popular belief, bungee jumping is not yet a thing of the past. Acapulco keeps it going at **Hackett Bungy Paradise** on Condesa Beach (☎ **744/484-7529**) with jumps during the day and during the night.

Deep Sea Fishing

You can't talk about Acapulco without talking about deep-sea fishing. Trips can be made through **Fish-R-Us** (mentioned below) or through the boat cooperative across from the zócalo. Call to book in advance (☎ **744/482-1099**).

Golf

For golf, you can either go to the **Club de Golf Acapulco** located off the Costera by the Convention Center (☎ **744/484-0781**) or the **Acapulco Princess,** which is much nicer, located in the Diamante section of town (☎ **744/469-1000**).

Horseback Riding

Horseback riding has become a popular activity in Acapulco over the past few years, so you'll encounter many Mexicans strolling the beaches and asking if you'd like to go horseback riding. Before you hop in that saddle, be warned that prices can easily climb past $400 for a 1-hour gallop on a beach full of people. For great horseback riding, hit up the stretch of beach in **Pie de la Cuesta** along Acapulco's northwest coast, and organize a ride through direct contact with people along the beach—I recommend doing so around sunset.

Scuba Diving & Snorkeling

Scuba diving and snorkeling around **Roqueta Island** are among the most popular activities in Acapulco. One of the best companies is **Fish-R-Us** (Costera Miguel Alemán #100; ☎ **877/3-fish-r-us** or 744/482-8282; www.fish-r-us.com) which is NAUI-affiliated and offers scuba diving, deep sea fishing, water skiing, and even swim lessons. PADI-certified **Divers of Mexico** organizes dives, among other trips (☎ **744/482-1398,** www.funfishing factory.com).

Acapulco Scuba Center (Tlacopanacha 13-14, Paseo del Pescador in downtown Acapulco; ☎ **744/480-1962;** www.acapulco scuba.com), is another popular company (NAUI- and PADI-certified). Their website is more informative than some of the others and they offer daily tours (including a night dive) for divers of all levels. You can plan a 2-hour scuba-diving excursion with someone right on the beach for about $400 to $500 or you can pay around $700 for a half-day trip including transportation to and from your hotel.

Spectator Sports

Bullfighting is one of the more exciting, unique activities a person can witness while in Acapulco. It's not recommended for vegetarians or animal rights activists, though, and personally, I'd avoid wearing red, just in case any sort of accidental running-of-the-bulls breaks out.

The best time to witness one of these fights is during Fiesta Brava, the time from December to April (also considered high season in town). The bullring is located up a hill from Caletilla Beach. Tickets can be purchased through a travel agency for about $200 to $400 (they often include transportation), or general admissions tickets can be purchased at the stadium (☎ **744/483-9561**), which are significantly cheaper (more like $50). The action begins at 5:30pm on Sundays.

Tennis

The **Club de Tenís Hyatt Acapulco** (☎ **744/484-1225**) is open from 7am to 11pm. You can rent a court for $80 per hour during the day or $130 per hour at night, and equipment can be rented for an extra cost. Lessons are also available.

Watersports

Arrangements for motorized sports like **jet-skiing** and **water-skiing** can be taken care of through direct contact with people on most beaches, especially Condesa and Hornitos beaches. Most people will charge between $350 and $700 for an hour rental. **Parasailing** costs about $200 to $300 for about 5 minutes of airtime—which is almost great enough to make the cost worth it.

Wencho's Aquatic Sports, a shady area with hammocks by the rocks to the right of the beach bars on Condesa beach can take care of most of your watersports needs. There, one can ride a **catamaran** (about $500 per hr.) or a **banana boat** ($50), rent a **kayak** (about $200 per hr.), or try **windsurfing** ($400 per hr.). Two-hour **snorkel** and **scuba** trips are also available through Wencho for $300 and $500, but a day trip through one of the companies mentioned earlier is much more worthwhile.

For a little more adventure, try the **Shotover Jet** (Centro Comercial Plaza Marbella Local 17; ☎ **744/484-1154;** www.shotoverjet.com.mx/acapulco.html). The Shotover Jet promises to create an exciting, thrilling spin-filled ride through the Puerto Marques Lagoon, but despite the peaceful, natural setting, don't expect a ride through the park: 360-degree turns and fancy boat maneuvers leave customers remembering the ride much more than the lagoon.

Shopping

Acapulco is not the best place in the country for shopping. Options consist mostly of festive Mexican clothing, phallic mugs, Acapulco T-shirts, and hammocks. Being such a center of tourism, souvenir shops are everywhere, along with stores where expensive bathing suits and beachwear can be purchased. But for anyone who is looking for cool handmade Mexican crafts by local artisans, look elsewhere.

For starters, there's **Sanborn's,** where one can find magazines in English, music, and clothing. There is one a couple of blocks from the zócalo (Costera Miguel Alemán 209; ☎ **744/484-2025**) but there are a couple others along the Costera in the Hotel Zone (Costera Miguel Alemán and Escuder; ☎ **744/482-6167**).

Then there is **Galería Diana** (Av. Costera Miguel Alemán 1926; ☎ **744/481-4021),** a beautiful, new shopping mall that transported me from slightly seedy Acapulco to a cleaner, newer place I didn't want to leave. Some stores that can be found here are: Zara, Puma, and Mango, along with a trusty Starbucks, a few lingerie stores, and a slot machine casino. There is also a nice **Cinépolis** movie theater inside.

Across the street is the outdoor **Diana Artisan Market** (a block from the Emporio Hotel near the Diana Statue on Av. Costera Miguel Alemán). Unfortunately, I wouldn't really describe it as an artisan's market, although there are tons of crafts to choose from. Inside this confined, stuffy labyrinth of shops you can find hammocks, T-shirts, shoes, silver, Mexican blouses, wooden sculptures, bikinis, and a whole bunch of junk. If you're looking for an artisan market, this is the closest thing you can get to one in Acapulco.

Plaza Bahía (Av. Costera Miguel Alemán 125; ☎ **744/485-6939**) is another nice shopping center, but again, it doesn't stock anything too interesting. The best thing about it is the **Aca Bol in Plaza Bahía** bowling alley, open daily from noon to 1:30am.

Road Trip: Taxco

Nestled in the rolling hills of Guerrero state, Taxco—about 3 1/2 hours from Acapulco—exerts a definite small-town charm through its steep, meandering cobblestone streets, gorgeous vistas of white stone houses with red-tiled rooftops, and surrounding green, mountainous landscape. Known as the "Silver City" for its history as a silver mining capital, Taxco (*tahs*-koh) is also the perfect example of a town where Mexico's rich history and culture has been vigilantly preserved. It's easy to forget Mexico's colonial history while you're splashing around in the water and sipping piña coladas at one of the country's overpopulated beach resort towns. While there's nothing wrong with using a vacation to simply relax, Taxco is a great reminder that sometimes a little history can make a place that much more beautiful.

And Taxco is indeed beautiful; the town sits at nearly 1,515m (4,969 ft) on a hill among hills, and almost any angle of the town is worth photographing. It's all so picturesque, in fact, that it almost seems fake. One of the coolest things about Taxco, though, is that's it is decidedly authentic—many of the people who live here hail from generation-old Taxco families.

Getting There & Getting Around

GETTING INTO TOWN

BY BUS You can take the bus from the **Ejido/Central Camionera station** (Ejido 47) in Acapulco, which takes about 4 hours. Buses also frequently depart from the **Central de Autobuses del Sur** station in Mexico City and take about 2½ to 3 hours.

Taxco has two bus stations. The **Estrella de Oro** buses arrive at its own station, **Terminal Estrella de Oro** located on the southern edge of town along Avenida de los Plateros in Barrio Pedro Martin. **Estrella Blanca** and **Flecha Roja** buses arrive at the **Autobuses Estrella Blanca** station located on the northeastern end of town on Avenida de los Plateros in Barrio Mora. Taxis from the bus stations to the central zócalo cost about $20.

BY CAR Getting to Taxco by car isn't so difficult. (It's driving around Taxco when you arrive that is challenging.) To drive from Acapulco to Taxco (296km/185 miles) you can take Highway 95D, which is the toll road through Iguala to Taxco, or you can take Highway 95, the old two-lane road that is slower and more windy but still in good condition.

To get to Taxco from Mexico City, take Paseo de la Reforma to Chapultepec Park where you will merge with Periférico. This will take you to Highway 95D on the south end of town. From the Periférico, take the Insurgentes exit and merge until you come to a sign for Cuernavaca/Tlalpan. You can choose either Cuernavaca Cuota (which has a toll) or Cuernavaca Libre (which is free). Continue south around Cuernavaca to the Amacuzac interchange and keep going straight ahead for Taxco. The drive should take about 3½ hours.

GETTING AROUND

BY CAR I highly encourage anyone who thinks having a car in Taxco is a good idea to re-think. Locals couldn't agree more. The majority of cars you'll see here are small white Volkswagens because they are the only cars that can really maneuver the tiny and extremely steep streets. Parking is a whole other problem, since it is extremely difficult to find parking spaces.

The taxis in town are cheap enough to get you anywhere you want to go and collective buses operate as well, so skip the driving and leave it to the locals and experts.

BY BUS There are a bunch of white VW vans, known as *burritos,* that circle throughout town, picking up and dropping off passengers along the route. These minibuses operate from 7am to 9pm and cost about $5.

Combi buses can take you to many of the local attractions for much cheaper than a taxi. They tend to do pick-ups at the Estrella Blanca bus station, where you can get more information on prices and schedules.

BY FOOT Walking is the absolute best way to explore Taxco. The town is extremely pedestrian-friendly, although some of the streets are so steep and narrow that it can be a little scary. Streets and sidewalks are one in the same here, so cars whiz by pedestrians sometimes with less than a foot of distance between each other. My advice: Be careful when rounding corners and do your best to get lost in the beautiful tiny streets. Also, be prepared: Walking around Taxco can be quite a workout.

Basics

NEIGHBORHOODS Taxco is too small to have different neighborhoods. The center of town is known as **Plaza Borda,** where you can find the central zócalo and the **Santa Prisca Church.** You can see this church from most vantage points in Taxco. Silver shops and restaurants surround Plaza Borda and extend up into the cobblestone streets that sprawl out from the beautiful, shady zócalo area.

TOURIST INFO & OFFICES The **State of Guerrero Dirección de Turismo** (☎/fax **762/622-6616** or 662-2274) has an office at the arches of the main highway on Av. de los Plateros 1 (on the north end of town). It is open Monday through Friday from 8am to 3:30pm and Saturday from 8am to noon. You can get there by taking a Zócalo-Arcos combi bus from Plaza Borda. Get off at the arch over the highway.

Sleeping

Taxco is a such a beautiful, small town that, although you can probably catch all the sights in a couple of days, it's worth staying longer so that you can get lost in the tiny streets and leave room to take some side trips. While there aren't any actual "hostels" in town, the sleeping options are cheap enough that you should be able to find a great deal.

CHEAP

→ **Hotel Los Arcos** ★★ Located just around the corner from the Plaza Borda, this is a gorgeous little hotel with a charming setting. When you walk in, you'll be able to tell instantly that Hotel Los Arcos was not always a hotel. In fact, the hotel is a converted 17th-century monastery, and this history comes across via its inner courtyard, with beautiful columns and furniture surrounding an old fountain. The rooms are very pretty, although minimalist in their decorations, matching the monastery personality. Inside all seems quiet, but it can get loud at night if you're located street-side. The charm of this hotel matches the colonial charm of the town and it's in a prime location for wandering and sightseeing. *Juan Ruiz de Alarcón no. 4, Taxco.* ☎ *762/622-1836. Fax 762/622-7982. www.hotellosarcos.net. $350 double, $400 triple, $450 quad, $500 junior suite (up to 6 people). No credit cards. In room: TV w/cable, fans.*

→ **Hotel Posada San Javier** ★★★ Tranquility and beauty are the underlying themes at this detail-oriented hotel. From the outside, the hotel seems very small but inside it seems much larger—due partly to luxurious bonuses like a courtyard and pool area that you'd expect from a much more expensive hotel. The atmosphere throughout is quiet and peaceful and, especially after a couple glasses of wine in

Taxco Sleeping & Eating

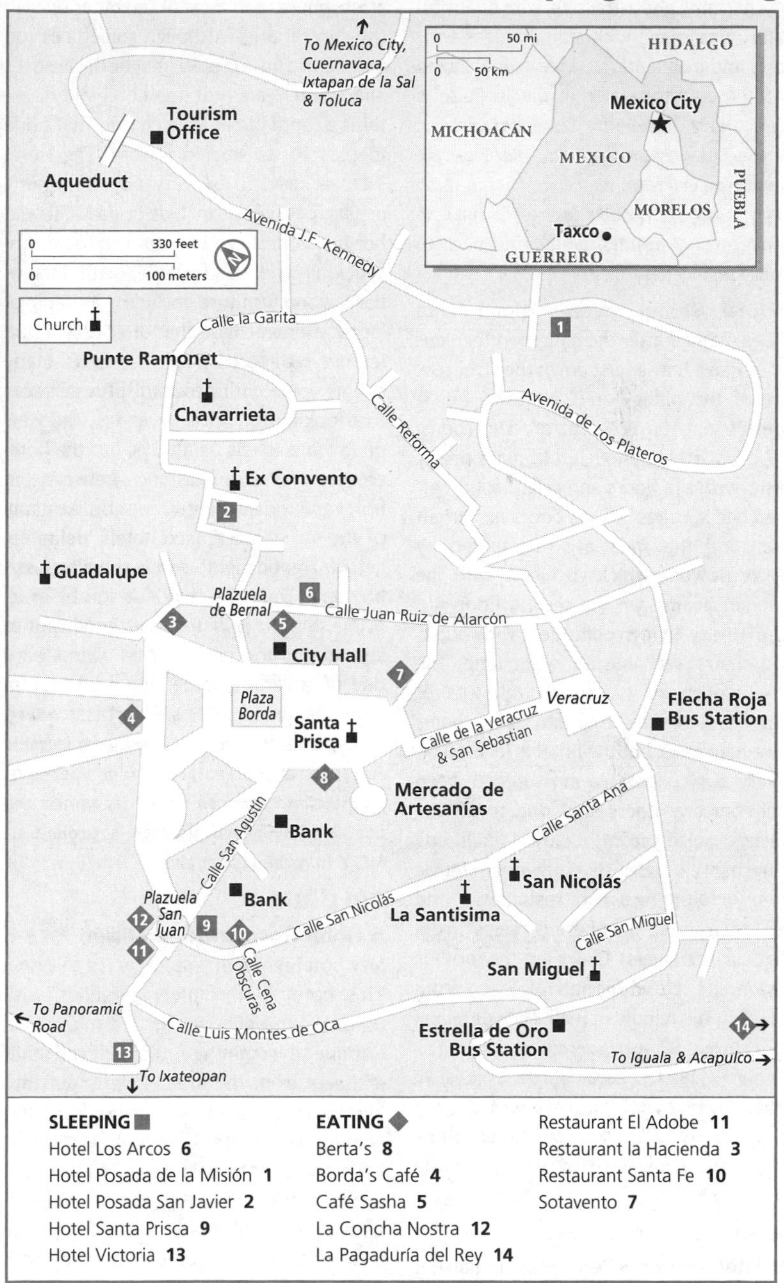

its restaurant, extremely romantic. Rooms are charming and attractive, with beautiful bathrooms, some with stained glass windows and iron lanterns. The view of Taxco and the countryside from the Jr. Suite is particularly excellent. *Estacadas no. 32. ☎ 762/662-3177 or -0231. Fax 762/622-2351. posadasanjavier@hotmail.com. $450–$500 single, $480–$540 double (up to 5 people). No credit cards. Amenities: Restaurant; pool. In room: Kitchenette.*

→ **Hotel Santa Prisca** ★ Hotel Santa Prisca, named after the church in the center of Plaza Borda (just down the street), is one of the older hotels in town, but it doesn't feel run down at all. The rooms are comfortable enough, although pretty basic, with tile floors and bright solid-colored bed spreads. All the doors are bright blue, and the walls are punctuated by pretty flowers, which go nicely with the wooden beams. On the second floor is a cute library/living room area, with books and chairs available for quiet time. The inner courtyard is pretty, with lots of plants and a central fountain. Some rooms have balconies, but the hotel is located on a very busy corner, so most people keep their balcony doors shut due to all the wacky noise from below (including chugging VW bugs, barking dogs, music from surrounding bars or restaurants, and the occasional, incoherent yelps from Mexican teenagers). Check out the roof for a stunning, close-up view of Taxco from smack in the middle of it all. *Cena Obscuras no. 1, Taxco. ☎ 762/622-0080 or -0980. Fax 762/622-2938. $400–$780 single, $550–$880 double, $620–$980 triple, $980 room #25 (up to 5 people). AE, DISC, MC, V. Amenities: Restaurant; laundry service; safety security box at reception.*

DOABLE

→ **Hotel Victoria** ★ Perched on a small hill down a private road just off the busy Plazuela San Juan, this hotel has a different atmosphere than most of the other ones in the central area. Although sometimes too quiet and a little creaky (maybe because it's almost 90 years old), the hotel still maintains a lot of old Mexico charm. That's due in part to its storied history: The Hotel Victoria used to be very popular among artists (past guests include Frida Kahlo and her husband Diego Rivera). The rooms are spacious and comfortable, with lots of dark, wood furniture, including a couple of large wooden chairs that offer only a thin leather seat to cushion your buns. Many rooms come with beautiful little terraces overlooking the floral verandas. The view of Taxco is lovely as always, but the hotel creates a sense of distance between the hotel and the bustling streets. Unlike many of the street-side Taxco hotels, definitely getting a good night's rest is actually possible here. Though it may not still be in its prime, the Hotel Victoria is a good spot to spread out and take a siesta after a hard day of silver shopping. For a little extra cash, the junior suites are worth it. *Carlos J. Nibbi 5 and 7, up narrow street from Plazuela San Juan. ☎ 762/622-0004. Fax 762/622-0010. www.victoriataxco.com. $500—$800 single and double, $600–$900 triple, $900–$950 quad. AE, MC, V. In room: TV w/cable.*

SPLURGE

→ **Hotel Posada de la Misión** ★★★ If any hotel is worth a splurge, it's this one. This hotel is absolutely gorgeous, with unique, museum-worthy displays on antique silver mining equipment and other artifacts from the area. Care is put into every detail; each wall in every room has something beautiful to look at. Rooms have some of the best views of Taxco and are beautiful from top to bottom, with extremely comfortable beds and large beautiful terraces. Some even come with their own fireplaces and bars. The service here is impeccable all around, but the downside is that it's a bit of a walk or a very cheap taxi ride to the Plaza Borda area. The Estrella de Oro bus even makes a special stop outside the hotel. *Cerro de la Misión 32. ☎ 800/00-TAXCO or 762/622-0063. Fax 762/622-2198. www.posadamision.com. $2,000 single, $2,200 double, $2,500 triple. Prices include breakfast and taxes. AE, DISC, MC, V. Amenities: Restaurant; bar; piano bar; coffee shop; convention halls; Estrella de Oro ticket counter; gallery; Jacuzzi; pool; spa; theater; travel agency. In room: TV w/cable, bar (not stocked), fireplace (in some rooms), hair dryer.*

Eating

Most of the restaurants in Taxco are scattered throughout the streets that branch away from the Santa Prisca Church. The prices are a little high because Taxco caters mostly to tourists but overall, the food is pretty good, and it's worth paying the price for any seat with such great views.

CHEAP

MTV Best → **Café Sasha** ★★★ INTERNATIONAL/VEGETARIAN Sasha's is the perfect place for any meal. The atmosphere is young, trendy, hippylike and comfortable. Perhaps that's why students from the local language university love it here. One room has low, comfy couches to sink into and relax while the other has a few small tables near to the large, airy windows that overlook the narrow street below. As for the food—it's really tasty and fresh, and offers dishes with a more Eastern touch of flavor than most Mexican restaurants. Try the curry Thai crepes stuffed with vegetables and peanut, coconut curry sauce for dinner. It's been named "the best vegetarian dish in Taxco." You can even order a chai tea, a rarity in Mexico. Sasha, a half-Mexican ex-pastry chef, is a native of Chicago but found her way to Taxco and never left. After tasting some of the house-brewed mescal at the end of a meal, I think it's hard for *anyone* to leave here. Come on a Sunday night to add some live music to that mescal. *Juan Ruiz de Alarcon #1, across from Hotel Los Arcos. ☎ 762/627-6464. www.cafesasha.com. Main courses $30–$79. No credit cards. Daily 8am–closing.*

→ **La Concha Nostra** ★★ MEXICAN/ITALIAN For anyone who likes Botticelli's painting *The Birth of Venus,* this relaxed bar/restaurant has you covered. The Boticelli painting is the muse behind the romantic restaurant decor. A couple of tables nestled in the tight window-balconies overlooking Plazuela San Juan enhance the romantic, arty vibe. The food itself, especially the signature lasagna, is also a work of art. La Concha Nostra is a great place all day long, whether you come for breakfast or to grab a couple of drinks and listen to the live music on Saturday nights. *Plazuela de San Juan, upstairs in the Casa Grande. ☎/fax 762/622-7944. laconchanostra@hotmail.com. Main courses $24–$70. No credit cards. Daily 7:45am–1am.*

→ **Restaurant Santa Fe** ★ MEXICAN Locals recommend Santa Fe as a good, cheap place to eat, and that's an apt description. Colorful checkered tablecloths and antique photos of Taxco adorn the walls of this small restaurant that's been around for 52 years. The simple décor offsets the simple but good and cheap, slightly *picante* Mexican fare like tacos and enchiladas. Just be warned that the street noise can make things a little loud, especially when a car goes by blasting reggaeton. *Hidalgo no. 2, Taxco. ☎ 762/622-1170. Main courses $18–$85. MC, V. Daily 8am–10pm.*

DOABLE

→ **Restaurant La Hacienda** ★ MEXICAN This restaurant is positioned right at a corner where every car that's turning has to practically do a three-point turn, which means you'll probably be inhaling exhaust and trying to talk over broken mufflers all through the meal. That is, unless you ask to be seated in the upstairs dining section, which makes such a difference. That way, you can sit on a terrace eating your meal with the towers of Santa Prisca Church right there with you, minus the exhaust. The food is decent (try the Mexican tortilla soup that combines tortillas, avocados, cheese, and tomatoes with your own preference of chile pepper) but it's really the (upstairs) atmosphere that makes this place worth a starlit meal. *In Hotel Agua Escondida, next to Plaza Borda. ☎ 744/469-1016. Main courses $32–$98. AE, DISC, MC, V. Daily 7am–11pm.*

→ **Sotavento** ★★ ITALIAN/INTERNATIONAL This is one of the nicer restaurants in town and within easy walking distance of good ol' Santa Prisca. The standouts on the sophisticated, unusual menu are the salads. The delicious Sotavento salad comes with lettuce, tomato, hard boiled egg, tuna, shrimp, garlic bread, and a goddess dressing (who doesn't like a little touch of goddess with their meal?). Rounding out the menu are entrees like a mediocre lemon chicken, a tasty prime rib, and fruity or chocolaty crepes for dessert. There are three seating options available: inside, where it is quiet and the walls are covered in large modern paintings; outside, where guests can people-watch to the sound of traffic that spills out from beneath the balcony; and finally, a dimly lit, peaceful and romantic courtyard inside the restaurant with a pretty fountain. The hip music piped throughout switches languages every song, adding a chic sensibility to the restaurant. *Benito Juárez no. 12, next to the City Hall. ☎ 762/627-1217. Main courses $43–$145. DISC, MC, V. Daily 1pm–midnight.*

SPLURGE

→ **La Pagaduría del Rey** ★★★ MEXICAN This is one of the most beautiful and elegant restaurants in Taxco—and the food is just as incredible as the stunning terrace view of town. It's hard to go wrong with any dish, especially with help from the friendly servers. The lime soup has a very subtle, interesting flavor and the *panuchos de cochinta* (tortillas with fried beans, onion, very tasty meat, and tomato sauce) are delicious. Your best bet is to come here for a few hours for lunch, and enjoy the view while you slowly munch on as many different dishes as possible, all in the comfort of the shade. Getting here requires a car or taxi (there is plenty of parking) but it's worth the trip. *H. Colegio Militar no. 8, Barrio de Bermeja, Taxco. ☎ 762/627-3381 or -3449. Main courses $45–$265. AE, DISC, MC, V. Daily 8am–11pm.*

CAFES & TEAROOMS

→ **Borda's Café** ★ CAFE Directly across from the Santa Prisca church, and up some stairs, this little cafe greets diners with photos of James Dean, Marilyn Monroe, and Elvis. I'm still not sure why the first two stars make a cameo on the cafe's walls, but I take it the owner is a big Elvis fan, judging by his Elvis hairstyle and chest hair. Grab one of the seven tiny circular tables (tiny meaning about the size of a large stool), and order a coffee or cappuccino; you can also order food like burgers and hotcakes depending on the time of day. *Plaza Borda #6A, Taxco. ☎ 762/622-3018. Coffee and snacks $16–55. No credit cards. Daily 9am–11pm.*

→ **Restaurant El Adobe** ★★ CAFE You can practically get lost in one of the frothy cappuccinos served at this quaint café—they're that good. Mexican jazz music plays to help you slowly wake up and ease your way into the day. The calming atmosphere also helps: The brick walls and dim lighting—the whole place is lit only by natural light that spills from two large windows—create an overall cozy feeling.

Cheers to Berta

Don't leave Taxco without trying a **Berta,** "the drink of Taxco." A Berta is prepared with tequila, lemon, honey, and soda water and is served in a long glass with frappe ice, making it as cool and refreshing as the Taxco mountain air. It's sweet enough to enjoy, yet infused with enough tequila to melt away any negative thoughts. For the real deal, go to (surprise, surprise) **Berta's** (no phone; in the Plaza Borda next to the Santa Prisca Church), opened in the 1930s by Señora Berta, who became famous for this drink. Most believe a trip to Taxco is not complete without sipping one of Berta's finest Bertas from a balcony overlooking the plaza. There is no better Berta in town.

Breakfast is tops here (the usual but delicious hotcakes, Mexican-style eggs, and fruit), though they also serve lunch and dinner and are known for their meats and cheeses, as well as their extensive wine list. *Plazuela de San Juan #13.* ☎ *762/622-1416.* ☎*/fax 762/622-1683. Breakfast $15–$36. MC, V. Daily 8am–11:30pm.*

Partying

Nightlife is not Taxco's forte, but there are definitely some good places to go if you find yourself in the mood to party. Though Taxco isn't the place to go if you're looking to party all night, it can certainly keep you from going to bed after dinner.

In addition to the bars and clubs reviewed below, a number of restaurants morph into fun places to get a drink at night. **La Concha Nostra,** Plazuela de San Juan, upstairs in the Casa Grande (☎ **762/622-7944**), is one example of a restaurant/bar that has a young following after dinner time is over. **Café Sasha,** Juan Ruiz de Alarcon #1, across from Hotel Los Arcos (☎ **762/627-6464**), is another, especially after a little of the delicious, cinnamon-flavored mescal served up here starts to enter people's bloodstreams and the crowd becomes friendlier and friendlier.

If you're in a dancing mood, **Casablanca** (see below) can get you up and moving, but so can a couple of other places. For pop, top 40, and the occasional reggaeton song, go to **Ibiza,** Av. de los Plateros #34 Altos (☎ **762/622-2689**), or **Onyx** (located in the same building as La Concha Nostra). **Heaven Windows** is also a popular nightclub, but many locals have never heard of it. It's located high in a mountain in the **Hotel Monte Taxco,** Av. Lomas de Taxco s/n, Fracc. Lomas de Taxco (☎ **762/622-1300**), so you'll need a taxi to get there. At Windows, they play anything from merengue to '70s and '80s hits. On Saturdays, the hotel even has a fireworks display.

CLUBS

→ **Casablanca** ★★★ There are a few dancing options in town, but this is one of the best. It boasts a spacious main bar area dotted with modish white couches and black tables, a good-sized dance floor, and a balcony area where you can see the stars and sit on long cushioned benches between songs. In addition to great drinks, you can order foods to munch on all night. The crowd is a mix of locals and tourists, with two-for-one Thursdays being the most popular night to party in town. Sometimes they have live music, but most people come for the swanky, no-cover, chill atmosphere that gets a little sassier as the night wears on. (A DJ plays techno and lounge early on, and then it transitions to reggaeton, eventually finishing the evening with more Mexican rhythms.) It's open from 7pm to

3am because the neighbors don't like to hear the loud music all night. That's a small town for ya. *Plazuela de San Juan #15 Altos, Taxco.* ☎ *762/622-1666. No cover.*

BARS & LOUNGES

→ **Acerto Bar/Lounge** ★ This place is easy to find if you're standing in Plaza Borda—just look away from the Santa Prisca church and then look up. I stopped by for an early dinner but was encouraged by the waiter to take a couple of tequila shots and ended up staying later than I'd planned. That's the power of "house blood" as the waiter called it—a tasty tequila chaser with tomato, orange, carrot, and chile pepper juice. The appealing list of drinks and late-night music helps a bit to offset the restauranty vibe, touristy crowd, and early closing hours. Since it is open daily only from noon to 11:30pm, just be prepared to stumble out before it has a chance to get really interesting. *Plaza Borda no. 12.* ☎ *762/622-0064. No cover.*

→ **La Estación** ★★ If you don't want to dance, but you want to play, come to this cool sports bar. It offers billiards and darts every day, as well as a pool table—hard to come by in town. It also functions as an Internet bar, so you can drink all you want while e-mailing or chatting with friends online. Basically, this is a laid-back place that never really gets crazy, except when there is a big soccer game screened on one of the big screen TVs. In case sports doesn't do it for you, there's live music on Saturdays, too. *Real de Cuauhtemoc #8.* ☎ *762/627-2113. No cover.*

Sightseeing

The most beautiful and interesting sightseeing in Taxco can be seen by merely walking the steep cobblestone streets and admiring the colonial style buildings. That said, there are still a number of small museums worth visiting and festivals worth attending; read on for info on the best.

FESTIVALS/EVENTS

Festivals of Santa Prisca and San Sabastian: The town celebrates Santa Prisca and San Sebastian with festivities and fireworks. Jan 18 and 20.

Holy Week: Taxco hosts one of the most moving celebrations of this week in all of Mexico, with daily processions—the biggest being on Thursday—of villagers carrying statues of saints, followed by self-flagellating penitents who carry large wooden crosses while they walk, chained at the ankles, carrying bundles of thorny branches. You'll also be able to catch

Meet (& Eat) the Beetles

Poor little jumil bugs—they've been eaten in Mexico since Aztec times, and, since **Jumil Day** became a traditional local holiday back in the 1940s, they're eaten in vast numbers in Taxco, on the first Monday of November after the Day of the Dead. Each year on this holiday, locals wind their way up to the mountain park of Huisteco where they camp out together and embark on a quest to collect the jumil bugs, a local beetle that migrates to the hill to reproduce. I hear the bugs are actually quite good, especially mashed up in salsa, but couldn't get over the initial exoskeleton *crunch* and the fact that I'd be eating a creepy, crawly bug. Go for it if you're brave, though: The jumil is believed to give you energy and life for another year. It's also said that, to be considered a true Taxcoan, you must eat jumil and that once you have, the magic of Taxco will have you in its grasp and you will always come back.

Taxco Partying, Sightseeing & Playing Outside

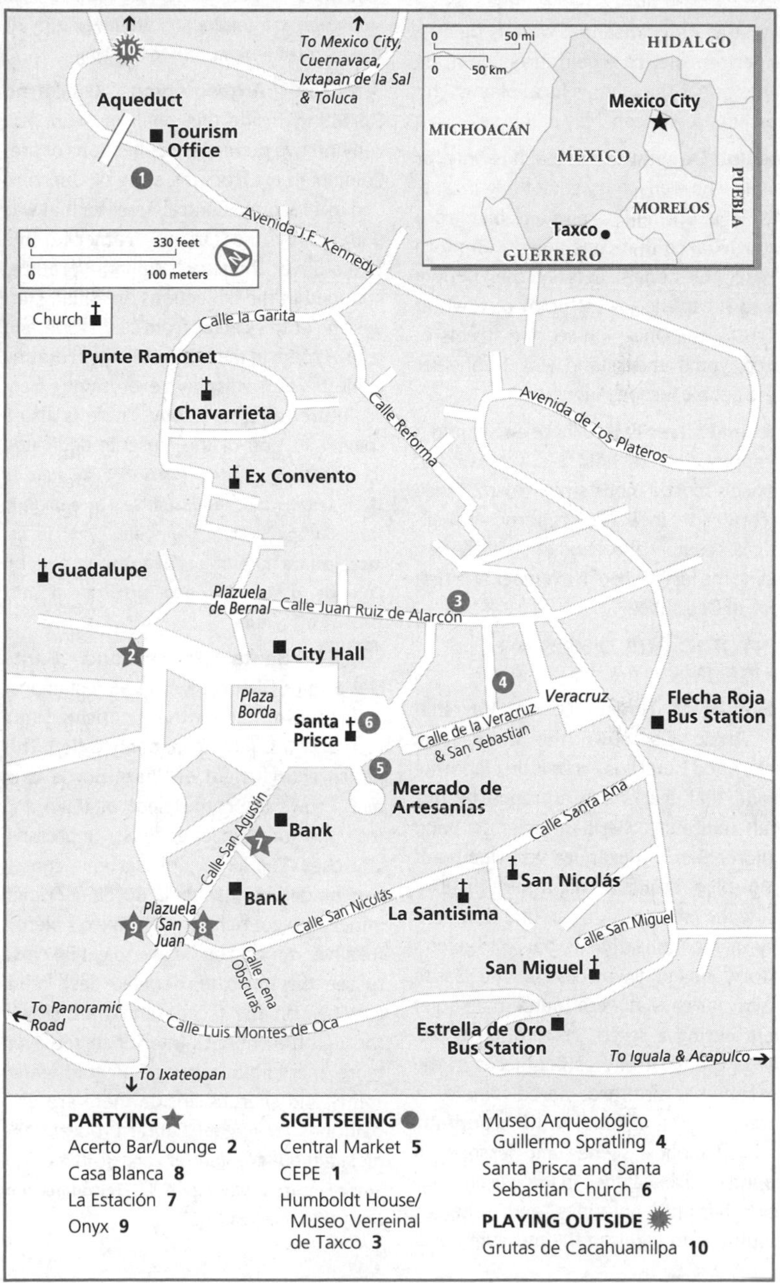

reenactments of Christ's procession to the cross. Holy week begins the week before Easter.

Jornadas Alarconianas: Various theatrical performances are held throughout the city to honor the famous local playwright, Juan Ruiz de Alarcon. May and June.

Red Bull Downhill: This event is only for people who want to try something insane. This is a downhill mountain bike race through Taxco that runs down 198m (653 ft.) of cobblestone streets and then 1,800m (5,940 ft.) to the lowest point of town at Cerro Atachi. Once you see the streets of Taxco, you'll understand why I consider these people insane. August.

National Silver Fair: Where else would it be appropriate to hold a silver fair but Mexico's most famous silver town? Taxco celebrates its local ore properly, with silver craft competitions and other activities. During the last week of November and first week of December.

HISTORIC BUILDINGS & MUSEUMS

→ **Humboldt House/Museo Virreinal de Taxco** Just down the street from Sasha's and Hotel Los Arcos is an elaborate facade that marks the entrance to this small museum. German scientist and explorer Baron Alexander von Humboldt (1769–1859) spent the night here in 1803. Inside the museum, you can find 18th-century memorabilia that is part of Taxco's history, including pieces of the Santa Prisca church that were found in a secret room during a recent restoration there. One of the most interesting pieces in the museum is a rare three-tiered *tumelo,* or wooden burial mound, with beautifully depicted biblical scenes and lessons all around it. Also included in the museum are some baroque paintings and religious sculptures. In addition the museum has a beautiful courtyard area and garden where theatrical events take place. *Calle Juan Ruiz de Alarcón 12.* ☎ *762/622-5501. Admission $20 adults, $15 students with ID. Tues–Sat 10am–6pm; Sun 10am–4pm.*

→ **Museo Arqueológico Guillermo Spratling** Inside this small museum you will find two permanent collections of pre-Columbian art from the state of Guerrero and from around Central America that was donated by the famous "Father of the Taxco Silver Industry," William Spratling. Included in the collections are small statues and pottery made from clay, stone, and jade. A room in the lower floor has rotating exhibits that display everything from sculpture to photography. There is also a special section of the museum dedicated to Spratling. *Calle Porfirio A. Delgado 1.* ☎ *762/622-1660. Admission $24, free on Sun. Tues–Sat 9am–5pm; Sun 9am–3pm. To get here, behind the Santa Prisca Church, go down Calle de la Veracruz, and turn left on Calle Porfirio a Delgado.*

FREE → **Santa Prisca and Santa Sebastián Church** ★★ It's almost impossible to visit Taxco without noticing Santa Prisca, as it is more commonly called. This parish church right on Plaza Borda is in many ways the centerpiece of town and it's one of Mexico's most impressive churches. The large pink Baroque church was funded by José de la Borda, a French miner who got rich through Taxco's plentiful silver mines. You'll have to get up close to see the intricate, detailed deep-relief carvings on the facade and walk slowly through the church's interior to see even more incredible carvings of gold-leafed saints and cherubs. Inside there are also paintings by Miguel Cabrera, one of the most famous colonial-era artists in Mexico. *Plaza Borda.* ☎ *762/622-0184. Free admission. Daily 6:30pm–8pm.*

Playing Outside

Taxco is near one of the most amazing natural wonders in the Americas: MTV Best **Las Grutas de Cacahuamilpa** ★★ (Parque Nacional "Grutas de Cacahuamilpa"; ☎ **734/346-1716;** admission $50 adults (includes guided tour); daily 10am–5pm), known as the Cacahuamilpa caves, is a site you simply must visit. The caves, which are part of a national park, are located only about a 20-minute drive through the countryside outside of Taxco. Or you can hop on a combi from the Estrella Blanca bus station (p. 541), which leaves about every hour.

Once at Las Grutas, plan on taking a 2- to 3-hour guided trek through the dark caves. During this walk through the caves, a guide will point out many different rock formations that have striking resemblances to famous landmarks and people. My favorite formation shows the silhouettes of two people about to kiss, and when the guide moves the flashlight around them, it seems as if the two people go from holding hands to making out. Warning: I hope you don't mind bats. For guided tours of the caves and nearby attractions, try **Viajes Sibely** (Miguel Hidalgo 24, ☎ **762/622-8080**).

Shopping

People from all over the world come to Taxco with one thing on their minds: **silver.** Let's just say that none of them leave empty-handed. Whether you're looking for something special or just shooting to stock up on cheap silver, you can spend a good deal of time in Taxco simply perusing the hundreds of silver shops that sprawl through the big and small streets surrounding the Plaza Borda and all around town. Some of the most popular shops are the ones right around the zócalo area, but the prices here will be steeper than the ones found at smaller shops out of the central area of town.

While a couple stores stand out, many of the stores have the same exact pieces. That said, don't buy the first thing you fall in love with. Keep looking around and see if you find it for cheaper, just ask for the cards of the stores where you found something you liked.

No matter where you buy your silver, prices in Taxco's shops are among the cheapest you can find, and the quality and variety of silver is top-notch. As for which stores to go to, it's hard to say. One of my favorite stores is **Dulce Plateros** ★★ (Cuauhtémoc no. 3 ☎ **762/622-2330**), where there is an incredible selection of both modern pieces and antique ones. I fell in love with an antique William Spratling bracelet here that is adorned with amethysts and turquoise that cost around $2,300 (but if you're a good haggler, you can probably get any price down).

Another store I stumbled into that had a great selection of shiny earrings and beautiful small-scale pieces was **Plateria San Rafaels** ★ (Benito Juárez no.89 ☎ **762/622-0371** or 622-1516). Small silver earrings cost anywhere from $100 to $800, but most are on the cheaper side compared to the overly crowded stores around the Santa Prisca Church.

For a unique piece of silver craftsmanship that goes beyond jewelry, you have to check out the pieces done by **Wolmar Costillas** ★★ (Juan Ruíz de Alarcón #7 ☎ **762/624-3030** or 624-3050), son of one of the most famous silversmiths in the area. His handmade pieces include incredible anthropomorphic bowls and vases that sometimes take on the shape of different birds, while other times they might have an alligator crawling up the side. Though the goods are a little pricey they are truly one of a kind and well worth it.

You can get the cheapest possible silver at the **silver market** that takes place by the

Estrella Blanca bus station on Saturdays from 9am to 4pm. Here, the artists themselves sell their work, rather than the stores, so it is dirt cheap and full of options. Be prepared for large, overzealous crowds.

One place worth visiting for a taste of local life is the **Mercado Central.** Providing a good break from the silver shopping, this market is located to the right of the Santa Prisca church, behind and below Berta's. The multi-leveled market weaves its way through tiny stairwells and streets. Go down the stairs from the street and just wander all the way in. Anything from old beat-up electronics to herbs and chile peppers is sold here. You'll be bumping into people, stepping on things, and probably coming to a complete standstill in the traffic. How people actually shop here amazes me. It's crowded and people can get a little pushy, but it's nice to feel like just another local trying to get some errands done.

Around the back, behind the Santa Prisca church and in front of the Archaeology Museum are a bunch of little stands where people sell hand-painted clay pottery and mugs as well as cheap non-silver jewelry and hand-carved wooden bowls.

For a cool little mask shop and "bazaar," there is a place called **Casa La Jaula** a short walk from Santa Prisca Church on Calle de la Veracruz #4. The store and a few stores in the same area have crafts made by local artisans in all different materials and for all different purposes. I especially liked the traditional masks.

Tip: Most silver shops will offer you a nice little discount if you can pay in cash rather than with a credit card. So either come armed with hard cash or be prepared to make an ATM run (ATMs are everywhere) once you've settled on buying a piece. Also, make sure it has a .925 stamped on it somewhere. This indicates that it is the highest quality sterling silver (and not a knock-off) and ensures that unless you try and destroy the silver, it shouldn't fall apart on you.

Ixtapa & Zihuatanejo

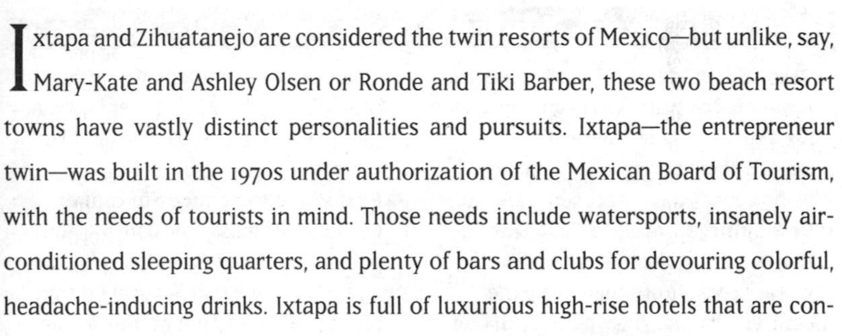

Ixtapa and Zihuatanejo are considered the twin resorts of Mexico—but unlike, say, Mary-Kate and Ashley Olsen or Ronde and Tiki Barber, these two beach resort towns have vastly distinct personalities and pursuits. Ixtapa—the entrepreneur twin—was built in the 1970s under authorization of the Mexican Board of Tourism, with the needs of tourists in mind. Those needs include watersports, insanely air-conditioned sleeping quarters, and plenty of bars and clubs for devouring colorful, headache-inducing drinks. Ixtapa is full of luxurious high-rise hotels that are constantly multiplying in number, while Zihuatanejo—the lazy twin—remains true to its fishing village roots, with a busy, scenic and often fishy-smelling port that is surrounded by many cheap hotels and bungalows both in the center of town and on the beach. As is the case with most twins, Ixtapa and Zihuatanejo get along quite well, but every visitor leaves with their own idea of which one was hotter.

The name Zihuatanejo ("Zihua" to the locals) comes from the Nahuatl word "Cihuatlan," which means "the place of women"—so perhaps fisherman originally came to this fishing port seeking to catch more than just mahimahi. The fishing tradition lives on, especially during competitions and festivals throughout the year that reel in some of the biggest names in the sports fishing industry. This is also a popular place for middle-aged expats, who live by the Zihuatanejo motto "another day in Paradise." (Indeed, this was Andy Dufresne's beach town of choice in *The Shawshank Redemption;* never mind that they filmed that scene in the Virgin Islands.) Zihua feels like a place for drinking a chilled coconut without a care in the world. The Centro town area also has plenty of wonderfully cheap restaurants and hotels, as well as a growing variety of bars, lounges, and clubs.

Nearby, Ixtapa is teeming with outdoor activities and has its own commercial center with banks, shops, Internet cafes, restaurants, and bars. Ixtapa is situated on a beautiful stretch of white-sand beach with an awesome view of rock formations that seem to float in the horizon. However, the area's natural beauty is somewhat obscured by the row of large looming hotels on Playa Palmar; there's no getting around the fact that the town is a carefully crafted and controlled artificial environment that Mexican tourism officials happily pimp out to travelers. But hey, it looks good. For a taste of local culture, Ixtapa is close enough to Zihuatanejo (20 min. on Hwy. 200) that it's easy to hop back and forth between the two very different spots.

Whatever brings you here—the fish, the people, the nightlife—you have a good chance of finding your sliver of paradise on at least one end of the highway.

Best of Ixtapa & Zihuatanejo

- **Best Affordable Hotel: Apartamentos Amueblados Valle** is a cheap way to feel like you're crashing at a friend's apartment, without having to worry about being a good guest. See p. 560.
- **Best Splurge Hotel: La Casa Que Canta** is altogether unforgettable. If you are capable of coughing up the cash, you'll be singing your way to one of the best hotel-stays in all of Mexico (and possibly, your life). See p. 564.
- **Best Restaurant to Catch a Sunset: Kau-Kan** is an imaginative restaurant built into the curvy hillside overlooking Zihuatanejo Bay that cleverly makes the sunset a natural backdrop to cause swooning from every table. See p. 567.
- **Best Piña Colada: Shiva Bar** got its start because it invented the piña colada, so why shouldn't it continue to capitalize on that? No matter how many they make here, the drink tastes like perfection. See p. 570.
- **Best Place to Seduce Someone:** Consider the music, the dancing, the palm trees, the stars, and the alcohol, and you can see that **Varuna Lounge** is one make-out session waiting to happen. See p. 572.
- **Best Place to Listen to Quality Live Music: Chez Ben** is one of the most sophisticated bar/lounge/restaurants in town, and its guest musicians take it to the next level. Everything produced by this upstairs haven—the food, the atmosphere, the music—contributes to a gratifying experience. See p. 573.

Getting There & Getting Around

Getting into Town

BY PLANE Both **AeroMexico** (☎ **755/554-2018;** www.aeromexico.com) and **Mexicana** (☎ **755/554-2208;** www.mexicana.com) offer daily flights to Ixtapa/Zihuatanejo from Mexico City and Guadalajara, making it fairly easy to find a flight. Flights are available year-round from U.S. gateways, but your best bet is to transfer in Mexico City. In addition to **AeroMexico** and **Mexicana,** other airlines making flights to Ixtapa/Zihuatanejo are: **Continental** (☎ **800/231-0856;** www.continental.com), **American** (☎ **800/433-7300;** www.aa.com), Mexicana's **Click Mexicana** (☎ **800/11-CLICK;** www.click

mx.com), **Delta** (☎ **800/221-1212;** www.delta.com), **Interjet** (☎ **551/102-5555;** www.interjet.com.mx), and Ryanair-affiliated **Viva Aerobús** (www.vivaaerobus.com). Most flights are indirect, but airlines such as **Alaska Airlines** (☎ **800/252-7552**), **America West** (☎ **800/235-9292**), **Continental** (☎ **800/523-3273**), and **Frontier** (☎ **800/432-1359**), offer direct service from select U.S. cities about once a week.

The budget carrier **Interjet** flies to Ixtapa, and **Click** flies to Zihuatanejo from other destinations in Mexico.

Once you arrive at the **Ixtapa-Zihuatanejo Airport** (☎ **755/554-2070**), you will be about 11km (7 miles) (15 min.) away from Central Zihuatanejo. A taxi ride from the airport will cost around $80 to $140 to Zihuatanejo and $120 to $180 to Ixtapa—taxis can be found just outside the arrival terminal at the Official Airport Transportation counter. Beware of people that try to help you find taxis, carry your luggage, or offer free transportation; instead go directly to the Official Airport Transportation counter for assistance.

A cheaper alternative to taxis are *colectivos,* or minivans that transport groups of people to their respective hotels, available for about $30 to $60 and found outside the baggage claim. The colectivos often make several stops and can take longer than private taxis, but they are safe and may cut transportation costs in half.

BY BUS There are two bus terminals in Zihuatanejo: The **Central de Autobuses** (across from the Pemex station and hospital on Paseo Zihuatanejo at Paseo la Boquita; ☎ **755/554-3477**) and the **Estrella de Oro** station a block away (☎ **755/554-2175**). Transportation at the Central de Autobuses is provided by several companies and offers service to/from Mexico City, Puerto Escondido, and Acapulco, among other places.

First-class **Estrella de Oro buses** (www.autobus.com.mx) have daily service to Acapulco and Mexico City. The buses range in class and price, with tickets to Acapulco costing around $120 for first-class service and tickets to Mexico City costing around $425. Surprisingly, the buses are extremely punctual, clean, and comfortable. The nicest are the Diamante buses, which offer complimentary snacks, separate male/female bathrooms, and seats that completely recline. Tickets can be purchased in advance through the website.

BY CAR You can certainly drive into town, but there is no real reason to have a car unless you plan on making day trips to nearby beaches or towns. There are plenty of taxis and buses to get you between Ixtapa and Zihuatanejo and the two places are very pedestrian-friendly. If you choose to rent a car while you're here, look for **Hertz** at the airport (☎ **800/654-3131** in the U.S., or 755/554-2952) and **Budget** (☎ **800/527-0700** in the U.S., or 755/553-0397). Rates range from $300 to $700 a day, depending on the season and type of car. Also, be prepared to pay an extra $150 for theft insurance at the rental car agencies.

Getting Around

BY BUS Taking a taxi is the most efficient and reliable way to get around this area, but you'll certainly save a bit by taking buses instead. Buses here are called *camionetas* and are large white vans rather than actual buses. These shuttle between Ixtapa and Zihuatanejo, making numerous stops along the Bulevar Ixtapa in Ixtapa, including a stop right by the Señor Frog's (p. 570). You can board and disembark the bus at any point along its route, and you just hail one like a cab.

The main destination of each bus is listed on its front windshield, but, when in doubt, don't hesitate to ask the driver if you're on the right bus. The cost is around $5 to $8, depending on how far you're going. In Zihuatanejo, the main bus stop is near the corner of Morelos/Paseo Zihuatanejo and Juárez (about 3 blocks north of the artisan market, near Elektra).

BY TAXI Taxis are the easiest way to get around and between Ixtapa and Zihuatanejo. There are three main taxi companies operating in the area: **APAAZ** (☎ **755/554-3680**), **UTAAZ** (☎ **755/554-4583**), and **UTZI** (☎ **755/554-4763**). All three share standardized flat rates determined by distance. It's wise to confirm those rates before leaving anywhere in the taxi. Within Zihuatanejo, the flat rate is $18. A trip to Playa La Ropa will cost about $30. Going to the neighborhoods on the outskirts of the town of Zihuatanejo will cost closer to $50. The oft-traveled trip between Ixtapa and Zihuatanejo (along Hwy. 200) could cost between $50 and $100 and takes 15 to 20 minutes. Taxis from Ixtapa or Zihuatanejo to Troncones, Barra de Potosí, or Playa Larga could cost anywhere between $200 and $350. Note that there is a 50% fee added to rides after 10pm.

Paying a taxi driver by the hour is common, especially for a day trip to somewhere like Troncones, which doesn't have many cabs available. Hiring a cab driver could also come in handy for sightseeing excursions; just be prepared to negotiate the hourly rate.

You can hail a taxi from any street corner in Zihuatanejo. In Ixtapa, try The Commercial Center (or if you're staying in a hotel here, arrange a cab with the front desk).

BY BICYCLE You can get around by bicycle, but be careful if you choose to venture off-course or onto the highway. Cars zip by at unreasonable speeds on major highways and drivers aren't accustomed to sharing the roads with bikers. And be aware of potholes and suspicious characters off the main roads. Though this area isn't particularly dangerous, there are plenty of poor neighborhoods that lack pay phones and police officers.

For rentals, try **Tropical Bikes** where you can rent mountain bikes for about $200 for the day (or $40 an hr.). It's near the Bancomer, La Puerta Plaza 12, Loc. 6 in Ixtapa (☎ **755/554-6894**).

A 4.3km ($2^3/_4$ miles) *ciclopista* (bike path) connects Ixtapa and Zihuatanejo, but beware that much of that ride is in the scorching heat along the highway.

BY FOOT For the most part, your feet are all you'll need to get around Zihuatanejo, as the downtown area is a small grid of streets. If you want to get to Ixtapa, however, you'll need to take a taxi or a *camioneta.* Once in Ixtapa, you can get around by foot; the best most scenic walking routes are along the beach between hotels. Otherwise, you'll need to head into downtown Zihuatanejo for a more interesting stroll.

Basics

Orientation: Ixtapa & Zihuatanejo Neighborhoods

The two main neighborhoods in Ixtapa and Zihuatanejo are—brace yourself—Ixtapa and Zihuatanejo. Central Ixtapa extends from the Marina de Ixtapa to the Centro Comercial while Zihuatanejo's neighborhoods tend to vary slightly from beach to beach.

Ixtapa is mainly a stretch of beach lined with hotels. There are no neighborhood boundaries, and in fact, there is nothing neighborhood-like about the area. Ixtapa is all about big resort hotels and tourism. The main strip of hotels is along **Playa Palmar/Palmar Beach,** with a commercial center at one end (with many bars, restaurants, and shops) and more expensive restaurants at the other end of the strip.

Zihuatanejo, on the other hand, has a clearly defined downtown area called **Zihuatanejo Centro.** Although it is considered a small fishing village, the downtown area has lots of restaurants, stores, and bargain silver vendors. This area branches off of **Playa Municipal/ Municipal Beach** and is fairly contained. If you follow the coastline from **Playa Municipal** to **Playa Madera** and then you keep going, you'll get to the **Playa La Ropa** section of town, which has some of Mexico's most beautiful resorts and some of the finer restaurants in the area. Most of the beaches in the downtown area are disconnected, but it is possible to walk from one end of the bay to the other, passing every beach along the way. The area around Playa La Ropa isn't as pedestrian-friendly as the **Centro** and, for the most part, the hotels here are much more expensive than Centro hotels and hotels and bungalows along Playa Madera.

Tourist Info & Offices

If you just want brochures, maps, books, and so on, go to the **State Tourism Office** (Paseo de las Golondrinas 1-A, Bulevar Ixtapa s/n, Ixtapa; ☎ **755/553-1967**) located in the La Puerta shopping center (open Mon–Fri 8am–8:30pm and Sun 8am–2pm). For more personalized information or advice, the administrative office of the **Zihuatanejo Tourism Office** is located off the main square in central Zihuatanejo by the basketball court at Alvarez (no phone). The administrative office is in City Hall (☎ **755/554-2355**). Go through the gates, up the stairs to the second floor, make a left and walk down to the end of the long hallway, and it's on the right side. The staff is friendly, though you may have to wait for assistance.

American Express Tours: From horseback riding to local fishing to day trips to Acapulco, American Express Tours has created numerous well-organized, memorable trips that take care of you from the first minute to the last. Call ☎ **755/544-6242** for info.

Adventours: Offers an assortment of ecological tourism activities including kayak, bike, and nature walk tours. For something different, there's even crocodile-watching. Call ☎ **755/553-1069** for info.

Catcha L'Ola: Surf lessons, surf paraphernalia, surf rentals, surf trips. Surf's up. (Centro Comercial Local 12, Ixtapa. ☎ **755/ 553-1384.**)

Recommended Websites

- **www.ixtapa-zihuatanejo.com**: This is a comprehensive website with all the information you need, from money-exchange information to recommended ways to relax, to city maps.
- **www.weheartzihua.com**: An up-to-date and easy to navigate site with reviews of fancy restaurants and places to hear live music. Take a second to read the "don't miss" sections of each review, which give good inside tips.
- **www.zihuatanejo.net**: If you ever search Ixtapa or Zihuatanejo on the Internet, you are guaranteed to come up with several pages produced by ZihuaRob—he's that good a source of info on the area.
- **www.zihua.net**: Find tons of recommendations for hotels, restaurants, and community events as well as information on getting to nearby destinations, like Barra de Potosí and Troncones.

Ixtapa & Zihuatanejo Nuts & Bolts

Banks You can find a **Bancomer,** Plaza Don Juan corner of Andador Punta San Esteban (☎ **755/553-0535**), in the La Puerta Centro shopping center, or **Banamex** in Zihuatanejo (Cuauhtémoc 4). There are many banks located in Zihuatanejo Centro, one across the street from Tomales Y Atole Any's (p. 566). Banks are open Monday to Friday from 9am to either 3 or 5pm and on Saturdays from 10am to 1pm.

Embassies & Consulates **U.S. Citizens** who need to replace a passport, get funds, or need assistance in the case of a medical or natural disaster or emergency, among other things, should come here. The office is located in Hotel Fontan in Ixtapa (Bulevar Paseo de Ixtapa; ☎ **755/553-2100,** emergencies ☎ **755/557-1106**) on the Ground floor at the entrance of the circular driveway. Elizabeth Williams is the Consular Agent.

Emergencies Call ☎ **065** from any telephone. You can also call the **municipal tourism office** (☎ **755/554-2355,** ext. TURISMO) or the **municipal police** (☎ **755/554-2040**).

Internet/Wireless Hot Spots There are a few places to access the Internet in the shopping center in **Ixtapa.** One is just to the left of Señor Frog's (Paseo de Ixtapa s/n Block 11 Lot 5, inside the La Puerta shopping center). The other is at **Dolfy's Internet Café** (on the second floor, inside the Lost Patios Shopping Center along Bulevar Ixtapa in Suite 108; ☎ **755/553-1177**). In Zihuatanejo, you'll find Internet cafes on almost every street. One I liked was across the street from **Apartamentos Amueblados de Valle** (between Ejido and Nicolas Bravo). You can also try **Zihuatanejo Bar Net** (Agustín Ramírez 9, on the first floor of Hotel Zihuatanejo Centro; ☎ **755/553-1177**). The Internet costs about $400 to $500 an hour in Ixtapa, and about $150 to $200 an hour in Zihuatanejo.

Laundry **Lavanderia del Centro** is directly across the street from **Apartamentos Amueblados de Valle** on Calle Vincente Guerrero 17, Zihuatanejo Centro (☎ **755/554-9791**). It is open Monday through Saturday 8am to 8pm and Sunday 10am to 4pm. You'll be charged according to the weight of your laundry, but a full-service job, (washing, drying, and folding, available after 24 hr.), costs around $35 for about 6kg (13 lb.) of clothing. Self-service washing costs around $5 to wash and dry about 1kg (up to 2 lb.) of laundry. An 8kg load (just under 18 lb.) will cost less than $40 to wash and dry yourself.

Luggage Storage You can store your luggage in **Angela's Hostel** (p. 559) for free if you're a guest there (the front desk is open 24 hr.) or for $20 per day, per piece of luggage.

Pharmacies There are pharmacies every couple of blocks in Zihuatanejo Centro including the **Farmacias Coyuca** (☎ **755/554-5390**) chain, with one located at Vincente Guerrero on the corner of Nicolás Bravo. They are open 24 hours, and they deliver. In Ixtapa try **Farmacia Cielito Lindo** (inside the La Puerta shopping center, Loc. 3 and 4; ☎ **755/553-2170**).

Post Office The post office, or **Servicio Postal** (☎ 755/554-2192), is located at Avenida Correos on the corner of Calle Telgrafitos in downtown Zihuatanejo.

Safety You'll feel relatively safe in Zihuatanejo and Ixtapa. A few good rules of thumb: Don't be on the beach at night, don't wear ostentatious items or otherwise flaunt money, don't get too drunk, and always have an emergency phone number at hand.

Telephone Tips The telephone area code is **755.**

Sleeping

Generally, there are more high-end luxury hotels in Ixtapa (think family-oriented high-rises) and cheaper options in Zihuatanejo (bungalows, hostels, cheaper hotels), but you can find budget and luxury accommodations in both areas if you know where to look.

In **Ixtapa,** a row of large, expensive hotels are cramped along Playa Palmar, each with its own set of organized outdoor activities, and you'll find plenty of restaurants, bakeries, and gelato stands to keep you happy. Many families stay at these hotels, but so do large or small groups of friends and the inevitable newlyweds. You'll find lots of quality hotels here, all very similar, with all-you-can-eat buffets, curvy overcrowded pools, and access to the beaches where all hotel guests blend, making Ixtapa feel at times like one big bloated resort.

Zihuatanejo, on the other hand, has much more authentic Mexican character. Hotels generally have a bit more pizzazz, even the old cruddy ones. While many hotels and bungalows have access to some of the nicest beaches in the area, Zihuatanejo tempts many-a-traveler to leave the beach behind and take a stroll past the plentiful eateries and sweaty fishermen. The real draw of Zihuatanejo is the combined atmosphere of its beaches and its fishing village charm; most accommodations take advantage of this duality.

If saving money is your priority, try and book a stay at one of the area's hostels or apartments/bungalows, which have kitchens and cost very little. For great beachside seafood and one of the nicest beaches in town, the hotels along **Playa La Ropa** range in cost but offer the same gorgeous beach and sunsets as some of the most expensive hotels in town.

The bottom line is that whatever you're looking for, it exists somewhere between Ixtapa and Zihuatanejo.

Hostels

MTV Best → **Angela's Hostel** ★★ ZIHUATANEJO CENTRO This is an excellent place to stay for socializing, getting drunk, and meeting young surfers or surfer-wannabes. Since it's in the heart of Zihuatanejo Centro, it's within walking distance from a couple of beaches (although not the best ones). The hostel claims to cater to students, international backpackers, and surfers, and those are exactly the three types of people that can be found here. The rooms are surprisingly well-decorated for a hostel, with funky colors and interesting artwork, but don't expect hot water in the showers. Most of the rooms have twin beds, although there is a dorm-style room with bunk beds that can accommodate more people (not available in Dec). The rooms can get stuffy, but that just inspires people to take advantage of the hammocks hanging in the lobby downstairs. And since the hostel isn't very big, a large percentage of the people staying here simply spend most of their time hanging out at the fun, welcoming bar across the street called Barracruda's (p. 570). ***Note:*** This hostel will be temporarily closed for renovations in mid-2007, so call ahead. *Pedro Ascencio 10, Zihuatanejo Centro. ☎ 755/554-5084. www.zihuatanejo.com.mx/angelas. $90 per person (dorm-style room), $210–$270 private rooms. Free airport/bus terminal pick-up for groups. No credit cards. Amenities: Internet; 2 communal kitchens; no hot water; luggage storage; front door shuts at 9pm but each guest has keys; quiet hours after 11pm. In room: Ceiling fans, TV (some rooms).*

Cheap

→ **America Hotel** ★ ZIHUATANEJO CENTRO For the most part, this is just another cheap hotel option in the area. It faces a small pedestrian street/sidewalk, which gets little car traffic, though you'll hear people outside enjoying the many cute cafes and restaurants just downstairs, including an organic coffee shop and a few Mexican equivalents of a "diner." The rooms lack natural light and the decor is mostly in the "functional" category, with lots of creaky wicker armchairs and a nondescript desk. Though the place is somewhat sterile, even conjuring to mind a hospital, the owners will do what they can to make sure visitors are comfortable. Plus, they have a very cheap suite that accommodates six to eight people, which is great for a group of friends who prioritize location over distinctiveness. *H. Galeana 16, Zihuatanejo Centro. ☎ 755/554-4337. Fax 755/554-4338. zihuamerica7@hotmail.com. $400–$500 singles and doubles, $600–$700 rooms for 4, $1,200 suites. No credit cards. Amenities: Restaurant and bar downstairs. In room: A/C (optional), TV w/cable, ceiling fan, fridge.*

MTV Best → **Apartamentos Amueblados Valle** ★★ ZIHUATANEJO CENTRO The rooms at this small, centrally located alternative to a hotel are well furnished and very homey, with an eat-in kitchen (with dishes), and a few benchlike couches. The one-bedroom apartments accommodate up to three people and the two-bedroom apartments easily fit four people. All rooms create a very happy and bright atmosphere, with roosters crowing in the background and floral fabrics that match the colorful tiles in the kitchen. They don't all have air-conditioning but the fans are good enough. Since the rooms are right in the center of downtown Zihuatanejo, but not on a loud busy street, it's easy to try all the nearby restaurants and bars without having to go very far. The restaurant downstairs is a good place to hit up for fruit smoothies and a banana pancake breakfast. *Vincente Guerrero 33, between Ejido and Nicolas Bravo, Zihuatanejo Centro. ☎ 755/554-2084 or 554-4154. Fax 755/554-3220. www.zihuatanejo.net/valle. $600–$800 1-bedroom apts. Ask about long-term stay discounts during low season. No credit cards. In room: A/C (in some rooms), fans, kitchenette.*

→ **Casa Gloria María** ★★ PLAYA LA ROPA This is a great place for anyone low-maintenance who just wants a clean bed, a kitchen, and constant beach access. It's also the most affordable housing directly on Playa La Ropa. Though the rooms here are far from fancy, they come with outdoor kitchenettes (with stoves and large fridges) and a small deck area only a few feet from the beach. The vibe is much like what you'd expect at a luxurious campsite, minus the tents—guests often spill out of their rooms onto their sandy patios for a drink, and get to chatting with each other.

Ixtapa & Zihuatanejo Sleeping & Eating

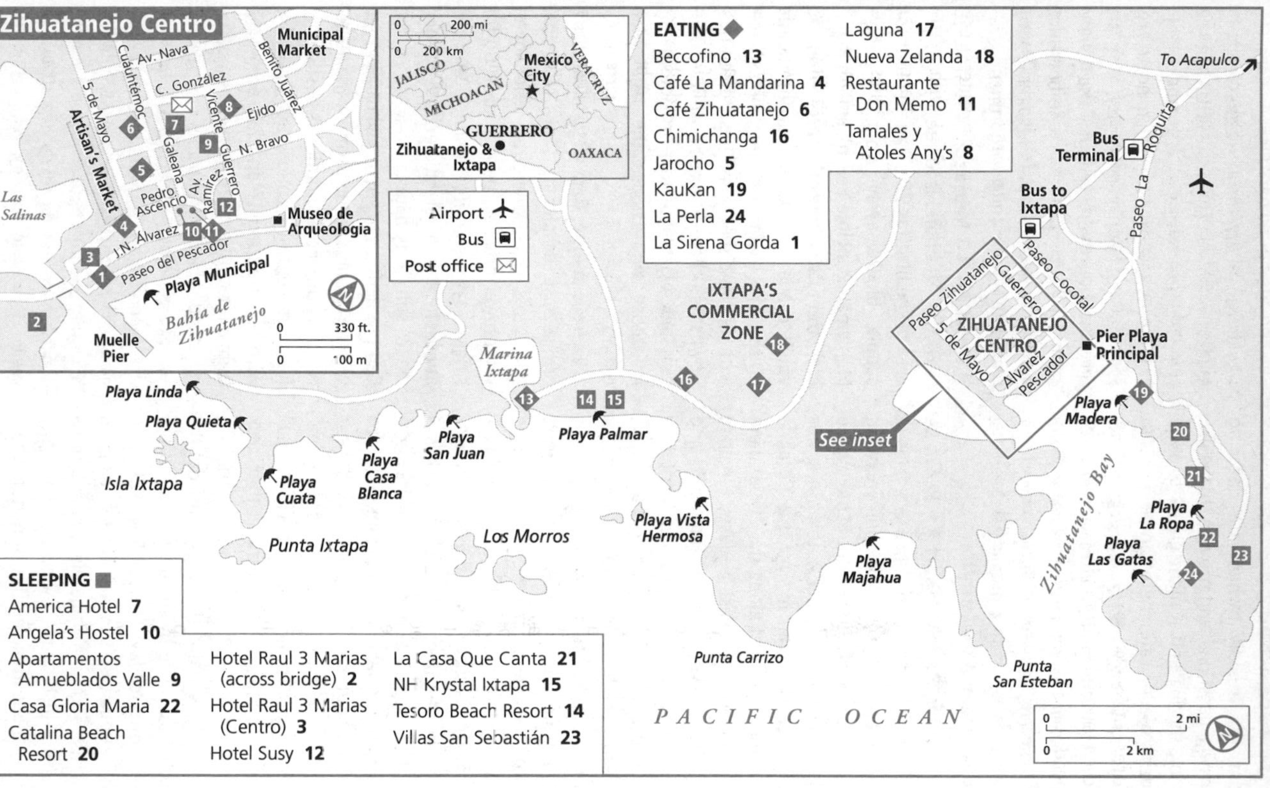

Everything is very clean and both linens and towels are changed daily. Most important, the friendly owners are eager to answer questions, and provide things like book sharing and a night guard to keep guests feeling safe and at home. *Playa La Ropa, Zihuatanejo. ☎ 755/554-2055 or 554-3510. www.zihuatanejo.net/casagloriamaria. Low season $900 room with 2 twin beds for up to 4 people; high season, $1,200 room with 2 twin beds for up to 4 people. Ask for group deals. In room: A/C, kitchenette.*

➔ **Catalina Beach Resort** ★★ PLAYA LA ROPA This resort in Zihuatanejo is a great place for a group of friends who want to access Playa La Ropa without paying the big bucks that the other hotels along this beach charge. Built in 1952, the Catalina was the first hotel along the Zihuatanejo Bay shoreline. Past guests include Elizabeth Taylor, George Hamilton, and Mick Jagger. Although not the cleanest or most beautiful hotel in the area anymore, guests get a lot more space for their buck here compared to similarly priced hotels in the downtown area. The bungalows with ocean views can easily fit four people inside. Rooms have a large spacious balcony that is shared with the other bungalows on the floor, and each room has a section to itself with reclining chairs and a hammock. A taxi into Zihuatanejo Centro costs about $30. Camionetas also pass through (look for one that says "La Ropa" to get here). The hotel organizes many outdoor activities and has a travel tour desk for planning day/weekend excursions.

One long staircase brings you from the reception office by the main road all the way down to Playa La Ropa. The walk up to this staircase, surrounded by tropical plants and unfortunately many-a-mosquito, will be quite the workout for any non-athletes reading this; why not take a break halfway up at the breezy two-level restaurant/bar that has a shady view of the Bay and a tempting bar? *Playa La Ropa s/n, Zihuatanejo. ☎ 877/287-2411, 755/554-2137, or 554-9321, ext. 25. Fax 755/554-9327. www.catalina-beach-resort.com. $750–$1,030 small casita with 2 double beds or 1 king-size bed, $990–$1,620 deluxe bungalow with large terrace and 2 queen-size beds. A/C, meal plans extra. AE, DC, MC, V. Amenities: Restaurant; 3 bars; beach access; pool. In room: A/C (some rooms), TV w/cable, fridge with freezer.*

➔ **Hotel Raul 3 Marías** ★ ZIHUATANEJO CENTRO This hotel is located in a pretty area of the bustling Zihuatanejo Centro, a couple blocks away from the Playa Municipal (Principle Beach), and on a quieter street than some other area hotels, so you'll evade the area's raucous nightly noises. The rooms are clean but sparse, with all white sheets and basic amenities. Downstairs there is a worthwhile restaurant called Garrobos that provides meals for those who choose the meal plan option.

There is another Raul 3 Marías across a bridge past the pier on Playa Municipal (Municipal Beach) where they offer somewhat lower prices (around $250–$400 for singles, $350–$600 for doubles) and the atmosphere is a lot quieter and calmer, while still a 15-minute walk from the Center's action. For anyone who's like Raul with three Marías around and wants to get his party on, the first option is best due to its more central location. But for those with just one special María, hop across the bridge for a little more privacy and peace of mind. *Juan N. Alvarez 52, Centro. ☎ 755/554-6706. www.ixtapa-zihuatanejo.net/r3marias/gar_r3_i.htm. $450–$950 singles, $150–$200 per extra person. AE, DC, MC, V. Amenities: Restaurant; doctor on call; laundry service; room service; safety deposit box. In room: TV w/cable, balcony, ceiling fan, hot water, kitchen.*

→ **Hotel Susy** ★ ZIHUATANEJO CENTRO Susy's like that friend everyone has who is not really that exciting (and yeah, a little ugly), but she's *always* there to listen if you've had a bad day. This cute, cheap hotel situated on a quiet street in downtown Zihuatanejo is *"muy sencillo"* as the Mexicans describe it, meaning simple and humble. The rooms are small, making it hard to cram more than a couple people in there. All hotel rooms face a pretty little courtyard that tends to be quiet, but ask for a room with a balcony in order to get a little more space. You probably won't want to hang out too long in your room anyways; Hotel Susy is just across the street from the archaeology museum, as well as the beach and within a couple blocks of many restaurants, bars, Internet cafes, and shops. *Juan Alvarez 3, corner of V. Guerrerp and Juan Alvarez, Zihuatanejo Centro. ☎ 755/554-2339. Fax 755/554-3299 or 554-4739. $340–$780 double. MC, V. In room: TV.*

Doable

→ **NH Krystal Ixtapa** ★★ IXTAPA Upon arrival at the NH Krystal, visitors are given a tropical fruit punch sans alcohol. That drink pretty much sums up the place. The hotel—like the virgin fruit drink—is fun and has a lot going on, but it lacks a punch of excitement that could make your vacation a little more memorable. Like the Tesoro resort next door, the Krystal has poolside and beachside activities, but there seems to be less of an urgency and/or desire for guests to participate. If you're up for a night of dancing and worried about stumbling home in a drunken stupor, have no fear—**Christine's,** the big nightclub in Ixtapa that's popular with tourists, is literally right in front of the Krystal. This hotel is also the closest you'll get to the commercial zone of Ixtapa and, at the very least, provides great food, decent accommodations (the rooms are spacious if basic), and wonderful views of the ocean. *Bulevar Ixtapa s/n, Ixtapa. ☎ 800/231-9860, or 755/553-0333. Fax 755/553-0216. www.nh-hotels.com. $1,190 standard room. AE, DC, MC, V. Amenities: 5 restaurants; lobby bar; nightclub; car rental; gym; laundry service; massage; pool; racquetball court; room service; salon; travel agency. In room: A/C, TV w/cable, hair dryer, minibar.*

→ **Tesoro Resort** ★★★ IXTAPA When it comes to vacations, Tesoro means business. Located next to all the other highrise hotels on Playa Palmar, this all-inclusive resort definitely takes good care of its guests and makes sure they know how to find a good party. It's so big that personalized service gets lost in the mix, though. The hotel boasts a curvy pool overflowing with happy people, direct access to the beach, and multiple restaurants to choose from without leaving the building. Yet the lengthy activities list, including pool games and bingo, is a bit much. The energy at this hotel is *always* up, as is the volume of the '80s/'90s pump-up, work-out-with-Jane-Fonda, music. Be prepared to take part in almost every activity or the freakishly upbeat party-motivator-like employees will make fun of you.

Rooms are bright and very cool, as in they take the air-conditioning to the next level. Four people can fit comfortably in the two double beds. When night falls and vacationers are too lazy to walk anywhere else, the hotel arranges for a van to bring hotel guests to the bars and clubs that are only a 5- to 10-minute walk away. *Bulevar*

Ixtapa s/n Lot 5, Zona Hotelera. ☎ 866/99-TESORO, or 755/555-0600. www.tesororesorts.com. Around $1,000 for standard room with 2 double beds, year-round. AE, DC, MC, V. Amenities: 2 restaurants; 2 bars (1 in the pool); 24-hr. snack bar; complete activities program; golf course; gym; pool; theme parties and nightly entertainment. In room: A/C, TV w/cable, hair dryer, minibar, phone, safety deposit box.

➔ **Villas San Sebastián** ★★ PLAYA LA ROPA This hotel is located in the same area as the Catalina Beach Resort and La Casa Que Canta, but is on the other side of the road and not directly attached to the beach. But never fear, the beach is near (only a short walk away). The recently renovated rooms here are very attractive and don't reflect the low rates. Yellow walls, wicker lamps, and large fragments of wood incorporated tactfully into the furniture add a slightly rustic touch to the otherwise sunny rooms. The slightly secluded villas offer excellent views of the ocean and rooms, complete with pretty, tiled bathrooms, you don't mind hanging out in, unlike some of the cheaper hotels in town.

There are several villas to choose from, so make sure you ask which are available and what the options are. Some come with their own outdoor bar (sweet), some with kitchens. Some even connect with a shared kitchen and balcony by the pool so that you and your friends can be divided between two rooms but still be close. The great rooms and the great views make the slightly distant, off-center location of this hotel worth it. *Lote 112, Playa La Ropa, Zihuatanejo. ☎ 755/554-4154 or 553-8258. $1,135–$1,675 1br villa, $1,785–$2,755 2br villas. No credit cards. Amenities: Pool. In room: A/C, TV w/cable, kitchenette (include coffeemaker and blender), phone, safety deposit box.*

Splurge

MTV Best ➔ **La Casa Que Canta** ★★★ PLAYA LA ROPA La Casa Que Canta (The Home that Sings) sings louder and more beautifully than any of the other hotels on Playa La Ropa—or in Zihuatanejo, for that matter. It is hands-down the most beautiful, most romantic, most charismatic, and most detail-oriented hotel in the area. As such, it's not surprising that designer Betsey Johnson loves it so much, or that it was named one of the Small Luxury Hotels of the World (www.slh.com). Guests look, feel, and smell like royalty when they stay here, but they pay for this royal treatment. From the Frida Kahlo–inspired paintings on the furniture to the flower petal designs on the beds, all the little luxuries come with a hefty price tag attached.

Each room features a shelf full of books and a basket of magazines to choose from. Every evening, fresh fruit will magically appear, and the complimentary minibar (no, it's not an oxymoron) is restocked. Their gourmet restaurant, tucked away by the infinity pool overlooking the Bay of Zihuatanejo, is a perfect place to eat—if only so that you can be waited on by the incredibly attentive staff. If you can't afford to splurge on this one, at least come for an unforgettable sunset-dinner here. ***Note:*** Two private residences are also available: El Murmullo and El Ensueño. They cost a lot more but come with their own chefs and pools. *Camino Escénico a Playa Ropa s/n Zihuatanejo. ☎ 888/523-5050, 755/555-7000, or 555-7030. Fax 755/554-7900. www.lacasaquecanta.com. $3,135–$7,345 double. AE, MC, V. Amenities: Restaurant; bar; fitness center; laundry service; freshwater pool; saltwater pool; room service; spa. In room: A/C, TV w/cable and DVD player, bath robes, ceiling fans, hair dryer, complimentary minibar, safety deposit box, telephone.*

Eating

When traveling through Ixtapa and Zihuatanejo, be prepared for inordinate amounts of delicious, fresh fish. (Zihuatanejo is still a major fishing port, after all.) In Zihuatanejo, Playa Municipal (also known as Playa Principal) is the best place to head to for cheap restaurants; there you can literally watch fisherman prepare their catch of the day on the beach while you're eating. (Just don't sit too close to the fish prep area, as the smell can be a bit much.) For cheap Mexican enchiladas, tacos, pozole, and consistently delicious seafood, sample as many of the restaurants in the Zihuatanejo Centro area as possible. For something a little fancier, head to one of the waterside romantic restaurants in Ixtapa or one of the edgier restaurants along the road parallel to Playa La Ropa.

Cheap

➔ **Chimichanga** ★★ MEXICAN/STEAK Because it's tucked away on the second floor—far away from the street vendors you'll encounter at street level—this restaurant is a much quieter and calmer alternative to the buzzing restaurants inside most of the area's hotels. The restaurant is also bright and breezy, with some nice modern artwork on the walls. According to the menu, Chimichanga claims to have "No doubt the best meat in Ixtapa/Zihuatanejo," and, true enough, this is a good place for anyone craving a juicy slab of meat. Breakfast is great, too; I recommend the banana pancakes or one of the hearty breakfast combos, which come with your choice of eggs (including Mexican style, which can be *un poco picante*) or a traditional Mexican steak and pepper dish, with fresh tropical fruit, freshly squeezed juice, and yummy coffee. *Bulevar Ixtapa (across from Hotel Emporio on the 2nd floor).* ☎ *755/553-1705. vasiliky@prodigy.net.mx. Main courses $25–$135. AE, DC, MC, V. Daily 8am–closing.*

➔ **La Perla** ★★ SEAFOOD With so many palapa-style, beachside restaurants to choose from, it can be tough to pick the best one. Let me make it easy for you: Go to La Perla. Towards the southern end of Playa La Ropa (in the opposite direction from La Casa Que Canta), look for the red and white umbrellas set up in the sand among small trees. Hungry beach bums can dine on fresh fish while digging their feet into the sand, or they can opt for a more traditional restaurant atmosphere under the thatched roof near the bar. The menu includes oysters, shrimp, lobster, octopus, red snapper—called *huachinango* in Mexico—dorado tuna, and whatever else the fishermen catch. The fish can be fried, battered, or grilled, and it is not rare to catch the fishermen bringing their fresh catches right from their boats and into the kitchen. The menu has no surprises and the service can be slow, but there are worse places to wait for a meal than on the sands of Playa La Ropa. *Playa La Ropa, Zihuatanejo.* ☎ *755/554-2700. Breakfast $40–$65, main courses $75–$240. AE, DISC, MC, V. Daily 9am–10pm. From Camino a Playa La Ropa road, go right at the fork in the road at the southern end of Playa La Ropa and look for the sign in the parking lot.*

➔ **La Sirena Gorda** ★★ MEXICAN If the fat mermaids that adorn the nooks and crannies of this popular restaurant (on the Paseo del Pescador) don't whet your appetite, I don't know what will. Many small hand-crafted wooden ships hang from the ceilings, and mermaid paintings scattered throughout appear to watch guests devour every piece of their food. Locals come here for a glorious breakfast of eggs, hot cakes (pancakes), fruit and granola, or their well-known seafood tacos. For dinner, try one of the daily specials that vary based on what's caught by the local fishermen in the port just beyond the entrance of the restaurant. You might feel like a fat mermaid when you leave, but in a good way. *Paseo del Pescador 90, next to the pier. ☎ 755/554-2687. Breakfast $20–$55, main courses $45–$120. MC, V. Thurs–Tues 8:30am–10:30pm.*

→ **Nueva Zelanda** ★ MEXICAN This popular restaurant, mysteriously named after far away New Zealand, successfully churns out delectable breakfast favorites at all hours of the day. Nueva Zelanda calls itself a "cafeteria" but it looks very much like a diner, with Mexican flare. I recommend the *tortas,* which are like a Mexican panini with ham, tomato, onion, refried beans, and guacamole on warm, soft bread that is extremely fresh. They serve breakfast all day and have milkshakes, fruit smoothies, and a drink called a *licuado* that is basically a mix of the two, made with a choice of tropical fruit. The food is decent and the service is fast, served up to the strains of the Beach Boys and other up-tempo tunes. You'll find a second location in Zihua Centro across from the America Hotel (p. 560). *Manzana 2, Lote 19 Local #1, Ixtapa, in commercial center. ☎ 755/553-0838. Breakfast and main courses $28–$99. No credit cards. Daily 8am–9:30pm.*

→ **Restaurante Don Memo** ★★ INTERNATIONAL This restaurant isn't exactly eye candy (it's kind of weird to eat surrounded by so many surrealist paintings of Jesus), but the food is surprisingly delicious and the portions are certainly large. Standouts include the rib-eye steak and spaghetti with meat sauce. Most important, the vibe is definitely friendly and communal. The bar counter was donated from an older, famous restaurant that went out of business—it's now a piece of Zihuatanejo history. You can even sit at the Barracruda bar across the sidewalk and have Don Memo's food brought over there since both owners are friends. *Pedro Ascencio 35, Zihuatanejo Centro, next to Angela's Hostel. ☎ 755/559-7000. Main courses $40–$50. No credit cards. Daily 4pm–midnight.*

→ **Restaurantes Mexicanos Tamales Y Atoles Any** ★★ MEXICAN Any is the place most locals will send you to for *pozole,* though many admit that there are better places for this Mexican soup. Still, this is an easy, popular, and tasty standby for anyone in the Centro, and one of the only places that offers pozole on a regular basis. They offer other menu items, too, but the real draw is the pozole, and the best day to taste it is Thursday, between 3 and 6 in the afternoon. During this time, diners congregate to choose one of three sizes and two colors (white is not spicy and green is *muy picante*). The pozole is then brought out on a platter with radishes, chile peppers, avocados, limes, onions, cheese, pork rind, and tortilla chips. Every eager pozole-eater adds their own amounts of these ingredients, to their liking. A complimentary shot of mescal comes with the order.

The place could use a few upgrades in the style department, as the colorful striped tablecloths and the wall's cheesy mural of cartoonlike Mexicans cooking is a tacky combo. But after downing some delicious mescal, who really cares about the walls? *Vicente Guerrero 38, corner of Ejido, in front of Banamex, Col. Centro Zihuatanejo. ☎ 755/554-7373 or 554-7303. Breakfast $35–$80, main courses $30–$90. AE, DISC, MC, V. Daily 9am–11pm.*

Doable

→ **Jarocho** ★★ SOUTHERN MEXICAN "Jarocho" is a word that expresses the fusion of Spanish, African, and indigenous cultures in the gulf region of Mexico, and this restaurant rightly prides itself on offering a menu that captures the central flavors of Mexico's gastronomic history. The dishes come loaded with flavor, literally—they're accompanied by chile pepper salsas in varying degrees of picante-ness. I thought the *huachinango en estilo verracruzana* (red snapper, Veracruz-style, with peppers, tomatoes, and capers) was the best I had in town. Other good dishes include shrimp cooked in foil with tomato and onion, chipotle chile, acuyo leaves, white wine, and fish sticks. Pair any of the flavorful dishes with one of their fresh salads and complimentary fresh bread with chorizo-flavored butter, and you've got yourself a delicious Mexican meal.

In addition to the more-upscale-than-usual food, this restaurant has a more refined personality than most of the other restaurants in downtown, laid-back Zihua. It's casual, but still nice enough for your fancy clothes. Christmas lights hang from the back wall and an iron chandelier hangs from the ceiling. The windows, with their bamboo bars, keep the dancing and live music indoors (guitar, samba, bossa nova, salsa, and rumba tunes turn this place into a sassy display of hip-swinging, during high season only). *H. Galena, corner of Nicolas Bravo, Centro Zihuatanejo. ☎ 755/544-7497. Main courses $80–$300. MC, V. Daily 2pm–11pm. Closed Mon during low season.*

➜ **Laguna** ★★ MEXICAN/ITALIAN Situated among the congested shops and bars of the Commercial Center, this might be the only place in town where six friends can order "Baked Piglet" and get an entire piggy, cooked and cut, to share for $240. If that doesn't entice you to eat at this place, maybe the large thatched roof and the water trickling down a stone wall in the back of the restaurant will do the job; it gives the restaurant a pleasant tropical feel. (Unfortunately, the tropical atmosphere comes complete with bugs that feast on guests' feet throughout the meal.)

While the dining experience here attempts to be tranquil and serene, the music from Señor Frog's next door (not the most considerate of neighbors) spills over into the open dining area and creates an awkward juxtaposition. But the food is first-rate, from the spaghetti carbonara (with bacon, ham, and a white cream sauce) to the always fresh seafood. *Paseo de Ixtapa, Hotel Zone, next to Señor Frog's. ☎ 755/553-1103. lagunaixtapa@hotmail.com. Main courses $75–$250. MC, V. Daily noon–midnight.*

Splurge

➜ **Beccofino** ★★ NORTHERN ITALIAN If you were to compare all the restaurants in Ixtapa to sailboats, than Beccofino would be a yacht with its own surrounding marina. This upscale restaurant has become a sanctuary for couples seeking romantic shelter and a refined Italian menu. Guests sit on the teak wood deck, jutting onto the water, and eat seafood-pasta dishes, like the delicious homemade spinach tagliolini with shrimp and black pepper, and the house specialty ravioli. Anyone who likes seafood and Italian dishes will find something here—plus all meals go well with a selection from the extensive wine list or, occasionally, complimentary shots of limoncello after the meal. If you want to bump your dining experience up a notch from the Mexican restaurants you've already sampled, this is a good choice; it's also a popular place for breakfast. *Veleros No. 6 Locales 7 & 8 Marina Plaza, Ixtapa. ☎ 755/553-1770 or 553-2109. beccofino@prodigy.net.mx. Breakfast $50–$70, main courses $144–$278. AE, MC, V. Daily 9am–midnight.*

MTV Best ➜ **Kau-Kan** ★★ NUEVA COCINA It sounds Asian, but isn't: Like almost every restaurant in the area, this one specializes in seafood. Still, it offers up edgier dishes than usual, like tasty fresh tuna rolls stuffed with sea bass tartar or grilled mahimahi filet with pumpkin seed sauce and pineapple. Though considered by some food magazines to cook "the best food in town," I would give Kau-Kan runner-up status. Mainly, Kau-Kan stands out because of what it does differently with the same fish that everyone else is using. But there are a few missteps; I ordered a potato stuffed with lobster and shrimp in a creamy basil and garlic sauce that was overcooked.

This is a popular place for tourists since it offers a great sunset photo-op over the restaurant's balcony. Kau-Kan is situated on the winding road that connects the center of town with the most famous beach in town (La Ropa), which gives it a unique position over the Bay. Be warned that it's not very easy to get to on foot. *Carretera Escenica, Lote No. 7, Zihuatanejo. ☎ 755/554-8446. Fax 755/554-5731. kaukan@prodigy.net.mx. Main courses $145–$340. AE, DISC, MC, V. Daily 5–11pm.*

Cafes & Tearooms

➔ **Anatma** ★★ CAFE From the outside, this looks like nothing more than a small coffee shop where people can sit both inside and out while sipping a drink and people-watching. Yes, it's a great place for breakfast and snacks, including fruit, waffles, smoothies, coffee drinks, sandwiches, and salads. But it's also one of the most important social centers in town: Its motto is "finding the unknown" and, judging by all the artwork and writing on display, that unknown could be just about anybody. The general vibe calls to mind the common area of a camp or dorm room (there's actually a CD player with stacks of CDs to choose from, along with lots of books). Anatma even hosts poetry readings, art shows, movie-nights, and very small-scale theatrical productions that are open to anyone who wants to participate. *Andador H. Galeana, Zihuatanejo Centro. ☎ 755/102-4155. Food $25–$40, coffee drinks $10–$20. No credit cards. Daily 8:20am–11:30pm.*

➔ **Café La Mandarina** ★★ CAFE Shopping can be exhausting, so thank god for this lovely cafe directly next to the bustling Artisan market. It's the perfect little place for a mid-afternoon pick-me-up, a full breakfast, or a sweet dessert. The walls are covered with cubist artwork and old French cafe billboards, and, while Mexican MTV plays overhead, coffee-sippers can sit and watch all the tourists pass by as they sip. In addition to coffee drinks, the cafe makes a badass (meaning delicious) frozen cappuccino in a large bowl-like glass, topped with frozen whipped cream and chocolate sprinkles, along with crepes (try the tropical ones or the "favorite" crepes, with chocolate, nuts, and sugar). *Av. 5 de Mayo 9E, Zihuatanejo Centro. ☎ 755/554-4618. crepe_mty@yahoo.com. Breakfast $34–$56. No credit cards. Daily 9am–midnight.*

MTV Best ➔ **Café Zihuatanejo** ★★ CAFE This is the best coffee house in Zihuatanejo and, surprisingly, the coffee it brews is even organic. The place just opened up in late 2006, so it's still figuring out its identity. When I visited, it had a bar-like atmosphere mixed with the chilled out bohemian-chic quality of a hip cafe that doesn't try too hard to be anything but itself. Though very narrow, with a long coffee bar inside and seating on high stools or at the bar inside, and small square tables outside, it's comfy. The chill earthy music they play only adds to the relaxing environment. While the music was in a language I didn't understand, the cafe definitely spoke my language when it comes to coffee—their iced vanilla frappuccino, for instance, is absolutely delicious. *Cuauhtémoc 170 Local B, Colonia Centro, Zihuatanejo.* ☎ *755/554-3890.* *café_zihuatanejo@hotmail.com. Coffee drinks $20. No credit cards. Daily 8am–noon.*

Partying

Zihuatanejo and Ixtapa are not necessarily the biggest party towns in Mexico, but after a few nights here, most visitors realize that bigger isn't necessarily better. The two resorts team up to provide enough bars and dance clubs that you won't feel cheated out of nightlife options nor overwhelmed by them. The gay scene is still somewhat young; while many bars are gay friendly, there are only a few openly gay bars and clubs in the area.

In Ixtapa, a few high-tech nightclubs like **Alebrije** and **Christine** provide large dance floors for vacationers to shake it, and the area also boasts a couple of more plush loungelike outdoor clubs. And it wouldn't be spring break at a Mexican beach resort without large touristy bar/clubs like **Señor Frog's** and **Carlos 'n' Charlie's,** home of ridiculously colorful, large, watered-down slushy drinks—both have outposts here.

Zihuatanejo has a mish-mash of possibilities. For real dancing (which includes good ol' gringo-esque grinding, as well as salsa and merengue), go to Ixtapa. But for the best piña coladas, live music, or bars where people can actually hear themselves, go to Zihuatanejo, which also offers a number of sports bars, like **Zorro's** and **Coconut's.** For many people, a night out in Zihua means ending up at one of the bars in the Centro playing silly drinking games and mingling with a mixed crowd of expats, locals, and tourists. Just be careful who you party with and how you party with them: Zihuatanejo is a very small town, so if you're swapping spit with someone at a bar on a Tuesday night you'll probably run into them again by Thursday night.

Clubs

➜ **Carlos 'n Charlie's** ★★ Like nearby Señor Frog's, Carlos 'n Charlie's is like a giant fun-house for drinking, full of random objects that pop out at all angles. It might be a little off-the-wall at times (both literally and figuratively speaking), but between the tropical drinks, the jokester atmosphere, and the upbeat music, Carlos and Charlie are great party hosts, both night and day. Come for the fun drinks or the dance floor that's always ready for gringo/gringa moves. But stay for the location; the dance floor overlooks the beach and turns what could be an ordinary night at a bar into a real beach resort vacation, complete with gently rolling waves, a starry sky, and lots of sweaty, sunburned people drinking irresponsibly. *Bulevar Ixtapa, by Best Western Posada Real, on beach side of street.* ☎ *755/553-0085. Cover around $100 after 9pm, free Sun–Fri in low season.*

➜ **Christine** ★★ This is one of the most popular clubs for tourists in the Ixtapa area, due largely to the fact that it is almost as easy to find as the beach. Located directly in front of the NH Krystal hotel, which owns the club, Christine is well-known for its midnight light show, but most people go simply to get their dance on. It's not the coolest, most beautiful nightclub (yes, there is a large disco ball) but with two bars, an amphitheater-like setup with the dance floor as the stage, and loud thumping Latin, pop, and disco beats, all anyone needs to do when they get here is follow the flashing lights to the dance floor and join in. ***Note:*** No sneakers, sandals, or shorts are allowed.

Wednesdays are salsa/merengue nights with no cover and buy one drink, get one free drink deals. *In front of the NH Krystal, Bulevar Ixtapa, Ixtapa.* ☎ *755/553-0456. www.christine-ixtapa.com. Cover free–$280.*

→ **Señor Frog's** ★ There are no surprises at this popular, colorful, somewhat crazy night or day spot. This bar has become a staple in Mexico's beach resorts, with an unfailing ability to attract swarms of young people to its funky, warehouse party atmosphere. An elevated dance floor awaits the crowds beneath a large movie screen playing music videos that accompany the blasting pop, '80s, and rock music. Although the space doesn't seem conducive to dancing, people have figured out how to work around the long benchlike tables and make it happen. Objects (like a car with a surfboard) hang upside down from the ceiling and one of the interactive walls asks onlookers to vote for their favorite superhero. Come here with a game face on: The waiters are itching to get you obnoxiously drunk. *Bulevar Ixtapa, in the La Puerta Center, Ixtapa.* ☎ *755/553-2282.*

Bars & Lounges

→ **Barracruda's** ★★ Expats and young wanderers from the nearby Angela's Hostel (p. 559) love the relaxed, friendly environment of this hole-in-the-wall bar. Barracruda's has two things that no other bar in the area has: a bar counter filled with seashells and sand and lit with Christmas lights, and "The Ring Game." This game involves a ring attached to a long string that hangs in the door-less doorway: You simply swing the string with the ring at the right angle so that it catches on a nail that is hammered into a wooden beam. The game is strangely contagious, perhaps because it's a great way to make new friends. (Though the drinks don't hurt, either.) *Pedro Ascencio no. 14, Zihuatanejo Centro.* ☎ *755/554-4075. No cover.*

→ **Jungle Bar** ★★ This is a great place to start the night, wherever else it might lead. (Most people plan on leaving early, but just end up staying.) It claims to be the "friendliest bar in town," which might be a little ambitious, but you'd have trouble proving them wrong. The crowd here tends to consist of young travelers and surfers, who are drawn by the reggae and pop music that keeps the energy upbeat and happy, along with the cheap drinks. Cold beer is $10, there are happy hours from 7 to 9pm, Tuesdays are Hookah Nights, Thursdays are Ladies Nights with free vodka, gin, and rum (turning most ladies into animals suitable for this jungle). Live music and guest DJs come throughout the week. Throw sports games, movies, and live events into the mix, and you have a crowd-pleasing concoction. *Augustin Ramirez 3, Zihautanejo Centro.* ☎ *755/108-6286. http://lajunglazihua.com. No cover. Closed during off season.*

MTV Best → **Shiva Bar** ★★★ It all started with a piña colada. A bartender made one of his famous piña coladas for a mysterious Italian man; the Italian man proposed that they open a bar together; and thus Shiva was born. For anyone who thinks all piña coladas are created equal, the Shiva Bar bartenders will prove that theory wrong with a piña colada so good, I consider it a liquid masterpiece. Beverages aside, this became my favorite bar in Zihua for its extremely chill vibe that could get just lively enough when a good band and lively crowd combine forces. The red walls, with white and black furniture, create an attractive environment that is more modern and chic-looking than most places in the area. Live music is performed on Fridays (blues and jazz) and Saturdays (acoustic rock) and birthday boys and girls get special free domestic drinks all night. But beware of a flaming shot called a *cucaracha* that might come creeping your

Ixtapa & Zihuatanejo Partying, Sightseeing & Playing Outside

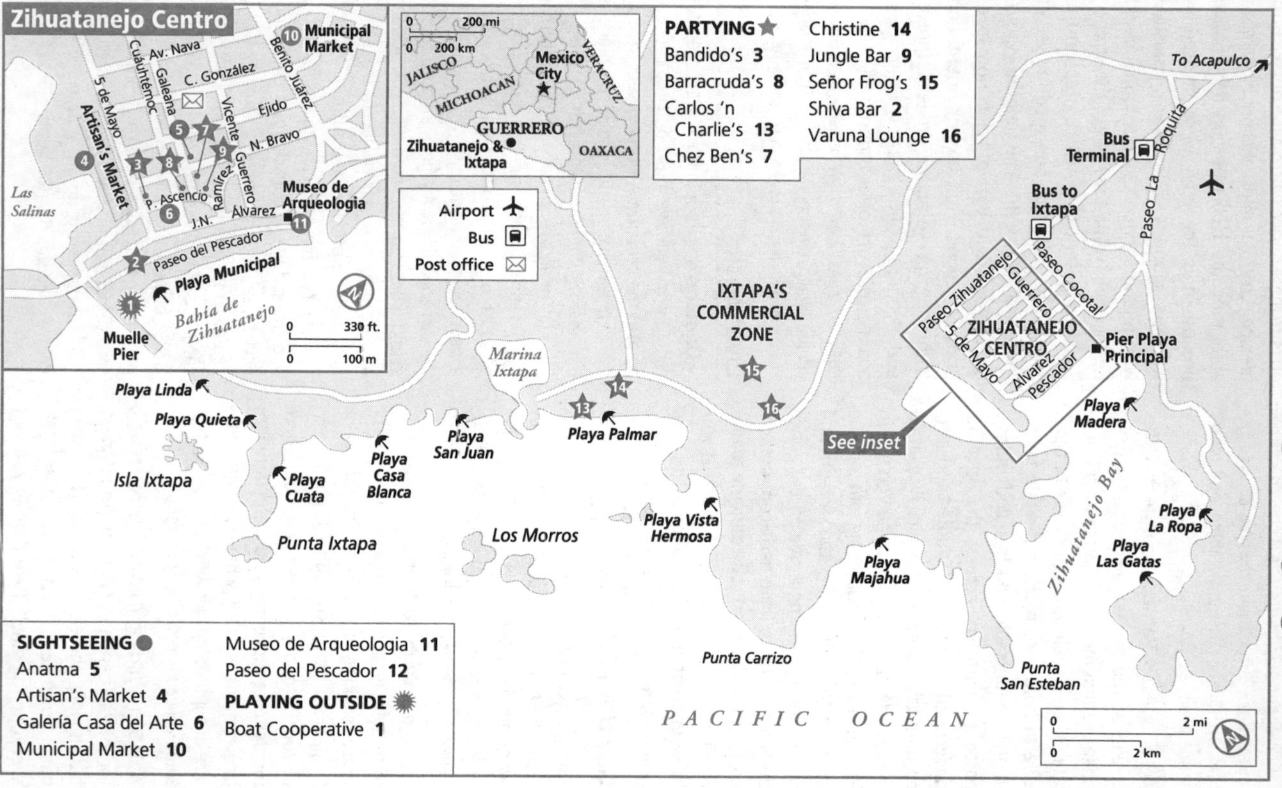

way—nasty for the recipient, but highly entertaining for everyone else. *Paseo del Pescador 31, Zihuatanejo, between Evira's and Mediterrano, close to the pier.* ☎ *755/108-2501, 111-1813, or 100-7781. shiva_bar_mex@hotmail.com. No cover.*

MTV Best → **Varuna Lounge** ★★ This is one of the sexiest places to party in Ixtapa/Zihuatanejo. It's better to get here late, when people are half-drunk but still able to hold a conversation while laying in the comfortable couches and pillow-patches scattered across the ground, underneath palm trees. Candles and long curtains are draped every which way, making some people want to put the "lounge" in lounge here. After sprawling out on the cushions for a bit, muster the strength and motivation to join the locals on the dance floor for anything from hard-core (almost professional-looking) salsa dancing to hip-hop and any other music they throw at you. Dress up to fit in. *Bulevar Ixtapa s/n, in front of Hotel Barceló, Ixtapa.* ☎ *755/553-3138.*

Gay Bars & Clubs

Though machismo culture in Mexico has kept most of the Ixtapa and Zihua gay scene in the closet, luckily a few places have developed a growing following. Below are the best options.

→ **Ange's Club & Disco** ★ Ange's factory-style venue is a decent option for those seeking a gay bar in the area. Compared to 5x8+1, this disco is less in-your-face, but just as open. Come here for dancing, drinking, and entertainment in a unique setting where all lifestyles are accepted. *Bulevar Aeropuerto Acapulco, Zihuatanejo Km 2.* ☎ *755/559-3269.*

→ **5x8+1 Wilde's Club** ★ There aren't a ton of gay bars and clubs in Zihuatanejo, but luckily there's this one. This sassy bar welcomes "everyone, absolutely everyone to come!" Take that as you will. The mathematical equation in the club's name symbolizes 41 men who were part of an elite male dance club on the outskirts of Mexico City. At midnight on November 20th, 1901, the club was raided by police because half the men were dressed in women's clothing. They were punished with public service so that people could heckle them while they swept the streets. Some were sent to penal colonies in the Yucatán but all were punished for secret "perverse" interests. This anything-goes, dance-your-tight-butt-off club now celebrates freedom of sexual orientation with transvestite shows, male strippers, and "coming out" parties, and racy, avant-garde art often adorns the walls. *Calle La Laja, Zihuatanejo.* ☎ *755/101-2505. edmundoomar@hotmail.com. Transvestite shows and strippers on Fri, Sat, and Sun.*

Live Music

→ **Bandido's** ★ People flock to this restaurant/bar to hear live music and eat a decent meal at the same time. Don't expect to be in the company of many locals; the place is like an anthill teeming with hungry tourists. Mid-day, it acts as an easy lunch option for tired tourists who spent their morning scouting out the goods at the surrounding artisan shops, but the energy picks up when the sun goes down. As the night goes on, the drink orders go up, the music gets louder, and even some locals come out from their hiding places and join in the fun.

The menu has Mexican staples like tacos and quesadillas, but it also has club sandwiches, salads, and burgers, showing that it caters to its popular tourist following and can please families with little kids. Saturday is the biggest night, when local musicians play music that ranges in style from salsa to traditional folk music from the area, and the *turistas* eat it up. *Av. 5 de mayo 8, Col. Centro Zihuatanejo.* ☎ *755/553-8072. www.*

zihuatanejo.net/bandidos. No cover, but must buy food or drink. Main courses $85–$180.

MTV Best → **Chez Ben** ★★★ This French-restaurant-meets-chic-Mexican-lounge is a perfect solution for anyone seeking to escape the ground level buzz of Zihuatanejo. The second-floor lounge is a virtual oasis of style. Owner Ben, a French chef and restaurant connoisseur, provides delicious, fresh French food (made primarily with three of his favorite ingredients: garlic, fresh herbs, and white wine), and takes pride not only in the cooking but in the exceptional service and atmosphere. Every night, there is live music that ranges from rock and salsa to acoustic and flamenco guitar. Whatever brings you here—the exquisite food, the delicious wine, the impeccable service, or the talented musicians—will most likely bring you back. *Nicolas Bravo 47, 2nd floor, Zihuatanejo Centro. ☎ 755/108-6028. No cover.*

Heading to the Beach

There are plenty of beaches, or *playas,* to choose from between Ixtapa and Zihuatanejo. Though all beaches in the area are technically public, some hotels have created artificial barriers closing off some areas. Also note that, though all beaches in Zihuatanejo are safe for swimming, beaches in Ixtapa have strong undertows and so are more dangerous.

Extending for about 3km (2 miles), **Playa Palmar** is the main tourist beach in Ixtapa. Most of the hotels located on Bulevar Ixtapa have direct access to this beach, which can get quite crowded during high season. It is chock-full of volleyball nets, sunbathers, and kids building sandcastles. There are plenty of watersports activities to partake in and the beach is surprisingly clean, despite its popularity.

Playa Linda, meaning "beautiful beach," is true to its name. It's located about 16km (10 miles) north of the central Ixtapa area, and is the main spot for catching ferries to outlying areas. It's the best spot for watersport activities in Ixtapa; perhaps that's why some consider it their favorite beach in the area.

Club Med and Qualton Club have largely claimed **Playa La Quieta,** on the mainland across from Isla Ixtapa. **Playa las Cuatas,** a pretty beach and cove a few miles north of Ixtapa, and **Playa Majahua,** an isolated beach just west of Zihuatanejo, are both being transformed into resort complexes, too.

Zihuatanejo has some of the most beautiful beaches in the area. **Playa Municipal,** the town beach, is not one of them, but it is still nice to walk up and down the **Paseo del Pescador** and watch the fishermen come back here at the end of the day. **Playa Madera** (Wood Beach) just east of Playa Municipal, is open to the surf but generally peaceful. There is no real reason you would need to or want to visit this one but I won't stop you if you're curious.

In Zihuatanejo, across the bay from Playa la Ropa, **Playa Las Gatas** is a gorgeous, Caribbean-like beach. It's accessible by a ferry ($30 round-trip) leaving from the pier on Playa Municipal every 10 minutes from 9am to 5pm. Las Gatas is great for watersports like snorkeling and scuba diving (tons of operators are on the beach and will approach you about arranging outings). The transparent water is calm and gorgeous, which means it's also great for swimming. There are plenty of restaurants to choose from, too, if you work up an appetite after working out. Small pangas run to Las Gatas from the Zihua town pier, a 10-minute trip. The captains will take you across whenever you wish between 8am and 4pm. Usually the last boat back leaves Las Gatas at 6:30pm.

My favorite beach in Zihua, though, is **Playa La Ropa** ★ and I'm not alone in thinking this: The scene can get very crowded on Sundays when locals flock here. Some of the area's nicest hotels, including La Casa Que Canta (p. 564), are located on or a short walk from this beach. Plus, the swimming is great—the waves are usually gentle, and the sand soft. The beach is even lined with excellent restaurants like La Perla (p. 565), so you won't go hungry.

The best beach for horseback riding is **Playa Larga,** between Zihua and the airport, because its long stretch of beach is less developed than some of the other ones in the area. Plus, there is a lot more natural vegetation here and great scenery.

Sightseeing

Festivals & Events

Zihuatanejo and Ixtapa mostly host fishing tournaments and fishing-related festivals, but once in a while something different pops up.

The **"Zihuatanejo On the Fly" Annual All-Release Fly Fishing Sailfish Tournament** is one of the popular fishing tournaments in the area. Zihuatanejo is famous for its fishing, so fishermen from around the world come to show off their skills. www.bajafly.com/Zihuatanejo.htm. Mid to late January.

The Zihuatanejo International Guitar Festival is one of the most popular in Zihuatanejo, and is a perfect way to enjoy the town's laid-back atmosphere. Talented musicians from around the world play at a number of venues throughout town, including local bars/restaurants. Reservations are a must for dinner shows and can be made online or purchased at Rick's Bar, Coconut's, or Sanka Grill. Ticket prices range from $75 to $150, depending on the venue. Visit www.zihuafest.info for more information. Early March.

Major Attractions

There isn't much "sightseeing" in Ixtapa or Zihuatanejo. Your best bet is to just wander through the Centro area of Zihuatanejo and see the town. The beach resorts are the main attraction in Ixtapa, though there's some outdoor-mall-type shopping in town (see "Shopping," below).

The only true museum in Zihua is the **Museo de Arqueología de la Costa Grande,** Paseo del Pescador 7 (no phone; Tues–Sun 9am–6pm), which is located right next to Playa Municipal. The tiny museum is worth a quick visit for anyone who is curious about the history of the region. It traces the history of the region known as La Costa Grande, which includes the area between Acapulco and Ixtapa/Zihuatanejo, from pre-Hispanic times through the colonial era and has a small but interesting collection of pottery and stone artifacts. It's also dirt cheap, costing just $5 for students and $10 for non-students.

There are also several galleries worth visiting in the area by Paseo del Pescador. My favorite gallery is **Galería Casa del Arte,** Cuauhtémoc 19 Centro, Zihuatanejo (☎ **755/544-6064;** www.galeriacasadelarte.com). It has original paintings by Mexican artists, as well as sculpture. The wide-ranging art (good news: it's on sale) is as beautiful as the owners and employees who work this place.

Playing Outside

You'll find plenty of outdoor activities to keep you busy in Ixtapa and Zihua. In addition to the listings below, **sunset cruises, sailboats, windsurfing,** and **kayaking** are all popular activities here. Some activities can be arranged directly on each beach. **Jet-skiing** costs about $350 for 20 minutes, a 15-minute **banana boat** ride costs around $150, and a **parasailing** ride costs around $200.

The sunsets can be absolutely stunning here, so taking a sunset catamaran ride is definitely worth it. **Picante Cruises** (☎ **755/554-2694;** picante@picante cruises.com) offers a number of cruises at all hours of the day. Sign up at one of the stands on **Playa La Ropa, Playa Las Gatas,** or **Isla Ixtapa.**

One adventure tour company to try is **Adventours** (☎ **755/101-8556;** www.ixtapa-adventours.com/index.html), which does a guided bike tour of Ixtapa Island, a kayak and snorkel tour of Playa Las Gatas, and a bird- and crocodile-watching tour of Aztlán Ecological Park. All tours last around 4 hours and cost between $560 and $760 per person.

BICYCLING A bicycle path starts at the **Marina Ixtapa** and runs along the golf club for 4.3km (2¾ miles). It then continues to **Playa Linda** and runs along **Aztlán Park** for 3.9km (2½ miles). Another path, also 4.3km (2¾ miles) long, connects the tourist parts of Ixtapa and Zihuatanejo. See the "Getting Around: By Bicycle" section on p. 556 for information on how and where to rent mountain bikes for this trip. ***FYI:*** Security officers patrol the bike paths here, so don't be alarmed if you see men with machine guns along the way.

BIRD-WATCHING Tons of local travel agencies (including Adventours, above) offer organized bird-watching trips. The cheapest option you'll be offered involves going out via boat to Playa Linda (see "Boat & Snorkel Tours" below for info) and having a guide take you around **Los Morros,** a cluster of small islands by **Playa Palmar** in Ixtapa.

BOAT & SNORKEL/SCUBA TOURS

Boat tours are the easiest, fastest way to get to the best snorkeling and scuba diving in the area. I recommend taking a trip to **Isla Ixtapa,** where they have some great beaches for swimming and snorkeling, as well as parasailing. Book a trip through local travel agencies, or go on your own by catching a boat from **Playa Linda.** Boats leave for Isla Ixtapa (where the Club Med is) every 10 minutes between 9am and 5pm (a round-trip costs a whopping $30). (Before hopping on the boat, take a little stroll by the river to see crocodiles and iguanas of all different sizes in the **Popoyote Estuary**.) Once on the beach, there are plenty of places to rent snorkel gear. Just make sure to get out of those flippers on time to catch the last ferry at 5pm (subject to change; check the ticket window).

Otherwise, most of the area beaches offer local scuba and snorkel trips on the spot, including gear. On **Playa Las Gatas,** I recommend exploring the coral reefs through **Carlo Scuba,** PADI dive center, Playa Las Gatas Zihuatanejo (☎ **755/554-6003;** www.carloscuba.com), which is midway down the beach in a little open hut. It costs about $500 for a one-tank dive and $800 for two dives (price includes lunch and equipment). Or try **Ixtapa Aqua Paradise,** Shopping Center Los Patios, Local 137 in front of Fontan Hotel (☎ **755/553-1510;** info@ixtapaaquaparadise.com;

PADI certified), which operates half-day scuba tours and certification classes for both experienced and inexperienced divers. Prices range from $230 to $800 depending on experience level and time (some courses last up to 4 days).

FISHING Zihuatanejo is famous for its fishing (see the Fly Fishing Sailfish Tournament, above), so there are plenty of ways to get behind a fishing rod and give it a shot. Just beware that, while fish is cheap to eat in Zihua, it can be paradoxically pricey to catch. The best way to organize a fishing excursion is to arrange for one with the **Zihuatanejo Boat Cooperative** (☎ **755/554-2056**), which is located right next to the pier on Playa Municipal. Trips cost between $1,300 and $3,000 depending on how long the trip is, how big the boat is, and how many people are going. **Mar y Tierra Ixtapa** (☎ **755/553-7141;** ed_kunze@zihuatanejo.net) does a number of different fishing excursions, ranging in price from $3,750 to $4,900. You can also contact the **Zihuatanejo Tourism Office** (p. 557) or travel agency through your hotel to learn more about day or half-day fishing excursions.

GOLF There are some beautiful golf courses in the area. Try the **Club de Golf Ixtapa Palma Real** (Apartado Postal 105, Blvd. Ixtapa s/n; ☎ **755/553-1062**) in front of the Sheraton Hotel. It is an 18-hole course and slightly cheaper than some of the other courses. The greens fee is around $750 (price varies according to season) with tee-time beginning at 7am. Players get to drive and putt among very pretty coconut plantations and natural lagoons.

HORSEBACK RIDING This is a must in this area. Beaches like **Playa Linda** offer rides, but I was most happy with my ride with **Rancho El Palmar** (☎ **755/558-2138,** 113-9803, or 556-2795). They offer an hour-long jaunt along **Playa Larga** (see p. 574) with barely any other tourists in sight. The ride, including pick up and drop off at your hotel, costs about $300.

SURFING The closest surfing spot is **Playa Las Gatas** (p. 573) but for the best surfing, head to **Playa Petalco** about an hour and a half away by car, or to **Troncones,** which you can read more about in the "Road Trip" section. Contact **Catcha L'Ola** (Centro Comercial Kiosko L. 12, Ixtapa; ☎ **755/553-1384;** www.ixtapasurf.com) for lessons and rentals.

Shopping

Scattered around Zihuatanejo and Ixtapa are plenty of souvenir shops that all sell the same T-shirts, bags, and crafts. But there are also a number of small jewelry stores, small clothing boutiques, and some leather shops. To find something unique, all you need to do is wander up the streets off Calle 5 de Mayo, away from the Artisan Market.

The commercial center in Ixtapa has many shops that sell expensive bathing suits and beach accessories. Then there is the **Artisan's Market** along Calle 5 de Mayo, which has a very colorful assortment of trinkets, jewelry, T-shirts, hats, bags, and some actual handmade crafts.

Another market worth checking out is the **municipal market** on Avenida Benito Juarez. Many locals do their shopping here, where bags of fresh herbs and chile peppers are sold alongside cheap sandals and fresh fish.

On the opposite side of the street from the artisan's market are some very nice stores with good quality sculptures,

Barra de Potosí: An Escape from Paradise

Nestled in the southern end of Playa Larga, about 20 to 30 minutes south of the Ixtapa-Zihuatanejo airport and 45 minutes from Zihuatanejo Centro, is **Barra de Potosi.** This small beachside village lies on a sanctuary lagoon framed by palm trees, sand bars, and gentle blue-green water. People come here to get away from it all and swing peacefully in hammocks, with no noisy chatter or traffic (or even crashing waves) to interrupt each moment. Though there's horseback riding, kayaking, and bird-watching opportunities on offer, for most visitors, the most strenuous thing they'll do during a stay here is just getting out of the hammock to eat. It's worth the effort, as Barra de Potosí has some excellent seafood palapa restaurants, run by families that catch their own fish and practically cook it right in the open. Try **Enramada Elva** (☎ **755/544-9081**), **Enramada Las Brisas,** or **Enramada Nayito.**

For those who plan on staying awhile, there are a few small, modest hotels like **Playa Calli** (Playa Blanca, Barra de Potosí ☎ **755/556-6333;** www.berniesbedandbreakfast.com), where doubles run for about $900 to $1,200, or **Villa Don Manuel** (Playa Blanca, Barra de Potosí; ☎ **755/559-7612;** www.zihuatanejo.com.mx/villadonmanuel), where doubles cost about $800 to $1,000 per night, including breakfast.

Getting here requires a somewhat twisty ride through coconut plantations where wild horses snack beside the road, but it's worth it. I recommend taking a taxi, since there is no real public transportation and the last leg of the trip is unmarked and full of crater-size potholes that could turn a trip to paradise into a nightmare. Taxis should cost around $200 to $350, depending on one's negotiating skills. For more information on Barra de Potosi, check out www.barrapotosi.com or contact the State of Guerrero Tourism Office (p. 557).

paintings, dishes, and crafts. Try **Arte Mexicano Nopal,** Av. 5 de Mayo 56, Zihuatanejo Centro (☎ **755/554-7530**), for some interesting sculptures and wooden crafts. For painted pots, vases, bowls, clocks, and the like, **Rosimar,** Calle Cuautémoc, corner of Ejido (☎ **755/554-2864;** artesaniasrosimar_ixtapazih@hotmail.com), has hand-painted pieces overflowing out of every nook and cranny. Ask to see the rooms in the back where they have antique-looking pieces that are slightly more unique and beautiful. **Lupita's Boutique** on the corner of Calle Vicente Guerrero and Calle Juan N. Álvarez 16 (☎ **755/554-2238;** lupita@zihuatanejo.net), has elegant Mexican attire with hand embroidered cotton and satin from around Guerrero, along with handmade accessories. Lupita does alterations and international shipments, but it'll cost a pretty penny.

For jewelry, I like **Pancho's,** Cuauhtémoc 15, Zihuatanejo Centro (☎ **755/554-5230**), where you can find a nice selection of silver from Taxco. Along Calle Cuauhtemoc are a number of worthwhile, tiny jewelry shops, including **Alberto's,** Cuauhtémoc 12 at Calle Nicolas Bravo (☎ **755/554-2162**), or **Platería Benito** (no phone; Cuauhtémoc 6). The jewelry doesn't vary drastically, so it's worth taking a stroll through each shop, comparing items and prices before deciding what to buy.

Road Trip: Troncones

Hunkering down in Ixtapa and Zihuatanejo not only gives you two resort towns to play in, you'll have several great nearby road trip destinations—including **Acapulco** (see Chapter 11), less than 3 hours away. Even closer is the still-not completely-discovered surfer's town of **Troncones,** only an hour away.

Getting There & Getting Around

There are a couple of ways to get to Troncones from Zihuatanejo. One way is by taxi, but this will probably cost about $250 to $500 (depending on where you leave from). **Taxi Express** (☎ **755/553-2868**) is one company that makes trips out to Troncones. The much cheaper option is taking a collective bus from one of the many pick-up points offered by **ETASA** (☎ **755/553-6313** or 553-7030; www.costagrande.net/etasa/en), which costs about $100 per person.

If you're driving, take Highway 200 going north towards Lazaro/Cardenas. At the turnoff for Troncones, go left and continue down the road to the beach. At the intersection with the frontage road, you can go left or right, but most of the hotels are on the right.

Note that if you rent a car, you'll have to navigate through a series of potholes the size of swimming pools off the main roads. And if you get stuck with a flat tire or a rental car buried in mud, be forewarned that there is very little help available. It is probably safest to travel by taxi (or the cheaper bus option).

Once in town, rent a bicycle to go up and down the long, pot-holed dirt road that connects the highway to every hotel on the beach (you can ask your hotel about bike rentals). If you plan on renting a car, get a four-wheeler and make sure your hotel has parking available. But really the best way to explore small Troncones is to just walk around (preferably with a surfboard, if you want to fit in).

Sleeping

There are a number of hotel options in the area. For those who want to be right on the best section of beach, stay at **The Inn Manzanillo Bay** (close to the beach, marked by signs once off Hwy. 200; ☎ **755/553-2884;** www.manzanillobay.com), a very attractive little hotel with small but pleasant rooms that surround a small pool. People come from all the hotels in Troncones for a meal here since the chef is a graduate from the California Culinary Institute. Room rates range from $1,080 to $1,500, depending on which room, how many people, and time of year. The hotel offers plenty of surf lessons and other water sport activities. It is surprisingly luxurious for what it costs.

Another option is **Mi Casa Es Su Casa** (☎ **755/553-2910;** www.micasasucasa.ws or www.troncones.com.mx/micasasucasa), which is more central to the main beach area and costs about $1,026 for up to two people or $1,520 for up to four people.

Eating

El Burro Borracho (on the beach; ☎ **755/553-2834;** daily 11:30am–10pm) is a great place to take a break from all the surfing you'll be doing and grab a bite to eat right on the beach. It's one of the most popular joints in town—the food is decent and a bit overpriced, but the atmosphere is just right. Plan to meet a lot of fellow surfers here at night.

Playing Outside

The beautiful thing about Troncones is that there isn't much to do besides eat, surf, and sleep. For a true surfer, that is enough. If you don't think that simplicity is beautiful, then you don't belong. Most of the frequent visitors are surfers who would rather keep the place unknown. Unfortunately for them, Troncones is beginning to get some of the attention it deserves—though the virgin sand of **Manzanillo Bay** remains untouched by the developers who had their way with Ixtapa.

There are a number of ways to get your surf on in Troncones. The most popular stop for both beginners and advanced surfers is the **Inn at Manzanillo Bay** (☎ **755/553-2884,** fax 755/553-2883; www.manzanillo bay.com). They have their very own (albeit tiny) surf shop, with boards for $220 per day and surf lessons for $500 per session, which includes transportation to the best surf spots and access to the great left break in the water that advanced surfers love. The best way to top off a day of surfing is with an excellent meal and a cold drink back at the Inn.

For those seeking thrills from more than a surfboard, consider **Costa Nativa Eco-Tours** (☎ **755/556-3616;** costanativa@ hotmail.com), which will take you hiking, mountain biking, cave exploring, or kayaking—hardcore types can do all on the same day. This company was started by Alejandro, a local surfer, who will also show you jungles and banks that are completely littered with trash; it's a unique opportunity to see both the beauty and the reality of Troncones—and to help clean up. This is a fun and fulfilling day.

Another option: Hop into a kayak on Barra de Potosí through **Zoe Kayak Tours** (☎ **755/553-0496;** www.zoekayaktours. com) for a peaceful and scenic paddle through the saltwater lagoon. The tour is approximately 6 miles long (4 hrs.) on flat water that will have you paddling through mangrove channels, tunnels, and back bays. Kayak tours hit the water at 9am, with four routes available for $800 (traveler's checks are okay, but no credit cards). An optional lunch is available for an extra charge. Make reservations at least 24 hours in advance.

Costa Chica

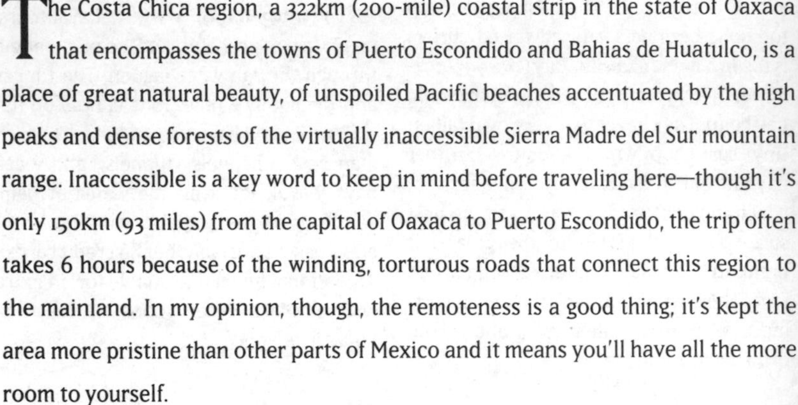

The Costa Chica region, a 322km (200-mile) coastal strip in the state of Oaxaca that encompasses the towns of Puerto Escondido and Bahias de Huatulco, is a place of great natural beauty, of unspoiled Pacific beaches accentuated by the high peaks and dense forests of the virtually inaccessible Sierra Madre del Sur mountain range. Inaccessible is a key word to keep in mind before traveling here—though it's only 150km (93 miles) from the capital of Oaxaca to Puerto Escondido, the trip often takes 6 hours because of the winding, torturous roads that connect this region to the mainland. In my opinion, though, the remoteness is a good thing; it's kept the area more pristine than other parts of Mexico and it means you'll have all the more room to yourself.

Puerto Escondido is a good option if you want hip nightlife, awesome hotel and dining values, and some of the best coffee shops in Mexico. Huatulco has the same unspoiled nature and laid-back attitude as Puerto Escondido, but with a difference—in the midst of all the natural splendor, you'll also encounter more upscale hotels and modern roads and facilities. You can really base yourself at either beach town, though—just be sure to get out and explore the outdoor options in the area. From the beaches in between the two towns, including the unofficial nude beach at Zipolite, to the turtle sanctuaries surrounding Puerto Angel, plenty of road trip options await you along this small, but beautiful, coast.

Best of Costa Chica

- **Best Value Hotel:** Run by bodybuilder Sam Castillon and his wife Sherry, the **Misión de los Arcos** is the best value in Huatulco because you'll get the sort of style and amenities appropriate to a five-star hotel for much better prices. Naturally, there's a great on-site gym, but more surprising is the excellent attached restaurant (with the best breakfast in town) and Internet cafe with Wi-Fi service. See p. 586.
- **Best Splurge Hotel:** Boasting a fabulous location on a cliff overlooking the sea, the stunning Moorish-designed **Quinta Real** in Huatulco commands exceptional views, especially from the balconies of the higher rooms. The view's not bad in the upstairs Skybar, either, where you can gape at all the Mexican bombshells and hot guys. See p. 589.
- **Best Place to Eat Crawfish and Watch the Sunset:** Head out to **Copalita Beach** in Huatulco to try the cook's wonderful recipes for *chacales* (crawfish), *frijoles de la olla* (soupy beans), or grilled fish. Since the beach faces west, it's one of the best places in Huatulco to watch the sunset, so try to time your visit for the late afternoon. See p. 593.
- **Best Place to Eat Grasshoppers:** The menu at Huatulco's funky French fusion restaurant **L'echalote** includes food from all over the world, from Vietnamese egg rolls to French soufflé, made by some very adept Franco-Swiss and Laotian owners. But the only must try is the fried grasshopper burrito. It's crunchy but, strangely, *good.* See p. 591.
- **Best Beachy Bar: La Crema,** a loungey bar with signature big drippy candles, bamboo-covered walls, outside seating, and a hip alternative play list, manages to be both comfortable and cool. Live music in high season and 375 kinds of booze up the ante, making it the best spot to imbibe in Huatulco. See p. 591.
- **Best Snorkeling at a Remote Bay.** The beach at Bahia de **San Agustín** is a 20-minute drive down a rutted dirt road from Huatulco, but it's well worth the trip. A village of about 100 live here in rustic palapas and someone will happily rent you snorkeling gear or boogie boards while they cook your lunch. The water is crystal clear and the snorkeling superb—it's literally swimming with tons of tropical fish. See p. 592.
- **Best Hostel for Not Sleeping:** With its mixed dorm rooms and backpackers from all over the world playing pool, watching the World Cup, sharing stories, and just hanging out, Puerto Escondido's **Hotel Mayflower** is great for socializing, but not for sleeping. But who cares when you can always take a nap on the beach right nearby? See p. 600.
- **Best Place to Watch Surfing:** At **La Flayita Beach Bar** in Puerto Escondido you can sprawl in a bean bag chair and share a hookah of fruity tobacco with new friends, while sipping smoothies or something harder. The ex-Chilango proprietors have installed groovy canvas rocking lounges under palapas on the beach as well, and even offer a hose to wash off the sand and salt as well as changing rooms—*que raro!* See p. 607.
- **Best Break for Newbie Surfers: La Punta** has some of the same characteristics as Puerto Escondido's main beach **Zicatela,** but because the waves are usually smaller, you can avoid a harsher rip. Since the waves tend to be a bit slower, Punta's great for bodyboarding, too. See p. 612.

- **Best Classy Restaurant:** In Puerto Escondido, **Hotel Santa Fe**'s delicious vegetarian dinners include a baked and batter-less chile relleno with a sauce to die for. They also offer a perfectly cooked whole *huachinango* (red snapper) and homemade pasta. See p. 606.

- **Best Breakfast:** I once drove the 2 hours from Huatulco just to stock up on the Danish pastries at **El Cafecito Cafe** on Zicatela Beach. Although this spot now offers cinnamon rolls and other breakfast goodies, the custardy *danesa* is still my fave. See p. 606.

Huatulco

Huatulco is made up of nine bays, with 36 beaches strung along 35km (22 miles) of coastline. Three-quarters of the region's 21 hectares (52 acres) have been earmarked for regeneration and preservation by FONATUR, Mexico's Tourism Development arm. Undeveloped stretches of pure white sand and isolated coves await the promised growth of Huatulco, but it's not catching on as rapidly as Cancún, the previous resort planned by FONATUR. At the moment, there really isn't a *town* of Huatulco, only a sprawling resort area which actually consists of three sections: Santa Cruz, Crucecita, and Tangolunda Bay (see "Orientation" below).

About 30 years ago, Huatulco used to be the first stop on a Hippie Trail that included the southern Pacific Coast's beaches, the coffee plantations/magic mushroom towns inland to the east, and Chiapas state to the south. That is now history. Most of the bays themselves remain pristine, as does the inland jungle, but the hippie vibe is gone. Where once one fishing operation existed per beach, there are now wall-to-wall palapas selling "stuffed pineapple" for $120 a pop.

On the upside, if you can afford to stay here (or score a decent package deal), you can stay in complete luxury—the hotels boast magnificent views, first-class amenities, and top-notch service. The luxury hotels tend to attract wealthier tourists, so there is a greater discrepancy between rich and poor than in Puerto Escondido—yet you won't feel closed off from locals like you may in a mega resort town like Cancún. Maybe it's the lack of day-trippers, or maybe it's the genuine friendliness of the locals, but there is a great sense of community here, even though there's no real town center.

Although there is plenty of partying here during high season and during events like Semana Santa, the typical tourist seems much more interested in eco-tourism and nature than in pounding back tequila. There are great opportunities not only for surfing, swimming, or just relaxing on the beach, but also for white-water rafting, kayaking, horse-back riding, hiking, rock climbing, mountain biking, and tree-top canopy touring. Then there's the 20,000-hectare (49,400-acre) "eco-archaeological" park, El Botazoo, at Punta Celeste (p. 594), home to great hiking (best seen on a guided tour).

Getting into Town

BY PLANE **Mexicana** (☎ **800/531-7921** in the U.S., or 958/581-9007 in Mexico) connects Huatulco directly with Chicago, Denver, and Houston, as well as Manchester, England. Flights from Los Angeles, Miami, San Antonio, San Francisco, San Jose, and Toronto connect by way of Mexico City.

If you're traveling to Huatulco from elsewhere in Mexico, you'll find cheap

Green Huatulco

Huatulco is the first community in the Americas to get Certified Status under the international **Green Globe Community Destination Standard** (www.greenglobe.org). That makes the community a world leader in sustainable community development. The Huatulco Wildlife and Marine Park was declared a National Protected Area in 1998. Initiatives of their local Green Team include community waste management and recycling campaigns, as well as Green Globe sustainable tourism seminars for students, tour guides, and locals. Huatulco also tries to promote local culture through events such as cuisine and dance festivals, sea turtle ceremonies, and programs to encourage nearby indigenous communities to sell their handicrafts. Kids are educated not to litter and there are even big recycle bins in front of some of the luxury hotels. The city is so clean (especially in contrast to many other areas of Mexico), that you'll never see an abandoned plastic bag or bottle anywhere.

fares on Mexicana's budget airline **Click** (☎ **958/587-0223;** www.clickmx.com).

From Huatulco's international airport (airport code: HUX; ☎ **958/581-9004**), about 20km (12 miles) northwest of the Bahías de Huatulco, private **taxis** charge $400 to Crucecita, $420 to Santa Cruz, and $480 to Tangolunda. **Transportes Terrestres** (☎ **958/581-9014**) colectivos fares are $80 to $100 per person. When returning, make sure to ask for a taxi, unless you have a lot of luggage. Taxis to the airport run $400, but unless specifically requested, you'll get a Suburban, which costs $540.

BY CAR Because Huatulco is so spread out, you may want to consider renting a car in order to fully explore the area. **Hertz** (☎ **958/581-9092**) and **Thrifty** (☎ **958/587-0010**) both have offices at the airport. Call in advance to be sure someone is at either agency when your flight arrives. **Budget** has an office in town (Calle Ocotillo 404, at Jazmín, La Crucecita; ☎ **958/587-0010**), as well as in Puerto Escondido—it may be possible to arrange a drop-off there (or vice versa).

Coastal Highway 200 leads to Huatulco (via Pochutla) from the north and is generally in good condition. The drive from Puerto Escondido takes just under 2 hours. The road is well maintained, but it doesn't have lights and does have giant topes and many curves, so do *not* drive it after sunset. Allow at least 6 hours for the trip from Oaxaca City, along mountainous Highway 175.

BY BUS There are three bus stations in Crucecita, all within a few blocks, but none in Santa Cruz or Tangolunda. The **Gacela** and **Estrella Blanca** station, at the corner of Gardenia and Palma Real, handles service to Acapulco, Mexico City, Puerto Escondido, and Pochutla. The **Cristóbal Colón** station (☎ **958/587-0261**) is at the corner of Gardenia and Ocotillo, 4 blocks from the Plaza Principal. It serves destinations throughout Mexico, including Oaxaca, Puerto Escondido, and Pochutla. The **Estrella del Valle** station, on Jasmin between Sabali and Carrizal, serves Oaxaca. See "Basics," p. 10, for bus company info.

BY BOAT A cruise-ship dock in nearby Santa Cruz Bay opened in 2005. Only time will tell if this will be a blessing or a curse. The new dock handles up to two 3,000-passenger cruise ships at a time.

Getting Around

It's too far to walk between La Crucecita, Santa Cruz, and Tangolunda, but **taxis** are inexpensive and easy to find. Taxi stands are available in La Crucecita opposite the Hotel Grifer and on the Plaza Principal. Taxis can also be found at the Darsena or cruising the streets in Santa Cruz, along the Calle Monte Alban (at Infonavit) in Chahué, and in front of the Hotel Barceló and Hotel Crown Pacific in Tangolunda. The fare between Santa Cruz and Tangolunda is about $25; between Santa Cruz and Crucecita, $20; between Crucecita and Tangolunda, $30.

You can hire a **water taxi** (panga) for around $500 per day at the marina in Santa Cruz to take you to some of the more inaccessible bays. And there is **colectivo** service between towns for $50.

There is **minibus service** between towns; the fare is $5. In Santa Cruz, catch the bus across the street from Castillo Huatulco; in Tangolunda, in front of the Grand Pacific; and in La Crucecita, kitty-corner to the Hotel Grifer.

Basics

ORIENTATION

The overall resort area is called **Bahías de Huatulco** and includes nine bays. The town of **Santa María de Huatulco,** the original settlement in this area, is 27km (17 miles) inland. **Santa Cruz Huatulco,** usually called Santa Cruz, was the first developed area on the coast. It has a central plaza with a bandstand kiosk, which has been converted into a cafe that serves regionally grown coffee. It also has an artisans' market on the edge of the plaza that borders the main road, a few hotels and restaurants, and a marina where bay tours and fishing trips set sail. **Juárez** is Santa Cruz's 4-block-long main street, anchored at one end by the Hotel Castillo Huatulco and at the other by the Meigas Binniguenda hotel. Opposite the Hotel Castillo is the marina, and beyond it are restaurants in new colonial-style buildings facing the beach. The area's banks are on Juárez. It's impossible to get lost and you can take in almost everything at a glance. This bay is the site of Huatulco's new cruise-ship dock.

About 3km (2 miles) inland from Santa Cruz is **Crucecita,** a planned city that sprang up in 1985. It centers on a lovely grassy plaza. This is the residential area for the resorts, with neighborhoods of new stucco homes mixed with small apartment complexes. Crucecita has evolved into a lovely, traditional town where you'll find the area's best, and most reasonably priced, restaurants, plus some shopping and several less expensive hotels.

Until other bays are developed, **Tangolunda Bay,** 5km (3 miles) east, is the focal point of development. Over time, half the bays will have resorts. For now, Tangolunda has an 18-hole golf course, as well as the Las Brisas, Quinta Real, Barceló Huatulco, Royal, Casa del Mar, and Camino Real Zaashila hotels, among others. Small strip centers with a few restaurants occupy each end of Tangolunda Bay. **Chahué Bay,** between Tangolunda and Santa Cruz, is a small bay with a beach club, and other facilities under construction along with houses and a few small hotels.

VISITOR INFORMATION

The **State Tourism Office,** or Oficina del Turismo (Bulevar Benito Juárez s/n; ☎ **958/581-0176;** www.baysofhuatulco.com.mx), has an information module in Tangolunda Bay, near the Grand Pacific hotel. It's open Monday to Friday from 8am to 5pm.

RECOMMENDED WEBSITES

- **www.tomzap.com**: For information about local events, traveler's hotel and restaurant reviews, and lots of useful links, head to this site.
- **www.costachica.net/zipolite/english/index.html**: A great site to hit up before exploring Puerto Angel and its nearby communities.

Huatulco Nuts & Bolts

Banks **HSBC** (☎ **958/587-0884**) is at Bugambilia 1504 in La Crucecita. **Bancomer, Bancrear,** and **Banco Bital** are along Bulevar Santa Cruz in Santa Cruz and all will change money during business hours. Although hours vary, most banks are open Monday through Friday from 9am to 4pm, with shorter hours on Saturday.

Emergencies For local **police,** call ☎ **958/587-0675;** for transit police call ☎ **958/587-0192;** and for Red Cross, call ☎ **958/587-1188** or 587-1548. For medical emergencies, **Dr. Javier Velasco** (☎ **958/587-0246** or 044/958-587-6230) speaks English and doesn't overcharge. **CMH Hospital** (☎ **958/587-0104**) is at Av. Flamboyan 205.

Internet/Wireless Hot Spots There are several Internet cafes in La Crucecita, including the **Café Misión de los Arcos** (Av. Gardenia 902; ☎ **958/587-0165**), which is also a free Wi-Fi hot spot. Another Café Misión is on the ground-floor level of the Hotel Plaza Conejo (Av. Guamúchil 208, across from the main plaza; ☎ **958/587-0054,** -0009). You can go online as well as make long distance or local calls, receive and send faxes, and get your messages at **El Telefonito** (Bugambilia 501; ☎ **958/587-1796;** and at Carrizal corner of Chacat; ☎ **958/587-1684**). There are Wi-Fi hot spots at the airport as well as at many hotels (some are free only if you are staying there). Why not drop by the beautiful Quinta Real (see "Sleeping" below) for a drink, bring your laptop, and log on for free?

Laundry **Centro de Lavado Express** (Bugambilia 402, La Crucecita; ☎ **958/587-2737**) has a $65 minimum to do your laundry in 1 day, so take in a few kilos to get your money's worth. It's open Monday to Saturday 10am to 6pm.

Libraries & Bookstores Your best bet for English books and magazines is the **Café Misión de los Arcos** (Av. Gardenia 902; ☎ **958/587-0165**), which also has a good book exchange system. It's open daily 8am to 11pm. Also try **Coconuts** (see "Shopping," below).

Pharmacies **Farmacia del Carmen,** just off the central plaza in La Crucecita (☎ **958/587-0878**), is one of the largest drugstores in town. If it doesn't have what you need, someone on staff will order it. **Farmacia La Clínica** (☎ **958/587-0591**) at Sabalí 1602, La Crucecita, offers 24-hour service and delivery.

Post Offices The correo, at Bulevar Chahué 100, Sector R, Crucecita (☎ **958/587-0551**), is open Monday through Friday from 8am to 3pm, Saturday from 9am to 1pm.

Safety Huatulco is much safer than the streets (or beaches) of big towns like L.A. or Miami, but you should still take common sense safety precautions: Don't walk in unlit areas of the beach at night with valuables; don't leave valuables on the beach; and don't pull out big wads of cash when shopping.

Telephone Tips The telephone area code is **958.**

Sleeping

While there are some good doable choices in Huatulco, it's hard to find a really cheap place here that is decent. There are no hostels, and the closest hammock to rent is at Playa San Augustin, 45 minutes north on the Carretera and another 45-minute drive down a dirt track to the beach. That said, there are more economical and smaller hotels in the soon-to-be-developed Bahía de Chahué area, close to the Bahía de Santa Cruz neighborhood, and you can find traditional Mexican block-style and cheap rooms in La Crucecita.

If you spring for a splurge hotel anyplace in Mexico, this is a good place to do so; Huatulco excels at expensive accommodations. There are about a dozen four- and five-star hotels in the "Zona Hoteleria" of Bahía de Tangolunda. Most offer package deals, so ask around before booking.

CHEAP

→ **Hotel Bahía Huatulco** This small, clean hotel next to Oceano (see "Shopping" below) has views of the ocean from the second- and third-floor rooms, and has a beautiful if small rooftop terrace, also with great views. There's a pool, though it's such a short walk to the ocean, why opt for chlorine? In addition, it's right across from Papaya (see "Partying" below)—that means you won't have to stumble far to return back to your room after an evening of excess. *Bulevar Benito Juárez, Lote 7, Chahué. ☎/fax 958/587-1464. www.hotelBahiahuatulco.com. $450 single, $550 double, $700 suite. MC, V. Amenities: Breakfast room; laundry; pool; safe box; travel info; wheelchair accessible; Wi-Fi. In room: A/C, cable TV.*

MTV Best → **Misión de los Arcos** ★★★ This hotel is the best value you're going to find in La Crucecita. Its whitewashed stuccoed structure is in the style of some of the five-star hotels down the road and features fountains in a central garden, French windows, and earth-colored tiles on the floors. There's no pool, but you can use the Castillo Beach Club at Chahué Bay, open daily from 9am to 7pm. The affable owners Sam and Sherry Castillon live on-site, and know just about everything you may want or need in Huatulco. Sam is a bodybuilder so there's an on-site gym with great beach equipment on hand—free for guests. The hotel is kitty-corner to La Crucecita's central plaza, so it's very convenient to shops, bars, and restaurants. However, the attached restaurant Terra-Cotta (see "Eating" below) is worth a visit—it's popular with locals from businessmen to surfers. *Gardenia 902, at Tamarindo, La Crucecita. ☎ 958/587-0165. Fax 958/587-1904. www.misiondelosarcos.com. $400–$650 single, $350–$700 double, $750–$950 suite. Higher rates at Christmas and Easter. AE, MC, V. Amenities: Restaurant; full gym; laundry service; shuttle to beach club; travel desk; Wi-Fi. In room: A/C, cable TV, hair dryer, safe.*

→ **Posada Primavera** This six-room hotel, just a few blocks north of the main plaza, has clean, simply furnished rooms. The upstairs rooms have higher ceilings with windows looking out onto the neighborhood. I'll admit you won't get anything fancy here, but you also can't beat the

Huatulco

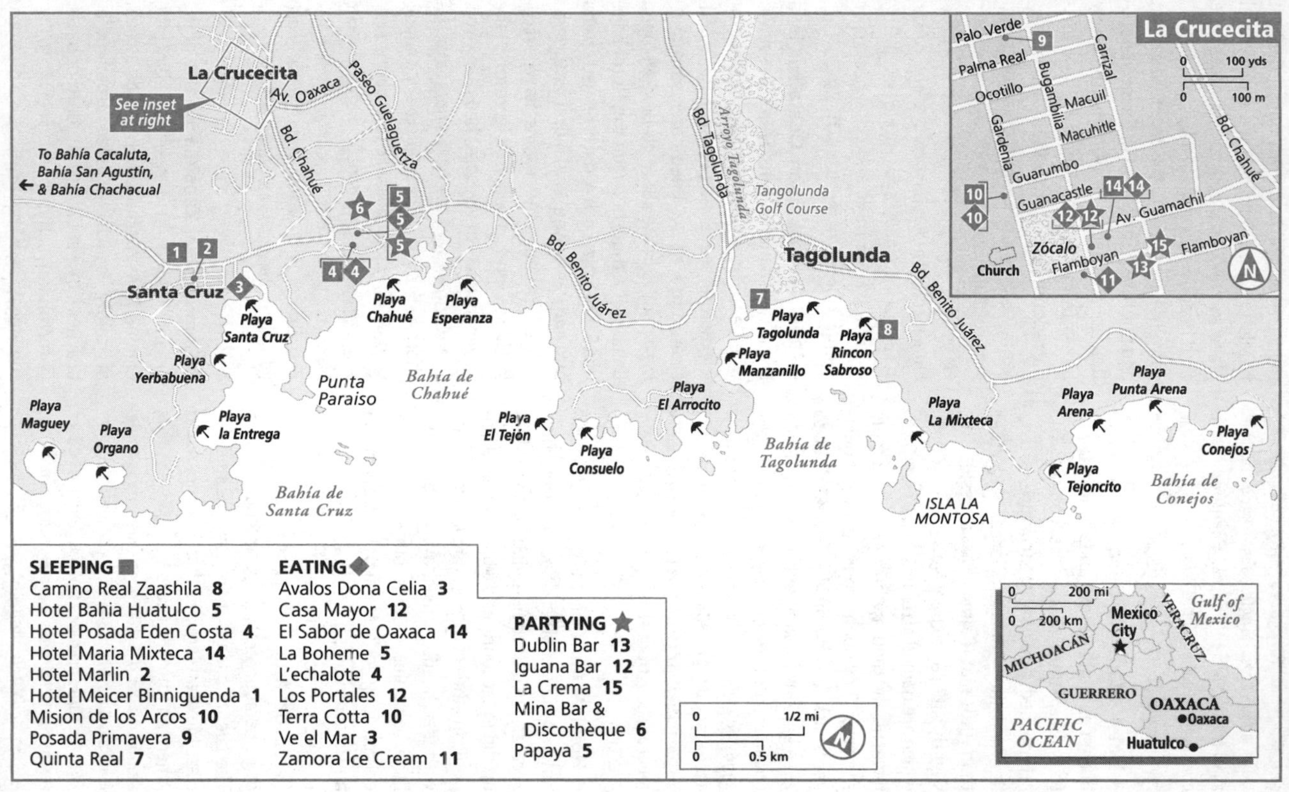
La Crucecita
See inset at right
Av. Oaxaca
Paseo Guelaguetza
Bd. Chahué
To Bahía Cacaluta, Bahía San Agustín, & Bahía Chachacual
Santa Cruz
Playa Santa Cruz
Playa Yerbabuena
Playa Maguey
Playa Organo
Playa la Entrega
Punta Paraiso
Bahía de Santa Cruz
Playa Chahué
Playa Esperanza
Bahía de Chahué
Bd. Benito Juárez
Playa El Tejón
Playa Consuelo
Playa El Arrocito
Bd. Tagolunda
Arroyo Tagolunda
Tangolunda Golf Course
Tagolunda
Playa Tagolunda
Playa Manzanillo
Playa Rincon Sabroso
Bahía de Tagolunda
Bd. Benito Juárez
Playa La Mixteca
ISLA LA MONTOSA
Playa Arena
Playa Punta Arena
Playa Tejoncito
Playa Conejos
Bahía de Conejos
La Crucecita
Palo Verde
Palma Real
Ocotillo
Bugambilia
Carrizal
Macuil
Macuhitle
Gardenia
Guarumbo
Guanacastle
Av. Guamachil
Zócalo
Flamboyan
Church
Bd. Chahué
0 100 yds
0 100 m
SLEEPING
Camino Real Zaashila 8
Hotel Bahia Huatulco 5
Hotel Posada Eden Costa 4
Hotel Maria Mixteca 14
Hotel Marlin 2
Hotel Meicer Binniguenda 1
Mision de los Arcos 10
Posada Primavera 9
Quinta Real 7
EATING
Avalos Dona Celia 3
Casa Mayor 12
El Sabor de Oaxaca 14
La Boheme 5
L'echalote 4
Los Portales 12
Terra Cotta 10
Ve el Mar 3
Zamora Ice Cream 11
PARTYING
Dublin Bar 13
Iguana Bar 12
La Crema 15
Mina Bar & Discothèque 6
Papaya 5
0 1/2 mi
0 0.5 km
0 200 mi
0 200 km
Gulf of Mexico
Mexico City
VERACRUZ
MICHOACÁN
GUERRERO
OAXACA
Oaxaca
PACIFIC OCEAN
Huatulco

price. *Palo Verde 309, between Bugambilia and Gardenia. ☎ 958/587-1167. Fax 958/587-1169. $200–$270 single, $250–$300 double, $380 triple. No credit cards. Amenities: Fax in common area. In room: TV, fans.*

DOABLE

➔ **Hotel María Mixteca** Surfers on a budget as well as Mexican families stay at this sister-hotel to the Las Palmas. The refurbished three-story structure is livelier, and the rooms are larger and cuter than those at Palmas (as a result, it's slightly more expensive). The rooms, which are named after Mixteca towns, also have newly tiled bathrooms with ample showers. They open around central courtyards; ask for one on the second floor to get a balcony looking out on the street. *Av. Guamúchil 204. ☎ 958/587-2337 or 958/587-2336. Fax 958/587-2338. $480–$800 single, $520–$900 double, $600–$1,000 triple. AE, MC, V. Amenities: Internet; room service; safe; tobacco shop; travel-agency services. In room: A/C, TV.*

➔ **Hotel Marlin** This very pink stuccoed hotel in quiet Santa Cruz has some blue accents, including one giant blue stuffed marlin in the lobby and a blue mosaic-tiled pool in the center. Rooms are clean, with tiled headboards above the beds and little balconies looking out at the ever-encroaching jungle. Though there aren't any beach views, it's only a 5-minute walk to one. The hotel has a decent restaurant (Jardín del Arte) with a basic menu of hot dogs, hamburgers, pizzas, and quesadillas. The clientele leans more towards middle-class Mexican families than European and American tourists. *Paseo Mitla 107, Bahía de Santa Cruz. ☎ 958/587-0055. www.oaxaca-mio.com/marlin.htm. $850–$1,950 single/double. Rates include breakfast. MC, V. Amenities: Bar; restaurant; laundry service; safe. In room: A/C, cable TV, telephone.*

➔ **Hotel Meicer Binniguenda** ★ This modern-colonial hotel was one of the first hotels in Santa Cruz, but it's still a good place to stay. Its clean rooms sport blue tiled headboards and each has a little balcony looking out onto the beautiful garden and pool area. The rooms in the newer section are the best. The hotel is just a few blocks from the water, and has free transportation every hour to the beach club at Santa Cruz—there's even poolside room service. *Bulevar Santa Cruz 201, Santa Cruz. ☎ 958/587-0077 or -0078. Fax 958/587-0284. binniguenda@prodigy.net.mx. $800 single, $800–$1,200 double, $900 triple. AE, MC, V. Amenities: Restaurant; laundry service; pool; shuttle to beach. In room: A/C, TV, safe.*

➔ **Hotel Posada Eden Costa** Run by a French husband and his Southeast Asian wife, and attached to their restaurant (L'echalote, see "Eating" below), this small, clean, and well-designed hotel, surrounding a pool, is in the about-to-be-developed Bahía de Chahué, between the Hotel Zone and Santa Cruz. Each room is named after a bird and has a sweet wall mural featuring a winged creature. All rooms have Wi-Fi, kitchens, and small refrigerators; the larger rooms have sofa beds as well. There's no view of the ocean but it's only a short walk away. *Calle Zapoteco s/n, Chahué. ☎ 958/587-2480. www.edencosta.com. $450 single, $800–$2,500 double. Rates include breakfast. No credit cards. Amenities: Restaurant; bar; beach club access; pool; Wi-Fi. In room: A/C, fans, fridge, kitchen.*

SPLURGE

➔ **Camino Real Zaashila** ★★ One of the original hotels in Tangolunda Bay, the Camino Real Zaashila is on a wide stretch of sandy beach secluded from other beaches by small rock outcroppings. Unfortunately, the hotel seems to be showing its age: The furniture is a bit worn, tiles are cracked, pillows lumpy, and pools need resurfacing and painting. However the lush tropical garden setting and ocean views from the room's individual balconies or terraces still make it a great place to stay, if not a great value. Rooms on the lower levels have individual infinity pools, and a 120m (390-ft.) main pool spans the beach, with shelves for lounging built into its shallow edges. *Bulevar Benito Juárez 5, Bahía de Tangolunda. ☎ 958/581-0460. www.camino-zaashila.com. $1,650–$2,650 double, $3,500 suite. AE, DC, MC, V. Amenities: 3 restaurants; lobby bar w/live music; large outdoor pool; room service; lighted tennis court; beachside watersports center; outdoor whirlpool. In room: A/C, TV, minibar, safe.*

MTV Best → **Quinta Real** ★★★ Double Moorish domes mark this romantic, relaxed hotel, known for its richly appointed cream-and-white decor and complete attention to detail. From the welcoming reception area to the luxurious beach club below, the staff emphasizes excellence in service. Lower suites have dipping pools; the presidential suites, which face more toward the ocean, have outdoor showers, large living rooms with bedrooms attached on either side, and bigger infinity pools. All rooms are elegant and comfortably stylish with overstuffed Mexican furniture, original art, and whirlpool tubs. The infinity pools, where young couples with perfect bodies sun around palapas, are prime hanging out spots. A short walk leads to the semi-private beach, which also has small palapas where you can relax with a drink after swimming. If you're just too exhausted to walk back up to your room a shuttle bus will take you. There's a Skybar as well as a bar off the lobby equipped with two computers and Wi-Fi; the on-site restaurant has romantic outdoor seating where you'll see newlyweds snuggling, as well as Mexican movie-star-look-alike bombshells nibbling food. *Paseo Benito Juárez Lt. 2, Bahía de Tangolunda. ☎ 888/561-2817 in the U.S. or 958/581-0428 in Mexico. www.quintareal.com. $2,800–$2,950 master suite. AE, DC, MC, V. Amenities: Restaurants; bar; beach club with 2 outdoor pools; Internet; laundry service; in-room massage; room service. In room: A/C, TV, bathrobes, hair dryer, minibar, safe.*

Eating

Although Huatulco has some simple yet decent beachside restaurants—good for easy dishes like grilled fresh fish—the restaurants in town are often mediocre. Prices for certain snacks have also risen ridiculously in the last few years; avoid the pineapples stuffed with cheese, bacon, corn, and seafood hawked at La Entrega—they're disgusting, and expensive.

Perhaps the best place to eat around town is at any of the palapas in San Agustín or Copalita (see "Heading to the Beach," below) where you can snorkel while waiting for your fish to be grilled. A number of more upscale restaurants are scattered around Santa Cruz and throughout the hotel strip, but the main place to go for a proper sit down meal is in La Crucecita.

CHEAP

→ **Los Portales** MEXICAN The food at this simple, small spot won't win any awards, but it's a good pit stop for refueling. The tacos and al pastor are tasty if unexciting. And though I was served fish that was a bit too mushy, the avocado/hot red sauce and fresh salsa cruda that accompanied made up for it. Bonus: You can always get a 2am breakfast here after drinking too much at the neighboring Iguana Bar (see "Partying," below). *Bugambilia 603, La Crucecita opposite the main square. ☎ 958/587-0142 or 958/587-0070. Main courses $30–$150. MC, V. Daily 7am–2am.*

→ **Ve el Mar** ★★ SEAFOOD This is probably the best seafood restaurant in town. The ceviche is a little disappointing—the current style along the coast unfortunately seems to favor a very ketchup-y sauce—but the grilled huachinango was pretty darn good, and the prices are reasonable. The restaurant is next to the very cool palapa-roofed outdoor Church of the Holy Cross. Ask the restaurant to turn on the fresh water so you can shower after your dip and before chowing down. *Manzana 20, Lote 10, Sector A, Santa Cruz.* ☎ *958/587-0364. Main courses $40–$120. No credit cards. Daily 10am–8pm.*

DOABLE

→ **El Sabor de Oaxaca** ★ MEXICAN Although this may be the best place in the area to have traditional Oaxacan food, if you're just arriving from the capital and taste some of the exquisite cuisine there, you may be disappointed. On the other hand, if you've just arrived in Mexico, you may think the dishes here are the best you've ever eaten. Four types of mole are on the menu, including Oaxaquena, Colorodito, Amarillo, and Verde at $110 each. The menu also features less expected spaghetti and hamburgers. A mix of tourists and locals come to pig out on the mixed grill for two: Oaxacan beef filet, pork tenderloin, chorizo, and pork ribs. Breakfasts are similarly hearty: eggs, bacon, ham, beans, toast, and fresh orange juice. *Av. Guamúchil 206, La Crucecita.* ☎ *958/587-0060. Main courses $50–$170. AE, MC, V. Daily 7am–11pm.*

→ **Restaurant Avalos Doña Celia** SEAFOOD Although Huatulco resident Doña Celia has moved from her original palapa restaurant where she cooked for years to this newer building, her food remains just as delicious. Among her specialties are *filete empapelado* (foil-wrapped fish baked with tomato, onion, and cilantro) and *filete almendrado* (fish filet covered with batter, beer, and almonds). Split the large plate of ceviche with a friend, and try the *platillo a la huatulqueño* (shrimp and young octopus fried in olive oil with chile and onion). The restaurant is basic, but the food is good enough to explain its popularity. *Bahía de Santa Cruz.* ☎ *958/587-0128. Main courses $40–$250. MC, V. Daily 8:30am–11pm.*

→ **Terra-Cotta** ★ INTERNATIONAL/MEXICAN Right next door to the Misión de los Arcos (see "Sleeping," above) and run by the same owners, this is the perfect place to indulge in stuffed French toast, homemade waffles, thick hot cakes, or *huevos divociados* (two eggs separated by chilaquiles). The decor here is pleasant with a slightly earthy feel; it opens onto a pretty park and is just kitty-corner to the main square. In the afternoon you can get great banana splits or espresso at the adjoining **Café Choco-Latte,** which is also a Wi-Fi hot spot. An added bonus is the adjacent Internet cafe, which has English magazines, books, and CDs and DVDs to rent. *Gardenia 902, at the Hotel Misión de los Arcos.* ☎ *958/587-0165. Breakfast $150–$600; main courses $40–$130. AE, MC, V. Daily 8am–midnight.*

SPLURGE

→ **La Boheme** ★★ FRENCH Come here for French cuisine in an old-world Parisian setting—think lush fabrics and fancy silverware. Despite the fancy decor, French Chef Olivier, formerly at the Quinta Real, presents the food here in a simple, traditional bistro style. Standouts on the menu include classic *coq au vin* (chicken fricassee), herbed frogs' legs, and roasted duck in mango sauce, but everything is delicious. *Paseo Chahué, Manzana 3, Sector "M," Chahué.* ☎ *958/587-2250. Main courses $180–$280. MC, V. Wed–Mon 2–11pm.*

MTV Best → **L'echalote** ★★ INTERNATIONAL This funky, yet simple French fusion restaurant offers food from France, Mexico, Thailand, Spain, Italy, China, América Latina, and North Africa, all made with recipes from the Franco-Swiss and Laotian owners. You definitely won't run out of options on the menu, which features everything from Vietnamese egg rolls, to French soufflé, to chicken liver salad. There's even a crunchy fried grasshopper burrito. *Calle Zapoteco s/n, at Eden Costa Hotel, Bahía de Chahué. ☎ 958/587-2480. Main courses $180–$220. AE, MC, V. Daily 2pm–midnight.*

CAFES & SWEETS

→ **Casa Mayor** ★ COFFEE HOUSE Casa Mayor has the best gourmet coffee in town, hands down. This family-owned business is fanatical about Oaxacan coffee being prepared correctly, so they export 80 to 100 tons of certified organic coffee a year. They also have full breakfasts, which are just okay (my huevos rancheros were covered with cream—*eww*) and snacks, salads, and cocktails. The real reason to come is the coffee, though—you won't get a bottomless cup, since each coffee serving is brewed individually, but the friendly staff lets patrons linger. *Bugambilia 603, 2f al Flamboyant (enter through Los Portales, next to Onix), La Crucecita. ☎ 958/587-1881. Coffee $2. No credit cards. Daily 8am–8pm.*

→ **Zamora Ice Cream** DESSERT First off, I should admit that I had a fair share of ice cream in Huatulco—hey, it *is* the beach. The folks at Zamora hand-make lots of unique flavors, like guayaba, but most people stop by for the banana splits—you can even order one for breakfast. I have to admit I liked the tubs of plain ole' Nestlé ice cream at the Café Internet next to Terra-Cotta (p. 590) even more, though. *Bugambila s/n, at Flamboyant. No phone. Ice cream $2. No credit cards. Daily 9am–10pm.*

Partying

Okay, so we've already established that you are in a place of mind-blowing and stunning natural beauty. Now, let's tackle the beautiful people: You'll find them at any of the discos near the Zona Hoteleria at night, though the La Crema bar is really the hippest spot around.

BARS/CLUBS

→ **Dublin Bar** Blink and you'll think you're in Ireland at this cool pub that serves Guinness on tap (at $75 a pop, a bit more expensive than you'd find in Dublin). There's even a dartboard and backgammon to go along with your pint. This is definitely a chill place—grab a seat on one of the comfy sofas, relax to the play list of '80s U.K. tunes, and leave the crazy partying to nearby La Crema. *Carrizal 504, La Crucecita. ☎ 044/985-589-2633.*

→ **Iguana Bar** This bar is on the bland side—but it's a good, cheap place for young partiers to get a bit liquored up before heading out to the town's clubs. It faces the main plaza of La Crucecita, so the people-watching seriously competes with the basic rock, tropical music, and TV sports that often play in the background. You can stumble next door to Los Portales Tacos and Grill (see "Eating," above) to get grounded if you over-indulge. *Bugambilias 603, La Crucecita. ☎ 958/587-0142 or 958/587-0070.*

MTV Best → **La Crema** ★★ This Loungey bar is the coolest in town. A young, glamorous set comes both to drink—they have 375 different kinds of booze on hand—and eat pub grub like pizza. It's intimate and comfortable, with candlelit sofa areas inside and stucco-covered booths with high wooden tables outside. There's live music during high season and a hip alternative-music play list all other times. *Carrizal 503, La Crucecita. ☎ 958/587-0702.*

CLUBS

→ **Mina Bar/Discothèque** At press-time, the bands on heavy rotation at Mina Bar were Shakira, the Black Eyed Peas, and Robbie Williams—in other words, don't come expecting authentic Mexican salsa or rumba. If you just want to dance to American tunes, though, it's a good time. Tourists in cowboy hats and tight jeans get down with locals in animal print tank tops, both on the big dance floor and in the plush booths lining the interior. *Mixie 770, Chahué. ☎ 958/587-2731. www.todohuatulco.com/la_mina.*

→ **Papaya** ★ This popular, 350-person capacity disco has a giant aquarium behind the bar complete with bikini-clad girls 'n' guys submerged for your viewing pleasure. The "Sexy show" a la *Coyote Ugly* has women in tight pants and cowboy hats dancing on the bar, and special events include everything from foam dancing to body painting to a Miss University Contest. The play list is pure disco. *Calle Zapoteca s/n, Bahía de Chahué. ☎ 958/583-4911. $80 cover.*

Heading to the Beach

The nine bays that make up this resort town are, from north to south: San Agustín, Chachacual, Cacaluta, Maguey, Organo, Santa Cruz, Chahué, Tangolunda, and Conejos. Each have their share of beautiful beaches. For about $150 one-way, pangas from the marina in Santa Cruz will ferry you to most of the surrounding beaches.

The beach by the cruise ship dock in **Santa Cruz** obviously isn't the best place for swimming. **La Entrega,** also in Santa Cruz bay, is a better option. It's so-named because it was where Mexican President General Vicente Guerrero disembarked, before being taken overland to Oaxaca to be executed. Now it is pretty much a tourist trap unless you get there before noon; giant tour buses tend to arrive in the afternoon.

The beautiful **El Maguey** and **Organo** beaches have great swimming and snorkeling. Avoid visiting between noon and 3pm when booze cruises come through, though.

Tangolunda Bay beach, fronting the best hotels, is wide and beautiful. Theoretically, all beaches in Mexico are public; however, nonguests at Tangolunda hotels may have difficulty entering the hotels to get to the beach.

Chahué Bay's beach will probably soon become more restricted with all the new developments planned, but for now it's totally public. Be careful swimming here, since there's a strong undertow. The beach club is free if you stay at Hotel Posada Eden Costa (p. 588), or $20 if not, and they have volleyball and drinks.

My favorite beach, MTV Best **San Agustín** ★★, is at the farthest-north bay in town. The snorkeling is superb due to a large stand of white coral that is protected by the bay and rocks at the entrance to the bay. They swear they've never seen a shark here, but the place is teeming with cardumon ciruljanos, mariposas, payaso, golondrinas, tigres, globos, and many other kinds of tropical fish. In high season the beach may be packed on the weekends with people from nearby pueblos.

The food at the palapas here is better and somewhat less pricey than at the beaches closer to town. **Charly's** (in the middle of the beach; no phone) offers tasty fresh seafood like *caldo de pescado,* a spicy red soup filled with vegetables. Charly and his wife María de Rosario also rent fins, snorkels, or boards for $50 for the day. This is also one of the few places you can still rent a hammock (or a tent) for the night for about $20; they also have very rustic cabañas with beds, and primitive showers and WCs.

To get to San Agustín, the turn-off is on the road north to Puerto Angel just past the airport. It's another 20-minute drive down a rutted dirt road (by taxi $200 each way; by colectivo $12 to the turn-off, then $15 to the beach; or by water taxi, $150 per hr.).

Fifteen minutes south of Conejos Bay is the magnificent Best **Copalita Beach** ★★ next to the Copa River. It's a great place to visit during the afternoon because the sun stays out here later—which means it's also a good spot to stay and see the sun set. It's not good for swimming but is an excellent surf spot when it breaks. There's also great fishing and diving here and a number of good palapa options.

Sightseeing

FESTIVALS/EVENTS

The international **Musica del Mar** (Turismo Conejo; ☎ **958/587-0009** or 555/554-2201; www.musicadelmar.com; $100) is held annually for a week in late November, and draws everything from techno to classical to jazz performances. Another annual musical event is **Musica por la Tierra** (www.esmas.com/espectaculos/musica), which brings mostly Latin rock stars like El Tri, Molotov, Moena, and other Mexican rock en Español groups to town.

Adventure Competitions and Fishing Tournaments are also held here annually, including the **Extreme Adventure Competition** (www.camdex.com.mx) which had 12 teams fighting each other kayaking, rappelling, swimming, trekking, and mountain biking. It's held annually in mid-November.

TOURS

Huatulco's major attraction is its coastline—a magnificent stretch of pristine bays bordered by an odd blend of cactus and jungle vegetation right at the water's edge. The only way to really grasp its beauty is to take a cruise of the bays, stopping at **Organo** or **Maguey Bay** for a dip in the crystal-clear water and a fish lunch at a palapa restaurant on the beach.

One way to arrange a bay tour is to go to the **boat-owners' cooperative** (☎ **958/587-0081**) in the red-and-yellow tin shack at the entrance to the marina. Prices are posted, and you can buy tickets for sightseeing, snorkeling, or fishing. Beaches other than La Entrega, including Maguey and San Agustín, are noted for offshore snorkeling. They also have palapa restaurants and other facilities. Several of these beaches, however, are completely undeveloped, so you will need to bring your own provisions. Boatmen at the cooperative will arrange return pickup at an appointed time. Prices run about $150 for 1 to 10 persons at La Entrega, and $350 for a trip to Maguey and Organo bays. The farthest bay is San Agustín; that all-day trip will run $800 in a private panga.

Another option is to join an organized daylong bay cruise. Any travel agency can easily make arrangements. Cruises are about $300 per person, with an extra charge of $50 for snorkeling-equipment rental and lunch. One excursion is on the *Tequila,* complete with guide, drinks, and on-board entertainment. Another, more romantic option is the *Luna Azul,* a 13m (43-ft.) sailboat that also offers bay tours and sunset sails. Call the Hotel Chahué at ☎ **958/587-0945** or -1145 for reservations.

Ecotours are growing in both popularity and number throughout the Bays of Huatulco. The mountain areas surrounding the Copalita River are also home to other natural treasures worth exploring, including the **Copalitilla Cascades.** Thirty kilometers (19 miles) north of Tangolunda at 395m (1,296 ft.) above sea level, this group of waterfalls—averaging 20 to 25m (66–82 ft.) in height—form natural whirlpools and clear pools for swimming. The area is popular for horseback riding and rappelling, too.

An all-day **Coffee Plantation Tour** takes you into the mountains east of Huatulco, touring various coffee plantations. You'll learn how Oaxacan coffee is cultivated and learn about life on the plantations. Lunch and refreshments are included. Cost for the day is $500; contact Paraíso Tours (☎ **958/581-0218;** paraisohuatulco@prodigy.net.mx) for reservations.

Another highly recommended guide for both hiking and bird-watching is Laura Gonzalez, of **Nature Tours Huatulco** (☎ **958/583-4047;** lauriycky@hotmail.com). Choices include a hike around the 50,000-acre Botazoo Ecological Park, near **Punta Celeste** with views of the river, open sea, and forest, for sightings of terrestrial and aquatic birds. The 3½-hour tour can be made in the early morning or late afternoon, and costs $450. (***Note:*** The Botazoo is unfortunately closed as we go to print, but it's worth inquiring with a tourguide.) An 8-hour excursion to the Ventanilla Lagoons takes you by boat through a mangrove to view birds, iguanas, and crocodiles. The cost is $800, and lunch is included. Tours include transportation, binoculars, specialized bird guide, and beverages.

Playing Outside

Huatulco is an outdoor-lover's paradise. There are plenty of bird-watching, mountain biking, horseback riding, hiking, and rock climbing options to be had. And if you're into watersports they've got it all: diving, snorkeling, kayaking (white water as well as ocean), and fishing. But if you want to surf, head north to Puerto Escondido (p. 596) since there's a limited amount here—the only breaks are at the river mouth of La Boca, in Copalita Bay.

In addition to the options below, check out "Sightseeing" earlier in this chapter for info on arranging adventure tours.

DIVING & SNORKELING

At San Sebastian or Isla Cacaluta (at the mouth of Bahía Cacaluta) you'll spot several different species of puffer fish, conch, King Angelfish, Cortez Angelfish, jewel fish, goat fish, blue-faced damsels, and the Crown of Neptune sea urchin (be careful where you step!).

You can learn to dive with the PADI-certified instructors at the **Centro de Buceo Sotavento** (Plaza Oaxaca, Local 18 in front of the main plaza, La Crucecita, ☎ **958/587-2166;** or at Condos las Conchas, Tangolunda, ☎ **958/587-0051;** or Bahía de Chahué, Sector M, Manzana 7, ☎ **958/587-1389**). Or try **Hurricane Divers** (☎ **958/587-1107**), located at the corner of Benito Juárez and Chahué. They offer scuba diving and snorkeling excursions, packages, instruction, as well as equipment sales and repair.

I recommend diving **El Naufragio,** the 50-year-old shipwreck below the lighthouse. There are also a number of fantastic dive sites at Bahías El Organo and El Maguey. Isla Cacaluta, at the mouth of Bahía Cacaluta, is great for snorkeling and you can do a deep dive on the open-ocean side. Playa El Indio on Chachacual Bay also has great snorkeling over coral in crystal clear water. The farther you get from the Río Copalita river mouth at Bahía El Conejo, the better the visibility; it's worth arranging a half- or full-day charter out farther.

FISHING

Huatulco is a great place to fish because there's not much commercial fishing nor are there many sport-fishing boats in the water. **Richard's Tackle** (www.richardtackleshop.com.mx) will take you out fishing for $500 per person per hour; or you can go with your friends (five persons per boat) for $4,000 for the day (8–10 hr.), including tackle. **The Sociedad Servicios**

Rancho Tangolunda

My favorite adventure tour operator in this area is Best **Rancho Tangolunda** ★★ (Carretera Federal 200 Km 256, about .5km/⅓ mile inland from Conejo Bay, Jabalina Community; ☎ **958/584-7814;** www.ranchotangolunda.com). It offers **horseback riding** for $450 per person through the jungle to the beach, or up in the mountains through the lush rainforest. You can also try out their zip line canopy tour ($300 per person)—it's quite the adrenaline kicker to step off a 12m-high (40-ft.) platform and literally swing between the trees. You can also go **white-water rafting** on the Copalita River, **kayaking** on the river or ocean, **hiking,** or **rock climbing;** it may be a bit more expensive than other tour operators, but it's worth it.

Turisticos Bahía Tangolunda (Marina Santa Cruz) takes people out for about $400 for a 3-hour trip. You can save money by bringing your own tackle; or by booking a trip through a travel agent such as **Aventuras Huatulco** (La Crucecita; ☎ **958/587-0054** or 958/587-1529).

GOLF & TENNIS

The 18-hole, par-72 **Tangolunda Golf Course** (☎ **958/581-0037**) is adjacent to Tangolunda Bay. It has **tennis** courts as well. The greens fee is $730, and carts cost $370. Tennis courts are also available at the **Barceló hotel** (☎ **958/581-0055**).

HORSEBACK RIDING

Guided **horseback riding** through the jungles and to Conejos and Magueyito beach makes for a wonderful way to see the natural beauty of the area. The ride lasts 3½ hours, with departures at 9:45am and 1:45pm, and costs $450. Contact **Caballo del Mar Ranch** (☎ **958/589-9387**).

Shopping

Huatulco is not exactly a shopper's dream; if you want fine arts, crafts, and textiles, you'll find more options in the bigger colonial cities inland. Shopping is concentrated in the **Santa Cruz Market,** by the marina in Santa Cruz, and in the **Crucecita Market,** on Guamúchil, a half-block from the plaza. Both are open daily 10am to 8pm (no phones).

Among the prototypical souvenirs, you may want to search out regional specialties, which include Oaxacan embroidered blouses and dresses, and *barro negro,* pottery made from dark clay exclusively found in the Oaxaca region. Also in Crucecita is the Plaza Oaxaca, adjacent to the central plaza. Its clothing shops include **Poco Loco Club/Coconut's Boutique** (☎ **958/587-0279**), for casual sportswear; and **Mic Mac** (☎ **958/587-0565**), for beachwear and souvenirs. **Coconuts** (☎ **958/587-0057**) has English-language magazines, books, and music.

If you're looking for something a bit more esoteric than the typical souvenir shop item and feel like a cup of tea, try the tearoom/yoga shop **Oceano** (Bulevar Benito Juárez s/n, Bahía de Chahué; ☎/fax **958/587-2724;** www.oceanohuatulco.com). In addition to stocking many New Age items that are difficult to find elsewhere, they offer "ceremonies, blessings, and meditation" classes every 3 months, taught by a visiting Buddhist monk.

The Manteleria Escober (Cocotillo 217, La Crucecita; ☎ **958/587-0532;** mantel escovar@prodigy.net.mx) sells woven tablecloths, blouses, and other textiles, as well as pottery and knickknacks. **The Museo de Artesanías Oaxaqueñas** (Calle Flamboyan 216, La Crucecita; ☎ **958/587-1513**) also stocks handicrafts from around the state, including hand-woven tablecloths, ceramics, painted tin objects, and rugs.

La Probadita (Bugambilia 501, La Crucecita; ☎ **958/587-1641** and 587-1196; www.laprobadita.com.mx) sells Oaxacan liquors and other drinks, as well as chocolate, mole, fried grasshoppers, and local cheeses.

Puerto Escondido

Puerto Escondido, or "Puerto" as the locals call it, literally means "hidden port." The name refers to the way the beach is tucked in between two points, hiding it from hurricanes that spin out around the bay on the storm track north. And although it's been a destination for hippies and surfers for many years, Puerto has remained hidden, escaping the over-development of Acapulco to the north and the big luxury hotels and ongoing development of Huatulco to the south. Best of all, prices are still happily lagging behind the country's other costal resort towns.

Often referred to as "gringolandia," by Europeans around Puerto Angel, Puerto Escondido has a healthy population of French and Italian expats as well as English-speaking immigrants. As a result, you'll have no problem meeting fellow tourists—if you're a solo traveler, in fact, you'll probably make friends within just a few hours. It also means that, in addition to great Mexican food, you'll find restaurants with a decidedly European epicurean slant—which translates into some of the best food on the coast.

Puerto's location makes it an ideal jumping-off point for ecological explorations of neighboring jungle and estuary sanctuaries, as well as indigenous mountain settlements. Increasingly, it attracts those seeking both spiritual and physical renewal, with abundant massage and bodywork services, and yoga classes. Surfing continues to be the main draw, though. During summer when there's a swell, the town is filled with surfers from all over the world and their hangers-on. Ah, *la vida surfista*: to sit on the beach with a *danesa* (a custardy Danish pastry) and cappuccino, watching the boys and girls stroll by, and count the innumerable piercings and tattoos on parade.

Getting into Town

BY AIR **Aerocaribe** (☎ **954/582-2023** or 954/582-2024) and **Aerovega** (☎ **954/582-0151**) operate daily flights to and from Oaxaca and Mexico City on small planes. Aerocaribe runs a morning and evening flight during high season; the fare is about $1,500 each way to Oaxaca. Aerovega flies to and from Oaxaca once daily. The price is about $1,000 each way. Budget carrier options include **Aero Tucan** (☎ **954/582-3461;** www.aero-tucan.com), which operates a flight from Oaxaca to Puerto Escondido at 10am daily, and **Click** (☎ **800/11-CLICK;** www.clickmx.com), which operates daily flights from Oaxaca and Mexico City to Puerto Escondido.

The Puerto Escondido airport (airport code: PXM) is about 3km (2 miles) northeast of the town center near Playa Bacocho. You can catch a taxi to town from right outside the airport for about $30. A cheaper option is to take a colectivo ($22 per person). **Aerotransportes Terrestres** sells colectivo (minibus) tickets to the airport through **Turismo Dimar Travel Agency** (☎/fax **954/582-0737** or -2305) on Avenida Pérez Gasga (the pedestrian-only zone) next to Hotel Casa Blanca.

Budget Rent-a-Car (☎ **954/582-0312** or 954/582-0315; budget33@hotmail.com, in town on Calle Juárez at Highway 200, Bachoco) is the only U.S.-based rental agency at the Puerto Escondido airport. It doesn't mean that someone will be there to meet your flight unless you make your reservation in advance; also double-check that they will be there when you drop your car off.

If flights to Puerto Escondido are booked, you might consider flying into Huatulco. It may be cheaper, and could work well if your destination is Puerto Angel, between Puerto Escondido and Huatulco. From the Huatulco airport, there is frequent bus service between Pochutla (near Puerto Angel) and Puerto Angel (see "Road Trips," p. 614). Thrifty and Hertz both have rental car service out of the Huatulco airport (See "Getting There," under Huatulco), but neither have a drop-off policy in Puerto Escondido, so you may need to drive the 2 hours back to fly out.

BY BUS Buses run frequently to and from Acapulco and Oaxaca, and south along the coast to and from Huatulco and Pochutla, the transit hub for Puerto Angel. Puerto Escondido's several bus stations are all within a 3-block area. For the **Gacela** and **Estrella Blanca** lines, the station in Puerto is just north of the intersection of Coastal Highway 200 and Pérez Gasga. First-class buses go from here to Pochutla, Huatulco, Acapulco, Zihuatanejo, and Mexico City.

A block north at Hidalgo and Primera Poniente is **Transportes Oaxaca Istmo,** in a small restaurant. Several buses leave daily for Pochutla, Salina Cruz (5 hr.), and Oaxaca (10 hr. via Salina Cruz) from here.

The terminal for **Líneas Unidas, Estrella del Valle,** and **Oaxaca Pacífico** is 2 blocks farther down on Hidalgo, just past Oriente 3. From Primera Norte 207, **Cristóbal Colón** buses (☎ **954/582-1073**) serve Salina Cruz, Tuxtla Gutiérrez, San Cristóbal de las Casas, and Oaxaca.

BY CAR From Oaxaca, Highway 175 via Pochutla is the least bumpy road. The 265km (165-mile) trip takes 5 to 6 hours. Highway 200 from Acapulco (403km/250 miles) is also a good road and should take about 5 hours to travel. Because it has no shoulders and is open range for livestock, and has been the site of numerous car and bus hijackings and robberies in recent years, do not travel it at night. As elsewhere, beware of *topes,* or speed bumps, while driving.

From Salina Cruz to Puerto Escondido is a 5-hour drive, past the Bahías de Huatulco and the turnoff for Puerto Angel. The road is paved but can be potholed and rutted during the rainy season.

Relax if you get stuck behind a bus between Huatulco and Puerto Angel since there really is no place to pass, and the road becomes straighter with passing lanes after the Puerto Angel/Pochutla turn-off. The trip from Huatulco to Puerto Escondido takes a bit over 2 hours; you can easily hire a taxi for a fixed rate of about $350 an hour. It takes about 45 minutes to the Puerto Angel turn-off.

Coming from Puerto Escondido, you will see the Highway 175 turn-off, which is a winding road passing through La Ventanilla, Mazunte, San Sebastianillo, and Zipolite, before arriving in Puerto Angel. If your destination is Puerto Angel or Zipolite, it's faster to continue on Highway 200 to the second Puerto Angel/Pochutla intersection and turn right to drive the 6km (3/4 miles) to town.

Getting Around

BY PUBLIC TRANSPORTATION

Almost everything is within walking distance in central Puerto Escondido. But **taxis** around town are inexpensive—about $17 from Playa Zicatela to Puerto Angelito (though they may charge an extra $10 at night). Taxis can be reached at ☎ **954/582-0990,** or **954/582-0955.** Colectivos (see "Getting into Town," above) are another cheap, safe option.

Buses running up and down the main stretches of town (on the east side of the Highway 200) are $4. On the west side, it is easier to just walk or take a taxi around town (especially at night).

The best way to visit the different beaches in the area is to hire a *lancha* or **water taxi;** you'll find operators along all the beaches in town. Most charge about $22 per person from Bahia Principal to Puerto Angelito. During certain times of the year and low tide, though, it's possible to simply walk from the Playa Principal to the beach of Puerto Angelito.

Basics

ORIENTATION

Looking out on the Bahía Principal and its beach, to your left you'll see the eastern end of the bay, consisting of a small beach, **Playa Marineros,** followed by rocks jutting into the sea. Beyond this is **Playa Zicatela,** unmistakably the main surfing beach. Zicatela Beach has come into its own as the most popular area for visitors, with restaurants, bungalows, surf shops, and hotels, well back from the shoreline. The west side of the bay, to your right, is about 1.5km long (1 mile), with a lighthouse and a long stretch of fine sand. Beaches on this end are not quite as accessible by land, but hotels are overcoming this difficulty by constructing beach clubs reached by steep private roads and jeep shuttles.

The town of Puerto Escondido has roughly an east-west orientation, with the long Zicatela Beach turning sharply southeast. Residential areas behind Zicatela Beach tend to have unpaved streets; the older town, with paved streets, is north of the Carretera Costera (Hwy. 200). The streets are numbered; Avenida Oaxaca divides east *(oriente)* from west *(poniente),* and Avenida Hidalgo divides north *(norte)* from south *(sur).*

South of this is the original **tourist zone,** through which Avenida Pérez Gasga makes a loop. Part of this loop is a paved pedestrians-only zone, known locally as the Adoquín, after the hexagonal bricks used in its paving. Hotels, shops, restaurants, bars, travel agencies, and other services are all here. In the morning, taxis, delivery trucks, and private vehicles may drive here, but at noon it closes to all but foot traffic.

Avenida Pérez Gasga angles down from the highway at the east end; on the west, where the Adoquín terminates, it climbs in a wide northward curve to cross the highway, after which it becomes Avenida Oaxaca.

The beaches—Playa Principal in the center of town and Marineros and Zicatela, southeast of the town center—are connected. It's easy to walk from one to the other, crossing behind the separating rocks. Puerto Angelito, Carrizalillo, and Bacocho beaches are west of town and accessible by road or water. Playa Bacocho is where you'll find the few more expensive hotels.

TOURIST INFO & OFFICES

The State Tourist Office, **SEDETUR** (☎ **954/582-0175**), is less than 1km (½ mile) from the airport at the corner of Carretera Costera and Bulevar Benito Juárez. It's open Monday through Friday from 9am to 5pm, Saturday from 9am to 2pm. A kiosk at the airport is open for incoming flights during high season.

RECOMMENDED WEBSITES

- **www.elsoldelacosta.com**: Has articles on everything from the town's Day of the Dead celebrations to long-boarding contests, as well as general lists of things to do in and around Puerto.
- **www.ifope.com**: Check out this site, created by an organization representing foreign nationalities in town, to get to know the international community in Puerto Escondido. They have links to info on volunteer work in the area, as well as good general info for planning your stay.

Puerto Escondido Nuts & Bolts

Banks **Banamex** (Perez Gasga 314; ☎ **954/582-0626**), **Bancomer, Bancrear,** and **Banco Bital** all have branches in town, and will change money during business hours. There are also ATMs scattered around town (the **HSBC** ATM next to the Hotel Las Palmas on the Adoquín is open 24 hr.), as are currency-exchange offices (one to try is the **Perez Gasga** next to the Hotel Casa Blanca; ☎ **954/582-1928**).

Emergencies **Hospital Unidad Médico** (Quirúrgica del Sur, Av. Oaxaca 113; ☎ **954/582-1288**), offers 24-hour emergency services and has English-speaking staff and doctors. **IFOPE** (☎ **044/954-540-3816;** www.ifope.com) can help you get out of jail or airlifted to Mexico City in case of a dire medical emergency. To call the **tourist police,** call ☎ **954/582-3439;** the police office is located on Gasga up the hill west of the tourist corridor. To report a fire, call ☎ **954/582-3538.**

Internet/Wireless Hot Spots There are more than 52 Internet cafes in Puerto. Wi-Fi hot spots include the **Hotel Nayar,** the **Hotel Santa Fe,** and the **Olas Altas,** where you can pay $20 per hour to sit in the common areas and go online with your laptop, or nothing if you are a guest of the hotels (just ask for the password). One Internet cafe to try is **Cyber-café** (☎ **954/582-0357**) on Zicatela at the entrance to the Bungalows & Cabañas Acuario, Calle de Morro s/n. It's open daily from 8am to 9pm and costs $15 for 15 minutes, $30 for a half-hour, and $50 per hour.

Laundry **Lavanderia Mango Club** (☎ **954/582-0406;** Mon–Sat 8am–8pm) is on Anador Libertad, just up from the Adoquín across the street from the Hotel Mayflower. Cost for 1 day service is $12 per kilo. **Lavamatico del Centro** (no phone; Mon–Sat 8am–8pm, Sun 8am–5pm) is an alternative on Perez Gasga 2 blocks up the hill.

Libraries **The IFOPE Library** (Bulevar Benito Juárez 10, Fracc. Rinconada) has over 4,000 titles in English, Spanish, German, French, and Italian, as well as over 200 videotapes and DVDs for loan. Short-term memberships are available for visitors. It's open Wednesday to Saturday from 10am to midnight. There's also a book exchange at **Casa Babylon** (p. 607) and **PJ's Book Bodega** (p. 608).

Pharmacies **Farmacia San Lucas** (Perez Gasga s/n, just east of the Adoquín; ☎ **954/582-3581** or 044/954-588-4018 for emergencies) is fully stocked and staffed by the knowledgeable (and English-speaking) Dr. Mario Francisco de Alba Gonzales. His wife Lupe Gonzales runs a sister **Farmacia La Moderna** (☎ **954/582-0698** or 582-2780) at Zicatela beach (Calle de Morro s/n) and also speaks English.

Post Offices The correo (☎ **954/582-0959**) is at the corner of Av. Oaxaca 101 at Avenida 7 Norte. It is open Monday through Friday from 8am to 3pm.

Safety At press-time, there was a shortage of police in Puerto. Take common sense precautions, though, and you'll be fine—be especially careful with valuables on the beach, don't venture into unlit areas at night alone, and don't carry valuables at night. Beware "tourist police" who dress all in black and drive a white pick-up, they are just as likely to shake you down as help you.

Telephone Tips The local area code is **954.**

Sleeping

As the surfing industry has grown, so has Puerto Escondido. Ten years ago, the main beach here, Zicatela, had nothing more than an unpaved stretch of cabañas with a few spots to hang a hammock. Today, it's become the center of the huge surfing scene in the region and enjoys all the restaurants, bars, and hotels that come with the scene.

That said, the hotel industry in Puerto still isn't *really* built up. The only luxury hotel here, the Santa Fe, is very understated. Puerto also remains one of the cheapest beach towns in Mexico, with a variety of accommodations. In addition to lots of camping-outside options, there are tons of cabaña and more standard hotel options. Rates for hotels vary considerably according to the season; be sure to ask for discounted rates during low season in September and October.

The Adoquín, or tourist zone, attracts not only surfers and spring-breakers but also vacationing Mexican families. You may find more modest prices here than in Zicatela, but expect less charming, more chainlike accommodations. The main commercial part of town north of the Carretera also has many economical hotels, but that's because they aren't on the beach. The Bacocho Beach suburb boasts many of the town's higher-end hotels.

HOSTELS

MTV Best → **Hotel Mayflower** ★★ Run by French-Canadian Minnie Dahlberg, this combination hostel/hotel is party central for the international backpacker set. It's located a few steps up from the center of the Adoquín and sprawls over several floors in a concrete three-story building; yet the outdoor spaces that are scattered throughout (perfect for chatting, reading, sleeping, or escaping roommates) create a homey feel. The clean but hostel-like dormitory-style rooms come with shared bathrooms, but the private rooms have private baths. A sign on the rooftop terrace warns "no sleeping or having sex on the billiard table." Everything else is no holds barred, though: On any given day, you can find Brits on the rooftop going nuts over a soccer game, Israelis cooking kosher in the communal kitchen, and Americans lounging in the hammocks outside. *Anador Libertad s/n, at the Adoquín.* ☎ *954/582-0367 or -0422. minniemay7@hotmail.com. $85–$120 dorm room, $200–$300 private room. MC, V accepted online to reserve rooms only, 10% discount with cash. Amenities: Breakfast room; communal kitchen; laundry service; shared bathrooms in hostel section; sheets; towels; travel info; communal TV. In room: Fans, security boxes.*

CHEAP

In addition to the below options, consider staying at **Bungalows Acali** (Calle del

Puerto Escondido

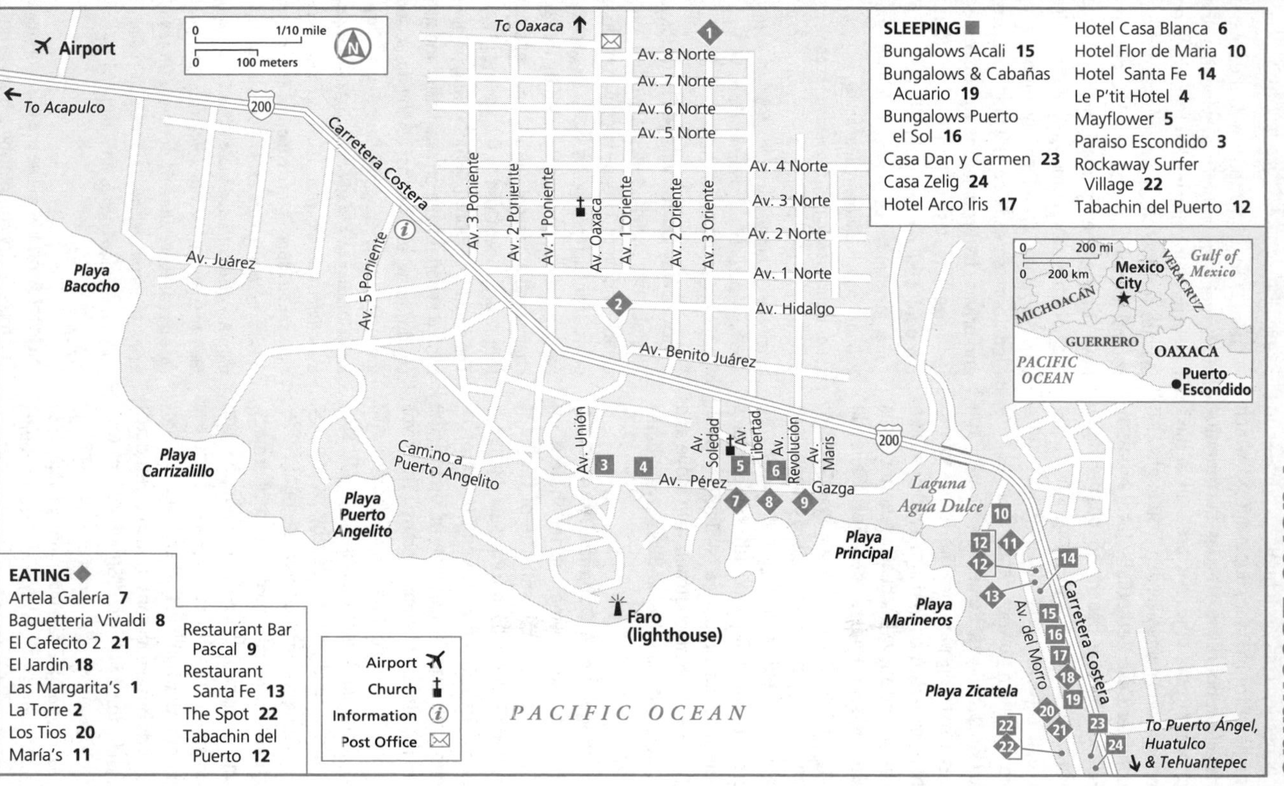

Morro s/n; ☎ **954/582-0278;** www.puertoconnection.com/acali.html; $360–$500 single with up to four people; MC, V), which has clean but rustic cabañas, surrounding a pretty pool and enclosed in a lush banana and mango garden. You might also consider **Casa Zelig** (Calle Jacaranda s/n, behind Zicatela beach; no phone; monica.alba@libero.it; $50–$100 single; no credit cards), a very cheap place with a cool Italian owner and a roster of European clients. Remember though: You get what you pay for: The four cabañas here are tightly packed into a rather airless compound above the beach. A better bet is **Bungalows Puerta del Sol** (Calle de Morro s/n, Zicatela Beach; ☎ **954/582-2922;** $295 and up single, $295–$395 double; no credit cards). These bungalows front a beautiful patio with tropical trees and flowers around a swimming pool. There is a common kitchen with stove and fridge, and shared as well as private bathrooms.

→ **Bungalows & Cabañas Acuario** ★★ One of the original surfer hotels on Zicatela beach, and still one of the most popular, especially during surf competitions, the Acuario gives you the option of either staying in a cabaña or one of the small, pleasant, clean rooms. The two-story hotel and bungalows (some with kitchens and air-conditioning) all surround a tiled pool shaded by palms. The adjoining commercial area has public telephones, a money exchange, a pharmacy, and a snack bar. The well-equipped gym on-site costs an extra $10 per day, $150 per month. **Central Surf** where you can rent boards or take lessons, is also located just inside the hotel (see "Shopping," p. 612). *Calle del Morro s/n, Playa Zicatela. ☎ 954/582-0357 or 954/582-1027. $660 double, $800 double with A/C, $500–$1,500 suites. Discounts available in low season. MC, V. Amenities: Bar with snacks; gym; Internet cafe; shared fridge; Jacuzzi; laundry service; pool; safe; surf shop; shared TV. In room: A/C (in some), fans.*

→ **Casa Dan y Carmen** ★★ At the far end of Zicatela on a bluff overlooking the beach, this charming inn has hammocks on private terraces, lush gardens, and some rooms with amazing views. The cabañas have either garden or beach views, and the top floor has a sweeping view of the entire bay. All rooms are elegantly simple with tiled floors, screens, ceiling fans, kitchens, and private bathrooms, and can be rented for longer term visits. There is a 17m (56-ft.) lap-pool and honor-system library, too. *Calle Jacaranda 14, between Jazmin and Palmas, above Zicatela Beach. ☎ 954/582-2760. www.casadanycarmen.com. $200–$275 cabaña for 1–4 people. No credit cards. Amenities: Laundry service; safe in office; sheets; towels; TV in common room; Wi-Fi. In room: Fans, kitchen with fridge.*

→ **Rockaway Surfer Village** Facing Playa Zicatela, this surfer's sanctuary offers very clean—and very cheap—accommodations geared for surfers. Rooms face a large open central patio, a pool surrounded by lounge chairs, and a tropical garden, and, let's not forget, are super close to the surfing break. The concrete-floored, bamboo, and palapa-roofed cabañas have private baths and air-conditioning as well as ceiling fans and mosquito nets. *Calle del Morro s/n, Playa Zicatela. ☎ 954/582-0668. Fax 954/582-2420. www.hotelrockaway.com. $120 single, $120–$550 double, $600–$1,000 cabañas. Rooms with private bath are more expensive, and weekly/monthly discounts available. Amenities: Bar in high season; kitchens in some cabañas; pool; safe box in office; shared bathrooms (in some); 24-hr. fridge; wheelchair friendly. In room: TV (in some), fridge/kitchen (in some).*

DOABLE

→ **Hotel Arco Iris** ★ The upstairs rooms in this three-story colonial-beach-style hotel have amazing views of Zicatela and the sea, although the pounding of the waves can get a bit insistent. An attractive shady garden surrounds the hotel and leads to the pool in the rear. Each room has a hammock on its terrace, mosquito nets, and traditional Oaxaca-woven bedspreads. **La Galera** bar on the third floor has a great view of the Mexican Pipeline, sunset views, and a lively happy hour daily from 5 to 7pm, with live music during high season. *Calle del Morro s/n, Playa Zicatela. ☎ 954/582-0432. Fax 954/582-2963. www.oaxaca-mio.com/arcoiris.htm. $600–$700 single, $600–$800 double with kitchen. Rates 10%–20% higher at Easter and Christmas and include breakfast during low season. MC, V. Amenities: Restaurant; bar; drugstore; Internet; medical services; outdoor pool; tour desk; cable TV in game room; Wi-Fi.*

➔ **Hotel Casa Blanca** In the middle of the Adoquín, this hotel feels somewhat closed-in (ask for the rooms with balconies overlooking the Adoquín for better people-watching and air), but it's great in terms of value and size. The small courtyard pool and adjacent palapa restaurant are good places to relax with a drink or a book from the small book-exchange library. The comfortable and simply furnished rooms offer a choice of bed combinations, but all have at least two beds and a fan, and some have both air-conditioning and a minifridge. *Av. Pérez Gasga 905, Adoquín. ☎ 954/582-0168. $240–$280 single, $400–$950 double. Discounts available in off season. MC, V. Amenities: In-room massage; money exchange; pool; room service; safe; tour desk. In room: TV, fans.*

➔ **Hotel Flor de María** Though not right on the beach, this hotel is a welcoming place to stay. This cheery, three-story hotel faces the ocean, which you can see from the rooftop. Built around a garden courtyard, each room is colorfully decorated with beautiful *trompe l'oeil* still lifes and landscapes. Two rooms have windows with a view, and the rest face the courtyard. All have double beds with orthopedic mattresses. The roof has a small pool, a shaded hammock terrace, and an open-air bar (5–9pm during high season) with a TV that receives American channels—all in all, a great sunset spot. The hotel is about .5km (1/3 mile) from the Adoquín, 60m (197 ft.) up a sandy road from Marineros Beach on an unnamed street at the eastern end of the beach. *Playa Marinero s/n. ☎ 954/582-0536. Fax 954/582-2617. pajope@hotmail.com. $350–$600 double. MC, V. Amenities: Restaurant; bar; exercise equipment; laundry service; pool. In room: Fans, no phone.*

➔ **Le P'tit Hotel** This three-story hotel, tucked away next to the river at the far west end of the Adoquín, has clean and light if somewhat worn rooms, communal patios with palapa roofs, and a small pool. Some have balconies (ask for #14 or #18 for a view of the sea as well as a kitchen). At press-time, the French owners were slated to open a bistro on-site. *Anador Soledad 379, at bottom of Adoquín. ☎ 954/582-3178. www.oaxaca-mio.com/leptit.htm. $250–$350 single, $450–$600 double, $550–$700 triple. No credit cards. Amenities: Bar with snacks; kitchen (in some); safe box in office. In room: A/C (in some), TV, fans, fridge.*

➔ **Paraíso Escondido** ★★ This small, modern colonial-style hotel is a step away from gallery-status—the owner has decorated it with an eclectic collection of Mexican folk art, paintings, masks, stained glass, Mixtex stone sculptures, antiques, and religious art. Situated on a street a couple of blocks from the Adoquín and Playa Principal, the hotel has a lovely pool and restaurant surrounded by gardens and a fountain, with a great view of the bay. The spotless and large rooms have built-in desks, handcrafted furniture, and a small balcony or terrace. The suites have fancier decor than the rooms, with recessed lighting, desks set into bay windows, living areas, and larger private balconies. *Calle Unión 10. ☎ 954/582-0444. $450 single, $600–$770 double, $1,500 suite. No credit cards. Amenities: Restaurant; bar; outdoor pool; tour desk. In room: A/C.*

➔ **Tabachin del Puerto** ★★ I love the funky cool India-meets-Mexico style of this two-building, three-story hotel tucked behind the Santa Fe (the owners of the two hotels are brothers). One is pink with white balusters a la New Delhi; the other is blue. Rooms are decorated in a fantastic swirl of murals, with elaborate bed headboards made entirely of tile, folk art antique chests, and even some marble floors. Each spotless room is equipped with its own kitchen, fridge, and bathroom. An open-air dining area serves delicious, organic, and eclectic food such as *egg fooyoung* (Chinese omelets) for breakfast. This hotel fills up fast in the winter months, mostly with Europeans, so make reservations early. *Calle de Morro s/n, up the Hotel Santa Fe driveway, Zicatela Beach. ☎/fax 954/582-1179. www.tabachin.com.mx. $600 single, $800 double including breakfast; discount by the week. MC, V. Amenities: Breakfast room; laundry service; wheelchair friendly; Wi-Fi. In room: A/C, TV, kitchen with fridge, safe boxes, stove, toasters.*

SPLURGE

MTV Best ➔ **Hotel Santa Fe** ★★★ If Puerto Escondido is the best beach value in Mexico, then the Santa Fe is without a doubt one of the best hotel values in Mexico. It boasts a winning combination of unique Spanish-colonial style, a welcoming staff, and comfortable rooms. The hotel has grown up with the surfers who came to Puerto in the 1960s and 1970s and nostalgically return today. It's about 1km (1/2 mile) southeast of the town center, off Highway 200, at the curve in the road where Marineros and Zicatela beaches join—a prime sunset-watching spot. The three-story hacienda-style buildings have clay-tiled stairs, archways, and blooming bougainvillea. They surround two courtyard swimming pools. The ample but simply stylish rooms feature large tile bathrooms, colonial furnishings, handwoven fabrics, Guerrero pottery lamps, and both air-conditioning and ceiling fans. Most have a balcony or terrace, with ocean views from upper floors. Bungalows are next to the hotel; each has a living room, kitchen, and bedroom with two double beds. The restaurant (see "Eating," below) is one of the best on the southern Pacific coast. *Calle del Morro s/n, at Bulevar Zicatela, Playa Zicatela. ☎ 954/582-0170 or -0266. www.hotelsantafe.com.mx. $1,050–$5,000 single, $1,200–$5,000 double, $1,550–$1,800 junior suite, $1,150–$1,750 bungalow. AE, MC, V. Amenities: Restaurant; bar; boutique; laundry; massage; pools; tour service. In room: A/C, cable TV, fans, safe.*

Eating

Puerto Escondido has some of the best and healthiest food on the Pacific coast. Because it is a popular destination for Europeans, you won't be limited to Mexican restaurants and fresh seafood—though the Veracruz-style fish, shrimp, and whole grilled snapper *(Tikin-Xic)* here are all great bets. You'll also find great French and Italian food (even decent pizza), wonderful baked goods, and natural/health food (even homemade tofu, a rarity in Mexico).

The town's many outdoor cafes are ideal spots to just sit back and watch it all, especially the ones around Zicatela Beach and on the Calle del Morro. A decent place for a late-night snack is **The Spot** (no phone) a taco stand on Zicatela Beach next to Rockaway. For a good comida corrida, try **Las Margaritas Restaurante** (Norte s/n, next to the Farmacia de Cristo;

☎ **954/582-0212;** nothing over $80; no credit cards; Mon–Sat 8am–3pm), where you can watch women hand-make *tlayudas* (giant white corn tortillas) on the comal before you stuff yourself with them.

Zicatela's late-night market **Abarrotes Merlin** (☎ **954/582-1130**) is a good place to buy a *cahuama* (quart of beer) or a bottle of wine and has a small grocery selection and other supplies like batteries. You can get a baguette sandwich to go at **Vivaldi** (Av. Perez Gasga s/n, Adoquin; ☎ **954/582-0800**), or **El Gourmet** (Calle Orcas 12, Rinconada; ☎ **954/588-3256**), which stocks imported cheese and cold cuts as well as prepared dishes—perfect for picnics on the beach.

CHEAP

➜ **Benito's Pizzeria** PIZZA Come here for the best pizza in Puerto, with a creative use of toppings—including capers, spicy tomato sauce, as well as cheese-free pizza—all baked in a brick oven. There's great guacamole, too—hey, you are in Mexico. *Perez Gasga s/n, at the beginning of the Adoquín. No phone. Pizza around $100. No credit cards. Daily 11am–10pm.*

➜ **La Torre** STEAK In an out of the way area across from a mall, this casually elegant place, complete with white linen tablecloths, is worth seeking out if you like meat. They offer barbecue specials on different nights, including *costillos de cerdo* (pork ribs), filet mignon, rib-eye steak, and burgers—any local can surely tell you all the details. *Benito Juárez 427, La Rinconada. ☎ 954/582-1119. Main courses $40–$100. No credit cards. Tues–Sun 4–10pm.*

➜ **Los Tios** MEXICAN This typical Mexican palapa restaurant on the beach offers everything from seafood to hot dogs. If the food is somewhat unremarkable, the view certainly isn't—the restaurant offers the best spot in town to set up your camera and capture a perfect shot of the Mexican pipeline. *Calle de Morro s/n. ☎ 954/582-2879. Main courses $15–$100. No credit cards. Wed–Mon 8am–10pm.*

DOABLE

➜ **Arte La Galería** INTERNATIONAL/SEAFOOD At the east end of the Adoquín, La Galería offers a satisfying range of eats in a cool, creative setting. Dark-wood beams tower above, contemporary works by local artists grace the walls, and jazz music plays. Specialties are homemade pastas and brick-oven pizzas, but burgers and steaks are also available. Cappuccino and espresso, plus desserts such as baked pineapples, finish the meal. La Galería has a second location in Playa Zicatela (next to the Arco Iris Hotel, see above; no phone). Beautifully decorated with tiny mosaic tiles on the bar and in the bathrooms, the second Galería serves up the same great fare in a beautiful garden setting. *Av. Pérez Gasga s/n. ☎ 954/582-2039. Main courses $30–$130. No credit cards. Daily 8am–midnight.*

➜ **María's Restaurant** INTERNATIONAL ★ This first-floor, open-air, hotel dining room near the beach is always good. Popular with the locals, the menu changes daily and features specials such as María's fresh homemade pasta dishes. María's is in the Hotel Flor de María, just steps from the center of town and up a sandy road from Playa Marinero on an unnamed street at the eastern end of the beach. *Playa Marinero s/n. ☎ 954/582-0536. Main courses $50–$140. MC, V. Daily 8–11:30am, noon–2pm, and 6–10pm. Closed May–July and Sept.*

➜ **Restaurant Bar Pascal** ★★ FRENCH/INTERNATIONAL At this restaurant owned by a French expat named, you guessed it, Pascal, the grilled food is exquisite. The whole red snapper comes with your choice of four sauces (try the exquisite grilled onion sauce) and fresh grilled veggies. For meat eaters, there's thick steak with heaps of potatoes and veggies. Local expatriates, mooning couples, and Mexican families sit outside on the plank wood floor placed directly on the sand, soaking in the gorgeous view of the bay and, often, the sounds of live son and rumba music. *Andador Gloria, steps down from the Adoquín, Playa Principal. ☎ 044/954-103-0608. Main courses under $120. MC, V. Daily for dinner.*

→ **Tabuchin del Puerto** ★ DINER It's worth the short walk up the driveway next to the Hotel Santa Fe for the Oaxacan, international, and vegetarian homemade breakfasts at this restaurant in the Tabuchin Hotel. The chef grows almost all of the fruits, vegetables, and coffee that he uses for his breakfasts, so you can rest assured that everything will be good and fresh. *Calle de Morro s/n, at the Tabuchin Hotel. ☎ 954/582-1179. Main courses $100. MC, V. Daily 7am–noon.*

SPLURGE

MTV Best → **Restaurant Santa Fe** ★★★ VEGETARIAN/SEAFOOD When Robin Cleaver built the Hotel Santa Fe (see earlier) 30 years ago, he decided to open a restaurant for vegetarians since he was one. It used to be one of the only veggie spots in town, but no longer; it still remains the best, though. Chef Nicolas Rojas and his excellent staff prepare amazing chile rellenos (baked not fried, with a delicate sauce), homemade pasta (the stuffed manicotti shells are especially good), fresh salads, perfectly grilled seafood like a red snapper, and even some vegan dishes. It's well worth it to have a meal here even if you can't afford the hotel, or at least sip a drink in the second floor bar to watch the sunset. *Calle del Morro s/n, at Bulevar Zicatela, Playa Zicatela. ☎ 954/582-0170. Main courses $40–$175. AE, MC, V. Daily 7am–11pm.*

CAFES

→ **Baguetteria Vivaldi** BAKERY This bakery has crepes and sweet rolls as well as full breakfast, but the main draw is their baguettes, and the sandwiches made with them. The end result is like a sub, but so much better. *Av. Perez Gasga s/n. ☎ 954/582-0800. Breakfast $26–$45, baguettes $28–$42. No credit cards. Daily 7am–11pm.*

MTV Best → **El Cafecito 2** ★★★ BAKERY Though I once drove hours just to get one of Carmen's *danesas* (a custardy flaky sweet roll) at its original location, now I don't need to. Carmen's has a new, larger location midway down Zicatela Beach just opposite the break, with a second location a couple of blocks up from Carrizalillo Beach. Both are the best places in town to sit down for a delicious full breakfast or simply pick up some baked goods like cinnamon rolls, brownies, or carrot and chocolate cake. I still love the sweet rolls best, though. *Calle del Morro s/n, Playa Zicatela. ☎ 954/582-0516. Main courses $16. No credit cards. Wed–Mon 6am–10pm.*

→ **El Jardín** ★★★ COFFEE HOUSE Italian owner Franco di Benedetto and his wife Adriana Vasquez Rios serve up some of the tastiest, healthiest, and most unusual cuisine on the coast—plus you'll get good portions for cheap prices. The emphasis is on vegetarian food—everything from homemade tofu, to *gado gado* (Indonesian salad), to amazing enchiladas verdes, to pretty decent pizza appears on the menu. Try the "Reyes de Rey" salad with brown rice and tofu; you can't find anything like it for 100 miles at least. The extensive drink menu includes fruit smoothies, espresso drinks, herbal teas, and a complete juice bar. The cafe rests under a slightly elevated palapa, so you can sit and watch the world stroll by along Zicatela beach. *Calle del Morro 310, Playa Zicatela. No phone. Main courses $40–$110. No credit cards. Daily 10am–11pm.*

Partying

Although surfers are stereotyped as wild party animals, the reality is that surfers are jocks. Since the best breaks happen at 7am, surfers mostly go to bed early, which kind of puts a damper on late-night partying. That can't really be said for all the surfer wannabes in Puerto, though, including gangs of Mexican kids blasting everything from rap to banda to norteno to techno on their car stereos, European girls who come to watch the surfers, *jarochos* (Verucruz natives, whom you may find carousing at 4am), and *boludos* (Argentineans who come for the surf but are known for their partying).

Add together all those sufer wannabes, the heat, and a whole lot of low-cut swimwear, and you get one of the most sexually charged towns in the world. Especially during holidays like Semana Santa, there will be huge parties on the beaches around town. Sometimes bands will just show up in town and there'll be an impromptu beach party at the **Piedra Iguana** (Calle de Morro s/n; no phone), an open-air club at the end of Calle de Morro where people meet after hours to play music, party, whatever.

When musicians pass through town, live music ranging from reggaeton to son to salsa to acoustic is featured in a variety of bar/clubs such as Casa Babylon. Some bars change location every 6 months (even the Son y Rhumba). Most don't have telephones and schedules are irregular, so look for flyers or check with the tourist kiosk (ask for Gina—she's up on nightlife happenings) at the far end of the Adoquín.

Hotels like the **Cabo Blanco** (p. 608) often feature DJs on Monday nights (although this day may vary, so ask around before going). **Pascal's** (no phone) on the main Adoquín has a live combo playing Latin folk and rumba on the weekend.

If you really want to get down, try **El Tractor** a *muy Mexicana* cantina, and get a *cabalitto* (shot glass), a *taro* (stein), or mescal. Of course, you can also drink while grooving to the music on the beach for free. Just try not to end up passed out on the beach at dawn with your pockets picked clean; see "Safety" under "Nuts & Bolts" above for safety tips.

BARS

→ **Barfly** Perched on the second floor rooftop terrace above Bananas restaurant (p. 608), the Barfly attracts everyone from surfers to geeks to slumming Mexican yuppies. The space is open and breezy, with a bar stocked with a wide selection of booze and a kitchen that churns out decent pizza. Surf videos are projected onto the bar's white walls, and punctuate a decidedly red decor. The music is a decent mix of rock and salsa—but who needs great music when you can chat up the sweet waiters and waitresses instead? *Calle del Morro s/n, Playa Zicatela. No phone.*

MTV Best → **Casa Babylon** ★★★ This hip spot on Zicatela beach is open as a cafe during the day—when it's a great place to play games like backgammon, swap books, and chat with new friends. At night, it transforms into a live music venue—once the reggae, cumbia, or salsa music starts blasting, the Casa instantly transforms into a place packed with sweating, gyrating, beautiful bodies. The party gets so hopping, it often spills out onto the street and beach. Locals swear that the bartenders are the best in Puerto—I can personally attest to the fact that they make the best mojitos. *Calle del Morro s/n. No phone.*

MTV Best → **La Flayita Beach Bar** ★★ This very cool hot pink palapa bar right on Zicatela beach features hookahs that you can share with friends. Buy a handful of various fruit-flavored tobaccos (for $80), plop down on one of the bean bag chairs, and fire up a bowl. They also have a full bar, smoothies, and a place outside to rinse off salt water and even changing rooms (during the day). Just down from the pipeline, it's an excellent spot to watch surfing, and for $50 minimum (this minimum is only charged during high season), you can sit in the groovy '50s modern furniture on the beach under a mini palapa all day and half the night. *Zicatela beach s/n.* ☎ *044/954-103-0761.*

CLUBS

→ **Wipeout** Despite the name, you won't wipe out if you come to this multi-level disco looking for a good time. On weekends, it fills up with local Mexican teens as well as tourists who come to dance to a range of *loud* techno music until very late—like 4am. Recently, it's been trying to change its image to become more of a lounge than a disco, so the scene might be slightly mellower when you visit. *Perez Gasga s/n.* ☎ *954/582-2302.*

LIVE MUSIC

In addition to the places reviewed in full below, check out **Rock Away** (Rockaway Hotel, Calle del Morro s/n, Playa Zicatela; ☎ **954/582-0668**), which has live music twice a week during high season. It gets packed with a rowdy crowd of surfers and their hangers on. **The Split Coconut** (Vista Hermosa Hotel, 2a. Orienta y 1a. Sur; ☎ **954/582-1222**) has live music on Friday, karaoke on the first Sunday of the month, and TV sports on other nights—plus there's always good barbecue.

→ **Cabo Blanco Hotel** Other hotels in Puerto offer similar dinner and dancing deals as the package at Cabo Blanco, but the music can be mediocre. The dinner here is all you can eat on Mondays, and the music is always good, especially the reggae on Fridays. *Calle del Morro s/n.* ☎ *954/582-0337. Closed May–Nov.*

Flicks 101

Cine Mar at **PJ's Book Bodega and Music Shop** (Calle del Morro s/n, next to Hotel Olas Altas, Zicatela; ☎ **954/582-2288**) has an outdoor screen showing nightly flicks, which you can watch from the comfort of beach chairs. Owner Paul Yacht also sells and exchanges used books and rents videos from the space. It's open every day except Wednesday; movies are screened from 7 to 11:30pm. An Italian movie called *Puerto Escondido* is shown every day at **Bananas** (Zicatela Beach downstairs from Barfly; ☎ **954/582-0005**) at 6pm; guess what it's about?

→ **El Son y Rhumba** ★★ This is one of the best places in town for live Latina and folk music. Owner Maika sings and jams with other local musicians, including well known flamenco guitarists or classical violinists, on a regular basis. The performers apparently have as good a time as the crowd—reportedly, they sometimes get so loaded they can barely stand. Fortunately, there's a good spot for unwinding by the pool. *Calle del Morro s/n, across from Hotel Santa Fe.* ☎ *954/582-3709. Cover $12.*

Heading to the Beach

Playa Principal, where small boats are available for fishing and tour services, and **Playa Marineros,** adjacent to the town center on a deep bay, are the best swimming beaches in the area. Beach chairs and sun shades rent for about $20, but that fee may be waived if you order food or drinks from the restaurants that offer them.

Although it's a bit farther north, my favorite swimming beach is the beautiful cove of **Playa Carrizalillo.** It's a great place for body boarding. You can rent boards on the beach for $50 including fins, or at **Central Surf** (Calle de Morro s/n; ☎ **954/582-2285;** www.centralsurf.com) for a 24-hour period. Just be careful to watch for jelly fish since they're abundant here.

MTV Best **Playa Zicatela** ★★★ which has lifeguards, adjoins Playa Marineros and extends southeast for several kilometers. The surfing part of Zicatela, with large curling waves, is about 2.5km (1½ miles) from the town center. Due to the size and strength of the waves, it's not a swimming beach, and only experienced surfers should attempt to ride the powerful waves; there's a lifeguard on-site. See "Surfing" below for more info.

At the far south end of Zicatela is MTV Best **La Punta** ★★, which has an awesome point break. It's somewhat gentler than the main break and so is a good place for intermediate surfers to practice. The curl is somewhat reminiscent of the break at Malibu, but minus all the aggressive locals. There's also a lifeguard stand manned by volunteers here.

Sightseeing

FESTIVALS/EVENTS

The third annual **Festival de Blues** (www.puertoblues.com) brings musicians from Canada and the States together for great blues music every weekend in January and February.

In February, there's also the Costa Alegre version of **Carnaval,** which is developing into a wild and crazy affair—slowly inching closer to the scale of festivities in places like Mazatlan (see chapter 10).

TOURS

Puerto Escondido is basically a beach town without notable museums or churches; the sights to be seen are mostly in the natural world. Following is a list of tour operators in the area in order to help you see them all.

Ecotours

Fishermen keep their colorful *pangas* (small boats) on the beach beside the Adoquín. A **fisherman's tour** around the coastline in a panga costs about $390, but a ride to Zicatela or Puerto Angelito beaches is only $50. Most hotels offer or will gladly arrange tours to meet your needs.

Laguna Manialtepec is located 12km (7 miles) west of Puerto Escondido and is home to magnificent red and white mangroves; from mid-November through March, there are 250 species of local and migratory birds here, such as cormorants, herons, ibis, parrots, egrets, ducks, jacanas, hummingbirds, and various kinds of hawks, among other birds.

A wonderful way to tour Laguna Manialtepec and other area lagoons is to go out by kayak with Gustavo Boltjes of **Rutas de Aventura** (contact Roberto Lepe at the Hotel Santa Fe; ☎ **582/0170-0266;** $200–$400 per person). When the water is high enough, you can paddle through natural corridors formed by the mangrove roots and spot crocodiles along the way.

Hidden Voyages Ecotours operates kayak tours to Manialtepec as well, hosted by naturalist and birder Michael Malone, an expert at explaining tropical biology to English speaking tourists. Tours are held from December through March, and are best booked in advance via the **Dimar Travel Agency** on the Adoquín (☎ **954/582-0734;** viajesdimar@hotmail.com; daily 8am–10pm).

Another popular day tour offered is to **Chacahua Lagoon National Park,** about 65km (40 miles) west of Puerto. It costs $380 per person to go out with Hidden Voyages, and a bit more with Rutas de Aventura. With either agency, you'll visit a beautiful sandbar and the area's two main lagoons, which has incredible bird life and rare flora, including black orchids. Overfished until recently, Chacahua is now the center of an eco-tourism movement that has helped recover much marine (including many crocodiles) and plant life.

In addition to offering tours to the Chachahua and Manialtepec Lagoons, **Lalo Ecotours** (☎ **954/582-2468,** cell 044/954-103-7852; laloecotours@hotmail.com) offers a nighttime tour to see phosphorescent plankton that appears at certain times of the year. It's pretty amazing to dip your arm in the water and watch it glitter and flash through the water. Rumor has it that some participants have stripped and jumped in to bathe their entire bodies in the phosphorescent light.

Another exceptional provider of ecologically oriented tour services here is **Ana's Eco Tours** ★★, Calle Futuro 214, Costa Chica (☎ **954/582-2001;** ana@anasecotours.com). Ana Marquez was born in the nearby mountain village of Jamiltepec, and has an intimate knowledge of the customs, people, flora, and fauna of the area. She and her expert guides lead small groups on both eco-adventures and cultural explorations. Tours into the surrounding mountains include a 5-hour horseback excursion up to the jungle region of the Chatino natives' **healing hot springs,** or to **Nopala,** a Chatino mountain village, and a neighboring coffee plantation. An all-day trip to **Jamiltepec** (a small, traditional Mixtec village) offers the opportunity to experience day-to-day life in an authentic village. It includes a stop at a market, church, and cemetery, and visits to the homes of local artisans.

Other Tours

Gina Machorro (at the Oaxaca tourist kiosk at the end of the Adoquín; ☎ **954/582-0276;** ginainpuerto@yahoo.com; call or e-mail for prices) offers a gastronomic 2-hour **walking tour** to Puerto market, where you'll buy food to cook later on; Gina not only teaches you how to cook, but she also lectures on the history of food in Oaxaca state.

Gina offers tours farther outside town, too, including to the **Mixtec ceremonial center** just east of Puerto Escondido. The site covers many acres, with about 10 pyramids and a ball court, with the pyramids appearing as hills covered in vegetation. A number of large carved stones have been found. Situated on a hilltop, it commands a spectacular view of Puerto Escondido and the Pacific coast. The large archaeological site spans several privately owned plots of land, and is not open to the public except on tours with Gina.

NESTING RIDLEY TURTLES

The beaches around Puerto Escondido and Puerto Angel are nesting grounds for the endangered Ridley turtle. During the summer, tourists can sometimes see the turtles laying eggs or observe the hatchlings trekking to the sea.

Escobilla Beach near Puerto Escondido and **Barra de la Cruz Beach** near Puerto Angel seem to be the favored nesting grounds of the Ridley turtle. In 1991, the Mexican government established the Centro Mexicano la Tortuga, known locally as the **Turtle Museum.** On view are examples of all species of marine turtles living in Mexico, plus six species of freshwater turtles and two species of land turtles. The center (no phone) is on **Mazunte Beach** ★, near the town of the same name. Hours are Tuesday through Saturday 10am to 4:30pm, and Sunday 10am to 2pm; admission is $25. The museum has a unique shop that sells excellent naturally produced shampoos, bath oils, and other personal-care products. All are made and packaged by the local community as part of a project to replace lost income from turtle poaching. You can volunteer at the center, too; see p. 617 for info.

Spa Stop

For terrific massage services—the ideal answer to a day spent in pounding surf—**Espacio Meditativo Temazcalli,** Calle Temazcalli, corner with Avenida Infraganti (☎ **954/582-1023;** www.temazcalli.com), is the place to go. A variety of therapeutic massages range in price from $150 to $320. There are also body treatments ($270–$330) and facials ($270), designed to minimize the effects of too much sun. The center is a tranquil haven, lushly landscaped, with the sound of the nearby ocean prevalent in the treatment areas. On full moon nights, they feature a special group temazcal (steam bath) ceremony, a truly fascinating experience.

Buses go to Mazunte from Puerto Angel about every half-hour, and a taxi ride is around $55. You can fit this in with a trip to Zipolite Beach (see "Puerto Angel," p. 614). Buses from Puerto Escondido don't stop in Mazunte; you can cover the 65km (40 miles) in a taxi or rental car.

Playing Outside

Puerto is all about being outside. Not only does some of the best surfing in the world exist here, but there's also great body boarding, fishing, diving, and even sky diving opportunities. Read on for info on the best options:

BODY BOARDING

Body boarding, a type of wave riding that involves using a body board, is huge here. Puerto has produced a lot of young champions; a local 14-year-old body boarder weaned on these waves just won a national competition. Lessons are available from several different teachers (see "Surfing" below), and most operators use special boards constructed with carbon fiber (or PVC) rods inserted to make them stiffer and more maneuverable than average body boards.

DIVING

Jorge with **Aventura Submarina** (Av. Pérez Gasga 601A, in front of the tourism office; ☎ **954/582-2353**) will take qualified divers to the Coco trench offshore Puerto. He speaks fluent English and is a certified scuba instructor, and charges $550 for a two-tank dive, with a refresher scuba course at no extra charge. Jorge can also arrange activities such as deep-sea fishing, surfing, and trips to other swimming beaches.

FISHING

Omar Sport Fishing (Tercera Poniente at Cuatro Norte; ☎ **954/549-1490;** or at Pto. Angelito Beach; ☎ **044/954-559-4406;** www.oaxaca-mio.com/omarsportfishing.htm) offers fresh- and saltwater fishing on a catch and release basis (you can keep what you can eat). They promise to find you sailfish, marlin, or tuna. They also offer **swimming with dolphin** tours where you can bring your snorkel gear and play with schools of dolphins if you are a good enough swimmer. Omar even sells boogie boards from $290 to $3,000 for professional boards with tubes inside them, as well as rash guards and other beach gear.

SKY DIVING

If surfing the pipeline just isn't exciting enough for you, take to the skies. Every winter, sky dive champ Antonio hits town with **Skydive Puerto Escondido** (at the Arco Iris Hotel, Calle del Morro s/n; ☎ **954/544-1708;** www.skydivecuautla.com). He promises "one minute of freefall jumping from 14,000 feet" while you're attached to him with a harness. Call or visit the website for prices.

SURFING

Unlike other parts of the world, the surf in Puerto is best in the summer. Although the breaks can change yearly it's always breaking somewhere in the vicinity, with waves that can challenge surfers of all abilities almost every day of the year. Puerto is most famous for the powerful Mexican pipeline, which has some of the fastest and most hollow waves in the world—even when the waves are small they hold their perfect shape. **Playa la Punta Zicatela** (see "Heading to the Beach," above) has the most perfect point break. You can go out through an opening cut in the cliff by the waves to drop into the line-up, and ride the left break a quarter of a mile. Although on most days it's not as strong or heavy (or vertical!) as the pipeline, beware when it breaks big, as the same rips and currents exist here.

World-class surfing competitions are held in Puerto in August, September, and November at Zicatela Beach.

The Salinas brothers at **Central Surf** (see "Shopping," p. 612) ★★ teach surfing as well as rent and sell boards and other paraphernalia. The brothers, who have been surfing for over 20 years, include Angel Salinas, notorious for surfing while wearing a wrestler's mask, as well as Roberto and Rene Salinas, all of whom have surfed their entire lives and won many competitions. These guys know it all, the breaks, the waves, the tides—they guarantee that even the most inexperienced surfers will stand up after a lesson, or they don't have to pay. Surfers with some experience pay $250 an hour; if you are a complete beginner, a lesson will cost you $350 an hour with a 2-hour minimum—all lessons include transportation to the appropriate beach for your level and all equipment.

MTV U How to Say "Surf's Up" in Spanish

Want to learn Spanish and get in some surfing at the same time? Then check out **Instituto de Lenguajes Puerto Escondido,** Carretera Costera (in front of Bodega de Cemento Cruz Azul; ☎ **954/582-2055;** www.puertoschool.com/index.html), which offers both surfboard rentals and language classes.

Raul Martin Tellez of **Escuela de Surf** (☎ **954/588-2552** or 954/588-5405) teaches surfing using some soft top boards. He charges $400 per hour including the board. Neto at **SURF,** Perez Gasga 506 (in front of Representacion de Colotepec), also teaches surfing, but in a more laid-back style. He doesn't have soft top boards, but does have cheaper rentals than elsewhere in town. **Oddyboards** at the point (La Playa Punta Zicatela; ☎ **954/540-1980**) makes, sells, and rents surfboards as well as providing lessons and rentals.

If you need to repair your board, ask for Mike at **Squall** (Perez Gasga s/n; no phone) or Central Surf. He has been fixing dings for the last 15 years.

Shopping

BOOKSTORES

Publicaciones Fabian (corner of Av. Oaxaca and Calle 1 Norte in the main part of town), has English language newspapers and magazines as well as a few paperback novels. English books are also available at **Acuario Books** (Perez Gasga 405D; ☎ **954/582-0127**) and the **Book Exchange** at Café Casa Babylon on Zicatela Beach. Also check out **PJ's Book Bodega** and **Cine Mar** (both on p. 608) at the south end of Zicatela.

IFOPE (International Friends of Puerto Escondido; www.ifope.com) has a lending library with books, videotapes, and DVDs.

BOUTIQUES

Although Oaxaca city is probably the best place in the country to shop for a variety of textiles and folk art, the same can't be said for Oaxaca state's beach cities. The majority of shops here all have the same sorts of things: sarongs, beach towels, bikinis, shell art, beaded necklaces, boogie boards, and swim equipment.

The charming **Bazar Santa Fe** (Calle de Morro at Bulevar Zicatela; ☎ **954/582-0170**), at the entrance to the Hotel Santa Fe, is probably the exception to this rule, but it ain't cheap. The owner was a former antiques buyer and collector, and his taste comes through in his shop's wares. There is a fine collection of antique gold earrings; hand-carved gourds with flowers, devils, birds, and larger painted ones from Tehuantepec; old hand-blown glass pitchers from Puebla; and authentic masks used in folkloric dances—all are pricey. Clothes include beautiful beaded blouses, huipils, and tehana costumes, some as much as $7,000.

Farther down Playa Zicatela, check out the exotic beachwear from Mexico, India, and Indonesia at the **Luna Jaguar** (Calle del Morro s/n; no phone) including embroidered and sequined skirts, tops, scarves, and handbags, as well as tropical jewelry.

For more practical beachwear and surf equipment, there's a row of shops just before the Hotel Acuario, but the oldest and best surf shop in town is **Central Surf** (just inside the hotel, Calle del Morro s/n; ☎ **954/582-2285;** www.centralsurf.com). Board rental is $100; boogie boards (fins included) rent for $50 for a 24-hour period. They also offer surf lessons (p. 612) and beach equipment. At neighboring shop **Crickets** (☎ **954/582-1872**) you can get swim trunks, bikinis, rash guards, fins, T-shirts, and even tongue studs and other jewelry.

Bikini Brazil ★ (Calle del Morro s/n; ☎ **954/582-2285** or 582-0568) now has locations at either end of Playa Zicatela. If you've got the body, the nerve, and the money to burn, get a string bikini from the place that perfected them. Go for it, but remember you're visiting a basically conservative, Catholic country. You *will* get whistles, stares, and propositions if you sport one.

The Adoquín is still considered the main shopping area for arts and crafts, although it takes a bit of looking to get past the typical tourist beach town T-shirt shop. The long standing **Casa di Bambole** (Av. Perez Gasga 707; ☎ **954/582-1331**) carries hand-woven bags from Chiapas and Guatemala, large woven hammocks in silk and cotton, wool vests, reggae hats, and crocheted hacky sacks. The prices are reasonable to somewhat expensive.

An alternative to the bikini shops at Zicatela is **Tribu Bazar** (Perez Gasgas s/n; no phone), which has crocheted bikinis from India for $300 as well as Indian skirts and camisole tanks. Various booths at the **Tianguis de Artesanías Guelaguetz** (on the stairs leading up the Hotel Hacienda, Av. Perez Gasga s/n; no phone) sell hand-woven "matrimonial" size hammocks for $250, simple white dresses and pants, hand-embroidered blouses, and huipils at reasonable prices.

Also on the Adoquín, **Plateria Ixtlan** (Perez Gasga s/n; ☎ **954/582-1672;** mariasilvia78@hotmail.com) has hippie-ish bracelets, necklaces, and earrings made on the premises, with good quality silver and semi-precious stones. The owner specializes in amber and coral, and can make a piece of jewelry according to your own design, within limits.

A bit farther down the street, **Arte Huitzi** (Perez Gasga s/n; ☎ **954/582-3525**; www.artehuitzi.aero) sells amber and silver handmade jewelry, beautiful hand-woven shirts, and gorgeous if expensive huipiles. **Oro de Monte Alban** (Perez Gasgas s/n, at Marina Nacional; ☎ **954/582-0530**) has more traditional settings of gold and silver jewelry, as well as some fashioned into Aztec designs.

MARKETS

The **Benito Juárez Mercado** (covering several square blocks between Calles 9a Norte and 3a Poniente) in the center of town east of the highway is an important part of life in Puerto and sells a variety of indigenous wares. Check it out on market days, Wednesday, Saturday, and Sunday.

Road Trips: Puerto Angel & Playa San Agustínillo

Puerto Angel

About midway between Puerto Escondido (80km/50 miles southeast) and Huatulco (50km/31 miles), you will find the turn-off from Carretera Federal 200 to Pochutla to the east and the small fishing village of Puerto Angel to the west. It's about another 6km (3¾ miles) on Highway 175 into town.

If you arrive by bus in Pochutla from either direction, and your driver won't drop you at the intersection, you may disembark at one of several bus stations that line the main street of Pochutla; walk 1 or 2 blocks toward the large sign reading Posada Don José. The buses to Puerto Angel are in the lot just before the sign.

Puerto Angel is a good jumping off point to the international backpacking nude beach of Zipolite and the eco-tourism destinations of Mazunte, San Augustínillo, and Playa Ventanilla; read on for info. Once in Puerto Angel, it's easiest to get to these outlying towns and beaches by taxi, for about $20 to and from these destinations, or colectivo, for a bit less money. Taxis can take you to the Huatulco airport or Puerto Escondido for about $400.

Though the town is popular with vacationing Mexican families, you may find that Puerto Angel locals are not quite as friendly as the locals at other beach towns along the coast. Maybe they're getting a bit tired of the nudity and drug use at nearby Zipolite (See-poh-*lee*-the), or maybe it's the repeated hurricane damage and the after-affects of a 1999 earthquake, which drove some of the best accommodations out of business. Although its small bay and several inlets offer calm swimming and snorkeling (especially compared to the open sea beaches farther north), there's also really not much to do in town. It's a good place to base yourself at night so that you can see the surrounding attractions by day, though.

The town center is only about 4 blocks long, oriented more or less east-west. The main beach, to one side of the pier leading from a public bathroom and tourist kiosk, is **Playa Principal,** where you can watch fishermen leaving early in the morning, mending their nets, or later cleaning their catch. A large navy base is toward the west end of town, just before the creek crossing toward **Playa Panteón** (Cemetery Beach). The safest swimming beach, it can be reached down a stone walkway built into the side of a sheer cliff leading downward. It has the usual palapas where you can sit all day for the price of a beer (or two) and even lifeguards.

SLEEPING

On a magnificently secluded and safe beach a few miles outside of town, you'll find the **Hotel Bahía de la Luna** (Hwy. 175

about halfway to Pochutla; ☎ **958/589-5020;** www.bahiadelaluna.com; $500–$770 single, $600–$1,300 double; weekend packages available; no credit cards). Several rustic palapa-roofed adobe bungalows on cliffs above the beach are tucked back into the jungle and grouped around a kitchen, outdoor bar, and patio area here. It's an incredibly romantic spot, and ideal for couples. Several ocean-going kayaks as well as adjustable masks and fins are available for use by guests. The amiable Swiss expat chef will cook your breakfast, which is included in the rates. The surrounding beautiful bay, called La Boquilla, is accessible either by water taxi from Puerto Angel ($200) or down a rough dirt road by car.

In Puerto Angel itself, the **Hotel Villa Florencia** (Bulevar Virgilio Uribe s/n; ☎ **958/584-3044;** villaserenaoax@hotmail.com; $180 single, $270–$360 double; no credit cards) is clean and tastefully decorated with local art and crafts. It is a quiet place with an excellent Italian restaurant; popular and centrally located on the main street in town. Another good choice is the **Buena Vista** (☎ **958/584-3104;** www.labuenavista.com; $230 single, $350–$450 double; no credit cards). It features poolside rooms on a hillside just west of Arroyo del Aguaje—though it takes some energy to climb the several flights to the upstairs lobby and then up to one of the five bungalows, it's worth it for the wonderful views, comfortable public spaces with hammocks, and lushly shaded outdoor areas.

EATING

Both the **Hotel Villa Florencia** and the **Buena Vista** (see above) have good restaurants (with almost nothing over $100); **Lulu's** at Hotel Villa Florencia specializes in Italian as well as delicious chiles rellenos stuffed with seafood. Or take a water taxi to **Hotel Bahía de la Luna** (see above) for lunch or dinner (just be sure to call before making the trip).

The **Rincon del Mar** (no phone) between the Playa Principal and Playa Panteon on the boardwalk, is a good place to have drinks and watch the sunset. There's good barbecue and a salad bar at **El Almendro** (Domicilio Conocido; no phone) on the side street behind the Villa Florenzia. On the Playa Pantheon, **Suzy's** has decent Mexican food and the **Eclipse** has good seafood, including dishes like avocado stuffed with tuna or shrimp—both are simple palapa establishments without exact addresses or phones.

Zipperless in Playa Zipolite

MTV Best **Playa Zipolite** ★★ and the village that has grown up behind it are 6km (3¾ miles) down a paved road from Puerto Angel. It's a 30-minute walk or a $20 taxi ride (it's less for a colectivo).

The main reason people come to "Zipa" is for the nude beach, at the west end of town behind a large rock outcropping. It's tolerated if not loved by the locals. Though nudity is *not* legal in Mexico and police sometimes patrol, most are more interested in looking for drugs than busting people for not wearing clothes. **Playa del Amore,** the south section of the beach, is where most of the nude action takes place.

Although all of Zipolite beach may be fine for surfing, there are drownings every year because of a strong undertow. Watch for flags showing the swimming conditions before jumping in: Red means don't go in, yellow means be cautious, and green means go—basically, the signs work just like traffic signals.

SLEEPING & EATING

Fifteen years ago, there were only a bunch of palapas on a sandy road along the beach here, but now you'll find four Internet cafes (the best is **Danydoquin,** at the south end of the main road, Roca Blanca), cheap restaurants (you can get a comida corrida for $20), even a library and a laundry.

You can still rent a hammock on the beach for as little as $20 a night, but now there are more accommodation choices, too. Although some of the accommodation places in town have websites, none have addresses or telephones—they're all on one stretch of land in town, though, so they'll be easy to find. Expect to pay extra for fans, mosquito nets, and security boxes (it's a good idea to use one as there have been robberies), and don't expect flush toilets or hot water.

Palapas Las Rockas is a cool place with third and fourth floor palapas going for $50 per person, including a full-size bed, solar closet for drying your swimsuit, and even a balcony with a view. The owner Susanna will cook her husband's catch of the day for you, too.

Another option is **Shambala** at the far end of the beach on the cliff. It has altars for meditation, wonderful views, and good vegetarian food. Cabañas are $75 per person, and a hammock is $10. They also have luggage storage and a safe box. **Lo Cosmico** (www.locosmico.com), just east of Shambala, charges $50 for a hammock and $150 to $350 for a cabaña.

On the hill above and behind the beach, **Las Casitas** (www.las-casitas.net) has great individual casita/cabañas, some with their own kitchens, for $150 to $600 (for four people). The cabins are built of adobe, wood, palm leaves, bamboo, and reeds. They use only solar energy, which means no reading after dark.

If this all sounds too rustic for you, book a room at one of the five standard hotels in the area; the best is **Posada Navidad** (☎ **958/584-3358;** tachueletas@hotmail.com.) They charge $200 for doubles with a fan, and rooms include a mosquito net and use of the security box in the office.

PARTYING

There are a couple of discos by Zipolite—**La Puesta** (no phone) on Roca Blanca and **Zipolipas** (no phone) in the center of the village, which both attract large groups in high season. At the **Iguana Izul** (in the middle of the beach; no phone) or **Shambala** (see above), there are great New Year's Eve parties, along with other events during high season.

Playa San Agustínillo

Traveling north on the two-lane Carretera 175, you'll come to another hot surf break and a beach of spectacular beauty, called Playa San Agustínillo. (A few more kilometers north is Playa Mazunte; see p. 610).

Before reaching the beach, look for a cobbled double-track going uphill on the west side of the road, and you'll find Mario's **Rancho Cerro Largo** ecohotel (Apartado Postal 121, Pochutla; no phone; ranchocerrolargomx@yahoo.com.mx; $450–750 single, $600–850 double; rates include breakfast and dinner; no credit cards). Built in the jungle on hills coming up from the sea are several palapa-roofed bungalows, some of adobe, others completely open air with sleeping lofts and mosquito nets and fans. The mostly vegetarian dinner is hearty and tasty—think delicious fish soup with tons of veggies, black beans a la olla, homemade brown bread, fresh salad, and ginger tea. Breakfast often includes fresh juice, homemade yogurt, fresh fruit, eggs, and pancakes. Beer and mezcal are available on an honor system basis. Return guests include people in the film industry, as well as travelers from all over the world.

Volunteer Opportunities

In Puerto Escondido, volunteers are needed for the **IFOPE Community Assistance Committee** (www.ifope.com; send inquiries under the "contact" button) which identifies and addresses needs in the local communities. This includes working with the local AIDS Clinic, helping at a remote rural boarding school for indigent children, and supporting local health services as well the local school for students with special needs.

Pina Palmera (Carretera Zipolite-Mazunte, Oaxaca; ☎ **958/584-3173;** fax 958/584-3145; www.pinapalmera.org) is a nonprofit organization that is actively working with volunteers from countries all over the world as well as locals to help lobby for rights for people with disabilities. In a beautiful jungle setting just behind Zicatela Beach, the nonprofit sells goods made by residents from recycled paper, and features living quarters for disabled residents and volunteers. Volunteers from Northern Europe, Canada, and the States have to make a 6-month commitment or else pay for their own food and lodging elsewhere. But you need only work 5 hours a day, which leaves plenty of extra time to go to the beach.

There are a number of volunteer options in the area to help release turtles. One is at **Mazunte** (see p. 610 under "Puerto Escondido"). Not that many years ago, slaughtering turtles was Mazunte's major source of income, but now it's one of the top turtle nesting spots in the world. That's because a 1990 prohibition against killing sea turtles caused the town to shift from turtle slaughter to promotion, and now, in addition to being home to the **National Mexico Turtle Center,** the town accepts volunteers who are willing to take the time to ensure that eggs are hatched and the turtles make it out to sea properly. Or you can try to volunteer at Playa Ventanilla, 1.5km (about 1 mile) east of Mazunte. The **Cooperativa Ventanilla** (1km/⅔ mile down the dirt path marked by a "La Ventanilla" sign) here runs lancha tours (for about $40) through the nearby lagoon to see crocodiles and a wide variety of birds, and includes a stop at the cooperative's crocodile project and a small museum. Coop members and volunteers patrol the beaches to make sure poachers don't get any fresh turtle eggs; volunteers then collect eggs for incubation and, after about 45 days, the workers release the newly hatched baby turtles into the sea.

Closer to both playas San Agustínillo and Mazunte, you'll spot numerous signs for local guesthouses, which rent rooms for an average of $50 to $100 a night, often with a home-cooked meal included. **Casa Pan de Miel** (Carretera 175, first turn right past the Turtle Museum when driving south from Mazunte; ☎ **958/589-5844;** www.casapandemiel.com; $850–$1,300 double, extra person $250 each; no credit cards) is on a cliff-top overlooking the ocean and has four beautiful and self-contained suites, each with terraces. There's also a lap pool and a dining area under a large palapa (meals are available but not included in the rates).

While in the area, be sure to drop by the **library** (Carreterra 175 s/n; bibliotecasanAustanilla@hotmail.com; Mon–Sat 2–5pm). Its entire collection of books in many languages comes from donations, and the space is home to an informal classroom and a computer room; ask about possible volunteer options here.

Oaxaca

There is no place quite like Oaxaca; even saying the name—Wa-*ha*-ka—feels exotic. That's because in Oaxaca, perhaps more than any other place in the country, the soul of Mexico endures. Sixteen indigenous groups, speaking 18 different languages, coexist in the state and the colonial city, also named Oaxaca, making it Mexico's true melting pot. Not counting nearby Chiapas, the state of Oaxaca also has the largest Indian population in the country, so indigenous culture here has a much stronger presence than in other parts of Mexico. For years, Oaxaca has relied on tourists who come to explore its villages where Indians live the same as they did centuries ago, with few modern conveniences—though the number of visitors has dropped since political uprisings in late 2006 (see the box on p. 619 for info), I've no doubt that the region will rebound entirely with time.

For now, the decline in visitors simply serves to enhance the city's quirky, intimate vibe, and Oaxaca remains as beautiful as ever. Consider the area's natural attractions: Seated in a valley and ringed by mountains, Oaxaca City is dotted with low-rise colonial buildings that feature a rainbow of striking colors, from burnt orange to vermillion and sky-blue. The city also boasts striking sites like the Iglesia de Santo Domingo, one of Mexico's most spectacular baroque churches, and is a short day trip away from Monte Albán, Mitla, and Yagul—three of Mexico's most intriguing, and surprisingly underrated, architectural sites.

Oaxaca's colorful landscape is matched by its vibrant art scene. The indigenous artist community here is Mexico's strongest—the markets, filled with everything from black polished pottery to weavings featuring ancient motifs, are renowned throughout the world. Oaxaca may not have Mexico's most happening nightlife, but that's not the point of visiting here: Come instead for the shopping, for Oaxaca's first-class museums, dance performances, and restaurants, and, most important, for the general laid-back spirit.

Because of Oaxaca's diverse mix of people and attractions, the most common word used to describe the state has long been "magical." When the Spanish conquistador Cortez first came to Oaxaca, he proclaimed it a land too mountainous for travel, much less for invasion. But after a few years, the magic of the place had seduced him, too, and he asked to be named the Marquis of Oaxaca. I believe that today's visitors, like Cortez, can't help but surrender to the allure of Oaxaca. Smell the roasting cacao and coffee beans, taste the roasted chicken drenched in *pasilla* pepper sauce, lose yourself in the music of trova or swing to salsa, and I guarantee you'll be calling Oaxaca magical, too.

Politics 101

From 2006 to early 2007, Mexico was bitterly split between the industrial north, which supported the newly elected President **Felipe Calderon,** and the poor and indigenous south, including Oaxaca, which supported the populist politics of **Lopez Obrador** (who claimed to have won the 2006 presidential election). Adding to the problems, a separate movement began in Oaxaca in early 2006 by the **Oaxaca Teachers Union,** who petitioned for better pay and working conditions. As the protestors started calling for the removal of **Governor Ruiz,** striking teachers were joined by other groups who shut down highways, took over radio stations, burned buses, and blocked off the zócalo, covering the city's historical buildings with political graffiti.

I visited Oaxaca during the height of the protests in summer 2006, and was touched by the teachers' plight. Somehow they endured months of living on the streets through the torrential rains of summer with nothing more than tarps to protect them. With no income, how did they even manage to eat, I wondered?

Yet, because of their protests, schools virtually shut down throughout the state. The tourist trade plummeted 75%. Beautiful colonial buildings were defaced. Even locals became afraid to venture out at night. When I spoke to some hotel owners, who were barely hanging on since their places were empty for months, tears came to their eyes. Finally in October 2007, then president Vicente Fox sent thousands of federal troops into the city, who used tear gas and water cannons to clear the zócalo.

Now peace has returned to the city, and gradually things are returning to normal. Businesses have reopened, at least, those that could survive. The State Department repealed its travel advisory, issued in 2006. Tourists are trickling in. Things may be okay now, but it bears mentioning that nothing has changed in the underlying conditions that brought on the protests, and, in fact, resentment of the government may be higher now than before. No one is sure what the teachers will do next time they want a raise. And the upcoming municipal elections, slated for 2007, could stir up bitter feelings.

So, if you want to plan a trip to Oaxaca, before you go do a little research to make sure all is still peaceful there. Oaxaca is waiting for you. Just make sure that you see it in the best possible conditions, and exercise caution.

Best of Oaxaca

- **Best Hostel: Paulina Youth Hostel** is set in a colonial building that has been renovated in a clean and modern minimalist style. Unlike other hostels, the dorms here are actually spacious—though you'll probably want to hang out in the very social dining area. See p. 625.
- **Best Art Hotel:** Local contemporary artist Rolando Rojas and his wife Claudia remodeled a family home to create a minimalist meets colonial design in the **Casa Catrina.** The rooms are each built according to one color scheme and feature the work of local artists. Bonus: You'll get the best hotel breakfast in town, and the **Bar El Catrin** in the basement features the inn's exclusive, award-winning mezcal "Mistique." See p. 628.
- **Best Splurge Restaurant:** Located in a fabulous modern take on a centuries-old courtyard, **Los Danzantes** is a great place to hang out, sample owner Hugo D'Acosta's excellent Baja wines, and munch everything from grasshopper soup to duck tacos. Though it's pricey, the hip factor makes it worthwhile—the place is populated with intellectuals and artists as well as we more humble *turistas.* See p. 632.
- **Most Romantic Place to Eavesdrop: El Asador Vasco,** perched on a second floor balcony, not only provides a voyeuristic experience of life below you, it's also one of the most romantic restaurants around the zócalo. The food can be hit or miss, but the view and ambience are always fantastic. See p. 631.
- **Best Bar to Relax in Between Drinks:** Squished between Los Perros and Fandango is **La Embajada,** a cool juice bar run by two Argentinian and Italian women. They've declared the bar to be "international laid-back territory" and it is indeed an island of peace—a good place to take a break between drinks (or while away the hours if you don't want to drink). See p. 638.
- **Best Place to Meet Locals:** Everyone in town hits the **Tlayudas del Libres** at some point during a night of drinking to get grounded with Dona Martha's famously amazing tlayudas. Her huge hand-made tortillas are crisped directly on live coals, plastered with black beans and salsa, and topped with *tasajo.* Waiting for one gives you the perfect opportunity to strike up a conversation with a similarly tlayuda-addicted Oaxaquenen. See p. 636.
- **Best Dance Club:** Housed in a beautiful colonial building, **La Candela** is a nightlife institution that's deserved of its rep. If the live salsa and merengue bands here don't get you to shake it, nothing will. See p. 639.
- **Best Garden in the Middle of a City:** The magnificent **Jardín Etnobotanico** covers 1.6 hectares (4 acres) behind the Iglesia Santo Domingo with medicinal, edible, ornamental, industrial, and ceremonial varieties of plants. With more than 9,000 flowering species alone, as well as the most extensive and complete collections of cacti and agaves from the State of Oaxaca, it's definitely worth a visit. See p. 645.
- **Best Church Interior:** The interior of the **Iglesia de Santo Domingo** church is literally awesome, with well-preserved and maintained ornate plaster statues and flowers that are carved with great depth and dimension. The extravagantly gilded walls and ceiling contain the work of the best artists of the 16th and 17th centuries when it was built (yes it took 100 years for the Dominican friars to finish it). See p. 643.

- **Best Art Library in Mexico: Instituto de Artes Graficas de Oaxaca** is one of the foremost art libraries in the world, with nearly 30,000 volumes of beautiful art books from the collection of Francisco Toledo. With books on art, architecture, archaeology, photography, movies, crafts, literature, and design, and a permanent collection of over 5,000 graphic works, you can spend all day here getting inspired. Best of all, it's free and open for anyone. See p. 644.
- **Best Store for Textiles:** The remarkable **"Los Baules" de Juana Cata** sells indigenous textile art from all over the state. The store's knowledgeable owner has traveled the world to collect rugs, blankets, shawls, skirts, and indigenous costumes; his wares are in private collections as well as museums, so you know you'll be buying something quality here. See p. 648.
- **Best Archaeological Site:** Atop a mountain that the Zapotec leveled sits the amazing site of **Monte Albán,** once a metropolis of 30,000. Dating from 500 B.C., these days, it's one of the most important sites in the country. See p. 650.

Getting There & Getting Around

Getting into Town

BY PLANE

Continental Express Jet (☎ **800/231-0856** in U.S.; www.continental.com) has direct and connecting service to/from Houston. **Mexicana** (☎ **951/516-8414** or 800/531-7921 in U.S.; www.mexicana.com) and **AeroMexico** (☎ **951/516-1066** or 800/237-6639 in U.S.; www.aeromexico.com.mx) have several flights daily to and from Mexico City, and connecting flights to/from the U.S.

Aeroputo Internacional de Oaxaca Xoxocotlan (OAX; tourist info booth ☎ **951/511-5040**) is 8km (5 miles) south or 20 minutes away from the center city. You can buy a ticket for a private cab ($100 to the centro) at the window on your left as you exit the airport. The van service **Transportes Aeropuerto Oaxaca** (☎ **951/514-4350**) provides shuttles from the airport to town. It doesn't take reservations by phone, so drop by Monday through Saturday from 9am to 2pm or 5 to 8pm to buy your ticket and arrange hotel pickup. The cost is $30 from downtown hotels, $55 and up from outlying hotels, and more if you have extra luggage.

BY CAR

It's a 5-hour drive from Mexico City on the toll road, Highway 135D, which begins at Cuacnoapalan, about 80km (50 miles) southeast of Puebla, and runs south, terminating in Oaxaca; the one-way toll is $290. The old federal Highway 190 winds through the mountains and offers spectacular views, but it takes a much longer 9 to 10 hours. Be warned that many people who have traveled on the coastal highway linking Oaxaca to Puerto Escondido or Huatulco say that if they had it to do over, they'd fly. If you're motion sick at all, the mountainous curves along the road will absolutely wreck you. See "By Car" under "Getting Around" later in this chapter for more tips on driving.

BY BUS

ADO and its affiliates handle most of the city's first-class and deluxe bus service. Your options are: first class (ADO), with almost hourly departures to Mexico City and a one-way fare of $340; deluxe (ADO GL) with seven or more departures per day for $400 one-way; and executive class (UNO), with five-plus departures per day for a $550 one-way fee. First-class and deluxe buses to and from Mexico City use the *autopista* (superhighway toll road) which takes 6 hours; some cheaper buses take as long as 9 hours because they travel along the winding old Highway 190.

Around the Day of the Dead, Holy Week, and Christmas, you should reserve a seat in advance, since buses fill up quickly. Visit www.adogl.com.mx and www.uno.com.mx for specific schedules and to make reservations. You can also buy tickets ahead of time at one of the offices of **Ticket Bus** (20 de Noviembre 103-D, near the corner of Hidalgo, 1 block from the zócalo; ☎ **951/515-5000;** Mon–Sat 7am–11pm, Sun 9am–4pm).

Almost all buses from Mexico City leave from Mexico City's TAPO (east) bus station (p. 85) and arrive at Oaxaca's **ADO station** (Calzada Niños Héroes de Chapultepec 1036 at Calle Emilio Carranza; ☎ **951/513-0529**), a short distance north of the center of town. If you're taking a second-class ADO bus from destinations along the Pacific coast, you'll arrive at the **Central Camionera de Segunda Clase** (second-class bus terminal) next to the Abastos Market, 10 blocks southwest of the zócalo. Cabs are on hand at both stations to take you to your final destination.

BY SUBURBAN

The **Viajes Atlántida** agency (La Noria 101, near Armenta y López; ☎ **951/514-7077;** daily 5:30am–11:30pm), runs suburban service eight times daily to Pochutla. The ride takes 5 hours and costs $140. From Pochutla, you can then catch a colectivo to Puerto Escondido, Huatulco, or Puerto Angel (the trip there takes 1–2 hr.).

Getting Around

BY PLANE

For flights from Oaxaca to elsewhere in Mexico, try the air taxi service offered by **Aero Tucan** (Alcalá 201-204; ☎ **951/501-0530** or 951/501-0532; Bulevar Santa Cruz, Huatulco; ☎ **958/587-2427** or 954/582-3461; www.aero-tucan.com). Scrape together $1,090 for a one-way trip to Oaxaca from Puerto Escondido or Huatulco, and you'll save yourself the torturous and dangerous 6-hour trip by car (9 hr. by bus). The planes are new, if small, and a flight on one only takes 30 minutes (flights usually leave at 10am, afternoon flights are also available). Check your hotel before booking, since discounts are available through the Oaxaca Hotel Group (www.oaxaca-hotel-group.com).

Another air taxi service to try is **Aerovega** (☎ **951/516-4982**), which flies a six-passenger twin-engine Aero-Commander to and from Puerto Escondido and Bahías de Huatulco once daily (twice if there are enough passengers).

Click, a Mexicana affiliate (☎ **800/122-5425;** www.clickmx.com), has service to/from Mexico City. **Aviacsa** (☎ **800/006-2200** or 951/514-5187; www.aviacsa.com) connects Oaxaca to Mexico City and Acapulco.

BY BUS

Buses to the outlying villages of Guelatao, Teotitlan del Valle, Tlacolula, and Mitla leave from the second-class station just north of the Abastos Market. Colectivos leave for nearby villages from Calle Mercaderes, on the south side of the Abastos Market.

BY TAXI

You can easily arrange a taxi to get to some of Oaxaca's outlying villages. Most taxi drivers have set hourly rates (about $150 per hr.) for touring the Oaxacan valleys. **Pablo Garcia** who works for **Taxi Express** (☎ **951/568-4648** or cell 044/951-117-2462) doesn't speak much English but is completely trustworthy and, for $150 per hour, will escort you to any bar or club in Oaxaca state—he knows them all. If he's booked, Sebastian Chino of **Chino Tours**

(☎ **951/508-1220**) and **Eric Ramirez** (☎ **951/171-9295**) are other excellent drivers.

BY CAR

You don't really need to rent a car since everything is within walking distance in town. It's also much cheaper to get to outlying villages by bus or taxi (rental cars in Oaxaca cost about $1,200 per day). However, if you must rent a car, your best bet is to reserve one before you leave home with an online agency, or try **Arrendadora Express** (20 de Noviembre 103-B; ☎ **951/516-6776**).

Basics

Orientation

Oaxaca's east—west axis is **Independencia.** When streets cross Independencia and the north—south axis, **Alcalá/Bustamante,** their names change. The city's center is the **zócalo,** a large square surrounded by portales, and the **Alameda,** a smaller plaza attached to the northwest part of the zócalo. Oaxaca's cathedral faces the Alameda; the Palacio del Gobierno faces the zócalo. A few blocks to the north is the **Plaza de Santo Domingo.** Most of the historic district's shops, hotels, and restaurants are situated between the zócalo and the Alameda. Two of the streets that run from Santo Domingo toward the zócalo—**Alcalá** and **Cinco de Mayo**—are partially pedestrian streets.

Tourist Info & Offices

The **State Tourist Office** (Calle Independencia 607, corner of Garcia Vigil; ☎/fax **951/516-0123**) is open daily from 8am to 8pm. The information booth at the airport keeps the same hours. The **Oficina de Turismo (Municipal Tourist Office)** is at García Vigil 517; it's open Monday through Friday from 9am to 3pm and 6 to 9pm.

Recommended Websites

- **www.mexicodesconocido.com**: Click on this site for many informative articles on Oaxacan art, history, and culture.
- **www.noticias-oax.com.mx**: The website of the newspaper *Noticias Oaxaca* is a great place to read about political goings-on in Oaxaca, as well as to find out about current festivals and other events (in Spanish).

OAXACA

Oaxaca Nuts & Bolts

Banks **Banamex, Banfa, Bancomer, Bancrear,** and **Banco Bital** all have branches in town, and all will change money during business hours. Most banks are open Monday through Friday from 9am to 4pm, with shorter hours on Saturday; Banfa stays open later during the week. Two of the most convenient branches are Banamex's at Perez Gasga 314 (☎ **951/582-0626**) and Banfa's at Garcia Vigil at Matamoros (☎ **951/516-8253**).

Cellphone Providers & Service Centers There is a **Telcel** office on Valerio Trunjano 400 (☎ **951/514-8566**), where for $200 you can buy a new SIM card to put in your existing cellphone. Or you can buy a new phone for $300, which comes loaded with $100 of time on it, for roughly $5 per minute.

Embassies The **U.S. Consular Agency** is at Alcalá 407, Int. 20 (☎/fax **951/514-3054**, emergency cell 044/951-547-1185). Hours are Monday through Friday from 10am to 3pm. The **Canadian consulate,** Pino Suárez 700-11B (☎ **951/513-3777**), is open daily from 11am to 2pm.

Emergencies **Hospital Molina** is at Garcia Vigil 317, Centro (☎ **951/516-5468**); office hours are Monday through Friday noon to 2pm and 4 to 8pm. The phone number for police is ☎ **951/516-0400.** The phone number for general emergencies is ☎ **060.**

Internet/Wireless Hot Spots Many of the city's hotels, including Hotel Vertiz, Aitana, Oaxaca Inn, Fiesta Inn, San Felipe Misión, and the Misión de Los Angeles, have Wi-Fi in their outdoor cafes, so you can have a cup of coffee, take your laptop, and log on. Wi-Fi is even available at the airport.

There are over 20 Internet access services and cybercafes in the downtown area. Many are on the Alcalá and around the zócalo and the Plaza Santo Domingo. In addition to **Nouveau** (see "Eating," p. 630), try **Café Punto Com** (Garcia Vigil 206; ☎ **951/501-1026;** Mon–Sat 7am–11pm), which will burn CDs, make digital prints and color laser copies, and provide the usual Internet services. **PlanetX** (Porfirio Diaz 102, Centro; ☎ **951/516-9855** or 044/951-547-1034) offers professional computer repair services as well as Internet and Wi-Fi service. Expect to pay around $10 an hour at Internet cafes; printing pages is $1 to $2 per page.

Laundry Laundromats are all over town; laundry is usually priced by the kilo ($20–$40). You can get your clothes washed in one day at **Azteca Lavanderia** (Av. Hidalgo 404; ☎ **958/514-7951;** Mon–Sat 8am–8pm, Sun 10am–2pm). They will also deliver to your hotel.

Luggage Storage You can store your luggage at most hotels; even the hostels will keep your backpack in their safe areas. You can also check your bags at the First Class bus station for a nominal fee.

Pharmacies **Farmacia Nino Dioss,** Garcia Vigil 317-1 (☎ **958/516-4242** or 958/516-1726), is open Monday to Friday from 9am to 10pm and Sunday from 10am to 6pm; it offers a 30% discount on medicine.

Post Offices The *correo* is at the corner of Independencia and Alameda Park. It is open Monday through Friday from 8am to 5pm, Saturday from 9am to 1pm. The phone number is ☎ **951/516-2661. PAKMAIL** (Garcia Vigil 504 at Allende; ☎ **951/516-8196** or 501-0925; www.pakmail.com.mx) has services with DHL, UPS, FedEx, MultiPack, as well as boxes and other packing materials for shipping.

Safety Although Oaxaca is generally very safe, you need to use caution while going out at night. Be aware of people around you and watch for pickpockets in the markets. Be careful in bars (especially if you're a single women) and keep abreast of the current political situation by checking http://travel.state.gov/travel.

Telephone Tips The Oaxaca area code is **951.**

Sleeping

You'll find a plethora of hostels and reasonably priced to expensive hotels in Oaxaca; hoteliers lowered prices starting in 2006 and continued to do so in 2007, so lots of deals are also on hand.

Most hostels and hotels listed here are in the Centro—the hood that's most convenient for tourists. In addition to staying at one of these accommodations in town, you can also camp or stay in a rustic yu'u accommodation outside of town. See p. 650 for info.

Hostels

→ **Hostal Fernanda** ★ Not only does this place have a great location, clean accommodations, and a friendly vibe going for it, it also has Fernanda, a hip Oaxaqueña owner. She designed her hostel to include boldly painted dormitory-style rooms, complete with the sort of perks, like fresh linens and a pretty front tea room that's perfect for lounging, that are missing from other hostels. Though I could hardly tear myself away from this place, they even make it easy to get away by offering bike rentals. *Jesus Carranza 112, between Garcia Vigil and Porfirio Diaz. ☎ 951/516-2104. www.hostalfernanda.com. $80 per person per bunk. No credit cards. Amenities: Breakfast room; Internet; kitchen; safe; shared bathrooms; sheets; telephone (in common room); towels; travel info; 24-hr. hot water; TV (in common room).*

→ **Hostel Luz de Luna Nuyoo** This hostel is run by two brothers, Juan Carlos and Eduardo Mayoral, who are musicians as well as rock climbers. You'll get standard bunk rooms here, all of which are on the musty side, but there are also cabañas and private rooms for one to six people. If the bedrooms don't rock your world, you can always give the rock climbing wall on the roof a whirl; the brothers host climbs outside of town, too. *Juárez 101. ☎ 951/516-9576. emayoral71@hotmail.com. $70 bunks, $200 private room. No credit cards (reservations are made via e-mail paid in advance). Amenities: Breakfast room; Internet; shared bathrooms; sheets; towels.*

→ **La Casa Nostra** Backpackers galore come here, yet other than a great, central location and a small cheap cafe, with a pool table and Ping-Pong table, there's not much to recommend La Casa Nostra. Though it's a bit cluttered, and could use a coat of paint, it's not *especially* dirty—the sheets are worn, but clean—and it's only $80 a bed! The cheap prices extend to the bar and restaurant, where beers are two for $20, mezcal is two for $30, and pizza is $45. Party down. *504 Independencia. ☎ 951/514-939. la_casanostra@hotmail.com. $80 per person in the co-ed dorm rooms, $220–$250 private room, shared bathrooms. No credit cards. Amenities: Restaurant; bar; kitchen with small fridge; safe; sheets. In room: Fans.*

MTV Best → **Paulina Youth Hostel** ★★ In a colonial building that has been renovated in a modern minimalist style, this hostel is built around a high-walled central garden and boasts a large cafeteria-style dining area that faces outward. The whole operation is airy, casual, and spotless, especially the spacious bunk dorms, which have larger than usual iron bunk beds and windows. The rooms with double beds are equally comfortable. The only drawback here is that there's no kitchen, but that hardly matters since so many restaurants are nearby. *Valerio Trujano 321. ☎ 951/516-2005. www.paulinahostel.com. $280 single, $300 double, $450 triple, $600 4-person room. MC, V. Amenities: Bar; dining room; 3:30am curfew; Internet at $1 per hour; laundry nearby; shared bathrooms; sheets; towels; travel desk. In room: Lockers.*

Cheap

→ **Casa Cué** This 1950s modern hotel is 2 blocks from the zócalo and right across from the market—it can get loud, but double-glazed windows block out most of the noise. The standard rooms are attractively furnished and well lit, and bathrooms have glass shower stalls and hot water. Junior suites are large and come with a sofa, coffee table, and writing table; most hold two double beds (some have one king and one double). The large suites with two bedrooms are perfect for groups. There's a lovely terrace on top of the three-story building (put on your sneaks, 'cause there isn't an elevator) with a view of the city and the mountains; the bar gets hopping with a mix of both young backpackers and older travelers. *Aldama 103. ☎/fax 951/516-1336. www.mexonline.com/casacue.htm. $650–$720 double, $790–$920 junior suite, $960–$1,300 suite. AE, MC, V. Amenities: Restaurant; bar; car-rental desk; laundry and dry cleaning service; room service; spa with exercise equipment; tour info. In room: A/C, TV.*

→ **Hotel Azucenas** ★ This pleasant two-story colonial hotel was built at the turn of the 19th century but doesn't feel old, perhaps because of the energy of the owners. Touches like mosaic-framed windows and a rooftop terrace, with chairs and views of the city and mountains, create a warm vibe. And everything is spotless, from the freshly tiled bathrooms to the simple rooms with desks. The downstairs rooms have small balconies over the street; but you'll need to head to the rooftop for the best views. The building's thick walls serve to keep the rooms quiet and cool, but they also mess with the Wi-Fi—it only works in the outdoor areas. *Calle Aranda 203, at Matamoros. ☎ 951/514-7918 or 800/882-6089 in U.S. www.hotelazucenas.com. $500 single, $550 double, $625 triple. Amenities: Bar; breakfast room; coffee/tea available all day long; laundry service nearby; travel services; Wi-Fi in common areas. In room: TV, fans, hair dryer (shared), iron.*

→ **Hotel Casa Arnel** ★ A cross between a hotel and a hostel, this family-run spot has been catering to budget travelers for 35 years. Yet the house stays fresh because of quirky touches like the center garden, which is filled with cages of squawking parrots, and an honor system library stocked with English paperbacks. The hotel also has three rooftop terraces with views of the church and the mountains, and lots of hammocks for lounging on. Though it's within walking distance from the long-distance bus terminal, it's a bit of a trek from town, way out in the Colonia Jalatlaco hood. You may have to spring for the occasional cab, but what does that matter if you're saving on the price of a room? *Col. Jalatlaco 404. ☎/fax 951/515-2856. www.casaarnel.com.mx. $120–$220 single, $350–$500 double. Rates rise 30% for holidays. No credit cards. Amenities: Internet; laundry service; luggage storage; safe; shared bathrooms (in dorms); travel info; Wi-Fi for $3 per day. In room: Hair dryer (shared).*

MTV Best → **Las Bugambilias** ★★ This B&B is tucked away in a cool modern house decorated with contemporary and folk art and antiques; there's even an art gallery. The arty vibe extends to all nine rooms, which boast a pleasing minimalist design. Though this may not be the best place to do tequila shots, it is a great place to relax the morning after drinking—the meditation room works wonders for the alcohol-soaked mind and body. A gourmet Oaxacan breakfast is served daily from the fantastic **La Olla** restaurant (see "Eating," below). *Reforma 402, at Constitution. ☎ 951/516-1165 or 877/OAX-CASA in U.S. $550 double (includes breakfast), $1,150 2-room suite. MC, V. Amenities: High-speed Internet; partial kitchen; laundry service; library; Vonage*

Downtown Oaxaca Sleeping & Eating

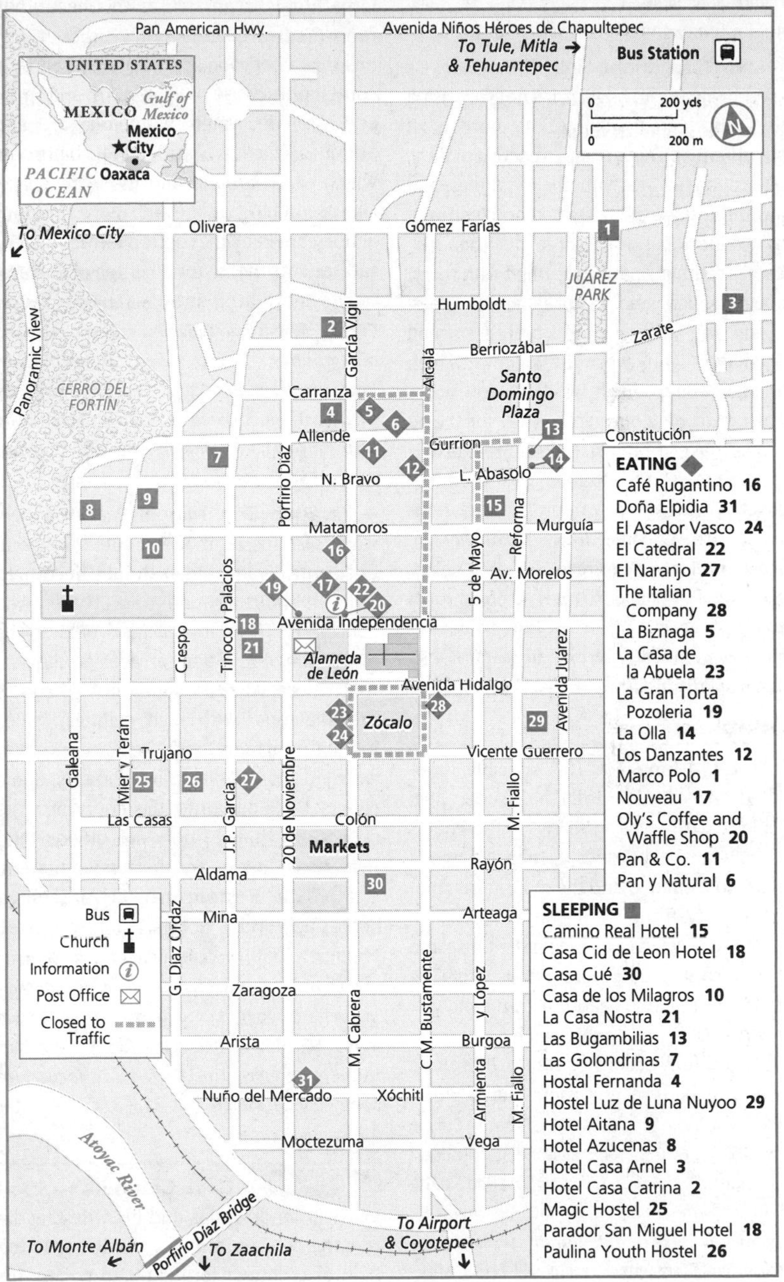

phone in office; travel info; TV (in common room); wheelchair accessible room. In room: A/C (in some), fans, hair dryer, safe, VCR, Wi-Fi.

→ **Las Golondrinas** Since it translates as "The Swallows" in English, it's not surprising that this clean, if slightly tatty, hotel is all about nature. Don't come expecting a party, but to commune with the swallows and those that love them. Owned and managed by Guillermina and Jorge Velasco, the hotel's rambling patios are filled with roses, bougainvillea, and mature banana trees. Inside, the 30 rooms are simply furnished and have slightly worn tile, some with high arched ceilings; most windows and doors open onto the courtyards. A few of the 30 rooms have a king-size bed. Breakfast is served between 8 and 10am in a small tile-covered cafe in a garden setting; non-guests are welcome. *Tinoco y Palacios 411, between Allende and Bravo. ☎ 951/514-3298. $550 double, $430–$570 triple. No credit cards except for deposit. Amenities: Internet at computer kiosk; laundry service; safe; travel info. In room: Private bath.*

OAXACA

Doable

→ **Hotel Aitana** ★★ This stylishly renovated 17th-century hotel has super high ceilings with vigas in many of the rooms and a beautiful outdoor terrace with views of Santo Domingo and the mountains ringing the city. Although it's on a loud street, all the rooms face away from the noise and many front a courtyard restaurant. The floors are made of beautiful green and yellow *cantera* (limestone), which accentuate the beautifully decorated rooms. Most hold two twin beds; a few rooms have either two doubles or a king. *Sabino Crespo 313. ☎ 951/516-39205. www.mexonline.com/aitana.htm. $560–$1,400 single, $600–$1,610 double, $720–$1,820 triple. MC, V. Amenities: Restaurant; bike rental; laundry service; medical service; messenger service; Wi-Fi in restaurant area. In room: Hair dryer, safe.*

→ **La Casa de los Milagros** ★ If you hate large hotels, then stay at this beautifully renovated early-20th-century B&B—it only has three bedrooms. All are inspired by a contemporary use of light, color, and space and are decorated with folk art and antiques. One has a garden in its bathroom which winds around into the living space. Guests itching for even more outdoor action can enjoy the rooftop terrace or venture out to the historic center of Oaxaca, only a short stroll away. *Matamors 500C, at Crespo. ☎ 951/501-2262. www.mexonline.com/milagros.htm. $850–$1,000 single/double. Rates include breakfast. MC, V. Amenities: Breakfast room; kitchen; laundry next door; travel info; TV (in common room); Wi-Fi in outdoor areas. In room: Fans, safe.*

→ **Parador San Miguel** Part of a new wave of midsize, modern hotels in town, this centrally located, tastefully decorated hotel is built around a pretty outside courtyard. There are gardens outside the first-floor rooms, and terraces on the second where you can sunbathe. All rooms are spacious, with high ceilings, hand-loomed curtains and bedspreads, and wrought iron Mexican headboards. Some rooms look out onto the courtyard; the second and third floors are quieter, and they boast desks and better ventilation. The on-site **Restaurante El Andariego** serves up good, if not particularly special, Mexican food. *Independencia 503. ☎ 951/514-9331. www.mexonline.com/paradorsanmiguel.htm. $925–$1,500 double, $1,500–$2,200 suite. AE, MC, V. Amenities: Restaurant; bar; laundry services. In room: A/C, TV, Jacuzzi (in some rooms), stereo.*

Splurge

MTV Best → **Casa Catrina** ★★★ Local artist Rolando Rojas and his wife Claudia remodeled her family's home with the help of architect Jorge Ruiz to create this minimal-meets-colonial space. They definitely succeeded. The walls of this light and open B&B are sealed with a traditional *nopal* (prickly pear) mixture and are simply luminous; when the light hits them a certain way, the flat finish seems to sparkle. The rooms are built according to one color scheme and each features the work of one artist. Indeed, the B&B functions almost like a gallery, built to exhibit the owners' amazing collection of art.

Two of the rooms here open onto a rooftop terrace with views of the Santo Domingo church. Breakfast (included in the price) is maybe the best I had at a hotel in town; the *tamal de amarillo* (yellow tamale) was wonderful, as were the crepes filled with chicken and raja chiles. The downstairs **Bar El Catrin** (see "Partying," p. 635) gets kicking nightly, perhaps because it features the inn's exclusive mescal "Mistique," which has been rated the best in Oaxaca. In case you sample too much, the spa's *temazcal* (steam bath) ceremony is a great way to detox before bed. *Garcia Vigil 703. ☎ 951/514-5322 or 800/728-9098 in the U.S. www.mexicoboutiquehotels.com/casacatrina. $1,440–$2,890 single/double. Rates include breakfast and temazcal for 2. AE, MC, V. Amenities: Bar; breakfast room; Internet; laundry service; massage service; shuttle service to airport; spa; Wi-Fi. In room: A/C, TV, hair dryer, safe, minibar.*

→ **Casa Cid de Leon** ★★ This hotel is a reflection of the owner Leticia Cid de Leon's lively personality. Each room has a theme that is interpreted by Lety's abundant collection of eclectic art—it virtually covers every surface. In her quest to share her life with her guests, guests are allowed, and even encouraged, to touch mementos from her wedding, gifts from her grandchildren, coral art she found in the street, and pieces of china.

The hotel is located in a colonial building in the heart of the city, and what's great about that is that you can sit on the hotel's terrace at night and do some serious people-watching. Once you tire of that, know that the four rooms here are *large;* some are on two levels—perfect for that freshman year reunion you've been planning. Breakfast (included in the rate) is served at a large table on the rooftop terrace by the friendly and attentive staff. *Av. Morelos 602. ☎ 951/514-1893 or 800/728-9098 in the U.S. www.mexicoboutiquehotels.com/ciddeleon. $2,120–$3,500 suite. Breakfast included in rates. AE, MC, V. Amenities: Breakfast room; laundry service; salon service; shuttle to airport; spa. In room: A/C, TV, bathrobe, fans, hair dryer.*

→ **Hotel Camino Real** ★★★ Though set in a 16th-century former convent, this beautifully appointed, luxurious hotel oozes a lot of romance. The great location—between the zócalo and the beautiful Santo Domingo Church—certainly helps, as does the stunning decor; color and textiles are used brilliantly, hidden corridors boast faded frescoes, and beautiful ironwork abounds. Although most of the rooms face into the several adjoining courtyards (one with a pool), it still feels a bit claustrophobic. I promise that it's not too overbearing, though (you *won't* feel like you've entered a convent). The former chapel is now a store; you can see a miniversion of the annual *Guelaguetza* (p. 640) performed there weekly. *Cinco de Mayo 300. ☎ 951/501-6100, or 800/722-6466 in the U.S. www.caminoreal.com/oaxaca. $3,500–$3,800 deluxe, $5,150 junior suite. Discounts in low season. AE, MC, V. Amenities: Restaurant; 2 bars; car-rental desk; health club (free access nearby); laundry service; large outdoor swimming pool; 24-hr. room service; Wi-Fi. In room: A/C, TV, hair dryer, minibar, safe.*

Eating

Traditional Oaxacan food is some of the best in Mexico. If the city only churned out its famous moles, a regional staple that often contains more than 32 ingredients, including chiles, seeds, spices, and chocolate—it'd still be one of the leading culinary destinations in the country. But it's not just about mole: In the last 10 years, Oaxacan cuisine has come a long way in terms of creative re-interpretation. Food here is now world class, on par perhaps with Singapore or other global culinary centers. A number of dishes, for instance, creatively use a wide variety of chiles, many of which you won't find in other parts of the country.

In addition to mole, you must try *tlayudas,* a foot-wide tortilla smeared with mashed beans and then filled with pork, beef, and veggies. Street stalls cook them (as well as their fillings) by placing them directly on hot coals. The result is a smoky, crunchy delight. Other must eats include *quesillo* (salty Oaxacan string cheese), *tamales de mole* (tamales steamed in banana leaves), or the famous *chapulines* (fried grasshoppers prepared with salt and lemon). According to legend, even a tiny bit of a *chapulin* will guarantee your return to Oaxaca, so be brave and try one.

Good restaurants are scattered all over the city, as well as in the markets and even inside hotels and some B&Bs. Cafes (called coffee houses) abound in every part of the city as well; look for them tucked into corners of bookstores, or in "plazas," which are often colonial homes that have been converted into shops.

Plenty of coffee shops also surround the zócalo. Dine at one of the cafes or restaurants here, though, and you'll literally pay for the view of the centuries' old architecture as well as the perfect people-watching. To save money but still enjoy the ambience, you can always bring in tacos or fresh fruit and veggies from one of the markets southeast of the zócalo (see "Shopping," p. 647) and simply dine on one of the many benches there.

For more cheap eats, visit a c*omedores familiares,* or one of the city's smaller, family-owned courtyard restaurants; these don't really advertise except by word-of-mouth, but search around, and you may find a full home-cooked comida corrida at one for under $30. Another option for cheap grub is the city's many food stands, which are spread all around town. Check out "The People's Food" box below for a crib sheet on what to order at one of these stands.

As usual in Mexico's more traditional cities, people here eat the main meal of the day *(comida)* from 2:30 or 3pm, and a lighter supper *(cena)* at 8 or 9pm. Although restaurants serving lunch and dinner may open at 1pm, most people don't show up to eat until later.

Cheap

➔ **Doña Elpidia** MEXICAN Though it's a bit out of the center towards the red-light district, this place is worth finding if you like home-style cooking. For a meal just like what you'd get in a Mexican home, go for their comida corrida of vegetable or pasta soup, a meat or enchilada course, rice, and dessert. Lots of locals come here for their mid-day main meal, so it's gotta be good. You can either sit outside, at tables strewn behind the overgrown garden, or in the comfy yet simple interior area. *Miguel Cabrera 413, between Arista and Nuño del Mercado. ☎ 951/516-4292. Fixed-price lunch $50. No credit cards. Daily 1–5pm.*

➔ **La Gran Torta Pozoleria** MEXICAN Got a hankering for pozole? Then come to this self-described "casa del pozole" right in the middle of town, because it serves big steaming bowls of the hominy soup full of chayote and other vegetables. You can order pozole meatless or with chicken, pork, or beef. They also have hamburgers, burritos, quesadillas, enchiladas, and other typical snacks. But trust me and stick with the pozole; they've been cooking it since 1950 with good reason. It's not a fancy place; you dine under portales surrounding the main patio within view of the kitchen in back, but who cares when the food's this good? *Porfirio Diaz 208. No phone. Main courses $60. No credit cards. Wed–Mon 5–11pm.*

➔ **Oly's Coffee and Wafflehouse** DINER If you're homesick for whole-wheat waffles, bagels, muffins, and sandwiches, this is the place for you. The wheaty carbs (hard to come by in Mexico) and everything else on offer are homemade; they also serve frittatas, steamed eggs, and espresso. You'll dine in an outdoor patio that'll likely be full of a healthy mix of tourists and kids from the school down the street. *Garcia Vigil 304. ☎ 951/516-5805. olyscoffee@hotmail.com. Nothing over $80. No credit cards. Mon–Sat 8am–8pm; Sun 8am–2pm.*

Doable

MTV Best ➔ **El Asador Vasco** ★★ CONTINENTAL/MEXICAN This is one of the most romantic restaurants around the zócalo, mainly because its beautiful balcony offers such a great view. Bring the hottie you met at La Candela (p. 639) last night and they'll be duly impressed; even if the food isn't always amazing, the view and the ambience make up for it. The menu boasts Basque and Oaxacan specialties, as well as chiles rellenos, mole, carne asada, and "continental" cuisine such as snapper filet cooked in olive oil and chile. But the best bets are the light dinners, especially the soups and salads. There's a good wine list, and sometimes there's great live music, too. *Portal de Flores 11. ☎ 951/514-4755. Main courses $80–$180. MC, V. Daily 1–11:30pm.*

➔ **El Catedral** MEXICAN Set inside the first floor of a colonial home, on the edge of the zócalo, El Catedral looks formal but isn't. In fact, it's a bit of a pick up spot; Claudia Rojas was working here as a waitress when she met Rolando Rojas (p. 640), so who knows whom you'll meet when you drop by? The owner and chef serves up tasty food, including cheese tamales; baked plantains filled with *picadillo* (ground beef with spices); and a delicious mousse made with local chocolate, with a slight coffee kick. There's dancing to live tropical music in the bar Friday to Saturday from 9pm to 1am. *Garcia Vigil 105, at Morelos. ☎ 951/516-3285. www.restaurantecatedral.com.mx. Main courses $100–$150. AE, MC, V. Wed–Mon 8am–11pm.*

➔ **El Colibri** MEXICAN A favorite of upwardly mobile Mexican families, this is one of the most tried and true restaurants in town. Though it's somewhat lacking in style (it looks like a stuffy VIP lounge), it compensates with big and tasty portions of food. Avoid the "international cuisine" and you'll be okay. Instead, stick with the Mexican menu, which features *enfrijoladas* (black bean tortillas), tostadas, and an excellent *sopa azteca* (cheese, tomato, and beef soup). *Héroes de Chapultepec 903, Col. Reforma. ☎ 951/515-8087. Main courses $100–$150. AE, MC, V. Daily 1–10pm.*

➔ **El Naranjo** ★★★ MEXICAN This restaurant was closed for a long time and has now opened with a new owner. (Former chef Iliana de la Vega has left Oaxaca.) At presstime, the new owner had hired a chef to design a new menu that will focus on contemporary dishes. Call ahead for hours and other info. In previous years, the restaurant prepared a different one of

Oaxaca's seven *moles* each day of the week, tweaking the traditional recipes a bit to reduce the fat and bring out the flavors. *Trujano 203.* ☎ *951/514–1878. Main courses $80–$150. AE, MC, V. Mon–Sat 1–10pm (hours vary, call ahead).*

➔ **La Biznaga** ★★ MEXICAN This rad restaurant near the Iglesia Santo Domingo attracts a hip, arty crowd for its nouvelle interpretation of traditional Oaxacan food. It's set in a brightly colored, minimalist open courtyard surrounded by contemporary art from the adjacent **Orion Carte** gallery. On my last visit, the tamales, wrapped in the hoya santo leaf and filled with flor de calabasa or *quesino* (a type of Oaxacan string cheese) were divine; the deep-fried tortilla "cones" filled with *flor de Jamaica* (dried hibiscus) and flavored with chipotle chiles, were equally great. For dessert, chef Fernando Lopez Velarde serves up a mole with fruit, salad, and fresh goat cheese, as well as ice cream flavored with mescal—two tasty twists on the traditional. There's an espresso bar as well as a bar with harder stuff; both are great places to hang out after visiting the nearby Jardín Etnobotanico. ***Just be warned:*** You may hang out a while longer than you anticipated, since service here is rather casual. *Garcia Vigil 512.* ☎ *951/516-1800. www.labiznaga.org. Main courses $80–$150. MC, V. Mon–Sat 1–10pm; Sun 2–6pm.*

OAXACA

➔ **La Casa de la Abuela** MEXICAN This typical Oaxacan restaurant, frequented by artists like Rolando Rojas and tourists alike, overlooks the zócalo. The location is nice, but the real draw is that the menu features so many Oaxacan moles, any of which are definitely the thing to get. I learned my lesson when I ordered something else—the chiles rellenos were a mess. The menu also features fried grasshoppers for the *Fear Factor* contestants reading this. *Portal de Flores 11, next to the Asador Vasco.* ☎ *951/516-3544. Main courses $100–$150. MC, V. Daily 1–11:30pm.*

MTV Best ➔ **La Olla** ★★ OAXACAN For another delicious spin on authentic Oaxacan food, try La Olla. The distinguishing factor here is that chef and owner Pilar Cabrera likes to cook a mixture of "not so traditional Mexican with natural food." That means the stress is on healthy, freshly prepared vegetarian food. Take the mole, which is made *en casa;* the small *chile pasilla,* a chile which comes filled with mashed black beans and an amazing sauce, for $75; and the rich soup, which is poured into a bowl with an aguacate leaf and little chunks of Oaxacan cheese. The flan and *arroz con leche* (rice with milk) are so good, they might make you want to weep. To wash down those tears, order a big *jarra* made with fruit juice or juice of the nopal. *Reforma 402.* ☎ *951/516-6668. www.laolla.com.mx. Main courses $100–$150. AE, MC, V. Tues–Sat 8am–10pm.*

➔ **Marco Polo** ★ SEAFOOD This is *the* place in town to get your seafood fix before heading to the beach. All the whole fish specials, baked or marinated in chile guajillo (or several other ways) are excellent, as are the ceviche and shrimp specials. The desserts, especially the bananas baked in cream, condensed milk, and egg nog, are wonderfully indulgent. If the weather's nice, you can eat on the lovely covered patio of this breakfast-and-lunch-only place, which fronts the park known as Paseo Juarez. *Pino Suárez 806.* ☎ *951/513-4308. Main courses $90–$150. AE, MC, V. Wed–Mon 8am–6pm.*

Splurge

MTV Best ➔ **Los Danzantes** ★★★ MEXICAN This place exudes hipness and its clientele—a mix of intellectuals and artists as well as more humble *turistas*—knows it. Architect Alejandro d'Acosta and

The People's Food

If restaurants seem empty in Oaxaca during your visit, it could be that everyone's at the covered market eating at stalls. These are simply the best places in town to try cheap tacos, tamales, tlayudas, and quesadillas. Some of Oaxaca's best food is at the **Mercado Abastos** (p. 649). The **Comedor Familiar Abuelita** (restaurant stall #101) here is a fourth-generation stand that serves delicious *tlayudas al tasajo* (dried beef), as well as black mole and yummy quesadillas for early morning shoppers (it's open 7am–3pm). Also look for special breads, such as *pan de yema con mantequilla* (eggy butter bread) at the bakery **Linda,** at stall #206, and for some of the best tamales in the city, try anything at **Tamales Leti**—especially the black mole, black bean, and sweet pineapple tamales. Horacio Reyes, the chef at **Hacienda de los Laureles,** recommends the **Florecita** stand, where you can sample things like enfrijoladas and empanadas, but **La Guerita** has amazing huitlacoche empanadas as well. Finally, don't miss the women with big baskets of fried grasshoppers sprinkled in lime juice, salt, chile, or garlic, at the entrance to the market. The grasshoppers they sell come in all different sizes; the smaller ones have perhaps a more delicate flavor but worse texture.

The **Mercado Benito Juárez** (p. 649) offers plenty of tasty options as well. There you can try tacos at **Aguas Casilda** or **La Abuelita;** hit up **Chaguita** for one of its famous fruit ices made granita style; or try the aguas frescas at **Casilda** (yes, their water is purified).

Look for **"the tamale lady"** who sets up in front of a farmacia on Avenida Hidalgo and 20 de Noviembre at about 7:30pm. Her salsa verde tamales are tremendously delicious (and people here know it—she can run out of food in an hour, so don't be late!). At night, the best and most famous stand for tlayudas is **Tlayudas del Libres** (Calle Libres at Abasolo; see "Partying," on p. 635).

his brother, owner-partner Hugo d'Acosta (an excellent vintner in Baja California) redesigned what was a centuries-old courtyard into its current multi-tiered state by employing a wall of 12m-high (40-ft.) stacks of adobe to fantastic effect. There's a lovely minimalist raised platform area that offers a more intimate lounge-style bar with comfy but cool sofas to complement the more formal downstairs space. A big pleated canvas roof can cover everything in case of rain. Art exhibitions, video installations, and performance art (not of the karaoke variety) occur regularly.

As an added bonus, the food here is great. It can get expensive if you keep eating small portions. But if you stick to the special $55 menus, which were offered at press time and include soup, salad, entree, fruit water, cafe, and a tiny cup of mescal (2–6pm Mon–Fri only), you'll do just fine. If you feel like splurging, come for dinner and try the grasshopper soup, huitlacoche ravioli in red sauce, duck tacos, salmon wrapped in banana leaves, or mussel casserole. Or simply spring for something off the fantastic liquor list, which includes spectacular choices from Los Danzantes' In Vino Veritas winery, as well as their own brand of mescal. *Alcalá 403, inside the Casa Vieja Plaza. ☎ 951/501-1184 or 501-1187. www.losdanzantes.com. Main courses $200. AE, DISC, MC, V. Daily 11am–midnight.*

OAXACA

Cafes

→ **Caffé Rugantino** COFFEE This student hang-out excels at literally homemade desserts like mocha cake and brownies—a local Spanish woman whips up the snacks sold here in the comfort of her own home. The shop also sells good black teas, cappuccino, flavored drinks, and coffees (amaretto, almond, vanilla, and so on) for all those planning late-night study (or date) sessions. *Garcia Vigil 605-A. ☎ 951/501-0568. Main courses $10–$28. No credit cards. Mon–Fri 8am–10pm.*

→ **The Italian Company** COFFEE The zócalo is bursting with numerous cafes, but this fairly new one (part of a chain) has delicious decaf cappuccino, something still difficult to come by in Mexico. Also on order are tasty desserts like cookies. I recommend snagging one of the corner tables under the entryways so that you can watch all the vendors and cruising tourists from a comfortable distance. *Portales 1. No phone. www.italiancoffee.com. Main courses $50. Daily 8am–11pm.*

→ **Nouveau** COFFEE A student hang-out across the street from the University Mesoamerica, Nouveau has Wi-Fi as well as bagels, croissants, and espresso. It looks pretty Starbucksy downstairs, but make a beeline for the loft upstairs and you'll find a charming spot where you and your laptop

OAXACA

Chocolate *Sin Azucar*

For years I tried Mexican chocolate in all forms and varieties but just couldn't get into it. The slight grittiness of the sugar and the what-is-that flavor just didn't do it for me. That is, until I sampled the real deal at **La Soledad** (Mina 212; ☎ **951/516-3807;** www.chocolatedeoaxaca.com.mx) one morning with the chef from Hacienda de las Laureles, Horacio Reyes, as my guide. At the back bar here you can try different varieties of thick steaming mugs of hot chocolate, including bitter and vanilla. Experiment with varying ratios of sugar to chocolate (I prefer 52% cacao to 48% sugar; apparently men like a higher ratio of chocolate to sugar, which is of course better for your health). Then get brave and try it straight with no sugar—it's actually quite delicious. In between sips and bites, manager Edgardo Chavez Pomo explained to me that before the Spaniards arrived in Mexico, cocoa was eaten with no sugar added, in all its bitter glory. It was also used as money for barter; only kings *ate* it. The cocoa used at La Soledad actually comes from Chiapas and Tabasco where apparently most modern-day locals, like their ancestors, don't eat it. *Que lastima.*

Once you're done salivating over the goods at La Soledad, wander the neighborhood around the covered markets, especially along Mina south of the **20 de Noviembre Market.** You'll find many shops there dedicated to chocolate, where you can not only sample and buy chocolate and mole, but watch the beans being ground in large antique metal grinders. Many of these stores have wooden shelves from floor to ceiling filled with chocolate, mole, and even chocolate-flavored mescal. By the time I left, I was reeling from the aphrodisiac (and caffeine-loaded) effects of the stuff. Or try the **Chocolate Mayordomo** chain, which has seven stores all over the city (including on the corner of Mina and 20 Noviembre, and Calle Morelos 804; www.mayordomo.com); or **Como Agua Pa' Chocolate** (Hidalgo 612; ☎ **951/516-2917**), a restaurant that specializes in dishes made of the stuff.

can chill all day with the friendly students and a cuppa joe. *Garcia Vigil 205. ☎ 951/516-0333, ext. 116. Main courses $50. No credit cards. Mon–Fri 10 am–11pm.*

➔**Pan & Co.** ★★ COFFEE It smells really, really good in here. The area around the Iglesia Santo Domingo is literally buzzing with little cafes filled with hungry church and gallery cruisers, but this bakery is one of the best. It boasts a selection of Italian breads (focaccia with onion, garlic, olive, and rosemary), large tarts (berry, chocolate "tip brownie," streusel, apple), and pastries, including croissants, Danishes, muffins, and pain au chocolate. For something less sweet but just as good, you can also try one of the inexpensive sandwiches like chicken pesto, tuna, veggie, and ricotta toasted with olives and pesto. *Allende 107-B. No phone. www.panetco.com. Snacks $10–$40. No credit cards. Daily 8am–3pm. Also at Aldama 209-D (☎ 951/501-1672) and Belisario Dominguez 612 (☎ 951/513-7104). Mon–Sat 7am–9pm at Aldama and Dominguez locations.*

➔**Pan y Natural** COFFEE You'll get great coffee and a great location at this beautiful open air cafe near the Iglesia Santo Domingo. Not a coffee fan? You can find solace in the huge selection of teas here (including amaretto, ruit, flor de jazmin, chai and guyaba, and more standard green and black). I recommend resisting the sweet snacks here, though, and grabbing one of the superior pastries from Pan & Co. across the street. *Allende 106. No phone. Pastry, coffee $10–$50. No credit cards. Mon–Sat 8am–8pm.*

OAXACA

Partying

Oaxaca may look like a conservative, Catholic town, but its nightlife, which starts around 10pm and goes on often until 2 or 3am, certainly isn't. This remains a place where 3-day-long street parties happen fairly regularly, and where you can pub crawl all night long around the centro's many bars and *antros* (clubs). Yet the heart of the centro also boasts quiet places where you can get away from too much alcohol and noise, like La Embajada (p. 638) or Bar del Borgo (p. 635). And the city has many great restaurants, like Los Danzantes (see "Eating," p. 630) that have cool bars to hang out in and listen to music or performance art.

Oaxaca also has an abundance of cantinas, usually male-only drinking holes, that allow women. Although I don't recommend traveling alone to cantinas in other parts of Mexico, especially if you're a woman, I felt pretty safe visiting cantinas in the touristy neighborhoods where La Farola and Casa de Mezcal are located. See "Appendix A" for more info on cantinas before you decide to visit one of these rowdy establishments, though.

South of the zócalo, in the area around the covered markets (Las Casa and Diez Ordaz streets), is the red light district. Because of high unemployment rates, more locals than ever are being forced into prostitution and you'll see plenty of them working the streets here. (As long as they are registered, prostitutes can work semi-legally in Oaxaca.)

You'll have to head to the outskirts of town to find the city's strip clubs (once called *antros*—that term has now been adopted as the cool way to say nightclub).

Bars & Cantinas

➔**Bar del Borgo** This quiet, cosmopolitan bar that serves both alcohol and caffeinated concoctions is the perfect antidote to its neighbors the Freebar and La Tentación. It's a good place to take a break from dancing and get a dose of

Late Night Grub

After drinking all night, head straight to MTV Best **Tlayudas del Libres** ★★ (Libres 200; no phone; daily 8pm–very late) and try **Dona Martha's** famously amazing *tlayudas.* Her huge handmade tortillas are crisped directly on live coals, then plastered with black beans (seasoned with avocado leaf) and salsa and topped with *tasajo* (half-dried salted beef). During the wee hours, so many people line up to sample the tlayudas (though I hear the pickled pigs' feet are pretty good, too) that the tipsy, friendly crowd spills over the sidewalk onto the street.

Other great places to get grounded at night include **Tacos Alvaro** (Porfirio Diaz at Quetzalcoatl; no phone), a popular street stand that has been around for years, serving people at all times of the night who station themselves at impromptu tables on the sidewalk; **Tacos Sierra** (on Morelos, a half-block west of Alcalá; no phone), an Oaxacan institution that churns out simple tacos filled with pork and spicy salsa; and **El Mesón** (Hidalgo 805, northeast corner of the zócalo; no phone), which sells delicious tacos *de la parrilla* (grilled) and *frijoles de olla* (boiled in a clay pot).

sanity until, that is, about 10pm when they pump up the volume and the mescal starts to flow among the backpackers and avant-garde locals. The walls are decorated with local art, which you may be able to score for a song. *Matamoros 100. No phone.*

→ **Bar El Catrin** Journey down to the basement of the Casa Catrina (p. 628) and you'll enter what seems like a private hangout space created by owners Rolando and Claudia Rojas for their friends. Decorated with local art and Rojas's sculptures, the bar exclusively sells the export-only, award-winning "Mistique" mescal. While having *una copa,* you can sample the great food—featuring everything from fondue to cold cuts—or simply discuss art and politics with the writers, singers, and artists who frequent the place. On any given night, you might stumble into a special auction held to benefit art institutions, live music, or karaoke (usually on holidays like Independence Day; and at a charge of $195 including buffet dinner). *Garcia Vigil 703.* ☎ *951/514-5322 or 516-0519.*

→ **Fandango** Hope you cultivated some inner peace at La Embajada (p. 638), cause now you're gonna spill it all over the dance floor at this smoky macho rock bar next door. From the messy wall collages to the futbol videos or soundless films playing in the background to the sloshed clientele, this place perfects stinky bar ambience. Have a few drinks and you'll feel right at home. *Across the street from Bar 502, Porfirio Diaz on corner of Allende. No phone.*

→ **La Casa de los Perros** At this very cool space, dominated by a long modern bar running its length, you won't find any *perros* (dogs), just beautiful young tattooed things. Actually, the clean, white, and minimalist space *is* named after the bulldogs that live here, but they don't make many appearances. Instead, a healthy mix of Swiss, German, French, Dutch, and North American muchachitas (and –chos), and hip locals come to dance to the mostly electronic and ambient mix on their tiny dance floor, or lounge in the groovy back room. *Porfirio Diaz 500, at Allende. No phone.*

Downtown Oaxaca Partying & Sightseeing

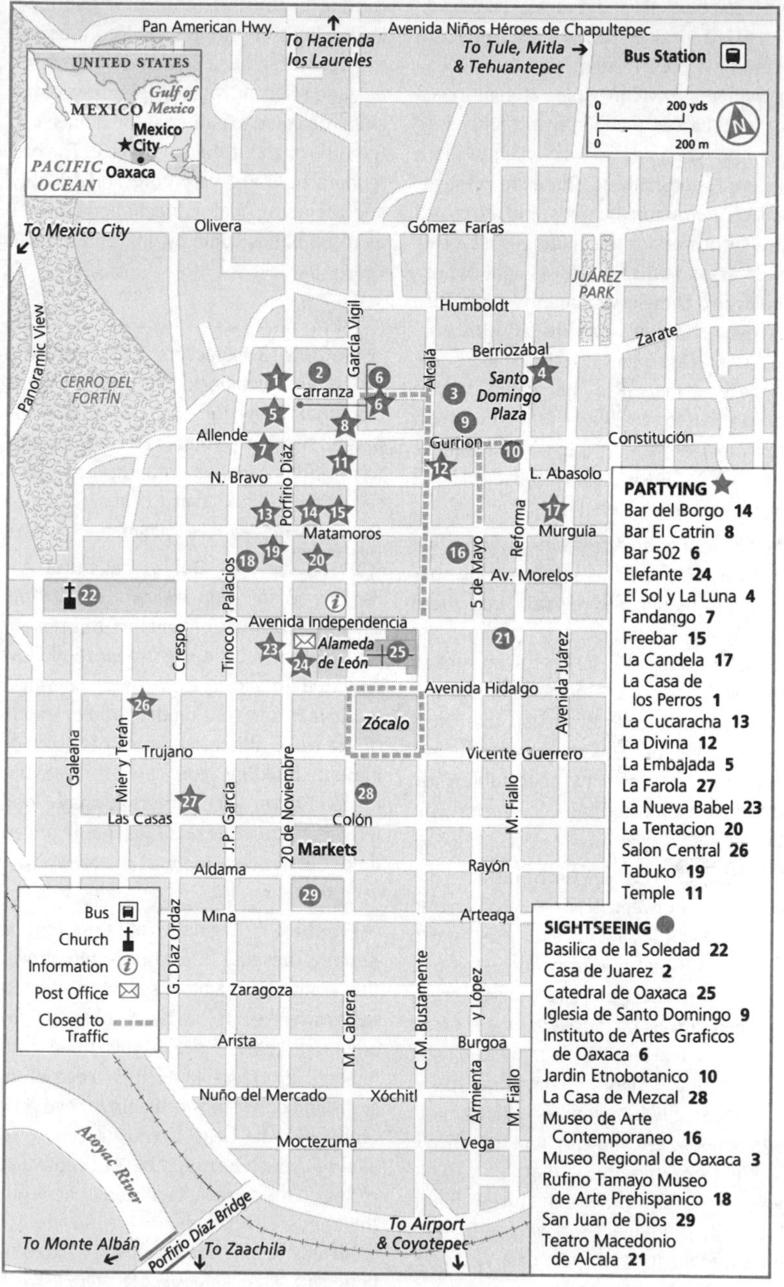

→ **La Casa de Mezcal** Opened in 1935, and just a block from the zócalo, La Casa de Mezcal is a Mexican rarity: a relatively safe cantina, although it still feels a *little* creepy for women traveling solo. It features a beautiful carved wood bar and jukeboxes from the '50s updated with slightly more modern Mexican music. There are great 70-year-old murals on the walls, and the crowd consists of working and middle-class locals on dates, as well as the occasional obnoxious drunk. They serve tamarindo, hibiscus, and even chocolate martinis, all with mezcal. Try at least one, since they make some of the best mezcal in the region. If that doesn't do if for you, know that they have a great stock of *toblada,* too, which is similar to tequila but made from wild agave. *Miguel Cabrera 209. ☎ 951/516-2191.*

→ **La Cucaracha** A less fancy alternative to La Casa Mezcal, this small cantina specializes in tequila and mezcal. Since there are over 100 varieties at $17 a shot, just watch out that you don't end up on the floor with the place's namesake. The bar also features regular live music in a small performance space, as well as dancing in a separate room, so tiny that tables are perched on a loftlike catwalk. *Porfirio Dias 301A. ☎ 917/501-1636.*

MTV Best → **La Embajada** ★★ Squished between Los Perros and Fandango is this cool juice bar run by two Argentinean and Italian women—it's one of the town's best places to take a break between drinks (or to take a longer break if you don't drink). You simply can't get more laid-back than this communal space, which basically functions as a living room with sofas where you can hook up on Wi-Fi. What's even better is that you can eat here, too; the menu features South American–style meat sandwiches for $30, and cafe for $20. *Porfirio Diaz 501. No phone. www.laembajada.blogspot.com.*

→ **La Farola** Although this is the oldest cantina in town, it looks new and fancy inside. Built in 1916, it's entered the modern age with a huge screen that plays futbol, and today attracts cellphone-wielding kids who come to gather at the tables scattered throughout the huge space. The bartenders here are very cute and friendly, and the occasional mariachi band as well as troba bands come by. *J. P. Garcia 300-A. ☎ 951/516-6974.*

Clubs

→ **Elefante** Backpackers and those who lust after them flock to this after-hours club that goes until 5am. It gets really packed with very young clubbers groovin' to reggaeton, monumento, hip-hop, some salsa, and '80s dance music. *20 de Noviembre 110, Centro. No phone.*

MTV Best → **El Sol y La Luna** ★★ Famous as the club where Mexican folk singer Lila Downs got her start, this restaurant/club attracts a slightly more mellow crowd than most. Latin, jazz, or world music fans hang out on the patio or in one of the three adjoining rooms of the colonial-era building. You can also see flamenco here. The international food (crepes, pizza, steaks) is reasonably priced if not outstanding. *Reforma 502. ☎ 951/514-8069. Cover $25–$50.*

→ **Freebar** ★ Regulars call this joint *la pescera,* because the young, hip crowd that comes here almost seems to swim in their own sweat in the two-room goldfish-bowl-size space. Once it gets filled with hipsters grooving to techno, reggaeton, salsa, and dance music, the tiny space generates definite heat. If you have time to admire your surroundings in between ogling all the dancers on display, check out the animal heads hanging behind the bar (with Day of the Dead candy sprinkled in between). *Matamoros 100C, at Garcia Vigil. ☎ 951/514-3834.*

Best → **La Tentación** ★★★ A restaurant during the day, this place morphs into one of the town's most popular clubs at night. When it gets really hopping, it feels like the whole city is here either standing in line to get in, trying to salsa on the dance floor, or chatting at the bar or in the narrow hallways. Earlier in the night, the not-huge and not really attractive space fills up with very young men who come out to cruise. Rap videos play overhead on small monitors, though the play list switches between dance, rap, and alternative tunes. Around 10pm on weekends, the DJ also blasts salsa, merengue, and cumbia before the live band plays. *Matamoros 101. ☎ 951/514-9521. Cover $35.*

→ **Tabuko** Instant karma's gonna get you at this Buddhist-themed club, where if you've been good, maybe you'll be rewarded with a date home. I'm not sure if Buddha would approve of the vastness of his visage above the dance floor, but lots of 18-year-old locals and foreign visitors, who pack into this trying-a-bit-too-hard club, don't seem to mind. Things really heat up when there's live merengue, salsa, or cumbia playing. During the week, the mix gears more toward the alternative. Oh yeah, and there's even karaoke. Fortunately, a back room offers a bit of respite from the resultant drunken warbling. *Porfino Diaz 219, at Matamoros. No phone.*

Gay Bars

→ **Bar 502** Ring the bell and the door will open (you hope) into this prominent gay club with the best house music in town. It has a late license so you can dance all night. Follow three simple rules and you'll do fine: Don't check your attitude at the door; arrive after midnight; and stay until dawn. *Porfirio Diaz 502. ☎ 951/516-6020.*

Live Music

Best → **La Candela** ★★★ Housed in a beautiful colonial building, this nightlife institution will get you to shake your salsa booty or nothing will. The great music here includes live salsa and merengue on the weekends. *Murguía 413, corner Pino Suarez. ☎ 951/514-2010. Cover varies, around $30.*

→ **La Divina** If you're into heavy metal alternative music, or guitar jams (with a touch of Manu Chao) this place, well, rocks. The five-room club's decor is a bit surreal, with the divine theme threading it's way through the small spaces. It gets especially wild and crazy on weekends, when there's live music. *Gurrion 104, at Alcalá. ☎ 951/582-0508.*

→ **La Nueva Babel** An open forum that plays Cuban and Latino music, this small, hip, and intimate boho club has jazz on the weekends as well as the occasional poetry reading. Don't be surprised if people around you spontaneously burst into song—it's that sort of place. *Porfiro Diaz 25. No phone. Cover $25.*

→ **Salon Central** Come here during the week, and you'll be greeted by a young hip art crowd; on the weekends, it gets more touristy. Featuring independent film screenings and obscure-but-worth-it live music, this club's walls also host art from established and not so well known artists. *Hidalgo 302. ☎ 951/514-2042. Cover $30–$50.*

→ **Temple** ★★ This Italian restaurant becomes a hip jazz spot playing everything from traditional quartets to funk/acid jazz on Wednesdays, Fridays, and Saturdays when guest artists jam in the cool, narrow space. The bar boasts blue-class lighting, exposed brick walls, and industrial window fans, all evoking the sort of joint you'd find somewhere in SoHo, New York. The food excels at regional cuisine, tweaked to a higher level—stand-out dishes include the grilled prawn stuffed with eel or squash blossom soup with goat cheese. *Garcia Vigil 409A.* ☎ *951/516-8676. www.restaurantetemple.com.*

Performing Arts

Two blocks east of the zócalo, the **Teatro Macedonio de Alcalá** (Independencia at Armenta y López; ☎ **951/516-8312;** open only for events; prices vary from $50–$300) holds 1,300 people and hosts concerts and performances in the evening. Check out the marble stairway and Louis XV vestibule, if you can get inside. Check the door to see if any events are posted.

On the last 2 Mondays in July, Oaxaca holds the **Fiesta Guelaguetza.** In the villages of central Oaxaca, a *guelaguetza* (literally, a gift) is a celebration by a family in need of assistance to hold a wedding or some other community celebration. Guests bring gifts, which the family repays when they attend other guelaguetzas. The Fiesta Guelaguetza, begun in 1974, brings dancers from all the state's various ethnic groups to Oaxaca. The fiesta is also an opportunity to show off traditional clothing and dance—the matter is treated with intense civic pride. Some 350 different *huipiles* (traditional Maya blouses) and other costumes are on display during the performances.

In years past, dance performances took place in the stadium that crowns the Cerro del Fortín each Monday from 10am to 1pm. At press time, however, that stadium was closed and a new main location for the festival was not yet announced. Tickets are usually available through Ticketmaster, though, so you can check for details there.

Oaxacan Art History 101

Not only is Oaxaqueno **Francisco Toledo** the most important living Mexican graphic artist, he also happens to have brought art to the people of Oaxaca in many different ways. Some of his projects in Oaxaca include the **Ethno Botanical Garden** (p. 645), the **Instituto de Artes Graficas de Oaxaca** (IAGO), and the **library** at IAGO (p. 644). Working with other artists, Toledo was also instrumental in the establishment of the **Museo de Arte Contemporáneo de Oaxaca (MACO)** (p. 644). Born in the town of Juchitan de Zaragoza in 1940, Toledo studied in Mexico City and later Paris but has been living in Oaxaca for years; his wife founded and runs a wonderful avant-garde boutique known simply as **Tienda Q** in downtown (p. 649).

Because Oaxaca is an artists' colony in every sense, the artists here aren't limited to Toledo. Other well-known artists hailing from here have included the late **Rufino Tamayo,** a world-renowned painter whose work can be viewed at the Rufino Tamayo Museo (p. 644), **Rodolfo Morales, Rodolfo Nieto,** and **Francisco Gutierrez** who, in spite of their deaths at an early age, left work considered fundamental to the country's art history.

One standout contemporary artist in Oaxaca is **Rolando Rojas,** whose work is made with oil, watercolor, lithography metal, wood, and bronze. You can hang out at his bar, El Catrin (p. 636) or better yet stay at his wonderful B&B, Casa Catrina (p. 628) to experience his work as well as that of other local artists.

Even if you don't attend the dances, you can enjoy the festival atmosphere that engulfs the city. On the Sunday nights before the Guelaguetza, university students present an excellent program in the Plaza de la Danza at the Soledad church. The production, the *Bani Stui Gulal,* is an abbreviated history of the Oaxaca valley. The program begins at 9pm; arrive early, because the event is free and seating is limited.

Sightseeing

Oaxaca has tons of fabulous churches, museums, galleries, and historic buildings. Fortunately, the city is so centralized that you can easily explore most sites on foot. To help you get oriented when you first arrive, I recommend taking a walking tour through the historic center. **Academic Tours** (☎ **951/518-4728;** www.academictoursoaxaca.com; call for rates and schedules) can arrange daily half-day tours of the zócalo and its chocolate mills, with some museums, galleries, and a church or two thrown in. **Linda Ridgecliff** also offers tours (ridgecliff@hotmail.com; at 10am on Tues or Sat, in front of the cathedral, $95 per person for a 2-hr. tour); all the proceeds go to Estancia, a children's charity. See "Playing Outside" below for more recommendations on companies that can arrange tours.

Once you have your bearings, it's fun to explore the city your own; wander Oaxaca's streets, and you're bound to come across an interesting church, museum, or gallery, and of course there are a million little boutiques and cafes along the way to distract you from sightseeing. Just don't forget to spend some quality time in the zócalo—this traffic-free square is the best place in town for relaxing while getting a feel for the town.

Break Time

During Oaxaca's festivals, sidewalk stands near the cathedral sell *buñuelos* (thin, crisp, sweet fritters), along with hot *ponche* (a steaming fruit punch) or *atole* (a cornstarch-based hot drink). The buñuelos are served in cracked dishes; it's customary to smash them on the sidewalk for good luck, so go for it!

Festivals/Events

Lots of people come to Oaxaca solely for its exuberant traditional festivals, especially Holy Week, the Guelaguetza (see "Performing Arts," above for info), Días de los Muertos, the Night of the Radishes (yes, you read that correctly), and Christmas. Make hotel reservations at least 2 months in advance if you plan to visit during these times.

Holy Week (Semana Santa): This week is celebrated all over Mexico (see "Basics," p. 10), but the ceremonies in Oaxaca are particularly beautiful and moving. As in San Miguel de Allende, there are processions where hundreds of the faithful walk from church to church to pray at each one. On Good Friday, there are *encuentros:* Groups depart from various churches, carrying religious figures through the surrounding neighborhoods, then "encounter" each other back at the church. Throughout the week, each church sponsors concerts, fireworks, fairs, and other entertainment. Early April.

Fiesta Nacional de Mezcal: Booths, replete with shelves of mescal, line the streets of Oaxaca during this celebration to all things mescal. Free tastings help everyone get blasted and fireworks rocketing overhead add to the celebratory mood. July 17 to 24.

Días de Los Muertos: Here's another festival that's celebrated across Mexico, but which Oaxaca excels at. During this macabre holiday that honors saints and deceased children on one day, and deceased adults on another, markets brim with skull candy and special breads and food shaped like coffins and bones. Elaborate altars are erected and embellished with the favorite dishes, drinks, and cigarettes of the deceased. People also decorate tombstones and spend the night partying at cemeteries. Try to take one of the nocturnal cemetery tours offered around this time. Hotel Casa Arnel (☎ **951/515-2856**) runs one. One feature of the holiday that's unique to Oaxaca is that here, it's customary for young men to dress up in ghoulish outfits and dance in the streets. November 1 and 2.

Fiesta de la Virgen de Guadalupe (Festival of the Virgin of Guadalupe): The December Festivals begin on the 12th with this festival and continue on the 16th with a *calenda,* or procession, to many of the older churches in the *barrios,* all accompanied by dancing and costumes. Festivities continue on the 18th with the **Fiesta de la Soledad** in honor of the Virgen de la Soledad, patroness of Oaxaca state. A large fireworks construction known as a *castillo* is erected in Plaza de la Soledad. When it is ignited, look out.

La Noche de Rábanos (the Night of the Radishes): Calling all radish lovers—each December 23, Oaxaqueños build fantastic sculptures out of enormous radishes, flowers, and cornhusks in celebration of their favorite root vegetable. Displays on three sides of the zócalo are set up in the early afternoon, and by 6pm, when the show officially opens, lines to see the figures are 4 blocks long. This homage to the radish leads off the city's more standard Christmas festivities; at about 8:30pm on December 24, churches organize processions with music, floats, enormous papier-mâché dancing figures, and crowds bearing candles, all of which converge on the zócalo. Late December.

Churches

→ **Basílica de Nuestra Señora de la Soledad** ★★ Though it's not as ornate or gilded as other churches in town—it actually feels a bit frayed at the edges—this church is nonetheless the religious heart of town. Since it's home to a beautiful pearl-encrusted statue of the Virgin of Solitude, the church is the best place to pay homage to the patroness of the State of Oaxaca. Pilgrims from all over the state flock here in December for the Fiesta de la Soledad (see above).

Though in need of repair, the church's concave facade offers a nice twist on most of Mexico's religious architecture. A small charming museum behind the church tells the Virgin's story through its hand-painted panels; it also contains all sorts of statues, religious paintings, a glass casket with a Santo Entierro used in Semana Santa ceremonies, a stuffed cat, mixed tapes, and odd religious knick-knacks. One of the best perks of a visit here, though, is the nearby ice cream stands—it's practically a tradition to indulge in a cone when visiting the Basílica. *Independencia 107 at Galeana. No phone. Suggested admission $30. Mon–Sat 10am–2pm and 4–6pm; Sun 11am–2pm. Basilica: Daily 7am–2pm and 4–9pm.*

FREE → **Catedral de Oaxaca** ★ This cathedral was built in 1553 and reconstructed in 1773. Its elaborate 18th-century baroque facade is an excellent example of the Oaxacan style. The central panel above the door depicts the assumption of the Virgin. Note the heavy, elaborate frame around the picture and the highly stylized wavelike clouds next to the cherubs—these elements, repeated in other churches in the region, are telltale signs of Oaxacan baroque. The interior isn't as interesting as the outside—it was plundered of most of its goods during the Wars of Reform. *In front of Parque Alameda. No phone. Free admission. Daily 7am–9pm.*

MTV Best FREE ➔**Iglesia de Santo Domingo** ★★★ There are 27 churches in Oaxaca, but none can equal the splendor of this one's interior, started in the 1550s by Dominican friars but finished a century later. The ornate statues and flowers carved from wood and then covered with plaster are amazingly well-preserved and maintained, and the extravagantly gilded walls and ceiling contain the work of the city's best artists. It's nice to sit and meditate in the silent Chapel of Christ, and get lost in the amazing patterns along the walls. Or check out the ceiling by the choir loft—it depicts the genealogical tree of the Dominican order, which starts with Don Domingo de Guzmán, (Saint Dominic). The original retabla was reconstructed in the 1950s from wood completely covered in gold leaf—as is much of this church. Don't leave without checking out the beautiful botanical gardens in the back; see the "Jardín Etnobotanico" box for info. *Alcalá s/n at Gurrión. No phone. Free admission. Daily 8am–1pm and 4–10:30pm.*

FREE ➔**San Juan de Dios** This oldest church in Oaxaca, built in 1521 or 1522 of adobe and thatch, and reconstructed in the mid-1600s, has an exterior that's sweetly simple. The interior has an ornate altar with paintings by Urbano Olivera on the ceiling. The glass shrine to the Virgin near the entrance is especially revered by Oaxaqueños. Many of the faithful visiting here are vendors (or buyers) at the nearby markets. *20 de Noviembre s/n, corner of Aldama and Arteaga. No phone. Free admission. Daily 6am–11pm.*

Museums & Galleries

➔**Casa de Juárez** If you want a crash course in the life of Mexico's ex-president Benito Juárez, stop by the house where he first lived upon arriving in the city as a

Free & Easy

There's lots to do for free in Oaxaca. Many of the city's beautiful churches and museums are always free, or sections are free, like the **Biblioteca** at the **Jardín Etnobotanico** (p. 645), where you'll be charged nada to browse the beautiful selection of art books. Other museums, like the **Basílica de la Soledad** (see above) are technically free, though they do ask for a small donation. Still want more museums? Check out the free **Museo de Filatelia** (Reforma 504; ☎ **951/516-8028;** www.mufi.org.mx), an architecture museum which doesn't charge admittance, or the **Centro Fotografico Alvarez Bravo** (Murgula 302; ☎ **951/516-9800**), a museum devoted to rotating photography exhibits.

Just because you're broke doesn't mean you can't go shopping, either; the **Galería Quetzalli, MARO, Amante,** and **Librería Granen Porrua** (see "Shopping," p. 647) make for great browsing. You can still drink, too. At **Museo del Mezcal** (Independencia 601; ☎ **951/501-2700** or Morelos 907 B; ☎ **951/514-6330**), you'll get free tastings of "La Reliquia" as well as crema de mezcal (kind of like Baileys, with different flavors) along with your admission fee. There are other free tasting rooms around the city, including **Don Agave** (Cinco de Mayo 210 or Aldam 209; ☎ **951/517-7349**). At most, you can sample booze from 10am until 8pm.

servant boy. Though the house disappointingly doesn't have any of his personal effects or any original furniture, it does show how a typical 19th-century household would have looked. Read the information provided in each room and you'll be an expert in about 20 minutes. *García Vigil 609. ☎ 951/516-1860. Admission $30. Tues–Sat 10am–7pm; Sun 10am–5pm.*

MTV Best FREE → **Instituto de Artes Graficas de Oaxaca/IAGO** ★★★ One of the foremost art libraries in the world, built up from the collection of Francisco Toledo (p. 640), is housed in this restored colonial house in downtown Oaxaca. To best take advantage of the long narrow rooms here, the books are stacked in neat floor to ceiling shelves. Ladders are provided to help you fully peruse the beautiful art books from all over the world, including Asia, Mongolia, India, Africa, Tibet, Europe, America, and Mexico. In addition to a permanent collection of over 5,000 graphic works, IAGO has a 20,000 volume library of works on art, architecture, archaeology, photography, movies, crafts, literature, and design. There's also a tiny temporary exhibition gallery, a book shop of hard-to-find publications, and two patios (a restaurant is located on one of them). Although you can't check out a book, the library is free and open for anyone to come in and browse or study. You can read in the small plaza as well. This place is simply not to be missed if you like art at all. *Alcalá 507. No phone. Free admission. Daily 10am–8pm.*

→ **Museo de Arte Contemporáneo de Oaxaca** ★★ The MACO is in an 18th-century building known as the Casa de Cortez but the name is misleading—it was never Cortez's estate. The museum was actually started in 1992 with the help of Francisco Toledo, and exhibits the work of contemporary artists primarily from Oaxaca state, which has produced some of Mexico's most famous painters—such as Toledo, Rodolfo Morales, Rodolfo Nieto, and Francisco Gutierrez. It also has workshops in the back with art classes and has a small yet helpful bookstore, as well as a cafe. *Alcalá 202, between Murguía and Morelos. ☎ 951/514-2228. Admission $10. Wed–Mon 10:30am–8pm.*

→ **Museo Regional de Oaxaca** ★★★ Housed in the ex-convent of Iglesia Santo Domingo, this is the most ambitious, if not the premier, museum in the city. The government spent millions on renovations and it shows; from the magnificent stairs, to the arches, to the cupolas, the place is now a visual orgy of stone detail work and heavy-hitting colonial-era murals. As for the actual exhibits on display, they encompass a somewhat overwhelming project displaying the course of human development in the Oaxaca valley from the earliest times through the 20th century. Rooms are dedicated to the present-day ethnographic makeup of Oaxaca and a brief history of the efforts of the Dominican order in the region. But if you're already yawning as you read this, skip straight to the artifacts from Monte Albán's Tomb 7—they'll prove enlightening if you plan to visit Monte Albán as a side trip. Discovered in 1932, this tomb contained 12 to 14 corpses and some 500 pieces of jewelry and art, made of 3.6kg (8 lb.) of gold as well as turquoise, conch shell, amber, and obsidian. The larger collection of artifacts from Monte Albán showcases the Olmec and Teotihuacan influence in ceramics and carvings. *Gurrión at Alcalá. ☎ 951/516-2991. Admission $43. Tues–Sun 10am–7:45pm.*

→ **Rufino Tamayo Museo de Arte Prehispánico de México** ★ You shouldn't spend all your time in Oaxaca gawking at the works of art inside its museums and galleries. You'll also want to take time to

A Garden Tour

Housed in the "backyard" of the Iglesia de Santo Domingo, the magnificent MTV Best **Jardín Etnobotanico** ★★★ covers 1.6 hectares (4 acres) of medicinal, edible, ornamental, industrial, and ceremonial varieties of plants. It has more than 9,000 flowering species alone, as well as the most extensive and complete collections of cacti and agaves from the State of Oaxaca in the country. It's another project of artist Francisco Toledo (and the ProOax organization that he leads) along with Luis Sarate and Alejandro d'Avila, who decided that the garden should attempt to show the connection between the diverse cultures of Oaxaca and its plant life. To really understand how the garden succeeds in doing this, you need to take a tour with one of the volunteer guides; it's included in the admission fee. The guides (mostly students earning credit) are quite knowledgeable and will show you plant seeds that can be used as soap (you can grind them up in one of the many fountains and wash your hands); trees used by ancient travelers to make paper; plant fiber used to make shoes, hats, and clothing; plants that can be eaten as sweets or taken medicinally; or plants that can be used as dyes, paints, or even as gourds for cooking or washing. There's also an extensive underground system of water reclamation that is beautifully incorporated via patios into the overall design of the garden, which is framed by the massive walls of the church. A Spanish language library that specializes in the natural sciences is also on-site and is open Monday through Friday 9am to 10pm and Saturday 9am to 2pm. It's located at Reforma s/n, at the corner of Constitucion.

Call ☎ **951/516-7672** or e-mail jetnobot@prodigy.net.mx for info. Tours in English are Tuesday, Thursday, and Saturday at 11am. The garden is open Monday to Friday from 9am to 8pm, and Saturday from 9am to 2pm. Admission is $50 or $25 for students or teachers; but remember to tip the volunteer guides—they are well worth it.

step outside and appreciate the beautiful colonial buildings many of these works are housed in. The building of the Museo de Arte Prehispánico is one such example—it's one of the finest examples of Spanish architecture from the colonial period.

Once you've checked out the exterior of the museum, try to spend at least some time inside. Most of the artifacts displayed here were donated by Oaxaqueno Rufino Tamayo, one of the leading Mexican artists of the 20th century. Yet the sheer amount of pre-Hispanic art can be a bit much; over 1,000 pieces cover the pre-Classic period up to the Aztec era, including regions from Nayarit to Chiapas, as well as the Gulf Coast. Hang in there, though, and you'll be rewarded with a deeper knowledge of the diversity and variety of styles of pre-Columbian art in Mexico. The collection of art by Tamayo himself is, not surprisingly, also strong. *Av. Morelos 503, between Tinoco y Palacios and Porfirio Díaz.* ☎ *951/516-4750. Admission $30. Mon and Wed–Sat 10am–2pm and 4–7pm; Sun 10am–3pm. Closed holidays.*

Playing Outside

Several eco-tourism outfits offer adventure tours that take you around town and to the surrounding Sierra Norte mountain range. **Zona Bici** (García Vigil 406;

☎ **951/516-0953;** boccaletti@prodigy.net.mx) conducts bike tours in the city as well as in the valley. Another bike touring company, used by many of the area hotels, is **Bicicletas Pedro Martinez** (Aldama 418; ☎ **951/514-5935;** www.bicicletaspedromartinez.com), which can rent you bikes or take you on tours in or outside of town. They also offer guided hiking trips for non-bikers.

A 7-day premier mountain biking trip is offered through **Rio y Montana's Sierra Norte de Oaxaca** (Bravo 210-1; ☎ **951/514-8271** or 866/591-5336 in the U.S.; www.rioymontana.com) through the cloud forests of the Sierra Norte. The 70-mile, 7-day trip (50%–70% on single-track) includes a night in Oaxaca and then visits some *pueblos mancomunados* (craft villages), as well as nearby Monte Albán and Teotitlán. One day of the tour features a 1,200m (4,000-ft.) downhill ride into Lachatao, an ancient town with a 16th-century church built by Spanish Dominican priests. The trip includes stays in everything from rustic cabañas to four-star hotels, hand-cooked meals, airport transports, gear (except the bike)—but you have to shell out for it (it's $6,540–$16,350 for a single room, half of that per person for double occupancy).

From the rural guesthouse MTV Best **Casa Sagrada** ★★ (Alcala 203; ☎ **951/516-4275;** www.casasagrada.com) perched high on a hill overlooking Teotilán and the entire valley of Oaxaca, you can get outside on a

OAXACA

MTV U Make Your Cake & *Habla Español*, Too

Pilar, owner of **La Olla** (see "Eating," above), offers Oaxacan cooking classes in the city. You can also arrange cooking classes in nearby Teotitlán through La **Mano Mágica** (p. 648). The 6-hour class here includes a trip to the local market, a class and garden tour, and a four-course gourmet meal taught by native Zapotec chef Reyna Mendoza. There's always someone on hand who provides cultural commentary as well as English translations.

Horacio Reyes from **Hacienda Los Laureles** ★ (Hidalgo 21, San Felipe del Agua; ☎ **951/501-5300;** www.mexicoboutiquehotels.com/loslaureles; $600 per person) takes students to the market to buy ingredients (like seasonal vegetables) and drink hot chocolate before instructing them on how to make his delicious mole. Hacienda also happens to be as great a place for resting as for eating—this former hacienda incorporates gardens into some of its spacious rooms, and features a full service spa with temazcal services.

Oaxaca has about a half-dozen language schools. With prior notice, most can arrange home stays with a Mexican family for students looking for total immersion. With little notice, most can arrange a week of classes for visitors to brush up their language skills. The **Instituto Cultural Oaxaca A.C.,** Av. Juárez 909 (Apdo. Postal 340, 68000 Oaxaca, Oax.; ☎ **951/515-3404;** www.instculturaloax.com.mx), has the biggest name and perhaps the least flexibility. Besides language skill, classes focus on Oaxaca's history and archaeology. The **Instituto de Comunicación y Cultura,** Alcalá 307–312 (68000 Oaxaca, Oax.; ☎/fax **951/516-3443;** www.iccoax.com), provides group and private instruction and uses music, art, and handicrafts to get students into the swing of things. Classes are small. **Becari Language School,** Manuel Bravo 210 (68000 Oaxaca, Oax.; ☎ **951/514-6076;** www.becari.com.mx) was founded in 1994, and gets raves from students for having lots of flexibility and small classes.

horse, a bike, or your own two feet. Run by Mary Jane Gagnier de Mendoza and her husband, local weaver Arnulfo Mendoza, this operation is a great way to really get away from typical tours and experience the countryside first hand. They excel at riding tours, like a 2-hour tour over ancient paths and through exotic flora, including candelabra cacti. All rides can include a picnic lunch or a four-course gourmet meal of regional Oaxacan cuisine. The half-day program includes transport, an outdoor activity (either horseback riding, mountain biking, or hiking), a temazcal, and a meal, for $950 per person. Overnight stays, including two full meals, are $1,300 per person.

Shopping

In my opinion, the state of Oaxaca makes the highest quality Mexican textiles and other crafts in the country. That makes shopping in its capital pretty fabulous. Most of the town's shops, bookstores, galleries, and boutiques are located in the 10-block area running north on Garcia Vigil from the zócalo toward Santo Domingo and encompassing the streets around it. The Alcalá, partially a pedestrian street running pretty much up the center of town from the Alameda parallel to Garcia Vigil, also has many great shops. The area around Santo Domingo (p. 643) is home to high-quality crafts shops—and the prices may reflect that. Better bargains can be found in the markets south of the zócalo or in the villages outside of town (see "Road Trips," below for info). Store hours are generally from 10am to 2pm and 4 to 7pm Monday through Saturday.

Bookstores

In addition to **Librería Granen Porrua** (see below), one of the best bookstores in Oaxaca, if not all of Mexico, is **Amate** ★★ (Alcalá 307-2, Plaza Alcalá; ☎ **951/516-6960**). In addition to stocking many guidebooks in English, they are one of the few places in town that stock a full catalog of "world" music CDs. The **Librería Universitaria** (Guerrero 108; ☎ **951/516-4242**) stocks a few books about Oaxaca in English. And you can find books on history, literature, archaeology, and anthropology, mostly in Spanish, in the upstairs section of **Provedora Escolar** (Independencia 1001; ☎ **951/516-0489**).

MTV Best → **Librería Granen Porrua** ★★ Part of a complex within a colonial courtyard, this bookstore carries an extensive collection of literature, travel, and art books; for those experiencing *Cosmo*-withdrawal, there are also magazines (most are in Spanish). I counted at least 15 books about Frida Kahlo, so you can also get your fix on surrealist art here. Hundreds of CDs are for sale, too, including an entire collection of regional, Mexican, classical, and Latin American discs. Most of the books are in Spanish but there's a small English collection (though what does that matter if you're looking for art books?).

Adjoining the bookstore is a **boutique** with a beautiful selection of rebozos from Santa María del Rio and other villages around Oaxaca City, as well as traditional skirts from the Isthmus and other regions. They also sell Francisco Toledo sketchbooks; delicate, original, and finely solid-beaded evening bags; as well as cochineal dyes in liquid or powder form (from a worm in the nopal), straw hats, and precious lithographs made by children. There's even a restaurant serving up tamales, chorizo, and other delicious local specialties. *M. Alcalá 104, between Independencia and Morelos.* ☎ *951/516-9901 or 516-8038.*

Craft Shops & Galleries

➔ **Artesanías e Industrias Populares del Estado de Oaxaca** This government store stocks the FONART (El Fondo Nacional para el Fomento de las Artesanías) selection of high-quality crafts, including masks, ceramics, jewelry, metalworking, wood-carving, rugs, baskets, clothing, furniture, and cutlery. All profits here go toward developing artisans in the state. The staff speaks English and will ship anywhere. *García Vigil 809, at Cosijopi.* ☎ *951/514-4030.*

➔ **Corazón del Pueblo** This highly recommended store is full of Huichol yarn paintings, exquisite tin objects, Virgin of Guadalupe mirrors, frames, milagros, carved and painted wood figurines, weavings, tablecloths, and shawls that are hard to find elsewhere. *Alcalá 307-9, at Murguía.* ☎ *951/516-6960 or 951/514-1808.*

➔ **Daniela Espinosa** This small, coolly designed shop carries modern jewelry by designer Daniela Espinosa. On sale are mostly large contemporary pieces that feature silver with quartz, crystal, or other stones, ranging in price from $300 to $7,000. *Alcalá 403 (interior 5).* ☎ *951/514-2019.*

➔ **Galería Arte de Oaxaca** This gallery, representing some of the state's leading contemporary artists, is housed in a bright blue colonial two-story building with rooms centered around an interior courtyard. The gallery also represents up-and-coming artists and sells everything from works on paper to oil paintings; the prices are reasonable compared to U.S. galleries. *Murguía 105.* ☎ *951/514-0910, -1532.*

➔ **Galería Quetzalli** Behind the church of Santo Domingo, this minimalist-style gallery represents some of the big names in Mexican art—think Francisco Toledo and José Villalobos—as well as up-and-coming artists. There's also a restaurant with a patio where you can eat surrounded by great contemporary art. Quetzalli has a gallery at Murguía 400, too. *Constitución 104-1.* ☎ *951/514-0030 or 951/514-2606. www.quetzalli.com.*

➔ **La Mano Mágica** ★★ As the owner of one of the first and best folk art shops in Oaxaca, Mary Jane Arnulfo Mendoza has a knack for finding the best of the best. Come here to contemplate prize-winning wool and silk rugs, some with gold and silver threads, woven by her husband Arnulfo Mendoza, and inspired by 19th-century *sarapes* (multicolored blankets) and classic Mexican tapestry. Each of the rooms in the gallery specializes in rugs; glass, lacquer, and ceramics; plus there's gallery space for books and fine art. In the back rooms, you can find well-chosen pieces of regional folk art, including some of the best and most elaborate tin work in town. The space even hosts live performances, artisan demonstrations, and other annual events. *Alcalá 203, between Morelos and Matamoros.* ☎ *951/516-4275. tienda_q@prodigy.net.mx.*

MTV Best ➔ **"Los Baules" de Juana Cata** ★★★ Tucked inside two rooms in the colonial "plaza" where Los Danzantes (p. 632) is located, this remarkable store stocks indigenous textile art from all over the state. The knowledgeable owner Remigio Mestas Revilla has traveled all over the world; his wares are in private collections as well as museums. In his opinion, a textile is closely connected to the personality of its weaver; since it takes 2 weeks or a year to make a piece, everything the weaver feels during that period is expressed in that piece. Skirts, pants, shawls, rugs, blankets, and indigenous costumes from most of the 26 regions of the state are all on sale—but all are on the expensive side, unfortunately. If you can't leave without a piece of Remigio, rest assured that the store sells some less expensive things, like a cool collection of felt hats. *Alcalá 403-2.* ☎ *951/501-0552. cbram@prodigy.net.mx.*

➔**MARO** ★ The regional association of craftswomen of Oaxaca, or Mujeres Artesanas de la Región de Oaxaca, sell their high-quality crafts from all over the state here. They do so in an effort to organize against industrialization, fight mass production, and to preserve the artistic process as it's practiced by the various ethnic groups of Oaxaca. Things are well priced and—befitting the store's credo—the quality of the goods is high. *5 de Mayo 204, between Murguía and Morelos.* ☎ *951/516-0670.*

➔ **Monedas de Oaxaca y Antiguedades** This well-established shop specializes in old and new reproductions of antique traditional silver filigree hoop earrings with beads and stones. The shop is also filled with books, paintings, carved wooden frames, *nichos* (kind of portable altars), new and antique embroidered skirts, and traditional blouses. *Abasolo 107, between Reforma and Cinco de Mayo.* ☎ *951/516-3935.*

MTV Best ➔ **Tienda Q** ★★★ This very hip and innovative design shop makes ultra modern clothes, rugs, cushions, and purses utilizing traditional weaving and embroidery techniques. Quirky color combinations are employed with original results. Francisco Toledo's wife's felt shawls and other clothing, as well as the DOSA line of clothing from Korean designer Christina Kim, are carried exclusively here. You'll find *guayaberas* (traditional men's shirts) from Mérida and Indian tie-dyed shirts, as well as porcelain by Jan Handrix, wool rugs by Matthew Brown, and other jewelry and glass designed by local artists. Only organic materials are used. The shop floor is covered in small, smooth river rocks, which makes at least a peek inside worthwhile if you can't afford to shop here—the goods range from US$50 to US$500. *Manuel Bravo 109.* ☎ *951/514-8880.*

MARKETS

The main market area, just south of the zócalo, is generally open daily from 8am to 5pm. Here you'll find the **Benito Juárez Market** (between Calles Las Casas, Cabrera, Aldama, and 20 de Noviembre), the **20 de Noviembre Market** (south of the Benito Juárez Market, across Aldama), and the **Mercado de Artesanía** (1 block south and 1 block west of the 20 de Noviembre). The **Mercado Abastos** (10 blocks west of the zócalo, between Calle Mercaderes and the Periférico) is most active on Saturday, when indigenous villagers come to town to sell and shop. Dried chiles, herbs, vegetables, crafts, bread, and even burros are all for sale at this bustling market.

The Benito Juárez Market has several stalls where vendors sell beautiful indigenous clothing. You'll find a lot of great skirts, including some in the Chine Oaxaquena style (stall number #320), fabulous Tehuana outfits from the Isthmus—the sort that Frida Kahlo wore—(stall #13 off Las Casas), as well as hand-woven rebozos from Luz María (at Local #369). There's a whole aisle of leather goods, including many styles of huaraches. You can also find crafts and of course vegetables, flowers, herbs, meat, and cheeses.

The Mercado de Artesanía sells mostly textiles and articles of clothing from Oaxaca's seven regions at cheap prices. The 20 de Noviembre Market has a lot of food stalls, as well as some arts and crafts. On the south side, along Mina, are stores selling chocolate and mole paste. Both busy areas are surrounded by small shops that sell everything from cellphones to chocolate.

Road Trips: Oaxaca Area

Two of the most important archaeological sites in Mexico are the ruins at **Monte Albán** (30 min. east of Oaxaca) and **Mitla** (1 hr. west). Because it's so close to Oaxaca City, Monte Albán can feel crowded with busloads of tourists; Mitla is much mellower.

There are also a number of craft villages in all directions around the surrounding valley. You can drive to all of them as day trips, or visit via tour companies. Try **Eric Ramirez** (☎ **951/562-17654,** cell 044/951-171-9295; oaxaquenconnections@hotmail.com), a wonderful and knowledgeable tour guide and driver. Not only does he know every little detail about Oaxaca's valley towns and archaeology, he also speaks English fluently and will take you to meet his grandmother (and try her home cooking!) in Tlacolula.

Lobhi Tour and Travel Agency (Dr. Aurelio Valdivieso 106, Centro; ☎ **951/516-2700;** lobhitour@yahoo.com) is a full-service travel agency that can also arrange tours outside the city for either a half-day (3–4 hr. for $180 per person not including admission fees) or a full-day (7–9 hr. for $300 per person, minimum six people). Private tours are also available to archaeological sites, churches, ex-convents, and museums. **Viajes Xochitlan** (Manuel Bravo 210-A; ☎ **951/514-3628** or 514-3271; www.xochitlan-tours.com.mx) has tours to many archaeological sites and markets in the valley. Finally, another good English-speaking guide is **Juan Montes Lara** (☎ **951/515-7731;** jmonteslara@yahoo.com). He conducts tours for small groups throughout Oaxaca as well as Chiapas; it's best to contact him in advance.

One of your best options for accommodations outside of town are **yu'us,** cabin or camping lodgings in authentic rural villages. The Tourist Yu'u program was created by SEDETUR (Independencia 607; ☎ **951/516-0123**), the state tourism agency, in areas that have been deforested or have other environmental problems, as a way to bring in much needed tourist income. The nine villages around Oaxaca that have yu'us are so tiny that there are no other lodgings available; each manages its own nursery too to help with reforestation. Staying at one is extremely cheap ($40 per night for shared cabin or camping), and you'll get a much more authentic experience than you would staying in, say, the Hotel Camino Real. One yu'u to try is the one in **Teotitlán del Valle** (p. 656).

MTV Best Monte Albán ★★

Monte Albán sits on a mountaintop that was literally leveled by the Zapotecs around 500 B.C. in order to build the massive and mystical city—this huge metropolis once held 30,000 people. Since it rises from the middle of the valley floor, there's an amazing view from the top, encompassing two valleys and the distant mountains.

Very few original structures remain here; they've either been obscured beneath newer construction or had their stones reused for other buildings. The great scope of the operation, though, makes this one of the most spectacular archaeological sites in Mexico. Excavations have revealed more than 170 tombs, numerous ceremonial altars, stelae, pyramids, and palaces, all highlighting various cultures. First influenced by contemporary cultures such as the Olmecs—you can see their influence in early sculptures—and later the Maya, Monte Albán also became a center of Zapotec culture. At its height in A.D. 300 under Zapotec control, it rivaled Teotihuacán as a major force in Mesoamerica. But around A.D. 800, Monte Albán's significance in Zapotec society

Oaxaca Area

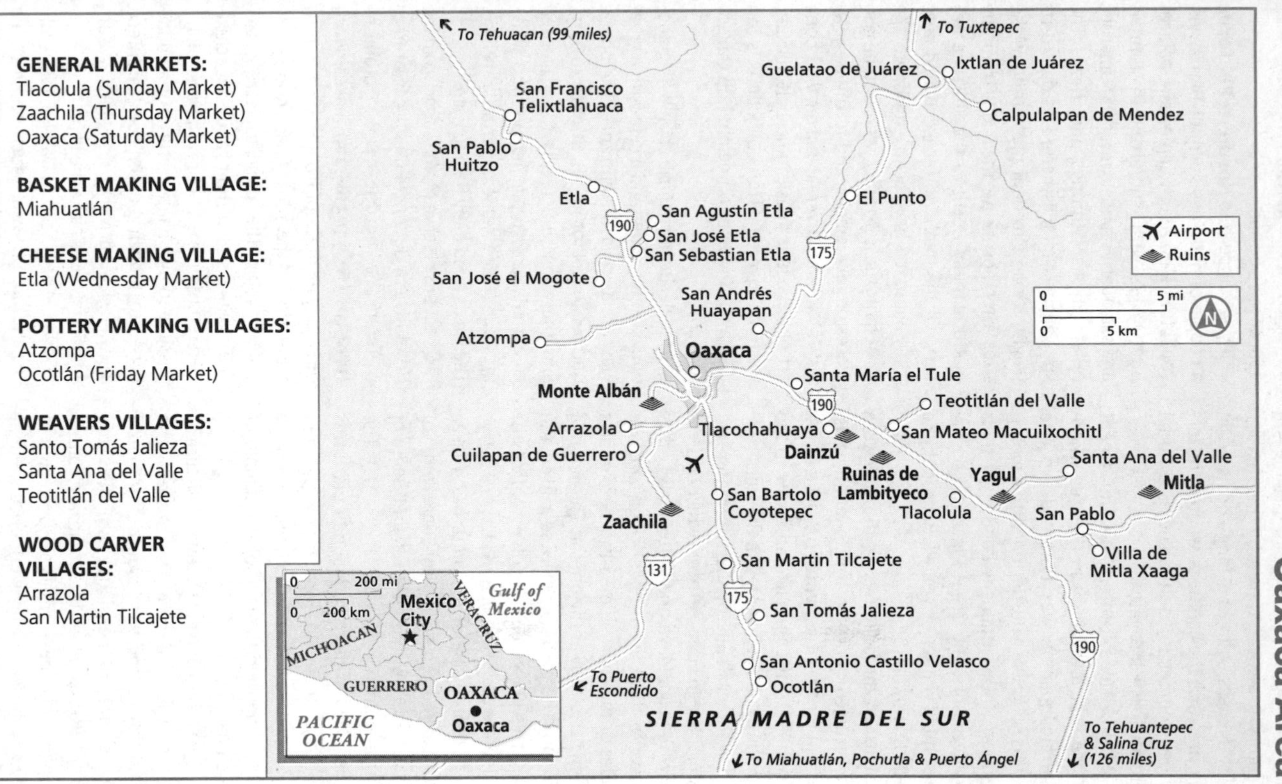
GENERAL MARKETS:
Tlacolula (Sunday Market)
Zaachila (Thursday Market)
Oaxaca (Saturday Market)
BASKET MAKING VILLAGE:
Miahuatlán
CHEESE MAKING VILLAGE:
Etla (Wednesday Market)
POTTERY MAKING VILLAGES:
Atzompa
Ocotlán (Friday Market)
WEAVERS VILLAGES:
Santo Tomás Jalieza
Santa Ana del Valle
Teotitlán del Valle
WOOD CARVER VILLAGES:
Arrazola
San Martin Tilcajete
To Tehuacan (99 miles)
To Tuxtepec
Guelatao de Juárez
Ixtlan de Juárez
Calpulalpan de Mendez
San Francisco Telixtlahuaca
San Pablo Huitzo
Etla
El Punto
190
San Agustín Etla
San José Etla
San Sebastian Etla
175
Airport
Ruins
San José el Mogote
San Andrés Huayapan
0
5 mi
0
5 km
Atzompa
Oaxaca
Santa María el Tule
Monte Albán
190
Teotitlán del Valle
Arrazola
Tlacochahuaya
San Mateo Macuilxochitl
Cuilapan de Guerrero
Dainzú
Santa Ana del Valle
Ruinas de Lambityeco
Yagul
Mitla
San Bartolo Coyotepec
Tlacolula
Zaachila
San Pablo
Villa de Mitla Xaaga
San Martin Tilcajete
131
175
San Tomás Jalieza
190
San Antonio Castillo Velasco
To Puerto Escondido
Ocotlán
SIERRA MADRE DEL SUR
To Miahuatlán, Pochutla & Puerto Ángel
To Tehuantepec & Salina Cruz (126 miles)
0
200 mi
0
200 km
Mexico City
VERACRUZ
Gulf of Mexico
MICHOACAN
GUERRERO
OAXACA
Oaxaca
PACIFIC OCEAN

began to wane; by the beginning of the 13th century, it was taken over by the Mixtecs. (The Mixtecs, who had long coexisted in the area with the Zapotecs, wanted the territory in order to use the site as a burial ground for their royalty.)

Monte Albán centers on the **Great Plaza,** which was built in the area where the mountaintop was flattened. No one seems to know who flattened the mountaintop; it was either the Zapotec or their predecessors. The Great Plaza will be the first thing you see as you walk through the ticketing station.

Most of the buildings at the site were constructed along a north-south axis, except for the **Observatorio,** close to the Great Plaza. It points like an arrow to the southwest in alignment with the stars.

On the east side of the site is the ball court **Juego de Pelota,** which differs slightly from Maya and Toltec ball courts because there are no goal rings, and the sides of the court slope. Also these courts aren't as creepy as the ones at Chichén Itzá (p. 301), where winners were sacrificed; the Zapotecs played ball to solve conflicts or celebrate the defeat of a rival.

The south side of the plaza has a large **platform** that bore several stelae, most of which are now in the National Museum of Anthropology in Mexico City (p. 117). The west side has more ceremonial platforms and pyramids. On top of the pyramid substructure are four columns that may have supported the roof of the temple at one time.

The earliest and best known structure at Monte Albán is **Los Danzantes** (The Dancers) on the west side of the plaza. These large stone slabs, with distorted naked figures carved into them, are mainly copies, since the originals are protected in the site museum. They were once thought to be dancers because of their fluid movement, but it's now thought that they could be captives or warriors because they appear to be bound.

If you wander the **Northern Platform,** a couple of buildings north of Danzantes, you'll find a maze of temples and palaces interwoven with subterranean tunnels and sanctuaries, and covered in numerous reliefs, glyphs, paintings, and friezes. The site's highest altar is here, and due to its height, it's an excellent place to view the site. After absorbing the view from the platform, head north to the site's **cemetery.** Of the tombs so far excavated here (only about 10% have been excavated), the most fantastic is **Tomb 7,** where some 500 pieces of gold, amber, and turquoise jewelry, as well as silver, alabaster, and bone art objects, fans, masks, and belt buckles, were discovered. The collection is on display at the Museo Regional de Oaxaca (p. 644).

A small site museum, a shop with guidebooks on the ruins, and a cafe with a great view are all near the entrance. The phone number to call for info is ☎ **951/516-1215,** and the admission fee is $40. Licensed guides charge $150 per person for a walking tour. Video camera permits are $50. The site is open daily 8am to 6pm.

Direct buses serve Monte Albán from the Hotel Riviera del Angel (Mina 518, at Mier y Terán; ☎ **951/516-5327**). Autobuses Turisticos (☎ **951/516-1215**) makes seven runs daily on the hour from 8:30am. Return service leaves the ruins at 11am, noon, 1, 2, 3, 4, and 5:30pm. The round-trip fare is $40. The ride takes a half-hour, and your scheduled return time is 2 hours after arrival. It's possible to take a later return for an additional $10 (though you won't be guaranteed a seat—ask the driver). During high season, additional buses make the trip.

If you're driving from Oaxaca, take Calle Trujano out of town, which becomes the road to Monte Albán, about 10km (6 miles) away.

Monte Albán

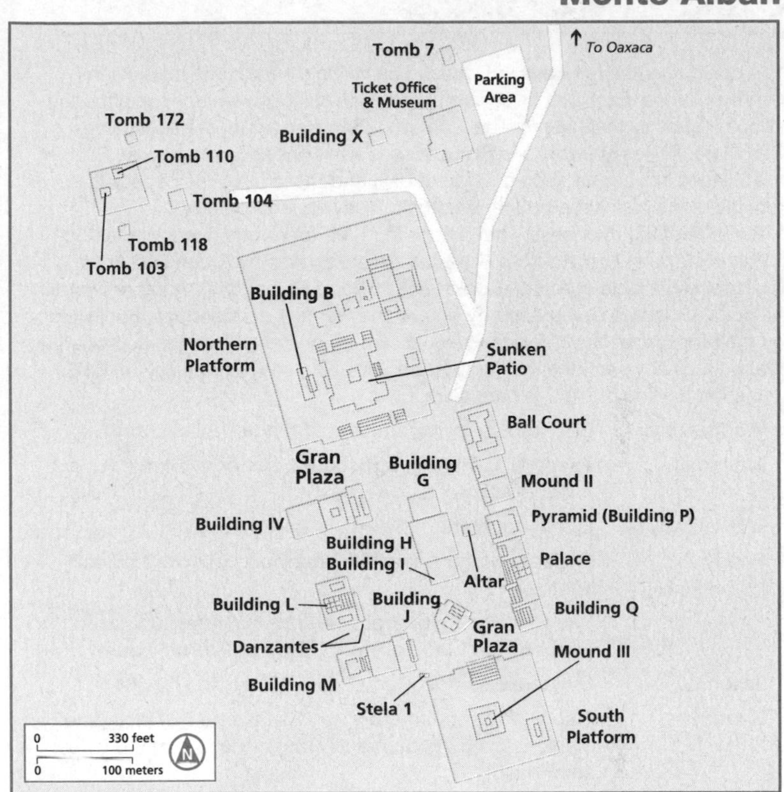

South of Monte Albán

Many crafts villages or villages of architectural or historical interest lie south of Monte Albán; you can reach them all by colectivo or bus (see the "Oaxaca's Market Villages," box below). **Arrazola** (24km/15 miles southwest of Oaxaca) is famous for its woodcarvings, especially that of the master folk artist Manuel Jiménez.

Cuilapan, about 15km (9⅓ miles) southwest of Oaxaca, is where the Ex-Convento de Santiago Apostol, a **monastery** built by Dominican friars, was started in 1550. Parts of the convent and church were never completed due to political complications in the late 16th century. The roof of the monastery has fallen in, but the cloister and the church remain. The church, which is still in use, is being restored. There are three naves with lofty arches, large stone columns, and many frescoes. It is open daily from 10am to 6pm; entry is $55, plus $40 for a video camera. The bus from the second-class station stops within a few hundred feet of the church.

Farther on from Cuilapan, 24km (15 miles) southwest of Oaxaca, **Zaachila** has a lively **Thursday market** where baskets and pottery are sold for local household use. Behind the town's church is the entrance to a small **archaeological site** containing several mounds and platforms

Oaxaca's Market Villages

You could spend a full week in Oaxaca just visiting the various markets in nearby villages. Each has its specialty; you can still tell women of neighboring villages apart by their wares: The women of San Bartolo favor headscarves; San Marcos likes ribbons; and San Lucas is keen on *rebozos* (shawls). Each of the villages has a market on a different day, and these have their specialties, too, including cheese, produce, livestock, weaving, and pottery.

If you're trying to choose what village to hit up for goods, a good reference guide is *Mexican Folk Art from Oaxacan Artist Families* by Arden and Anya Rothstein (available at Amate Books, see "Shopping," p. 647). Another wonderful book is *Oaxaca Celebration* by Mary Jane Gagnier de Mendoza, published by the Museum of New Mexico Press (pick it up online or from the author at La Mano Magica, where she may autograph it for you, see "Shopping," p. 647).

Market days in the villages are as follows:

Wednesday	Etla: known for its cheese; 15km (9⅓ miles) north.
Thursday	Zaachila: ruins and agriculture; pottery; 16km (10 miles) southwest.
	Ejutla: agriculture; 64km (40 miles) south.
Friday	Ocotlán: pottery, textiles, and food; 30km (19 miles) south.
	San Bartolo Coyotepec: ceramic figurines; unglazed earthenware black pottery; 12km (7½ miles) south.
Saturday	Oaxaca: Abastos Market (see "Shopping," p. 647).
Sunday	Tlacolula: agriculture and crafts (see below) including blankets from Teotilan and Santa Ana; 31km (19 miles) southeast.

You can get to any of these craft villages by bus from the second-class station (p. 621). But be warned that on market days, passengers cram these buses. If you get off a bus between destinations—say, at Cuilapan (see above) on the way to Zaachila—but want to continue to the next place, return to the highway and hail a passing bus.

It's also possible to take a colectivo from the south end of the Abastos market, where on Calle Mercaderes you'll see maroon-and-white colectivo taxis. The town they're going to is written on the door, trunk, or windshield. Posted metal signs also give destinations. Colectivos fill up relatively fast and are an economical way to reach the villages, but go early; by afternoon there'll be a wait. Or check with one of the tour operators mentioned earlier.

and two interesting tombs. The artifacts found here now reside in the National Museum of Anthropology in Mexico City, but **Tomb 1** contains carvings that are worth checking out. The site and tombs are open daily from 9am till 4pm, and the entrance fee is $30.

South Along Highway 175

San Bartolo (15km/9⅓ miles south on Carretera 175) is where Mexico's famous earthenware **black pottery** is made. Native Doña Rosa invented the technique—smoking the pottery during firing to make it black and then rubbing the fired pieces with a piece of quartz to produce a sheen. Her son, **Valente Nieto Real,** took over the tradition after her death. The family's home and factory is a few blocks off the main road; you'll see the sign as you enter town. It's open daily from 9am to 5:30pm.

San Martín Tilcajete, about 15km (9⅓ miles) past San Bartolo, is one of the best spots to pick up fantastic surreal *alebrijes*—brightly painted animals and imaginary beasts that often take on the form of little space monsters. (They're also produced in **Arrazola,** see above.) This place is full of **woodcarvers** who produce them from the wood of the copal tree, which has a sweet odor (its resin is used to make incense). Wander from house to house to see the amazing collections and you'll probably come across one that you can buy at a bargain price.

About 2km (1 mile) beyond San Martín, you'll see a sign on the left for **Santo Tomás Jalieza,** a village of **weavers** who use strap looms to make blankets, sashes, and other woven products, all sold at reasonable prices. The village cooperative runs a market in the middle of town. Prices are fixed; you'll find the greatest variety of goods on Friday.

If you travel 20 minutes farther on Carretera 175, you'll come to **Ocotlán,** where the **Aguilar sisters** (Josefina, Guillermina, Irene, and Concepción) and their families produce red clay pottery figures that are prized by collectors, and which are much cheaper here than in the capital. You'll see their row of home-workshops on the right as you enter the town. You can't miss them—there are pottery figures on the fence and roof. (Don't go around town asking for the Aguilar family. Most of the town's inhabitants are named Aguilar.)

Ocotlán is also the home of **Rodolfo Morales,** a Mexican surrealist painter who, upon becoming wealthy and famous, took an active role in aiding his hometown with renovation projects. Two projects worth visiting are the parish church and former convent. Inside the convent, which is now a community museum, you can see some original Dominican decorations. On market day on Friday, the town fills up; it's a great market and worth checking out.

The Road to Mitla

The archaeological sites, markets, and craft villages east of Oaxaca on the Pan American Highway (Hwy. 190) en route to Mitla are less crowded than the villages closer to Monte Albán, but no less worthy of seeing.

If you can afford to do so, hire a taxi (p. 622) or rent a car to get here. Going on your own is the best option because you'll want to veer off the highway to check out many of the small and somewhat out of the way stops along the way. If you take a tour, just ask which sites it includes. To get to the highway, go north from downtown to Calzada Niños Héroes and turn right. This feeds directly on to the highway. All the sites that follow are listed in order, from west (Oaxaca) to east (Mitla).

SANTA MARIA DEL TULES On the road to Mitla, about 8km (5 miles) east of Oaxaca, is one of the largest trees in the world, and it's worth a stop here just for the tour given by very young (around 8-years-old) volunteers. The volunteers will lead you around the base of the 36m-diameter (118-ft.) **El Tule Tree** (a Montezuma cypress, akin to the bald cypress). The guides will then shine mirrors on various parts of it to illustrate sections that resemble elephants, dolphins, crocodiles—or whatever else their imagination dreams up. My favorite guide pointed out one section that, I have to admit, looked a lot like "Monica Lewinsky's butt." Over 2,000 years old, the tree stands in a churchyard just off the main road and looks every bit its age, the way large cypresses tend to do. There's a $25 admission fee that goes toward the care of the tree by a private foundation. It is open daily from around 9am to 5pm, but hours vary according to which kids show up as guides.

Six kilometers (3¾ miles) down the road is the **Iglesia de San Jerónimo Tlacochahuaya** (no phone) a surreally beautiful 18th-century church. Follow the sign a kilometer into town after the turnoff. Inside the church are an elaborately carved altar and a crucifix fashioned out of a ground paste made from the corn plant. The murals decorating the walls, a mix of Spanish and Indian aesthetics, were the work of local 18th-century artists. Make a point of seeing the beautifully painted baroque organ in the choir loft. The church is usually open daily from 10am to 2pm and 4 to 8pm.

DAINZU'S ZAPOTEC RUINS Three kilometers (2 miles) farther, visible from the highway (26km/16 miles from Oaxaca), you'll see a sign pointing to the right. It's less than a kilometer (under a mile) to the ruins, which were first excavated in the 1960s. Dainzú is a pre-Classic site that dates from between 700 and 600 B.C. Increasingly sophisticated building continued until about A.D. 300. The site occupies the western face of a hill, presumably for defense. The main building is a platform structure whose walls were decorated with carvings resembling Monte Albán's Danzantes. These carvings are now in a protective shed; a caretaker will unlock it for interested parties. These figures show Olmec influence but differ from the Danzantes because they wear the trappings of the "ball game," which make them in all likelihood the earliest representations of the ball game in Mexico. And, in fact, a partially reconstructed ball court sits below the main structure. The site provides an outstanding view of the valley. Admission is $30 and it's open daily 8am to 6pm.

TEOTILAN DEL VALLE Famous for its beautiful woolen loomed rugs, this town is another 2km (1¼ miles) east and then 3km (2 miles) from the highway. The prosperous town, once one of the most important in Zapotec culture, is lined with homes and shops of weavers. Early Dominican friars brought sheep (and wool) here; the designs on many of today's rugs are of ancient cultural motifs as well as animals. Most weavers, who are also expert spinners, dyers, and merchants, sell out of their homes and give demonstrations; it's fun to visit and watch as well as buy. An added bonus is that the prices are considerably lower than in Oaxaca. Just beware of rugs made with acrylic, or not made in the region. Famous weaver Arnulfo Mendoza's lodge Sagrada Corazon is located here on a hill high above town.

The 17th-century **Templo de la Preciosa Sangre de Cristo** (Calle Hidalgo, a block east of Calle Juárez; no phone; free admission) church here is worth a visit. As was customary in Mexico, early friars used pre-Hispanic construction stones to build the church. The original material peeks through in spots where the plaster is scraped away to reveal stones with carved figures. Teotitlán also has a small community museum, **Museo Comunitario Balaa Xtee Guech Gulal** (Calle Hidalgo, 1 block east of Juárez; ☎ **951/524-9123;** admission $10; daily 10am–6pm) opposite the artisans' market and adjacent to the church. The museum has exhibits on natural dye-making, using herbs, plants, and cochineal (a red dye derived from insects) that are employed in rug weaving, as well as Zapotec carvings. There's a wall outside the museum from a temple that once stood here.

On the right on the main street as you approach the main part of town, in a red brick building, is the **Restaurant Tlamanalli** (Av. Juárez 39; ☎ **951/524-4006;** main courses $50–$100; no credit cards; Mon–Fri 1–4pm), run by Abagail Mendoza and her sisters. Here you'll find some of the best food in the whole valley, prepared from scratch in the traditional Zapotec village way—and lighter in flavor than what you'll find in Oaxaca city.

LAMBITYECO'S Continuing on the highway eastward for 3km (2 miles) is the turnoff (watch carefully, it's not marked clearly) for the small archaeological site of Lambityeco (no phone; admission $30; daily 8am–5pm). There are six progressively larger temples built on top of each other here. In the middle of a carving of a nobleman and his wife is the tomb where they were buried. In the nearby **Palacio de Cocijo** (no phone; admission $30) is an impressive pair of beautifully executed and preserved stucco carvings depicting the **Rain God** Cocijo wearing a large headdress.

TLACOLULA Onward 1.5km (almost 1 mile) past Lambityeco (now about 30km/19 miles from Oaxaca), this town has a bustling Sunday market and a baroque-style chapel, the **Capilla del Mártir.** With its stunning display of wrought iron, almost life-size sculptures of the 12 apostles, and the convoluted baroque interior, it is an incredible example of Mexico's religious architecture. A few years ago, a secret passage was found in the church, leading to a room that contained valuable silver religious pieces that had been hidden during the Revolution of 1916.

The town is small and sleepy, except on Sunday, market day. But no matter what day you come here, do yourself a favor and go straight to the main square for a tlayuda and ice cream from the famous **Neveria Rosita** (☎ **965/512-0573**). This place was started by two sisters in 1941 and now has a branch in Los Angeles dubbed "Oaxacalifornia." The fruit flavored ices are my favorite. There are also several reasonable cafeterias in town with quite good comida corrida.

YAGUL A fortress city built on a hill overlooking the valley, Yagul (☎ **951/516-0123;** admission $40, still cameras free, video cameras $50; daily 8am–5:30pm) is a couple of kilometers farther on down the highway. It's about a kilometer on from the left-side turnoff. Because it's much less visited than other area attractions, it is a favorite among locals. It's also a good place for a picnic because it's so intimate.

The city is divided into two sections: the fortress at the top of the hill and the palaces lower down. If you climb up the hill, you get an amazing view across the entire valley. The center plaza is surrounded by four temples. In the center is a ceremonial platform, and under it is the **Triple Tomb.** The door of this somewhat eerie tomb is a large stone slab decorated on both sides with beautiful hieroglyphs. The tomb may be open for viewing; if there are two guards, one can leave the entrance to escort visitors; if not, you can tip one $10 and get him to open it for you.

There's a beautifully restored Zapotec **ball court** down the hill from the main structure. North of the plaza is the **palace** structure built for the chiefs of the city. As you wander through its maze of rooms and patios decorated with painted stucco and stone mosaics, you'll probably find yourself serenaded by neighborhood birds. Ceremonial mounds and tombs decorated in the same geometric patterns found in Mitla (see below) are visible around the grounds.

Mezcal Tours

Remember that you're in mezcal country now. Even more important, the several distilleries dotting the road to Mitla have tasting rooms. **Mezcal Beneva** (Carretera Oaxaca 190 Km 42.5, San Pablo Villa de Mitla; ☎ **951/514-7005;** www.mezcalbeneva.com) has guided tours showing the distilling process, followed by free samples, including a 6-year-old Gran Reserva that's definitely worth trying. Another distillery to try is **Pensamiento Mezcal** (Km 32 Carretera 190; ☎ **951/956-2001**), which has flavors like mint, orange, blackberry, lime, guava, and coconut.

Mitla ★

Less grand in scale than Monte Albán, **Mitla (☎ 951/568-0316;** admission $40, with video camera $50; daily 8am–5pm) is nonetheless a powerful site—it actually blossomed as Monte Albán's society was on the decline, and so is quite different architecturally. Mitla is 46km (29 miles) from Oaxaca, the site is 4km (2½ miles) from the highway; the turnoff terminates at the ruins by the church. By bus, it's less than a kilometer up the road from the town square (you can hire a cab in the square).

The complex of structures here was first built by the Zapotecs around 600 B.C. and then taken over by the Mixtecs in the late 10th century—although locals dispute this, pointing out that people here don't speak Mixtec, but Zapotec. At the time of the Spanish Conquest, society here was still flourishing, and many of the buildings were used through the 16th century. The Spaniards built their cathedral **(San Pablos Mitla)** on top of the Zapotec structure, using it as a foundation for the church and stones pulled from the temples as its walls.

The elaborate workmanship on display is pretty much unequaled in Mexico. Each line of the geometric design covering the walls of many of the structures is worth contemplation. All the designs have meanings that go far beyond pleasing the eye; a cross signifies the four directions north/south/east/west; a jagged line design means water; and others indicate the Feathered Serpent Quetzalcoatl. Look for these designs on blankets woven in the area.

Mixtec architecture is based on a quadrangle surrounded on three or four sides by patios and chambers, usually rectangular. Many of the roofs, now gone, were made of adobe covered with a nopal plaster. Today, there are five groups of buildings, divided by the Mitla River. The most important buildings are on the east side of the ravine.

Mitla comes from the Nahautl word for "place of the dead," and the name fits if you go to the **Grupo de las Columnas;** here you can literally climb down into a tomb—an event that manages to be simultaneously claustrophobic, creepy, and cool. **La Columna de la Muerte** ("The Column of Death") is in the bottom of another of the buildings; legend has it that if you wrap your arms around it, you can calculate how many years you have to live by how much space remains between your fingers. Just remember that the indigenous people several centuries ago were much smaller than we are, so don't freak if your fingers touch.

Appendix A: Mexico in Depth

History 101

Pre-Hispanic Civilizations

The earliest "Mexicans" were Stone Age hunter-gatherers from the north, descendants of a race that had probably crossed the Bering Strait and reached North America around 12,000 B.C. They arrived in what is now Mexico by 10,000 B.C. Sometime between 5200 and 1500 B.C., in what is known as the **Archaic period,** they began practicing agriculture and domesticating animals.

THE PRE-CLASSIC PERIOD (1500 B.C. to A.D. 300) Eventually, agriculture improved enough to support large communities and free some of the population from agricultural work. A civilization emerged that we call the **Olmec**—an enigmatic people who settled the lower Gulf Coast in what is now Tabasco and Veracruz. Anthropologists regard them as the mother culture of Mesoamerica because they established a pattern for later civilizations in a wide area stretching from northern Mexico into Central America. The Olmec developed the basic calendar used throughout the region, established a 52-year cycle (which they used to schedule the construction of pyramids), established principles of urban layout and architecture, and originated the cult of the jaguar and the sanctity of jade.

The Maya civilization began developing in the late pre-Classic period, around 500 B.C. Our understanding of this period is sketchy, but Olmec influences are apparent everywhere. The Maya perfected the Olmec calendar and, somewhere along the way, developed an ornate system of hieroglyphic writing and early architectural concepts. Two other civilizations began the rise to prominence around this time: the people of Teotihuacán, just north of present-day Mexico City, and the Zapotec of Monte Albán in the valley of Oaxaca.

THE CLASSIC PERIOD (A.D. 300–900) The flourishing of these three civilizations marks the boundaries of this period—the heyday of pre-Columbian Mesoamerican artistic and cultural achievements. These include the pyramids and palaces in Teotihuacán; the ceremonial center of Monte Albán; and the temple complexes and pyramids of Palenque and Calakmul.

The inhabitants of **Teotihuacán** (100 B.C. to A.D. 700), near present-day Mexico City, built a city that, at its zenith, is thought to have had 200,000 or more inhabitants. It was a well-organized city, covering 30 sq. km (12 sq. miles), and built on a grid with streams channeled to follow the city's plan.

Farther south, the **Zapotec,** influenced by the Olmec, raised an impressive civilization in the region of Oaxaca. Their two principal cities were **Monte Albán,** inhabited by an elite class of merchants and artisans, and **Mitla,** reserved for the high priests.

THE POST-CLASSIC PERIOD (A.D. 900–1521) Warfare was a more conspicuous activity of the civilizations that flourished in this period. Social development was impressive but not as cosmopolitan as the Maya, Teotihuacán, and Zapotec societies. In central Mexico, a people known as the **Toltec** established their capital at Tula in the 10th century. They revered a god known as **Tezcatlipoca,** or "smoking mirror," who later became an Aztec god. The Toltec maintained a large military class divided into orders symbolized by animals. At its height, Tula may have had 40,000 people, and its influence spread across Mesoamerica. By the 13th century, however, the Toltec had exhausted themselves, probably in civil wars and in battles with the invaders from the north.

Of those northern invaders, the **Aztec** were the most warlike. At first they served as mercenaries for established cities in the valley of Mexico—one of which allotted them an unwanted, marshy piece of land in the middle of Lake Texcoco for their settlement. It eventually grew into the island city of Tenochtitlán. Through aggressive diplomacy and military action, the Aztec soon conquered central Mexico and extended their rule east to the Gulf Coast and south to the valley of Oaxaca.

During this later period, the Maya civilization flourished in northern Yucatán, especially in cities such as Chichén Itzá and Uxmal.

The Conquest

In 1517, the first Spaniards arrived in what is today known as Mexico and skirmished with Maya Indians off the coast of the Yucatán Peninsula. One of the fledgling expeditions ended in shipwreck, leaving several Spaniards stranded as prisoners of the Maya. The Spanish sent out another expedition, under the command of **Hernán Cortez,** which landed on Cozumel in February 1519. Cortez inquired about the gold and riches of the interior, and the coastal Maya were happy to describe the wealth and splendor of the Aztec empire in central Mexico. Cortez promptly disobeyed all orders of his superior, the governor of Cuba, and sailed into the Gulf of Mexico, landing at what is now Veracruz.

MEXICO IN DEPTH

Dateline

- **10,000–1500 B.C.** Archaic period: hunting and gathering; later, the dawn of agriculture: domestication of chiles, corn, beans, avocado, amaranth, and pumpkin. Mortars and pestles in use. Stone bowls and jars, obsidian knives, and open-weave basketry developed. Possible dating of the cave paintings of central Baja, believed to have been created by nomadic indigenous tribes.
- **1500 B.C.–A.D. 300** Pre-Classic period: Olmec culture develops large-scale settlements and irrigation methods. Cities spring up. Olmec influence spreads over other cultures in the Gulf Coast, central and southern Mexico, Central America, the lower Mexican Pacific Coast, and the Yucatán. Several cities in central and southern Mexico begin the construction of large ceremonial centers and pyramids. The Maya develop several city-states in Chiapas and Central America.
- **A.D. 300–900** Classic period: Broad influence of Teotihuacán culture and the establishment there of a truly cosmopolitan urbanism. Satellite settlements spring up across central Mexico and as far away as Guatemala. Trade and

Cortez arrived when the Aztec empire was at the height of its wealth and power. **Moctezuma II** ruled over the central and southern highlands and extracted tribute from lowland peoples. His greatest temples were literally plated with gold and encrusted with the blood of sacrificial captives. Moctezuma was a fool, a mystic, and something of a coward. Despite his wealth and military power, he dithered in his capital at Tenochtitlán, sending messengers with gifts and suggestions that Cortez leave. Meanwhile, Cortez blustered and negotiated his way into the highlands, always cloaking his real intentions. Moctezuma, terrified by the military tactics and technology of the Spaniard, convinced himself that Cortez was in fact the god Quetzalcoatl making his long-awaited return. By the time the Spaniards arrived in the Aztec capital, Cortez had gained some ascendancy over the lesser Indian states that were resentful tributaries to the Aztec. In November 1519, Cortez confronted Moctezuma and took him hostage in an effort to leverage control of the empire.

In the middle of Cortez's dangerous game of manipulation, another Spanish expedition arrived with orders to end Cortez's authority over the mission. Cortez hastened to meet the rival's force and persuade them to join his own. In the meantime, the Aztec chased the garrison out of Tenochtitlán, and either they or the Spaniards killed Moctezuma. For the next year and a half, Cortez laid siege to Tenochtitlán, with the help of rival Indians and a decimating epidemic of smallpox, to which the Indians had no resistance. In the end, the Aztec capital fell, and when it did, all of central Mexico lay at the feet of the conquistadors.

The Spanish Conquest started as a pirate expedition by Cortez and his men, unauthorized by the Spanish crown or its governor in Cuba. The Spanish king legitimized Cortez following his victory over the Aztec and ordered the forced conversion to Christianity of this new colony, to be called **New Spain.** Guatemala and Honduras were explored and conquered, and by 1540, the territory of New Spain included possessions from Vancouver to Panama. In the 2 centuries that followed, Franciscan and Augustinian friars converted millions of Indians to Christianity, and the Spanish lords built huge feudal estates on which the Indian farmers were little more than serfs. The silver and gold that Cortez looted made Spain the richest country in Europe.

THE COLONIAL PERIOD

Hernán Cortez set about building a new city upon the ruins of the old Aztec capital. To do this he collected from the Indians the

cultural interchange with the Maya and the Zapotec flourish. The Maya perfect the calendar and improve astronomical calculations. They build grandiose cities at Palenque, Calakmul, and Cobá, and in Central America.

- **900** Post-Classic period begins: More emphasis is placed on warfare in central Mexico. The Toltec culture emerges at Tula and replaces Teotihuacán as the dominant city of central Mexico. Toltec influence spreads to the Yucatán, forming the culture of the Itzaés, who become the rulers of Chichén Itzá.
- **909** This is the date on a small monument at Toniná (near San Cristóbal de las Casas), the latest date yet discovered, symbolizing the end of the Classic Maya era.
- **1325–1470** Aztec capital Tenochtitlán is founded; Aztecs begin military campaigns in the Valley of Mexico and then thrust farther out, subjugating the civilizations of the Gulf Coast and southern Mexico.
- **1516** Gold found on Cozumel during aborted Spanish expedition of Yucatán Peninsula arouses interest of Spanish governor in Cuba, who sends Juan de Grijalva on an expedition,

continues

tributes once paid to the Aztec emperor, many of these rendered in labor. This arrangement, in one form or another, became the basis for the construction of the new colony. But diseases brought by the Spaniards decimated the native population over the next century and drastically reduced the pool of labor.

Cortez soon returned to Spain and was replaced by a governing council, and, later, the office of viceroy. Over the 3 centuries of the colonial period, 61 viceroys governed Mexico. Spain became rich from New World gold and silver, chiseled out by Indian labor. The colonial elite built lavish homes in Mexico City and in the countryside. They filled their homes with ornate furniture, had many servants, and adorned themselves in imported velvets, satins, and jewels.

A new class system developed. Those born in Spain considered themselves superior to the *criollos* (Spaniards born in Mexico). Those of other races and the *castas* (mixtures of Spanish and Indian, Spanish and African, or Indian and African) occupied the bottom rungs of society. It took great cunning to stay a step ahead of the avaricious Crown, which demanded increasing taxes and contributions from its fabled foreign conquests. Still, wealthy colonists prospered enough to develop an extravagant society.

However, discontent with the mother country simmered for years over social and political issues: taxes, royal monopolies, the bureaucracy, Spanish-born citizens' advantages over Mexican-born subjects, and restrictions on commerce with Spain and other countries. In 1808, Napoleon invaded Spain and crowned his brother Joseph king in place of Charles IV. To many in Mexico, allegiance to France was out of the question; discontent reached the level of revolt.

INDEPENDENCE

Fittingly, the mestizos whom the Spanish so aggressively created would ultimately be the source of their expulsion from this rich land. In 1810, the Mexican war for independence began, led by the mixed-blood generation, in conjunction with the criollos. The rebellion began when **Father Miguel Hidalgo** gave the *grito,* a cry for independence, from his church in the town of Dolores, Guanajuato. The uprising soon became a full-fledged revolution, as Hidalgo and Ignacio Allende gathered an "army" of citizens and threatened Mexico City. Although Hidalgo ultimately failed and was executed, he is honored as "the Father of Mexican Independence." Another priest, José María Morelos, kept the revolt alive with several successful campaigns

followed by another led by Hernán Cortez.

- **1519** Conquest of Mexico begins: Hernán Cortez and troops make their way along Mexican coast to present-day Veracruz.
- **1521** Conquest is complete after Aztec defeat at Tlatelolco.
- **1521–24** Cortez organizes Spanish empire in Mexico and begins building Mexico City on the ruins of Tenochtitlán.
- **1532** Cortez launches the first exploration to Baja, then believed to be an island. The expedition is unsuccessful, with ships intercepted by pirates.
- **1534** The *Concepción* makes landfall near present-day La Paz, under charge of a group of mutineers; most are killed by the indigenous inhabitants of the area.
- **1539** Capt. Ulloa explores the entire perimeter of the Sea of Cortez, establishing that Baja is not an island, as believed, but a peninsula.
- **1541** Cortez is recalled to Spain, never to return to Mexico.
- **1565** Trade routes between Acapulco and Manila are established, with Baja becoming an important stopping point along this route, which lasted for over 250 years. It was also the site of ongoing pirating, which

through 1815, when he, too, was captured and executed.

After the death of Morelos, prospects for independence were rather dim until the Spanish king who replaced Joseph Bonaparte decided to make social reforms in the colonies. This convinced the conservative powers in Mexico that they didn't need Spain after all. With their tacit approval, Agustín de Iturbide, then commander of royalist forces, changed sides and declared Mexico independent and himself emperor. Before long, however, internal dissension brought about the fall of the emperor, and Mexico was proclaimed a republic.

Political instability engulfed the young republic and Mexico waged a disastrous war with the United States and lost half its territory. A central figure was **Antonio López de Santa Anna,** who assumed the leadership of his country no fewer than 11 times and was flexible enough in those volatile days to portray himself variously as a liberal, a conservative, a federalist, and a centralist. He probably holds the record for frequency of exile; by 1855 he was finally left without a political comeback and ended his days in Venezuela.

Political instability persisted, and the conservative forces, with some encouragement from Napoleon III, hit upon the idea of inviting in a Hapsburg to regain control (as if that strategy had ever worked for Spain). They found a willing volunteer in Archduke Maximilian of Austria, who accepted the position of Mexican emperor with the support of French troops. The ragtag Mexican forces defeated the French force—a modern, well-equipped army—in a battle near Puebla (now celebrated annually as **Cinco de Mayo**). A second attempt was more successful, and Ferdinand Maximilian Joseph of Hapsburg became emperor. After 3 years of civil war, the French were finally induced to abandon the emperor's cause; Maximilian was captured and executed by a firing squad near Querétaro in 1867. His adversary and successor (as president of Mexico) was **Benito Juárez,** a Zapotec Indian lawyer and one of the great heroes of Mexican history. Juárez did his best to unify and strengthen his country before dying of a heart attack in 1872; his impact on Mexico's future was profound, and his plans and visions bore fruit for decades.

The Porfiriato & the Revolution

A few years after Juárez's death, one of his generals, **Porfirio Díaz,** assumed power in a coup. He ruled Mexico from 1877 to 1911, a period now called the "Porfiriato." He stayed in power by imposing repressive measures

becomes an embarrassment to the Spanish crown.

- **1535–1821** Viceregal period: Sixty-one viceroys appointed by King of Spain govern Mexico. Control of much of the land ends up in the hands of the Catholic Church and the politically powerful.
- **1697–1767** Jesuit Mission period of Baja, during which 20 missions were established for the purpose of converting the indigenous populations to Christianity.
- **1810–21** War of Independence: Miguel Hidalgo starts movement for Mexico's independence from Spain but is executed within a year; leadership and goals change during the war years, but Agustín de Iturbide outlines a compromise between monarchy and republic.
- **1822** First Empire: Iturbide ascends throne as Emperor of Mexico, loses power after a year, and loses life in an attempt to reclaim throne.
- **1824–64** Early Republic period, characterized by almost perpetual civil war between federalists and centralists, conservatives and liberals, culminating in the victory of the liberals under Benito Juárez.
- **1833–47** Mexican-American War results in the

continues

and courting the favor of powerful nations. Generous in his dealings with foreign investors, Díaz became, in the eyes of most Mexicans, the archetypal *entreguista* (one who sells out his country for private gain). With foreign investment came the concentration of great wealth in few hands, and social conditions worsened.

In 1910, Francisco Madero called for an armed rebellion that became the **Mexican Revolution** (La Revolución in Mexico; the revolution against Spain is the Guerra de Independencia). Díaz was sent into exile; while in London, he became a celebrity at the age of 81, when he jumped into the Thames to save a drowning boy. He is buried in Paris. Madero became president but was promptly betrayed and executed by **Victoriano Huerta.** Those who had answered Madero's call responded again—to the great peasant hero **Emiliano Zapata** in the south, and to the seemingly invincible **Pancho Villa** in the central north, flanked by **Alvaro Obregón** and **Venustiano Carranza.** They eventually put Huerta to flight and began hashing out a new constitution.

For the next few years, the revolutionaries Carranza, Obregón, and Villa fought among themselves; Zapata did not seek national power, though he fought tenaciously for land for the peasants. Carranza, who was president at the time, betrayed and assassinated Zapata. Obregón finally consolidated power and probably had Carranza assassinated. He, in turn, was assassinated when he tried to break one of the tenets of the Revolution—no reelection. His successor, Plutarco Elias Calles, learned this lesson well, installing one puppet president after another, until **Lázaro Cárdenas** severed the puppeteer's strings and banished him to exile.

Until Cárdenas's election in 1934, the outcome of the revolution remained in doubt. There had been some land redistribution, but other measures took a back seat to political expediency. Cárdenas changed all that. He implemented massive redistribution of land and nationalized the oil industry. He instituted many reforms and gave shape to the ruling political party (now the **Partido Revolucionario Institucional,** or PRI) by bringing a broad representation of Mexican society under its banner and establishing mechanisms for consensus building. Most Mexicans practically canonize Cárdenas.

MODERN MEXICO

The presidents who followed were noted more for graft than for leadership. The party's base narrowed as many of the reform-minded elements were marginalized. Economic progress, a lot of it in the

loss of huge amounts of territory to the U.S. by Mexico. In 1847 Mexico City falls to U.S. troops. The Treaty of Guadalupe Hidalgo was signed in 1848, in which Mexico conceded not only the Río Grande area of Texas but part of New Mexico and all of California for a payment of US$25 million and the cancellation of all Mexican debt.

- **1849** The California Gold Rush lures many Mexicans and Indians from the Baja peninsula to seek their fortunes in California, reducing Baja's already scarce population, and transforming it into a haven for outlaws, pirates, and renegades.
- **1864–67** Second Empire: The French invade Mexico in the name of Maximilian of Austria, who is appointed Emperor of Mexico. Juárez and the liberal government retreat to the north and wage war with the French forces. The French finally abandon Mexico and leave Maximilian to be defeated and executed.
- **1872–76** Juárez dies, and political struggles ensue for the presidency.
- **1877–1911** Porfiriato: Porfirio Díaz, president/dictator of Mexico for 33 years, leads country to

form of large development projects, became the PRI's main basis for legitimacy. In 1968, the government violently repressed a democratic student movement. Police forces shot and killed an unknown number of civilians in the Tlatelolco section of Mexico City. Though the PRI maintained its grip on power, it lost all semblance of being a progressive party. In 1985, a devastating **earthquake in Mexico City** brought down many of the government's new, supposedly earthquake-proof buildings, exposing shoddy construction and the widespread government corruption that fostered it. The government's handling of the relief efforts also drew heavy criticism. In 1994, a political and military **uprising in Chiapas** focused world attention on Mexico's great social problems. A new political force, the Ejército Zapatista de Liberación Nacional, or EZLN (Zapatista National Liberation Army), has skillfully publicized the plight of the peasant.

In the years that followed, opposition political parties grew in power and legitimacy. Facing pressure and scrutiny from national and international organizations, and widespread public discontent, the PRI had to concede defeat in state and congressional elections throughout the '90s. The party began choosing its candidates through primaries, instead of through appointment. But in the presidential elections of 2000, **Vicente Fox,** candidate for the Partido Acción Nacional (National Action Party, or PAN), won by a landslide. It couldn't have been otherwise. For many voters this election was an experiment to see if their votes would really count. They voted for the most prominent opposition candidate to see if in fact he would be allowed to assume the presidency. For Mexicans, a government under the PRI was all that they had ever known.

During Fox's presidency, the three main political parties had to adjust to the new realty of power sharing. The old government party, the PRI, still had a large infrastructure for getting out the vote and still controlled the local governments of several states. Fox's center-right PAN, had control of the presidency and the most seats in the legislature. While the center-left PRD (Partido de la Revolución Democrática, or Democratic Revolution Party) controlled the city government of Mexico City as well as a few southern states. Many observers anticipated gridlock. But the three parties, to their credit, handled the transition better than expected.

But by the end of Fox's term, the situation turned ugly, and Mexico's experiment with pluralistic democracy faced a difficult

modernization by encouraging foreign investment in mines, oil, and railroads. Mexico witnesses the development of a modern economy and a growing disparity between rich and poor. Social conditions, especially in rural areas, become desperate.

- **1911–17** Mexican Revolution: Francisco Madero drafts revolutionary plan. Díaz resigns. Leaders jockey for power during period of great violence, national upheaval, and tremendous loss of life.
- **1920** U.S. Prohibition, in which the manufacture, sale, and consumption of alcoholic beverages is made a federal offense, is a boon to Baja, with Americans rushing across the border into Tijuana and northern Baja to buy liquor and drink in cantinas. It also initiates an era of organized crime and sees the establishment of casinos and brothels.
- **1917–40** Reconstruction: Present constitution of Mexico is signed; land and education reforms are initiated and labor unions strengthened; Mexico expropriates oil companies and railroads. Pancho Villa, Emiliano Zapata, and presidents Alvaro Obregón and Venustiano Carranza are assassinated.

continues

crisis. The Fox administration showed no finesse in dealing with the legislature and failed to pass most of its initiatives. In the off-year elections of 2004, PAN lost many seats in the legislature and several governorships.

The main beneficiary was the PRI, which looked to be in an excellent position for the presidential election of 2006, but not for long. In 2005, the party's leader, Roberto Madrazo, sought to become the party's nominee without going through primary elections. His power plays worked to make him the nominee but splintered the party badly and reminded voters of the old days when their votes didn't count for anything.

Meanwhile, the PRD's choice of nominee seemed inevitable. Mexico City mayor Andrés Manuel López Obrador (AMLO for short) was without question the most important figure in the party. He was tremendously popular for creating programs, such as a pension for the city's elderly. And his popularity soared when he became the target of political dirty tricks to make him ineligible to run for president. He was genuinely interested in helping the poor, but there was something unsettling about the way he would take political opposition personally. He dismissed a large demonstration in Mexico City against kidnapping and other crimes as the work of his political enemies and not as the expression of local citizens to highlight the need to feel safe in their city.

The PAN ended up having the only meaningful primary elections, which resulted in an underdog candidate, **Felipe Calderón,** becoming the party nominee. He is a social conservative and a devout Catholic who believes in privatization and market forces.

A bitter campaign between AMLO and Calderón, followed by an incredibly close election in the summer of 2006, made for a serious crisis. So close was the election that it took over a month for the elections tribunal to declare Calderón the winner. AMLO refused to recognize the verdict and launched a protest that lasted another month. Supporters in his party even tried to physically prevent Calderón from taking office by occupying the legislative chambers. All of this ended up diminishing AMLO's popularity.

The crisis shows that Mexico must continue to strengthen its political institutions. PAN now has the most seats in the legislature, but not a majority. To pass legislation it will need to compromise with the other parties. The PRD has the second highest number of seats. It must put AMLO behind it if it doesn't want to be marginalized. And

- **1940** Mexico enters contemporary period of political stability and makes steady economic progress. Quality of life improves, although problems of corruption, inflation, national health, and unresolved land and agricultural issues continue.
- **1952** The Territory of Northern Baja California becomes Mexico's 29th state.
- **1973** Carretera Transpeninsular (Hwy. 1) opens, connecting Tijuana to Cabo San Lucas. This leads to serious growth in Baja, and the following year, Baja California Sur becomes Mexico's 30th state.
- **1994–97** Mexico, Canada, and the United States sign the North American Free Trade Agreement (NAFTA). An Indian uprising in Chiapas sparks countrywide protests over government policies concerning land distribution, bank loans, health, education, voting, and human rights.
- **2000** Mexico elects Vicente Fox, of the PAN party, president.
- **2006** PAN party candidate Felipe Calderón wins the presidential election against PRD candidate Andrés Manuel Lopez Obrador by a very small margin. Massive protests result.

the PRI must learn from its mistakes and move towards democracy and transparency. But at the moment, its legislators enjoy the role of powerbrokers between the government and a powerful opposition party. It will be the key player in deciding what gets accomplished in the next few years.

Culture 101

The Land & Its People

Mexico stretches nearly 3,200km (1,984 miles) from east to west and more than 1,600km (1,000 miles) north to south. Only one-fifth the size of the United States, its territory includes trackless deserts in the north, dense jungles in the south, thousands of miles of lush seacoast and beaches along the Pacific and Caribbean, and the central highlands, crisscrossed by mountain ranges.

Mexico has more than 100 million inhabitants, and 22 million of them live in the capital, Mexico City. Over the last few decades, the rate of population growth has been steadily declining, from 3.2% per year in the 1970s to 1.6% at present. Mexico City has the slowest growth rate in the country, at less than 1% per year.

By most measurements, the disparity between rich and poor has increased in the last 30 years. Cycles of boom-and-bust seem to weigh heavier on the poor than on the rich. The middle class also seems to have had a rough ride of it, especially during the monetary crisis of 1994. And, as a result, the ranks of the poor grow while the concentration of wealth increases (as it does in many other countries).

There is no other industrialized country in the world with such a mixed-race population as Mexico. The idea of the Cosmic Race, a blend of European, indigenous Indians, and Africans, was first spoken of with pride by Education Minister Jose Vasconselos in 1908. The unique mixture of Old World and New World, evident not only via genes, but also culture and mores, exists nowhere else in such numbers. And for most Mexicans, this mixture is a point of pride—one that shows that they are unlike anybody else. Having said that, there is still some unstated racism in Mexico. *Morenos* (dark-skinned Indios) are often not-so-subtly discriminated against, and to call someone an Indio is considered an insult in some circles.

But in the face of all of this, Mexican society maintains its cohesiveness. It is amazingly resilient, due in some part to the way Mexicans live. They place a high value on family and friends, social gatherings, and living in the present; the uncertain prospects of the future take a back seat. In Mexico, there is always time to meet with friends for a drink or a cup of coffee or attend a family get-together. The many high-spirited public celebrations that Mexico is so famous for are simply another manifestation of this attitude.

Entertainment & Sports

This country loves a good party. Any time of the year, there's probably a festival going on someplace in Mexico, from Day of the Dead celebrations to carnaval. See "Basics" p. 10 for specific info on celebrations.

A general festive spirit always surrounds spectator sports events here, too. **Bullfights, *charreadas*** (rodeos), and **fútbol** (soccer) are all popular. For info on fútbol matches, visit the Mexican National Team's website at www.femexfut.org.mx. **Baseball** is becoming more so, now that the Liga Mexicana de Beisbol (www.lmb.com.mx) represents 16 teams throughout the country. **Pelota mixteca** is a modern

MEXICO IN DEPTH

Maya Herbs & Homeopathics: A User's Guide

While you're traveling through Mexico, ample opportunities abound to try local herbs, whether diced in your guacamole, swirled in a smoothie, or slathered luxuriously over your whole body at one of the many Maya spas. Here is a user's guide to all of the naturally enhancing bounty that the jungles of Mexico's Caribbean coast produce:

Achiote (annatto or bitter orange): This brilliant red seed of the annatto plant is a staple in the best Yucatecan marinades. Look for it in the ruby colored fish Tikin Xic, and also on grilled chicken. Usually it is combined in a sauce with bitter orange, chiles, and other arousing spices. Bitter orange is used by Maya medicine men as a cure for many nervous disorders, and is thought to stimulate positive activity while simultaneously halting panicky thoughts.

Albahaca (sweet basil): This international favorite is used in purifying temazcals, or steam baths, as well as green salads and dressings. Albahaca is also used by shamans, or Maya medicine men, as a remedy for colds and stomach problems.

Amaranto (amaranth): A favorite of smoothie joints and health conscious cafes, this sweet spice is also used in alegria candy. If you see *mole amaranto* on a menu, try it—it's a rare, delicious dish.

Ajonjolí (sesame seed): Ground sesame seeds make the base of many of the best moles, as well as topping the savory sandwich rolls *cemitas*, and sweetening a host of other pastries. Keep an eye out for teas made from these leaves, which are known as a natural tranquilizer.

Anís (anise): Found in the sweet-smelling liqueur of the same name, this intoxicating seed is also an ingredient in many aphrodisiac lotions and potions found in specialty stores and small stalls.

Avena: This grain is most often served in a delicious porridge with milk, cinnamon, and raisins for a light breakfast.

Berros (watercress): This nutrient rich green is found floating in soups and blended into drinks; it's also used as a remedy for kidney and lung problems.

Chaya: An iron-laden herb that only grows wild in the Yucatán, and has been used in Maya recipes since ancient times. Look for it in chaya water, a refreshing blend of lemon, honey, ice, and chaya, as well as sprinkled in crepes, tamales, and the popular "poison eggs." Chaya is widely believed to detoxify the blood, and is a powerful antioxidant. It's an acquired taste, but give it more than a few tries, and you'll come around to its bittersweet goodness.

Cilantro (coriander, Chinese parsley): Most people love or hate this pungent herb; there is no middle ground. If you find yourself in the latter group, you may have a difficult time in Mexico, since it is an ingredient in everything from guacamole and salsa to ceviche and gazpacho.

interpretation of the pre-Hispanic ball game, which means no one gets sacrificed after the game—it's most frequently played in Oaxaca state. ***Lucha libre,*** or Mexican wrestling, is almost every bit as ridiculous as it looks in the movie *Nacho Libre*—it's less a sport and more an opportunity for men to don strange costumes and masks and pummel each other in a ring. Check out www.luchawiki.org for info on matches.

Corteza de maguey or mixiote (century plant): Often used as a packet for chicken or fish, instead of a banana leaf, these delicate herbs are known as *mixiotes.*

Epazote (wormseed): Wormseed is considered a key ingredient in the best refried beans. It's also believed to help cure *turista,* the diarrhea that many tourists experience, as well as to kill off most parasites. So if you were trying to resist those beans for your own good, give in—they may actually help.

Hierba buena (spearmint): You will recognize the refreshing smell of this herb as spearmint, especially if you are lucky enough to stay at a resort that puts Hierba buena (also known as Yerba buena) in its free toiletries. A key ingredient of any temazcal, the herb will make your lungs feel as if you've smoked a whole pack of menthol cigarettes the next day. This versatile herb is also a favorite after-sun soother, it's drunk in hot or iced teas, and it's thought to cure upset stomachs.

Manzanilla (chamomile): Chamomile tea in Mexico is the most delicious in the world. If you're a tea drinker, or just like to chill out, you owe it to yourself to try a pot of this mellow brew. Chamomile is also used in many calming and soothing spa treatments and shower gels.

Pápalo: This unusual herb is most commonly served grated and sprinkled on *tortas,* the Mexican version of a sub sandwich. The name originates from the Maya word for butterfly.

Pepicha: This invigorating green herb is frequently used to balance out the hotter habanero in green salsas.

Romero (rosemary): Used as one of the main aromatherapy agents in purifying temazcal baths, as well as a seasoning on pan de ajo and other savory breads, rosemary is readily available as a natural cure for every ailment from stomach ulcers to soaking sprained ankles. Maya shamans also prescribe rosemary tonics as remedies for shock and memory loss.

Toronjil (gentle balm): This tall, lemon-scented herb can be found at many family restaurants brewed into tea, and is a popular home remedy for weight control and nervous system disorders. It is also one of the herbs in the purifying temazcal.

Verbena and Lipia (lemon verbena): Another of the main ingredients of temazcal steam baths, this fragrant plant is used in many relaxing teas, ointments, and lotions—it's thought to calm the nerves.

—Sara Lieber

MEXICO IN DEPTH

Social Mores

American and English travelers (often called *gringos* by locals) have often observed that Mexicans have a different conception of time and that life in Mexico obeys slower rhythms. This is true, and yet few observers go on to explain what the consequences of this are for the visitor to Mexico. This is a shame, because an imperfect appreciation of this difference causes a good deal of misunderstanding between tourists and locals.

As the pace of life for Americans, Canadians, and others has quickened, they have come to skip some of the niceties of social interaction. When walking into a store, many Americans simply smile at a clerk and launch right into a question or request. The smile, in effect, replaces the greeting. In Mexico, it doesn't work that way. Mexicans misinterpret this American manner of greeting. After all, a smile when there is no context can be ambiguous; it can convey amusement, smugness, or superiority.

One of the most important pieces of advice to keep in mind while in Mexico is always to give a proper greeting when addressing Mexicans. Don't try to abbreviate social intercourse. Mexican culture places a higher value on proper social form than on saving time. A Mexican must at least say *"¡Buenos días!"* or its equivalent to show proper respect. When an individual meets up with a group, he will greet each person separately, which can take quite a while. For us, the polite thing would be to keep our interruption to a minimum and give a general greeting to all.

Mexicans, like most people, will consciously or subconsciously make quick judgments about individuals they meet. Most divide the world into the *bien educado* (well raised and cultured), and the *mal educado* (poorly raised). Unfortunately, many visitors are reluctant to try out their Spanish, preferring to keep exchanges to a minimum. Don't do this. To be categorized as a foreigner isn't a big deal. What's important in Mexico is to be categorized as one of the cultured foreigners and not one of the barbarians. This makes it easier to get the attention of waiters, hotel desk clerks, and people on the street.

Religion, Myth & Folklore

Mexico is predominantly Roman Catholic, a religion introduced by the Spaniards during the conquest of Mexico. Despite its preponderance, the Catholic faith in many places in Mexico (Chiapas and Oaxaca, for example) has pre-Hispanic undercurrents. You need only visit the *curandero* section of a Mexican market (where you can purchase copal, an incense agreeable to the gods; rustic beeswax candles, a traditional offering; the native species of tobacco used to ward off evil; and so on) or attend

What Not to Wear

Although you'll likely hang at many seaside resorts during your stay in Mexico, keep in mind that the resorts also are the home and place of business for many Mexicans. Wearing swim trunks or a *pareo* skirt wrapped around your bikini is okay while you're on your way to the beach, but we recommend that you put on a shirt or a sundress when you plan to explore the town. You can still go casual, but Mexicans frown upon tourists who can't tell the difference between beach and town attire—especially true when it comes to going into any church wearing inappropriate clothing.

When it comes to club wear, the dress code throughout most of Mexico isn't nearly as froufrou or pretentious as in places like New York or London. Most clubs will let you in with whatever you're wearing (as long as you're not barefoot or topless). Jeans, tanks, and sandals are the norm, but why be boring? Now is as good a time as any to wear those quirky threads you bought at the *mercado*. To fit in with the metropolitan Mexico City crowd, though, think tight and black. Outfits there are chic and far from conservative, regardless of gender.

How to Be Cool

Hablas español? If not, learn a little. Mexicans are so invariably polite and hospitable that it is downright rude for tourists not to even *try* to speak rudimentary Spanish. If you want to almost blend in and get along, also do the following:

- Always greet everyone you encounter during the day (see above). If you're passing an acquaintance on the street, you can say (or they may) *"Adios"* instead of *"Hola."* This expression literally means "Go with God."
- Do not take pictures of people without asking permission; also don't take pictures during Mass.
- Do not speak English loudly if someone doesn't understand.
- Don't pee in the street—it's not only rude, you can be fined.
- Do not criticize Mexico in any way. That includes comparing it to the U.S. or Canada or anywhere else pejoratively.

a village festivity featuring pre-Hispanic dancers to understand that supernatural beliefs often run parallel with Christian ones in Mexico.

Mexico's complicated mythological heritage from pre-Hispanic religion is full of images derived from nature—the wind, jaguars, eagles, snakes, flowers, and more—all intertwined with elaborate mythological stories to explain the universe, climate, seasons, and geography. Most groups believed in an underworld (not a hell), usually containing 9 levels, and a heaven of 13 levels—which is why the numbers 9 and 13 are so mythologically significant. The solar calendar count of 365 days and the ceremonial calendar of 260 days are significant as well. How one died determined one's resting place after death: in the underworld (*Xibalba* to the Maya), in heaven, or at one of the four cardinal points. For example, men who died in battle or women who died in childbirth went straight to the sun. Everyone else first had to make a journey through the underworld.

Machismo

Probably the most familiar and least understood social issue in Mexico is the concept of *machismo,* which roughly translates as "a cult of masculinity." Machismo is an imported idea, brought to Mexico by Spanish conquistadors, who in turn learned it from the Moors who occupied Spain in the 8th century. The original Spanish version had a strong element of medieval chivalry attached to it, but when it came to Mexico, it was warped by the situation of invasion and conquest in which it manifested itself. Part of the mandate of the invaders was to create a new mixed-blood race *(mestizos);* hence rape was viewed as a legitimate colonizing tool, a way to "civilize" the locals. While some mestizos were accepted into society, the majority of the offspring of these unions were rejected by both locals and pure-blood Spanish.

The Spanish set up a 16-level list of how "pure" a mixed-blood child was, and manliness was included in this. To be manly meant not having any "feminine" traits—sincerity, nurturing, kindness, or honesty. Being macho also meant controlling one's family with an iron fist, never revealing one's feelings to anyone else, and being able to stoically endure any deprivations or social inequities. This mentality poisoned Mexican society for hundreds of

A Maya Wedding

Not that you're planning to get married while in Mexico, but in case you fall in love with the beaches here as much as with that guy or girl you eventually want to call the one, know that this is a great place to come back to tie the knot. Maya weddings are an increasingly popular way to have a non-traditional (by American and European standards, that is) ceremony. Since ceremonies are conducted by a shaman entirely in the indigenous Maya language, you avoid saying trite vows and just leave it to the shaman to envelop you in good luck. The typical ceremony, which my husband and I underwent on the beach at Playa del Carmen, begins with the beating of drums and the long, low bleat of conch shells. The shaman then offers incense and bowls of flower petals, candles, cacao, tortillas, and corn as symbolic gifts for what the bride and groom bring to each other. At my wedding, the shaman even unexpectedly threw the flower petals in our faces. It all resulted in the least boring wedding imaginable, because we learned about an ancient culture in the process of getting married.

Ready to settle down right away? Under a treaty between the United States and Mexico, Mexican civil marriages are automatically valid in the United States. You need certified copies of birth certificates, driver's licenses, or passports; tourist cards (provided when you enter Mexico); and results of blood tests performed in Mexico within 15 days before the ceremony. Check with a local, on-site wedding planner through your hotel to verify all the necessary requirements and obtain an application well in advance of your desired wedding date, or contact the Mexico Tourism Board (☎ **800/446-3942;** www.visitmexico.com) for information. **Yaxche restaurant** (www.mayacuisine.com) or **Ajua Weddings** (www.ajuaweddings.com) can hook you up with all the info you need to plan your own Maya wedding, too.

—Liza Monroy

years, gradually fading after the 1910 Revolution that marked the final rejection of all things Spanish.

That doesn't mean machismo is gone, of course. Any man who exhibits feminine characteristics is still often viewed as weak, homosexual, or controlled by a woman. But to be fair, some educated elites say that to be macho means to support one's family, to be a strong upright member of society, and to be protective and productive.

One bizarre aspect of machismo is the saint-harlot view of women that it propagates. While most Mexican men revere their mothers, some are less protective and respectful of women whom they are not related to. This sexist double standard is a relic of centuries of Catholic teachings. Because of the country's Catholic background, the Virgin of Guadalupe is the most recognized and beloved icon in Mexican culture. She is considered to be the ultimate Mother, endlessly forgiving, suffering, and patient and, obviously, she's someone who's hard to live up to.

Art & Architecture 101

Mexico's artistic and architectural legacy reaches back more than 3,000 years. Until the conquest of Mexico in A.D. 1521, art, architecture, politics, and religion were intertwined. Although the European conquest influenced the style and subject of

Mexican art, this continuity remained throughout the colonial period.

Pre-Hispanic Forms

Mexico's **pyramids** were truncated platforms crowned with a temple. Many sites have circular buildings, such as El Caracol at Chichén Itzá, usually called the observatory and dedicated to the god of the wind. El Castillo at Chichén Itzá has 365 steps—one for every day of the year. The Temple of the Magicians at Uxmal has beautifully rounded and sloping sides. Evidence of building one pyramidal structure on top of another, a widely accepted practice, has been found throughout Mesoamerica.

Throughout Mexico, carved stone and mural art on pyramids served a religious and historic function rather than an ornamental one. **Hieroglyphs,** picture symbols etched on stone or painted on walls or pottery, functioned as the written language of the ancient peoples, particularly the Maya. By deciphering the glyphs, scholars allow the ancients to speak again, providing us with specific names to attach to rulers and their families, and demystifying the great dynastic histories of the Maya. For more on this, read *A Forest of Kings* by Linda Schele and David Freidel, and *Blood of Kings* by Linda Schele and Mary Ellen Miller. Good hieroglyphic examples appear in the site museum at Palenque.

Pre-Hispanic cultures left a wealth of fantastic painted **murals and cave paintings,** most of which are remarkably preserved, in the central mountain region concentrated in the San Francisco de la Sierra and Santa Martha mountains. Most depict a combination of faceless human forms and animal forms, in apparent depictions of ritualistic ceremonies. Their origin remains a mystery. Over 300 cave paintings are concentrated in an area known as the Great Wall, in the San Francisco de la Sierra—it's the largest concentration of ancient rock paintings in the world.

Spanish Influence

With the arrival of the Spaniards, new forms of architecture came to Mexico. Many sites that were occupied by indigenous groups at the time of the conquest were razed and in their place appeared Catholic churches, public buildings, and palaces for conquerors and the king's bureaucrats. In the Yucatán, churches at Izamal, Tecoh, Santa Elena, and Muná rest atop former pyramidal structures. Indian artisans, who formerly worked on pyramidal structures, were recruited to build the new buildings, often guided by drawings of European buildings. Frequently left on their own, the indigenous artisans implanted traditional symbolism in the new buildings: a plaster angel swaddled in feathers, reminiscent of the god Quetzalcoatl, and the face of an ancient god surrounded by corn leaves. They used pre-Hispanic calendar counts—the 13 steps to heaven or the nine levels of the underworld—to determine how many florets to carve around church doorways.

To convert the native populations, New World Spanish priests and architects altered their normal ways of teaching and building. Often before a church was built, an open-air atrium was constructed to accommodate large numbers of parishioners for services. *Posas* (shelters) at the four corners of churchyards were another architectural technique unique to Mexico, again to accommodate crowds. Because of the language barrier between the Spanish and the natives, church adornment became more explicit. Biblical tales came to life in frescoes splashed across church walls. Christian symbolism in stone supplanted that of pre-Hispanic ideas as the natives tried to make sense of it all.

Tips for Digital Travel Photography

- **Take along a spare camera—or two.** Even if you've been anointed the "official" photographer of your travel group, encourage others in your party to carry their own cameras and provide fresh perspectives—and backup. Your photographic "second unit" may include you in a few shots so you're not the invisible person of the trip.
- **Stock up on digital film cards.** At home, it's easy to copy pictures from your memory cards to your computer as they fill up. During your travels, cards seem to fill up more quickly. Take along enough digital film for your entire trip or, at a minimum, enough for at least a few days of shooting. At intervals, you can copy images to CDs. Many camera stores and souvenir shops offer this service, and a growing number of mass merchandisers have walk-up kiosks you can use to make prints or create CDs while you travel.
- **Share and share alike.** No need to wait until you get home to share your photos. You can upload a gallery's worth to an online photo sharing service. Just find an Internet café where the computers have card readers, or connect your camera to the computer with a cable. You can find online photo sharing services that cost little or nothing at **www.clickherefree.com**. You can also use America Online's Your Pictures service, or commercial enterprises that give you free or low-cost photo sharing: Kodak's EasyShare gallery (**www.kodak.com**), Yahoo! Photos (**www.photos.yahoo.com**), Snapfish (**www.snapfish.com**), or Shutterfly (**www.shutterfly.com**).
- **Add voice annotations to your photos.** Many digital cameras allow you to add voice annotations to your shots after they're taken. These serve as excellent reminders and documentation. One castle or cathedral may look like another after a long tour; your voice notes will help you distinguish them.
- **Experiment!** Travel is a great time to try out new techniques. Take photos at night, resting your camera on a handy wall or other support as your self-timer trips the shutter for a long exposure. Try close-ups of flowers and crafts, or maybe the exotic cuisine you're about to consume. Discover action photography—shoot the countryside from buses or cars. With a digital camera, you can experiment and then erase your mistakes.

—From *Travel Photography Digital Field Guide*, 1st edition (John Wiley & Sons, 2006)

Baroque became even more baroque in Mexico and was dubbed **churrigueresque** or **ultrabaroque.** Exuberant and complicated, it combines Gothic, baroque, and plateresque elements.

Almost every major town in the country has the remains of a **mission** nearby. About 2 hours from Loreto in Baja, in a section of the old Camino Real used by Spanish missionaries and explorers, is **Misión San Francisco Javier,** one of the best-preserved, most spectacularly set missions in the country—high in a mountain valley beneath volcanic walls. Founded in 1699 by the Jesuit priest Francisco María Píccolo, it was the second mission established in

California, completed in 1758. The original building of the **Misión Santa Rosalía de Mulegé,** founded in 1706 by Father Juan de Ugarte and Juan María Basaldúa, was completed in 1766, but in 1770, a flood destroyed nearly all the common buildings, and the mission was rebuilt on the site it occupies today, on a bluff overlooking the river. Although not the most architecturally interesting of the country's missions, it remains in excellent condition and still functions as a Catholic church, although mission operations halted in 1828.

When Porfirio Díaz became president in the late 19th century, the nation's art and architecture experienced another infusion of European sensibility. Díaz idolized Europe, and he commissioned a number of striking European-style public buildings, including many opera houses. He provided European scholarships to promising young artists who later returned to Mexico to produce Mexican-subject paintings using techniques learned abroad.

In Baja, Díaz granted the Compañía de Boleo (part of the Rothschild family holdings) a 99-year lease to the rich deposits of copper in the area surrounding Santa Rosalía in exchange for the company building a town, the harbor, public buildings, and establishing a maritime route between the port and Guaymas, meant to create employment for Mexican workers. The architectural influence of Santa Rosalía is decidedly European, and no more so than in its church, the **Iglesia de Santa Barbara,** a structure of galvanized steel designed by Gustave Eiffel (of Eiffel Tower fame) in 1884. It was originally created for the 1889 Paris World Expo, where it was displayed as a prototype for what Eiffel envisioned as a sort of prefab mission. The structure eventually made its way to Santa Rosalía in 1897, where its somber gray exterior belies the beauty of the intricate stained-glass windows viewed from inside.

The Advent of Mexican Muralism

As the Mexican Revolution ripped the country apart between 1911 and 1917, a new social and cultural Mexico was born. In 1923, Minister of Education José Vasconcelos was put in charge of educating the illiterate masses. As one means of reaching people, he invited **Diego Rivera** and several other budding artists to paint Mexican history on the walls of the Ministry of Education building and the National Preparatory School in Mexico City. Thus began the tradition of painting murals in public buildings, which you will find in towns and cities throughout Mexico.

A Taste of Mexico

Authentic Mexican food differs dramatically from what is frequently served in the U.S. under that name. Food here is a blend of thousands of years of culinary fusion, and is far more sophisticated than your local Taco Bell will lead you to believe. There are lots of regional differences, but some generalizations can be made. Mexican food usually isn't pepper-hot when it arrives at the table (though many dishes must have a certain amount of piquancy, and some home cooking can be very spicy, depending on a family's or chef's tastes). Chiles and sauces add piquant flavor after the food is served; you'll never see a table in Mexico without one or both of these condiments. Mexicans don't drown their cooking in cheese and sour cream, a la Tex-Mex, and they use a great variety of ingredients. But the basis

Comfort Food Mexican Style

All over Mexico, but especially in Oaxaca, you can tell what you're ordering by paying attention to the word's prefix or suffix. All food that's dipped in beans, tomatoes, or mole sauces will start with an "en" and end in "ada." The "en/ada" portion indicates the type of sauce the tortilla wrapped around it is dipped in. Here are some examples:

Enfrijoada: A tortilla dipped in bean sauce (or mashed beans)

Enchilada: Tortillas wrapped around cheese, chicken, or some beans or other meat

Enmolada: Tortillas dipped and rolled in mole

Entomatada: A tortilla dipped in tomato sauce and wrapped around cheese

Empanada: Little pockets of corn bread, with various fillings; the tortilla is dipped in a sauce made of whatever is in the middle

of Mexican food is simple—tortillas, beans, chiles, squash, and tomatoes—the same as it was centuries ago, before the Europeans arrived.

Many food writers have said that Mexico City is the most exciting culinary city in the world, surpassing Singapore and Paris but with none of the attitude, pretense, or the cost. We completely agree, but should add that the good grub isn't limited just to Mexico City.

For tips on eating and drinking safely in Mexico, see "Health & Safety" in "Basics".

The Basics

TORTILLAS Traditional tortillas are made from corn that's boiled in water and lime, and then ground into *masa* (a grainy dough), patted and pressed into thin cakes, and cooked on a hot griddle known as a *comal.* In many households, the tortilla takes the place of fork and spoon; Mexicans merely tear them into wedge-shaped pieces, which they use to scoop up their food. Restaurants often serve bread rather than tortillas because it's easier, but you can always ask for tortillas. A more recent invention from northern Mexico is the flour tortilla, which is seen less frequently in the rest of Mexico.

ENCHILADAS The tortilla is the basis of several Mexican dishes, but the most famous of these is the enchilada. The original name for this dish would have been *tortilla enchilada,* which simply means a tortilla dipped in a chile sauce. There's also the *entomatada* (tortilla dipped in a tomato sauce) and the *enfrijolada* (a bean sauce). The enchilada began as a very simple dish: A tortilla is dipped in chile sauce (usually with ancho chile) and then into very hot oil, and then is quickly folded or rolled on a plate and sprinkled with chopped onions and a little *queso cotija* (crumbly white cheese) and served with a few fried potatoes and carrots. You can get this basic enchilada in food stands across the country. I love them, and if you come across them in your travels, give them a try. In restaurants you get the more elaborate enchilada, with different fillings of cheese, chicken, pork, or even seafood, and sometimes in a casserole.

TACOS A taco is anything folded or rolled into a tortilla, and sometimes a double tortilla. The tortilla can be served either soft or fried. Flautas and quesadillas are species of tacos. For Mexicans, the taco is the quintessential fast food, and the *taquería* (taco stand)—a ubiquitous sight—is a great place to get a filling meal. See the section "Eating Out: Restaurants,

Taquerías & Tipping," below, for information on taquerías.

FRIJOLES An invisible "bean line" divides Mexico: It starts at the Gulf Coast in the southern part of the state of Tamaulipas and moves inland through the eastern quarter of San Luis Potosí and most of the state of Hidalgo, then goes straight through Mexico City and Morelos and into Guerrero, where it curves slightly westward to the Pacific. To the north and west of this line, the pink bean known as the *flor de mayo* is the staple food; to the south and east, including all of the Yucatán, the standard is the black bean.

In private households, beans are served at least once a day and, among the working class and peasantry, with every meal, if the family can afford it. Mexicans almost always prepare beans with a minimum of condiments—usually just a little onion and garlic and perhaps a pinch of herbs. Beans are meant to be a contrast to the heavily spiced dishes. Sometimes they are served at the end of a meal with a little Mexican-style sour cream.

Mexicans often fry leftover beans and serve them on the side as *frijoles refritos. Refritos* is usually translated as "refried," but this is a misnomer—the beans are fried only once. The prefix "re" actually means "well" (as in thoroughly).

TAMALES You make a tamal by mixing corn masa with a little lard, adding one of several fillings—meats flavored with chiles (or no filling at all)—then wrapping it in a corn husk or in the leaf of a banana or other plant, and finally steaming it. Every region in Mexico has its own traditional way of making tamales. In some places, a single tamal can be big enough to feed a family, while in others they are barely 7.5cm (3 inches) long and 2.5cm (an inch) thick.

CHOCOLATE The Maya were the first people to have harvested cacao beans around 250 A.D. The seeds were roasted, ground, and mixed with chile, water, and cornmeal and then frothed into a drink that had significant religious overtones. It was a beverage of the powerful, mainly sipped by soldiers, priests, rulers, and rich merchants. During the Aztecs' heyday, cacao beans were also used as money. The chocolate drink that was so popular among the Aztecs and Maya was a bitter caffeinated jolt; it took the Spanish to dream up adding sugar to it.

Today **hot chocolate** is still a major part of Mexican cuisine, often drunk in the morning during winter and commonly associated with Day of the Dead rituals. For drinking purposes, chocolate is sold in round tablets containing sugar and

children of the corn

It's impossible to overstate the importance that corn has played in the Americas, and continues to play today in Mexico. Corn is the basis for much Mesoamerican food, so to call it a Mexican staple is to negate that it's been a staple for all humans on this continent. The Aztec name for corn was *toconayo,* meaning "our flesh." According to Popul Vuh, the Maya religious text, corn was what the gods used to make man. Today, it's safe to say that just about any Mexican meal will use corn in some way, either as a backdrop or in a feature role. Assorted corn dishes in Mexican cuisine include tortillas, tacos, chimichangas, enchiladas, tamales, tortilla soup, tostadas, nachos, burritos, and gorditas, to name just a few.

cinnamon. These are melted in slowly heated milk and then whipped using a *molinillo,* a wooden mixer with a hollowed out knob-end notched with grooves. After the chocolate/sugar tablet melts, the molinillo is placed in the liquid and then one rubs the handle quickly, spinning the head and frothing the chocolate. This is done three times for best results.

Not all chocolate here is drunk of course. Oaxacan **mole negro,** for example, depends greatly on the use of unsweetened chocolate to achieve a uniquely bitter flavor.

CHILES There are more than 300 different chile varieties in Mexico. Strips of chile are called *rajas,* and they're great stuffed in tacos. Generally, chiles are like dogs: the smaller they are, the more likely they'll bite you. The most common is the **jalapeño,** usually seen on every restaurant table *en escabeche* (pickled in vinegar). About 2.5 to 5cm (1–2 inches) long, they can be green, yellow, or red, and can be grilled and stuffed. When jalapeños are smoked and dried, they can be marinated in a vinegar *adobo* sauce. They are then known as **chile chipotle.** The **chile poblano** is about 13cm (5 inches) long, dark green, and mild in spiciness. When the poblano is dried, it turns deep red and is known as **chile ancho.**

The **chile serrano** is short, thin, and green and often presented in vinegar. If it's dried, it turns red and is called **chile japones.** It is very spicy and best when mixed into soups and moles. The **chile pequin** is blisteringly hot and used for making Tabasco sauce. Maybe the hottest chile is **chile habanero,** often found in the Yucatán. Be very careful when putting one of these in your mouth. **Chile de arbol** grows on trees (hence the name) and is small and dark green when fresh, turning orange when dried. It is also very hot. The **chile pasilla** is long, thin, dark green when fresh and almost black when dried. It's used in soups as a garnish and is not particularly spicy.

A note about salsa: It can be fresh, cooked, fruity, bitter, sour, sweet, bland, hot, basic, or acidic. The variations are endless and new ones are constantly being invented by Mexican chefs. From **Labna** in Cancún (p. 197) where Yucatecan flavors rule (think habanero and red onions) to the 30 different types of salsa at Cabo's **Felix** (p. 400), you'll never find the same thing done exactly the same way twice.

CACTUS Two types of cacti might pop up in your Mexican meals. The first is **nopales,** the peeled, sliced, and diced leaves of a nearly spineless cactus. They are much like okra, slightly slimy if not rinsed, but have a unique flavor, a mix of asparagus, sorrel, and green pepper. They can be sautéed and used in salsas, eggs, stews, and salads. **Tunas,** the fruit of the prickly pear cactus, are fleshy red globes that are kiwilike in flavor and texture. They are eaten fresh or used in drinks. To remove the small spines on the skin, just singe over a low fire.

MOLE The word *molli* means "stew or sauce" in Nahuatl, the Aztec language. While it's associated with Oaxaca, mole actually has many distinct regional variations. Some say that mole originated in 17th-century Puebla, when a nun had to make a special meal for some VIPs and had nothing but leftovers to work with. Others claim that mole was invented when a priest accidentally tipped his whole spice tray over into a stew he was making.

Today, mole sauce is served over rice and chicken, enchiladas, potatoes, turkey, eggs, pork, or fish. Its creation is an insanely labor-intensive process. (As a result, many restaurants don't include it on their menus.) Many recipes have 30-plus ingredients, and many require either dry frying or grinding or both.

There are many different types of moles and chocolate is only sometimes used as a key ingredient. A partial list of the ingredients commonly used in moles includes pureed roasted chiles (guajillo, serrano, jalapeño, arbol, and poblano), pumpkin seeds, sesame seeds, chocolate, cilantro, cloves, raisins, cinnamon, tomatoes, garlic, cumin, lettuce, chayotes, green beans, peanuts, almonds, allspice, potatoes, onion, avocado leaf, and carrots . . . the list just goes on and on.

The sweet mole poblano of Puebla is often considered to be the national dish of Mexico. Yet Oaxaca also has many good moles—seven different styles, to be exact, including *mole colorado* (red), *amarillo* (yellow), *verde* (green), and perhaps the most famous mole, *negro* (black), which includes chocolate. Veracruz's mole verde is known for its green chiles and tomatillo base; Guerrero's mole verde has pumpkin seeds.

If you're a mole fan, by all means plan a trip to Mexico in mid-October—the annual Mole Festival in the small town of San Pedro Atocpan is a great place to sample thousands of varieties of mole.

Mealtime

MORNING The morning meal, known as *el desayuno*, can be something light, such as coffee and sweet bread, or something more substantial: eggs, beans, tortillas, bread, fruit, and juice. It can be eaten early or late and is always a sure bet in Mexico. The variety and sweetness of the fruits are remarkable, and you can't go wrong with Mexican egg dishes.

MIDAFTERNOON The main meal of the day, known as *la comida* (or *el almuerzo*), is eaten between 2 and 4pm. Stores and businesses close, and most people go home to eat and perhaps take a short afternoon siesta before going about their business. The first course is the *sopa*, which can be either *caldo* (soup) or *sopa de arroz* (rice) or both; then comes the main course, which usually is a meat or fish dish prepared in some kind of sauce and served with beans, followed by dessert. Typical desserts include *flan*, a vanilla custard cake with a sugar shell; *arroz con leche* (rice pudding); and *nieve* (ice cream).

Although restaurants serving lunch and dinner may open at 1pm, most people don't show up to eat until later. But this doesn't necessarily hold true in beach cities, where the clientele are mainly tourists who are used to eating earlier.

EVENING Between 8 and 10pm, most Mexicans have a light meal called *la cena*. If eaten at home, it is something like a sandwich, bread and jam, or perhaps a couple of tacos made from some of the day's leftovers. At restaurants, the most common thing to eat is *antojitos* (literally, "little cravings"), a general label for light fare. Antojitos include tostadas, tamales, tacos, and simple enchiladas. Large restaurants offer complete meals as well.

Eating Out: Restaurants, Taquerías & Tipping

Avoid eating at those inviting sidewalk restaurants you'll see around the country's main plazas. These places usually cater to tourists and don't need to count on getting any return business—hence, they can charge more. But they are great for nursing a coffee or beer and people-watching.

The country's hotel restaurants also do not impress for the most part. Yes, they feed you until you're stuffed, especially at the feast-like breakfast buffets. But you should venture beyond your hotel walls for a more interesting and authentic meal.

Most nonresort towns have one or two restaurants (though sometimes one is a coffee shop) that serve as social centers for the locals. These establishments over time become virtual institutions, and change comes very slowly. The food is usually good

Huitla-wha?

The skinny on Mexico's fave eats

Huitlacoche, calabaza, pastor, oh my! If you're used to burritos and fajitas from Taco Hell you may be left wondering, *What is this stuff?* Well, we're here to help you decipher Mexican cuisine. Many of the dishes described below can be found at street carts as well as top restaurants. Also check out the "Menu Terms" listed in Appendix B for info on other menu items.

- ***Al pastor:*** Pork marinated in different spices and cooked on a rotisserie, and often stuffed inside tacos and burritos. Hands-down the most popular type of tacos.
- ***Atole*:** Corn meal toasted and boiled with milk or water to make a thin porridge-like drink, seasoned with cinnamon, brown sugar, chocolate, or nuts. Usually served for breakfast.
- ***Barbacoa*:** Lamb, onion, cilantro, and red chili sauce on corn tortillas.
- ***Birria*:** A goat stew that is very commonly used as a hangover cure.
- ***Carne asada*:** A grilled beef dish, common in Northern Mexico regions like Baja—kind of like barbecue.
- ***Ceviche*:** Any mix of white fish, shrimp, or octopus, marinated and "cooked" in lemon, green chilis, onions, vinegar, cilantro, and often served with salt crackers or fried tortilla strips.
- **Chalupas:** The chalupas in Mexico are far from the mass-market, drive-thru version you may be accustomed to. The original version, a tostada platter heaped with shredded pork, onion, and pepper, hails from Puebla.
- ***Chilaquiles:*** Tortillas, fried up with red salsa, eggs, and cheese. This is a common (and very filling) breakfast meal.
- ***Chile relleno*:** A long poblano chile, stuffed with cheese, dipped in a batter, deep-fried, and served with a mild red sauce.
- ***Chiles en nogada:*** A roasted mild chile poblano stuffed with a meat filling (usually containing raisins and pomegranate seeds) and topped with a white almond sauce. It's *very* rich. Because of the colors—red, green, and white, like the flag—it's associated with both Independence Day as well as Christmas, but it's technically only in season from August through November.
- ***Churros*:** Kind of like a long more-delicious doughnut, churros are fried dough sticks covered in sugar. They can be ordered with a filling, like *cajeta* (caramel) or chocolate. They're so good accompanied by hot chocolate that some places are devoted solely to serving *churros con chocolate*.
- ***Elote*:** Corn on a stick with creamy mayo, *queso fresco* (sprinkled cheese), and chile. A fantastic snack.
- **Flan:** Originally from Spain, this is an egg custard dish, flavored with vanilla, and topped (or bottomed) by a caramel crust.
- ***Flor de calabaza*:** Flor de calabaza are zucchini blossoms, commonly stuffed in quesadillas.
- ***Huaraches*:** Nope, not the shoes. This popular street-snack is a thick corn tortilla that's topped with steak, cheese, and salsas. It may be as big as a loafer but it's far tastier.

- ***Huchinango a la Veracruzana:*** Veracruz-style red snapper is grilled or broiled fish topped with a sauce of tomato, onion, and, most notably, green olives and capers.
- ***Huevos albanil*****:** Eggs poached in a green (or red) salsa that's blended with black beans, often served with nopales.
- ***Huevos rancheros:*** Fried eggs accompanied by corn tortillas and chile sauce.
- ***Huitlacoche:*** This is the mushroom that grows upon ears of corn—it's viewed as a blight by American farmers, but in Mexico it's seen as a delicacy. Don't be turned off by its black color and soft texture; it's wonderful sautéed and used in crepes, tacos, eggs, and pasta dishes.
- ***Mixiote*****:** Corn tortillas with spiced lamb, onion, and cilantro.
- **Mole:** A spicey chocolate-based sauce topped with sesame seeds. A signature dish of Puebla and Oaxaca, it's most popular on chicken (*pollo con mole*). See above for more info.
- ***Molletes*****:** Toasted French bread with refried beans, melted cheese, and *salsa Mexicana* (pico de gallo).
- **Nopales:** These shredded cactus veggies don't sting. Think exotic green beans that are super high in iron and slightly slimy. See above for more info.
- ***Pambazo*****:** As delish as the name is fun to say. It's a fried roll accompanied with potato, chorizo (chicken is common, too), lettuce, onion, cream, and cheese.
- ***Pescado mojo de ajo:*** Fish in a slow-cooked garlic-oil sauce.
- ***Pozole*****:** A stew of pork, onions, hominy (made from dried corn kernels), oregano, raw radish, cabbage, and lime, built around a deep rich broth.
- ***Queso fundido*****:** This rich melted cheese dish comes in a bowl, with or without *chorizo* (spicy sausage) or sometimes other additions like mushrooms. The best is served with thin warm flour tortillas, which makes it kind of like fondue.
- ***Sopa de tortilla*****:** Day-old tortillas dipped in chicken broth, pasilla chilies, onion, garlic, and tomatoes, and topped with *queso freso*, avocado, and lime.
- ***Sopes*****:** Somewhere between a *masa* pie and thick tortilla, these are open-faced palm-sized "boats" that are filled with just about anything you'd put in a taco or a burrito.
- ***Torta*****:** Not to be confused with the Italian word for cake, tortas are typical Mexican sandwiches, served on a fluffy, toasted roll. Try a *torta de pollo,* a delicious combination of shredded chicken, cheese, tomato, avocado, beans, lettuce, and mayonnaise.
- ***Tostada*****:** Large toasted corn tortilla topped with refried beans, cream, chicken, lettuce, and chili sauce.

standard fare, cooked as it was 20 years ago; the decor is simple. The patrons have known each other and the staff for years, and the *charla* (banter), gestures, and greetings are friendly, open, and unaffected. If you're curious about Mexican culture, eating and observing the goings-on is fun.

During your trip, you're going to see many ***taquerías* (taco joints).** These are generally small places with a counter or a few tables set around the cooking area; you get to see exactly how the cooks make their tacos before deciding whether to order. Most tacos come with a little chopped onion and cilantro, but not tomato and lettuce. Find one that seems popular with the locals and where the cook performs with brio (a good sign of pride in the product). Sometimes there will be a woman making the tortillas right there (or working the *masa,* the dough). You will never see men doing this—men may do all other cooking and kitchen tasks, and work with prepared tortillas, but they will never be found working masa.

For the main meal of the day, many restaurants offer a multicourse blue-plate special called ***comida corrida*** or ***menú del día.*** This is the least expensive way to get a full meal during the day. We recommend having a comida corrida at lunchtime and snacking on antojitos or grabbing street stand food for dinner in order to save money.

Tips are about the same as in the United States. You'll sometimes find a 15% **value-added tax** on restaurant meals, which shows up on the bill as "IVA." This is a boon to arithmetically challenged tippers, saving them from undue exertion.

In Mexico, you need to ask for your check; it is generally considered inhospitable to present a check to someone who hasn't requested it. If you're in a hurry to get somewhere, ask for the check when your food arrives.

To summon the waiter, wave or raise your hand, but don't motion with your index finger, which is a demeaning gesture that may even cause the waiter to ignore you. Or if it's the check you want, you can motion to the waiter from across the room using the universal pretend-you're-writing gesture.

Most restaurants do not have **non-smoking sections;** when they do, we mention it in the reviews. But Mexico's wonderful climate allows for many open-air restaurants, usually set inside a courtyard of a colonial house, or in rooms with tall ceilings and plenty of open windows.

Bebidas

You'll find shops selling *jugos* (juices) and *licuados* (smoothies) made from several kinds of tropical fruit as well as *aguas frescas*—water flavored with hibiscus, melon, tamarind, or lime—all over Mexico. Pepsi and Coca-Cola here taste the way they did in the United States years ago, thick and syrupy, before the makers started adding corn syrup.

Coffee

Mexico's centuries-old method of growing coffee in the shade is organic and Fair Trade and bird friendly. Shade-grown coffee plantations provide an important stop in the corridor from North to South America for migratory birds. As the demand for coffee has grown, some growers have started to use agrochemicals and to grow coffee plants in the sun for faster production, but the plantations in Oaxaca, Veracruz, and Chiapas still use the same methods that they have for years.

Mexico is the number one exporter of organic coffee to the United States (and

Watering Holes

Just as there are plenty of things to drink in Mexico, there are a huge variety of places *to* drink. You'll have your choice of everything from standard sports bars to gay clubs and bars. Then there's the distinctly Mexican phenomenon of **cantinas,** bars traditionally only frequented by men—very loud men. These are mostly located in inland towns like San Miguel de Allende, so before visiting bars there, look for signs that prohibit women *("no mujeres").* At some cantinas, you can enter only if accompanied by a guy; a rare few allow women to enter on their own.

Most drinking spots in Mexico don't require so much advance planning, though. Here's a brief list of Spanish words to keep in mind so that you can crash different parties, depending on your mood:

- *Antros:* Dance club
- *Para tirar rostro:* To see and be seen spot
- *Rock en vivo:* Live rock venue
- *Club de playa:* Beach club
- *Para llevar:* A bar with drinks to go

the world) and supplies 25% of Fair Trade coffee. That doesn't mean that the growers here are getting rich, however; more and more have abandoned their farms to make the long trek to the U.S. in search of a living wage. About 80% of the growers are small farmers and the coffee-growing areas are some of the poorest in Mexico, with inadequate health and education facilities. Indeed in Chiapas one is more likely to get a cup of Nescafe instead of locally grown beans since the product is too expensive to drink. The Zapatistas in Chiapas gained some of their early support from the Maya growers in the area and their political organization has helped to make the practice of shade-grown coffee even more ingrained.

Once it was hard to find decent coffee in Mexico but that situation has changed for the better in the last 5 years. You'll now find excellent choices throughout all the towns and cities featured in this book. Starbucks outlets are starting to pop up here and there but they're not dominating the scene yet. One encouraging sign is that eco-tourism outlets and organic coffee farms are starting to band together, particularly around Oaxaca, to offer hikes, plantation visits, and bike tours into the farmlands where coffee is grown.

Pulque

Made by hollowing out the center of the agave plant and fermenting its juice, *pulque* is a native beverage that some say was invented to be used in religious rituals. The exact origins of pulque, however, remains an ancient Aztec secret. What we do know is that it's difficult to preserve, which is why it's not exported like tequila or mezcal—or maybe that's because it's such an "acquired" taste. So be forewarned, you might not like it . . . but it's worth trying! In pulquerias today, it comes in a variety of high-octane flavors like strawberry, coffee, and guava and plays a role in the modern ritual of getting your drink on.

Mezcal

Mezcal is, in essence, a distilled pulque, and it must be made from at least 80%

The Do-It-Yourself Guide to Mexican Cocktails

La Michelada

The Michelada is a lighter, more masculine version of a bloody mary. It's good in the morning as a hangover cure with any light Mexican beer, as well as a darker Negro Modelo.

4 drops Tabasco sauce

¼ teaspoon Worcestershire sauce

A few dashes of salt and ground pepper

Juice of 1 lime wedge

1 bottle of beer

Sea salt

Combine above ingredients in a glass and pour beer to top. Serve with a wedge of lime in a salted glass.

Margarita

1½ ounce tequila

½ ounce triple sec

1 ounce lime juice

Salt

Rub the rim of a cocktail glass with lime juice, and dip in salt. Shake all ingredients with some ice, strain into a glass, and serve. For a frozen margarita, add a few handfuls of ice to the mixture and blend until smooth and slushy.

Piña Colada

1 cup coconut milk

1cup pineapple juice

1 cup rum

4 tablespoons white sugar

8 ice cubes

In a blender, combine coconut milk, pineapple juice, rum, sugar, and ice. Blend until smooth. Pour into glasses, and serve immediately.

agave. It can come from eight different agaves, but the most commonly used is Agave Angustifolia Haw. (Tequila, on the other hand, need only be 49% agave, but it comes from only one species of the plant, see below.) Mezcal is most associated with Oaxaca, since that state produces more than 60% of Mexican mezcal.

While tequila is made by steaming agave, the mezcal process involves roasting agave on charcoal in underground ovens—this produces a unique smoky flavor. The addition of a pickled worm, the larva of a moth that lays its eggs in agave, used to be added to young, clear mezcal to bring out a distinctive flavor, and to indicate that the liquor has a high alcohol content.

The Mexican government has tried to stop this practice recently, though. Today, premium versions of mezcal may be aged in oak casks for months and sell for $200 or more a bottle and they rarely have worms in the bottom.

Tequila

For most fans of agave drinks, tequila is the real deal—by law, it's a product of one specific agave variety, agave Tequiliana Weber (blue agave), and hails specifically from the highlands of Jalisco state. The center for making spirits in Jalisco is around the little town of Tequila—hence the name—just outside Guadalajara. Excellent blue agave distilled liquor is produced elsewhere but by law cannot be labeled tequila. Look for the NOM designation on the label, a federal registry number, to make sure you're getting the real deal.

Are you accustomed to lick, shoot, and suck? Well, get out of the habit 'cause that ain't really how it's done down here—tequila is meant to be savored, not slurped. Here's what you need to know to avoid being pegged as a tourist. Typically, the shot glass of the fiery potion is accompanied by a second one filled with *sangrita*—a spiced tomato juice concoction. The tequila is delicately sipped from its shot glass, followed by equally small sips of sangrita. *Muy sutil* (very subtle).

Beer

There are really only two major beer brewers in Mexico: Femsa (formerly Cuauhtemoc and Moctezuma) and Cerveceria Modelo. The first makes Carta Blanca, XX, Indio, Noche Buena, Chihuahua, Sol, Superior, and Tecate. The latter makes Corona, Modelo, Negro Leon, and Pacifico. Most of these have a 4.5% alcohol by volume content and are "clara" or light lagers. There are dark versions made as well—Negra Modelo is the most popular.

Fairly recently, a small brewery in Monterrey has started putting out beer that is a wonderful sign of the future. Especialidades Cervesas makes five different Casta brand beers: Bruna (a pale ale), Dorada (using German hops), Milenia (high alcohol and bottle conditioned), Morena (a dark ale), and Triguera (wheat beer). They will cost more but are worth the money. Of course, your choice of brew is up to you, but try to buy the locally produced brand whenever possible. My overall favorite everywhere is Modelo for both clear and dark varieties. After that (in declining order), I like Victoria, Indio, Pacifico, XX, and Tecate. If the only choices on hand are Carta Blanca, Sol, and Corona, you might as well ask for water instead.

Appendix B: Useful Terms & Phrases

Most Mexicans are very patient with foreigners who try to speak their language; it helps a lot to know a few basic phrases. Below are some simple phrases for expressing basic needs, followed by some common menu items.

Pronunciation Guide

Spanish is a straightforward language with a simple alphabet. If foreign letters (k and w) are counted, the alphabet has 27 letters (ñ, in addition to the English alphabet).

Spanish also has two double letters: ll (elle), pronounced like y in English "yes," and rr (erre), pronounced like an English r trilled by vibrating the end of the tongue against the hard palate, just above the upper teeth. There is also ch, as in chipmunk.

Pronunciation Guide

VOWELS

a	**ah as the a in father: abajo** (ah-*bah*-hoh)
au	**ow as in cow: automático** (ow-to-*mah*-tee-koh)
ay	**aye as in "All in favor, say aye": hay** (aye)
e	**eh to rhyme with the e in Nestlé: espera** (ehs-*peh*-rah)
i	**ee as in feed: pasillo** (pah-*see*-yoh)
o	**oh as in boat: modismo** (moh-*dees*-moh)
oy	**oy as in boy: hoy** (oy)
u	**oo as in the word coo: buscar** (boos-*kahr*)

CONSONANTS

b	**as in bean, but softer with less explosion than in English: buscar** (boos-*kahr*)
c	**before e and i as English initial s; ce is pronounced as seh: necesito** (neh-seh-*see*-toh); **ci is pronounced as see: cinco** (*seeng*-koh); **before a, o, u as English k, but softer with less explosion: caballero**

	(kah-bah-*yeh*-roh); **consejo** (kohn-*seh*-hoh); **Cuba** (*koo*-bah)
cu	**in combination with a, e, i, o pronounced like the qu in quick: cuándo** (*kwahn*-doh); **cuestión** (kwehs-*tyohn*)
d	**as the d in day, but softer with less explosion than in English. Some final ds can be pronounced as the th in the: usted** (oo-*stehth*). **If you pronounce Spanish d like the English d, you will be understood: ciudad** (see-oo-*dahd*); **de** (deh)
f	**as in fox: favor** (fah-*vohr*)
g	**before e and i as English h; ge is pronounced like he in hen: emergencia** (eh-mehr-*hehn*-syah); **gi is pronounced like English he: puerta giratoria** (*pwehr*-tah hee-rah-*tohr*-yah) **before a, o, u as initial hard g in English as in gate: llegar** (yeh-*gahr*); **tengo** (*tehn*-goh); **seguridad** (seh-goo-ree-*dahd*)
h	**silent; hizo** (*ee*-soh), **hasta** (*as*-tah); **hi before a vowel is pronounced like English y: hielo** (*yeh*-loh)
j	**as English h in hot: equipaje** (eh-kee-*pah*-heh)
k	**as in English: kilómetro** (kee-*loh*-meh-troh)
l	**as in English: ala** (*ah*-lah)
ll	**as the initial y in yeah: llegada** (yeh-*gah*-dah)
m	**as in English: aeromozo** (eh-roh-*moh*-soh)
n	**as in English: negocios** (neh-*goh*-syohs)
ñ	**as ny in canyon: cañón** (kahn-*yohn*)
p	**as in English but softer: pasaporte** (pah-sah-*pohr*-teh)
q	**qu is pronounced as k: máquina** (*mah*-kee-nah)
r	**as in English but more clipped: puerta** (*pwehr*-tah)
rr	**as a trilled r sound, vibrating the end of the tongue against the area just above the top teeth: perro** (*peh*-rroh). **A single r that starts a word is pronounced like the double r: rayos X** (*rrah*-yohs *eh*-kees)

Hey You

Spanish has two words for "you"—*tú,* spoken among friends and familiars, and *Usted* (abbreviated Ud. or Vd.), used among strangers or as a sign of respect toward elders and authority figures. When speaking with a stranger, expect to use Usted, unless you are invited to do otherwise. The second-person familiar plural form *(vosotros)* is rarely used, and then only in Spain, Argentina, and Chile. *Ustedes* (abbreviated Uds. or Vds.) is used instead, even among friends, especially in Latin America.

s	**as in English: salida** (sah-*lee*-dah)
t	**as in English but softer: tranvía** (trahn-*vee*ah)
v	**as in English: vuelo** (*vweh*-loh)
w	**as in English: waflera** (wah-*fleh*-rah)
x	**like English x: próximo** (*prohk*-see-moh)**; in some old names and some names of Native American origin, like h: Don Quixote** (dohn kee-*hoh*-teh)**, México** (*meh*-hee-koh) **spelled with j in Spain; before a consonant, like s: Taxco** (*tahs*-koh)
y	**as in English: yo** (yoh)**; by itself, as the ee sound in bead: y** (ee)
z	**like English s: aterrizaje** (ah-teh-rree-*sah*-heh)

Gender, Adjectives, Modifiers

Each noun takes a masculine or feminine gender, most often accompanied by a masculine or feminine definite article (el or la). Definite articles ("the"), indefinite articles ("a," "an"), and related adjectives must also be masculine or feminine, singular or plural, depending on the noun they're modifying.

THE DEFINITE ARTICLE ("THE")

	Masculine	Feminine
Singular	***el*** perro (the dog)	***la*** mesa (the table)
Plural	***los*** perros (the dogs)	***las*** mesas (the tables)

Basic Greetings

Essential Terms

English	Spanish	Pronunciation
Good day	**Buen día**	bwehn *dee*-ah
Good morning	**Buenos días**	*bweh*-nohs *dee*-ahs
How are you?	**¿Cómo está?**	*koh*-moh eh-*stah*
Very well	**Muy bien**	mwee byehn
Thank you	**Gracias**	*grah*-syahs
You're welcome	**De nada**	deh *nah*-dah
Goodbye	**Adiós**	ah-*dyohs*
Please	**Por favor**	pohr fah-*vohr*

An Abbreviated Take on Abbreviations

Common address abbreviations include *Apdo.* (post office box), *Av.* or *Ave.* (*avenida;* avenue), *Blv.* (*bulevar;* boulevard), *c/* (*calle;* street), *Calz.* (*calzada;* boulevard), *Dept.* (apartments), and *s/n* (*sin número;* without a number).

The C on faucets stands for *caliente* (hot), and F stands for *fría* (cold). PB *(planta baja)* means ground floor, and most buildings count the next floor up as the first floor (1).

English	Spanish	Pronunciation
Yes	**Sí**	see
No	**No**	noh
Excuse me	**Perdóneme**	pehr-*doh*-neh-meh
I'm sorry, I don't understand.	**Lo siento, no entiendo.**	loh *syehn*-toh no ehn-*tyehn*-doh
Do you speak English?	**¿Habla usted inglés?**	*ah*-blah oo-*sted* een-*glehs*
Is there anyone here who speaks English?	**¿Hay alguien aquí que hable inglés?**	eye *ahl*-gyehn ah-*kee* keh *ah*-bleh een-*glehs*
I speak a little Spanish.	**Hablo un poco de español.**	*ah*-bloh oon *poh*-koh deh eh-spah-*nyohl*
I don't understand Spanish very well.	**No (lo) entiendo muy bien el español.**	noh (loh) ehn-*tyehn*-doh mwee byehn el eh-spah-*nyohl*

Useful Phrases

English	Spanish	Pronunciation
I would like	**Quisiera**	key-*syeh*-rah
Give me	**Déme**	*deh*-meh
Do you have . . . ?	**¿Tiene usted . . . ?**	tyeh-neh oo-*sted*
a dictionary	**un diccionario**	oon deek-syoh-*nah*-ryoh
postcard	**Tarjeta postal**	tar-*heh*-tah poh-*stahl*
insect repellent	**Repelente contra insectos**	reh-peh-*lehn*-teh *cohn*-trah een-*sehk*-tohs
How much is it?	**¿Cuánto cuesta?**	*kwahn*-toh *kweh*-stah
Who?	¿Quién? ¿Quiénes?	*Kyehn? Kyeh*-nehs?
When?	**¿Cuándo?**	*kwahn*-doh
What time is it?	**¿Qué hora es?**	keh *oh*-rah ehs
There is (Is there . . . ?)	**(¿)Hay (. . . ?)**	eye
Good	**Bueno**	*bweh*-noh
Bad	**Malo**	*mah*-loh
Better (best)	**(Lo) Mejor**	(Loh) meh-*hohr*
More	**Más**	mahs
Less	**Menos**	*meh*-nohs
No smoking	**Se prohibe fumar**	seh proh-*ee*-beh foo-*mahr*
May I see your menu?	**¿Puedo ver el menú (la carta)?**	*pweh*-doh vehr el meh-*noo* (lah *car*-tah)
The meal is good.	**Me gusta la comida.**	meh *goo*-stah lah koh-*mee*-dah
The check, please.	La cuenta, por favor.	lah kwehn-tah pohr fa-vorh
What do I owe you?	**¿Cuánto le debo?**	*kwahn*-toh leh *deh*-boh
I want (to see) . . .	**Quiero (ver) . . .**	*kyeh*-roh (vehr)
a room	**un cuarto** or **una habitación**	oon *kwar*-toh, *oo*-nah ah-bee-tah-*syohn*
for two persons	**para dos personas**	*pah*-rah dohs pehr-*soh*-nahs
with (without) bathroom	**con (sin) baño**	kohn (seen) *bah*-nyoh

English	Spanish	Pronunciation
We are staying here only . . .	**Nos quedamos aquí solamente . . .**	nohs keh-*dah*-mohs ah-*kee* soh-lah-*mehn*-teh
one night.	**una noche.**	*oo*-nah *noh*-cheh
one week.	**una semana.**	*oo*-nah seh-*mah*-nah
We are leaving . . . tomorrow.	**Partimos (Salimos) . . . mañana.**	pahr-*tee*-mohs (sah-*lee*-mohs) mah-*nya*-nah
Do you accept . . . ? credit cards?	**¿Acepta usted . . . ? tarjetas de credito?**	ah-*sehp*-tah oo-*sted* tar-*he*-tas de cre-*dee*-to
Is there a laundromat . . .? near here?	**¿Hay una lavandería . . .? cerca de aquí?**	eye *oo*-nah lah-*bahn*-deh-*ree*-ah *sehr*-kah deh ah-*kee*
Please send these clothes to the laundry.	**Hágame el favor de mandar esta ropa a la lavandería.**	*ah*-gah-meh el fah-*vohr* deh mahn-*dahr eh*-stah *roh*-pah a lah lah-*bahn*-deh-*ree*-ah
What's up?	Que Pedo?	*Kay*- pay-doh
See you later.	Hasta luego.	*ahs*-tah *lway*-goh
Are you married / single?	¿Usted es casado -a / soltero -a?	oos-*tehd* ehs kah-*sah*-doh -dah / sohl-*teh*-roh -rah
I'm married.	Soy casado -a.	soy kah-*sah*-doh -dah
I'm single.	Soy soltero -a.	soy sohl-*teh*-roh -rah
What are you studying?	¿Qué estudia?	keh ehs-*too*-dyah
I'm a student.	Soy estudiante.	soy ehs-too-*dyahn*-teh
Where are you from?	¿De dónde es?	deh *dohn*-deh ehs
I'm Canadian.	Soy Canadiense.	soy kah-nah-dee-*ayn*-seh
I'm American.	Soy Americano.	soy ah-may-ree-*kah*-noh
May I have your phone number / e-mail please?	¿Me puede dar su número de teléfono/ dirección de e-mail, por favor?	meh *pweh*-deh dar soo *noo*-meh-roh deh teh-*leh*-foh-noh/ dee-reck-*syohn* deh e-mail, porh fah-*vohr*
What kind of music do you like?	¿Qué tipo de música le gusta?	keh *tee*-poh deh *moo*-see-kah leh *goos*-tah
Cheers!	Arriba, abajo, al centro, padentro	a-*ree*-bah, a-*baa*-ho, ahl-*sayn*-chro, pah-*dayn*-chro
Another please.	**Otra por favor.**	*oh*-chra, pohr fah-*vohr*
Can you take a picture of us?	**¿Nos tomas una foto?**	*nohs toe*-mahs *oo*-nah *foe*-toe
Dude, Man	**Guey**	*way*
Cool	**Chingon**	*cheeng*-on
Quart of beer	**Cahuama**	ka-*wah*-ma
Weed	**Motito**	mo-tee-to
Let´s party.	**Vamonos de peda.**	vah-mown-nohs *thay* pay-*dah*
I flirted with him (her)	**Me lo (la) ligue**	*may low (lah) lee*-gay
I hooked up	**Me lo (la) agarre**	*may low (lah) ah*-garr-ay

USEFUL TERMS & PHRASES

NUMBERS

1	**uno** (*ooh*-noh)
2	**dos** (dohs)
3	**tres** (trehs)
4	**cuatro** (*kwah*-troh)
5	**cinco** (*seen*-koh)
6	**seis** (sayes)
7	**siete** (*syeh*-teh)
8	**ocho** (*oh*-choh)
9	**nueve** (*nweh*-beh)
10	**diez** (dyehs)
11	**once** (*ohn*-seh)
12	**doce** (*doh*-seh)
13	**trece** (*treh*-seh)
14	**catorce** (kah-*tohr*-seh)
15	**quince** (*keen*-seh)
16	**dieciseis** (dyeh-see-*sayes*)
17	**diecisiete** (dyeh-see-*syeh*-teh)
18	**dieciocho** (dyeh-*syoh*-choh)
19	**diecinueve** (dyeh-see-*nweh*-beh)
20	**veinte** (*bayn*-teh)
30	**treinta** (*trayn*-tah)
40	**cuarenta** (kwah-*ren*-tah)
50	**cincuenta** (seen-*kwen*-tah)
60	**sesenta** (seh-*sehn*-tah)
70	**setenta** (seh-*tehn*-tah)
80	**ochenta** (oh-*chehn*-tah)
90	**noventa** (noh-*behn*-tah)
100	**cien** (syehn)
200	**doscientos** (do-*syehn*-tohs)
500	**quinientos** (kee-*nyehn*-tohs)
1,000	**mil** (meel)

English	Spanish	Pronunciation
I'm hungry (thirsty).	**Tengo hambre (sed).**	*tehn*-go *ahm*-bray/said
I don't feel well.	**No me siento bien.**	*No may see*-en-toe *be*-yen
I am going to throw up.	**Voy a vomitar.**	*boy* a *bomb*-ee-tar

TRANSPORTATION TERMS

English	Spanish	Pronunciation
Where is . . . ?	**¿Dónde está . . . ?**	*dohn*-deh eh-*stah*
the station	**la estación**	lah eh-stah-*syohn*
a hotel	**un hotel**	oon oh-*tehl*
a gas station	**una gasolinera**	*oo*-nah gah-soh-lee-*neh*-rah
a restaurant	**un restaurante**	oon res-tow-*rahn*-teh
the toilet	**el baño**	el *bah*-nyoh
a good doctor	**un buen médico**	oon bwehn *meh*-dee-coh
the road to . . .	**el camino a/hacia . . .**	el cah-*mee*-noh ah/*ah*-syah
To the right	**A la derecha**	ah lah deh-*reh*-chah
To the left	**A la izquierda**	ah lah ees-*kyehr*-dah
Straight ahead	**Derecho**	deh-*reh*-choh
Airport	**Aeropuerto**	ah-eh-roh-*pwehr*-toh
Flight	**Vuelo**	*bweh*-loh
Rental car	**Arrendadora de autos**	Ah-rehn-da-doh-rah deh ow-tohs
Bus	**Autobús**	ow-toh-*boos*
Bus or truck	**Camión**	ka-*myohn*
Lane	**Carril**	kah-*reel*
Nonstop (bus)	**Directo**	Dee-*rehk*-toh
Intercity	**Foraneo**	Foh-rah-*neh*-oh
Luggage storage area	**Guarda equipaje**	gwar-dah eh-kee-*pah*-heh
Arrival gates	**Llegadas**	yeh-*gah*-dahss
Originates at this station	**Local**	loh-*kahl*
Originates elsewhere	**De paso**	deh *pah*-soh
Stops if seats available	**Para si hay lugares**	*pah*-rah see eye loo-*gah*-rehs
First class	**Primera**	pree-*meh*-rah
Second class	**Segunda**	seh-*goon*-dah
Nonstop (flight)	**Sin escala**	seen ess-*kah*-lah
Baggage claim area	**Recibo de equipajes**	reh-see-boh deh eh-kee-*pah*-hehss
Ticket window	**Taquilla**	tah-*kee*-yah
Where can I get a taxi?	**¿Dónde puedo pedir un taxi?**	d*ohn*-day P*way*-doh *pay*-deer Oohn *tax*-ee
How do I get there?	**¿Como llego ahí?**	*koh*-moh *yay*-go *ah*-yee
How much time does it take?	**¿Cuanto tiempo se hace allá?**	*kwan*-toe *tee*-ehm-poe say *ah*-say *ah*-ya
Can I get it cheaper?	**¿No me lo deja mas barato?**	*no* may *low day*-ha *mahs bar*-ah-toe
How much does it cost?	**¿Cuánto cuesta?**	*kwan*-toe *kways*-tah

SIZE

English	Spanish	Pronunciation
small	**pequeño -a**	peh-*keh*-nyoh / peh-*keh*-nyah
medium	**mediano -a**	meh-*dyah*-no / meh-*dyah*-na
big	**grande**	*grahn*-deh
fat	**gordo -a**	*gohr*-doh / *gohr*-dah
wide	**ancho -a**	*ahn*-cho / *ahn*-cha
narrow	**angosto -a**	ahng-*goh*-stoh / ahng-*goh*-stah

TIME

Time in Spanish is referred to, literally, by the hour. "What time is it?" translates literally as "What hour is it? / What hours are they?"

English	Spanish	Pronunciation
What time is it?	**¿Qué hora es?**	keh *oh*-ra ehs
At what time?	**¿A qué hora?**	ah *keh oh*-rah
For how long?	**¿Por cuánto tiempo?**	pohr *kwahn*-toh *tyehm*-poh
It's one o'clock.	**Es la una en punto.**	ehs lah *oo*-nah ehn *poon*-toh
It's two thirty.	**Son las dos y media.**	sohn lahs *dohs* ee *meh*-dyah
It's two fifteen.	**Son las dos y cuarto.**	sohn lahs *dohs* ee *kwahr*-toh
It's noon.	**Es mediodía.**	ehs *meh*-dyoh *dee*-ah
It's midnight.	**Es medianoche**	ehs meh-dyah-*noh*-cheh
It's early.	**Es temprano**	ehs tehm-*prah*-noh
It's late.	**Es tarde**	ehs *tahr*-deh
In the morning	**de la mañana**	deh lah mah-*nyah*-nah
In the afternoon	**de la tarde**	deh lah *tahr*-deh
At night	**de la noche**	deh lah *noh*-cheh
Dawn	**la madrugada**	lah mah-droo-*gah*-dah

DAYS OF THE WEEK

English	Spanish	Pronunciation
Sunday	**el domingo**	ehl doh-*meeng*-go
Monday	**el lunes**	ehl *loo*-nehs
Tuesday	**el martes**	ehl *mahr*-tehs
Wednesday	**el miércoles**	ehl *myehr*-koh-lehs
Thursday	**el jueves**	ehl *hweh*-vehs
Friday	**el viernes**	ehl *vyehr*-nehs
Saturday	**el sábado**	ehl *sah*-bah-doh
today	**hoy**	oy
tomorrow	**mañana**	mah-*nyah*-nah
yesterday	**ayer**	ah-*yehr*
the day before yesterday	**anteayer**	ahn-teh-ah-*yehr*
one week	**una semana**	*oo*-nah seh-*mah*-nah
next week	**la próxima semana**	lah *prohk*-see-mah seh-*mah*-nah
last week	**la semana pasada**	lah seh-*mah*-nah pah-*sah*-dah

Local Nicknames

- ***Jarochos:*** People from Veracruz, usually folks who like to sing and play *jarana* or regional ballads on a ukulele or marimba.
- ***Guyabos:*** People from the state of Morelos.
- ***Yucatecos:*** Folks from the Yucatán peninsula.
- ***Boludo/boluda:*** An Argentinian fun-loving guy or gal.
- ***Oaxaqueños:*** Oaxacan locals.
- ***Parece Guacamaya:*** People who are chatterboxes, named so after the guacamaya, which is an Orn Macaw that squawks endlessly. It's only used with women (why aren't there negative stereotypes for men, huh?).
- ***Gordo/gorda* (fatty) or *flaco/flaca* (skinny):** Both are used freely and not considered insulting, though it's more desirable to be a gordo/gorda than a flaco/flaca.

MONTHS OF THE YEAR

English	Spanish	Pronunciation
January	**enero**	eh-*neh*-roh
February	**febrero**	feh-*breh*-roh
March	**marzo**	*mahr*-soh
April	**abril**	ah-*breel*
May	**mayo**	*mah*-yoh
June	**junio**	*hoo*-nee-oh
July	**julio**	*hoo*-lee-oh
August	**agosto**	ah-*gohs*-toh
September	**septiembre**	sehp-*tyehm*-breh
October	**octubre**	ohk-*too*-breh
November	**noviembre**	noh-*vyehm*-breh
December	**diciembre**	dee-*syehm*-breh
next month	**el mes entrante**	ehl *mehs* ehn-*trahn*-teh
last month	**el mes pasado**	ehl *mehs* pah-*sah*-doh

SEASONS OF THE YEAR

English	Spanish	Pronunciation
spring	**la primavera**	lah pree-mah-*veh*-rah
summer	**el verano**	ehl veh-*rah*-noh
autumn	**el otoño**	ehl oh-*toh*-nyoh
winter	**el invierno**	ehl een-*vyehr*-noh

THE WEATHER

English	Spanish	Pronunciation
It's so ____	Es tan ____	Ehs *tahn*
Is it always so ____?	¿Siempre es tan ____?	*syehm*-preh ehs tahn
sunny	soleado	soh-leh-*ah*-doh
rainy	lluvioso	yoo-vee-*oh*-soh
cloudy	nublado	noo-*blah*-doh

humid	húmedo	*o*-meh-doh
warm	caliente	kah-*lyehn*-teh
cool	frío	*free*-oh
windy	ventoso	vehn-*toh*-soh

Food Glossary

Bebidas/Drinks

English	Spanish	Pronunciation
Alcoholic	**con alcohol**	kohn ahl-koh-*ohl*
neat / straight	**sencillo**	sehn-*see*-yoh
on the rocks	**en las rocas**	ehn lahs *roh*-kahs
with (seltzer or soda) water	**con agua (de seltzer o de soda)**	kohn *ah*-wah (deh sehlt-*sehr* oh deh *soh*-dah)
Beer	**cerveza**	sehr-*veh*-sah
Wine	**vino**	*vee*-noh
White wine	**vino blanco**	*vee*-noh *blahn*-koh
Red wine	**vino tinto**	*vee*-noh *teen*-toh
Tea	**té**	teh
Coffee	**café**	kah-*feh*
Cappuccino	**cappuccino**	kah-poo-*chee*-noh
Espresso	**café expreso**	kah-*feh* ehs-*preh*-soh
Iced coffee	**café helado**	kah-*feh* heh-*lah*-doh
Fruit juice	**jugo de fruta**	*hoo*-goh deh *froo*-tah
Soda	**soda**	*soh*-dah

Carnes/Meats

English	Spanish	Pronunciation
Beef	**carne de res fresca**	*kahr*-neh deh rrehs *frehs*-cah
Chicken	**pollo**	*poh*-yoh
Goat	**cabra fresca**	*kah*-brah *frehs*-kah
Lamb	**cordero fresco**	kohr-*deh*-roh *frehs*-koh
Pork	**cerdo fresco**	*sehr*-doh *frehs*-koh

Mariscos/Seafood

English	Spanish	Pronunciation
Clams	**las almejas**	lahs ahl-*meh*-hahs
Fish	**el pescado**	ehl pehs-*kah*-doh
Flounder	**la platija**	lah plah-*tee*-hah
Octopus	**el pulpo**	ehl *pool*-poh
Oysters	**las ostras**	lahs *ohs*-trahs
Sea bass	**el róbalo**	ehl *roh*-bah-loh
Seafood	**los mariscos**	lohs mah-*rees*-kohs
Shark	**el tiburón**	ehl tee-boo-*rohn*
Shrimp	**los camarones**	lohs kah-mah-*roh*-nehs
Squid	**el calamar**	ehl kahl-ah-*mahr*

Vegetables

English	Spanish	Pronunciation
Artichoke	**alcachofa**	ahl-kah-*choh*-fah
Bean sprouts	**brotes de soja**	*broh*-tehs deh *soh*-ha
Beans	**frijoles**	free-*hoh*-lehs
Broccoli	**brócoli**	*broh*-koh-lee
Carrot	**zanahoria**	sah-nah-*oh*-ryah
Celery	**apio**	*ah*-pyoh
Corn	**maíz**	mah-*ees*
Cucumber	**pepino**	peh-*pee*-noh
Eggplant	**berenjena**	beh-rehn-*heh*-nah
Lettuce	**lechuga**	leh-*choo*-gah
Olives	**aceitunas**	ah-seh-*too*-nahs
Onion	**cebolla**	seh-*boh*-yah
Peppers	**pimiento, chile**	pee-*myehn*-toh, *chee*-leh
hot	**picante**	pee-*kahn*-teh
mild	**suave**	soo-*ah*-veh
poblano	**poblano**	poh-*blah*-noh
jalapeno	**jalapeño**	hah-lah-*peh*-nyoh
habanero	**habanero, habañero**	ah-bah-*neh*-roh, ah-bah-*nyeh*-roh
chipotle	**chipotle**	chee-*poht*-leh
cayenne	**pimienta de Cayena**	pee-*myehn*-tah deh kah-*yeh*-nah
pcascabeles	**cascabeles**	kahs-kah-*beh*-lehs
Potato	**papa, patata**	*pah*-pah, pah-*tah*-tah
Spinach	**espinaca**	ehs-pee-*nah*-kah
Squash	**zapallo**	sah-*pah*-yoh
Sweet corn	**maíz dulce**	mah-*ees dohl*-seh
Tomato	**jitomate (Mexico)**	hee-toh-*mah*-teh

Fruits

English	Spanish	Pronunciation
Apple	**manzana**	mahn-*zah*-nah
Banana	**plátano, banana**	*plah*-tah-noh, bah-*nah*-nah
Blackberries	**zarzamora, mora negra**	sahr-sah-*moh*-rah, *moh*-rah *neh*-grah
Carambola, star fruit	**carambola**	kah-rahm-*boh*-lah
Cherry	**cereza**	seh-*reh*-sah
Citron	**cidra**	*see*-drah
Coconut	**coco**	*koh*-koh
Cranberry	**arándano rojo**	ah-*rahn*-dah-noh *roh*-hoh
Grapefruit	**toronja**	toh-*rohn*-hah
Grapes (green, red)	**uvas (verdes, rojas)**	*oo*-vahs (*vehr*-dehs, *rroh*-hahs)
Guava	**guayaba**	wah-*yah*-bah
Honeydew	**melón**	meh-*lohn*

English	Spanish	Pronunciation
Lemon	**limón amarillo**	lee-*mohn* ah-mah-*ree*-yoh
Lime	**limón verde**	lee-*mohn vehr*-de
Melon	**melón**	meh-*lohn*
Orange	**naranja**	nah-*rahn*-hah
Palm fruit	**fruta de palma**	*froo*-tah deh *pahl*-mah
Peach	**melocotón, durazno**	meh-loh-koh-*tohn*, doo-*rahs*-noh
Pineapple	**piña**	*pee*-nyah
Strawberry	**fresa**	*freh*-sah
Watermelon	**sandía, melón de agua**	sahn-*dee*-ah, meh-*lohn* deh *ah*-wah

Menu Terms

In addition to the below menu items, check out Appendix A for info on more common Mexican food.

Spanish	Pronunciation	Definition
Arepas	ah-*reh*-pahs	savory stuffed cornmeal patties
Arroz con pollo	ah-*rrohs* kohn *poh*-yoh	rice with chicken and vegetables
Bife de lomo	*bee*-feh deh *loh*-moh	filet mignon
Buñuelos	boon-yoo-*eh*-lohs	round, thin fritters dipped in sugar (may also be savory)
Butifarra	boo-tee-fah-rrah	spiced pork breakfast sausage
Camarones al ajillo	kah-mah-*roh*-nehs ahl ah-*hee*-yoh	garlic shrimp stew
Carne en polvo	*kahr*-neh ehn *pohl*-voh	seasoned ground beef
Carnitas	kahr-*nee*-tahs	slow-cooked pork served with corn tortillas
Chicharrón	chee-chah-*rrohn*	deep-fried pork skin
Chorreados	choh-rreh-*ah*-dohs	Corn pancakes with sour cream
Empañadas/ empanadas	ehm-pah-*nyah*-dahs/ ehm-pah-*nah*-dahs	turnovers filled with meat and/or cheese, beans, potatoes
Enchiladas	ehn-chee-*lah*-dahs	Pastries stuffed with cheese, meat, or potatoes
Escabeche	hs-kah-*beh*-cheh	spicy fish stew
Gorditas	gohr-*dee*-tahs	Thick, fried corn tortillas stuffed with cheese, beans, and/or meat
Helado	eh-*lah*-doh	ice cream
Menudo	meh-*noo*-doh	tripe stew
Mole poblano	*moh*-leh poh-*blah*-noh	chicken with bitter chocolate/chile sauce
Olla de carne	*oh*-yah deh *kahr*-neh	beef stew with yucca, squash, and pumpkin
Panqueques	pahn-*keh*-kehs	dessert crepes with caramel and whipped cream

Survival Slang

A lot of the Spanish you'll hear on the streets won't necessarily be in your pocket dictionary. Here are some of the most commonly used slang words you'll overhear and their definitions:

- ***Chilango:*** This demonym (a term that refers to a group of inhabitants of a place—how's that for an SAT word?) used to be considered derogatory. These days it's an accepted term—there's even a magazine called *Chilango*. It still can be considered slanderous, though, if it's used by someone from outside Mexico City to refer to the city's residents.
- ***Qué onda?:*** Literally "what wave?" Translates to "whaddup?"
- ***Guey*****:** Dude.
- ***Naco*****:** Low-class, trashy. It's best not to use this word as a foreigner; depending on the context, it can be interpreted to have negative racial connotations.
- ***Fresa:*** Preppy, rich, innocent. Also used to mean cool—depends on the context.
- ***No mames!*****:** Are you freakin' kidding me! Literally means "Don't suck off me."
- ***Qué padre:*** *So* cool.
- ***Chévere:*** Cool or very good; used for places, people, situations. ***Pedro es chévere!*** translates as "Pedro is cool!"
- ***Pinche*****:** While it actually refers to a cook's helper, this word serves as an "enhancer" of sorts—usually added in front of *naco, cabron,* and *guey* for emphasis. In that sense it serves the same purpose as "effing" in the U.S. For instance: ***Pinche guey! Pinche cabron!*** These terms can be used jokingly/affectionately, in the right company.
- ***No pasa nada.*** Don't worry, nothing will happen. Equivalent to Jamaican "no problem, man" (in other words, there may be a problem . . .).
- ***A todo mal, mezcal. A todo bien, mescal también*****:** If everything's bad, (drink) mescal. If it's good, drink it too (anyway).

Spanish	Pronunciation	Definition
Papas rellenas	*pah*-pas Re-*hey*-nas	fried mashed potatoes, stuffed with meat
Patas de pavo rellenas	*pah*-tahs deh *pah*-voh reh-*yeh*-nahs	stuffed turkey legs
Pollo a la brasa	*poh*-yoh ah lah *brah*-sah	spit-roasted chicken
Pollo frito	*poh*-yoh *free*-toh	fried chicken
Puerco en adobo	*pwehr*-koh ehn ah-*doh*-boh	pork in chile sauce
Quesadillas	keh-sah-*dee*-yahs	Tortillas with cheese
Rellenos	rreh-*yeh*-nohs	Bits of meat or cheese breaded with yucca or potato paste and deep fried

Spanish	Pronunciation	Definition
Ropa vieja	*roh*-pah *vyeh*-hah	stewed shredded beef
Salmorejo de jueyes	sahl-moh-*reh*-hoh deh *hweh*-yehs	crab in tomato and garlic sauce
Seco de chancho	*seh*-koh deh *chahn*-cho	pork stew
Sopa de pavo	*soh*-pah deh *pah*-voh	turkey soup
Sopapillas	soh-pah-*pee*-yahs	puffed up crisps of a pie crust–like dough, drizzled with honey and sprinkled with powdered sugar
Tacos	*tah*-kohs	Traditional Mexican tacos are made with ground tongue
Tamales	tah-*mah*-lehs	Chicken, pork, or potatoes with chiles in cornmeal steamed inside a banana leaf or corn husk
Tortas	*tohr*-tahs	Sandwiches with meat and/or cheese, garnished with vegetables

Appendix C: Useful Numbers & Websites

Airlines Serving Select Mexican Destinations

See the "Basics" chapter, p. 10 for info on budget airlines that service Mexico.

Aeroméxico
☎ 800/237-6639
www.aeromexico.com
Acapulco, Cancún, Huatulco, Los Cabos, Ixtapa-Zihuatanejo, Puerto Vallarta

Air Canada
☎ 888/247-2262
www.aircanada.ca
Cancún, Cozumel, Puerto Vallarta

Alaska Airlines
☎ 800/252-7522
www.alaskaair.com
Cancún, Ixtapa-Zihuatanejo, Los Cabos, Puerto Vallarta

American Airlines
☎ 800/223-5436
www.aa.com
Acapulco, Cancún, Cozumel, Ixtapa-Zihuatanejo, Los Cabos, Puerto Vallarta

America West Airlines
☎ 800/327-7810
www.americawest.com
Acapulco, Cancún, Ixtapa-Zihuatanejo, Los Cabos, Puerto Vallarta

ATA Airlines
☎ 800/435-9282
www.ata.com
Cancún, Ixtapa-Zihuatanejo, Puerto Vallarta

British Airways
☎ 800/247-9297
www.britishairways.com
Flights from London to Cancún

Continental Airlines
☎ 800/537-9222
www.continental.com
Acapulco, Cancún, Cozumel, Ixtapa-Zihuatanejo, Los Cabos, Puerto Vallarta

Delta Air Lines
☎ 800/221-1212
www.delta.com
Cancún, Los Cabos, Puerto Vallarta

Frontier Airlines
☎ 800/432-1359
www.frontierairlines.com
Cancún, Ixtapa-Zihuatanejo, Los Cabos, Puerto Vallarta

United Airlines
☎ 800/538-2929
www.united.com
Cancún, Los Cabos

It's Easy Being Green

Each time you take a flight or drive a car CO_2 is released into the atmosphere. You can help neutralize this danger to our planet through "carbon offsetting"—paying someone to reduce your CO_2 emissions by the same amount you've added. Carbon offsets can be purchased in the U.S. from companies such as **Carbonfund.org** (www.carbonfund.org) and **TerraPass** (www.terrapass.org), and from **Climate Care** (www.climatecare.org) in the U.K.

Although one could argue that any vacation that includes an airplane flight can't be truly "green," you can go on holiday and still contribute positively to the environment. You can offset carbon emissions from your flight in other ways. Choose forward-looking companies that embrace responsible development practices, helping preserve destinations for the future by working alongside local people. An increasing number of sustainable tourism initiatives can help you plan a family trip and leave as small a "footprint" as possible on the places you visit.

We can all help conserve fuel and energy when we travel. Here are a few simple ways you can help preserve your favorite destinations:

- Whenever possible, choose nonstop flights; they generally require less fuel than those that must stop and take-off again.
- If renting a car is necessary on your vacation, ask the rental agent for the most fuel efficient one available. Not only will you use less gas, you'll save money at the tank.
- At hotels, request that your sheets and towels not be changed daily. You'll save water and energy by not washing them as often, and you'll prolong the life of the towels, too. (Many hotels already have programs like this in place.)
- Turn off the lights and air-conditioner (or heater) when you leave your hotel room.

Serviced Through Aeroméxico

Mexicana
☎ 800/531-7921
www.mexicana.com
Acapulco, Cancún, Cozumel, Huatulco, Ixtapa-Zihuatanejo, Los Cabos, Puerto Vallarta

Northwest Airlines
☎ 800/225-2525
www.nwa.com
Seasonal flights to Acapulco, Cancún, Cozumel, Los Cabos, Puerto Vallarta

US Airways
☎ 800/428-4322
www.usairways.com
Cancún, Cozumel

Where to Get More Information

Local **tourist information offices** offer all kinds of information to travelers, including brochures, maps, and destination-specific magazines and posters. If you want them to mail information to you, allow four to six weeks for the mail to reach you.

- **Acapulco's State of Guerrero Tourism Office** (Costera Miguel Aleman 4455, Centro Internacional Acapulco, Acapulco, Guerrero, located on the Costera side of the convention center; ☎ 744/484-4416; Fax: 744/484-4583; www.acapulco.gob.mx). Note that

Frommers.com: The Complete Travel Resource

It should go without saying, but we highly recommend **Frommers.com**, voted Best Travel Site by *PC Magazine.* We think you'll find our expert advice and tips; independent reviews of hotels, restaurants, attractions, and preferred shopping and nightlife venues; vacation giveaways; and an online booking tool indispensable before, during, and after your travels. We publish the complete contents of over 128 travel guides in our **Destinations** section covering nearly 3,800 places worldwide to help you plan your trip. Each weekday, we publish original articles reporting on **Deals and News** via our free **Frommers.com Newsletter** to help you save time and money and travel smarter. We're betting you'll find our new **Events** listings (http://events.frommers.com) an invaluable resource; it's an up-to-the-minute roster of what's happening in cities everywhere—including concerts, festivals, lectures and more. We've also added weekly **Podcasts, interactive maps,** and hundreds of new images across the site. Check out our **Travel Talk** area featuring **Message Boards** where you can join in conversations with thousands of fellow Frommer's travelers and post your trip report once you return.

the Web site is currently available in Spanish only.

- **Cancún Convention and Visitors Bureau** (Kukulkán Km 9, "Cancún Center," first floor, Hotel Zone-Cancún, Quintana Roo, México 77500; ☎ 998/881-2745 or 881-2774; www.cancun.info).
- **Huatulco Hotels Association** (Bulevar Benito Juárez 8, Local 1, Interior Hotel Crown Pacific, Bahía de Tangolunda, Bahías de Huatulco, Oaxaca, 70989; ☎ 866/416-0555 from the U.S. or 958/581-0486; Fax: 958/581-0487; www.hoteleshuatulco.com.mx; www.hotels.baysofhuatulco.com.mx).
- **Huatulco State Tourism Office** (Bulevar Benito Juárez s/n, Bahía de Tangolunda, Bahías de Huatulco, Oaxaca, 70989; ☎ 958/581-0176 or 581-0177; www.oaxaca.gob.mx/sedetur). The Web site offers information about the whole state of Oaxaca, including some information on Huatulco; however, the information is in Spanish and not very consumer-oriented.
- **Isla Mujeres Tourism Office** (Av. Rueda Medina 130, Isla Mujeres, Quintana Roo, Mexico, 77400, across from the main pier between Immigration and Customs; ☎ 998/877-0767; www.isla-mujeres.com.mx).
- **Ixtapa Tourism Office** or Subsecretaría de Fomento Turístico (Centro Comercial La Puerta, Locales 2, 3, 8, and 9, Ixtapa, Guerrero, 408880; ☎ 755/553-1967; Fax: 755/553-1968).
- **Los Cabos Tourism Office** (Bulevar Mauricio Castro, Plaza San José, Locales 3 and 4, Col. 1 de Mayo, Cabo San Lucas, BCS; ☎ 624/146-9628; www.visitcabo.com or www.loscabos.gob.mx). You can try to call the office for information, and who knows, someone may even be there to answer the phone; however, you're better off visiting the Web site.
- **Puerto Escondido State Tourism Office** (SEDETUR, Bulevar Benito Juárez s/n, Fraccionamiento Bacocho, Puerto Escondido, Oaxaca, 71980; ☎ 954/582-0175; www.oaxaca.gob.mx/sedetur).
- **Puerto Vallarta Tourism Board and Convention and Visitors Bureau** (Local 18, Planta Baja, Zona Comercial Hotel Canto del Sol, Zona Hotelera Las

Glorias, Puerto Vallarta, Jalisco, 48310; ☎ 888/384-6822 from the U.S., and 01-800/719-3276 from Mexico or 322/224-1175; Fax: 322/224-0915; www.visitpuertovallarta.com).

- **State of Jalisco Tourism Office in Puerto Vallarta** (Centro Comercial Plaza Marina, Locales 144 and 146, Marina Vallarta, Puerto Vallarta, Jalisco, 48321; ☎ 322/221-2676 or 221-2677; Fax: 322/221-2678).
- **Zihuatanejo Tourism Office or Dirección de Turismo Municipal** (in the city-hall building in Zihuatanejo; ☎ 755/554-2001, ask for the tourism office; presidencia@ixtapa-zihuatanejo.com).

A

G

INDEX

INDEX

Q

R

T

U

V

INDEX